KU-781-356

Marketing Communications

P

Pearson

At Pearson, we have a simple mission: to help people make more of their lives through learning.

We combine innovative learning technology with trusted content and educational expertise to provide engaging and effective learning experiences that serve people wherever and whenever they are learning.

From classroom to boardroom, our curriculum materials, digital learning tools and testing programmes help to educate millions of people worldwide – more than any other private enterprise.

Every day our work helps learning flourish, and wherever learning flourishes, so do people.

To learn more, please visit us at **www.pearson.com/uk**

About the authors

Chris Fill BA, MSc, is a Director of Fillassociates. He was a Principal Lecturer at the University of Portsmouth, and Senior Examiner and Fellow at The Chartered Institute of Marketing. He now works with the Institute of Practitioners in Advertising on special projects. He has authored over 35 textbooks, published papers in many leading academic journals, and is internationally recognised for his contribution to marketing communications.

Sarah Turnbull PhD, MBA, MSc, FCIM, FHEA is Director of the DBA programme at the University of Portsmouth and a Principal Lecturer in Marketing. She leads the DBA course in Portsmouth and Reutlingen, Germany and is a Fellow of The Chartered Institute of Marketing. Prior to joining academia she worked in a number of global advertising agencies and spent eight years as Account Director on the Emirates account in Dubai. Her research on advertising practice and creativity has been published in leading academic and professional journals. She serves on the Editorial Review Board of the *International Journal of Advertising* and is regularly invited to speak about advertising at practitioner and academic events internationally.

We thank you for reading our book, and if you have any comments, observations, suggestions or opinions, please feel free to contact either of us: Sarah can be reached through sarah.turnbull@port.ac.uk., and Chris through chris@chrisfill.com.

New to this edition

Each of the chapters has been revised and brought up-to-date. Three new chapters have been developed for this edition in order to reflect contemporary marketing communications. These are:

- **Chapter 2 Marketing communications: issues, influences and disruption**

  This chapter considers the various issues and influences that impact marketing communications, many of which have caused disruption and changes to the conventional processes, procedures and strategies. These include international issues, developments in technology, ethics and moral behaviour, and industry related developments. Links are made to other chapters where topics are developed.

- **Chapter 4 Classical theories and interpretations of buyer behaviour**

  This chapter opens with a consideration of ideas relating to consumer journeys. It then examines classical theories and concepts associated with buyer behaviour, a core platform on which marketing communications is built.

- **Chapter 5 Contemporary interpretations of buyer behaviour**

  Building on the previous chapter, this one introduces various ideas and strategies associated with contemporary perspectives of buyer behaviour. In particular, issues concerning perceived risk, and the impact of the internet and mobile usage on buyer behaviour are reviewed.

Each chapter contains new examples of marketing communications practice, drawn from around the world. Many of these are presented through Viewpoints.

Each chapter has a new case study. Many of these concern campaigns for well-known brands, and most have achieved national and international acclaim. Many of these cases have been written by either agencies or clients, demonstrating the practical orientation of the book. Cases situated at the end of each chapter contextualise your learning in the real world.

All of the scholars' papers have been reviewed and the number of papers included has been increased, with key academic papers discussed to help take your study further.

Eighth edition

Marketing Communications

touchpoints, sharing and disruption

Chris Fill and Sarah Turnbull

Pearson

Harlow, England • London • New York • Boston • San Francisco • Toronto • Sydney • Dubai • Singapore • Hong Kong
Tokyo • Seoul • Taipei • New Delhi • Cape Town • São Paulo • Mexico City • Madrid • Amsterdam • Munich • Paris • Milan

PEARSON EDUCATION LIMITED
Kao Two, Kao Park
Harlow, Essex
CM17 9SR
United Kingdom
Tel: +44 (0)1279 623623
Web: www.pearson.com/uk

First published under the Prentice Hall Europe imprint 1995 (print)
Second edition published 1999 (print)
Third edition published 2003 (print)
Fourth edition published 2006 (print)
Fifth edition published 2009 (print)
Sixth edition published 2013 (print and electronic)
Seventh edition published 2016 (print and electronic)
Eighth edition published 2019 (print and electronic)

© Prentice Hall Europe 1995, 1999 (print)
© Pearson Education Limited 2003, 2006, 2009 (print)
© Pearson Education Limited 2013, 2016, 2019 (print and electronic)

The rights of Chris Fill and Sarah Turnbull to be identified as authors of this work have been asserted by them in accordance with the Copyright, Designs and Patents Act 1988.

The print publication is protected by copyright. Prior to any prohibited reproduction, storage in a retrieval system, distribution or transmission in any form or by any means, electronic, mechanical, recording or otherwise, permission should be obtained from the publisher or, where applicable, a licence permitting restricted copying in the United Kingdom should be obtained from the Copyright Licensing Agency Ltd, Barnard's Inn, 86 Fetter Lane, London EC4A 1EN.

The ePublication is protected by copyright and must not be copied, reproduced, transferred, distributed, leased, licensed or publicly performed or used in any way except as specifically permitted in writing by the publishers, as allowed under the terms and conditions under which it was purchased, or as strictly permitted by applicable copyright law. Any unauthorised distribution or use of this text may be a direct infringement of the authors' and the publisher's rights and those responsible may be liable in law accordingly.

All trademarks used herein are the property of their respective owners. The use of any trademark in this text does not vest in the author or publisher any trademark ownership rights in such trademarks, nor does the use of such trademarks imply any affiliation with or endorsement of this book by such owners.

Pearson Education is not responsible for the content of third-party internet sites.

ISBN: 978-1-292-23497-7 (print)
       978-1-292-23501-1 (PDF)
       978-1-292-23500-4 (ePub)

British Library Cataloguing-in-Publication Data
A catalogue record for the print edition is available from the British Library

Library of Congress Cataloging-in-Publication Data
Names: Fill, Chris, author. | Turnbull, Sarah, Dr., author.
Title: Marketing communications : touchpoints, sharing and disruption / Chris
   Fill and Sarah Turnbull.
Description: Eighth Edition. | New York : Pearson, [2019] | Revised edition
   of Marketing communications, 2016.
Identifiers: LCCN 2018058829| ISBN 9781292234977 (print) | ISBN 9781292235011
   (pdf) | ISBN 9781292235004 (epub)
Subjects: LCSH: Communication in marketing. | Marketing channels. | Sales
   promotion. | Branding (Marketing)
Classification: LCC HF5415.123 .F55 2019 | DDC 658.8/02—dc23
LC record available at https://urldefense.proofpoint.com/v2/url?u=https-3A__lccn.loc.gov_2018058829&d=DwIFAg&c=
0YLnzTkWOdJIub_y7qAx8Q&r=5GhAeyYynXlbVOzAbvhIak8zLCrKyUyNZdaUjp_AR_qlbXFjWAsA1hwmzOLfY1Gs&m=
5DOAKhqCEQQ81oNp6n7cEdfcJLm3hINg1kkp2vytx6o&s=Rf4UrbVbV8ehj2ZUXYP2aFiu7exzGzZw89y6hHGCM4E&e=

10 9 8 7 6 5 4 3 2 1
23 22 21 20 19

Cover image © themacx/iStock/Getty Images Plus
Cover type based on © Epifantsev/iStock/Getty Images Plus

Print edition typeset in 9.5/12pt Avenir LT Pro by Pearson CSC
Printed in Slovakia by Neografia

NOTE THAT ANY PAGE CROSS REFERENCES REFER TO THE PRINT EDITION

Brief contents

For Karen ... always for you (CF)
For Simon, Daisy and Bea (ST)

Contents

Part 3 The marketing communications mix

13 Advertising: role, forms and strategy

14 Public relations: principles and practice

Supporting resources

Visit **www.pearsoned.co.uk/fill** to find valuable online resources

Companion Website for students

- Selected additional viewpoints to contextualise your learning.
- Links to video resources to illustrate and reinforce both practical and academic material.
- Online glossary.
- Practice multiple choice quizzes help assess your understanding.

For instructors

- Complete, downloadable Instructors' Resource Guide.
- PowerPoint slides that can be downloaded and used for presentations
- Video and web links to assist teaching preparation

Also: The Companion Website provides the following features:

- Search tool to help locate specific items of content
- E-mail results and profile tools to send results of quizzes to instructors
- Online help and support to assist with website usage and troubleshooting

For more information please contact your local Pearson Education sales representative or visit **www.pearsoned.co.uk/fill**

Preface

Why study marketing communications?

Marketing communications provides a core activity for all organisations, large and small, commercial, government, charities, educational and other not-for-profit and third-sector organisations and their various audiences. The goal is to foster engagement so that all interested parties can understand the intentions of others and appreciate the value of the goods and services offered.

The world of marketing communications continues to change, and some of these changes have caused major disruption. Technology is the principal driver of this change, the effects of which can be seen in new forms of buyer behaviour, changing organisational structures, new ways of delivering marketing communications, and of course different expectations, experiences, forms of measurement and revised organisational performance.

Many of these changes and their impact are explored in this book. It is not possible to cover them all in depth but many of the key academic and practitioner reactions to these developments are examined.

Your career and employability

Whether you follow a career in marketing, marketing communications or any other business discipline you will need to apply a range of skills necessary for analysing and solving problems, and for communicating ideas and solutions to colleagues and clients. This requires the ability to think critically and to apply core concepts and ideas to new situations.

When you are in your final year and starting to apply for jobs, you will need to demonstrate to potential employers that you are 'employable' and that you have the characteristics, skills and potential that help distinguish you as the individual they need to employ.

Employability is a core focus of this book. Critical thinking is developed through questions and tasks, positioned in the Viewpoint features, and Review questions, which are positioned at the end of each chapter. These questions and activities are designed to encourage you to reflect on what you have just read and thereby improve and deepen your learning.

Critical thinking is also developed through the use of theories, concepts and frameworks. These can be found in each of the chapters. In certain chapters we present a range of theories and approaches, without specifying one that is correct. You should consider the different approaches and formulate your own opinion, making a judgement about which is more appropriate and note the reasons for your decision.

The cases studies included in this book are all drawn from the world of marketing communications. Many are written by agencies and practitioners. A large number of these cases have won awards, and national and international recognition. Readers are encouraged to consider the cases from a critical perspective and to think about the actions and decisions that agencies and clients have taken. The review questions that follow the cases are designed to help you apply your learning and understanding of the case itself, and with regard to the content of the chapter in which it is located. There are many additional case studies with questions available on the student website.

If you have access to the online learning resources you will find a range of multiple-choice questions. Answers are provided, so use these to test your understanding and make sure your learning is on track. These questions enable you to reflect on your learning and on where additional work is required.

In terms of employability, employees who can think flexibly and apply concepts and theories in new and perhaps strange situations to analyse and solve problems will be much more valuable to their employer. This book helps you to develop these skills. What is more, use of this book and the online resources will allow you to gain experience in using evidence to support and assess arguments. Employers value these problem-solving skills and the more you demonstrate your abilities the greater the number of opportunities that will come your way.

The aim of this book

This is the eighth edition of *Marketing Communications* and we have developed it to reflect current issues and practices in marketing communications.

The book is positioned as an academic resource about marketing communications. The practitioner element however, is acknowledged as an important distinguishing feature of this book (Rossiter and Percy, 2013) and is reinforced in this edition. The support and endorsement provided by the Institute of Practitioners in Advertising (IPA) has been continued and is much appreciated.

This book:

- Recognises the complexity of marketing communications and considers the strategic, tactical and operational aspects. Above all else, this book considers marketing communications from a contextual standpoint. This means that no one single theory is used to explain all marketing communications activities. Indeed, several theories are presented for some of the topics, and readers are encouraged to consider multiple interpretations.
- Offers a blend of academic and practitioner materials. The goal is to enable you to see the practical application of theories and concepts. This real-world orientation is designed to encourage you to reflect on your learning, to apply it to the real world, and to use real-world examples to understand marketing communications issues and problems, to help you develop your career.

In particular, this book has been written to help you in four main ways:

1. To understand and appreciate the variety of ways in which organisations use marketing communications.
2. To identify and understand some of the key theories and concepts associated with marketing communications.
3. To appreciate the way in which academic materials can be used to interpret practical aspects of marketing communications.
4. To develop insights into the reasoning behind the marketing communications activities used by organisations.

Marketing communications is a complex subject and draws on a variety of disciplines. This book has been written in the hope of disentangling some of the complexity so that you can enjoy the subject, be stimulated to want to know more and wish to engage further with the exciting and fast-changing world of marketing communications.

Additional resources

Web support

Students and lecturers who adopt this text have access to a range of support materials and facilities. Readers are invited to use the website designed for *Marketing Communications*, not only as a source of additional material but also as an interactive forum to explore and discuss marketing communications issues, academic and practitioner developments, and to improve learning. The site accommodates the needs of student readers and lecturers.

Student resources

- Additional learning materials including selected viewpoints from the previous edition.
- Annotated weblinks.
- Full online glossary.
- Multiple-choice questions.

Lecturer resources

- Instructors' Resource Guide.
- PowerPoint slides for each chapter.
- Annotated weblinks.

A test bank of multiple-choice questions has been developed for use by students and lecturers. In addition, there are links to a range of related sites and, an online glossary is available.

For lecturers and tutors not only is there an Instructors' Resource Guide containing a range of slides and exercises in downloadable format, but there is also a password protected section of the website for their use. From this site a much larger range of resources can be downloaded.

Structure of the text

There are three main parts to the book:

Part 1 Introduction to marketing communications

- **Chapters 1 to 6**
  This part introduces readers to the subject from a general perspective and provides a platform upon which the subject is explored. Following an introduction, the topics covered include a new chapter on the various issues and influences that impact marketing communications, communication theory, and two new chapters on classical and contemporary buyer behaviour. The final chapter in this part considers ideas about how marketing communications works.

Part 2 Managing marketing communications

- **Chapters 7 – 12**
  This part explores some of the managerial aspects associated with marketing communications. The core content concerns the various aspects of *strategy* and how organisations should develop their marketing communications in the light of their contextual positions. Consideration is then given to the role and nature of objectives and positioning, before exploring some of the issues associated with the communication industry, the financial implications associated with managing marketing communications, and the issues associated with the evaluation and measurement of marketing communications. The part concludes with two chapters that review the important topics of branding and integration within marketing communications.

Part 3 The marketing communications mix

- **Chapters 13 – 22**
  The marketing communications mix material constitutes by far the largest part of the book. This content is, of course, crucial to most courses on marketing communications. Unlike other texts, the approach here is focused on the three elements of the communication mix, namely the disciplines, content and the media.

Cases

Each of the 22 cases are new to this edition. These have been written by a variety of people including client organisations and marketing communications agencies.

Chapter 1	Introducing marketing communications
Case	Fearless Girl
Chapter 2	Marketing communications : issues, influences and disruption
Case	Channel 4 Paralympics
Chapter 3	Communication: theory and practice
Case	How L'Oréal Paris *Age Perfect* transformed its fortunes by showing older women that they are still 'worth it'
Chapter 4	Classical theories and interpretations of buyer behaviour
Case	How Sixt challenged car hire culture, and changed its fortunes
Chapter 5	Contemporary interpretations of buyer behaviour
Case	Help to Buy
Chapter 6	How does marketing communications work?
Case	Costa: creating a nation of coffee lovers
Chapter 7	Marketing communications: strategies and planning

These cases refer either to broad issues concerning a particular topic, or focus on a specific issue that is included in the chapter to which the case is assigned. Some cases refer to several campaigns undertaken for a specific brand or company, while others consider a specific campaign and associated activities. Several of these cases have won awards either at the IPA Effectiveness Awards or at Cannes. There are review questions at the end of each chapter that refer directly to the designated case.

Reference

Rossiter, J.R. and Percy, L. (2013) Observations: how the roles of advertising merely appear to have changed, *International Journal of Advertising*, 32(3), 391–98.

Authors' acknowledgements

This book could not have been written without the support of a wide range of brilliant people from marketing communication agencies, brands, industry bodies and academia. Contributions range from those who provided information and permissions, to those who wrote cases, viewpoints and answered questions, and those who have liaised with others. Finally, there are those who have read and reviewed drafts, made constructive comments and provided moral support and encouragement. Our thanks are offered to all of you.

Amy Ostermayr	Sixt
Andrew Orr	FreemanXP
Anna Stumpf	Anderson University
Bilyana Petrova	J. Walter Thompson: Brussels
Brock Vaughters	Anderson University
Carl Bratton	Direct Line Group
Daniel Sherrard	Grey London
Elly Fenlon	AMV BBDO
Eloise Augustine	former student at Buckinghamshire New University
Emily Ellis	McCann London
Fermín Paús	Danone Argentina
Hannah Smith	Vizeum & Kerry Foods
Harriet Rich	Brands2Life
James M. Crick	Loughborough University
Jemima Monies	adam&eveDDB
Jordan Maddern-Bell	easyjet
Justin Bairamian	BBC Creative
Kathryn Patten	IPA
Katie Kershaw	easyjet
Kay Heenan	IPA
Kevin Chesters	Ogilvy
Lars Samuelsen	UNCLEGREY
Marian Brannelly	Ascential Events
Mark Stockdale	The Effectiveness Partnership
Mathew Waksman	Karmarama Communications
Matt Box	George P Johnson Experience Marketing (UK)
Matt Buttrick	Grey London
Matt Gladstone	Grey London
Nic Pietersma	Ebiquity
Oliver Pople	Grey London
Rachel Walker	WRCS
Ray Sylvester	Anderson University (IN)
Rebecca Clay	PHD
Robin Forrester	IPA

Rosa Stanley	WRCS
Sharon Whale	Oliver
Signe Jost	Bolia.com
Sophie Somers	John Lewis & Partners
Stephen Tisdalle	State Street Global Advisors
Tim Elkington	IAB UK
Tom Patterson	Now
Vasileios Kourakis	L'Oréal UK
Will Hodge	Karmarama Communications

Other organisations

In addition to the named individuals there are several organisations who have provided images, case studies, support, or their permission which has enriched our book. These include Affinity, Bolia.com, Channel 4, Costa, John Lewis, L'Oréal Paris, Narellan Pools, Sixt, WARC, Emirates, Cannes Lions.

The list of individuals and organisations involved with this book is extensive. We have tried to list everyone but if anyone has been omitted then we offer our sincere apologies.

Many people have given their time and energies either to writing or cajoling others to write Cases and Viewpoints for this edition. The fruits of their labour are on show here and we would like to express our gratitude to you all for your support. These contemporary insights into practice make this book unique.

Above all, we would like to thank the team at Pearson and their associates who have taken our manuscript, managed it and published it in this form. In particular, we would like to thank Eileen Srebernik, Editor, Business & Economics, for her continued support with this book. We would also like to thank Anita Atkinson and her production team for successfully managing the project. Thank you all.

Publisher's acknowledgements

Text

9 Procter & Gamble: Tagline of Ariel, Procter & Gamble. **10 Taylor & Francis Group:** Rossiter, J.R. and Percy, L. (2013) Observations: How the roles of advertising merely appear to have changed, *International Journal of Advertising*, 32(3), 391–98. **11 Pearson Education:** *From Essentials of Marketing Communications*, Pearson Education (Fill, C. 2011) figure 1.3, p. 10, reproduced by permission of Pearson Education Ltd. **13 Westburn Publishers Ltd:** From Redefining the nature and format of the marketing communications mix, *The Marketing Review*, 7 (1), 45–57 (Hughes, G. and Fill, C. 2007), reproduced by permission of Westburn Publishers Ltd. **15 Badger & Winters:** Tagline of Badger & Winters. **15 Emerald Publishing Limited:** Andersson, P. (1992) Analysing distribution channel dynamics, *European Journal of Marketing*, 26(2), 47–68. **25 State Street Global Advisors:** Stephen Tisdalle, Chief Marketing Officer, State Street Global Advisors. **36 Forbes Media LLC:** Sicular, S. (2013) Gartner's Big Data Definition Consists of Three Parts, Not to Be Confused with Three "V"s, *Forbes*, 27 May. Retrieved 3 July 2017 from https://www.forbes.com/sites/gartnergroup/2013/03/27/gartners-big-data-definition-consists-of-three-parts-not-to-be-confused-with-three-vs/#3cd0a72c42f6 **37 Garry King:** Gary King, 2017. **42 American Marketing Association:** Holbrook, M.B. (1987) Mirror, mirror, on the wall, what's unfair in the reflections on advertising? *Journal of Marketing*, 51 (July), 95–103. **46 Pearson Education:** *Longman Business English Dictionary*, p 15, Pearson Education Limited. **65 American Marketing Association:** Park, E., Rishika, R., Janakiraman, R., Houston, M.B., and Yoo, B. (2018) Social dollars in online communities: the effect of product, user, and network characteristics, *Journal of Marketing*, 82, (January), 93–114. **65 Crowell-Collier Publishing Company:** Theodorson, S.A. and Theodorson, G.R. (1969) *A Modern Dictionary of Sociology*, New York: Cromwell. **67 Matt Buttrick:** Matt Buttrick – Planning Director at Grey London. **71 Rowman & Littlefield Publishing Group:** Mallen, B. (1977) *Principles of Marketing Channel Management*, Lexington, MA: Lexington Books. **72 Pearson Education:** *From Essentials of Marketing Communications*, Pearson Education (Fill, C. 2011) figure 2.2, p. 39. **72 Pearson Education**: *From Essentials of Marketing Communications*, Pearson Education (Fill, C. 2011) figure 2.4, p. 41. **73 Pearson Education:** *From Essentials of Marketing Communications*, Pearson Education (Fill, C. 2011) figure 2.3, p. 39. **74 Bilyana Petrova:** Bilyana Petrova, an Account Manager at J. Walter Thompson, Brussels. **77 The University of Chicago Press:** Hamilton, R., Vohs, K.D. and McGill, A.L. (2014) We'll be honest, this won't be the best article you'll ever read: the use of dispreferred markers in word-of-mouth communications, *Journal of Consumer Research*, 41, June, 197–212. **77 Emerald Publishing Limited:** Stokes, D. and Lomax, W. (2002) Taking control of word of mouth marketing: the case of an entrepreneurial hotelier, *Journal of Small Business and Enterprise Development*, 9(4), 349–57. **77 John Wiley & Sons, Inc:** Kawakami, T., Kishiya, K. and Parry, M.E. (2014) Personal word of mouth, virtual word of mouth and innovation use, *Journal of Product Innovation Management*, 30(1), 17–30. **78 Emerald Publishing Limited:** Mazzarol, T., Sweeney, J.C. and Soutar, G.N. (2007) Conceptualising word-of-mouth activity, triggers and conditions: an exploratory study, *European Journal of Marketing*, 41(11/12), 1475–94. **78 The European Marketing Academy:** Helm, S. and Schlei, J. (1998) Referral potential –potential referrals:

an investigation into customers' communication in service markets, *Proceedings of 27th EMAC Conference, Marketing Research and Practice*, 41–56. **79 Simon & Schuster:** Rogers, E.M. (1962) *Diffusion of Innovations*, 1st edn, New York: Free Press. **82 SAGE:** Haenlein, M. and Libai, B. (2017) Seeding, referral, and recommendation: creating profitable word-of-mouth programs, *California Management Review*, 59(2), 68–91. **83 Taylor & Francis Group:** Branchik, B.J. and Chowdhury, T.G. (2017) Men seeing stars: celebrity endorsers, race, and the male consumer, *Journal of Marketing Theory and Practice*, 25(3), Summer, 305–22. **83 Oxford University Press:** McCracken, G. (1989) Who is the celebrity endorser? Cultural foundations of the endorsement process, *Journal of Consumer Research*, 16 (December), 310–21. **84 Journal of Marketing Theory and Practice:** Adapted from Branchik, B.J. and Chowdhury, T.G. (2017) Men seeing stars: celebrity endorsers, race, and the male consumer, *Journal of Marketing Theory and Practice*, 25(3), Summer, 305–22. **88 Simon & Schuster:** Rogers, E.M. (1986) *Communication Technology: The New Media in Society*, New York: Free Press. **91 McGraw-Hill Companies:** From Hawkins et al. (1989) *Consumer Behavior: Implications for Marketing Strategy* (9780256063318), 4th edn. Used with permission of the McGraw-Hill Companies. **93 Emily Ellis:** Emily Ellis – McCann London Vasileios Kourakis – L'Oreal UK. **101 Stuart Hogg:** Hogg, S. (2018) Customer journey mapping: The path to loyalty, *Think with Google*, February, retrieved 23 February 2018 from https://www.thinkwithgoogle.com/marketing-resources/experience-design/customer-journey-mapping/ **101 McKinsey & Company:** Exhibit from "The consumer decision journey", June 2009, *McKinsey Quarterly*, www.mckinsey.com. Copyright (c) 2018 McKinsey & Company. All rights reserved. Reprinted by permission. **102 McKinsey & Company:** Exhibit from "The consumer decision journey", June 2009, McKinsey Quarterly, www.mckinsey.com. Copyright (c) 2018 McKinsey & Company. All rights reserved. Reprinted by permission. **102 Harvard Business School Publishing:** Rawson, A., Duncan, E. and Jones, C. (2013) The truth about customer experience, *Harvard Business Review*, September, 90–98, retrieved 21 August 2014 from http://hbr.org/2013/09/the-truth-about-customer-experience/ **102 McKinsey & Company:** Edleman and Singer, M. (2015) The new consumer decision journey, *McKinsey Quarterly*, October, retrieved 13 July 2017, from http://www.mckinsey.com/business-functions/marketing-and-sales/our-insights/the-new-consumer-decision-journey **103 McKinsey & Company:** Exhibit from "The new consumer decision journey", October 2015, McKinsey & Company, www.mckinsey.com. Copyright (c) 2018 McKinsey & Company. All rights reserved. Reprinted by permission. **105 McGraw-Hill:** Hawkins, D., Best, R. and Coney, K. (1989) *Consumer Behaviour*, Homewood, IL: Richard D. Irwin. **120 Pearson Education:** From *Essentials of Marketing Communications*, Pearson Eduaction (Fill, C.2011) figure 3.5, p. 72. **120 Pearson Education:** From *Essentials of Marketing Communications*, Pearson Eduaction (Fill, C. 2011) figure 3.6, p. 72. **121 Pearson Education:** From *Essentials of Marketing Communications*, Pearson Eduaction (Fill, C.2011) figure 3.7, p. 74. **125 Pearson Education:** Webster, F.E. and Wind, Y. (1972) *Organisational Buying Behaviour*, Englewood Cliffs, NJ: Prentice Hall. **127 Pearson Education:** Based on Webster, F.E. and Wind, Y. (1972) *Organisational Buying Behaviour*, Englewood Cliffs, NJ: Prentice Hall. **127 B2B Marketing:** Anon (2017) How Tate & Lyle Sugars achieved ROI of 183% on its campaign to reach decision-makers with its new range of beverage syrups, *B2B Marketing*, 16 November. Retrieved 20 August 2018 from https://www.b2bmarketing.net/en-gb/resources/b2b-case-studies/awards-case-study-how-tate-lyle-sugars-achieved-roi-183-its-campaign **130 Matt Gladstone:** By Grey London Principal Authors: Rachel Walker and Oliver Pople Contributing Author: Matt Gladstone. **138 Allied Business Academies:** Bahmanziari, T. and Odom, M.D. (2015) Prospect theory and risky choice in the ecommerce setting: evidence of a framing effect, *Academy of Accounting and Financial Studies Journal*, 19(1), 85–106. **144 Nestlé:** KitKat. **146 Taylor & Francis Group:** Liu, X., Burns, A. C., Hou, Y. (2017) An Investigation of Brand-Related User-Generated Content on Twitter, *Journal of Advertising*, 46(2), 236–47. **147 American Marketing Association:** Hirschmann, E.C. and Holbrook, M.B. (1982)

Hedonic consumption: emerging concepts, methods and propositions, *Journal of Marketing*, 46 (Summer), 92–101. **151 Association for Consumer Research:** Cooper-Martin, E. and Holbrook, M.B. (1993) Ethical consumption experiences and ethical space, *Advances in Consumer Research,* 20(1), 113–18. **151 Springer:** Szmigin, I., Carrigan, M., O 'Loughlin, D.O. (2007) Integrating ethical brands into our consumption lives, *Brand Management*, 14(5), May, 396–409. **152 Sage:** Maffesoli, M. (1996) *The Time of Tribes*, London: Sage. **154 Taylor & Francis Group:** Hamilton, K. and Hewer, P. (2010) Tribal mattering spaces: social-networking sites, celebrity affiliations, and tribal innovations, *Journal of Marketing Management,* 26(3–4), 271–89. **154 Harvard Business School Publishing:** Ariely, D. (2009) The end of rational economics, *Harvard Business Review*, July–August, 78–84. **154 Unilever:** Persil. **158 Institute for Government:** MINDSPACE, Influencing behaviour through public policy, Institute for Government. https://38r8om2xjhhl25mw24492dir-wpengine. netdna-ssl.com/wp-content/uploads/2015/07/MINDSPACE.pdf **160 IPA Advertising Effectiveness Awards:** This case study is an edited version of a paper submitted to the IPA Advertising Effectiveness Awards 2016. It has been reproduced here with the kind permission of the IPA, WARC, and Ogilvy and Mather. **170 Rebecca Clay:** Rebecca Clay, Media Director at PHD. **171 GfK Verein:** Kozinets, R.V. (2014) Social brand engagement: a new idea, GfK *Marketing Intelligence Review*, 6(2), November, 8–15. **172 GfK Verein:** Kozinets, R. V. (2014). Social Brand Engagement: A New Idea, GfK *Marketing Intelligence Review*, 6(2), 8–15. doi: https://doi.org/10.2478/gfkmir-2014-0091 **172 The Advertising Research Foundation:** Schivinski, B., Christodoulides, G. and Dabrowski, D., (2016) Measuring consumers' engagement with brand-related social-media content: development and validation of a scale that identifies levels of social-media engagement with brands, *Journal of Advertising Research*, 56(1), 1–18. **183 Springer Verlag:** Day, G. (2000) Managing market relationships, *Journal of the Academy of Marketing Science*, 28, 1, Winter, 24–30. **183 Pearson Education:** *From Essentials of Marketing Communications*, Pearson Education (Fill, C. 2011) table 8.1, p. 190. **185 B2B Marketing:** Anon (2017) How Fujitsu's sales/marketing success helped establish a key client partnership, *B2B Marketing Awards*, 16 November. Retrieved 24 December 2017 from https://www.b2bmarketing.net/en-gb/resources/b2b-case-studies/awards-case-study-how-fujitsus-salesmarketing-success-helped-establish **188 UBM Company:** CMI (2015) What is content marketing? Content Marketing Institute, retrieved 17 February 2015 from http://contentmarketinginstitute.com/what-is-content-marketing/ **188 Millward Brown UK Ltd.:** Brown, G. (1991) *How Advertising Affects the Sales of Packaged Goods Brands*, Warwick: Millward Brown, Used with kind permission. **191 McGraw-Hill:** Olsen, J.C. and Peter, J.P. (1987) *Consumer Behavior,* Homewood, IL: Irwin. **192 McGraw-Hill:** Belch, G.E. and Belch, M.A. (2004) *Advertising and Promotion: An Integrated Marketing communications Perspective*, 6th edn, Homewood, IL: Richard D. Irwin. **193 Emerald Publishing Limited:** Goldsmith, R.E. and Lafferty, B.A. (2002) Consumer response to websites and their influence on advertising effectiveness, *Internet Research: Electronic Networking Applications and Policy*, 12(4), 318–28. **194 University of Bath School of Management:** Heath, R. and Feldwick, P. (2008) 50 years using the wrong model of TV advertising, *International Journal of Market Research*, 50(1), 29–59. **194 Sage Publishing:** Witkin, H.A., Moore, C.A., Goodenough, D.R. and Cox, P.W. (1977) Field dependent and field independent cognitive styles and their educational implications, *Review of Educational Research*, 47, 1–64. **194 Sage Journals:** Heath, R., Hyder, P. (2005) Measuring the hidden power of emotive advertising, *International Journal of Market Research*, 47(5), 467–86. **197 Mathew Waksman:** Will Hodge-Karmarama Communications. **209 Emerald Publishing Limited:** Beane, T.P. and Ennis, D.M. (1987) Market segmentation: a review, *European Journal of Marketing*, 21(5), 20–42. **210 Haymarket Media:** Based on Edwards, H. (2011) Work towards an 'Ideal Self', *Marketing*, 2 February, p. 21. **213 Pearson Education:** *From Essentials of Marketing Communications*, Pearson Education (Fill, c. 2011) figure 4.2, p. 99. **214 Fidor Bank:** Fidor Bank Slogan. **215 Pearson Education:**

From Essentials of Marketing Communications, Pearson Education (Fill, c. 2011) figure 4.3, p. 102. **216 Pearson Education:** *From Essentials of Marketing Communications*, Pearson Education (Fill, c. 2011) figure 4.4, p. 102. **219 Honda:** Honda's Tagline. **219 Johnnie Walker's:** Johnnie Walker's Tagline. **234 Fermín Paús:** Fermín Paús, Sr Brand Manager at Danone. **247 NTC Business Books:** Dutka, S. (1995) *Defining Advertising Goals for Measured Advertising Results,* 2nd edn, New York: Association of National Advertisers. **252 Tom Patterson:** Petplan uses explicit objectives By Tom Patterson – a Planner at Now **259 Emerald Group Publishing:** Herstein, R. and Mitki, Y. (2008) How El Al Airlines transformed its service strategy with employee participation, *Strategy & Leadership*, 36(3), 21–5. **259 Neal:** Neal (1980). **262 Revlon:** Revlon Slogan. **273 The Incorporated Society of British Advertisers Ltd:** The ISBA In-House Agency Survey 2017. **274 Sharon Whale:** Sharon Whale, Chief Executive Officer UK Group, Oliver. **274 The Incorporated Society of British Advertisers Ltd:** The ISBA In-House Agency Survey 2017. **275 WARC:** WARC (2018). Used with permission from WARC. **276 Alan Mitchell:** Mitchell, A. (2012) Face it, your consumers hate you, *Marketing*, 28 March 2012, 30–2. **278 IPA:** IPA (2015) Admission. Industry Guide. IPA, retrieved 10 May 2015 from www.theadmission.co.uk/industry-guide **289 Nielsen:** Nielsen, cited by Tan (2018). **293 Harvard Business School Publishing:** From Ad spending: growing market share, *Harvard Business Review* January/February, pp. 44–8 (Schroer, J. 1990), Reprinted by permission of *Harvard Business Review*. Copyright (c) 1990 by Harvard Business School Publishing Corporation; all rights reserved. **293 Harvard Business School Publishing:** Jones, J.P. (1990) Ad spending: maintaining market share, *Harvard Business Review*, January/February, 38–42. **294 Harvard Business School Publishing (HBSP):** From Ad spending: maintaining market share, *Harvard Business Review* January/February, pp. 38–42 (Jones, J.P. 1990), Reprinted by permission of Harvard Business Review. Copyright (c) 1990 by Harvard Business School Publishing Corporation; all rights reserved. **294 Emerald Publishing Limited:** West, D. and Prendergast, G.P. (2009) Advertising and promotions budgeting and the role of risk, *European Journal of Marketing*, 43(11/12), 1457–76. **305 Institute of Practitioners in Advertising (IPA):** IPA (2014) *How to Evaluate the Effectiveness of Communications Plans*, IPA .**306 WARC:** Lee, D.H. and Park, C.W. (2007) Conceptualization and measurement of multidimensionality of integrated marketing communications, *Journal of Advertising Research*, 47(3), 222–36. Used with permission from WARC. **309 Dr Sarah Turnbull:** Turnbull, S. (2011) The creative development process within U.K. advertising agencies: an exploratory study, Unpublished PhD Thesis, University of Portsmouth. **312 McGraw-Hill:** Based on Peter M Chisnall, *Marketing Research 7e*, p. 228–31, McGraw-Hill, 2005. **318 WARC:** Gordon, W. (1992) Ad pre-testing's hidden maps, *Admap*, June, 23–7. **320 International Association for Measurement and Evaluation of Communication:** Reproduced by kind permission of the International Association for Measurement and Evaluation of Communication (AMEC). **321 International Association for Measurement and Evaluation of Communication:** AMEC (2015). Changes from the original Barcelona Principles 2010 to the Barcelona Principles 2015. AMEC. Reproduced by kind permission of the International Association for Measurement and Evaluation of Communication (AMEC) Retrieved 10 January 2018 from https://amecorg.com/how-the-barcelona-principles-have-been-updated/ **322 International Association for Measurement and Evaluation of Communication:** Reproduced from Macnamara, J. (2014) Breaking the PR measurement and evaluation deadlock: a new approach and model, AMEC International Summit on Measurement, 'Upping the Game', Amsterdam, 11–2. Reproduced by kind permission of the International Association for Measurement and Evaluation of Communication (AMEC). **322 Jim Macnamara:** *Evaluating Public Communication: Exploring New Models, Standards, and Best Practice*, Jim Macnamara, Routledge 2017. **323 Academy of Management:** Pearson, C.M. and Mitroff, I. (1993) From crisis prone to crisis prepared: a framework for crisis management, *Academy of Management Executive*, 7(1), 48–59. **325 Institute of Practitioners in Advertising (IPA):** IPA (2014) *How to Evaluate the Effectiveness of Communications Plans*, IPA **326 Tim Elkington:** By Tim Elkington, Chief

Digital Officer, IAB UK. **328 WARC:** WARC/MMA (2017). The State of the Industry: Mobile Marketing in EMEA 2017. Retrieved 10 February 2018 from https://www.warc.com/content/article/the_state_of_the_industry_mobile_marketing_in_emea_2017/111576 **329 Adjust GmbH, adjust Inc:** Mobile Application Advertising Measurement Guidelines (2017). **331 Christine Moorman:** Moorman, C. (2015). CMO Survey report: highlights and insights. Retrieved 5 May 2018 from https://cmosurvey.org/wpcontent/uploads/sites/15/2017/04/The_CMO_Survey-Highlights_and_Insights-Aug-2015.pdf **331 WARC:** Buckley, E. (2013) The business return from social media, *Admap,* retrieved 10 April 2015 from www.warc.com/Content/ContentViewer.aspx?MasterContentRef=24ca6283–696c-4822-9dd4-dc62db9807b3&q=the+business+return+for+social+media&CID=A99742&PUB=ADMAP **332 Taylor & Francis Group:** Murdough, C. (2009) Social media measurement: it's not impossible, *Journal of Interactive Advertising,* 10(1), 94–9. Used with the kind permission of the Academy of Marketing. **341 Sage Publishing:** Chernatony de, L. (2009) Towards the holy grail of defining 'brand', *Marketing Theory,* 9(1), 101–5. **344 John Wiley & Sons, Inc:** Cohen, R.J. (2014) Brand personification: introduction and overview, *Psychology and Marketing,* 31(1), 1–30. **346 Kogan Page:** Jean-Noël Kapferer, *The New Strategic Brand Management,* 9780749465155, p259, Kogan Page (Kapferer, J.-N. 2012). **348 Emerald Publishing Limited:** Arora, R. and Stoner, C. (2009) A mixed method approach to understanding brand personality, *Journal of Product & Brand Management,* 18(4), 272–83. **354 American Marketing Association:** Brakus, J.J., Scmitt, B.H. and Zarantonello, L. (2009) Brand experience: what is it? How is it measured? Does it affect loyalty? *Journal of Marketing,* 73 (May), 52–68. **356 Taylor & Francis Group:** Keller, K.L. (2009) Building strong brands in a modern marketing communications environment, *Journal of Marketing Communications,* 15(2–3), 139–55 Used with permission. **357 Taylor & Francis Group:** Keller, K.L. (2009) Building strong brands in a modern marketing communications environment, *Journal of Marketing Communications,* 15(2–3), 139–55. **360 California State University:** Bizzi, L. (2018). The hidden problem of Facebook and social media at work: What if employees start searching for other jobs? *Business Horizons,* 61(1), 23–33. Mihaylo College of Business & Economics, California State University, Fullerton, 800 N. State College Blvd., Fullerton, CA, U.S.A. **361 Emerald Group Publishing Limited:** Mary Welch, Paul R. Jackson, (2007) Rethinking internal communication: a stakeholder approach, *Corporate Communications: An International Journal,* 12(2), 177–98, https://doi.org/10.1108/13563280710744847 **361 International Association of Business Communicator:** Grossman, R. (2005) Sometimes it pays to play the fool, *Business Communicator,* 6, 3. **362 Mentor Books:** McLuhan, M. (1964) *Understanding Media: The Extensions of Man,* New York: Mentor. **362 Taylor & Francis Group:** White, C., Vanc, A. and Stafford, G. (2010) Internal communications, information satisfaction, and sense of community: the effect of personal influence, *Journal of Public Relations Research,* 22(1), 65–84. **364 American Marketing Association:** Keller, K. L. (1993). Conceptualizing, measuring, and managing customer-based brand equity. *Journal of Marketing,* 1–22. **364 Simon & Schuster:** David, A. (1991). Managing brand equity. Capitalizing on the value of a brand name. New York: The Free Press. **365 Sage Publishing:** Feldwick, P. (1996) What is brand equity anyway, and how do you measure it? *Journal of Market Research,* 38(2), 85–104. **365 Millward Brown:** Adapted from Haigh (1997), Millward Brown (2018) and Pirrie (2006). **368 Rachel Walker:** McVitie's: Waking the sleeping giant by Principal author: Daniel Sherrard Contributing Authors: Rachel Walker, Matt Gladstone **377 Taylor & Francis Group:** Kliatchko, J.G. and Shultz, D.E. (2014) Twenty years of IMC, *International Journal of Advertising,* 33(2), 373–90. **378 Taylor & Francis Group:** Kerr, G. and Patti, C. (2015) Strategic IMC: From abstract concept to marketing management tool, *Journal of Marketing Communications,* 21(5), 317–39. **378 Emerald Publishing Limited:** Eagle, L., Kitchen, P.J. and Bulmer, S. (2007), Insights into interpreting integrated marketing communications: a two-nation qualitative comparison, *European Journal of Marketing,* 41(7/8), 956–70. **378 Taylor & Francis Group:** Luxton, S., Reid, M., and Mavondo, F. (2015) Integrated marketing communication capability and brand performance, *Journal of Advertising,* 44(1), 37–46. **385 Henry Stewart Publications:** Bird, J. (2016) Switching off TV, turning on touchpoints: New ways to communicate in a new world, *Journal of Brand Strategy,* 5(3), Winter, 266–74. **386 Emerald Publishing Limited:** Melewar, T.C., Foroudi, P., Gupta, S., Kitchen, P.J., Foroudi, M.M. (2017) Integrating identity, strategy and communications for trust, loyalty and commitment, *European Journal of Marketing,* 51(3), 572–604. **389 Taylor & Francis Group:** Kliatchko, J.G. and Shultz, D.E. (2014) Twenty years of IMC, *International Journal of Advertising,* 33(2), 373–90. **389 Journal of Marketing:** Batra, R. and Keller, K.L. (2016) Integrating marketing communications: new findings, new lessons, and new ideas, *Journal of Marketing*: AMA/MSI Special Issue, 80, (November), 122–45. **393 MHE:** Schultz (1993: 17), *Integrated Marketing Communications,* 1993, McGraw Hill Professional. **393 A-B, Budweiser:** Budweiser tagline. **394 Taylor & Francis Group:** Kliatchko, J. (2008) Revisiting the IMC construct: a revised definition and four pillars, *International Journal of Advertising,* 27(1), 133–60. **395 Institute of Practitioners in Advertising (IPA):** IPA (2011) *New Models of Marketing Effectiveness: From Integration to Orchestration,* WARC.(2011). **399 Emerald Publishing Limited:** Finne, A. and Grönroos, C. (2017) Communication-in-use: customer-integrated marketing communication, *European Journal of Marketing,* 51(3), 445–63. **401 Crain Communications Inc:** www.adage.com/lp/top15/#introw **403 Elly Fenlon:** Elly Fenlon, AMV BBDO. **417 Taylor & Francis Group:** Richards, J.I. and Curran, C. M. (2002) Oracles on 'advertising': searching for a definition, *Journal of Advertising,* 31(2), 63–77. **417 Taylor & Francis Group:** Richards and Curran (2002). **417 Mobile Marketing Association:** MMA (2015) The mobile native ad formats, *Mobile Marketing Association,* retrieved 1 June 2015 from www.mmaglobal.com/files/documents/the_mobile_native_ formats_final.pdf **420 Pearson Education:** Adapted from De Pelsmacker, P., Geuens, M. and Van Den Berg, J. (2016). *Marketing Communications. A European Perspective* (6th ed). Pearson Education. **422 Association for Consumer Research:** Based on John T. Cacioppo and Richard E. Petty (1984), "The elaboration likelihood model of persuasion", in NA – *Advances in Consumer Research Volume 11,* eds. Thomas C. Kinnear, Provo, UT: Association for Consumer Research, Pages: 673–75. **428 WARC:** Ehrenberg, A.S.C. (1997) How do consumers come to buy a new brand? *Admap,* March, 20–4. **431 WARC:** Vaughn, R. (1980) How advertising works: a planning model, *Journal of Advertising Research,* October, 27–33. **432 Professor John R. Rossiter:** Adapted from Rossiter and Percy (1997). Used with kind permission. **434 Apple Inc:** Apple Tagline. **435 International Journal of Hospitality Management.:** Shulga, L. V., Busser, J. A., & Bai, B. (2018). Factors affecting willingness to participate in consumer generated advertisement. *International Journal of Hospitality Management.* **436 California Management Review:** Based on Berthon, P.R., Pitt, L. F. and Campbell, C. (2008) 'Ad lib: when customers create the ad', *California Management Review,* 50(4), 6–30. **436 Taylor & Francis Group:** Campbell, C., Pitt, L.F., Parent, M. and Berthon, P.R. (2011) Understanding consumer conversations around ads in a Web 2.0 world, *Journal of Advertising,* 40(1), 87–102. **438 Lars Samuelsen:** By Lars Samuelsen, Matthew Gladstone, Mark Stockdale. **446 CIPR Public Relations Centre:** CIPR (2018). FAQs. CIPR.co.uk. Retrieved 20 May 2018 from https://www.cipr.co.uk/content/policy/ policy/lobbying/faqs **446 Houghton, Mifflin Company:** Grunig, J. and Hunt, T. (1984) *Managing Public Relations,* New York: Holt, Rineholt & Winston. **446 Pearson Education:** Cutlip, S.M., Center, A.H. and Broom, G.M. (1994) *Effective Public Relations,* Englewood Cliffs, NJ: Prentice Hall. **448 Elsevier:** Gregory, A. (2004) Scope and structure of public relations: a technology driven view, *Public Relations Review,* 30(3), 245–54. **450 James E. Grunig:** Grunig, J. and Hunt, T. (1984) *Managing Public Relations,* New York: Holt, Rineholt & Winston. Used with kind permission. **452 Taylor & Francis:** Seong-Hun Yun (2006) Toward public relations theory-based study of public diplomacy: testing the applicability of the excellence study, *Journal of Public Relations Research,* 18(4), 287–312, DOI: 10.1207/ s1532754xjprr1804_1 **453 Harriet Rich:** Pestaurant by Harriet Rich, Joint Managing Director, Brands2Life. **461 International Thomson Press:** Moloney, K. (1997) Government and lobbying activities, in *Public Relations: Principles and Practice* (ed. P.J. Kitchen), London: International Thomson Press. **462 CIPR Public Relations Centre:** CIPR (2018). FAQs. CIPR. co.uk. Retrieved 20 May 2018 from https://www.cipr.co.uk/content/policy/policy/lobbying/ faqs **462 John Wiley & Sons, Inc:** Hill, M.D., Kelly, G.W., Lockhart, G.B. and Ness, R.A. (2013) Determinants and effects of corporate lobbying, Financial Management, 42(4), 931–57. **462 Springer:** Bauer, T. (2014) Responsible lobbying: a multidimensional model, *Journal of Corporate Citizenship*, 14(53), 64. **463 Emerald Publishing Limited:** Strauss, N. (2018). The role of trust in investor relations: a conceptual framework. *Corpo-rate Communications: An International Journal*, in-press. **463 Pearson Education:** Cutlip, S.M., Center, A.H. and Broom, G.M. (1999) *Effective Public Relations*, 8th edn, Englewood Cliffs, NJ: Prentice Hall. **463 The Investor Relations Society:** UK Investor Relations Society (2018) retrieved 23 March 2011 from www.ir-soc.org.uk/ **468 BBC:** BBC. **468 Local World:** Corn-wallLive. **468 Herald & Times Group:** The Herald. **469 National Trust:** Lanhydrock National Trust. **471 Palgrave Macmillan Ltd:** Coombs, W.T. (2007) Protecting organization reputa-tions during a crisis: the development and application of situational crisis communications theory, *Corporate Reputation Review* 10(3), 163–76. **483 WARC:** Based on Poon, D.T.Y., Prendergast, G. and West, D. (2010) Match game: linking sponsorship congruence with communication outcomes, *Journal of Advertising Research*, 4(80), 214–26. **486 Psychology & Marketing:** Meenaghan, T., McLoughlin, D. and McCormack, A. (2013) New challenges in sponsorship evaluation actors, new media, and the context of praxis, *Psychology & Marketing*, 30(5), 444–60. **486 IEG Sponsorship Report:** Esp Properties Special Report (2018). What Sponsors Want & Where Dollars Will Go in 2018. IEG Sponsorship Report. Retrieved 15 January 2018 from http://www.sponsorship.com/IEG/files/f3/f3cfac41-2983-49be-8df6-3546345e27de.pdf **491 Elsevier:** Based on Farrelly, F., Quester, P. and Burton, R. (2006) Changes in sponsorship value: competencies and capabilities of successful spon-sorship relationships, *Industrial Marketing Management*, 35(8), November, 1016–26. **493 James M. Crick:** By James M. Crick Lecturer, Loughborough University. **495 Vodafone Group Plc:** Vodafone (2017). Vodafone Comedy Festival unveils its most exciting and diverse line-up yet! 14 June, Retrieved 10 December 2017 from https://n.vodafone.ie/ aboutus/press/vodafone-comedy-festival-unveils-its-most-exciting-and-diverse-line-up-yet. html **498 IEG Sponsorship Report:** Burton and Chadwick (2017) Used with permission: http://www.sponsorship.com/IEG/files/f3/f3cfac41-2983-49be-8df6-3546345e27de.pdf **511 Pearson Education:** *From Essentials of Marketing Communications*, Pearson Educa-tion (Fill, C. 2011) figure 11.1, p. 280. **513 EUGDPR.org:** eu.gdpr (2018).GDPR Key Changes. Retrieved 2 May 2018 from https://www.eugdpr.org/key-changes.html **532 Emerald Publishing Limited:** Brehmer, P.O. and Rehme, J. (2009) Proactive and reactive: drivers for key account management programmes, *European Journal of Marketing*, 43(7/8), 961–84. **532 Emerald Group Publishing Ltd:** Brehmer, P.O. and Rehme, J. (2009) Proactive and reactive: drivers for key account management programmes, *European Journal of Mar-keting*, 43(7/8), 961–84. **533 John Wiley & Sons:** Hennessey, D.H. and Jeannet, J.-P. (2003) *Global Account Management: Creating Value*, Chichester: Wiley. **535 Direct Line Group:** Carl Bratton (Direct Line Group); Ann Constantine (Direct Line Group); Nic Pietersma (Ebiq-uity). **544 Butterworth-Heinemann:** Peattie, S. and Peattie, K.J. (1994) Sales promotion, in *The Marketing Book* (ed. M.J. Baker), 3rd edn, London: Butterworth-Heinemann. **545 Emerald Publishing Limited:** Lee, C.H. (2002) Sales promotions as strategic communica-tions: the case of Singapore, *Journal of Product and Brand Management*, 11(2), 103–14. **546 American Marketing Association:** Guyt, J.Y. and Gijsbrechts, E. (2014) Take turns or march in sync? The impact of the National Brand promotion calendar on manufacturer and retailer performance, *Journal of Marketing Research*, LI (December), 753–72. **547 Mars, Incorporated:** Snickers Tagline. **552 American Marketing Association:** Stilley, K.M., Inman, J.J. and Wakefield, K.L. (2010b) Spending on the fly: mental budgets, promotions, and spending behavior, *Journal of Marketing*, 74(3), 34–47. **559 Palgrave Macmillan:** Based on Hallberg, G. (2004) Is your loyalty programme really building loyalty?

Why increasing emotional attachment, not just repeat buying, is key to maximizing programme success, *Journal of Targeting Measurement and Analysis for Marketing*, 12(3), 231–41.Hallberg (2004). **561 Haymarket Media:** Adapted from McLuhan, R. (2000) Fighting for a new view of field work, *Marketing*, 9 March, 29–30. Reproduced from Marketing magazine with the permission of the copyright owner, Haymarket Business Publications Limited. **561 Elsevier:** Drèze, X., Hoch, S.J. and Purk, M.E. (1994) Shelf management and space elasticity, *Journal of Retailing*, 70(4), 301–26. **565 Guardian Media Group:** Behrman, D. (2012) Work: better business: acts of kindness, *Guardian*, 13 April, 2. **566 Andrew Orr:** By Andrew Orr, Client Services Director, TRO. **578 Taylor & Francis Group:** Chen, H. and Haley, E. (2014) Product placement in social games: consumer experiences in China, *Journal of Advertising*, 43(3), 286–95. **578 Westburn Publishers Ltd:** Kandhadai, R. and Saxena, R. (2014) Brand placement: new perspectives and a comprehensive definition, *The Marketing Review*, 14(3), 231–44. **579 Journal of Marketing Management:** Simon Hudson & David Hudson (2006) Branded entertainment: a new advertising technique or product placement in disguise?, *Journal of Marketing Management*, 22(5–6), 489–504, DOI: 10.1362/026725706777978703. Reproduced with permission. **590 Laurence King Publishing Ltd:** Stewart, B. (2007). *Packaging Design*, London, Laurence King. **591 Emerald Publishing Limited:** Wells, L.E., Farley, H. and Armstrong, G.A. (2007) The importance of packaging design for own-label food brands, *International Journal of Retail and Distribution Management*, 36(9), 677–90. **592 The Coca-Cola Company:** Coca-Cola Tagline. **594 Brand Licensing Europe:** Brand Licensing Europe (2018). Brand Licensing Handbook 2018, retrieved 20 February, 2018 from, https://ubm.brandlicensing.eu/licensinghandbook/ **594 The Marketing Management Association:** Ervelles, S., Horton, V. and Fukawa, N. (2008) Understanding B2C brand alliances between manufacturers and suppliers, *Marketing Management Journal*, 18(2), 32–46. **595 Sage Publishing:** Weidmann, K.-P. and Ludwig, D. (2008) How risky are brand licensing strategies in view of customer perceptions and reactions? *Journal of General Management*, 33(3), 31–52. **596 Dr Ray Sylvester Anderson:** Dr Ray Sylvester Anderson University, USA. **600 NFL Enterprises LLC:** NFL Enterprises LLC Tagline. **619 The Association:** Venkat, R. and Abi-Hanna, N. (1995) Effectiveness of visually shocking advertisements: is it context dependent? *Administrative Science Association of Canada Proceedings*, 16(3), 139–46. **619 Cambridge University Press:** Dahl, D.W., Frankenberger, K.D. and Manchanda, R.V. (2003) Does it pay to shock? Reactions to shocking and nonshocking advertising content among university students, *Journal of Advertising Research*, 43(3), 268–81. Used with kind permission from WARC. **625 Professor John R. Rossiter:** Rossiter, J.R. and Percy, L. (1997) *Advertising and Promotion Management*, 2nd edn, New York: McGraw-Hill. **628 Taylor & Francis Group:** Kim, B.H., Han, S. and Yoon, S. (2010) Advertising creativity in Korea: scale development and validation, *Journal of Advertising*, 39(2), 93–108. **629 Pearson Education:** Goodenough, W.H. (1981) *Culture, Language, and Society*, Menlo Park, CA: Benjamin/Cummings. **630 Emerald Publishing Limited:** Dan, V. and Ihlen, Ø. (2011) Framing expertise: a cross-cultural analysis of success in framing contests, *Journal of Communications Management*, 15(4), 368–88. **633 Journal of Consumer Marketing:** Based on Caroline Papadatos, (2006) The art of storytelling: how loyalty marketers can build emotional connections to their brands, *Journal of Consumer Marketing*, 23(7), 382–84, https://doi.org/10.1108/07363760610712902 Permanent link to this document: https://doi.org/10.1108/07363760610712902 **638 Adam&EveDDB:** This case is endorsed by Adam&EveDDB. **647 Taylor & Francis Group:** Sundar, S.S. and Limperos, A.M. (2013) Uses and Grats 2.0: new gratifications for new media, *Journal of Broadcasting and Electronic Media*, 57(4), 504–52. **650 Adweek:** Goodwin, T. (2014) Is vagueness killing advertising? *Adweek*, 30 November, retrieved 23 January 2015 from www.adweek.com/news/advertising-branding/vagueness-killing-advertising-161638 **650 Atchison Topeka and Santa Fe Limited:** England, E. and Finney, A. (2011) Interactive media – what's that? Who's involved? ATSF White Paper – Interactive Media UK, retrieved 27 October 2014 from www.atsf.co.uk/atsf/interactive_media.pdf **653 Taylor & Francis Group:** Vlasic, G.

and Kesic, T. (2007) Analysis of customers' attitudes toward interactivity and relationship personalization as contemporary developments in interactive marketing communications, *Journal of Marketing Communications*, 13(2), 109–29. **664 Millward Brown:** Fitch, D. (2007) Outdoor advertising, retrieved 20 January 2008 from www.millwardbrown.com/Sites/MillwardBrown/Content/News/EPerspectiveArticles.aspx?id=%2f200711010001 **673 Atchison Topeka and Santa Fe Limited:** England, E. and Finney, A. (2011) Interactive media – what's that? Who's involved? ATSF White Paper – Interactive Media UK, retrieved 27 October 2014 from www.atsf.co.uk/atsf/interactive_media.pdf **683 Taylor & Francis Group:** Boerman, S.C., Kruikemeier, S., and Borgesius, F.J.Z. (2017) Online behavioral advertising: a literature review and research agenda, *Journal of Advertising*, 46(3), 363–76. **687 Taylor & Francis Group:** Yang, M., Roskos-Ewoldsen, D.R., Dinu, L. and Arpen, L.M. (2006) The effectiveness of in-game advertising: comparing college students' explicit and implicit memory for brand names, *Journal of Advertising*, 35(4), 143–52. **688 Human Kinetics, Inc:** Hwang, Y., Ballouli, K., So, K., and Heere, B. (2017) Effects of brand congruity and game difficulty on gamers' response to advertising in sport video games, *Journal of Sport Management*, 31, 480–96. **688 Taylor & Francis, Ltd:** Cauberghe, V. and de Pelsmacker, P. (2010) Advergames: the impact of brand prominence and game repetition on brand responses, *Journal of Advertising*, 39(1), 5–18. **692 Search Engine Journal:** Davies, D. (2017) The death of organic search (as we know it), *Search Engine Journal*, 29 March. Retrieved 11 December 2017 from https://www.searchenginejournal.com/death-organic-search-know/189625/ **693 Elsevier:** Kietzmann, J.H., Hermkens, K., McCarthy, I.P. and Silvestre, B.S. (2011) Social media? Get serious! Understanding the functional building blocks of social media, *Business Horizons*, 54(3), 241–51. **693 Elsevier:** Kaplan, A.M. and Haelein, M. (2010) Users of the world unite! The challenges and op-portunities of social media, *Business Horizons*, 53, 59–68. **693 Elsevier:** Kietzmann, J.H., Hermkens, K., McCarthy, I.P. and Silvestre, B.S. (2011) Social media? Get serious! Understanding the functional building blocks of social media, *Business Horizons*, 54(3), 241–51. **700 Journal of Marketing Communications:** Based on Wood, N.T. and Burkhalter, J.N. (2014) Tweet this, not that: a comparison between brand promotions in microblogging environments using celebrity and company-generated tweets, *Journal of Marketing Communications*, 20(1–2), 129–46. **701 Red Herring Communications:** Juvertson, S. (2000) *What is Viral Marketing?* Draper Fisher Juvertson website, retrieved 12 March 2006 from www.dfj.com/cgi-bin/artman/publish/printer_steve_may00.shtml **701 John Wiley & Sons:** Eckler, R. and Rodgers, S. (2010) Viral advertising: a conceptualization. Paper presented at the Annual Meeting of the Association for Education in Journalism and Mass Communication, Denver, CO. **701 Fermín Paús:** Fermín Paús Formerly Soberana Sr. Brand Manager at Heineken. **704 Elsevier:** Fournier, S. and Avery, J. (2011) The uninvited brand, *Business Horizons*, 54, 193–207. **706 Westburn Publishers Ltd:** Dwivedi, Y.K., Rana, N.P., Alryalat, M.A.A. (2017) Affiliate marketing: An overview and analysis of emerging literature, *Marketing Review*, 17(1), Spring, 33–50. **707 Mary Ann Liebert, Inc:** Rosa, P.J., Morais, D., Gamito, P., Oliveira, J., and Saraiva, T. (2016) *The Immersive Virtual Reality Experience, Cyberpsychology, Behavior, and Social Networking*, 19(3), 209–16. **709 Hannah Smith:** Vizeum & Kerry Foods. **717 McGraw-Hill:** McLuhan, M. (1966) *Understanding Media: The Extensions of Man*, New York: McGraw-Hill. **717 McGraw-Hill:** McLuhan, M. (1966) *Understanding Media: The Extensions of Man*, New York: McGraw-Hill. **718 Eloise Augustine:** Eloise Augustine. **725 WARC:** Plessis, E. du (1998) Memory and likeability: keys to understanding ad effects, *Admap*, July/August, 42–6. **727 WARC:** Adapted from Ephron, E. (1997) Recency planning, *Admap*, February, 32–4. Used by permission of WARC. **728 The Nielsen Company:** Adapted from setting frequency levels: an art or a science?, *Marketing and Media decisions*, 24(4), pp. 9–11 (Ostrow, J.W. 1984), The Nielsen company. **731 WARC:** WARC (2013) Automated TV buying moves closer, retrieved 14 November 2014 from www.warc.com/LatestNews/News/Automated_TV_buying_moves_closer.news?ID=31820 **732 Kenneth Kulbok:** Kenneth Kulbok, LinkedIn Programmatic. **737 WARC:** Taylor, J., Kennedy, R., Mcdonald, C.,

Larguinat, L., El Ouarzazi, Y. and Haddad, N. (2013) Is the multi-platform whole more powerful than its separate parts? *Journal of Advertising Research*, 53(2), 200–11. **743 IPA:** IPA Effectiveness Awards 2016.It has been reproduced here with the kind permission of the IPA, WARC, Narellan Pools, and their agency who wrote the original paper.

Photographs

5 Transport Accident Commission: Used with permission from Transport Accident Commission. **6 Transport Accident Commission:** Used with permission from Transport Accident Commission. **9 Procter & Gamble:** Used with permission from Procter & Gamble. **16 All Paws Rescue NZ:** All Paws Rescue – Helping those in need no matter the breed! **23 Emirates SkyCargo:** Emirates SkyCargo. **25 State Street Global Advisors Media:** Sculpture by Kristen Visbal; commissioned by State Street Global Advisors. **26 State Street Global Advisors Media:** Sculpture by Kristen Visbal; commissioned by State Street Global Advisors. Façade used with permission of NYSE Group, Inc. **32 Shutterstock:** Andrew Krasovitckii/Shutterstock. **39 Shutterstock:** filip robert/Shutterstock. **44 Shutterstock:** Barry Barnes/Shutterstock. **47 Shutterstock:** Tomislav Pinter/Shutterstock. **53 Shutterstock:** Sohel Parvez Haque/Shutterstock. **57 Shutterstock:** Howard Davies/Alamy Stock Photo. **66 Shutterstock:** kurhan/Shutterstock. **68 British Heart Foundation:** British Heart Foundation. **69 British Heart Foundation:** British Heart Foundation. **76 Shutterstock:** Rawpixel.com/Shutterstock. **81 Shutterstock:** POC/Shutterstock. **85 Getty Images:** David M. Benett/Getty Images for Zoella Beauty. **86 Getty Images:** pixelfit/Getty Images. **93 Shutterstock:** MDOGAN/Shuttertsock. **94 Shutterstock:** Andrea Raffin/Shutterstock. **106 Alamy:** Emmanuel LATTES/Alamy Stock Photo. **107 Shutterstock:** gcpics/Shutterstock. **107 Shutterstock:** m.syafiq/Shutterstock. **108 Shutterstock:** g0d4ather/Shutterstock. **111 Alamy:** Carolyn Jenkins/Alamy Stock Photo. **122 Chipotle Mexican Grill:** Chipotle Mexican Grill. **131 Sixt rent a car:** Sixt rent a car. **131 Sixt rent a car:** Sixt rent a car. **139 McDonald's:** McDonald's. **148 Shutterstock:** Shutterstock. **149 Shutterstock:** Pecold/Shutterstock. **153 Morling Sthlm Ab:** Morling Sthlm Ab. **156 Department for Communities and Local Government:** Department for Communities and Local Government. **158 The Institute for Government:** The Institute for Government. **160 Shutterstock:** Serhii Krot/Shutterstock. **161 Crown copyright:** Help to Buy. **162 Crown copyright:** Help to Buy. **163 Crown copyright:** Help to Buy. **170 Alamy:** Clynt Garnham Food & Drink/Alamy Stock Photo. **178 Freepik:** Freepik.com **178 Shutterstock:** dovla982/Shutterstock. **182 Shutterstock:** Kinga/Shutterstock. **189 Alamy:** Justin Kase z12z/Alamy Stock Photo. **190 IKEA:** © Inter IKEA Systems B.V. **198 Costa Coffee:** Costa Coffee. **199 Costa Coffee:** Costa Coffee. **210 123RF:** faithie/123RF. **211 Getty Images:** Jamie McDonald/Getty Images. **214 Fidor Bank:** Fidor Bank. **217 Shutterstock:** Michal Zarzycki/Shutterstock. **220 Alamy:** Denis Michaliov/Alamy Stock Photo. **222 Shutterstock:** Ian Langsdon/EPA/Shutterstock. **230 Shutterstock:** S-F/Shutterstock. **234 Juan Camilo Gomez:** Juan Camilo Gomez. **235 Juan Camilo Gomez:** Juan Camilo Gomez. **243 123RF:** simon gurney/123RF. **252 Shutterstock:** Joe Pepler/Shutterstock. **256 Alamy:** Richard Levine/Alamy Stock Photo. **257 easyJet:** easyJet. **260 Getty Images:** Handout/Getty Images. **261 Getty Images:** Suhaimi Abdullah/Stringer/Getty Images. **262 Shutterstock:** Anton_Ivanov/Shutterstock. **263 Shutterstock:** Quanthem/Shutterstock. **267 Shutterstock:** Nor Gal/Shutterstock. **274 Shutterstock:** Kzenon/Shutterstock. **278 WPP plc:** WPP plc. **281 Cannes Lions:** Cannes Lions. **284 Shutterstock:** YKTR/Shutterstock. **287 Shutterstock:** Marquisphoto/Shutterstock. **298 Shutterstock:** Piotr Swat/Shutterstock. **310 Simon Culverhouse:** Simon Culverhouse, www.storyboardace.co.uk. **308 Shutterstock:** ImageFlow/Shutterstock. **313 Alamy:** Guy Bell/Alamy Stock Photo. **326 IAB UK:** IAB UK. **329 Shutterstock:** Yayayoyo/Shutterstock. **334 Shutterstock:** Grzegorz Czapski/

Shutterstock. **335 AP Images:** AP Images for Whirlpool/AP Images. **342 The Lego Group:** The Lego Group. **343 The Lego Group:** The Lego Group. **345 PrettyGreen:** PrettyGreen. **349 The Mary Rose:** The Mary Rose. **353 Emirates Group:** Emirates Group. **354 Shutterstock:** EvrenKalinbacak/Shutterstock. **363 Cheetos:** Cheetos. **368 Alamy:** Chris Bull/Alamy Stock Photo. **380 Shutterstock:** idiltoffolo/Shutterstock. **384 Shutterstock:** Iakov Filimonov/Shutterstock. **386 Alamy:** Zoonar GmbH/Alamy Stock Photo. **389 Shutterstock:** Zety Akhzar/Shutterstock. **393 Budweiser:** Budweiser. **396 IKEA:** © Inter IKEA Systems B.V. **400 Shutterstock:** casejustin/Shutterstock. **403 Shutterstock:** Jstone/Shutterstock. **415 This Girl Can:** This Girl Can. **415 This Girl Can:** This Girl Can. **423 PepsiCo:** PepsiCo. **423 Twitter Inc:** Screenshot © Twitter Inc. **424 Twitter Inc:** Screenshot © Twitter Inc. **429 Shutterstock:** Rob Wilson/Shutterstock. **434 Shutterstock:** Bon Appetit/Shutterstock. **438 Alamy:** Bernie Epstein/Alamy Stock Photo. **440 Bolia International:** Bolia International. **440 Bolia International:** Bolia International. **448 123RF:** Sergii Gnatiuk/123RF. **448 123RF:** Tobi/123RF. **449 Twitter Inc:** Screenshot © Twitter Inc. **449 Twitter Inc:** Screenshot © Twitter Inc. **453 Brands2life:** Brands2life. **453 Brands2life:** Brands2life. **458 Shutterstock:** Polhansen/Shutterstock. **458 Shutterstock:** stefano cellai/Shutterstock. **468 123RF:** Marcin Jucha/123RF. **473 The Swedish Number:** The Swedish Number. **474 The Swedish Number:** The Swedish Number. **480 Telefónica UK Limited:** Telefónica UK Limited. **482 STV:** STV. **487 McDonald's:** McDonald's. **493 Shutterstock:** Nayladen/Shutterstock. **496 Alamy:** WENN Rights Ltd/Alamy Stock Photo. **502 The Emirates Group:** The Emirates Group. **503 The Emirates Group:** The Emirates Group. **503 The Emirates Group:** The Emirates Group. **511 The British Army:** The British Army. **514 Shutterstock:** Stas Ponomarencko/Shutterstock. **518 Unilever:** Unilever. **521 IKEA:** © Inter IKEA Systems B.V. **522 Shutterstock:** NextNewMedia/Shutterstock. **523 Shutterstock:** Chendongshan/Shutterstock. **536 U K Insurance Limited:** U K Insurance Limited. **536 U K Insurance Limited:** U K Insurance Limited. **544 Shutterstock:** Designs by Jack/Shutterstock. **546 Shutterstock:** WAYHOME studio/Shutterstock. **554 Nestlé:** Nestlé. **555 Nestlé:** Nestlé. **562 Alamy:** Tribune Content Agency LLC/Alamy Stock Photo. **564 Alamy:** Jim West/Alamy Stock Photo. **566 TRO Group:** TRO Group. **567 TRO Group:** TRO Group. **570 Discover Northern Ireland:** Discover Northern Ireland. **571 Discover Northern Ireland:** Discover Northern Ireland. **572 Discover Northern Ireland:** Discover Northern Ireland. **579 Costa Coffee:** Costa Coffee. **582 Ofcom:** Ofcom 2018. **585 WTM London:** WTM London. **591 123RF:** Keith Homan/123RF. **592 Nestlé:** Nestlé. **595 Britvic PLC:** Britvic PLC. **596 Getty Images:** Kevin Winter/Staff/Getty Images Entertainment/Getty Images. **600 Alamy:** PCN Photography/Alamy Stock Photo. **615 AUDI AG:** AUDI AG. **617 McCann:** Print advertisement created by McCann, Brazil for Salvation Army. **621 Tagline of Badger & Winters:** Tagline of Badger & Winters. **634 Shutterstock:** d_odin/Shutterstock. **638 Shutterstock:** Pajor Pawel/Shutterstock. **639 Shutterstock:** Elena Rostunova/Shutterstock. **653 WCRS:** Rankin/WCRS. **663 H.O.G:** © 2018 H-D. **663 Alamy:** Justin Kase zninez/Alamy Stock Photo. **663 Shutterstock:** Jevanto Productions/Shutterstock. **665 Ocean Outdoor UK Limited:** Ocean Outdoor UK Limited. **669 123RF:** Stanisic Vladimi/123RF. **670 John Lewis & Partners:** John Lewis & Partners. **674 Metro Trains Melbourne:** Metro Trains Melbourne. **675 Metro Trains Melbourne:** Metro Trains Melbourne. **676 Metro Trains Melbourne:** Metro Trains Melbourne. **686 L'Oréal:** L'Oréal. **690 Google LLC:** Google LLC. **688 ADVERGAMING:** ADVERGAMING. **691 Getty Images:** David Becker/Stringer/Getty Images North America/Getty Images. **695 PowWowNow:** PowWowNow. **701 Fermín Paús:** Fermín Paús Formerly Soberana Sr. Brand Manager at Heineken. **708 Shutterstock:** SeventyFour/Shutterstock. **718 Shutterstock:** KerdaZz/Shutterstock. **733 Getty Images:** Anthony Devlin – PA Images/Getty Images. **735 Alamy:** VStock/Alamy Stock Photo. **743 Shutterstock:** Jodie Johnson/Shutterstock.

Introduction to marketing communications

Part 1 establishes the scope and contextual aspects of marketing communications. It provides an underpinning for the other chapters in this book.

Chapter 1 sets out an introductory perspective on marketing communications and presents some of the key concepts. From a consideration of the scope, role and tasks of marketing communications it explores ideas associated with engagement and the way the marketing communications mix is configured.

Chapter 2 examines some of the key issues and influences that impact marketing communications. It explores international marketing communications and the influence that technology is having on brand communications. Additionally, the chapter considers some of the ethical and moral issues associated with marketing communications and how recent developments within the industry are affecting communications.

Chapter 3 explores issues concerning communications theory. In particular it examines a range of theoretical interpretations and communications that reflect developments in the media and the way marketing communications is thought to work. In addition, this chapter highlights the influence of people, their behaviour and the interactional elements within the communications process.

Chapter 4 is the first of two chapters that explore the impact of consumer behaviour on marketing communications. The first considers issues associated with consumer journeys, before examining perception, learning and attitudes. It then examines traditional, academic approaches to both consumer and organisational buyer behaviour.

Chapter 5 explores some of the more contemporary approaches to buyer behaviour. It opens with a consideration of the nature and types of perceived risk that customers experience when purchasing products and services. We then review the way digital media has changed people's behaviour. This is followed with an exploration of hedonic, ethical and tribal consumption before concluding with a review of behavioural economics. In all of these approaches the implications for marketing communications is considered.

The final chapter in this part introduces ideas about how marketing communications might work. Rather than trust a single approach, five separate approaches are presented. These reflect the diverse thinking and developing knowledge about how marketing communications might work. These five are the sequential, attitude, relationship, significant value and cognitive processing approaches.

01

Introducing marketing communications

Marketing communications is concerned with the methods, processes, meanings, perceptions and actions that audiences (consumers and organisations) undertake with regard to the presentation, consideration and actions associated with products, services and brands.

Aims and learning objectives

The primary aim of this chapter is to introduce some of the key concepts associated with marketing communications. In addition, readers are encouraged to consider the scope and purpose of marketing communications, and to develop an appreciation of the key characteristics of the communications mix.

The learning objectives are to enable readers to:

1. examine definitions of marketing communications;
2. explore ideas about how engagement underpins the key role of marketing communications;
3. discuss the scope and tasks of marketing communications;
4. consider ways in which the environment can influence the use of marketing communications;
5. understand the nature and configuration of the marketing communications mix.

Introduction

Marketing communications is used to engage audiences. It is a complex activity that is used by organisations with varying degrees of sophistication and success. For example, global brands may develop campaigns to run across multiple territories and in multiple languages, while in contrast, a local firm may produce a one-off radio ad to air on the local radio station.

While organisations may use marketing communications in different ways, to achieve different goals, and to pursue their own marketing and business objectives, engaging audiences is key to the success of any campaign. This book will help you to understand *why* organisations use marketing communications and *how* campaigns are developed and implemented, drawing on academic and practitioner views.

The opening sentence contains the word 'engage'. 'Engagement' refers to the nature of the communications that can occur between people, and between people and technology. There is no universally agreed definition of the term 'engagement', and it is used in many different contexts. Marketing communications is closely aligned to an educational context and Li et al. (2013) refer to three types of engagement taken from a learning perspective. These are cognitive, relational and behavioural engagement. Cognitive engagement refers to the degree to which individuals are engrossed and intellectually involved in what they are learning (messages). Relational engagement refers to the extent to which individuals feel connected with their environment, while behavioural engagement reflects the extent to which individuals feel involved and participate in activities.

All three of these aspects of engagement can be activated using marketing communications. A range of communication tools are available to first expose, and then sometimes to gain the attention, captivate, and then enable interaction with an audience. It is often achieved through a blend of intellectual and emotional content. Engagement may last seconds, such as the impact of a funny video ad, an emotional TV ad, a witty radio commercial or an interactive billboard. Alternatively, engagement may be protracted and last hours, days, weeks, months or years, such as an exhibition, a festival sponsorship or brand experience.

Viewpoint 1.1
Meet Graham

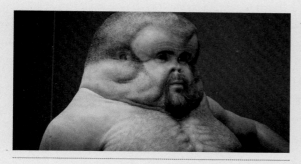

Image 1.1 Graham was put on display as part of an interactive exhibition
Source: Used with permission from Transport Accident Commission.

Engaging audiences in road safety messages has always been challenging. For more than 25 years the Transport Accident Commission (TAC) in Australia pioneered shock advertising campaigns that had been successful in reducing road accidents. However, audiences had become desensitised to shock messages and accidents were increasing.

To find a way to cut through and engage audiences, TAC developed a unique campaign, 'Meet Graham', a direct response campaign featuring 'Graham', a sculpture, showing what humans would need to look like to survive a car crash. Developed by an artist in collaboration with a trauma surgeon and a road safety engineer, Graham created a stark visual experience to highlight the inability of the human body to withstand road accidents.

Graham was put on display as part of an interactive exhibition that toured Australia and visitors were invited to experience Graham for themselves using Tango, Google's augmented reality technology. Bringing audiences face-to-face with Graham allowed them to explore his anatomy and see for themselves what would happen to the body in a crash scenario. To extend the reach of the campaign, TAC developed a visitor website that allowed visitors to explore Graham online in 360 degrees.

Image 1.2 Meet Graham created a new way to engage audiences with road safety
Source: Used with permission from Transport Accident Commission.

Graham created a unique experience that engaged visitors directly with the safety message. The provocative sculpture encouraged interaction and discussion around road safety. More than 287,000 visitors saw Graham close up at the exhibitions and the campaign website saw over 10 million visitors in five days and 1.2 billion global impressions in the first week of launch. Graham was integrated into school curriculums to educate future drivers about road safety.

Graham has engaged audiences not only in Australia, but around the world. By developing a creative campaign that encouraged audiences to experience road safety messages in person and to share online, Graham launched a global conversation.

Meet Graham has won numerous industry awards, including a host of Lions trophies, which are seen as the most coveted awards globally for creative and marketing communications. In 2017, the campaign won two Grand Prix, eight Gold Lions, fifteen Silver Lions and four Bronze Lions.

Sources: Deighton (2018); Graham reaches millions as TAC vulnerability campaign goes global (2016); Meet Graham (2017).

Insight

Meet Graham illustrates how organisations are using marketing communications to engage audiences. Experiential approaches such as this allow audiences to engage in person with the organisation and messages, and extend the length of engagement. The integration of the campaign online provided additional opportunities to extend the reach and length of the interaction with audiences.

Question: Using Li et al's (2013) three types of engagement, consider what types of engagement were achieved by Meet Graham.

Task: Find examples of three other recent campaigns that have used unique ways to engage with audiences and discuss how the strategy encouraged engagement.

Organisations such as Apple and Google, John Lewis and Aldi, HSBC and Santander, Samsung and Sony, Ryanair and easyJet, Chanel and L'Oréal, Boeing and Airbus, Oxfam and Shelter, and Merlin and Disney all operate across different sectors, markets and countries and use a variety of marketing communications activities to engage with their various audiences. These audiences consist not only of people who buy their products and services but also of people and organisations who might be able to influence them, who might help and support them by providing, for example, labour, finance, manufacturing facilities, distribution outlets and legal advice or who are interested because of their impact on parts of society or the business sector in particular.

The organisations mentioned earlier are all well-known brand names, but there are hundreds of thousands of smaller organisations that also use marketing communications to engage their audiences. Each of these organisations, large or small, is part of a network of companies, suppliers, retailers, wholesalers, value-added resellers, distributors and other retailers, which join together, often freely, so that each can achieve its own goals.

Scholars' paper 1.1
What does engagement mean?

Hollebeek, L.D. (2011) Demystifying customer brand engagement: exploring the loyalty nexus, *Journal of Marketing Management*, 27(7–8), 785–807.

Consumer brand engagement is a relatively recent concept and this paper explains the nature of the construct and provides a contemporary definition. The author makes a clear distinction between direct and indirect brand interactions, which are important considerations for marketing communications.

Defining marketing communications

There is no universally agreed definition of marketing communications. This lack of consensus can in part be explained by the vast number of ways marketing communications is used. For example, we see some campaigns using sales promotion and personal selling to drive sales, whereas other marketing communications activity may use sponsorship or public relations to build brand image. The different ways marketing communications is used has led to a number of orientations being identified. Table 1.1 identifies some of the main orientations that have developed and the range of uses.

The origin of many definitions rests with a promotional outlook, based on the traditional conceptualisation of the 4Ps framework by McCarthy (1960), which saw the purpose of 'promotion' as an activity to persuade people to buy products and services. The focus was on products, one-way communications, and the perspective was short-term.

Table 1.1 The developing orientation of marketing communications

Orientation	Explanation
Information and promotion	Communications are used to persuade people into product purchase, using mass-media communications. Emphasis on rational, product-based information.
Process and imagery	Communications are used to influence the different stages of the purchase process that customers experience. A range of tools is used. Emphasis on product imagery and emotional messages.
Integration	Communications resources are used in an efficient and effective way to enable customers to have a clear view of the brand proposition. Emphasis on strategy, media neutrality and a balance between rational and emotional communications.
Relational	Communications are used as an integral part of the different relationships that organisations share with customers. Emphasis on mutual value and meaning plus recognition of the different communications needs and processing styles of different stakeholder groups.
Experience	In some contexts, communications are used to develop unique customer experiences. These involve both integration and relational elements necessary for consistency and meaning.

The expression 'marketing communications' emerged as a wider range of tools and media evolved and as the scope of the tasks these communications activities were expected to accomplish expanded.

In addition to awareness and persuasion, new goals such as developing understanding and preference, reminding and reassuring customers became accepted as important aspects of the communications effort. Direct marketing activities heralded a new approach as one-to-one, two-way communications began to shift the focus from mass to personal communications efforts. Now a number of definitions refer to an integrated perspective. This view has gathered momentum since the mid-1990s and is even an integral part of the marketing communications vocabulary. (This topic is discussed in greater depth in Chapter 12.)

However, this transition to an integrated perspective raises questions about the purpose of marketing communications. For example, should the focus extend beyond products and services; should corporate communications be integrated into the organisation's marketing communications; should the range of stakeholders move beyond customers; what does integration mean and is it achievable? With the integrative perspective, a stronger strategic and long-term orientation has developed, although the basis for many marketing communications strategies appears still to rest with a 'promotional mix' orientation.

Some of these interpretations fail to draw out the key issue that marketing communications provides added value, through enhanced product and organisational symbolism. They also fail to recognise that it is the context within which marketing communications flows that impacts upon the meaning and interpretation given to such messages. Its ability to frame and associate offerings with different environments is powerful.

In an age where the word 'integration' is used to express a variety of marketing and communications-related activities, where interaction and relationship marketing is the favoured paradigm (Grönroos, 2004), marketing communications now embraces a wider remit. Rather than simply provide product information, marketing communications now forms an integral part of an organisation's overall communications and relationship management strategy. This perspective encompasses communications as one-way, two-way, interactive and dialogic approaches, necessary to meet the varying needs of different audiences. The integration stage focuses on the organisation, whereas the next development may have its focus on the relationships that an organisation has with its various audiences. Above all else, marketing communications should be an audience-centred activity.

Two definitions are proposed: one short and memorable, the other deeper, more considered and involving. First, the short definition:

> **Marketing communications is an audience-centred activity, designed to engage audiences and promote conversations.**

This definition focuses marketing communications on generating engagement and conversations as outputs of the activity. The longer definition that follows has three main themes:

> **Marketing communications is a process through which organisations and audiences attempt to engage with one another. Through an understanding of an audience's preferred communications environments, participants seek to develop and present messages, before evaluating and responding. By conveying messages that are relevant and significant, participants are encouraged to offer attitudinal, emotional and behavioural responses.**

The first concerns the word *engage*. By recognising the different transactional and collaborative needs of the target audience, marketing communications can be used to engage with a variety of audiences in such a way that one-way, two-way, interactive and dialogic communications are used that meet the needs of the audience (Chapters 3 and 12). It is unrealistic to believe that all audiences always want a relationship with your organisation/brand, and, for some, one-way communications are fine. Messages, however, should encourage individual members of target audiences to respond to the focus organisation (or product/brand). This response can be immediate through, for example, purchase behaviour, use of customer carelines or use of the FAQs on a web page. Alternatively it can be deferred as information is assimilated and considered for future use. Even if the information is discarded at a later date, the communications will have attracted attention and consideration of the message.

The second theme concerns the *audiences* for, or participants in, marketing communications. Traditionally, marketing communications has been used to convey product-related information to customer-based audiences. Today, a range of stakeholders have connections and relationships of varying dimensions, and marketing communications needs to incorporate this breadth and variety. Stakeholder audiences, including customers, are all interested in a range of corporate issues, sometimes product-related and sometimes related to the policies, procedures and values of the organisation itself. Marketing communications should be an audience-centred activity and in that sense it is important that messages be based on a firm understanding of both the needs and environment of the audience. To be successful, marketing communications should be grounded in the behaviour and information-processing needs and style of the target audience. This is referred to as 'understanding the context in which the communications event is to occur'. From this base it is easier to present and position brands in order that they are perceived to be different and of value to the target audience.

The third theme from the definition concerns the *response*. This refers to the outcomes of the communications process, and can be used as a measure of whether a communications event has been successful. There are essentially three key responses: attitudinal, emotional and behavioural. Attitudinal responses can be seen in changes to audiences' attitudes towards brands, services or issues. For example, communications activity may be aimed towards improved consumer attitudes towards the quality perceptions of a brand. Emotional responses seek to drive emotional engagement with the brand or organisation. Campaigns seeking to elicit emotional responses use emotional messaging, which is discussed further in Chapter 19. Behavioural responses can occur when campaigns seek to change audiences' behaviours and the case study in Chapter 20 provides a good example of how an organisation used marketing communications as a means to change behaviours around trains.

Viewpoint 1.2
#ShareTheLoad

Image 1.3 #ShareThe Load became a social movement for change in India
Source: Used with permission from Procter & Gamble.

Marketing communications can bring about behavioural change. As well as changing purchasing behaviour and ways in which consumers use brands and services, it can also effect societal change. Recognising the challenges faced by their audiences, many brands are using their marketing communications skills to help improve the lives of consumers around the world.

Ariel launched 'Share the Load' in India to tackle the issue of gender inequality in the home. Despite the increasing equal contribution women were making to family incomes in India, women still carried the sole responsibility for the household washing. This traditional view of women's role in the home was endorsed by research which showed that 87 per cent of men saw household washing as a women's job. To address this, Ariel decided to start a national conversation around domestic responsibility.

Share the Load encouraged men and dads across India to take responsibility for the washing chores. The campaign developed branded content and included celebrity endorsements, partnerships with clothing brands and launched 'His and Her' packaging. Additionally, the campaign tied up with matchmaking websites asking men to make a declaration of their willingness to share the load.

Ariel challenged stereotypical attitudes towards women and invited a cultural debate around gendered norms. The campaign not only raised the problem of gender inequality, but through #ShareTheLoad provided a solution.

The campaign sparked a national conversation and earned media worth $9.5 million. Facebook engagement increased by 225 per cent, the campaign trended nationally on Twitter and, more importantly, over 3.7 million men in India made the pledge to 'Share the Load' in their homes, demonstrating a change in how men viewed the responsibility of household chores across the country.

The campaign also saw sales of Ariel increase by 60 per cent and Share the Load was awarded a Bronze and Glass Lion at Cannes.

Sources: Ariel Share The Load: a social movement to remove the cultural stain of gender (2017); Coffee (2016); Turnbull (2018).

Insight

This example reflects the three main themes of the current definition of marketing communications. First, Ariel sought to engage audiences with the issue of gender inequality within Indian households and start a conversation about sharing domestic responsibility. Second, the campaign was centred around the target audience and demonstrated how communications need to understand the context of the environment. Third, #Sharetheload encouraged a response from audiences.

Question: Considering the definition of marketing communications, explain what type of response Share the Load aimed to achieve.

Task: Find an example of another campaign that has used marketing communication tools to bring about social change.

The engaging role of marketing communications

Marketing communications allows brands to engage with audiences in order to pursue their marketing and business objectives. These objectives will vary between organisations and may be to drive brand awareness, knowledge or purchase intention. As we have seen from the viewpoints already shared in this chapter, marketing communications can be used to achieve a range of attitudinal and behavioural objectives.

The reason to use marketing communications may vary according to the prevailing situation or context but the essential goal is to provoke an audience response. For Rossiter and Percy (2013: 392) this response is only about selling products and services. They see the role of advertising as unquestionably about selling 'more of the branded product or service, or to achieve a higher price that consumers are willing to pay than would obtain in the absence of advertising'.

To get to the point of purchase, however, several communications effects may need to have been achieved. So, the response might be geared to developing brand values, attitudes, preferences and the positive thoughts an individual might have about a brand. This is grounded in a 'thinking and feeling orientation', a combination of both cognitive thoughts and emotional feelings about a brand.

Another type of response might be one that stimulates an audience to act in particular ways. Referred to as 'behavioural' or sometimes 'brand response', the goal is to 'encourage particular audience behaviours'. For example, these might include trying a piece of cheese in a supermarket, encouraging visits to a website, sampling a piece of music, placing orders and paying for goods and services, sharing information with a friend, registering on a network, opening letters, signing a petition or calling a number. Brands with a Facebook presence can utilise call-to-action buttons. These link to any destination on or off Facebook and include: Book Now, Contact Us, Use App, Play Game, Shop Now, Sign Up, and Watch Video. All of these are an integral part of an engagement strategy (Anon, 2014). Figure 1.1 depicts the two key drivers of engagement. Apart from generating cash flows, the underlying purpose of these responses can be considered to be a strategic function of developing relationships with particular audiences and/or for (re)positioning brands.

Engagement, therefore, can be considered to be a function of two forms of response. The quality of engagement cannot be determined, but it can be argued that marketing communications should be based on driving a particular type of response that captivates an individual. For example, Petplan used television to develop new brand values and then switched to behavioural advertising to drive responses to call centres and their website. This activity was supported with an online competition via Facebook, inviting pet owners to join in with the campaign and to submit a photo of their pet to form the basis of a user-generated version of the advert. Over 28,000 owners entered their pets into the Facebook competition, demonstrating not only their positive feelings towards the campaign, but also a growing affinity with the Petplan brand.

Where engagement occurs, an individual might be said to have been positively captivated and, as a result, opportunities for activity should increase. Engagement acts as a bridge, a mechanism through which brands and organisations link with target audiences and through which the goals of all parties can be achieved. In other words, there is mutual value.

An extension of the engagement process can be seen in the way many brands now focus on developing customer experiences. This requires linking together the various points at which customers interact with brands so that there is consistency in their brand experiences. Today there is a multitude of media channels, which represents a major challenge for those seeking to interlink their communications. For example, many retailers attempt to manage the multichannel environment but do so by treating each channel as an independent entity, a silo approach.

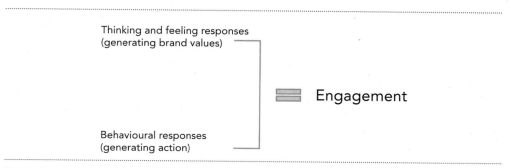

Figure 1.1 The two key drivers of engagement
Source: From *Essentials of Marketing Communications*, Pearson Education (Fill, C. 2011) Figure 1.3, p. 10, reproduced by permission of Pearson Education Ltd.

Some retailers have moved to a customer-centric focus and have tried to link the channels so that customer perception of the brand is less disjointed and more consistent with the desired perceptions (Patel, 2012). Brands are increasingly using technology, such as apps, to provide a more streamlined approach to their communications with customers. The use of technology as a facilitator is discussed in more depth in Chapter 2.

Successful engagement indicates that understanding and meaning have been conveyed effectively, that the communications have value. Counting the number of likes, viewers, readers or impressions says little about the quality of the engagement and the value that it represents to individuals. At one level, engagement through one-way communications enables target audiences to understand product and service offers, to the extent that the audience is sufficiently engaged to want to enter into further communications activity. At another level, engagement through two-way or interactive communications enables information that is relationship-specific (Ballantyne, 2004) to be exchanged. The greater the frequency of information exchange, the more likely collaborative relationships will develop.

As if to emphasise the appropriateness of the term 'engagement' the concept is now being tested as an alternative measurement to impressions, clicks and page views. Ideas of 'engaged time', the amount of time that individuals spend on a web page, is a metric being considered by several organisations. A key measurement metric at ScribbleLive is user engagement minutes, or UEMs. These represent the amount of time a person spends 'engaged' with their content (Dana, 2012). Similarly, Turnbull and Jenkins (2016) highlighted how Facebook reactions can be used to evaluate the success of Facebook campaigns beyond likes or shares. All of this suggests that the primary role of marketing communications is to engage audiences.

The scope of marketing communications

At a basic level, marketing communications, or 'promotion' as it was originally known, is used to communicate elements of an organisation's offering to a target audience. This offer might refer to a product, a service or the organisation itself as it tries to build its reputation. However, this represents a broad view of marketing communications and fails to incorporate the various issues, dimensions and elements that make up this important communications activity. Duncan and Moriarty (1997) and Grönroos (2004) suggest that in addition to these 'planned' events there are marketing communications experienced by audiences relating to both their experience from using products (how tasty is this smoothie?) and the consumption of services (just how good was the service in that hotel, restaurant or at the airport?) In addition to these there are communications arising from unplanned or unintended brand-related experiences (empty stock shelves or accidents). These dimensions of marketing communications are all represented in Figure 1.2 (Hughes and Fill, 2007).

Figure 1.2 helps demonstrate the breadth of the subject and the complexity associated with the way audiences engage with a brand. Although useful in terms of providing an overview, this framework requires elaboration in order to appreciate the detail associated with each of the elements, especially planned marketing communications. This book builds on this framework and in particular considers issues associated with both planned and unplanned aspects of marketing communications.

Planned marketing communications incorporates three key elements: tools, media and content (messages). The main communications tools are advertising, sales promotion, public relations, direct marketing, personal selling and added-value approaches such as sponsorship, exhibitions and field marketing. Content can be primarily informative or emotional but is usually a subtle blend of both dimensions, reflecting the preferences and

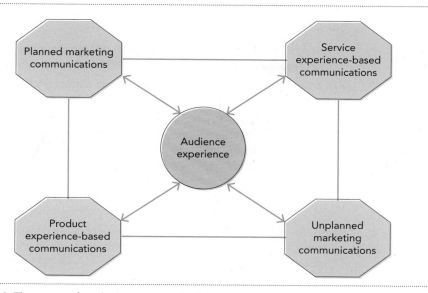

Figure 1.2 The scope of marketing communications
Source: From Redefining the nature and format of the marketing communications mix, *The Marketing Review*, 7 (1), 45-57 (Hughes, G. and Fill, C. 2007), reproduced by permission of Westburn Publishers Ltd.

needs of the target audience. To help get these messages through to their audiences, organisations have three main routes:

1. They can pay for the use of particular media that they know their target audiences will use – for example, magazines, websites or television programmes.
2. They can use their own assets to convey messages, such as their buildings, employees, vehicles and websites, which they do not have to pay to use.
3. They can encourage people to talk and share ideas about their brand, often through social media, which involves relatively little cost.

In reality brands use a mixture of these three routes.

Unplanned marketing communications involves messages that have not been anticipated. These may be both positive and negative, but the emphasis is on how the organisation reacts to and manages the meaning attributed by audiences. So, comments by third-party experts, changes in legislation or regulations by government, the actions of competitors, failures in the production or distribution processes or – perhaps the most potent of all communications – word-of-mouth comments between customers, all impact on the way in which organisations and brands are perceived and the images and reputations that are developed. Many leading organisations recognise the influence of word-of-mouth communications and actively seek to shape the nature, timing and speed with which it occurs. (This topic is discussed in more detail in Chapter 3.) Increasingly, interactive media, and the Internet in particular, are used to 'talk' with current, potential and lapsed customers and other stakeholders.

The tasks of marketing communications

Bowersox and Morash made a significant contribution in their 1989 paper when they demonstrated how marketing flows, including the information flow, can be represented as a network that has the sole purpose of satisfying customer needs and wants.

Communications are important in these exchange networks as they can help achieve one of four key tasks:

1. Communications can *inform* and make potential customers aware of an organisation's offering. They can also provide knowledge and understanding about a brand.

2. Communications may attempt to *persuade* current and potential customers of the desirability of entering into an exchange relationship.

3. Communications can also be used to *reinforce* experiences. This may take the form of *reminding* people of a need they might have or reminding them of the benefits of past transactions with a view to convincing them that they should enter into a similar exchange. In addition, it is possible to provide *reassurance* or comfort either immediately prior to an exchange or, more commonly, post-purchase. This is important, as it helps to retain current customers and improve profitability, an approach to business that is much more cost-effective than constantly striving to lure new customers.

4. Finally, marketing communications can act as a *differentiator*, particularly in markets where there is little to separate competing products and brands. Mineral water products, such as Perrier and Highland Spring, are largely similar: it is the communications surrounding the products that has created various brand images, enabling consumers to make purchasing decisions. In these cases it is the images created by marketing communications that enable people to differentiate one brand from another and position them so that consumers' purchasing confidence and positive attitudes are developed.

Therefore, communications can inform, persuade, reinforce and build images to differentiate a product or service, or to put it another way, DRIP (see Table 1.2).

At a higher level, the communications process not only supports the transaction, by informing, persuading, reinforcing or differentiating, but also offers a means of exchange itself, for example communications for entertainment, for potential solutions and concepts for education and self-esteem. Communications involve intangible benefits, such as the psychological satisfactions associated with, for example, the entertainment associated with engaging and enjoying advertisements (Schlinger, 1979) or the experiences within a sponsored part of a social network.

Communications can also be seen as a means of perpetuating and transferring values and culture to different parts of society or networks. For example, it is argued that the way women are portrayed in the media and stereotypical images of very thin or 'size zero' women are dysfunctional in that they set up inappropriate role models. The form and characteristics of the communications process adopted by some organisations (both the deliberate and the unintentional use of signs and symbols used to convey meaning) help to provide stability and continuity. Dove, for example, understood this and successfully

Table 1.2   DRIP elements of marketing communications

Task	Sub-task	Explanation
Differentiate	Position	To make a product or service stand out in the category
Reinforce	Remind, reassure, refresh	To consolidate and strengthen previous messages and experiences
Inform	Make aware, educate	To make known and advise of availability and features
Persuade	Purchase or make further enquiry	To encourage further positive purchase-related behaviour

Scholars' paper 1.2
Is advertising harmful to women?

Badger, M., Bronstein, C. and Lambiase, J. (2018) #WomenNotObjects: Madonna Badger takes on objectification, *Advertising & Society Quarterly,* **19(1).**

This paper is based on an interview with Madonna Badger who founded Badger & Winters, a New York-based agency. She reveals how she became aware of advertising's potential harm to women and explains her campaign to stop the objectification of women in advertising, #WomenNotObjects. (This campaign is discussed further in Chapter 19.)

repositioned itself based on natural beauty, using a variety of ordinary people for its communications.

Other examples of intangible satisfactions can be seen in the social and psychological transactions involved increasingly with the work of the National Health Service (NHS), charities, educational institutions and other not-for-profit organisations, such as housing associations. Not only do these organisations recognise the need to communicate with various audiences, but they also perceive value in being seen to be 'of value' to their customers.

The notion of value can be addressed in a different way. All organisations have the opportunity to develop their communications to a point where the value of their messages represents a competitive advantage. This value can be seen in the consistency, timing, volume or expression of the message. Heinonen and Strandvik (2005) argue that there are four elements that constitute communications value. These are the message content, how the information is presented, where the communications occur and their timing: in other words, the all-important context within which a communications event occurs. These elements are embedded within marketing communications and are referred to throughout this book.

Communications can be used for additional reasons. The tasks of informing, persuading, reinforcing and differentiating are primarily activities targeted at consumers or end-users. Organisations do not exist in isolation from each other, as each one is a part of a wider system of corporate entities, where each enters into a series of exchanges to secure raw material inputs or resources and to discharge them as value-added outputs to other organisations in the network.

The exchanges that organisations enter into require the formation of relationships, however tenuous or strong. Andersson (1992) looks at the strength of the relationship between organisations in a network and refers to them as 'loose or tight couplings'. These couplings, or partnerships, are influenced by the communications that are transmitted and received. The role that organisations assume in a network and the manner in which they undertake and complete their tasks are, in part, shaped by the variety and complexity of the communications in transmission throughout the network. Issues of channel or even network control, leadership, subservience and conflict are implanted in the form and nature of the communications exchanged in any network.

Viewpoint 1.3
The Pedigree Child Replacement Programme

Image 1.4 The Pedigree Child Replacement Programme sought to connect 'Empty Nesters' with abandoned dogs
Source: All Paws Rescue - Helping those in need no matter the breed!

Pedigree identified that fewer dogs were being adopted from shelters in Auckland. Data revealed that of the 3,338 dogs that had entered Auckland city shelters, only 671 of them had found homes to adopt them. To address this growing problem, Pedigree launched a campaign to raise awareness of the increasing number of dogs needing homes and to encourage New Zealanders to adopt a dog.

Identifying 'Empty Nesters' as a key target audience because of their high disposable income and with no children living at home, Pedigree launched a multiple-channel campaign aimed at increasing dog adoption numbers. The campaign used a straight-talking humorous approach aimed at encouraging the target audience to replace their children with dogs.

The 'Pedigree Child Replacement Programme' sought to connect lonely parents, whose children had grown up and left home, with abandoned dogs. Targeting these Empty Nesters in a blunt tone of voice and with a mix of TV, cinema, Skype, radio and online films, the campaign drove audiences to replacethem.co.nz. The website allowed lonely parents to match the characteristics of their child with similar characteristics of abandoned dogs looking for homes in the shelters.

To further extend the campaign, digital sites were used at airports to encourage parents to replace their children as soon as they had left the country. To drive conversations and add to the comedic value of the campaign, parents were given the chance to convert their children's old stuff into useful accessories for their new pet. So, examples were given of how their children's old bedspreads could make a nice new dog bed or children's old clothes could be converted into a dog jacket.

The suggestion that Empty Nesters could replace their child with a similar looking dog resonated comically with both the target audience and the media. The Pedigree Child Replacement Programme was covered on national TV news stations and the campaign saw an increase of 824 per cent in enquiries about dog adoption through shelters. In addition to being the most successful dog adoption campaign for the last decade and winning three Gold and two Silver Lions at Cannes, the sales of Pedigree dog food increased by 16 per cent over the campaign period.

Sources: Gianatasio (2017); Jardine (2017); The Child Replacement Programme (2017).

Insight

The Pedigree Child Replacement Programme highlights how brands are using marketing communications as a means to differentiate themselves against competitors. This campaign allows Pedigree to position themselves as a caring brand that shares similar values to the target audience. As well as showing empathy, the campaign allows audiences to engage with the brand directly through the adoption appeal.

Question: Consider which of the DRIP elements apply to The Pedigree Child Replacement Programme. Using the list provided in Table 1.2 make a list of all the tasks and sub-tasks that apply and explain each.

Task: Find three other recent campaigns and make a list of the DRIP elements that apply to each. Provide an explanation of each task and sub-task.

Delivering consumer experiences

Providing experiences that directly engage consumers has become a key aspect of marketing and, as highlighted throughout this book, customer and brand experiences are increasingly becoming a central feature of marketing communications campaigns.

As customers interact with brands through a variety of touchpoints in multiple channels and media, their purchasing journeys have become exceedingly complex. Marketing communications is used to manage and enhance customer experiences during these journeys. Indeed, the establishment of customer experience managers at many major organisations, such as KPMG, Amazon and Google, is recognition of the growing importance of this aspect of marketing (Lemon & Verhoef, 2016). These researchers believe that customer experience is considered to be a multidimensional construct, involving a customer's responses to a brand's cognitive, emotional, behavioural, sensorial and social components (Schmitt, 1999), during their entire purchase journey. Managing experiences during the entire journey is considered to be an opportunity to create a competitive advantage, something that cannot be copied by competitors. (The customer journey is considered in more detail in Chapters 4 and 22.)

Experiences can create memorable and shareable brand moments. The Art Institute of Chicago for example created a unique experience for visitors. To launch their van Gogh exhibit, the museum reconstructed van Gogh's bedroom and invited visitors to book an overnight stay for a truly immersive experience of the artist's life and work (Chapter 17). As well as offering museum visitors the once-in-a-lifetime chance to sleep in van Gogh's bedroom, the opportunity created a shareable experience.

One explanation for the growth in brand experiences is undoubtedly its disruptive ability. Unlike online ads, face-to-face experiences are hard to block and experiential activity can create an immediate connection with audiences (Smith and Hanover, 2016). Experiences provide an opportunity for brands to interact directly with audiences and the Meet Graham campaign featured in this chapter highlights how effective experiential approaches can be in engaging consumers (Viewpoint 1.1).

Brand experiences are not just about face-to-face events however. Marketing communications campaigns can deliver experiences online and through apps. This book shares a number of examples of how brands have created virtual experiences for consumers; Cheetos Museum (Chapter 11), Dumb Ways to Die (Chapter 20) and Google Sheep View (Chapter 14). These experiential campaigns illustrate how marketing communications is helping to deliver brand experiences.

Experiences are personal and can act as a differentiator for brands. Marketing communications can help to deliver these personal experiences. The Swedish Tourist Association provided audiences with a highly personal experience of chatting to a 'random Swede'. The Swedish Number, featured in Chapter 14, created the world's first telephone number for a country, connecting callers to Swedes to talk about anything related to Sweden. The personal nature of such experiences helps to build relationships with customers and can form a lasting bond with the brand.

Even when the experience is delivered on a larger scale, such as the Emirates pre-match safety demonstration stunt performed live in front of 57,000 fans at an SL Benfica match (Chapter 15), it provides audiences with a memory of the brand that will be remembered and talked about long after the event.

Brands can create an experience at any point in the customer journey. Smith and Hanover argue brand experiences can drive customer purchase (Smith and Hanover, 2016). Chapter 17 provides an example of how experiential marketing was used to create a unique sales promotion. Snickers developed HUNGERITHM, an algorithm that changed the price of Snickers bars in response to the mood on the Internet and allowed consumers to track price changes and download coupons.

Experiences are seen to add value to target audiences (Smilansky, 2017). Experiences are searched for, talked about and shared by consumers. Marketing communications plays a vital role in delivering these brand experiences to audiences and providing the means by which they can be talked about and shared.

Environmental influences

The management of marketing communications is a complex and highly uncertain activity. This is due in part to the range of issues and influences that impact marketing communications. We explore many of these in Chapter 2 but here consideration is given to the overall influence of the environment.

The environment can be considered in many different ways, but for the purposes of this opening chapter, three categories are considered: the internal, external and market environments. The constituents of each of these are set out in Figure 1.3.

Internal influences

The internal environment refers primarily to the organisation and the way it works, what its values are and how it wants to develop. Here various forces seek to influence an organisation's marketing communications. The overall strategy that an organisation adopts should have a huge impact. For example, how the organisation wishes to differentiate itself within its target markets will influence the messages and media used and,

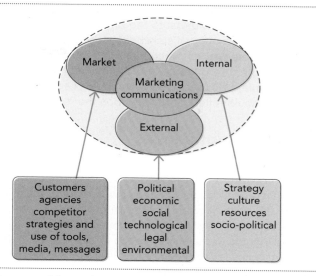

Figure 1.3 The environmental forces that shape marketing communications

of course, the overarching positioning and reputation of the company. Brand strategies will influence such things as the way in which brands are named, the extent to which sales promotions are an integral part of the communications mix and how they are positioned. The prevailing organisational culture can also be extremely influential. A hierarchical management structure and power culture usually leads to a subservient, risk-averse culture. This can lead to communications that are largely oriented to significant selling points and product benefits, rather than oriented to engaging audiences emotionally.

The amount of money available to a marketing communications budget will influence the media mix or the size of the sales force used to deliver messages. Apart from the quality and motivation of the people employed, the level of preferences and marketing skills deployed can impact on the form of the messages, the choice of media, and the use of agencies and support services. Finally, the socio-political climate of the firm shapes not only who climbs the career ladder fastest, but how and to which brands scarce marketing resources are distributed.

The ethical culture of the organisation can impact marketing communications practice. Organisational attitudes towards truth telling, vulnerable groups, privacy and respect, taste and decency, and incentives, bribery and extortion will influence how marketing communications is undertaken. (Each of these ethical issues is discussed in more depth in Chapter 2.)

Scholars' paper 1.3
Opportunities to act unethically

Schauster, E. and Neill, M. (2017) Have the ethics changed? An examination of ethics in advertising and public relations agencies, *Journal of Media Ethics*, 32(1), 45–60.

This study examines perceptions of ethical responsibility among advertising and public relations executives. The findings highlight how there are greater opportunities for industry executives to act unethically and identify native advertising, paid endorsement and digital ad fraud as key ethical concerns.

Marketing communications is sometimes perceived as only dealing with communications that are external to the organisation. It should be recognised that good communications with internal stakeholders, such as employees, are also vital if, in the long term, favourable images, perceptions and attitudes are to be established successfully. Influences through the workforce and the marketing plan can be both positive and effective. For example, staff used in B&Q and Halifax advertising are intended to project internal values that should reflect positively upon the respective brands.

Market influences

Market influences are characterised by partial levels of control and typified by the impact of competitors. Competitors occupy particular positions in the market and this shapes what others claim about their own products, the media they use, the geographic coverage of the sales force and their own positioning. Intermediaries influence the nature of business-to-business marketing communications. The frequency, intensity, quality and overall willingness to share information with one another are significant forces. Of course, the various agencies an organisation uses can also be very influential, as indeed they should be. Marketing research agencies (inform about market perception, attitudes and behaviour), communications agencies (determine what is said and then design how it is said, what is communicated) and media houses (recommend media mixes and when it is said) all have considerable potential to influence marketing communications.

However, perhaps the biggest single market group consists of the organisation's customers and network of stakeholders. Their attitudes, perceptions and buying preferences and behaviours, although not directly controllable, (should) have a far-reaching influence on the marketing communications used by an organisation. Chapter 2 considers the impact of the marketing communications industry on the management of brand-based communication.

External influences

As mentioned earlier, the external group of influencers are characterised by the organisation's near lack of control. The well-known PESTLE framework is a useful way of considering these forces. (Political forces, which can encompass both legal and ethical issues and voluntary controls are discussed further in Chapter 2.)

Economic forces, which include demographics, geographics and geodemographics, can determine the positioning of brands in terms of perceived value. For example, if the government raises interest rates, then consumers are more inclined not to spend money, especially on non-staple products and services. This may mean that marketing communications needs to convey stronger messages about value and to send out strident calls-to-action.

Social forces are concerned with the values, beliefs and norms that a society enshrines. Issues to do with core values within a society are often difficult to change. For example, the American gun culture or the once-prevalent me-orientation with respect to self-fulfilment set up a string of values that marketing communications can use to harness, magnify and align brands. The current social pressures with regard to obesity and healthier eating habits forced McDonald's to introduce new menus and healthier food options. As a result, its marketing communications has not only to inform and make audiences aware of the new menus but also to convey messages about differentiation and positioning and provide a reason to visit the restaurant.

Technological forces have had an immense impact on marketing communications. New technology continues to advance marketing communications and has already led to more personalised, targeted, customised and responsive forms of communications. What was once predominantly one-way communications, based upon a model of information provision and persuasion, has given way to a two-way model in which integration with audiences, and where sharing and reasoning behaviours are enabled by digital technology, are now used frequently with appropriate target audiences. Chapter 2 discusses the impact of Big Data, data management platforms, programmatic technologies, mobile and data privacy in more depth.

Legal forces may prevail in terms of trademarks and copyrights, while environmental forces might impact in terms of what can be claimed and the associated credibility and social responsibility issues. For example, compliance with data protection laws such as the recently introduced General Data Protection Regulation (GDPR) are important considerations.

Marketing communications has evolved in response to changing environmental conditions. For example, direct marketing is now established as a critical approach to developing relationships with buyers, both consumer and organisational. New and innovative forms of communications through social media, digital technologies such as near-field technologies, plus sponsorship, ambient media and content marketing, all suggest that effective communications require the selection and integration of an increasing variety of communications tools and media, as a response to changing environmental contexts. Chapter 2 examines related issues associated with consolidation and convergence that are impacting marketing communications.

The marketing communications mix

In the recent past there have been several major changes in the communications environment and in the way organisations can communicate with their target audiences. Digital technology has given rise to a raft of different media at a time when people have developed a variety of new ways to spend their leisure time. These phenomena are referred to as *media* and *audience fragmentation* respectively, and organisations have developed fresh combinations of the communications mix in order to reach their audiences effectively. For example, there has been a dramatic rise in the use of direct-response media as direct marketing has become a key part of many campaigns. The Internet and digital technologies have enabled new interactive forms of communications, where receivers can be more participative and assume greater responsibility for their contribution in the communications process.

Successful marketing communications involves managing various elements according to the needs of the target audience and the goals the campaign seeks to achieve. Originally the elements that made up the marketing communications mix were just the tools or disciplines, namely advertising, sales promotions, public relations, direct marketing and personal selling. These were mixed together in various combinations and different degrees of intensity in order to attempt to communicate meaningfully with a target audience.

This mix was used at a time when brands were developed through the use of advertising to generate 'above-the-line' mass communications campaigns. The strategy was based around buying space in newspapers and magazines, or advertising time (called spots) in major television programmes that were watched by huge audiences (20+ million people). This strategy required media owners to create programmes (content) that would attract brand owners because of the huge, relatively passive audiences. By interrupting the audience's entertainment, brand owners could talk to (or at) their markets in order to sell their brands.

Since the days of just two commercial television stations there has been a proliferation of media. Although the use of television is actually increasing, audiences, especially young adults, no longer use television as their main source of information or entertainment. When considered together with falling newspaper and magazine readership, it is clear that consumers are using media for a variety of purposes. These include a need to explore and discover new activities, people, experiences and brands, to participate in events and communities, to share experiences and information, and to express themselves as individuals. This reveals that people seek active engagement with media.

We now have a huge choice of media and leisure activities, and we decide how and when to consume information and entertainment. People are motivated and able to develop their own content, be it through text, music or video, and consider topics that they can share with friends on virtual networks. Media and messages are therefore key to reach consumers today, not the tools. More direct and highly targeted, personalised communications activities using direct marketing and the other tools of the mix now predominate. This indicates that, in order to reach audiences successfully, it is necessary to combine not just the tools, but also the media and the content and messages.

So, in addition to the five principal marketing communications tools, it is necessary to add the media, or the means by which advertising and other marketing communications messages are conveyed. Tools and media should not be confused as they have different characteristics and seek to achieve different goals. Also, just in case you were thinking something is missing, the Internet is a medium, not a tool.

To complete the trilogy, messages need to be conveyed to the target audience. Increasingly referred to as content, four forms can be identified: informational, emotional, user-generated and branded content. These are explored in Chapter 19 and the case study on John Lewis in the same chapter shows how some brands are using emotional messages in order to connect with consumers. Previously organisations were primarily responsible for the origin and nature of the content about their brand. Today an increasing number of messages are developed by consumers, and shared with other consumers.

The marketing communications mix depicted in Figure 1.4 represents a shift in approach. Previously the mix represented an *intervention*-based approach to marketing communications, one based on seeking the attention of a customer who might not necessarily be interested, by interrupting their activities. The shift is towards *conversation*-based marketing communications, where the focus is now on communications with and between

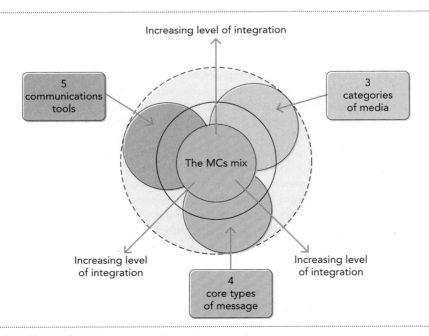

Figure 1.4 The marketing communications mix

members of an audience who may even have contributed content to the campaign. This has a particular impact on direct marketing, interactive communications and, to some extent, personal selling. Figure 1.4 depicts the marketing communications mix at the core of three overlapping elements: tools, media and content. The dashed lines serve to illustrate the varying degree of integration and coordination between the three elements. The wider the circle, the higher the level of integration and the more effective the marketing communications mix.

Viewpoint 1.4

How audiences influence B2B communications

Image 1.5 Emirates SkyCargo's advertising positions the airline as experts in handling perishable cargo
Source: Emirates SkyCargo.

Brands such as Emirates SkyCargo operate in a business-to-business (B2B) marketing environment and their marketing communications differs in a number of ways from business-to-consumer (B2C) approaches.

For all B2B brands, it is important to consider some of the key differences that will influence their communication decisions.

The number of decision-makers needs to be considered. In consumer markets a single person very often makes the decision, whereas in organisational markets decisions are made by many people within a buying centre. This means that a variety of different individuals need to be reached and influenced and this may involve the use of different media and message strategies.

The balance of the communications mix is likely to differ. The role of advertising and sales promotions in B2B communications is primarily to support the personal selling effort. This contrasts with the mix that predominates in consumer markets where personal selling plays a relatively minor role and is only significant at the point of purchase in some product categories such as cars. Direct marketing and exhibitions are also frequently used.

The content of B2B messages tends to be more rational and information based than in B2C, reflecting the higher level of risk involved in the purchase decision. Target audiences are usually experts in their field and therefore are more familiar with technical information.

In B2B, evaluation of communications is often based on the measurement of sales volume, value, number of enquiries and market share.

Insight

The way in which the marketing communications mix is configured for consumer markets is very different from the mix used for business markets. The tools, media and messages used are all different as the general contexts in which they operate require different approaches. Business markets favour personal selling, exhibitions and direct marketing.

Question: Consider what the communication goals might be for a B2B brand such as Emirates SkyCargo and how these might influence the choice of marketing communications elements used.

Task: Find two other examples of B2B advertising and make a list of the characteristics of the target audience for the campaign.

Key points

- Definitions have evolved as communications have developed. Here marketing communications is defined as:

  a process through which organisations and audiences engage with one another. Through an understanding of an audience's preferred communications environments, participants seek to develop and present messages, before evaluating and acting upon any replies. By conveying messages that are relevant and significant, participants are encouraged to offer attitudinal, emotional and behavioural responses.

- Engagement is considered to be the main role of marketing communications. By engaging audiences it becomes easier to provoke relevant conversations.

- Engagement is an activity that involves two-way interactions between a consumer and an organisation. This has three dimensions: cognitive, emotional and behavioural engagement. Engagement may last a second, a minute, an hour, a day or even longer.

- The scope of marketing communications embraces an audience-centred perspective of planned, unplanned, product and service experiences.

- The tasks of marketing communications are based within a need to differentiate, reinforce, inform or persuade audiences to think and behave in particular ways.

- The internal, market and external environments all influence the use of marketing communications and need to be considered by organisations when planning communications.

- The marketing communications mix consists of various tools, media and messages that are used to reach, engage and provoke audience-centred conversations. The five tools, three categories of media and four types of message can be configured in different ways to meet the needs of target audiences.

Case study

Fearless Girl

By Stephen Tisdalle, Chief Marketing Officer, State Street Global Advisors

Image 1.6 Fearless Girl was part of an integrated marketing campaign
Photo: Sculpture by Kristen Visbal; commissioned by State Street Global Advisors.

To say that the tremendous success of the Fearless Girl campaign was unexpected to us at State Street Global Advisors would be an understatement. After all, it's not often that a B2B financial services brand is involved in a big viral marketing campaign. In fact, we originally applied for a permit to keep the Fearless Girl statue installed in New York for just seven days. While we knew this had the potential to be an impactful campaign, we didn't fully anticipate the scale of the viral spread or that, more than a year after launch, her impact and influence would still be expanding.

The story of Fearless Girl begins with a simple truth: research shows that companies with women in leadership outperform those without.[i] Yet, women continue to be under-represented in senior leadership roles. In 2017, one in four Russell 3000 Index companies did not have a single woman on their board.[ii]

Taking a bold stand for change

As the world's third largest asset manager, responsible for investing approximately $2.5 trillion[iii] on behalf of our clients across the globe, State Street Global Advisors pays close attention to these statistics. For us, encouraging companies in our investment portfolio to adopt good governance practices – including increasing board diversity – is a means to drive long-term value of clients' investments.

After launching a gender diversity index and exchange-traded fund (ETF) in 2016, offering the ability to invest in companies with a strong track record of promoting women to senior leadership positions, in 2017 our leaders decided to take the bold step of calling on portfolio companies to increase the number of women on their boards. As one of the largest shareholders, we were prepared to engage these companies, offer guidance on how to go about increasing diversity and, if needed, use our proxy voting power to effect change.

We needed a way to raise broad awareness about the power of women in leadership and about our related investment offerings in the environmental, social and governance (ESG) space. Those were the marketing objectives that led to Fearless Girl. Working with our advertising agency McCann, we developed the idea to place a bronze statue of a little girl – a daring and confident girl, hands on hips and head held high – in the heart of New York's financial district.

But, it's important to note, we didn't just install a statue and hope for the best. We built an integrated marketing campaign to maximise the impact.

A global viral conversation ignites

We installed the statue overnight on the eve of International Women's Day. At daybreak, we quickly took photos and video footage of Fearless Girl, then rushed to a makeshift editing studio in a nearby hotel to finish editing digital content. By 7 a.m., the *Wall Street Journal* had added a photo of the statue to the exclusive article they'd published at midnight, and we'd posted our launch video with behind the scenes footage on our social media and web properties.

The only paid advertising we did for this campaign was paid search. We focused instead on earned and shared media – print, broadcast and digital news coverage, and a series of social media posts. We created #FearlessGirl and invited people to lend their voices to our fight for women in leadership. Within the first 12 hours Fearless Girl had over one billion Twitter impressions[iv] and we were seeing conversations across six continents. Key social media influencers, media personalities and celebrities joined the conversation almost immediately. As the social media firestorm spread, the experiential element of the campaign kicked in. People started flooding to the site to take their own photos, and Fearless Girl was mobbed with girls and women doing her power pose. With this campaign, we created a unifying message that transcended the statue's place on Wall Street, becoming a rallying cry for fearless women and girls everywhere.

Other parts of the campaign launched that day included a major speech by our then-CEO Ron O'Hanley at a prestigious corporate governance conference, an email blast to our clients, a blog post by one of our female leaders, and a joint event with a client where investment managers gathered to talk about how to get more women into financial services. But the amplification of our message went beyond our own planned activities. Within 36 hours, a Wikipedia page about Fearless Girl appeared. And multiple Change.org petitions were launched by people urging lawmakers to make the statue permanent – one attracting over 40,000 signatures. This is a powerful example of a substantive campaign going viral, leading to advocacy at scale with influencers helping to amplify our message exponentially.

Just over a month later, the campaign had 3.3 billion Twitter impressions and 405 million Instagram impressions.[v] By year's end the campaign had won the highest accolade at the Cannes Festival of Creativity – just one of 18 Cannes Lions awarded to the campaign – as well as a record number of Clio Awards and numerous other industry honours.

Sculpture by Kristin Visbal.
NYSE façade used with permission of NYSE Group, Inc.

Image 1.7 Fearless Girl was placed in the heart of New York's financial district
Photo: Sculpture by Kristen Visbal; commissioned by State Street Global Advisors.
Façade used with permission of NYSE Group, Inc.

A lasting impact

The campaign delivered real business impact for us as well. Average daily trading volumes of the gender diversity ETF increased by around 170 per cent,[vi] with web page views for the fund increasing 450 per cent. State Street Global Advisors home page traffic doubled. In the three weeks following launch, there were about 43.4 million impressions on radio and TV with a specific State Street mention,[vii] and about 140 million impressions on print and digital media.[viii] Our share of voice compared to competitors shot from 8 per cent to more than 37 per cent.[ix]

We asked our media buying agency to give us an estimate of what it would have cost to purchase these impressions. They told us it would have cost between US$27–38 million. Needless to say, we spent far less. All in, we spent less than $250,000 to create the bronze statue and get a permit from the City of New York.

Perhaps the most important impact of the campaign is what it has enabled us to do with companies in our portfolio. The notoriety of Fearless Girl gave us a platform for engagement with companies on gender diversity and board leadership issues. We reached out to more than 1200 companies with no women on their boards in 2018 urging them to take action. Of those, 301 have added a female director to the board and 28 more have committed to doing so. Now, we are extending our voting policy to companies in additional regions and encouraging them to disclose the level of gender diversity at all levels of management, not just boards.

We are pleased that the statue moved to a new home in front of the New York Stock Exchange in December 2018 – providing a permanent reminder that women in corporate leadership positions are good for business. Fearless Girl taught us all about the power of diversity. But, as a marketer, she taught me something else: that with an authentic message and experience you can do so much more than promote a product. You can start a conversation. You can inspire people to action. And maybe you can even change the world.

Notes

i Why diversity matters, McKinsey, February 2015; Women on boards: global trends in gender diversity on corporate boards, MSCI, November 2015; Is gender diversity profitable? Peterson Institute for International Economics, February 2016.
ii State Street Global Advisors Asset Stewardship Team.
iii AUM reflects approximately $32.45 billion (as of December 31, 2018), with respect to which State Street Global Advisors Funds Distributors, LLC (SSGA FD) serves as marketing agent; SSGA FD and State Street Global Advisors are affiliated.
iv Spreadfast Intelligence.
v Spreadfast Intelligence.
vi Bloomberg Finance L.P., 7 April 2017.
vii TVeyes.
viii Vocus.
ix Radian6, 731 March 2017.

Review questions

Fearless Girl case questions

1. Evaluate the main role of marketing communications in the Fearless Girl campaign.
2. Using the DRIP framework identify and explain the key tasks that marketing communications was required to accomplish for State Street Global Advisors.
3. Examine the main elements of the marketing communications mix that were used in this campaign.
4. Appraise the main forces in the external environment that influenced the shape, nature and characteristics of the campaign.
5. Explain who were the key target audience for the campaign and how they influenced the choice of marketing communications mix used.

General questions

1. Define marketing communications. What are the key elements in the definition?
2. How might the contribution of the tools differ from those of the media within a marketing communications programme?
3. Discuss the way in which the elements of the mix compare across the following criteria: control, communications effectiveness and cost.
4. Evaluate the ways in which engagement might vary across campaigns.
5. Explain how marketing communications might differ within consumer and business marketing strategies.

References for Chapter 1

Andersson, P. (1992) Analysing distribution channel dynamics, *European Journal of Marketing*, 26(2), 47–68.

Anon (2014) Facebook adds more features, WARC, retrieved 15 December 2014 from https://www.warc.com/newsandopinion/news/facebook_adds_more_features/34024

Ariel Share The Load: a social movement to remove the cultural stain of gender (2017) Cannes Archive, retrieved 10 January 2018 from http://www.canneslionsarchive.com/Home/PublicHome

Badger, M., Bronstein, C. and Lambiase, J. (2018) #WomenNotObjects: Madonna Badger takes on objectification, *Advertising & Society Quarterly*, 19(1), retrieved 1 May 2018 from https://muse.jhu.edu/article/689167

Ballantyne, D. (2004) Dialogue and its role in the development of relationship specific knowledge, *Journal of Business and Industrial Marketing*, 19(2), 114–23.

Bowersox, D. and Morash, E. (1989) The integration of marketing flows in channels of distribution, *European Journal of Marketing*, 23(2), 58–67.

Coffee, P. (2016) Research and analysis pointed us to the fact that while Indian women are increasingly contributing equally to the family income, the burden of household chores still lies on them, *Adweek*, 25 February, retrieved 10 January 2018 from http://www.adweek.com/brand-marketing/ad-day-fathers-touching-apology-his-daughter-highlights-struggles-working-mothers-169871/

Dana (2012) Introducing User Engagement Minutes. ScribbleLive, retrieved 11 January 2018 from https://www.scribblelive.com/blog/2012/10/31/introducing-user-engagement-minutes/

Deighton, K. (2018) Meet Graham's creators, the Aussie duo that rewrote the 'shock & awe' road safety creative for the most awarded campaign of 2017, The Drum, 1 February, retrieved 10 April 2018 from http://www.thedrum.com/news/2018/02/01/meet-graham-s-creators-the-aussie-duo-rewrote-the-shock-awe-road-safety-creative-and

Duncan, T.R. and Moriarty, S. (1997) *Driving Brand Value*, New York: McGraw-Hill.

Gianatasio, D. (2017) Kids Leaving Home? Try This 'Child Replacement Program,' Says Fun Pedigree Campaign, *Adweek*, 22 March, retrieved 10 January 2018 from http://www.adweek.com/creativity/kids-leaving-home-try-this-child-replacement-program-says-fun-pedigree-campaign/

Graham reaches millions as TAC vulnerability campaign goes global (2016) *TAC*, 25 July, retrieved 10 January 2018 from http://www.tac.vic.gov.au/about-the-tac/media-room/news-and-events/current-media-releases/graham-reaches-millions-as-tac-vulnerability-campaign-goes-global

Grönroos, C. (2004) The relationship marketing process: communication, interaction, dialogue, value, *Journal of Business and Industrial Marketing*, 19(2), 99–113.

Heinonen, K. and Strandvik, T. (2005) Communication as an element of service value, *International Journal of Service Industry Management*, 16(2), 186–98.

Hollebeek, L.D. (2011) Demystifying customer brand engagement: exploring the loyalty nexus, *Journal of Marketing Management*, 27(7–8), 785–807.

Hughes, G. and Fill, C. (2007) Redefining the nature and format of the marketing communications mix, *The Marketing Review*, 7(1), 45–57.

Jardine, A. (2017) Replace your grown-up kids with a dog, says this Pedigree campaign, *AdAge*, 20 March, retrieved 15 February 2018 from http://creativity-online.com/work/pedigree-child-replacement-program–trophy/51315.

Lemon, K.N. and Verhoef, P.C. (2016) Understanding customer experience throughout the customer journey, *Journal of Marketing*, AMA/MSI Special Issue, 80 (November), 69–96.

Li, T., Berens, G. and de Maertelaere, M. (2013) Corporate Twitter channels: the impact of engagement and informedness on corporate reputation, *International Journal of Electronic Commerce*, 18(2), 97–126.

McCarthy, E.J. (1960) *Basic Marketing: A Managerial Approach*, Homewood, IL: Irwin.

Meet Graham (2017) *Cannes Archive*, retrieved 10 January 2018 from http://www.canneslionsarchive. com/Home/PublicHome

Mohr, J. and Nevin, J. (1990) Communication strategies in marketing channels, *Journal of Marketing*, 54 (October), 36–51.

Patel, D. (2012) Brands are placing multimedia at the heart of the in-store experience, 6 September 2012, retrieved 7 January 2014 from www.brandrepublic.com/opinion/1148554/ Think-BR-Brands-placing-multimedia-heart-in-store-experience/?DCMP=ILC-SEARCH

Rossiter, J.R. and Percy, L. (2013) How the roles of advertising merely appear to have changed, *International Journal of Advertising*, 32(3), 391–8.

Schauster, E. and Neill, M. (2017) Have the ethics changed? An examination of ethics in advertising and public relations agencies, *Journal of Media Ethics*, 32(1), 45–60.

Schlinger, M. (1979) A profile of responses to commercials, *Journal of Advertising Research*, 19, 37–46.

Schmitt, B.H. (1999) *Experiential Marketing*, New York: The Free Press.

Smilansky, S. (2017) *Experiential Marketing: A Practical Guide to Interactive Brand Experiences*, London: Kogan Page.

Smith, K. and Hanover, D. (2016) *Experiential Marketing: Secrets, Strategies, and Success Stories From the World's Greatest Brands*, Hoboken: Wiley.

The Child Replacement Programme (2017) *Cannes Archive*, retrieved 10 January 2018 from http://www.canneslionsarchive.com/Home/PublicHome

Turnbull, S. (2018) Using labels and accessories as creative advertising media: insights from Cannes Lions 2017, *Current Trends in Fashion Technology and Textile Engineering*, 3(2), 1–2.

Turnbull, S. and Jenkins, S. (2016) Why Facebook Reactions are good news for evaluating social media campaigns, *Journal of Direct, Data and Digital Marketing Practice*, 17(3), 156–8.

Marketing communications: issues, influences and disruption

The way in which organisations use marketing communications is influenced by a range of factors. These can embrace political, economic, societal, technological, legal and environmental issues.

Understanding the relative impact of these influences and the consequences, especially if something goes wrong, can be critical to a brand's long-term health.

Aims and learning objectives

The aims of this chapter are to develop understanding about some of the various issues that are associated with marketing communications, and the influences that frame much of contemporary marketing communications practice.

The learning objectives are to enable readers to:

1. explore some of the issues associated with international marketing communications;
2. examine the impact that technology is having on marketing communications;
3. discuss some of the ethical and moral issues associated with marketing communications;
4. consider the extent to which the marketing communications industry influences marketing communications.

Introduction

The increasing number of influences on marketing communications means that the way in which organisations use marketing communications varies considerably. This is because not only are firms striving to achieve different objectives, with varying levels and types of resources, but also because they are subject to a huge range of influences, many of which are disruptive, and all of which vary in their degree of impact.

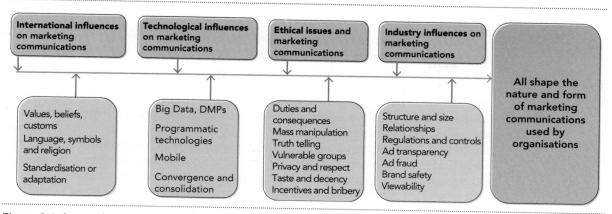

Figure 2.1 Some of the issues and influences that shape marketing communications

We appreciate that there are a host of external and internal influences, some of which were considered in Chapter 1 using the PESTLE framework. In this chapter however, and because of space limitations, we consider some of the more pertinent issues that influence marketing communications. These are represented in Figure 2.1.

The first topic to be considered is the dynamics associated with operating in global and international environments. We then review some of the influences that technology has brought and, in particular, examine some of the issues associated with digital and interactive communications.

Our next topic concerns issues associated with changing cultural and social values. Brought about partly through the huge amount of data that is driven largely through the use of social media, organisations are increasingly faced with ethical and moral issues, particularly with regard to their use of marketing communications.

We conclude the chapter with a consideration of the issues and influences brought about by a changing communications industry. Again, we recognise there are many but we highlight three areas: structural changes, the evolving form and nature of industry relationships, including challenges arising directly from online advertising, and the regulations used to control marketing communications.

International issues and influences

For organisations operating in international markets there are a host of economic, cultural, social, legal, educational, attitudinal and religious differences that may need to be considered. Brand managers might be conversant with the marketing environment at home but, as they move outside the country or region, it is likely that their knowledge and understanding of market characteristics, such as prices, market channels, finance, customer behaviour and knowledge, media and competitors, will be less informed.

Developing marketing communications for overseas markets has always been seen as particularly challenging for organisations. Understanding the differences in consumers' beliefs and values and interpreting the sometimes subtle nuances that exist between cultures has challenged brand managers for decades (Melewar et al., 2000). The complexities of creating international or global campaigns and the decreased level of control that often accompanies international campaign development, provides additional uncertainty. It is not unsurprising that the risks associated with international campaigns are seen to be higher than those for their home country.

Even when campaigns are created for single country use, given the global nature of media, particularly digital platforms, it is likely that communications will be seen in a number of countries. Brands therefore need to consider how their messages will be received by different cultures and ethnic identities, even if the campaign is only to be used in their home country.

Culture is an important consideration. The values, beliefs, customs and symbols of particular societies are referred to as culture and provide individuals with their identity. It is culture that provides guidance on what is deemed to be acceptable behaviour and influences behaviours and lifestyle. Marketing communications needs to ensure that culture is respected, otherwise there is a danger that campaigns will be seen as offensive and this is likely to have a negative effect on the organisation. Campaigns are often adapted to meet the local market needs to ensure the imagery and language adhere to cultural norms. Turnbull et al. (2016) highlight the importance of meeting cultural norms when advertising in Middle East Islamic markets. For example, they suggest advertisers need to avoid showing food being served using the left hand and suggest women are shown modestly dressed.

Other aspects of culture, such as language, symbols and religion are equally important considerations for marketing communications. Language is a symbolic device used to share meaning in society and therefore the words and style of language used in campaigns needs to consider how other members of that society will receive the message. Translating advertising from one language to another can be problematic and advertisers need to ensure that the campaign message is retained and understood by the local market.

Organisations need to be mindful of the imagery used in advertising, public relations and direct mail campaigns, to avoid infringing a culture's aesthetic codes. The clothing of models for use in international marketing communications material can be particularly problematic, and it is not uncommon for some photography and film to be shot several times with models wearing different clothing to align with local dress codes.

Religion has always played an important part in shaping the values and attitudes of society and is an important cultural consideration. Care needs to be taken not to offend religious beliefs and their associated artefacts. Turnbull et al. (2016) suggest organisations need to consider Islamic ethics when developing messages for Muslim audiences. They argue advertising needs to be mindful of both the socio-cultural and religious sensitivities in Muslim countries and when targeting Muslim consumers. Imagery such as statues is seen as being insensitive to Islamic tradition and to be avoided. Other considerations, such as avoiding comparative advertising and respect for elders are highlighted.

Image 2.1 Global thinking requires local cultural awareness

Observing local cultural values is an important dimension of international marketing communications
Source: Andrew Krasovitckii/Shutterstock.

Although many organisations go to great lengths to ensure that they get their communications right, with some pre-testing their messages across countries, blunders are not uncommon. Fromowitz (2017) highlights a number of brands that have caused offence to consumers by getting messages wrong. In one case, Food Basics, a Canadian grocery store, ran a campaign to reach out to the Sikh community to celebrate Baisakhi, a Sikh religious holiday. The campaign featured halal chicken, which is a Muslim product and forbidden for practising Sikhs. This was seen as offensive by many Sikhs, who felt the grocery chain did not understand the difference between Sikhs and Muslims.

Tylee (2017) highlights the challenges that advertisers have running campaigns globally. He suggests that brands struggle to maintain a global status and at the same time meet the needs of different consumers. He reports on some global brands that have managed to produce strong global campaigns, such as Procter & Gamble (P&G), Heineken and Unilever. Although there are numerous challenges and risks, the rewards for successful global campaigns are well documented and researched (Agrawal, 1995; Melewar et al., 2000; Melewar and Vemmervik, 2004). As well as the potential cost savings that can be gained from global campaigns, there are significant benefits from brands being able to run much larger-scale campaigns.

The dilemma facing organisations is whether to have one single creative platform that can run globally across markets, or to adapt messages to meet the needs of each individual market.

Standardisation versus adaptation

The extent to which organisations should adapt their communications messages to suit local requirements has been an ongoing debate among academics for over four decades (Fastoso and Whitelock, 2007; Kanso et al., 2015; Melewar et al., 2000; Turnbull et al., 2016). Since Levitt (1983) published his seminal work on global branding, declaring the world had become a global marketplace, the issue of whether to standardise communication messages or adapt campaigns to meet the needs of local markets has been a topic that has received significant discussion and remains unresolved.

Standardisation

Standardisation offers two key advantages for brands. First, there is the potential for significant cost efficiencies associated with adopting a uniform approach to marketing communications. Organisations can save on creative development and production costs by using the same creative ideas and creative assets across markets. This makes better use of resources and because of the economies of scale leveraged, organisations have the opportunity to spend more on the creative production. This means that there is the potential for much larger-scale campaigns.

The second key advantage of a standardised approach is that it presents a consistent global brand to consumers. In whatever country consumers see a brand message, it will be the same; message consistency and the prospect of horizontally integrated campaigns is very compelling and it is not hard to understand why so many global brands opt for a standardised approach.

While standardisation offers a number of potential advantages such as cost savings and message synergy, a number of problems are also identified with adopting this strategy. Kanso et al. (2015) highlight the cultural differences of consumers across markets, different lifestyles, language diversity, alternative market infrastructures and government regulations as some of the impediments to standardisation. Some authors have warned against standardisation and argue that ignoring local tastes and culture does not provide competitive advantage (Navarro et al., 2010).

Adaptation

Adapting messages to meet the needs of local markets provides an alternative approach for organisations. The argument in favour of this approach highlights the different needs of consumers and argues that even if suitable advertising stimuli could be identified as having universal appeal, it is unlikely that consumers across international boundaries share similar experiences, abilities or potential to process information in a standardised way, or to ascribe similar sets of meaning to the stimuli they perceive. Using ideas and message concepts developed centrally may be inappropriate for local markets and less effective at engaging audiences.

Adaptation takes into account the different cultural environment of each local market. Messages are developed to suit the local values and native language is used. This may mean for example, that in some Middle East countries Arabic calligraphy may replace typefaces in advertising copy. This strategy also ensures that local advertising regulations are taken into account when campaigns are developed.

The strategic choice of whether to standardise or adapt marketing messages is a complex one and in practice few organisations operate at either end of the spectrum. Most brands tend to use a 'middle of the road' or contingency approach (Melewar et al., 2000). This means that there is a degree of standardisation that occurs and organisations will try to make cost savings whenever possible by using existing creative material across markets.

Some organisations choose to adopt a strategy of 'glocalisation'. This means that the organisation develops a global creative platform centrally and then allows the local markets to adapt or localise the creative. This has the advantage of offering a more consistent brand style across markets and is also tailored to local culture.

Global consumer culture theory

An alternative theory that has emerged to explain strategies for global marketing in recent years is global consumer culture theory (GCCT) (Arnould and Thompson, 2005). The theory of GCCT argues that the globalisation of markets has led to the emergence of a global consumer culture, with consumers who share similar beliefs and consumption values. These consumers are not bound by where they live and so this market segment exists across borders.

An extension of GCCT is used in marketing communications to develop positioning strategies for brands (Alden et al., 1999). The authors argue that global consumers have shared behaviours and symbols and this makes it possible for brands to develop positioning strategies to target them. Alden et al. (1999) propose global consumer culture positioning (GCCP) as a strategy organisations can use to identify their brand as a symbol of global culture. Taylor and Okazaki (2015) outline two alternatives to GCCP; local consumer culture positioning (LCCP) and foreign consumer culture positioning (FCCP). They explain LCCP to be when an organisation avoids making any association with shared global cultural meanings and instead draws on local cultural meanings within their message. A study of advertising from the USA and Japan identified that GCCP is frequently being used as a positioning strategy by brands (Taylor and Okazaki, 2015). The findings highlighted how GCCP appeals in the USA used symbols of global culture such as luxury goods and well-known sports brands. Similarly, global symbols such as Pokémon and soccer players were identified in GCCP appeals for advertising in Japan.

The suggestion here is that standardisation of advertising may be an effective route for more global brands. The identification of a global culture allows organisations to use language and symbols that appeal to a wider cultural base. Developing a position and messages that are likely to appeal across borders allows organisations to take advantage of global media and has the potential to save costs.

Scholars' paper 2.1
Cultural issues affect global consumers

Meyer, M. (2017) Cultural Behaviour Determinants of the Global Consumer, *Handel Wewnêtrzny,* **1, 230–39.**

Although this paper should not be considered particularly insightful, it does provide an easily digestible overview of the cultural behaviour determinants of the global consumer. The paper includes some practical actions global marketing managers should consider.

See also:

Tian, K. and Borges, L. (2011) Cross-Cultural Issues in Marketing Communications: An Anthropological Perspective of International Business, *International Journal of China Marketing,* 2(1), 110–126.

Levitt, T. (1983) The globalization of markets, *Harvard Business Review,* May/June, 61, 92–102.

Technological issues and influences

Technological developments have always had an impact on marketing communications. From the creation of the printing press, to the development of radio, and then television, which enabled brands to get closer to their audiences. In the past 20 years it has been the Internet that has had not only a huge and significant influence but has also disrupted many established marketing communications practices.

More recently marketing communications has been radically influenced by advancement in digital technologies. These influences include the high frequency with which many individuals use mobile devices daily, increasing consumer engagement with social media and the growing number of interactive facilities that now pervade modern lifestyles. For example, the number of devices used in households has increased enormously in recent years. Tablets, mobiles and 'phablets' have become more accessible and their functionality supports new lifestyles. Part of this involves interacting with TV through these devices, particularly among younger audiences.

These effects can be considered in two contexts. One, of course, concerns consumers or users. Their behaviour has changed to accommodate these developments and these are explored in Chapter 5. The other concerns the communications industry, and in particular clients and the agencies that work on their behalf to reach and influence specific audiences. At a broad level, technology has enabled several aspects of marketing communications strategy and media planning to be automated. This is explored in Chapter 22, but here consideration is given to the influence of technology on the industry side, clients and agencies.

Marketing communications practitioners now have access to technologies that deliver a range of specific benefits. These are set out in Figure 2.2. Technological advances can be considered to be features, and once applied, they can give rise to benefits. For example, Big Data, which is considered below, is essentially a feature. It's only through analysis of the data that the benefit of more accurate, and faster audience targeting emerges.

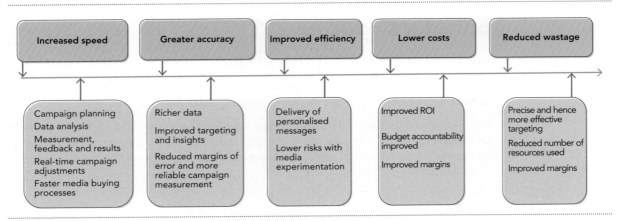

Figure 2.2 Benefits of using contemporary technologies within marketing communications

Big Data

One of the pivotal technological developments concerns Big Data. This term is used to describe the huge volumes of structured and unstructured data that is created each day.

Big Data has been defined as 'high-volume, velocity and variety information assets that demand cost-effective, innovative forms of information processing for enhanced insight and decision making' (Sicular, 2013). Embedded in this is the 3Vs concept first used to describe the three dimensions of Big Data (Laney, 2001):

1. **Volume** refers to the enormity of data that organisations collect from a variety of sources.
2. **Velocity** concerns the near real-time speed at which the data is created, stored, analysed and visualised.
3. **Variety** refers to the structured and unstructured data formats that characterise Big Data. Sources of data can be seen as streaming data (first-party owned sources), social media data (second-party data) and publicly available data (third-party data).

These 3Vs have subsequently been supplemented with a range of further Vs:

- **Veracity** concerns the accuracy of the data and the subsequent analyses that are undertaken.
- **Variability** refers to the extent to which the data is liable to change its meaning.
- **Visualisation** concerns making sure that complex data is presented in an easy to understand and comprehensible format.
- **Value** refers to the benefits created for organisations. The main value lies within the processing and analysis of raw primary data.

For marketing communications the utilisation of Big Data is having an enormous impact. It can help clients understand consumers with detail not previously known, including knowledge of their actual, real behaviours, not those that are claimed, which are gleaned from surveys and questionnaires. Big Data can be used to segment and target audiences as narrowly as a single person, and provide insight into the media used as individuals move through purchase journeys. In addition, communication strategy is now focused on an audience first basis, whereas previously it was founded on fitting a media channel around a brand (O'Hara, 2015). Big Data can be used not only to measure a purchase click but also to determine how relevant the ads were that the individual consumer was exposed to on a particular journey. All of these and other outputs from the use of Big Data are considered in later chapters.

Data management platforms

Big Data is harnessed by data management platforms (DMPs) so that clients and agencies can centralise the control of all of their audience and campaign data. DMPs use first- and third-party data from online, mobile and offline sources. They collect, classify, analyse and transfer data to other platforms such as those used for targeted advertising, content customisation and campaign management.

Among the many benefits, this enables clients to implement customised re-targeting campaigns based on specific activities and behaviours. They can also optimise their websites so that content is customised for different customers, and measure campaign performance. In addition, DMPs enable audience segmentation and targeting, media integration, as well as real-time campaign and audience analytics. DMPs have spurred the technological revolution by focusing on the need to understand what the data reveals. That means it is the way we analyse data, not the data itself which is critical (King, 2017).

Programmatic technologies

Programmatic technologies are concerned with the automatic buying of digital advertising space, using data from a DMP, to decide which ads to buy and how much to pay for them. This is often undertaken in real time. When looked at in terms of traditional approaches when publishers ran campaigns, programmatic reverts the management and measurement to the advertiser (Rogers, 2017).

In particular programmatic enables advertisers to target very exact audiences, at precisely the right time, in the right context and with the right creative message. In addition, campaigns can be adjusted or optimised, based on real-time information, to re-target audiences and to deliver more appropriate messages (see Viewpoint 2.1). Media budgets can also be optimised to reflect changing campaign conditions. (More information about programmatic media buying can be found in Chapter 22.)

Viewpoint 2.1
Johnson & Johnson use data to uncover fresh insights

Johnson & Johnson (J&J) a multinational medical devices, pharmaceutical and consumer packaged goods manufacturing company, used data analysis to uncover a fresh insight about mothers. Conversations were observed on social media, across tablet devices, early in the morning. These were happening after getting their babies back to sleep, and they were happening worldwide. This was a moment when mum was able to reconnect with the world after being completely immersed in their child's life for the last few hours.

The use of data and technology provided J&J with an opportunity to create relevant video content, optimised for tablet devices, in order to engage their target audiences at a precise moment. With greater understanding of audience behaviours, motivations and media consumption, data insights can inform the strategic approach across both media and creative to create more powerful connections.

Sources: Rahman (2016); WARC (2016).

Insight

Here we can see that J&J used marketing communications and technology in a very precise way. Using data based on social media usage they identified an opportunity to open conversations with a target audience. They communicated with a particular audience, at a particular time with relevant content. There was little waste due to the targeting and delivery through programmatic technology.

Question: What's not to like about this campaign?

Task: Find another example of precise targeting through programmatic and DMP platforms.

Mobile

Of all the new technologies, it is the rise of the mobile, and the rise of the smartphone in particular, that has arguably had the greatest impact on the media landscape, and on marketing communications. Consumers now spend much longer (an extra four hours) each day with media than in the pre-mobile era, and stay connected to the Internet for longer using mobile devices. Seven in ten UK adults use a smartphone and a major part of their usage is geared to social media.

Mobile's 'always on' and roaming capability presents advertisers with an opportunity to focus on micro-moments, and to meet consumers' desires at the right moment, at the right time and in the right place.

Mobile screens engage users through sight, sound, touch, movement and depth. As a result they can deliver immersive, multi-sensory experiences that are on-demand, personalised and seamless. This in turn presents a range of opportunities for advertisers to integrate content and entertainment. Advertising utilising traditional formats is of course routine, but add the enormous rise in the use of video, add the developing augmented and virtual reality technologies, plus product placement, in-game advertising and sponsorship, and it can be seen that mobile has become the dominant screen.

Consolidation and convergence

Technology has forced media channels together and as a result many organisations are moving into unfamiliar markets. This is evidenced by deals such as Facebook's purchase of WhatsApp and Instagram, Apple's takeover of Beats Music, and Amazon's acquisition of the video game live-streaming service Twitch.

This means that while previously these companies operated in separate sectors, convergence has brought them into direct competition with one another. Convergence and integration activity can be seen through consoles such as the PS4 and Xbox One, which now host streaming apps such as Netflix, Amazon and Now TV, all accessed through the home screen.

Some organisations seek to package different technologies together and in doing so offer high levels of cross-functionality. For example, Virgin and BT offer phone, mobile phone, broadband and TV services packages as one solution. This provides advertisers with access to potentially lucrative audiences.

Image 2.2 Mobile advertising

The growth of mobile advertising has been enormous, as it is always on, ubiquitous and can be used to reach consumers at the right moment, at the right time and in the right place.
Source: filip robert/Shutterstock.

Traditional content providers such as *The Times* and the *Guardian*, which started life as broadsheet newspapers, now deliver content online and through video, and radio-style podcasts. Google and Facebook attract huge audiences and are continually expanding their range of services. For example, Facebook has developed its mobile offering, following the purchase of Instagram and WhatsApp. In 2017 they announced the launch of *Watch,* their video hub designed to compete with rivals Snapchat, Twitter, YouTube, Pinterest, and TV networks Hulu, YouTube TV and DirecTV Now.

Reference has been made to some of the major organisations that are influencing the world of marketing communications. Companies such as Google, Facebook, Amazon and Microsoft are reconfiguring themselves to compete in new markets, introducing new advertising platforms, investing heavily in innovation and driving technological change. Facebook and Google, according to Group M, ended 2017 with an 84 per cent share of all digital media investments, excluding China (Ritson, 2017a).

We have only referred to a limited number of ways in which technology has influenced marketing communications. Other developments include social media, voice and chatbots, augmented and virtual realities, apps and viral marketing, all of which are considered in Chapter 21. What is common to all of these technology-enabled marketing communications is the change in consumer behaviour that they generate. These changes are explored in Chapter 5 but for clients and agencies they have disrupted the way they use marketing communications. The impacts have been felt in terms of strategy and planning, tactics, more precise segmenting and targeting of audiences, more effective use of budgets and reduction in the amount of waste, real-time optimisation, more media-based experimentation, and highly tuned measurement and campaign management. In addition, there are changes in agency structures, operations and the skill sets required to deliver optimal returns for their clients. These are also explored in later chapters.

The final comment at this stage is reserved for the way in which technology has brought to the surface a number of ethical issues. These include concerns associated with data privacy, taste and decency associated with gender issues and misplaced ads, plus deception and misrepresentation, which are explored in the next section.

Scholars' paper 2.2
The impact of technological advances

Malthouse, E.C. and Li, H. (2018) Opportunities for and pitfalls of using Big Data in advertising research, *Journal of Advertising,* 46(2), 227–35.

This editorial paper provides a very helpful insight into some of the issues associated with managing Big Data within an advertising context. The authors define Big Data by examining how it is, or will be, created in advertising environments. Among other things they propose a conceptual framework for understanding the different types of digital advertising touch points that create Big Data.

See also:

Garaus, M., Wagner, U. and Back, A.-M. (2017) The effect of media multitasking on advertising message effectiveness, *Psychology & Marketing,* 34(2), February, 138–56.

Ethical and societal influences

Ethics is the study of morality. This involves those practices and activities that are importantly right and wrong (De George, 1999). Marketing as a discipline is not 'exempt' from the moral considerations that apply to human affairs in general. As organisations seek advantage in increasingly competitive markets, so they must be held accountable for the decisions and actions they undertake.

Duties and consequences

Two major schools of thought can be distinguished in ethics, which broadly lie on either side of the means/ends debate. The first is concerned with *duties,* and argues that some actions are always bad and others always good. The second approach focuses on *consequences,* holding that whether an act is good or bad depends on what happens as a result of taking that action, no matter what the action is. Utilitarianism is a well-known form of this approach, seeking to identify actions that (very broadly) can be expected to result in the greatest good for the greatest number.

This distinction oversimplifies a very complex and long-running debate and also overlooks the many sophisticated variants and hybrid theories that have been developed. Neither approach on its own offers a practical and foolproof guide to ethical decision-making. As has been suggested above, a simple and apparently unarguable duty-based rule such as 'Always tell the truth in marketing communications' may cause problems as soon as we start to plan a campaign. Is it our duty to provide a detailed and reasoned discussion of all of the reasons for and against buying the product, whatever the medium we are using? Must we refrain from using ironic statements that are plainly designed to entertain, rather than inform? In practical terms, it can be difficult to forecast all of the consequences of a proposed action, however concerned one may be to achieve a balanced assessment.

The teleological approach

The practical difficulties associated with the application of simple rules or methods to complex real-life situations have led to alternative ideas for judging the ethical implications of proposed business actions. Jackson (1996), for example, explains how a focus on moral virtues in business life can provide a much more practical basis for assessing good conduct in business. The concept of virtues seeks to express those qualities and dispositions in a person that will help to ensure a good life, often seeking a 'mean' between two undesirable poles. Finding the 'mean', however, is far from straightforward. Murphy (1999) argues that a virtues approach is appropriate and useful in analysing the ethics of organisations as well as individuals, and discusses five virtues which are particularly relevant to the ethical conduct of international marketing: integrity, fairness, trust, respect and empathy.

Sternberg (2000) proposed that business ethics should be based upon the *purpose* of the company, a teleological perspective. This involves distributive justice, which refers to the principle by which rewards are allocated in proportion to the contribution made to organisational ends. The teleological approach recognises that 'long-term owner value' is not the same thing as that of short-term rewards, as the pursuit of long-term value may require very different actions from a policy designed to maximise, say, the next dividend payment. The requirement to behave with 'common decency' firmly excludes actions on the part of the firm such as lying, cheating, stealing and coercion, no matter how expedient or financially attractive they may seem in the short term: these things are always unethical. An intelligently self-interested firm will generally not wish to pursue activities that give it a bad reputation among customers, suppliers, potential recruits and the media, because to do so would be to fail to maximise long-term owner value. This is not to say that individual employees may have no other reasons for this restraint, but rather to suggest that the teleological principle will often provide sufficient reason to behave ethically in business.

The teleological principle requires that stakeholder interests be acknowledged and taken into account, because not to do so would be a violation of the principle. Importantly, it also provides guidance on *how* those interests are to be taken into account, by assessing their impact on the long-term interests of the owners of the firm.

Ethical issues in marketing communications

Consideration is now given to some of the particular ethical issues that relate directly to marketing communications. These are set out in Table 2.1 and then explored in the remaining part of this section.

Advertising as mass manipulation

Vance Packard's famous book about mass communications, *The Hidden Persuaders* (1960), had a major impact. His concern was what he saw as the manipulative, widespread use of psychological techniques in advertising, among other disciplines. Packard's book provided a powerful expression of a point of view that is often found in press and academic commentaries on advertising, sometimes linked to more fundamental political critiques of the capitalistic society in which advertising takes place. Forty years later, a similar concern is evident in Klein's (2000) account of the anti-capitalist protests that have taken place in several cities internationally. One of the strands of this diverse movement has been concern about the dominance of global brands in everyday life.

Pollay's (1986) review of social science commentaries on advertising drew together a wide range of material into a general framework. This synthesis suggested that advertising was seen – by social scientists – as a powerful and intrusive means of communication and persuasion, whose (unintended) effects could be to reinforce materialism, cynicism, irrationality, selfishness and a number of other undesirable outcomes. Holbrook's (1987) response was to suggest that the 'conventional wisdom or prevailing opinion' represented in the Pollay model was unfairly critical of a much more diverse reality.

Associated with this perspective is the argument that the advertising industry has annoyed consumers, accelerated consumption to unacceptable levels, polluted cities and even jeopardised its own existence. Brodsky (2017) argues that the existing urban infrastructures for many cities have become increasingly stretched. Public services for energy, education, health, waste-management, safety, are failing to keep pace with growing populations who seek ever more comfortable lifestyles.

This presents an opportunity for brands to move away from communications framed around the promotion of conspicuous consumption, to one that is a 'regenerative force in

Table 2.1 Areas of ethical concern in marketing communications

Issue	Explanation
Mass manipulation	The use of advertising, primarily, to manipulate people into buying products they do not want. This view is often used when reviewing the use of advertising in political critiques of capitalistic society.
Truth-telling	The need to present audiences with factually correct and transparent information, and not to lie, deceive or misrepresent a company or an offering's attributes.
Vulnerable groups	To recognise and communicate sympathetically with people (groups) who are unable to make informed decisions. These include children, pregnant women, elderly people, the recently bereaved and people who are ill.
Privacy and respect	To respect the wish of some people not be sent direct communications and to refrain from using communications that are annoying, harassing or that cause unwarranted distress or shock.
Taste and decency	The use of communications that do not either deliberately or inadvertently offend audiences.
Incentives, bribery and extortion	The use of bribes and extortion is an attempt to cheat and violate distributive justice. Incentives and the use of corporate hospitality can be considered inappropriate use of marketing communications.

the economy of cities'. For Brodsky this means using a brand's various media touchpoints not just as messengers but also as a means of helping to deliver public utility services. This approach to communications enables constructive engagement that can reconnect people, brands, communications agencies and local government. He cites the Indian energy company Halonix, which used LED billboards to communicate its brand and help tackle Delhi's ugly reputation as India's rape capital. Using an online poll, the public helped identify and prioritise the streets and areas in most need of improved lighting.

Halonix then installed a variety of lighting solutions, which featured their brand name, but at the same time their brand was framed meaningfully around supplementing Delhi's energy grid, assisting the efforts of the police force and contributing to a reduction in the number of rape crimes. The campaign proved so successful that the Indian population expressly requested that the campaign be rolled out nationally.

Truth-telling

The general ethical requirement to tell the truth applies to all forms of marketing communications. There are numerous legal and voluntary deterrents to deter lying and deceit. Although most organisations wish to comply there remains plenty of scope for judgement in respect of which aspects of the truth are to be presented in marketing communications and how they are to be conveyed.

We do not expect a salesperson to lie to us, but few expect a full and balanced account of the advantages and disadvantages of our entering into a transaction, if only for practical reasons associated with time and space. The aim of a salesperson is to sell a company's products, not to provide buyer guidance (Sternberg, 2000). Both buyer and seller have their own interests and it is normally up to either party to look after these interests during the purchase process. Thus there is no ethical requirement that customers should ensure that the transaction is profitable for the seller, nor that the seller must go to great lengths to ensure that the buyer is making a wise and prudent purchase. It is also usually important for the seller to make it plain in some way that selling is actually taking place. The Market Research Society, for example, defines the unacceptable practice of 'sugging' – selling under guise (of conducting research). The distinction between selling and giving independent advice is also embodied in the regulations relating to the marketing of financial services in the UK.

The practice of PR is also likely to raise many truth-telling issues. The purpose of PR is to create and manage relationships between a firm and its various stakeholders. This requires an ethical balance between placing an undue emphasis on the positive aspects of the firm's actions and representing the best interests of the organisation. Firms that make a habit of using PR techniques to mislead stakeholder groups are in effect consuming, in the short term, the trust upon which their long-term profitable existence may depend.

Associated with this is the epidemic of fake and false news. False news is driven by foreign state organisations while fake news is perpetuated by opportunists encouraging clickbait and false ad measurements and, of course, payments (Schiff, 2017). Facebook has been at the centre of this controversy claiming to be a platform not a publisher, and hence not responsible.

Misrepresentation and 'puffery'

On the same spectrum as truth-telling, but not at the same end, is the problem of deliberate or reckless misrepresentation in selling. Chonko (1995) defines misrepresentation as occurring when salespeople make incorrect statements or false promises about a product or service. The dividing line is not always absolutely clear, as a salesperson for example, can be expected to show enthusiasm for the product, which may result in some degree of exaggeration.

Misrepresentation or deception in advertising is usually condemned by codes of practice, if not by actual statute. It is standard practice for organisations to assume responsibility to avoid false and misleading advertising and sales promotions that use deception or manipulation. Much advertising, however, contains some degree of what might be called 'embellishment' or 'puffery'. This is the enthusiastic use of language and images to convey the most optimistic view of the product or service being portrayed. Chonko (1995) points out that the American Federal Trade Commission regards puffery as acceptable because such statements are not likely to be relied upon by consumers in making their choice. However, this places great reliance upon being able to identify those parts of marketing communications that *are* likely to be relied upon. Similar issues are raised by the visual images created for advertising, which naturally seek to show the product or endorser in the most appealing way. Children's toys are often referred to in this context as exaggerated images may have a greater potential to delude.

Vulnerable groups

There are a number of vulnerable groups to which marketing communications campaigns are targeted. Typically, but not exclusively, these include children, pregnant women, elderly people, the recently bereaved and people who are ill. Many countries have strict controls on the content and timing of advertising to children but appear to avoid advertising issues related to other vulnerable groups.

The often-discussed tragic problems resulting from the sale of baby milk products in some developing countries had much to do with marketing and associated communications from the seller that did not take adequate account of the reality of life in developing countries. For example, greater attention should have been given to the likelihood that in this environment, the product would be made up with water from a contaminated source or that the product would be over-diluted by users who were unfamiliar with it.

Viewpoint 2.2
Communicating with vulnerable groups

Image 2.3 The front of a William Hill betting shop
All William Hill outlets are carefully managed so that there are no images of gaming machines
Source: Barry Barnes/Shutterstock.

Research has found that it is common for TV and magazine ads, in South Africa, to carry misleading health and nutrition claims. Advertisers have been found to use various persuasive techniques to tempt vulnerable groups who are unable to make informed decisions about the products they buy. For example, it was found that over 50 per cent of ads in magazines that primarily target poor, black people were for unhealthy and starchy foods. Conversely, affluent, non-black groups were presented with ads for slimming foods and dietary supplements. Many ads also made false claims about the nutritional health value of food.

Staff at the bookmaker William Hill, are trained to recognise vulnerability triggers. These can indicate that customers are gambling excessively. Timed pop-ups are used to advise online customers to take a break. There are also facilities for people to pre-set limits on their spending.

The window space at William Hill's outlets is also carefully managed, with no images of gaming machines. In addition, approximately 20 per cent of all window space is committed to responsible gambling messages, a policy that is extended to TV adverts, and 10 per cent of print ad space. The company also developed a gaming machine algorithm. This is used to identify players who display 'markers of harm', one of which is a change in gambling patterns. Customers are encouraged to sign up to a linked card, which allows the identification of patterns of play. When the markers indicate dangerous behaviour, they are sent responsible gambling messages.

Sources: Abrahams et al. (2016); Mchiza (2017); Mchiza et al. (2013); ReadWriteThink (2009); Rogers (2016).

Insight

These examples offer two perspectives. The first reveals the deliberate exploitation of a vulnerable group and the second shows the awareness and informed way in which a brand manages vulnerable people. It may be argued that not enough is done and there is no overall accountability but it does demonstrate organisational awareness, insight and responsibility.

Question: If you were a manager for a brand that could easily attract vulnerable groups, how would you ensure that your brand acted responsibly?

Task: Find a different bookmaker and ascertain the extent to which they care about vulnerable groups/gamblers.

Privacy and respect

One aspect of the duty-based view of ethics referred to at the beginning of this section is the importance of treating others as ends in themselves, rather than merely as means: in other words, not merely using others, but treating them with the respect they deserve as fellow human beings. The number of potential applications in the world of marketing communications include:

- avoiding the annoyance and harassment that can result from the inappropriate application of high-pressure sales techniques;
- respecting the wish that some may have at some times to be private, not to be approached with sales calls, and not to be sent direct unsolicited communications;
- refraining from causing unwarranted distress or shock by ensuring that the content of any marketing communication 'remains within generally accepted boundaries of taste and decency'.

Privacy-related concerns fall into two main categories: unwelcome sales approaches (e.g. silent tele-selling calls) and concerns about Big Data. Marr (2017) refers to issues regarding data privacy and who is allowed to access our personal data. He also refers to data security and whether those entrusted to keep our data private can do that. The evidence in the light of several major breaches of data security, such as the hacking at Talk Talk, the NHS and the King's Fund, and the misuse of personal data by Cambridge Analytica/Facebook, suggests that all is not as secure as it might be.

Finally, reference is made to data discrimination and whether it is acceptable to discriminate against people based on data we have on them, especially those who already have access to fewer resources and information than the majority.

In the first case, the ethical response is the same as for sales harassment: ethical firms will refrain as far as possible from making unwelcome approaches, for reasons of enlightened self-interest. They will, for example, support and encourage the development of general schemes through which individuals can signify their general wish not to be contacted. They will also seek out and use mailing lists that are a very close match with their target segments, which will both make the mailing more effective and also reduce the chance of the mailing piece being seen as 'junk'. They will also provide a clear means for those who do not wish to be contacted to indicate their wish.

An ethical company can also respond to the second and more general concern about privacy, both by offering clear opportunities to individuals to have their details excluded from files and also by ensuring as far as possible that information about individuals used in direct marketing has been ethically collected, processed and stored (e.g. such that it is still up to date, thus minimising the risk of, say, causing distress by inadvertently mailing to deceased people). Sometimes, even these efforts may not be enough to avoid causing offence inadvertently, and an ethical firm will ensure that it has in place clear and effective systems to receive and respond to the complaint.

Taste and decency

Communications that annoy or alienate target audiences are unlikely to be effective, and issues regarding the taste and decency in the content of marketing communications have undoubtedly evolved. For example, the portrayal of women in early TV advertisements now seems so obviously inappropriate and could not be reused today. The 'Are You Beach Body Ready' ads represent a contemporary example of advertising that fails the taste and decency test.

Effective (and ethical) advertisers wish to treat their audiences with respect, if only because in a competitive market they cannot afford to behave otherwise. Concerns are expressed not only about the portrayal of women in advertising, but also about the way in which advertising images may carelessly stereotype people, groups, cultures and regions for narrow commercial purposes (Borgerson and Schroeder, 2002). Ethical advertisers seek to understand their target audiences well enough to be able to communicate effectively, without giving inadvertent offence. This understanding is also very important in a cross-cultural context, where the risk of giving offence inadvertently is much higher. The point is obviously true for international or global marketing.

The same concerns may apply to a charity: those appealing for funds to help alleviate distressing problems around the world may be tempted to make use of shocking real-life images of the situations that they encounter. Being aware of the ever-present risk of 'compassion fatigue' on the part of donors, as well as the possibility of causing unwarranted distress to some recipients of the message, most charity fund-raising communications remain within limits of taste and decency for what are likely to be purely prudential reasons.

Public service organisations can also consider the use of shocking imagery to communicate important messages: adverts against drinking and driving have for many years been deliberately hard-hitting, for reasons that most would accept as justifiable.

Incentives, bribery and extortion

The payment of bribes affects marketing communications as they may well involve sales staff. Bribes are unofficial, and usually illegal, payments to individuals 'to dishonestly give money to someone to persuade them to do something that will help you'. These payments may be to secure orders, for example, or to expedite deliveries.

There is a distinction between extortion and bribery: extortion is demanded by the would-be receiver, while bribery is offered by an individual or organisation wishing to buy influence. Organisations need to consider the impact on their image, and wider relationships, of taking part in bribery or extortion. These illegal practices have harmful effects on local economies and are likely to be regarded negatively by most stakeholders. The normal conduct of business relies heavily upon trust and the rule of law, both of which are undeniably jeopardised by corruption.

Sales staff operating at the customer interface can be exposed to opportunities for both bribery and extortion. Management can frame an organisational culture whereby sales recruitment, training and briefing systems are designed to encourage ethical behaviours. If neglected, however, a cultural vacuum may provide an uncertain context for individual employees, in which inexperienced or opportunistic staff may start to take decisions that are ethically unsound and against the long-term interest of the company.

For Sternberg (2000), offering a bribe is an attempt to cheat and a violation of ordinary decency, while taking a bribe is a violation of distributive justice: decisions are made because of the bribe, rather than the relevant merits of the business offering. These are difficult questions in practice, which may involve hard choices, including the choice of whether to take part in markets in which corruption is endemic.

The use of gifts and entertainment such as corporate hospitality may be intended to reward past behaviours. They can equally be regarded as an attempt to shape future purchasing or influencing behaviours. Most organisations have established policies, which limit the amount and frequency with which gifts and entertainment can be accepted.

Associated unethical practices concern corruption, collusion and anti-competitive behaviours. Viewpoint 2.3 provides an example about corruption in the German car manufacturing industry.

Viewpoint 2.3

German car manufacturers admit corruption

Image 2.4 Protests against diesel engines increase

Following the admissions about emissions fraud, consumer rejection of diesel engines has increased
Source: Tomislav Pinter/Shutterstock.

Germany had a reputation for engineering excellence and reliability, one that spanned a range of products, including watches, aircraft, cameras, tanks and cars. This positioning was threatened in 2015 when a little-known group of environmentalists asked the question: why are diesel cars in the US much less polluting than those in Europe?

Their research found that Volkswagen had deliberately recalibrated the emissions tests on 11 million diesel cars (Porsche, Audi and VW) and in doing so had been responsible for the release of huge amounts of illegal and deadly exhaust gases into the atmosphere. This alone has allegedly cost Volkswagen $25 billion in fines, refits and compensation.

In the following year a number of European truck makers, including Daimler and VW, were served with one of the largest fines for price fixing and suppressing new technologies.

In 2017 Volkswagen and Daimler wrote separately to EU competition authorities declaring that Daimler, BMW and Volkswagen had been involved in a cartel for the previous two decades. This arrangement enabled price fixing and component coordination, all at the expense of consumers, suppliers and the environment. Volkswagen estimated that there were over 60 working groups focused on different components.

At a time when the car industry is in transition, and moving from diesel and petrol to electric, hydrogen and hybrid formats, when sales of diesel cars are falling, and investment in driverless cars is increasing, these revelations threaten the German car manufacturing industry.

Sources: Charter (2017); Merenda and Irwin (2018).

Insight

The ramifications of this exposure have been enormous and rightly threaten the wellbeing and reputation of the German car industry. The actions of the individuals responsible for the deceit and cover up represent a deliberate strategy of exploitation designed to corrupt, collude and defy market and societal norms. The motives were embedded in their corporate and personal objectives, but a question concerning whether this shields a culture of industrial misrepresentation remains unanswered.

Question: To what extent is it in a society's interest to disband organisations who practise deviant behaviour on this scale?

Task: Using the web, find out what has happened to VW as a result of these revelations.

Scholars' paper 2.3
Management and relationships influences

Martínez-Martínez, I.J., Aguado, J-M., and Boeykens, Y. (2017) Ethical implications of digital advertising automation: the case of programmatic advertising in Spain, *El Profesional de la Información*, 26(2), 201–10.

This paper considers the use of programmatic advertising and some important questions regarding the level of implementation and the ethical implications derived from the implementation of this new technology. The authors report that these new technologies give rise to complex processes with important ethical and reputational implications. They identify a major contradiction between professionals' views and users' perceptions.

See also:

Pollay, R.W. (1986) The distorted mirror: reflections on the unintended consequences of advertising, *Journal of Marketing*, 50 (April), 18–36.

Fulgoni, G.M. (2016) Fraud in digital advertising: a multibillion-dollar black hole, *Journal of Advertising Research*, June, 122–25.

Industry influences

Having considered some of the international, technological and ethical influences on marketing communications, we now consider how these have impacted the marketing communications industry and the knock-on effect these are having on the management of brand-based communications.

We start with a look at the changes in the structure and configuration of the industry, the importance of industry relationships, and finish with a view of industry regulation, including issues associated with online advertising and expenditures. This content should be considered along with Chapter 9.

The UK marketing communications industry

Over the last 15 years the size of the industry has increased in response to changes in technology, the growth in the number of marketing communications activities, and with it the real value of advertising, sales promotion, public relations and direct marketing.

The configuration of the agency services industry partly reflects the moves made by the larger agencies to consolidate their positions. They have attempted to buy either smaller, often medium-sized competitors, in an attempt to protect their market shares or provide an improved range of services for their clients, particularly in areas of digital and content.

This has led to an industry characterised by a small number of very large agencies, many owned by holding companies that dominate the industry landscape. As shown in Figure 2.3, these six 'supergroups' now own the world's largest agency networks and can be said to represent the majority of creative and media agencies. Within these giant organisations structural changes are made to better meet customer needs, to reduce costs and improve efficiencies. For example, WPP consolidated five of its branding agencies into one, under a new name *Superunion*. The move was engineered to reduce costs, but it also provides global clients with improved service. A similar restructuring was undertaken when media agencies *Maxus* and *MEC* were merged into *Wavemaker*. *WPP Health & Wellness* was also created by bringing together its four large healthcare agencies (O'Reilly, 2018).

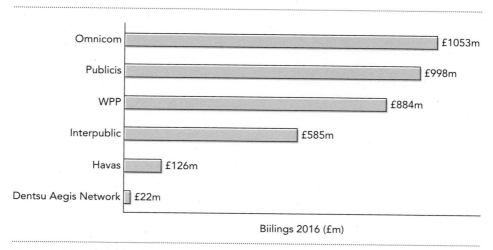

Figure 2.3 Top holding companies ranked by advertising billings

In contrast to these large agency networks there are an even greater number of very small agencies. These smaller agencies have formed as the result of people formerly employed in large agencies becoming frustrated with having to work within tight margins and increased administration, or spotting niche opportunities, and then leaving and setting up their own fledgling businesses.

Broadly speaking, the industry consists of a few very large group of agencies, some big agencies, a large number of very small agencies and relatively few medium-sized agencies. Although ownership has been an important factor driving industry development, the current preference for loose, independent networks has enabled some large organisations to offer clients an improved range of services and the small agencies a chance to work with some of the bigger accounts.

Developments in technology, most noticeably automation, has brought a renewed phase of restructuring. This manifests itself as merger and acquisition activity as the larger players acquire digital start-ups that show promise and provide a strong strategy fit.

Client organisations also exert influence and shape the industry. For example, P&G, the world's largest advertiser, had invested heavily in digital media advertising for several years. In 2017 P&G cut hundreds of millions of dollars in digital advertising and also cut its global agency roster from 6,000 to 2,500 (Hercher, 2018), saving around $750 million in agency fees and production costs. This was a response to online fraud, invisible inventory, bot traffic and over-targeting individuals to cap the frequency at which messages are presented to viewers across each channel. Yet, despite these cutbacks P&G's performance in the final quarter improved, supporting the case that there is too much waste within the digital advertising arena. In February 2018 P&G announced a further cut of $400 million by 2021 (Neff, 2018).

The rise of automation within media buying has brought a number of changes. These include clients, such as P&G and Unilever, starting their own trading desks, agencies having to reskill and develop new ways of working, while several major consultancies have started to acquire media buying businesses.

Viewpoint 2.4

Amazon disrupts shelf space

Such is the dominance of Amazon that the way a product is presented and perceived, including its ratings and reviews, has become critical to a brand's success, on and off the Amazon site. For example, Amazon does not sell cars, but worked with Hyundai to offer test drives to Prime Now customers in California.

Amazon's advertising business has grown to the point that it threatens the dominance of Google and Facebook. Its power affects ad agencies who are offering specialised services to help brands piggyback on Amazon's universe. Two WPP ad agencies provide a service that helps organisations to spend their advertising budgets specifically across 'the Amazon ecosystem'.

What is interesting are the relative advantages held by the big three, Google, Facebook and Amazon. Google knows what people are searching for; Facebook knows what people are interested in and who they are connected to; Amazon knows specifically what products and how frequently customers are purchasing. The point being that Amazon has a massive amount of consumer purchase data.

Now that the power of its sales strategy is established, Amazon has shifted its focus to the other end of the customer journey. It is now working to improve the increasingly important role of how people discover and learn about their range of offerings. Amazon urges agencies to view product pages and images as 'brand marketing vehicles'. If they are not well maintained then all of the preparatory work is wasted.

Amazon now encourages companies to buy more ads through its own media group. It does this by drawing a connection between people seeing an ad and then making a purchase. More than half of the consumers in the USA now start online product searches on Amazon, compared with 28 per cent on search engines, and 16 per cent on retailer websites.

Sources: Maheshwari (2017); Thomas (2017).

Insight

There can be little doubt that Amazon have disrupted most of the markets that they have entered. Their practices appear to have lowered prices, squeezed margins and with affiliate marketing practices and associated networking, strangled many smaller operators, such as small, independent book shops. Amazon have now embarked on disrupting the agency and advertising market.

Question: Is Amazon predominantly a publisher, a client, agency, or just a platform? Justify your response.

Task: Make notes itemising the positive contribution Amazon has made to society.

Relationships

There are a vast number of relationships that form between the various stakeholders but of these we consider those between clients and agencies. The quality of the relationship between an agency and a client very often determines the length of the contract and the strength of the solutions advanced for a client.

There are a number of client–agency relationships that have flourished over a very long period of time, some for several decades. There are some agencies that have retained specific clients over long periods of time, such as JWT, who have held the Shell account for nearly 50 years, Rolex for over 60 and Unilever for over 100 years. It should be said that there are a huge number of other accounts who also have excellent relationships that have lasted a long time.

These, however, appear to be in the minority as Antoniewicz (2017) reports research by R3 that the average length of client–agency relationships is now 3.2 years. Many relationships appear to founder as clients abandon agencies and search for better, fresher solutions, because a contract expires, the client needs change, or owing to takeovers and mergers between agencies, which require that they forfeit accounts that cause a conflict of interest. Clients are seeking more control over their creative and media activities, witnessed by their use of fewer agencies and customising their approach to media and marketing (Spanier, 2017).

From a contextual perspective these buyer/seller relationships can be seen to follow a pattern of inception, development, maintenance and dissolution stages (Fam and Waller, 2008). During this relationship lifecycle, clients and agencies enter into a series of interactions (West and Paliwoda, 1996) or exchanges through which levels of trust and commitment develop. Hakansson (1982) identified several contexts, or atmospheres, within which relationships develop. These contexts had numerous dimensions: closeness/distance, cooperation/conflict, power/dependence, trustworthiness and expectations. Therefore, the client–agency relationship should be seen in the context of the network of organisations and the exchanges or interactions that occur in that network. It is through these interactions that the tasks that need to be accomplished are agreed, resources made available, strategies determined and goals achieved.

The quality of a client–agency relationship is a function of trust, which is developed through successive exchanges and which fosters confidence. According to Hobbs (2017) the level of trust is falling following much publicised evidence of dubious supply chains and agency kick-backs. Several major clients, including Pepsi, have responded to their distrust with the media supply chain by bringing both creative and media buying expertise in-house. The benefits include making significant cost savings through opportunities to create content for others, and to use these revenues to reduce their own communications costs. Ritson (2017b) predicts that a primary attraction of this move is to manage auto-mated media planning and buying, to the point that it becomes an internal competency, and from there, a source of differentiation.

Perhaps the biggest issue concerns the ownership of data. This reflects the increasing prominence and importance of programmatic advertising, and the criticality of data and customer relationship management. Marketers are becoming more reluctant to share their data with agencies and tech platforms, and as a result they want to own their data.

The way in which clients use multiple agencies to fulfil the whole range of communications tasks does not encourage the establishment of strong relationships nor does it help the cause of integrated marketing communications. The use of roster agencies means that marketing teams have to manage more agencies, often with reduced resources. This means that agencies get a smaller share of the available budget, which in turn does not help agencies feel comfortable (Child, 2007).

Poor relationships between agencies and clients are likely to result from a lack of trust and falling commitment. As it appears that communications are a primary element in the formation and substance of relational exchanges, clients might be advised to consider the agencies in their roster as an extended department of the core organisation and use internal marketing communications procedures to assist the development of identity and belonging.

The marketing communications industry has experienced major disruption as a result of recent technological and social developments. These are driving constituent organisations to find new, more effective and efficient ways of achieving their goals within a changing environment.

Scholars' paper 2.4
Client-agency relationships

Gambetti, R., Biraghi, S., Schultz, D.E. and Graffigna, G. (2016) Brand wars: consumer–brand engagement beyond client–agency fights, *Journal of Strategic Marketing,* **24(2), 90–103.**

This paper reveals the conflict that exists in the relationship between clients and agencies. The study reveals the lack of a 'relationship culture' between agency and client, with each blaming the other for inhibiting consumer–brand engagement.

See also

Zolkiewski, J., Burton, J. and Stratoudaki, S. (2008) The delicate power balance in advertising agency-client relationships: partnership or battleground? The case of the Greek advertising market, *Journal of Customer Behaviour,* 7(4), 315–32.

Turnbull, S. (2016). From pitch to ditch: the client/ad agency life cycle, *The Marketing Review,* 16(2), 111–27.

Kim, D.M. (2016) Media groups' management strategies: business areas, platform strategies, content distribution strategies and business strategies, *Journal of Digital Convergence,* 14(2), February, 157–67.

Advertising regulations

The UK advertising industry is controlled and regulated in two main ways. One of these is through legislation and the other, the majority, is through voluntary self-controls. Indeed, the UK is regarded as having one of the best self-regulation frameworks in the world. All advertising is governed by codes of practice that have been established to protect the consumer and ensure advertising is honest, legal, decent and truthful. These codes of practice are maintained by the Committees of Advertising Practice (CAP) and must be followed by all advertisers, media and agencies. The codes are enforced by the Advertising Standards Authority (ASA) and regulate all forms of advertising, including banner and display ads, paid-for search, company websites and networking sites such as Twitter and Facebook, commercial email and SMS text message ads, in-app ads and online behavioural advertising (OBA).

The ASA has been regulating ads for over 50 years and administers the UK Advertising Codes (ASA, 2018). Providing general guidance on self-regulation to industry about what is responsible advertising, the ASA protects consumers from misleading, harmful or offensive ads. There are codes for advertising to specific audiences, such as children and special guidance on advertising alcohol, health, motoring, gambling and financial products. Any complaints about advertising are handled by the ASA. While some complaints such as a minor mistake on an ad are resolved with the advertiser quickly, others undergo a formal investigation by the ASA Council who will rule on the issue. They will decide if the Advertising Codes have been breached and if ads are seen to have broken the rules they are required to be changed or withdrawn.

In its first year of operation the ASA received less than 100 complaints. Nowadays, with the increasing number of media channels and adverts, both on and offline, the ASA handles over 30,000 complaints a year.

Advertising on social media sites, brand owners' own websites and video-on-demand (VOD) have been added to the ASA's remit in the last decade. In 2009, the ASA agreed a co-regulatory agreement with Ofcom to regulate ads that appear on VOD services to ensure that VOD ads met the same standards as TV advertising (ASA, 2012).

Online advertising has been covered by the ASA since 1995 when the ASA's remit was extended to capture 'non-broadcast electronic media' such as banner ads and paid-for search. However, it was not until 2010 that the ASA extended its remit to cover brand owners' websites and advertising on social networking sites like Facebook and Twitter. The ASA had been receiving an increasing number of complaints against

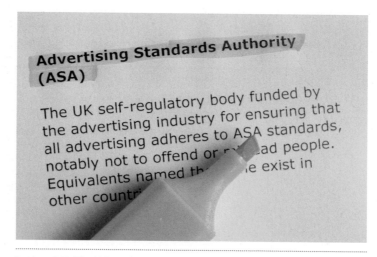

Image 2.5 The ASA

The ASA regulates ads to ensure they are legal, decent, honest and truthful
Source: Sohel Parvez Haque/Shutterstock.

internet ads, but because most of the complaints related to ads appearing on brands' own websites, they were not subject to the ASA standards. Extending the ASA regulations to cover websites owned by brands has brought advertising on these sites in line with other media.

The remit of the ASA has certainly expanded over the last five decades and no doubt will continue to grow as the media arena changes and new forms of advertising emerge (ASA, 2018).

The point is, therefore, that new forms of media have proved challenging for all sectors of the marketing communications industry. It is not just the brand owners and the agencies that have had to adapt to the new media arena, but other stakeholders such as the regulatory bodies. The increased volume and complexity of advertising across platforms has forced the ASA to redefine its scope and remain agile in order to respond to emergent advertising forms and media.

The social and technological changes outlined earlier in this chapter not only influence consumers but have forced agencies and their clients to adapt their practices. For example, the World Federation of Advertisers reported that a survey of the top 35 multinational companies with a total annual marketing budget of over $30 billion, identified a list of priority issues that were of concern (Anon, 2017).

At the top of the list was transparency, with over 70 per cent stating that they had amended their media agency contracts. Brand safety was the second most important issue. Seventy-four per cent of respondents had suspended investment in ad networks where there was unnecessary risk to their brands, and others had plans to limit investment in networks that do not permit the use of third-party verification. Other priority issues included ad fraud, and viewability, with over a third of firms devising their own viewability criteria. See Table 2.2 for an explanation of these terms.

As a response to some of these issues P&G announced in 2017 that they now require all of their media suppliers to provide validated and accredited third-party measurement verification (Pritchard, 2017). It might be that the development of blockchain technologies can provide the disruptive force necessary to overcome these 'priority issues'. (Blockchain technologies are considered in Chapter 22.)

Trends in communications expenditure

The amount of financial resources made available by clients has always influenced the overall level of communication activity. The amount of investment varies according to client perceptions about the strength of the economy and the goals they wish to achieve.

Table 2.2 Key terms associated with online advertising issues

Issue	Explanation
Transparency	The ability to openly measure the cost, performance and pricing of digital advertising.
Brand safety	Ensuring that online ads appear in an appropriate and conforming context. The aim is to avoid placing ads in environments (e.g. offensive or inappropriate) that could potentially damage a brand's reputation.
Ad fraud	A financial scam based on driving fake hits and fake leads to generate inaccurate and misleading advertising performance outcomes. Types of ad fraud include click fraud, search ad fraud, ad stacking, keyword stuffing, domain spoofing and pixel stuffing.
Viewability	An online advertising metric that aims to track only those impressions that can actually be seen by users. An ad is considered viewable if at least half of a display ad has the chance to be seen in the viewable portion of a browser window for at least one continuous second.

With recession comes inevitable cutbacks, and with growth comes lagged increases in communication investment.

In addition to the overall amount there is an important question about where this resource is used. How should a budget be deployed across different disciplines? Which media channels should be used to convey messages? There has been considerable speculation in recent years that offline advertising revenues were about to plummet as organisations move their 'spend' into online and mobile, collectively referred to in the statistics as internet. Although many organisations have increased their digital and interactive investments considerably and have reduced these offline the impact has not been as great as some commentators had feared. In 2018 total media expenditure in the UK grew. Although some areas such as print have seen expenditure decline, the growth in internet spend has increased the overall advertising expenditure (WARC, 2018).

What is also of interest is the way in which the communications mix has been changing over the past 20 years. For a long time spend on media advertising dominated the marketing budget of consumer brands. Sales promotion became a strong influence but spend on this tool has stagnated, although it revives as recessions take hold. Today, television, sponsorship, direct marketing and above all else, digital activities, now attract the most investment. The reasons for this shift are indicative of the increasing attention and accountability that management is attaching to marketing communications. Increasingly, marketing managers are being asked to justify the amounts they invest/spend on their entire budgets, including advertising and sales promotion. Senior managers want to know the return they are getting for their communications investments, in order that they meet their business objectives and that scarce resources can be used more efficiently and effectively in the future. Programmatic advertising now provides these figures for managers, which indicate the possible returns on their investments, where investments should be made, and reduces wastage and inefficiencies. (To read more on this see Chapter 22.)

Key points

- Organisations using marketing communications in international markets need to observe and openly respect local and regional cultures. These concern the values, beliefs, customs, symbols, language and religious properties and characteristics that provide individuals and societies with their identity.

- A fundamental decision for firms operating in the global marketplace concerns whether to standardise communication messages or adapt campaigns to meet the needs of local markets.

- Global consumer culture theory holds that the globalisation of markets has led to the emergence of a global consumer culture, with consumers who share similar beliefs and consumption values. These consumers are not bound by where they live and so this market segment exists across borders.

- The rapid development of digital technologies continues to have a profound effect on the way organisations use marketing communications. The impact of Big Data, data management platforms, programmatic technologies and mobile, amongst others, has impacted consumer behaviour and the nature, shape and structure of the communications industry.

- Organisations need to be aware of a variety of ethical and societal issues in order that they demonstrate a consumer orientation and operate with appropriate values. These influences concern mass manipulation, telling the truth, communicating with vulnerable groups, observing individual rights to privacy and respect, communicating and behaving tastefully and with decency, and avoiding situations where accusations of incentives, bribery and extortion could be levelled.

- The structure and shape of the marketing communications industry is evolving and influences the nature of the services offered, their cost and the quality of delivery. Relationships between clients and agencies are of critical importance and influence the level of trust and commitment.

- Issues concerning online advertising are increasing and are of particular concern to clients. These include transparency, viewability, brand safety and ad fraud.

- The advertising industry is self-regulated. Codes of practice are maintained by the Committees of Advertising Practice (CAP) and enforced by the Advertising Standards Authority (ASA).

Channel 4 Paralympics
One of the most accessible campaigns ever seen

Image 2.6 Channel 4 supported The Paralympic Games 2016

C4 wanted to challenge perceptions of disability

Source: Howard Davies/Alamy Stock Photo.

Channel 4 is a commercially funded, publicly owned UK TV channel. The channel is committed to championing diversity, inclusivity and inspiring change in people's lives. As part of Channel 4's Diversity Charter, 2016 was declared their Year of Disability and the channel was determined to use the year to improve representation of disabled people on and off screen.

Channel 4 had broadcast coverage of the debut 2012 Paralympic Games in London and the Rio 2016 Games offered a chance to further demonstrate the channel's commitment to diversity. The channel saw an opportunity to make the Rio 2016 Paralympics more than just a sporting event and decided to use the Games as a platform to start a conversation about disability and to change public attitude. Rio 2016 brought a number of challenges, including a four-hour time difference and no host nation advantage, which the 2102 Games had provided. The biggest challenge, however, was the attitude of British audiences towards disability. Research had shown that only a quarter of Brits were interested in the Paralympic Games, compared to more than a third who showed an interest in the Olympics.

Research undertaken by Scope identified that 67 per cent of the UK public felt uncomfortable speaking to a disabled person. The research identified that this discomfort was mainly because they didn't know anyone who was disabled to talk to. The research highlighted that one fifth of 18–34 year-olds had avoided speaking to a disabled person because they were uncertain about how to communicate with them. Channel 4 needed to find a way to engage audiences in the Paralympics and in doing so make Britain feel comfortable with disability. The campaign had an overarching goal of turning disability into a celebration of activity in all walks of life and three key communications objectives were set:

1. Increase audience ratings for the 2016 Rio Paralympics.
2. Drive positive perceptions of Channel 4 as a channel that champions diversity and inclusivity.
3. Challenge perceptions of disability in the UK.

The strategy was led by the channel's core values of innovation and diversity. Channel 4 wanted the campaign to be a positive, life-affirming celebration of the ability of disabled people. The channel developed an integrated strategy with inclusivity at the heart of the campaign.

The centrepiece of the campaign was a three-minute film, featuring 140 disabled people. The film was premiered across broadcast and social media channels simultaneously. Social media was used to encourage sharing and the film trended within the first 10 minutes of release. The soundtrack to the film, *Yes I Can*, was released as a single to extend the campaign reach. Signed, subtitled and audio-described versions of the film were created and distributed across platforms to create Channel 4's most accessible advertising campaign ever.

As well as the accessibility of the creative, Channel 4's media strategy was built around inclusivity. The campaign used innovative audio-enabled posters as one form of media and featured the use of artificial intelligence (AI) on Facebook to provide access for the partially sighted. Accessibility was at the core of the media planning.

To extend the reach of the message, Channel 4 invited brands to participate in the campaign by launching a competition to give away £1 million of commercial airtime. Brands were encouraged to feature disability in their advertising campaigns and were rewarded with airtime from the channel.

Channel 4 partnered with international broadcasters to extend the reach of the campaign to global audiences. In Australia, the channel teamed up with Channel 7 to run the film as part of the official Paralympic Games promotion.

The campaign delivered against its objectives. First, Channel 4 wanted to increase audience ratings. Coverage of the 2016 Rio Paralympic games was watched by 27.2 million people. That is, half of the UK's population tuned in to watch the games. The viewing share among younger audiences aged 25–34 increased by 5 per cent in comparison to London 2012. Additionally, audience data showed that Channel 4 was the most viewed channel during the Rio games between 11 p.m. and 1 a.m. Second, Channel 4 wanted to drive positive perceptions of their commitment to diversity and inclusivity. The campaign also delivered on this and enhanced the reputation of the channel as a champion of disability. Campaign evaluation showed that half of those who could recall the launch campaign said they had a better impression of the channel as a result. Third, Channel 4 had set out to challenge perceptions of disability. Campaign data revealed that by the opening of the 2016 Paralympic Games, two-thirds of the population recalled seeing the campaign and 49 per cent said it made them feel more positive towards disabled people. The survey also showed that three-quarters of the UK population reported the campaign helped them feel more comfortable talking about disability and to disabled people. The campaign succeeded in changing attitudes to disability in the UK.

The success of Channel 4's 2016 Rio Paralympic Games campaign, *Yes I Can*, extends beyond the objectives set. The technological innovation and cross-platform video strategy had delivered the most accessible marketing communications campaigns ever seen and redefined media 'reach'. The campaign not just spoke about inclusivity, but it was inclusive. All aspects of the creative and media strategy were driven by the goal to reach everyone in the UK. An indication of the cultural impact of the campaign comes from *Yes I Can* being the most shared Olympic/Paralympic campaign globally. The campaign has been referenced by the US State Department and used as part of a UN initiative for disabled people. Additionally, Channel 4's coverage of the 2016 Rio Paralympic Games has been included in the UK school curriculum for media studies.

Sources: Best Topical Campaign – C4 Paralympics (n/d); Channel 4 Paralympics (2017); The story behind how Channel 4 changed minds on disability (2018).

Review questions

Channel 4 Paralympics case questions

1. Identify the range of influences that might have impacted Channel 4's decision to engage with the Rio Paralympic Games.

2. To what extent did the *Yes I Can* campaign utilise digital technology?

3. What advertising regulations might Channel 4 have had to work within?

4. Discuss the ways in which the *Yes I Can* campaign met the ethical parameters set out in this chapter.

5. Explain how the campaign succeeded in changing attitudes to disability in the UK.

General questions

1. What are the practical problems of adopting either a standardisation or adaptation strategy towards international marketing communications?

2. Why is it both difficult and important for an organisation to take account of individual privacy when designing and implementing its marketing communications?

3. How might the misuse of Big Data lead to problems for individual organisations?

4. Explore the way the agency services industry might reconfigure as technology adopts a more voice-based platform.

5. How effective would it be if the level of voluntary controls over marketing communications were reduced in favour of increased legislation?

References for Chapter 2

The authors wish to acknowledge Richard Christy whose contribution to previous editions has been used to underpin the ethics section in this chapter.

Abrahams, Z., Temple, N.J., Mchiza, Z.J. and Steyn, N.P. (2016) A study of food advertising in magazines in South Africa, *Journal of Hunger & Environmental Nutrition*, 12(3), 429–41.

Agrawal, M. (1995) Review of a 40-year debate in international advertising: practitioner and academician perspectives to the standardization/adaptation issue, *International Marketing Review*, 12(1), 26–48.

Alden, D.L., Steenkamp, J.B.E. and Batra, R. (1999) Brand positioning through advertising in Asia, North America, and Europe: the role of global consumer culture, *The Journal of Marketing*, 63(1), 75–87.

Anon (2017) Global marketers make media management changes, WARC, 17 August, retrieved 17 August from https://www.warc.com/NewsAndOpinion/News/Global_marketers_make_media_management_changes/39147?utm_source=DailyNews&utm_medium=email&utm_campaign=DailyNews20170817

Antoniewicz, S. (2017) The five rules of successful client-agency relationships, *The Drum*, 14 June, retrieved 1 April 2018 from http://www.thedrum.com/opinion/2017/06/14/the-five-rules-successful-client-agency-relationships

Arnould, E.J. and Thompson, C.J. (2005) Consumer culture theory (CCT): twenty years of research, *Journal of Consumer Research*, 31(4), 868–82.

ASA (2012) Guidance on advertising for providers of video-on-demand services, ASA, 2 July, retrieved 30 August 2018 from https://www.asa.org.uk/resource/advertising-in-video-on-demand-services.html

ASA (2018) Our history, retrieved 20 August 2018 from www.asa.org.uk/about-asa-and-cap/our-history.html

Best Topical Campaign – C4 Paralympics (n/d) *Newsworks*, retrieved 30 March 2018 from https://www.newsworks.org.uk/write/MediaUploads/2014%20Research%20Planning/Case%20Studies/2015/channel_4_OMD.pdf

Borgerson, J.L. and Schroeder, J. (2002) Ethical issues of global marketing: avoiding bad faith in visual representation. *European Journal of Marketing*, 36(5–6), 570–94.

Brodsky (2017) Urban brand-utility: turning brand comms into a network of creative, urban resiliency, *Brand Quarterly*, Tuesday 15 August, retrieved 15 August 2017 from http://www.brandquarterly.com/urban-brand-utility-regenerative-strategy-can-turn-brand-communications-network-creative-urban-resiliency?

Channel 4 Paralympics (2017) Cannes Archive, retrieved 10 January 2018 from http://www.canneslionsarchive.com/Home/PublicHome

Charter, D. (2017) Why 'Made in Germany' is now a badge of dishonour, *The Times*, Saturday 29 July, 32–3.

Child, L. (2007) How to manage your relationship, *Marketing Agency* (December), 4–7.

Chonko, L.B. (1995) *Ethical Decisions in Marketing*, Thousand Oaks, CA: Sage.

De George, R.T. (1999) *Business Ethics*, 5th edn, Englewood Cliffs, NJ: Prentice-Hall.

Fam, K.S. and Waller, D.S (2008) Agency-client relationship factors across life-cycle stages, *Journal of Relationship Marketing*, 7(2), 217–36.

Fastoso, F. and Whitelock, J. (2007) International advertising strategy: the standardisation question in manager studies: patterns in four decades of past research and directions for future knowledge advancement, *International Marketing Review*, 24(5), 591–605.

Fromowitz, M. (2017) Hall of shame: more multicultural brand blunders. *Campaign-live*, retrieved 10 January 2018 from https://www.campaignlive.com/article/hall-shame-multicultural-brand-blunders/1423941

Fulgoni, G.M. (2016) Fraud in digital advertising: a multibillion-dollar black hole, *Journal of Advertising Research*, June, 122–25.

Gambetti, R., Biraghi, S., Schultz, D.E. and Graffigna, G. (2016) Brand wars: consumer–brand engagement beyond client–agency fights, *Journal of Strategic Marketing*, 24(2), 90–103.

Garaus, M., Wagner, U. and Back, A.-M. (2017) The effect of media multitasking on advertising message effectiveness, *Psychology & Marketing*, 34(2), February, 138–56.

Hakansson, H. (1982) *International Marketing and Purchasing of Industrial Goods: An Interaction Approach*, Chichester: John Wiley.

Hercher, J. (2018) Procter & Gamble plans to keep slashing marketing costs, *adexchanger*, 23 January, retrieved 24 January 2018 from https://adexchanger.com/online-advertising/procter-gamble-plans-keep-slashing-marketing-costs/

Hobbs, T. (2017) The big debate: is it the beginning of the end for the 'big five' agency holding groups? *Marketing Week*, 17 October, retrieved 12 January 2018 from https://www.marketingweek.com/2017/10/17/big-debate-big-five-agency/

Holbrook, M.B. (1987) Mirror, mirror, on the wall, what's unfair in the reflections on advertising? *Journal of Marketing*, 51 (July), 95–103.

Jackson, J.C. (1996) *An Introduction to Business Ethics*, Oxford: Blackwell.

Kanso, A., Nelson, R. A. and Kitchen, P. J. (2015) Meaningful obstacles remain to standardization of international services advertising: new insights from a managerial survey, *International Journal of Commerce and Management*, 25(4), 490–511.

Kim, D.M. (2016) Media groups' management strategies: business areas, platform strategies, content distribution strategies and business strategies, *Journal of Digital Convergence*, 14(2), February, 157–67.

King, G. (2016) Big Data is not actually about the data, *The Washington Post*, 20 May, retrieved 5 July 2017 from https://www.washingtonpost.com/blogs/post-live/wp/2016/05/05/meet-professor-gary-king/?utm_term=.d0aafa16ee2e

Klein, N. (2000) *No Logo*, Knopf Canada, Picador.

Levitt, T. (1983) The globalization of markets, *Harvard Business Review*, May/June, 61, 92–102.

Maheshwari, S. (2017) As Amazon's influence grows, marketers scramble to tailor strategies, *New York Times*, 31 July, retrieved 9 August 2017 from https://www.nytimes.com/2017/07/31/business/media/amazon-advertising.html?emc=edit_th_20170801&nl=todaysheadlines&nlid=53305755&_r=0

Malthouse, E.C. and Li, H. (2018) Opportunities for and pitfalls of using Big Data in advertising research, *Journal of Advertising*, 46(2), 227–35.

Marr, B. (2017) The complete beginner's guide to Big Data everyone can understand, *Forbes*, 14 March, retrieved 31 July 2017 from https://www.forbes.com/sites/bernardmarr/2017/03/14/the-complete-beginners-guide-to-big-data-in-2017/#3ac1f9f07365

Martínez-Martínez, I.J., Aguado, J-M., and Boeykens, Y. (2017) Ethical implications of digital advertising automation: the case of programmatic advertising in Spain, *El Profesional de la Información*, 26(2), 201–10.

Mchiza, Z. (2017) How marketers target poor illiterate people with unhealthy food ads, *The Conversation*, 15 February, retrieved 30 July 2017 from http://theconversation.com/how-marketers-target-poor-illiterate-people-with-unhealthy-food-ads-70285

Mchiza, Z.J., Temple, N.J., Steyn, N.P., Abrahams, Z. and Clayford, M. (2013) Content analysis of television food advertisements aimed at adults and children in South Africa, *Public Health Nutrition*, 16(12), 2213–20.

Melewar, T.C., Turnbull, S. and Balabanis, G. (2000) International advertising strategies of multinational enterprises in the Middle East, *International Journal of Advertising*, 19(4), 529–47.

Melewar, T.C. and Vemmervik, C. (2004) International advertising strategy: a review, reassessment and recommendation, *Management Decision*, 42(7), 863–81.

Merenda, M.J. and Irwin, M. (2018) Case study: Volkswagen's diesel emissions control scandal, *Journal of Strategic Innovation and Sustainability*, 13(1), 53–62.

Meyer, M. (2017) Cultural behaviour determinants of the global consumer, *Handel Wewnêtrzny*, 1, 230–39.

Murphy, P.E. (1999) Character and virtue ethics in international marketing: an agenda for managers, researchers and educators, *Journal of Business Ethics*, 18, 107–24.

Navarro, A., Losada, F., Ruzo, E. and Díez, J.A. (2010) Implications of perceived competitive advantages, adaptation of marketing tactics and export commitment on export performance, *Journal of World Business*, 45(1), 49–58.

Neff, J. (2018) P&G will cut another $400 million in agency, production costs, *AdAge*, 22 February, retrieved 8 March 2018 from http://adage.com/article/cmo-strategy/p-g-cut-400-million-agency-produc/312488/?utm_source=breaking_news_alerts&utm_medium=newsletter&utm_campaign=adage&ttl=1519930942&utm_visit=1192849

O'Hara, C. (2015) What role should agencies play in Data Management? *Adexchanger*, 2 February, retrieved 22 August 2018 from https://adexchanger.com/data-driven-thinking/what-role-should-agencies-play-in-data-management/

O'Reilly, L. (2018) WPP consolidates five branding agencies into 'Superunion', *The Wall Street Journal*, 24 January, retrieved 24 January 2018 from https://www.wsj.com/articles/wpp-consolidates-five-branding-agencies-into-superunion-1516707001

Packard, V. (1960) *The Hidden Persuaders*, Harmondsworth: Penguin.

Pollay, R.W. (1986) The distorted mirror: reflections on the unintended consequences of advertising, *Journal of Marketing*, 50 (April), 18–36.

Pritchard, M. (2017) *Better Advertising Enabled by Media Transparency*, IAB Annual Leadership Meeting, Hollywood, retrieved 3 January 2018 from https://www.youtube.com/watch?v=NEUCOsphol0

Rahman, S. (2016) Marketing in moments that matter, *CIM Exchange*, 30 August, retrieved 22 January 2018 from https://exchange.cim.co.uk/blog/marketing-in-moments-that-matter/

ReadWriteThink (2009) Persuasive techniques in advertising, retrieved 11 August 2018 from http://www.readwritethink.org/files/resources/lesson_images/lesson1166/PersuasiveTechniques.pdf

Ritson, M. (2017a) Why you should fear the 'digital duopoly' in 2018, *Marketing Week*, 5 December, retrieved 15 December 2017 from https://www.marketingweek.com/2017/12/05/ritson-digital-duopoly-2018/

Ritson, M. (2017b) Media buying's deadly sins – and why agencies are too late to save their souls, *Marketing Week*, 3 October, retrieved 12 January 2018 from https://www.marketingweek.com/2017/10/03/mark-ritson-media-buying/

Rogers, C. (2016) Marketers need to understand the widening scope of vulnerability to avoid alienating customers, *Marketing Week*, 9 June, retrieved 30 July 2017 from https://www.marketingweek.com/2016/06/09/marketers-need-to-understand-the-widening-scope-of-vulnerability-to-avoid-alienating-customers/

Rogers, C. (2017) What is programmatic advertising? A beginner's guide, *Marketing Week*, 27 March, retrieved 31 July 2017 from https://www.marketingweek.com/2017/03/27/what-is-programmatic/

Schiff, A. (2017) Fake Russian ads could have very real implications for Facebook, *Adexchanger*, 20 September, retrieved 24 January 2018 from https://adexchanger.com/platforms/fake-russian-ads-real-implications-facebook/?

Sicular, S. (2013) Gartner's Big Data definition consists of three parts, not to be confused with three 'V's, *Forbes*, 27 May, retrieved 3 July 2017 from https://www.forbes.com/sites/gartnergroup/2013/03/27/gartners-big-data-definition-consists-of-three-parts-not-to-be-confused-with-three-vs/#3cd0a72c42f6

Spanier, G. (2017) Brands take control from agencies, *Campaign*, 8 June, retrieved 12 January 2018 from https://www.campaignlive.co.uk/article/brands-control-agencies/1435797

Sternberg, E. (2000) *Just Business*, 2nd edn, Oxford: Oxford University Press.

Thomas, L. (2017) Amazon's growing advertising clout threatens the dominance of Google and Facebook, says analyst, *CNBC*, Tuesday 4 April retrieved 9 August 2017 from https://www.cnbc.com/2017/04/04/bmo-capital-amazon-upgraded-google-downgraded.html

Taylor, C.R. and Okazaki, S. (2015) Do global brands use similar executional styles across cultures? A comparison of US and Japanese television advertising, *Journal of Advertising*, 44(3), 276–88.

The story behind how Channel 4 changed minds on disability (2018) *Campaign*, 17 January, retrieved 30 March 2018 from https://www.campaignlive.co.uk/article/story-behind-channel-4-changed-minds-disability/1450209

Tian, K. and Borges, L. (2011) Cross-Cultural Issues in Marketing Communications: An Anthropological Perspective of International Business, *International Journal of China Marketing*, 2(1), 110–26.

Turnbull, S. (2016) From pitch to ditch: the client/ad agency life cycle, *The Marketing Review*, 16(2), 111–27.

Turnbull, S., Howe-Walsh, L. and Boulanouar, A. (2016) The advertising standardisation debate revisited: implications of Islamic ethics on standardisation/localisation of advertising in Middle East Islamic States, *Journal of Islamic Marketing*, 7(1), 2–14.

Tylee, J. (2017) The lost art of global marketing, *Campaign IQ.* Q3, 68–70.

WARC (2016) Strategy in 2016: Moment Marketing, WARC, retrieved 26 October 2017 from http://content.warc.com/read-strategy-moment-marketing-from-the-warc-toolkit-2016

WARC (2018) Adspend Database, WARC, retrieved 30 August 2018 from www.warc.com/Pages/ForecastsAndData/InternationalDataForecast.aspx?Forecast=DatabaseAndCustomTables&isUSD=True

West, D.C. and Paliwoda, S.J. (1996) Advertising client–agency relationships, *European Journal of Marketing*, 30(8), 22–39.

Zolkiewski, J., Burton, J. and Stratoudaki, S. (2008) The delicate power balance in advertising agency-client relationships: partnership or battleground? The case of the Greek advertising market, *Journal of Customer Behaviour*, 7(4), 315–32.

Communication: theory and practice

Communications are concerned with receiving, interpreting and sending messages, but are essentially about sharing meaning with others. Only by using messages that reduce ambiguity, and which share meaning with audiences, can it be hoped to stimulate meaningful interaction and dialogue. To create and sustain valued conversations the support of influential others is often required. These may be people who are experts, those who share common interests, those who have relevant knowledge or people who have access to appropriate media channels.

Aims and learning objectives

The aims of this chapter are to introduce communications theory and to set it in the context of marketing communications.

The learning objectives are to enable readers to:

1. understand the linear model of communications and appreciate how the various elements link together and contribute to successful communications;
2. examine the characteristics of the influencer, interactional, relational and network forms of communications;
3. explain the influence of opinion leaders, formers and followers;
4. examine the nature and characteristics associated with word-of-mouth communications;
5. describe the processes of adoption and diffusion as related to marketing communications.

An introduction to the process of communications

It was established in Chapter 1 that the use of marketing communications is partly an attempt by an organisation/brand to create and sustain conversations with its various audiences. It is also necessary to encourage members of these audiences to talk among themselves about a brand. As communications are the process by which individuals share meaning, each participant in the communications process needs to be able to interpret the meaning embedded in the messages, and be able to respond in appropriate ways.

Successful marketing communications requires an appreciation of the nature and characteristics of the target audience. Most campaigns require that information is transmitted *to*, *with* and *among* key participants. Indeed, communication within online communities and social networks has proven to be rich in content yet complex. Understanding this complexity is important, as it is through knowledge and understanding of the communications process that participants are likely to achieve their overall objective of sharing meaning. This can lead to sustainable dialogue and the development of significant relationships. As Park et al. (2018: 111) demonstrate, there are 'substantial benefits from harnessing the power of social networks'.

This chapter starts with a consideration of the linear, influencer, interactional, relational and network models of communication. Time is then spent exploring the nature and issues associated with word-of-mouth communications and concludes by looking at the way products, services and ideas are adopted by individuals and markets.

A linear model of communications

Wilbur Schramm (1955) developed what is now accepted as the basic model of mass communications, shown in Figure 3.1. The components of the linear model of communications are:

1. Source: the individual or organisation sending the message.
2. Encoding: transferring the intended message into a symbolic style that can be transmitted.
3. Signal: the transmission of the message using particular media.
4. Decoding: understanding the symbolic style of the message in order to understand the message.
5. Receiver: the individual or organisation receiving the message.
6. Feedback: the receiver's communications back to the source on receipt of the message.
7. Noise: distortion of the communications process, making it difficult for the receiver to interpret the message as intended by the source.

This is a linear model, one that emphasises the 'transmission of information, ideas, attitudes, or emotion from one person or group to another (or others), primarily through symbols' (Theodorson and Theodorson, 1969). The model and its components are straightforward, but it is the quality of the linkages between the various elements in the process that determine whether a communications event will be successful.

Source/encoding

The source is an individual or organisation, which identifies a need to transmit a message. It then selects a combination of appropriate words, pictures, symbols and music to represent the message to be transmitted. This is called 'encoding'.

The source is a part of the communications process, not just the generator of detached messages. Patzer (1983) determined that the physical attractiveness of the communicator, particularly if they are the source, contributes significantly to the effectiveness of persuasive communications. This observation can be related to the use, by organisations, of

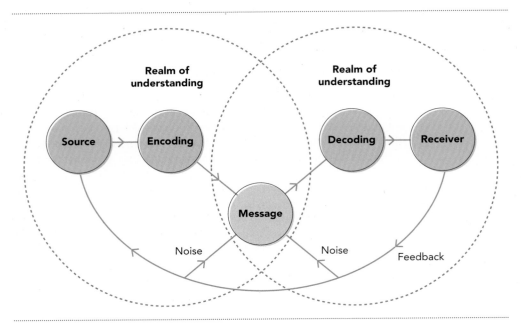

Figure 3.1 A linear model of communications
Source: Based on Schramm (1955) and Shannon and Weaver (1962).

spokespersons and celebrities to endorse products. Spokespersons can be better facilitators of the communications process if they are able to convey conviction, if they are easily associated with the object of the message, if they have credible expertise and if they are attractive to the receiver, in the wider sense of the word.

This legitimate authority has been developed in many television and video advertisements by the use of the 'white coat', black-framed glasses or product-specific clothing, as a symbol of expertise. Dressing the spokesperson in a white coat means that they are immediately perceived as a credible source of information ('they know what they are talking about'), and so are much more likely to be recognised and believed. Northampton General Hospital decided to reinstate the use of white coats after it was reported that patients did not realise they had seen a doctor (Spoors, 2015).

Image 3.1 Doctor wearing a white coat.

Doctors wear white coats for hygiene reasons but they also signal authority and trigger recognition
Source: kurhan/Shutterstock.

The source of a message is an important factor in the communications process. A receiver who perceives a source lacking conviction, authority, trust or expertise is likely to discount any message received from that source, until such time as credibility is established.

The purpose of encoding is to create a message that is capable of being understood and acted upon by the receiver. By understanding people's behaviour, their decision-making processes and key contextual issues, messages can be encoded so that audiences can understand (decode), learn and act on (and share) messages.

There are a number of reasons why the source/encoding link might break down. For example, the source may fail to diagnose a particular situation accurately. By not fully understanding a stakeholder's problem or level of knowledge, inappropriate information may be included in the message, which, when transmitted, may lead to misunderstanding and misinterpretation by the receiver. By failing to appreciate the level of education of the target receiver, a message might be encoded in words and symbols that are beyond the comprehension of the receiver.

Signal

Once encoded, the message must be put into a form that is capable of transmission. It may be oral or written, verbal or non-verbal, in a symbolic form or in a sign. Whatever the format chosen, the source must be sure that what is being put into the message is what is required to be decoded by the receiver.

The channel is the means by which the message is transmitted from the source to the receiver. These channels may be personal or non-personal, formal or informal. Personal channels involve face-to-face contact and word-of-mouth communications, which can be extremely influential. Non-personal channels are characterised by mass-media advertising, which can reach large audiences.

Information received directly from personal influence channels is generally more persuasive than information received through mass media. This may be a statement of the obvious, but the reasons for this need to be understood. First, the individual approach permits greater flexibility in the delivery of the message. The timing and power with which a message is delivered can be adjusted to suit the immediate 'selling' environment. Second, a message can be adapted to meet the needs of the customer as a chat, conversation or sales call progresses. This flexibility is not possible with mass-media messages, as these have to be designed and produced well in advance of transmission and often without direct customer input.

Viewpoint 3.1

Encoding messages and 'Stayin' Alive'

Matt Buttrick, Planning Director at Grey London

In the UK, over 60,000 cardiac arrests occur outside of hospital every year and only an average of 7 per cent (4,200) survive to be discharged from hospital. However, if someone can step in before emergency services arrive and perform CPR (getting the blood circulating again by performing chest compressions and rescue breaths), survival rates can double.

With ambulances struggling to get through crowded road networks, and the number of people calling 999 increasing all the time, the British Heart Foundation (BHF), the UK's number one heart charity, felt compelled to mobilise the public to step in and fill the time before ambulances arrived.

Previously CPR instruction had been complex, intimidating and sparsely communicated, let alone understood. 82 per cent of adults didn't even know if CPR was the right response, and BHF research showed that 73 per cent of adults claimed they were unfamiliar with the CPR procedure.

A new simplified 'Hands-only CPR' approach was devised, one not requiring mouth-to-mouth, or the 'kiss of life' as it was once known. Just pushing hard and fast in the middle of the chest to the tempo of 100 BPM is all that is required until help arrives.

The BHF decided to create an army of knowledgeable bystanders ready to apply CPR wherever they were. The challenge was to teach this behaviour, not just drive awareness. Using laughter to defuse fear, the campaign team searched for a song that was at the right tempo, 100 BPM. The answer was the Bee Gees hit, 'Stayin' Alive'!

We selected Vinnie Jones to lead the campaign, and as someone famed for violence (football and Hollywood) he provided the humour as he pushed hard and fast to 'Stayin' Alive'!

We'd created a funny and memorable 'dance' that brought together five elements to maximise 'cut through':

1. A 100 BPM soundtrack with universal appeal: 'Stayin' Alive' by The Bee Gees.
2. A well-known character famous for toughness and hurting people: Vinnie Jones, football and Hollywood.
3. A sticky phrase that conveyed the key action: hard and fast.
4. A tone that would challenge traditional government first aid messaging: the comedic and the serious.
5. A script that clearly walked the five steps of hands-only CPR.

Using TV to reach 80 per cent of the population at least once, the 'Vinnie' film became the most shared online video in launch week, at the time. The film was used on Twitter, an app was developed and Vinnie T-shirts were sold in the BHF's 700 nationwide stores.

Image 3.2 Vinnie – Hands-only CPR
Source: British Heart Foundation.

The 'Vinnie' campaign was amplified through major PR coverage, it was parodied on the biggest TV shows and was even recreated in LEGO as part of the promotion for *The LEGO Movie* where famous UK ads were spoofed and pulled together for a special ad break.

The campaign was a huge success. Post-tracking told us that we created an extra 6 million people who were now more likely to perform 'Hands-only CPR'. We know that 30 lives were saved as a direct result of people seeing the ad, due to the letters we have received.

Image 3.3 Vinnie is now used for NHS training
Source: British Heart Foundation.

This Viewpoint is based on a case study written by Matt Buttrick, when he was Planning Director at Grey London.

Insight

These lives were saved because the way in which the message was encoded not only conveyed the right information but it also engaged the audience sufficiently that they learned a new behaviour easily. Research indicates that the likeability element of the campaign message enabled it to become easily understood and 'sticky' as it resonated with people and was passed on to others.

Neuro-linguistic programming (NLP) suggests people learn in three key ways: through pictures and images (visually); through chants and rhythm (auditory); and through gestures and body movements (kinaesthetically). 'Vinnie' combined all three and it was this that helped to communicate effectively, maximise reach, and enable a mass audience to learn a new behaviour.

Question: How might the Vinnie campaign illustrate encoding, signalling and decoding?
Task: Find another campaign that you feel demonstrates good message encoding.

Decoding/receiver

Decoding is the process of transforming and interpreting a message into thought. This process is influenced by the receiver's realm of understanding, which encompasses the experiences, perceptions, attitudes and values of both the source and the receiver. The more a receiver understands about the source and the greater their experience in decoding a source's messages, the more able the receiver will be to decode and attribute the intended meaning to the message.

Feedback/response

The set of reactions a receiver has after seeing, hearing or reading a message is known as the *response*. These vary from sending a text or email, visiting a website, calling an enquiry telephone number, redeeming or downloading a coupon or even buying the product, to storing information in long-term memory for future use.

Feedback is that part of the response that is sent back to the sender, and it is essential for successful communications. The need to understand not just whether the message has been received but also 'which' message has been received is vital. For example, the receiver may have decoded the message incorrectly and a completely different set of responses may have been elicited. If a suitable feedback system is not in place then the source will be unaware that the communications have been unsuccessful and is liable to continue wasting resources. This represents inefficient and ineffective marketing communications.

Scholars' paper 3.1

Mass communication – uncut

Schramm, W. (1962) Mass communication, *Annual Review of Psychology*, 13(1), 25–84.

This is a seminal paper. Schramm explores mass communications and the various elements that influence or constitute the mass communications process. This paper provides an excellent insight into the theoretical development of the topic, at which point the linear model of communications was possibly at its highest point of popularity. You will be surprised at the range of elements considered by Schramm.

Feedback through mass-media channels is generally much more difficult to obtain, mainly because of the inherent time delay involved in the feedback process. There are some exceptions, namely the overnight ratings provided by the Broadcasters' Audience Research Board (see www.barb.co.uk) to the television contractors, but as a rule feedback is normally delayed and not as fast. Some commentators argue that the only meaningful indicator of communications success is sales. However, there are many other influences that affect the level of sales, such as price, the effect of previous communications, the recommendations of opinion leaders or friends, poor competitor actions or any number of government or regulatory developments. Except in circumstances such as direct marketing, where immediate and direct feedback can be determined, organisations should use other methods to gauge the success of their communications activities. For example, the level and quality of customer enquiries, the number and frequency of store visits, the degree of attitude change, customer lifetime value, and the ability to recognise or recall an advertisement. All of these represent feedback, but, as a rough distinction, the evaluation of feedback for mass communications is much more difficult than the evaluation of interpersonal communications.

Noise

A complicating factor, which may influence the quality of the reception and the feedback, is noise. Noise, according to Mallen (1977), is 'the omission and distortion of information', and there will always be some noise present in all communications. Management's role is to ensure that levels of noise are kept to a minimum, wherever it is able to exert influence.

Noise occurs when a receiver is prevented from receiving all or part of a message in full. This may be because of either cognitive or physical factors. For example, a cognitive factor may be that the encoding of the message was inappropriate, thereby making it difficult for the receiver to decode the message. In this circumstance it is said that the realms of understanding of the source and the receiver were not matched. Another reason noise may enter the system is that the receiver may have been physically prevented from decoding the message accurately because the receiver was distracted. Examples of distraction are that the telephone rang, or someone in the room asked a question or coughed. A further reason could be that competing messages screened out the targeted message.

Realms of understanding

The concept of the 'realm of understanding' was introduced earlier. It is an important element in the communications process because it is a recognition that successful communications are more likely to be achieved if the source and the receiver understand each other, that is they share meaning. This understanding concerns attitudes, perceptions, behaviour and experience: the values of both parties to the communications process. Therefore, effective communications are more likely when there is some common ground, a realm of understanding between the source and receiver.

The more organisations understand their receivers, the more confident they become in constructing suitable messages. Repetition and learning are important elements in marketing communications. Learning is a function of knowledge and the more we know, the more likely we are to understand.

Issues associated with the linear communication process

The linear, sequential interpretation of the communications process was developed at a time when broadcast media dominated marketing communications. Today, when interactive, and social media in particular, is taking an increasing share of overall media activity, the linear model is not a suitable model with which to interpret contemporary communications. Issues concerning media and audience fragmentation, the need to consider social and relational dimensions of communications and the impact of interactive communications has reduced the overall applicability of the linear model.

Contemporary technologies provide opportunities for interaction and dialogue with customers. With conventional (linear) media the tendency is for monologue or at best delayed and inferred interaction. Traditionally, providers implant their messages into the various environments frequented by their targets. Interactive media communications tend to make providers relatively passive, as it is the audience that become the active participants.

The linear view of communications holds that the process consists essentially of one step. Information is directed and shot at prospective audiences, rather like a bullet is propelled from a gun. The decision of each member of the audience whether to act on the message is the result of a passive role or participation in the process. Organisations can communicate with different target audiences simply by varying the message and the type and frequency of channels used.

The linear model has been criticised for its oversimplification, and it certainly ignores the effect of personal influences on the communications process and the potential for misunderstanding and information deviance. To accommodate these issues two further models are introduced, the influencer model and the interactional model of communications.

The influencer model of communications

The influencer model depicts information flowing via media channels to particular types of people (opinion leaders and opinion formers) to whom other members of the audience refer for information and guidance. Through interpersonal networks, opinion leaders not only reach members of the target audience who may not have been exposed to the message, but may reinforce the impact of the message for those members who did receive the message (see Figure 3.2). For example, feedback and comments on Tripadvisor.com assist others when making travel plans, and constitute opinion leadership. However, professional travel bloggers, editors of travel sections in the Sunday press and television presenters of travel programmes fulfil the role of opinion former and can influence the decision of prospective travellers through their formalised knowledge.

Originally referred to as the 'two-step model', this approach indicates that the mass media do not have a direct and all-powerful effect over their audiences. If the primary function of the mass media is to provide information, then personal influences are necessary to be persuasive and to exert direct influence on members of the target audience.

The influencer approach can be developed into a multi-step model. This proposes that communications involve interaction among all parties to the communications process (see Figure 3.3). This interpretation closely resembles the network of participants who are often involved in the communications process.

Interactional model of communications

The models and frameworks used to explain the communications process so far should be considered as a simplification of reality and not a true reflection of communications in practice. The linear model is unidirectional, and it suggests that the receiver plays a passive role in the process. The influencer model attempts to account for an individual's role in the communications process. These models emphasise individual behaviour but exclude any social behaviour implicit in the process.

The interactional model of communications attempts to assimilate the variety of influences acting upon the communications process. This includes the responses people give

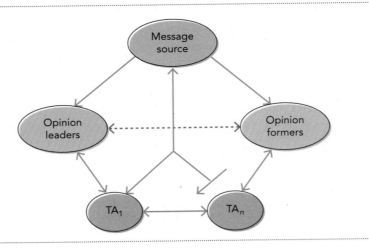

Figure 3.2 The influencer model of communications
Source: From *Essentials of Marketing Communications*, Pearson Education (Fill, C. 2011) Figure 2.2, p. 39.

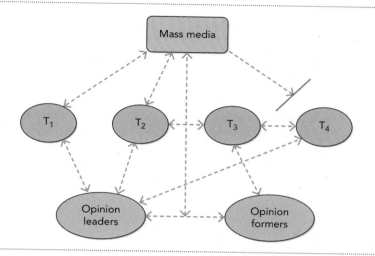

Figure 3.3 Multi-step variation of the influencer model of communications
Source: From *Essentials of Marketing Communications*, Pearson Education (Fill, C. 2011) Figure 2.3, p. 39.

to communications received from people and machines. Increasingly communications are characterised by attributing meaning to messages that are shared, updated and a response to other messages. These 'conversations' can be termed interactional and are an integral part of society. Figure 3.4 depicts the complexity associated with these forms of communications.

Interaction is about actions that lead to a response. The development of direct marketing helped make a significant contribution to the transition from what is essentially

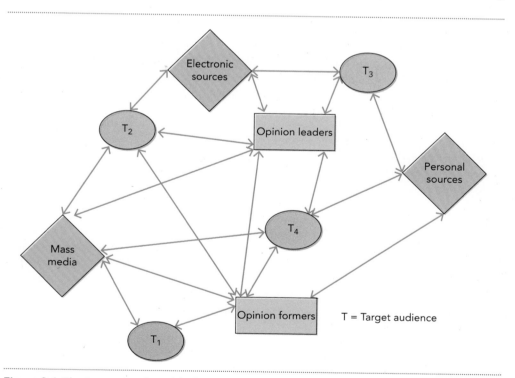

Figure 3.4 The interactional model of communications
Source: From *Essentials of Marketing Communications*, Pearson Education (Fill, C. 2011) Figure 2.4, p. 41.

one-way to two-way and then interactive-based communications. Digital technology, and social media in particular, has progressed this interaction process. As we discuss later in this chapter, the impact of influencers in the communication process has been significant.

Prominent users of influencer marketing initiatives are fashion and beauty brands. They use image-led channels such as Facebook and Instagram to engage customers, with a falling number using Twitter as their primary platform. This is because increasing numbers of people prefer interaction through visual means, and this invariably means the use of video and short film formats. These enable the telling of stories, connection with audiences and the sharing of engaging content. What is interesting is that, from an influencer-marketing perspective, Twitter is no longer considered appropriate, due to a reluctance to construct text and interact through 280 words (Eyal, 2017).

Viewpoint 3.2

Brands use celebrity influencers through Instagram

Bilyana Petrova, Account Manager at J. Walter Thompson, Brussels

Instagram, now owned by Facebook Inc., has recently seen a sharp increase in usage, and in the direct promotion of products and services. Instagram has evolved from being a space to share your photos and interact with users to become a serious money-making tool for celebrities and brands. In 2018, the social network announced the start of the so-called 'Paid partnership with [brand X]' posts which make it clearer if the influencer was paid to post or not.

Although they are not allowed to sell anything directly, celebrities usually manage to create an interesting way of presenting and recommending a product or service. A mandatory communication element is to always acknowledge and tag the brand by making a direct link with its Instagram profile. Hashtags do help too. Sometimes, they also give a direct promo code with a specific percentage discount.

For example, by collaborating with some of the most famous celebrity influencers, Airbnb managed to obtain exposure and reach a potential audience of around 1 billion users. Their main goal was really simple – to make the company a global phenomenon in the hospitality industry. Mariah Carey was the first major celebrity to book accommodation through the website and this was an opportunity that the brand was not going to miss. In a sponsored Instagram post, which received more than 45,000 likes, Carey tagged Airbnb both in the photo and caption. This particular case marked the start of the company's influencer marketing strategy. Airbnb began to focus on major events such as the Super Bowl and Coachella, by giving free apartments to celebrities in return for posts, which extended the brand's visibility and increased their engagement rate on Instagram and traditional media.

In 2016, Chanel, one of the most iconic French brands, invited top world Instagram influencers to visit the brand's flower fields in southern France, prior to launching their new fragrance Chanel No. 5 L'Eau. Instagrammers such as Julie Sariñana (with over 4 million followers in 2018), and others, attended the event and documented (on Instagram) every single detail of the Chanel tour. Two hashtags #newchanel5 and #chanelgrasse were created to help users find the new branded content. In addition, they aimed to inspire the generation of users' own posts around the new fragrance. The results were astonishing with over 1,600 pieces of content created (both user & influencer generated) and more than one million likes in the first month of the campaign.

Sources: Anon (2016); Anon (2017a); Ingram and Bartz, (2017).

This Viewpoint was written by Bilyana Petrova, formerly a student at Coventry University.

Insight

Instagram's format reflects users' preference for using a visual vocabulary rather than text. Airbnb and Chanel's successful use of celebrity influencers, through Instagram, is partly because the celebrities have a strong online presence, a huge fan base, which represents enormous reach, and they communicate their day-to-day activities on a regular basis. Most celebrity influencers, such as Mariah Carey and Julie Sariñana, are considered by their fans to be extremely trustworthy, based on the fans' perception and interpretation of the celebrities' identity cues (behaviour, comments, ability and attributes) that are of particular interest to followers. Brands strive to be associated with celebrities because they want to transfer the 'celebrity trust' and other associations to their brand. This refers to McCracken's (1989) theory of meaning transfer, which is considered later in this chapter.

Question: If visual communications are currently the preferred communication format, how might 'voice' work for celebrity endorsements?

Task: Find a fashion brand that uses Instagram and list the ways it uses the network to communicate with its followers.

However, interaction alone is not a sufficient goal, simply because the content of the interaction could be about a radical disagreement of views, an exchange of opinion or a social encounter.

Ballantyne refers to two-way communications with audiences first as a 'with' experience, as manifest in face-to-face encounters and contact centres. Second, he distinguishes a higher order of two-way communications based on communications 'between' parties. It is this latter stage that embodies true dialogue where trust, listening and adaptive behaviour are typical. These are represented in Table 3.1.

Table 3.1 Communications matrix

Direction	Mass markets	Portfolio/mass-customised	Networks
One-way. Planned communications designed to inform and persuade. Medium to high wastage.	Communications 'to'. Planned persuasive messages aimed at securing brand awareness and loyalty; e.g. communications of USPs and ESPs.	Communications 'for'. Planned persuasive messages with augmented offerings for target markets; e.g. communicating targeted lifecycle products, guarantees, loyalty programmes.	
Two-way. Formal and informal with a view to listening and learning. Minimal wastage.		Communications 'with'. Integrated mix of planned and interactively shared knowledge; e.g. face-to-face, direct (database), contact centres, interactive B2B Internet portals.	Communications 'between'. Dialogue between participants based on trust, learning and adaptation with co-created outcomes; e.g. key account liaison, expansion of communities, staff teamwork.

Source: Ballantyne (2004).

A key question emerges: what is interaction and what are its key characteristics? If we can understand the dynamics and dimensions of interactivity then it should be possible to develop more effective marketing communications. In this context interactivity can be considered from one of two perspectives. One is the technology, tools and features (e.g. multimedia, www, online gaming) that provide for interaction. The second, according to Johnson et al. (2006), is the added value that interactivity is perceived to bring to the communications process.

Arising out of interaction is dialogue. This occurs through mutual understanding and a reasoning approach to interactions, one based on listening and adaptive behaviour. Dialogue is concerned with the development of knowledge that is specific to the relationship of the parties involved. Ballantyne refers to this as 'learning together' (Ballantyne, 2004: 119).

The adoption of dialogue as the basis for communications changes an organisation's perspective with its audiences. Being willing and able to enter into a dialogue indicates that there is a new emphasis on the relationships organisations hold with their stakeholders. In other words, for meaningful dialogue to occur there must first be interaction.

The influencer model is important because it demonstrates the importance of people in the communications process. Successful communications, however, are often determined by the level of interactivity the communications encourage.

Word-of-mouth communications

Person-to-person conversations about products, services and brand-related marketing messages and meanings are naturally occurring events. Indeed, many argue that word-of-mouth (WoM) communication is the most powerful way of communicating marketing messages (Fulgoni and Lipsman, 2017).

Increasingly organisations use word of mouth as an integral part of their marketing communications and deliberately encourage people to have positive conversations

Image 3.4 Word of mouth communication is an integral part of social media
Source: Rawpixel.com/Shutterstock.

about their particular brand. They do this because WoM communication is considered to be the primary driver of purchasing decisions. Shih et al. (2013) refer to a Nielsen survey of online consumers, which found that whereas only 33 per cent of consumers trust online advertisements, 90 per cent trust recommendations from friends and 70 per cent trust eWoM (electronic WoM). It should also be noted that, in addition to the impact on purchasing, eWoM has also been found to impact e-reputation (Castellano and Dutot, 2017).

WoM communications are traditionally characterised as informal, unplanned and unsolicited conversations. These recommendations provide information and purchasing support and serve to reinforce an individual's purchasing decisions. At the heart of this approach is the source credibility that is assigned to people whose opinions are sought after, trusted and used in the purchase decision process. Those who provide information in WoM communications can be characterised as informal experts who are unbiased, trustworthy and who can be considered to be objective. Personal influence is important and can enrich the communications process. Unlike advertising, where messages are primarily linear, unidirectional and formal, WoM communications are interactive, bidirectional and more believable. Or, as Hamilton et al. (2014: 197) put it, the 'opinions of other consumers are appreciated because they are more likely to include negative information about a product or service than one could find in formal marketing communications'.

Scholars' paper 3.2
So why am I talking about this brand?

Berger, J. and Schwartz, E.M. (2011) What drives immediate and ongoing word of mouth? *Journal of Marketing Research*, XLVIII (October), 869–80.

These researchers consider the psychological drivers of WoM and how companies can design more effective WoM marketing campaigns. Whereas most of the research in this area looks at the consequences of WoM, the focus here is on what causes WoM, how the product itself can shape what is discussed, and how WoM may vary over different time horizons. They distinguish between immediate and ongoing WoM. This paper should be considered in terms of updating Dichter's 1966 paper.

Definition and motives

Stokes and Lomax (2002) define WoM communications as 'interpersonal communication regarding products or services where the receiver regards the communicator as impartial'. This simple definition was developed from some of the more established interpretations that failed to accommodate contemporary media and the restrictions concerning the perceived independence of the communicator.

Kawakami et al. (2014: 17) define WoM as 'the exchange of information and evaluative beliefs between adopters and potential adopters regarding a product in which the communications content is not created or sponsored by the product manufacturer or related marketing organisations'. They also make the point that WoM can occur between people who know each other personally (pWoM) and between people who have never met each other in real life, which they refer to as virtual (vWoM). Weisfeld-Spolter et al. (2014) identify several different formats of eWoM, which suggests that there needs to be care when referring to eWoM.

People like to talk about their product (service) experiences for a variety of reasons that are explored in the next section. By talking with a neighbour or colleague about the good experiences associated with a holiday, for example, the first-hand 'this has actually happened to someone I know' effect can be instrumental in the same views being passed on to other colleagues, irrespective of their validity or the general impression people have of other holidays and destinations. Mazzarol et al. (2007) identify the 'richness of the message' and the 'strength of the implied or explicit advocacy' as important triggers for WoM. Palmer (2009) brings these together and refers to WoM as information people can trust as it comes from people just like them and it helps them make better decisions.

Helm and Schlei (1998: 42) refer to WoM as 'verbal communications (either positive or negative) between groups such as the product provider, independent experts, family, friends and the actual or personal consumer'. As discussed later, organisations use eWoM techniques in a commercial context in order to generate brand-based conversations around a point of differentiation. Where WoM used to be a one-to-one conversation, the digital influence makes this a one-to-many communication when product reviews are posted online or when blogs or videos go viral.

One important question that arises is: why do people want to discuss products or advertising messages? Bone (1995) as cited by Stokes and Lomax (2002) refers to three elements of WoM (see Table 3.2).

Dichter (1966) determined that there were four main categories of output WoM.

1. *Product involvement* People, he found, have a high propensity to discuss matters that are either distinctly pleasurable or unpleasurable. Such discussion serves to provide an opportunity for the experience to be relived, whether it be the 'looking for' or the 'use' experience, or both. This reflects the product and service experience elements of marketing communications, identified as part of the scope of the topic, in Chapter 1.

2. *Self-involvement* Discussion offers a means for ownership to be established and signals aspects of prestige and levels of status to the receiver. More importantly, perhaps, dissonance can be reduced as the purchaser seeks reassurance about a decision.

3. *Other involvement* Products can assist motivations to help others and to express feelings of love, friendship, and caring. These feelings can be released through a sense of sharing the variety of benefits that products can bestow.

4. *Message involvement* The final motivation to discuss products is derived, according to Dichter, from the messages that surround the product itself, in particular the

Table 3.2 Elements of word-of-mouth communications

Element of WoM		Explanation
Direction	Input WoM	Customers seeking recommendation prior to purchase
	Output WoM	Expression of feelings as a result of the purchase experience
Valence		The positive or negative feelings resulting from the experience
Volume		The number of people to which the message is conveyed

Source: After Bone (1995).

advertising messages and, in the B2B market, seminars, exhibitions and the trade press, which provide the means to provoke conversation and so stimulate WoM recommendation.

Marketing communications can be used to stimulate conversations, by using these motivations as an anchor for messages.

People who identify very closely with a brand and who might be termed 'brand advocates' often engage in WoM communications. Advocacy can be demonstrated not only through WoM communications but also through behaviour – for example, by wearing branded clothing or using tools and equipment.

These motivations to discuss products and their associative experiences vary between individuals and with the intensity of the motivation at any one particular moment. There are two main persons involved in this process of WoM communications: a sender and a receiver. Research indicates that the receiver's evaluation of a message is far from stable over time and accuracy of recall decays (expectedly) through time. What this means for marketing communications is that those people who have a positive product experience, especially in the service sector, should be encouraged to talk as soon as possible after the event (Christiansen and Tax, 2000). Goldsmith and Horowitz (2006) found that risk reduction, popularity, reduced costs, access to easy information, and even inspiration from offline sources such as cinema, TV and radio were some of the primary reasons why people seek the opinions of others online.

Opinion leaders

Katz and Lazarsfeld (1955) first identified individuals who were predisposed to receiving information and then reprocessing it to influence others. Their studies of American voting and purchase behaviour led to their conclusion that those individuals who could exert such influence were more persuasive than information received directly from the mass media. These opinion leaders, according to Rogers (1962), tend 'to be of the same social class as non-leaders, but may enjoy a higher social status within the group'. Williams (1990) uses the work of Reynolds and Darden (1971) to suggest that they are more gregarious and more self-confident than non-leaders. In addition, they have a greater exposure to relevant media content and, as a result, have more knowledge/familiarity and involvement with the product class, are more innovative and more confident of their role as influencer (leader) and appear to be less dogmatic than non-leaders (Chan and Misra, 1990).

The importance of opinion leaders in the design and implementation of communications plans should not be underestimated. Litterio et al. (2017) refer to individuals who stand out because they have the potential to influence buying behaviour in their network.

Opinion leadership can be simulated in advertising by the use of product testimonials. Using ordinary people to express positive comments about a product to each other is a very well-used advertising technique. However, while the importance of these individuals is not doubted, a major difficulty exists in trying to identify just who these opinion leaders and innovator communicators are.

Nisbet (2005) provides a useful insight into the background of opinion leadership. He observes that opinion leadership has been previously defined as exhibiting three primary dimensions: social embeddedness (Weimann, 1994), information-giving (Rogers, 2003), and information-seeking (Keller and Berry, 2003) behaviours. Table 3.3 sets out some of the main characteristics associated with opinion leaders.

Table 3.3 Characteristics associated with opinion leaders

Characteristic	Explanation
Social gregariousness	Refers to an opinion leader's level of social embeddedness because they tend to have more social ties, more friends, and more social contacts than non-leaders.
Efficacy and trust	Opinion leaders have a higher self-confidence and self-reliance than non-leaders, although it is noted that they generally have lower confidence in political systems.
Values and satisfaction	Opinion leaders are less concerned with material gain and financial success than non-leaders. They tend to exhibit higher levels of social responsibility, political tolerance, civic-mindedness, and environmental concern.

Opinion formers

Opinion formers are individuals who are able to exert personal influence because of their authority, education or status associated with the object of the communications process. Like opinion leaders, they are acknowledged and sought out by others to provide information and advice, but this is because of the formal expertise that opinion formers are adjudged to have. For example, community pharmacists are often consulted about symptoms and medicines, and film and theatre critics carry such conviction in their reviews that they can make or break a new production.

Popular television soap operas such as *General Hospital* (USA), *Alles was zählt* (Germany), *Shortland Street* (New Zealand) and *Coronation Street* (UK), all of which attract huge audiences, have been used as vehicles to draw attention to and open up debates about many controversial social issues, such as contraception, abortion, drug use and abuse, and serious illness and mental health concerns.

The influence of opinion formers can be great. For example, dentists may be a recognised source of expertise for all matters concerning oral hygiene and dentistry, and so toothpaste brands often carry their testimonials and recommendations as this enhances a brand with increased credibility. This principle of using the endorsement of experts in a product category to help form the beliefs of a target audience is an established practice. This is because the credibility of opinion formers is vital for communications effectiveness. If there is a suspicion or doubt about the impartiality of the opinion former, then the objectivity of their views and comments is likely to be perceived as tainted and not believed so that damage may be caused to the reputation of the brand and those involved.

Many organisations constantly lobby key members of parliament in an effort to persuade them to pursue 'favourable' policies. Opinion formers are relatively easy to identify, as they need to be seen shaping the opinion of others, usually opinion followers.

Opinion followers

The majority of consumers can be said to be opinion followers. The messages they receive via the mass media are tempered by the opinions of the two groups of personal influencers just discussed. Some people actively seek information from those they believe are well informed, while others prefer to use the mass media for information and guidance (Robinson, 1976). However, this should not detract from the point that, although followers, they still process information independently and use a variety of inputs when sifting information and responding to marketing stimuli.

Viewpoint 3.3

Marriott use influencers through Snapchat

Image 3.5 Marriott use influencers to attract guests, especially in the younger market, through Snapchat
Source: POC/Shutterstock.

In order to engage young consumers, the hotel and hospitality company, Marriott, used the mobile-messaging platform, Snapchat. This platform gave them the ability to communicate with a younger audience, one that is not familiar with the Marriott brand.

Marriott released four 'snapisodes', a term used to describe advertisements they have created for Snapchat. These were three-minute, influencer-oriented productions designed to capture teenagers and build its Snapchat presence. The campaign saw Marriott launch a vertical video series on the app. Called 'Six Days, Seven Nights', it featured four influencers who each documented their adventures in Dubai, New York, Seoul and Berlin. One of these influencers, an actress and social-media influencer with more than 100,000 followers on Snapchat, was Jen Levinson, who was a notoriously picky eater. One of her goals was to try everything from frogs' legs to currywurst in Berlin.

Among the key performance indicators that Marriott used was the length of engagement. How many times people watched the content, and whether they were watched all the way through. The 'Six Days, Seven Nights' campaign had the highest view-through average across any advertising campaign for any brand in any sector, on Snapchat.

Sources: Anon (2017b); Flynn (2017); www.wearesocial.net

Insight

Marriott, just like most other organisations, use other people to speak on their behalf. In this example, the use of the short-film format reflected their target audience's preference for a visual vocabulary. The messages from these influencers may be direct or implicit but they are all intended to influence positively the thoughts or behaviour of the target audience.

Question: Why was the Marriott story delivered across a series of short films, not just one?

Task: Find two examples of brand ambassadors and then make a list of the other brands they endorse. Are there any similarities across each list?

Developing brands with word-of-mouth communications

So far in this section WoM communications have been examined as naturally occurring, unplanned conversations. This is not entirely correct, as most organisations deliberately plan to reach their audiences using WoM principles. There are a variety of methods that organisations use to influence their audiences, all in the name of WoM. Of these, three main forms of WoM can be identified: voluntary, prompted and managed.

1. *Voluntary WoM* – can be considered to be the most natural form of interpersonal conversation, free from any external influence, coercion or intent. This still occurs among genuine opinion leaders, formers and followers for reasons considered earlier.

2. *Prompted WoM* – occurs when organisations convey information to specific opinion leaders and formers, with the intention of deliberately encouraging them to forward and share the information with their followers. The goal is to prompt conversations among followers based around the credibility bestowed on the opinion leader. This outward perspective can be counterbalanced by an inward view. For example, some organisations use various elements of social media, such as blogs, online communities and forums, to prompt consumer-to-consumer conversations and then listen, observe and revise their approaches to the market.

3. *Managed WoM* – occurs when organisations target, incentivise and reward opinion leaders for recommending their offerings to their networks of followers. In these situations opinion leaders lose their independence and objectivity within the communications process, and become paid representatives of a brand. As a result, the credibility normally attached to these influencers diminishes and the essence of freely expressed opinions about products and brands is removed.

Haenlein and Libai (2017) have categorised the different WoM programmes according to the purpose of the programme. Three main formats are identified: seeding, referrals and recommendations. These can be seen in Table 3.4. These researchers advance a new measurement approach, one that considers the customer equity developed as a lifetime value that these WoM programmes contribute.

Table 3.4 Major types of WOM programmes

Program archetype	Program form	Description
Seeding programs	Product seeding	Acclerate the overall adoption of a wider group by getting a (typically new) product into the hands of a small group of people (the 'seeds')
	Viral marketing	Encourage a seed of individuals to share and spread a marketing message through electronic channels
Referral programs	Referral reward	Incentivise existing customers (mainly in B2C settings) to make product recommendations by providing rewards that depend on turning a referral into a sale
	Business reference	Use references from client firms in a B2B setting when trying to influence specific potential customers favourably to become new customers
	Affiliate marketing	Pay a monetary incentive (based on sales or clicks) for referring a person to a certain site via online links
Recommendation programs	Narrowband recommendations	Encourage recommendations through the social network of the specific individual (e.g., Facebook)
	Broadband recommendations	Encourage recommendations through dedicated (review) sites (e.g., TripAdvisor, Amazon)

Note: A WOM program is a marketing initiative that aims to trigger a WOM process by targeting a certain number of individuals and incentivizing them to spread WOM. WOM=word of mouth. B2C=business to consumer; B2B=business to business.

Source: Haenlein and Libai (2017), Table 1, p. 71.

The term eWoM is used here as the electronic version of the spoken endorsement of a product or service, where messages are targeted at key individuals who then voluntarily pass the message to friends and colleagues. In doing so they endorse the message and provide it with a measure of credibility. The use of eWoM is an intentional attempt to influence consumer-to-consumer communications using professional marketing methods and technologies to prompt conversations (Kozinets et al., 2010).

Scholars' paper 3.3
WoM, influencers and networks

Haenlein, M. and Libai, B. (2017) Seeding, referral, and recommendation: creating profitable word-of-mouth programs, *California Management Review,* 59(2), 68–91.

This paper provides an accessible insight into the various programmes and issues associated with the organisational use of WoM programmes. In particular, it focuses on the need for improved measurement methods and a shift from measuring conversations and impressions to one that accounts for lifetime value.

See also:

Litterio, A.M., Nantes, A., Larrosa, J.M. and Gómez, L.J. (2017) Marketing and social networks: a criterion for detecting opinion leaders, *European Journal of Management and Business Economics*, 26(3), 347–66.

Kozinets, R.V., de Valck, K., Wojnicki, A.C. and Wilner, S.J.S. (2010) Networked narratives: understanding word-of-mouth marketing in online communities, *Journal of Marketing*, 74 (March), 71–89.

Celebrity endorsers

Traditionally brands were built partly through offline communications directed to opinion leaders, when they could be identified, and through opinion formers. Sporting and entertainment celebrities have been used as brand ambassadors for a long time, and as Branchik and Chowdhury (2017: 319) state, the 'use of celebrity endorsers in advertising is frequent, growing, and costly'. They are used to enable audiences to develop positive associations between the personality of the ambassador and a brand. A celebrity endorser is defined as 'any individual who enjoys public recognition and who uses this recognition on behalf of a consumer good by appearing with it in an advertisement' (McCracken, 1989: 310).

McCracken (1989) believes that celebrity endorsement works through the theory of meaning transfer. Consumers make an overall assessment of what a celebrity 'represents' to them, based on their perception and interpretation of the celebrity's identity cues. These cues relate to their behaviour, comments, ability and attributes that are of particular interest to the consumer. McCracken (1989: 315) refers to their public image as demonstrated in 'television, movies, military, athletics, and other careers'.

Jin and Phua (2014) found that celebrities who use Twitter to endorse brands are invariably perceived by their followers as fellow social media users. This helps make their endorsements more credible and trustworthy than if they had appeared in television or print advertisements. In addition, their research found that the celebrities who endorse

Table 3.5 Theories used to interpret the use of celebrity endorsement

Theory	Explanation
Meaning transfer	Products and services have culturally imbued meanings for those who consume them. Celebrity endorsers enable and accelerate the transfer of these meanings.
Source credibility	Celebrities (sources) who are perceived as both experts and trustworthy are considered credible. Their influence on a consumer's beliefs, opinions, attitudes and/or ultimate behaviour occurs through the process of 'internalisation'. This occurs when receivers accept a source's influence in terms of their personal attitude and value structures.
Source attractiveness	Developed by McGuire (1985), this approach is based on the familiarity, likeability, and/or similarity of the endorser to persuade recipients.
Product match-up	Based on a congruence between products and their celebrity endorsers in order to communicate an effective and unified message to targeted buyers.

Source: Adapted from Branchik and Chowdhury (2017).

a large number of brands through eWoM are likely to lose trust as they are perceived to be 'tweeters for hire'.

The meaning assigned to a celebrity is transferred from the celebrity endorser to the product when the two are paired in a commercial message. The meaning transfer model is the most frequently used in this context, but as Branchik and Chowdhury (2017) observe, three other models are applied to celebrity endorsements. These are source credibility, source attractiveness, and product match-up (see Table 3.5).

Brand development now incorporates the use of social media and bloggers (and vloggers in particular), who play an increasingly critical role in the dissemination of brand-related information. More detailed information about the use of social media can be found in Chapter 21, but here it is important to establish the way in which brands can be developed through WoM marketing communications.

Opinion formers such as journalists, find or receive information about brands through press releases and social media feeds. They then relay the information, after editing and reformatting, to their readers and viewers through their particular media. Accordingly, brand-related information is targeted at journalists, with the intention that their messages will be forwarded to their end-user audience through media channels.

Bloggers are now an important and influential channel of communication. They are so influential that when social-media influencer Kylie Jenner tweeted that she doesn't open Snapchat any more, the comment drew similar replies from her 24.5 million followers. Snap Inc.'s shares fell by 7.2 per cent, wiping out $1.3 billion in market value (Anon, 2018).

Bloggers do not share the same characteristics as journalists. For example, the number of bloggers in any one market can be counted in terms of tens of thousands of people in contrast to the relatively small, select number of opinion formers. The majority of bloggers have an informal interest in a subject, whereas opinion formers are deemed to have formal expertise. Bloggers, however, are not tied to formal processes or indeed an editor. As a result, bloggers do not have to be objective in their comments and are not constrained by any advertising messages. Most importantly, bloggers conduct conversations among themselves and their followers, whereas journalists receive little feedback. (See Viewpoint 3.4 and Chapter 21.)

Viewpoint 3.4
Fashionable vloggers

Image 3.6 Zoella – an established hairstyling vlogger.
Source: David M. Benett/Getty Images for Zoella Beauty.

Zoella, a vlogger, started in 2009, filming herself giving make-up tips in her bedroom. Since then she has accumulated 10.5 million followers on Instagram, and 7 million on Twitter. Her hair styling tutorials are based on trends in social media and Google data about current hair styling talking points. Unilever then enable followers to purchase the brands. She earns, it is thought, £50,000 a month from her lifestyle channels alone. She also has a beauty range in Superdrug which, when it launched in 2015, sold out on the first day.

As a 15-year-old, Izy Hossack developed a food-based blog, 'Top with Cinnamon', and she now has more than 250,000 Instagram followers. Her blog is notable for the recipes, which avoid trendy foods and unending salads, and which promotes full-flavour recipes, including a range of vegetarian dishes. She is noted for her friendly yet direct writing style, and for the quality of the photography and videos. Her influence in social media led to a publisher offering a book deal to feature her recipes, advertisers who place ads on her website attempting to reach her followers, and of course a growing array of people attracted to her recipes and food ideas. She has been described as 'the new Nigella' and published her new book *The Savvy Cook* just before her 20th birthday.

Organisations use bloggers to reach and influence their target audiences. For example, Unilever developed a YouTube channel 'All Things Hair' to advertise their brands such as Toni & Guy, Dove and VO5.

Sources: Essuah, (2017); Rivalland (2014); Robinson and Malm (2015); Swift (2014); Williams (2017).

Insight

These two vloggers reflect many of the opinion leadership characteristics identified prior to the digital era. They have informal influence as they are from the same group as non-leaders but their success has elevated their social status. They certainly have more knowledge and familiarity with the product category than non-leaders and they demonstrate innovation and confidence.

Question: Is blogging just a means of self-expression?

Task: Find three different blogs, one each in the fashion, travel and sport categories. Make a list of their similarities and differences.

To conclude this section on WoM communications, three elements concerning the potential of any one WoM recommendation to change behaviour or dissuade from doing so can be identified. According to Bughin et al. (2010) these are what is said, who says it and where it is communicated.

The primary driver is the content of a message, what is said. The message must address important product or service features. For example, in skin care, functional aspects such as packaging and ingredients create more powerful WoM communications than emotional messages about how a product makes people feel.

The second driver concerns the person sending the message. Opinion leaders or influentials embody trust and competence. As a result, they generate three times more WoM messages than non-influentials. Each leader-based message has four times more impact on a recipient's purchasing decision.

The third driver is about the environment and power with which WoM messages circulate. Compact, trust-based networks enable low reach, but messages in this type of environment have great impact, relative to those circulated through dispersed communities. This is because there is often a high correlation between people whose opinions we trust and the members of networks we most value.

Amplification

Marketing communications is about enabling relevant brand-based conversations. It might be claimed that an effective communications programme should therefore be based on the number, as well as the quality, of conversations. There are several circumstances when this logic does not tie together, but in principle the volume, diversity and perhaps the dispersion of conversations can be indicative of a successful communications event.

In essence therefore, WoM communications are about amplifying a message so that it reaches as many people as possible. Today, the interaction of people through various media, and social media in particular, can lead to an exponential increase in the number of conversations. Indeed, viral marketing programmes (considered in more detail in Chapter 21) can be generated either by the judicious and deliberate seeding of content around the Internet, or spontaneously, as a result of a cultural spark. In both cases a message is amplified and reaches a much wider audience than would normally be expected.

Image 3.7 Social media amplifies word of mouth communication
Source: pixelfit/Getty Images.

Amplification involves both the cognitive and behavioural elements of the engagement concept. This means saving reviews about a brand, either as thoughts and feelings about a brand, or actions such as a brand trial, experience or purchase, and then sharing it with a network of contacts, friends and family. In social media the use of sponsored stories, embedded tweets and social ads using trending content all serve to amplify messages.

The use of and measurement of both online and offline WoM communications are recognised as important although not always undertaken or prioritised as highly as they should (Leggatt, 2014). Groeger and Buttle (2014: 1186) use social networking analysis to investigate the effectiveness of eWoM. One of their findings concerns the possible overstatement of WoM conversations. They refer to standard metrics for these campaigns, which assume that reach equates to the number of campaign-related conversations. They argue that this approach does not recognise that some people may be exposed multiple times to campaign-related messaging. What this means is that campaigns could be 'significantly less efficient in terms of cost-per-conversation' than is normally understood and that 'multiple exposures mean that the total number of campaign-related conversations cannot be regarded as equivalent to the number of individuals reached'.

Scholars' paper 3.4
Three paradoxes of electronic WoM

Lin, Z. and Heng, C.-S. (2015) The paradoxes of word of mouth in electronic commerce, *Journal of Management Information Systems*, 32(4), 246–84.

This paper provides an interesting theoretical review of WoM. Written from an information systems perspective the authors challenge conventional wisdom and identify three paradoxes associated with e-commerce.

Relational approaches to communications

The previous model accounts for social behaviour but does not account for the context within which the behaviour occurs. Communications events always occur within a context (Littlejohn, 1992) or particular set of circumstances. It is the context which not only influences the form of the communications but also affects the nature and the way the communications are received, interpreted and acted upon. There are a huge number of variables that can influence the context, including the disposition of the people involved, the physical environment, the nature of the issue, the history and associated culture, the goals of the participants and the expected repercussions of the dialogue itself.

Littlejohn identifies four main contextual levels: interpersonal, group, organisational and mass communications. These levels form part of a hierarchy whereby higher levels incorporate the lower levels but 'add something new of their own'.

The relational approach means that communications events are linked together in an organised manner, one where the events are 'punctuated' by interventions from one or more of the participants. These interventions occur whenever the participants attempt cooperation or if conflict arises.

Soldow and Thomas (1984), referring to a sales negotiation, state that a relationship develops through the form of negotiations rather than the content. An agreement is necessary about who is to control the relationship or whether there will be equality. Rothschild (1987) reports that 'sparring will continue' until agreement is reached or the

Table 3.6 Layers of social penetration

Characteristic	Explanation
Orientation	The disclosure of public information only.
Exploratory affective exchange	Expansion and development of public information.
Affective exchange	Disclosure, based upon anticipated relationship rewards, of deeper feelings, values and beliefs.
Stable exchange	High level of intimacy where partners are able to predict each other's reactions with a good level of accuracy.

Source: Taylor and Altman (1987).

negotiations are terminated. In other words, without mutual agreement over the roles of the participants, the true purpose of the interaction, to achieve an exchange, cannot be resolved.

An interesting aspect of relational communications theory is social penetration (Taylor and Altman, 1987). Through the disclosure of increasing amounts of information about themselves, partners in a relationship (personal or organisational) develop levels of intimacy, which serve to build interpersonal relationships. The relationship moves forward as partners reveal successive layers of information about each other and, as a greater amount or breadth of information is shared, confidence grows. These levels can be seen to consist of orientation, exploratory affective exchange, affective exchange and stable exchange (see Table 3.6). These layers are not uncovered in a logical, orderly sequence. It is likely that partners will return to previous levels, test the outcomes and rewards and reconsider their positions as the relationships unfold through time. This suggests that social penetration theory may lie at the foundation of the development of trust, commitment and relational exchanges between organisations.

Relationships need not be just dyadic, as the interactional approach suggests, but could be triadic or even encompass a much wider network or array of participants. Through this perspective a 'communications network' can be observed, through which information can flow. Participants engage in communications based upon their perception of the environment in which the communications occur and the way in which each participant relates to the others.

Rogers (1986) identifies a communications network as 'consisting of interconnected individuals who are linked by patterned communications flows'. This is important, as it views communications as transcending organisational boundaries. In other words, it is not only individuals within an organisation that develop patterned communications flows but also individuals across different organisations. These individuals participate with one another (possibly through exchanges) and use communications networks to achieve their agenda items.

The extent to which individuals are linked to the network is referred to as *connectedness*. The more a network is connected, the greater the likelihood that a message will be disseminated, as there are few isolated individuals. Similarly, the level of integration in a network refers to the degree to which members of the network are linked to one another. The greater the integration, the more potential channels there are for a message to be routed through.

Systems theory recognises that organisations are made of interacting units. The relational approach to communications is similar to systems theory. The various 'criss-crossing' flows of information between reciprocating units allow individuals and groups to modify the actions of others in the 'net', and this permits the establishment of a pattern of communications (Tichy, 1979).

Communications are an integral part of relationship marketing, and within this collaborative context, interaction and dialogue are essential factors.

Scholars' paper 3.5

Let's get relational

Soldow, G.F. and Thomas, G.P. (1984) Relational communication: form versus content in the sales interaction, *Journal of Marketing,* **48 (Winter), 84–93.**

This was the first paper that attempted to develop ideas about face-to-face communications, which until that point had been well established. Soldow and Thomas introduced the concept of relational communications, which refers to that part of a message beyond the actual content which enables participants to negotiate their relative positions. Thus, the message sender can bid for dominance, deference, or equality. The message receiver, in turn, can accept the bid or deny it.

See also:

Fazal-e-Hasan, S.M., Lings, I.N., Mortimer, G. and Neale, L. (2017) How gratitude influences customer word-of-mouth intentions and involvement: the mediating role of affective commitment, *Journal of Marketing Theory and Practice*, 25(2), (Spring), 200–11.

Process of adoption

An interesting extension to the concept of opinion followers and the discussion on WoM communications is the process by which individuals become committed to the use of a new product. Rogers (1983) has identified this as the process of adoption and the stages of his innovation decision process are represented in Figure 3.5. These stages in the adoption process are sequential and are characterised by the different factors that are involved at each stage (e.g. the media used by each individual).

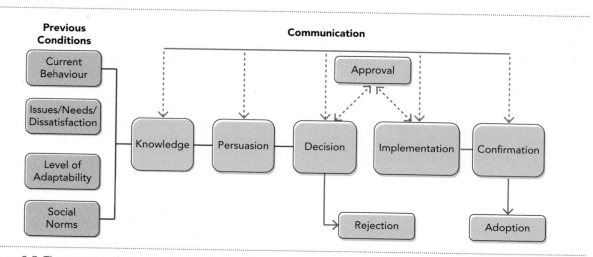

Figure 3.5 The stages in the innovation decision-making process of adoption

1. *Knowledge*

   The innovation becomes known to consumers, but they have little information and no well-founded attitudes. Information must be provided through mass media to institutions and people whom active seekers of information are likely to contact. Information for passive seekers should be supplied through the media and channels that this group habitually uses to look for other kinds of information (Windahl et al., 1992).

   Zoe washes her hair regularly, but she begins to notice changes to the condition of her hair and deposits on her comb. She becomes aware of conversations on social media for this condition and notices ads and sponsored content for the use of DIY treatments involving aloe vera, as well as hair restoration brands.

2. *Persuasion*

   The consumer becomes aware that the innovation may be of use in solving known and potential problems. Information from those who have experience of the product becomes very important.

   Zoe notices that the makers of a particular hair growth treatment use a serum containing aloe vera. Claims are made that not only does the serum reduce the amount of hair loss, but it also aids hair gain. Online recommendations and testimonials boost Zoe's confidence and trust in DIY treatments and this serum in particular. Modelling behaviour predominates.

3. *Decision*

   An attitude may develop and may be either favourable or unfavourable, but as a result a decision is reached whether to trial the offering or not. Communications need to assist this part of the process by continual prompting.

   Zoe is prepared to believe (or not to believe) these messages and the claims made by others on the use of the serum. She thinks that this is a potentially very good solution (or not). She intends trying the DIY serum treatment as she was given a free sample (or because it was on a special price deal).

4. *Implementation*

   For the adoption to proceed in the absence of a sales promotion, buyers must know where to get it and how to use it. The product is then tested in a limited way. Communications must provide this information in order that the trial experience be developed.

   Zoe tries the DIY serum treatment.

5. *Confirmation*

   The innovation is accepted or rejected on the basis of the experience during trial. Planned communications play an important role in maintaining the new behaviour by dispelling negative thoughts and positively reaffirming the original 'correct' decision. McGuire (1989), as reported in Windahl et al. (1992), refers to this as *post-behavioural consolidation*.

   It works. Zoe's hair condition improves. She reads an article that reports that large numbers of people are using these types of products satisfactorily. Zoe resolves to buy and use the serum in the future.

This process can be terminated at any stage and, of course, a number of competing brands may vie for consumers' attention simultaneously, so adding to the complexity and levels of noise in the process. Generally, mass communications are seen to be more effective in the earlier phases of the adoption process for products that buyers are actively interested in, while more interpersonal forms are more appropriate at the later stages, especially trial and adoption. This model assumes that the stages occur in a predictable sequence, but this clearly does not happen in all purchase activity, as some information that is to be used later in the trial stage may be omitted, which often happens when loyalty to a brand is high or where the buyer has experience in the marketplace.

Process of diffusion

The process of adoption in aggregate form, over time, is diffusion. According to Rogers (1983), diffusion is the process by which an innovation is communicated through certain channels over a period of time among the members of a social system. This is a group process and Rogers again identified five categories of adopters. Figure 3.6 shows how diffusion may be fast or slow and that there is no set speed at which the process occurs. The five categories are as follows:

1. *Innovators*

   These groups like new ideas and have a large disposable income. This means they are more likely to take risks associated with new products.

2. *Early adopters*

   Research has established that this group contains a large proportion of opinion leaders and they are, therefore, important in speeding the diffusion process. Early adopters tend to be younger than any other group and above average in education. Internet activity and use of publications are probably high as they actively seek information. A high proportion of early adopters are active bloggers. This group is important to the marketing communications process because they can determine the speed at which diffusion occurs.

3. *Early majority*

   The early majority are usually composed of opinion followers who are a little above average in age, education, social status and income. Although not capable of substantiation, it is probable that web usage is high and they rely on informal sources of information and take fewer publications than the previous two groups.

4. *Late majority*

   This group of people is sceptical of new ideas and only adopts new products because of social or economic factors. They take few publications and are below average in education, social status and income. Their web usage may be below average.

5. *Laggards*

   This group of people is suspicious of all new ideas and is set in their opinions. Lowest of all the groups in terms of income, social status and education, this group takes a long time to adopt an innovation.

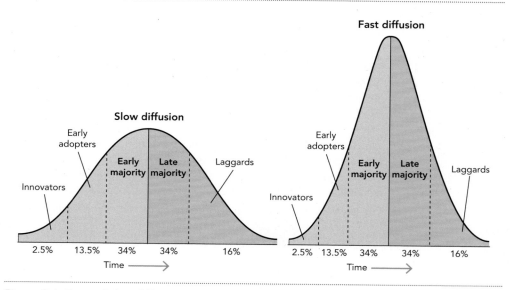

Figure 3.6 Fast and slow diffusion of an innovation
Source: From Hawkins et al. (1989) *Consumer Behavior*, 4th edition. Used with permission of the McGraw-Hill Companies.

This framework suggests that, at the innovation stage, messages should be targeted at relatively young people in the target group, with a high level of income, education and social status. This will speed WoM recommendation and the diffusion process. Mahajan et al. (1990) observe that the personal influence of WoM communications does not work in isolation from the other communications tools and media. Early adopters are more likely to adopt an innovation in response to 'external influences' and only through time will the effect of 'internal influences' become significant. In other words, mass-media communications need time to work before WoM communications can begin to build effectiveness. However, digital developments circumvent the need to use mass media, which means that viral communications and social networks alone can lead to substantial WoM penetration.

Key points

- The linear or one-way communications process suggests that messages are developed by a source, encoded, transmitted, decoded and meaning applied to the message by a receiver. Noise in the system may prevent the true meaning of the messages from being conveyed, while feedback to the source is limited. The effectiveness of this communications process is determined by the strengths of the linkages between the different components.

- There are two particular influences on the communications process that need to be considered. First, the media used to convey information have fragmented drastically as a raft of new media have emerged. Second, people influence the communications process considerably, either as opinion leaders or formers or as participants in the word-of-mouth process.

- The influencer model depicts information flowing via media channels to particular types of people (opinion leaders and opinion formers; see p. 79) to whom other members of the audience refer for information and guidance. Through interpersonal networks, opinion leaders not only reach members of the target audience who may not have been exposed to the message, but may reinforce the impact of the message for those members who did receive the message.

- Increasingly communications are characterised by attributing meaning to messages that are shared, updated and a response to other messages. These 'conversations' can be termed 'interactional' and are an integral part of society. The interactional model of communications attempts to assimilate the variety of influences acting upon the communications process and account for the responses (interactions) people give to messages received from people and machines.

- Opinion leaders are members of a peer group who have informal expertise and knowledge about a specific topic. Opinion formers have formal expertise bestowed upon them by virtue of their qualifications, experience and careers. Opinion followers value and use information from these sources in their decision-making processes. Marketing communications should, therefore, target leaders and formers as they can speed the overall communications process.

- Word-of-mouth (WoM) communications are 'interpersonal communications regarding products or services where the receiver regards the communicator as impartial'. WoM is an increasingly important form of effective communications. It is relatively cost-free yet very credible, and embodies the increasingly conversational nature of marketing communications.

- The process of adoption in aggregate form, over time, is diffusion. It is a group process by which an innovation is communicated through certain channels over a period of time among the members of a social system. Five particular groups, each with distinct characteristics, can be identified.

Case study

How L'Oréal Paris *Age Perfect* transformed its fortunes by showing older women that they are still 'worth it'

Emily Ellis, McCann London, Vasileios Kourakis, L'Oréal UK

Image 3.8 L'Oreal Paris launched a campaign to revitalise their Age Perfect brand.
Source: MDOGAN/Shuttertsock.

L'Oréal Paris *Age Perfect* is an anti-ageing moisturiser targeted at 55–65-year-old women. The other big players include Olay Regenerist, No7 Protect and Perfect, and Nivea Q10. L'Oréal Paris also market the 'Revitalift' anti-ageing skincare range, targeted at women in their 40s.

When the market dropped by 5 per cent in value sales, *Age Perfect* witnessed a 14 per cent fall in the same period. In particular there was a large loss of approximately 75,000 shoppers aged 55+ from the female mass skincare market, equating to a yearly loss of £1.3 million. As the over-55 shopper spends three times as much on skincare per year than the under-55 shopper she was a crucial consumer to win back.

There were other difficulties facing the L'Oréal Paris *Age Perfect* brand.

- The skincare category is critical to the overall success of L'Oréal Paris.
- L'Oréal Paris has a marketing culture that thrives on new product news. On this occasion we didn't have any.

Our 55–65-year-old UK consumers regarded the brand as aloof, and presenting an unattainable level of beauty.

To respond to these issues we set out a series of objectives. Our main commercial objective was to increase the *Age Perfect* market value share from 5.5 per cent to 6.5 per cent by the end of the campaign. This meant we needed to get 40,000 new shoppers to buy at least one *Age Perfect* product.

Because no-one was talking to them on *their* terms, our target audience felt undervalued and misunderstood, and they regarded the brand as cold and indifferent. Our communications objective was therefore to increase brand affinity within our core target market.

Research found that 70 per cent of women in this group felt invisible, 72 per cent felt they were misrepresented in advertising, and a staggering 87 per cent said they were invisible in the eyes of the beauty industry. So we did some social listening, and realised that 55+ women are actually living life to the max. In fact, many older women are becoming entrepreneurs, rediscovering their love lives, and exploring the world. So, while the world may see 'tired and old', she's actually feeling more 'rock and roll' than ever. The creative insight from this was that at a time in her life when she's most confident, paradoxically she feels increasingly invisible.

Our big idea was simple, having uncovered that she's still got it – enjoying her freedom, having the time of her life and achieving great things – we wanted to celebrate 55+ women as fabulous, not fading and as bold, not old.

Flipping our product name '*Age Perfect*' on its head, our campaign line 'The Perfect Age' was born.

We needed a perfect spokesmodel, someone who would fulfil two roles: she had to be relatable to our UK audience and she had to have the ultimate Perfect Age attitude. We knew the ideal woman: Helen Mirren. Not only a national treasure, she was already breaking stereotypes about older women and making the most of The Perfect Age. So we championed her, and her attitude, right across the media mix.

We launched with a huge PR event to introduce her as our new spokesmodel, while starting a conversation about the campaign.

We released our Helen Mirren behind the scenes content films on Facebook and YouTube, where she discussed what The Perfect Age and 'You're worth it' means to her. In these, Helen describes the beauty of growing older and living The Perfect Age. She contrasts this with the paralysing insecurities that many women feel when they're young, that she says disappear as you get older.

She also opens up about her own experience of self-doubt in a profession in which she is constantly

Image 3.9 Helen Mirren became the brand ambassador for Age Perfect as she related perfectly to the brand's UK audience and she had the ultimate Perfect Age attitude. *Source*: Andrea Raffin/Shutterstock.

critiqued and criticised publicly. She encourages women to overcome their doubt, rediscover their worth and ultimately 'free their fabulous'.

In order to reach our business objective, The Perfect Age couldn't *just* be about an attitude – we wanted her to look as fabulous as she was feeling. For our product messaging we used traditional, highly visible media to create desire for our product: with statement OOH (out-of-home) locations such as the Kings Road, as well as TV spots, press, cinema and in-store. The TV advert was also shown on Facebook and YouTube where it had fantastic engagement with over 2 million views, but more importantly some fantastic comments around our choice of spokesmodel, our lack of retouching and the whole notion of embracing The Perfect Age.

We knew our audience were far more rock and roll than society would have us think, so we wanted to give them the opportunity to smash the stereotype. We partnered with Gransnet to create sponsored threads, which were designed to give her a voice. This created campaign engagement, with hundreds of responses that showed these women were embracing The Perfect Age.

Inspired by the response on Gransnet, we wanted to give 55+ women the chance to tell their stories in person and to a much larger audience. We took to the streets and asked: 'what's the most outrageous thing you do now, that you didn't dare do before?' The answers surprised us and showed there was a huge appetite to ridicule age old stereotypes.

For example:

Jenny: age 60 – 'I am a member of the mile-high club . . . I don't know how many.'

Janie: age 68 – 'I surf; I don't mean on the internet . . . we call ourselves the silver surfers.'

Fiona: age 70 – 'I started to do a striptease . . . '

We used the best responses to create a short film that was seeded on Facebook and YouTube. This was the first time that L'Oréal Paris had featured 'real' 55+ women in their content, which was essential if we were to prove to our target audience that we were a brand for her. With over 3 million views, it was clear our audience loved it.

The results of the campaign were astonishing. Market share grew from 5.5 per cent to 6.9 per cent during the campaign. It brought in nearly 50,000 more 55+ shoppers into the *Age Perfect* range, overshooting the client objective by 25 per cent. It also increased shoppers for all the other age brackets too. The result was a total shopper increase of over 78,000 women – equating to nearly £1.4 million in incremental sales for L'Oréal Paris.

We grew our target audience of 55+ women by 23 per cent vs the market growth of 4 per cent and the total market by 25 per cent vs the market growth of just 2 per cent.

To improve brand affinity KPIs among our core target market, the metric *model of femininity she can relate to* saw a huge increase from 15 per cent in pre-campaign testing to 21 per cent in May 2015. The metric L'Oréal Paris as *experts in mature skincare*, also increased by 6 per cent in the same period. Furthermore, we saw evidence to support the power of our insight. The metric *L'Oréal Paris enables women of my age to be more visible in society* shifted from 30 per cent to 39 per cent.

This case study is an edited version of a paper submitted to the IPA Effectiveness Awards 2016. It has been reproduced here with the kind permission of the IPA, WARC, L'Oreal Paris, and the agency McCann London.

Review questions

L'Oréal Paris case questions

1. Discuss the way in which the Perfect Age message was encoded. Could it be improved and if so how?

2. Make brief notes explaining how consumer insight assisted the development of the Perfect Age campaign.

3. How might the Perfect Age campaign be interpreted through the influencer model of communications?

4. Which of the linear, influencer and interactional models best illustrates how communications worked for L'Oréal Paris?

5. Discuss ways in which the Perfect Age message might be interpreted through the process of adoption.

General questions

1. Name the elements of the linear model of communications and briefly describe the role of each element.

2. How do opinion leaders differ from opinion formers and opinion followers?

3. What are the three elements of word-of-mouth communications identified by Bone?

4. If voluntary is one form of WoM, what are the other two and how do they differ?

5. Using a product of your choice, show how the stages in the process of adoption can be depicted.

References for Chapter 3

Anon (2016) How Chanel wins on Instagram, *MediaKix*, 24 May, retrieved 9 April 2018 from http://mediakix.com/2016/05/instagram-marketing-case-study-chanel-fashion-beauty/#gs.4ENletU

Anon (2017a) Airbnb's celebrity-focused Instagram marketing strategy, *MediaKix*, 30 July, retrieved 9 April 2018 from http://mediakix.com/2017/07/airbnb-marketing-celebrity-instagram-influencers/#gs.3TEFLks

Anon (2017b) Marriott sees Snapchat success, WARC, 9 August, retrieved 11 August 2017 from https://www.warc.com/NewsAndOpinion/News/Marriott_sees_Snapchat_success/39104?utm_source=DailyNews&utm_medium=email&utm_campaign=DailyNews20170809

Anon (2018) Snapchat royalty Kylie Jenner helped erase $1.3 billion in one tweet, *Adage*, 22 February, retrieved 23 February 2018 from http://adage.com/article/digital/snapchat-royalty-kylie-jenner-helped-erase-1-3-billion-tweet/

Ballantyne, D. (2004) Dialogue and its role in the development of relationship specific knowledge, *Journal of Business and Industrial Marketing*, 19(2), 114–23.

Berger, J. and Schwartz, E.M. (2011) What drives immediate and ongoing word of mouth? *Journal of Marketing Research*, XLVIII (October), 869–80.

Bone, P.F. (1995) Word of mouth effects on short-term and long-term product judgments, *Journal of Business Research*, 32(3), 213–23.

Branchik, B.J. and Chowdhury, T.G. (2017) Men seeing stars: celebrity endorsers, race, and the male consumer, *Journal of Marketing Theory and Practice*, 25(3), Summer, 305–22.

Bughin, J., Doogan, J. and Vetvik, O.J. (2010) A new way to measure word-of-mouth marketing, *McKinsey Quarterly*, Issue 2.

Castellano, S. and Dutot, V. (2017) Investigating the influence of e-word-of-mouth on e-reputation, *International Studies of Management & Organization*, 47, 42–60.

Chan, K.K. and Misra, S. (1990) Characteristics of the opinion leader: a new dimension, *Journal of Advertising*, 19(3), 53–60.

Christiansen, T. and Tax, S.S. (2000) Measuring word of mouth: the questions of who and when, *Journal of Marketing Communications*, 6, 185–99.

Dichter, E. (1966) How word-of-mouth advertising works, *Harvard Business Review*, 44 (November/December), 147–66.

Essuah, I. (2017) Meet Izy Hossack, the 'new Nigella', *Viva*, Wednesday 16 August, retrieved 20 September 2017 from http://www.viva.co.nz/article/food-drink/young-cook-izy-hossack/

Eyal, G. (2017) Why 280 characters won't save Twitter, *AdAge*, 21 November, retrieved 22 November 2017 from http://adage.com/article/digitalnext/280-characters-save-twitter/311348/

Fazal-e-Hasan, S.M., Lings, I.N., Mortimer, G. and Neale, L. (2017) How gratitude influences customer word-of-mouth intentions and involvement: the mediating role of affective commitment, *Journal of Marketing Theory and Practice*, 25(2), (Spring), 200–11.

Flynn, K. (2017) Brands are creating Snapchat 'Shows' with dreams of getting on Discover, *MashableUK*, 30 March, retrieved 20 September 2017 from http://mashable.com/2017/03/30/snapchat-marriott-rewards-shows/#IlmBtlP6TmqP

Fulgoni, G.M. and Lipsman, A. (2017) The downside of digital word of mouth and the pursuit of media quality, *Journal of Advertising Research*, 57(2), 127–31.

Goldsmith, R.E. and Horowitz, D. (2006) Measuring motivations for online opinion seeking, *Journal of Interactive Advertising*, 6(2), 3–14, retrieved 5 April 2010 from www.jiad.org/article76

Groeger, L. and Buttle, F. (2014) Word-of-mouth marketing: towards an improved under-standing of multi-generational campaign reach, *European Journal of Marketing*, 48(7/8), 1186–208.

Haenlein, M. and Libai, B. (2017) Seeding, referral, and recommendation: creating profitable word-of-mouth programs, *California Management Review*, 59(2), 68–91.

Hamilton, R., Vohs, K.D. and McGill, A.L. (2014) We'll be honest, this won't be the best article you'll ever read: the use of dispreferred markers in word-of-mouth communications, *Journal of Consumer Research*, 41, June, 197–212.

Helm, S. and Schlei, J. (1998) Referral potential – potential referrals: an investigation into customers' communication in service markets, Proceedings of 27th EMAC Conference, *Marketing Research and Practice*, 41–56.

Ingram, D. and Bartz, D. (2017) FTC demands endorsement info from Instagram 'influencers', *Reuters*, 13 September, retrieved 9 April 2018 from https://www.reuters.com/article/us-usa-ftc-celebrities/ftc-demands-endorsement-info-from-instagram-influencers-idUSKCN1BO2TE

Jin, S.A.A. and Phua, J. (2014) Following celebrities' tweets about brands: the impact of Twitter-based electronic word-of-mouth on consumers' source credibility perception, buying intention, and social identification with celebrities, *Journal of Advertising*, 43(2), 181–95.

Johnson, G.J., Bruner II, G.C. and Kumar, A. (2006) Interactivity and its facets revisited, *Journal of Advertising*, 35(4), 35–52.

Katz, E. and Lazarsfeld, P.F. (1955) *Personal Influence*, Glencoe, IL: Free Press.

Kawakami, T., Kishiya, K. and Parry, M.E. (2014) Personal word of mouth, virtual word of mouth and innovation use, *Journal of Product Innovation Management*, 30(1), 17–30.

Keller, E.B. and Berry, J.L. (2003) *The Influentials: One American in Ten Tells the Other Nine How to Vote, Where to Eat, and What to Buy*, New York: Simon & Schuster.

Kozinets, R.V., de Valck, K., Wojnicki, A.C. and Wilner, S.J.S. (2010) Networked narratives: understanding word-of-mouth marketing in online communities, *Journal of Marketing*, 74, (March), 71–89.

Leggatt, H. (2014) Marketers struggle to measure offline word-of-mouth marketing, *BizReport: Social Marketing*, 28 April, retrieved 5 August 2014 from www.bizreport.com/2014/04/marketers-struggle-to-measure-offline-word-of-mouth-marketin.html

Lin, Z. and Heng, C-S. (2015) The paradoxes of word of mouth in electronic commerce, *Journal of Management Information Systems*, 32(4), 246–84.

Litterio, A.M., Nantes, A., Larrosa, J.M., and Gómez, L.J. (2017) Marketing and social net-works: a criterion for detecting opinion leaders, *European Journal of Management and Business Economics*, 26(3), 347–66.

Littlejohn, S.W. (1992) *Theories of Human Communication*, 4th edn, Belmont, CA: Wadsworth.

Mahajan, V., Muller, E. and Bass, F.M. (1990) New product diffusion models in marketing, *Journal of Marketing*, 54 (January), 1–26.

Mallen, B. (1977) *Principles of Marketing Channel Management*, Lexington, MA: Lexington Books.

Mazzarol, T., Sweeney, J.C. and Soutar, G.N. (2007) Conceptualising word-of-mouth activity, triggers and conditions: an exploratory study, *European Journal of Marketing*, 41(11/12), 1475–94.

McCracken, G. (1989) Who is the celebrity endorser? Cultural foundations of the endorse-ment process, *Journal of Consumer Research*, 16 (December), 310–21.

McGuire, W.J. (1985) Attitudes and Attitude Change, in *Handbook of Social Psychology* (eds G. Lindzey and E. Aronson), Vol 2, New York: Random House, 233–346.

McGuire, W.J. (1989) Theoretical foundations of campaigns, in, *Public communication campaigns,* 2nd edn (eds R.E. Rice and C.K. Atkin), Newbury Park, CA: Sage Publications, 43–65.

Nisbet, E.C. (2005) The engagement model of opinion leadership: testing validity within a European context, *International Journal of Public Opinion Research*, 18(1), 1–27.

Palmer, I. (2009) WoM is about empowering consumers in shaping your brand, *Admap*, 504, retrieved 2 June 2010 from www.warc.com/admap

Park, E., Rishika, R., Janakiraman, R., Houston, M.B. and Yoo, B. (2018) Social dollars in online communities: the effect of product, user, and network characteristics, *Journal of Marketing*, 82 (January), 93–114.

Patzer, G.L. (1983) Source credibility as a function of communicator physical attractiveness, *Journal of Business Research*, 11, 229–41.

Reynolds, F.D. and Darden, W.R. (1971) Mutually adaptive effects of interpersonal communication, *Journal of Marketing Research*, 8 (November), 449–54.

Rivalland, M. (2014) Student blogger may be the next Nigella, *The Times*, 2 August, 16.

Robinson, J.P. (1976) Interpersonal influence in election campaigns: two step flow hypothesis, *Public Opinion Quarterly*, 40, 304–19.

Robinson, M. and Malm, S. (2015) The house that 7 million followers on YouTube bought, *Mail Online*, 17 February, retrieved 30 May 2015 from www.dailymail.co.uk/news/

Rogers, E.M. (1962) *Diffusion of Innovations*, 1st edn, New York: Free Press.

Rogers, E.M. (1983) *Diffusion of Innovations*, 3rd edn, New York: Free Press.

Rogers, E.M. (1986) *Communication Technology: The New Media in Society*, New York: Free Press.

Rogers, E.M. (2003) *Diffusion of Innovations*, 5th edn, New York: Free Press.

Rothschild, M. (1987) *Marketing Communications*, Lexington, MA: D.C. Heath.

Schramm, W. (1955) How communication works, in *The Process and Effects of Mass Communications* (ed. W. Schramm), Urbana, IL: University of Illinois Press, 3–26.

Schramm, W. (1962) Mass communication, *Annual Review of Psychology*, 13(1), 25–84.

Shannon, C. and Weaver, W. (1962) *The Mathematical Theory of Communication*, Urbana, IL: University of Illinois Press.

Shih, H.P., Lai, K.H. and Cheng, T.C.E. (2013) Informational and relational influences on electronic word of mouth: an empirical study of an online consumer discussion forum, *International Journal of Electronic Commerce*, 17(4), 137–65.

Soldow, G.F. and Thomas, G.P. (1984) Relational communication: form versus content in the sales interaction, *Journal of Marketing*, 48 (Winter), 84–93.

Spoors, N. (2015) NGH to bring back white coats after patients did not realise they had seen a doctor, *Northampton Chronicle & Echo*, 28 July, retrieved 26 November 2017 from http://www.northamptonchron.co.uk/news/ngh-to-bring-back-white-coats-after-patients-did-not-realise-they-had-seen-a-doctor-1-6871846

Stokes, D. and Lomax, W. (2002) Taking control of word of mouth marketing: the case of an entrepreneurial hotelier, *Journal of Small Business and Enterprise Development*, 9(4), 349–57.

Swift, J. (2014) Unilever pilots multi-brand advertising with YouTube beauty channel, *Campaignlive*, retrieved 3 April 2018 from www.campaignlive.co.uk/news/

Taylor, D. and Altman, I. (1987) Communication in interpersonal relationships: social penetration theory, in *Interpersonal Processes: New Directions in Communication Research* (eds M.E. Roloff and G.R. Miller), Newbury Park, CA: Sage, 257–77.

Theodorson, S.A. and Theodorson, G.R. (1969) *A Modern Dictionary of Sociology*, New York: Cromwell.

Tichy, N. (1979) Social network analysis for organisations, *Academy of Management Review,* 4, 507–19.

Weimann, G. (1994) *The Influentials: People Who Influence People,* Albany, NY: State University of New York Press.

Weisfeld-Spolter, S., Sussan, F. and Gould, S. (2014) An integrative approach to eWOM and marketing communications, *Corporate Communications: An International Journal,* 19(3), 260–74.

Williams, K. (1990) *Behavioural Aspects of Marketing,* Oxford: Heinemann.

Williams, Z. (2017) Zoe Sugg: the vlogger blamed for declining teenage literacy, *Guardian,* Friday 24 February, retrieved 20 September 2017 from https://www.theguardian.com/culture/2017/feb/24/zoe-sugg-zoella-the-vlogger-blamed-for-declining-teenage-literacy

Windahl, S., Signitzer, B. and Olson, J.T. (1992) *Using Communication Theory,* London: Sage.

Classical theories and interpretations of buyer behaviour

Understanding the way in which people perceive their world, the way they learn, develop attitudes and respond to marketing communications stimuli is fundamental if effective communications are to be developed. In the same way, recognising the ways in which people make decisions and the factors that impact upon the decision process also influences the effectiveness of marketing communications.

This is the first of two chapters considering different aspects of buyer behaviour.

Aims and learning objectives

The aims of this chapter are to consider some of the classical interpretations associated with the way information is processed by people, and their decision-making processes. We consider the implications of this knowledge for the way marketing communications can be used.

The learning objectives are to enable readers to:

1. explore ideas concerning the format and shape of customer purchase journeys;

2. appreciate the primary elements associated with information processing: perception, learning, attitudes;

3. explain how information is used by both consumers and organisations when making purchase decisions;

4. consider the importance of involvement in consumer decision-making and the impact on marketing communications.

Introduction

People consume products and services not only because of the utilitarian value but also because of what they represent, their meaning and symbolic value. In other words, people make purchase decisions, either knowingly or subconsciously, about their identity and how they might wish to be seen.

Marketing communications is about managing promises: their creation, delivery and realisation. It makes sense, therefore, to understand the way buyers think and behave, in order that these promises remain realistic and effective. Understanding the ways in which buyers make decisions, the factors that impact upon the decision process and their preferred identities, influences the effectiveness of marketing communications (Mikolajová and Olšanová, 2017). In particular, it can affect message structure, content, integration and media scheduling. In this chapter, and indeed the book, reference is made to both buyers and audiences. This is because, although all buyers constitute an audience, not all audiences are buyers.

Customer journeys

The whole process of customer purchasing is often referred to as a journey. In an ideal world, Hogg (2018) suggests that the journey people take to becoming loyal customers would be 'a straight shot down a highway: See your product. Buy your product. Use your product. Repeat.' This encapsulates the initial stages of problem awareness, the search for solutions, decision-making and then through to post-purchase experience and reflection.

There are numerous, largely practitioner-based ideas, about what constitutes a journey. The customer decision journey was once conceptualised as a linear format, often represented by a (sales) funnel as set out in Figure 4.1 (Court et al., 2009). This approach was used to portray the way customers identified a problem, how they considered a certain set of brands, and then their systematic reduction of the number of feasible solutions until a purchase was made (McNeal, 2013).

Today, the complexity of the media landscape, the variety of buying opportunities and the huge volume of data that is available have made the linear interpretation redundant. Now a non-linear explanation, such as a circular or even a jigsaw format, is necessary in order to express the multiplicity of paths customers use to make purchase decisions. Hogg (2018) suggests the journeys can be considered as 'a sightseeing tour with stops, exploration, and discussion along the way—all moments when you need to convince people to pick your brand and stick with it instead of switching to a competitor'.

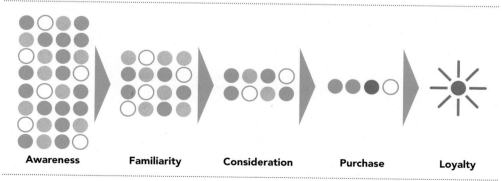

Figure 4.1 The traditional funnel metaphor
Source: Court et al. (2009) used with the kind permission of McKinsey.

This complexity means that organisations have less time, fewer resources per journey format, and hence less control than they thought they used to have. Court et al. (2009) argue that there are four distinct phases to the contemporary customer decision journey:

1. initial consideration;
2. active research and evaluation of potential purchases;
3. closure through the selection and purchase of a brand;
4. post-purchase, the overall experience of the brand as a solution and shaping of future purchases.

Figure 4.2 sets out the way in which these elements work together.

Traditionally organisations attempt to isolate one key journey and from that build a business model. This is no longer a feasible approach and attempts to manage the various consumer/brand touchpoints in order to improve efficiency and customer satisfaction at individual parts of the journey is equally questionable. Rawson et al. (2013: 92) believe that customer satisfaction is not a factor of these multiple, yet individual interactions, it is the 'cumulative experiences across multiple touchpoints and in multiple channels over time' that influence the overall experience and levels of customer satisfaction. Indeed, it is the sum of all the different types and forms of engagement with a brand that appears to be critical. Customers now interact with brands through an increasingly complex web of channels and media. As a result attention has shifted from understanding touchpoints and customer satisfaction to one that is focused on managing customer experience (Lemon and Verhoef, 2016).

Subsequent to these developments McKinsey found that organisations, using digital technologies to design and continuously optimise decision journeys, can now respond to customers as they make purchasing decisions and they can also 'actively shape those decision journeys' (Edelman and Singer, 2015). Many leading organisations use journeys

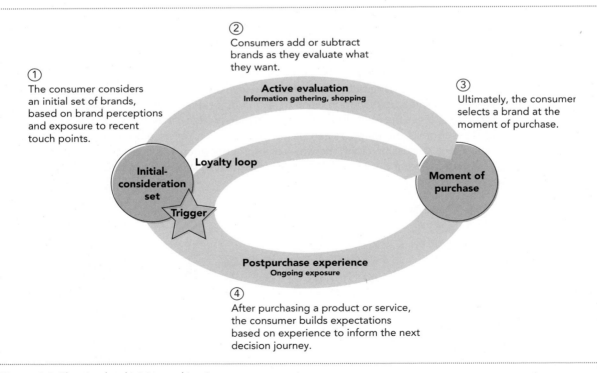

Figure 4.2 The circular decision-making journey
Source: Court et al. (2009) used with the kind permission of McKinsey.

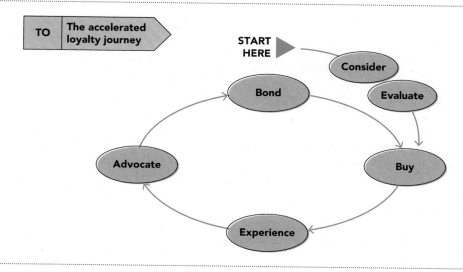

Figure 4.3 The accelerated loyalty journey
Source: Edelman and Singer (2017) used with the kind permission of McKinsey.

to deliver value to the customer (as well as the brand), and achieve this by radically compressing or eliminating the consideration and evaluation phases. Consumers are consequently projected into the loyalty phase of the relationship. The purchase journey is now configured differently, as in Figure 4.3.

People are becoming less responsive to mass communications and expect a more personalised experience, regardless of the sector in which they are purchasing. Their attention spans are decreasing but their search activities are more detailed. This means that brands must deliver a more relevant experience at each point on their customer purchase journey and that requires being helpful, timely and more of a customer companion, rather than aloof, interruptive and instrumental (Sciuto, 2017).

This and Chapter 5 consider some of the key issues that impact the use of marketing communications at various points within these customer journeys. This chapter considers issues relating to the classical interpretation of the way people are thought to process information and make decisions, and it assumes rational decision-making. Chapter 5 considers uncertainty in decision-making and some contemporary, less orthodox, or perhaps more realistic approaches to understanding consumer behaviour.

Viewpoint 4.1

Nestlé Waters funnel their marketing through customer journeys

Nestlé Waters wanted to better manage their customer relationships and to do this it was necessary to understand the purchase funnel or journey that their customers were using.

Search is one of the first steps on a purchase journey and it is now as critical as shelf space in a supermarket. If a brand is not on a shelf it is not going to be bought, and the same applies to

search. If a consumer searches for sparkling water then a Nestlé Waters brand has to show up early in the results. With this in mind Nestlé Waters created their own e-commerce subscription channel, ReadyRefresh, a first touchpoint for their customers and a direct means of assisting their journeys.

Rather than develop content and then fit it around different touchpoints, Nestlé Waters decided they would create specific content for each touchpoint, as this drives relevance. So, a prospective customer in the research phase might get branded messages about the benefits of a brand, such as Poland Spring. As they move closer to purchase, the messaging evolves to one that is more of a call-to-action and they are driven to the ReadyRefresh site. Content also changes in response to other influences. For Nestlé Waters one of these is heat. If temperatures exceed 85 degrees the message focus switches to beating the heat.

Internal changes were also made to better organise around the customer journey. For example, digital specialists were integrated into all the brand teams. Then, their performance teams and media agencies began to be briefed together. This resulted in the integration of the brand and performance teams into one.

It was also important to use data more effectively. Each of their teams only had partial data visibility due to the siloed nature of the data

sources. This led to uncoordinated and overlapping internal activities, and inconsistent conversations with customers. Working with partners and new data management tools they were able to combine data from digital touchpoints. This provides a more even and unified view, which in turn presents opportunities to be more relevant to customers. For example, by sharing data they are able to find prospective customers whose behaviours mimic those of their current customers. By reaching out to similar customers, they are more likely to reach prospects who are more likely to respond, and they avoid interrupting people who would not be receptive to Nestlé Waters' messages.

Nestlé Waters are now able to re-target and re-engage customers who are higher in the funnel and send them to ReadyRefresh at the right moment. For example, those who are looking for home delivery options. As a result, they now find more qualified consumers, and have cut their customer acquisition costs by over 30 per cent.

Source: Sciuto (2017).

Insight

The essence of this Viewpoint is that to be effective marketing communications needs to be aligned with the various touchpoints along the purchase journeys that customers undertake. This requires shaping content to be compatible with each touchpoint. It also means that brand management issues concerning internal communication, team structures and data management are an integral part of this process.

Question: Consider whether communicating with customers at touchpoints is the optimal use of marketing communications resources.

Task: Locate a brand of your choice and make a list of the likely touchpoints in a customer journey.

The classical interpretation of buyer behaviour is based on a largely rational view of the way people access and process information, make purchasing decisions and then rationalise their actions. Two core elements, information processing and decision-making are considered in turn.

Scholars' paper 4.1
Customer experiences and complex journeys

Lemon, K.N. and Verhoef, P.C. (2016) Understanding customer experience through the customer journey, *Journal of Marketing AMA/ MSI Special Issue,* **80 (November), 69–96.**

This helpful paper provides an interesting and thought-provoking view on customer experience and the customer journey, largely from a social media perspective. The authors track the development of customer experience and examine the increasingly complex nature of customer behaviour.

Information processing

Marketing communications is an audience-centred activity, so it is vitally important to understand the way in which people process information throughout their purchase journeys. Traditionally, awareness has been considered an integral part of information processing. However, this important topic is considered as part of an organisation's objectives and positioning activities and is considered in Chapter 8. Here three main information-processing issues are considered: perception, learning and attitudes.

Perception

Perception is concerned with how individuals see and make sense of their environment. It is about how individuals select, organise and interpret stimuli, so that they can understand their world.

Perceptual selection

The vast number of commercial messages received each day need to be filtered, as individuals cannot process them all. The stimuli that are selected result from the interaction of the nature of the stimulus with the expectations and the motives of the individual. Attention is an important factor in determining the outcome of this interaction: 'Attention occurs when the stimulus activates one or more sensory receptor nerves and the resulting sensations go to the brain for processing' (Hawkins et al., 1989).

The nature of the stimuli, or external factors such as the intensity and size, position, contrast, novelty, repetition and movement, are factors that have been developed and refined by marketing communicators to attract attention. Animation is used to attract attention when the product class is perceived as bland and uninteresting, such as margarine or teabags. Unexpected camera angles and the use of music can be effective methods of gaining the attention of the target audience, as used successfully in the Ibis ad, 'Everybody's Famous', supported by Martin Solveig's 'Everybody'. Sexual attraction, as promoted through perfume ads, can be a powerful means of capturing the attention of audiences and, when associated with a brand's values, can be a very effective method of getting attention.

The expectations, needs and motives of an individual, or internal factors, are equally important. Individuals see what they expect to see, and their expectations are normally based on past experience and preconditioning. From a communications perspective, the presentation of stimuli that conflict with an individual's expectations will invariably receive more attention.

Individuals see what they want or need to see. If they are considering the purchase of a new car, there will be heightened awareness of car advertisements and a correspondingly lower level of awareness of unrelated stimuli. Selective attention allows individuals to expose themselves to messages that are comforting and rewarding. For example, reassurance is often required for people who have bought new cars or expensive technical equipment and who have spent a great deal of time debating and considering a purchase and its associated risk. Communications congratulating the new owner on their wise decision often accompany post-purchase emails and literature such as warranties and service contracts. If potentially harmful messages do get through this filter system, perceptual defence mechanisms help to screen them out after exposure.

Image 4.1 The way we perceive brand packaging impacts our attitudes. Here soy sauce is intentionally packed in a 'fish shaped' container, helping shoppers to understand the contents and framing their attitude
Source: Emmanuel LATTES/Alamy Stock Photo.

Perceptual organisation

For perception to be effective and meaningful, the vast array of selected stimuli needs to be organised. The four main ways in which sensory stimuli can be arranged are: figure–ground, grouping, closure and contour.

Figure–ground

Each individual's perception of an environment tends to consist of articles on a general background, against which certain objects are illuminated and stand proud. Williams (1981) gives the examples of trees standing out against the sky and words on a page. This has obvious implications for advertisers and the design and form of communications, especially advertisements, to draw attention to important parts of a message, most noticeably the price, logo, endorser, or company/brand name.

Grouping

Objects that are close to one another tend to be grouped together and a pattern develops. Grouping can be used to encourage associations between a product and specific attributes. For example, food products that are positioned for a health market are often displayed with pictures that represent fitness and exercise, the association being that consumption of the food will lead to a lifestyle that incorporates fitness and exercise, as these are important to the target market.

Closure

When information is incomplete, individuals make sense of the data by filling in the gaps. This is often used to involve consumers in the message and so enhance selective attention.

Advertisements for American Express charge cards or GM credit cards ('if invited to apply'), for example, suggest that ownership denotes membership, which represents exclusiveness and privilege.

Television ads that are run for 60 seconds when first launched are often cut to 30, 15 or even 7 seconds later in the burst. The purpose is two-fold: to cut costs and to keep reminding the target audience. This process of reminding is undertaken with the assistance of the audience, who recognise the commercial and mentally close the message even though the advertiser only presents the first part.

Contour

Contours give objects shape and are normally formed when there is a marked change in colour or brightness. This is an important element in package design and, as the battle for shelf space in retail outlets becomes more intense, so package design has become an increasingly important aspect of attracting attention. The Coca-Cola bottle and the packaging of the Toblerone bar are two classic examples of packaging that conveys the brand.

Image 4.2 Toblerone and Coke Bottle

These are two major examples of the way distinctive packaging and the use of a significant contour can assist brand recognition and understanding
Sources: (a) gcpics/Shutterstock (b) m.syafiq/Shutterstock.

These methods are used by individuals in an attempt to organise stimuli and simplify their meanings. They combine in an attempt to determine a pattern to the stimuli, so that they are perceived as part of a whole or larger unit. This is referred to as *gestalt psychology*.

Perceptual interpretation

Interpretation is the process by which individuals give meaning to the stimuli once they have been organised. As Cohen and Basu (1987) state, by using existing categories, meanings can be given to stimuli. These categories are determined from the individual's past experiences and they shape what the individual expects to see. These expectations, when combined with the strength and clarity of the stimulus and the motives at the time perception occurs, shape the pattern of the perceived stimuli.

Colour can also be used to influence the way a product or category is perceived. So, the sensitive skincare category is often associated with green due to the link with nature. Blue is linked to trust, red (appetite) and yellow (flavour) with fast food (Candy and Bullen, 2017).

Brands use specific colours as means of identification and symbolic association. For example, luxury grocer Fortnum & Mason has used 'eau de nil' as its signature shade (of turquoise) throughout the brand's 300-year history, and it is regarded as a central element in their customers' visual experience (Hosea, 2017).

The degree to which each individual's ascribed meaning is realistic is dependent upon the levels of distortion that may be present. Distortion may occur because of stereotyping:

the predetermined set of images which we use to guide our expectations of events, people and situations. Another distortion factor is the halo effect that occurs when a stimulus with many attributes or dimensions is evaluated on just a single attribute or dimension. Brand extensions and family branding strategies are based on the understanding that if previous experiences with a different offering are satisfactory, then risk is reduced and an individual is more likely to buy a new offering from the same 'family'.

Marketing and perception

We have seen that individuals select and interpret particular stimuli in the context of the expectations arising from the way they classify the overall situation. The way in which individuals perceive, organise and interpret stimuli is a reflection of their past experiences and the classifications used to understand the different situations each individual frames every day. Individuals seek to provide a context within which their role becomes clearer. Shoppers expect to find products in particular situations, such as rows, shelves or display bins of similar goods. They also develop meanings and associations with some grocery products because of the utility and trust/emotional satisfaction certain pack types evoke. The likelihood that a sale will be made is improved, if the context in which a purchase transaction is undertaken does not contradict a shopper's expectations.

Marketing communications should attempt to present products (objects) in a frame or 'mental presence' (Moran, 1990) that is recognised by a buyer, such as a consumption or purchase situation. A product has a much greater chance of entering a consideration set if the situation in which it is presented is one that is expected and relevant. A new pack design however, can provide differentiation and provoke people into reassessing their expectations about what constitutes appropriate packaging in a product category. See Viewpoint 4.2 where Heineken used this concept of framing.

Viewpoint 4.2

Heineken 0.0 – perceptual taste?

Image 4.3 The Heineken 0.0 bottle
Source: g0d4ather/Shutterstock.

Heineken, the second biggest beer company in the world, launched 'Heineken 0.0', a non-alcoholic beer with just 69 calories per bottle. Heineken had recognised that there was an emerging market of people who want to drink beer but don't want the alcoholic content. These include those in training or following fitness regimes, pregnant women, slimmers and those about to drive.

The beer sector faces several challenges. Lager sales were falling, craft beers were gaining popularity and other alcoholic drinks were getting a foothold in the market. Many consumers are pursuing healthier lifestyles or 'clean living', so alcohol does not fit. As if to substantiate this, a Mintel report in 2016 showed that 19 per cent of UK adults do not drink alcohol, while 32 per cent said they had limited or reduced the amount of alcohol they consume. The European non-alcoholic beer market had been growing at about 5 per cent per year for the previous four years. In Spain zero-strength beer already had a 10 per cent market share.

Although the bottle and overall presentation of Heineken 0.0 is the same as the main brand, it was necessary to associate the new drink with the alcohol-free category. This was achieved by changing the colour of its 'iconic' label from green to blue. This also helped consumers to recognise the brand. To convince consumers that Heineken 0.0 was suitable for everyone and at all drinking occasions the tag line 'Open to all' was used.

There are many different alcohol-free beers and the public's overall perception is that their taste is not very good. It was important, therefore, that Heineken, who had spent two years refining the taste and flavour, were able to convince the public that this product was different to the others in the sector. The launch campaign, which included TV, digital and experiential activity, also included a sampling strategy delivered through supermarkets and pubs. The goal was to help people test the product and in doing so change perceptions about taste.

Sources: Gianatasio (2017); Roderick (2017); Williams-Grut (2017).

Insight

By framing the label to align the new product with the established colour code of the category and the parent brand, Heineken were better able to manage perceptions of their brand within the non-alcoholic beer sector. In doing so Heineken was able to realign consumer perceptions with the established quality associations of Heineken. Perceptions were managed not just through one-way communication but through tastings and sampling.

Question: Why did Heineken choose not to refer to the taste of 0.0 in the launch?

Task: Find another low-alcohol beer and show how they manage perceptions of their product.

Javalgi et al. (1992) point out that perception is important to product evaluation and product selection. Consumers try to evaluate a product's attributes using the physical cues of taste, smell, size and shape. Sometimes no difference can be distinguished, so the consumer has to make a judgement on factors other than the physical characteristics of the product. This is the basis of branding activity, where a personality is developed for the product that enables it to be perceived differently from its competitors. The individual may also set up a separate category or consideration set in order to make sense of new stimuli or satisfactory experiences.

Scholars' paper 4.2
Simply a cosmetic perception

Schivinski, B. and Dabrowski, D. (2016) The effect of social media communication on consumer perceptions of brands, *Journal of Marketing Communications*, **22(2), 189–214.**

This paper considers the impact of social media content driven by firms and content driven by users. They find that user-generated social media communication has a positive influence on both brand equity and brand attitude, whereas firm-created social media communication affected only brand attitude. This paper also provides a useful literature background for a range of concepts including brand attitude, brand equity, and both firm and user generated content.

See also:

Guthrie, M.F. and Kim, H.-S. (2009) The relationship between consumer involvement and brand perceptions of female cosmetic consumers, *Journal of Brand Management*, 17(2), 114–33.

The concept of positioning products in the mind of each consumer is fundamental to marketing strategy and communications. (This topic is examined in greater depth in Chapter 8.)

Learning

There are two mainstream approaches to learning. These are behavioural and cognitive, and their core characteristics are set out in Table 4.1.

Behavioural learning

The behavourist approach to learning views the process as a function of an individual's acquisition of responses. There are three factors important to behavioural learning: association, reinforcement and motivation. However, it is the basic concept of the stimulus–response orientation that will be looked at in more detail.

For learning to occur all that is needed is a 'time–space proximity' between a stimulus and a response. Learning takes place through the establishment of a connection between

Table 4.1   Types of learning

Type of learning		Explanation
Behavioural	Classical	Individuals learn to make associations or connections between a stimulus and their responses. Through repetition of the response (the behaviour) to the stimulus, learning occurs.
	Operant	Learning occurs as a result of an individual operating or interacting with the environment. The response of the individual is instrumental in getting a positive reinforcement (reward) or negative reinforcement (punishment). Behaviour that is rewarded or reinforced will be continued, whereas behaviour that is not rewarded will cease.
Cognitive		Assumes that individuals attempt to actively influence their immediate environment rather than be subject to it. They try to resolve problems by processing information from past experiences (memory) in order to make reasoned decisions based on judgements.

a stimulus and a response. Marketing communications are thought to work by the simple process of people observing messages and being stimulated/motivated to respond by requesting more information or purchasing the advertised product in search of a reward. Behaviour is learned through the conditioning experience of stimulus and response. There are two forms of conditioning: classical and operant.

Classical conditioning

Classical conditioning assumes that learning is an associative process that occurs between a stimulus and a response, within an existing relationship. By far the best-known examples of this type of learning are the experiments undertaken by the Russian psychologist Pavlov. He noticed that dogs began to salivate at the sight of food. He stated that this was not taught, but was a reflex reaction. This relationship exists prior to any experimentation or learning. The food represents an unconditioned stimulus and the response (salivation) from the dogs is an unconditioned response.

Pavlov then paired the ringing of a bell with the presentation of food. Shortly the dogs began to salivate at the ringing of the bell. The bell became the conditioned stimulus and the salivation became the conditioned response (which was the same as the unconditioned response).

From an understanding of this work it can be determined that two factors are important for learning to occur:

1. To build the association between the unconditioned and conditioned stimulus, there must be a relatively short period of time.
2. The conditioning process requires that there be a relatively high frequency/repetition of the association. The more often the unconditioned and conditioned stimuli occur together, the stronger will be the association.

Image 4.4 We learn about brands when messages evoke positive associations
Source: Carolyn Jenkins/Alamy Stock Photo.

Classical conditioning can be observed operating in each individual's everyday life. An individual who purchases a new product because of a sales promotion may continue to buy the product even when the promotion has terminated. An association has been established between the sales promotion activity (unconditioned stimulus) and the product (conditioned stimulus). If product quality and satisfaction levels allow, long-run behaviour may develop despite the absence of the promotion. In other words, promotion need not act as a key purchase factor in the long run.

Advertisers attempt to frame the way their products/services are perceived by using images and emotions that are known to evoke positive associations and reactions from consumers. Image advertising seeks to develop the associations that individuals have when they think of a brand or an organisation, hence its reputation. Messages of this type show the object with an unconditioned stimulus that is known to evoke pleasant and favourable feelings. So, the puppet 'Aleksandr Orlov' is the face for comparethemarket.com, Gary Lineker is associated with Walkers crisps, Ellie Goulding with Pantene, and Virat Kohli represents Philips India. The product becomes a conditioned stimulus eliciting the same favourable response.

Operant conditioning

This type of learning, sometimes known as *instrumental conditioning,* occurs as a result of an individual operating or acting on some part of the environment. The response of the individual is instrumental in getting a positive reinforcement, which strengthens a behaviour by providing an outcome that an individual finds rewarding. For example, if your fitness coach praises you each time you complete your set routines (a reward) you will be more likely to repeat this behaviour, and strengthen the behaviour of completing your routines.

Alternatively a negative reinforcement can strengthen behaviour because it prevents or removes an unpleasant experience. For example, should you fail to complete your routines, your fitness coach will make you do extra press-ups. As a result you will complete your routines to avoid extra press-ups, and so strengthen the behaviour of completing your set routines (McLeod, 2015).

Behaviour that is rewarded or reinforced will be continued, whereas behaviour that is not rewarded will cease.

B.F. Skinner was a pioneer researcher in the field of operant conditioning. His research showed that rats learned to press levers in order to receive food. He went on to demonstrate that the rats learned to press a lever when a light shone (discriminative stimulus). This highlights the essential feature of this form of conditioning, that reinforcement follows a specific response.

Many organisations use reinforcement in their communications by stressing the benefits or rewards that a consumer can anticipate receiving as a result of using a product or brand. For example, airlines offer air miles, Tesco offer 'reward points' and Nectar offer a reward of money savings. Reinforcement theories emphasise the role of external factors and exclude an individual's ability to process information internally. Learning takes place either through direct reinforcement of a particular response or through an associative conditioning process. However, operant conditioning is a mechanistic process that is not realistic, as it serves only to simplify an extremely complex procedure.

Cognitive learning

This approach to our understanding of learning assumes that individuals are capable of and attempt to control their immediate environments. They are seen as active participants in that they try to resolve problems by processing information that is pertinent to each situation. Central to this process is memory. Just as money can be invested in short-, medium-, and long-term investment accounts, so information is memorised for different periods of time. These memories are sensory, short-term and long-term, set out in Figure 4.4

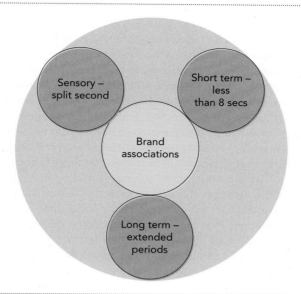

Figure 4.4 Memory and information storage

Sensory storage refers to the period in which information is sensed for a split second. If an impression is made the information is transferred to short-term memory where it is rehearsed before transfer to long-term memory. Short-term memory lasts no longer than approximately eight seconds and a maximum of four or five items can be stored in short-term memory at any one time. Readers will probably have experienced being introduced to someone at a social event only to forget the name of the guest when they next meet them at the same event. This occurs because the name was not entered into long-term memory. Information can be stored for extended periods in long-term memory. This information is not lying dormant, however, it is constantly being reorganised and recategorised as new information is received.

There are four basic functions by which memory operates. The first is *rehearsal*, where information is repeated or related to an established category. This is necessary so that the second function, *encoding*, can take place. This involves the selection of an image to represent the perceived object. Once in long-term memory it is *categorised and stored,* the third function. *Retrieval* is the final function, a process by which information is recovered from storage.

Cognitive learning is about processing information in order that problems can be resolved. These information-handling processes can range from the simple to the complex. There are three main processes: iconic, modelling and reasoning.

Iconic rote learning involves understanding the association between two or more concepts when there is an absence of a stimulus. Learning occurs at a weak level through repetition of simple messages. Beliefs are formed about the attributes of an offering without any real understanding of the source of the information. Advertisers of certain products (low value, frequently purchased) will try to remind their target audiences repeatedly of the brand name in an attempt to help consumers learn. Through such repetition, an association with the main benefits of the product may be built, if only via the constant reminders by the spokesperson.

Learning through the *modelling* approach involves the observation and imitation of others and the associated outcomes of their behaviour. In essence, a great deal of children's early learning is developed in this way. Likewise, marketing communicators use the promise of rewards to persuade audiences to act in a particular way. By using positive images of probable rewards, buyers are encouraged to believe that they can receive the same outcome if they use the particular product. For example, clothing advertisements often depict the model receiving admiring glances from passers-by. The same admiration is the reward 'promised' to those who wear the same clothing. A similar approach was used by Kellogg's to promote their Special K breakfast cereal. The commercial depicted a (slim) mother and child playing on a beach. The message was that it is important to look after yourself and to raise your family through healthy eating, an outdoor life and exercise.

Reasoning is perhaps the most complex form of cognitive learning. Through this process, individuals need to restructure and reorganise information held in long-term memory and combine it with fresh inputs in order to generate new outputs. Financial services providers have to convey complex information, strictly bounded by the Financial Services legislation and the Financial Conduct Authority. So, brands such as PayPal and Hiscox convey key points about simplicity and specialist services respectively, to differentiate their brands. This enables current and potential customers to process detailed information about these brands and to make judgements or reason that these brands reach acceptable (threshold) standards.

Of all the approaches to understanding how we learn, cognitive learning is the most flexible interpretation. The rational, more restricted approach of behavioural learning, where the focus is external to the individual, is without doubt a major contribution to knowledge. However, it fails to accommodate the complex internal thought processes that individuals utilise when presented with various stimuli.

It is useful to appreciate the way in which people are believed to learn and forget as there are several issues which are useful to media planners in particular. Cognitive theory has underpinned much of the research that has been undertaken to explain how marketing and communication works.

Decay

The rate at which individuals forget material assumes a pattern, as shown in Figure 4.5. Many researchers have found that information decays at a negatively decelerating rate. As much as 60 per cent of the initial yield of information from an advertisement has normally decayed within six weeks. This decay, or wear-out, can be likened to the half-life of radioactive material. It is always working, although it cannot be seen, and the impact of the advertising reduces through time. Like McGuire's (1978) retention stage in his hierarchy of effects model (see Chapters 6 and 13), the storage of information for future use is important, but with time, how powerful will the information be and what triggers are required to promote recall?

Advertising wear-out is thought to occur because of two factors. First, individuals use selective perception and mentally switch off after a critical number of exposures. Second, the monotony and irritation caused by continued exposure lead to counter-argument to both the message and the advertisement (Petty and Cacioppo, 1979). Advertisements

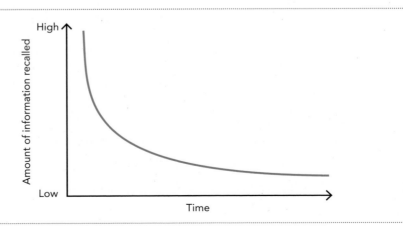

Figure 4.5 A standard decay curve

for alcoholic drinks such as Carlsberg and Stella Artois attempt to prevent wear-out by using variations on a central theme to provide consistency yet engage audiences through interest and entertainment.

Scholars' paper 4.3
Learning about brands

Heath, R. (2001) Low involvement processing – a new model of brand communication, *Journal of Marketing Communications,* **7, 27–33.**

At the beginning of the noughties, Heath began publishing papers about low-involvement processing and how we learn about brands through communications. He subsequently changed the terminology to low- and high-attention theory. Since then he has published a stream of papers on this topic, one which contradicts the traditional rational view of brand choice. Heath offers a new and different perspective on how consumers are influenced by advertising. This paper provides an insight into the literature and his thinking. It also serves to link various concepts, many of which are covered in this chapter.

Attitudes

Attitudes are predispositions, shaped through experience, to respond in an anticipated way to an object or situation. Attitudes are learned through past experiences and serve as a link between thoughts and behaviour. These experiences may relate to the product itself, to the messages transmitted by the different members of the channel network (normally mass media communications) and to the information supplied by opinion leaders, formers and followers.

Attitudes tend to be consistent within each person: they are clustered and very often interrelated. This categorisation leads to the formation of stereotypes, which is extremely useful for the design of messages as stereotyping allows for the transmission of a lot of information in a short time period without impeding learning or the focal part of the message.

Attitude components

Attitudes are hypothetical constructs, and classical psychological theory considers attitudes to consist of three components:

1. **Cognitive component (learn).** This component refers to the level of knowledge and beliefs held by individuals about a product and/or the beliefs about specific attributes of the offering. This represents the learning aspect of attitude formation.

   Marketing communications is used to create attention and awareness, to provide information and to help audiences learn and understand the features and benefits a particular product/service offers.

2. **Affective component (feel).** By referring to the feelings held about a product – good, bad, pleasant or unpleasant – an evaluation is made of the object. This is the component that is concerned with feelings, sentiments, moods and emotions about an object.

Marketing communications is used to induce feelings about the product/service such that it becomes a preferred brand. This preference may be based on emotional attachment to a brand, conferred status through ownership, past experiences and longevity of brand usage or any one of a number of ways in which people can become emotionally involved with a brand.

3. **Conative component (do).** This is the action component of the attitude construct and refers to an individual's disposition or intention to behave in a certain way. Some researchers go so far as to suggest that this component refers to observable behaviour. Marketing communications therefore, should be used to encourage audiences to do something. For example, text, visit a website, phone a number, take a coupon, book a visit, press red (on a remote control unit) for interactivity through digital television.

This three-component approach to attitudes, set out in Figure 4.6, is based upon attitudes towards an object, person or organisation. The sequence of attitude formation is generally considered to be learn, feel and do. However, this approach to attitude formation is limited in that the components are seen to be of equal strength. A single-component model has been developed where the affective component is the only significant component.

Attitudes impact on consumer decision-making, and the objective of marketing communications is often to create a positive attitude towards a product and/or to reinforce or change existing attitudes. An individual may perceive and develop a belief that British Airways has a friendly and informal in-flight service and that the service provided by Lufthansa is cold and formal. However, both airlines are perceived to hold a number of different attributes, and each individual evaluates these attributes in order that an attitude can be developed. It is necessary, therefore, to measure the strength of the beliefs held about the key attributes of different products.

An understanding of attitude components and the way in which particular attributes can be measured not only enables organisations to determine the attitudes held towards them and their competitors, but also empowers them to change the attitudes held by different stakeholders. For more on changing attitudes see Chapter 6.

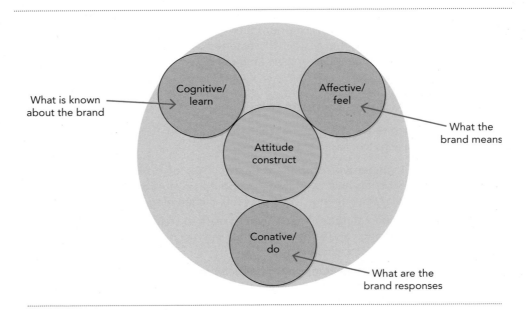

Figure 4.6 The three-component attitude model

Intentions

Ajzen and Fishbein (1980) reasoned that the best way of predicting behaviour was to measure an individual's intention to purchase (the conative component). Underlying intentions are an individual's attitude towards the act of behaviour and the subjective (or social) norm. In other words, the context within which a proposed purchase is to occur is seen as important to the attitude that is developed towards the object.

The subjective norm concerns the relevant feelings others are believed to hold about the proposed purchase, or intention to purchase. Underpinning the subjective norm are the beliefs held about the people who are perceived to 'judge' the actions an individual might take. Would they approve or disapprove, or look favourably or unfavourably upon the intended action?

Underpinning the attitude towards the intention to act in a particular way are the strengths of the beliefs that a particular action will lead to an outcome. Ajzen and Fishbein argue that it is a individual's attitude to the act of purchasing, not the object of the purchase, that is important. For example, a manager may have a positive attitude towards a particular type of expensive office furniture, but a negative attitude towards the act of securing agreement to purchase it.

The theory of reasoned action recognises the interrelationship of the three components of attitudes, but that it is not attitude alone but the intention to act or behave that precedes observable behaviour that should be the focus of attention. Intentions are determined by beliefs about the probable outcomes that a behaviour will lead to (an attitude), together with subjective norms, which are the perceived social pressures from significant others (Yap and Gaur, 2016).

Scholars' paper 4.4

I like your attitude but it's time to change

Ajzen, I. (1991) The theory of planned behavior, *Organizational Behavior & Human Decision Processes*, 50(2), December, 179–211.

Following on from the theory of reasoned action, published in 1980, Ajzen's paper shows how behaviour change is best managed by understanding and influencing three core beliefs. These are attitudes towards the behaviour and the subjective norm, and perception about behavioural control.

This paper also demonstrated that advertising that provides or attempts to influence audiences through the provision of knowledge and information alone do not work.

See also:

Yap, S.-F. and Gaur, S.S. (2016) Integrating functional, social, and psychological determinants to explain online social networking usage, *Behaviour & Information Technology*, 35(3), 166–83.

Decision making

Much of marketing communications has been oriented towards influencing decision-making processes used by customers. This requires identifying the right type of information, to be conveyed at the right time, in the appropriate format, in order to engage with the target audience.

There are two broad types of customer, consumers and organisational buyers, and each is considered to follow particular rational, sequential and logical pathways when making purchase decisions. The consumer decision-making process is depicted in Figure 4.7 and the organisational process later in this chapter in Figure 4.11. The consumer pathway consists of five stages, and marketing communications can impact any or all of these stages with varying levels of potential effectiveness.

Consumer purchase decision-making process

There are many factors that impact on decision-making, including the time available, levels of perceived risk, the degree of involvement a buyer has with the type of product and past experience, to name a few. Perceived risk and involvement are explored later. Three types of problem-solving behaviour can be identified (extended problem solving, limited problem solving and routinised response) and are considered here. However, it should be noted that in reality buyers do not follow these decision steps.

Extended problem solving (EPS)

Consumers considering the purchase of a car or house undertake a great deal of external search activity and spend a lot of time reaching a solution that satisfies, as closely as possible, the evaluative criteria previously set. This activity is usually associated with products that are unfamiliar, where direct experience and hence knowledge are weak, and where there is considerable financial risk.

Marketing communications should aim to provide a lot of information to assist the decision process. The provision of information through sales literature, such as brochures and leaflets, websites for determining product and purchase criteria in product categories where there is little experience, access to salespersons and demonstrations and advertisements, are just some of the ways in which information can be provided.

Limited problem solving (LPS)

Having experience of a product means that greater use can be made of internal, memory-based search routines and the external search can be limited to obtaining up-to-date information or to ensuring that the finer points of the decision have been investigated.

Marketing communications should attempt to provide information about any product modification or new attributes and convey messages that highlight those key attributes known to be important to buyers. By differentiating the product, marketing communications provides the buyer with a reason to select that particular product.

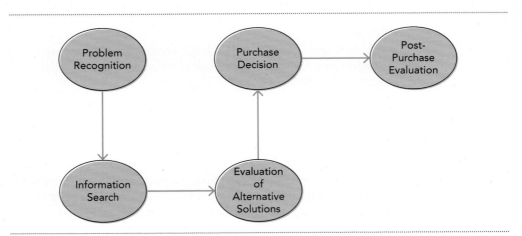

Figure 4.7 A consumer's decision-making framework

Routinised response behaviour (RRB)

For a great number of products the decision process will consist only of an internal search. This is primarily because the buyer has made a number of purchases and has accumulated a great deal of experience. Therefore, only an internal search is necessary, so little time or effort will be spent on external search activities. Low-value items that are frequently purchased fall into this category – for example, toothpaste, soap, tinned foods and confectionery.

Communicators should focus upon keeping the product within the consideration set or getting it into the set. Learning can be enhanced through the repetition of messages, but repetition can also be used to maintain attention and awareness.

Involvement theory

One of the factors thought to be key to brand choice decisions is the level of involvement a consumer has with either the product or the purchase process. Involvement is about the degree of personal relevance and risk perceived by consumers when making a particular purchase decision (Rossiter et al., 1991). This implies that the level of involvement may vary through time as each member of the target market becomes more (or less) familiar with the purchase and associated communications. At the point of decision-making, involvement is high or low, not somewhere on a sliding scale or on a continuum between two extremes.

High involvement

High involvement occurs when a consumer perceives an expected purchase that is not only of high personal relevance but also represents a high level of perceived risk. Cars, washing machines, houses and insurance policies are seen as 'big ticket' items, infrequent purchases that promote a great deal of involvement. The risk described is financial but, as we saw earlier, risk can take other forms. Therefore, the choice of perfume, suit, dress or jewellery may also represent high involvement, with social risk dominating the purchase decision. Consumers therefore devote a great deal of time to researching these intended purchases and collect as much information as possible in order to reduce, as far as possible, levels of perceived risk.

Low involvement

A low-involvement state of mind suggests that an intended purchase represents little threat or risk. Low-priced items such as washing powder, baked beans and breakfast cereals are bought frequently. Purchase and consumption experience of the product class and the brand provides purchase cues, so little information or support is required. Items such as alcoholic and soft drinks, cigarettes and chocolate are also normally seen as low-involvement, but they induce a strong sense of ego risk associated with the self-gratification that is attached to the consumption of these products.

Two approaches to decision-making

We now consider two main approaches to consumer decision-making; high and low involvement.

High-involvement decision-making

If an individual is highly involved with the initial purchase of a product, EPS is the appropriate decision sequence, as information is considered to be processed in a rational, logical order. Individuals who are highly involved in a purchase are thought to move through the process shown in Figure 4.8. When high-involvement decision-making is present, individuals perceive a high level of risk and are concerned about the intended purchase. The essential element in this sequence is that a great deal of information is sought initially and an attitude is developed before a commitment or intention to trial is determined.

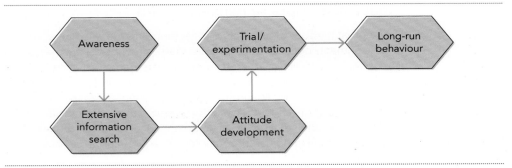

Figure 4.8 Decision-making process where there is high involvement
Source: From *Essentials of Marketing Communications,* Pearson Education (Fill, C. 2011) Figure 3.5, p. 72.

Information search is an important part of the high-involvement decision-making process. Because individuals are highly motivated, information is actively sought, processed and evaluated. Many media sources are explored, including websites, the mass media, word-of-mouth communications and point-of-sale communications. As individuals require a lot of information, print media used to be the primary media where high involvement was identified. Today, websites are the primary source of large volumes of detailed information. Unlike print, these sites can also be updated quickly but both types enable visitors to search and process information at a speed they can control.

Low-involvement decision-making

If an individual has little involvement with an initial purchase of a product, LPS is the appropriate decision process. Information is processed cognitively but in a passive, involuntary way. Processing occurs using right-brain thinking so information is stored as it is received, in sections, and this means that information is stored as a brand association (Heath, 2000). Advertisements for Andrex toilet tissue featuring a puppy are stored as the 'Andrex Puppy' without any overt thinking or reasoning. Because of the low personal relevance and perceived risk associated with this type of processing, message repetition is necessary to define brands and create meaningful brand associations. Individuals who have a low involvement with a purchase decision choose not to search for information and are thought to move through the process shown in Figure 4.9.

Communications can assist the development of awareness in the low-involvement decision-making process. However, as individuals assume a passive problem-solving role, messages need to be shorter than in the high-involvement process and should contain less information. Broadcast media are preferred as they complement the passive learning posture adopted by individuals. Repetition is important because receivers have little or no

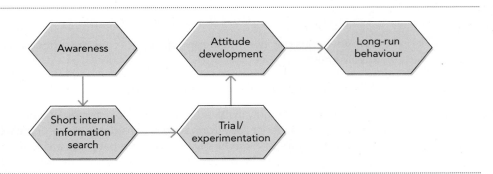

Figure 4.9 Decision-making process where there is low involvement
Source: From *Essentials of Marketing Communications,* Pearson Education (Fill, C. 2011) Figure 3.6, p. 73.

motivation to retain information, and his or her perceptual selection processes filter out unimportant information. Learning develops through exposure to repeated messages, but attitudes do not develop at this part of the process (Harris, 1987).

Where low involvement is present, each individual relies upon internal, rather than external, search mechanisms, often prompted by point-of-purchase displays.

Impact on communications

Involvement theory is central to our understanding of the way in which information is processed and the way in which people make decisions about product purchases. We have established in the preceding section that there are two main types of involvement, high and low. These two types lead directly to two different uses of marketing communications. In decisions where there is high involvement, attitude precedes trial behaviour. In low-involvement cases this position is reversed.

Where there is high involvement, consumers seek out information because they are concerned about the decision processes and outcomes. This can be because of the levels of uncertainty associated with the high costs of purchase and usage, inexperience of the product (category) – often due to the infrequency of purchases – the complexity of product and doubts about its operational usefulness. Because they have these concerns, people develop an attitude prior to behaviour. Informational ads that require cognitive processing are recommended.

Where there is low involvement, consumers are content to select any one of a number of acceptable products and often rely on those that are in the individual's consideration set. Low involvement is thought to be a comfortable state, because there are too many other issues in life to have to make decisions about each one of them, so an opportunity not to have to seek information and make other decisions is welcome. See Figure 4.10, which indicates the marketing communications strategies best suited for each level within both involvement sequences. Emotional or transformational ads are recommended.

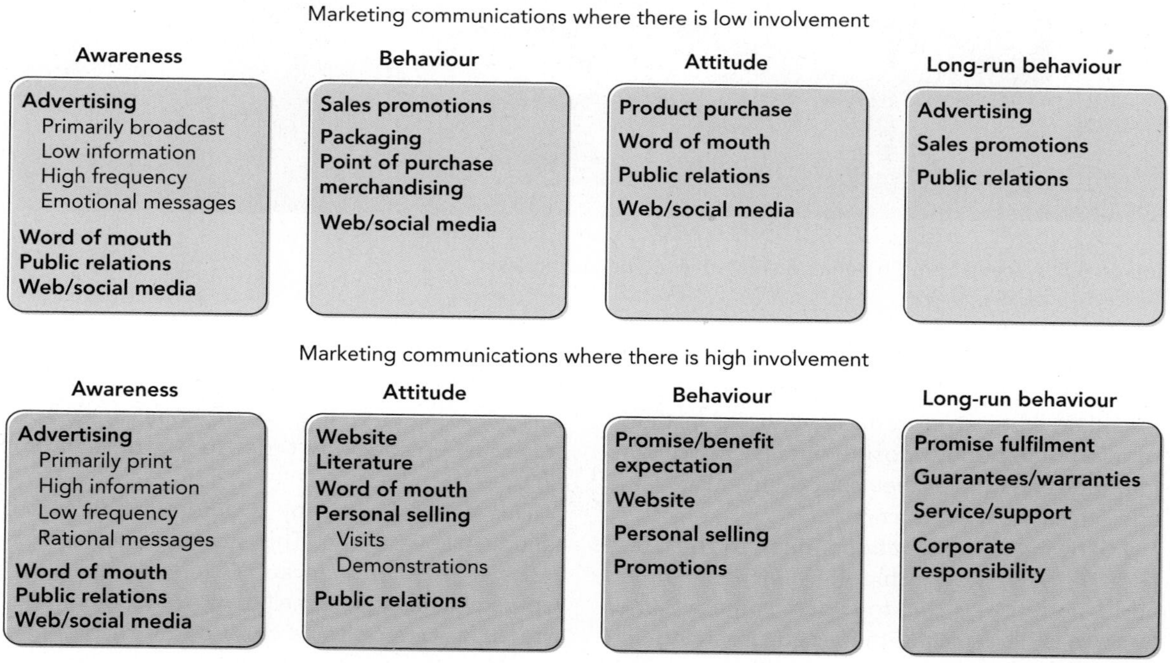

Marketing communications where there is low involvement

Awareness
Advertising
 Primarily broadcast
 Low information
 High frequency
 Emotional messages
Word of mouth
Public relations
Web/social media

Behaviour
Sales promotions
Packaging
Point of purchase
 merchandising
Web/social media

Attitude
Product purchase
Word of mouth
Public relations
Web/social media

Long-run behaviour
Advertising
Sales promotions
Public relations

Marketing communications where there is high involvement

Awareness
Advertising
 Primarily print
 High information
 Low frequency
 Rational messages
Word of mouth
Public relations
Web/social media

Attitude
Website
Literature
Word of mouth
Personal selling
 Visits
 Demonstrations
Public relations

Behaviour
Promise/benefit
 expectation
Website
Personal selling
Promotions

Long-run behaviour
Promise fulfilment
Guarantees/warranties
Service/support
Corporate
 responsibility

Figure 4.10 Approaches to marketing communications for the two levels of involvement
Source: From *Essentials of Marketing Communications*, Pearson Education (Fill, C. 2011) Figure 3.7, p. 74.

Planning communications based on involvement is not as straightforward as the preceding material might suggest. There are various factors that might influence the outcomes. For example, some individuals who are cognitively capable of processing information may not always be able to process information in information-based ads because they are overloaded. In these circumstances they are more likely to develop positive attitudes towards affective or transformational ads. Ranjbariyan and Mahmoodi (2009) also found that people under time pressure are more prone to use transformational ads as they pick up visual cues to help their decision-making.

Viewpoint 4.3
Changing attitudes the Chipotle way

Image 4.5 A scene from Chipotle's animated film, *The Scarecrow*
Source: Chipotle Mexican Grill.

The restaurant chain Chipotle Mexican Grill have used a series of award-winning animations to differentiate themselves from conventional fast food retailers. Chipotle's positioning is 'Food With Integrity' and reflects their support for sustainable and ethical food production.

Following the animations 'Back to the Start' and 'The Scarecrow', Chipotle launched 'Farmed and Dangerous'. This four-part comedy series was available on Hulu, the video-streaming service and satirised their competitors' and their supply chains. In addition to the parody of the processed food industry, viewers were invited to play trivia games on their smartphones, based on individual episodes, in order to win prizes from Chipotle.

This was followed by a different animation called 'A Love Story'. This story involves a boy and a girl, called Ivan and Evie, who start out separately managing small orange and lemonade stands. In spite of Ivan's crush on Evie, competition drives them to grow their businesses into big brands. They soon realise that their expansion into mass-produced food and money has been made at the expense of quality and companionship.

One of the key characteristics of their animations is the absence of any overt branding. This is because Chipotle's strategy was to change beliefs about the product category, ethical fast-food, and it was not their direct aim to change attitudes towards their brand. Although it is generally understood that these animations increased sales for the Chipotle brand, and won awards and increased publicity for the brand and the creators of the animations, attitude change to Chipotle might be considered to be peripheral.

Sources: Bellman et al. (2017); Wong (2016).

Insight

The use of short video-based animations in a low-involvement category suggests that Chipotle have tried to move audiences into high involvement. By encouraging thought about the category issues (mass production of fast processed foods), Chipotle have tried to benefit by a positive association through the changed beliefs about the category.

Question: To what extent is this approach to attitude change likely to be successful in non-food sectors?

Task: View each of the Chipotle ads and count the number of references or mentions of Chipotle.

The material presented so far in this section is based on classical research, theoretical development and is supported by empirical research. However, much of the knowledge has been developed in a non-digital era, and that raises questions about the depth of its validity in the contemporary world. Foley et al. (2009) undertook research that showed that people organise product categories according to the level of risk associated with brand-choice decisions and the level of reward, together with the enjoyment people derive from the decisions they make. They also found that the types of categories people organise lead to different patterns of decision-making. Four main product categories were identified:

1. *Routine.*

   In this category people perceive low risk and low reward. Brand-choice decision-making is therefore characterised by inertia and decision-making is robotic.

2. *Burden.*

   People perceive high risk and low reward. Search is extensive and decision-making improved if someone can assist.

3. *Passion.*

   Risk is high and reward is high because people are emotionally engaged with these types of products and services. The symbolism and meaning attached to brands in the category is high, reflected in high ego and social risks.

4. *Entertainment.*

   People use this category where risk is low but reward can be high. This means that decision-making can be a pleasant, if brief, experience.

Each of these categories has implications for the communications strategies necessary to reach people and be effective. For example, consideration of the type of website that best suits each of these categories provides immediate insight into how having an understanding or insight into the target audience can shape marketing communications.

Scholars' paper 4.5
A no-brainer

Hsu, M. (2017) Neuromarketing: inside the mind of the consumer, *California Management Review,* **59(4), 5–22.**

This paper provides a useful insight into human neuroscience and brain-based methods of understanding consumer behaviour. It provides a framework and practical guidance on how managers can use brain-based methods to understand customers and generate actionable insights.

See also:

Chengwei, L., Vlaev, I., Fang, C., Denrell, J. and Chater, N. (2017) Strategizing with biases: making better decisions using the mindspace approach, *California Management Review,* 59(3), Spring, 135–61.

Organisational decision-making process

In order to function, organisations need to buy materials, parts, general supplies and services from a range of other organisations. Although referred to as *business-to-business marketing,* the term 'organisational marketing' is used here to reflect the wide range of organisations involved with such activities.

The term 'buyphases' was given by Robinson et al. (1967) to the several stages of the organisational buying decisions, as depicted in Figure 4.11. However, considering the buying process in terms of these neat steps is also misleading, again owing to the various forces acting on organisations.

Just like consumers, organisational buyers make decisions that vary with each buying situation and buyclass. Buyclasses, according to Robinson et al. (1967), comprise three types or contexts: new task, modified rebuy and straight rebuy (see Table 4.2).

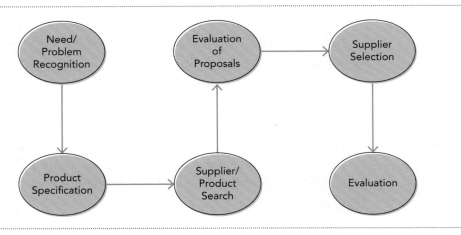

Figure 4.11 The buyphases of organisational buying decisions

Table 4.2 The main characteristics of the buyclasses

Buyclass	Degree of familiarity with the problem	Information requirements	Alternative solutions
New buy	The problem is fresh to the decision-makers.	A great deal of information is required.	Alternative solutions are unknown, all are considered new.
Modified rebuy	The requirement is not new but is different from previous situations.	More information is required but past experience is of use.	Buying decision needs new solutions.
Rebuy	The problem is identical to previous experiences.	Little or no information is required.	Alternative solutions not sought or required.

Some readers may have noticed how these phases bear a strong resemblance to the extended, limited and routinised responses identified earlier with respect to the consumer market.

Organisational buying, according to Webster and Wind (1972), is 'the decision making process by which formal organisations establish the need for purchased products and services and identify, evaluate and choose among alternative brands and suppliers'. Of particular significance is the relationship that develops between organisations that enter market exchange transactions. As mentioned previously, the various networks that organisations belong to will influence the purchase decisions that other organisations in the network make. However, before exploring these issues, it is necessary to review the context in which organisational decisions are made.

One way of examining the context is to compare organisational decisions with those made in consumer markets. There are far fewer buyers in the organisational context than in the consumer market, although there can be a number of people associated with a buying decision in an organisation. Orders are invariably larger and the frequency with which they are placed is much lower. It is quite common for agreements to be made between organisations for the supply of materials over a number of years. Similarly, depending upon the complexity of the product (photocopying paper or a one-off satellite), the negotiation process may also take a long time.

Many of the characteristics associated with consumer decision-making processes can be observed in the organisational context. Organisational buyers however, make decisions which ultimately contribute to the achievement of corporate objectives. To make the necessary decisions, a high volume of pertinent information is often required. This information needs to be relatively detailed and is normally presented in a rational and logical style. The needs of the buyers are many and complex and some may be personal. Goals, such as promotion and career advancement within the organisation, coupled with ego and employee satisfaction combine to make organisational buying an important task, one that requires professional training and the development of expertise if the role is to be performed optimally.

Reference has been made on a number of occasions to organisational buyers, as if these people are the only representatives of an organisation to be involved with the purchase decision process. This is not the case, as very often a large number of people are involved in the purchase decision. This group is referred to as either the decision-making unit (DMU) or the buying centre.

Buying centres vary in size and composition in accordance with the nature of each individual task. Webster and Wind (1972) identified a number of people who make up the buying centre.

Users are people who not only initiate the purchase process but also use the product, once it has been acquired, and evaluate its performance. *Influencers* very often help set the technical specifications for the proposed purchase and assist the evaluation of alternative offerings by potential suppliers. *Deciders* are those who make purchasing decisions. In repeat buying activities the buyer may well also be the decider. However, it is normal practice to require that expenditure decisions involving sums over a certain financial limit be authorised by other, often senior, managers. *Buyers* (purchasing managers) select suppliers and manage the process whereby the required products are procured. As identified previously, buyers may not decide which product is to be purchased but they influence the framework within which the decision is made. *Gatekeepers* have the potential to control the type and flow of information to the organisation and the members of the buying centre. These gatekeepers may be technical personnel, secretaries or telephone switchboard operators.

The size and form of the buying centre is not static. It can vary according to the complexity of the product being considered and the degree of risk each decision is perceived to carry for the organisation. Different roles are required and adopted as the nature of the buying task changes with each new purchase situation (Bonoma, 1982). It is vital for seller organisations to identify members of the buying centre and to target and refine their messages to meet the needs of each member of the centre.

The task of the communications manager and the corresponding sales team is to decide which key participants have to be reached, with which type of message, with what frequency, and to what depth contact should be made. Just like individual consumers, each member of the buying centre is an active problem-solver and processes information so that personal and organisational goals are achieved.

Social selling

An increasing number of sales professionals and organisations are using social selling to build relationships with buyers and other members in buying centres. At its heart, Forrester claim that social selling involves a formal programme designed to develop a sales professional's personal brand across the relevant networks, share content, identify contacts, listen to needs, and to connect and engage with buyers (Fently, 2017). Within this, Schriber (2017) identifies three core activities:

1. **Smarter targeting:** using the rich data available on social media platforms sales professionals can identify and qualify leads using 'signals of intent'. These could be job changes, as people are more inclined to make risky decisions when they enter a new role. Social posts are an indicator of top-of-mind questions, and recruitment patterns are a signal of investment and opportunities.

2. **Better understanding:** instead of opening conversations with a typical 'Can I ask you a few questions?', the social selling approach starts with a more informed and direct question, such as 'I noticed that you've been thinking about . . . '. This is achieved by following social media threads in advance. This also involves understanding who is in the buying centre.

3. **Closer engagement:** strong relationships are characterised by continuity of contact and dialogue. If sales professionals can provide information that is of value to the buyer then the relationship will continue. This requires establishing themselves as a trusted acquaintance, and invariably buyers feel obligated to remain engaged. Through use of technology, such as email tracking, reps are able to sense whether the information they are providing is of value.

Sellers need to establish and then maintain relationships with buyers and increasingly this is accomplished through formalised social selling programmes.

Influences on the buying centre

Three major influences on organisational buyer behaviour can be identified as stakeholders, the organisational environment and those aspects that the individual brings to the situation, as set out in Table 4.3.

Table 4.3   Major influences on organisational buying behaviour

Stakeholder influences	Organisational influences	Individual influences
Economic conditions	Corporate strategy	Personality
Legislation	Organisational culture and values	Age
Competitor strategies	Resources and costs	Status
Industry regulations	Purchasing policies and procedures	Reward structure and systems
Technological developments	Interpersonal relationships	
Social and cultural values		
Inter-organisational relationships		

Source: Based on Webster and Wind (1972).

Stakeholders develop relationships between the focus organisation and other stakeholders in the network. The nature of the exchange relationship and the style of communication will influence buying decisions. If the relationship between organisations is trusting, mutually supportive and based on a longer-term perspective (a relational structure) then the behaviour of the buying centre may be seen to be cooperative and constructive. If the relationship is formal, regular, unsupportive and based on short-term convenience (a market, structure-based relationship) then the purchase behaviour may be observed as courteous yet distant.

Viewpoint 4.4
Reaching sweet decision-makers

Tate & Lyle Sugars (T&L) produces sugar, syrups and sauces in a variety of formats and flavours and is a leading supporter of Fairtrade.

The development of beverage syrups for the out-of-home foodservice market was a key strategy. The target market was the UK's largest coffee chains, quick-service restaurants and European coffee roasters.

The real issue facing T&L was not one of product quality as T&L has historic expertise in syrup production and is the only mainstream supplier of Fairtrade beverage syrups. The challenge lay in reaching the range of key decision-makers, including food and beverage buyers and procurement directors. Once reached, they had to be able to influence them sufficiently to encourage them to switch suppliers. These decision-makers are notoriously difficult to reach, partly because everyone wants to talk to them, and they receive countless requests from a multitude of suppliers every day. Typically in this category, contract lengths are

long and as there are multiple decision-makers, it is hard to drive engagement.

In order to break through to these decision-makers and generate leads, thought was given to how get noticed without being sidelined by well-intentioned gatekeepers. When consideration was given to traditional postal processes, the question was what gets opened first . . . bank statements, invoices, trade press publications? These get opened by assistants but a handwritten, stamped addressed envelope would be passed through to the named decision-maker.

This was the first touchpoint, and handwritten, signed, stamped and addressed letters from the relevant T&L salespersons were sent announcing that something exciting would be arriving in a couple of days.

The follow-up to each target was a high-value, premium T&L branded box, which included mini samples, a bespoke brochure, a business card, and an engaging and compelling animated video that revealed the key benefits of the T&L beverage syrup range.

Following the video box was another handwritten letter, before the sales team telephoned the lead, fed the details into their CRM system and continued the lead conversion process.

Once all boxes had been delivered, the video content was cut into bite-size pieces and seeded in highly targeted and sponsored LinkedIn ads that were placed on the target's feed, and extended to their colleagues.

The campaign integrated traditional lead generation techniques, new technologies and social media for a total cost of just £33,570 and within a few months the T&L's sales team were in discussions with 61 per cent of the target accounts, over double the 30 per cent target, sales were up by over 250 per cent and a campaign ROI of 183 per cent achieved.

Source: Anon (2017).

Insight

The problem of how to reach the key decision-makers is an issue faced by most B2B organisations. In this case a mixture of direct mail, product sampling and social media was sufficient to break through the barriers and reach not only the decision-makers but a range of others in the DMU.

Question: Which of the buyclasses (Table 4.2) does this example best fit?

Task: Find another example where direct mail and social media were used to good effect.

Without doubt the major determinant of the organisational environment is the cost associated with switching from one supplier to another (Bowersox and Cooper, 1992). When one organisation chooses to enter into a buying relationship with another organisation, an investment is made in time, people, assets and systems. Should the relationship with the new supplier fail to work satisfactorily, then a cost is incurred in switching to another supplier. It is these switching costs that heavily influence buying decisions. The higher the potential switching costs, the greater the loss in flexibility and the greater the need to shape the relationship at the outset.

Behaviour within the buying centre is also largely determined by the interpersonal relationships of the members of the centre. Participation in the buying centre has been shown to be highly influenced by the perceptions individuals have of the personal consequences of their contribution to each stage in the process. The more that individuals think they will be blamed for a bad decision or praised for a good one, the greater their participation, influence and visible DMU-related activity (McQuiston and Dickson, 1991). The nature and dispersal of power within the unit can influence the decisions that are made. Power is increasingly viewed from the perspective of an individual's ability to control the flow of information and the deployment of resources (Stone and Gronhaug, 1993). This approach reflects a network approach to, in this case, intra-organisational communications.

Key points

- Classical theory suggests that there are five stages to the general process whereby buyers make purchase decisions and implement them. These are problem recognition, information search, alternative evaluation, purchase decision and post-purchase evaluation. Organisations use marketing communications in different ways in order to influence these different stages.

- Perception is concerned with how individuals see and make sense of their environment. The way in which individuals perceive, organise and interpret stimuli is a reflection of their past experiences and the classifications used to understand the different situations each individual frames every day.

- There are three factors important to the behavourist approach to learning: association, reinforcement and motivation. Behaviour is learned through the conditioning experience of a stimulus and a response.

- Cognitive learning considers learning to be a function of an individual's attempt to control their immediate environment. Cognitive learning is about processing information in order that problems can be resolved. Central to this process is memory.

- Information-handling processes can range from the simple to the complex. There are three main processes: iconic, modelling and reasoning.

- Attitudes are predispositions, shaped through experience, to respond in an anticipated way to an object or situation. Attitudes are learned through past experiences and serve as a link between thoughts and behaviour. Attitudes tend to be consistent within each individual: they are clustered and very often interrelated. Attitudes consist of three interrelated elements: the cognitive, affective and conative, otherwise referred to as learn, feel, do.

- Marketing communications can be used to influence the attitudes held by a target market. When developing campaigns, consideration needs to be given to the current and desired attitudes to be held by the target audience. The focus of communications activities can be on whether the audience requires information (learning), an emotional disposition (feeling) or whether the audience needs to be encouraged to behave in a particular way (doing).

- Buyers do not follow the general purchase decision sequence at all times and three types of problem-solving behaviour are experienced by consumers. These are extended problem solving, limited problem solving and routinised response. The procedure may vary depending upon the time available, levels of perceived risk and the degree of involvement a buyer has with the type of product.

- Involvement is about the degree of personal relevance and risk perceived by individuals in a particular purchase situation. Individuals experience involvement with products or services to be purchased.

- The level of involvement may vary through time as each member of the target market becomes more (or less) familiar with the purchase and associated communications. At the point of decision-making, involvement is either high or low.

- The organisational buying decision process consists of six main stages or buyphases. These are need/problem recognition, product specification, supplier and product search, the evaluation of proposals, supplier selection and evaluation.

- There are a wide variety of individuals involved in organisational purchase decisions. There are *users, influencers, deciders, buyers* and *gatekeepers*. All fulfil different functions, all have varying degrees of impact on purchase decisions and all require different marketing communications in order to influence their decision-making.

How Sixt challenged car hire culture, and changed its fortunes

Principal authors: Rachel Walker and Oliver Pople, Grey London
Contributing author: Matt Gladstone, Grey London

Image 4.6 Sixt used outdoor media in the impressive space at Canary Wharf tube station to reach their target audience.
Source: Sixt rent a car.

Sixt, a global car hire company with branches in over 105 countries, launched into the UK in 1998. It is currently fifth largest, in a market led by household names – Europcar, Enterprise, Avis, Hertz – which together account for 80 per cent of the market.

The company had concentrated on building its network and in 2014 had 47 UK locations, which compares poorly against Europcar and Enterprise who each have around 300. There has been no substantial investment to build the brand, witnessed by no media spend in 2012, 2013 or 2014. In contrast the competition were supporting their brands

consistently, and one of them – Enterprise – had spent £7.5 million across those three years.

Spontaneous awareness for Sixt was low at 5 per cent. Even when prompted, 72 per cent of people didn't recognise Sixt's name. The brand was nowhere near being top of mind, as it was mentioned first by only 1 per cent of people. Consideration was also low. Only 11 per cent would consider Sixt.

Strong awareness matters in this market for three reasons:

- Consumers have very small consideration sets. Nearly half of consumers look at only one or two brands. So unless you're the first or second brand people think of, you'll struggle.

- Consumers hire direct, not via price comparison sites. If people shopped on price comparison sites, small brands might passively enter consideration lists through competitive prices. But in fact only 18 per cent of people shop that way. By far the most common way to rent a car is via a brand's own web-site, which accounts for 41 per cent of car rentals.
- Consumers stick with familiar brands, the leading reason for brand choice is 'Used them before'.

In order to break into the top four Sixt had to over-come the small consideration sets and lack of aware-ness. To achieve these goals the UK team were given £500,000 and three months.

The business goal was to grow revenue by 13 per cent, in London, over the campaign period. The attitu-dinal objectives were to raise spontaneous awareness in London by +4 per cent, and to raise consideration in London by +4 per cent. To assist the strategy we created a new image statement against which to mea-sure success: 'Premium cars at economy prices'.

The real point of difference is that Sixt offers a higher proportion of premium marques such as BMW, Audi and Mercedes in its fleet than its com-petitors, 50 per cent at Sixt, and 25 per cent with competitors. And they are available in every car category – even economy – at competitive prices. Its cars are also on the road for less than six months on average, ensuring latest models, in great condition. So consumers normally get a better model at Sixt than at a competitor, at the same price.

Initially we considered competing on the existing battlefields of price, service and travel inspiration, but none of these felt like battles we could win.

To raise awareness of Sixt's premium fleet, at competitive prices, seemed an obvious role for com-munications. However, a message that claimed 'pre-mium cars at economy prices' was more likely to be attributed to competitors, than to Sixt.

There was another, bigger stumbling block. People just weren't interested. Even though peo-ple might dream of *owning* a premium car, when it comes to *renting* it's a different matter. Rental car enjoyment doesn't cross most people's minds.

So premium cars – even at ordinary prices – were an irrelevant offer. Hire cars just weren't part of the fun. Our biggest barrier was cultural. Sixt's only hope of breaking through the Big Four's 80 per cent share stranglehold, was to shift how people thought about the category.

We know that when people book hire cars, they are driven by their heads. But when they sit behind the wheel, the heart takes over and their emotions kick in.

No one was talking about how the car makes you feel, and the powerful untapped emotions that are released when driving a premium rental car. This was the space that Sixt could occupy and use to disrupt the market.

This powerful insight was turned into a creative based on celebrating the swagger you feel when you drive a premium car, which hasn't broken the bank. Our campaign line became 'Drive Smug', to unapol-ogetically express this emotional benefit. Executions celebrated smugness, with ballsy humour.

If our media body language was to convey a confi-dent swagger befitting the Drive Smug creative idea, we couldn't use shy, retiring media. On the contrary, given the creative idea's flagrant self-congratulation, we needed a loud, proud and very public campaign. The media strategy was to sacrifice reach for domi-nation. This required focus.

Our audience was Londoners, for two reasons. First, 60 per cent of Sixt's locations are in London and second, Londoners are less likely to own cars, and more likely to rent. Further, a core audience was chosen: young (25–45) affluent men and women who work and play hard, taking frequent trips.

Competitors were mainly using TV. To appear as big as the genuinely big brands, we selected less-er-used media, which we could dominate. A takeover of a tube station became the lead activity. Not only was the mindset of a London commute the perfect primer to inspire a better type of travel, we could also reach young professionals who, travelling by tube, were potentially not car owners.

Image 4.7 Sixt used Drive Smug to communicate the emotional benefit
Source: Sixt rent a car.

Far from the dark, dingy places you might picture when you think of the London Underground, Canary Wharf station is a new, gleaming, impressive space, befitting a premium brand. Using ticket barriers, pillars, wall panels and escalator wraps, the creative was unmissable for commuters arriving for, or leaving, their city jobs.

To reach more of our target audience across all of London, we ran a one-day cover wrap in the *Evening Standard.* In addition to banners, Sixt took over the *Evening Standard* home page for one month.

The marketing team was inspired to take the idea into owned channels. On Facebook, Instagram and Twitter, marketing teams ran a social media campaign called Smugshot, inviting people to send in their smug selfies.

The Drive Smug campaign promoted a premium image, and unsurprisingly Sixt's luxury car transactions grew significantly during the campaign, to reach a record peak. London's revenue grew 54 per cent, showing strong improvement compared to the year before and comfortably beat the campaign target.

Eighty-one per cent of people exiting Canary Wharf recognised the advertising. This rose to 96 per cent of those passing through twice a day. Remarkably, the brand became the *first* brand mentioned by 21 per cent of people who passed through Canary Wharf, a level equal with Hertz and Avis. This was a significant improvement over the control stations, where it was only mentioned first by 4 per cent.

One in six (16 per cent) of frequent users of Canary Wharf station said they would look into Sixt next time they wanted to hire a vehicle. Ten per cent said they would search for Sixt online. Consideration increased by 24 percentage points, bringing Sixt level with Hertz.

Whereas previously consumers had attributed Sixt's brand promise to its competitors, now Sixt owned it.

This case study is an edited version of a paper submitted to the IPA Effectiveness Awards 2016. It has been reproduced here with the kind permission of the IPA, WARC, Sixt and their agency Grey London.

Review questions

Sixt case questions

1. What is a consideration set and how was this a significant factor in Sixt's marketing communications?

2. Identify the purchase journey a prospective car renter might follow. How did Sixt's communications complement the journey?

3. Explain how Sixt's marketing communications can be understood in terms of learning theory.

4. Explain how Sixt's marketing communications can be interpreted in the light of attitude theory.

5. Discuss the relevance of high- and low-involvement theories in the car rental market.

General questions

1. Make brief notes explaining each of the following: buyclasses, buying centre, EPS, LPS and RRB.

2. Describe the high- and low-involvement decision-making processes. How does this help the practice of marketing communications?

3. Explain the principles of perceptual organisation.

4. What is the DMU and how might marketing communications be adjusted to meet the needs of the DMU?

5. Make brief notes explaining the differences between classical and operant conditioning.

References for Chapter 4

Ajzen, I. (1991) The theory of planned behavior, *Organizational Behavior & Human Decision Processes*, 50(2), December, 179–211.

Ajzen, I. and Fishbein, M. (1980) *Understanding Attitudes and Predicting Social Behavior.* Englewood Cliffs, NJ: Prentice-Hall.

Anon (2017) How Tate & Lyle Sugars achieved ROI of 183% on its campaign to reach decision-makers with its new range of beverage syrups, *B2B Marketing*, 16 November, retrieved 20 August 2018 from https://www.b2bmarketing.net/en-gb/resources/b2b-case-studies/awards-case-study-how-tate-lyle-sugars-achieved-roi-183-its-campaign

Bellman, S., Rask, A. and Varan, D. (2017) How Chipotle used unbranded content to increase purchase intention by changing beliefs about ethical consumption, *Journal of Marketing Communications*, 4 October.

Bonoma, T.V. (1982) Major sales: who really does the buying? *Harvard Business Review*, May/June, 113.

Bowersox, D. and Cooper, M. (1992) *Strategic Marketing Channel Management*, New York: McGraw-Hill.

Candy, N. and Bullen, V. (2017) How brands can use colour to impact subconscious decision-making, *Admap*, July–August.

Chengwei, L., Vlaev, I., Fang, C., Denrell, J. and Chater, N. (2017) Strategizing with biases: making better decisions using the mindspace approach, *California Management Review*, 59(3), Spring, 135–61.

Cohen, J. and Basu, K. (1987) Alternative models of categorisation, *Journal of Consumer Research*, March, 455–72.

Court, D., Elzinga, D., Mulder, S. and Vetvik, O.J. (2009) The consumer decision journey, *McKinsey Quarterly*, June, retrieved 15 January 2015 from www.mckinsey.com/insights/marketing_sales/the_consumer_decision_journey

Edelman, D.C. and Singer, M. (2015) The new consumer decision journey, *McKinsey Quarterly*, October, retrieved 13 July 2017, from http://www.mckinsey.com/business-functions/marketing-and-sales/our-insights/the-new-consumer-decision-journey

Fently, K. (2017) Social selling: a new B2B imperative, Forrester, June, retrieved July 2017 from https://hootsuite.com/resources/white-paper/social-selling-b2b-imperative

Foley, C., Greene, J. and Cultra, M. (2009) Effective ads in a digital age, *Admap*, 503 (March), retrieved 2 June 2010 from https://www.warc.com/content/paywall/article/admap/effective_ads_in_a_digital_age/89223

Gianatasio, D. (2017) Heineken 0.0's first ads prove you can have fun without alcohol, *AdWeek*, 5 July, retrieved 12 August 2017 from http://www.adweek.com/brand-marketing/heineken-0-0s-first-ads-prove-you-can-have-fun-without-alcohol/

Guthrie, M.F. and Kim, H-S. (2009) The relationship between consumer involvement and brand perceptions of female cosmetic consumers, *Journal of Brand Management*, 17(2), 114–33.

Harris, G. (1987) The implications of low involvement theory for advertising effectiveness, *International Journal of Advertising*, 6, 207–21.

Hawkins, D., Best, R. and Coney, K. (1989) *Consumer Behaviour*, Homewood, IL: Richard D. Irwin.

Heath, R. (2000) Low-involvement processing, *Admap*, March, 14–16.

Heath, R. (2001) Low involvement processing – a new model of brand communication, *Journal of Marketing Communications*, 7, 27–33.

Hogg, S. (2018) Customer journey mapping: the path to loyalty, *Think with Google*, February, retrieved 23 February 2018 from https://www.thinkwithgoogle.com/marketing-resources/experience-design/customer-journey-mapping/

Hosea, M. (2017) How brands are using colour to influence purchase decisions and change perceptions, *Marketing Week*, 8 September, retrieved 9 September 2017 from https://www.marketingweek.com/2017/09/08/brands-colour-influence-purchase-decisions/

Hsu, M. (2017) Neuromarketing: inside the mind of the consumer, *California Management Review*, 59(4), 5–22.

Javalgi, R., Thomas, E. and Rao, S. (1992) US travellers' perception of selected European destinations, *European Journal of Marketing*, 26(7), 45–64.

Lemon, K.N. and Verhoef, P.C. (2016) Understanding customer experience through the customer journey, *Journal of Marketing AMA/MSI Special Issue*, 80 (November), 69–96.

McGuire, W. (1978) An information processing model of advertising effectiveness, in *Behavioural and Management Science in Marketing* (eds H.J. Davis and A.J. Silk), New York: Ronald Press, 156–80.

McLeod, S. (2015) Skinner – Operant Conditioning, *SimplePsychology*, retrieved 23 February 2018 from https://www.simplypsychology.org/operant-conditioning.html

McNeal, M. (2013) A never-ending journey, *Marketing Insights*, Fall, retrieved 21 August 2014 from https://www.ama.org/publications/MarketingInsights/Pages/trader-joes-retail-customer-experience-consumer-behavior-marketing-metrics-big-data.aspx

McQuiston, D.H. and Dickson, P.R. (1991) The effect of perceived personal consequences on participation and influence in organisational buying, *Journal of Business*, 23, 159–77.

Moran, W. (1990) Brand preference and the perceptual frame, *Journal of Advertising Research*, October/November, 9–16.

Mikolajová, K. and Olšanová, K. (2017) How to engage children into the world of traditional car brands? Exploration of specific touchpoints between future buyers in the car industry and established brands, *Central European Business Review*, 6(3), 27–40.

Petty, R.E. and Cacioppo, J.T. (1979) Effects of message repetition and position on cognitive responses, recall and persuasion, *Journal of Personality and Social Psychology*, 37 (January), 97–109.

Ranjbariyan, B. and Mahmoodi, S. (2009) The influencing factors in ad processing: cognitive vs. affective appeals, *Journal of International Marketing and Marketing Research*, 34(3), 129–40.

Rawson, A., Duncan, E. and Jones, C. (2013) The truth about customer experience, *Harvard Business Review*, September, 90–98, retrieved 21 August 2014 from http://hbr.org/2013/09/the-truth-about-customer-experience/

Robinson, P.J., Faris, C.W. and Wind, Y. (1967) *Industrial Buying and Creative Marketing*, Boston, MA: Allyn & Bacon.

Roderick, L. (2017) Four challenges Heineken needs to overcome to make its non-alcoholic beer a success, *Marketing Week*, 19 May, retrieved 12 August 2017 from https://www.marketingweek.com/2017/05/19/heineken-non-alcoholic-beer/

Rossiter, J.R., Percy, L. and Donovan, R.J. (1991) A better advertising planning grid, *Journal of Advertising Research*, October/November, 11–21.

Schivinski, B. and Dabrowski, D. (2016) The effect of social media communication on consumer perceptions of brands, *Journal of Marketing Communications*, 22(2), 189–214.

Schriber, J. (2017) How B2B sellers are offering personalization at scale, *Harvard Business Review*, 12 July, retrieved 19 July 2017 from https://hbr.org/2017/07/how-b2b-sellers-are-offering-personalization-at-scale

Sciuto, A. (2017) How Nestlé Waters reclaimed the customer relationship, *Think with Google*, November, retrieved 3 December 2017 from https://www.thinkwithgoogle.com/marketing-resources/omnichannel/nestle-personalized-customer-relationship/

Stone, R.N. and Gronhaug, K. (1993) Perceived risk: further considerations for the marketing discipline, *European Journal of Marketing*, 27(3), 39–50.

Webster, F.E. and Wind, Y. (1972) *Organisational Buying Behaviour*, Englewood Cliffs, NJ: Prentice Hall.

Williams, K.C. (1981) *Behavioural Aspects of Marketing*, London: Heinemann.

Williams-Grut, O. (2017) People are drinking less booze — so Heineken is launching a 0.0% beer, *Business Insider*, 12 May, retrieved 12 August 2017 from http://uk.businessinsider.com/heineken-alcohol-free-lager-0-0-drinking-rates-decline-2017-5?r=US&IR=T

Wong, Y.S. (2016) Chipotle's new ad is a surprisingly sweet animation about love and greed, *Taxi*, 11 July, retrieved 14 November 2017 from http://designtaxi.com/news/387087/Chipotle-s-New-Ad-Is-A-Surprisingly-Sweet-Animation-About-Love-And-Greed/

Yap, S.-F. and Gaur, S.S. (2016) Integrating functional, social, and psychological determinants to explain online social networking usage, *Behaviour & Information Technology*, 35(3), 166–83.

Contemporary interpretations of buyer behaviour

Many aspects of the classical interpretations of the ways in which people process information and make purchasing decisions, considered in the previous chapter (Chapter 4), are still valid. Since these theories were established however, there have been many changes to purchase behaviours induced by society, culture and technology. Here we consider some of these changes and present some contemporary interpretations of buyer behaviour.

Aims and learning objectives

The aims of this chapter are first to consider the impact of fear and uncertainty on purchase decision-making and second, explore some contemporary interpretations of buyer behaviour.

The learning objectives are to enable readers to:

1. understand how perceived risk can influence the use of marketing communications;
2. identify changes in consumer behaviour that have been influenced by digital, largely mobile, technologies;
3. consider hedonic consumption as a way of understanding consumer buyer behaviour;
4. appraise the principal issues associated with ethical consumption;
5. explore tribal consumption as a viable explanation of certain purchase behaviours;
6. suggest ways in which marketing communications can be influenced by an understanding of behavioural economics.

Introduction

The classical approaches to understanding information processing and decision-making, considered in Chapter 4, are based largely on the premise that consumers undertake rational thinking and work with full information. This does not reflect reality and people consume products and services not only because of the utilitarian value that is offered, but also because of what they represent, their meaning and symbolic value. In other words, people make purchase decisions, either knowingly or subconsciously, about their identity and how they might wish to be seen.

This chapter considers some different explanations and interpretations of consumer behaviour. These contemporary perspectives reflect the disruptive impact that technology and societal forces have brought, and which require marketing communications be used in new and innovative formats. No longer can the provision of information alone, through mass media channels, be a suitable foundation for a campaign. These new approaches require a strong emotional base, using a variety of media all used in a seamless format, and increasingly in an 'always-on' format.

Before examining these different perspectives, consideration is given to issues concerning the perception of risk and uncertainty experienced by consumers when making purchase decisions. The presence of uncertainty is evidence that people do not have full information. This uncertainty can be reduced through the judicious use of marketing communications.

Fear, uncertainty and perceived risk

Perceived risk is an integral aspect of consumer behaviour, and as Maziriri and Chuchu (2017) indicate it helps explain information-searching behaviour and consumer purchase decision-making.

Of the many emotions experienced by individuals fear is an underlying driver of consumer behaviour. Fear is generated by the presence or anticipation of a specific danger or threat. People do not perceive the same risks although many are shared within cultural groups, if only to maintain a particular way of life.

Research shows that anxiety and fear can make consumers more risk averse, and the use of scarcity appeals are less likely to be successful. Dunn and Hoegg (2014) report that fear can also motivate individuals to connect with others, as demonstrated by troops on a battlefield (Marshall, 1947) and the victims of natural disasters (Fried, 1963). People try to manage the fear they perceive by sharing experiences and affiliating with others.

The threat of fear induces a sense of risk or uncertainty. The concept of perceived risk, first proposed by Bauer (1960), concerns the negative and positive consequences that are perceived to arise from a purchase decision, whether that might be not to buy or to buy.

Risk is perceived because a buyer has little or no experience of the performance of the product or the decision process associated with the purchase. As Chang and Hsiao (2008) state, perceived risk includes two factors. The first can occur prior to a purchase and the second subsequent to a purchase when an individual experiences the unfavourable consequences of a purchase (Cox and Rich, 1967).

Risk is related not only to brand-based decisions but also to product categories, an especially important aspect when launching new technology products, for example. The level of risk an individual experiences varies through time, across products, and is often a reflection of an individual's propensity to manage risk. Settle and Alreck (1989) suggest that there are five main forms of risk that can be identified and Stone and Gronhaug (1993) added time as a further factor. These are set out in Table 5.1 using the purchase of a smartphone to illustrate each element.

Table 5.1   Types of perceived risk

Type of perceived risk	Explanation
Performance	Will this smartphone perform properly?
Financial	Can I afford that much or should I buy a less expensive version?
Physical	Is the smartphone built to the required safety standards . . . will it catch fire?
Social	Will my friends and colleagues approve?
Ego	Will I feel cool about using this smartphone?
Time	Can I afford the right amount of time to search for a good smartphone?

Sources: Derived from Settle and Alreck (1989) and Stone and Gronhaug (1993).

These forms of risk were determined for an offline purchasing context. The development of online shopping and e-commerce has driven new types of risk. Security risk concerns the uncertainty perceived in revealing personal, private and financial information. It also refers to the concerns about being attacked electronically and the theft of credit card and other financial information. Privacy risk embraces uncertainties concerning the collection and use, by website sellers, of personal, private and financial data, and whether they will distribute to third parties, without the owner's consent.

What constitutes risk is a function of the contextual characteristics of each situation, the individuals involved, and the nature of the product under consideration. Indeed, it is possible to use contextual risk to frame communications when launching new products.

A major reason to use marketing communications, therefore, is to reduce levels of perceived risk and increase levels of trust. By providing extensive and relevant information a buyer's risks can be reduced substantially. The use of mass media, social media, word-of-mouth, websites and sales representatives, for example, are popular ways to set out the likely outcomes from purchase and so reduce the levels of risk. Brand loyalty can also be instrumental in reducing risk when launching new products. The use of guarantees, third-party endorsements, money-back offers (some car manufacturers offer the opportunity to return a car within 30 days or exchange it for a different model) and trial samples (as used by many haircare products) are also well-used devices to reduce risk.

Many websites and direct-response magazine ads seek to reduce a number of different types of risk. Companies offering wine for direct home delivery, for example, try to reduce performance risk by providing information about each wine being offered. Financial risk is reduced by comparing the 'special' prices with those in the high street, social risk is approached by developing the brand name associations trying to improve credibility and time risk is reduced through the convenience of home delivery.

Assurance structures are designed to reduce perceived online risk and to promote trust and purchase intentions. Bahmanziari and Odom (2015: 87) refer to assurance structures as 'statements, promises, guarantees, logos, symbols and any other structural components of a website intended by the vendor to reduce perceptions of risk in transacting on their website'. Certificates and symbols, representing support and credibility, provided by third-party financial organisations, plus WebTrust seals and retailer disclosures concerning security, privacy and cookies usage policies, are examples of assurance structures in practice.

Some of the more commonly used assurance structures are depicted at Table 5.2.

A contemporary source of uncertainty lies with the increasing proliferation of fake news and misinformation. The reasons for this are many but one of these is 'clickbait'. Online publishers rely on advertising revenue and some are tempted to publish sensationalist headlines within social media. These drive user clicks and visits, and this can attract

Table 5.2   Assurance structures used to reduce online perceived purchasing risk

Risk reducing assurance structure	Explanation
Payment security	High visibility of third-party certification, logos and symbols.
Provision of product and service information	Provision of pictures, details about sizes and variants, material components and product comparison, designed to enable buyers to develop a more complete idea of the quality and outward appearance of the product. Branding and logos can also reduce risk. Promise of customer service and 24/7 accessibility.
Ease of communication	Provision of a variety of easy-to-use communication channels for buyers to 'talk' with the vendor, including 'chat' facilities.
Vendor's reputation	Customer reviews, third-party and WoM endorsements, awards and achievements.
Guarantees	Product quality, product performance, money-back offers and free returns.
Experience with the website	Interaction with well-known brand, previous product purchases, provision of loyalty programmes, frequency of access and usage.

Viewpoint 5.1

McDonald's challenge fake news about their brand

Image 5.1 McDonald's tackled the problem of myths with satire

In order to reduce the impact of fake news and misinformation about their brand, McDonald's used satirical advertising and employed vloggers to tell the story as they saw it.
Source: McDonald's.

In an age of misinformation McDonald's has long been the subject of malicious rumour mongering about the quality of its food. Back in 2009 McDonald's ran a TV ad 'Big nothing', which provided compelling rational information about their food within an emotionally engaging wrapper. They also made substantial business changes, including many in the supply chain. Although these measures helped restore consumer confidence in the short term, the myths soon returned.

This time the rumours were propelled by social media. Fake Twitter accounts were tweeting about cancer-causing 'pink slime', while 'clickbait' sites were seducing millions into watching YouTube videos based on these false claims. On top of this consumers were sharing the misinformation.

Consumer perceptions and trust in McDonald's food quality started to decline steeply, resulting in fewer store visits and declining revenue. Research and social listening highlighted the problem – a knowledge vacuum. Advertising had reassured consumers that McDonald's food originated from wholesome farms and that the end product was good. What they didn't know was what happened in the middle.

McDonald's sought to tackle the specific myths that were proving damaging, and address myths in general. Conventional measures would not be good enough so they used satire. Using mimicry and exaggeration McDonald's sought to focus on the myths and rumours while the humour enabled them to poke fun at the culture of fake news and all who are drawn in by it.

To address some of the most sensational myths, such as deformed cows, McDonald's used a variety of playful visual techniques in their advertising, including the use of Plasticine animation, and cute drawings by a child.

McDonald's also drove user-generated content, to get inside the online world that rumours and myths inhabit. They allowed YouTube personalities to access McDonald's farms, factories and restaurant kitchens to find out for themselves how McDonald's makes and prepares its food. These vloggers then posted their thoughts and findings on their own channels, quite independently of McDonald's.

Post-campaign research found that use of satire had worked. The campaign had a positive impact on consumers' food-quality perceptions, and many of them now stopped to think about whether to believe and share questionable information. In addition, the openness and transparency of the vlogger content improved perception and levels of brand trust.

Source: Bullmore and Moore (2017).

Insight

A central role of marketing communications is to reduce risk and uncertainty. Here we can see that providing rational and factual information can be a constructive approach to tackling this issue. McDonald's have shown that the use of satire can also be an effective way of changing perceptions and reducing the level of risk and uncertainty. One of the more unsavoury aspects of social media is the amplification of myths and misinformation, and is something that brands are having to deal with on a more frequent basis.

Question: How likely is it that the use of satire will have a longer-lasting impact on reducing the potency of myths than the conventional approach of rational, factual information?

Task: Find one other brand that has used satire to counter the influence of fake news.

advertising. As rumours, myths and plain mistruths are often placed adjacent to legitimate journalism in newsfeeds, they become difficult to distinguish. As a result peoples' levels of uncertainty and perception of risk about a brand can flourish (Bullmore and Moore, 2017). See Viewpoint 5.1 to see how McDonald's coped with this problem.

User-generated content in the form of product reviews is increasingly seen as a strong way to improve brand trust. This is partly because of the perceived objectivity provided by these reviewers. TripAdvisor is probably one of the better-known examples but care has to be taken as the reviews can often be fake. For example, it is known that restaurant reviews have been written by critics who have never visited the restaurant (Turner, 2017).

She also reports how a journalist set up a pretend restaurant in his garden shed, photographed fake food and posted it online. He then registered the 'restaurant' on TripAdvisor and posted flattering yet fictitious reviews. It was not long before 'The Shed' became London's premier restaurant.

Scholars' paper 5.1
Well, it must be risky

Stone, R.N. and Gronhaug, K. (1993) Perceived risk: further considerations for the marketing discipline, *European Journal of Marketing,* **27(3), 39–50.**

Readers interested in consumer behaviour and marketing communications should understand the basic principles associated with perceived risk. This is the seminal paper in this area, although the concept was introduced 33 years before by Bauer. This paper provides an insight into the literature and issues associated with perceived risk and references the uncertainty experienced by consumers when making purchasing decisions.

See also:

Maziriri, T. and Chuchu, T. (2017) The conception of consumer perceived risk towards online purchases of apparel and an idiosyncratic scrutiny of perceived social risk: a review of literature, *International Review of Management and Marketing,* 7(3), 257–65.

Boshoff, C., Schlechter, C. and Ward, S.-J. (2011) Consumers' perceived risks associated with purchasing on a branded website: the mediating effect of brand knowledge, *South African Journal of Business Management,* 42(1), 45–54.

In Chapter 4, consideration was given to what might be called 'the rational and cognitive approach' to both information processing and decision-making. These ideas are informative and enable us to build an organised understanding. Indeed, organisations often install logical buying procedures as a means of controlling and managing the procurement process.

Many organisations recognise that the linear, logical journey that consumer decision follows is no longer relevant. As a result they now consider issues concerning customer experience, and focus on maximising engagement opportunities at particular 'touchpoints' on a consumer journey. There is a view that this approach misses the bigger picture of a consumer's overall decision journey (Rawson et al., 2013). As will be seen shortly, implicit decision-making concerns the emotional value that people attach to the various options they are faced with when making a decision. Damasio (1996) argues that when faced with time pressures or too many options, complex decisions are resolved by choosing an option that evokes the greatest number of positive emotional associations (Kent-Lemon, 2013). These implicit heuristics, it is argued, are the emotional shortcuts we use every day, when it is not possible, due to the available time or energy required, to use rational analysis.

A number of alternative views about consumer decision-making and behaviour have been advanced. First we consider some of the behavioural changes that digital and mobile technologies in particular have generated among consumers. Next, we explore ideas associated with *hedonic consumption, ethical consumption,* then *tribal consumption* and finally *behavioural economics (BE).* Now although BE is not new, it has received increased attention recently. Each of these have implications for the way marketing communications should be used.

Digital and mobile influences on buyer behaviour

Although the title to this section refers to digital, this is really about the impact mobile technologies and devices (tablets and smartphones), have had on people and their behaviour. Several years ago mobile marketing was first considered to deliver several key benefits: personalisation, interactivity, localisation and ubiquity (Bauer, 2015). These have not changed and it is therefore unsurprising that investment in mobile marketing activities has grown significantly in recent years.

Research indicates that mobile marketing communications generally elicit negative attitudes, largely annoyance and irritation. However, for consumers who hold positive attitudes towards mobile marketing they are more likely to follow up and enquire about commercial messages (Kushwaha and Agrawal, 2016). Mobile has had an enormous impact on behaviour and has helped to reshape the way in which we communicate with one another, and with organisations. Figure 5.1 sets out some of the core behaviours induced by mobile marketing.

Usage

Mobiles are personal, multifunctional devices that can engage sight, sound, touch and movement. They enhance consumer lives and impact daily behaviour and media consumption patterns. Parrett (2016) reports that 81 per cent of UK adults own a smartphone, and 73 per cent of people report that they use their phone within an hour of waking up (Barley, 2016).

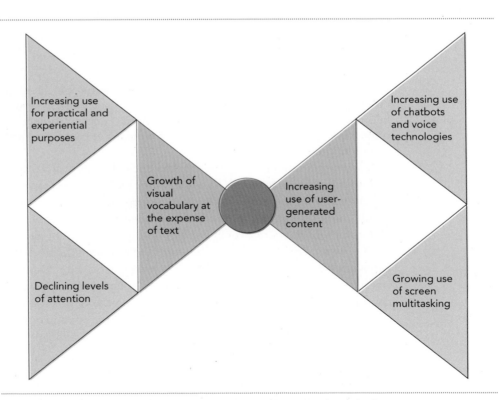

Figure 5.1 New consumer behaviours induced through usage of mobile devices

A key behaviour is a user's typically constant referral to their mobile device during each day. Mobiles are always on and therefore are taken everywhere. So, in addition to reaching consumers through timely media meshing activities, the GPS location-based targeting opportunities enable advertisers to deliver contextually relevant messages, to the right people, at precisely the right time.

Mobile is data rich and enables advertisers to know a huge amount about a user's mobile and related behaviours. This ranges from their general search and usage behaviour, a user's location, the nature and time of their content consumption, and the environment in which it was consumed. When this is combined with programmatic buying, advertisers are able to use this real-time data to deliver timely, personalised and contextually relevant content (Graves, 2016).

Mobile devices are used for work reasons, social engagement and relationships, entertainment, accessing information and m-commerce. Gevelber (2016) refers to micro-moments, those points within a day when people turn to their devices in response to four issues: I-want-to-know, go, do and buy (see Figure 5.2).

Understanding and anticipating these micro-moments has become an integral part of a brand's digital strategy. This enables brands to be available at the precise time when people need help. By connecting consumers to the answer they are seeking at the time (moment) they need it, the overall positive digital experience serves to enhance brand perception and reputation.

In addition to these micro-moments, there is evidence that consumers are increasingly seeking experiences rather than owning material possessions (Schultz, 2015). Many advertisers, therefore, are looking to deliver meaningful brand experiences and are attempting to shield themselves from being seen to use 'advertising'. As Kingston (2015) argues, the use of video and virtual reality can help deliver such experiences.

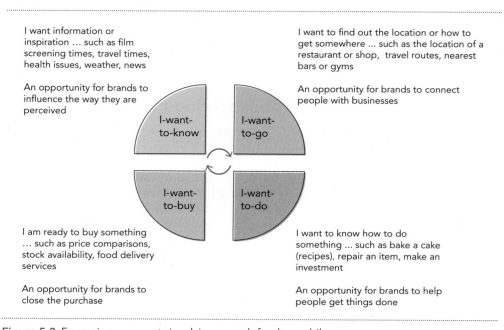

Figure 5.2 Four micro-moments involving a reach for the mobile

Source: Micro-moments derived from Lisa Gevelber: www.thinkwithgoogle.com/consumer-insights/mobile-search-consumer-behavior-data/

Viewpoint 5.2
KitKat generate the right experiences

The slogan used by the chocolate brand KitKat is 'Take a Break'. When it was understood that mobile technology had changed the way people took a break, the management team undertook research and as a result adapted their communications.

72 different types of break were identified. This meant that the brand could deliver content to complement particular breaks. For example, video content for those taking a 'music break' on YouTube, or listicles for those having a 'funny break' on Buzzfeed. Whatever type of break the consumer was taking, KitKat could deliver a consistent campaign message but in a variety of reformatted ways that best suited the audience.

Source: Havill and Coelho (2016).

Insight

This example demonstrates understanding and application of micro-moments, namely the four I-want-to-know, go, do and buy moments. By appreciating how consumers perceive the KitKat brand and the associations they have with the Take a Break slogan, communications were shaped for a 'do' moment. Note should be made of the number of creative executions that were developed and the flexibility this provided.

Question: Should knowledge about how a brand is used always influence marketing communications?

Task: Find another brand whose marketing communications is influenced by consumer usage.

Multitasking and layering media

The net amount of time consumers spend with media has remained reasonably constant but media multitasking has become a significant new behaviour for over 90 per cent of adults at least once each week (Ofcom 2016). Sometimes referred to as multiscreening, the phrase refers to the use of mobile devices while watching television. Two particular behaviours have been identified, media meshing and media stacking.

Media meshing refers to the simultaneous use of media devices in order to improve or enhance the main media (TV) experience, in other words, interact or communicate about the content of a TV programme. This offers opportunities for advertisers to reach target audiences. For example, it is possible to create specific content to enhance the cross-device media experience.

Media stacking refers to undertaking media activities that are unrelated to the principal media experience. This is more frequent and more common than media meshing. Here the opportunities for advertisers are less obvious but it is possible to target messages across media channels in a frequent and consecutive format.

Interestingly, research found that brands that use television ads were found to drive higher sales in the two-hour slot around the time of the ad broadcasts. This is compared with brands that are not advertised on television (Liaukonyte et al., 2015). The authors apply constructs from consumer psychology to further untangle these effects, differentiating between action-, emotion-, information-, and imagery-focused ads. See also Scholars' paper 5.2.

Attention levels

The surge in use of social media has had a profound impact on the way people process information. Not only has it challenged and reshaped the nature of interpersonal relationships, it has also increased the amount of time spent using mobiles. Information processing is now quicker, with content digested in bite-sized formats. The downside of this is that attention spans have fallen to as little as four seconds. The issue for advertisers is that they have a very small window in which to get a consumer's attention and keep them engaged in order to message them effectively.

Visual vocabulary

A major way to overcome the attention span issue is to use a visual vocabulary. As technology launches increasingly high-quality cameras and screens, mobile has enabled consumers to communicate through visuals, and so satisfy short attention spans. Facebook, for example, has been registering over 300 million images a day, while 70 per cent of all social media interactions involve visuals (Noyes, 2018). The growth of Instagram for example, is based primarily on the predominant visual user experience. The frequent use of emojis, selfies and memes to communicate in short form echoes the ingrained preference for visual communications, rather than text (Barley, 2015).

The growth in the use of video also reflects the preferred visual messaging format. Mobile usage has driven people to consume content across a variety of channels, and their behaviour varies across media. This means that 30-second TV ads do not work across mobile display, Facebook, Instagram and Snapchat, as consumers use mobile to consume video differently to the way they watch TV ads. For example, they do not listen when viewing video content on mobile, and they use the screen in vertical format, different to the landscape TV ad format. Many advertisers use subtitles or even create video that does not need sound (Barley, 2015).

It is important that advertisers develop content that is right for a specific platform and they also have to ensure that it is in the right format (Bailey, 2016). Many advertisers now use simple visual messaging in preference to long-form text content, avoiding the previous approach which required audiences to concentrate in order to decode the message. Many agencies incorporate a content matrix when developing campaign plans. These set out guidelines on consumer behaviour for each platform and for each format across all specified channels. This enables clients to understand the content they need to produce before a TV ad is shot. This can include a video that works without audio, a vertical video, short-form video and GIFs. As a rule social media based video hubs such as Facebook's Watch, provide a very different experience to that of TV. Watch and others provide a quick and reactive visual experience, whereas TV and premium video provide a visual and audio experience, which is consumed passively, and over a longer period (Liyakasa, 2017).

Chat

Another behaviour emerging partly as a response to declining attention spans, is the increasing use of chat. These began in categories where online decision-making was sufficiently complex to warrant the assistance of the client. Initially, conversations with humans could be triggered from a website and these supported the online sales process. These soon evolved into 'chat' based on text exchanges. These can be used to provide information, clarify issues and help potential buyers focus on the key buying criteria.

Today, chatbots are being used increasingly. These are computer programs, which conduct a conversation via auditory or textual methods designed to simulate how a human would behave as a conversational partner. In other words, chatbots simulate a human interface with digital and interactive technologies and make it easier for online and mobile users to interact with brands.

For example, Exodus who offer adventure and alternative experience-based holidays, introduced a 'Live Chat' facility, available 24/7, enabling online users the opportunity to discuss their holiday ideas with their experts. Online sales increased by 14 per cent and 25 per cent of online sales are generated through Live Chat.

The software supporting chatbots is developing rapidly and their range of skills is expanding. This is reflected in the name 'virtual assistants'. In time it is anticipated that the majority of consumers will use voice to make purchases, or to add items to a list via voice, rather than writing them down on a notepad. Amazon's Alexa, Apple's Siri and Microsoft's Cortana are examples of this emerging technology. These already respond to voice and text commands and can make lists, schedule appointments, order taxis, open software and activate smart devices, with varying degrees of success.

Consumer behaviour will adapt to harmonise with the benefits offered by virtual assistants. The shopping experience will also evolve, and so a challenge for brands will be to develop the right shopping experience through voice and to communicate effectively with both consumers and perhaps, virtual assistants. (For more on voice and associated technologies, see Chapter 21.)

User-generated content

The prominence and significance of user-generated content (UGC) has been increasing throughout the digital era. The use of mobile devices to access social media has fuelled this growth such that UGC from social media is an important source of Big Data. UGC can be observed in a variety of sources. These according to Liu et al. (2017: 237) include 'tweets or Facebook pages, pictures (Pinterest), blogs, microblogs, and product reviews (Amazon, Yelp). Previous empirical findings show that UGC has significant effects on brand images, purchase intentions, and sales'.

Brands now have to listen to and consider UGC in order to use marketing communications in an effective, empathetic and timely manner. Deeper consideration is given to UGC in Chapter 19 but the point here is that mobile usage combined with frequent access to social media has increased the nature and volume of UGC, and this in turn influences the nature of a brand's own marketing communications.

All of these mobile-induced new behaviours have had a strong influence on marketing communications. The way in which campaigns are planned and implemented, the use of real behavioural data rather than claimed attitudes and intended behaviours, the focus on visual rather than text based communications, the forging of new forms of media integration, and personalised messaging are changes that we explore elsewhere in this book.

Scholars' paper 5.2
Is mobile marketing irritating?

Kushwaha, G.S. and Agrawal, S.R. (2016) The impact of mobile marketing initiatives on customers' attitudes and behavioural outcomes, *Journal of Research in Interactive Marketing,* **10(3), 150–76.**

This paper considers customers' behavioural outcomes based on their actual attitudinal responses to mobile marketing initiatives. It provides useful background information about previous research in this area and is one of the first to investigate attitudes and behaviour rather than just the benefits and usage of mobile marketing.

See also:

Segijn, C.M., Voorveld, H.A.M. and Smit, E.G. (2017) How related multiscreening could positively affect advertising outcomes, *Journal of Advertising,* 46(4), 455–72.

Hedonic consumption

Consumption is recognised as a socio-cultural experience, and is more than an individual cognitive process. With this in mind the classical approaches to buyer behaviour explored in Chapter 4 might be considered to represent utilitarian consumption. Consumers in these situations place more emphasis on the practicality, functionality, usefulness and fulfilment of basic needs. People in utilitarian consumption situations tend to be goal oriented (Strahilevitz and Myers 1998) and their decisions involve thoughts about the consequences of the purchase (Batra and Ahtola 1990). This perspective ignores the sense-making, identity construction, group membership and affiliation issues associated with socio-cultural experiences (Arnould and Thompson, 2005) that are associated with consumption. We now consider three other forms of consumption: hedonic, ethical and tribal consumption.

An alternative approach considers a range of products and services that can evoke high levels of involvement based on the emotional impact that consumption provides buyers. This is referred to as 'hedonic consumption', and Hirschman and Holbrook (1982) describe this approach as 'those facets of consumer behaviour that relate to the multisensory, fantasy and emotive aspects of one's experience with products'. People in hedonic consumption situations therefore, are far more pleasure oriented (Strahilevitz and Myers 1998). They emphasise experiential enjoyment, pleasure and fun, and make decisions based largely on their feelings (Pham 1998).

With its roots partly in the motivation research and partly in the cognitive processing schools, this interpretation of consumer behaviour seeks to explain how and why buyers experience emotional responses to the act of purchase and consumption of particular products.

Historical imagery occurs when, for example, the colour of a dress, the scent of a perfume or cologne, or the aroma of a restaurant or food can trigger an individual's memory to replay an event. In contrast, *fantasy imagery* occurs when a buyer constructs an event, drawing together various colours, sounds and shapes to compose a mental experience

Image 5.2 Music festivals
Attendance at music festivals represents hedonic consumption
Source: Shutterstock.

of an event that has not occurred previously. Consumers imagine a reality in which they derive sensory pleasure. Some smokers were encouraged to imagine themselves as 'Marlboro Men': not just masculine, but as idealised cowboys (Hirschman and Holbrook, 1982).

Because of the high emotional values associated with these purchase decisions, feelings of guilt can set in, even before consumption occurs. Unsurprisingly, purchase justification based on the personal nature of the benefits gained is troublesome, if only from the association with being wasteful or because of the difficulty associated with their largely self-rewarding purchase goals (Kim and Kim, 2016).

The advertising of fragrances and luxury brands is often based on images that encourage individuals to project themselves into a desirable or pleasurable environment or situation: for example, those which foster romantic associations. Some people form strong associations with particular fragrances and use this to develop and maintain specific images. Advertising is used to create and support these images and, in doing so, enhance the emotional benefits derived from fragrance brand associations. Hedonics are closely related and influence the simultaneous perception of fragrances.

Viewpoint 5.3
Parfums De Versailles fantasises its growth

France is considered by Chinese consumers to be a luxury destination that produces high quality exports. They associate the country with high fashion, culture and high quality. As China has become a major economy, it has also adopted a more international and outward-looking orientation. With this change the number of affluent citizens has also increased. China's 350 million middle-class consumers are increasing their spend on luxury fragrances. These individuals are considered to be very discriminating and value special, quality products that tell an individual story and which add to their sense of self and their understanding of the world. With this background,

Image 5.3 French aristocracy sets the tone for the Parfums De Versailles campaign
Source: Pecold/Shutterstock.

French luxury brand, Parfums De Versailles (PDV), recognised China as a key market for their long-term growth.

In a market often known for poorer quality goods and fakes it is critical that genuine luxury brands such as PDV are trusted. The discerning Chinese consumers desire quality products and one way of reaching and establishing trust is through the consistent use of engaging stories.

Using formulas from the 17th and 18th centuries the fragrances used by Parfums De Versailles were originally and exclusively only available at the Palace of Versailles. It was here that a number of French kings famously indulged their extravagant passion for cosmetics. PDV's positioning strategy was built on this history and prestige to engage with the Chinese luxury spenders' desire to feel 'treated like royals'. The campaign tone was that Chinese consumers should be treated like 'royalty' and that they could experience this premium luxury through the PDV range.

In China gaming is viewed not just as a mass-market approach but a key way to engage with wealthy consumers. PDV used a high-quality mobile-based multiplayer game to promote interaction between Chinese consumers and the brand. The adventure game was set in the luxurious Palace of Versailles and involved a 'Royal character' who had to accumulate points and different value coins. The game became a platform for the brand's communication strategy as before playing, the brand's story and promotional content was conveyed.

Within two weeks the game had created a buzz with over 50 articles written about the game and in excess of 200 gamers in a single day. This activity drew in 'Fashion Xi', a fashion video channel which reported on the campaign. Their video received 1.72 million views.

Source: Benji (2017).

Insight

PDV have deliberately enabled Chinese individuals to project themselves into a desirable environment, and one that fosters fantasies of a French royalty lifestyle. The associations are then set between the romance of the royal scenario and the brand. What is interesting is that by understanding the Chinese culture PDV have been able to engage the wealthy target audience through game play. This is not something that would normally be possible with a wealthy European audience.

Question: To what extent does the mobile game help reflect hedonic consumption?

Task: Find another fragrance brand campaign and determine the fantasy associated with its positioning.

Hedonic contamination

Films and television programmes are considered to provide hedonic value to many consumers (Hirschman and Holbrook, 1982). Such entertainment content however, is often preceded by commercial marketing messages, which can irritate consumers even though they are designed to persuade audiences (Danaher and Rossiter, 2009).

This type of pre-entertainment commercial exposure can damage the overall entertainment experience to the extent that not only do audiences experience a more negative hedonic experience and their attitudes toward the entertainment programme itself are lowered but it has even been found to affect the taste of concessions consumed as part of a theatrical experience (Russell et al. 2017). This concept is referred to as hedonic contamination. This particular case not only challenges the accepted role and benefits of pre-entertainment messaging but also suggests that the configuration of marketing programmes related to where hedonic experiences are known to exist need to be reconsidered.

Scholars' paper 5.3
Hedonic consumption is not a fantasy

Hirschman, E.C. and Holbrook, M.B. (1982) Hedonic consumption: emerging concepts, methods and propositions, *Journal of Marketing*, 46(3), 92–101.

This is the seminal paper used by Hirschman and Holbrook to introduce their groundbreaking ideas about hedonic consumption.

See also

Sharma, A., Kumar, V. and Borah, S.B. (2017) Ritualization: a strategic tool to position brands in international markets, *Journal of International Marketing*, 25(2), 1–24.

There are a number of challenges with the hedonic consumption approach, namely measurement factors of reliability and validity; nevertheless, appreciating the dreams, ideals and desires of the target audience can be an important contribution to the creation of promotional messages.

Ethical consumption

There has been substantial interest in ethical consumption, from both a consumer and a wider business perspective. Burke et al. (2014) refer to the considerable growth of ethical consumerism such that the UK market value reached £47.2 billion.

Crane and Matten (2003) consider ethical consumption be the conscious and deliberate choice to make certain consumption choices due to personal and moral beliefs. Davies and Gutsche (2016) observe that ethical consumption embraces a range of terms including sustainable, moralistic, green, organic and fairtrade consumption. They settle on Cooper-Martin and Holbrook's (1993: 113) definition of ethical consumption, which encompasses 'consumption experiences that are affected by the consumer's ethical concerns'.

Ethical consumers choose to purchase goods and services that reflect their moral, ethical and social concerns. As Szmigin et al. (2007: 399) rightly point out, 'ethical consumption is as much part of the active social process of consumption with its material and symbolic dimensions as any other form of consumption'.

Why buy ethically?

Ethical consumption, sometimes referred to as conscious consumption, might be considered to be undertaken by consumers who are active information seekers, and who engage with a wide range of media, including the Internet, to be better informed. Burke et al. (2014) refer to several reasons why people make positive decisions to buy ethically. These are often guided by social norms and moral principles that serve to reinforce personal values:

- a willingness to comply with others in buying ethically reputable products;
- a belief that ethical products are of a higher quality ;
- an opportunity to communicate social position, status and wealth;
- awareness and concern about health and environmental risks;
- disenchantment and cynicism regarding aggressive marketing and unethical practices such as abuses of data privacy and child labour;
- the deliberate boycotting of brands with questionable ethical practices.

The growth in ethical consumption is partly a result of brands recognising the market potential and positioning themselves appropriately. This involves them providing improved information about the availability of ethical alternatives to mainstream products and services. Supermarkets now provide a wider range of ethical products, which in turn allows them to be perceived in-store as suitable alternatives to mainstream products. Improvements to labelling and better access to product information via online or mobile devices all help to reduce uncertainty, concerns about product attributes, and the effort required to purchase ethical products. Ethical consumption behaviour has been shown to be strengthened by participation in online communities (Gummerus et al., 2017).

It is clear that ethical consumption is undertaken by a relatively small number of consumers, the others choosing to not be involved because of the low levels of awareness, premium prices, and the cognitive complexity resulting from the difficulty involved with discriminating on issues such as ethical integrity (Carrigan et al., 2004).

Communication in an ethical market

Genuinely ethical brands need to distinguish and differentiate themselves from competitors to ensure that they deliver both the functional and the symbolic needs of customers. This requires an understanding of their customers' values and then communicating appropriately. Here functionality refers to a brand's ability to satisfy utilitarian needs, while the symbolic dimensions are those aspects of a brand that enable consumers to express something about themselves.

Szmigin et al. (2007) isolate four dimensions against which a number of ethical goods are positioned and have become integrated into mainstream consumption. These are distinction, hedonism, love and aesthetics. These are summarised below.

Distinction – the choice of ethical brands can reflect lifestyle choices and can make statements about personal identity. Ethical consumption can enable a conspicuous response to the marketplace, as it allows consumers to distinguish themselves through proactive purchasing and rejection. Fairtrade consumers pay more for products, often make a greater effort to purchase them, and they also engage in extensive search activities to ensure the ethical validity of their purchases. Ethical brands need to provide reassurance that the goods are genuinely ethical and to this extent trademarks and other visual identifiers can play an important role.

Hedonism – ethical hedonism requires actions that drive pleasure and prevent pain. Consumers who purchase ethical brands, might be regarded as acting hedonistically, both in relation to their own feelings of purchase pleasure, such as doing the right thing, and feelings of self-respect. This, Szmigin et al. (2007) argue, can provide feelings of pleasure and brands should endeavour to provide signals that generate hedonistic associations normally expected from mainstream products.

Love – the longer-term notion of love can be seen as one of caring, and advertising often depicts this using 'images of people together as couples and families, conveying the understanding that the purchase of a brand will act as a defence from being alone'. Ethical consumption can be used to signal deep feelings of concern for significant others. In advertising, ethical brands use love in messages about doing the right thing for your family, and taglines indicating that this product is 'for people who care'.

Aesthetics – the production of things that are aesthetically pleasing, useful and non-exploitative is culturally established. Ethical consumption can reflect an aesthetic experience and this dimension is often observed in advertising for ethical brands. Communication needs to incorporate consumer culture where the aestheticisation of the everyday is expected. They see a need for ethical brands to 'develop their visual and aesthetic representations alongside mainstream brands'.

Tribal consumption

Another approach to understanding consumption concerns the concept of individualism and tribes. Cova (1997) identifies two schools of thought about consumption and identity. The Northern school believe that consumption enables individuals to reveal their self-identity in society. People consume as an end in itself as this allows them to *take* meaning for their lives through what they consume. Here consumption is a means of individual differentiation.

The Southern school believe that it is important to maintain a culture's social fabric. As society reconfigures itself into groups of people that, according to Maffesoli (1996), reflect primitive tribes, so the role of consumption evolves into a means of linking people to multiple communities, or tribes. Here consumption is a means of offering value to a tribe (Cooper et al., 2005).

Maffesoli (1996) considers contemporary culture to be one not based on individualism, but one defined by 'fluidity, occasional gatherings and dispersal'. This might be likened to a fragmentation of social groupings (Hamilton and Hewer, 2010), many of

Scholars' paper 5.4
Thriving networks and tribal identities

Hamilton, K. and Hewer, P. (2010) Tribal mattering spaces: social-networking sites, celebrity affiliations, and tribal innovations, *Journal of Marketing Management*, 26(3–4), 271–89.

Further to the exploration of tribes in consumer behaviour, these authors use ideas about tribal identities and fandom to explore Web 2.0. They argue that social networks that focus on iconic celebrities provide a rich context to consider the interaction, connectivity, and creativity of the fans that populate them.

See also:

Cova, B. and Cova, V. (2001) Tribal aspects of postmodern consumption research: the case of French in-line roller skaters, *Journal of Consumer Behaviour*, 1(1), 67–76.

which are transient. According to Jenkins (2006), tribes represent a participatory culture where business and social interests and affiliations come together.

The term 'tribe' refers to communities characterised by people who share emotions, experiences, lifestyles and patterns of consumption. In order that these tribes are able to effect tribal communion (Cova et al., 2007) so that members can reaffirm their identity, various emblems, sites, recognition or support are used. Products and services are not consumed for their utility value, or for the sense of individual identification. Their consumption is considered to be important for the 'linking value' they provide within a tribal network. Tribes serve to link people who share passions and interests, examples of which, according to Hamilton and Hewer (2010), include brands such as Harley-Davidson, Saab, Star Trek and the X-Files, adrenalin activities such as skydiving, dancing, river rafting, or a variety of sports, or even sports stars and celebrities. Tribes are loosely interconnected communities (Cova and Cova, 2001) where bonding and linking represent key activities designed to retain tribal membership. See Image 5.4.

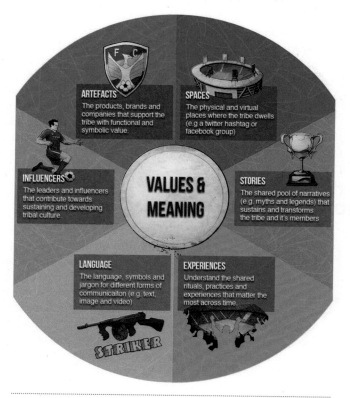

Image 5.4 The Tribal Map
Source: Morling Sthlm Ab.

Tribes proliferate on the Internet, thanks mainly to its power to aggregate communities who share similar interests. These e-tribes have the same characteristics as traditional communities, namely shared rituals and traditions, a similar consciousness of kind, and an obligation, or sense of duty, to the community and to its individual members (Muniz and O'Guinn, 2001). Kozinets (2008) established that there were eight Es that can be associated with e-tribes. These are set out in Table 5.3.

Table 5.3   Eight Es of e-tribes

E reference	Explanation
Electronic	e-tribes communicate via the medium of the Internet
Enculturating	e-tribe members learn and adopt the language, practices, rituals and values of the community
Emotive	e-tribes generate a high level of emotional involvement from members
Expressive	e-tribe members engage in creative, product work
Empowered	e-tribe members gain great satisfaction from the agentic potential of their practices
Evangelical	e-tribe membership can be compared with a quasi-religious or spiritual experience
Emergent	e-tribes are self-generated, emerging on their own rather than under the control of a company
Entangled	Network boundaries overlap and merge

Source: Hamilton and Hewer's (2010) adaption of Kozinets (2008).

According to Hamilton and Hewer, this listing indicates the breadth and complexity of the virtual tribal environment and the openness and opportunities that people have to explore, work, play and become immersed and passionate about interests, which Kozinets et al. (2008) relate to the intimate feelings people experience in childhood.

The recognition and acceptance of e-tribes and tribal consumption for marketing communications practitioners is not clear cut. Indeed, some commentators warn against outright tribal intrusion and recommend activities that encourage a tribe's social and linking behaviours, simply because these are critical for members. Organisations should aim to become listeners and to work 'with' tribes by fostering conversations and enabling them to function through the provision of 'play-rich mattering spaces' (Hamilton and Hewer, 2010: 285).

Behavioural economics

Just as ideas about tribal consumption are a rejection of 'rational man' perspectives, so behavioural economics is grounded in the belief that people are 'fundamentally irrational in their decision-making and motivated by unconscious cognitive biases' (Ariely, 2009). The final issue to be considered under the banner of contemporary or alternative approaches to understanding consumer behaviour, therefore, concerns the emerging popularity of the concept called 'behavioural economics'. One of the interesting points about behavioural economics is that it challenges established thinking, and another is that it is not a million miles from the idea of low-attention processing.

Behavioural economics has emerged following decades of frustration with classical economic theory. Conventional economic theory suggests that people make rational choices in their decision-making and even seek to maximise their opportunities and minimise expenditure. The 'rational man' makes the best possible decisions, on the basis of maximising benefits and minimising costs, in order to obtain the most advantageous and efficient economic outcome. The classical view of economics is reflected in advertising that is essentially informational in nature and which promotes a USP. The Persil slogan 'washes whiter' typifies the traditional perspective of advertising: one core message, we are better, faster, safer or cleaner than the rest.

The idea that people follow a sequential decision-making process is a long way from the truth. Early researchers Kahneman and Tversky (1979) wrote a paper called 'Prospect theory'. This showed that the decisions people make are not always rational or indeed optimal. The degree to which people take risks was shown to be influenced by the way in which choices are framed. This means that decisions are related to the context in which the choices are considered and decisions made. These were a complete contradiction to the rational-man perspective that classical economists had used to underpin their work.

Classical economics assumes rational decision-making and that, in general, markets and institutions are self-regulating. The collapse of the banks and much of the financial sector in 2008, however, casts serious doubt on the efficacy of this view. Behavioural economics, therefore, challenges the conventional view about the way people and organisations behave. Indeed, the central platform on which behavioural economics is constructed is behaviour. This moves advertising and marketing communications forward because the focus is no longer on attitudes, beliefs and opinions, USPs, or even on what people intend to do, but on how they behave, what they actually do. The utilisation of behavioural economics in advertising is reflected in the use of emotional content that seeks to embrace audiences and develop brand associations.

In order to change existing behaviours, or encourage new ones, people need to be presented with a choice that makes decision-making feel effortless, even automatic, or as Gordon (2011) puts it, 'a no-brainer'. Thaler and Sunstein (2008) refer to this as 'choice architecture'. This posits that there is no neutral way to present a choice. People choose according to what is available, not what they absolutely want. What is also important is that they do not expend much energy or thought when they make a choice, and they use *heuristics* or rules of thumb to assist them. As mentioned earlier, these heuristics are thought to be rooted in emotional drivers. See Viewpoint 5.4 for some examples of BE in action.

Scholars' paper 5.5
Behavioural economics gains traction

Tversky, A. and Kahneman, D. (1974) Judgment under uncertainty: heuristics and biases, *Science (New Series)*, 185, 1124–31.
Kahneman, D. and Tversky, A. (1979) Prospect theory: an analysis of decision under risk. *Econometrica*, 47, 263–91.

These papers represent an important step towards the establishment of behavioural economics. The authors demonstrate that decisions are not always optimal and that risk taking is influenced by the way choices are framed.

See also:

Thaler, R.H. (1990) Anomalies: saving, fungibility, and mental accounts, *The Journal of Economic Perspectives*, 4, 193–205.

Tversky, A. and Kahneman, D. (1981) The framing of decisions and the psychology of choice, *Science*, 211 (4481), 453–58.

Both Kooreman and Prast (2010) and Grapentine and Altman Weaver (2009) agree that people's behaviour is often not congruent with their intentions, that they are sensitive to the way choices are presented to them, and that they have limited cognitive abilities. However, not everyone agrees that BE is a good step forward. For example, Mitchell (2010) puts forward a number of doubts about the validity of the concept.

So, purchase decisions are not made deliberatively and consciously by evaluating all permutations and outcomes. Decisions are made around choices that are based on comparison, rather than absolutely. These decisions are based on what is available rather than scanning the whole market or options and, as Gordon says, in terms of 'how this makes me feel' both emotionally and instinctively, but not rationally.

One of the main areas in which behavioural economics impacts upon advertising and brand communications is choice architecture. Indeed, the Institute of Practitioners in Advertising (IPA, 2010) has embraced behavioural economics and observed its relevance to campaign planning, purchase decisions, brand experiences, how behaviour can be changed, and the way that choice works in complex situations. All of these can be reflected in the advertising and brand communications.

Viewpoint 5.4
BE drives action and behaviour

Image 5.5 Burnt clock used in a fire safety campaign

A print campaign that featured a single powerful image of a burnt clock in the context of a real home. The ad was designed to look as if it was forensic evidence retrieved from a home that had been on fire. The goal was to provide a visual stimulus between the need to change our clocks (twice a year) and the need to test smoke alarms
Source: Department for Communities and Local Government.

Various organisations have adopted behavioural economics, partly as a result of the IPA championing it through the provision of visibility, information and insight. Here are a few examples:

Fire safety – attitudes and intentions often have a very weak correlation to actual behaviour in real life. This can be seen when people say testing their smoke alarms is important, but in reality too many don't actually follow through and test. As a result over 100 people die in house fires in England each year, in dwellings where there was a non-working fire alarm.

There have been many previous attitudinal campaigns designed to encourage and motivate people to test their alarms. This campaign used the ideas of behavioural economics and focused on changing behaviour by decreasing the perceived effort required to test the alarms. The campaign nudged people into testing their smoke alarms by piggybacking on existing behaviours, namely the twice-yearly clock change.

Hyundai – consumer fear at the huge depreciation incurred when buying a new car prompted Hyundai into reframing the choice car buyers face. Instead of shying away from the issue, Hyundai offered new car buyers a guaranteed price for their car, valid for four years after purchase. Television advertising was used to communicate the deal and so reduce perceived risk.

Department of Health – advised the government, when developing the regulatory framework for e-cigarettes, that it is much easier to substitute a similar behaviour than to eliminate an entrenched one, such as smoking. By considering vaping devices as a positive means to help people quit smoking, there are now over 2.3 million people vaping.

Uber – on a more negative note, it has been reported that Uber has experimented with video game techniques, graphics and non-cash rewards of little value. The purpose was to nudge drivers into working longer and harder, and sometimes at hours and locations that are less lucrative for them. For example, Uber alerts drivers, when they try to log off, that they are very close to hitting an important target, to encourage them to stay on.

Sources: Gino (2017); Huntley and Hoad (2014); McCormick (2011); Partington (2017).

Insight

This Viewpoint hints at the breadth of ways and range of situations in which behavioural economics can be used. Decisions are made around choices that are based on comparison, rather than absolutely, and are based on what is available rather than scanning the whole market for options. The impact for marketing communications is enormous as it frames the ways in which people understand what is to be done, when and how.

Question: To what extent, and in which situations does classical economics have a role to play in contemporary marketing communications?

Task: Choose three product categories and make notes about the way BE might be applied to enhance communications.

Table 5.4 Elements of behavioural economics

BE element	Explanation
How	Helping people to make a decision by presenting easy methods can encourage action now, rather than in the future. For example, paying for tickets for a festival online is easier than being in a queue on the telephone. Schemes that require people to opt out are more likely to generate the desired behaviour, than requiring people to make the choice to opt in.
When	When required to do something disagreeable, people are more likely to delay making a decision or taking action – for example, to stop smoking, to complete an income tax return form, or start an essay.
Where	Although price and perceived value can be important, it can be location and convenience that shape a decision. Questions such as 'Do I have to go there to do this or should I do it here where it is convenient?' can often influence behaviour.
Availability	Items that appear to be scarce have a higher value than those items that are plentiful. For example, recorded music is abundant and virtually free, yet live music is relatively expensive, as it is scarce.
Price	The price of an item leads people to give it a value. So, people who pay more for a product/service often perceive increased benefit or gain. However, price needs to be contextualised and supported by other indicators of value.
Task duration	People prefer to complete parts of a task rather than try to finish in a single attempt. Therefore, the way a task is presented can influence the behaviour and the number of people completing the task. Filling in forms seems less daunting with the opportunity to save and return. Colour coding antibiotic pills might ensure more people complete the treatment and avoid repeat visits, further illness and lost days from work.

Sources: Based on Gordon (2011); IPA (2010).

To conclude this chapter we draw attention to the increasing use of behavioural economics within the public sector. A significant aspect of government activity is to manage or influence people's behaviour. Much of this has traditionally been implemented through legislation, regulation or taxation. However, new approaches are required to influence many of the new challenges facing government, such as those associated with chronic health conditions. This necessitates influencing people sufficiently so that they change their behaviour, their lifestyles or their existing habits.

The UK government published a report in 2010 designed to make this happen. The report helped to make the case for the establishment of the Behavioural Insights Team at the heart of the UK Government, and it continues to be used by the Behavioural Insights Team as a framework to aid the application of behavioural science to the policy-making process.

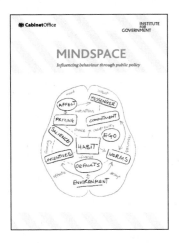

Image 5.6 The Cover of the
MINDSPACE Report
Source: The Institute for Government.

The report sets out nine of the most robust influences on our behaviour, which are captured in the simple mnemonic – MINDSPACE. The essence of these are described in Table 5.5.

These illustrate some of the main tools at the disposal of individuals and policy-makers in influencing behaviour. They are presented as the most robust effects that policy-makers should understand and, if appropriate, use. For an example of their application see the case study at the end of this chapter.

Table 5.5   The elements of MINDSPACE

Element	Explanation
Messenger	We are heavily influenced by who communicates information
Incentives	Our responses to incentives are shaped by predictable mental shortcuts, such as strongly avoiding losses
Norms	We are strongly influenced by what others do
Defaults	We go with the flow of pre-set options
Salience	Our attention is drawn to what is novel and seems relevant to us
Priming	Our acts are often influenced by sub-conscious cues
Affect	Our emotional associations can powerfully shape our actions
Commitments	We seek to be consistent with our public promises, and reciprocate acts
Ego	We act in ways that make us feel better about ourselves

Source: https://www.behaviouralinsights.co.uk/publications/mindspace/

Key points

- Consumers and organisational buyers experience risk when making purchasing decisions. This risk is perceived and concerns the uncertainty of the proposed purchase and the outcomes that will result from a decision to purchase a product. Five types of perceived risk can be identified. These are ego, social, physical, financial and performance risks.

- Individuals and groups make purchasing decisions on behalf of organisations. Different types of risk can be experienced, relating to a range of organisational and contextual issues. Marketing communications has an important task to reduce risk for consumers and organisational buyers.

- The growing use of mobile has had an enormous impact on behaviour and this has reshaped the way in which we communicate with brands and organisations and one another.

- Some of the key behaviours induced by the Internet and mobile technologies include constant referral as they are always on, a reduction in attention spans, an increase in the use of visual communications, dual (multi) screen usage, and a growth in user-generated content.

- Some products and services can evoke high levels of involvement based on the emotional impact that consumption provides the buyer. This is referred to as *hedonic consumption,* and refers to behaviour that relates to the multi-sensory, fantasy and emotive aspects of an individual's experience with products. *Historical imagery* and *fantasy imagery* are two aspects of hedonic consumption.

- Ethical consumption is considered to be the conscious and deliberate choice to make certain consumption choices due to personal and moral beliefs. There are four dimensions against which a number of ethical goods are positioned and have become integrated into mainstream consumption. These are distinction, hedonism, love and aesthetics.

- Tribes are loosely interconnected communities where bonding and linking represent key activities designed to retain tribal membership. Tribes serve to link people who share passions and interests and 'tribal consumption' refers to consumption of products and services, not for their utility value, or for the sense of individual identification. Their consumption is considered to be important for the 'linking value' they provide within a tribal network.

- Tribes proliferate on the Internet, thanks mainly to its power to aggregate communities who share similar interests. These e-tribes have the same characteristics as traditional communities, namely shared rituals and traditions, a similar consciousness of kind, and an obligation, or sense of duty, to the community and to its individual members.

- Behavioural economics is grounded in the belief that people make irrational rather than rational decisions and the central platform is about actual behaviour, not attitudes or opinions. People choose according to what is available, not what they absolutely want.

Help to Buy

Nudging aspiring homeowners to realise that Help to Buy was here to help

Image 5.7 The Help to Buy financial scheme was designed to help young people get into the UK housing market.
Source: Serhii Krot/Shutterstock.

In 2012 fewer homes were built in England than at any time since the 1920s, with just over 100,000 completed in the year compared to a projected requirement of 240,000. A lack of planning permission, the economic climate and issues surrounding the availability of mortgages were regarded as the key influences. In addition, many people aspiring to enter the UK housing market couldn't afford the required deposit for a mortgage, despite being able to afford the monthly repayments. This situation was not only a barrier to buying a house, but also stood in the way of social mobility.

It was clear the housing market was cyclical, developers weren't developing due to a number of factors, renters couldn't buy without more affordable deposits, and lenders wouldn't lend without a reduction in risk. It was time for state intervention to give the housing market and 'generation rent' a step up the property ladder.

The Help to Buy scheme

The government wanted to stimulate the new-build market and vowed to tackle this situation with two initiatives under their 'Help to Buy' umbrella brand, launched in 2013. Both were inclusively open to first-time buyers and existing homeowners looking to move on to a bigger place, and were available for as little as a 5 per cent deposit. The two schemes were as follows:

1. Help to Buy Equity Loans – a scheme that offered up to 20 per cent of the cost of a new-build home, only requiring a 5 per cent cash deposit and a 75 per cent mortgage to make up the rest.

Cova, B. and Cova, V. (2001) Tribal aspects of postmodern consumption research: the case of French in-line roller skaters, *Journal of Consumer Behaviour,* 1(1), 61–76.

Cova, B., Kozinets, R.V. and Shankar C.A. (2007) *Consumer Tribes,* Oxford: Butterworth-Heinemann.

Cox, D.F. and Rich, S.U. (1967) Perceived risk and consumer decision making – the case of telephone shopping, in *Consumer Behaviour* (ed. D.F. Cox) Boston, MA: Harvard University Press.

Crane, A. and Matten, D. (2003) *Business Ethics: A European Perspective, Managing Corporate Citizenship and Sustainability in the Age of Globalization,* Oxford University Press: Oxford.

Damasio, A.R. (1996) The somatic marker hypothesis and the possible functions of the prefrontal cortex, *Transactions of the Royal Society (London),* 351(1346), 1413–20.

Danaher, P.J. and Rossiter, J.R. (2009) Comparing perceptions of marketing communication channels, *European Journal of Marketing,* 45(1–2), 6–42.

Davies, I.A. and Gutsche, S. (2016) Consumer motivations for mainstream 'ethical' consumption, *European Journal of Marketing,* 50(7/8), 1326–47.

Dunn, L. and Hoegg, J. (2014) The impact of fear on emotional brand attachment, *Journal of Consumer Research,* 41 (June), 152–68.

Fried, M. (1963) Grieving for a lost home, in *The Urban Condition: People and Policy in the Metropolis* (ed. Leonard J. Duhl) New York: Basic Books, 151–71.

Gevelber, L. (2016) Mobile has changed search intent and how people get things done: new consumer behavior data, *Think with Google,* September, retrieved 8 August 2017 from https://www.thinkwithgoogle.com/consumer-insights/mobile-search-consumer-behavior-data/

Gino, F. (2017) Uber shows how not to apply behavioral economics, *Harvard Business Review,* 13 April, retrieved 20 October 2017 from https://hbr.org/2017/04/uber-shows-how-not-to-apply-behavioral-economics

Gordon, W. (2011) Behavioural economics and qualitative research – a marriage made in heaven? *International Journal of Market Research,* 53(2), 171–85.

Grapentine, T.H. and Altman Weaver, D. (2009) What really affects behaviour? *Marketing Research,* 21(4), Winter, 12–17.

Graves, S (2016) Location, location, location: why where you are is as important as the message, *Campaign,* 17 June, retrieved 8 August 2017 from http://www.campaignlive.co.uk/article/location-location-location-why-important-message/1399110#zbUl1YSkeFPBlMdM.99

Gummerus, J., Liljander, V. and Sihlman, R. (2017) Do ethical social media communities pay off? An exploratory study of the ability of Facebook ethical communities to strengthen consumers' ethical consumption behavior, *Journal of Business Ethics,* 144(3), 449–65.

Hamilton, K. and Hewer, P. (2010) Tribal mattering spaces: social-networking sites, celebrity affiliations, and tribal innovations, *Journal of Marketing Management,* 26(3–4), 271–89.

Havill, A.L. & Coelho, K. (2016) Kit-Kat: 72 different break types, WARC, retrieved 8 August 2017 from http://www.warc.com/Content/ContentViewer.aspx?MasterContentRef=b897e18c-4be9-49ae-bacb-fadb3da501d4&q=cross+channel&CID=A109014&PUB=WARC-AWARDS-MEDIA

Hirschman, E.C. and Holbrook, M.B. (1982) Hedonic consumption: emerging concepts, methods and propositions, *Journal of Marketing,* 46(3), 92–101.

Huntley, A. and Hoad, A. (2014) Fire safety – IPA effectiveness awards 2014, retrieved 15 January 2015 from www.ipa.co.uk/page/fire-safety-2014-ipa-effectiveness-awards-shortlist-interview\#.VLffpUesUh8

IPA (2010) *Behaviour Economics: Red Hot or Red Herring?* London: IPA.

Jenkins, H. (2006) *Fans, Bloggers and Gamers: Essays on Participatory Culture,* New York: New York University Press.

Kahneman, D. and Tversky, A. (1979) Prospect theory: an analysis of decision under risk, *Econometrica, 47,* 263–91.

Kent-Lemon, N. (2013) Researching implicit memory: get to the truth, *Admap,* May, retrieved 16 January 215 from www.warc.com/Content/ContentViewer.aspx?ID=dd4e fd93-d775-42b3-bcdb-569f914b74a7&MasterContentRef=dd4efd93-d775-42b3-bcdb-56 9f914b74a7&Campaign=admap_may13

Kim, S. and Kim, J. (2016) The influence of hedonic versus utilitarian consumption situations on the compromise effect, *Marketing Letters, 27,* 387–401.

Kingston, H. (2015) Using uncommon sense is the key to mobile advertising, *Campaign,* 8 December, retrieved 20 January 2018 from www.campaignlive.co.uk/article/1376073/ using-uncommon-sense-key-mobile-advertising#

Kooreman, P. and Prast, H. (2010) What does behavioural economics mean for policy? Challenges to savings and health policies in the Netherlands, *De Economist,* 158(2), June, 101–22.

Kozinets, R.V. (2008) e-Tribes and marketing: the revolutionary implications of online communities, Seminar presented at Edinburgh University Business School, 24 November 2008.

Kozinets, R.V., Hemetsberger, A. and Schau, H.J. (2008) The wisdom of crowds: collective innovation in the age of networked marketing, *Journal of Macromarketing,* 28(4), 339–54.

Kushwaha, G.S. and Agrawal, S.R. (2016) The impact of mobile marketing initiatives on customers' attitudes and behavioural outcomes, *Journal of Research in Interactive Marketing,* 10(3), 150–76.

Liaukonyte, J., Thales T, and Wilbur, K.C. (2015) Television advertising and online shopping, *Marketing Science,* 34(3), 311–30.

Liu, X., Burns, A.C. and Hou, Y. (2017) An investigation of brand-related user-generated content on Twitter, *Journal of Advertising,* 46(2), 236–47.

Liyakasa, K. (2017) Facebook faces challenges and opportunities with 'Watch', *adexchanger. com,* 11 August retrieved 18 August 2017 from https://adexchanger.com/digital-tv/ facebook-faces-challenges-opportunities-watch/

Maffesoli, M. (1996) *The Time of Tribes,* London: Sage.

Marshall, S.L.A. (1947) *Men Against Fire,* New York: Morrow.

Maziriri, T. and Chuchu, T. (2017) The conception of consumer perceived risk towards online purchases of apparel and an idiosyncratic scrutiny of perceived social risk: a review of literature, *International Review of Management and Marketing,* 7(3), 257–65.

McCormick, A. (2011) Behavioural economics: when push comes to nudge, *Marketing,* 19 May, retrieved 27 April 2012 from www.brandrepublic.com/features/1070184/ Behavioural-economics-When-push-comes-nudge/?DCMP=ILC-SEARCH

Mitchell, A. (2010) Behavioural economics has yet to deliver on its promise, *Marketing,* 15 September, 28–9.

Muniz, A.M. and O'Guinn, T.C. (2001) Brand community, *Journal of Consumer Research,* 27(4), 412–23.

Noyes, D. (2018) The top 20 valuable Facebook statistics, *Zephoria,* 4 January, retrieved 20 January 2018 from https://zephoria.com/top-15-valuable-facebook-statistics/

Ofcom (2016) *Adults' media use and attitudes,* retrieved 2 November 2016 from http:// stakeholders.ofcom.org.uk/binaries/research/media-literacy/adults-literacy-2016/2016-Adults-media-use-and-attitudes.pdf

Parrett, G. (2016) Smartphone ownership peaks as one in three check their phones in the middle of the night, Deloitte, 26 September, retrieved 20 January 2018 from https://www2.deloitte.com/uk/en/pages/press-releases/articles/smartphone-ownership-peaks.html

Partington, R. (2017) What is behavioural economics? *Guardian*, 9 October, retrieved 4 December 2017 from https://www.theguardian.com/world/2017/oct/09/what-is-behavioural-economics-richard-thaler-nobel-prize

Pham, M. (1998) Representativeness, relevance, and the use of feelings in decision making, *Journal of Consumer Research*, 25(2), 144–59.

Rawson, A., Duncan, E. and Jones, C. (2013) The truth about customer experience, *Harvard Business Review*, September, 90–98, retrieved 21 August 2014 from http://hbrorg/2013/09/the-truth-about-customer-experience/.

Russell, C.A., Russell, D., Morales, A. and Lehu, J-M. (2017) Hedonic contamination of entertainment: how exposure to advertising in movies and television taints subsequent entertainment experiences, *Journal of Advertising Research*, 57(1), March, 38–52.

Schultz, B. (2015) Not just millennials: consumers want experiences, not things, *AdAge*, 18 August, retrieved 20 January 2018 from http://adage.com/article/digitalnext/consumers-experiences-things/299994/

Segijn, C.M., Voorveld, H.A.M. and Smit, E.G. (2017) How related multiscreening could positively affect advertising outcomes, *Journal of Advertising*, 46(4), 455–72.

Szmigin, I., Carrigan, M. and O 'Loughlin, D.O. (2007) Integrating ethical brands into our consumption lives, *Brand Management*, 14(5), May, 396–409.

Settle, R.B. and Alreck, P. (1989) Reducing buyers' sense of risk, *Marketing Communications*, January, 34–40.

Sharma, A., Kumar, V. and Borah, S.B. (2017) Ritualization: a strategic tool to position brands in international markets, *Journal of International Marketing*, 25(2), 1–24.

Stone, R.N. and Gronhaug, K. (1993) Perceived risk: further considerations for the marketing discipline, *European Journal of Marketing*, 27(3), 39–50.

Strahilevitz, M. and Myers, J. (1998) Donations to charity as purchase incentives: how well they work may depend on what you are trying to sell, *Journal of Consumer Research*, 24(4), 434–46.

Thaler, R.H. (1990) Anomalies: saving, fungibility, and mental accounts, *The Journal of Economic Perspectives*, 4, 193–205.

Thaler, R. and Sunstein, C. (2008) *Nudge: Improving Decisions About Health, Wealth and Happiness*, New York: Yale University Press.

Turner, J. (2017) Online reviews are a five-star world of fakery, *The Times*, Saturday 9 December, 31.

Tversky, A. and Kahneman, D. (1974) Judgment under uncertainty: heuristics and biases, *Science* (New Series), 185, 1124–31.

Tversky, A. and Kahneman, D. (1981) The framing of decisions and the psychology of choice, *Science*, 211 (4481), 453–58.

Chapter 06

How does marketing communications work?

Any attempt to understand how marketing communications might work must be made with an understanding of actual consumer behaviour. However, the complexity and inherent contradictions associated with the rich mosaic of people's perceptions, emotions, attitudes, information and patterns of behaviour makes this important task challenging and, at times, inconclusive.

Aims and learning objectives

The aims of this chapter are to explore some of the theoretical concepts associated with ideas about how marketing communications might work and to consider the complexities associated with understanding how clients can best use marketing communications.

The learning objectives are to enable readers to:

1. explore ideas concerning engagement and the role of marketing communications;
2. explain how marketing communications works through sequential processing;
3. understand how marketing communications can be used to influence attitudes;
4. appraise the way relationships can be shaped through the use of marketing communications;
5. consider ways in which marketing communications might develop significant value;
6. examine the role marketing communications might play in helping people process information.

Introduction

All campaigns, regardless of purpose, use a range of tools, media and messages to achieve their objectives. Some are successful, some drive moderate performances, and some wither and are never seen again. What is not clear is just how these elements work together and how marketing communications might actually work.

This chapter explores this interesting topic, and introduces a number of concepts and frameworks that have contributed to our understanding. Ideas about how advertising works dominate the literature, whereas ideas about how marketing communications is thought to work appear to be of secondary importance, which is strange when so much energy is put into exploring integrated marketing communications. It is clear that there is no single, universally agreed explanation about how marketing communications works. This chapter therefore, presents a variety of explanations and interpretations about how marketing communications might work.

Engagement and the role of marketing communications

In Chapter 1 the term 'engagement' was introduced to explain the role of marketing communications. 'Engagement', rather like 'integrated marketing communications', is a term that is used regularly, yet inconsistently by commentators, journalists and academics. For example, engagement is referred to as customer engagement, consumer engagement and consumer brand engagement. In addition, we can observe the term being used within other disciplines, for example, social, employee, political and stakeholder engagement.

'Customer engagement' is normally considered to be a state of mind that refers to a post-consumption event and which spurs trust and word-of-mouth activity. What is agreed is that it is important to understand the different locations and channels where customers' engagement takes place (Braun et al., 2017).

In a communications context, which is often pre-consumption, engagement requires that there must first be some attention or awareness, be that overt or at a low level of processing. Engagement can be considered to consist of two main elements: intellectual and emotional (Thomson and Hecker, 2000). The intellectual element is concerned with audiences engaging with brand communications on the basis of processing rational, functional information. The emotional element is concerned with audiences engaging and aligning themselves with a brand's values on the basis of emotional and expressive information.

It follows that marketing communications should be based on the information-processing styles and needs of audiences, their preferred media and their likely purchase journeys. Effective communications reflect a suitable balance between the need for rational information to meet intellectual needs, and expressive types of communications to meet the emotional needs of different audiences. These ideas are important foundations and will be returned to later.

Brakus et al. (2009) refer to engagement as a form of (brand) experience. They believe engagement consists of two dimensions both evoked by brand-related stimuli, including the design, packaging, identity, communications and environment. One dimension concerns the sensations, feelings and cognitions experienced individually and subjectively as an internal response. The second concerns the behavioural responses the stimuli prompt. From this the primary role of marketing communications may be considered to be the engagement of audiences in one of two ways:

1. To drive a response to the message itself, often reflected in building awareness and brand associations, cultivating brand values or helping to position brands in markets, or the minds of people in target audiences. This can be considered to be a long-term or brand-building exercise (Binet and Field, 2013).

2. To drive a response to the brand itself. This might be to encourage clicks, likes, calls to a particular number, visits to a website, shop or showroom, or participation in a game, discount scheme or other form of entertainment. These requests within a message are referred to as a *call-to-action*. This can be considered to be a short-term or activation exercise (Binet and Field, 2013).

When engagement occurs an individual might be said to have been positively captivated, and as a result opportunities for further communications activity increase. Engagement not only involves attention-getting, awareness and involvement but it also encompasses the decoding and processing of information at a conscious or subconscious level, so that meaning can be attributed to a message, at an appropriate time.

Successful engagement suggests that understanding and meaning have been conveyed effectively. At one level, engagement through one-way communications enables target audiences to understand, for example, product and service offers, to the extent that the audience is sufficiently engaged to want further communications. This is what advertising does well. At another level, engagement through two-way, or interactive, communications enables information that is relationship-specific (Ballantyne, 2004) to be exchanged. Advertising is not always able to generate or sustain this frequency or type of information exchange so other elements of the communications mix are often used to support these relationship needs. See Viewpoint 6.1 for an example of how engagement can be generated.

Viewpoint 6.1
Engaging jacket potatoes
Rebecca Clay, Media Director at PHD

Image 6.1 McCain's ready baked jacket potatoes.
Source: Clynt Garnham Food & Drink/Alamy Stock Photo.

When McCain developed their innovative Ready Baked Jackets (RBJs) that cooked in five minutes in the microwave, their communications strategy had to generate awareness, stimulate trial and drive conversations. These three specific communications tasks were matched with paid, owned and earned media. Awareness and appetite appeal had a bias towards paid-for media, trial was matched with owned, and conversations utilised earned media.

A heavyweight TV campaign, and an extensive press and outdoor campaign were used to generate awareness. Engagement occurred when people were making their way home thinking about what to have for dinner. Over 20 large-format digital screens were switched on at 4 p.m. each evening across the campaign. TV spots were bought at 9 p.m., a time when people thought it too late to cook a potato for an hour in the oven.

A realistic fibreglass heated potato was built into bus shelters to warm up cold hands in a freezing February and to deliver the comforting warmth of a jacket potato. Consumers were able to collect a 50p-off coupon from bus shelters, at the press of a button, so they could try RBJs for themselves.

Owned media was used to drive the trial once people had been made aware of the product. A 'money-back guarantee' was issued across all product packaging. This meant that potential customers could be reassured that if they weren't satisfied with the product they wouldn't have to pay. An online display running across MSN and AOL networks drove traffic straight through to a sponsored section on mySupermarket.co.uk where consumers could purchase the product. Behaviourally targeted placements were activated when consumers were browsing products that are used as jacket potato toppings, such as grated cheese or baked beans.

Foodie and convenience food sceptics, some writing for national newspapers, became powerful advocates, once they had tasted the product. McCain also secured TV editorial, gaining further endorsement and advocacy from some of Britain's best-loved TV celebrities such as Matthew Wright on Channel 5's *The Wright Stuff*, and Holly Willoughby and Phillip Schofield on ITV's *This Morning*.

RBJs passed the Good Housekeeping Institute tests, and the GHI endorsement was used across all communications and packaging, lending an extra layer of credibility to the product. The Facebook brand page drove awareness, over 100,000 likes and, most importantly, it started and fuelled conversations from consumers about RBJs. Positive reviews of the new product were positioned so that they were the first thing visitors to the page would see.

This Viewpoint is based on a case study written by Rebecca Clay, when she was Media Director at PHD.

Insight

This extract demonstrates the variety of objectives that can be used by organisations. It should also be seen that different types of objectives are an integral part of a strategy and are used to shape, guide and measure the success of campaigns.

Question: How and when might consumers have been engaged by McCain's use of marketing communications?

Task: Make a list of other ways McCain might have engaged their audiences.

Ideas about engagement and relationships have been developed by Kozinets (2014). He refers to social brand engagement (SBE), where the relationship widens from person–brand to person–person–brand. He argues that brands are evolving into social brands, where SBE is regarded as 'meaningful connection, creation and communication between one consumer and one or more other consumers, using brand or brand-related language, images and meanings' (p. 10). He identifies four core strategies: customer care, co-creation, communing and listening, and communication and sharing. See Figure 6.1 and Scholars' paper 6. 2 for more information about these ideas.

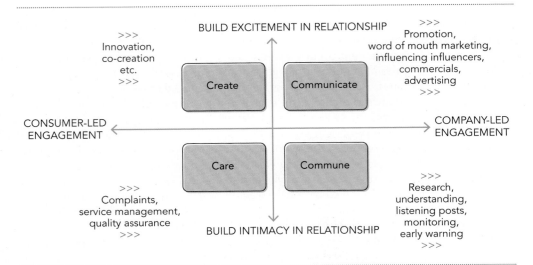

Figure 6.1 Strategies to leverage social brand engagement
Source: Kozinets (2014).

Schivinski et al. (2016) consider engagement within a social media context. Their interesting perspective considers three levels of engagement: consumption (of media content), contribution (sharing of content) and creation (the publication of brand-related content).

They define engagement within this context as 'A set of brand-related online activities on the part of the consumer that vary in the degree to which the consumer interacts with social media and engages in the consumption, contribution, and creation of media content' (p. 66). This is helpful as it serves to emphasise that engagement occurs at different stages and is not just about (brand) response.

Scholars' paper 6.1

And now for something completely different – social brand engagement

Kozinets, R.V. (2014) Social brand engagement: a new idea, *GfK Marketing Intelligence Review*, **6(2), November, 8–15.**

The author explores ideas about social brand engagement. He tracks the development and role of brands and how they now assume a social rather than just an individual role. This is an easily accessible conceptual consideration of what is an emerging topic.

See also:

Braun, C., Hadwich, K. and Bruhn, M. (2017) How do different types of customer engagement affect important relationship marketing outcomes? An empirical analysis, *Journal of Customer Behaviour*, 16(2), 111–44.

Scheinbaum, A.C. (2016) Digital engagement: opportunities and risks for sponsors, *Journal of Advertising Research*, December, 341–45.

How does marketing communications work?

The main thrust of this chapter is to consider how marketing communications works in order to achieve successful engagement. Despite years of research and speculation by a great many people, there is no single model that can be presented as the definitive way marketing communications works. From all the work undertaken in this area, however, mainly with regard to advertising, a number of views have been expressed, and the following sections attempt to present some of the more influential perspectives.

For a message to be communicated effectively, it should be meaningful (and of value) to the participants in the communications process. Messages need to be targeted at the right audience, be capable of gaining attention, and be understandable, relevant and acceptable. For effective communications to occur, messages should be designed that fit the context in which the messages are 'processed'.

Engagement can be encouraged by helping audiences to understand the essence of a message with minimal effort. This can be achieved through framing. Goffman (1974) refers to frames as mental brackets, lenses or picture frames, which serve to focus on a few salient dimensions within a message. These serve to structure communication and to simplify sensemaking (Giorgi and Weber, 2015), because any distracting or contradictory dimensions are eliminated so the focus is on the interpretation intended by the source. (See Chapter 19 for a more detailed consideration of framing.)

In terms of communication theory, framing assists the encoding and decoding process. On its own, however, framing does not explain how marketing communication works. In the sections that follow, a number of different interpretations about how marketing communications works are considered, each in a different context.

For an interpretation of how advertising might work, this chapter should be read in conjunction with Chapter 13. Here five different interpretations of how marketing communications is considered to work are presented (see Figure 6.2).

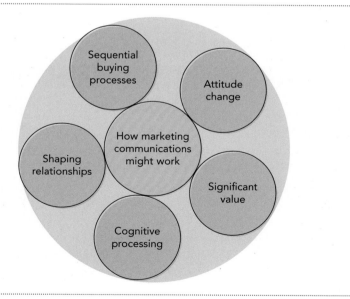

Figure 6.2 Five interpretations of how marketing communications works

HMCW interpretation 1: sequential models

Various models have been developed to assist our understanding of how communications tasks are segregated and organised effectively. Table 6.1 shows some of the better-known models. These models were developed primarily to explain how advertising worked. However, the principle of these hierarchical models also applies to marketing communications. The context for all of these sequential models is the general purchase process.

AIDA

Developed by Strong (1925), the AIDA model was designed to represent the stages that a salesperson must take a prospect through in the personal selling process. This model shows the prospect passing through successive stages of attention, interest, desire and action. This expression of the process was later adopted, very loosely, as the basic framework to explain how persuasive communications, and advertising in particular, was thought to work.

Hierarchy of effects models

An extension of the progressive, staged approach advocated by Strong emerged in the early 1960s. Developed most notably by Lavidge and Steiner (1961), the hierarchy of effects models represent the process by which advertising was thought to work and assume that there is a series of steps a prospect must pass through, in succession, from unawareness to actual purchase. Advertising, it is assumed, cannot induce immediate behavioural responses; rather, a series of mental effects must occur, with fulfilment at each stage necessary before progress to the next stage is possible.

The information-processing model

McGuire (1978) contends that the appropriate view of the receiver of persuasive advertising is as an information processor or cognitive problem-solver. This cognitive perspective becomes subsumed as the stages presented reflect similarities with the other hierarchical models, except that McGuire includes a retention stage. This refers to the ability of the receiver to understand and retain information that is valid and relevant. This is important,

Table 6.1   Sequential models of marketing communications

Stage	AIDA[a]	Hierarchy of effects[b]	Information processing[c]
		Awareness	Presentation ↓
Cognitive			Attention
		↓	↓
	Attention	Knowledge	Comprehension
	↓	↓	↓
	Interest	Liking	Yielding
		↓	
Affective		Preference	
	↓	↓	↓
	Desire	Conviction	Retention
Conative	↓	↓	↓
	Action	Purchase	Behaviour

Sources: [a]Strong (1925); [b]Lavidge and Steiner (1961); [c]McGuire (1978).

because it recognises that marketing communications messages are designed to provide information for use by a prospective buyer when a purchase decision is to be made at some time in the future.

Difficulties with the sequential approach

For a long time, the sequential approach was accepted as the model upon which advertising should be developed. Questions arose, however, about what actually constitutes adequate levels of awareness, comprehension and conviction, and how it can be determined which stage the majority of the target audience has reached at any one point in time.

The model is based on a logical and sequential movement of consumers towards a purchase via specified stages. The major criticism is that it assumes that the consumer moves through the stages in a logical, rational manner: learn, then feel and then do. This is obviously not the case, as anyone who has taken a child into a sweetshop can confirm. There has been a lot of research that attempts to offer an empirical validation for some of the hierarchy propositions, the results of which are inconclusive and at times ambiguous (Barry and Howard, 1990). Among these researchers is Palda (1966), who found that the learn–feel–do sequence cannot be upheld as a reflection of general buying behaviour and provided empirical data to reject the notion of sequential models as an interpretation of the way advertising works.

The sequential approach sees attitude towards the product as a prerequisite to purchase, but there is evidence that a positive attitude is not necessarily a good predictor of purchase behaviour. Ajzen and Fishbein (1980) found that what is more relevant is the relationship between attitude change and an individual's intention to act in a particular way. It seems therefore, reasonable to suggest that what is of potentially greater benefit is a specific measure of attitude *towards* purchasing or *intentions* to buy a specific product. Despite measurement difficulties, attitude change is considered a valid objective, particularly where there is high involvement.

All of these models share the similar view that the purchase decision process is one in which individuals move through a series of sequential stages. Each of the stages from the different models can be grouped in such a way that they are a representation of the three attitude components, these being cognitive (learn), affective (feel) and conative (do) orientations. This could be seen to reflect the various stages in the buying process, especially those that induce high involvement in the decision process but do not reflect the reality of low-involvement decisions.

Scholars' paper 6.2
Let's do it in sequence

Lavidge, R.J. and Steiner, G.A. (1961) A model for predictive measurements of advertising effectiveness, *Journal of Marketing*, 25(6), October, 59–62.

Published in the *Journal of Marketing* in 1961, this paper was pivotal in changing the way we considered that advertising works. Up until then advertising research and measurement was very much oriented to techniques and methods. This paper asked the question: what is advertising supposed to do and what function should it have? The answer was broadly that advertising should help consumers move through the various steps in the purchasing process. Lavidge and Steiner then made the link to the attitude construct, upon which much work has been done and so many ideas have subsequently emerged.

HMCW interpretation 2: changing attitudes

Attitude change has been regarded by many practitioners as the main way to influence audiences through marketing communications. Although it is recognised that product and service elements, pricing and channel decisions all play an important part in shaping the attitudes held, marketing communications has a pivotal role in conveying each of these aspects to the target audience and in listening to responses. Branding (Chapter 11) is a means by which attitudes can be established and maintained in a consistent way, and it is through the use of the communications mix that brand positions can be sustained. The final point that needs to be made is that there is a common thread between attributes, attitudes and positioning. Attributes provide a means of differentiation, and positions are shaped as a consequence of the attitudes that result from the way people interpret the associated marketing communications.

Environmental influences on the attitudes people hold towards particular products and services are a consequence of many factors. First, they are a reflection of the way different people interpret the marketing communications surrounding them. Second, they are an expression of their direct experience of using them and, third, they are the result of the informal messages and indirect messages received from family, friends and other highly credible sources of information. These all contribute to the way people perceive (and position) products and services and the feelings they have towards them and towards competing products. Managing brand attitudes is very important, and marketing communications plays an important part in changing or maintaining the attitudes held by a target audience. There are a number of ways in which attitude change can be implemented through marketing communications.

Influencing the components of the attitude construct

As outlined in Chapter 4, attitudes are made up of three components: cognitive, affective and conative. Marketing communications can be used to influence each of these elements, namely the way people think, feel or behave towards a brand.

Cognitive component

When audiences lack information, misunderstand a brand's attributes or when their perception of a brand is inappropriate, the essential task of marketing communications is to give the audience the correct or up-to-date information. This enables perception, learning and attitude development based on clear truths. This informational approach appeals to a person's ability to rationalise and process information in a logical manner. It is important that the level and quality of the information provided is appropriate to the intellectual capabilities of the target audience. Other tasks include showing the target audience how a brand differs from those of competitors, establishing what the added value is and suggesting who the target audience is by depicting its members in the message.

Both advertising and public relations are key tools, and the Internet, television and print are key media for delivering information and influencing the way people perceive a brand. Rather than provide information about a central or popular attribute of an offering, it is possible to direct the attention of an audience to different aspects of an object and so shape its beliefs about a brand in ways that are different to those of competitors. So, some crisp and snack food manufacturers used to communicate the importance of taste. Now in an age of increasing chronic obesity, many of these manufacturers have lowered the salt and fat content in their products and appeal to audiences on the basis of nutrition and health. They have changed the focus of attention from one attribute to another.

Although emotion can be used to provide information, the overriding approach is informational.

Scholars' paper 6.3
Do I really need to get your attention?

Heath, R. and Feldwick, P. (2008) 50 years using the wrong model of TV advertising, *International Journal of Market Research,* **50(1), 29–59.**

For several years Heath (and Feldwick) have challenged the dominance and pervasiveness of the information-processing approach and believe that attention is not necessary for ads to be effective. Readers should find this paper helpful because it sets out the arguments and history associated with information processing. The authors argue that people can be influenced by advertising, even when they cannot recall ads. Decision-making is founded on emotions triggered through associations made at subconscious levels.

Affective component

Rational, logical information may not be enough to stimulate behaviour, in which case marketing communications can be used to convey a set of emotional values that will appeal to and, hopefully, engage a target audience.

When attitudes to a brand or product category are discovered to be either neutral or negative, it is common for brands to use an emotional rather than rational or information-based approach. This can be achieved by using messages that are unusual in style, colour and tone and, because they stand out and get noticed, they can change the way people feel and their desire to be associated with that object, brand or product category. There is often great use of visual images and the appeal is often to an individual's senses, feelings and emotional disposition. The goal is to help people feel, 'I (we) like, I (we) desire (aspire to), I (we) want or I (we) belong to' whatever is being communicated. Establishing and maintaining positive feelings towards a brand can be achieved through reinforcement and to do this it is necessary to repeat the message at suitable intervals.

Creating positive attitudes used to be the sole preserve of advertising, but today a range of tools and media can be used. For example, product placement within films and music videos helps to show how a brand fits in with a desirable set of values and lifestyles. The use of music, characters that reflect the values of either the current target audience or an aspirational group, a tone of voice, colours, images and, increasingly, brand experience, all help to create a particular emotional disposition and understanding about what a brand represents or stands for.

Perhaps above all else, the use of celebrity endorsers is one of the main ways attitudes are developed. The role for marketing communications is to stimulate desire for the object by helping to make an association (celebrity and brand) which is based on an emotional disposition towards the celebrity. This approach focuses on changing attitudes to the communications (attitudes to the ad) rather than the offering. Fashion brands are often presented using a celebrity model and little or no text. The impact is visual, inviting the reader to make positive attitudes and associations with the brand and the endorser.

Marmite uses an emotional approach based on challenging audiences to decide whether they love or hate the unique taste. The government has used a variety of approaches to change peoples' attitude to drink driving, smoking, vaccinations, tax, pensions and the use of rear seat belts, to name but a few of their activities. The government will often use an information approach, but in some cases use an affective approach, based on dramatising the consequences of a particular behaviour to encourage people to change their attitudes and behaviour. The overriding strategy is therefore emotional.

Conative element

In some product categories people are said to be inert because they are comfortable with a current brand, have little reason to buy into a category, do not buy any brand or are just reluctant to change. In these situations, attitude change should be based on provoking behaviour. The growth and development of direct marketing, through both online and mobile-based communications, are based partly on the desire to encourage people to do something rather than undertake passive attitude change that does not necessarily result in action or a sale. Accordingly, a conative approach stimulates people to try, test, trial, visit (a showroom or website) a brand, usually free and often without overt commitment.

Sales promotion, personal selling and direct marketing are the key tools used to drive behavioural change. For example, sales promotions are geared to driving behaviour by getting people to try a brand, direct marketing seeks to encourage a response and hence engage in interaction, and salespeople will try to close a customer to get a sale. Advertising can be used to raise awareness and lead people to a store or website.

In addition to these approaches, experiential marketing has become increasingly popular, as it is believed that direct experience of touching, feeling or using a product helps establish positive values and develop commitment. For example, many car manufacturers offer opportunities to test-drive a car not only for a few hours but for several days. They have test circuits where drivers can spend time driving several different cars in the range across different terrains. The overriding strategy in this context is to provoke customers into action and to get them to experience the brand in use. See Viewpoint 6.2 to see how a range of tools and media were used to change attitudes towards the Fitbit brand.

Viewpoint 6.2

Changing attitudes through a fitness experience

Image 6.2 The Fitbit Fifty Challenge

A gruelling cycling and running event helped serious athletes change their attitudes to the Fitbit brand
Source: Freepik.com and dovla982/Shutterstock.

The market leader in the consumer activity tracking market is Fitbit. The brand's position in the performance training sector is not as strong, as Fitbit was not considered to be a leading brand for serious athletes. To help change these attitudes Fitbit had developed a new activity tracker, *Surge*. This is very different to Fitbit's other trackers, and most other fitness wristbands. The *Surge* features all the functions of the other Fitbits and adds many extra sports-related features. It was designed to look more watch-like than the other Fitbits.

The goal was to raise product awareness about *Surge*, to establish it as a major competitor to TomTom, Garmin and Polar devices, and to increase purchase consideration among the target audience. To achieve these goals it was necessary to change the attitudes held by serious athletes towards Fitbit.

The campaign strategy centred on creating an event around which *Surge* would be the sole featured activity tracker. To accomplish this a range of health and fitness titles were used to announce, inform and recruit participants for a 50-hour endurance cycling and running challenge. The route was a return trip from Buckingham Palace to Edinburgh Castle, something that had never previously been attempted.

The critically acclaimed technology website Alphr supported the event. Both video and written content about the Fitbit *Surge* was developed for print and online channels and deployed before, during and post-challenge. Social media platforms allowed participants to create organic and original content as the event unfolded.

Source: Anon (2016).

Journalists from the Dennis publishing house travelled with the athletes for the 800 miles to cover night and day shoots, capturing the on- and off-road struggle. A deal was also brokered with a local radio network and Olympian Greg Whyte reported on the event, gave fitness tips and encouraged locals to turn out and cheer on the teams.

Following the event, research found that 54 per cent of the audience had visited fitbit.com, 40 per cent of the audience had recommended Fitbit to someone else, 24 per cent planned to upgrade their fitness tracker, and three out of four considered Fitbit as the next brand purchase for wearable fitness tech.

Insight

Changing brand attitudes is a complex activity and cannot be achieved by simply using advertising and messaging. Fitbit used Dennis, a media company with a variety of magazine titles across a range of activities. The campaign featured experience marketing, radio, print and online media, public relations, advertising, website, user-generated content and the use of an opinion former, plus associated word-of-mouth communication.

Question: How does this campaign demonstrate how marketing communications can be used to change each of the three elements of the attitude construct?

Task: Make brief notes outlining other ways in which attitudes towards a brand of your choice might be changed.

HMCW interpretation 3: shaping relationships

So far in this chapter the way marketing communications might work has been considered in terms of progressing the buying process, and by changing or influencing attitudes. Here we explore ideas that marketing communications works by influencing relationships. To do this, we shall look first at ideas about the relationship lifecycle, and then consider how marketing communications can support an audience's preferred mode of exchange. The context for this approach is the buyer–seller relationship.

The customer relationship lifecycle

Customer relationships can be considered in terms of a series of relationship-development phases: customer acquisition, development, retention and decline. Collectively these are referred to as the *customer relationship lifecycle*. The duration and intensity of each relationship phase in the lifecycle will inevitably vary and it should be remembered that this representation is essentially idealistic. A customer relationship cycle is represented in Figure 6.3.

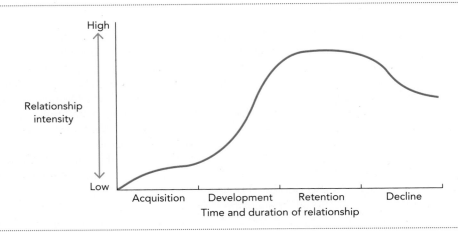

Figure 6.3 The customer relationship cycle

Table 6.2   Customer acquisition events

Acquisition event	Explanation
Search	Buyers and sellers search for a suitable pairing.
Initiation	Both parties seek out information about the other before any transaction occurs.
Familiarisation	The successful completion of the first transaction enables both parties to start revealing more information about themselves.

Marketing communications plays an important role throughout all stages of the customer lifecycle. Indeed, marketing communications should be used to engage with audiences according to each audience's relational needs, whether transactional and remote, or collaborative and close.

Customer acquisition

The acquisition phase is characterised by three main events: search, initiation and familiarisation. See Table 6.2.

The logical sequence of acquisition activities moves from search and verification through the establishment of credentials. The length of this initiation period will depend partly on the importance of the buying decision and the complexity of the products, and partly upon the nature of the introduction. If the parties are introduced by an established and trusted source, certain initiation rites can be shortened.

Once a transaction occurs, buyers and sellers start to become more familiar with each other and gradually begin to reveal more information about themselves. The seller receives payment, delivery and handling information about the buyer, and as a result is able to prepare customised outputs. The buyer is able to review the seller's products and experience the service quality of the seller.

During the acquisition phase, marketing communications needs to be geared towards creating awareness and providing access to the brand. Included within this period will be the need to help potential customers become familiar with the brand and to help them increase their understanding of the key attributes, possible benefits from use and to know how the brand is different from and represents value that is superior to the competition.

Customer development

The development phase is characterised by a seller attempting to reduce buyer risk and enhancing credibility. This is achieved by encouraging cross-selling. This involves a buyer consuming other products, increasing the volume of purchases, engaging buyers with other added-value services, and by varying delivery times and quantities. The buyer's acquiescence is dependent upon their specific needs and the degree to which the buyer wishes to become more involved and whether it is worth developing deeper relationships with the seller.

In order to reduce risk, a number of messages will need to be presented through marketing communications. Depending on the forms of risk that are present, marketing communications needs to engage by communicating messages concerning warranties and guarantees, finance schemes, third-party endorsements and satisfied customers, independent testing and favourable product performance reports, awards and the attainment of quality standards, membership of trade associations, delighted customers, growth and market share, new products, and alliances and partnerships, all of which have the potential to reduce risk and improve credibility.

Customer retention

The retention phase is the most profitable, where the greatest level of relationship value is experienced. The retention phase will generally last as long as both the buyer and seller are able to meet their individual and joint goals. If the relationship becomes more involved, greater levels of trust and commitment between the partners will allow for increased cross-buying and product experimentation and, for B2B relationships, joint projects and product development. The essence of relationship marketing is for organisations to identify a portfolio of customers with whom they wish to develop a range of relationships. This requires the ability to measure levels of retention and also to determine when resources are to be moved from acquisition to retention and back to acquisition activities.

The length of the retention phase will reflect the degree to which the marketing communications is truly interactional and based on dialogue. Messages need to be relational and reinforcing. Incentive schemes are used extensively in consumer markets as a way of retaining customers and minimising customer loss (or churn, defection or attrition).

Customer decline

Customer decline is concerned with the closure of a relationship. Termination may occur suddenly as a result of a serious problem or episode between the parties. The more likely process is that the buying organisation decides to reduce its reliance on the seller because its needs have changed, or an alternative supplier who offers superior value has been found. The buyer either formally notifies the established supplier or begins to reduce the frequency and duration of contact and moves business to other, competitive organisations.

The termination process, therefore, may be sharp and sudden, or slow and protracted. Marketing communications plays a minor role in the former but is more significant in the latter. During an extended termination, marketing communications, especially direct marketing in the form of web marketing, telemarketing and email, can be used to deliver orders and profits. These forms of communications are beneficial, because they allow for continued personal messages but do not incur the heavy costs associated with field selling (B2B) or advertising (B2C). Social media activity can be eased back to reflect the increasing lack of interaction.

This cycle of customer attraction (acquisition), development, retention and decline provides a customer- rather than a product-oriented approach to explaining how marketing communications might work. The car manufacturer Audi developed the Audi Customer Journey. This is used to chart the ownership cycle and then to superimpose optimised brand communications for each owner. This approach is reflected in Audi's loyalty rate, which has grown consistently since the 'Journey' was introduced.

Scholars' paper 6.4
Relationship-based communications

Grönroos, C. (2004) The relationship marketing process: communication, interaction, dialogue, value, *Journal of Business and Industrial Marketing,* **19(2), 99–113.**

This is a classic paper and one that all students of marketing communications should experience first-hand. Grönroos considers relationship marketing as a process and then explores ideas about planned and integrated marketing communications. He observes that, if the interaction and planned communications processes are successfully integrated and geared towards customers' value processes, a relationship dialogue may emerge. There are a large number of interesting issues in this paper.

See also:

Gummesson, E. (2017) From relationship marketing to total relationship marketing and beyond, *Journal of Services Marketing,* 31(1), 16–19.

Influencing value exchanges

In Chapter 1 reference was made to transactional (market) and collaborative exchanges. It is within this framework of different forms of exchange that ideas about how engagement might be established through a relationship marketing perspective are now considered.

A useful way of considering these types of exchanges is to see them at either end of a continuum, as set out in Figure 6.4. At one end of the continuum are transactional exchanges. These are characterised by short-term, commodity- or price-oriented exchanges, between buyers and sellers coming together for one-off exchanges independent of any other or subsequent exchanges. Both parties are motivated mainly by self-interest. Movement along the continuum represents increasingly valued relationships. Interactions between parties are closer, more frequent and stronger. The focus moves from initial attraction, to retention and to mutual understanding of each other's needs.

At the other end of the continuum is what Day (2000) refers to as *collaborative exchanges*. These are characterised by a long-term orientation, where there is complete

Image 6.3 Collaborative exchanges
Source: Kinga/Shutterstock.

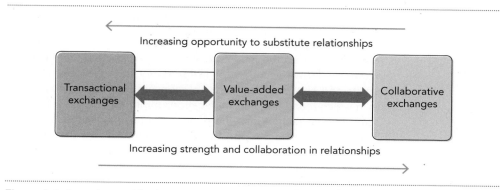

Figure 6.4 A continuum of value-oriented exchanges
Source: Adapted from Day (2000).

Table 6.3 The characteristics of transactional and collaborative exchanges

Attribute	Transactional exchange	Collaborative exchange
Length of relationship	Short-term – abrupt end	Long-term – a continuous process
Relational expectations	Conflicts of goals, immediate payment, no future problems (there is no future)	Conflicts of interest, deferred payment, future problems expected to be overcome by joint commitment
Communications	Low frequency of communications, formal, mass-media communications	Frequent communications, informal, personal, interactive communications
Cooperation	No joint cooperation	Joint cooperative projects
Responsibilities	Distinct responsibilities, defined obligations	Shared responsibilities, shared obligations

Source: From *Essentials of Marketing Communications,* Pearson Education (Fill, C. 2011) Table 8.1, p. 190.

integration of systems and processes and the relationship is motivated by partnership and mutual support. Trust and commitment underpin these relationships, and these variables become increasingly important as collaborative exchanges become established.

These two positions represent extremes. In the middle there are a range of exchanges where the interaction between customers and sellers is based around the provision and consumption of perceived value. The quality, duration and level of interdependence between buyers and sellers can vary considerably. The reasons for this variance are many and wide-ranging, but at the core are perceptions of shared values and the strength and permanence of any relationship that might exist.

Perceived value may take many forms and be rooted in a variety of attributes, combined in different ways to meet segment needs. However, the context in which an exchange occurs between a buyer and a seller provides a strong reflection of the nature of their relationship. If the exchange is focused on the product (and the price) then the exchange is considered to be essentially transactional. If the exchange is focused around the needs of customers and sellers, the exchange is considered to be collaborative. The differences between transactional and collaborative exchanges are set out in Table 6.3 and provide an important starting point in understanding the nature of relationship marketing.

Relationship marketing can be characterised by the frequency and intensity of the exchanges between buyers and sellers. As these exchanges become more frequent and more intense, so the strength of the relationship between buyer and seller improves. It is this that provided the infrastructure for a perspective on marketing which is based on relationships (Rowe and Barnes, 1998), rather than the objects of a transaction, namely products and services. Using this relationship framework, it is possible to superimpose ways in which marketing communications might be considered to work.

Transactional exchanges, where the relationship has little value for the buyer, and possibly the seller, are best supported with communications that do not seek to build a relationship but are generally oriented towards engaging through the provision of product and price (attribute-based) information. Communications are essentially a monologue as the buyer does not wish to respond, so the one-way or linear model of communications predominates. The communications might coincide with purchase cycles but are generally infrequent and regularised. These communications are one-sided, so an asymmetric pattern of communications emerges as they are driven by the seller. In many cases the identity of the buyer is unknown, so it is not possible to personalise messages and media channels and the largely informational messages are delivered through mass-communications media. These communications are formal and direct.

Collaborative exchanges, on the other hand, reflect the strong bond that exists between a buyer and a seller. Marketing communications, therefore, should seek to engage buyers by maintaining or strengthening the relationship. This means that communications patterns are irregular, informal, frequent and indirect. This is because buyers and sellers, working collaboratively, seek to provide mutual value. It means there are frequent interactions, often through dialogue, as one party responds to the other when discussing and resolving issues and challenges. The communications flow is symmetrical, messages are indirect and personalised as the identities are known. See Figure 6.5 for a visual interpretation of this spectrum and Table 6.4 for an explanation of the terms used.

Key to these ideas is the notion of dialogue. The adoption of dialogue as the basis for communications changes an organisation's perspective of its audiences and signals a transition from transactional relationships. Being willing and able to enter into a dialogue indicates that there is a new emphasis on the relationships organisations hold with their stakeholders. Kent and Taylor (2002) argue that there are five main features of a dialogical orientation. These are presented in Table 6.5 where it can be seen that many aspects of dialogue require interaction as a precursor. In other words, for dialogue to occur there must first be interaction and it is the development and depth of the interaction that leads to meaningful dialogue.

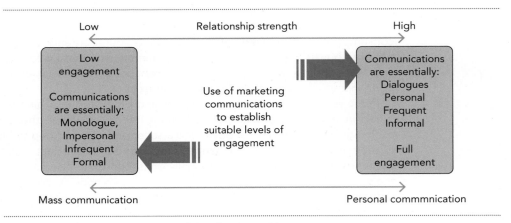

Figure 6.5 Achieving engagement through relationships

Table 6.4   Elements of relational marketing communications

Elements	Explanation	Transactional exchanges	Collaborative exchanges
Content	The extent to which the content of the message is intended to change behaviour (direct) or attitudes and beliefs (indirect)	Direct	Indirect
Formality	The extent to which communications are structured and routinised (formal) or spontaneous and irregular (informal)	Formal	Informal
Individuality	The extent to which recipients are identified by name	Impersonal	Personal
Frequency	How often do communications events occur?	Infrequent	Frequent
Audience	The size of the target audience for a communications event	Mass	Personal
Interaction	The level of feedback allowed or expected	Monologue	Dialogue

Source: Based on Mohr and Nevin (1990).

Table 6.5   The five features of a dialogical orientation

Role	Explanation
Mutuality	The recognition of the presence of organisational stakeholder relationships
Propinquity	The temporality and spontaneity of organisation–stakeholder interactions
Empathy	Support for stakeholder interests and their goals
Risk	Willingness to interact with others on their terms
Commitment	The extent to which an organisation actually interprets, listens to and practises dialogical communications

Source: Kent and Taylor (2002). Used with permission.

A word of caution is necessary, however, as not everyone believes relationship marketing is an outright success. For example, Rapacz et al. (2008: 22) suggest that relationship marketing has become 'stuck in a rut'. They argue that audits of the relationship marketing practices used to support many leading brands indicate that relationship marketing is not working. The goal, Rapacz et al. suggest, should be commitment to the brand rather than the relationship itself. They refer to the over-promise of one-to-one marketing, the difficulties and inefficiencies associated with databases and CRM technology, and to issues

Viewpoint 6.3
Fujitsu build relationships through collaboration

Fujitsu's main business is the manufacture of computing products. It operates a key accounts division but often assumed a secondary role within the relationship with the client. A growth opportunity was spotted by changing this into a relationship of equals, partly by presenting itself as an innovative and agile digital partner. The strategy was built on using its technologies to deliver business benefits. So, rather than just 'sell to', Fujitsu sought to change the relationship to one that was based on 'sell through' and 'sell with'.

Fujitsu's Alliance Programme (AP) started informally when, as a supplier with no real presence to a large logistics firm, they created a small campaign 'Fresh thinking to unlock value'. The idea was to show the logistics company the potential that existed if the two companies worked together, especially if the sales and marketing teams operated as an integrated unit.

The outcome was that Fujitsu and the logistics business co-created several market-changing products in just 18 months. The marketing support focused on generating a single set of integrated communications that delivered consistent messages exploring business benefits first, and then technology solutions.

The logistics client ran a health and safety programme, which included their 'Driver drowsiness' project. This features a FEELythm collar, which monitors the driver's heart rate and vibrates when drowsiness is detected, alerting the driver in the process. Fujitsu created a series of videos featuring ordinary drivers, not company executives, discussing the project features. Posters were created using stills from the videos,

underlining the collaboration between the two companies. The logistics company reused this material in a poster campaign aimed at its own staff. Social media enabled frequent conversations not only within the partnership but as a means of developing relationships with clients as projects unfolded.

Other projects included one that introduced a new process for the replenishment of duty-free flight trolleys, removing 20 per cent of human capital costs. Another was a technology solution that detected potential collisions between workers and forklift trucks in warehouses.

This partnership alone resulted in £16 million worth of UK contracts, and €55 million worth of contracts closed across the region, which includes Europe, the Middle East, India and Asia (EMEIA).

Fujitsu have since developed this concept into a formal AP and have successfully changed the relationship with many of its existing client–supplier deals. The AP aims to build long-lasting sustainable partnerships, in order to create opportunities for both parties to access new markets, increase market presence and win joint customers.

Source: Anon (2017).

Insight

Although this example considers collaboration at a corporate level, the principle of working together and building a relationship to achieve marketing goals still applies. The use of frequent, informal messages within a dialogue-based framework typifies many of the attributes associated with relational based communications.

Question: Discuss the ways in which the Fujitsu AP-based campaigns worked in order to develop relationships.

Task: Find two other campaigns and list three elements that demonstrate the development of relationships.

concerning loyalty programmes. The result of their critique is that they advocate the use of a variety of marketing communications techniques to generate increased brand commitment. They use the Jack Daniel's brand and their use of storytelling, to make their point about good practice. If communications are disciplined, entertaining, benefit-oriented and multifaceted, there will be greater commitment to a brand.

Ideas about how marketing communications works must be founded, in part, on the notion and significance of the level of interaction and dialogue that the organisation and its stakeholders desire. One-way communications, as reflected in traditional, planned, mass-media-based communications, still play a significant role, especially for audiences who prefer transactional exchanges. Two-way communications based on interaction with audiences who desire continuing contact, or dialogue for those who desire a deeper, more meaningful relationship, will form an increasingly important aspect of marketing communications strategy in the future.

HMCW interpretation 4: developing significant value

Marketing communications involves utilising a set of tools and media to convey messages to, with and among audiences. Depending upon the context in which a message is created, delivered and interpreted, a brand and the individual have an opportunity to interact. Marketing communications messages normally pass individuals unobserved. Those that are remembered contain particular characteristics (Brown, 1991; Fletcher, 1994). These would appear to be that the offering must be different or new, that the way the content (of a message) is executed is different or interesting, and that it proclaims something that is personally significant to the recipient in their current context.

The term 'significance' means that the content is meaningful, relevant (e.g. the individual is actually looking to buy a new car or breakfast cereals tomorrow or is planning to gather information on a new project) and is perceived to be suitably credible. These three characteristics can be tracked from the concept of ad likeability, considered in Chapter 10, which many researchers believe is the only meaningful indicator of the effectiveness of an advertisement.

To be successful, therefore, it is necessary for marketing communications messages to:

- present an offering that is new to the receiver;
- be interesting and stimulating;
- be personally significant.

The object referred to in the first element refers to both products and services (or an offering that is substantially different from others in the category) and to organisations as brands. The net effect of all these characteristics might be that any one message may be *significantly valuable* to an individual.

Content that announces new brands or new attributes may convey information that is perceived to be significantly different. As a result, individuals may be intrigued and interested enough to want to try the brand at the next purchase opportunity. For these people there is a high level of personal relevance derived from the message, and attitude change can be induced to convince them that it is right to make a purchase. For them the message is significantly valuable and as a result may well generate a purchase decision, which will, from a market perspective, drive a discernible sales increase.

The vast majority of marketing communications, however, are about offerings that are not new or that are unable to proclaim or offer anything substantially different. The content of these messages is either ignored or, if interest is aroused, certain parts of the message are filed away in memory for use at a later date. The question is: if parts are filed away, which parts are filed and why and how are they retrieved?

Marketing communications can provide a rationale or explanation for why individuals (cognitive processors) have bought a brand and why they should continue buying it. Normally, advertising alone does not persuade, it simply reminds and reassures individuals. To put it another way, individuals use advertising and public relations to remind themselves of preferred brands or to reassure themselves of their previous (and hence correct) purchase behaviour. Sales promotions, personal selling and direct marketing are then used by organisations to help consumers behave in particular ways.

Consumers, particularly in fast-moving consumer goods (FMCG) markets, practise repertoire buying based on habit, security, speed of decision-making and, to some extent, self-expression. The brands present in any single individual repertoire normally provide interest and satisfaction. Indeed, advertising needs to ensure that the brand remains in the repertoire or is sufficiently interesting to the individual that it is included in a future repertoire. Just consider the variety of messages used by mobile phone operators. These are continually updated and refreshed using particular themes, all of which are intended to be visually and cognitively engaging.

We know that messages have two main elements, an informational and an emotional component, and that each message should balance these elements according to the prevailing context of the target audience. Marketing communications that delivers significant value, therefore, can be considered to have either informational content or emotional content that is of value.

Significant value – informational content

Messages that consistently deliver relevant and meaningful content are considered to have a positive and cumulative influence on purchase decision-making. This understanding has given rise to the contemporary practice called '*content marketing*'. The Content Marketing Institute advises that the purpose is to attract and retain customers by consistently 'creating and curating relevant and valuable content with the intention of changing or enhancing consumer behavior' (CMI, 2015), and that its focus is on owned, not paid-for, media. Content marketing is concerned with delivering information that consistently informs and boosts an audience's knowledge. The rise in popularity of customer magazines is a reflection of the growth in content marketing.

Content enables positioning and provides a means by which individuals perceive value. For example, Netflix used to be a platform through which people could watch television programmes and films. This model was easily imitated by others. The solution was to create original content that was only available through Netflix, such as *House of Cards*, its first, and more recently *A Series of Unfortunate Events* and *The Crown*. The result was that people chose Netflix over its competitors because the content represented significant value (Clark, 2015). Netflix builds on the perceived value using data to promote its

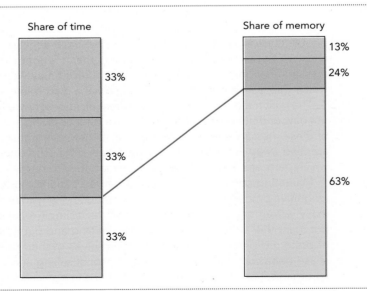

Figure 6.6 The creative magnifier
Source: From Brown (1991). Used with kind permission.

core content. For example, before a series of *House of Cards* was released, one or two trailers were made to build the buzz. Netflix made 10 different cuts of a trailer and served individuals, through social media, a trailer that was compatible with their previous viewing behaviour (Williams, 2017).

Significant value – emotional content

Messages, in particular advertising messages that are interesting, immediately relevant or interpreted as possessing a deep set of personal meanings (all subsequently referred to as 'likeable' (see Chapter 13)), are stored in long-term memory.

Research shows repeatedly that only parts of an advertisement are ever remembered – those parts that are of intrinsic value to the recipient and are sometimes referred to as 'the take-out'. Brown (1991) refers to this selectivity as the creative magnifier effect. Figure 6.6 illustrates the effect that parts of a message might have on the way a message is remembered.

Image 6.4 The Andrex puppy

The Andrex puppy was probably of significant value, as it may have been the key element that audiences took away from the Andrex ads
Source: Justin Kase z12z/Alamy Stock Photo.

The implication of this is that messages work best through the creation of emotional interest and likeable moments, from which extracts are taken by individuals and stored away in memory. It might also be reasonable to suggest that the other elements of the mix are also capable of enabling individuals to take extracts. For example, the size of a sales promotion offer, or the tone of a sales presentation, the professionalism of a direct mail piece or the immediacy of an online promotion might all give due reason for an individual to generate a take-out. Interest is generated through fresh, relevant ideas where the brand and the messages are linked together in a meaningful and relevant way. This in turn allows for future associations to be made, linking brands and marketing communications messages in a positive and experiential way.

Marketing communications is used to trigger emotionally based brand associations and experiences for people, not only when seated in front of a television, or with a tablet or laptop, or when reading a magazine, text or mobile messages, but also when faced with purchase decisions. Of all low-value FMCG decisions 70 per cent are said to be made at the point of purchase. All forms of marketing communications, but principally advertising, can be used to generate brand associations, which in turn are used to trigger advertising messages or, rather, 'likeable' extracts.

Viewpoint 6.4
The 'hook story' drives significant value

Image 6.5 Home scene from a 'Wonderful Everyday' IKEA ad
Source: © Inter IKEA Systems B.V.

When IKEA UK addressed the issues surrounding the weakness of their brand it was a designer who prompted thought about the practicalities of home life. These were then developed into a brand strategy called 'Wonderful Everyday', more of which can be seen in Viewpoint 12.4. The following represents the agency's thinking about how the idea about 'The Hook' emerged.

'Wrestling kids into their outdoor clothes every morning takes time and causes arguments. However, in Sweden, the challenge is compounded by the fact that harsh winters mean layer upon layer of snowsuits, hats, gloves, scarves and thick boots. Every snowy day brings tears and tantrums when it's time to get dressed to go out.

In Älmhult, an IKEA designer explained that the solution to these daily arguments was a simple coat hook. Not a special coat hook, just a standard, run-of-the-mill coat hook that costs about €1.

The secret? Simply putting the coat hook at your child's height. This way they can be like mummy or daddy, they can take their clothes from their own hook and get dressed for themselves.

With the kids now keen to get dressed for themselves, the process of leaving the house in winter becomes quicker and much less fraught. This not only stops arguments and tantrums, but also gives you 10 more minutes in the morning to enjoy together.

All of a sudden, this wasn't just a coat hook after all.'

This hook can be considered to be of significant value to audiences. This inspiration led to a series of campaigns that helped re-establish the brand in the UK. This, it can be argued, was because the ads provided audiences with something that was significant to them, such as a stress-free home life, happy children/families, memorable events, even fantasies. There is one particular event or scene, in each ad, that audiences magnify and remember disproportionately to the other elements that make up each of the ads.

Sources: Gianatasio (2016); Stewart (2017); Tiersen and Mackay (2017).

Insight

The principle of significant value is based on the notion that people magnify a single pleasurable element from an ad and store this as a link to the brand in their memories. Here significant value could be attributed to the scene where the child gets their own coat and the family harmony is maintained. Associations are then made between this emotional and pleasurable scene and IKEA.

Question: How might the success of ads be evaluated in the light of the significant value criteria?

Task: View three different ads from 'Wonderful Everyday' and determine the elements that might represent significant value. What is common among these elements?

The brand, its packaging, sales promotion, interactive media, point of purchase, outdoor media and, increasingly, social media, all have an important role to play in providing consistency and interest, prompting recall and recognition. Integrated marketing communications is important, not just for message take-out or likeable extracts, but also for triggering recall and recognition and stimulating relevant brand associations.

Content delivered through pertinent and relevant information, or as a result of what individuals take out emotionally from an advertisement, represents significant value. Marketing communications, therefore, can be considered to work by delivering either significant information or emotional take-outs that are relevant and meaningful.

HMCW interpretation 5: cognitive processing

Reference has already been made to whether buyers actively or passively process information. In an attempt to understand how information is used, cognitive processing tries to determine 'how external information is transformed into meanings or patterns of thought and how these meanings are combined to form judgments' (Olsen and Peter, 1987).

By assessing the thoughts (cognitive processes) that occur to people as they read, view or hear a message, an understanding of their interpretation of a message can be gained, which is useful in campaign development and evaluation (Greenwald, 1968; Wright, 1973). These thoughts are usually measured by asking consumers to write down or verbally report the thoughts they have in response to such a message. Thoughts are believed to be a reflection of the cognitive processes or responses that receivers experience and they help shape or reject communications.

Researchers have identified three types of cognitive response and have determined how these relate to attitudes and intentions. Figure 6.7 shows these three types of response, but readers should appreciate that these types are not discrete; they overlap each other and blend together, often invisibly.

Product/message thoughts

These are thoughts that are directed to the product or communications. Much attention has been focused on the thoughts that are related to the message content. Two particular types of response have been considered: counter-arguments and support arguments.

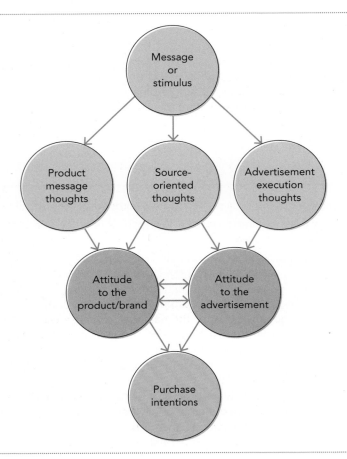

Figure 6.7 A model of cognitive processing
Source: Lutz et al. (1983).

A counter-argument occurs when the receiver disagrees with the content of a message. According to Belch and Belch (2004):

> The likelihood of counter-argument is greater when the message makes claims that oppose the beliefs or perceptions held by the receiver. Not surprisingly, the greater the degree of counter-argument, the less likely the message will be accepted. Conversely, support-arguments reflect acceptance and concurrence with a message. Support-arguments, therefore, are positively related to message acceptance.

Advertisements and general communications should encourage the generation of support arguments.

Source-oriented thoughts

A further set of cognitive responses is aimed at the source of the communications. This concept is closely allied to that of source credibility, where, if the source of the message is seen as annoying or untrustworthy, there is a lower probability of message acceptance. Such a situation is referred to as *source derogation*, the converse as a *source bolster*. Those responsible for communications should ensure, during the context analysis (see Chapter 7), that receivers experience bolster effects to improve the likelihood of message acceptance.

Message-execution thoughts

This relates to the thoughts an individual may have about the overall design and impact of the message. Many of the thoughts that receivers have are not always product-related but are related emotionally to the message itself. Understanding these feelings and emotions is important because of their impact upon attitudes towards the message, most often an advertisement, and the offering.

Attitudes towards the message

It is clear that people make judgements about the quality of commercial communications. These include advertisements, their creativity, the tone and style in which they or the website, promotion or direct mail piece have been executed. As a result of their experiences, perceptions and the degree to which they like a message, people form an attitude towards the message itself. From this base an important stream of thought has developed about cognitive processing.

Lutz's work led to the attitude-towards-the-ad concept, which has become an important foundation for much of the related marketing communications literature. As Goldsmith and Lafferty (2002: 319) argue, there is a substantial amount of research that clearly indicates that advertising that promotes a 'positive emotional response of liking an ad is positively related to subsequent brand-related cognitions (knowledge), brand attitudes and purchase intentions'. Similar work by Chen and Wells (1999) shows that this attitude-towards-the-ad concept applies equally well with various digital media and e-commerce in particular. They refer to an attitude-towards-the-site concept and similar ideas developed by Bruner and Kumar (2000) conclude that the more a website is liked, so attitudes improve towards the brand and purchase intentions. A word of caution, however, is required. Rossiter and Percy (2013) dismiss the attitude-to-the-ad concept as an irrelevant mediator of advertising effectiveness.

Despite this view the overwhelming evidence makes it seem highly reasonable therefore, to conclude that attitudes-towards-the-message (and delivery mechanism) impact on brand attitudes, which in turn influence consumers' propensity to purchase. It is also known that an increasing proportion of advertisements attempt to appeal to feelings and emotions, simply because many researchers believe that attitudes towards both the advertisement and the product should be encouraged and are positively correlated with purchase intention. Similarly, time and effort are invested in the design of sales promotion instruments, increasing attention is given to the design of packaging in terms of a pack's communications effectiveness, and care is taken about the wording in advertorials and press releases. Perhaps above all else, more and more effort is being made to research and develop websites with the goal of designing them so that they are strategically compatible, user-friendly and functional, or to put it another way – liked.

Low attention processing

Just as a word of caution was offered with regard to the continuum of marketing relationships, so an alternative view needs to be mentioned with regard to cognitive processing. The cognitive processing model assumes that people attend to and process information in a logical rational way. Sometimes referred to as the 'information processing (IP)' model, the approach assumes that messages are processed and stored in memory, and later retrieved and updated. (See Chapter 4 for more information on this topic.)

This processing approach is related to both informational and emotional messages. The latter were considered to be a consequence of people's thoughts and that by understanding what we think then we can understand everything (Heath and Hyder, 2005). Unfortunately psychologists such as Zajonc (1980) and Damasio (2000) upset this thinking, because their research showed that this was the wrong way round and that it was feelings and emotions (affect) that shaped our thoughts, at all times. This meant that advertising might be effective through mere exposure, rather than having to attend to, and cognitively process, a message.

In 2001 Heath published his 'Low Attention Processing Model', previously referred to as the Low *Involvement* Processing Model. The core characteristics of the Low Attention Processing (LAP) Model are summarised by Heath and Hyder in Table 6.6.

The prevailing view is that messages need only be seen, that is attended to, just once or twice. This is known as *high-attention processing* (HAP). What the LAP model says is that advertising can exploit low-attention processing when an individual is able to see the ad several times. The argument, based around empirical research, is that advertising messages can be processed with low attention levels. Typically, people watch television passively (Krugman, 1965) and today many multitask with other media, so their attention to ads can be extremely low. As a result, people may not have any conscious recall of 'receiving' a message yet make decisions based on the emotions and the associations made at a low level of consciousness. According to Heath and Feldwick (2008), ad messages do not necessarily need to create impact and they do not need to deliver a proposition or functional benefit. What is important is that a creative 'influences emotions and brand relationships' (p. 45).

If this view is accepted then cognitive processing does not explain how marketing communications works, or at least diminishes the power of the conventional view that advertising works through information processing.

Cognitive styles

Unsurprisingly, individuals do not share the same way of processing information. Referred to as brain lateralisation theory, various studies have demonstrated that the left side of the brain tends to specialise in rational, analytic and sequential information processing. The right side specialises in visual, intuitive and simultaneous information processing (Armstrong, 1999).

The term 'cognitive styles' is given to the different ways people receive, organise and process information (Messick, 1972). In effect, 'cognitive styles' refers to the differences in the way groups of people consistently 'perceive, think, solve problems, learn, take decisions and relate to others' (Witkin et al., 1977). The dominant style is stable through time and contexts, and importantly is independent of an individual's level of intelligence (Vinitzky and Mazursky, 2011).

Table 6.6 Core characteristics of the Low Attention Processing Model

Characteristic	Explanation
Intuitive choice	Intuitive decision-making is more common than considered choice, so emotions will be more influential.
Information acquisition	Intuitive decision-making dampens information seeking and minimises the need to attend to ads.
Passive and implicit learning	Brand information is acquired through low level of attention by passive learning and implicit learning.
Enduring associations	Associations are developed and reinforced through time and linked to the brand through passive learning. These associations can activate emotional markers, which in turn influence decision-making.
Semi-automatic	Learning occurs semi-automatically, regardless of the level of attention paid.

Source: Heath and Hyder (2005).

Understanding cognitive styles is important for many disciplines because they influence the way individuals behave. In marketing, insight into cognitive styles is important particularly for multinational organisations. This is because matching advertising formats to consumers' style (analytical versus imagery) improves advertising performance (Thompson and Hamilton, 2006). Comparative-style ads were shown to be more effective when consumers used analytical processing, whereas non-comparative ads were more effective when consumers used imagery processing (Armstrong et al., 2012). For example, research cited by Cuia et al. (2013: 17) has found that East Asians emphasise right-brain processing as more receptive to transformational or symbolic advertising. Westerners tend to emphasise left-brain processing and as a result informational advertising is more effective (Chan, 1996).

The principles of cognitive style have been distilled into a 'thinking and feeling' dimension and used to shape advertising strategy. (These are explored in Chapter 13.)

Comment

In this chapter, five different interpretations about how marketing communications might work have been considered. None of them are completely wrong or completely right. Indeed, it is safe to conclude that marketing communications works in different ways in different contexts, and that traces of several of these interpretations can be found in most campaigns.

For example, the sequential interpretation includes the principle of attitude change, while some would argue that cognitive processing underpins all of these approaches. Some of these approaches evolved in the pre-digital era and, therefore, it might be unsafe to suggest that they are equally applicable or relevant today. For example, it could be argued that marketing communications needs to include more emphasis on listening to audiences, customers and tribes in social networks, yet this aspect is not explicit in any of the models presented here.

Scholars' paper 6.5

B2B communications: models, interactivity and social media

Gilliland, D.I. and Johnston, W.J. (1997) Towards a model of marketing communications effects, *Industrial Marketing Management*, 26, 15–29.

This paper provides a useful counterbalance to the wealth of consumer-oriented papers about marketing communications. As the title describes, the authors develop a well-respected model that explains how marketing communications works in a business-to-business context.

See also:

Murphy, M. and Sashi, C.M. (2018) Communication, interactivity, and satisfaction in B2B relationships, *Industrial Marketing Management*, 68, January, 1–12.

Andersson, S. and Wikström, N. (2017) Why and how are social media used in a B2B context, and which stakeholders are involved? *Journal of Business & Industrial Marketing*, 32(8), 1098–1108.

Key points

- Marketing communications should be used to complement an organisation's marketing, business and corporate strategies. Such harmonisation serves to reinforce core messages, reflect the mission and provide a means of using resources efficiently yet at the same time reinforce the business strategy.

- The primary role of marketing communications is to engage audiences by either driving a response to the message itself, or encouraging a response to the brand itself, referred to as a *call-to-action*.

- There are five main ways in which marketing communications can be considered to work. These are the sequential buying process, attitude change, shaping relationships, developing significant value and cognitive processing.

- The sequential approach assumes that marketing communications needs to take consumers through the decision-making process in a series of logical steps.

- Attitude change has been regarded by many as the main way to influence audiences through marketing communications. Marketing communications can be used to focus one of the three elements of the attitudinal construct: that is, the cognitive, affective or conative component.

- Relationship marketing can be characterised by the frequency and intensity of the exchanges between buyers and sellers. As these exchanges become more frequent and more intense, so the strength of the relationship between a consumer and a brand improves.

- Customer relationships can be considered in terms of a series of development phases: customer acquisition, development, retention and decline. Collectively these are referred to as the *customer relationship lifecycle*. The duration and intensity of each phase in the lifecycle vary.

- Marketing communications is used to trigger brand associations and experiences for people.

- Those messages that are remembered contain particular characteristics. These are that the product must be different or new, that the way the message is executed is different or interesting, and that the message proclaims something that is personally significant to the individual in their current context.

- The term 'significance' means that the message is meaningful, relevant and is perceived to be suitably credible. This is based on the concept of ad likeability, which many researchers believe is the only meaningful indicator of ad effectiveness. The net effect of all these characteristics might be that any one message may be *significantly valuable* to an individual.

- The cognitive processing model assumes that people attend to and process information in a logical rational way. Three types of cognitive response and how these relate to attitudes and intentions have been determined. These are attitudes towards the product, attitudes towards the message and attitudes towards the ad and its execution.

- There is a substantial amount of research that indicates that marketing communications (advertising) that promotes a 'positive emotional response of liking an ad is positively related to subsequent brand-related cognitions (knowledge), brand attitudes and purchase intentions'.

- Marketing communications works because liking an ad is positively related to subsequent brand-related cognitions (knowledge), brand attitudes and purchase intentions. The attitude-towards-the-ad concept applies equally well with interactive media, e-commerce (attitude-towards-the-site), sales promotion and personal selling.

Costa: creating a nation of coffee lovers

Matthew Waksman and Will Hodge, Karmarama Communications

Image 6.6 Part of Costa's communications featured their baristas in order to show their skill and passion.
Source: Costa Coffee.

Costa was established as a family business in 1971 by two Italian brothers, and comprised 40 coffee shops when Whitbread bought it in 1995 and kick-started expansion.

In 2008 Costa was the Number 2 player in the UK coffee shop market. Facing fierce competition, and the worst recession since WW2, Costa decided not to resort to discounting, but to embark on a brand development programme designed to establish Costa as the UK's Number 1 coffee shop brand. This approach was founded on the principle that in a recession consumers tend to reserve their restricted disposable income for their favourite brands, and it is the Number 2 brand that gets hit.

Over the following four-year period, Costa sought to get coffee shop visitors to choose Costa over Starbucks. This involved increasing preference by stealing Starbuck's customers, by convincing them that Costa's coffee is better. This was anchored on independent blind taste tests which revealed a strong preference for Costa. Seventy per cent of people, who saw themselves as lovers of coffee, preferred Costa to Starbucks. In addition, Costa's artisan, hand-made approach from bean to cup was an in-shop performance. This was seen as clearly superior to Starbucks 'baristas' who make cappuccinos by pressing buttons. That is why their machines face away from customers. As consumers didn't know this they remained perfectly happy with their Starbucks offering, but it was these two insights that provided a valuable platform for marketing communications.

What followed was the '7/10 coffee lovers, like you, think Costa is better' campaign. It was tested in the national and local press, online, radio and outdoors. Costa then took the message to a wider audience with the category's first TV ads. This reasserted the message that 'not all coffees are created equal', playing up the skill and craft of the Costa barista and implicitly compared Starbucks' button-pushing baristas to monkeys. Before these brand communications started, consumers preferred Starbucks. The Monkeys campaign in particular drove a dramatic sales and footfall increase right from the start of the campaign, so by the time the campaign finished research showed consumers preferred Costa. Communications had made Costa brand leader.

The next phase was about getting more people to visit Costa and keep them coming back, as consumers were still more likely to recommend Starbucks. Now communications had to increase brand preference by creating brand love for Costa. This was achieved by convincing people of the passion and care at Costa. This needed a change from the aggressive 7/10 approach, which signified opposition (why we're better than the competition). Now we needed to proposition (why we're special). Whereas a product focus lends itself to the comparative nature of opposition, for proposition, we needed something more engaging. Baristas were the answer as they allowed us to move from product to people, building on 7/10, showing *how* we make it better.

We showed baristas as not only more skilled but also more passionate and we did this when we created 'Coffee Heads', a love song, delivered by a Costa barista to a customer. Symbolically and semiotically, we filled it with love: heart motifs, romantic lighting, red velvet and the track 'I was made for loving you'.

Throughout this phase we extended our love theme. In product-led point of sale we communicated a heartfelt benefit and highlighted preference through the tactical use of press. While the love message increased brand warmth, the campaign significantly impacted the likelihood that Starbucks' customers would visit Costa.

At this stage the coffee shop market was looking up. Usage rose with 75 per cent of consumers buying coffee out of home in the previous three months. Consumer confidence nearly reached pre-recession levels. The Costa brand was strongly differentiated and trusted.

But a fresh, unexpected challenge was emerging. Just as towns had protested against Tesco, campaign groups were turning on Costa. Costa even had to halt its expansion in Totnes due to high-profile resistance. Costa's challenge was its size. It needed to be seen as a high-street institution, not an invader. Only then could it maintain preference and continue its expansion with the public's blessing.

Communications now needed to convey the relevance of Costa as a part of people's lives. This was accomplished by leveraging the power of Christmas and seasonal moments to create emotional affinity. We knew that emotional campaigns drive long-term profitability and resonant Christmas campaigns also deliver emotional affinity. We investigated why people buy festive drinks from coffee shops at Christmas. Unlike supermarkets or gift retailers, we realised coffee shops were not at the heart of the big day, although that didn't make their festive role any less special. They offered instead little moments of festive joy throughout the seasonal run up. So we set out to make Costa festive moments the most fun, starting with a range of charming, interactive cups. The trouble was, Starbucks had 'owned' coffee shop Christmas for years.

Despite this we felt their cups fell short on emotional impact and as cups were a free media and a driver of advocacy, we couldn't ignore them.

We believed a character-led rather than graphic-led approach would be more powerful. But to turn cups into characters meant the logo couldn't be front and centre, unlike on Starbucks' festive cups. Changing Costa's iconic cups at all was a major step both operationally and from a branding perspective. Now we were considering making the logo less prominent. But whereas Starbucks' cups were an exercise in seasonal branding, we were after brand affinity. Costa's advertising heroed the role as festive-fun-bringer with six-sheets up and down the country in battlegrounds close to competitors.

We offered prizes on social channels for a picture of customers with their cup. The cups were designed to make a fun photo. When you held them to your lips, you gave the cups' character a face. To maximise the power of engagement, we used advertising to showcase fans' snaps to others.

Just as the 7/10 campaign showed customers that coffee lovers go to Costa, our user-generated content was incorporated within our out-of-home ads, which showed Christmas lovers go to Costa.

Image 6.7 Christmas advertising
Source: Costa Coffee.

Costa's cups charmed Brits who found them more appealing than Starbucks', even though Starbucks had been established since 2007 and this was year one for Costa. So we stayed with the idea and evolved the campaign the following year.

The social successes led us to seek new ways to engage, including vlogger Tanya Burr. She unveiled the cups to 2.4 million subscribers, generating 650,000+ views. By 2015, people were openly valuing and anticipating our cups.

By investing heavily in brand communications from 2008 to 2015, Costa expanded from 695 stores to over 2000, more than Starbucks, Pret and Nero combined. Communications drove the brand to Number 1 status on both turnover and preference for six straight years. The communications generated an average incremental profit of £3.81 for every £1 of advertising spent and Costa became the nation's favourite coffee shop brand.

This case study is an edited version of a paper submitted to the IPA Effectiveness Awards 2016. It has been reproduced here with the kind permission of the IPA, WARC, Costa and their agency, Karmarama, who wrote the original paper.

Review questions

Costa case questions

1. How did Costa use marketing communications to change attitudes (preference) towards the brand?

2. To what extent is Costa's marketing communications influenced by transactional or collaborative exchange-based relationships?

3. What justification is there to argue that Costa's communications is best interpreted through the concept of significant value?

4. Discuss ways in which Costa seeks to engage audiences.

5. Explain how Costa's use of media might be said to complement ideas about attitude development.

General questions

1. Sketch the customer relationship lifecycle and show how marketing communications can be used to influence each of the stages.

2. Describe the creative magnifier effect. Why is it important?

3. Cognitive processing consists of three main elements. Name them.

4. Write brief notes outlining the difference between three sequential models and evaluate the ways in which they are considered to work.

5. Why might cognitive processing not be an entirely acceptable approach?

References for Chapter 6

Ajzen, I. and Fishbein, M. (1980) *Understanding Attitudes and Predicting Social Behavior,* Englewood Cliffs, NJ: Prentice Hall.

Andersson, S. and Wikström, N. (2017) Why and how are social media used in a B2B context, and which stakeholders are involved? *Journal of Business & Industrial Marketing,* 32(8), 1098–1108.

Anon (2016) Dennis partners with Fitbit to launch the Fitbit Fifty challenge, *Dennis,* 19 August, retrieved 20 March 2018 from http://www.dennis.co.uk/dennis-partners-fitbit-fifty/

Anon (2017) How Fujitsu's sales/marketing success helped establish a key client partnership, B2B Marketing Awards, 16 November, retrieved 24 December 2017 from https://www.b2bmarketing.net/en-gb/resources/b2b-case-studies/awards-case-study-how-fujitsus-salesmarketing-success-helped-establish

Armstrong, S. (1999) The influence of individual cognitive style on performance in management education, in *Proceedings of the 4th Annual Conference of the European Learning Styles Information Network* (eds J. Hill, S. Armstrong, M. Graff, S. Rayner and E. Sadler-Smith), Preston: University of Central Lancashire, 31–50.

Armstrong, S.J., Cools, E. and Sadler-Smith, E. (2012) Role of cognitive styles in business and management: reviewing 40 years of research, *International Journal of Management Reviews,* 14, 238–62.

Ballantyne, D. (2004) Dialogue and its role in the development of relationship specific knowledge, *Journal of Business and Industrial Marketing,* 19(2), 114–23.

Barry, T. and Howard, D.J. (1990) A review and critique of the hierarchy of effects in advertising, *International Journal of Advertising,* 9, 121–35.

Belch, G.E. and Belch, M.A. (2004) *Advertising and Promotion: An Integrated Marketing Communications Perspective,* 6th edn, Homewood, IL: Richard D. Irwin.

Binet, L. and Field, P. (2013) *The Long and the Short of It: Balancing Short and Long-Term Marketing Strategies,* London: Institute of Practitioners in Advertising.

Brakus, J.J., Schmitt, B.H. and Zarantello, L. (2009) Brand experience: what is it? How is it measured? Does it affect loyalty? *Journal of Marketing,* 73(3), 52–68.

Braun, C., Hadwich, K. and Bruhn, M. (2017) How do different types of customer engagement affect important relationship marketing outcomes? An empirical analysis, *Journal of Customer Behaviour,* 16(2), 111–44.

Brown, G. (1991) *How Advertising Affects the Sales of Packaged Goods Brands*, Warwick: Millward Brown.

Bruner, G.C. and Kumar, A. (2000) Web commercials and advertising hierarchy of effects, *Journal of Advertising Research*, January/April, 35–42.

Chan, D. (1996) Cognitive misfit of problem-solving style at work: a facet of person–organisation fit, *Organisational Behavior and Human Decision Processes*, 68, 194–207.

Chen, Q. and Wells, W.D. (1999) Attitude toward the site, *Journal of Advertising Research*, September/October, 27–37.

Clark, A. (2015) How to measure success in content marketing, *ScribbleLive*, retrieved 14 February 2015 from http://media.dmnews.com/documents/105/scribblelive_white paper_measur_26084.pdf

CMI (2015) What is content marketing? *Content Marketing Institute*, retrieved 17 February 2015 from http://contentmarketinginstitute.com/what-is-content-marketing/

Cuia, G., Liub, H., Yang, X. and Wang, H. (2013) Culture, cognitive style and consumer response to informational vs. transformational advertising among East Asians: evidence from the PRC, *Asia Pacific Business Review*, 19(1), 16–31.

Damasio, A.A. (2000) *The Feeling of What Happens*, London: Heinemann.

Day, G. (2000) Managing market relationships, *Journal of the Academy of Marketing Science*, 28(1), Winter, 24–30.

Fletcher, W. (1994) The advertising high ground, *Admap*, November, 31–4.

Gianatasio, D. (2016) Ikea just made one of its loveliest ads yet about the beauty of everyday life, *Adweek*, 22 April, retrieved 1 November 2017 from http://www.adweek.com/creativity/ikea-just-made-one-its-loveliest-ads-yet-about-beauty-everyday-life-171002/

Gilliland, D.I. and Johnston, W.J. (1997) Towards a model of marketing communications effects, *Industrial Marketing Management*, 26, 15–29.

Giorgi, S. and Weber, K. (2015) Marks of distinction: framing and audience appreciation in the context of investment advice, *Administrative Science Quarterly*, 60(2), 333–67.

Goffman, E. (1974) *Frame Analysis*, Cambridge, MA: Harvard University Press.

Goldsmith, R.E. and Lafferty, B.A. (2002) Consumer response to websites and their influence on advertising effectiveness, *Internet Research: Electronic Networking Applications and Policy*, 12(4), 318–28.

Greenwald, A. (1968) Cognitive learning, cognitive response to persuasion and attitude change, in *Psychological Foundations of Attitudes* (eds A. Greenwald, T.C. Brook and T.W. Ostrom), New York: Academic Press, 197–215.

Grönroos, C. (2004) The relationship marketing process: communication, interaction, dialogue, value, *Journal of Business and Industrial Marketing*, 19(2), 99–113.

Gummesson, E. (2017) From relationship marketing to total relationship marketing and beyond, *Journal of Services Marketing*, 31(1), 16–19.

Heath, R. (2001) Low involvement processing – a new model of brand communication, *Journal of Marketing Communications*, 7, 27–33.

Heath, R. and Feldwick, P. (2008) 50 years using the wrong model of TV advertising, *International Journal of Market Research*, 50(1), 29–59.

Heath, R. and Hyder, P. (2005) Measuring the hidden power of emotive advertising, *International Journal of Market Research*, 47(5), 467–86.

Kent, M.L. and Taylor, M. (2002) Toward a dialogic theory of public relations, *Public Relations Review*, 28(1), 21–37.

Kozinets, R.V. (2014) Social brand engagement: a new idea, *GfK Marketing Intelligence Review*, 6(2), November, 8–15.

Krugman, H.E. (1965) The impact of television advertising: learning without involvement, *Public Opinion Quarterly*, 29 (Fall), 349–56.

Lavidge, R.J. and Steiner, G.A. (1961) A model for predictive measurements of advertising effectiveness, *Journal of Marketing*, 25(6), October, 59–62.

Lutz, J., Mackenzie, S.B. and Belch, G.E. (1983) Attitude toward the ad as a mediator of advertising effectiveness, *Advances in Consumer Research*, 10(1), 532–9.

McGuire, W.J. (1978) An information processing model of advertising effectiveness, in *Behavioral and Management Science in Marketing* (eds H.L. Davis and A.J. Silk), New York: Ronald/Wiley, 156–80.

Messick, S. (1972) Beyond structure in search of functional modes of psychological process, *Psychometrica*, 37, 357–75.

Mohr, J. and Nevin, J.R. (1990) Communication strategies in marketing channels, *Journal of Marketing*, October, 36–51.

Murphy, M. and Sashi, C.M. (2018) Communication, interactivity, and satisfaction in B2B relationships, *Industrial Marketing Management*, 68, January, 1–12.

Olsen, J.C. and Peter, J.P. (1987) *Consumer Behavior*, Homewood, IL: Irwin.

Palda, K.S. (1966) The hypothesis of a hierarchy of effects: a partial evaluation, *Journal of Marketing Research*, 3, 13–24.

Rapacz, D., Reilly, M. and Schultz, D.E. (2008) Better branding beyond advertising, *Marketing Management*, 17(1), 25–9.

Rossiter, J.R. and Percy, L. (2013) How the roles of advertising merely appear to have changed, *International Journal of Advertising*, 32(3), 391–8.

Rowe, W.G. and Barnes, J.G. (1998) Relationship marketing and sustained competitive advantage, *Journal of Market-Focused Management*, 2(3), 281–9.

Scheinbaum, A.C. (2016) Digital engagement: opportunities and risks for sponsors, *Journal of Advertising Research*, December, 341–45.

Schivinski, B., Christodoulides, G. and Dabrowski, D. (2016) Measuring consumers' engagement with brand-related social-media content: development and validation of a scale that identifies levels of social-media engagement with brands, *Journal of Advertising Research*, 56(1), 1–18.

Stewart, R. (2017) Ad of the day: Ikea's 'Wonderful Everyday' returns in colourful Fantasia-style spot, *The Drum*, 21 October, retrieved 1 November 2107 from http://www. thedrum.com/news/2017/10/21/ad-the-day-ikeas-wonderful-everyday-returns-colourful-fantasia-style-spot

Strong, E.K. (1925) *The Psychology of Selling*, New York: McGraw-Hill.

Thompson, D.V. and Hamilton, R.W. (2006) The effects of information processing mode on consumers' responses to comparative advertising, *Journal of Consumer Research*, 32, 530–40.

Thomson, K. and Hecker, L.A. (2000) The business value of buy-in, in *Internal Marketing: Directions for Management* (eds R.J. Varey and B.R. Lewis), London: Routledge, 160–72.

Tiersen, L. and Mackay, K. (2017) Ikea and the pursuit of everyday wonder: how the retailer revived its fortunes, *Campaign*, 16 October, retrieved 1 November 2017 from https://www.campaignlive.co.uk/article/ikea-pursuit-everyday-wonder-retailer-revived-its-fortunes/1447274

Vinitzky, G. and Mazursky, D. (2011) The effects of cognitive thinking style and ambient scent on online consumer approach behavior, experience approach behavior, and search motivation, *Psychology & Marketing*, 28(5), 496–519.

Williams, D. (2017) 4 Content marketing lessons to learn from Netflix, Entrepreneur: Europe, 17 May, retrieved 22 August 2018 from https://www.entrepreneur.com/article/294050

Witkin, H.A., Moore, C.A., Goodenough, D.R. and Cox, P.W. (1977) Field dependent and field independent cognitive styles and their educational implications, *Review of Educational Research*, 47, 1–64.

Wright, P.L. (1973) The cognitive processes mediating the acceptance of advertising, *Journal of Marketing Research*, 10 (February), 53–62.

Zajonc, R.B. (1980) Feeling and thinking: preferences need no inferences, *American Psychologist*, 39, 151–75.

Managing marketing communications

Part 2 is concerned with a variety of subjects related to the management of marketing communications and associated activities.

Chapter 7 explores the nature of communications strategy and considers the interrelationship between strategy and planning. The first section of this chapter considers ideas about strategy and contains four distinct approaches to marketing communications strategy. The second section of the chapter introduces the marketing communications planning framework and highlights significant issues and linkages.

Chapter 8 examines the nature of objectives and positioning in marketing communications and considers both academic and practitioner (IPA) approaches to the nature of communication-based objectives.

The nature and characteristics of the UK marketing communications industry is the focus of Chapter 9. This material specifically examines the strategic and operational issues of communications agencies and their interaction with client organisations. It also considers some of the financial issues, including agency remuneration, and budgeting, with regard to the management of marketing communications activities.

Chapter 10 examines the ways in which the performance of marketing communications activities can be evaluated. In effect, these two chapters consider how much should be invested in the engagement process and how the engagement process should be measured.

Chapter 11 focuses on the role marketing communications can play in building product/service brands. Consideration is given to the development and delivery of brand associations, the role of marketing communications in business-to-business contexts, and the importance of engaging with employees and enabling them to communicate a brand's or organisational values to external audiences.

The final chapter in this part is about integrated marketing communications. This chapter challenges ideas about the nature and validity of the 'integrated' view of marketing communications. Four separate interpretations about what integrated marketing communications might be are presented. This is a core chapter because it bridges the contextual elements and the application of the various disciplines. The notion that integrated marketing communications (IMC) is a valid and realistic concept is explored and readers are encouraged to consider the arguments for and against this approach. Its position at the end of the management part of the book is designed to encourage readers to reflect on what should be integrated and what integration incorporates.

02

Marketing communications: strategies and planning

Marketing communications strategy refers to a brand's thematic platform, its overall positioning, and their customers' and other stakeholders' preferred approach to communications. Marketing communications strategies should at all times be aligned with the organisation's business and marketing strategies.

Marketing communications plans are concerned with the timing and resources associated with the delivery of ongoing programmes and campaigns designed to articulate a brand's marketing communications tactics and strategy.

Campaign planning is concerned with the strategies and tactics principally associated with advertising and is increasingly becoming an automated process.

Aims and learning objectives

The aims of this chapter are to develop understanding about the elements and concepts associated with marketing communications strategy and planning, and a planning framework within which to implement these strategies.

The learning objectives are to enable readers to:

1. examine the meaning of strategy within a marketing communications context;
2. evaluate several interpretations of marketing communications strategy: positioning, audience, platforms and configuration;
3. explain a planning framework and consider the different elements and linkages involved in the development of marketing communications plans;
4. discuss the elements and issues associated with campaign planning.

Introduction

The word 'strategy' can conjure a number of diverse meanings and images. In a communications context, strategy can also be considered in various ways and at different levels. However, in order to explore and appreciate the role and nature of communications strategy it is helpful to consider the broad dimensions of the strategy concept.

The management literature on strategy is extensive, yet there seems to be little agreement or consensus about what it is, what it means or how it should be developed. A detailed discussion about this topic is beyond the scope of this book but interested readers should see Scholars' paper 7.1. Strategy encompasses the design, implementation and evaluation of a course of action that leads to the satisfaction or achievement of previously set objectives. Strategy, objectives, tactics and implementation are discrete activities but they are all an integral part of strategy.

Scholars' paper 7.1
What is strategy?

Andrews, K. (1987) *The Concept of Corporate Strategy*, Homewood, IL: Richard D. Irwin.

Ansoff, H.I. (1965) *Corporate Strategy*, New York: McGraw-Hill.

Chaffee, E. (1985) Three models of strategy, *Academy of Management Review*, 10(1), 89–98.

Kay, J. (1993) The structure of strategy, *Business Strategy Review*, 4(2), 17–37.

Mintzberg, H. and Waters, J.A. (1985) Of strategies, deliberate and emergent, *Strategic Management Journal*, 6(3), 257–72.

These are classic publications from the 'early' strategy literature. They provide an insight into some of the principal ideas and approaches.

See also:

Van Alstyne, M.W., Parker, G.G. and Choudary, S.P. (2016) Pipelines, platforms, and the new rules of strategy, *Harvard Business Review*, April, 54–60.

Hagiu, A. and Altman, E.J. (2017) Finding the platform in your product: four strategies that can reveal hidden value, *Harvard Business Review*, 95(4), July/August, 94–100.

At a very broad level traditional marketing communications strategies can be considered to be linear. These reflect marketing strategies which, essentially, consist of adding value to a product as it moves through a value chain of supplier/distributor participants towards the end user. Marketing communications strategies tend to echo this 'pipeline' effect (Van Alstyne et al., 2016) as they either focus on consumers or distributors.

Emerging marketing strategies combine a 'pipeline' approach with a new 'platform' strategy, as evidenced by Apple, Airbnb and Uber, among others. For example, Apple's operating system constitutes a platform that enables both app developers and app users to be connected, which in turn creates a two-sided market. This is because both participants can generate value through the iPhone 'platform'. Van Alstyne et al. (2016) refer to 'network effects', which are driven as the number of developers and users increases. Marketing communications strategies in this context can be considered to be a platform, one that anchors the essence of a brand's promise, which it makes not only to its customers but a range of participants. The communications can be networked and stimulated to interact, independently of the source.

We begin with a contextual and audience perspective on which to build marketing communications strategy. This is used in preference to a production orientation, which is founded purely on a resource base. From this, four different interpretations of marketing communications strategy are considered. The chapter closes with an exploration of a framework within which to plan, develop and implement marketing communications strategies.

Reference to the central tenets of strategy as a 'pipeline' or 'platform' should be maintained as readers move through this chapter.

Marketing communications strategies

The prevailing approach to marketing communications strategy has traditionally been founded upon the configuration of the 'promotional' mix. Strategy was interpreted as a mix of the tools and, hence, the resources an organisation deploys. This inside-out form of strategy is essentially resource-driven. Unfortunately, this represents a production rather than a market orientation and as such is restricted and discredited.

A market orientation to strategy requires a consideration of the needs of the audience first, and then a determination of the various messages, media and disciplines necessary to accomplish the strategy: an outside-in approach. This is demonstrated in the Sr Toronjo case at the end of this chapter.

Just as general strategy has been interpreted in different ways, so there are various explanations regarding what is marketing communications strategy. Broadly, marketing communications strategy concerns the overall approach used to realise marketing and communications objectives, within an audience-related context. However, this is a broadbrush perspective, especially as the phrase 'overall approach' can be interpreted in different ways.

Here, four main explanations are considered. They are drawn from the academic literature and practitioner experience and comment. These four are marketing communications as a position, as an audience, as a platform and as a configuration or pattern. These should not be considered to be discrete or exclusive interpretations, as aspects of each can be observed within the others. See Figure 7.1 and note that these strategic forms are loosely aligned with Mintzberg's interpretation of strategy, featured in Scholars' paper 7.1.

MC strategy interpretation 1: positioning strategies

The process of market analysis and evaluation leading to planned strategies designed to meet prescribed and measurable goals is well established. It is argued that this enables finite resources to be used more efficiently as they can be directed towards markets that hold, potentially, greater value than other markets. This approach involves three main activities: market segmentation, target market selection and positioning (otherwise referred to as STP).

Market segmentation is the means by which organisations define the broad context within which their strategic business units (SBUs) and products are offered. Market

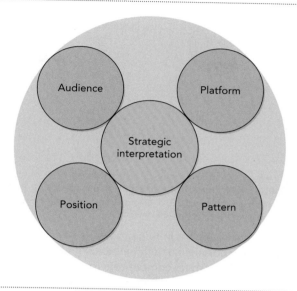

Figure 7.1 Four interpretations of marketing communications strategy

segmentation is the division of a mass market into identifiable and distinct groups or segments, each of which has common characteristics and needs and displays similar responses to marketing actions. Through this process specific target segments can be selected and marketing plans developed to satisfy the individual needs of the potential buyers in these chosen segments. The development, or rather identification, of segments can be perceived as opportunities and, as Beane and Ennis (1987) suggest, 'a company with limited resources needs to pick only the best opportunities to pursue'.

This process of segmentation is necessary because a single product is unlikely to meet the needs of all customers in a mass market. If it were, then a single type of toothpaste, chocolate bar or car would meet all of our needs. This is not so, and there are a host of products and brands seeking to satisfy particular buyer needs.

Having identified a market's various segments, the next step is to select particular target markets. These represent the best marketing potential and, once selected, require that resources are concentrated on these and no others. Targeted segments, therefore, constitute the environment and the context for a marketing communications strategy and activities. It is the characteristics of the target segment and their perception that should shape an audience-centred marketing communications strategy. Edwards (2011) suggests that rather than refer to a *target* audience, a static interpretation of people, it is better to consider them on an emotional journey, and that we all fluctuate between four different emotional states.

The *actual* self represents who we really are on a day-to-day basis, and perhaps this is the static person that the term 'target audience' refers to. There are times, however, when we move into a *worry* state, and times when we daydream and move into a *fantasy* self. Closest to our actual self is the *idealised* self, that person we would like to be, the person we strive to become. Marketing communications, as well as other elements of the marketing strategy, can be shaped to engage people according to their perceptions of themselves and their emotional states (see Figure 7.2).

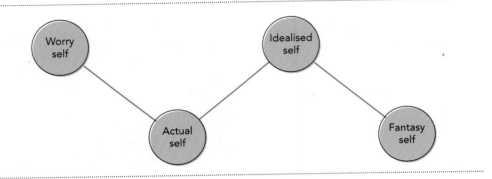

Figure 7.2 A journey of four emotional stages
Source: Based on Edwards (2011). Reproduced from *Marketing* magazine with the permission of the copyright owner, Haymarket Business Publications Limited.

The final element in this process is *positioning*. Reference to the DRIP model emphasises the importance of differentiation and the need to communicate a brand's core point(s) of difference with its competitors (see Chapter 1). Positioning is about audiences understanding the claimed differences.

As noted in the earlier discussion about strategy, positioning is an integral concept, and for some the essence of strategy. Wind (1990) stated quite clearly that positioning is the key strategic framework for an organisation's brand-based communications, as cited by Jewell (2007). All products and all organisations have a position in the minds of audiences. The task, therefore, is to manage actively the way in which audiences perceive brands. This means that marketing communications strategy should be concerned with achieving effective and viable positions so that target audiences understand what the brand does, what it means (to them) and can ascribe value to it. This is particularly important in markets that are very competitive and where mobility barriers (ease of entry into and exit from a market, e.g. plant and production costs) are relatively low.

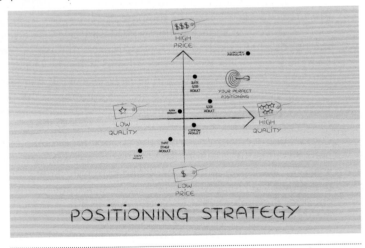

Image 7.1 Positioning is an integral concept of strategy
Source: faithie/123RF.

Positioning is about visibility and recognition of what a product/service/organisation represents to a buyer. In markets where the intensity of rivalry and competition are increasing and buyers have greater choice, the fast identification and understanding of a product's intrinsic values become critical. Channel members have limited capacities, whether this is the level or range of stock they can carry or, for retailers, the amount of available shelf space that can be allocated. An offering with a clear identity and orientation to a particular target segment's needs not only will be stocked and purchased, but can warrant a larger margin through increased added value.

Viewpoint 7.1

A swinging strategy at Li-Ning

Image 7.2 Chinese gymnasts delivering the Li Ning salute

Source: Jamie McDonald/Getty Images.

Li-Ning is China's largest sportswear brand, founded by Li Ning, the famous Chinese Olympian gymnast and hero. At the 2008 Bejing Olympic games he lit the cauldron to signal the opening of the event. The act of lighting the torch, in front of a worldwide audience and dressed in the Li-Ning branded clothing, helped fuel the meteoric growth of the brand. This informal communication sidelined accredited Olympic sponsors such as Adidas.

The brand has subsequently experienced a dramatic fluctuation in its fortunes. A failed attempt to take on Adidas in the USA, increasingly intense competition from both international brands such as Nike and Adidas, and domestically from ANTA Sports and Peak Sport led to considerable financial losses, and at one point Li-Ning lost 80 per cent of its market value.

Li-Ning's initial strategy involved targeting fashionable, fast-growing areas of sport in China, such as basketball. Using Western sports stars such as NBA basketball superstar Dwayne Wade, the goal was to attract younger consumers with a mid-range pricing strategy. The danger of this approach was that older, loyal customers would feel excluded.

Li-Ning positioned itself as a high-quality brand, equivalent to the international brands, but did not support this with a suitable pricing strategy.

The subsequent turnaround involved a shift in positioning to one that embraced its roots in China and Chinese sports. This meant developing a different set of brand values to those introduced by the international brands. Three core values, sports legacy, Chinese health and wisdom, were utilised. None of these are capable of being copied or eroded by the international competitors. The brand's sports legacy involves associating Li-Ning with what people can do with sports, which is to gain both physical and mental wellbeing. So, rather than using sport to win and be better than the competition, as exemplified by Nike and their 'I can do' orientation, Li-Ning associates with inner and outer harmony through team sports, a 'We' orientation.

Instead of following Nike and Adidas down the technology and innovation positioning, Li-Ning associated itself with Chinese health, which incorporates traditional Chinese medicine, acupuncture and an appreciation of how the body works. The advantage of this positioning is that it appeals to both the serious and fun sports enthusiast. To differentiate Li-Ning and divert attention away from the values associated with its international competitors, Li-Ning taps into ancient Chinese wisdom, with China's expertise in physical training and sports performance, particularly martial arts, being emphasised.

Rather than go after large team sponsorships they targeted the Indian, Filipino, and Malaysian teams at the 2016 Rio Olympic games. They supported the gymnastics, basketball and badminton squads, which are popular sports in those markets.

Li-Ning's 2016 financial results reflect a change in fortunes with revenue growth of 13 per cent and a 13 per cent increase in gross profit.

Sources: Anon (2016a); Fan and Murata (2015); Kwok (2014); Sauer (2017).

Insight

Li-Ning's strategic positioning demonstrates the need for consistency. The luxury positioning was not compatible with mid-range pricing, and resulted in a financial performance that was under expectations.

Their subsequent strategy demonstrates greater consistency and one that cannot be copied. It also appeals at an emotional level, as the Chinese health and wisdom positioning can be used to resonate with both serious and amateur sports enthusiasts.

Question: What, if any, is the value of continuing the association of the founder with the Li-Ning brand?

Task: Find two other sports brands and compare their approach to the Chinese market.

It is generally accepted that positioning is the natural conclusion to the sequence of activities that constitute a core part of strategy. Market segmentation and target marketing are prerequisites to successful positioning. Having established that marketing communications should be an audience-centred rather than a product-centred activity, it can be concluded with some confidence that marketing communications strategy is essentially about positioning. For new products and services, marketing communications needs to engage target audiences so that they can understand what the brand means, how it differs from similar offerings and, as a result, position it in their minds. For the vast majority of products and services that are already established, marketing communications strategy should be concerned with either developing a strong position or repositioning it in the minds of the target audiences. Chapter 8 explores the positioning concept and the different strategies used by organisations to position their brands.

MC strategy interpretation 2: audience strategies

Consumer purchase decisions can be characterised, very generally, by a single-person buying centre, whereas organisational buying decisions can involve a large number of different people fulfilling different roles and all requiring different marketing communications messages. In addition to this there are other stakeholders who have an interest in a brand's development – for example, suppliers and the media. It follows from this that communications with these three very different audiences should be radically different, especially in terms of what, where, when and how a message is communicated. Three audience-focused marketing communications strategies emerge:

- *Pull strategies* – these are intended to influence end-user customers (consumers and B2B).
- *Push strategies* – these are intended to influence marketing (trade) channel buyers.
- *Profile strategies* – these are intended to influence a wide range of stakeholders, not just customers and intermediaries.

These are referred to as the '3Ps' of marketing communications strategy and can be considered to be generic strategies thanks to their breadth. *Push* and *pull* relate to the direction of communications in a marketing channel: pushing communications down through a marketing channel or pulling consumers/buyers into a channel via retailers, as a result of receiving communications. They do not relate to the intensity of communications and

Table 7.1 An audience interpretation of marketing communications strategy

Target audience	Message focus	Communications goal
Consumers	Product/service	Purchase
End-user B2B customers	Product/service	Purchase
Channel intermediaries	Product/service	Developing relationships and distribution network
All relevant stakeholders	The organisation	Building reputation

only refer to the overall approach. *Profile* refers to the presentation of an organisation as a whole and the reputation that it bestows on its brands. The identity is said to be 'profiled' to various other target stakeholder audiences, which may well include consumers, trade buyers, business-to-business customers and a range of other influential stakeholders. Normally, profile strategies do not contain or make reference to the specific products or services that the organisation offers. See Table 7.1 for a further explanation of each of these three dimensions.

A pull strategy

If messages designed to position a brand are to be directed at targeted, end-user customers, then the intention is invariably to generate increased levels of awareness, change and/or reinforce attitudes, reduce risk, encourage involvement and ultimately provoke a motivation within the target group. This motivation is to stimulate action so that the target audience expect the offering to be available to them when they decide to enquire, experiment or make a repeat purchase. This approach is a *pull (positioning)* strategy and is aimed at encouraging customers to 'pull' products through the channel network (see Figure 7.3). This usually means that consumers go into retail outlets (shops) to enquire about a particular product and/or buy it, or to enter a similar transaction direct with the manufacturer or intermediary through direct mail or the Internet. B2B customers are encouraged to buy from dealers and distributors while both groups of consumers and B2B customers have opportunities to buy through direct marketing channels where there is no intermediary.

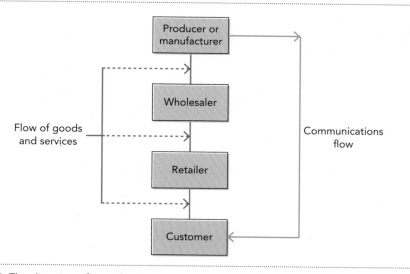

Figure 7.3 The direction of a marketing communications pull strategy
Source: From *Essentials of Marketing Communications*, Pearson Education (Fill, C. 2011) Figure 4.2, p. 99.

Viewpoint 7.2

Fidor puts customers at the heart of their strategy

Image 7.3 Fidor bank's strategy was built on communities and flexibility
Source: Fidor Bank.

Fidor is a digital bank, which has grown remarkably since it was set up in Germany in 2009. It was created in the aftermath of the banking and financial crisis, and the huge public dissatisfaction with bankers and banking practices. The focus of the bank's entire strategy has always been on customers and their needs. This meant that products and services had to be adapted to them rather than bend or amend offerings to different segments.

As a result, Fidor have built a reputation for developing innovative new financial products, some based on crowd financing deals and peer-to-peer loans. The bank's online community provides the marketplace for these facilities. For example, customers can post requests to borrow money and other customers can make offers to lend to them. The community also provides opportunities for customers to ask money-related questions, to provide savings ideas, to consider financial services or evaluate providers, and to suggest new products and services. Its interest rates are linked to its Facebook page. So, for every 2,000 likes that the bank receives, 0.05 per

cent is added to the interest rate, rising to a maximum of 0.5 per cent.

Fidor's strategy is also built around an ability to adapt quickly to changing market conditions. With new entrants such as Starling, Monzo and Atom Bank speed of change is crucial. To help with this Fidor has placed 'technology enablement' at its core, a principle that shapes what it does, in order to provide customers with choice and remain competitive. This is achieved by using technology to bring new products and services to the market at a rapid rate.

'Banking with Friends' is Fidor's slogan. This echoes the anchoring role that customers and bank employees play within the Fidor community. Indeed, Fidor's marketing communications are based on the core strategy of openness and transparency, again based largely on and around the community.

At the outset Fidor targeted potential early adopters, in order to listen and discover their priorities and to shape and refine the initial offering. Since then, the bank has sought to use an integrated approach, which incorporates a variety of marketing channels, spread across multiple platforms. These include social media, public relations, events, online and mobile marketing. An important part of the Fidor concept is consistent communication across social media platforms such as Twitter, Facebook and YouTube, plus online chat. The internal team at Fidor is also an integral part of its innovation and communications activities.

Sources: Anon (2016b); William-Smith (2017); www.fidorbank.uk/about-fidor/group

Insight

This example sets out an important distinction. Marketing strategy is different to marketing communications strategy. In this case the customer-focused marketing strategy is echoed by the marketing communications strategy. For example, the strategy of openness and transparency is based largely around the community, and 'Banking with Friends' complements this neatly.

Question: To what extent does Fidor's communications reflect a platform strategy as presented at the beginning of this chapter?

Task: Find another new bank and compare their approach to communications with those exhibited by Fidor.

A push strategy

A second group or type of target audience can be identified on the basis of their contribution to the marketing channel and these organisations do not consume the products and services they buy, but add value before selling the product on to others in the demand chain. The previous strategy was targeted at customers who make purchase decisions related largely to their personal (or organisational) consumption of products and services. This second group buys products and services, performs some added-value activity and moves the product through the marketing channel network.

The 'trade' channel has received increased attention in recent years as the strategic value of intermediaries has become both more visible and questioned in the light of the Internet. As the channel networks have developed, so has their complexity, which impacts upon the marketing communications strategies and tools used to help reach marketing goals.

A push communications strategy concerns an attempt to influence other trade channel organisations and, as a result, encourage them to take stock, to allocate resources (e.g. shelf space) and to help them to become fully aware of the key attributes and benefits associated with each product with a view to adding value prior to further channel transactions. This strategy is designed to encourage resale to other members of the network and contribute to the achievement of their own objectives. This approach is known as a push strategy, as it is aimed at pushing the product down through the channel towards the end-users for consumption (see Figure 7.4).

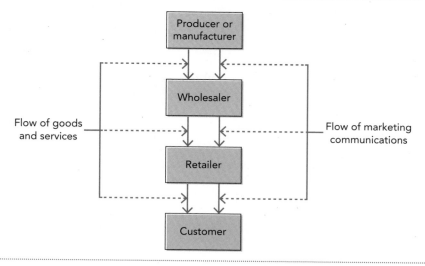

Figure 7.4 The direction of a marketing communications push strategy
Source: From *Essentials of Marketing Communications*, Pearson Education (Fill, C. 2011) Figure 4.3, p. 102.

A profile strategy

The strategies considered so far concern the need for dialogue with customer audiences (pull) and trade channel intermediaries (push). However, there is a whole range of other stakeholder audiences, many of whom need to know about and understand the organisation rather than actually purchase its products and services (see Figure 7.5). This group of stakeholders may include financial analysts, trade unions, government bodies, employees or the local community. It should be easy to understand that these different stakeholder groups can influence the organisation in different ways and, because of this, need to receive (and respond to) different types of messages. Thus, the financial analysts need to know about financial and trading performance and expectations, and the local community may be interested in employment and the impact of the organisation on the local environment, whereas the government may be interested in the way the organisation applies health and safety regulations and pays corporation, VAT and other taxes. It should also be remembered that consumers and business-to-business customers may also be more interested in the organisation itself and so help initiate an umbrella branding strategy.

Traditionally these organisation-oriented activities have been referred to as *corporate communications,* as they deal more or less exclusively with the corporate entity or organisation. Products, services and other offerings are not normally the focus of these communications. It is the organisation and its role in the context of the particular stakeholders' activities that are important. Communications used to satisfy this array of stakeholder needs and the organisation's corporate promotional goals are developed through what is referred to as a *profile strategy*, a major element of which is corporate branding.

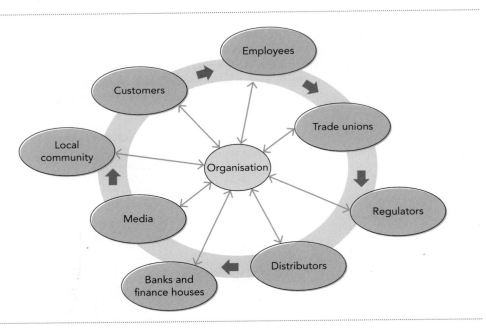

Figure 7.5 The direction of a marketing communications profile strategy
Source: From *Essentials of Marketing Communications*, Pearson Education (Fill, C. 2011) Figure 4.4, p. 102.

Viewpoint 7.3

Allianz raise their profile

Image 7.4 Allianz profile their brand through sponsorship and stadium naming rights.
Source: Michal Zarzycki/Shutterstock.

Allianz SE Group is the largest insurer in the world. The Munich based company has 142,000 employees worldwide, helping 85 million customers in more than 70 countries. In the UK, Allianz Insurance offers commercial, car, home, pet and musical insurance, all distributed through a network of brokers and partners. It is this network that has provided a strategic challenge for Allianz. Despite being the largest property and casualty insurer in the world, UK consumer awareness of the brand was poor, as the business was conducted largely through brokers.

In an attempt to raise the Allianz profile, research was undertaken internally to unlock the brand's DNA. The deep and passionate expertise of its staff within a range of insurance categories, combined with their genuine enthusiasm, provided a platform on which to raise the profile in the UK. The ensuing four-year campaign featured high-profile examples of work in which Allianz was involved. These included space and satellite technology, movies (James Bond films), their previous involvement in the construction of the Golden Gate Bridge in San Francisco, their official road-safety partnership status with Formula 1, and that they are the only insurer to have their own road safety research institute.

In addition to professional development and scholarship programmes for its broker partners, sponsorship in sport and the arts is an ongoing integral part of the profile strategy. For example, Allianz were the official core sponsor of the 2016 Rio Paralympic Games on Channel 4.

Allianz have the naming rights to the Munich football stadium, which they insured during its construction. The Allianz Arena is the home of both FC Bayern Munich and TSV 1860 Munich. There is now a growing family of stadiums, including the Allianz Stadium in Sydney, the Saracens' Allianz Park rugby stadium in London, the Allianz Riviera in Nice, and the most recent stadium, the Allianz Parque in São Paulo.

These facilities are used to enable staff and customers to experience a range of activities and even to buy merchandise. This fosters brand ambassadors and advocates who use word-of-mouth communications and user-generated social media-based content to further raise the Allianz profile.

Sources: Degun (2016); Simms (2017); www.allianz.co.uk

Insight

Allianz had previously concentrated their communications on their distributors, a push strategy. As competitive conditions have changed they have had to refocus their attention on stakeholder audiences and this requires a profile strategy. The complexity of the markets in which they operate negate the use of detailed product-information-based communications. Here the pipeline approach to strategy is predominant.

Question: To what extent should Allianz and other insurers seek to increase brand knowledge when brokers and online agents provide the contact point and necessary insurance expertise?

Task: Develop an outline plan concerning ways in which social media could be used to extend the profile of the Allianz brand.

A *profile* strategy focuses an organisation's communications upon the development of stakeholder relationships, corporate image and reputation, whether that be just internally, just externally or both. To accomplish and deliver a profile strategy, public relations, including media relations, sponsorship and corporate advertising, become the pivotal tools of the marketing communications mix.

Within each of these overall strategies, individual approaches should be formulated to reflect the needs of each particular case. So, for example, the launch of a new shampoo product will involve a push strategy to get the product onto the shelves of the appropriate retailers. The strategy would be to gain retailer acceptance of the new brand and to position it as a profitable new brand to gain consumer interest. Personal selling supported by trade promotions will be the main marketing communications tool. A pull strategy to develop awareness about the brand will need to be created, accompanied by appropriate public relations work. The next step will be to create particular brand associations and thereby position the brand in the minds of the target audience. Messages may be primarily functional or expressive, but they will endeavour to convey a brand promise. This may be accompanied or followed by the use of incentives to encourage consumers to trial the product. To support the brand, carelines and a website will need to be put in place to provide credibility as well as a buyer reference point and an opportunity to interact with the brand.

The 3Ps provide a generic approach to marketing communications strategy. To provide more precision and utility it is possible to combine the positioning approach considered previously with each of these 3Ps.

Scholars' paper 7.2
The benefits of keeping the ivories clean

Haley, R.I. (1968) Benefit segmentation: a decision-oriented research tool, *Journal of Marketing*, 32 (July), 30–5.

Russell Haley's paper is a classic as it demonstrates some pioneering research through which he identifies four distinct types of customer: those who bought toothpaste for white teeth (sociables); those who wished to prevent decay (worriers); those who liked the taste and refreshment properties (sensors); and, finally, those who bought on a price basis (independents). Each of these groups has particular demographic, behaviouristic and psychographic characteristics from which different brands have developed, all of which require audience-focused brand communications.

MC strategy interpretation 3: platform strategies

A brand's communications should express its promise, and much of this is achieved through a brand's values and differential claims. In order to maintain brand authority and legitimacy, it is critical to maintain consistency in these communications. This requires a brand to be anchored, to have a set of grounded principles through which the brand is presented at all times. This anchoring has a central role in developing the core images stakeholders have of a brand.

Many organisations, in conjunction with their agencies, determine a strategic theme or platform to anchor their brands. These platforms concern the essence of the promise a brand makes to its customers. For example, this promise may be that the brand delivers happiness (Coca-Cola), safety (Volvo – cars), whiteness (Persil – washing powder), winning mentality (Nike), extra-long life (Duracell – batteries), value (Aldi and Lidl – supermarkets), reliability (Kia – cars), adrenalin rush (Red Bull), or any number of things.

Marketing communications strategy should be developed thematically and consistently around an agreed core theme, or a platform. If stakeholders do not discern any core messages then the brand will not be positioned clearly and the resultant diffused or confused messages might lead to underperformance.

Strategy and the Institute of Practitioners in Advertising

Utilising some of the findings of the IPA's research into successful campaigns, three main platforms can be identified. These are based on an advertising-led creative platform, a brand concept or need-state platform, and platforms based on conversation and participation.

Creative platforms are strategies based on a big, core advertising-led idea that enables audiences to recognise the idea across different media and touchpoints. These campaigns might share the same 'look and feel', response mechanic, competition, brand icon across channels, or central idea that is disseminated through the most appropriate media. A classic example of the advertising-led platform was P&O's use of a flag as its visual identity across all channels, including on-board communications, advertising and customer communications.

Brand concept platforms are characterised by their roots within a brand. This means they can be communicated using a variety of different creative expressions over time, something an advertising-led idea cannot accomplish.

These types of campaigns can be disaggregated into those based on tangible product attributes and those founded on more intangible conceptual ideas. Tangible campaigns identify a specific occasion (e.g. a birthday celebration), a tightly defined target audience (e.g. first-time mothers) or a specific 'point of market entry' (e.g. a new product).

Intangible campaigns are developed from emotional concepts, which allow them a high degree of creative inconsistency, are used across a range of tools and, unlike the advertising-led platforms, last a long time. Honda's 'The Power of Dreams' and Johnnie Walker's 'Keep Walking' campaigns are recognised as great examples of the use of this type of strategic platform (Cox et al., 2011).

Participation platforms represent a more recent strategic approach, thanks mainly to the interactive properties of digital media. This enables brands and audiences to interact, engage in dialogue and conversations and participate in a range of events, actions and communities.

This platform aims to integrate a brand into people's life patterns in a way that is significant and relevant to them. Audiences are invited to participate in a centrally driven brand idea, which is then played back through public media in order to involve others. For example, BT (telecoms) invited audiences to suggest storylines for the relationship that was developing, and later sagging, between its ad-brand couple.

More information about these platform strategies can be seen in Chapter 12 about integrated marketing communications.

Image 7.5 Johnnie Walker have used a walking platform

The Scottish whisky brand has focused its communications around a brand concept platform. This features the striding man with a walking cane.

Source: Denis Michaliov/Alamy Stock Photo.

MC strategy interpretation 4: configuration strategies

The configuration approach to marketing communications strategy gives emphasis to the structural aspects associated with the design of a message, and the way it is conveyed and received. This approach seeks to maximise the effectiveness of a communications activity by matching goals and resources with an audience's needs. This might involve varying the frequency with which a message is received by the target audience, continuity issues; others involve managing the formality, permanence or direction of a message. Communications strategies designed to get the attention of the audiences are common-place, while others seek to be immersed or provide continual presence. This approach to communications strategy involves the configuration of four facets of communications: the frequency, direction, modality and content of communications (Mohr and Nevin, 1990).

Frequency

The amount of contact between members of a communications network can impact on effectiveness. Too much information (too frequent, aggregate volume or pure repetition) can overload people and have a dysfunctional effect and affect learning. Too little information can undermine the opportunities for favourable performance outcomes by failing to provide the necessary operational information, motivation and support. As a consequence, it is important to identify the current volume of information being provided and to make a judgement about the desired levels of communications and optimise learning opportunities.

Direction

Direction refers to the horizontal and vertical movement of communications within a network. Each network consists of people who are dependent on others, but the level of dependence will vary, so that the distribution of power and influence is unequal.

Communications can be unidirectional in that they flow in one direction only. For example, information from a major food retailer, such as Aeon in Japan, Pão de Acucar in Brazil, or Metro in Canada, to small food manufacturers might be considered to be unidirectional because the small food manufacturers perceive little reason to respond, as these supermarkets represent a source of power. Communications can also be bidirectional: that is, to and from organisations and influential opinion leaders and formers.

Modality

Modality refers to the method used to transmit information and there is a wide variety of interpretations of the methods used to convey information. Modality can be seen as communications that is formal, planned and regulated, or informal, unplanned and spontaneous, such as word-of-mouth communications and water-cooler conversations.

Content

This refers to what is said. Frazier and Summers (1984) distinguish between direct and indirect influence strategies. Direct strategies are designed to change behaviour by specific request (recommendations, promises and appeals to legal obligations). Indirect strategies attempt to change another person's beliefs and attitudes about the desirability of the intended behaviour. This may take the form of an information exchange, where the source uses discussions about general business issues to influence the attitudes of the receiver. Social networks and online communities serve to influence consumer attitudes and change behaviour.

Exchange relationship

Communications strategies work within particular contexts, often characterised by the nature of the prevailing relationships and associated exchanges, the level of trust and support experienced by those in the communications network, and aspects of power as perceived by organisations in a B2B environment.

According to Stern and El-Ansary (1988), the nature of the exchange relationship structures the way communications should be used. Collaborative exchanges have a long-term perspective and high interdependence and involve joint decision-making. By contrast, market, or transactional exchanges are ad hoc and hence have a short-term orientation where interdependence is low.

Climate

Climate refers to the degree of mutual supportiveness that exists between participants. Anderson et al. (1987) used measures of trust and goal compatibility in defining communications climate.

Power

Dwyer and Walker (1981) showed that power conditions within a marketing channel can be symmetrical (with power balanced between members) or asymmetrical (with a power imbalance).

Two specific forms of communications strategy can be identified. The first is a combination referred to as a 'collaborative communications strategy' and includes higher-frequency, more bidirectional flows, informal modes and indirect content. This combination is likely to occur where there are collaborative structures, supportive climates or symmetrical power. The second combination is referred to as an 'autonomous communications strategy' and includes lower-frequency, more unidirectional communications, formal modes and direct content. This combination is likely to occur in channel conditions of market structures, unsupportive climates and asymmetrical power.

Communications strategy should, therefore, be built upon the characteristics of the situation facing each communications episode. Not all audiences share the same conditions, nor do they all possess the same degree of closeness or collaborative expectations. By considering the nature of the channel conditions and then developing communications strategies that complement them, the performance of the focus organisation and other members can be considerably improved, and conflict and tension substantially reduced.

Although the configuration approach is often associated with marketing-channel-based communications, the principles can be observed in consumer markets. Stern and El-Ansary (1992) stress consideration of information flows and movement, and, in particular, the timing and permanence of the communications flows. In addition, work by Mohr and Nevin (1990) takes into account the various facets of communications and the particular channel structures through which communications are intended to move.

Viewpoint 7.4

Embraer configures a new strategy

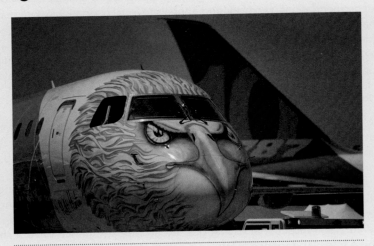

Image 7.6 The Profit Hunter

Embraer painted the nose cones of its new fleet with the image of an eagle to symbolise the brand's values
Source: Ian Langsdon/EPA/Shutterstock.

Embraer, the Brazilian manufacturers of regional aircraft with a range up to 2,000 miles, was the little known yet fourth largest aircraft manufacturer in the world, behind Boeing, Airbus and Bombardier. The challenge was to change awareness and perception of the Brazilian brand.

The strategies pursued by the established competitors tended to focus on specific tangible attributes such as fuel burn and low emissions. Embraer needed to find a different strategy and positioning as they did not have the budget to compete on this basis. This meant they had to stop selling 'metal' and convey a bolder personality, within which a solutions-based message could be conveyed. The target audience consisted of c-suite, analysts, the media and operators of 70 airlines across 50 countries in existing and new markets, including leasing companies.

The new aircraft were very cheap to operate, extremely light and capable of generating extra revenue for airline operators. This led to the new personality

'The Profit Hunter'. To convey this the nose-cone of the aircraft was painted as a golden eagle. This symbolised how the aircraft adapted perfectly to its environment, was able to fly longer distances efficiently, and like an eagle, was recognised as a hunter.

The eagle was painted by an employee of Embraer. As well as an engineer he was also an artist and the 20-night-long process was captured with a stop-motion camera. This went viral. The CEO then launched the new aircraft to the world as a profit-hunting machine. This made worldwide headlines.

All the communications channels used for the campaign were re-envisioned partly as a way of expressing the Embraer brand through its use of technology and 'digital first' principles.

FleetSmart, based on three core principles – Design Smart, Experience Smart and Business Smart, expressed the competitive philosophy of the business, and represented the competitive positioning strategy. It encapsulated Embraer's approach to creating solutions designed to help airlines and lessors optimise their operational efficiency, drive passenger preference and sustain profitability.

The campaign was launched at Le Bourget Airshow, and used various offline and online marketing channels to deliver the FleetSmart messages. These included press and online display advertising, outdoor displays at airports, a new website, social media, a live TV channel streamed on social media, blogs, virtual reality experiences of flying Profit Hunter, a market outlook report, brochureware, and customer events.

The campaign exceeded all the communication objectives but also delivered above expectation against the business goals as 50 orders were placed, worth over $3 billion, representing a broadening of the operational franchise.

Sources: Anon (2017a); Reid, (2017); www.gravitylondon.com

Insight

The strategy behind the Profit Hunter campaign was about delivering a new competitive positioning, one that distinguished Embraer in the market. Once formulated the new emotional positioning was delivered through a campaign that embraced a range of offline and online channels. Many of the features of the configuration approach can be observed here.

Question: To what extent might the new Embraer positioning be defended against copycat strategies?

Task: Make a list of the similarities between the Profit Hunter campaign and the different elements of the configuration approach.

Scholars' paper 7.3

Configuration and communications

Mohr, J. and Nevin, J.R. (1990) Communication strategies in marketing channels, *Journal of Marketing*, **October, 36–51.**

Written at a time when there was little published material on marketing communications strategy, this paper shed new light on strategy within marketing channels. Now the contingency principles presented by Mohr and Nevin have relevance in terms of the configuration approach to marketing communications strategy. All marketing communications students should read this paper.

Planning marketing communications

The context in which a communications event occurs not only shapes what and how messages are developed and conveyed, but also influences the interpretation and meaning ascribed to communications. In other words, the goals can be missed if the marketing communications is not entirely effective. The development of marketing communications plans helps to minimise errors and provide for efficiency and effectiveness.

There are a number of contexts that influence or shape marketing communications. All marketing managers (and others) should understand these contextual elements and appreciate how they contribute and influence the development of marketing communications programmes. In addition, there are a number of other elements and activities that need to be built into a programme in order that it can be implemented. These elements concern the goals, the resources, the communications tools to be used and measures of control and evaluation. Just like the cogs in a clock, these elements need to be linked together if the plan is to work. Planning frameworks aim to bring together the various elements into a logical sequence of activities. The rationale for decisions is built on information generated at previous levels in the framework. It also provides a checklist of activities that need to be considered.

However, there needs to be a word of caution as sometimes unforeseen events can lead to serious disruption of marketing communications plans. For example, companies working in the holiday industry set out detailed marketing communications plans accounting for economic conditions and forecasts. Unfortunately these plans can be disrupted by a number of different crises, such as terrorism and outbreaks of civilian unrest or even war, extreme weather conditions such as volcanic ash clouds, hurricanes, heavy rain and snow, or health issues such as illness and disease.

To help students and managers comprehend the linkages between the elements and to understand how these different components complement each other, the rest of this chapter deals with the development of marketing communications plans. To that extent it will be of direct benefit to managers seeking to build plans for the first time or for those familiar with the activity to reconsider current practices. Second, the material should also be of direct benefit to students who are required to understand and perhaps prepare such plans as part-fulfilment of an assessment or examination in this subject area.

Scholars' paper 7.4
Understanding the marketing planning process

Horáková, H., Švarcová, M. and Volf, L. (2017) Marketing planning process – reflection on the complex of activities that affect all aspects of business life, *Marketing Science & Inspirations*, 12(2), 43–53.

Marketing communications occurs within the scope of a marketing plan. This paper sets out the basic elements of the marketing plan. The key out-take of this paper is to understand that marketing planning and marketing communications planning are two separate yet similar and interrelated activities.

The marketing communications planning framework

The principal tasks facing those managing marketing communications are to decide:

- Who should receive the brand's messages.
- What is to be achieved.
- What the messages should say.
- How the messages are to be delivered.
- What actions the receivers should take.
- What image of the organisation/brand receivers are expected to retain.

- How much is to be spent establishing this new image.
- How to control the whole process once it has been implemented.
- What was achieved.

Note that more than one message is transmitted and that there is more than one target audience. This is important, as recognition of the need to communicate with multiple audiences and their different information requirements, often simultaneously, lies at the heart of marketing communications. The aim is to generate and transmit messages that present the organisations and their offerings to their various target audiences, encouraging them to enter into a dialogue. These messages must be presented consistently and they must address the points stated above. It is the skill and responsibility of the marketing communications planner to blend the communications tools and to create a mix that satisfies these elements.

Figure 7.6 presents the marketing communications planning framework (MCPF). This represents a sequence of decisions that marketing managers undertake when preparing, implementing and evaluating communications strategies and plans. It does not mean that this sequence reflects reality; indeed, many marketing decisions are made outside any recognisable framework. However, as a means of understanding the different components, appreciating the way in which they relate to one another and bringing together various aspects for work or for answering examination questions leading to a qualification, both academic and professional, this approach has many advantages and has been used by a number of local, national and international organisations.

Marketing communications activities should seek to satisfy particular objectives through the explicit and deliberate development of a communications strategy. The MCPF will be used to show, first, the key elements, second, some of the linkages and, third, the integrated approach that is considered good practice.

This framework reflects the deliberate or planned approach to strategic marketing communications. The processes associated with marketing communications, however, are not linear, as depicted in this framework, but integrative and interdependent. To that extent, this approach recognises the value of stakeholder theory and the requirement to build partnerships with buyers and other organisations networked with an organisation.

Other 'decision sequences' have been advanced, in particular one by Rothschild (1987) and another by Engel et al. (1994). One of the difficulties associated with these frameworks is that they fail to bring strategy into the development of the promotional mix.

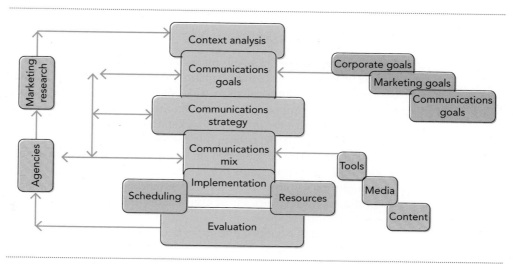

Figure 7.6 A marketing communications planning framework (MCPF)

These frameworks rely on the objective and task approach, whereby plans are developed for each of the individual communications tools, and then aggregated to form strategy.

Another framework, the SOSTAC approach (situation, objectives, strategy, tactics, action, control), was developed by Smith (2003). This is a robust system, and moves closer than most of the others to help formulate suitable marketing communications plans. However, as SOSTAC is multi-purpose and is intended for application to a variety of planning situations, there is a danger that the communications focus is lost at the situation analysis phase when used for developing marketing communications plans. This can lead to a reiteration of a SWOT (strengths, weaknesses, opportunities, threats) and/or a general marketing plan, with subsequent problems further down the line in terms of the justification and understanding of the communications strategy and mixes that need to be deployed. In addition, the SOSTAC model does not give sufficient emphasis to the need to identify and understand the characteristics of the target audience, which is so important for the development of coherent marketing communications.

The MCPF approach presented here is not intended to solve all the problems associated with the formulation of such plans, but it is sufficiently robust to meet the needs of employers and examiners, and is recommended.

Elements of the plan

Marketing communications plans should consist of the following elements. These elements are now considered in turn:

- Context analysis (developed from a communications perspective).
- Communications objectives.
- Marketing communications strategy.
- Coordinated communications mix (tools, media and content).
- Resources (human and financial).
- Scheduling and implementation.
- Evaluation and control.
- Feedback.

Context analysis

Analysing the context in which marketing communications events occur is a necessary, indeed vital, first step in the planning process. Bloxham and Sylvester (2013) stress the importance of a context analysis (CA) within a media context, and state that an understanding of the context in which media are used and messages consumed is necessary in order to optimise the impact of marketing communications. This can be seen clearly in Viewpoint 7.5 about TfL, later in this chapter.

Bosiljevac (2015) argues that an understanding of context helps bridge the work of strategists, creatives and the media team, in order to create customer relevancy. This might be in terms of really understanding the audience and saying something insightful, or finding a point of connection that complements the audience's pattern of media usage.

The purpose of a context analysis is to understand the key market and communications drivers that are likely to influence (or are already influencing) a brand (or organisation) and either help or hinder its progress towards meeting its long-term objectives. This is different from a situation analysis, because the situation analysis considers a range of wider organisational factors, most of which are normally considered in the development of marketing plans (while the communications focus is lost). Duplication is to be avoided, as it is both inefficient and confusing.

The compilation of a CA is very important, as it presents information and clues about what the promotional plan needs to achieve. Information and market research data about target audiences (their needs, perception, motivation, attitudes and decision-making characteristics), the media and the people they use for information about offerings, the marketing objectives and time scales, the overall level of financial and other resources that are available, the quality and suitability of agency and other outsourced activities, and the environment in terms of societal, technological, political and economic conditions, both now and at some point in the future, all need to be considered.

At the root of the CA is the marketing plan. This will already have been prepared and contains important information about the target segment, the business and marketing goals, competitors and the time scales in which the goals are to be achieved. The rest of the CA seeks to elaborate and build upon this information so as to provide the detail in order that the plan can be developed and justified.

The CA provides the rationale for the communications plan. It is from the CA that the marketing objectives (from the marketing plan) and the marketing communications objectives are derived. The type, form and style of the message are rooted in the characteristics of the target audience, and the media selected to convey messages will be based on the nature of the tasks, the media habits of the audience and the resources available. The main components of the CA are set out in Table 7.2.

Communications objectives

The role of communications objectives in the planning process is important for a number of reasons. First, they provide a balance to the plan and take away the sole emphasis on sales that inevitably arises. Second, they indicate positioning issues, third, they highlight the required balance of the mix, fourth, they provide time parameters for campaigns and, finally, they provide a crucial means by which particular marketing communications activities are evaluated.

Table 7.2 The main elements of the context analysis

Context element	Dimensions
The customer context	Segment characteristics Levels of awareness, perception and attitudes towards the brand/organisation Levels of involvement and types of perceived risk DMU characteristics and issues Media usage
The business context	Corporate and marketing strategy and plans Brand/organisation analysis Competitor analysis
The internal context	Financial constraints Organisation identity Culture, values and beliefs Marketing expertise Agency availability and suitability
The external context	Who are the key stakeholders and why are they important? What are their communications needs? Social, political, economic and technological restraints and opportunities

Ideally, communications objectives should consist of three main elements:

1. Corporate objectives.

   These are derived from the business or marketing plan. They refer to the mission and the business area that the organisation believes it should be in.

2. Marketing objectives.

   These are derived from the marketing plan and are output-oriented. Normally these can be considered as sales-related objectives, such as market share, sales revenues, volumes, ROI and profitability indicators.

3. Marketing communications objectives.

   These are derived from an understanding of the current context in which a brand exists and the future context in the form of where the brand is expected to be at some point in the future. These will be presented as awareness levels, perception, comprehension/ knowledge, attitudes towards and overall degree of preference for the brand. The choice of communications goal depends on the tasks that need to be accomplished. In addition, most brands need either to maintain their current brand position or to reposition themselves in the light of changing contextual conditions.

These three elements constitute the communications objectives and they all need to be set out in SMART terminology (see Chapter 8). What also emerges is a refinement of the positioning that managers see as important for success. Obviously, not all plans require express attention to positioning (e.g. government information campaigns) but most commercial and brand-oriented communications programmes need to communicate a clear position in their market. Thus, at this point the positioning intentions are developed and these will be related to the market, the customers or some other dimension. The justification for this will arise from the CA.

Marketing communications strategy

As noted earlier, the communications strategy can take many different forms, but should always be customer-, not method/media-oriented. Therefore, strategy depends on whether the target audience is a customer segment, a distributor or dealer network or whether other stakeholders need to be reached. In addition, it is imperative that the strategy be geared to the communications needs of the target audience that is revealed during the customer and business context analyses. This will show what the task is that marketing communications needs to fulfil. Having established who the audience is, push, pull or profile-dominated strategies can be identified. The next step is to determine the task that needs to be accomplished. This will have been articulated previously in the marketing communications objectives, but the approach at this stage is less quantitative and softer.

The DRIP tasks of marketing communications can be used to suggest the strategy being pursued. For example, if a new brand is being launched, the first task will be to inform and differentiate the brand for members of the trade before using a pull strategy to inform and differentiate the brand for the target, end-user customers. An organisation wishing to signal a change of strategy and/or a change of name following a merger or acquisition may choose to use a profile strategy and the primary task will be to inform of the name change. An organisation experiencing declining sales may choose to remind customers of a need or it may choose to improve sales through persuasion.

Coordinated communications mix

Having formulated, stated and justified the required position, the next step is to present the basic form and style of the key message that is to be conveyed. Is there to be a lot of copy or just a little? Is there to be a rational or emotional approach or some weighting between the two? What should be the tone of the visual messages? Is there to be a media blitz? It is at this point that those responsible for the development of these plans can be imaginative and try some new ideas. Trying to tie in the message to the strategic orientation is the important part, as the advertising agency will refine and redefine the message and the positioning.

From this the communications mixes need to be considered *for each* of the strategies proposed: that is, a mix for the consumer strategy, a mix for the trade strategy and a distinct mix for the communications to reach the wider array of stakeholders.

The choice of methods should clearly state the tools and the media to be used. A short paragraph justifying the selection is very important, as the use of media in particular is to a large extent dependent upon the nature of the goals, the target audience and the resources. The key is to provide message consistency and a measure of integration.

Resources

This is a vitally important part of the plan, one that is often avoided or forgotten about. The resources necessary to support the plan need to be determined and these refer not only to the financial issues but to the quality of available marketing expertise and the time that is available to achieve the required outcomes.

Project management software such as Prince2, and Gantt charts and other planning aids, are best used to support this part of the plan. Preferably, actual costs should be assigned, although percentages can be allocated if being written for examination purposes. What is important is the relative weighting of the costs, and a recognition and understanding of the general costs associated with the proposed communications activities.

It must be understood that the overall cost of the strategy should be in proportion to the size of the client organisation, its (probable) level of profitability and the size and dynamics of the market in which it operates.

Scheduling and implementation

The next step is to schedule the deployment of the methods and the media. Events should be scheduled according to the goals and the strategic thrust. So, if it is necessary to communicate with the trade prior to a public launch, those activities tied into the push-positioning strategy should be scheduled prior to those calculated to support the pull strategy.

Similarly, if awareness is a goal then, if funds permit, it may be best to use television and posters first before sales promotions (unless sampling is used), direct marketing, point of purchase and personal selling.

Evaluation and control

Unless there is some form of evaluation, there will be no dialogue and no true marketing communications. There are numerous methods to evaluate the individual performance of the tools and the media used, and for examination purposes these should be stated. In addition, and perhaps more meaningfully, the most important measures are the communications objectives set in the first place. The success of a promotional strategy and the associated plan is the degree to which the objectives set are achieved.

Feedback

The planning process is completed when feedback is provided. Not only should information regarding the overall outcome of a campaign be considered, but so should individual aspects of the activity. For example, the performance of the individual tools used within the campaign, whether sufficient resources were invested, the appropriateness of the strategy in the first place, any problems encountered during implementation and the relative ease with which the objectives were accomplished are all aspects that need to be fed back to all internal and external parties associated with the planning process.

This feedback is vitally important because it provides information for the CA that anchors the next campaign. Information fed back in a formal and systematic manner constitutes an opportunity for organisations to learn from their previous campaign activities, a point often overlooked and neglected.

Viewpoint 7.5

The TfL London Olympic campaign – a strategic success

Image 7.7 TfL used marketing communications strategically

The successful management of the volume and flow of people around London during the 2012 Olympic Games was a critical success factor.

Source: S-F/Shutterstock.

Managing the transport infrastructure for the London 2012 Olympics was a critical activity. At the time the London transport network carried over 25 million journeys daily, very close to capacity. Forecasting indicated that there would be over 3 million incremental journeys per day and that 300 junctions and 187 public-transport 'hotspots' would be affected during the Games. A solution was required to reduce demand and spread it across less-congested routes and times.

The challenge was to develop a communications strategy that would engage sufficient travellers and prompt them to modify their own journeys. Research showed that the risk of personal journey disruption was a more effective message than contributing to the success of the Games. This insight led to the core message platform for the behavioural strategy, 'Get ahead of the Games'.

Three core audiences were identified; people making non-Olympic journeys (background demand), businesses, and ticket holders. As everyone's journey is unique, the strategy focused on using marketing communications to 'push' travellers and businesses towards various online planning tools held at www.getaheadofthegames.com. Individuals could then see the likely impact of the Games on their journeys and the better journey options.

Audience 1: background demand

This audience consisted of regular London travellers making non-Olympic journeys, whether by public transport or car. The goal required that 30 per cent of them changed their travel habits on any given day. Many needed to be encouraged to make alternative plans as they were reluctant to adapt and were unmotivated to help the broader Olympic effort.

This was overcome by the use of advertising, direct marketing and 106 million emails sent to the most at-risk people. Travellers were also encouraged to subscribe via Twitter for real-time updates.

Audience 2: businesses

Businesses with London workforces had to encourage their employees to change their travel arrangements. This required the adoption of new working practices, travel times and policies. Those with road-based supply chains would be affected by restrictions and potentially contribute to congestion, unless they made changes.

Face-to-face events and direct marketing (direct mail and e-CRM) was used to 'reach the few to influence the many', with activity targeting key intermediaries and nominated Olympic Liaison Officers. The communication theme was based on 'keep on running', in line with the overall strategy.

Awareness was raised via a conference in November 2010, followed by several high-profile events, direct mail, including a letter from Lord Coe, and paid-for advertising in business environments. Specific advertising and bulletins were targeted at businesses making freight deliveries. At the same time, data released to satnavs and the freight industry alerted drivers of congestion. The London Lorry Control Scheme was also relaxed to allow 'out of hours' deliveries.

Audience 3: ticket holders

As it was important that visitors use public transport, not cars, travel information was provided on the Games website. This helped potential visitors make informed travel decisions before applying for tickets. Travel advice was subsequently directed to successful purchasers via email. The use of One-Day Travelcards and travel information were dispatched with each ticket.

Despite record demand, transport reliability was maintained. Over 99.5 per cent of scheduled services ran during the Games. The total cost of the Travel Demand Management campaign was £30 million and the Olympics passed without major disruption. In fact, media, competitors, spectators and other nations universally declared them a huge success.

Sources: Anon (2012); Hanley (2012); Storey (2014); Topham and Gibson (2012).

Insight

The unusual nature of the transport task should not mask the strategic nature of the marketing communications undertaken by TfL and their agency, M&C Saatchi. This Viewpoint sets out the various strategy and planning activities undertaken and can also be considered to be a very good example of strategic integration. Note the identification and segmentation of particular audiences and the development of audience-centred communication, all aimed at driving a level of behavioural response.

Question: Are objectives or strategy the most important part of the planning framework?

Task: Using the TfL material above, identify content that fits the different elements of the MCPF.

Links and essential points

It was mentioned earlier that there are a number of linkages associated with different parts of the marketing communications plan. It is important to understand the nature of these links as they represent the interconnections between different parts of the plan and the rationale for undertaking the CA in particular. The CA feeds the items shown in Table 7.3.

Table 7.3 Linkages within the MCPF

MCPF	Elements explanation
Objectives	From the marketing plan, from the customer, stakeholder network and competitor analysis and from an internal marketing review
Strategic balance between push, pull and profile	From an understanding of the brand, the needs of the target audiences, including employees and all other stakeholders, and the marketing goals
Brand positioning	From users' and non-users' perceptions, motivations, attitudes and understanding about the brand and its direct and indirect competitors
Message content and style	From an understanding about the level of involvement, perceived risk, DMU analysis, information-processing styles and the positioning intentions
Promotional tools and media	From the target audience analysis of media habits, involvement and preferences, from knowledge about product suitability and media compatibility, from a competitor analysis and from the resource analysis

For example, research undertaken by Interbrand for Intercontinental Hotels, to find out what influenced the brand experience of hotel guests, discovered that one of the key factors was the hotel concierge. As a result, the role of the concierge became a central element in the communications strategy, influencing the campaign goals, positioning and message strategy (Gustafson, 2007). The objectives derived from the CA feed decisions concerning strategy, tools and media, content, scheduling and evaluation.

The marketing communications strategy is derived from an overall appreciation of the needs of the target audience (and stakeholders) regarding the brand and its competitive position in the market. The communications mix is influenced by the previous elements and the budget that follows. However, the nature of the tools and the capacity and characteristics of the media influence scheduling, implementation and evaluation activities.

Scholars' paper 7.5
Planning Renault's expansion

Caemmerer, B. (2009) The planning and implementation of integrated marketing communications, *Marketing Intelligence & Planning*, 27(4), 524–38.

Students of marketing communications should read this paper, simply because it illustrates the tasks involved in the planning and implementation of integrated marketing communications. Using a case study approach based on Renault's attempt to expand their market share in Germany, the paper considers the range of tasks involved in planning an integrated marketing communications campaign. These include the context analysis and the identification of marketing communications opportunities; choosing the right marketing communications agency; campaign development and implementation, including the selection of the marketing communications mix, creative execution and media planning; campaign evaluation; planning of follow-up campaigns; and managerial coordination between all tasks and parties involved to ensure integration of marketing communications initiatives throughout the campaign.

The MCPF provides a view of the planning activities and sequence of actions necessary to develop and implement a marketing communications activity. At the end of Chapter 22, readers can see how this framework is reworked into the activities necessary for media planning.

Key points

- There are many different views of what constitutes strategy, partly because it is a multi-dimensional concept.
- Marketing communications strategy is not just about the mix, and should start with an audience-centred orientation.
- Marketing communications strategy should be concerned with the overall direction of the programme and target audiences, the fit with marketing and corporate strategy, the key message and desired positioning the brand is to occupy in the market, plus the resources necessary to deliver the position and accomplish the goals.
- There are four core ways of interpreting marketing communications strategy. These are the positioning, audience, platform and configuration approaches. Each of these emphasise particular elements and issues but they are not mutually discrete. Aspects of each can be found in the others.
- The positioning approach is derived from the STP process.
- The audience approach is referred to as the '3Ps' of marketing communications strategy.
- The platform approach can be advertising-led (around a creative idea), brand-led (around a core brand characteristic) or take the form of a participatory platform.
- The configuration approach requires managing the structural elements of an intended communications event, within the prevailing relationship, climate and power context, where appropriate.
- To manage efficiently and perhaps more effectively, marketing communications should be implemented through the use of a planning framework.
- The framework consists of a number of elements, which are presented sequentially, but in reality often happen simultaneously. Key to understanding the planning framework are the linkages between the various elements.

Sr Toronjo

Fermín Paús, Sr Brand Manager at Danone

Colombia is located in the northwest of South America, a region that is close to the equator line and is characterised by its tropical weather and vegetation. Colombian people are happy, optimistic and have a passion for dancing and music. In addition, Colombia has an enormous variety of flavours that can be found in the different fruits and vegetables that Colombians consume daily.

The soft drinks category is not isolated from this phenomenon and apart from the global traditional flavours (cola, orange and lemon) you could find apple, grapefruit, pineapple, grape and tamarind soft drinks. Due to the relevance of local flavours,

the market is diversified and the competition fierce. Two players dominate the market: The Coca-Cola Company and a local company called Postobón (Pepsi), which leads the local flavours game, with the exception of grapefruit. Grapefruit represents around 4 per cent of the total soft drinks market and has experienced growth above industry average in the last few years.

Quatro, a Coca-Cola Company brand, has been the leader with 100 per cent market share of the grapefruit flavour since it was launched in 1996. Postobón has tried for 20 years to gain traction in this segment with the launch of Toronja Postobón,

Image 7.8 Mr Grapefruit: a new Colombian reaggaeton singer
Source: Juan Camilo Gomez.

Speed Toronja and Hit; however, these launches could not achieve the necessary level of relevance to compete. In contrast, Quatro, with its humorous and witty tone, connects well with consumers. It targets young adults (20–29 years), for whom this flavour is more appealing, and focuses its communication on common situations: home, university and work settings.

In 2014, Postobón decided to try again but this time they totally changed their approach to compete in this segment. The first step was to define, analyse and understand the consumer target. Postobón decided to target the Z generation, youth between 15 and 19 years old and the entry-level consumer of the grapefruit segment. By doing so, the company was planning to recruit an entire new generation, not an easy job. They were born in the digital world, are massive consumers of any type of online content and have a very short attention span. As mentioned before, Colombians love to dance and this generation loves 'reggaeton', one of the most popular music genres in Latin America. Reggaeton singers are very influential and this generation is passionate about their lifestyle.

Regarding soft drinks preferences, the Z generation is willing to change their brand repertoires and try everything. Thus, there was a good opportunity to launch a new beverage to capture at least 25 per cent of the grapefruit segment in the first year. The main problem was that they are reluctant to engage with a new brand, specially a soft drink. In this way, a differentiated strategy was essential to accomplish the volume target.

After two years of work, the strategy was finally shaped and the new product ready to see the light in 2016. The strategy was called 'the celebrity project' and is based on a new global trend: social celebrities. When celebrities become famous online, they usually use their massive organic reach to create a brand and launch products, achieving incredible business results. So, why not bring this idea to the launch of a new soft drink? The strategy consisted of two stages. The company aimed to create a new celebrity, a super-cool reggaeton singer. And once he becomes famous, he will launch his own beverage. The name chosen for both the celebrity and the beverages was 'Sr Toronjo' (Mr Grapefruit).

Postobón presented Mr Grapefruit as a 'new Colombian reggaeton singer who has an acid touch and loves parties. His music mixes urban rhythms; his lyrics are funny and spread the happy side of life'. He always wears a mask that has a grapefruit shape and it totally covers his face to create mystery and attract youth attention. His face looks like an emoji and is constantly changing to reflect expressions and emotions.

The new character was launched totally unbranded through traditional and digital media and after a month on air, he had already attracted the attention of young people all over the country. His first song 'Sácalo' (Get it out) reached 2 million views on YouTube. Radio stations, entertainment shows, music channels, news channels and international media like MTV were talking about this new singer.

Mr Grapefruit became a national phenomenon and people were asking who this singer was. The company took advantage of this situation and decided to launch a second single, 'Who I am?' Using the excuse of the presentation of this new single, Mr Grapefruit launched his new soft drink; with his name and face printed on each bottle. Postobón describes the new beverage as a 'unique experience with an irreverent tone, fresh, young and daring. It has an acid touch that you will enjoy until the end'.

The media mix used for the second stage of the campaign gave the brand important national coverage. It used TV commercials, radio spots, out-of-home positions across the main Colombian cities, print, digital, experiential, public relations and point of sale materials. In relation to the content, Postobón decided to shift the message towards more product-centric pieces leaving the new character in second place.

The Mr Toronjo case has achieved interesting results. In the first months, more than 11 million units were sold and Postobón captured 38 per cent market

Image 7.9 The products featured the image of Mr Grapefruit when the brand was launched.
Source: Juan Camilo Gomez.

share of the grapefruit segment in only nine months, easily passing the initial goal of 25 per cent in the first year. The 38 per cent market share remains stable.

Moreover, Sr Toronjo has become a national celebrity. He has more than twelve songs produced with more than 24 million views on YouTube and he often performs at massive concerts around the country. Regarding social media interaction, the new brand achieved more than 20 million interactions, with a 6.5 per cent engagement rate and has a fan community close to 300,000.

These results could be explained by a differentiated positioning strategy together with disruptive creativity and connection planning. There is now a new brand that sings, gives interviews and dances, a totally out of the box approach. The Mr Toronjo case shows that tackling risk and breaking the rules can bring incredible sales results and a stronger consumer connection. With more than 15 global awards, it has become one of the most awarded cases in Latin America and worldwide in 2016 and 2017, including the Latin America Advertiser of the Year.

Source: Anon (2017b); Anon (2017c); Villegas (2017); www.behance.net

Review questions

Sr Toronjo case questions

1. Explain the role strategy plays in marketing communications, using the Mr Toronjo case to illustrate your points.
2. Evaluate which of the four interpretations of strategy presented in this chapter, might best be used to explain the success of the Mr Toronjo campaign.
3. Discuss the extent to which the Mr Toronjo campaign might be interpreted as an advertising-led creative platform, a brand-concept platform, or a platform based on conversation and participation.
4. Which type of engagement best explains the Mr Toronjo approach to marketing communications?
5. Identify the elements of the marketing communications mix used to implement the Mr Toronjo launch.

General questions

1. Compare strategy with planning. In what ways might planning be the same as strategy?
2. Make notes for your friend in which you explain the differences between an advertising-led and a brand-led platform for marketing communications strategy.
3. Explain the configuration approach to marketing communications strategy.
4. Sketch the marketing communications planning framework – from memory.
5. Following on from the previous question, check your version of the MCPF with the original and then prepare some bullet-point notes, highlighting the critical linkages between the main parts of the framework.

References for Chapter 7

Anderson, E., Lodish, L. and Weitz, B. (1987) Resource allocation behaviour in conventional channels, *Journal of Marketing Research*, February, 85–97.

Andrews, K. (1987) *The Concept of Corporate Strategy*, Homewood, IL: Richard D. Irwin.

Anon (2012) Delivering transport for the London 2012 Games, Olympic Delivery Authority, October, retrieved 14 April 2016 from http://learninglegacy.independent.gov.uk/documents/pdfs/transport/london-2012-report-lowres-withlinks.pdf

Anon (2016a) Li Ning gains branding opportunity at the Rio Olympics, SGK, 12 August, retrieved 22 September 2017 from http://www.sgkinc.com/insights-marketing/marketing-blog/Li-Ning-Gains-Branding-Opportunity-at-the-Rio-Olympics

Anon (2016b) Rising out of crisis, *Catalyst,* 4 May, retrieved 17 July 2017 from http://exchange.cim.co.uk/editorial/rising-out-of-crisis/

Anon (2017a) Embraer increases share of audience by 624% with challenger brand multichannel campaign, *B2B Marketing Awards,* 30 October, retrieved 24 December 2017 from www.b2bmarketing.net/en-gb/resources/b2b-case-studies/awards-case-study-embraer-increases-share-audience-624-challenger-brand

Anon (2017b) Sancho BBDO y Sr. Toronjo: el éxito fue concebir un producto que canta, baila y se bebe, *Adlatina,* 9 October, retrieved 16 April 2018 from http://www.adlatina.com/publicidad/sancho-bbdo-y-sr-toronjo-%E2%80%9Cel-%C3%A9xito-fue-concebir-un-producto-que-canta-baila-y-se-bebe%E2%80%9D

Anon (2017c) Juan Camilo Gómez: Valoramos más los Effie que el resto de los premios, *Marketers,* 9 September, retrieved 16 April 2018 from http://www.marketersbyadlatina.com/articulo/2880-juan-camilo-g%C3%B3mez%E2%80%9Cvaloramos-m%C%A1s-los-effie-que-el-resto-de-los-premios%E2%80%D

Ansoff, H.I. (1965) *Corporate Strategy,* New York: McGraw-Hill.

Beane, T.P. and Ennis, D.M. (1987) Market segmentation: a review, *European Journal of Marketing,* 21(5), 20–42.

Bloxham, M. and Sylvester, A.K. (2013) Media research: planning for context, *Admap,* April, retrieved 13 July 2014 from www.warc.com/Content/ContentViewer.aspx?ID=7e94ad81-00d2-4696-ab8e-e8077187bbeb&MasterContentRef=7e94ad81-00d2-4696-ab8e-e8077187bbeb&Campaign=admap_apr13&utm_campaign=admap_apr13.

Bosiljevac, J. (2015) Advertising in context: create context and relevancy, *Admap,* May.

Caemmerer, B. (2009) The planning and implementation of integrated marketing communications, *Marketing Intelligence & Planning,* 27(4), 524–38.

Chaffee, E. (1985) Three models of strategy, *Academy of Management Review,* 10(1), 89–98.

Cox, K., Crowther, J., Hubbard, T. and Turner, D. (2011) *New Models of Marketing Effectiveness: From Integration to Orchestration,* WARC.

Degun, G. (2016) British Paralympians star in first Channel 4 ad-funded Shorts series on linear TV, *Campaign,* 7 July, retrieved 1 November 2017 from https://www.campaignlive.co.uk/article/british-paralympians-star-first-channel-4-ad-funded-shorts-series-linear-tv/1401538

Dwyer, R. and Walker, O.C. (1981) Bargaining in an asymmetrical power structure, *Journal of Marketing,* 45 (Winter), 104–15.

Edwards, H. (2011) Work towards an 'ideal self', *Marketing,* 2 February, 21.

Engel, J.F., Warshaw, M.R. and Kinnear, T.C. (1994) *Promotional Strategy,* 8th edn, Homewood, IL: Richard D. Irwin.

Fan, K. and Murata, P. (2015) Revitalizing a national icon, *Millward Brown,* retrieved 30 January 2015 from www.millwardbrown.com/docs/default-source/insight-documents/case-studies/Firefly_MB_Li_Ning_Case_Study_2013.pdf?sfvrsn=4

Frazier, G.L. and Summers, J.O. (1984) Interfirm influence strategies and their application within distribution channels, *Journal of Marketing,* 48 (Summer), 43–55.

Gustafson, R. (2007) Best of all worlds, *Marketing: Brands by Design,* 14 November, 11.

Hagiu, A. and Altman, E.J. (2017) Finding the platform in your product: four strategies that can reveal hidden value, *Harvard Business Review,* 95(4), July/August, 94–100.

Haley, R.I. (1968) Benefit segmentation: a decision-oriented research tool, *Journal of Marketing,* 32 (July), 30–5.

Hanley, C. (2012) London 2012 Travel Demand Management, Journeys, 1 November, retrieved 3 September 2018 from https://www.yumpu.com/en/document/view/18199965/london-2012-travel-demand-management-lta-academy

Horáková, H., Švarcová, M. and Volf, L. (2017) Marketing planning process – reflection on the complex of activities that affect all aspects of business life, *Marketing Science & Inspirations*, 12(2), 43–53.

Jewell, R.D. (2007) Establishing effective repositioning communications in a competitive marketplace, *Journal of Marketing Communications*, 13(4), 231–41.

Kay, J. (1993) The structure of strategy, *Business Strategy Review*, 4(2), 17–37.

Kwok, D. (2014) China's Li Ning stumbles from gold medal position to no man's land, *Reuters*, Monday 1 September, retrieved 31 January 2015 from https://www.reuters.com/article/lining-outlook/chinas-li-ning-stumbles-from-gold-medal-position-to-no-mans-land-idUSL-4N0QR13020140901

Mintzberg, H. and Waters, J.A. (1985) Of strategies, deliberate and emergent, *Strategic Management Journal*, 6(3), 257–72.

Mohr, J. and Nevin, J.R. (1990) Communication strategies in marketing channels, *Journal of Marketing*, October, 36–51.

Reid, D. (2017) Embraer claims its biggest ever jet is 'profit hunter' for airlines, *CNBC*, 19 June, retrieved 24 December 2017 from https://www.cnbc.com/2017/06/19/embraer-claims-its-biggest-ever-jet-is-profit-hunter-for-airlines.html

Rothschild, M. (1987) *Marketing Communications*, Lexington, MA: DC Heath.

Sauer, A. (2017) Li Ning on the past: brand founders and the need to recede, Brand Channel, 31 March, retrieved 22 September 2017 from http://www.brandchannel.com/2017/03/31/li-ning-033117/

Simms, J. (2017) Raising your profile, *Catalyst*, January, 6, 11–13.

Smith, P.R. (2003) *Great Answers to Tough Marketing Questions*, 2nd edn, London: Kogan Page.

Stern, L. and El-Ansary, A.I. (1988) *Marketing Channels*, Englewood Cliffs, NJ: Prentice-Hall.

Stern, L. and El-Ansary, A.I. (1992) *Marketing Channels*, 4th edn., Englewood Cliffs, NJ: Prentice-Hall.

Storey, R. (2014) Olympic Delivery Authority/Transport for London: securing Gold at London 2012, *Institute of Practitioners in Advertising*, retrieved 14 April 2016 from www.warc.com/Pages/Search/WordSearch.aspx?Sort=ContentDatepercent7c1&q=storey*+TFL

Topham, G. and Gibson, O. (2012) London 2012: campaign seeks to cut commuter numbers during Games, *Guardian*, Monday 30 January, retrieved 14 April 2016 from www.theguardian.com/sport/2012/jan/30/london-olympics-2012-cut-commuter

Van Alstyne, M.W., Parker, G.G. and Choudary, S.P. (2016) Pipelines, platforms, and the new rules of strategy, *Harvard Business Review*, April, 54–60.

Villegas, J. (2017) Sorprendente guerra de la Toronja, *Brand Experts*, 9 May, retrieved 16 April 2018 from: https://expertosenmarca.com/marketing/sorprendente-guerra-de-la-toronja/

William-Smith, H. (2017) Customers hungry to feel valued: Fidor Bank, 9 May, retrieved 17 July 2017 from http://fst.net.au/news/customers-hungry-feel-valued-fidor-bank

Wind, Y.J. (1990) Positioning analysis and strategy, in *The Interface of Marketing and Strategy* (eds G. Day, B. Weitz and R. Wensley), Greenwich, CT: JAI Press, 387–412.

Marketing communications: objectives and positioning

The setting of formalised marketing communications objectives is important for three main reasons. They provide guidance about what is to be achieved, when, and measurement of how successful an event has been.

Objectives form a pivotal role between the business/marketing plans and the marketing communications strategy. The way in which a product or service is perceived by buyers is the only positioning that really matters.

Aims and learning objectives

The aims of this chapter are to establish the role and characteristics of marketing communications objectives and to explore the concept of positioning.

The learning objectives are to enable readers to:

1. explore the different types of organisational objectives;
2. appreciate the relationship between corporate strategy and communications objectives;
3. determine the components of SMART-based objectives;
4. examine the differences between sales- and communications-based objectives;
5. understand the concept of positioning and the principles of perceptual mapping;
6. explain the main types of positioning strategies.

Introduction

Research shows clearly that successful marketing communications utilise a clear set of objectives (Patti et al., 2017). Research also shows that there is considerable variation in the extent to which practitioners actually set objectives. Furthermore, it is apparent that it is not established practice to set detailed objectives that are used to measure the outcomes of a campaign.

There are many different opinions about what it is that marketing communications seeks to achieve. The conflicting views have led some practitioners and academics to polarise their thoughts about what constitutes an appropriate set of objectives. First, much effort has been spent trying to determine what 'promotion' and marketing communications activities are supposed to achieve; second, how should the success of a campaign be evaluated; and finally, how best to determine the degree of investment that should be made in each of the areas of the communications mix?

The process of resolving these different demands that are placed on organisations has made the setting of 'promotional' objectives very complex and difficult. It was termed by Kriegel, way back in 1986, as 'a job of creating order out of chaos', and as Patti and his colleagues observe, things have not changed much since then. This perceived complexity has led a number of managers to fail to set suitably comprehensive communication objectives or to set the wrong ones. Many of those who do set them do so in such a way that they are inappropriate, inadequate or merely restate the marketing objectives. The most common marketing communications objectives set by managers are sales-related, such as increases in market share, return on investment, sales volume increases and improvements in the value of sales made after accounting for the rate of inflation.

Such a general perspective ignores the influence of the other elements of the marketing mix and implicitly places the entire responsibility for sales performance with communications. This is not an accurate reflection of the way in which businesses and organisations work. In addition, because sales tests are too general, they are an insufficiently rigorous test of promotional activity, and there is no real evaluation of promotional activities. Sales volumes vary for a wide variety of reasons:

- competitors change their prices;
- buyers' needs change;
- changes in legislation may favour the strategies of particular organisations;
- favourable third-party communications become known to significant buyers;
- general economic conditions change;
- technological advances facilitate improved production processes;
- economies of scale, experience effects and, for some organisations, the opportunity to reduce costs;
- the entry and exit of different competitors.

These are a few of the many reasons why sales levels fluctuate. Therefore, the notion that marketing communications is entirely responsible for the sales of an offering, is clearly unacceptable, unrealistic and incorrect.

The role of objectives

Objectives play an important role in the activities of individuals, social groups and organisations because they:

1. provide direction and an action focus for all those participating in the activity;
2. set up a framework through which the variety of decisions relating to an activity can be made in a consistent way;
3. set out the time period in which the activity is to be completed;
4. communicate the values and scope of the activity to all participants;
5. offer a means by which the success of an activity can be evaluated;

It is generally accepted that the process of developing corporate strategy demands that a series of objectives be set at different levels within an organisation (Johnson et al., 2017). This hierarchy of objectives consists of mission, strategic business unit (SBU) or business objectives, and functional objectives, such as production, finance or marketing goals.

The first level in the hierarchy (mission) requires that an overall direction be set for the organisation. If strategic decisions are made to achieve corporate objectives, both objectives and strategy are themselves constrained by an organisation's mission. Mission statements should be a vision that management has of what the organisation is trying to achieve in the long term. A mission statement outlines who the organisation is, what it does and where it is headed. A clearly developed, articulated and communicated mission statement enables an organisation to define whose needs are to be satisfied, what needs require satisfying, and which products and technologies will be used to provide the desired levels of satisfaction. The mission should clearly identify the following:

- the customers/buyers to be served;
- the needs to be satisfied;
- the products and/or technologies by which these will be achieved.

In some organisations these points are explicitly documented in a mission statement. These statements often include references to the organisation's philosophy, culture, commitment to the community and employees, growth, profitability and so on, but these should not blur or distract attention from the organisation's basic mission. The words 'mission' and 'vision' are often used interchangeably, but they have separate meanings. Vision refers to the expected or desired outcome of carrying out the mission over the agreed period of time.

The mission provides a framework for the organisation's objectives, and the objectives that follow should promote and be consistent with the mission. While the word 'mission' implies a singularity of purpose, organisations have multiple objectives because of the many aspects of the organisation's performance and behaviour that contribute to the mission, and should, therefore, be explicitly identified. Many of these objectives however, will conflict with each other. In retailing, for example, if an organisation chooses to open larger stores, then total annual profit should rise, but average profit per square metre will probably fall. Short-term profitability can be improved by reducing investment, but this could adversely affect long-term profitability. Organisations have long-term and short-term objectives.

At the SBU level, objectives represent the translation of the mission into a form that can be understood by relevant stakeholders. These objectives are the performance requirements for the organisation or unit, which in turn are broken down into objectives or targets that each functional area must achieve, as their contribution to the unit objectives. Marketing strategies are functional strategies, as are the strategies for the finance, human resource management, production and other departments. Combine or aggregate them, and the SBU's overall target will, in reductionist theory, be achieved.

The various organisational objectives are of little use if they are not communicated to those who need to know what they are. Traditionally, such communications have focused on employees, but there is increasing recognition that the other members of the stakeholder network need to understand an organisation's purpose and objectives. The marketing objectives developed for the marketing strategy provide important information for the communications strategy. Is the objective to increase market share or to defend or maintain the current situation? Is the product new or established? Is it being modified or slowly withdrawn? The corporate image is shaped partly by the organisation's objectives and the manner in which they are communicated. All these impact on the objectives of the communications plan.

Scholars' paper 8.1
So, just what is the value of marketing?

Hanssens, D.M. and Pauwels, K.H. (2016) Demonstrating the value of marketing, *Journal of Marketing*: **AMA/MSI Special Issue, 80 (November), 173–90.**

This paper considers some of the issues facing organisations in their attempt to place an economic value on marketing. Among these is the reality that the scope and objectives of marketing differ widely across organisations. This is an interesting paper as it provides a useful context in which to start exploring the role and nature of marketing objectives.

The role of brand communications objectives and plans

Many organisations fail to set realistic (if any) communications or campaign objectives. There are several explanations for this behaviour, but one of the common factors is that managers are unable to differentiate between the value of communications as an expense and as an investment. The value of these objectives, however, can be seen in terms of the role they play in communications planning, evaluation and brand development.

The databank created by the Institute of Practitioners in Advertising consists of data concerning over 1,200 successful campaigns, recorded since 1980. This clearly shows that those campaigns that set clear and appropriate objectives are more successful than those that do not (Binet and Field, 2007). As a result of this data a large proportion of UK agencies appear to be setting a hierarchy of goals for the campaigns they develop.

The setting of marketing communications objectives is important for three main reasons:

1. They provide *a means of communications and coordination* between groups (e.g. client and agency) working on different parts of a campaign. Performance is improved if there is common understanding about the tasks and the individual elements of the mix that an integrated campaign has to accomplish.

2. Objectives constrain the number of options available to an organisation. Campaign objectives act as *a guide for decision-making* and provide a focus for decisions that follow in the process of developing and implementing communications plans. This is also important during campaigns as programmatic technologies allow for budgets and media to be switched as low-performing aspects of a campaign are identified.

3. Objectives provide *a benchmark* so that the relative success or failure of a programme can be evaluated. Again, this can be used during as well as at the end of a campaign.

There is no doubt that organisations need to be flexible, to be able to anticipate and adjust to changes in their environments. This principle applies to the setting of campaign objectives. To set one all-encompassing objective and expect it to last the year (or whatever period is allocated) is both hopeful and naive; multiple objectives are necessary.

Viewpoint 8.1
Goals galore

Image 8.1 Leeds Castle
Source: simon gurney/123RF.

Different brands encounter different situations, and arising from this are a rich variety of goals.

Leeds Castle set a campaign goal to encourage repeat visits, particularly during the winter period, by emphasising the different events that take place at the castle all year round.

notonthehighstreet.com aimed to improve consumer understanding not only of the wide range of their offering but to also attract a bigger variety of customers over the Christmas period.

VisitScotland attempted to inspire tourists to visit the country during winter. The campaign was

Sources: Various.

designed to appeal to all of the senses, reversing preconceptions of dreariness and presenting Scotland as a romantic and exciting destination, with an emphasis on luxury.

China's shower gel market segment has 11 brands and 93 variants. Unilever's Dove had been dormant for five years. Its campaign aim was to challenge market leader Olay and grow market share from 2 per cent to 3.4 per cent. This meant persuading 4 million Chinese women to buy Dove Body Wash.

The Shangri-La Hotels and Resorts campaign, 'It's in our nature', set a goal of achieving an extra $90 million in room revenues, and this meant that it had to sell 10 more rooms per hotel per night.

Country Life's campaign goals were to correct the misperception that their main rival 'Anchor' was a British brand, and to enable consumers to make an informed butter choice.

When the B2B market in Singapore started to recover from the 2008 recession, HP and Intel joined forces to accomplish two main goals. The first was to generate new business leads by an incremental positive 30 per cent over the previous year. The second was to change their image from being perceived as cold and corporate to a more personable and approachable profile. A target of a 1:3 return on investment was set.

Insight

The point here is that organisations have a variety of goals that reflect the individual context of their brands at a particular moment. So, there are different types of goals, each established for different reasons, but they are all used to underpin the communications strategies that evolve from them. What these objectives do not do is provide a clear means of campaign measurement.

Question: If goals are designed to focus activities, are they the most important element of marketing communications or is something else more important?

Task: Make a list of the different types of goals that might be used for marketing communications.

The academic literature suggests that a combination of sales and communications objectives is optimal. Practitioners appear to use a variety of approaches and demonstrate inconsistency in their use and format. Consideration is given first to the academic interpretations before turning to the practitioner views. The content of campaign objectives has also been the subject of considerable debate. Academics refer to two distinct schools of thought: those that advocate sales-related measures, sometimes referred to as activation by practitioners, as the main factors, and those that advocate communications-related measures as the main orientation.

The sales school

As stated earlier, many managers see sales as the only meaningful objective for campaigns. Their view is that the only reason an organisation spends money on communications is to sell its product or service. Therefore, the only meaningful measure of the effectiveness of 'the spend' are the sales results.

These results can be measured in a number of different ways. Sales turnover is the first and most obvious factor, particularly in business-to-business markets. In consumer markets and the fast-moving consumer goods sector, market share movement is measured regularly and is used as a more sensitive barometer of performance. Over the longer term, return-on-investment measures are used to calculate success and failure. In some sectors the number of products sold, or volume of product shifted, relative to other periods of activity, is a common measure. There are a number of difficulties with this view. One of these has been considered earlier: that *sales result from a variety of influences,* such as the other elements in the marketing mix, competitor actions and wider environmental effects, such as the strength of a currency, changing social preferences or the level of interest rates.

A second difficulty rests with the concept of *adstock* or *carryover.* The impact of promotional expenditure may not be immediately apparent, as the receiver may not enter the market until some later date, but the effects of the promotional programme may influence the eventual purchase decision. This means that, when measuring the effectiveness of a campaign, sales results will not always reflect its full impact.

Sales objectives do little to assist the media planner, copywriters and creative team associated with the development of a communications programme, despite their inclusion in campaign documents such as media briefs.

Sales-oriented objectives are, however, applicable in particular situations. For example, where direct action is required by the receiver in response to exposure to a message, measurement of sales is justifiable. Such an action, a behavioural response, can be solicited in direct-response advertising. This occurs where the sole communications are through a particular channel, such as a website, television or print.

The retail sector can also use sales measures, and it has been suggested that packaged-goods organisations, operating in mature markets with established pricing and distribution structures, can build a databank from which it is possible to isolate the advertising effect through sales. For example, when supermarkets use celebrity chefs such as Jamie Oliver, Nigella Lawson and James Martin they can monitor the stock movements of the ingredients used in 'celebrity recipe' commercials. Not only does this enable supermarkets to evaluate the success of particular campaigns, recipes and particular celebrities, but they can also learn to anticipate demand and stock ingredients in anticipation of particular advertisements being screened. Despite this cause-and-effect relationship however, it can be argued that this may ignore the impact of changes in competitor actions and changes in the overall environment. Furthermore, the effects of an organisation's own corporate advertising, adstock effects, and other family brand promotions need to be accounted for if a meaningful sales effect is to be generated.

The sales school advocate the measure on the grounds of simplicity. Any manager can utilise the tool, and senior management does not wish to be concerned with information which is complex or unfamiliar, especially when working to short lead times and accounting periods. It is a self-consistent theory, but one that may misrepresent consumer behaviour and the purchase process (perhaps unintentionally), and may result in less than optimal investment in marketing communications.

The communications school

There are many situations where the aim of a communications campaign is to enhance the image or reputation of an organisation or product. Sales are not regarded as the only goal. Consequently, promotional efforts are seen as communications tasks, such as the creation of awareness, or positive attitudes towards the organisation or a product. To facilitate this process, receivers have to be given relevant information before the appropriate decision processes can develop and purchase activities become established as a long-run behaviour.

Various models have been developed to assist our understanding about how these promotional tasks are segregated and organised effectively. AIDA and other hierarchy of effects models were considered earlier at some length and need not be repeated here. One particular model, however, was developed deliberately to introduce clear objectives into the advertising development process: DAGMAR.

DAGMAR

Russell Colley (1961) developed a model for setting advertising objectives and measuring the results. This model was entitled 'Defining Advertising Goals for Measured Advertising Results – DAGMAR'. Colley's rationale for what is effectively a means of setting communications-oriented objectives was that advertising's job, purely and simply, is to communicate to a defined audience information and a frame of mind that stimulates action. Advertising succeeds or fails depending on how well it communicates the desired information and attitudes to the right people at the right time and at the right cost.

Colley proposed that the communications task be based on a hierarchical model of the communications process: awareness–comprehension–conviction–action (see Table 8.1).

Awareness

Awareness of the existence of a product or an organisation is necessary before purchase behaviour can be expected. Once awareness has been created in the target audience,

Table 8.1   A hierarchy of communications

Stage	Explanation
Awareness	Awareness of the existence of a product or brand is necessary before any purchase will be made.
Comprehension	Audiences need information and knowledge about the product and its specific attributes. Often the audiences need to be educated and shown either how to use the product or how changes (in attributes) might affect their use of the product.
Conviction	By encouraging beliefs that a product is superior to others in a category or can confer particular rewards through use, audiences can be convinced to trial the product at the next purchase opportunity.
Action	Potential buyers need help and encouragement to transfer thoughts into behaviour. Providing call-free numbers, website addresses, reply cards, coupons and salespeople helps people act upon their convictions.

Source: Based on Colley (1961).

it should not be neglected. If there is neglect, an audience may become distracted by competing messages and the level of awareness of the focus product or organisation may decline. Awareness, therefore, needs to be created, developed, refined or sustained, according to the characteristics of the market and the particular situation facing an organisation at any one point in time (see Figure 8.1).

In situations where a buyer experiences high involvement and is fully aware of a product's existence, attention and awareness levels need only be sustained. Communications efforts need to accomplish other tasks in a consumer's purchase journey.

Where low levels of awareness are found, getting attention needs to be a prime objective so that awareness can be developed in the target audience. Where low involvement exists, the decision-making process is relatively straightforward. With levels of risk minimised, buyers with sufficient levels of awareness may be prompted into purchase with little assistance from the other elements of the mix. Recognition and recall of brand names and corporate images are felt by some (Rossiter and Percy, 1987) to be sufficient triggers to stimulate a behavioural response. The requirement in this situation would be to refine and strengthen the level of awareness in order to provoke interest and stimulate a higher level of involvement during recall or recognition.

Where low levels of awareness are matched by low involvement, the prime objective has to be to create awareness of the product in association with the product class. It is not surprising that organisations use awareness campaigns and invest a large proportion of their resources in establishing their brand or corporate name. Many brands seek to establish 'top-of-mind awareness' as one of their primary objectives for their advertising spend.

It is interesting to observe that most advertising programmes still include awareness as an objective. The logic is clear: if the ad is not seen, it is not going to be effective. However, in the light of the low attention processing theory, are high-awareness goals necessary and, more important, are they a waste of financial resources? Heath (2009) and colleagues would argue that they are, but convincing a client, or agency even, that driving high levels of awareness is not necessary is likely to be problematic.

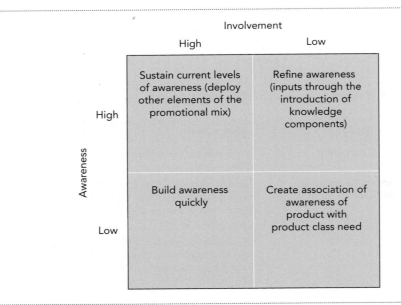

Figure 8.1 An awareness grid

Comprehension

Awareness on its own is, invariably, not enough to stimulate purchase activity. Knowledge about a product (or what the organisation does) is necessary, and this can be achieved by providing specific information about key brand attributes. These attributes and their associated benefits may be key to the buyers in the target audience or may be key because the product has been adapted or modified in some way. This means that the audiences need to be informed and educated about the change and shown how their use of the product may be affected. For example, in attempting to persuade people to try a different brand of mineral water, it may be necessary to compare the product with other mineral water products and provide an additional usage benefit, such as environmental claims.

Conviction

Having established that a product has particular attributes that lead to benefits perceived by the target audience as important, it is then necessary to establish a sense of conviction. By creating interest and preference, buyers are moved to a position where they are convinced that one particular product in the class should be tried at the next opportunity. To do this, an audience's beliefs about a product need to be shaped, and this can be accomplished by using messages that demonstrate a product's superiority over its main rival or by emphasising the rewards conferred as a result of using the product. For example, the reward of social acceptance associated with many fragrance, fashion clothing and accessory advertisements, and the reward of self-gratification associated with many confectionery messages, such as those by associated with Cadbury's 'Flake', 'Galaxy' by Mars, and Mondelēz International's 'Terry's Chocolate Orange'.

High-involvement decisions are best supported with personal selling and sales promotion activities, in an attempt to gain conviction. Low-involvement decisions rely on the strength of advertising messages, packaging and sales promotion to secure conviction.

Action

A communications programme is used to encourage buyers to engage in purchase activity. Advertising can be directive and guide buyers into certain behavioural outcomes: for example, to click on an offer, to send a response text, use of free phone numbers (0800 in the United Kingdom), direct mail activities, reply cards and coupons. However, for high-involvement decisions the most effective tool in the communications mix at this stage in the hierarchy is personal selling. Through the use of interpersonal skills, buyers are more likely to want to buy a product or service than if the personal prompting is absent. The use of direct marketing activities by Avon Cosmetics, Tupperware, Betterware and suppliers of financial and double-glazing services, has been instrumental in the sales growth experienced by organisations in these markets.

Colley's dissatisfaction with the way in which advertising agencies operated led him to specify the components of a good advertising objective: 'A specific communications task to be accomplished among a defined audience, to a given degree, in a given period of time' (Dutka, 1995). An analysis of this statement shows that a communications objective should contain four distinct elements:

1. a specific communications task;
2. a defined audience;
3. a stated degree of change;
4. a time period in which the activity is to occur.

Colley's statement is very clear – it is measurable and of assistance to creative teams. Indeed, DAGMAR revolutionised the approach taken by advertisers to the setting of objectives. It helped move attention from the sales effect to the communications effect school and has led to improved planning processes.

Scholars' paper 8.2
First time to set advertising goals

Patti, C.H., Hartley, S.W., van Dessel, M.M. and Baack, D.W. (2017) Improving integrated marketing communications practices: a comparison of objectives and results, *Journal of Marketing Communications*, 23(4), 351–70.

This paper considers the role and nature of marketing communications objectives within a practitioner context. It utilises Colley's four elements of suitable marketing communications objectives.

See also the seminal book on this subject:

Colley, R. (1961) *Defining Advertising Goals for Measured Advertising Results*, New York: Association of National Advertisers.

Many of the difficulties associated with sequential models (as presented in Chapter 6), are also applicable to DAGMAR. In addition to problems of hierarchical progression and measurement, are issues concerning the sales orientation, restrictions upon creativity and short-term accountability. These are set out in Table 8.2.

Table 8.2   Issues associated with DAGMAR

Stage	Explanation
Hierarchical progression	The rational and sequential movement of consumers towards a purchase via specified stages of learn, then feel and then do does not sit with actual consumer behaviour.
Measurement	The primary measurement difficulty concerns what constitute adequate levels of awareness, comprehension and conviction, and how can it be determined which stage the majority of the target audience has reached, at any one point in time.
Sales orientation	The sales school believe that the completion of communications tasks may not result in sales, and as they believe sales are the only valid measure, working through DAGMAR is a waste of resources.
Restrictions on creativity	It is argued that creative flair can be lost because attention passes from looking for the big idea to concentration on measures of recall, attitude change and awareness. It is agreed that the creative personnel are held to be more accountable under DAGMAR and this may well inhibit some of their work.
Short-termism	There are four primary time-related factors that work against the successful implementation of DAGMAR, and similar approaches. First, there is a trend within many commercial organisations to shorten the accounting reporting period, usually to 13 weeks. This is implemented in order to inform investors and other stakeholders of progress and development. Second, the shortening length of time that many managers stay in a job makes this communications approach impractical, as it is not long enough for all of the communications tasks to be progressed or completed. Sales measures present a much more readily digestible benchmark of performance, which helps to satisfy the accounting period requirements. Third, managers do not have enough time to spend analysing levels of comprehension or preference and to convert them into formats that are going to be of direct benefit to them and their organisations. Sales tests are straightforward and easy to implement and comprehend. Fourth, the introduction of programmatic technologies means that the automatic real-time optimisation of campaigns makes brand development over the longer term unattractive and seemingly unnecessary.

The approach adopted by the communications school is not universally accepted. Those who disagree argue that it is too difficult and impractical to translate a sales objective into a series of specific communications objectives. Furthermore, what actually constitutes adequate levels of awareness and comprehension and how can it be determined which stage the majority of a target audience has reached at any one point in time? Details of measurement, therefore, throw a veil over the simplicity and precision of the approach taken by the communications-orientation school.

From a practical perspective, it should be appreciated that most successful marketing organisations do not see the sales and communications schools as mutually exclusive. They incorporate both views and weight them according to the needs of the current task, their overall experience, the culture and style of the organisation, and the agencies with whom they operate.

Derivation of campaign objectives

It has been established that specific campaign objectives need to be set up if a suitable foundation is to be laid for the many communications-oriented decisions that follow. Campaign objectives are derived from understanding the overall context in which the communications will work. Comprehending the contexts of the buyer and the organisation allows the objectives to be identified: the *what* that is to be achieved. For example, objectives concerning the perception that different target customers have of a brand, the perception that members of a performance network have of the organisation's offerings, the reactions of key stakeholders to previous communications and the requirements of the current marketing plan all impact upon the objectives of the communications plan. Therefore, campaign objectives evolve principally from a systematic audit and analysis of the key communications contexts, and specifically from the marketing plan and stakeholder analysis.

Three main streams of objectives can be distinguished, as set out in Figure 8.2. The first concerns issues relating to market share/sales volume, profitability and revenue. The second concerns issues relating to the buyers of the product or service offered by the organisation. The third stream relates to the image, reputation and preferences that other stakeholders have towards the organisation.

All these objectives are derived from an analysis of the current situation. The marketing communications brief that flows from this analysis should specify the sales-related

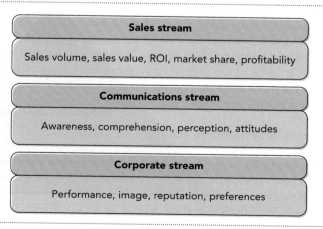

Figure 8.2 The three streams of objectives

Viewpoint 8.2
Petplan uses explicit objectives

Image 8.2 Petplan's new branding approach was aimed at consumers
Source: Joe Pepler/Shutterstock.

Tom Patterson, Planner at Now

Petplan provide specialist insurance cover for pets. Following three decades of strong growth that had cemented Petplan as market leader, several issues threatened the brand. These included a levelling-off of the number of pets in the UK, a fall in the number of owners buying pet insurance and a number of new market entrants such as Tesco Bank, More Th>n, Direct Line and Sainsbury's Finance. These competed on low prices, supported by large advertising budgets. Petplan found itself drawn into a cost-driven environment, and had begun to play the same low-cost game.

In addition to this, Petplan had always relied heavily on intermediaries with 60 per cent of sales driven through vets, breeders and charities. The number of direct sales, however, was growing and sales through partners declining. In addition, comparison websites were beginning to play an

increasingly important role in purchasing. These sites were becoming a first port of call for consumers considering pet insurance and Petplan wasn't on them.

The shift away from intermediaries meant that Petplan needed to start communicating directly with end-user consumers. The strategy required repositioning Petplan as the consumers' premium brand of choice in the category, based on Petplan's expertise and heritage. To accomplish the strategy a clear set of business and marketing objectives were established.

The repositioning strategy involved an action plan, the results of which were considered against the objectives.

Business objectives

- Drive volume into the business by increasing penetration.

Outcome – direct sales grew and the volume of the customer base increased by 8.7 per cent over the course of the campaign. This equated to a 5 per cent increase in penetration.

- Drive value into the business by attracting higher-value customers.

Outcome – Petplan's value increased 11 per cent ahead of the volume increase. This was due to the increased number of premium policy sales, indicating that the communications were attracting higher-value customers. Brand share reached 29.4 per cent, up by over 5 per cent.

Marketing objectives

- Drive brand awareness levels to help combat the threat of comparison sites.

Outcome – spontaneous awareness increased to 26 per cent after two months of the campaign, up from a pre-campaign level of 15 per cent. Over the course of the year spontaneous awareness didn't drop back to pre-campaign levels.

- Drive people to the brand's direct channels.

  Outcome – call-centre volumes increased significantly, by 6.6 per cent, and call-centre sales were up 8.9 per cent on the previous year. Google Trends revealed 'interest' in Petplan rising over the year and showed the brand pulling away significantly from Tesco.

- Improve conversion rates of our direct channels.

  Outcome – visits to the website rose by 30.3 per cent and web sales increased by a staggering 29 per cent. More people than ever before went to Petplan directly, and more people than ever before were purchasing from them directly.

This Viewpoint is based on a case study written by Tom Patterson, when he was a Planner at Now.

Insight

This extract demonstrates the variety of objectives that can be used by organisations. It should also be seen that different types of objectives are an integral part of a strategy and are used to shape, and guide not only the tactics but also measure the success of a campaign.

Question: How might the presentation of these objectives have been improved in order to assist better measurement and review?

Task: Read the following section on SMART objectives and then review the extent to which the Petplan objectives (as presented here) could be improved.

SMART objectives

To assist managers in their need to develop suitable objectives, regardless of source, a set of guidelines has been developed, commonly referred to as SMART objectives. This acronym stands for specific, measurable, achievable, relevant, targeted and timed.

The process of making objectives SMART requires management to consider exactly what is to be achieved, when, where, and with which audience. This clarifies thinking, sorts out the logic of the proposed activities and provides a clear measure for evaluation at the end of the campaign:

- Specific – what is the actual variable that is to be influenced in the campaign? Is it awareness, perception, attitudes or some other element that is to be influenced? Whatever the variable, it must be clearly defined and must enable precise outcomes to be determined.

- Measurable – set a measure of activity against which performance can be assessed. For example, this may be a percentage level of desired prompted awareness in the target audience.

- Achievable – objectives need to be attainable, otherwise those responsible for their achievement will lack motivation and a desire to succeed.

- Realistic – the actions must be founded in reality and be relevant to the brand and the context in which they are set.

- Targeted and timed – which target audience is the campaign targeted at, how precisely is the audience defined and over what period are the results to be generated?

Multiple objectives rather than a single objective should be set. The primary objectives should be business-oriented, preferably around profit. Next, the appropriate behavioural objectives need to be established. From this point communications goals should be determined. Whatever the level, the objectives should be written in SMART format.

Positioning

The final act in the target marketing process of segmentation and targeting is positioning. Following on from the identification of potential markets, determining the size and potential of market segments and selecting specific target markets, positioning is the process whereby a brand is managed so that it is perceived by consumers/stakeholders to be clear, distinctive and desirable relative to competitive products (Kotler and Armstrong, 2017). In other words, a brand's position is a configuration of perceptions, impressions and feelings that exist *in the minds of consumers.*

Scholars' paper 8.3

Positioning is key

Ries, A. and Trout, J. (1972) The positioning era cometh, *Advertising Age*, 24 April, 35–8.

This is a classic paper that should be read by everyone associated with this subject. It was the first paper to outline the positioning concept. Ries and Trout argue that it is not what marketers do to a product itself, but how they influence the mind of a prospective customer. As the level of competition has extended so much, there is often little to choose between the actual products themselves. It should, therefore, be the role of marketing to differentiate on the basis of what customers think about them. Such differences might be real or merely perception.

This is an important aspect of the positioning concept. Positioning is not about a product (which is made in a factory) but what the buyer thinks about the product or organisation (which is formulated in an individual's mind). It is not the physical nature of the product that is important for positioning, but how the product is perceived that matters. This is why part of the context analysis requires a consideration of perception and attitudes, and the way stakeholders see and regard brands and organisations. Of course, this may not be the same as the way brand managers intend their brands to be seen or how they believe the brand is perceived.

This audience orientation is emphasised by Blankson and Kalafatis (2007). They considered the positioning strategies of several leading credit card providers from three perspectives. These were the banks' executives, the positioning strategies that were implemented and finally, but most important, the perception of the target audiences of the positioning strategies. In the words of the researchers: presumed practice, actual practice and perceived practice. One of the outcomes of their work was the need to manage the potential gulf that may occur when the presumed and actual positioning strategies drift away from the way audiences actually perceive the brand.

In the consumer market established brands from washing powders (Ariel, Daz, Persil) and hair shampoos (such as Sunsilk, Kerastase, Garnier), to cars (Renault, VW, Nissan) and grocery multiples (Sainsbury's, Aldi and Maxi ICA Stormarknad) each carry communications that enable audiences to position them in their respective markets.

The positioning concept is not the sole preserve of branded or consumer-oriented offerings or indeed those of the business-to-business market. Organisations are also positioned relative to one another, mainly as a consequence of their corporate identities, whether they are deliberately managed or not. The position an organisation takes in the mind of consumers may be the only means of differentiating one product from another. King (1991) argues that the high level of physical and functional similarity of products in the same class, means that consumer choice will be more focused on their assessment of the company rather than the product. It follows, therefore, that it is important to position organisations as brands in the minds of actual and potential customers.

Whatever the position chosen, either deliberately or accidentally, it is the means by which customers understand the brand's market position. It often provides signals to determine a brand's main competitors, or whether, as is often the case, customers fail to understand the brand or are confused about what the brand stands for.

Scholars' paper 8.4
The benefit of positioning

Fuchs, C. and Diamantopoulos, A. (2010) Evaluating the effectiveness of brand-positioning strategies from a consumer perspective, *European Journal of Marketing*, 44(11/12), 1763–86.

This paper considers the overall effectiveness of positioning strategies. The paper provides an interesting and readable review of the positioning literature. The results of the authors' research show that the success of a brand is influenced by the type of positioning strategy used. They also find that benefit-based positioning and surrogate (user) positioning generally outperform feature-based positioning strategies along the three effectiveness dimensions.

See also:

Rajkumar, K.B. and Abraham, M. (2017) Enlargement of positioning qualities: the emotional attribute, *International Journal of Marketing & Business Communication*, 6(2), 16–21.

The positioning concept

From the research data and the marketing strategy, it is necessary to formulate a positioning statement that is in tune with the overall communications objectives.

One of the roles of marketing communications is to convey information so that the target audience can understand what a brand stands for and differentiate it from other competing brands. Clear, consistent positioning is an important aspect of integrated marketing communications. So, the way in which a brand is presented to its audience influences the way it is going to be perceived. Therefore, accepting that there are extraneous reasons why the perception of a brand might not be the same as that intended, it seems important that managers approach the positioning task in an attentive and considered manner.

Generally there are two main ways in which a brand can be positioned: *functional* and *expressive* (or *symbolic*) positioning. Functionally positioned brands stress the features and benefits, while expressive brands emphasise the ego, social and hedonic satisfactions that a brand can bring.

In the context of washing powder, both approaches make a promise. The functional promise embraces whiter, cleaner and brighter clothes. The emotional approach considers clothes that we are confident to hang on the washing line (for all to see), dress our children in and send to school and not feel guilty, or dress ourselves in for a social evening or to complete a major business deal (symbolic).

Viewpoint 8.3
The Economist challenges prospective subscribers

Image 8.3 *The Economist* challenged potential subscribers

The Economist took to the streets in order to change perceptions held by consumers of the publication
Source: Richard Levine/Alamy Stock Photo.

In order to maintain growth, *The Economist* developed a market penetration strategy. This required attracting new customers to the brand and to do this they had to change the way new audiences perceived the weekly publication.

The Economist is an authoritative magazine, one that seeks to keep readers well-informed about the trends that will be shaping tomorrow's world. The publication generates great loyalty among its readership. Many non-readers, however, have either a lack of awareness of the title, or a misconception about the content. The task therefore, was to encourage new audiences to re-evaluate their understanding of the brand.

Research indicated that people attracted to *The Economist* have an open mind and are comfortable when challenged. The strategy that unfolded needed to target this segment, called the 'globally curious', with a challenging taste of the future today. This would help screen out the poor prospects yet flatter the curious, and in doing so, open up an opportunity to discuss subscriptions.

The 'Discomfort Future' strategy involved bringing to life articles and features that the publication was running. The first involved an ice cream stand that appeared as if *The Economist* was simply handing out free treats. Closer inspection revealed that the ice-cream was protein-enriched with locusts, mealworms and grasshoppers. Another version involved grubs and bugs being served as a crunchy topping for crepes. These enabled prospects to experience what many regard as the food of the future, and built on a topic featured in *The Economist*.

This principle of challenging people to revisit their perceptions of *The Economist* was used to highlight the food waste issue. *The Economist* served smoothies made from food that supermarkets had rejected. Another involved referencing new technology that can turn raw sewage into drinking water. To achieve this, a coffee trike was presented to suggest that its water supply was being provided directly from a portaloo.

The Discomfort Future campaign began in London but within a year it was deployed in Europe, then on to Brazil, the USA, Australia, South Africa, Singapore and China. Over 30,000 new subscriptions have been generated from this campaign with a return on investment of 171%. In addition, research found that in the UK, people who find the brand interesting rose by 24%, while those who found the content boring and dry fell by a third.

Sources: Anon (2017a); Staff (2017).

Insight

This example considers the various elements associated within marketing communications planning. These include setting out the issue, which is derived from the marketing plan, understanding the target's behaviour, formulating and implementing a strategy, setting objectives, implementing the plan and measuring the outcomes. Above all else it reveals how perception of a brand is connected to its positioning.

Question: Is this functional or emotional positioning? Justify your response. What might be the disadvantages of this positioning?

Task: Consider a different topic that *The Economist* might run, and suggest ways in which it might be converted into a campaign.

easyJet's communications at one time were almost exclusively oriented to its (low) price, a functional position. However, when this position was challenged and overtaken, the company's communications began to convey a closer association with premium carriers yet one that maintained its challenger spirit. Messaging switched to one that focused on championing the destination, selling Europe and associated experiences. This created a new long-term brand platform, 'Europe by easyJet', allowing the brand to create emotional affinity and be more aspirational in its look and feel.

Image 8.4 easyJet's positioning has evolved with the changing competitive conditions.

easyJet currently use an emotional positioning strategy, having moved away from one based on price and functionality.
Source: easyJet.

This expressive positioning used an emotional brand message, one that required a different media mix. The functional position used print, outdoor and digital, while the expressive position required heavy use of television (Anon, 2014).

Managing positions

The development and establishment of a position is a core strategic marketing communications activity. Positioning is one of two dynamics considered within communications strategy and is considered in Chapter 7. The first dynamic is concerned with who, in broad terms, is the target audience. End-user customers need to derive particular benefits based on perceived value from the exchange process. These benefits are very different from those that intermediaries expect to derive, or indeed any other stakeholder who does not consume the product or service.

The second dynamic concerns the way in which an audience understands the offering it is experiencing either through use or through communications. The way in which people interpret messages and frame objects in their minds is concerned with positioning, and as such is an integral part of marketing communications strategy.

In order that suitable positions be set, managers wishing to develop a position can be guided by the following process:

1. Determine the positions held by competitors. This will almost certainly require research to determine attitudes and perceptions and, possibly, the key attributes that consumers perceive as important. Use perceptual mapping.

2. From the above, it will be possible to determine which position, if any, is already held by the focus brand.

3. From the information gathered so far, will it be possible to determine a positioning strategy – that is, what is the desired position for the brand?

4. Is the strategy feasible in view of the competitors and any budgetary constraints? A long-term perspective is required, as the selected position has to be sustained.

5. Implement a programme to establish the desired position.

6. Monitor the perception held by consumers of the brand, and their changing tastes and requirements, on a regular basis.

Perceptual mapping

In order to determine how various offerings are perceived in a market, the key attributes that buyers use to perceive products in the market need to be established. A great deal of this work will have been completed as part of the research and review process prior to developing a communications plan. The next task is to determine perceptions and preferences in respect of the key attributes as perceived by buyers.

The objective of the exercise is to produce a perceptual map (brand and multidimensional maps) where the dimensions used on the two axes are the key attributes, as seen by buyers. This map represents a geometric comparison of how competing products are perceived (Sinclair and Stalling, 1990). Figure 8.4 shows that consumers consider national/international and popular/exclusive as key dimensions in the airline market. Each airline is positioned on the map according to the perception that buyers have of the strength of each attribute of each airline. By plotting the perceived positions of each brand on the map, an overall perspective of the market can be developed.

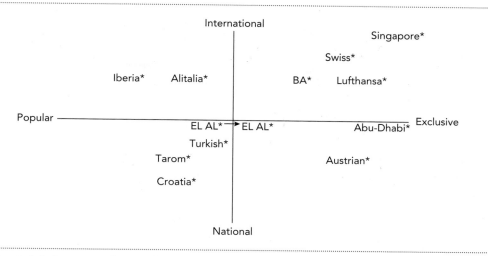

Figure 8.4 A perceptual map of airlines
Source: Herstein and Mitki (2008).

The closer airlines are clustered together, the greater the competition. The further apart the positions, the greater the opportunity to enter the market, as competition is less intense. From the map it can be seen that Croatia Airlines is perceived to be a strong national airline, whereas Swiss Air and Singapore Airlines are seen to be very international and exclusive. El Al was repositioned from being reasonably popular to one that was more exclusive, yet retained the same level of nationality. It may be that both Turkish and Tarom might find it less competitive if they attempted to become more popular and so provide a strong point of differentiation. Such a move, however, would only be endorsed if research showed that it would be acceptable to consumers, and profitable.

Substitute products are often uncovered by their closeness to each other (Day et al., 1979). It is also possible to ask buyers and other stakeholders what an ideal brand would consist of. This perfect brand can then be positioned on the map, and the closer an offering is to the ideal point, the greater its market share should be, as it is preferred over its rivals. These maps are known as *preference maps*.

By superimposing the position of an ideal brand on the map, it is possible to extend the usefulness of the tool. Perceptions of what constitutes the right amount of each key attribute can assist management in the positioning exercise. Marketing communications can, therefore, be designed to convey the required information about each attribute, thus adjusting buyers' perceptions so that they are closer to the ideal position, or to the position on the map that management wants the brand to occupy. For example, Austrian Airlines may wish to reposition by changing the perception that users have of its exclusivity and relative unpopularity. Following any necessary adjustments to the routes followed and services provided, marketing communications would emphasise the popularity and accessibility attributes and hope to move it away from its association with exclusivity.

Neal (1980) offered the following reasons why perceptual mapping is such a powerful tool for examining the position of products:

1. It develops understanding of how the relative strengths and weaknesses of different products are perceived by buyers.
2. It builds knowledge about the similarities and dissimilarities between competing products.

3. It assists the process of repositioning existing products and the positioning of new products.

4. The technique helps to track the perception that buyers have of a particular product, and assists the measurement of the effectiveness of communications programmes and marketing actions intended to change buyers' perceptions.

Perceptual mapping is an important tool in the development and tracking of marketing communications strategy. It enables brand managers to identify gaps and opportunities in the market and allows organisations to monitor the effects of past marketing communications. For example, in the early 1980s none of the available brands in the newly emerging lager market was seen as refreshing. All brands were perceived as virtually the same. Heineken saw the opportunity and seized the position for refreshment, and has been able to occupy and sustain the position ever since.

Positioning strategies

The development of positions that buyers can relate to and understand is an important and vital part of the marketing communications plan. In essence, the position adopted is a statement about what the brand is, what it stands for, and the values and beliefs that customers (hopefully) will associate with a particular brand. The visual images or the position statement represented in the strapline may be a significant trigger that buyers use to recall images and associations of the brand.

There are a number of overall approaches to developing a position. These can be based on factors such as the market, the customer or redefining the appeal of the brand itself.

To implement these three broad approaches, various strategies have been developed. The list that follows is not intended to be comprehensive or to convey the opinion that these strategies are discrete. They are presented here as means of conveying the strategic style, but in reality a number of hybrid strategies are often used.

Product features

This is one of the easier concepts and one that is more commonly adopted. The brand is set apart from the competition on the basis of the attributes, features or benefits that the brand has relative to the competition. For example, Red Bull gives you energy; Weetabix contains all the vitamins needed each day; and Audi proclaims Vorsprung durch Technik or 'advancement through technology'.

Image 8.5 Red Bull's positioning encapsulates its energy based brand values
Source: Handout/Getty Images.

Price/quality

This strategy is more effectively managed than others because price itself can be a strong communicator of quality. A high price denotes high quality, just as a low price can deceive buyers into thinking a product to be of low quality and poor value. Retail outlets such as Harrods and Aspreys use high prices to signal high quality and exclusivity.

At the other end of the retail spectrum, Matalan and Primark position themselves to attract those with less disposable income and to whom convenience is of greater importance. The price/quality appeal used to be best observed in Sainsbury's, 'where good food costs less' before it was changed, and with the alcoholic lager Stella Artois, which was positioned as 'refreshingly expensive'.

Image 8.6 A store's architecture signals the price/quality relationship
Source: Suhaimi Abdullah/Stringer/Getty Images.

Use

By informing markets of when or how a product can be used, a position can be created in the minds of the buyers. For example, Kellogg's, the breakfast cereal manufacturer, repositioned itself as a snack-food provider. Its marketing strategy of moving into new markets was founded on its over-dependence on breakfast consumption. By becoming associated with snacks, not only is usage increased, but the opportunity to develop new products becomes feasible. After Eight chocolate mints clearly indicate when they should be eaten. The hair shampoo Wash & Go positions the brand as a quick and easy-to-use (convenience) product, for those whose lifestyles are full and demanding.

Product class dissociation

Some markets are essentially uninteresting, and most positions have been adopted by competitors. A strategy used by margarine manufacturers is to disassociate themselves from other margarines and associate themselves with what was commonly regarded as a superior product, butter. The Dove moisturising bar is positioned as 'not a soap'.

User

A sensible extension of the target marketing process is to position openly so that target users can be clearly identified. Flora margarine was for men, and then it became 'for all the family'. Perfumes are not just endorsed by celebrities but some celebrities launch their own perfume brands, such as Jennifer Lopez, Katy Perry, Kate Moss, David Beckham and of course, Beyoncé, Britney Spears and Paul Smith. Some hotels position

Image 8.7 Revlon's 'Love is On' campaign

Revlon repositioned using a use and application-based strategy
around the slogan 'Love is On'
Source: Anton_Ivanov/Shutterstock.

themselves as places for weekend breaks, as leisure centres or as conference centres. Revlon repositioned to appeal to a younger customer segment and incorporated the slogan 'Love Is On' into each element in their marketing strategy. Using television, print and digital ads, with a new recording of the song 'Addicted to Love', the repositioning featured brand ambassadors Halle Berry, Emma Stone and Olivia Wilde (Mann, 2015).

Competitor

For a long time, positioning oneself against a main competitor was regarded as dangerous and was avoided. Saab contested the 'safest car' position with Volvo. Petplan (featured Viewpoint 8.2), repositioned itself against its competitors as the 'knowledge experts', based on its unrivalled experience in the market.

Benefit

Positions can also be established by proclaiming the benefits that usage confers on those who consume. Sensodyne toothpaste appeals to all those who suffer from sensitive teeth, and a vast number of pain relief formulations claim to smooth away headaches or relieve aching limbs, sore throats or some offending part of the anatomy.

Successful positioning can be difficult to accomplish, often because of the entrenched perceptions and attitudes held by buyers towards brands and the vast (media) resources required to make the changes. For example, although consumption of plant-based foods is increasing, research indicates that labelling food as vegetarian or vegan on menus and packaging can generate huge negative responses. Better to refer to these foods as healthy or delicious in order to provoke interest and purchase intention.

Quorn, once regarded as a good quality, trusted meat-free alternative for vegetarians, has moved to a positioning that associates it with good food that fits peoples' lifestyles. The result has been a 19 per cent rise in global sales (Burrows, 2017).

Image 8.8 The promotion of meat-free food

Promoting meat-free food as healthy and delicious is more likely to be successful than labelling it vegetarian.
Source: Quanthem/Shutterstock.

Heritage or cultural symbol

An appeal to cultural heritage and tradition, symbolised by age, particular heraldic devices or visual cues, has been used by many organisations to convey quality, experience and knowledge. Kronenbourg 1664, 'Established since 1803', and the use of coats of arms by many universities to represent depth of experience and a sense of permanence are just some of the historical themes used to position organisations.

Whatever the position adopted by a brand or organisation, both the marketing and communications mixes must endorse and support the position so that there is consistency throughout all communications. For example, if a high-quality position is taken, such as that of the Ritz-Carlton Hotel Company, then the product/service quality must be relatively high compared with competitors, the price must be correspondingly excessive and distribution synonymous with quality and exclusivity. Sales promotion activity will be minimal in order not to convey a touch of inexpensiveness, and advertising messages should be visually affluent and rich in tone and copy, with public relations and personal selling approaches transmitting high-quality, complementary cues.

The dimensions used to position brands must be relevant and important to the target audience and the image cues used must be believable and consistently credible. Positioning strategies should be developed over the long term if they are to prove effective, although minor adaptions to the position can be carried out in order to reflect changing environmental conditions.

Repositioning

Technology continues to develop rapidly, consumer tastes and behaviours are evolving, and new and substitute offerings enter the market. This dynamic perspective of markets means that the relative positions occupied by offerings in the minds of consumers will be challenged and shifted on a frequent basis. If the position adopted by an offering is strong, if it was the first to claim the position and the position is being continually reinforced with clear simple messages, then there may be little need to alter the position originally adopted.

There are occasions however, when offerings need to be repositioned in the minds of consumers/stakeholders. This may be due to market opportunities and development, mergers and acquisitions or changing buyer preferences, which may be manifested in declining sales. Research may reveal that the current position is either inappropriate or superseded by a competitor, or that attitudes have changed or preferences been surpassed; whatever the reason, repositioning is required if past success is to be maintained.

In the light of declining performance and a cultural shift in food and health values, McDonald's has gradually shifted its position in the market in order to reflect its food's improved taste and higher quality. Part of their repositioning is reflected in their corporate adoption of dark green. Apple moved from black to 'white' and 'moon grey' as the brand began to reposition around the idea of simplicity (Candy and Bullen, 2017).

Viewpoint 8.4
The AA reposition through celebration

In the fiercely competitive UK car breakdown and recovery market, the way a brand is perceived by British motorists can be critical in order to sustain a viable number of customers. In order to improve their competitiveness, the trustworthy AA brand embarked on a business transformation exercise. Part of this involved research that revealed that although 80 per cent are enthusiastic drivers, 25 per cent of UK drivers were much more interested in what goes on inside a car, not what goes on under the bonnet. It is the singing, the comedy, the banter, the arguments, the time for quiet reflection, the general entertainment possibilities away from email, texts and social media.

Traditionally brands in this market have focused on the anxiety and stress associated with a car breakdown, all relieved with the car recovery brand arriving promptly, solving the problem and sending the driver (and family) back on their journey with happy smiling faces. Using this new insight, the AA labelled this new group as

'freedom seekers' and used this as a platform to reposition the brand with a 'fun of driving' focus. So, out went the stress, inconvenience and recovery scenario, and in came a celebration of what happens when journeys go right. A celebration of the best of family moments, even when they might go wrong.

The £10 million ad campaign used to lead the repositioning featured a father driving to the airport with his amazingly talented toddler singing a full-throated rendition of 'Proud Mary'. Happily singing throughout the journey, even throughout an unexpected breakdown, the core message is that the rapid response of the AA means that your plans should never be derailed.

The 'Singing baby' ad was supported with outdoor, radio and digital advertising. It represented a 'wholesale shift in approach' for the AA, from its core strategy and positioning, through to tone of voice, look and feel, and even the way it describes its AA men and women.

Sources: Anon (2017b); Oakes (2017).

Insight

This Viewpoint demonstrates how firms in the same market can select different ways to position themselves. It also suggests that firms in some markets might position themselves in broadly the same way, and thus not provide any strong distinguishing signals for their audiences.

Question: To what extent is repositioning contingent on sound segmentation?

Task: Find two other car recovery brands and compare the way they position themselves.

Jewell (2007) draws attention to the need to consider repositioning from a customer's perspective, something that was neglected in the literature. He also shows that two key tasks need to be accomplished during a repositioning exercise. First, the old positioning needs to be suppressed so that customers no longer relate to it and, second, consumers need to learn the new position. These twin tasks are complementary, as interference or rather the deliberate weakening of the old position will help strengthen acceptance of the new position.

Repositioning, however, should not be confused with revitalisation. In many cases brands need to be revitalised and as Ritson (2017) points out, this requires understanding a brand's founder, its history and approach. This enables recognition and extraction of the 'brand DNA'. This presents the opportunity to ask the fundamental question, 'what does this DNA direct us to do now?' As Ritson says, this helps avoid past strategies and tactics, and enable contemporary approaches that are derived from a respect for, and connection with, the history of the brand.

Scholars' paper 8.5
Repositioning through interference

Jewell, R.D. (2007) Establishing effective repositioning communications in a competitive marketplace, *Journal of Marketing Communications*, 13(4), 231–41.

This paper considers positioning from a consumer's perspective, rather than through the traditional manufacturer's lens. Product positioning is important to marketers because it can influence consumers. The author proposes that successful repositioning should be based not only on the audience learning the new positioning but also on interfering with competitors' communications in order to inhibit messages about the previous positioning.

Key points

- Objectives provide direction and an action focus for all those participating in an activity. They are a means by which the variety of decisions relating to an activity can be made in a consistent way, and they set out the time period in which it is to be completed. In addition to communicating the values and scope of the activity to all participants, they also provide a means by which success can be evaluated.

- The use of objectives in the management process is vital if an organisation's desired outcomes are to be achieved. Each of the objectives, at corporate, unit and functional levels, contributes to the formulation of the communications objectives. They are all interlinked, interdependent, multiple and often conflicting.

- The various organisational objectives are of little use if they are not communicated to those who need to know what they are. Traditionally, such communications have focused on employees, but it is now recognised that other members of the stakeholder network need to understand an organisation's purpose and objectives.

- Communications objectives are derived from an initial review of the current situation and the marketing plan requirements. They are not a replication of the marketing objectives but a distillation of the research activities that have been undertaken subsequently.

- There are three main streams of objectives. The first concerns issues relating to the buyers of the product or service offered by the organisation. The second concerns issues relating to market share/sales volume, profitability and revenue. The third stream relates to the image, reputation and preferences that other stakeholders have towards the organisation.

- Communications objectives consist of two main elements: sales-oriented and communications-oriented. A balance between the two will be determined by the situation facing the organisation, but can be a mixture of both product and corporate tasks. These objectives, once quantified, need to be ranked and weighted in order that other components of the plan can be developed.

- The IPA has identified a hierarchy of brand communications objectives following its analysis of effective campaigns. These are business, behavioural and intermediate goals.

- To assist managers in their need to develop suitable objectives, a set of guidelines has been developed, commonly referred to as SMART objectives. This acronym stands for specific, measurable, achievable, relevant, targeted and timed.

- The position adopted is a statement about what the brand is, what it stands for and the values and beliefs that audiences (hopefully) will come to associate with the particular brand. Visual and text/copy images or the position statement represented in a strapline may be a significant trigger that buyers use to recall images and associations of the brand.

- There are two main ways in which a brand can be positioned: these are functional and expressive (or symbolic) positioning. Functionally positioned brands stress the features and benefits, and expressive brands emphasise the ego, social and hedonic satisfactions that can be associated with a brand.

- A perceptual map represents a geometric comparison of how competing products are perceived by customers, based on important attributes. Each product is positioned on the map according to the perception that buyers have of the strength of each attribute of each product. By plotting the perceived positions of each brand on the map, an overall perspective of the market can be developed and strategies formed to develop clearer, more rewarding positions.

- There are a number of overall approaches that can be used to develop a position. These can be based on factors such as the market, the customer or redefining the appeal of the brand itself. To implement these three broad approaches, various strategies have been developed. These include product features, price/quality, use, product class dissociation, user, competitor, benefit and heritage or use of cultural symbols.

Repositioning Axe

Image 8.9 Axe redefined masculinity
Source: Nor Gal/Shutterstock.

The market for men's grooming products has been changing. Firstly, there are more competitors, attracted partly by a greater proportion of men who are more willing to use them in their daily routines. Second, the digital environment has changed media usage and with it, has reformatted the 'mating' game.

Axe, or Lynx as it is known in some markets, is a major brand in the male grooming market. For some time, the brand's core values have been rooted in sexual attraction with a direct connection to female conquest. These values had been translated into a communications strategy that was based on equating a liberal application of its deodorant with sex or acquisition. While sales of Axe have continued to grow, in all of its markets, research indicated that Axe's brand equity was turning down. Axe's association with a stereotypical interpretation of masculinity was regarded by consumers as no longer valid and that this connection was not sustainable. Indeed, critics had argued that the brand's positioning, based primarily on the objectification of women, belonged to the past. Axe was seen as anachronistic, and as on a different path

to the one in which culture was headed. In addition, a host of new entrants to the market also signalled that the brand could no longer sustain its market share.

Unilever, who own Axe, had previously established a new value set for the entire business. The new corporate strategy was based around values associated with developing a sustainable business that benefits all stakeholders and society as a whole, not just itself and its shareholders with a myopic focus on profitability. All of these elements indicated that Axe was not fit for the future.

As a next step Unilever invested in research, encompassing 10 countries and 3,500 men. The goal was to gain an insight into the relationship men had with the brand. It also involved trying to understand the issues they experienced with masculinity and what it meant to them. Among the results was the insight that nearly 50 per cent of all men were afraid of appearing to be different for the fear of being judged. 98 per cent of men reported that they had been told to 'man up' at some point in their lives. The internal masculinity struggle that men face can contribute to bullying, violence and even suicide. The research also found that women actively rejected stereotypes of masculinity and that the Axe brand was failing to make a meaningful connection with women. Approximately 90 per cent of women said that they liked men who were 'true to themselves', a position directly opposite to that previously taken by Axe. These findings led Axe and their agency to label the current environment as 'toxic masculinity'.

Among the various campaign insights gleaned from the research was that individuality is aspirational, and brands that encourage consumers to be themselves rather than conforming are likely to be successful and grow. It was also found that diversity itself is not a brand differentiator, but it is a business necessity. Influencer marketing is becoming a critical element of mainstream strategies, and brands need to collaborate with these opinion leaders and formers. Marketers need to understand what consumers are searching for outside their core product area as this will feed an appropriate data strategy. From this, marketers should try to identify the problems their consumers have that their brand can help to solve.

In order to sustain its growth Axe needed to reposition the brand away from its associations with toxic masculinity to one that communicated two things. First that attraction is a connection, not a conquest, and second, a need to inspire men through their individuality.

The new work was themed 'Is it ok for guys?', and was part of Axe's 'Find Your Magic' positioning, which was launched originally in the USA before being rolled out globally. This featured, among other things, one man in high heels and another in a wheelchair. The 'Is it ok for guys?' campaign developed by 72andSunny Amsterdam, featured a new video (YouTube) which took these ideas further. For example, it asked 'Is it ok for guys to experiment with other guys?' in an attempt to identify what 'real manhood' means. The video started by showing how men privately struggle with masculinity, and used actual Google searches to reveal their anxiety about adhering to, and straying from, societal norms. The goal of the campaign was to highlight human individuality and to empower men to be the most attractive man they could be, namely themselves.

The campaign featured various brand ambassadors, including the musician John Legend. He became an integral part of an initiative to mentor musicians and film-makers with the aim of showcasing their work at the Toronto Film Festival. This was called the Axe Collective. To complement the campaign the brand also launched the Axe Collection, a premium range of grooming products.

Influencer marketing was key to the strategy. Activated through the 'Instagroom' platform, it harnessed data to create content in order to answer questions consumers were asking about male grooming on Google.

The campaign achieved 12 per cent organic reach, purchase consideration soared and the global growth rate of the brand tripled. Some of the content was not received well but this was to be expected when promoting diversity and using experimental approaches to creativity. The campaign generated over 39.3 million digital views and there were four billion media impressions in the first quarter after launch. Perhaps the biggest success was the campaign's ignition of a global debate about masculinity. There were 225,411 direct engagements with the film and more than 12,000 comments across all platforms. Perception of the brand shifted substantially. Over 30,000 posts referred to 'Find your magic' on social media, and overall positive sentiment for Axe rose from 14.74 per cent to 41.35 per cent.

Sources: Kemp (2017); Kirkpatrick (2017); Nudd (2017).

Review questions

Repositioning Axe case questions

1. Identify the type of objectives Axe might have set for its campaign.

2. What led Axe to consider changing their positioning and strategy?

3. Consider the probable reactions of Axe's competitors to the repositioning.

4. To what extent might images about anxiety and diversity reflect poorly on Axe by association?

5. Identify three strengths associated with the repositioning.

General questions

1. Write a brief report arguing the case both for and against the use of an increase in sales as the major objective of all promotional activities.

2. Why is positioning an important part of marketing communications? Use the Axe case to illustrate your response.

3. What is perceptual mapping?

4. Select three brands in any category of your choice and comment on the positions they have adopted.

5. What are the main positioning strategies?

References for Chapter 8

Anon (2014) Grand Prix: easyJet, Marketing Society Awards, *Marketing*, June, 7.

Anon (2017a) 'The Economist' raising awareness of food issues through 'gross', uncomfortable experiences, *Sustainable Foods*, 13 June, retrieved 17 July from http://www.sustainablebrands.com/news_and_views/marketing_comms/sustainable_brands/economist_expands_food_waste_campaign_new_york_lon

Anon (2017b) adam&eveDDB deconstruct The AA with a singing baby, *Creativepool*, 5 June, retrieved 14 July 2017 from http://creativepool.com/magazine/advertising/adameveddb-deconstruct-the-aa-with-a-singing-baby.14486

Barry, T. and Howard, D.J. (1990) A review and critique of the hierarchy of effects in advertising, *International Journal of Advertising*, 9, 121–35.

Binet, L. and Field, P. (2007) *Marketing in an Era of Accountability*, Henley: IPA-WARC.

Blankson, C. and Kalafatis, S.P. (2007) Positioning strategies of international and multicultural-orientated service brands, *Journal of Services Marketing*, 21(6), 435–50.

Burrows, D. (2017) How brands can tap into the 'flexitarian' trend, *Marketing Week*, 23 October, retrieved 9 November 2017 from https://www.marketingweek.com/2017/10/23/brands-effectively-tap-flexitarian-trend/

Candy, N. and Bullen, V. (2017) How brands can use colour to impact subconscious decision-making, *Admap*, July–August.

Colley, R. (1961) *Defining Advertising Goals for Measured Advertising Results*, New York: Association of National Advertisers.

Day, G., Shocker, A.D. and Srivastava, R.K. (1979) Customer orientated approaches to identifying product markets, *Journal of Marketing*, 43(4), 8–19.

Dutka, S. (1995) *Defining Advertising Goals for Measured Advertising Results*, 2nd edn, New York: Association of National Advertisers.

Fuchs, C. and Diamantopoulos, A. (2010) Evaluating the effectiveness of brand-positioning strategies from a consumer perspective, *European Journal of Marketing*, 44(11/12), 1763–86.

Hanssens, D.M. and Pauwels, K.H. (2016) Demonstrating the value of marketing, *Journal of Marketing*: AMA/MSI Special Issue, 80 (November), 173–90.

Heath, R. (2009) Emotional engagement: how television builds big brands at low attention, *Journal of Advertising Research*, March, 62–73.

Herstein, R. and Mitki, Y. (2008) How El Al Airlines transformed its service strategy with employee participation, *Strategy & Leadership*, 36(3), 21–5.

Jewell, R.D. (2007) Establishing effective repositioning communications in a competitive marketplace, *Journal of Marketing Communications*, 13(4), 231–41.

Johnson, G., Whittington, R., Regnér, P., Scholes, K. and Angwin, D. (2017) *Exploring Strategy*, 11th edn, Harlow: Pearson Education.

Kemp, N. (2017) How Axe redefined masculinity, *Campaignlive*, 10 April, retrieved 8 September 2017 from http://www.campaignlive.co.uk/article/case-study-axe-redefined-masculinity/1430092

King, S. (1991) Brand building in the 1990s, *Journal of Marketing Management*, 7, 3–13.

Kirkpatrick, D. (2017) Axe asks tough questions to fight toxic masculinity in brand pivot, *Marketing Dive*, 18 May, retrieved 9 September 2017 from http://www.marketingdive.com/news/axe-fights-toxic-masculinity-in-brand-pivot/443001/

Kotler, P. and Armstrong, G. (2017) *Principles of Marketing*, Global edn, New York: Pearson.

Kriegel, R.A. (1986) How to choose the right communications objectives, *Business Marketing*, April, 94–106.

Mann, R. (2015) Revlon promotes new positioning and product innovation, *The Moodie Report*, 14 April, retrieved 22 November 2017 from https://www.moodiedavittreport.com/revlon-promotes-new-positioning-and-product-innovation/

Neal, W.D. (1980) Strategic product positioning: a step by step guide, *Business (USA)*, May/June, 34–40.

Nudd, T. (2017) Axe tackles 'toxic masculinity' by revealing how deeply young men struggle with it, *Adweek,* 17 May, retrieved 8 September 2017 from http://www.adweek.com/brand-marketing/axe-tackles-toxic-masculinity-by-revealing-how-deeply-young-men-struggle-with-it/

Oakes, O. (2017) AA repositions brand towards 'fun of driving' with £10m ad campaign, *Campaignlive*, 2 June, retrieved 14 July 2017 from http://www.campaignlive.co.uk/article/aa-repositions-brand-towards-fun-driving-10m-ad-campaign/1435408

Patti, C.H., Hartley, S.W., van Dessel M.M. and Baack D.W. (2017) Improving integrated marketing communications practices: A comparison of objectives and results, *Journal of Marketing Communications*, 23(4), 351–70.

Rajkumar, K.B. and Abraham, M. (2017) Enlargement of positioning qualities: the emotional attribute, *International Journal of Marketing & Business Communication*, 6(2), 16–21.

Ries, A. and Trout, J. (1972) The positioning era cometh, *Advertising Age*, 24 April, 35–8.

Ritson, M. (2017) Burberry's luxury repositioning won't work, it's not in the brand DNA, *Marketing Week*, 15 November, retrieved 22 November 2017 from https://www.marketingweek.com/2017/11/15/mark-ritson-burberry-repositioning/

Rossiter, J.R. and Percy, L. (1987) *Advertising and Promotion Management*, Lexington, MA: McGraw-Hill.

Sinclair, S.A. and Stalling, E.C. (1990) Perceptual mapping: a tool for industrial marketing: a case study, *Journal of Business and Industrial Marketing*, 5(1), 55–65.

Staff (2017) How The Economist ramped up subscriptions by bringing gross stories to life, *Campaignlive*, 31 May, retrieved 17 July 2017 from https://www.campaignlive.co.uk/article/economist-ramped-subscriptions-bringing-gross-stories-life/1433484#S8xd-d411KjoYc6yz.99

The communications industry: structure, operations and finance

The communications industry has undergone significant changes over the last decade. Managing new digital media landscapes and embracing new forms of communications have been challenging for the industry. This has led to the emergence of new types of agencies, restructuring the way that some agencies manage their clients' business and an increase in clients using in-house and on-site agencies.

Aims and learning objectives

The aim of this chapter is to explore issues relating to the communications industry, including the structure, the types of organisations involved and the operations and processes used to develop marketing communications for clients.

The learning objectives are to enable readers to:

1. understand the nature and structure of the communications industry;
2. consider the role and characteristics of the main types of organisations involved in the industry;
3. examine the principal methods and operations used within agencies to meet their clients' needs;
4. explore relationships and methods of remuneration used within the industry;
5. appraise the role of the communications budget and trends in budgeting;
6 appreciate the different techniques used to set marketing communications budgets.

Introduction

The marketing communications industry consists of four principal actors or types of stakeholders. These are the media, clients, who fund the whole process, agencies, historically the most notable of which are advertising agencies, and finally the thousands of support organisations, such as production companies and fulfilment houses, that enable the whole communications process to function. At the centre of this theatre are consumers, audiences who engage with the output with varying levels of intensity and involvement.

It is the operations and relationships between these organisations and, increasingly, audiences that not only drive the industry but also form an important context within which marketing communications can be understood. Figure 9.1 sets out the main actor organisations in the industry.

Some organisations choose to manage their marketing communications 'in-house' – that is, do it themselves. This may be to keep costs low or to provide a good level of control over the messages and media. While this does offer advantages, there are also a number of challenges with operating an in-house agency. In particular, the organisation is unlikely to have the same access to creative talent and range of specialist skills that an external agency has. Additionally, running an in-house department will increase the organisation's fixed costs and often introduces political dimensions that can greatly impact on the objectivity and creativity. However, as the BBC Creative case study at the end of this chapter shows, more organisations are overcoming the challenges of setting up their own agency and have created highly effective in-house agencies.

The number of in-house agencies has increased over the last decade. According to a 2017 survey by the ISBA, almost 40 per cent of UK brand owners now have an in-house resource and 14 per cent plan to create one in the near future (ISBA, 2017). Figure 9.2 shows the popularity of having an in-house resource. As well as the potential to save costs and provide brand expertise, an in-house agency is seen to offer greater speed and agility than external agencies, allowing brands to react more quickly in the digital space (ISBA, 2017).

Brands such as Jaguar and Specsavers have had their own in-house creative resource for a number of years (Daldry, 2015). Channel 4 set up their own in-house agency, 4Creative, and have begun to challenge the assumption that in-house work is less creative with their award-winning campaigns, such as We're the Superhumans. Additionally, there are a growing number of brands operating their own in-house media departments, including BT,

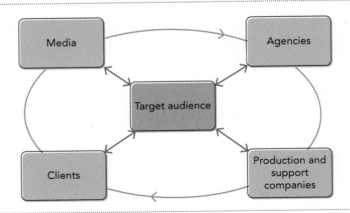

Figure 9.1 The key stakeholders in the marketing communications industry

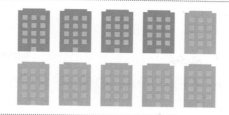

Figure 9.2 Four out of ten brand owners have an in-house agency
Source: ISBA (2017).

Unilever, Procter & Gamble, GlaxoSmithKline, Reckitt Benckiser, the COI and Anheuser-Busch (*Media Week*, 2005).

An alternative route is to use freelancers or self-employed consultants. Although each individual's skills may have been developed within a particular discipline, such as public relations or advertising, freelancers can provide flexibility and access to some experts through their network of personal contacts. Many in-house agencies include a number of freelancers, with a typical in-house team being made up of seven freelancers and seven full time staff (ISBA, 2017). However, it should be remembered that the use of freelancers and in-house facilities requires use of the client organisation's resources, if only to manage the freelancers. Crowdsourcing, the use of the public to generate creative advertising content, is an attempt by clients to circumnavigate the agency sector in order to find new material and cut costs. This form of user-generated content is explored in more detail later in the text (Chapter 19).

The use of external agencies is popular because they can provide objectivity, access to expertise and specialist technologies while at the same time allowing clients to concentrate on their core business activities. Indeed, this is the route taken by the vast majority of organisations, who regard the use of communications agencies in the same way as they do accountants, consultants, lawyers and other professionals. By outsourcing these activities, organisations buy experts whose specialist services can be used as and when required. This flexibility has proved to be efficient and effective for both client and agency. However, the decision to use an agency leads to further questions to be resolved: which types of agency and what do we want them to do, how many agencies should we use and what role should the client play in the relationship with the agency?

These may sound strange questions, but consider the question of strategy. Whose responsibility will it be to develop the marketing communications strategy and make decisions about positioning? Should the client decide on strategy or should this be part of the agency's task? Different client organisations will adopt different positions depending upon their experience, size and the nature of the task that needs to be undertaken. Another question concerns whether a single agency is required to deliver integrated marketing communications activities, whether a single agency should manage the integration process and sub-contract tasks to other specialist or group-based agencies (and in doing so act as lead agency) or whether a series of specialist agencies should be appointed, each reporting to the client.

Agencies are seen to provide access to creative talent that delivers high-quality creative work. While creative expertise has always been seen to be a key advantage of using an external agency, the increasing need to produce creative work quickly, particularly digital assets, has made the external agency model less attractive for some brand owners. Viewpoint 9.1 sets out a new agency model, the on-site agency that appears to be addressing some of the disadvantages of the traditional external agency model.

Viewpoint 9.1

On-site agencies: a new agency model

Sharon Whale, Chief Executive Officer UK Group, Oliver

Image 9.1 In-house agencies provide the speed and agility to respond quickly to market needs
Source: Kzenon/Shutterstock.

The in-house agency model is not a new phenomenon. Most large brands have had their own in-house agency for decades and in the US it is estimated that 58 per cent of brand owners have an in-house resource. Similarly, in the UK, brands such as Specsavers have been producing their own advertising since 1985, arguing that developing their creative in-house has a number of distinct advantages over using an agency, including brand knowledge.

Now, a new agency model has emerged. The on-site agency. And it is attracting a lot of interest in the industry, among brand owners and agencies. The on-site agency is an alternative, hybrid model that sees a third-party supplier running an agency within the brand owner's organisation. The ISBA have defined this new model as '*A team of people provided by an external partner to sit alongside the advertiser's own marketing team. Whilst they are dedicated to the advertiser's business and resident on their premises, they are employed by and report directly to the third-party agency*'.

On-site agencies are seen as hybrids of previous agency models and offer an alternative solution for brand owners to deliver creative solutions. The new model offers brand owners creative expertise right on their doorstep, providing the speed and agility to respond quickly to market needs. McDonald's We Are Unlimited agency in Chicago is an example of such an on-site agency. Unlimited is an omni-channel agency, populated with creative talent and strategists from the Omnicom Group, which services the McDonald's business. Having the agency on-site allows creative work to be produced quickly and ensures the agency team is familiar with the complexities of the McDonald's business.

A key advantage is the time saved. By getting the creative right the first time around, means fewer amends, fewer emails, fewer agency meetings and phone calls, and fewer layers of account management. That means greater cost efficiencies and more productive hours. This coupled with lower overhead costs, means clients get better work, faster and more cost effectively.

On-site agencies are a full-time concern for OLIVER, a company who has made it their business to build and operate on-site agencies for brand owners. The group has set up dedicated on-site agencies for a number of major brands, including Adidas, BMW, Britvic, 3M, Ryanair and Virgin.

OLIVER, who pioneered the on-site agency model in 2004, builds bespoke agencies within their clients' offices to provide greater proximity to brand owners' businesses. The model offers a viable alternative to clients setting up their own in-house agency and enjoys many of the same benefits as an in-house solution.

Sources: Daldry (2015); ISBA (2017); OLIVER (2018); We Are Unlimited (2018).

Insight

This highlights the ever-changing landscape of the marketing communications industry and shows how agencies can adapt themselves to meet clients' advertising needs. On-site agencies are emerging as a viable third way for brand owners to handle their marketing communications requirements.

Question: What would be the advantages and disadvantages for using an on-site agency?

Task: Visit OLIVER's website and make a list of the types of work the on-site agencies are handling for their clients.

Dimensions of the UK marketing communications industry

It is useful to consider the size and value of the industry by considering the sums of money spent by clients on marketing communications. Some of these figures are acknowledged to be estimates, and there is some evidence of 'double counting' (one or more sectors claiming part of the overall spend for itself). That said, however, the total spend for advertising in the UK is forecast to rise, to reach over £26 billion (WARC, 2018) (see Table 9.1).

Table 9.1 Total UK advertising expenditure (£million)

Media	2000 (£m)	2010 (£m)	2018 (£m) (forecast)
Newspaper	7,586.6	4,993.1	1,609.4
Magazines	3,055.5	1,660.0	572.2
Television	6,098.5	6,636.6	6,356.4
Radio	899.6	808.3	821.5
Cinema	140.0	284.8	380.4
Outdoor	1,054.3	1,361.3	1,482.2
Internet	231.6	6,331.5	15,236.9
Mobile	n/a	n/a	7,588.4
Total	19,066.1	22,075.5	26,459.0

Note: Mobile spend data is only available from 2011.
Source: WARC (2018). Used with permission from WARC.

The trend has been for increased expenditure online with advertisers moving budgets out of newspapers and magazines. While there has been considerable speculation that television expenditure would suffer from brands increasing their investment online, the impact has not been as great as some commentators feared.

Other areas of the marketing communications mix such as sponsorship have experienced significant growth. Global sponsorship advertising expenditure was estimated to be US$62.8 billion in 2017, meaning that since 2009 the global sponsorship market has grown by 42.7 per cent (WARC, 2017).

Publicly available figures regarding the size of the public relations, direct marketing and sales promotion industries are based on the size of the industry rather than what has been spent by each client. The Holmes report valued the global public relations (PR) agency industry at US$15 billion in 2016, an increase from $14.2 billion in 2015 (Sudhaman, 2017). The world's top 10 PR firms accounted for US$5.1 billion of the total value.

Although estimates vary, mainly because of problems of definition, the direct marketing industry has similarly experienced large growth, with the European industry estimated to be worth £14.2 billion (DMA, 2015). The growth in this sector is being driven largely by the growth in digital, with other forms of direct marketing, such as direct mail, seeing a decline in spend. In 2016, direct mail advertising expenditure in the UK fell to £1,713 million, representing a year-on-year decline of 10.4 per cent from 2015 (WARC, 2017).

Sales promotion is another area of the industry that is difficult to measure given that the breadth of activities attributable to sales promotion are many and varied. In 2013 the industry body, The Institute of Promotional Marketing (IPM), undertook a major research project to gain a better understanding of the size of the UK promotional marketing industry. The study identified that the total spend for the UK industry was £54.8 billion, although £40.4 billion of that value was price discounting. Despite this, the study showed that £14.4 billion was spent through agencies and on media and rewards (IPM, 2013).

Expenditure patterns do change, albeit at different rates, but, given the domination of advertising and sales promotion, the overall balance is unlikely to change dramatically in the short term. However, it is clearly important for those responsible for the future and current planning of marketing communications activities to monitor trends, particularly those in the fastest-growing sectors of the industry, in order to identify and target creative opportunities.

Having painted a picture of the size and dynamics of the industry, a word needs to be said about the consumer view of the industry. Here issues about ethics and morality surface, accompanied by a suggestion that the public view the industry with cynicism and distrust. The industry is aware of consumers' views of advertising, as the chief executive of the Advertising Association highlights, 'advertising is facing a problem, favourability has evaporated, the public's trust and confidence in [it] has fallen through the floor and the industry has missed a trick by failing to renegotiate its deal with society in which it operates' (Mitchell, 2012).

Agency types and structures

The marketing communications industry consists of a number of different types of organisations whose purpose is to enable clients to communicate effectively and efficiently with their target audiences. Essentially, clients appoint agencies to develop and implement campaigns on their behalf. To accomplish this, advertising agencies buy media time and space from media owners, public relations agencies place stories with the media for their clients' representation, and other agencies undertake a range of other communications activities on behalf of their clients.

Originally, advertising agencies undertook two main roles, creative message design and media planning and buying. The media component has subsequently been spun off to specialist agencies. However, the interest in and drive towards integrated marketing communications have helped agencies assume new, more independent roles in the communications industry. The development of digital media has had a profound impact on all areas of marketing communications and agencies are now being asked to provide services that meet the needs of these new media platforms. Clients want agencies to help develop blogger programmes, deliver digital content and design social media campaigns, and the industry has seen the emergence of a new wave of specialist agencies in response to this demand.

Scholars' paper 9.1

Can agencies survive in a digital world?

Deighton, J. (2017) Rethinking the profession formerly known as advertising: how data science is disrupting the work of agencies, *Journal of Advertising Research*, 57(4), 357–61.

The author highlights the challenge facing advertising agencies to survive in an increasingly IT-dominated marketing environment. He argues that the traditional role of advertising agencies has been to address communication problems for brands, whereas current marketing problems are being solved with IT solutions. The article questions the role of advertising agencies in the future.

See also:

Keegan, B.J., Rowley, J. and Tonge, J. (2017) Marketing agency–client relationships: towards a research agenda, *European Journal of Marketing*, 51(7/8), 1197–223.

Clients will typically work with a number of different agencies, each with its own area of expertise to develop communications ideas. Having a range of agencies on their roster provides the clients with access to different specialisms and they will brief agencies together to respond to their brief with an integrated marketing communications campaign. While many clients choose to manage this process themselves, some large holding groups such as WPP have identified a need to develop a new client servicing model. The 'horizontal' WPP service model allows clients access to all the specialist services within the holding group and draw on talent from across the group's vast agency networks. The WPP horizontal service model is a unique cross-group way of working and has proved successful with many clients, including Bayer, Colgate-Palmolive, Danone, Dell, Emirates, Ford, HSBC, Janssen J&J, Kimberly-Clark, Procter & Gamble, Shell and Vodafone (WPP, 2015).

Clients working with individual agencies can choose from a range of agency types. The IPA identifies 11 main types of agency that exist: full-service or integrated agencies, creative agencies, media agencies, digital agencies, search agencies, social media agencies, direct marketing agencies, branded content agencies, experiential agencies, healthcare agencies and outdoor or out-of-home (OOH) agencies (IPA, 2015). As shown in Table 9.2, the range of agencies provides a wide choice for brand owners. Whatever their marketing communications needs, there is a broad spectrum of agency services on offer, from the full-service agencies offering a complete range of services to small specialist agencies, offering niche skills.

The agencies and organisations set out so far in this chapter have their roots and core business firmly set within the advertising part of the communications industry. In addition to these

Image 9.2 The 'Horizontal' WPP service model allows clients to access talent from several hundred different companies operating out of more than 3,000 offices in 112 countries
Source: WPP plc.

Table 9.2   Types of agencies

Type of agency	Services offered
Full-service or integrated agencies	A full range of services, including strategic planning, research, creative development, production, media planning and buying, and evaluation services. Examples include agencies such as J. Walter Thompson and Leo Burnett.
Creative agencies	Provide specialist or niche services for clients such as copywriting, developing creative content and other artistic services. These agencies provide clients with an alternative source of ideas, new ways of thinking about a problem, issue or product.
Media agencies	Provide media services expertise. Offering media strategy and consulting services for both client advertisers and agencies. Their core business, however, is focused on the planning, scheduling, buying and monitoring of a client's media schedule. Examples include MediaCom.
Digital agencies	Specialise in their digital offering. Services range from digital media planning to creative services, such as web design and display advertising. Digital agencies provide search, social media, content and mobile campaigns.
Search agencies	Specialise in a range of services that help to drive traffic to an organisation's website. While the range of expertise they offer differs, most have expertise in pay-per-click advertising and search engine optimisation (SEO), as well as affiliate and social media marketing.
Social media agencies	Provide a range of services to organisations, including community management, channel monitoring and analysis, crisis management and a range of content development including blogging.
Direct marketing agencies	Specialise in creating and delivering campaigns through direct mail, telemarketing or through a variety of offline and online media, which are referred to as direct-response media.
Branded content agencies	Offer planning and development of digital content and commercials largely for the Internet. Most offer video production for viral advertising, product videos and films, and some offer app development.

Type of agency	Services offered
Experiential marketing agencies	Develop experiences for consumers, such as roadshows, product launches, live events, PR stunts, in-store sampling, pop-up showrooms and even guerrilla activity.
Healthcare agencies	Provide marketing communications solutions for the pharmaceutical and healthcare sector. While they offer a range of services that may be similar to other agencies such as campaign planning and development, their specialist knowledge of the healthcare, medical and medical device sectors make them attractive to clients.
Outdoor agencies/ out-of-home	Specialise in planning, buying, implementing and evaluating out-of-home media, such as ATMs, billboards, petrol pumps, tube posters, taxis, buses and a range of ambient media.

Source: (IPA, 2015).

there is a raft of other agencies, each specialising in a particular aspect of the marketing communications industry. So, there are agencies that provide sales promotion, public relations and sponsorship. Their structure and operations reflect the needs of their market specialism, and many are based on the principles through which the advertising agencies operate.

Selecting an agency

There has been much debate in recent years about the process used by clients when selecting a new agency. One of the main concerns raised by industry bodies such as the IPA and ISBA has been the costs involved. The 'pitch' process as it is called is an expensive one for agencies, with an average of £178,000 being spent by agencies on pitch costs a year (ISBA, 2013).

While the industry discussion has been centred around the pitch process, the academic literature has largely focused on the criteria used by organisations when choosing a new agency (Fam and Waller, 2008; van Rensburg et al., 2010). Studies provide evidence that creative skill, agency people, cost and experience are the key determinants of what agency an organisation selects (Turnbull and Wheeler, 2016).

Scholars' paper 9.2

Selecting a new agency

Turnbull, S. and Wheeler, C. (2016) Exploring advertiser's expectations of advertising agency services, *Journal of Marketing Communications*, 22(6), 587–601.

The authors identify the expectations clients have of the agency at the selection stage. The study, which was undertaken in the United Arab Emirates, identifies that clients expect agencies to offer craft skill such as creative ability; functionality, such as geographical or media capabilities; strategic perspective; and to feel an affinity towards the agency team. The authors conclude that not all expectations are made clear at the selection stage and this can be problematic once the relationship with the agency develops further. They provide recommendations for clients to adopt service level agreements (SLAs) with their agency to help make expectations more explicit.

See also:

Moeran, B. (2005) Tricks of the trade: the performance and interpretation of authenticity, *Journal of Management Studies*, 42(5), 901–22.

The process of selecting an agency, often referred to as the pitch process, as set out below appears to be rational and relatively straightforward. The reality, however, is that the process is infused with political and personal issues, some of which can be contradictory. Logically the process commences with a *search*, undertaken to develop a long list of potential agencies. This is accomplished by referring to industry publications such as *Campaign*, visiting agency websites and often with guidance from an intermediary. In some cases, personal recommendations or prior experience with an agency may help with this initial stage. As many as ten agencies could be included at this stage, although four or eight are to be expected.

Next, the client will make a request for information (RFI) from each agency. While there are a number of different formats used for this, the IPA provides a standardised template to help organisations. In addition to requesting information from the agency, the RFI provides the agency with details about why the organisation is reviewing the agency's account, the scope of the work, geographical regions to be covered and the type of agency it is looking for. At this stage the agency can evaluate whether there is a conflict of interest with any other clients. The RFI requires the agency to respond with details of its published financial accounts, HR policies and experience on similar brands and within the sector (IPA, 2009a).

The client will then request a *credentials meeting* (creds meeting) with each of the agencies. This is a crucial stage in the process, as it is now that the agency is evaluated for its degree of fit with the client's expectations and requirements. This provides the client with an opportunity to visit the agency offices, see the resources the agency can offer, meet with key agency personnel and see examples of current creative work. Following these meetings, the organisation will then decide on a shortlist of agencies, which usually results in between three to five agencies being invited to continue to the next stage in the process: the pitch presentation.

In the PR industry agencies are selected to pitch on the basis of the quality and experience of the agency people, the agency's image and reputation, and relationships with existing clients. In addition, Lankester (2014) reports that cost is an important consideration and suggests clients look for agencies offering to work on a project basis.

In advertising, those agencies that have made it to the shortlist will be given a brief by the organisation and invited to respond with a mix of strategic, creative and media recommendations, as required at a *pitch* presentation. The time given to agencies to prepare their recommendations varies and is often around six to eight weeks, although two-week deadlines are not unknown. Often during this time the agency will arrange to meet the client for a *chemistry meeting*. This provides an opportunity for the agency both to clarify the brief and to develop the potential relationship between the agency and the client (Turnbull and Wheeler, 2017).

The pitch presentation itself is about how the agency would approach the strategic and creative issues and the account is awarded to whichever agency produces the most suitable proposal. Suitability is a relative term, and a range of factors need to be considered when selecting an organisation to be responsible for a large part of a brand's visibility. A strategic alliance is being formed and, therefore, a strong understanding of the strategic objectives of both parties is necessary, as is an appreciation of the structure and culture of the two organisations.

The pitch has become infamous for its drama with some agencies adding theatrical elements to the meeting to impress potential new clients and demonstrate their creativity (Robinson, 2010). This has led to many pitch presentations becoming theatrical performances with clients treated to role-playing scenarios and displays to add a sense of drama to the occasion. To impress *Strictly Come Dancing*, who were looking to appoint a new partner, one agency choreographed its own routine to the *Strictly Come Dancing* theme tune and had the whole agency perform the dance when the client arrived for the pitch presentation (Swift, 2015).

The selection process is a bringing together of two organisations whose expectations may be different but whose cooperative behaviour is essential for these expectations to have any chance of materialising. For example, agencies must have access to comprehensive and often commercially confidential data about products and markets if they are to operate efficiently. Otherwise, they cannot provide the service that is expected. However, it should be noted that pitches are not mandatory, and as Jones (2004) reports, nearly one-third of clients move their accounts without involving pitches.

The immediate selection process is finalised when terms and conditions are agreed and the winner is announced to the contestants and made public, often through press releases and the use of trade journals such as *Campaign, Marketing* and *Marketing Week*.

This formalised process is now being questioned as to its suitability. The arrival of new media firms and the need to find communications solutions in one rather than eight weeks have meant that new methods have had to be found. Additionally, many agencies feel that they had to invest a great deal in a pitch with little or no reward if the pitch failed. Their response has been to ask for payment to pitch, which has not been received well by many clients. The pitching process also fails to give much insight into the probable working relationships and is very often led by senior managers who will not be involved in the day-to-day operations. One solution has been to invite agencies to discuss mini-briefs, which enables the client to see agency teams working together. Another approach promoted by the IPA is the use of workshops and trial projects (IPA, 2009b).

Viewpoint 9.2

Cannes Lions Awards

Image 9.3 The Cannes Lions are held every year in Cannes, France
Source: Cannes Lions.

Winning new business is a highly competitive business in adland. Agencies need to demonstrate they can offer the best service in the market. In particular, they need to convince clients they can produce compelling creative work.

One way to showcase their creative skill is to win awards. The Lions are one the most coveted global awards in the industry and are seen as a hallmark of an agency's creativity. Held in Cannes, France every year the Lions showcase the best creative work from around the globe. To win an award at the Lions places both the agency and the creative team who created the work among an elite group of Lions winners.

Lions are awarded for 26 categories, including the Creative eCommerce Lion, Social & Influencer Lion and Brand Experience & Activation Lion, all of which are judged, in part, on the commercial success of the creative work. Other categories include the Industry Craft Lion, which is judged on creative artistry, talent and skill, and a Sustainable Development Goals Lion, which celebrates creative solutions that tackle one of the United Nations' 17 Sustainable Development Goals.

Winning a Lion is seen as the ultimate achievement for an agency and provides prospective clients with evidence that they have the creative expertise to produce compelling and effective creative work.

Source: Cannes Lions (2018).

Insight

The key takeaway here is the value of creativity in the industry. Awards such as the Lions attract new clients for agencies. For clients, creativity can improve the effectiveness of their marketing communications. And for the creative teams who win awards, the value of their CV is undoubtedly increased.

Question: Why do agencies enter their work for awards? What value would a Cannes Lion bring to an agency?

Task: Imagine you are a prospective client looking for a new agency. Make a list of all the skills and experience you would expect to find in an agency. Rate the importance of each of these factors on a scale from 1–10.

Agency operations

Many communications agencies are generally organised on a functional basis. There have been moves to develop matrix structures utilising a customer orientation, but this is very inefficient and the low margins prohibit such luxuries. There are departments for planning, creative and media functions coordinated on behalf of the client by an account handler or executive.

The account executive fulfils a very important role, in that these people are responsible for the flow of communications between the client and the agency. The quality of the communications between the two main parties can be critical to the success of the overall campaign and to the length of the relationship between the two organisations. Acting at the boundary of the agency's operations, the account executive needs to perform several roles, from internal coordinator and negotiator to presenter (of the agency's work), conflict manager and information gatherer. Very often account executives will experience tension as they seek to achieve their clients' needs while trying to balance them with the needs of their employer and colleagues.

Once an account has been signed, a client brief is prepared that provides information about the client organisation (see Figure 9.3). It sets out the nature of the industry it operates in, together with data about trends, market shares, customers, competitors and the problem that the agency is required to address. This is used to inform agency personnel. In particular, the account planner will undertake research to determine market, media and audience characteristics and make proposals to the rest of the account team concerning how the client problem is to be resolved.

Briefing is a process that is common across all client–agency relationships in the communications industry. Regardless of whether working in direct marketing, sales promotion, advertising, public relations, media planning and buying or other specialist area, the brief has a special importance in making the process work and the outcomes significant. However, the importance of preparing a brief of suitable quality has for some been underestimated and studies show that client briefs are often inadequate (Koslow et al., 2006). This has led to a joint industry initiative to establish common working practices. The outcome of the process was a briefing template intended to be used by all across the communications agencies in the industry. Eight key headings emerged from the report and these can be seen at Figure 9.3.

Project management – Provide basic project details, e.g. timescales, contacts and people, project numbers

Where are we now? – Describe current brand details, e.g. background, position, competitors, key issues

Where do we want to be? – What needs to be achieved in terms of goals, e.g. sales, market share, ROI, shareholder value, awareness, perception, etc.?

What are we doing to get there? – What is the context in terms of the marketing strategy, overall communications strategy and campaign strategy?

Who do we need to talk to? – What is understood about the audiences the communications are intended to influence?

How will we know if we have arrived? – What will be measured, by whom, how and when to determine whether the activity has been successful?

Practicalities – Budgets, timings and schedules, creative and media imperatives

Approvals – Who has the authority to sign off the brief and the agency work?

Figure 9.3 A new briefing structure

In addition to the role of account handler, there is the role of the account planner. The account planner's role has been the subject of debate (Collin, 2003; Crosier et al., 2003; Grant and McLeod, 2007; Mackert and Munoz, 2011; Patwardhan et al., 2011). The general conclusion of these papers is that the role of account planner, which has been evolving since the beginning of the 1960s, has changed as the communications industry has fragmented and that a new role is emerging in response to integrated marketing communications (IMC) and media-neutral planning initiatives. (For more about IMC see Chapter 12.)

Scholars' paper 9.3
The planner's role

Jacobi, E.S., Freund, J. and Araujo, L. (2015) 'Is there a gap in the market, and is there a market in the gap? How advertising planning performs markets', *Journal of Marketing Management*, 31(1–2), 37–61.

This ethnographic study provides a rich insight into the role of a planner in a London advertising agency. The researchers work as part of the planning team to help develop a new energy/health drink for a UK brand. The study highlights the planners' role in translating data insights and commercial goals into advertising campaigns. Additionally, the findings show how planners mediate between clients and creatives during campaign development.

See also:

Haley, E., Taylor, R. and Morrison, M. (2014) How advertising creatives define excellent planning, *Journal of Current Issues & Research in Advertising*, 35(2), 167–89.

The traditional role of the account planner, which began in full-service agencies, was to understand the client's target consumers and develop strategies for the creative and media departments. As media broke away from full-service agencies, so the role of the account planner shifted to the creative aspect of the agency work. Media planners assumed the same type of work in media companies, although their work focused on planning the right media mix to reach the target audience. With the development of integrated perspectives and the move towards a broader view of a client's communications needs comes an expectation that the planning role will evolve into a strategic role. The role will be to work with a broad range of marketing disciplines (tools) and media, but not to brief creatives or media planners directly (Collin, 2003). Account planning is a strategically important activity in agencies, and a major source of power and conflict (Grant et al., 2012).

Creative teams comprise a copywriter and an art director, supported by a service team. This team is responsible for translating the brief into an advertisement. In a full-service agency, a media brief will also be generated, informing the media planning and buying department of the media and the type of media vehicles required. However, the vast majority of media planning work is now undertaken by specialist media agencies, media independents, and these will be briefed by the client, with some support from those responsible for the creatives.

In recent years, partly as a response to the growth of new media, a raft of small entrepreneurial agencies has emerged, to exploit the new opportunities arising from the digital media. Many of these are run without the control and structures evident in large, centralised agencies. While dedicated teams might theoretically be the best way to manage a client's project, the reality in many cases is the use of project teams comprising expert individuals working on a number of projects simultaneously. This is not a new phenomenon, but as a result many people are multitasking and they assume many roles with new titles. For example, the title *Head of Content* has arisen to reflect the significance of content issues in the new media market. Project managers assume responsibility for the implementation phase and the coordination of all aspects of a client's technological facilities. In addition, there are positions such as head of marketing, mobile, production and technology. The result is no hierarchies, flat structures and flexible working practices and similar expectations.

Viewpoint 9.3

Fancy a latte?

Image 9.4 adam&eveDDB have trained baristas to ensure agency staff get the perfect latte
Source: YKTR/Shutterstock.

adam&eveDDB have been awarded *Campaign*'s Advertising Agency of the Year for the last four consecutive years and in 2017 was ranked by the Gunn Report as the most awarded agency in the world. As well as creating some of the best advertising on the planet, it is now ranked as one of the best large UK agencies to work for.

The agency has been placed in *Campaign*'s top 5 of the Best Places to Work 2018. When you look at how well they look after their staff, it isn't surprising that adam&eveDDB is seen to be one of the best agencies to work for in the UK.

Where do we start? Staff in adam&eveDDB's London Paddington offices are certainly well catered for with trained baristas on hand to ensure agency staff get the perfect cafe latte throughout the day. And, on Friday evenings the agency serves alcoholic beverages to round off the week.

Source: Campaign (2018).

But it's not just about the drinks. The agency has a generous wellbeing package with complimentary access to an on-site doctor, physiotherapist, ergonomics specialist, nutritionist and exercise classes.

To top it all, every summer the agency organises Eden Fest, an all-day festival for employees. Staff are invited to attend and enjoy the entertainment which includes live music and craft workshops.

Interested? adam&eveDDB are always on the lookout for new talent. Their recruitment is committed to being inclusive and as well as the 'adam&everyone' diversity programme, the agency are members of the Stonewall Diversity Champions programme.

Insight

While working on the agency side of the business can mean long hours, the rewards are attractive. Benefits such as free beverages and health packages support staff wellbeing and help to retain talent in the agency.

Question: Consider the agency roles explained in this chapter. Which role would most interest you in an agency? Explain your choice.

Task: Look on the Brand Republic website for three entry-level jobs in advertising. Make a list of the skills required and write against each skill how you would evidence this on your own CV.

Agency remuneration

How to pay agencies fairly for their work has always been a topic of debate in the industry. Traditionally, advertising agencies were paid a commission by media owners for selling space in their publications. This commission was soon referred to as 'the line' and a figure of 15 per cent above the line emerged as the norm and was seen to be a fair reward for the efforts of the agency. However, the emergence of media independents, increasing disintermediation of the industry and drives for greater cost-efficiencies within client organisations has resulted in a wider range of remuneration agreements between agencies and their clients.

Table 9.3   The IPA's 10 forms of agency remuneration

Method	Explanation
Payment by results	PBR is based on the attainment of predetermined KPIs. Here both parties can win and results are transparent and measurable.
Value-based	Value-based approaches consider the agency's results in terms of outputs and outcomes. This can incorporate a base fee to cover the agency's cost of producing the outputs, with a mark-up, rather than discretionary bonus, based on actual performance metrics.
Retainers	A negotiated activity fee for a defined period (e.g. one year) is paid monthly in advance for agreed workloads and activities.
Project fees	Rather than an annual fee, fees are based on an individual project.
Variable fees	Fees are based on actual time spent on a client's account, paid after the activity has been incurred.
Scale fees + win bonus	Client pays a 'salary' based on sales (bonus included) or marketing budget plus a bonus if based on a marketing budget.
Consultancy and concept fees	This is a one-off fee designed to reward an agency for developing a creative concept.
Licensing fees	The client pays for concept development but at a reduced rate before paying a licence fee for the finished concept, once approved.
Output or 'off-the-shelf' rate fee	Used where the output can be readily measured and costed. Here a fixed price per unit of output is agreed, typically suited to the 'pay-per-click' approach.
Commission	A percentage (originally 15 per cent of the gross media cost within a full-service arrangement) is paid by media owners for the work placed with them by agencies on behalf of their client.

Source: IPA/ISBA/CIPS (2012).

According to the IPA there are 10 key remuneration methods used. These are explained in Table 9.3. Almost 90 per cent of creative agency agreements are based on fee payments and the rest are mainly hybrid arrangements that include some form of commission (Baskin, 2012). The development of more complex remuneration models such as *payment by results* (PBR) and *value-based remuneration* are seen to reflect the rise in digital media and the increasing involvement of clients' procurement departments. Each of these approaches is discussed below and it should be noted that it is very rare for a single method to be used within a single contract.

Agency remuneration has seen a number of significant developments over the years. In times of recession, marketing budgets are inevitably cut, which means less revenue for agencies. Increasing competition means lower profit margins if an agency is to retain the business, and if costs are increasing at the same time, the very survival of the agency is in question.

During the early 1990s there was a great deal of discussion and energy directed towards non-commission payment systems. This was a direct result of the recession, in which clients cut budgets, and there was a consequent reduction in the quantity of media purchased and hence less revenue for the agencies. Fees became more popular, and some experimented with payment by results. Interestingly, as that recession died and the economy lifted, more revenue resulted in larger commission possibilities, and the death throes of the commission system were quickly replaced by its resuscitation and revival. Most media agencies' agreements still have an element of commission (Singh, 2016).

Payment by results (PBR) has been popular over the last decade. In 2009 Coca-Cola introduced a new way by which its agencies were to be remunerated. It is referred to as a *value-based compensation model* and Tylee (2010) argues that it extends the PBR model. Agencies are promised profit mark-ups of 30 per cent if specific targets are met. If they are not, then only their costs are covered. Procter & Gamble also adopted a similar value-based reward programme (Williams, 2010).

However, the 2017 ISBA/Arc report, Paying for Advertising, identified that there has been a dramatic decrease in the use of PBR in recent years. The survey found that while most of the big global accounts are still using PBR, the overall number has reduced to just 43 per cent of agreements (Singh, 2016). With six out of ten PBR schemes resulting in no payout, it is not hard to imagine why this type of agreement is in decline (Singh, 2016). One of the inherent problems of PBR is the lack of control agencies have over the other marketing activities of the client and hence this payment option involves risk for the agency.

Fees have been around for a long time, either in the form of retainers or on a project-by-project basis. Indeed, many agencies charge a fee for services over and above any commission earned from media owners. The big question concerns the basis for calculation of fees (and this extends to all areas of marketing communications, not just advertising), and protracted, complicated negotiations can damage client–agency relationships.

The use of bonuses is widespread but, whereas the intention is to reward excellent work, some agencies see bonuses as a means by which fees are reduced and, as some clients refuse to pay, the impact on relationships can be far from positive (Child, 2007).

Viewpoint 9.4
Paying for the idea

Image 9.5 Paying agencies for ideas is one alternative to traditional remuneration models
Source: Marquisphoto/Shutterstock.

Finding a fair way to compensate agencies for their work has always been challenging.

Traditional payment models have been based on paying agencies for the amount of time agency personnel work on a client's account or the volume of media purchased. These payment structures have been controversial and many in the industry agree that more transparent and equitable payment models are needed.

Part of the problem lies in the client's view of an agency's function. If a client sees the agency primarily as a factory that spends time producing ads and coordinating campaigns, then possibly the traditional fee-based payment may be the best way to compensate the agency. If, however, the client regards the agency as an ideas business that can add value to the brand, then perhaps a better way to compensate the agency may be a type of royalty payment for the idea.

Thinking differently about the work that agencies do and seeing the creative idea as a product with a value encourages new agency payment models to be considered. Some organisations have already started to experiment with new ways of paying their agencies based on ideas. General Mills for example have moved away from traditional payment structures and have introduced a new payment model based around *thinking, making things* and *incentives*. Based on these three forms of compensation, agencies are rewarded for thinking on behalf of the client and compensated for any ideas that are liked. General Mills report that by changing the reward system paid to their agencies, they have seen an increase in the quality of creative work from their agencies.

While the payment for ideas seems a good solution to the agency compensation dilemma, it too is not without its challenges. For example, how do you value an idea? Should the client make a one-off payment for the idea, or be made to pay a usage fee for each time the idea is used?

Sources: Baskin (2012); Jensen (1995); Whiteside (2016).

Insight

This highlights the complexity and challenges of agency remuneration. The development of new payment structures such as the ideas model is a result of the dissatisfaction with traditional models of payment and reflects the changing nature of agency services. A move towards an ideas-based payment model shows that brands recognise the value of creativity and are incentivising agencies to deliver breakthrough ideas.

Question: What would be the advantages and disadvantages for both the client and agency of a payment for ideas model?

Task: Imagine you are an agency pitching for a new client in the food retailing sector. Consider which form of remuneration you would propose to them. Justify *why* this form of payment would be the most appropriate for both your agency and the client.

Budgeting for communications

One of the key questions associated with investing in marketing communications is: what is the right amount an organisation should spend on marketing communications? In addition, how should organisations divide this sum across their brands, regions, territories and various activities? These two questions underpin the setting of communications budgets and the allocation of the budget once it is agreed (Corstjens et al., 2011).

The rate at which advertising and associated media costs have outstripped the retail price index in developed economies was regarded as both alarming and troublesome. This disproportionate increase in the costs of advertising served to make it less and less attractive to some clients. Larger clients became more discerning and introduced procurement specialists to overview media purchasing. Unsurprisingly, this has spurred the increased use of other tools such as brand placement, sponsorship, event marketing, direct marketing and digital media platforms. However, major brands still commit large budgets to their advertising, as shown in Table 9.4.

Large investment and commitment are required over a period of years if long-term, high-yield performance is to be achieved. Many accountants and procurement managers, however, view communications from a different perspective. For a long time their attitude

Table 9.4   Top 10 UK advertisers in 2017

Brand	£million total (2017)
Sky UK	197.1
Procter & Gamble	196.8
BT	144.1
Unilever UK	116.8
McDonalds	96.2
Tesco	89.5
Reckitt Benckiser	88.2
Virgin Media	72.1
Lidl UK	71.1
Samsung UK	66.6

Source: Nielsen, cited by Tan (2018).

has been to consider these activities, and advertising in particular, as an expense, to be set against the profits of the organisation. Many see planned marketing communications as a variable, one that can be discarded in times of recession (Whitehead, 2008).

These two broad views of advertising and of all marketing communications activities, one as an investment to be shown on the balance sheet and the other as a cost to be revealed in the profit and loss account, run consistently through discussions about how much should be allocated to advertising and other brand communications spend. For management, the four tools of the communications mix are often divided into two groups. The first contains advertising, sales promotion and public relations, while the second group contains the financial aspects that relate to personal selling.

This division reflects not only a functional approach to marketing but also the way in which, historically, the selling and marketing departments have developed. This is often observed in older, more established organisations, those that find innovation and change seriously difficult and challenging. Accountability and responsibility for communications expenditure in the first group often fall to the brand or product manager. In the second group, this aspect is managed by sales managers who often, at national level, report to a sales director.

A variety of techniques are used to determine the correct allocation of funds to advertising, sales promotion, public relations, the field sales force and other marketing communications activities. In an era in which shareholder value is becoming increasingly prominent and a means of distinguishing between alternative strategic options, however, companies also need to consider how a brand's value might influence the budget setting.

The role of the communications budget

The role of the communications budget is the same regardless of whether the organisation is a multinational trading from numerous international locations, or a small manufacturing unit on an industrial estate outside a semi-rural community. Both types of organisations want to ensure that they achieve the greatest efficiency with each pound/euro/dollar they allocate to promotional activities. Neither can afford to be profligate with scarce resources, and each is accountable to the owners of the organisation for the decisions it makes.

There are two broad decisions that need to be addressed. The first concerns how much of the organisation's available financial resources (or relevant part) should be allocated to marketing communications over the next period. The second concerns how much of the total amount should be allocated to each of the individual disciplines of the communications mix.

Benefits of budgeting

The benefits of engaging in budgeting activities are many and varied, but in the context of marketing communications planning they can be considered as follows:

1. The process serves to focus people's attention on the costs and benefits of undertaking the planned communications activities.

2. The act of quantifying the means by which the marketing plan will be communicated to target audiences instils a management discipline necessary to ensure that the objectives of the plan are capable of being achieved. Achievement must be at a level that is acceptable and will not overstretch the organisation.

3. The process facilitates cross-function coordination and forces managers to ensure that the planned communications are integrated and mutually supportive. Additionally, it means campaigns can be monitored and management control asserted. This is particularly important in environments that are subject to sudden change or competitive hostility.

4. At the end of the campaign, a financial review enables management to learn from the experiences of the promotional activity in order that future communications can be made more efficient and the return on the investment improved.

The process of planning the communications budget is an important one. Certain elements of the process will have been determined during the setting of the campaign objectives. Managers will check the financial feasibility of a project prior to committing larger resources. Managers will also discuss the financial implications of the communications strategy (i.e. the push/pull positioning dimension) and those managers responsible for each of the individual tools will have estimated the costs that their contribution will involve. Senior management will have some general ideas about the level of the overall appropriation, which will inevitably be based partly upon precedent, market and competitive conditions and partly as a response to the pressures of different stakeholders, among them key members of the distribution network. Decisions now have to be made about the viability of the total plan, whether the appropriation is too large or too small and how the funds are to be allocated across the promotional tools.

Communications budgets are not formulated at a particular moment in a sequence of management activities. The financial resources of an organisation should be constantly referred to, if only to monitor current campaigns. Therefore, budgeting and the availability of financial resources are matters that managers are constantly aware of and able to tap into at all stages in the development and implementation of planned communications.

Difficulties associated with budgeting for communications

There are a number of problems associated with the establishment of a marketing communications budget. Of them all, the following appear to be the most problematic. First, it is difficult to quantify the precise amount that is necessary to complete all the required tasks. Second, communications budgets do not fit neatly with standard accounting practices. The concept of brand value is accepted increasingly as a balance sheet item, but the concept of investment in communications to create value has only recently begun to be accepted.

Third, the diversity of the tools and the means by which their success can be measured renders like-for-like comparisons null and void. Finally, the budget-setting process is not as clear-cut as it might at first appear.

There are four main stakeholder groups that contribute to the budget decision. These are the organisation itself, any communications agencies, the media and production or fulfilment houses whose resources will be used to carry designated messages, and the target audience. It is the ability of these four main stakeholders to interact, to communicate effectively with each other and to collaborate that will impact most upon the communications budget. However, determining the 'appropriate appropriation' is a frustrating exercise for marketing managers. The allocation of scarce resources across a communications budget presents financial and political difficulties, especially where the returns are not easily identifiable. The development and significance of technology within marketing can lead to disputes concerning ownership and control of resources. For example, in many companies, management and responsibility for the website rests with the IT department, which understandably takes a technological view of issues. Those in marketing, however, see the use of the website from a marketing perspective and need a budget to manage it. Tension between the two can result in different types of website design and effectiveness and this leads to different levels of customer support.

Budgeting – techniques and approaches

At a broad level there are a number of techniques used by organisations to determine the communications budget. The main models, proposed by different authors to determine the appropriation of the communications mix, are set out in Table 9.5.

Table 9.5   Principal budgeting methods and techniques

Budgeting technique	Explanation
Marginal analysis	Otherwise referred to as the advertising response function, this theoretical approach involves determining how many extra sales are generated from an extra unit of communications spend. A point will be reached when an extra pound/euro/dollar spent on communications will generate an equal amount (a single pound/euro/dollar's-worth) of revenue. At this point marginal revenue is equal to marginal costs, which represents the point of maximum communications expenditure and which generates maximum profit.
Arbitrary	Sometimes referred to as 'chairperson's rules', this approach is based on what the 'boss' decides. Simple but inappropriate as the boss may not have a clue what the optimal figure should be and these decisions, made on the hoof, lack consideration of customer needs, the demands of the environment or marketing strategy, and there is an absence of any critical analysis. Unfortunately this approach is often used by many small organisations.
Inertia	This approach involves 'let's keep it the same'. Here all elements of the environment and the costs associated with the tasks facing the organisation are ignored. Not recommended.
Media multiplier	In order to maintain the same impact in the next period, this approach requires that spend be changed by the rate at which media costs have altered. This assumes all previous decisions were sound and that marketing strategies and the environment remain unchanged. This is unlikely.
Percentage of sales	Here the budget is set at a level equal to some predetermined percentage of past or expected sales. However, as advertising is intended to create demand, not be the result of past sales, then it is likely that the next period's results will be similar, all things being equal. As no consideration is given to sales potential, this technique may limit performance.
Affordable	This requires each unit of output to be allocated a proportion of all the costs associated with the value-adding activities in production, manufacturing and distribution. After making an allowance for profit, what is left is what can be afforded to be spent on communications. The affordable technique is not in the least analytical, nor does it have any market or task orientation.

(continued)

Table 9.5   Principal budgeting methods and techniques (*Continued*)

Budgeting technique	Explanation
Objective and task	After attempting to determine the resources required to achieve each objective, these separate costs are aggregated into an overall budget. This focuses management attention on the goals to be accomplished. On the down side, this approach does not generate realistic budgets, in the sense that the required level of resources may not be available and the opportunity costs of the resources are not usually determined.
Competitive parity	Assuming advertising is the only effective factor influencing demand and that all others are self-cancelling, some organisations deliberately spend the same amount on advertising as their competitors – competitive parity. Unfortunately, this approach fails to consider the qualitative aspects of the advertising undertaken by the different players.
Advertising-to-sales (A/S) ratio	The underlying principle of the A/S ratio is that, in each industry, it is possible to determine the average advertising spend of all the players and to compare it with the value of the market. Therefore, it is possible for each organisation to determine its own A/S ratio and compare it with the industry average.
Share of voice (SOV)	Within any market the adspend of any one advertiser can be compared with the total spend of all competitors. This is known as share of voice (SOV). This figure can be compared with the share of market (SOM) that each player holds. If these percentages are equal then there is equilibrium. Variations above and below this represent strategic intent.

Marginal analysis suffers from a number of disadvantages. First, it assumes that communications can be varied smoothly and continuously. This is not the case. Second, it assumes that communications are the only influence upon sales. As discussed previously, sales are influenced by a variety of factors, of which planned communications are but one. Controllable and uncontrollable elements in the environment influence sales. Next, no account is taken of the other costs associated indirectly with the presentation of the offering, such as those allied to distribution. Each communications thrust will often be matched, or even bettered, by the competition. Furthermore, the actions of rivals may even affect the sales performance of all products in the same category.

The competitive parity approach fails to consider the qualitative aspects of the advertising undertaken by the different players. In addition, there are a number of disadvantages with this simple technique. The first is that, while information is available, there is a problem comparing like with like. For example, a carpet manufacturer selling a greater proportion of output into the trade will require different levels and styles of advertising and promotion from another manufacturer selling predominantly to the retail market. Furthermore, the first organisation may be diversified, perhaps importing floor tiles. The second may be operating in a totally unrelated market. Such activities make comparisons difficult to establish, and financial decisions based on such analyses are highly dubious.

Share of Voice (SOV) is used to compare adspend against total spend of all competitors. The relationship between SOV (share of voice) and SOM (share of market) is recognised by a number of authors, including Broadbent (1989), Buck (2001), Field (2009), Jones (1990) and Schroer (1990). When a brand's market share is equal to its share of advertising spend, equilibrium is said to have been reached (SOV = SOM). Increasing the SOV above the point of equilibrium generally raises SOM, while lowering SOV reduces SOM and reaches a new point of stability.

These concepts of SOV and SOM frame an interesting perspective of competitive strategy based upon the relative weight of advertising expenditure. Schroer (1990) reports that,

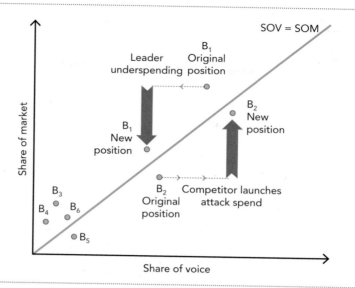

Figure 9.4 Strategy to gain market share by increasing adspend

Source: From Ad spending: growing market share, *Harvard Business Review*, January/February, pp. 44–48 (Schroer, J. 1990), Reprinted by permission of *Harvard Business Review*. Copyright © 1990 by Harvard Business School Publishing Corporation; all rights reserved.

following extensive research on the US packaged goods market (FMCG), it is noticeable that organisations can use advertising spend to maintain equilibrium and to create disequilibrium in a market. The former is established by major brand players maintaining their market shares with little annual change to their advertising budgets. Unless a competitor is prepared to inject a considerable increase in advertising spend and so create disequilibrium, the relatively stable high spend deters new entrants and preserves the status quo. Schroer claims that, if the two market leaders maintain SOV within 10 per cent of each other, then competitive equilibrium will exist. This situation is depicted in Figure 9.4. If a market challenger launches an aggressive assault upon the leader by raising advertising spend to a point where SOV is 20–30 per cent higher than the current leader, market share will shift in favour of the challenger.

The concepts of SOV and SOM have also been used by Jones (1990) to develop a new method of budget setting. He suggests that those brands that have an SOV greater than their SOM are 'investment brands', and those that have an SOV less than or equal to their SOM are 'profit-taking brands'.

Using data collected from an extensive survey of 1,096 brands across 23 different countries, Jones 'calculated the difference between share of voice and share of market and averaged these differences within each family of brands' (p. 40). By representing the data diagrammatically (see Figure 9.5), Jones shows how it becomes a relatively simple task to work out the adspend that is required to achieve a particular SOM. The first task is to plot the expected (desired) market share from the horizontal axis, then move vertically to the intersection with the curve and read off the SOV figure from the vertical axis.

It is interesting to note that the SOV concept commanded a reasonable profile in the early to mid-1990s but then subsided from view. Its revival by Binet and Field (2007) when communicating with advertising practitioners is helpful and commensurate with the emerging emphasis on accountability and the use of metrics. As these authors point out,

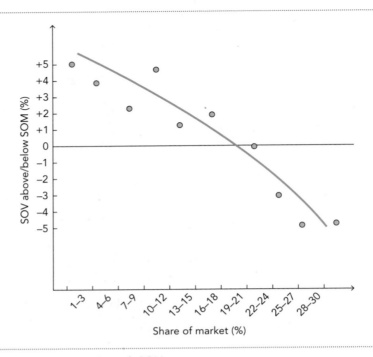

Figure 9.5 Curve comparing SOV with SOM

Source: From Ad spending: maintaining market share, *Harvard Business Review*, January/February, pp. 38–42 (Jones, J.P. 1990), Reprinted by permission of Harvard Business Review. Copyright © 1990 by Harvard Business School Publishing Corporation; all rights reserved.

marketing success is predicated on SOV rather than size of budget. In addition, the vast proportion of budget is invested in order to maintain or slow the decline of market share, rather than grow it.

Which methods are most used?

A major question, therefore, is which of these tools are used in practice, and which ones should be used? West and Prendergast (2009) found that approximately 28 per cent of their respondents claimed that their firms used judgemental budgeting methods, with a similar number claiming use of the objective and task processes. Measurement-based budgeting methods were reported by 20 per cent, sales 15 per cent and competitive by roughly 8 per cent. However, their key finding was that budgeting is not about methods, measurement or analysis. The real factors that influence budgets are 'personalities, organisation, timing, planning, the nature of the market and access to data'. They identify a 'cultural code' which permeates and shapes the budgeting strategy within organisations. An organisation's culture provides the decision-making frame within which budgets are developed, balanced, influenced and agreed.

A study of US advertisers by West et al. (2014) similarly found that budget-setting frequently combines both heuristics, such as maximum advertising/sales ratio, with analytics, such as marketing mix models. Their study suggests that the budgeting process is complex and decisions may not be purely rational. Heuristics are seen to provide checks on analytical techniques and assist organisations with managing risk. All organisations in the study were found to use at least two methods of budget setting.

It appears that over time a number of budgeting models and methods have been developed. A selected number, usually two, are then utilised within an organisation and its cultural framework, to produce a marketing communications budget.

Scholars' paper 9.4
How are budgets set?

West, D., Ford, J.B. and Farris, P.W. (2014) How corporate cultures drive advertising and promotion budgets: best practices combine heuristics and algorithmic tools, *Journal of Advertising Research*, 54(2), 149–62.

This article is based on research among US firms to examine the methods used to set advertising and promotions budgets. The study considers the influence of culture, risk and organisational experience on budgeting methods and highlights the difference between heuristic and algorithmic tools.

See also:

West, D. and Prendergast, G.P. (2009) Advertising and promotions budgeting and the role of risk, *European Journal of Marketing*, 43(11/12), 1457–76.

Budgeting for the other elements of the communications mix

The methods presented so far have concentrated on the FMCG sector. The assumption has been that only one product has been considered. In reality, a range of products will need investment for communications and the allocation decision needs to reflect the requirements of an organisation's portfolio of brands. Broadbent (1989) suggests that this situation and others (e.g. direct marketing, corporate advertising) require particular combinations of the approaches presented so far. The recommendation again is that no single method will help organisations to determine the optimal investment sum.

Sales promotion activities can be more easily costed than advertising in advance of a campaign. Judgements can be made about the expected outcomes, based upon experience, competitive conditions and the use of predictive software tools. The important variable with sales promotion concerns the redemption rate. How many of the extra packs, price deals and samples will customers demand? How much extra of a brand needs to be sold if all the costs associated with a campaign are to be covered? The production and fulfilment costs can also be determined, so in general terms a return can be calculated in advance of a sales promotion event. However, there are a large number of sales promotion activities and these will often overlap.

The costs of *public relations* activities can also be predicted with a reasonable degree of accuracy. The staffing and/or agency costs are relatively fixed and, as there are no media costs involved, the only other major factor is the associated production costs. These are the costs of the materials used to provide third parties with the opportunity to 'speak' on the organisation's behalf. As with sales promotion, if a number of public relations events have been calculated as a necessary part of the overall communications activities of the organisation, then the costs of the different tasks need to be anticipated and aggregated and a judgement made about the impact the events will make.

The cost of the *sales force* can be the highest of all the elements of the mix, especially in business-to-business situations. The budget for the sales force needs to include salaries, cars, expenses, training and development. Unlike other marketing communications tools, which have some degree of flexibility, communications through personal selling require the establishment of a relatively high level of fixed costs. In addition to these expenses are the opportunity costs associated with the lengthy period taken to recruit, train and release suitably trained sales personnel into the competitive environment. This process can take over 15 months in some industries, especially in the fast-changing, demanding and complex information technology markets.

Strategic investment to achieve the right sales force, in terms of its size, training and maintenance, is paramount. It should be remembered, however, that managing a sales force can be rather like turning an ocean liner: any move or change in direction has to be anticipated and actioned long before the desired outcome can be accomplished.

Budgeting for communications activities can vary in the degree of sophistication and usefulness. Of all the methods and different approaches, the one constant factor that applies to all concerns the objectives that have been set for the campaign. Each element of the communications mix has particular tasks to accomplish and it is these objectives that drive the costs of the promotional investment. If the ultimate estimate of the communications spend is too high, then the objectives, not the methods used, need to be revised.

Key points

- The communications industry consists of a variety of very large-, medium- and small-sized agencies, with many agencies owned by large global holding companies. Technology and new media channels have had a significant influence on shaping the structure of the industry.

- In 2018 UK media expenditure is expected to reach over £26 billion, with internet spend seeing the largest growth (WARC, 2018). Other sectors of the industry such as sponsorship and direct marketing have experienced high growth rates and are expected to continue to rise.

- Agencies broker or facilitate the communications needs of clients, while media houses plan, buy and monitor media purchases for their clients. Production facilitators ensure the processes work by making videos, providing fulfilment or staging events. All deliver specific value to the industry and have different roles to play.

- The IPA has identified 11 different types of agencies: full service or integrated, creative, media, digital, search, social media, direct marketing, branded content, experiential, healthcare, and outdoor or out-of-home (OOH) agencies.

- Clients use a fairly standardised process to select an agency which involves a search, a request for information and a credentials meeting. Shortlisted agencies often arrange chemistry meetings with the client team and a formal pitch presentation is used to make a final decision.

- Setting the marketing communications budget serves to focus people's attention on the costs and benefits of undertaking planned communications activities. The act of quantifying the means by which the marketing plan will be communicated to target audiences instils a management discipline necessary to ensure that the objectives of the plan are achievable. The process facilitates cross-function coordination and forces managers to ensure that the planned communications are monitored and controlled.

- Marginal analysis provides a theoretical basis to determine the 'right' budget. However, this approach is impractical so organisations use a variety of practical approaches. These include guesswork, a percentage of sales, what is affordable, inertia, and objective and task. The last is considered to be the most appropriate.

- Within any market the adspend of any one advertiser can be compared with the total spend of all competitors. This is known as share of voice (SOV). This figure can be compared with the share of market (SOM) that each player holds. If these percentages are equal then there is equilibrium. Variations above and below this represent strategic intent.

- For other elements of the communications mix different budgeting techniques are used. There are specific techniques available to determine the optimum sales force size and costs. The size of the public relations effort depends on usage, but the financial investment can be reduced to a judgement. Sales promotions are project-oriented and can be costed accordingly.

Case study

BBC Creative: solving the BBC's digital challenge

Image 9.6 The BBC decided to move away from the traditional agency model and took creative in-house
Source: Piotr Swat/Shutterstock.

The UK broadcasting industry is highly competitive, with broadcasters competing against each other for a share of increasingly fragmented audiences. While for commercial broadcasters such as Channel 4, Sky and ITV, higher audience ratings attract more advertisers, for a public service broadcaster such as the BBC, maintaining a share of audience is important to reassure licence fee payers they are getting value. BBC's marketing plays a key role in communicating this message to licence fee payers, ensuring they are aware of what programmes are available and how they are able to access and engage with them across multiple platforms.

The emergence of new forms of communication and digital channels, demanding digital assets and short-form content, presented new marketing communications challenges for the BBC. It had become clear that the traditional TV based model, taking a six-hour drama and creating a 60-second TV trail, which although still needed, was no longer enough to engage younger audiences. These audiences weren't consuming as much linear television and had moved away to digital and social channels. Producing content to reach these younger audiences on digital platforms had become expensive 'add-ons' within the existing agency model. Additionally, the process of producing marketing assets after programmes had been completed restricted opportunities to develop content for digital and social channels during production. The BBC recognised that the old creative model no longer worked.

The BBC has worked with some of the largest advertising agencies over the years, with all TV trails handled by one agency, Red Bee. With Red Bee's 10-year contract coming to an end, the BBC saw an opportunity to rethink the existing creative model. Other UK broadcasters, Channel 4, ITV and Sky, had already moved away from the traditional agency model and taken creative in-house, proving that highly effective, award-winning creative work can be achieved in-house. The BBC recognised that an in-house model would provide an opportunity to work more closely with commissioners and programme makers up front to produce marketing assets, while shooting programmes. Additionally, an in-house agency would save on agency fees and their profit mark-up, addressing the need to reduce costs within the BBC. The advantages of the in-house agency model appeared to offer a good solution to the BBC's creative challenge.

Cost was an important consideration, but while fees could be saved, the in-house model required additional headcount at a time when the BBC were looking to reduce overheads. There was also the consideration of attracting creative talent. The BBC knew that for their marketing communications to be successful, there was a need to develop compelling creative work that would engage audiences across platforms. This required attracting the best creative talent. The BBC offers creative talent an opportunity to work on some of the UK's most iconic brands such as *Eastenders*, the *BBC Proms*, and *The Apprentice* as well as cultural events such as the Olympics, guaranteeing their work would be seen by millions of people. The reputation of the BBC and the chance to work on bigger-scale projects that can influence culture and society was an attractive proposition to creatives and other team members. This attracted one of the UK's top creative teams and Cannes Lions winners, Aiden McClure and Laurent Simon to join the in-house team. And, in January 2016, BBC Creative was born.

BBC Creative now has 125 permanent staff and between 15–30 freelancers. Moving creative production in-house has saved the BBC £1.5 million net a year and this figure continues to rise as more work is brought in-house. As well as the cost savings, the BBC has seen a marked increase in the quality of the creative work and this has been recognised with a number of prestigious industry awards. In 2017, BBC Four's Friday Night Music Idents won Silver at The Clios for sound design and BBC Creative picked up 17 awards at The PromaxBDA UK Awards, including Best New Talent of the Year.

BBC Creative's 2017 Christmas ad, 'The Supporting Act' is an example of the agency's ability to develop a beautifully crafted ad. Built on BBC1's brand strategy, 'everything we share', the two-minute ad draws on insight that everyday life gets in the way of things and tells an emotional story of a 10-year-old girl and her dad at Christmas time. While the dad appears too busy to notice his daughter's preparations for her school talent show, he makes an unexpected appearance just as his daughter begins her act and saves the day when he is able to help her overcome her stage fright by leading her through the dance steps. The two-minute film is accompanied by four idents and a range of digital assets. The ad demonstrates BBC Creative's ability to develop compelling creative work that resonates with audiences, both in traditional TV trails and on digital platforms.

The film, 'The Supporting Act' has been recognised in industry with a Gold for Best Animation and Silver for Best TV over 60 seconds at the 2018 Creative Circle Awards. The Christmas film also won BBC Creative their first D&AD Pencil and Outstanding Promo at the 2018 EBU Connect Awards, with five further award nominations.

The BBC Creative Christmas ad is only one of the high-profile pieces of creative work that have come out of the in-house agency so far. Other work, such as, 'Sorry Not Sorry for Being Me' an out-of-home campaign for BBC Three's season celebrating the identity of young people in Britain, clearly demonstrates the agency's ability to develop engaging digital campaigns.

BBC Creative had 26 nominations for creative awards in the first quarter of 2018 for a number of campaigns, proving that this alternative creative model can deliver compelling creative.

Sources: BBC Creative (2018); ISBA (2017); Kiefer (2017); Swift (2016); Thom (2017).

Lankester, C. (2014) How to pick the right agency. *PR Week,* 31 July, retrieved 20 December 2017 from https://www.prweek.com/article/1306108/pick-right-agency

Mackert, M. and Munoz, I.I. (2011) Graduate account planning education: insights from the classroom, *Journal of Advertising Education,* 15(2), 35–9.

Media Week (2005) Keeping your options in-house, *Media Week,* 1 February, retrieved 10 May 2015 from www.mediaweek.co.uk/article/511893/keeping-options-in-house#AxOFltIL0Mu2icO4.99

Mitchell, A. (2012) Face it, your consumers hate you, *Marketing,* 28 March 2012, 30–2.

Moeran, B. (2005) Tricks of the trade: the performance and interpretation of authenticity. *Journal of Management Studies,* 42(5), 901–22.

OLIVER (2018) www.oliver.agency, retrieved 20 January 2018 from https://www.oliver.agency/

Patwardhan, P., Patwardhan, H. and Vasavada-Oza, F. (2011) Diffusion of account planning in Indian ad agencies: an organisational perspective, *International Journal of Advertising,* 30(4), 665–92.

Robinson, M. (2010) The pitch, *New Business: A Guide To Life On The Front-Line,* IPA, 32–5, retrieved 10 December 2014 from www.thegoodpitch.com/wp-content/uploads/2011/09/IPA_Life-on-the-front-line-Final.pdf

Schroer, J. (1990) Ad spending: growing market share, *Harvard Business Review,* January/February, 44–8.

Singh, S. (2016) The cost of advertising, *Campaign,* 22 August, retrieved 10 January 2018 from https://www.campaignlive.co.uk/article/cost-advertising-isba-arc-study-reveals-adlands-commercial-trends/1406152

Sudhaman A. (2017) Global PR industry now worth $15bn as growth rebounds to 7% in 2016. *Holmes Report,* 24 April, retrieved 1 March 2018 from https://www.holmesreport.com/long-reads/article/global-pr-industry-now-worth-$15bn-as-growth-rebounds-to-7-in-2016

Swift, J. (2016) Behind the BBC's new in-house agency: more perfect days to come? *Campaign,* retrieved 12 December 2017 from https://www.campaignlive.co.uk/article/behind-bbcs-new-in-house-agency-perfect-days-come/1382089

Tan, E. (2018) Sky overtakes P&G as UK's biggest spender as FMCG giant cuts traditional spend, *Campaignlive,* 23 April, retrieved 28 August 2018 from https://www.campaignlive.co.uk/article/sky-overtakes-p-g-uks-biggest-spender-fmcg-giant-cuts-traditional-spend/1462730

Thom, A. (2017) How to develop an in-house agency: lessons learned from the launch of BBC Creative, WARC, June, retrieved 12 December 2017 from https://www.warc.com/content/paywall/article/bestprac/how_to_develop_an_inhouse_agency_lessons_learned_from_the_launch_of_bbc_creative/111419

Turnbull, S. and Wheeler, C. (2016) Exploring advertiser's expectations of advertising agency services, *Journal of Marketing Communications,* 22(6), 587–601.

Turnbull, S. and Wheeler, C. (2017) The advertising creative process: a study of UK agencies. *Journal of Marketing Communications,* 23(2), 176–94.

Tylee, J. (2010) Will others follow Coke's remuneration model? *Campaign,* 19 February, 17.

van Rensburg, J.M., Venter, P. and Strydom, J.W. (2010) Approaches taken by South African advertisers to select and appoint advertising agencies, *South African Business Review,* 14(4), 25–36.

WARC (2017) Sponsor data North American, sponsorship advertising expenditure by type, WARC, 17 December, retrieved 10 January 2018 from https://www.warc.com/content/paywall/article/warc-datapoints/north_american_sponsorship_advertising_expenditure_by_type/117868

WARC (2018) Adspend database, WARC, retrieved 10 March 2018 from www.warc.com/Pages/ForecastsAndData/InternationalDataForecast.aspx?Forecast=DatabaseAndCustomTables&isUSD=True.

We Are Unlimited (2018) *WeAreUnlimited.com*, retrieved 10 January 2018 from http://weareunlimited.com/#how-we-do-it

West, D., Ford, J.B. and Farris, P.W. (2014) How corporate cultures drive advertising and promotion budgets: best practices combine heuristics and algorithmic tools, *Journal of Advertising Research*, 54(2), 149–62.

West, D. and Prendergast, G.P. (2009) Advertising and promotions budgeting and the role of risk, *European Journal of Marketing*, 43(11/12), 1457–76.

Whitehead, J. (2008) IPA backs ads in face of downturn, *Brand Republic*, 9 January, retrieved 20 April 2015 from www.brandrepublic.com/article/775516/ipa-backs-ads-face-downturn.

Whiteside, S. (2016) General Mills gives agencies new incentives, *WARC Event Reports*, retrieved 20 January 2018 from https://www.warc.com/content/article/event-reports/general_mills_gives_agencies_new_incentives/109541

Williams, T. (2010) Why agencies should call time on selling time, *Campaign*, 16 July, 12.

WPP (2015) *WPP Annual Report and Accounts*, retrieved 10 January 2018 from http://www.wpp.com/annualreports/2015/downloads-and-financials/2015-annual-report-pdf-and-financial-statements/

Evaluation and metrics

Evaluation is an important part of the marketing communications process. All activities need to be evaluated to understand the impact and effect that a campaign has on a target audience. There is also increasing pressure to measure the return on investment from all areas of marketing communications.

Aims and learning objectives

The aims of this chapter are to review the ways in which marketing communications activities can be evaluated.

The learning objectives are to enable readers to:

1. discuss the role of evaluation within marketing communications;
2. explore the value and methods of pre-testing and post-testing advertisements;
3. explain the main ideas behind different physiological measures of evaluation;
4. consider ways in which advertising and public relations can be evaluated;
5. review the issues associated with measuring the fulfilment of brand promises;
6. examine the metrics used to measure online, mobile and social media campaigns.

Introduction

All organisations should review and evaluate the performance of their various activities. Many organisations do use formal mechanisms to evaluate their campaigns, but there are many others who do not review and if they do it is informal, and ad hoc.

Evaluation allows an organisation to reflect on what happened and determine whether the communications objectives have been met. It provides an opportunity to evaluate which areas of the communications had the most, and the least, impact and make decisions about future campaigns. Evaluation also allows organisations to calculate the return

Table 10.1 Stakeholder requirements

Stakeholder	Requirement
Marketing Director	Did the campaign build market share? What was the ROI?
Sales Director	Did the campaign increase sales?
Finance Director	What was the ROI?
Brand Manager	Did the campaign improve image dimensions?
Media Manager	Do we look good against our peers? Is this new channel working for us?
Communications agency	Is the campaign delivering as planned? Is the mix right?
Agency channel specialists	Is the deployment optimal?

Source: IPA (2014).

on investment. As there is likely to be a range of stakeholders involved in the evaluation process it is important to consider the evaluation priorities of each group (IPA, 2014). Table 10.1 highlights the possible requirements of each stakeholder.

The evaluation of planned marketing communications consists of two distinct elements. The first element is concerned with the development and testing of individual messages. An advertising message has to achieve, among other things, a balance of emotion and information in order that the communications objectives and message strategy be achieved. To accomplish this, testing is required to ensure that the intended messages are encoded correctly and are capable of being decoded accurately by the target audience and the intended meaning ascribed to the message.

The second element concerns the overall impact and effect that a campaign has on a target audience once a communications plan has been executed. This post-test factor is critical, as it will either confirm or reject management's judgement about the viability of its communications strategy. The way in which the individual components of the communications mix work together needs to be understood so that strengths can be capitalised on and developed and weaknesses negated.

Prediction and evaluation require information about options and alternatives. For example, did sales presentation approach A prove to be more effective than B and, if so, what would happen if A was used nationally? Predictably, the use of quantitative techniques is more prevalent with this set of reasons.

This chapter considers the range of methods available to help managers evaluate their brand marketing communications. It starts with a review of the principles and need for measurement and evaluation. It then examines the traditional methods used to test and evaluate marketing communications activities. It also reviews some of the more contemporary approaches and the issues associated with the measurement and evaluation of online communications.

The role of evaluation in planned communications

The evaluation process is a key part of marketing communications. The findings and results of the evaluative process feed back into the next campaign and provide indicators and benchmarks for further campaign decisions. The primary role of evaluating the performance of a communications strategy is to ensure that the communications objectives have been met and that the strategy has been effective. The secondary role is to ensure that the strategy has been executed efficiently, and that the full potential of the individual tools and media has been extracted and that resources have been used economically.

Table 10.2   Four dimensions of IMC

Dimension of IMC	Explanation
Unified communications for consistent messages and images	Activities designed to create a clear, single position, in the target market, delivering a consistent message through multiple channels.
Differentiated communications to multiple customer groups	The need to create different marketing communications campaigns (and positions) targeted at different groups (in the target market) who are at different stages of the buying process. Sequential communications models based on the hierarchy of effects or attitude construct apply.
Database-centred communications	This dimension emphasises the need to generate behavioural responses through direct marketing activities created through information collected and stored in databases.
Relationship fostering communications for existing customers	The importance of retaining customers and developing long-term relationships is a critical element of marketing communications.

Source: Lee and Park (2007). Used with permission from WARC.

The prevalence and acceptance of the integrated marketing communications (IMC) concept (Chapter 12) suggests that its measurement should be a central aspect when evaluating marketing communications activities. One of the predominant issues surrounding the development of IMC is the challenges and lack of empirical evidence concerning the measurement of this concept. In an attempt to resolve this, Lee and Park (2007) provide one of the first multidimensional-scaled measures of IMC. Their model is based on four key dimensions drawn from the literature. These are set out in Table 10.2.

Each of these dimensions is regarded as a separate yet integral element of IMC. Lee and Park (2007) developed an 18-item scale, derived from the literature, to measure these dimensions. The use of this approach may advance our understanding of IMC and provide a substantial basis on which IMC activities can be measured. It is interesting to note that Lee and Park (2007) see IMC as a customer-only communications activity and choose to exclude other critical stakeholders from their measurement model.

Scholars' paper 10.1
Evaluating IMC

Porcu, L., Del Barrio-García, S. and Kitchen, P.J. (2017) Measuring integrated marketing communication by taking a broad organisational approach: the firm-wide IMC scale, *European Journal of Marketing,* **51(3), 692–718.**

This paper discusses the challenges of measuring integrated marketing communications (IMC) and presents a firm-wide conceptualisation of this multi-dimensional concept. The authors develop and validate a new scale to measure IMC and offer this for future research.

See also:

Patti, C.H., Hartley, S.W., van Dessel, M.M. and Baack, D.W. (2017) Improving integrated marketing communications practices: a comparison of objectives and results, *Journal of Marketing Communications*, 23(4), 351–70.

Advertising

The techniques used to evaluate advertising are by far the most documented and, in view of the relative sizes of the communications tools, it is not surprising that slightly more time is devoted to this tool. This is not to disregard or disrespect the contribution each of the communications tools can make to an integrated campaign. Indeed, it is the collective measure of success against the goals set at the outset that is the overriding imperative for measurement, as will be seen later.

Pre-testing unfinished ads

Advertisements can be researched prior to their release (pre-test) or after they have been released (post-test). Pre-tests, sometimes referred to as *copy tests*, have traditionally attracted more attention, stimulated a greater variety of methods and generated much controversy, in comparison with post-tests.

The effectiveness of *pre-testing*, the practice of showing unfinished commercials to selected groups of the target audience with a view to refining the commercial to improve effectiveness, is still subject to debate. Turnbull and Wheeler (2017), however, identified that pre-testing is used extensively by some brands, especially fast-moving consumer goods (FMCG) brands, during the creative development process to validate the advertising creative. The researchers found that pre-testing creative ideas provided a means of validating the creative ideas with consumers and was also used in some instances to resolve creative disagreements between the agency and client. The study found that in some cases up to 10 different creative ideas were put into pre-testing (Turnbull and Wheeler, 2017).

The methods used to pre-test advertisements are based upon either qualitative or quantitative criteria. The most common methods used to pre-test advertisements are concept testing, focus groups, consumer juries, dummy vehicles, readability, theatre and physiological tests. Focus groups are the main qualitative method used and theatre or hall tests the main quantitative test. Each of these methods will be discussed later. Many organisations use proprietary tools such as Millward Brown's Link global copy testing tool.

The primary purpose of testing advertisements during the developmental process is to ensure that the final creative work will meet the advertising objectives. Pre-testing ads at an earlier stage allows the agency and client to make changes before the costs become too high and commitment too final. Changes to an advertisement that are made too late may be resisted partly because of the sunk costs and partly because of the political consequences that 'pulling' an advertisement might have. Pre-testing also provides an opportunity to optimise ads before they go to air.

Once a series of advertisements has been roughed or developed, advertisers seek reassurance and guidance regarding which of the alternatives should be developed further. Concept tests, in-depth interviews, focus groups and consumer juries can be used to determine the better of the proposed ads, by using ranking and prioritisation procedures. Of those selected, further testing can be used to reveal the extent to which the intended message is accurately decoded. As the Millward Brown Viewpoint shows, pre-testing can also help refine the final TV edits. These comprehension and reaction tests are designed to prevent inappropriate advertisements reaching the finished stage.

Viewpoint 10.1
Does pre-testing kill creativity?

Image 10.1 Pre-testing can dismiss good ideas early in the process if they don't test well
Source: ImageFlow/Shutterstock.

Many clients see pre-testing as part of the creative development process and value the opportunity to gain insight at an early stage. However, clients are also aware of the dangers of being over-reliant on pre-testing and see that over-use can lead to formulaic creative solutions.

While pre-testing can be seen to reduce the risk of running creative work that doesn't perform well, the problem is that pre-testing could kill off really creative ideas altogether.

Creativity by definition means something new and unexpected and often this can make someone feel uncomfortable. Asking the consumer to judge ideas that are new is asking them to respond to something that may make them feel uncomfortable just because it's novel. Pre-testing also relies on consumers being able to express what they are thinking and this has sometimes been known to produce inaccurate responses. In particular, emotional advertising is seen to be difficult to test, even though it can deliver very good campaign results.

In some cases, the agency and client have been known to ignore pre-testing results and go with their gut instinct that an ad will work. Heineken's iconic and highly successful 'Refreshes the parts other beers cannot reach' campaign, which ran in the 1970s is a good example of this. The campaign did not perform well in pre-testing but despite this the marketing director decided to run the ad. The campaign resulted in a huge uplift in sales and the slogan quickly entered into popular culture.

Direct Line's campaign starring Winston Wolfe, better known for his gangster role in *Pulp Fiction*, is another good example of how brands need to trust their creative judgement. Although the ads performed quite well in pre-tests. Placing a gangster as the company spokesperson was always going to be a risky route to take and required a brave client to have faith that the creative idea would work.

Sources: Gwynn (2017); Murphy (2005); Turnbull (2011).

Insight

While pre-testing is not always able to accurately predict how an ad will perform in the market it does provide clients and agencies with some insight into how consumers will react and respond to advertising. In this sense the consumers act to validate the idea. However, pre-testing does not take place in the real world and therefore it does not always reflect how advertising will perform in the market.

Question: What are the advantages and disadvantages of pre-testing?

Task: Using the techniques outlined in this chapter for pre-testing ads, which method would you have used to pre-test Direct Line's ad campaign? Explain your reasons for this.

Concept testing

The concept test is an integral part of the advertising creative development process. The purpose is to reduce the number of alternative advertising ideas, to identify and build upon the good ideas, and to reject those that are judged by the target audience not to be suitable. While many clients see this as a valuable stage in the creative process, not least because it can identify potential problems with the creative route early, not all advertising undergoes pre-testing.

Concept testing can occur very early on in the creative development process. Agencies have been known to put creative ideas into concept testing before they are shown to the client to help the agency decide which route to propose. In most cases, however, concept testing occurs after initial ideas are shown to the client and an agreed route or number of routes are then tested with the target audience.

The agency prepares scamps or a storyboard (see Table 10.3) which is essentially a rough version of the ad used to illustrate the intended artwork and the messages to be used. There are varying degrees of sophistication associated with concept testing, from the use of simple cards with no illustrations to photomatics, which are films of individual photographs shot in sequence, and livematics, which are films very close to the intended finished message. Animatics and stealomatics are also used (see Table 10.3). Some storyboards will consist of as many as 20 sketches, depicting key scenes, camera and product shots, close-ups, along with background scenery and essential props. Which type of storyboard is used depends on the size of the advertiser's budget, the completion date of the campaign and the needs of the creative team.

Table 10.3   Terminology used in creative development

Term	Meaning
Animatics	Storyboards using animated footage to illustrate the narrative of the TV commercial.
Scamps	Roughly drawn television storyboards or press ads.
Stealomatic	A compilation of video material to show the intended tone of the television advert.
Storyboards	A sequence of illustrations that show the narrative of the television commercial.

Source: Turnbull (2011).

Table 10.4　Projective techniques

Projective technique	Explanation
Association	Free word association tests require respondents to respond with the first word that comes to mind in response to a stimulus word. Often used when naming brands.
Completion	Spontaneous sentence or storytelling completion are the most used methods. Responses can be graded as approval, neutral or disapproval, enabling attitudes towards brands to be determined.
Transformation	These are also known as 'expressible' techniques and involve techniques such as psychodrawing. This requires respondents to express graphically their inner feelings about a brand or event (e.g. a shopping trip, holiday or purchase process).
Construction	This approach can involve role playing where respondents are asked to act out their feelings towards a purchase, a brand, event or organisation.

Source: Based on Peter M. Chisnall, *Marketing Research* 7th edn., pp. 228–31, McGraw-Hill, 2005.

commences, details regarding the respondents' demographic and attitudinal details are recorded and they are asked to nominate their product preferences from a list. At the end of the viewing their evaluation of the programme is sought and they are also requested to complete their product preferences a second time.

There are a number of variations on this theme: one is to telephone the respondents a few days after the viewing to measure recall and another is to provide joysticks, push buttons and pressure pads to measure reactions throughout the viewing. The main outcome of this process is a measure of the degree to which product preferences change as a result of exposure to the controlled viewing. This change is referred to as the persuasion shift. This approach provides for a quantitative dimension to be added to the testing process, as the scores recorded by respondents can be used to measure the effectiveness of advertisements and provide benchmarks for future testing.

It is argued that this form of testing is too artificial and that the measure of persuasion shift is too simple and unrealistic. Furthermore, some believe that many respondents know what is happening and make changes because it is expected of them in their role of respondent. Those in favour of theatre testing state that the control is sound, that the value of established norms negates any 'role play' by respondents and that the actual sales data supports the findings of the brand persuasion changes in the theatre.

This technique is used a great deal in the USA, but has had limited use in the UK. Agencies are concerned that the simplistic nature of recording scores as a means of testing advertisements ignores the complex imagery and emotional aspects of many messages. If likeability is an important aspect of eventual brand success then it is unlikely that the quantitative approach to pre-testing will contribute any worthwhile information.

Physiological measures

A bank of physiological tests has been developed, partly as a response to advertisers' increasing interest in the emotional impact of advertising messages and partly because many other tests rely on the respondents' ability to interpret their reactions. Physiological tests are designed to measure the involuntary responses to stimuli that avoid the bias inherent in other tests. There are substantial costs involved with the use of these techniques, and the validity of the results is questionable. Consequently they are not used a great deal in practice, but, of them all, eye tracking is the most used and most reliable (see Table 10.5).

Table 10.5 Physiological tests

Pupil dilation

Pupil dilation is associated with action and interest and is used to measure a respondent's reaction to a stimulus. if the pupil is constricted then interest levels are low and energy is conserved. The level of arousal is used to determine the degree of interest and preference in a particular advertisement or package design.

Eye tracking

This technique requires the use of eye movement cameras that fire an infrared beam to track the movement of the eye as it scans an advertisement. The sequence in which the advertisement is read can be determined and particular areas that do or do not attract attention can be located.

Galvanic skin response

This measures the resistance the skin offers to a small amount of current passed between two electrodes. Response to a stimulus will activate the sweat glands, which in turn will increase the resistance. Therefore the greater the level of tension induced by an advertisement, the more effective it is as a form of communication.

Tachistoscopes

These measure the ability of an advertisement to attract attention. The speed at which an advertisement is flashed in front of a respondent is gradually slowed down until a point (about 1/100 second) is reached at which the respondent is able to identify components of the message. This can be used to identify those elements that respondents see first as a picture is exposed, and so facilitates the creation of impact-based messages.

Electro-encephalographs

This involves the use of a scanner that monitors the electrical frequencies of the brain. Hemispheric lateralisation concerns the ability of the left-hand side of the brain to process rational, logical information and the right-hand side handles visual stimuli and responds more to emotional inputs.

Brain activation measures the level of alpha-wave activity, which indicates the degree to which the respondent is aroused by and interested in a stimulus. Therefore, the lower the level of alpha activity, the greater the level of attention and cognitive processing. It would follow that, by measuring the alpha waves while a respondent is exposed to different advertisements, different levels of attention can be determined.

Image 10.3 Galvanic skin response process being used
Source: Guy Bell/Alamy Images.

On the surface, pupil dilation has a number of attractions, but it is not used very much as research has shown little evidence of success. The costs are high and the low number of respondents that can be processed limits the overall effectiveness. Eye tracking can be a useful means of reviewing and amending the layout of an advertisement. Galvanic skin response is flawed because the range of reactions and emotions, the degree of learning and recall, and aspects of preference and motivation are all ignored. When these deficiencies are combined with the high costs and low numbers of respondents that can be processed, it is not surprising that this method of pre-testing has little value. Similarly, other physiological tests such as tachistoscopes and electro-encephalographs, although used in academic research, are not widely used by clients or agencies in the creative development process.

Scholars' paper 10.2
What's new in Neuroscience?

Harris, J.M., Ciorciari, J. and Gountas, J. (2018) Consumer neuro-science for marketing researchers, *Journal of Consumer Behaviour*, 17(3), 239–52.

This paper provides a review of neuroscience techniques and includes an explanation of their function and use in marketing. The authors identify electroencephalography, eye tracking and implicit measurements as increasingly popular techniques of research used in marketing.

See also:

Plassmann, H., Ambler, T., Braeutigam, S. and Kenning, P. (2007) What can advertisers learn from neuroscience? *International Journal of Advertising*, 26(2), 151–75.

Post-testing

Testing advertisements that have been released is generally more time-consuming and involves greater expense than pre-testing. However, the big advantage with post-testing is that advertisements are evaluated in their proper environment, or at least the environment in which they are intended to be successful.

There are a number of methods used to evaluate the effectiveness of such advertise-ments, and of these enquiry, recall, recognition and sales-based tests predominate.

Enquiry tests

These tests are designed to measure the number of enquiries or direct responses stimu-lated by advertisements. Enquiries can take the form of returned coupons and response cards, requests for further literature or actual orders. They were originally used to test print messages, but some television advertisements now carry 0800 (free) telephone numbers. An increase in the use of direct-response media will lead to an increase in the sales and leads generated by enquiry-stimulating messages, so this type of testing will become more prevalent.

Enquiry tests can be used to test single advertisements or a campaign in which responses are accumulated. Using a split run, an advertiser can use two different advertisements and run them in the same print vehicle. This allows measurement of the attention-getting properties of alternative messages. If identical messages are run in different media then the effect of the media vehicles can be tested.

Care needs to be given to the interpretation of enquiry-based tests, as they may be mis-leading. An advertisement may not be effective simply because of the responses received. For example, people may respond because they have a strong need for the offering rather than the response being a reflection of the qualities of the advertisement. Likewise, other people may not respond despite the strong qualities of the advertisement, simply because they lack time, resources or need at that particular moment.

Recall tests

Recall tests are designed to assess the impression that particular advertisements have made on the memory of the target audience. Interviewers, therefore, do not use a copy of the advertisement as a stimulus, as the tests are intended to measure impressions and perception, not behaviour, opinions, attitudes or the advertising effect.

Normally, recall tests require the cooperation of several hundred respondents, all of whom were exposed to the advertisement. They are interviewed the day after an advertisement is screened, hence the reference to day-after-recall (DAR) tests. Once qualified by the interviewer, respondents are first asked if they remember a commercial for, say, air travel. If the respondent replies 'Yes, Virgin', then this is recorded as unaided recall and is regarded as a strong measure of memory. If the respondent says 'No', the interviewer might ask the question 'Did you see an advertisement for British Airways?' A positive answer to this prompt is recorded as aided recall.

These answers are then followed by questions such as, 'What did the advertisement say about British Airways?', 'What did the commercial look like?' and 'What did it remind you of?' All the answers provided to this third group of questions are written down word for word and recorded as verbatim responses.

The reliability of recall scores is generally high. This means that each time the advertisement is tested, the same score is generated. Validity refers to the relationship or correlation between recall and the sales that ultimately result from an audience exposed to a particular advertisement. The validity of recall tests is generally regarded by researchers as low.

Recall tests have a number of other difficulties associated with them. First, they can be expensive, as a lot of resources can be consumed by looking for and qualifying respondents. Second, not only is interviewing time expensive, but the score may be rejected if, on examination of the verbatim responses, it appears that the respondent was guessing.

It has been suggested by Zielske (1982) that thinking/rational messages appear to be easier to recall than emotional/feeling ones. Therefore, it seems reasonable to assume that recall scores for emotional/feeling advertisements may be lower. It is possible that programme content may influence the memory and lead to different recall scores for the same offering. The use of a preselected group of respondents may reduce the costs associated with finding a qualified group, but they may increase their attention towards the commercials in the knowledge that they will be tested the following day. This will inevitably lead to higher levels of recall than actually exist.

On-the-air tests are a derivative of recall and theatre tests. By using advertisements that are run live in a test area, it is possible to measure the impact of these test advertisements with DAR. As recall tests reflect the degree of attention and interest in the advertisement, this is a way of controlling and predicting the outcome of a campaign when it is rolled out nationally.

Recall tests are used a great deal, even though their validity is low and their costs are high. It is argued that this is because recall scores provide an acceptable means by which decisions to invest heavily in advertising programmes can be made. Agencies accumulate vast amounts of recall data that can be used as benchmarks to judge whether an advertisement generated a score that was better or less than the average for the product class or brand. Having said that, and despite their popularity, recall tests are adjudged to be poor predictors of sales (Lodish and Lubetkin, 1992).

Recognition tests

Recall tests are based upon the memory and the ability of respondents to reprocess information about an advertisement. A different way of determining advertising effectiveness is to ask respondents if they recognise an advertisement. This is the most common of the post-testing procedures for print advertisements.

Recognition tests are normally conducted in the homes of approximately 200 respondents. Once it has been agreed that the respondent has previously seen a copy of the magazine, it is opened at a predetermined page and the respondent is asked, for each advertisement, 'Did you see or read any part of the advertisement?' If the answer is yes, the respondent is asked to indicate exactly which parts of the copy or layout were seen or read.

Four principal readership scores are reported: noted, seen-associated, read most and signature, as set out in Table 10.6.

The reliability of recognition tests is very high, higher than recall scores. Costs are lower, mainly because the questioning procedure is simpler and quicker. It is also possible to deconstruct an advertisement into its component parts and assess their individual effects on the reader. As with all interviewer-based research, bias is inevitable. Bias can also be introduced by the respondent or the research organisation through the instructions given or through fatigue of the interviewer.

The validity of recognition test scores is said to be high, especially after a number of insertions. However, there can be a problem of false claiming, where readers claim to have seen an advertisement but, in fact, have not. This, it is suggested, is because when readers confirm they have seen an advertisement the underlying message is that they approve of and like that sort of advertisement. If they say that they have not seen an advertisement, the underlying message is that they do not usually look at that sort of advertisement. Krugman (1988) believes that readers are effectively voting on whether an advertisement is worth spending a moment of their time to look at. It might be that readers' memories are a reliable indicator of what the reader finds attractive in an advertisement and this could be a surrogate indicator for a level of likeability. This proposition has yet to be fully investigated, but it may be that the popularity of the recognition test is based on the validity rating and the approval that high scores give to advertisers.

Sales tests

If the effectiveness of advertisements could be measured by the level of sales that occurs during and after a campaign, then the usefulness of measuring sales as a testing procedure would not be in doubt. However, the practical difficulties associated with market tests are so large that these tests have little purpose. Counting the number of direct-response returns and the number of enquiries received are the only sales-based tests that have any validity.

Practitioners have been reluctant to use market-based tests because they are not only expensive to conduct but also historical by definition. Sales occur partly as a consequence of past actions, including past communications strategies, and the costs (production, agency and media) have already been sunk. There may be occasions where it makes little

Table 10.6   Principal readership scores

Readership scores	Explanation
Noted	The percentage of readers who remember seeing the advertisement.
Seen-associated	The percentage of readers who recall seeing or reading any part of the advertisement identifying the offering.
Read most	The percentage of readers who report reading at least 50 per cent of the advertisement.
Signature	The percentage of readers who remember seeing the brand name or logo.

political and career sense to investigate an event unless it has been a success, or at the very least reached minimal acceptable expectations.

For these reasons and others, advertisers have used test markets to gauge the impact their campaigns have on representative samples of the national market.

Simulated market tests

By using control groups of matched consumers in particular geographic areas, the use of simulated test markets permits the effect of advertising on sales to be observed under controlled market conditions. These conditions are more realistic than for tests conducted within a theatre setting and are more representative of the national market than the limited in-house tests. This market representation is thought by some to provide an adequate measure of advertising effect. Other commentators, as discussed before, believe that unless advertising is the dominant element in the marketing mix, there are usually too many other factors that can affect sales. It is therefore unfair and unrealistic to place the sole responsibility for sales with advertising.

Single-source data

With the advances in technology it is now possible to correlate consumer purchases with the advertisements they have been exposed to. This is known as *single-source data* and involves the controlled transmission of advertisements to particular households whose every purchase is monitored through a scanner at supermarket checkouts. In other words, all the research data is derived from the same households.

The advent of cable television has facilitated this process. Consumers along one side of a street receive one set of control advertisements, while the others on the other side receive test advertisements. Single-source data provides exceptionally dependable results, but the technique is expensive, is inappropriate for testing single advertisements, and tends to focus on the short-term effect.

Other methods of evaluation

There is a range of other measures that have been developed in an attempt to understand the effect of advertisements. Among these are tracking studies and financial analyses.

Tracking studies

A tracking study involves interviewing a large number of people on a regular basis, weekly or monthly, with the purpose of collecting data about buyers' perceptions of marketing communications messages – not just advertisements – and how these messages might be affecting buyers' perceptions of the brand. By measuring and evaluating the impact of a campaign when it is running, adjustments can be made quickly. The most common elements that are monitored, or tracked, are the awareness levels of an advertisement and the brand, image ratings of the brand and the focus organisation, and attributes and preferences.

Tracking studies can be undertaken on a periodic or continuous basis. The latter is more expensive, but the information generated is more complete and absorbs the effect of competitors' actions, even if the effects are difficult to disaggregate. A further form of tracking study involves monitoring the stock held by retailers. Counts are usually undertaken each month, on a pre- and post-exposure basis. This method of measuring sales is used frequently. Audited sales data, market share figures and return on investment provide other measures of advertising effectiveness.

Tracking studies are also used to measure the impact and effectiveness of online activities. These may be applied to banner ads, email campaigns and paid-for search engine placements and have for a long time been geared to measuring site visitors, clicks through or pages visited. Increasingly these studies are attending to the volume and value of traffic with regard to the behaviour undertaken by site visitors. Behaviour, or the more common term, *call-to-action,* can be considered in terms of the engagement through exchanges or transactions, the number of site or subscription registrations, the volume of downloads requested or the number of offline triggers such as 'call me buttons' that are activated.

Financial analysis

The vast amount of resources that are directed at planned communications and, in particular, advertising, requires that the organisation reviews, on a periodic basis, the amount and the manner in which its financial resources have been used. For some organisations the media spend alone constitutes one of the major items of expenditure.

Variance analysis enables a continuous picture of the spend to be developed and acts as an early warning system should unexpected levels of expenditure be incurred. In addition to this and other standard financial controls, the size of the discount obtained from media buying is becoming an important and vital part of the evaluation process.

Increasing levels of accountability and rapidly rising media costs have contributed to the development of centralised media buying. Under this arrangement, the promotion of an organisation's entire portfolio of brands, across all divisions, is contracted to a single media-buying organisation. Part of the reasoning is that the larger the account, the greater the buying power an agency has, and this in turn should lead to greater discounts and value of advertising spend.

The point is that advertising economies of scale can be obtained by those organisations that spend a large amount of their resources on the media. To accommodate this, centralised buying has developed, which in turn creates higher entry and exit barriers, not only to and from the market, but also from individual agencies.

Likeability

A major study by the American Research Foundation investigated a range of different pre-testing methods with the objective of determining which were best at predicting sales success. The unexpected outcome was that, of all the measures and tests, the most powerful predictor was likeability: 'how much I liked the advertisement'.

From a research perspective, much work has been undertaken to clarify the term 'likeability', but it certainly cannot be measured in terms of a simple Likert scale of 'I liked the advertisement a lot', 'I liked the advertisement a little', etc. The term has a much deeper meaning and is concerned with the following issues (Gordon, 1992):

> personally meaningful, relevant, informative, true to life, believable, convincing relevant, credible, clear product advantages, product usefulness, importance to 'me'; stimulates interest or curiosity about the brand; creates warm feelings through enjoyment of the advertisement.

The implication of these results is that post-testing should include a strong measure of how well an advertisement was liked at its deepest level of meaning.

Research by Smit et al. (2006) determined that there are four main elements associated with likeability. These are entertainment, relevance, clearness (or clarity) and pleasantness. Of these they found relevance to be the most important for changing viewers' opinions and entertainment for explaining how people process ads.

There are two main approaches to measuring likeability. One seeks to isolate what it is that viewers think and feel after seeing particular ads, that is how they feel. The other measures attitudes towards the ad itself. Essentially likeability is concerned with the affective element of the attitude construct. Indeed, some researchers argue that likeability is a suitable response to the cognitive processing school of thought where individuals are considered to be rational problem-solvers.

Marketing mix modelling

Marketing mix modelling (MMM), or econometric analysis, uses multivariate analysis to evaluate the impact of marketing communications. Using statistical analysis, MMM allows brands to isolate the effects of factors such as advertising, weather and competitive activity to quantify the effects of each on sales (IPA, 2014).

Consider, for example, an ice-cream brand that wanted to identify the effect of advertising on sales. Since there are many other factors that could account for an increase in sales, such as a rise in the temperature or a new distribution channel, it is necessary to separate the effects of the other influences in order to allow the advertising effect to be quantified.

Using MMM can assist in setting budgets and deciding when campaigns should run. For example, in the case of the ice-cream brand it can help to evaluate which season to advertise in. Analysis can also help brands to explore campaign weight, flighting, levels of coverage and frequency, and decide when diminishing returns on expenditure are likely to start (IPA, 2014).

While MMM can be a valuable tool to evaluate marketing communications it involves building econometric models using regression analysis and other sophisticated techniques. This requires specialist knowledge of statistical analysis and also requires data that is valid, since the model will only be as good as the data that went into it.

Public relations

The objectives that are established at the beginning of a campaign must form the basis of any evaluation and testing activity. However, much of the work of public relations (PR) is continuous, and therefore measurement should not be campaign-oriented or time-restricted but undertaken on a regular, ongoing basis. PR is mainly responsible for the identity cues that are presented to the organisation's various stakeholders as part of a planned programme of communications. These cues signal the visibility and profile of the organisation and are used by stakeholders to shape the image that each has of the focus organisation.

PR is, therefore, focused on communications activities, such as awareness, but there are others such as preference, interest and conviction. Evaluation should, in the first instance, measure levels of awareness of the organisation. Attention should then focus on the levels of interest, goodwill and attitudes held towards the organisation as a result of all the planned and unplanned cues used by the organisation.

Traditionally these levels were assumed to have been generated by PR activities. The main method of measuring their contribution to the communications programme was to collect press cuttings and to record the number of mentions the organisation received in the electronic media. These were then collated in a cuttings book that would be presented to the client. While this provides a simple means of measuring media coverage it is not an effective way to evaluate the overall value of a PR campaign.

The content of the cuttings book and the recorded media mentions can be converted into a different currency. The exchange rate used is the cost of the media that would have been incurred had this volume of communications or awareness been generated by advertising activity (advertising value equivalents, or AVEs). For example, a 30-second news item about an organisation's contribution to a charity event may be exchanged for a 30-second advertisement at rate card cost. The temptation is clear, but the validity of the equation is not acceptable. By translating PR into advertising currency, the client is expected not only to understand, but also to approve of, the enhanced credibility that public relations possesses. It is not surprising that the widely held notion that PR is free advertising, has grown so substantially when practitioners use this approach.

A further refinement of the cuttings book is to analyse the material covered. The coverage may be positive or negative, approving or disapproving, so the quality of the cuttings needs to be reviewed in order that the client organisation can make an informed judgement about its next set of decisions. This survey of the material in the cuttings book is referred to as a content analysis and has traditionally been undertaken using a qualitative approach (Macnamara, 2005). Content analysis has been subject to poor interpretation and reviewer bias, however well the task was approached. Today, increasingly sophisticated software is being used to produce a wealth of quantitative data reflecting the key variables that clients want evaluated.

Viewpoint 10.2
The Barcelona Principles

Image 10.4 The Barcelona Principles were updated in 2015
Source: Reproduced by kind permission of the International Association for Measurement and Evaluation of Communication (AMEC).

In 2010 the Barcelona Declaration of Measurement Principles was developed by the International Association for the Measurement and Evaluation of Communications (AMEC) in association with a number of industry bodies, including the Institute of Public Relations and the Public Relations Society of America.

The principles represent a significant landmark in public relations measurement since they challenge the premise of using advertising value equivalents (AVEs) and false multipliers as a means of evaluating public relations outcomes. The industry has traditionally used AVEs, which provide an equivalent cost of paid media, and false multipliers, which multiply the AVE by at least twice to provide a value on the earned media to measure public relations outcomes. The Barcelona Principles clearly state that AVEs should not be used as a measure of public relations value.

Sources: AMEC (2010, 2015); Manning and Rockland (2011).

The Barcelona Principles were updated in 2015 to recognise their broader application to communications in organisations and brands. The seven revised Barcelona Principles are as follows:

1. Goal Setting and Measurement are Fundamental to Communication and Public Relations.
2. Measuring Communication Outcomes is Recommended Versus Only Measuring Outputs.
3. The Effect on Organizational Performance Can and Should Be Measured Where Possible.
4. Measurement and Evaluation Require Both Qualitative and Quantitative Methods.
5. AVEs are not the Value of Communications.
6. Social Media Can and Should be Measured Consistently with Other Media Channels.
7. Measurement and Evaluation Should be Transparent, Consistent and Valid.

Insight

The Barcelona Declaration of Measurement Principles has set new standards for evaluating PR. The industry has been encouraged to move away from traditional measures such as AVEs and consider measuring the effect on outcomes rather than outputs. Among the principles is the need to measure social media communications.

Question: Why are AVEs seen to be an inappropriate measure of value for public relations? Discuss why some practitioners might still be using this method.

Task: Make a list of the reasons why it is important to set goals and measure campaign results.

Macnamara (2014) suggests that a key challenge to measuring and evaluating PR comes from the range of terminology used, particularly in social media evaluation, and the inconsistency with which terms are used. To clarify the metrics used across PR and social media communications, Macnamara (2014) provides definitions of outputs, outtakes and outcomes (see Table 10.7).

Macnamara (2008) provides a Macro Model of Public Relations Evaluation, which breaks activity into three stages: *inputs*, *outputs* and *outcomes*. The model differentiates between each PR activity and indicates appropriate formal and informal methods of evaluation for each stage (see Figure 10.1).

Table 10.7   Metrics used in public relations

Basic outputs	Outputs → outtakes	Outtakes → outcomes
Counts of press clippings	Unique visitors	Engagement
Audience	Views	Influence
Reach	Likes	Impact
Target audience reach	Followers	Awareness
Impressions	Fans	Attitudes
Opportunities to see (OTS)	Clickthroughs	Trust
Share of voice	Downloads	Loyalty
Cost per thousand (CPM)	Comments	Reputation
Hits	Tone	Relationships
Visits	Sentiment	Return on investment (ROI)

Source: Reproduced from Macnamara (2014).

Corporate image

The approaches discussed so far are intended to evaluate specific media activity and comment on the focus organisation. Press releases are fed into the media and there is a response that is measured in terms of positive or negative, for or against. This quality of information, while useful, does not assist the management of the corporate identity. To do this requires an evaluation of the position that an organisation has in the eyes of key members of the performance network.

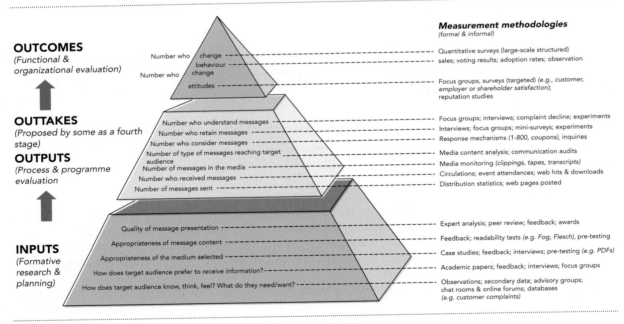

Figure 10.1 Macnamara's macro model of public relations evaluation
Source: Macnamara (2008). Used with permission.

The evaluation of the corporate image should be a regular exercise, supported by management. There are three main aspects. First, key stakeholders (including employees, as they are an important source of communications for external stakeholders), together with members of the performance network and customers, should be questioned regarding their perceptions of the important attributes of the focus organisation and the business they are in. Second, how does the organisation perform against each of the attributes? Third, how does the organisation perform relative to its main competitors across these attributes?

The results of these perceptions can be evaluated so that corrective action can be directed at particular parts of the organisation and adjustments made to the strategies pursued at business and functional levels. For example, in the computer retailing business, prompt home delivery is a very important attribute. If company A had a rating of 90 per cent on this attribute, but company B was believed to be so good that it was rated at 95 per cent, regardless of actual performance levels, then although A was doing a superb job it would have to improve its delivery service and inform its stakeholders that it was particularly good at this part of the business.

Crisis management

Crises normally follow a number of phases, during which different types of information must be communicated. When the crisis is over, a period of feedback and development for the organisation begins. 'What did we do?', 'How did it happen?', 'Why did we do that?' and 'What do we need to do in the future?' are typical questions that socially aware and mature organisations, which are concerned with quality and the needs of their stakeholders, should always ask themselves.

Pearson and Mitroff (1993) report that many organisations do not expose themselves to this learning process in the fear of 'opening up old wounds'. Those organisations that do take action should communicate their actions to reassure all stakeholders that the organisation has done all it can to prevent a recurrence, or at least to minimise the impact should the origin of the crisis be outside the control of management. A further question that needs to be addressed concerns the way the organisation was perceived during the different crisis phases. Was the image consistent? Did it change, and if so why? Management may believe that it did an excellent job in crisis containment, but what really matters is what stakeholders think – it is their attitudes and opinions that matter above all else.

The objective of crisis management is to limit the effect that a crisis might have on an organisation and its stakeholders, assuming the crisis cannot be prevented. The social system in which an organisation operates means that the image held of the organisation may well change as a result of the crisis event. The image does not necessarily become negative. On the contrary, it may be that the strategic credibility of the organisation could be considerably enhanced if the crisis were managed in an open and positive way. However, it is necessary that the image that stakeholders have of an organisation should be tracked on a regular basis. This means that the image and impact of the crisis can be monitored through each of the crisis phases. The management process of scanning the environment for signals of change, along with change in the attitudes and the perception held by stakeholders towards the organisation, make up a joint process that PR activities play a major role in executing.

Scholars' paper 10.3
Evaluation frameworks

Macnamara, J. (2018) A review of new evaluation models for strategic communication: progress and gaps, *International Journal of Strategic Communication,* **12(2), 180–95.**

This paper reports on a two-year study, which examined a number of evaluation frameworks and models used by practitioners. The author provides a valuable insight into the dimensions used to evaluate communications and identifies gaps for further research.

See also:

Macnamara, J. (2014) Breaking the PR measurement and evaluation deadlock: a new approach and model, AMEC International Summit on Measurement, 'Upping the Game', Amsterdam, 11–12.

Measuring the fulfilment of brand promises

Brands make promises and communicate them in one of two main ways. One is to make loud claims about the brand's attributes and the benefits these deliver to customers. This approach tends to rely on advertising and the strength of the brand to deliver the promise. The alternative is not to shout, but to whisper, and then surprise customers by exceeding their expectations when they experience the brand. This is an under-promise/over-deliver strategy, one which reduces risk and places a far greater emphasis on word-of-mouth communications and brand advocacy. This in turn can reduce an organisation's investment in advertising and lead to a redirection of communications effort and resources in order to improve the customer experience.

It follows therefore that there are measurable gaps between the image and perceptions customers have of brands and their actual experiences. Where expectations are exceeded, the promise gap is said to be positive. Where customers feel disappointed through experience of a brand, a negative promise gap can be identified. These gaps are reflected in the financial performance of brands.

The Promise Index, reported by Simms (2007), found that although 66 per cent of the brands surveyed had positive promise gaps, only 15 per cent had gaps that impacted significantly on business performance. Other research by Weber Shandwick found that the main factor for creating brand advocacy was the ability to 'surprise and delight customers'. This survey of 4,000 European consumers, reported by Simms, found that brand advocacy is five times more likely to prompt purchase than advertising.

A related metric, the Net Promoter Score (NPS), seeks to identify how likely an individual is to recommend a brand. Again, a key outcome is that brand growth is driven principally by surprising and delighting customers.

On the basis that brand advocacy is of major importance, two key marketing communications issues emerge. The first concerns how the marketing communications mix should be reformulated in order to encourage brand advocacy. It appears that advertising and mass media have an important role to play in engaging audiences to create awareness and interest. However, more emphasis needs to be given to the other tools and media in order to enhance each customer's experience of a brand beyond their expectations.

The second issue concerns identifying and communicating with passive rather than active advocates. Encouraging customers to talk about a brand means developing content that gives passive advocates a reason to talk about a brand. This means that the message component of the mix needs to be designed away from product attributes and towards stories and memorable events that can be passed on through all customer contact points. This in turn points to a greater use of PR, viral and the use of user-generated content, networks and communities, and the use of staff in creating brand experiences.

Online communications

Online research has grown as the internet population has soared and the measures used have developed through trial and experience. However, the notion that measurement of online communications is easy simply because all that is necessary is 'counting clicks' is misleading.

Ideas and approaches towards measuring the effectiveness of banner ads and websites, in whatever shape or form, have always been a cause of controversy. The notion that click-through or dwell time represents engagement or a sign of an embryonic relationship has now been dismissed by the majority.

However, a core activity still persists. This is the need to develop insights and understanding about the nature and characteristics of website visitors. From this it is necessary to develop visitor profiles so that media planners can optimise banner ad placement. Many organisations use free tools such as Google Analytics and Google Trends to analyse web traffic and search volume.

Changes to the transactional aspects associated with online display ads, the emergence of demand-side platforms that aggregate data from multiple sources, and the development of real-time bidding have all advanced the processes and means by which this core activity is undertaken and through which online advertising is measured and interpreted.

Attribution modelling is a current method used to evaluate digital ad placements. Also known as path to conversion analysis, this uses ad server or tag management system (TMS) data to evaluate interactions that occur online to measure the number and function of each channel (IPA, 2014). This works to attribute the channel's role within the consumer's online journey. The IPA identifies four key types of attribution models used and the advantages and disadvantages of each (see Table 10.8). The Last Click method is the easiest measure but does not take previous channels visited into account. Other methods such as Time Decay and Efficiency Score are seen to improve upon Last Click, but are seen as less robust than the Statistical method.

Table 10.8 Types of attribution models

Type of attribution	Advantages	Disadvantages
Last Click	Easy to calculate and monitor	Ignores previous channels and events
Time Decay	Fairer than last click	Overnight breaks distort. Still seen as arbitrary
Efficiency Score	More objective than last click and time decay	Cannot calculate granular metrics
Statistical	Seen as best approach. Can include unconverted users	Resource intensive

Source: IPA (2014).

Viewpoint 10.3
Measuring Digital Advertising: Moving Past the Click
By Tim Elkington, Chief Digital Officer, IAB UK

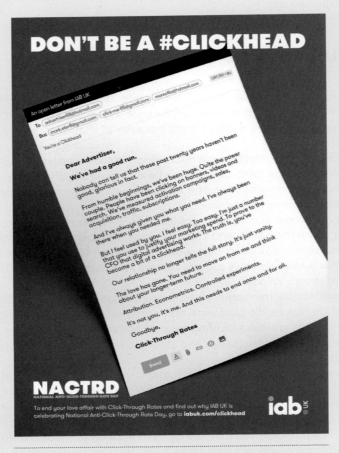

Image 10.5 The IAB sent an open letter to hundreds of marketers to launch the first annual 'National Anti-Click-Through Rate Day'
Source: IAB UK.

In 2017, £11.55bn was spent on digital marketing within the UK alone. This is a mature market, and a success story for UK industry. As such, IAB UK, the trade association for internet advertising, has moved beyond a purely growth focus, with their goal now to support a sustainable future for digital advertising.

This includes tackling issues that affect the long-term health of this industry. Issues like the way digital advertising is measured. Issues such as the over-reliance on click-through rates (CTR).

CTR is a relic of the early days of digital, but making it the central reporting focus can be misleading. To address this challenge, the IAB launched the first, annual 'National Anti-Click-Through Rate Day' on 12th February 2019.

As part of the campaign the organisation sent a "Dear John"-style open letter to hundreds of marketers, accusing them of becoming "clickheads", a tongue-in-cheek castigation of the industry's reliance on vanity metrics to measure the effectiveness of online media.

IAB UK also launched the IAB Measurement Toolkit, with research consultancy MTM, to help advertisers as they transition to more robust measurement approaches. This guide consolidates current best practices and provides guidance on measuring digital advertising in the context of other media. It sets out the main models and techniques that can be used to measure digital advertising and concludes with a set of practical templates and checklists for creating your own measurement strategy.

Some of the alternative techniques for measuring digital advertising covered within the guide include:

1. Brand Studies

   A collection of tools, often survey-led, to measure brand metrics over the life of the campaign, including awareness, familiarity, favourability, consideration and intent, both pre and post campaign, to measure uplift. Studies are most effective when used longitudinally, to provide quantitative evidence for the impact of longer-term brand activities.

2. Econometrics and Marketing Mix Modelling

   Statistical tools to quantify the cause and effect in economic data, these models predict how advertising channels, as well as external factors – like changes in weather – translate into incremental sales, enabling a deeper understanding of Return on Ad Spend (ROAS).

3. Attribution Modelling

   Statistical models to evaluate how different touchpoints contribute to a sale or action. Was it seeing the TV ad that drove a customer to buy your product, or was it being retargeted with that message on mobile? Channels are assigned credit based on their level of involvement, creating immediate actionable insights.

4. Controlled Experiment

   Take a clear, testable hypothesis, divide your subjects into a test group, who see the ad, and a control, who don't, then observe the impact over a defined time period. Controlled experiments work best when treated as part of an ongoing process of improvement, rather than as a one-off tool.

All four methodologies have their own limitations, however it's about deploying whichever methodology – or methodologies, plural - is right for your campaign objectives.

Used together, one technique can add an extra dimension to findings, with the right mix dependent on factors like the length and complexity of the product sales cycle, the balance of online/offline media spend, and the use of non-media based promotional tools.

This is why IAB UK is so keen to reduce the emphasis on CTR. It doesn't reflect the realities of modern digital marketing – but more importantly, it's just one signal, which can never hope to show the full, complex picture of awareness, consideration and purchase all on its own.

For further insight into the most appropriate and effective measurement strategies for your campaign, download the IAB Measurement Toolkit at: www.iabuk.com/measurement

Insight

This highlights the industry's over-reliance on click-through rates (CTR) and the need to consider alternative techniques to measure digital advertising. Using different methodologies to evaluate digital advertising can provide a more complete picture of the effectiveness of a campaign.

Question: Why do you think the industry has become over-reliant on click-through rates?

Task: Consider the alternative techniques provided by the IAB for measuring digital advertising. For each, list the advantages and disadvantages.

Mobile

Measuring mobile is challenging because much of the mobile analytics is held with the mobile platforms or applications themselves. This makes it difficult for brands to evaluate the success of their campaigns. In a survey of marketers across Europe, the Middle East and Africa, marketers reported measurement and metrics as the biggest barrier to mobile growth (WARC/MMA, 2017).

The survey by WARC/MMA (2017) highlights that engagement metrics such as video completion rates, social sharing and click-through rate (CTR) are used by the highest percentage of marketers to evaluate the effectiveness of mobile marketing. The findings highlight that engagement metrics and behavioural metrics are used more than business measures such as return on investment (ROI) (see Figure 10.2).

The context of how the user is interacting with the mobile device is seen to be an important analytic. Information about the location, time, proximity and mobile device allows the brand to understand where the consumers are seeing the content, at what time they are viewing it, how close they are to a kiosk or store and what device they are using. Although this information provides valuable data for brands there are also privacy issues to be considered and brands need to be sensitive of this (MMA, 2012).

There are a number of metrics used to measure mobile campaigns and some of the key definitions and terms are described in Table 10.9.

The IAB (2015) provides a framework for measuring mobile engagement, which identifies three categories of measurement: cognitive, behavioural and emotional. The IAB framework suggests each category can be measured using specific metrics. Cognitive engagement, for example, can use metrics such as campaign awareness, brand message recall, attribute recall and other measures, which identify how consumers are thinking differently about the brand or message. While a number of behavioural engagement metrics are identified, including view-throughs and location, the IAB suggests metrics such as movement (shakes or tilts) and calls are important for mobile. Metrics for emotional engagement include change in baseline brand perception, favourability and loyalty. Additionally, physiological response can be used to measure emotional engagement (IAB, 2015).

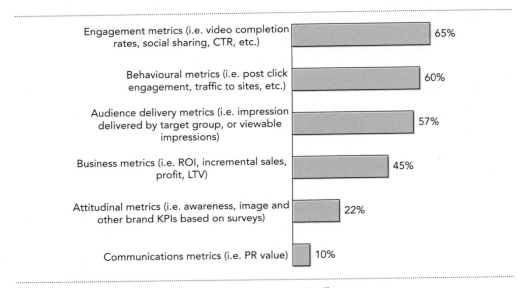

Figure 10.2 Metrics used by marketers to measure mobile effectiveness
Source: WARC/MMA, 2017. Used with the kind permission of WARC/MMA.

Table 10.9 Some key mobile advertising measurement definitions

Mobile measurement terms	Description
Ad Impressions	The response measurement for the number of ads delivered to an ad request.
Deferred Ad Impressions	These are ad impressions which take place while a user is off-line.
Session	This term refers to the period of time that a user interacts with an application.
Software Development Kit (SDK) Based Measurement	This measures the performance of common application functions, such as advertising delivery.
Tracked Ads	This term refers to the ads that have been measured.
User, Unique User	The individual person who is using the application and is seeing the ad messages.

Source: Mobile Application Advertising Measurement Guidelines (2017).

Viewpoint 10.4
Ad fraud: the top 5

Image 10.6 Ad fraud steals from the advertiser's budget
Source: Yayayoyo/Shutterstock.

Ad fraud is recognised to be an industry-wide problem and costs brands £billions every year. Some estimate that ad fraud costs brands 4 per cent of their budget, although this figure can be a lot higher. As well as the loss to ad budget, ad fraud makes it difficult for advertisers to accurately measure the impact of a mobile campaign and evaluate the return on investment.

Ad fraud steals budgets from the advertiser and many of the techniques used to commit the fraud are hard to detect as they generate installs which look genuine. In many cases the fraud is committed using real devices, which makes the fraud hard to identify.

The problem is so large that many companies now offer a range of proprietary tools to help advertisers spot the fraud. Adjust, a leading mobile measurement company, who provide analytics and measurement solutions for mobile apps globally, offer clients 'The Adjust Fraud Prevention Suite' to help them identify the five main types of ad fraud:

1. SDK spoofing (also known as 'replay attacks') is 'a type of fraud that consumes an advertiser's budget by generating legitimate-looking installs without any real installs occurring' (Muller, 2018).

2. Click injections, which 'trigger fraudulent clicks in the last second of an app's installation' (Muller, 2018).

3. Click spam, which occurs when the conversions are claimed by a source that had nothing to do with the install (Anon, 2018a: 13).

4. Fake installs, which occur when an attribution partner is tricked into tracking an install that hasn't taken place on a real device (Anon, 2018a).

5. Fake in-app purchases, which occur when 'an in-app purchase (or IAP) was made but no revenue was exchanged' (Anon, 2018a: 18).

Using proprietary tools to detect ad fraud allows activity to be blocked and allows organisations to evaluate campaigns and mobile use more effectively.

Sources: Anon (2018a); Anon (2018b).

Insight

Ad fraud impacts the whole ad industry. Advertisers are paying for advertising that they have not had and this is fraud. The measurement data advertisers receive is also flawed. Proprietary tools such as, 'The Adjust Fraud Prevention Suite' are helping to combat the problem.

Question: Why is ad fraud problematic for the evaluation of mobile campaigns?

Task: Visit adjust.com and identify the tools they have created to help combat each of the FIVE types of mobile ad fraud. For each, explain how the tools work.

Scholars' paper 10.4
Mobile and social metrics

Fulgoni, G.M. and Lipsman, A. (2017) Are you using the right mobile advertising metrics? How relevant mobile measures change the cross-platform advertising equation, *Journal of Advertising Research*, 57(3), 245–9.

This paper reports on the reliability of mobile metrics and highlights the issues related to using click-through rates, viewability, daily versus monthly reach and target reach efficiency. The authors suggest that marketers have started to measure the effectiveness of cross-platform campaigns to understand how digital and mobile contribute to campaign performance, rather than how each perform on their own.

See also:

Turnbull, S. and Jenkins, S. (2016) Why Facebook Reactions are good news for evaluating social media campaigns, *Journal of Direct, Data and Digital Marketing Practice*, 17(3), 156–8.

Social media

Measuring the effectiveness of social media campaigns has proved challenging for many organisations and there has been criticism of the misplaced reliance on counting the numbers of clicks, fans and followers as surrogate measures of social media activity (Owyang, 2011). What is more relevant is measuring what these fans and followers do, the outcomes of the social media activities.

Moorman (2015) identifies the main metrics used by marketers when evaluating social media. Although the survey shows more than 20 different metrics are employed, marketers report that hits/visits/page views, site traffic, click-through rates and numbers of friends, followers and likes are used most frequently (see Table 10.10).

Table 10.10 Social media metrics used

Metrics	Percentage using metrics
Hits/visits/page views	60.3%
Site traffic	51.4%
Click-through rates	47.9%
Number of friends, followers and likes	41.1%
Conversion rates (from visitor to buyer)	28.8%
Search volume (number of people searching for your brand)	28.4%
Repeat visits	25.3%
Social influence of friends, followers and likes	23.7%
Buzz indicators (web mentions)	21.4%
Virality (extent to which content/likes are shared)	19.1%
Brand sentiment ratings	16.7%
Share of voice (compared to other competitors' mentions)	16.0%
Net promoter score	16.0%
Number of inbound links	15.6%
Revenue per customer	15.6%
App download	14.8%
Sales levels	14.0%
Customer acquisition costs	12.5%
Online product/service ratings	10.9%
Metrics using analysis of online text	9.7%
Profits per customer	6.6%
Customer retention costs	6.2%
Abandoned shopping carts	5.8%

Source: Moorman (2015). With permission from Moorman (2015).

While 'hits' still appears to be one of the metrics most used, it is thought that a measure of the level of social influence exacted is more appropriate. This is because online influence can help attract and develop brand ambassadors, and also convey an intention to interact with consumers (McCormick, 2011).

In line with other forms of marketing communications, it is important to use metrics that allow objectives to be evaluated. Buckley (2013) argues that social media need to be measured against the business objectives set and need to demonstrate a return on investment (ROI). The author suggests using a variety of tools to evaluate social media as each has different functions (see Table 10.11).

Table 10.11 Measurement tools for social media

Evaluation	Function	Examples
Listening and monitoring	Overview of all public-related conversation online	Radian6, Crimson Hexagon, Sysomos, Netbase, Synthesio
Third-party-owned channel performance and competitor tracking	Tracking of owned and competitor channel performance	Simply Measured, Social Bakers
Social CMS analytics	Data available through the social content management solution	Buddy Media, Hootsuite
Platform analytics	Data available through the platform	Facebook Insights, YouTube Analytics

Source: Buckley (2013).

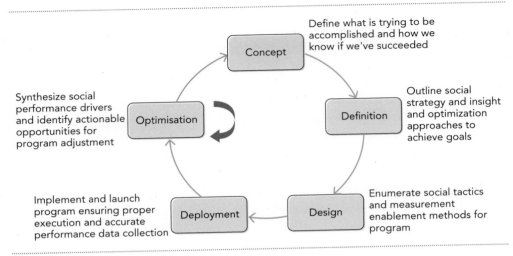

Figure 10.3 The core phases of the social media measurement process
Source: Murdough (2009). Used with the kind permission of the Academy of Marketing.

From this we should conclude that measurement should focus on the associated business outcomes arising from the deliberate use of social media. This might be related to the level of influence, leads or conversions, generating conversations and word of mouth, improving customer service and support, or stimulating ideas for brand development.

In order to be able to measure these business outcomes, it is necessary to develop a digital marketing strategy. The strategy and plan should contain the social media goals that are to be achieved (the objectives) and the ways in which performance is to be measured (the metrics), and how the data is to be collected and analysed (the tools or analytics). The goals can vary from selling more products and getting more traffic through the website, to increasing a fan base, reaching a specific audience, or getting established as an opinion leader.

Another key part of the social media strategy is the channel mix that is to be utilised to reach and engage audiences. Where the engagement takes place is the location for the information to be collected. So, if Facebook, Twitter and a blog are the core channels, then the tools and technologies associated with these channels are going to be the most appropriate: for example, Google Analytics and Hootsuite Analytics (Reid, 2012). At the end of the process the goal is to determine the return on investment. However, as several commentators observe, it can be difficult to derive an accurate ROI in social media.

Murdough (2009) suggests that certain core phases associated with the social media measurement process can be isolated. These are set out in Figure 10.3. Each of the phases requires a consideration of the goals and both the quantitative and qualitative measures that reveal insight and performance.

Key points

- The evaluation of a marketing communications plan is a key part of the planning process. The evaluation provides a potentially rich source of material for future campaigns.
- Evaluation consists of two distinct elements. The first element is concerned with the development and testing of individual messages. For example, a particular advertising campaign. The second element concerns the overall impact and effect that a campaign has on a target audience.

- Pre-testing is the practice of showing unfinished commercials to selected groups of the target audience with a view to refining the commercial to improve effectiveness. The most common methods used to pre-test advertisements are concept testing, focus groups, consumer juries, dummy vehicles, projective assessments, readability, theatre and physiological tests.

- Physiological tests are designed to measure the involuntary responses to stimuli and so avoid the bias inherent in other tests. As there are substantial costs involved with the use of such techniques they are not used a great deal in practice.

- Post-testing is the practice of evaluating ads that have been released. The most common methods are enquiry, recall, recognition and sales-based tests. The main advantage with post-testing is that advertisements are evaluated in their proper environment.

- Tracking studies involve interviewing a large number of people on a regular basis, weekly or monthly, with the purpose of collecting data about buyers' perceptions of marketing communications messages. Perceptions, attitudes and meanings attributed to campaigns can be tracked and adjustments made to campaigns as necessary.

- Other methods of evaluation include financial analysis, likeability and media mix modelling (MMM). Using media mix modelling requires sophisticated statistical analysis.

- Public relations (PR) has a number of established forms of measurement and evaluation based on quantitative and qualitative methods. While measurements such as AVEs have been widely used in the past, greater emphasis is being placed on measuring outcomes rather than just outputs.

- There are measurable gaps between the image and perceptions customers have of brands and their actual experiences. Where expectations are exceeded, the promise gap is said to be positive. Where customers feel disappointed through experience of a brand, a negative promise gap can be identified. These gaps are reflected in the financial performance of brands. The Promise Index and the Net Promoter Score (NPS) are two approaches to measuring the success of delivering brand promises.

- Online communications can be measured in a number of ways, although attribution models are commonly used. Four main types of attribution models exist: Last Click, Time Decay, Efficiency Score and Statistical.

- Engagement metrics such as video completion rates, social sharing and click-through rate (CTR) are used by the highest percentage of marketers to evaluate the effectiveness of mobile marketing.

- Marketers use a range of analytical tools to evaluate social media. The measures used most frequently are hits/visits/page views, site traffic, click-through rates and number of friends, followers and likes.

Case study

Care Counts Laundry Program

Image 10.7 Washing machines and dryers were installed in schools across America
Source: Grzegorz Czapski/Shutterstock.

The Care Counts Laundry Program is a philanthropic initiative from Whirlpool. A nationwide study of teachers in America revealed that one in five school-children didn't have access to washing machines. This meant that many children were missing school because they didn't have clean clothes to wear. The research showed that unclean clothes affected how students performed at school and their attitude to school. To address this issue, Whirlpool developed the Care Counts Laundry Program.

As the world's leading major home appliance company, Whirlpool has built a reputation around everyday care (i.e. cooking, cleaning and washing) and the Care Counts Laundry Program aligned with the organisation's corporate brand values.

The objectives of the programme were:

1. Increase awareness of the problem of children wearing dirty clothes to school. Research high-lighted that many children are bullied for not having clean clothes and this caused many of them to stay at home.

2. Educate media about the link between clean clothes and school attendance.

3. Encourage a national conversation in traditional media and on social around the issues to engage policy makers.

4. Inform audiences about the impact of the Care Counts Laundry Program.

The Care Counts Laundry Program installed washing machines and dryers in schools across America to provide students who didn't have access to washing machines with the opportunity to wash and dry their clothes when at school.

During the first year of the programme, Whirlpool collected data and video film to provide content

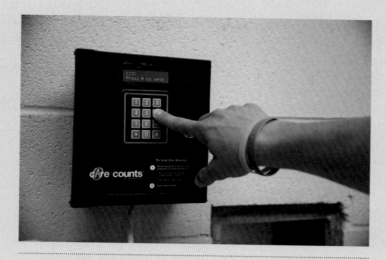

Image 10.8 Data was gathered using custom devices from the washing machines directly to Whirlpool's cloud database
Source: AP Images for Whirlpool/AP Images.

for a public relations campaign. Data was gathered using custom devices from the washing machines directly to Whirlpool's cloud database. This allowed the programme to record how many times individual students used the washing machines and dryers, and their school attendance. By tracking individual usage, the programme was able to evaluate the impact the machines were having on each student's attendance.

A documentary film was made, which featured teachers and students. Filming was undertaken before the start of the programme and during the year to show the impact the Care Counts Laundry Program was having on the school and social lives of the students.

At the end of the year and during the back-to-school season, when school stories are more in demand by the media, Whirlpool released the documentary film about the Care Counts Laundry Program to local and national news outlets. The film explained the issues related to children not having clean clothes and explained how the programme had helped many children attend school.

Media were provided with multimedia material, including the statistics from the programme and access to schoolteachers, officials and Whirlpool spokespeople who were made available for interviews.

The Care Counts Laundry Program built measurement into the campaign from the beginning. This meant that measureable results would be available at the end of the programme.

Media results

PR impressions: 378MM earned impressions.

PR stories: 600 earned stories, including ABC World News Tonight, Today.com, Parade, Business Insider, Huffington Post, U.S. News & World Report, NPR, The Atlantic's City Lab, BBC, Daily Kos and Upworthy. Four national broadcast stories resulted in 60 more in 18 states.

Conversations: Care Counts Laundry Program was noticed by The White House and the L.A. Mayor's Office. One of the teachers who had been featured on the programme was awarded ABC News' Person of the Week, providing additional coverage for the programme on national TV.

PR Coverage tone: the tone of coverage was also monitored and results showed that 100 per cent of the PR coverage had a positive or neutral tone. Additionally, 100 per cent of the PR coverage gave Whirlpool the credit for the Care Counts Laundry Program and 89 per cent included the results of the programme.

Brand results

The brand's own evaluation, Whirlpool 2016 Cross Media Results Report, carried out by Millward Brown, showed that media assets produced to support the programme increased purchase intent. Research also identified that 71 per cent of consumers who were aware of the programme linked it to Whirlpool.

Measuring the impact on participating students

- High-risk students who participated attended nearly two more days of school per month during the programme.

- An increase in participating student attendance rates from 82 per cent percent to 91 per cent.
- Teachers reported that 95 per cent of participants in the programme showed increased motivation in class and were more likely to participate in extracurricular activities and interact with peers.

Sources: Anon (2018c); Care Counts (2017); Gianatasio (2016).

The Care Counts Laundry Program has won a number of global awards, including Gold, Grand Prix and two Bronze Lions.

The success of the programme has led to requests from over 1,000 other schools in the US requesting Whirlpool to run the initiative in their district.

Review questions

Care Counts Laundry Program case questions

1. Why do you think the Care Counts Laundry Program built measurement into the campaign from the beginning? Explain your answer.

2. What specific measures were used to evaluate the success of the campaign?

3. Why was it important for the programme to collect data from the washing machines and dryers?

4. What measures were used to evaluate the PR results? Why do you think that AVEs were not measured?

5. What measures could be used to evaluate the impact on Whirlpool's corporate image?

General questions

1. Explain the difference between pre-testing and post-testing.

2. Explain why AVEs are seen to be a less effective method of measuring public relations outcomes. What other methods could be used to evaluate public relations outcomes?

3. What are the main challenges with measuring mobile ad effectiveness? Discuss what the industry could do to improve measurement in the future.

4. What are the challenges with measuring social media communications? Discuss why so many types of metrics are used to evaluate social media.

5. Many organisations fail to undertake suitable research to measure the success of their campaigns. Why is this and what can be done to change this situation?

References for Chapter 10

Adjust (2018) The Adjust Mobile Measurement Glossary, retrieved 1 May 2018 from https://www.adjust.com/glossary/

AMEC (2010) Barcelona summit, *AMEC*, retrieved 10 April 2015 from http://amecorg.com/2010/06/knowledge-share-barcelona-summit-2010/

AMEC (2015) Changes from the original Barcelona Principles 2010 to the Barcelona Principles 2015, AMEC, retrieved 10 January 2018 from https://amecorg.com/how-the-barcelona-principles-have-been-updated/

Anon (2018a) The bad, the ugly, and the truth of mobile ad fraud. *Adjust*, 18 April, retrieved 30 May 2018 from http://learn.adjust.com/rs/108-GAZ-487/images/An%20Expert%E2%80%99s%20Guide%20to%20Mobile%20Ad%20Fraud.pdf

Anon (2018b) Case Study: MyTona. *Adjust*, retrieved 30 May 2018 from https://www.adjust. com/resources/case-studies/mytona/

Anon (2018c) Whirlpool's Care Counts ™ Laundry Program helps improve student attendance, Whirlpool.com, retrieved 30 May 2018 from https://www.prnewswire.com/ news-releases/whirlpools-care-counts-laundry-program-helps-improve-student-attendance-300509897.html

Buckley, E. (2013) The business return from social media, *Admap*, retrieved 10 April 2015 from https://www.warc.com/content/paywall/article/admap/the_business_return_from_ social_media/99742

Care Counts (2017) *Cannes Lions Archive*, retrieved 30 May 2018 from http://www.can neslionsarchive.com/Home/PublicHome

Dichter, E. (1966) How word-of-mouth advertising works, *Harvard Business Review*, 44 (November/December), 147–66.

Flesch, R. (1974) *The Art of Readable Writing*, New York: Harper & Row.

Fulgoni, G.M. and Lipsman, A. (2017) Are you using the right mobile advertising metrics? How relevant mobile measures change the cross-platform advertising equation, *Journal of Advertising Research*, 57(3), 245–9.

Gianatasio, D. (2016). Ad of the day: Whirlpool put washers and dryers in schools, with remarkable results, *AdWeek*, 4 August, retrieved 30 May 2018 from https://www.adweek. com/brand-marketing/ad-day-whirlpool-put-washers-and-dryers-schools-remarkable-results-172785/

Gordon, W. (1992) Ad pre-testing's hidden maps, *Admap*, June, 23–7.

Gwynn, S (2017) Pretesting threatens to kill creativity in advertising. *Campaign*, 6 July, retrieved 10 November 2017 from https://www.campaignlive.co.uk/article/pretesting-threatens-kill-creativity-advertising/1438506

Harris, J.M., Ciorciari, J. and Gountas, J. (2018) Consumer neuroscience for marketing researchers, *Journal of Consumer Behaviour*, 17(3), 239–52.

IAB (2015) Mobile engagement framework and definitions, IAB Website, retrieved 7 February 2016 from http://www.iab.com/wp-content/uploads/2015/08/Engagement-Digital-Simplified-Final.pdf

IPA (2014) *How to Evaluate the Effectiveness of Communications Plans*, IPA.

Krugman, H.E. (1988) Point of view: limits of attention to advertising, *Journal of Advertising Research*, 38, 47–50.

Lee, D.H. and Park, C.W. (2007) Conceptualization and measurement of multidimensionality of integrated marketing communications, *Journal of Advertising Research*, 47(3), 222–36.

Lodish, L.M. and Lubetkin, B. (1992) General truths? *Admap*, February, 9–15.

Macnamara, J. (2005) Media content analysis: its uses, benefits and best practice methodology, *Asia Pacific Public Relations Journal*, 6(1), 1–34.

Macnamara, J.R. (2008) Research in public relations: a review of the use of evaluation and formative research, retrieved 10 April 2015 from http://195.130.87.21:8080/dspace/bitstream/123456789/233/1/Macnamara-research%20in%20public%20relations.pdf

Macnamara, J. (2014) Breaking the PR measurement and evaluation deadlock: a new approach and model, AMEC International Summit on Measurement 'Upping the Game', Amsterdam, 11–12.

Macnamara, J. (2018) A review of new evaluation models for strategic communication: progress and gaps, *International Journal of Strategic Communication*, 12(2), 180–95.

Manning, A. and Rockland, D.B. (2011) Understanding the Barcelona Principles, *The Public Relations Strategist*, 21 March, retrieved 10 April 2015 from www.prsa.org/Intelligence/ TheStrategist/Articles/view/9072/1028/Understanding_the_Barcelona_Principles\#. VW8qWM9VhBc

McCormick, A. (2011) Online influence, *Revolution*, September, 32–3.

MMA (2012) *The MMA Primer on Mobile Analytics*, Mobile Marketing Association, retrieved 10 June 2015 from http://www.mmaglobal.com/documents/mma-primer-mobile-analytics

Mobile Application Advertising Measurement Guidelines (2017).Accessed 7th January 2019 from http://mediaratingcouncil.org/Mobile%20In-App%20Measurement%20Guide-lines%20(MMTF%20Final%20v1.1).pdf

Moorman, C. (2015) CMO survey report: highlights and insights, retrieved 5 May 2018 from https://cmosurvey.org/wp-content/uploads/sites/15/2017/04/The_CMO_Survey-Highlights_and_Insights-Aug-2015.pdf

Muller, P. (2018) Mobile fraud trends to watch in 2018: SDK spoofing and click injections, *Mobile Marketer*, 2 April, retrieved 30 August 2018 from https://www.mobilemarketer.com/news/mobile-fraud-trends-to-watch-in-2018-sdk-spoofing-and-click-injections/520303/

Murdough, C. (2009) Social media measurement: it's not impossible, *Journal of Interactive Advertising*, 10(1), 94–9.

Murphy, C. (2005) Pre-testing: gut or numbers? *Brand Republic*, 15 June, retrieved 10 May 2015 from www.brandrepublic.com/article/480267/pre-testing-gut-numbers

Owyang, J. (2011) Number of fans and followers is NOT a business metric – what you do with them is, web-strategist.com, retrieved 9 May 2012 from http://www.web-strategist.com/blog/2011/11/17/number-of-fans-and-followers-is-not-a-business-metric-what-you-do-with-them-is/

Patti, C.H., Hartley, S.W., van Dessel, M.M. and Baack, D.W. (2017) Improving integrated marketing communications practices: a comparison of objectives and results, *Journal of Marketing Communications*, 23(4), 351–70.

Pearson, C.M. and Mitroff, I. (1993) From crisis prone to crisis prepared: a framework for crisis management, *Academy of Management Executive*, 7(1), 48–59.

Plassmann, H., Ambler, T., Braeutigam, S. and Kenning, P. (2007) What can advertisers learn from neuroscience? *International Journal of Advertising*, 26(2), 151–75.

Porcu, L., Del Barrio-García, S. and Kitchen, P.J. (2017) Measuring integrated marketing communication by taking a broad organisational approach: the firm-wide IMC scale, *European Journal of Marketing*, 51(3), 692–718.

Reid, A. (2012) Measuring social media: a step-by-step guide for newbies, business2community.com, retrieved 9 May 2012 from www.business2community.com/social-media/measuring-social-media-a-step-by-step-guide-for-newbies-0163705

Robson, S. (2002) Group discussions, in *The International Handbook of Market Research Techniques* (ed. R. Birn), London: Kogan Page.

Simms, J. (2007) Bridging the gap, *Marketing*, 12 December, 26–8.

Smit, E.G., van Meurs, L. and Neijens, P.C. (2006) Effects of advertising likeability: a 10-year perspective, *Journal of Advertising Research*, 46(1), 73–83.

Turnbull, S. (2011) *The creative development process within U.K. advertising agencies: an exploratory study*, Unpublished PhD Thesis, University of Portsmouth.

Turnbull, S. and Jenkins, S. (2016), Why Facebook Reactions are good news for evaluating social media campaigns, *Journal of Direct, Data and Digital Marketing Practice*, 17(3), 156–8.

Turnbull, S. and Wheeler, C. (2017) The advertising creative process: a study of UK agencies, *Journal of Marketing Communications*, 23(2), 176-94.

WARC/MMA (2017) The state of the industry: mobile marketing in EMEA 2017, retrieved 10 February 2018 from https://www.warc.com/content/article/the_state_of_the_industry_mobile_marketing_in_emea_2017/111576

Zielske, H.A. (1982) Does day-after recall penalise 'feeling' ads? *Journal of Advertising Research*, 22(1), 19–22.

Branding and marketing communications

Marketing communications plays an integral part in the development of positive brand associations that have meaning, relevance and purpose for customers. The images, associations and experiences that customers have with brands, and the brand identities that managers seek to create, need to be closely related if long-run brand purchasing behaviour is to be achieved.

Aims and learning objectives

The aims of this chapter are to explore how marketing communications assists the development and maintenance of brands that engage their respective target audiences.

The learning objectives are to enable readers to:

1. explore the meaning of the brand concept through definitions;
2. understand the variety of brand characteristics;
3. evaluate the significance of associations and personalities in branding;
4. discuss the way in which marketing communications can be used to build and support brands;
5. consider the branding issues within business-to-business, employee and interactive contexts;
6. appraise the nature and characteristics of brand equity.

Introduction

Brands are promises that frame the way they are positioned in the minds of stakeholders, and which shape their expectations. Ideally these expectations match the promises, which are realised or experienced through brand usage and performance. Brand performance can be experienced directly, perhaps through consumption, sampling or first-hand interpretation, or indirectly, through observations and comments made by other people and the media. Successful brands deliver consistently on their promises, by meeting or exceeding expectations, and in doing so reinforce the positioning and the credibility of the promise.

Successful brands, therefore, might be considered to encapsulate three core brand elements: promises, positioning and performance. These are depicted in Figure 11.1, as the three brand Ps (3BPs).

Central to the interaction of these 3BPs are communications. Communications are used to make the promise known (brand awareness), to position a brand correctly (brand attitude) and to encourage and realise brand performance (brand response). Unsurprisingly, advertising has a critical role to play in building and sustaining this interaction of branding elements (Dwivedi and McDonald, 2018).

Consistent brand performance, fulfilled brand promises and strong levels of customer satisfaction through time can help consumers to trust a brand. Trust, over time, leads to commitment (Morgan and Hunt, 1994) and is reflected in customers prioritising a brand within their buying repertoire for a product category. Accepting that consumers are active problem-solvers means that brands can be regarded as a way in which the amount of decision-making time and associated perceived risk can be reduced for buyers. This is because brand names provide information about content, taste, durability, quality, price and performance, without requiring a buyer to undertake time-consuming comparison tests with similar offerings or other risk-reduction approaches to purchase decisions.

In much of the literature, brands assume a myopic perspective: namely, one that is centred just on customers. In reality, brands encompass a range of stakeholders (Astrachan et al., 2018) and branding should be considered not only from managerial but also from service, relational and social perspectives (Brodie and de Chernatony, 2009).

Successful brands create strong, positive and lasting impressions, all of which are perceived by audiences to be of value to them personally. Individuals perceive brands without having to purchase or have direct experience of them. The elements that make up this

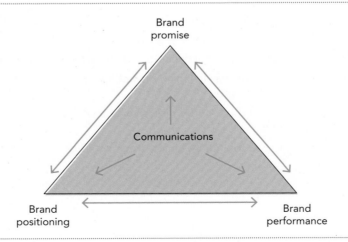

Figure 11.1 The triangulation of the 3BPs

impression are numerous, and research by de Chernatony and Dall'Olmo Riley (1998a) suggests that there is little close agreement on the definition of a brand. They identified 12 types of definition; among them is the visual approach adopted by Assael (1990) that a brand is the name, symbol, packaging and service reputation. The differentiation approach is typified by Kotler (2000), who argues that a brand is a name, term, sign, symbol or design, or a combination of these intended to identify the goods or services of one seller or group of sellers, and to differentiate them from those of competitors. Some of the more commonly quoted definitions are presented in Table 11.1.

In recent times there have been few significant developments in how a brand is defined Riley (2016). There has been increasing recognition of brand co-creation, explored later, and this has evolved into ideas about brand types and typologies. For example, Muzellec et al. (2012) consider how the brand as a concept may now be detached from being merely a physical embodiment. They explore the application of branding to the fictional and computer-synthesised worlds, using examples of virtual brands from books, films, video games and other multi-user virtual environments.

In 2009 de Chernatony suggested that, from a managerial perspective, there is a 'plethora of interpretations', which can lead to brand management inefficiencies. To support his argument, he identifies a spectrum of brand interpretations, ranging from differentiation through to added value. He suggests a brand might be defined as, 'a cluster of values that enables a promise to be made about a unique and welcomed experience'.

What these researchers have identified is that brands are a product of the work of managers who attempt to augment their products with values and associations that are recognised by, and are meaningful to, their customers. In other words, brands are a composite of two main logics: the first is an identity that managers wish to portray, while the second is images, construed by audiences, of the identities they perceive. The development of Web 2.0 and user-generated content in the form of blogs, wikis and social networks has added a new dimension to the managerial-driven perspective of brands. Consumers are assuming a greater role in defining what a brand means to them, and now they are prone to sharing this with their friends, family and contacts rather than with the organisation itself. What this means is that brand managers have reduced levels of influence over the way their brands are perceived and this in turn impacts on the influence they have in managing brand reputation.

Table 11.1 Brand definitions

Author	Brand definition
Alexander (American Marketing Association, 1960)	'A name, term, sign, symbol, or design, or a combination of them, intended to identify the goods or services of one seller or group of sellers and to differentiate them from those of competitors.'
Assael (1990)	'Name, symbol, packaging and service reputation.'
Schmitt (1999)	'A rich source of sensory, affective, and cognitive associations that result in memorable and rewarding brand experiences.'
Riezebos (2003)	'Every sign that is capable of distinguishing the goods or services of a company and that can have a certain meaning for consumers both in material and in immaterial terms.'
Keller (2008)	'Something that has actually created a certain amount of awareness, reputation, prominence . . . in the marketplace.'
American Marketing Association (2014)	'A customer experience represented by a collection of images and ideas; often, it refers to a symbol such as a name, logo, slogan, and design scheme.'
Aaker (2014)	This last definition refers to 'brand and branding': 'an organisation's promise to a customer to deliver what a brand stands for . . . in terms of functional benefits but also emotional, self-expressive and social benefits.'

It is important, therefore, to recognise that both managers and customers are involved in the branding process. In the past, the emphasis and control of brands rested squarely with brand owners. Today, this influence has shifted to consumers as they redefine what brands mean to them and how they differentiate among similar offerings and associate certain attributes or feelings and emotions with particular brands. Indeed, there is now a discussion about whether brands should be considered outside the narrow marketing perspective, since they are a construct of a wider realm of influences. For those interested in these issues see Brodie and de Chernatony (2009), and for developments in managerial aspects, see de Chernatony (2009) and de Lencastre and Côrte-Real (2010).

Viewpoint 11.1

Engaging brand tribes

Image 11.1 Lego invited kids to build a Kronkiwongi and share their creations online
Source: The Lego Group.

Brand tribes are groups of consumers who share loyalty and passion for a brand. The emotional connection they have with the brand is shared among the group and brands can build on these shared brand associations to strengthen brand value.

Lego has built a strong brand following and uses social media to engage fans. To drive social engagement, the brand has focused around two key brand associations, 'Build Together', which positions Lego as something that is fun to do with others and, 'Pride of Creation', which encourages children and parents to celebrate with pride their Lego creations.

The brand has communicated these associations in their social campaigns. The $100 campaign, named after the total cost of the campaign, was a competition asking Lego fans to create 'George' and post photos of him travelling on Facebook. Lego created a simple George character to launch the campaign and after only 20 minutes George was turning up all over the world and getting involved in all sorts of activities, including kissing a kangaroo in Australia. Although the campaign was launched in 2011, George continues to appear in unusual places around the globe. In May 2018, George appeared in Limerick eating a baked goats' cheese crostini.

The Kronkiwongi campaign is another example of how Lego have used social to engage Lego fans around the world. Lego asked kids to build an imaginary 'thing' called a Kronkiwongi and to explain how it could help other people. The campaign encouraged kids to use their imagination and parents were asked to share the creations online.

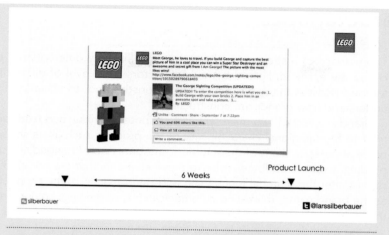

Image 11.2 Lego fans were invited to post images of George on Facebook
Source: The Lego Group.

Sources: Romero (2017); Saunders (2017).

Insight

This highlights how marketing communications can help to build brand associations. The co-creative nature of both campaigns remains true to the creativity of the brand itself and encourages parents to celebrate their child's creations by sharing. The continuation of George's travels so long after the campaign launch is testament to the level of engagement with Lego fans.

Question: Using the definitions of a brand provided in Table 11.1, which description best fits the Lego brand? Explain why.

Task: Find an example of a brand tribe and explain how the brand engages consumers socially.

Scholars' paper 11.1
How social media is disrupting brands

Holt, D. (2016) Branding in the age of social media, *Harvard Business Review*, 94(3), 40–50.

Holt suggests that conventional branding models are no longer relevant in an era of crowdculture. He suggests that an alternative, cultural branding model, where brands collaborate with crowdcultures and target novel ideologies is a more effective framework to use. The paper challenges conventional views of branding and provides some good examples to support his cultural branding model.

See also:

Dwivedi, A. and McDonald, R. (2018) Building brand authenticity in fast-moving consumer goods via consumer perceptions of brand marketing communications, *European Journal of Marketing*, 52(7/8), 1387–1411.

Brand characteristics

The essence of a strong brand is that it is sufficiently differentiated to the extent that it cannot be easily replicated by its competitors. This level of differentiation requires that a brand possess many distinctive characteristics and, to achieve this, it is important to understand how brands are constructed.

Brands consist of two main types of attributes: intrinsic and extrinsic. Intrinsic attributes refer to the functional characteristics of the product, such as its shape, performance and physical capacity. If any of these intrinsic attributes were changed, it would directly alter the product. Extrinsic attributes refer to those elements that are not intrinsic and, if changed, do not alter the material functioning and performance of the product itself: devices such as the brand name, marketing communications, packaging, colour, price and mechanisms that enable consumers to form associations that give meaning to the brand. Buyers often use the extrinsic attributes to help them distinguish one brand from another, because in certain categories it is virtually impossible for them to make decisions based on the intrinsic attributes alone.

Biel (1997) refers to brands being composed of a number of elements. The first refers to the functional abilities a brand claims and can deliver. The particular attributes that distinguish a brand are referred to as *brand skills*. He cites cold remedies and their skill to relieve cold symptoms, for six hours, twelve hours or all day.

The second element is the *personality* of a brand and its fundamental traits concerning lifestyle and perceived values, such as being bland, adventurous, exciting, boring or caring. Brand personification or the transformation into 'a character endowed with human-like characteristics' (Cohen, 2014) is not a new idea. It is, however, an important part of understanding how a brand might be imagined as a person and how a brand is different from other brands (people). See the section on brand associations later in this chapter for more information.

The third branding element is about building a *relationship* with individual buyers. People are said to interact with brands. A two-way relationship can be realistically developed when it is recognised that the brand must interact with the consumer just as much as the consumer must interact with the brand. Blackston (1993) argues that successful branding depends on consumers' perceptions of the attitudes held by the brand towards them as individuals. He illustrates the point with research into the credit card market, where different cards share the same demographic profile of users and the same conventional brand images. Some cards provide recognition or visibility of status, which by association are bestowed upon the owner in the form of power and authority. In this sense the card enhances the user. This contrasts with other cards, where the user may feel intimidated and excluded from the card because as a person the attitudes of the card are perceived to be remote, aloof, condescending and hard to approach. For example, respondents felt the cards were saying, 'If you don't like the conditions, go and get a different card', and 'I'm so well-known and established that I can do as I want'.

The implications for brand development and associated message strategies become clearer. In line with this thinking, Biel cites Fournier (1995), who considers brand/consumer relationships in terms of levels of intimacy, partner quality, attachment, interdependence, commitment and love.

Therefore, Biel sees brands as being made up of three elements: skills, personality and relationships. These combine to form what he regards as 'brand magic', which underpins added value.

A more recent approach to brand development work involves creating a brand experience. Tango was an early pioneer of this approach. Tango used roadshows to create indirect brand-related experiences, such as bungee jumping, trampolining and other fun activities. Pandora, the jewellery brand, has used a number of innovative experiential

Image 11.3 As part of Pandora's #ChristmasDelights campaign, the brand staged the Dance of the Sugar Plum Fairy (Benjamin, 2016)
Source: PrettyGreen.

activities. Much to the surprise of passers-by, the brand staged a performance of the Nutcracker ballet's Dance of the Sugar Plum Fairy, accompanied by a 50-person choir, at Birmingham New Street Station (Benjamin, 2016).

Kapferer (2012) refers to a brand identity prism and its six facets (see Figure 11.2). The facets to the left represent a brand's outward expression, while Kapferer argues that those

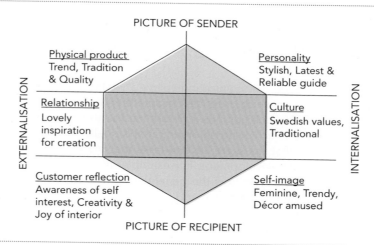

Figure 11.2 Brand identity prism for the Swedish magazine *Sköna hem*
Source: Farhana (2014). Used with permission.

Table 11.2   Brand facets

Brand facet	Explanation
Physique	Refers to the main physical strength of the brand and its core added value. What does the brand do and what does it look like (e.g. the Coca-Cola bottle)?
Personality	Those human characteristics that best represent the identity, best understood by the use of celebrity spokespersons who provide an instant personality.
Culture	A set of values that are central to a brand's aspirational power and essential for communications and differentiation.
Relationship	A brand's relationship defines the way it behaves and acts towards others. Apple exudes friendliness, IBM orderliness and Nike provocation. Important in the service sector.
Customer reflection	Refers to the way customers see the brand . . . for old people, for sporty people, clever people, people who want to look younger. This is an outward reflection.
Self-image	Refers to how individuals feel about themselves, relative to the brand. This is an inner reflection.

Source: Adapted from Kapferer (2012). Used with permission.

to the right are incorporated within the brand, an *inner expression* or *spirit* as he refers to it. Farhana (2014) refers to the facets 'Physique' (physical attributes) and 'Personality' (human characteristics), which portray the source. The 'Reflection' (image of target audience) and 'Self-image' (how the brand is perceived by the consumers) facets characterise the receiver of brand messages. The two central elements 'Culture' (values) and 'Relationship' (the way of conduct) form a source–receiver linkage.

These facets represent the key dimensions associated with building and maintaining brand identities and are set out in Table 11.2; they are interrelated and define a brand's identity, while also representing the means by which brands can be managed, developed and even extended. All brands consist of a mixture of intrinsic and extrinsic attributes and management's task is to decide on the balance between them. Indeed, this decision lies at the heart of branding in the sense that it is the strategy and positioning that lead to strong brands.

The task of marketing communications in branding

Marketing communications plays a vital role in the development of brands and is the means by which products become brands. The way in which marketing communications is used to build brands is determined strategically by the role that the brand is expected to play in achieving an organisation's goals. de Chernatony and Dall'Olmo Riley (1998b) argue that there are several tasks that marketing communications can play in relation to brand development. For example, they suggest the task during brand extensions is to show buyers how the benefits from the established brand have been transferred or extended to the new brand.

Dwivedi and McDonald (2018) identify the importance of marketing communications' role in positioning the brand. Ehrenberg (1974) argues advertising in particular can remind buyers and reinforce their perceptions and in doing so defend the market. However, above all of these, marketing communications has a primary task: namely, to build associations through which consumers identify, recognise, understand, assign affection, become attached and develop relationships with a brand. These associations can be many and varied but they are crucial to brand strength and equity.

Scholars' paper 11.2
Building brand relationships

Fournier, S. (1998) Consumers and their brands: developing relationship theory in consumer research, *Journal of Consumer Research,* **24(4), 343–73.**

Fournier argues that it is important to understand people's life experiences, as this frames the assortment of brands and the relationships they develop with brands. She argues that meaningful consumer brand relationships are shaped not by symbolism/functional category measures, or by involvement, but through the ego significance a brand offers an individual. This much-cited paper should be read by all involved in both academic and practitioner brand management.

See also:

Thompson, A.J., Martin, A.J., Gee, S. and Geurin, A.N. (2018) Building brand and fan relationships through social media, *Sport, Business and Management: An International Journal,* 8(3), 235–56.

Associations and personalities

Successful brands trigger associations in the minds of consumers, and these are not necessarily based on a function or utility. These associations enable consumers to construe an emotional connection with a particular brand.

McCraken (1986) found that consumers might search for brands with a personality that complements their self-concept. Belk (1988) suggested that brands offer a means of self-expression, whether this be in terms of who they want to be (a desired self), who they strive to be (an ideal self) or who they think they should be (an ought self). Brands, therefore, provide a means for individuals to indicate to others their preferred personality, as they relate to these 'self' concepts.

This emotional and symbolic approach is intended to provide consumers with additional reasons to engage with a brand, beyond the normal functional characteristics a brand offers (Keller, 1998), but which are so easily copied by competitors. Aaker (1997) refers to brand personality as the set of human characteristics that consumers associate with a brand. She developed the Brand Personality Scale, which consists of five main dimensions of psychosocial meaning, which subsume 42 personality traits. The dimensions are sincerity (wholesome, honest, down-to-earth), excitement (exciting, imaginative, daring), competence (intelligent, confident), sophistication (charming, glamorous, smooth) and ruggedness (strong, masculine).

Aaker's initial research was conducted in the mid-1990s and revealed that in the USA, MTV was perceived to be best on excitement, CNN on competence, Levi's on ruggedness, Revlon on sophistication and Campbell's on sincerity.

These psychosocial dimensions have subsequently become established as dimensions of brand personality. Aaker developed a five-point framework around these dimensions in order to provide a consistent means of measurement. The framework has been used frequently and cited many times by both academics and marketing practitioners. For example, Arora and Stoner (2009) report that various studies have found that consumers choose offerings that they feel possess personalities similar to their own personalities (Linville and Carlston, 1994; Phau and Lau, 2001). They prefer brands that project a personality that is consistent with their self-concepts. As Arora and Stoner (2009: 273) indicate, 'brand personality provides a form of identity for consumers that expresses symbolic meaning for themselves and for others'. Brand personality, therefore, can be construed as a means of creating and maintaining consumer loyalty, if only because this aspect is difficult for competitors to copy.

Scholars' paper 11.3

The personality of brands

Davies, G., Rojas-Méndez, J.I., Whelan, S., Mete, M. and Loo, T. (2018) Brand personality: theory and dimensionality, *Journal of Product & Brand Management,* **27(2), 115–27.**

This paper critiques the use of human personality as a theory to understand brand personality and suggests that human perception theory may be a better way of understanding brand personality. The authors provide a good review of the published measures of brand personality and suggest a new model featuring three key dimensions: sincerity, competence and status.

See also:

Keller, K.L. and Richey, K. (2017) The importance of corporate brand personality traits to a successful 21st century business, in *Advances in Corporate Branding* (eds J.M.T. Balmer, S. Powell, J. Kernstock and T.O. Brexendorf), London: Palgrave Macmillan, 47–58.

Ideas about brand personification are important when considering brand associations. Cohen (2014) identifies four different ways in which brand personification can be used. The first involves a brand being anthropomorphised or changed into a form with human-like characteristics. Kellogg's used 'Tony the Tiger' to represent their Frosties cereal brand. The second involves associating the brand with an object with human-like characteristics. These could be items used to illustrate brand attributes that speak to the viewer but which are not an integral part of the way the brand functions.

A third interpretation involves a real person, not an anthropomorphised animal or object, to represent or symbolise particular product benefits or values. This might be a character in an ad that depicts a service or brand attribute, but not the brand as a whole.

The fourth interpretation of 'brand personification' occurs when the brand itself is personified by the person who founded, built, owned or is known to be the dominant force in the life of the brand. This is accomplished by pairing the brand name with the brand personifier's likeness. Cohen suggests this might be a real photo, an artist's rendering, a caricature or perhaps that person's handwritten signature, or even just the person's name presented in a distinctive but consistent way (see Viewpoint 11.2, where Henry VIII's silhouette is featured in advertising for The Mary Rose Museum).

Viewpoint 11.2

A 500-year brand heritage

Image 11.4 The iconic silloutte of Henry VIII used by The Mary Rose Museum is a good example of brand personification
Source: The Mary Rose.

The Mary Rose Museum, in Portsmouth UK, is one of the most famous maritime museums in the world. Attracting more than 1.8 million visitors a year, the museum is home to the iconic *Mary Rose*, the flagship of Henry VIII's Tudor Navy.

As well as providing visitors with a spectacular view of this 500-year-old shipwreck, the museum offers a rare opportunity to see thousands of

Source: Anon (2018a).

artefacts that were recovered with the wreck, which sank suddenly off Portsmouth in 1545. As well as canons, longbows and other weaponry, museum visitors can immerse themselves in Tudor England with displays of some of the more common objects found aboard the ship, including surgeons' instruments, a backgammon set and nit combs.

The museum allows visitors to step back 500 years in time and experience the sights, sounds and smells of Tudor England.

Marketing communications plays a key role in reinforcing the museum's heritage and positioning the brand as a unique Tudor experience. To connect audiences with Tudor England the museum chose Henry VIII to personify the brand.

Henry VIII symbolises the Tudors and enables even very young audiences to associate the attraction with Tudor England. The campaign featuring Henry VIII's iconic silhouette triggers associations for audiences and these enable consumers to connect with the brand.

Insight

Brand personification helps audiences form brand associations. By pairing the *Mary Rose* with Henry VIII, who built the ship 500 years ago, it clearly positions the museum as a Tudor experience in the minds of the audience. As Henry VIII is the most notorious Tudor and a favourite with schoolchildren, he makes an authentic brand personifier.

Question: Why do you think The Mary Rose Museum chose to personify the brand with Henry VIII rather that a celebrity brand ambassador? Explain your answer.

Task: Use the brand identity prism in Figure 11.2 as a guide to interpret the identity of The Mary Rose Museum. Draw a brand identity prism for The Mary Rose Museum.

Brand ambassadors

Many brands appoint brand ambassadors to help audiences associate particular personality types with a brand and to assist brand positioning. Celebrities are often used to endorse brands because of their high media profile and their level of expertise in their particular field (Proctor and Kitchen, 2018). Social media influencers also act as brand ambassadors and while some brands such as American Express select influencers with followings up to 3 million, others, such as Lululemon, opt for a larger team of micro influencers (Anon, 2018b).

Using celebrities provides what Belch and Belch (2013) refer to as 'stopping power', or a way for an ad to stand out in a cluttered media environment and attract the attention of audiences. Belch and Belch also claim that celebrities are used because they can positively influence the attitudes and perceptions, feelings and intentions a consumer has about a brand. In other words, celebrities impact on the consumer decision-making process.

Brand ambassadors are used extensively in a variety of markets but they incur risk associated with an ambassador's behaviour and reputation, and the costs can be substantial. For example, Adidas quickly axed one of its global World Cup brand ambassadors, Luis Suárez, from its world-wide campaign, after the Uruguayan footballer striker bit Italy's Giorgio Chiellini during the tournament in Brazil (Joseph, 2014).

Delivering the brand associations

There are various strategic communications approaches to delivering brand associations. However, the initial decision to pursue one association strategy rather than another is partly a function of the size of the available financial resources. They are also partly a function of the context in which the communications are intended to work and the context in which audiences are most likely to interact with the brand and associated messages. However, as a general observation, five main ways to deliver brand associations can be identified (see Figure 11.3):

1. *Above-the-line communications:* should the budget be high, and the need for audience interaction low, then advertising will often be the main way through which brand name associations are shaped. The brand name itself will not need to be related to the function or use experience of the brand as the advertising will be used to create and maintain brand associations. Expressive propositions predominate.

2. *Through-the-line communications:* sometimes the brand strategy requires a behavioural response and so a direct marketing approach. Here some advertising is necessary but in combination with sales promotion, public relations, merchandising and online activity. A mix of functional and expressive associations can be observed.

3. *Below-the-line communications:* where resources are restricted and advertising is not an option, the brand name needs to be closely related to the function and use experience of the product. In the FMCG sector packaging should also play a significant role in building brand associations. Functional associations tend to predominate.

4. *On-the-line communications:* when engagement through a behavioural approach is preferred yet the audience is large and dispersed, a combination of both offline tools and linear and interactive media is used. Initially the penetration of advertising is used to get attention. This is followed by the complementary use of social media and online communications to build relevancy and action. Functional and expressive propositions can be used.

5. *Around-the-line communications:* whether resources are tight or freely available, there are circumstances when the sole use of a formal mix of brand-building tools and media is inappropriate. In these circumstances word-of-mouth communications and

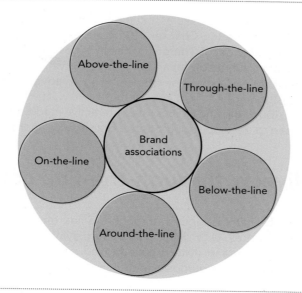

Figure 11.3 Five generic ways to deliver brand associations

brand experience are sufficient to propel a brand's visibility. Expressive propositions predominate, although both approaches are possible.

Each of these is now considered in turn.

Brand delivery: *above-the-line* communications

When there are sufficient resources, and competitive conditions are intense and margins small, advertising is often the primary means to help consumers to make brand associations. In line with ideas about engagement, two main approaches can be used: a rational or an emotional approach. When a rational approach is used, the functional aspects of a brand are emphasised and the benefit to the consumer is stressed. Very often product performance is the focus of the message and a key attribute is identified and used to position the brand. Typically, unique selling propositions (USPs) were often used to draw attention to a single superior functional advantage that consumers found attractive – for example, a washing powder that washes clothes whiter.

Many brands now try to present two or even three brand features as the USP has lost ground. For example, when Britvic launched Juice Up into the chilled fruit juice sector to compete with Sunny Delight, it used the higher fruit juice and lower sugar attributes as the main focus of the communications strategy. The rational approach is sometimes referred to as an *informative approach* (and complements functional positioning).

When an emotional approach is used, advertising should provide emotional selling points (ESPs). These can enable consumers to make positive brand associations based on both psychological and socially acceptable meanings; a psychosocial interpretation. Product performance characteristics are dormant while consumers are encouraged to develop positive feelings towards and associations with the brand. A further goal can be to create positive attitudes towards the advertising itself, which in turn can be used to make associations with the brand. In other words, the role of likeability (discussed in Chapter 10) becomes paramount when using an emotional advertising approach. Therefore, these types of advertisements should be relevant and meaningful, credible, and of significant value to the consumer. In essence, emotional advertising is about people enjoying an advertisement (and complements expressive positioning).

Above-the-line incorporates interactive media advertising with both display and search used to develop strong positive brand associations.

Brand delivery: *through*-the-line communications

As the name suggests, through-the-line offers a blend of above- and below-the-line approaches, with direct marketing playing a strong role in the communications mix. As many brand owners have moved away from using marketing communications for brand-building purposes and then used communications to change or motivate buyer behaviour, so the development of direct marketing has emerged.

Through-the-line communications involve the use of advertising to deliver a call-to-action. Often this is associated with sales promotions, events and merchandising, all of which reinforce behaviour. In consumer markets advertising is used to drive awareness as well as behaviour, but in business markets advertising has a relatively minor role to play, as greater emphasis is placed on email, trade shows and websites.

Brand associations in consumer markets are therefore driven by advertising, web promotions, direct mail and a functional brand name, all reinforced through brand experience and word-of-mouth communications. In business markets brand associations are normally developed through direct mail, telemarketing, personal selling, trade shows as well as the quality of the website and relationship potential. The name is not always important in terms of providing a functional association. A mix of functional and expressive associations can be observed.

Brand delivery: *below*-the-line communications

When the marketing communications budget is limited or where the target audience cannot be reached reasonably or effectively through advertising, then it is necessary to use various other communications tools to develop brand associations.

Direct marketing and public relations are important methods used to build brand values, especially when consumers experience high involvement. The Internet offers opportunities to build new dot-com brands and the financial services sector has tried to harness this method as part of a multichannel distribution policy. What appears to be important for the development of brands operating with limited resources is the brand name and the merchandising activities, of which packaging, labelling and point of purchase (POP) are crucial. In addition, as differentiation between brands becomes more difficult in terms of content and distinct symbolism, the nature of the service encounter is now recognised to have considerable impact on brand association. The development of loyalty schemes and helplines for FMCG, durable and service-based brands is a testimony to the importance of developing and maintaining positive brand associations.

The below-the-line route needs to achieve image transfer. Apart from the clarity of the brand name, which needs to describe the product functions, it is the packaging and associated labelling that shape the way a brand is perceived.

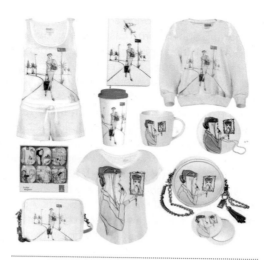

Image 11.5 Emirates have developed a range of merchandise to support their brand
Source: Emirates Group.

Brand delivery: *on*-the-line communications

As the multichannel environment becomes more complex and the opportunities to reach consumers become more challenging, so the need to deploy an array of tools and media becomes paramount.

If an audience is large and dispersed, and the financial resources are reasonably strong, advertising, using both linear and interactive media, can be used first to establish brand name awareness. The first phase often involves the use of emotional content delivered through conventional linear media. Sometimes interactive media are used initially to create brand presence. The second phase strengthens the association through frequency of interaction in interactive media environments. This can include games, competitions, communities and promotions that require consumers to return to the site on a reasonably frequent basis. Managed word-of-mouth communications and viral will also enable reach.

When engagement is routed through a behavioural approach, an element of direct marketing or sales promotion is used to enable responses and register consumer details by driving audiences to websites and social networks. The use of social media becomes an integral element either to enable the completion of the behavioural goals, or to maintain brand interest and frequent usage.

Although functional associations can be established in this way, expressive-based brand name associations are more common.

Brand delivery: *around*-the-line communications

Although not an entirely contemporary strategy, a further approach involves the development of brands without the use of formal communications tools or conventional media. The key to success is to seed the brand through word-of-mouth communications. Google is a good example of a brand that developed without advertising, sales promotion or direct marketing. The brand used some public relations, but its market dominance has been developed through word-of-mouth communications (often viral) and experience through usage strategies.

Communications through social media, in particular social networks, email, viral marketing, blogging and in some cases Twitter, have enabled people to pass on news and views about brands. When opinion leaders and formers are targeted with relevant and interesting brand-related material, they pass on information and views, usually with an exponential impact. Brand-based conversations among consumers enable the development of brand associations.

Brand experience has become an important factor both in marketing practice and in the marketing literature. These experiences are considered to be the 'internal responses (sensations, feelings and thoughts) and behavioural responses evoked by brand-related stimuli that are part of a brand's design and identity, packaging, communications and environments' (Brakus et al., 2009: 53).

Consumers experience brands in a number of ways, but perhaps the most common experiences occur at one of three distinct points. According to Arnould et al. (2002), cited by Brakus et al. (2009), these are when searching for brands, when they buy brands and when they consume them. Brakus et al. (2009) go on to demonstrate that brand experiences consist of four dimensions, all of which vary according to brand type and category. These are sensory, affective, intellectual and behavioural. Therefore, the sound management of these elements and dimensions can have a positive impact on developing the right brand associations.

Viewpoint 11.3
Bajaj V – the nation's bike

Image 11.6 Made from the metal of the INS Vikrant, the Bajaj V embodied the pride of India
Source: EvrenKalinbacak/Shutterstock.

They love their motorbikes in India. There are more motorbikes registered in India than cars and over a million are sold in the country every month.

Most motorbikes are used as a means of commuting to work and the purchase decision is largely made on value for money. Two brands have dominated the commuter motorcycle market, Hero Motors and Honda Motors, and with reluctance on the part of consumers to accept any product change, there seemed little scope for any new entrant to the market.

Bajaj Motorcycles, a leader in the sports bike sector, wanted to find a way to break into the commuter bike market. They knew that getting a foothold into the market would be a challenge. The last six years had already seen 22 of 24 new motorbike launches offering incremental product changes fail. The solution came in the form of national pride.

This national pride was drawn from the INS *Vikrant* – India's first aircraft carrier, that was operational during the 1971 Indo-Pakistani War. Despite the public outcry and legal attempts to save this national treasure, the warship had been decommissioned and turned into scrap. The outpouring of pride that was witnessed during the decommissioning gave Bajaj an idea. They decided to use the scrap metal to make a new motorcycle, the Bajaj V.

Made with the metal from the INS *Vikrant*, the Bajaj V embodied the pride of India. The brand story was built around the iconic warship and the bike became symbolic of the bravery of the men that had served on her.

The launch of the Bajaj V was supported by a digital campaign telling emotive stories of those in the Indian Navy that had served onboard and fought in the 1971 Indo-Pakistani War. First-hand accounts from the war heroes were posted onto YouTube and on a dedicated site.

Bajaj extended the pride-based content on their platforms to include stories about people from around India whose work has brought about changes in Indian Society. The website celebrates 'Invincible Indians' and shares 'stories that involve pride everyday'. Bajaj shares personal accounts from inspirational Indians such as Girish Bharadwaj, the 'Bridgeman', who has built 127 bridges to connect remote Indian villages, and women such as Vijaylaxmi Sharma or Didi (the Elder Sister), who fights against child marriage in Rajasthan. These Indians have been selected as brand ambassadors and two of these ambassadors have been recognised with Padma Shri awards, one of India's highest civilian honours.

The brand positioning and the emotional approach used in the campaign resonated with Indian audiences and 11,000 Bajaj V bikes were sold on the first day of the launch. After the first three months 100,000 bikes had been sold and the return on investment was $53 for every dollar spent through the campaign. The brand has an annual turnover of $240 million.

Sources: Anon (2018c); Bajaj V – the nation's bike (2017).

Insight

This case from India provides a good example of how brands can trigger powerful associations in the minds of consumers. The association made with the INS *Vikrant* through using the metal to build the motorbike, enables the consumer to construe an emotional connection with the Bajaj V brand. The use of brand ambassadors to help audiences associate pride with the brand further strengthens the brand positioning.

Question: In what way did Bajaj V deliver the brand association? Use Figure 11.4 to help justify your answer.

Task: Visit the Bajaj V website and view the brand ambassador videos. Explain why you think these individuals were selected as brand ambassadors.

In addition to these five forms of brand development, there are several additional mechanisms through which brand associations can be fostered. These include: co-branding, geographical identifiers, the use of ingredient brands, support services and award symbols.

Marketing communications is the means through which products can evolve into brands. People make associations immediately they become aware of a brand name. It is the brand manager's task to ensure that the associations made are appropriate and provide a sufficient means of differentiation. By communicating the key strengths and differences of a brand, by explaining how a brand enables customers to create value for themselves, by reinforcing and providing consistency in the messages transmitted, and by enabling consumers to experience brands, a level of integration can be brought to the way a brand is perceived by the target market.

Finally in this section, the importance of branding as a part of integrated marketing communications should not be forgotten and, for this, internal brand education is crucial. The way a brand relates internally to departments and individuals and the way the brand is articulated by senior management are important parts of brand education. Brands are not just external elements – they should form part of the way in which an organisation operates (Theurer et al., 2018). This is explored further in the section on employee branding later in this chapter.

Building brands with marketing communications

Having considered some of the main elements associated with the development of brands, they can now be brought together by a means provided by Keller (2009). He acknowledges the view that brands consist of both rational and emotional elements and that both need to be developed in sequence in order to create strong brand equity or value. He also recognises the importance of developing relevant brand associations.

Keller sees the brand-building processes as a series of steps within a pyramid (see Figure 11.4). The rational blocks are used to build up the left-hand side, and the blocks on the right-hand side reflect the emotional route.

There are four main steps in the brand-building process:

1. *Salience or awareness*: the first building block requires that customers are helped to identify with the brand, to enable them to make associations with a specific product class or customer need.

2. *Understanding*: customers then need to understand what the brand means and to do this links need to be established with various tangible and intangible brand associations.

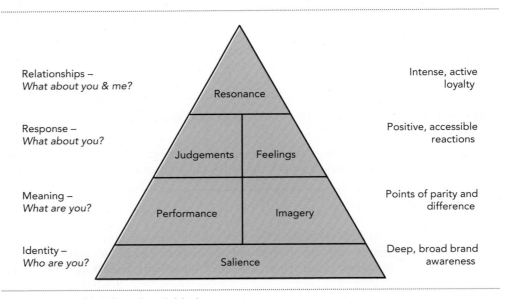

Figure 11.4 Building brands with blocks
Source: Keller (2009). Used with permission.

3. *Responses*: at this stage customers should be encouraged to provide responses in terms of their opinions and evaluations. Their feelings towards the brand reflect their emotional reaction towards the brand.

4. *Relationships*: the top of the pyramid represents the final step, the development of an active relationship between customers and the brand. This is referred to as *resonance*, which is the 'intensity or depth of the psychological bond that customers have with the brand, as well as the level of activity engendered by this loyalty' (Keller, 2009: 144).

Reaching the top of the pyramid does not end the brand development journey, as resonance itself has four dimensions: behavioural loyalty, attitudinal attachment, a sense of community or affiliation with other people about a brand, and active engagement.

Brand resonance is most likely to result when marketers create proper salience and breadth and depth of awareness. From this position 'points-of-parity and points-of-difference' (p. 143) need to be established, so that positive judgements and feelings can be made that appeal to both the head and the heart respectively.

What is clear is that Keller considers marketing communications to be an integral element in the way that the various steps and linkages within the brand development process are developed. An integrated approach to marketing communications is necessary in order that brand awareness can be created, that appropriate associations are fostered in order to link the brand image in consumers' memory; positive brand judgements or feelings are stimulated; and/or enabling a strong(er) connection between a consumer and the brand.

It is also advocated that interactive marketing communications is used as an integral brand-building component. This is because of its power and versatility across all of the building blocks of the pyramid. Readers interested in these concepts should see the paper presented in Scholars' paper 11.4.

Scholars' paper 11.4

Branding essentials

Keller, K.L. (2009) Building strong brands in a modern marketing communications environment, *Journal of Marketing Communications*, 15(2–3), 139–55.

This paper is a must-read for all marketing students and professionals. Keller explains how brands can be developed through various building blocks that form a pyramid, at the top of which is the goal of brand resonance. Keller argues that an understanding of consumer brand knowledge structures underpins the use of marketing communications, which when integrated should enable brand resonance to be achieved.

See also:

Yoo, B. and Donthu, N. (2001) Developing and validating a multidimensional consumer-based brand equity scale, *Journal of Business Research*, 52(1), 1–14.

Business-to-business branding

Branding has been used by a number of manufacturers (e.g. Intel, Caterpillar, Cisco, DuPont, FedEx, Teflon, Nutrasweet) to achieve two particular goals. Rich (1996) reports that the first goal is to develop an identity that final end-users perceive as valuable. For example, Intel has developed its microprocessors such that PCs with the Intel brand are seen to be of high quality and credibility. This provides PC manufacturers with an added competitive advantage. The second goal is to establish a stronger relationship with the manufacturer. Nutrasweet works with food manufacturers, advising on recipes, simply because the final product is the context within which Nutrasweet will be evaluated by end-users.

A business-to-business (B2B) brand is often tied closely to the company itself, as opposed to business-to-consumer (B2C) brands, which often distance themselves from the manufacturer or company name. For example, a Rolls-Royce power turbine is branded Rolls-Royce because of the perception of tradition, high quality, performance and global reach that are associated with the Rolls-Royce name. Marketing communications should be developed so that it incorporates and perpetuates the personality of the brand. Thus, all the Rolls-Royce advertising materials should be in corporate colours and contain the logo. All copy should be in the house style and reinforce brand perceptions.

Beverland et al. (2007) offer an alternative model to Kapferer's prism (above) in order to address the needs of the business market. Their approach (see Figure 11.5) uses five main dimensions upon which business brands are built: product, service, adaptation, logistics and advice.

The researchers argue that the tangible elements (product benefits) are normally more prominent at the beginning of a business relationship. However, as the relationship develops and as the decision-making becomes increasingly complex, so there is a shift away from the tangible to the intangible aspects and abstract associations.

Elsäßer and Wirtz (2017) identified that both rational brand quality and emotional factors influence customer satisfaction and brand loyalty in a B2B setting. While product quality, service quality and distribution quality are all important rational factors, emotional brand associations such as consistent advertising style, brand image, country-of-manufacture image and salesperson's personality were also found to influence satisfaction and loyalty.

Although not as high profile as in the consumer market, branding is a critical aspect in the B2B market. This, according to Hynes (2014), is because competitive advantage and differentiation is so difficult to establish, let alone maintain. B2B products are very often bought by groups that include people who are very knowledgeable about price points, product specifications and service offerings. This is partly due to their constant monitoring of the marketplace. In these circumstances the 'brand' is the single most important differentiating factor.

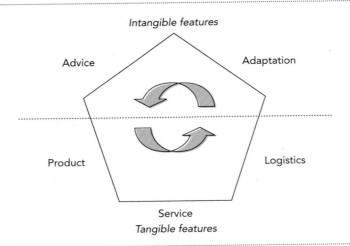

Figure 11.5 Five pillars of business branding

Branding in an interactive environment

The major difference between online and offline branding is the context in which the brand associations are developed, delivered and sustained. Both forms of branding are about developing and sustaining valuable relationships with customers, but online branding occurs in a virtual context. This context deprives consumers of many of the normal cues used to sense and interpret brands. Opportunities to touch and feel, to try on, and physically feel and compare products are largely removed and a new set of criteria has to be used to convey and interpret brand associations.

One of the strengths of the Internet is its ability to provide copious amounts of regularly updated information, available '24/7'. As a result, online brands tend towards the use of rational messages, using product attributes, quality and performance measures, third-party endorsements, comparisons and price as a means of brand differentiation and advantage. However, it should be remembered that online branding strategies are influenced by the nature of the brand itself. If the brand has a strong offline presence, then the amount of online branding work will be smaller than if it is a pure-play brand. Branding should be a part of an overall communications strategy, where online and offline work is coordinated.

All branding activities need to extend across all key consumer contact points, in both offline and online environments. Internet users generally exhibit goal-directed behaviour and experiential motivations. Goal-directed behaviour that is satisfied is more likely to make people want to return to a site. Therefore, it can be concluded (broadly) that satisfying experiential motivations makes people stay, and in so doing boosts the potency of an online brand.

Employee branding

Berry (1980) is widely credited as the first to recognise the term 'internal marketing', in a paper that sought to distinguish between product- and service-based marketing activities.

Employees are important to external stakeholders not only because of the tangible aspects of service and production that they provide, but also because of the intangible aspects, such as attitude and the way in which the service is provided: 'How much do they really care?' Images are often based more on the intangible than the tangible aspects of employee communications. Punjaisri et al. (2009) find that employee branding influences the extent to which employees identify with, and are committed to, a brand. They also provide empirical evidence concerning the positive impact of internal communications on the alignment of employee behaviour and their consistent delivery of the brand promise.

Management, on the other hand, is responsible for the allocation of resources and the process and procedures used to create value. Its actions effectively constrain the activities of the organisation and, either consciously or unconsciously, shape the nature and form of the communications the organisation adopts. It is important, therefore, to understand how organisations can influence and affect the communications process.

The role of employees has changed. Once they could be just part of the company fulfilling their core activity, but this role has been extended so that they are now recognised as brand ambassadors (Edinger-Schons et al., 2018). This is particularly important in service environments where employees represent an interface between an organisation's internal and external environments and where their actions can have a powerful effect in creating images among customers (Punjaisri and Wilson, 2017). It is evident that many people now recognise the strategic role of employees as brand ambassadors and their important contribution to brand equity (Gelb and Rangarajan, 2014). Within this context communications play a critical role (Punjaisri et al. 2009).

External communications

The quality of employees' external communications impacts on brand reputation and at one time this was closely controlled by management. Today, employees use social media so that they can have a positive influence on the perception of the organisation among key target audiences. In addition, it can be used to support opinion leadership, be an advocate for brands and products, as well as the overall organisation, and can influence profitability and brand equity.

Unfortunately, the use of social media by employees can also have a negative effect. This may include a decline in employee productivity, inconsistent messaging, legal action, regulatory audits and fines, various types of crises, cybercrime and the loss of confidential data, plus the exposure of company secrets, and security breaches.

Social media cannot be fully regulated, nor can they be monitored, controlled, or their impact halted or messages retracted. This means that organisations effectively surrender control and must resort to a proactive approach involving coaching, training, storytelling and informal communications in order to avoid these costly and protracted consequences.

Bizzi (2018) provides a number of recommendations to help organisations mitigate the risks of social media at work, including:

1. Agree a social media policy that encourages social media use at work and ensures employees state that opinions are their own and not those of the organisation.
2. Employ corporate social media staff to introduce and manage the organisation's social media policy.
3. Introduce social media training to inform employees of the benefits of social media.
4. Set up social media groups to encourage internal networking and relationships.
5. Reward employees for using social media to achieve organisational goals.

Internal communications

Research by Foreman and Money (1995) indicates that managers see the main components of internal communications falling into three broad areas: development, reward and vision for employees. These will inevitably vary in intensity on a situational basis.

All three of these components have communications as a common linkage. Employees and management (members) need to communicate with one another and with a variety of non-members, and do so through an assortment of methods. Communications with members, wherever they are located geographically, need to be undertaken for a number of reasons. These include the DRIP factors (Chapter 1), but these communications also serve the additional purposes of providing transaction efficiencies and affiliation needs (see Table 11.3).

Table 11.3 The roles of internal marketing communications

DRIP factors	To provide information To be persuasive To reinforce – reassure/remind To differentiate employees/groups
Transactional	To coordinate actions To promote the efficient use of resources To direct developments
Affiliation	To provide identification To motivate personnel To promote and coordinate activities with non-members

The values transmitted to customers, suppliers and distributors through external communications need to be reinforced by the values expressed by employees, especially those who interact with these external groups. Internal marketing communications is necessary in order that internal members are motivated and involved with the brand in such a way that they are able to present a consistent and uniform message to non-members. This is an aspect of integrated marketing communications and involves product- and organisation-centred messages. If there is a set of shared values, internal communications are said to blend and balance the external communications. This process, whereby employees are encouraged to communicate with non-members so that organisations ensure that what is promised is understood by customers, is referred to as 'living the brand', or 'employee branding'. Hiscock (2002) claims that employees can be segmented according to the degree and type of support they give a brand. He claims that, in the UK, 30 per cent of employees are brand neutral, 22 per cent are brand saboteurs and 48 per cent are brand champions, of whom 33 per cent would talk about the brand positively if asked, and 15 per cent do so spontaneously.

Welch and Jackson (2007) provide an interesting and helpful insight into some of the issues associated with understanding internal communications. Although they assume a stakeholder approach and refrain from considering any related marketing issues, they suggest that internal communications should be considered in terms of four dimensions: internal line management communications; internal peer communications; internal project communications; and internal corporate communications. These are intended to provide a typology of internal communications and are set out in Table 11.4.

Attention is given to the fourth dimension, internal corporate communications. Welch and Jackson believe that this refers to communications between an organisation's strategic managers and its internal stakeholders, with the purpose of promoting *commitment* to the organisation, a sense of *belonging* (to the organisation), *awareness* of its changing environment and *understanding* of its evolving goals (2007:186). These four goals are depicted in Figure 11.6.

These four goals serve to engage employees not only with their roles, tasks and jobs but also with the organisation. It is recognised that the internal environment incorporates the organisation's structure, culture, sub-cultures, processes, behaviour and leadership style and that this interacts with the external environment and provides context for the internal communications. Employees, especially 'the disgruntled within' (Grossman, 2005: 3), represent a real threat to organisations that do not make sure that external and internal messages are consistent and congruent.

Table 11.4 Internal communications matrix

Dimension	Level	Direction	Participants	Content
Internal line management communications	Line managers/ supervisors	Predominantly two-way	Line managers–employees	Employees' roles; personal impact, e.g. appraisal discussions, team briefings
Internal team peer communications	Team colleagues	Two-way	Employee–employee	Team information, e.g. team task discussions
Internal project peer communications	Project group colleagues	Two-way	Employee–employee	Project information, e.g. project issues
Internal corporate communications	Strategic managers/top management	Predominantly one-way	Strategic managers–all employees	Organisational/ corporate issues, e.g. goals, objectives, new developments, activities and achievements

Source: Welch and Jackson (2007). © Emerald Group Publishing Limited. All rights reserved.

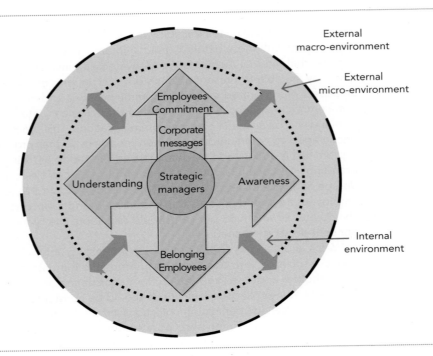

Figure 11.6 Internal corporate communications

Very often employees perceive the value of internal communications in terms of the richness of information and the media used to convey it. In other words, to quote McLuhan (1964), 'the medium is the message'. White et al. (2010) interpret media richness theory in terms of the different media used to communicate with employees. Email is invariably used for short and fast updates, important information is released through printed paper, while websites are used to alert staff to fresh information but also to archive it for retrieval as necessary. Above all else, interpersonal communications are the richest and most important form of communications to employees, as this strongly influences attitudes and behaviours.

Intellectual and emotional aspects

Employees are required to deliver both the functional aspects of an organisation's offering and the emotional dimensions, particularly in service environments. By attending to these twin elements it is possible that long-term relationships between sellers and buyers can develop effectively. Hardaker and Fill (2005) explore ideas concerning the notion that employees need to buy into organisational vision, goals and strategy and, as White et al. (2010: 67) confirm, 'employees want to know where their organization is headed and how they contribute to achieving the vision'.

This buy-in, or engagement, consists of two main components: intellectual and emotional (see Figure 11.7). The intellectual element is concerned with employees buying in and aligning themselves with the organisation's strategy, issues and overall direction. The emotional element is concerned with employees taking ownership of their contribution and becoming committed to the achievement of stated goals. Communications strategies should be based on the information-processing styles of employees and access to preferred media. Communications should reflect a suitable balance between the need for rational information to meet intellectual needs and expressive types of communications to meet the emotional needs of the workforce. It follows that the better the communications, the higher the level of engagement.

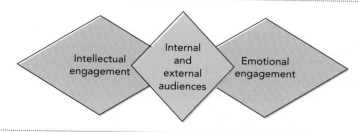

Figure 11.7 Brand engagement

The development of internal brands based around employees can be accomplished effectively and quickly by simply considering the preferred information-processing style of an internal audience. By developing messages that reflect the natural processing style and using a diversity of media that best complement the type of message and the needs of each substantial internal target audience, the communications strategy is more likely to be successful.

The key to successful employee branding hinges upon an organisation's ability to communicate desirable values and goals, as this helps employees to identify with the organisation. This in turn prompts employees to speak positively about the organisation and so influence external stakeholders.

Viewpoint 11.4
Cheetos Museum

Image 11.7 The Cheetos Museum engaged consumers with the brand
Source: Cheetos.

Cheetos was facing pressure as industry leader in the US and wanted to find a new reason to engage audiences with the brand.

The brand had noticed that consumers had started posting images of Cheetos that looked like other objects or people on Instagram and social platforms. To capitalise on this emerging trend and to engage with parents and their kids, the brand created the Cheetos Museum.

The museum featured real Cheetos that had been found, which looked like something familiar. The idea of celebrating the shape of the snack was seen to fit with the brand's mischievous personality. The launch was supported by a series of films that showed Cheetos that looked like a cat, Abraham Lincoln, the Statue of Liberty and the Loch Ness Monster.

Consumers were encouraged to send in photos of their Cheetos shapes to a microsite where images were framed and exhibited in the online gallery. The more unusual images were shared on social media and the most popular Cheetos were collected for the Museum, with a live exhibit in New York City's Grand Central Station. Audiences were invited to vote for their favourite shape to win $60,000.

The Cheetos Museum captivated the attention of consumers and media. The fan-curated website saw 127,717 unique images of Cheetos shapes uploaded from across all 50 states. One snack that looked similar to Harambe the gorilla even sold on eBay for $99,000.

Sources: Cheetos Museum (2017); Frederick (2017).

To communicate the brand, an integrated campaign was used, which included digital, social, experiential, point-of-sale and PR.

The Cheetos Museum was the brand's most successful social media campaign and led to the strongest sales week in the brand's history. The campaign generated over 23 million video views and trended on Facebook for two days. It generated more than 1 billion earned-media impressions and the microsite saw 1.47 million visits.

Insight

The development of this fan-curated museum shows how brands are collaborating with crowdculture as discussed in Holt's paper (2016) highlighted in Scholars' paper 11.1.

Brands are identifying new cultural behaviours on social platforms and developing marketing communications strategies to fit with these emerging trends.

Question: How would you define the Cheetos brand identity? Use the brand facets listed in Table 11.2 to guide your answer.

Task: Using Keller's brand-building stages shown in Figure 11.4, identify where you think the Cheetos brand should appear in the pyramid. Justify your answer.

Brand equity

The concept of brand equity has arisen from the increasing recognition that brands represent a value to both organisations and shareholders (Aaker, 1991; Keller, 1993). Brands as assets can impact heavily on the financial wellbeing of a company. Indeed, Perrey et al. (2015) refer to the evidence that strong brands can outperform the market by 73 per cent.

The original conceptualisation of brand equity was introduced by Aaker (1991) and Keller (1993) and included four dimensions: brand loyalty, brand awareness, perceived quality and brand associations. Each dimension of brand equity has been defined and highlights the multi-dimensional nature of the concept. Aaker (1991) argues that brand loyalty provides a measure of customer attachment to a brand and is a key component of brand equity. Brand loyalty is central to predicting future sales and the long-term success of a brand. Brand awareness is 'the likelihood that a brand name will come to mind and the ease with which it does so' (Keller, 1993: 3). Brand awareness is measured through brand recognition and brand recall. Perceived quality is defined as 'the customer's perception of the overall quality or superiority of a product or service' (Aaker, 1991: 85). Brand association is seen to be 'anything linked in memory to a brand' (Aaker, 1991: 109).

Lasser et al. (1995) identify two main perspectives of brand equity: financial and marketing. The financial view is based on a consideration of a brand's value as a definable asset, based on the net present values of discounted future cash flows (Farquahar, 1989). The marketing perspective is grounded in the beliefs, images and core associations consumers have about particular brands. Richards (1997) argues that there are both behavioural and attitudinal elements associated with brands and recognises that these vary between groups and represent fresh segmentation and targeting opportunities.

A further component of the marketing view is the degree of loyalty or retention a brand is able to sustain. Measures of market penetration, involvement, attitudes and purchase intervals (frequency) are typical. Feldwick (1996) uses a three-part definition to bring these two approaches together. He suggests brand equity is a composite of:

- *brand value*, based on a financial and accounting base;
- *brand strength*, measuring the strength of a consumer's attachment to a brand;
- *brand description*, represented by the specific attitudes customers have towards a brand.

Attempts to measure brand equity by academics and practitioners have to date been varied and have lacked a high level of consensus (Maio Mackay, 2001), although the spirit and ideals behind the concept are virtually the same. Table 11.5 sets out some of the approaches developed by practitioners/consultants. Table 11.6 sets out the major academic approaches (Mirzaei et al. 2011). As a means of synthesising these approaches the following are considered the principal dimensions through which brand equity should be measured:

- *brand dominance*: a measure of its market strength and financial performance;
- *brand associations*: a measure of the beliefs held by buyers about what the brand represents;
- *brand prospects*: a measure of its capacity to grow and extend into new areas.

Brand equity is considered important because of the increasing interest in trying to measure the return on promotional investments. This in turn aids the valuation of brands for balance sheet purposes. A brand with a strong equity is more likely to be able to preserve its customer franchise and so fend off competitor attacks. Farr (2006) determined that the top brands are characterised by four factors. They are all strong in terms of innovation, great customer experience, clear values and strong sector leadership.

Developing brand equity is a strategy-related issue and whether a financial, marketing or twin approach is adopted, the measurement activity can help focus management activity on brand development. However, there is little agreement about what is measured and how and when it is measured. Ambler and Vakratsas (1998) argue that organisations should not seek a single set of measures simply because of the varying circumstances and contextual factors that impinge on brand performance. In reality, the measures used by most firms share many common elements.

Table 11.5   Practitioner approaches to measuring brand equity

Source	Factors measured
BrandDynamics (Kantar Millward Brown)	Volume share, price premium, brand value growth
Brand Asset Valuator (Young and Rubicam)	Strength (differentiation and relevance), stature (esteem and knowledge).
EquiTrend	Salience, quality, satisfaction
Interbrand (Omnicom)	Economic profit, the role of the brand, brand strength.

Sources: Adapted from Haigh (1997), Millward Brown (2018) and Pirrie (2006).

Table 11.6 Academic approaches to measuring brand equity

Author/s	Dimensions	Perspective	Data used
Holbrook (1992)	Price premium	PMO	Price data
Kamakura and Russell (1993)	Brand intangible value and perceived quality	CMO	Scanner panel data
Simon and Sullivan (1993)	Market capitalisation	FMO	Published annual data
Park and Srinivasan (1994)	Attribute-based/non-attribute-based components (market share and price premium)	PMO	Survey/firm/expert judgement
Yoo and Donthu (2001)	Brand awareness, brand associations, perceived quality	CMO	Customer survey
Ailawadi et al. (2003)	Revenue premium	PMO	Retail sales data
Srinivasan et al. (2005)	Awareness, attribute perception biases, and non-attribute preferences	CMO	Survey/firm/expert judgement
Pappu et al. (2005)	Brand awareness, brand associations, perceived quality, brand loyalty	CMO	Customer survey
Sriram et al. (2007)	Brand choice utility	PMO	Store-level data
Shankar et al. (2008)	Offering value, relative brand importance	CMO	Customer survey/ financial data
Buil et al. (2008)	Brand awareness, perceived quality, brand loyalty, brand associations	CMO	Customer survey

Note: CMO=customer mindset outcomes, PMO=product market outcomes, FMO=financial market outcomes.
Source: From Developing a new model for tracking brand equity as a measure of marketing effectiveness, *The Marketing Review*, 11(4), 323–36 (Mirzaei, Gray and Baumann, 2011), reproduced by permission of Westburn Publishers Ltd.

Consumer-based brand equity (CBBE) is a widely used measure of brand equity by academics (Nam et al., 2011; Yoo and Donthu, 2001) and has been applied across a number of different domains to research the interrelationship between brand equity dimensions (Tasci, 2018).

Key points

- Brands are a composite of two main constructs: (1) an identity that managers wish to portray, and (2) images, construed by audiences, of the identities they perceive, as articulated through user-generated content in the form of blogs, wikis and social networks. It is important, therefore, to recognise that both managers and customers are involved in the branding process.
- Brands consist of two main types of attributes: intrinsic and extrinsic. Intrinsic attributes refer to the functional characteristics of the product such as its shape, performance and physical capacity. If any of these intrinsic attributes were changed, it would directly alter the product. Extrinsic attributes refer to those elements that are not intrinsic and if changed do not alter the material functioning and performance of the product itself: devices such as the brand name, marketing communications, packaging, price and mechanisms, which enable consumers to form associations that give meaning to the brand.

- Marketing communications can help customers make associations with brands with either a rational or an information-based approach, or alternatively with one based more on imagery and feelings. Brand associations can be developed in one of five main ways: above, through, below, on and around the line.

- Employees constitute a major stakeholder group and have many roles of varying complexity. Internal marketing communications is necessary in order to drive employees' engagement so that they are motivated and aligned with the brand strategy.

- Employees are required to deliver both the functional aspects of an organisation's offering and the emotional dimensions, particularly in service environments.

- The major difference between online and offline branding is the context in which the brand associations are developed and sustained. Both forms of branding are about developing and sustaining valuable relationships with consumers, but online branding occurs in a virtual context.

- Brand equity recognises the value of brands to organisations and shareholders. Brands can impact the financial wellbeing of a company and strong brands are recognised to outperform others in the market. There are two main ways of considering brand equity, namely financial and marketing perspectives.

Case study

McVitie's: waking the sleeping giant

Principal author: Daniel Sherrard
Contributing authors: Rachel Walker, Matt Gladstone

Image 11.8 McVitie's was seen as a British institution
Source: Chris Bull / Alamy Stock Photo.

The context

McVitie's, a long-established UK biscuit company, faced several challenges in 2013, which were preventing it from meeting its full potential. These concerned the biscuit category and the brand itself.

The sweet biscuits category is worth £2,500 million but both volume and value sales were flat, and there was increasing competition for shelf space. In-store space was being squeezed and the category was seeing significant distribution losses. Driven down by competitive promotions, all the big manufacturers had dropped their prices.

Although McVitie's was the largest player its market share (22 per cent) had been static since 2011. McVitie's had only 23 per cent spontaneous awareness and Cadbury was regarded by consumers as category leader. To put it another way, although McVitie's was market leader, it was not the Coke of Colas or the Colgate of toothpastes. Retailers, like consumers, saw McVitie's as an unwieldy portfolio of brands rather than a singular strong leader (see Image 11.9).

In the past many of these product brands had been supported by their own brand campaigns. In addition, media budgets had been stretched by media inflation. The outcome was that most McVitie's brands were with insufficient, or in some cases, no media support. McVitie's was the category leader, but it was neither behaving like one, nor being perceived as one. McVitie's was seen by consumers as a British institution, staid and boring.

There are certain benefits that come from not just *being* the market leader, but from being *seen* as the market leader, for example trade favour and being the default choice of consumers – and McVitie's was missing out. If it continued on the same path, the brand could start declining, as prices and distribution continued to be squeezed, the brand continued to lack sufficient support, and it continued to be outshone by newer kids on the block.

Strategy

McVitie's had to do something radically different to protect its business and more clearly exploit its leadership position, in order to grow. The first strategic decision was to establish a masterbrand, rather than support multiple product brands. This drives media and production efficiencies, but by pursuing a single proposition helps to make the McVitie's brand more famous and loved. By uniting our forces into one masterbrand, being more emotionally resonant and therefore more intuitively present in the minds of the shopper – and the trade – we would drive sales.

As such, we expected communications to work in the following way:

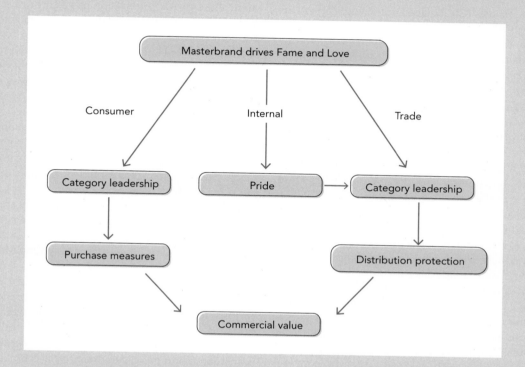

Historically, McVitie's campaigns had been rational and focused on ingredients. This was no longer viable and ethnographic research was commissioned. This revealed that while enjoyable, biscuits are incidental – a fleeting moment rather than a lasting experience. At an emotional level however, biscuits are rich in nostalgic, childhood memories of love, nurture and maternal care.

Like other small things – hugs, hot drinks, babies, puppies, kittens – biscuits can evoke powerful feelings. We found a rich vein of emotion associated with the love of small cute things, the emotions of care and nurture, which trigger our parenting instincts and make us feel fuzzy and warm.

We expressed this insight as follows:

Biscuits might be trivial, but they create powerful feelings of love, warmth, nurture & care.

These powerful feelings became the heart of our masterbrand campaign and served to unify the range and capture the heart of the market.

We needed a big, bold solution to embed the brand firmly into popular culture. The creative leap was to use adorable baby animals to embody the feeling of biscuits. Each biscuit would have its own cute animal representative.

We expressed this idea as:

Sweeet: Cute pain which evokes the utterly trivial yet emotionally powerful feeling of McVitie's biscuits.

In our main channels, TV and VOD, these cute critters magically emerge from McVitie's biscuit packets to give unsuspecting biscuit-eaters a Sweeet! surprise. The animals disappear once the biscuits are eaten – and normality is restored.

To further build consistency, all communications used the new blue and gold world that we created for McVitie's. Our new masterbrand tagline ran across everything.

All touchpoints reinforced the creative idea, creating an identity for McVitie's which cemented its role as category leader, for both consumers and trade.

We road-blocked peak-time TV with three different McVitie's TV ads (Chocolate Digestives, Digestives and Jaffa Cakes) airing simultaneously on different channels, during different well-loved programmes helping us get to the heart of the nation (*Coronation Street, Come Dine With Me, Sherlock*) as well as on YouTube.

TV was chosen to drive fame awareness with our mass audience, and to allow us to target key biscuit-eating moments at home on the sofa. Importantly, the rich storytelling format of TV allowed us to evoke the cute pain feeling and emotion that was central to the strategy and idea. We even launched our own epically sweet Christmas ad.

Digital advertising ran on sites that people visit on their biscuit breaks: Mail Online, Buzzfeed, Facebook, Twitter. Our digital ads worked like the bite-sized populist content on these sites, soliciting votes and shares. And we extended the joy with 'Sweeet' experiences pushed out through digital and social: 'Send a cuddle', 'Paw Cursor' and 'Release the Snuggles'.

Meanwhile PR created real-life Sweeet experiences to fuel media engagement including an adorable Cuddle Café and a Cuddle Vending Machine.

We needed our in-store communications to make McVitie's top of mind and convert to purchase. Cute animals featured on attention-grabbing formats: from 3D gondola headers with googly-eyed tarsiers in Morrisons, to lenticulars and retail-tainment in Asda.

Results

After years of static share McVitie's saw volume and value share grow. Penetration has also risen steadily from the start of the campaign – from 25.2 to 36.8 per cent to date.

People clearly loved the advertising, driving over four million unpaid views online – unprecedented for a UK biscuit brand. The advertising was highly memorable and emotionally engaging – performing above norms for emotional response.

It drove right through to the mainstream UK media and it even featured in *Time* magazine and on *Good Morning America*. The Sweeet campaign made people search for McVitie's content on YouTube for the first time in five years. As a result, we saw campaign recognition rise significantly and all of the fame measures grew as the brand became top of mind. Since the start of the campaign, both consumers and retailers have increasingly seen McVitie's as a leader.

The masterbrand campaign has galvanised the business to give its previously disparate brands and various teams a single focus and purpose. It has boosted morale internally, and even helped with recruiting new talent to the business. The masterbrand campaign has given the internal team a different conversation to have with the trade than simply price and promotion.

This case study is an edited version of a paper submitted to the IPA Effectiveness Awards 2016. It has been reproduced here with the kind permission of the IPA, WARC, McVitie's, and the authors Daniel Sherrard, Rachel Walker and Matt Gladstone who wrote the original paper.

Review questions

McVitie's case questions

1. Explain the brand promise offered by McVitie's.

2. How does the McVitie's brand structure assist consumers?

3. Apply Biel's concept of 'brand magic' to the McVitie's brand.

4. Identify the main ways in which the McVitie's brand might form brand associations.

5. Explain the different ways in which marketing communications can be used to deliver brand associations. Which of these might best apply to McVitie's?

General questions

1. Find three non-FMCG brands and evaluate how their brand strength has been developed without the aid of advertising. How might you improve the strength of these brands?

2. Write a short definition of internal marketing and explain how marketing communications needs to assume both internal and external perspectives.

3. What is the role of internal marketing communications?

4. How might online branding complement offline branding activities?

5. Discuss two approaches to brand equity.

References for Chapter 11

Aaker, D.A. (1991) *Managing brand equity. Capitalizing on the value of a brand name*, New York: The Free Press.

Aaker, D. (2014) *Aaker on Branding*, New York: Morgan James.

Aaker, J. (1997) Dimensions of brand personality, *Journal of Marketing Research*, 34 (August), 347–56.

Ailawadi, K.L., Lehmann, D.R. and Neslin, S.A. (2003) Revenue premium as an outcome measure of brand equity, *Journal of Marketing*, 67 (October), 1–17.

Ambler, T. and Vakratsas, D. (1998) Why not let the agency decide the advertising? *Market Leader*, 1 (Spring), 32–7.

American Marketing Association (1960) *Marketing Definitions: A Glossary of Marketing Terms*, Chicago, IL: American Marketing Association.

American Marketing Association (2018) *AMA Dictionary*, retrieved 10 January 2018 from https://www.ama.org/resources/Pages/Dictionary.aspx?dLetter=B

Anon (2018a) New TV advert, Maryrose.org, retrieved 30 May 2018 from https://maryrose.org/news/new-tv-advert/

Anon (2018b) How American Express, Lululemon, Red Bull & Maybelline win with brand ambassadors, *MediaKix*, retrieved 24 May 2018 from http://mediakix.com/2018/05/best-brand-ambassador-programs/#gs.ZWA9A20

Anon (2018c) Bajajauto.com, retrieved 27 May 2018 from https://www.bajajauto.com/motor-bikes/v#view360

Arnould, E.J., Price, L.L. and Zinkhan, G.L. (2002) *Consumers*, 2nd edn, New York: McGraw-Hill.

Arora, R. and Stoner, C. (2009) A mixed method approach to understanding brand personality, *Journal of Product & Brand Management*, 18(4), 272–83.

Assael, H. (1990) *Marketing: Principles and Strategy*, Orlando, FL: Dryden Press.

Astrachan, C.B., Botero, I., Astrachan, J.H. and Prügl, R. (2018) Branding the family firm: a review, integrative framework proposal, and research agenda, *Journal of Family Business Strategy*, 9(1), 3–15.

Bajaj V – the nation's bike (2017), *Cannes Archive*, retrieved 10 February 2018 from http://www.canneslionsarchive.com/Home/PublicHome

Belch, G.E. and Belch, M.A. (2013) A content analysis study of the use of celebrity endorsers in magazine advertising, *International Journal of Advertising*, 32(3), 369–89.

Belk, R. (1988) Possessions and the extended self, *Journal of Consumer Research*, 15, 2 (September), 139–68.

Benjamin, K. (2016) Event TV: Pandora delivers Christmas delights, *Campaign*, 21 December, retrieved 10 January 2018 from https://www.campaignlive.co.uk/ event-tv-pandora-delivers-christmas-delights/%7Bsubjects%7D/article/1419437

Berry, L.L. (1980) Services marketing is different, *Business*, May/June, 24–9.

Beverland, M., Napoli, J. and Yakimova, R. (2007) Branding the business marketing offer: exploring brand attributes in business markets, *Journal of Business and Industrial Marketing*, 22(6), 394–9.

Biel, A. (1997) Discovering brand magic: the hardness of the softer side of branding, *International Journal of Advertising*, 16, 199–210.

Bizzi, L. (2018) The hidden problem of Facebook and social media at work: what if employees start searching for other jobs? *Business Horizons*, 61(1), 23–33.

Blackston, M. (1993) A brand with an attitude: a suitable case for treatment, *Journal of the Market Research Society*, 34(3), 231–41.

Brakus, J.J., Schmitt, B.H. and Zarantonello, L. (2009) Brand experience: what is it? How is it measured? Does it affect loyalty? *Journal of Marketing*, 73 (May), 52–68.

Brodie, R.J. and de Chernatony, L. (2009) Towards new conceptualizations of branding: theories of the middle range, *Marketing Theory*, 9(1), 95–100.

Buil, I., de Chernatony, L. and Martinez, E. (2008) A cross-national validation of the consumer-based brand equity scale, *Journal of Product and Brand Management*, 17(6), 384–92.

Cheetos Museum (2017) Cannes Archive, retrieved 10 February 2018 from http://www. canneslionsarchive.com/Home/PublicHome

Christodoulides, G., de Chernatony, L., Furrer, O., Shiu, E. and Abimbola, T. (2006) Conceptualising and measuring the equity of online brands, *Journal of Marketing Management*, 22, 799–825.

Cohen, R.J. (2014) Brand personification: introduction and overview, *Psychology and Marketing*, 31(1), 1–30.

Cooper, A. and Simmons, P. (1997) Brand equity lifestage: an entrepreneurial revolution, TBWA Simmons Palmer, Unpublished working paper.

Davies, G., Rojas-Méndez, J.I., Whelan, S., Mete, M., and Loo, T. (2018) Brand personality: theory and dimensionality, *Journal of Product & Brand Management*, 27(2), 115–27.

de Chernatony, L. (2009) Towards the holy grail of defining 'brand', *Marketing Theory*, 9(1), 101–5.

de Chernatony, L. and Dall'Olmo Riley, F. (1998a) Defining a brand: beyond the literature with experts' interpretations, *Journal of Marketing Management*, 14, 417–43.

de Chernatony, L. and Dall'Olmo Riley, F. (1998b) Expert practitioners' views on roles of brands: implications for marketing communications, *Journal of Marketing Communications*, 4, 87–100.

de Lencastre, P. and Côrte-Real, A. (2010) One, two, three: a practical brand anatomy, *Brand Management*, 17(6), 399–412.

Dwivedi, A., and McDonald, R. (2018) Building brand authenticity in fast-moving consumer goods via consumer perceptions of brand marketing communications, *European Journal of Marketing*, 52(7/8), 1387–411.

Edinger-Schons, L.M., Lengler-Graiff, L., Scheidler, S. and Wieseke, J. (2018) Frontline employees as corporate social responsibility (CSR) ambassadors: a quasi-field experiment. *Journal of Business Ethics*, 1–15.

Ehrenberg, A.S.C. (1974) Repetitive advertising and the consumer, *Journal of Advertising Research*, 14 (April), 25–34.

Elsäßer, M., and Wirtz, B.W. (2017) Rational and emotional factors of customer satisfaction and brand loyalty in a business-to-business setting, *Journal of Business & Industrial Marketing*, 32(1), 138–52.

Farhana, M. (2014) Implication of brand identity facets on marketing communications of lifestyle magazine: case study of a Swedish brand, *Journal of Applied Economics and Business Research*, 4(1), 23–41.

Farquahar, P. (1989) Managing brand equity, *Marketing Research*, 1(9), 24–33.

Farr, A. (2006) Soft measure, hard cash, *Admap*, November, 39–42.

Feldwick, P. (1996) What is brand equity anyway, and how do you measure it? *Journal of Market Research*, 38(2), 85–104.

Foreman, S.K. and Money, A.H. (1995) Internal marketing: concepts, measurements and application, *Journal of Marketing Management*, 11, 755–68.

Fournier, S. (1995) A consumer–brand relationship perspective on brand equity, presentation to Marketing Science Conference on Brand Equity and the Marketing Mix, Tucson, Arizona, 2–3 March, Working paper 111, 13–16.

Fournier, S. (1998) Consumers and their brands: developing relationship theory in consumer research, *Journal of Consumer Research*, 24(4), 343–73.

Frederick, D. (2017) Instagram trend sparks idea for Cheetos Museum. *PR Week*, 30 June, retrieved 10 March 2018 from https://www.prweek.com/article/1438231/instagram-trend-sparks-idea-cheetos-museum

Gelb, B.D. and Rangarajan, D. (2014) Employee contributions to brand equity, *California Management Review*, 56(2), 95–112.

Grossman, R. (2005) Sometimes it pays to play the fool, *Business Communicator*, 6, 3.

Haigh, D. (1997) Brand valuation: the best thing to ever happen to market research, *Admap*, June, 32–5.

Hardaker, S. and Fill, C. (2005) Corporate service brands: the intellectual and emotional engagement of employees, *Corporate Reputation Review: an International Journal*, 8(1), 365–76.

Hiscock, J. (2002) The brand insiders, *Marketing*, 23 May, 24–5.

Holbrook, M.B. (1992) Product quality, attributes, and brand name as determinants of price: the case of consumer electronics, *Marketing Letter*, 3(1), 71–83.

Holt, D. (2016) Branding in the age of social media, *Harvard Business Review*, 94(3), 40–50.

Hynes, F. (2014) NEWS: top 20 most valuable B2B brands in world revealed, *B2B Marketing*, 16 September, retrieved 28 September from www.b2bmarketing.net/news/archive/news-top-20-most-valuable-b2b-brands-world-revealed

Joseph, S. (2014) Six lessons from the 2014 World Cup for marketers, *Marketing Week*, 14 July, retrieved 22 September 2014 from https://www.marketingweek.com/2014/07/14/six-lessons-from-the-2014-world-cup-for-marketers/

Kamakura, W.A. and Russell, G.J. (1993) Measuring brand value with scanner data, *International Journal of Research in Marketing*, 10(1), 9–22.

Kapferer, J.-N. (2012) *The New Strategic Brand Management*, London: Kogan Page.

Keller, K.L. (1993) Conceptualizing, measuring, and managing customer-based brand equity, *Journal of Marketing*, 57(1), 1–22.

Keller, K.L. (1998) *Strategic Brand Management: Building, Measuring, and Managing Brand Equity*, Upper Saddle River, NJ: Prentice Hall.

Keller, K.L. (2008) *Strategic Brand Management: Building, Measuring, and Managing Brand Equity*, Englewood Cliffs, NJ: Pearson Education.

Keller, K.L. (2009) Building strong brands in a modern marketing communications environment, *Journal of Marketing Communications*, 15(2–3), 139–55.

Keller, K.L., and Richey, K. (2017) The importance of corporate brand personality traits to a successful 21st century business, in *Advances in Corporate Branding* (eds J.M.T. Balmer, S. Powell, J. Kernstock and T.O. Brexendorf), London: Palgrave Macmillan, 47–58.

Kotler, P. (2000) *Marketing Management: The Millennium Edition*, Upper Saddle River, NJ: Prentice Hall.

Lasser, W., Mittal, B. and Sharma, A. (1995) Measuring customer based brand equity, *Journal of Consumer Marketing*, 12(4), 11–19.

Linville, P. and Carlston, D.E. (1994) Social cognition of the self, in *Social Cognition: Impact on Social Psychology* (eds P.G. Devine, D.L. Hamilton and T.M. Ostrom), San Diego, CA: Academic Press, 143–93.

Maio Mackay, M. (2001) Evaluation of brand equity measures: further empirical results, *Journal of Product & Brand Management*, 10(1), 38–51.

McCraken, G. (1986) Culture and consumption: a theoretical account of the structure and movement of the cultural meaning of consumer goods, *Journal of Consumer Research*, 13 (June), 71–84.

McLuhan, M. (1964) *Understanding Media: The Extensions of Man*, New York: Mentor.

Millward Brown (2018). Discovering your brand's meaningful difference, retrieved 30 November 2018 from https://www.millwardbrown.com/solutions/slick-sheets/millwardbrown_branddynamics.aspx

Mirzaei, A., Gray, D. and Baumann, C. (2011) Developing a new model for tracking brand equity as a measure of marketing effectiveness, *The Marketing Review*, 11(4), 323–36.

Morgan, R.M. and Hunt, S.D. (1994) The commitment–trust theory of relationship marketing, *Journal of Marketing*, 58 (July), 20–38.

Muzellec, L., Lynn, T. and Lambkin, M. (2012) Branding in fictional and virtual environments: introducing a new conceptual domain and research agenda, *European Journal of Marketing*, 46(6), 811–26.

Nam, J., Ekinci, Y. and Whyatt, G. (2011) Brand equity, brand loyalty and consumer satisfaction, *Annals of Tourism Research*, 38(3), 1009–30.

Pappu, R., Quester, P.G. and Cooksey, R.W. (2005) Consumer-based brand equity: improving the measurement – empirical evidence, *Journal of Product and Brand Management*, 14(3), 143–54.

Park, C.S. and Srinivasan, V. (1994) A survey-based method for measuring and understanding brand equity and its extendibility, *Journal of Marketing Research*, 31(2), 271–88.

Perrey, J, Freundt, T, and Spillecke, D. (2015) The brand is back: staying relevant in an accelerating age, *McKinsey*, May, retrieved 10 January 2018 from https://www.mckinsey.com/business-functions/marketing-and-sales/our-insights/the-brand-is-back-staying-relevant-in-an-accelerating-age

Phau, I. and Lau, K.C. (2001) Brand personality and consumer self-expression: single or dual carriageway? *Journal of Brand Management*, 8(6), 428–44.

Pirrie, A. (2006) What value brands? *Admap*, October, 40–2.

Proctor, T. and Kitchen, P.J. (2018) Celebrity ambassador/celebrity endorsement–takes a licking but keeps on ticking, *Journal of Strategic Marketing*, 1–15.

Punjaisri, K. and Wilson, A. (2017) The role of internal branding in the delivery of employee brand promise, in *Advances in Corporate Branding* (eds J.M.T. Balmer, S. Powell, J. Kernstock and T.O. Brexendorf), London: Palgrave Macmillan, 91–108.

Punjaisri, K., Evanschitzky, H. and Wilson, A. (2009) Internal branding: an enabler of employees' brand-supporting behaviours, *Journal of Service Management*, 20(2), 209–26.

Rich, M. (1996) Stamp of approval, *Financial Times*, 29 February, 9.

Richards, T. (1997) Measuring the true value of brands, *Admap*, March, 32–6.

Riezebos, R. (2003) *Brand Management: A Theoretical and Practical Approach*, Harlow: Pearson.

Riley, F.D.O. (2016) Brand definitions and conceptualizations: the debate, in *The Routledge Companion to Contemporary Brand Management* (eds F. Dall'Olmo Riley, J. Singh and C. Blankson), Abingdon: Routledge, 35–44.

Romero, V. (2017) Notes from #WebSummit: the secrets behind the Lego brand, *WebSummit*, 9 November, retrieved 5 May 2018 from https://medium.com/web-summelier/the-secrets-behind-the-lego-brand-fc936daea33

Saunders, L. (2017) Examining Lego's social success (and how it boosts ROI). *econsultancy*, 21 November, retrieved 10 January 2018 from https://econsultancy.com/blog/69592-examining-lego-s-social-success-and-how-it-boosts-roi

Schmitt, B.H. (1999) *Experiential Marketing: How to Get Customers to Sense, Feel, Think, Act, Relate to Your Company and Brands*, New York: Free Press.

Shankar, V., Azar, P. and Fuller, M. (2008) BRAN*EQT: a multicategory brand equity model and its application at Allstate, *Marketing Science*, 27(4), 567–84.

Simon, C.J. and Sullivan, M.W. (1993) The measurement and determination of brand equity: a financial approach, *Marketing Science*, 12(1), 28–52.

Srinivasan, V., Park, C.S. and Chang, D.R. (2005) An approach to the measurement, analysis, and prediction of brand equity and its sources, *Management Science*, 51(9), 1433–48.

Sriram, S., Balachander, S. and Kalwani, M.U. (2007) Monitoring the dynamics of brand equity using store-level data, *Journal of Marketing*, 71 (April), 61–78.

Tasci, A.D. (2018) Testing the cross-brand and cross-market validity of a consumer-based brand equity (CBBE) model for destination brands, *Tourism Management*, 65, 143–59.

Theurer, C.P., Tumasjan, A., Welpe, I.M. and Lievens, F. (2018) Employer branding: a brand equity-based literature review and research agenda, *International Journal of Management Reviews*, 20(1), 155–79.

Thompson, A.J., Martin, A.J., Gee, S. and Geurin, A.N. (2018) Building brand and fan relationships through social media, *Sport, Business and Management: An International Journal*, 8(3), 235–56.

Welch, M. and Jackson, P.R. (2007) Rethinking internal communications: a stakeholder approach, *Corporate Communications: An International Journal*, 12(2), 177–98.

White, C., Vanc, A. and Stafford, G. (2010) Internal communications, information satisfaction, and sense of community: the effect of personal influence, *Journal of Public Relations Research*, 22(1), 65–84.

Yoo, B. and Donthu, N. (2001) Developing and validating a multidimensional consumer-based brand equity scale, *Journal of Business Research*, 52(1), 1–14.

Integrated marketing communications

The principle of integrated marketing communications (IMC) has widespread support among practitioners and academics. The subject, however, remains controversial as it remains theoretically under-developed, empirically unproven and is used inconsistently.

Is IMC just a matter of rhetoric or does it deliver enhanced engagement opportunities and cut through?

Aims and learning objectives

The aims of this chapter are to explore the nature and characteristics of integrated marketing communications and to understand the complexities associated with developing and implementing IMC.

The learning objectives are to enable readers to:

1. appreciate the development and the various reasons for interest in IMC;
2. explain the conceptual background associated with IMC;
3. consider which elements should or need to be integrated;
4. examine how definitions of IMC have evolved;
5. discuss different interpretations of the IMC concept.

Introduction

The development of the integrated marketing communications concept (IMC) in the early 1990s represented a major step change for the industry. Up until that point the various tools, media and disciplines that make up the marketing communications industry tended to work in isolation, sometimes referred to as silos. The disruption caused by IMC stimulated changes in the way consumers were considered and the industry structured.

Much of the early IMC academic activity was led by Schultz et al. (1993) and Duncan and Everett (1993). This was at a time when organisations were beginning to see how ideas about integration could assist them to deliver messages more consistently and also enable them to restructure internally and reduce communications wastage and costs. These early ideas were driven by agencies such as Ogilvy who claimed they delivered 'Ogilvy Orchestration', whereas Young and Rubicam talked about their integration facility as the 'Whole Egg' (Keller, 2016). The essential underlying reason for the emergence of IMC was the appreciation that stakeholder relationships could be managed more effectively by using an array of communications tools, media and messages (Foroudi et al., 2017).

The next phase was characterised by an exploration of the nature, direction and content typified by definitions that introduced management, strategy and brand development into the IMC process. Shimp (2000), among others, supported the explicit introduction of these aspects to IMC. This approach often manifested itself as communications reinforcement, or saying the same thing in different ways (Keller, 2016).

The next step moved the IMC concept towards an audience- or customer-driven process, one that incorporates ideas concerning relationship marketing. Duncan and Mulhern (2004), cited by Reid (2005) and Grönroos (2004), have provided valuable insights into this dimension of IMC, one which Kitchen et al. (2004) refer to as the *outside-in* approach to IMC.

The wave of IMC enthusiasm was not entirely universal as authors such as Cornelissen and Lock (2000), Percy et al. (2001) and Spotts et al. (1998), to name but a few, have been critical of the concept and have doubted the merits inherent in the notion. This dichotomy of views revealed an inherent instability in the IMC concept, and the dearth of empirical research.

As part of his critique Cornelissen (2003) stated that IMC was a not a proven marketing theory, and as a concept was worthy of only symbolic value. This view was later refuted by Kitchen. It could be argued that nothing of real significance has developed to change that position. Luxton et al. (2015) refer to the large amount of conceptual work that has been undertaken around IMC but state that there has been little work to demonstrate the value of IMC to brands. Batra and Keller (2016) continue the conceptual approach although they call for empirical work to ground their bottom-up and top-down IMC models.

Kliatchko and Schultz (2014: 380) found that in practice the use of IMC as a marketing framework is limited. Terms such as 'fusion marketing', 'insight-driven marketing', 'holistic marketing', 'marketing as customer experience' and 'integrated business planning' are more common.

Unsurprisingly, therefore, there is no absolute agreement about what IMC is, what it encompasses or how it should be measured. Indeed, there is no universally agreed definition and, apart from some anecdotal comment, there is little practical evidence of the application of a strategic, customer-oriented IMC programme. There are numerous claims of IMC practice but these are little more than coordinated communications mix activities using themed messages (inside-out).

Readers interested in a fuller appraisal of IMC are referred to Batra and Keller (2016), Kliatchko and Schultz (2014) and Kitchen et al. (2004).

A strategic view

The strategic integration view suggests that IMC is more than simply the coordination of different marketing messages and channels, and that IMC needs to be embedded throughout a business or organisation, as a strategic driver of elements such as product and service attributes. Fuchs et al. (2000: 124) argue that IMC comprises an organisation's direction, product/market focus, resources, operational capabilities and organisational culture.

This view is reinforced more recently by Kerr and Patti (2013: 2) who state that strategic integration 'is the defining construct of IMC'.

Eagle et al. (2007: 961) propose six perspectives of IMC as follows:

1. coordination of communications disciplines;
2. a way to organise the business or firm;
3. a way to develop and direct brand strategy;
4. a way to deliver unified messages;
5. coordination of advertising and PR programmes; and
6. a strategic brand business process.

The principle underpinning these six perspectives is that they all reflect strategic integration.

Luxton et al. (2015) present the results of their empirical work in which they claim 'a firm's IMC capability contributes to brand performance by facilitating the development and implementation of more effective IMC campaigns resulting in positive brand-related market performance outcomes' (p. 43). In other words the emphasis is on building the strategic capability or infrastructure to enable successful IMC campaigns over the longer term.

Scholars' paper 12.1

IMC – meaning and practice

Keller, K.L. (2016) unlocking the power of integrated marketing communications: how integrated is your IMC program? *Journal of Advertising,* 45(3), 286–301.

Keller has written several interesting and helpful papers about IMC, and branding. This one considers seven IMC choice criteria that are designed to help marketers make a judgement about the effectiveness of their IMC programmes. These 7 'Cs' are founded on an understanding of how consumers make brand decisions and the different effects that the growing number of communications opportunities might have on consumers.

See also:

Kliatchko, J.G. and Schultz, D.E. (2014) Twenty years of IMC, *International Journal of Advertising,* 33(2), 373–90.

Cornelissen, J.P. (2003) Change, continuity and progress: the concept of integrated marketing communications and marketing communications practice, *Journal of Strategic Marketing,* 11 (December), 217–34.

The forces for IMC

The opportunities offered to organisations that contemplate moving to IMC are considerable and it is somewhat surprising that relatively few organisations have been either willing or able to embrace the full approach. The three main forces or drivers for IMC can be categorised as organisational, market and communication, see Figure 12.1.

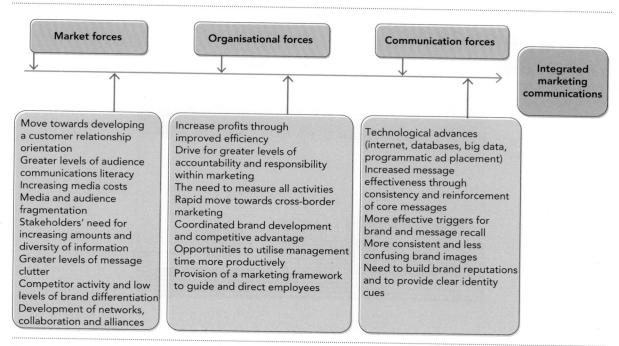

Figure 12.1 Forces driving organisations towards IMC

One of the main organisational drivers for IMC is the need to become increasingly efficient. Driving down the cost base enables managers to improve profits and levels of productivity. By seeking synergistic advantages through its communications and associated activities and by expecting managers to be able to account for the way in which they consume marketing communications resources, so IMC becomes increasingly attractive. At the same time, organisational structures are changing more frequently and the need to integrate across functional areas reflects a drive for efficiency.

From a market perspective, the predominant driver is the reorientation from transaction based marketing to relationship marketing. The fundamental principle is to turn clients who are essentially distinterested in a brand, apart from any fleeting interest in a product or price, into supporters and loyal advocates who not only buy frequently but who also speak favourably about the brand whenever opportunities arise.

From a communications perspective, the key driver is to meet the changing ways in which audiences use communications. This can be through the devices they use, their communication behaviours, or their shortening attention spans (see Chapter 5). The goal is to provide a series of triggers to enable buyers to form brand associations, understand a brand's values and consider the extent to which a brand might become or continue to be a part of their lives, however peripheral. By differentiating the marketing communications, often by providing clarity and simplicity, advantages can be attained.

An integrated approach should, at some level, attempt to provide a thematically coherent or consistent set of messages. These should be relatively easy to interpret and to assign meaning. This enables audiences to think about and perceive brands within a relational context, and so encourage behaviour as expected by the source. Those organisations that try to practise IMC understand that buyers refer to and receive messages about brands and companies from a wide range of information sources. Harnessing this knowledge is a fundamental step towards enhancing marketing communications.

Viewpoint 12.1
Burger integration

Image 12.1 Burger King made a peace offering to McDonald's

The McWhopper was a proposed mashup burger, to symbolise peace between Burger King and McDonald's.
Source: idiltoffolo/Shutterstock.

Burger King was in danger of being repositioned by other brands in the fast food category. Chipotle, in particular, were engaging young consumers with a message that echoed social responsibility, health and a shared purpose. The result was that Burger King was increasingly being sidelined as 'old fashioned'.

Burger King's response was to collaborate with Peace One Day. This is a global non-profit organisation, whose goal is to make United Nations Peace Day an annual day of non-violence and global unity. The goal of the collaboration was to increase brand consideration for Burger King and raise awareness of Peace Day 2015.

The campaign centred on an open, very public proposal to its arch competitor, McDonald's to make peace with Burger King. This was to be accomplished by a collaborative mash-up burger, combining key ingredients from each restaurant's signature product, the Big Mac and the Whopper. It was to be called the McWhopper. It would be prepared and served from a pop-up store in Atlanta, midway between the two headquarters (Chicago and Miami), on one day only, United Nations Peace Day, 21 September 2015.

The range of tools and media used to communicate the proposal was extensive. An open letter was published using both print media and online, plus social media. The proposal used outdoor media whilst the mcwhopper.com site used a range of co-branded assets, including joint staff uniforms, signage and the pop-up restaurant. An image of the proposed McWhopper was used as a central symbol across the whole campaign.

McDonald's were not impressed and declined the invitation. This prompted consumers to start making their own 'Peace Day' burger mashups on social media. In addition, a group of smaller fast-food chains including Denny's, Krystal, Wayback Burgers and Giraffas took up Burger King's idea of a mash-up burger for World Peace Day.

The results included 8.9 billion media impressions, and earned media value was estimated to be $138 million. McWhopper became the number one trending topic on both Facebook and Twitter, and drew over 10,000 DIY McWhopper reviews on YouTube PEACE ONE DAY. It was reported that there was a 40 per cent increase in Peace Day awareness in the USA, and worldwide awareness of Peace Day increased over 16 per cent.

Sources: Anon (2015); Pollack (2016); Richards and Nudd (2016); Tylee (2017).

Insight

This was a short-lived campaign with integration enabled around a clear, single-minded proposition. The central idea of the McWhopper provided a means for all the other elements, including the tools, media, agencies and other elements of the marketing mix, to be integrated. The McWhopper became a unifying campaign symbol, encapsulating social issues as well as driving brand awareness.

Integration should not only improve efficiency but, more importantly, enable more effective engagement. It would appear that engagement was achieved with consumers and a range of other stakeholders, including the media.

Question: Why did McDonald's reject the proposal?

Task: Find another campaign and determine which elements have been integrated.

Definitions of IMC

Table 12.1 sets out various definitions of IMC. From Schultz et al.'s (1993) original to those used today, the table reveals how the term has evolved. In much the same way, the very diversity of the term 'integration' has been highlighted by the Institute of Practitioners in Advertising (IPA). Their research into what is meant by integration, as practised by clients and agencies, reveals several different interpretations, leading them to the conclusion that the term is ambiguous in practice.

In order to provide clarity and insight into the way integration is considered and practised, the IPA have analysed over 1,400 cases submitted to the IPA Effectiveness Awards. The IPA searched for a common definition of integration, but it became clear that just as the academic definitions had evolved, so had working practices also developed.

Table 12.1 Evolving definitions of IMC

Author	Definition
Schultz, Tannenbaum and Lauterborn (1993)	A concept of marketing communications planning that recognises the added value of a comprehensive plan that evaluates the strategic role of a variety of communication disciplines (such as advertising, direct response, sales promotion, etc.) and combines them to provide clarity, consistency and maximum communication impact.
Duncan and Moriarty (1998)	A cross-functional process for creating and nourishing profitable relationships with customers and other stakeholders by strategically controlling or influencing all messages sent to these groups and encouraging purposeful dialogue with them.
Keller (2001)	Involves the development, implementation, and evaluation of marketing communications programmes using multiple communication options, where the design and execution of any communication option reflects the nature and content of other communication options that also make up the communication programme.
Kliatchko (2005)	The concept and process of strategically managing audience-focused, channel-centred and results-driven brand communication programmes over time.

(continued)

Table 12.1   Evolving definitions of IMC (*Continued*)

Author	Definition
Porcu et al. (2012)	The interactive and systemic process of cross-functional planning and optimisation of messages to stakeholders with the aim of communicating with coherence and transparency to achieve synergies and encourage profitable relationships in the short, medium and long-term.
Serić et al. (2015)	A tactical and strategic consumer-centric business process, boosted by advances in information and communication technology (ICT) which, on the basis of information obtained from customers' databases, delivers a clear and consistent message through the coordination and synergies of different communications tools and channels, in order to nourish long-lasting profitable relationships with customers and other stakeholders, and create and maintain brand equity.
Batra and Keller (2016)	The coordinated, consistent means by which firms attempt to inform, incent, persuade and remind consumers – directly or indirectly – about the products and brands they sell.
Melewar et al. (2017)	The strategic coordination of all the company's messages as well as the media used by an organisation to impact on the company's perceived value.

What is to be integrated?

The notion that some aspects of marketing communications should be integrated begs two questions. First, what is it that needs to be integrated, and, second, what are the means by which integration is achieved, in order that it can be recognised and measured?

While the origins of IMC might be found in the prevailing structural conditions and the needs of particular industry participants, an understanding of which elements should be integrated in order to achieve IMC needs to be considered. The problem with answering this question is that unless there is an agreement about what IMC is, then identifying appropriate elements is far from easy, practical or in anyone's best interests. Figure 12.2 shows some of the elements that need integrating.

The following represents some of the fundamental elements, but readers are advised to consider some of the other issues that have been raised in this chapter before confirming their views about this stimulating concept.

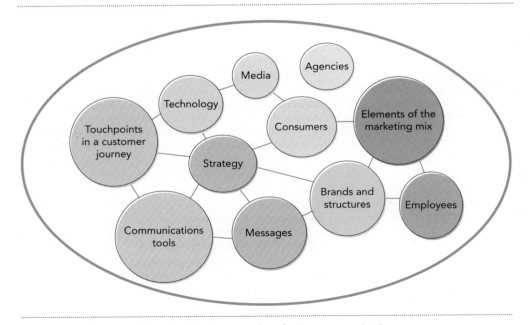

Figure 12.2 Elements that comprise integrated marketing communications

Communications tools or disciplines

One of the early and more popular views of IMC was that the messages conveyed by each of the 'promotional' tools should be harmonised in order that audiences perceive a consistent set of meanings within the messages they receive. One interpretation of this perspective is that the key visual triggers (design, colours, form and tag line) used in advertising should be replicated across the range of tools used, including POP and the sales force. At another level, integration is about bringing together the communications tools (Pitta et al., 2006). One such combination is the closer alliance of advertising with public relations. Increasing audience fragmentation means that it is more difficult to locate target audiences and communicate with them in a meaningful way. By utilising the power of public relations to get advertisements talked about, what the trade refers to as media equivalents, a form of communications consistency, or integration to some, becomes possible.

The use of direct marketing approaches has helped organisations to bring together the different tools such that they undertake more precise roles and reinforce each other. For example, the use of direct mail and telemarketing to follow through on an ad campaign was commonplace. Now web-based communications facilitate the linking together of customer care centres and sales promotions, through database applications, so that the same core message is conveyed.

Messages

A deeper perspective holds that the theme and set of core messages used in any campaign should first be determined and then deployed as an integrated whole across the communications mix (sometimes referred to as *synergy*). One of the differences is the recognition that mass-media advertising is not always the only way to launch consumer or business-to-business promotional activities, and that a consideration of the most appropriate mix of communications tools and media might be a better starting point when formulating campaigns.

Another perspective of IMC, provided by Duncan and Moriarty (1998), is that stakeholders (including customers) automatically integrate brand messages. This suggests that as long as the gaps between the different messages (in content and meaning) are acceptable, then management's task is to manage the process and seek to narrow any gaps that may be perceived.

What runs through both these approaches is the belief that all brand-related communications need to be moulded into one cohesive bundle, from which elements can be selected and deployed as conditions require.

Media

Integrating the media used within a campaign has been regarded as a foundation block of IMC. Indeed, early ideas about IMC were focused on the way different media, or channels as practitioners refer to them, could be synchronised in order to emphasise and amplify messages.

In the early part of the twenty-first century, media-neutral planning (MNP) emerged as one of the first attempts to require campaigns to use a more balanced mix of media. The traditional approach used a primary medium, very often television, and perhaps two or three secondary media, scheduled over a five-week campaign. The changing media landscape, the increasing penetration of new interactive technologies and new consumer behaviours mean that this approach is largely redundant, and a more contemporary mix has developed. At a general level this uses television not as an anchor but only where there is a specific role to build brand fame or associations over the longer term. An array of other media are used where a short-term direct response is the goal. There are no longer references to primary and secondary media. Instead there is a greater orientation to cross-media planning, where media particular to an audience is employed.

Some major client organisations (e.g. Mondelēz International, Kellogg's, Unilever and Procter & Gamble) have reduced their reliance on television over the past 10 years and have steadily increased their use of 'digital' or interactive media and other approaches.

Their goal has been to reduce costs and deliver consistent messages in an attempt to cut through the increasing clutter. It is interesting to note that in 2017 Procter & Gamble announced that they were no longer going to invest in digital communications at the same rate of increase as they had previously. This reflects their concern about transparency issues, advertising waste (too much staff and agency time devoted to advertising, plus viewability issues) and the fact that when they cut £100 million from their digital advertising, sales actually increased (Neff, 2017; Tesseras, 2017).

The role and nature of the media within marketing communications is explored in Chapters 20, 21, and 22.

Touchpoints

Associated with the media is the term 'touchpoints'. This has become a part of the marketing practitioners' lexicon. A touchpoint is any facility that enables a person to interact with a brand. This may occur through person-to-person interaction, through a website, an app or any form of marketing communications.

It makes sense therefore, to manage the specific touchpoints prospective customers are likely to encounter during the pre-purchase, purchase and post-purchase phases of a customer journey. Each touchpoint represents an opportunity not only to influence a person's journey to purchase, by providing information and appropriate emotional content, but also to give people a brand experience (Pantano and Viassone, 2015), which may be positive or negative. A touchpoint provides for continuing engagement through each stage of the purchase journey, and in doing so increases the likelihood of purchase.

To accomplish IMC it appears that the identification of suitable touchpoints within a purchase journey is a fundamental prerequisite. See Viewpoint 12.2 for an example of the use of touchpoints. For more information about purchase journeys see Chapter 4.

Viewpoint 12.2

Colgate use touchpoints to achieve an instant smile

Image 12.2 Colgate's Luminous White brand

The launch of Colgate's Luminous White brand was aimed at new and younger users
Source: Iakov Filimonov/Shutterstock.

Major brands are fully aware of the need to understand the purchase journeys undertaken by their consumers. As a result, they invest in research and use detailed consumer insights and knowledge of their market and competitors to develop and implement IMC programmes. These campaigns are based upon an understanding of each marketing communications touchpoint and how these interrelate within a customer journey.

When Colgate launched their Luminous White brand in Latin America, their goal was to grow market share by attracting new and younger users with the promise of 'instant white teeth'. This was to be achieved through two strategies. The first was to use the insight that a white smile is a must in today's world of social media. The second was to maintain a fashion/beauty platform to keep the sub-brand contemporary.

Colgate executed the idea that 'a white smile so instant, it makes everything else seem time-consuming', by demonstrating that tasks such as choosing the right dress to wear, or taking the perfect 'selfie' for use in social media now take 'longer than whitening your teeth' (with Colgate). This message was developed through 'tried and tested' media such as television and print, a website and online banner ads. They also activated the idea through touchpoints in social media and event marketing. Colgate also plotted the likely purchase journey and created engagement opportunities through further touchpoints at 'bus shelters, posters and outdoor billboards near stores; printed flyers; retailer e-commerce sites; window signage at stores; and multiple executions in stores such as pallet displays, end-of-aisle displays, on-shelf trays and counter displays' (p. 270).

Insight

Colgate plotted the purchase journey that their target audience would most likely take on the path to purchasing Luminous White Instant. This enabled Colgate marketers to highlight potential touchpoints and use these to communicate and engage with the target audience as they moved towards purchasing the brand. By linking touchpoints and messages at different stages of the purchase journey Colgate created an integrated programme.

Question: To what extent might the touchpoints used by customers in the same segment be so similar that all brands use the same configuration for the segment purchase?

Task: Think of a purchase journey you have undertaken, or are about to embark on, and plot the likely touchpoints.

Marketing mix

The elements of the marketing mix, however configured, also need to be integrated because they too communicate (Smith, 1996). The price and associated values, the product, in terms of the quality, design and tangible attributes, the manner and efficiency of the service delivery, and where and how it is made available, for example the location, website, customer contact centres, retailer/dealer reputation and overall service quality, need to be perceived by customers as coordinated and consistent.

These touchpoints with brands are aspects of a consumer's brand experience and are used to develop images that through time may shape brand reputations. Traditionally the marketing mix was expected to deliver the brand proposition. Now it is expected that all these elements will be coordinated to maximise impact and enable customers to experience the brand through pre-, actual and post-product use.

Brands and structures

Brands are themselves a form of integration. This means that organisations need to be sufficiently coordinated internally so that a brand can be perceived externally as consistent and uniform. As brands need to appeal to a number of different audiences (White, 2000), it is necessary to develop brands that appeal to diverse consumer groups. White refers to these new brands as 'chameleon' brands. They are characterised by their ability to adapt to different situations (audiences and media) yet retain a core proposition that provides a form of continuity and recognition. For example, a top-of-the-range speaker system may be seen by the owner as prestigious and technically superb, by a guest at a party as ostentatiously outrageous and overpriced, and by a friend as a product of clever design and marketing. All three might have developed their attitudes through different sources (e.g. social media, print, exhibitions, websites, online and offline retail stores, word of mouth) but all agree that the brand has a common set of values and associations that are important to each of them.

The presentation of chameleon brands requires high levels of integration, a need to develop a series of innovative messages based around a core proposition. The use of a single ad execution needs to be replaced by multiple executions delivered through a variety of media, each complementing and reinforcing the core brand proposition. This means that the audience is more likely to be surprised or reminded of the brand (and its essence) through a series of refreshingly interesting messages, thereby raising the probability that 'likeability' (see Chapter 10) will be strengthened, along with the brand and all relevant associations.

Many organisational structures have developed around a brand hierarchy. IMC can encourage new portfolios and with that different brand structures that bring various communication disciplines together in a single body or unit. By creating a single department out of which brand communications operate, cross-functional coordination between the disciplines is enabled.

Strategy

IMC is regarded by some as a means of using the communications mix in a more efficient and synergistic manner. At some level this can be true, but IMC requires a deeper understanding of how and where messages are created. At a strategic level, IMC has its roots in the overall business strategy of an organisation. Using Porter's (1980) generic strategies, if a low-cost strategy (e.g. Lidl) is being pursued, it makes sense to complement the strategy by using messages that either stress any price advantage that customers might benefit from or at least do not suggest extravagance or luxury. If using a differentiation focus strategy (e.g. Waitrose), price should not figure in any of the messages and greater emphasis should be placed on particular attributes and associations that convey added value and enable clear positioning. There is no right way (or formula) to establish IMC but there is a need to recognise that it has a strategic orientation and outputs.

Integration can be considered to be a core element of marketing communications planning as it can add value and deliver consistency, clarity and maximum communications impact (Melewar et al., 2017). Interestingly, these authors refer to IMC in the context of an organisation's overall strategy, identity and its relationships with various stakeholders. They assume a holistic perspective of IMC and reinforce the view that the perceived value of an organisation/brand can be influenced through the strategic management of messages and the media employed by an organisation. Specifically, they find 'that consumer attitudes towards a brand identity may be enhanced by pursuing a strategy that consistently integrates messages across controlled communication' (p. 586).

Employees

It is generally agreed that all customer-facing employees should adopt a customer focus and 'live' the brand. While this can be achieved partially through the use of training courses and documentation, it usually requires a change of culture and that means a longer-term period of readjustment and the adoption of new techniques, procedures and ways of thinking and behaving.

Image 12.3 IMC works more effectively when employees reinforce a brand's values
Source: Zoonar GmbH/Alamy Stock Photo.

Once the internal reorientation has begun (not completed), it is possible to take a message to external audiences. As long as they can see that employees are attempting to care about them as customers and do know what they are talking about in support of the products and services offered, then it is likely that customers (and other stakeholders) will be supportive. IMC should be concerned with the blend of internal and external messages so that there is clarity, consistency and reinforcement of an organisation's (or brand's) core proposition.

Technology

The use of technology, and in particular database technologies, has enabled marketing managers to have an improved view of customer behaviour, attitudes and feelings towards their brands. This has allowed more precise and insightful communications to be generated, and the subsequent feedback and measurement facilities have served to enrich the overall quality of customer communications.

The mere presence of technology, however, does not result in effective marketing communications. Technology needs to be integrated into not just the overall information systems strategy but also the marketing strategies of organisations. The recent surge of organisations using social media and mobile technologies provides clear evidence.

Technology is an enabler and to use it effectively requires integration. The effective use of technology can touch a number of areas within the IMC orbit. For example, technology can be used to develop effective websites, extranets and intranets, customer contact centres, databases, campaigns, fulfilment processes, CRM and sales force automation. If each of these applications is deployed independently of the others their impact will be limited. Developed within an integrated framework, the potential for effective marketing and customer service can be tremendous.

Agencies

Agencies play a critical role in marketing communications and IMC cannot be accomplished without the explicit involvement of all those working on the supply side. Agencies, however, complain that too many clients provide briefs that specify particular channels, rather than adopt open planning, which enables the development of integrated communications strategies (Bacon, 2017).

On the other hand, clients question the level of expertise that a single agency might have access to in order to deliver IMC. This is countered by the argument that agencies are a part of a wide network such as WPP and Dentsu, within which there is the expertise for a truly integrated campaign.

Apart from questions concerning the range of promotional services offered by individual agencies and whether these are all delivered by a single agency or through a network of interacting agencies, three particular issues arise: implementation, leadership and other remuneration.

Implementation

The implementation of IMC programmes, by agencies, has proved to be challenging. Most major brands operate with several agencies, each providing different skills. These are known as 'roster agencies' simply because different agencies can be brought into different campaigns to provide support when necessary. Unilever encourages its local teams to adopt its preferred agencies through the use of an internal website called The Agency List (Gwynn, 2017).

One problem facing clients seeking to implement an integrative programme is how best to manage an integrative approach. One way is to appoint a lead agency that assumes responsibility for integration. Another way is for the client to drive the programme forward and to involve the roster agencies. However, many client organisations appoint a lead agency and very often it is the generalist ad agency that is appointed.

Research by Mortimer and Laurie (2017) identified three main obstacles to the effective implementation of IMC. The first concerns the difficulty some clients have understanding IMC, which can lead to risk-avoiding behaviours, such as not attempting IMC. The second reason concerns the structural and political issues regarding the lack of influence that some marketing departments have over other parts of the organisation. The third and final reason refers to the absence of a clear role for agencies in the implementation of IMC.

Roles

This lack of a clear role relates to another issue concerning leadership, and whether an agency or the client should lead the implementation of IMC. The consensus appears to be that this is the client's role (Swain, 2004), mainly because clients are better positioned to make integration happen across their own organisation. However, Swain then points out that there is no agreement about who in the client organisation should be responsible for implementing IMC. Indeed, Kitchen et al. (2007) confirm the reluctance of both advertising and public relations agencies to provide for integrative working practices.

Remuneration

Remuneration has always been a contentious subject, and as a move to IMC requires a change in agency performance measures, it follows that a change in their method of remuneration is considered necessary. Closer integration of agencies within an IMC process will, among other things, bring changes in structure, operations, performance measures, remuneration and new responsibilities within the client relationship.

This list of elements that need to be integrated is not exclusive. There are other influences that are particular to individual organisations that could have been included. However, consideration of these various elements suggests strongly that what is being integrated is far more than just the tools, media and messages of the communications mix. Indeed, viewed holistically, integration is a strategic concept that strikes at the heart of an organisation's marketing and business orientation.

We see later in this chapter that at one level integration might be considered in terms of the frequency and consistency with which logos, colours and other identification marks are used across all elements of a campaign. This provides a relatively easy means to identify and measure integration. It can be argued, however, that the mere provision of identification marks does not make for a truly integrated campaign, and there is a lack of any real customer orientation.

Scholars' paper 12.2

Integration to drive trust, loyalty and commitment

Melewar, T.C., Foroudi, P., Gupta, S., Kitchen, P.J. and Foroudi, M.M. (2017) Integrating identity, strategy and communications for trust, loyalty and commitment, *European Journal of Marketing*, 51(3), 572–604.

Part of a special issue on integrated marketing communications, this paper considers the impact of IMC within the context of an organisation's overall strategy and its controlled and uncontrolled communications. The aim is to evaluate the potential of IMC to create trust and loyalty.

See also:

Mortimer, K. and Laurie, S. (2017) The internal and external challenges facing clients in implementing IMC, *European Journal of Marketing*, 51(3), 511–27.

Building IMC programmes

Having tried to define what IMC is and is not, and having considered the elements that might need to be integrated the next step is to explore ways in which these elements might be linked together in order to drive an integrative campaign. Some might argue that the quality of an integrated campaign can be seen in the achievement of the objectives. The outcomes, however, could have been achieved without any integration so other facets need to be considered.

By definition integrated campaigns consist of several tools, messages, and media. The way in which these elements of the communications mix are blended and the quality of the transition through the length of a campaign will impact on the quality of campaign integration. For example, the campaign used to launch Sensodyne Pronamel in the UK (a toothpaste brand) was in two phases. The first was designed to raise awareness of the issue of 'acid wear', and the second was to reveal the relevance of the issue to consumers. Across both phases dentists were involved in the campaign, either actively or passively, and this scheduling, combined with astute timing of the various components, enabled what some might argue to be an integrated campaign.

Research into IMC practice in Asia by Kliatchko and Schultz (2014: 382) found three key features of IMC practice that were common to both agency and client respondents:

1. use of multiple media in planning and delivering marketing communications messages;
2. primacy of consumer understanding as the kernel of marketing communications planning and execution;
3. use of proprietary frameworks or processes for IMC planning, including measurement tools, by both clients and agencies.

This is interesting because there appears to be no reference to the use of multiple tools or the role of the media, nor is there mention of the importance of the message within IMC.

The development of IMC programmes needs to be linked with the underlying activity that they are designed to influence, namely customer behaviour. This involves understanding the journey that customers undertake and ensuring that the campaign integrates a brand's full range of consumer touchpoints in order to achieve two principal outcomes. First, the generation of short-term purchases and second, to build long-term loyalty and brand value.

Viewpoint 12.3

Volvo apply integrative criteria

Image 12.4 Volvo have adopted a safety positioning for many years.
Source: Zety Akhzar/Shutterstock.

Car manufacturer Volvo have adopted and maintained safety as a core positioning element for a considerable period. They use print and TV ads, PR and corporate communications to communicate the 'safety superiority' message in a consistent manner. In addition, the message is conveyed through the company's website and other digital and interactive formats. Sponsorships with the American Trucking Associations are also used to promote various key safety outreach programmes for the trucking industry. Learning about Volvo is encouraged by using the same persuasive message reinforced in different ways across different communications.

Each communication option is used to address different brand objectives, all of which are needed to persuade consumers, drive sales and build brand equity. For example, while sponsorships are designed to improve the brand's visibility and contemporary status, Volvo's involvement with golf, cultural events and even an ocean race serve to raise salience and brand consideration. Sales promotions and financing programmes are used to encourage safety-concerned consumers to take action. By using different communication options, each with their own varied strengths and weaknesses, consumers' brand-related information needs are more likely to be met through the complementary nature of the communication options.

The cross-effect of integration refers to the enhanced experience a consumer has of a particular message, should they have been exposed to a previous yet different form of communication. For example, Volvo's use of sponsorships and advertising messages helped develop positive feelings and awareness about the brand, and these served to heighten brand predispositions and impressions when consumers evaluated a Volvo vehicle at a later date.

Source: Batra and Keller (2016).

Insight

These communication activities can be considered to assist the integration process because they support consistency, complementarity and cross-effects, criteria as set out by Batra and Keller (2016).

Question: If safety is a concern for all car brands what other positioning might distinguish Volvo more effectively?

Task: Make a list of other brands that have tried to use safety as their positioning focus.

Earlier in this chapter, reference was made to touchpoints as an integral element in any IMC programme. Batra and Keller (2016) have developed this principle and have identified seven criteria necessary for an effective integrated marketing communications programme. A fully integrated programme should perform well on each of these seven criteria: coverage, cost, contribution, commonality, cross-effects, complementarity and conformability. These authors, having researched the academic literature on IMC, present an overall framework, which seeks to match different communication platforms with the different stages consumers pass through on their purchase journey. This is presented in Figure 12.3. Readers interested in this idea are referred to Scholars' paper 12.3.

Although this framework has yet to be tested empirically, it represents an important contribution to the academic literature on IMC. This is because it highlights the need to understand the different touchpoints experienced by consumers on their purchase journeys, and to then match these with particular communication platforms.

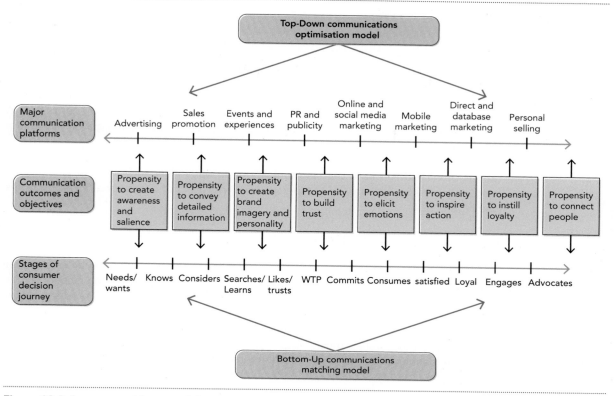

Figure 12.3 A conceptual framework for IMC
Source: Batra and Keller (2016). Used with the kind permission of the AMA.

Scholars' paper 12.3
Building better IMC programmes

Batra, R. and Keller, K.L. (2016) Integrating marketing communications: new findings, new lessons, and new ideas, *Journal of Marketing*, AMA/ MSI Special Issue, 80 (November), 122–45.

This is an important and accessible conceptual paper for readers interested in IMC. The authors offer advice concerning the ways in which traditional and new media (search, display, mobile, TV and social media) interact to affect consumer decision making. They then suggest ways in which an enhanced understanding of the consumer decision journey and how consumers process communications, might facilitate the development of more effective and efficient integrated marketing communication programmes. They outline a comprehensive framework featuring two models.

See also:

Kliatchko, J. (2008) Revisiting the IMC construct: a revised definition and four pillars, *International Journal of Advertising*, 27(1), 133–60.

Turner, P. (2017) Implementing integrated marketing communications (IMC) through major event ambassadors, *European Journal of Marketing*, 51(3), 605–26.

Interpretations of IMC

The lack of any agreement about how to define IMC is indicative of the debate, contradiction and perhaps vagueness of the concept. It is also reflective of an emerging concept, one that has had little chance to stabilise in the context of a rapidly changing media landscape and new forms of communications. Indeed, Kliatchko and Schultz (2014) found in their survey of senior marketing practitioners in the Asia Pacific area that the term 'IMC' is hardly used. Terms such as 'integrated thinking, integrated planning, integrated marketing, full service, 360 or simply integration' are much more common (p. 380).

Within these diverse views and perspectives of IMC, we now consider four interpretations of what IMC might be. Harmonisation, an early view and one that is still practised, followed by a review of the perspective, portfolio and relational interpretations (see Figure 12.4).

Interpretation 1: IMC as harmonisation

One of the early interpretations of IMC, indeed the leading view at the time, was that integration was a function of the harmonisation of the elements of communications. This involved communicating consistent messages through all forms of relevant media to target audiences. In this view, sometimes referred to rather dismissively as 'matching luggage', harmonisation represented a largely visual interpretation of IMC.

Typically brand colours, music, logos and straplines are placed and presented in a consistent manner across all media where the target audience encounters the brand. This content view aimed to achieve a 'one voice, one look' position. Despite being perceived as an advertising-led communications programme at this stage, other disciplines were incorporated into the process, so that sales promotion, public relations and, increasingly, direct marketing, all became part of the harmonised approach to IMC. Through harmonisation of all the elements of the marketing communications mix, the channels, as practitioners refer to them, represented the key integration factors. Schultz (1993: 17)

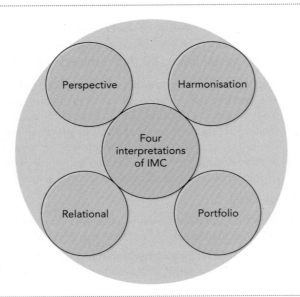

Figure 12.4 Four interpretations of IMC

refers to IMC as 'the process of developing and implementing various forms of persuasive communications programs with customers and prospects over time'. This customer-only perspective merely served to limit the scope, not only of IMC but of marketing communications as a whole.

Image 12.5 Budweiser's 'Bud Music 2017' campaign
Source: Budweiser.

A Budweiser campaign in China used multiple elements (celebrity, colour scheme, bottle, logo, slogans) across TV, online and outdoor executions. The campaign featured a popular singer and actor, Eason Chan, whose role was to position Budweiser as young, passionate and forward looking. What made this an example of matching luggage is that all the ads were linked together through the electronic music, colour, similar scenes in the ads, the message – 'this Bud's for you' and Eason Chan (Anon, 2017).

One of the issues, however, is that harmonisation represents a resource-driven view of IMC, an inside-out approach, which by definition is not audience-centred and lacks any strategic, structural or market view. Furthermore, harmonisation fails to consider the context in which communications are to occur and remains a predominantly advertising-led activity.

Interpretation 2: IMC as a perspective

According to Cornelissen (2003) the literature indicates that there are two main interpretations of IMC: a 'content' and a 'process' perspective respectively. This view is supported by Kerr and Patti (2015) who refer to two types of integration: executional (message or tactical) integration, and strategic (planning) integration.

The *content* or *executional* perspective assumes that message consistency is the major goal in order to achieve the 'one voice, one look' position. IMC works when there is consistency throughout the various materials and messages including benefits, tone, characters, theme-line, logo or other executional elements in all consumer communications (Petrison and Wang, 1996: 154). Interestingly, Delgado-Ballester et al. (2012) find that high levels of consistency are important when building new or unfamiliar brands, whereas moderate levels of consistency are suitable for established or familiar brands.

This is not a new practice, however, as Cornelissen points out that practitioners had been doing this long before the term 'IMC' surfaced. This view is also associated with the zero-based planning approach, which holds that the choice of tools and media should be based on effectiveness criteria rather than the specialist functions for which the planners and managers are responsible. This means that the various agencies and personnel responsible for campaign design and deployment do so without prejudice or bias towards a preferred tool or media.

The second interpretation refers to a *process* or *strategic* perspective. Here the emphasis is on a strategic and largely structural realignment of the communications disciplines within organisations. This is necessary in order that cross-functional systems and processes are in position to enable IMC.

The *process* or *strategic* perspective of IMC is rooted in the belief that real IMC can only be generated through an organisation's structure, control systems and management incentives (Kerr and Patti, 2015). This perspective seeks to dismantle the different marketing communication silos and structurally realign the various communications disciplines together in a single body or unit. By creating a single department, cross-functional coordination between the disciplines is enabled. From this position it is possible to create a culture of collaboration and a shared approach to achieving the corporate goals, establishing competitive advantage, and a sharing of the objectives, budgets and outcomes.

Research suggests that many organisations have made little attempt to restructure their marketing communications disciplines and that public relations and marketing remain as a clear divide. What has happened, however, is that there are much closer cross-functional relationships and systems and processes to support them. Some organisations are moving incrementally towards a process perspective on IMC.

In an attempt to develop our understanding of IMC, Lee and Park (2007) proposed a multidimensional model of IMC, based on four key dimensions. These have been drawn from the literature and, unlike Cornelissen, have attempted to measure IMC. Their four dimensions are concerned with a single message, multiple customer groups, database marketing and the need to use IMC to build customer relationships (a fuller account of these dimensions can be seen in Chapter 10).

Kliatchko (2008) suggests that IMC has several distinctive attributes and he refers to them as the 'four pillars of IMC'. These are stakeholders, content, channels and results. Figure 12.5 sets out the constituent elements within each of the pillars.

His argument is that these four elements can be observed at different levels of IMC and that at each level one of the elements tends to dominate.

It may be that a suitable theoretical basis upon which to develop IMC is emerging through the relationship marketing literature. We know that a relationship orientation requires a multidisciplinary approach to trigger interaction and dialogue (Grönroos, 2004). So, it may be that a deeper understanding of relational theory will help to advance the IMC concept and provide researchers with a surer footing upon which to explore the topic.

Regardless of whether a content or process perspective is adopted, the position remains that, until there is empirical evidence to support a theoretical base upon which to build IMC strategy and operations, the phrase will probably continue to be misused and used inconsistently.

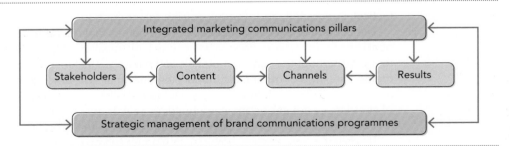

Figure 12.5 The four pillars of IMC
Source: Kliatchko (2008). Used with permission from WARC.

Table 12.2   Four platforms for integration

Form of integration	Explanation
No integration	No attempt is made to unify the tools in a consistent way.
Advertising-led integration	Based around a common creative platform.
Brand idea-led orchestration	Unification occurs around a shared brand concept or platform.
Participation-led orchestration	Characterised by a common dialogue, co-creation, experience or 'conversation' between brand and audience.

Source: IPA (2011). Used with permission from WARC.

Interpretation 3: IMC as a portfolio

Reference was made to the IPA's research and analysis of its Effectiveness Awards programmes. From an investigation of the various submissions for the best integrated campaign the IPA uncovered four distinct forms of integrated programmes (see Table 12.2).

Within each of these four forms of integration, the IPA observe various sub-categories. These are outlined in Table 12.3.

Table 12.3   Sub-categories of integration

Form of integration	Sub-category	Explanation
No integration	Single tool	Campaigns where there is no specific requirement to integrate other tools, media or marketing activity (such as packaging, on-pack promotions, in-store or website), into the advertising or marketing campaign.
	Pragmatically non-integrated	These campaigns use a wide variety of communication tools but there is no message integration. These campaigns tend to have no unifying concept, message or idea across any of the activities, and do not share a unifying strapline.
Advertising-led integration	Visual	These campaigns are only united by 'look and feel'. This is the so-called 'matching luggage' concept. These share the same visual identity but do not seek to integrate all campaign messages across channels.
	Promotion	Unification is achieved both visually and through a single promotional platform, competition or response mechanic.
	Icon	This refers to the use of the same brand icon across all tools and media – for example, by using the same celebrity in the store promotion, PR photo calls and events (e.g. Helen Mirren for L'Oréal Paris 'Age Perfect') or by developing a specific brand persona for use in all channels (e.g. Felix for Felix cat food).
	Idea	Here integration is achieved through one big advertising idea, which is disseminated through the most appropriate media.
Brand idea-led orchestration	Tangible	These campaigns are built on the more tangible foundations associated with a specific need-state, occasion, tightly defined target audience or a specific 'point of market entry' upon which to focus the activity and the channel orchestration.
	Intangible	Developed for higher-order, emotional engagement, these campaigns exhibit a high degree of creative inconsistency across time, while still retaining their orchestrating elements.
Participation-led orchestration		Here digital media are used to engage audiences in conversation and so improve brand and audience interaction. The goal is to *integrate brands into people's lives* in a way that is both relevant and valuable for the audience, rather than aiming a message out towards a target audience and hoping they will be receptive.

Source: Based on IPA (2011). Used with permission from WARC.

In many ways the revelation that there are different forms of integration should not be surprising, especially in the light of the multitude of definitions. What is interesting is the terminology used to identify the different forms. In particular, attention is drawn to the use of the word 'orchestration'. This is a term identified in the very early days by academics to explain the integration concept. Here we are, over 20 years later, and it is practitioners who are reviving the term. Perhaps of greater interest should be what the term 'orchestration' represents. In a musical context 'to orchestrate' means to arrange or compose music to be played by an orchestra in a predetermined order. The conductor then interprets the score in order to reproduce the composer's original ideas. This suggests a planned way of operating, one where there is some, but limited, flexibility. Another interpretation of the word 'orchestration' involves the organisation of an event to achieve a desired, again predetermined, effect or outcome. What is common to both of these ideas about orchestration is that there is a planned outcome. To what extent is integration more concerned with flexibility than planning, however, and what part of the difficulties associated with IMC are to be found rooted in planning and linear thinking?

Viewpoint 12.4
IKEA orchestrates a 'Wonderful Everyday'

Image 12.6 A scene from a television ad for IKEA's 'Wonderful Everyday'
Source: © Inter IKEA Systems B.V.

When the UK management team decided to re-evaluate its strategic direction in the light of the poor brand performance they found that the IKEA brand had never truly been 'properly' introduced to the UK market, they had never really told anyone who or what IKEA was. Research found that there was a lack of substance and meaning in the IKEA brand, and that even current loyal brand supporters saw little beyond durability and storage.

An IKEA designer observed how placing a child's coat hook at a child's height, not an adult's, enabled the child to partake of the going to school/out ritual independently. This sidestepped the numerous daily arguments and delays as children resisted the parental coercion. This everyday hook story (see Viewpoint 6.4) provided the critical insight about how to make this brand purpose relevant to UK consumers by associating IKEA with only one thing – to improve the 'everyday'. This became 'The Wonderful Everyday' a simple expression of the everyday benefit that IKEA helps deliver.

This expression became a strategic platform, one which allowed the brand's behaviour and communication to reflect the meaning and purpose of its founding principles, namely to 'to create a better everyday life for the many people'.

The Wonderful Everyday platform gave rise to a rich, broad and deep range of creative ideas, incorporating emotional storylines for 90, 60, and 20-second TV spots, CRM, PR, outdoor and a huge amount of content for social media. It has survived over four years and is still in position at the time of writing. The Wonderful Everyday approach has sidestepped the all too frequent short-term agency chop and change, and the associated new 'creative', as it has enabled the same group of seven agencies to keep united and deliver tighter, more effective and more transformative campaigns.

Since its launch in January 2014, and with no shift in media share of voice, The Wonderful Everyday has helped IKEA to deliver over 8 per cent year-on-year sales growth for three consecutive years to the end of 2016. By putting IKEA back in the heart of British homes, by attracting more shoppers to shop more frequently, and across a wider range of IKEA products, this platform has generated the highest incremental sales that IKEA UK has ever experienced from marketing communications. It reinforces the importance of taking a long-term approach to brand building.

Sources: Stewart (2016); Tiersen and Mackay (2017); Vizard (2017); www.ikea.com

Insight

The reinvigoration of the IKEA brand in the UK, led through the Wonderful Everyday, reflects the importance of consistency as advocated by Batra and Keller (2016) when implementing integrated marketing communications. In addition, it demonstrates how necessary it is to root an integrated programme in an understanding of consumer behaviour and to then infuse it with emotion and present the messages at appropriate touchpoints.

Question: With which of the four forms of integration identified by the IPA is the IKEA campaign best matched?

Task: Find two other furniture campaigns and determine the degree to which each might be integrated.

Interpretation 4: relational IMC

This interpretation has emerged naturally as marketing has become more relationship-aware and, as a result, more oriented towards relational issues. Relationships are dynamic and vary in strength and intensity through time. Some are referred to as *transactional exchanges*, characterised by short-term, product- or price-oriented exchanges between buyers and sellers coming together for one-off exchanges independent of any other or subsequent exchanges. Both parties are motivated mainly by self-interest.

Other relationships are characterised by relational exchanges or what Day (2000) refers to as *collaborative exchanges*. These are characterised by a long-term orientation, where ultimately there is complete integration of systems and processes and where the relationship is motivated by partnership and mutual support. Trust and commitment underpin these relationships, and these variables become increasingly important as relational exchanges become established. IMC therefore, needs to consider and adapt to these very different relational contexts. Each is considered in turn.

IMC and transactional marketing

The discussion so far has been based largely on the assumption that exchanges are (or should be) essentially collaborative in character and that customers are willing and eager to enter into a wide range of relationships. However, it appears that some, if not the majority of, exchanges are essentially transactional in character. Buyers do not always wish to enter into a deep, complex relationship with all suppliers, nor do some consumers wish to enter into a relationship with the supplier of their favourite chocolate bar, dishwasher tablets or frozen peas. As a result, these convenience-based exchanges are oriented towards a value based on the product, its price and overall availability and convenience. Depending upon the product category, after-sales and service support will be important but, by definition, customers in transactional mode do not wish to enter into any serious interaction, let alone dialogue.

The target-marketing process requires the development and implementation of a distinct marketing mix to meet the requirements of selected target markets. The elements are mixed together in such a way that they should meet the needs of the target segment. Each element of the marketing mix has a variable capacity to communicate (see Figure 12.6).

Therefore, it may be that traditional forms of marketing communications are sufficient to reach transactional customers. Messages that focus mainly on attributes, features and benefits, emotional values, price and availability will continue to be valid and improved if delivered through a coordinated mix of tools and media that are customer oriented. Using communications that contain a coordinated communications mix, which makes greater use of a range of tools and media that are neutral and seek to cut waste and improve efficiency, will be advantageous.

IMC and relationship marketing

As stated already, there is no universally agreed definition of IMC, and the development of this concept is strewn with attempts to pin it down and label it. What can be observed, however, is that the relationship-marketing paradigm has developed at the same time as IMC and that there are areas where the two concepts intertwine and reinforce each other.

One of the difficulties associated with IMC is that successful marketing communications results from an entirely planned approach. Planning is an essential aspect of managing marketing communications, but customers interact with products and services in different ways. They experience brands through their observation of others consuming them, through their own use, as well as through planned, unplanned and word-of-mouth communications.

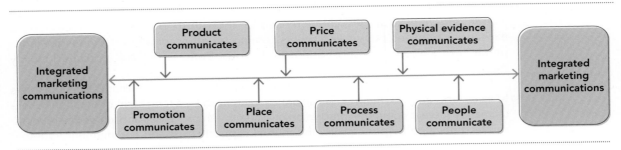

Figure 12.6 Each of the elements of the marketing mix communicates

It is the totality of this communications experience that impacts on relationship development. IMC therefore, has a critical role in the development of relationship marketing. This is because it is an important process, one that seeks to generate a response from customers, provoke interaction and then dialogue, which is a key characteristic of relationship marketing (Grönroos, 2004).

IMC has a potentially greater role to play within collaborative transactions and with customers who wish to become involved within mutually rewarding relationships. To date, IMC has been regarded as a concept that needs to be applied across an organisation's entire marketing communications and customer base. The suggestion is that aspects of IMC should be applied to both transactional and collaborative customers, but greater emphasis on interaction and dialogue should be given to communications with current and potential relationship-driven customers and other stakeholders.

To conclude this section on relational aspects of IMC it is appropriate to consider recent ideas about a customer perspective of IMC. Contemporary thinking holds that IMC needs to be considered from a customer-centric perspective, an outside-in perspective. IMC is no longer structured according to different communication instruments, but according to relationships, contents and processes. Digital and interactive media have enabled customer-to-customer communication, and as Bruhn and Schnebelen (2017) state, this has given rise to a new space of communication, the meaning space. This is an area that companies and brands do not control and allows customers to attribute meaning to the messages they perceive.

This idea of customer-centric IMC is also explored by Finne and Grönroos (2009, 2017). They concur with Bruhn and Schnebelen that much of what has been termed IMC is an inside-out view of the subject. To facilitate a change to an outside-in view Finne and Grönroos introduce the concept of relationship communication. In essence they argue that IMC should be based on the meaning a consumer attributes to all the messages they receive, regardless of the source.

To support this outside-in approach they offer the relationship communication model. This has two dimensions. A time dimension relates to a consumer's perception of a given relationship, using both historical and future factors. A situational dimension relates to a consumer's individual context, based on external and internal factors. They suggest that some or all of these factors may influence the meaning that consumers create out of marketing communication messages they perceive.

More recently (2017) these authors build on their earlier model to consider IMC in terms of the value recipients derive from the messages they perceive. This they argue is a truly customer-centric perspective of IMC.

They reason that customers integrate and make sense of messages regardless of their source (company, competitor, societal, customer-to-customer). All of these messages influence each other and merge within this process of integration. The outcome is communication-in-use, defined as 'a customer's integration and sense-making of all messages from any source, company-driven or stemming from other sources the customer perceives as communication, forming value-in-use for him or her for a specific purpose. In addition to traditional communication instruments, this definition encompasses all types of open sources' (p. 454).

Communication-in-use in turn influences the value of communication that a customer forms. The value of communication is the importance to the customer of what they perceive as communication (communication-in-use). It is this value of communication that influences how a customer perceives a brand, which can then influence their decision making.

This customer-centric approach is entirely new and radically different to the traditional view of what IMC is and how it may be practised. The managerial implications of this perspective are considerable.

Scholars' paper 12.4
A customer view of integrated communications

Finne, A. and Grönroos, C. (2017) Communication-in-use: customer-integrated marketing communication, *European Journal of Marketing,* **51(3), 445–63.**

This conceptual paper builds on the authors' 2009 paper about IMC within a relationship marketing context, listed below. The 2017 paper provides an interesting analysis of current ideas and approaches to IMC. From here a customer-driven view of marketing communications is developed using recent developments in relationship communication, customer-dominant logic and the notion of customer value formation as value-in-use.

See also:

Bruhn, M. and Schnebelen, S. (2017) Integrated marketing communication – from an instrumental to a customer-centric perspective, *European Journal of Marketing,* 51(3), 464–89.

Finne, A. and Grönroos, C. (2009) Rethinking marketing communication: from integrated marketing communication to relationship communication, *Journal of Marketing Communication,* 15(2–3), 179–95.

Viewpoint 12.5
Amex drives 'Small Business Saturday'

Image 12.7 Small Business Saturday

Amex founded and continue to support the Small Business Saturday initiative. However, they resist applying their logo and brand symbols to SBS advertising and promotional materials.
Source: casejustin/Shutterstock.

For small companies such as Green Apple Books in San Francisco 'Small Business Saturday' is critical because it can increase sales by as much as 20 per cent. Small Business Saturday happens every year on the Saturday after Thanksgiving. It has become a regular event but the original idea behind it was a deliberate attempt by American Express to help their small-business customers boost sales.

The idea was seeded at a time when the recession was deep and when there was a groundswell towards looking after 'local' needs. For AmEx, however, the challenge lay in getting consumers and small businesses to not only participate in the programme but to also help promote the idea. The answer lay in encouraging participation among various collaborative partners. These included YouTube, Foursquare and Twitter who provided free social-media support, FedEx who donated personalised signs, and business organisations from the US Chamber of Commerce to the National Federation of Independent Businesses who held events and promoted the day on their own.

The campaign had three core elements. The first was to enable small business owners and rally them to own the day. The second was to galvanise consumers to support the movement and to go out and shop in small businesses on Small Business Saturday. The third was to lobby Government officials to make it 'an official day'.

To enable small business owners and rally them to own the day, AmEx encouraged small businesses to participate with an advertising campaign, which featured small business owners being urged to unite to combine forces and fight back against the mega-sized retailers. In addition, a communications toolkit was created for small businesses to run and promote SBS. This included a logo and simple artwork for use as in-store displays. AmEx bought advertising 'space' on Facebook then offered it free to its small business account holders. The toolkit was distributed digitally via a hub that lived online, on both Facebook and AmEx's sites.

To galvanise consumers to support the movement and to go out and shop in small businesses on Small Business Saturday, consumers needed to be made aware of and understand their role: to shop. To do this a cross-platform advertising campaign designed to position Small Business Saturday as a national movement was developed. The commercial depicted a cross-section of shoppers making 'the pledge to shop small'. People who wanted to help their small-town communities were recognised as 'Neighborhood Champions'.

AmEx built an entirely separate website at ShopSmall.com for Small Business Saturday, where there are toolkit and social media materials for the SBS brand. AmEx built a community around Small Business Saturday and enabled the community to do some of the work for them. This has made it easy for participants to rally around a brand that is separate from the AmEx brand itself. It is important to recognise that although AmEx have driven the movement, participants are not required to sign up to AmEx. Their CEO went on the *Today* show and said, 'I don't care how you shop, where you shop or how you pay. . . this is the day to go out and support small businesses.' American Express has developed an entire brand around Shop Small and Small Business Saturday.

The campaign has evolved and grown in strength with each year's event. Following the launch in 2010, the US Senate officially recognised the movement in 2011. In 2012, it was estimated that $5.5 billion was spent at small independent businesses on the designated day. In 2013, over 1,450 neighborhood champions signed up to rally their communities to get involved and support small businesses. That year $5.7 billion in sales were generated. The cause-marketing campaign won two Cannes Grand Prix awards among many other industry accolades. It is now a cultural movement that has helped change the way consumers view and support small businesses.

Sources: Beechler (2014); Quittner (2016); www.adage.com/lp/top15/#introw; www.americanexpress.com

Insight

The SBS initiative has gained considerable momentum since its early days and is now an influential part of the commercial calendar in North America. At the root of the programme is participation among a growing network of stakeholders. Integration has been achieved through the small business owners combining resources and exerting pressure through a collaborative advertising campaign. The utilisation of social media around the new Shop Small brand has been a significant factor enabling integration.

Question: Write brief notes explaining why this campaign can be considered to be integrated marketing communications.

Task: Find two other campaigns, each demonstrating a relational interpretation of IMC.

Key points

- Integrated marketing communications (IMC) is concerned with the development, coordination and implementation of an organisation's various strategies, resources and messages.
- The role of IMC is to enable coherent, consistent and meaningful engagement with target audiences. In an age when consumers can touch brands across a range of channels it is important that each contact reinforces previous messages and facilitates the development of valued relationships.
- Definitions of IMC have evolved from a simple coordination of the disciplines and messages perspective to one that incorporates touchpoints, the development of relationships and mutual value. There is no single agreed definition or view of IMC.
- There has been a great deal of debate about the meaning and value of an integrated approach. Many agencies speak of integrated communications campaigns but the reality suggests different approaches, forms and interpretations. Most organisations achieve only partial or coordinated levels of communications activity.
- The interest in IMC has resulted from three main forces. These include market-based forces, those that arise from the changing communications landscape and those that are driven from opportunities within the organisation itself.
- A wide range of elements needs to be integrated. These include the communications tools, media and messages, plus the elements of the marketing mix, touchpoints, brands, strategy, consumers, employees, agencies and technology.
- Four interpretations of IMC can be identified. These are harmonisation, perspective, portfolio and relational. Each has its own origins and theoretical grounding.

Snickers: thinking like a Hollywood blockbuster
Elly Fenlon, AMV BBDO

Image 12.8 Rowan Atkinson was used in the Snickers campaign, partly because his Mr Bean character had global appeal.
Source: Jstone/Shutterstock.

'You're not you when you're hungry' (YNYWYH) was formulated as a response to hard times in 2009, where global share of value sales dramatically dropped, and competitors were encroaching on Snickers' position as the world's biggest chocolate bar. The strategy originated in a desire for a more focused approach to communications, and the logic that the way to arrest global decline would be through a united strategy across all markets.

The idea was built on a simple but powerful universal insight: that there is an unspoken code of conduct that must be abided by in order to stay part of the male pack. Being hungry can endanger your ability to abide by the code of conduct that keeps you as 'one of the guys'. Whether you become irritable, weak or dopey, there are certain universal symptoms of hunger that can stop a guy from keeping to the code. Snickers is the solution: as a filling, peanut-packed bar, Snickers can sort out hunger and restore your place in the pack.

The simplicity of the idea and universality of its insight meant widespread adoption by Snickers' many local markets, and in the years since launch YNYWYH has carved out worldwide fame and business success via locally produced executions. YNYWYH helped Snickers regain global market share of $376.3 million between 2009 and 2011, with the launch ad 'Game' creating 400 million media impressions and becoming the most successful Super Bowl ad at the time.

However, 2014 saw new headwinds. The global chocolate confectionery category only just managed to maintain volumes in a world increasingly concerned about sugar intake and bombarded by alternative snack options. Snickers' unfashionable format as a heavy duty 'bar' performed even worse than the category, with a 1.59 per cent drop in volume (representing around 60 million Snickers bars), meaning that market share by value fell by 1.81 per cent.

It was clear that in a changing consumer environment, we needed to re-think how we framed YNYWYH.

We needed to drive sales in order to regain market share. We knew that achieving this in the chocolate category meant increasing penetration. There are plenty of chocolate bars competing at the shelf so increasing penetration means being the most salient. Since everyone knows Snickers, our goal isn't about brand awareness but about delivering brand fame. Being famous is our single most important metric as it means being talked about by a higher proportion of those people who currently don't care about us. We know this dynamic means fame can deliver significantly and exponentially in terms of market share gains.

YNYWYH is, in many ways, the perfect tool to deliver fame in today's fractured, fragmented media landscape. Not one big idea, but a coherent framework for the creation of many smaller ones. A framework that creates momentum as consumers pick it up to use as their own – largely driven through the use of local celebrities in order to drive buzz and relevance.

However, in 2014, with category-wide decline especially affecting the UK, Russia and Australia, we needed to evolve our construct to match our changing business environment.

We wanted to complement the existing YNYWYH platform by adding a 'blockbuster' at the head of our 'long tail' of local, relevant and organic activity. Using a single execution and a single celebrity who commanded relevance and buzz across multiple markets, we felt that we could tackle the divergent issues facing a range of markets.

We needed to look outside of advertising for inspiration, if only to sidestep the copycats. Since our key objective was to create fame, we considered the biggest fame-driving industry in the world: Hollywood. The success of film franchises like *Star Wars*, the *Jurassic Park*s and *Harry Potter*s showed us that efficacy is not always locally bound. So how do they do it?

Analysis shows that films with more production budget usually create bigger box office, and to get the level of investment required, studios are relying ever more heavily on revitalising franchises that have proven track records. Notably, a number of the more successful franchises operate within fantasy worlds. We theorised that by creating a new world for the story, films are more aspirational, exciting, and are more easily transferred across markets as they are equally relatable to everyone. We also considered how the hype and buzz around these films must have contributed to their success – especially the latest instalment of *Star Wars*.

This was our breakthrough: to create fame in very different markets, we would adopt the model of global *entertainment*, not advertising.

Needing to create global fame, and a 'blockbuster', we naturally looked to the extensive and reliable reach of TV. Ideally to fill out the long tail our idea would translate online and locally, but first and foremost we needed to crack a film that would work in at least three markets with a celebrity who would be recognisable across country borders.

Enter Mr Bean. His last film *Holiday* was a worldwide box office success – taking millions of dollars in the Russian, Australian and UK box offices, among others. Rowan Atkinson's hit TV show has been shown in over 200 countries, spawned two films, and two animated series. His non-linguistic humour made him instantly global, and his schadenfreude approach to comedy made Mr Bean the perfect character for a YNYWYH film.

To launch the final Bean Kung Fu film, we emulated as many Hollywood techniques as we could. In the UK we partnered with ITV to create teaser trailers, before airing a cinematic 60-second cut of the film during *The X Factor*. Cinema spots were also booked to show off the film at its very best. Atkinson spoke at an internal conference, which boosted confidence within the business to take the film out to further markets. In China, we 'leaked' stories about Atkinson flying to Shanghai to film a new Kung Fu movie – with a signature new Kung Fu move – and he made an appearance on the popular *Tonight 80s Talk Show*. Mr Bean's new Kung Fu move, the 'Fist of Hunger' was so popular it got parodied by the press and transcended into 'meme' status. We also launched four short 'prequels' online, which documented Mr Bean's Kung Fu training, to extend the experience for keen fans. We ensured that Rowan was involved in the scripting and production of these to make them as authentically 'Mr Bean' as possible.

The film launched in the UK in October 2014. By summer 2015 it was running in 49 markets, and at time of writing it was in over 60 markets (and counting). A truly global film.

In 2015 the markets airing Bean collectively saw market share growth of 4.06 per cent. We also know that it fulfilled its global objective in its performance across all markets. In 2015 Bean Kung Fu helped Snickers to grow volume sales by 5.38 per cent, way ahead of the category. Value sales equally outpaced growth in the category at 9.91 per cent.

Sales performance in the UK lifted in the first week the film was aired. Russia saw an impressive 2.3 per cent uplift in penetration, and in the six months following launch, Australia saw an increase of 21 per cent in volume sales and a 14 per cent increase in value sales.

This case study is an edited version of a paper submitted to the IPA Effectiveness Awards 2016. It has been reproduced here with the kind permission of the IPA, WARC, Mars, and their agency AMV BBDO who wrote the original paper.

Review questions

Snickers case questions

1. What were the main driving forces leading Snickers to develop an integrated approach?

2. Prepare brief notes explaining the role and contribution of any four integration elements within the YNYWYH approach.

3. Consider the integration-related issues Snickers might have had to address when developing YNYWYH.

4. Consider which of the different interpretations of IMC best explains the YNYWYH approach.

5. How might Snickers have measured the success of their integrated approach to communications?

General questions

1. Consider the merits of the harmonisation and perspective views of IMC. Which do you believe is the most pragmatic?

2. Compare the ideas concerning the advertising-led and brand-idea orchestration found within the portfolio interpretation of IMC.

3. Explain how various definitions of IMC have evolved.

4. What are the structural issues that can accelerate or hinder the development of IMC?

5. Prepare the outline for an essay exploring whether IMC is a strategic approach or just a means to correct internal operational difficulties and reduce media costs.

References for Chapter 12

Anon (2015) McWhopper, *Cream*, September, retrieved 1 December 2017 from http://sites.wpp.com/wppedcream/2016/digital/mcwhopper/

Anon (2017) *The art of integration*, Kantar Millward Brown, retrieved 22 January 2018 from http://www.millwardbrown.com/documents/Reports/The_Art_of_Integration/default.aspx?access=yes

Bacon, J. (2017) Agencies are sceptical about 'integrated' client briefs, *Marketing Week*, 13 April, retrieved 2 December 2017 from https://www.marketingweek.com/2017/04/19/agencies-sceptical-integrated-client-briefs/

Batra, R. and Keller, K.L. (2016) Integrating marketing communications: new findings, new lessons, and new ideas, *Journal of Marketing*, AMA/MSI Special Issue, 80 (November), 122–45.

Beechler, D. (2014) 9 Key marketing lessons from American Express's Small Business Saturday, *Salesforce Marketing Cloud,* 14 November, retrieved 20 January 2015 from www.exacttarget.com/blog/9-key-marketing-lessons-from-american-expresss-small-business-saturday/

Bird, J. (2016) Switching off TV, turning on touchpoints: new ways to communicate in a new world, *Journal of Brand Strategy*, 5(3), Winter, 266–74.

Bruhn, M. and Schnebelen, S. (2017) Integrated marketing communication – from an instrumental to a customer-centric perspective, *European Journal of Marketing*, 51(3), 464–89.

Cornelissen, J.P. (2003) Change, continuity and progress: the concept of integrated marketing communications and marketing communications practice, *Journal of Strategic Marketing*, 11 (December), 217–34.

Cornelissen, J.P. and Lock, A.R. (2000) Theoretical concept or management fashion? Examining the significance of IMC, *Journal of Advertising Research*, 50(5), 7–15.

Day, G. (2000) Managing market relationships, *Journal of the Academy of Marketing Science*, 28(1), Winter, 24–30.

Delgado-Ballester, E., Navarro, A. and Sicilia, M. (2012) Revitalising brands through communication messages: the role of brand familiarity, *European Journal of Marketing* 46(1/2), 31–51.

Duncan, T. and Everett, S. (1993) Client perceptions of integrated marketing communications, *Journal of Advertising Research*, 3(3), 30–9.

Duncan, T. and Moriarty, S. (1998) A communication-based marketing model for managing relationships, *Journal of Marketing*, 62 (April), 1–13.

Duncan, T. and Mulhern, F. (2004) *A White Paper on the Status, Scope and Future of IMC Programs* (from the IMC symposium by the IMC programs at Northwestern University and University of Denver), New York: McGraw-Hill.

Eagle, L., Kitchen, P.J. and Bulmer, S. (2007) Insights into interpreting integrated marketing communications: a two-nation qualitative comparison, *European Journal of Marketing*, 41(7/8), 956–70.

Finne, A. and Grönroos, C. (2009) Rethinking marketing communication: from integrated marketing communication to relationship communication, *Journal of Marketing Communications*, 15(2–3), 179–95.

Finne, A. and Grönroos, C. (2017) Communication-in-use: customer-integrated marketing communication, *European Journal of Marketing*, 51(3), 445–63.

Foroudi, P., Dinnie, K., Kitchen, P.J., Melewar, T.C. and Foroudi, M.M. (2017) IMC anteced-ents and the consequences of planned brand identity in higher education, *European Journal of Marketing*, 51(3), 528–55.

Fuchs, P.H., Mifflin, K.E., Miller, D. and Whitney, J.O. (2000) Strategic integration: competing in the age of capabilities, *CA Management Review*, 42(3), 118–47.

Grönroos, C. (2004) The relationship marketing process: communication, interaction, dialogue, value, *Journal of Business and Industrial Marketing*, 19(2), 99–113.

Gwynn, S. (2017) Unilever launches site to publicise roster agencies, *Campaign*, 23 February, retrieved 22 January 2018 from https://www.campaignlive.co.uk/article/unilever-launches-site-publicise-roster-agencies/1424900

IPA (2011) *New Models of Marketing Effectiveness: From Integration to Orchestration*, WARC.

Keller, K.L. (2001) Mastering the marketing communications mix: micro and macro perspectives on integrated marketing communications programs, *Journal of Marketing Management*, 17, 819–47.

Keller, K.L. (2016) Unlocking the power of integrated marketing communications: how inte-grated is your IMC program? *Journal of Advertising*, 45(3), 286–301.

Kerr, G. and Patti, C. (2013) Strategic IMC: from abstract concept to marketing management tool, *Journal of Marketing Communications*, 21(5), 317–39.

Kitchen, P., Brignell, J., Li, T. and Spickett-Jones, G. (2004) The emergence of IMC: a theoret-ical perspective, *Journal of Advertising Research*, 44 (March), 19–30.

Kitchen, P.J., Spickett-Jones, G. and Grimes, T. (2007) Inhibition of brand integration amid changing agency structures, *Journal of Marketing Communications*, 13(2), 149–68.

Kliatchko, J. (2005) Towards a new definition of integrated marketing communications (IMC), *International Journal of Advertising*, 24(1), 7–34.

Kliatchko, J. (2008) Revisiting the IMC construct: a revised definition and four pillars, *Interna-tional Journal of Advertising*, 27(1), 133–60.

Kliatchko, J.G. and Schultz, D.E. (2014) Twenty years of IMC, *International Journal of Adver-tising*, 33(2), 373–90.

Lee, D.H. and Park, C.W. (2007) Conceptualization and measurement of multidimensionality of integrated marketing communications, *Journal of Advertising Research*, 47(3), September, 222–36.

Luxton, S., Reid, M. and Mavondo, F. (2015) Integrated marketing communication capability and brand performance, *Journal of Advertising*, 44(1), 37–46.

Melewar, T.C., Foroudi, P., Gupta, S., Kitchen, P.J. and Foroudi, M.M. (2017) Integrating iden-tity, strategy and communications for trust, loyalty and commitment, *European Journal of Marketing*, 51(3), 572–604.

Mortimer, K. and Laurie, S. (2017) The internal and external challenges facing clients in imple-menting IMC, *European Journal of Marketing*, 51(3), 511–27.

Neff, J. (2017) P&G slashes digital ads by $140m over brand safety. Sales rise any-way, *Adage*, 27 July, retrieved 30 November 2017 from http://adage.com/article/cmo-strategy/p-g-slashe/309936/

Pantano, E. and Viassone, M. (2015) Engaging consumers on new integrated multichannel retail settings: challenges for retailers, *Journal of Retailing and Consumer Services*, 25 (July), 106–14.

Percy, L., Rossiter, J.R. and Elliot, R. (2001) *Strategic Advertising Management*, New York: Oxford University Press.

Petrison, L. and Wang, P. (1996) Integrated marketing communication: examining planning and executional considerations, in *Integrated Communication: A Synergy of Persuasive Voices* (eds E. Thorson and J. Moore), Mahwah, NJ: Lawrence Erlbaum Associates, 153–66.

Pitta, D.A., Weisgal, M. and Lynagh, P. (2006) Integrating exhibit marketing into integrated marketing communications, *Journal of Consumer Marketing*, 23(3), 156–66.

Pollack, J. (2016) Blurred lines: 'cheeky' McWhopper wins media grand prix, *Adage*, 22 June, retrieved 1 December 2017 from http://adage.com/article/special-report-cannes-lions/cheeky-mcwhopper-wins-media-grand-prix/304637/

Porcu L., del Barrio-García S. and Kitchen, P.J. (2012) How integrated marketing communications (IMC) work? A theoretical review and an analysis of its main drivers and effects, *Comunicacion Sociedad*, 25(1), 313–48.

Porter, M.E. (1980) *Competitive Strategy: Techniques for Analyzing Industries and Competitors*, New York: Free Press.

Quittner, J. (2016) Small Business Saturday is no longer just an AmEx holiday, *Fortune*, 21 November, retrieved 16 July 2017 from http://fortune.com/2016/11/21/small-business-saturday-amex-holiday/

Reid, M. (2005) Performance auditing of integrated marketing communications (IMC) actions and outcomes, *Journal of Advertising*, 34(4), 41–54.

Richards, K. and Nudd, T. (2016) Y&R's 'McWhopper' for Burger King adds another Cannes Grand Prix, in Media, *Adweek*, 22 June, retrieved 1 December 2017 from http://www.adweek.com/brand-marketing/yrs-mcwhopper-burger-king-adds-another-cannes-grand-prix-media-172164/#/

Schultz, D.E., Tannenbaum, S.L. and Lauterborn, R. (1993) *Integrated Marketing Communications: Putting It Together and Making It Work*, Lincolnwood, IL: NTC Business Books.

Serić, M., Saura, I.G., and Došen, Đ.O. (2015) Insights on integrated marketing communications: implementation and impact in hotel companies, *International Journal of Contemporary Hospitality Management*, 27(5), 958-979.

Shimp, T.A. (2000) *Advertising Promotion: Supplemental Aspects of Integrated Marketing Communications*, 5th edn, Fort Worth, TX: Dryden Press, Harcourt College Publishers.

Smith, P. (1996) Benefits and barriers to integrated communications, *Admap*, February, 19–22.

Spotts, H.E., Lambert, D.R. and Joyce, M.L. (1998) Marketing déjà vu: the discovery of integrated marketing communications, *Journal of Marketing Education*, 20(3), 210–18.

Stewart, R. (2016) Ikea gives its 'Wonderful Everyday' campaign the John Lewis treatment in nostalgic film, *The Drum*, 21 April, retrieved 16 November 2017 from http://www.thedrum.com/news/2016/04/21/ikea-gives-its-wonderful-everyday-campaign-john-lewis-treatment-nostalgic-film

Swain, W.N. (2004) Perceptions of IMC after a decade of development: who's at the wheel, and how can we measure success? *Journal of Advertising Research*, 44(1), March, 46–65.

Tesseras, L. (2017) P&G's Marc Pritchard: We are 50% of the way to cleaning up digital, *Marketing Week*, 20 June, retrieved 30 November from https://www.marketingweek.com/2017/06/20/pg-marc-pritchard-clean-up-digital/

Tiersen, L. and Mackay, K. (2017) Ikea and the pursuit of everyday wonder: how the retailer revived its fortunes, *Campaign*, 16 October, retrieved 1 November 2017 from https://www.campaignlive.co.uk/article/ikea-pursuit-everyday-wonder-retailer-revived-its-fortunes/1447274

Turner, P. (2017) Implementing integrated marketing communications (IMC) through major event ambassadors, *European Journal of Marketing*, 51(3), 605–26.

Tylee, J. (2017) Creativity is king, *Campaign*, 16 June, 11.

Vizard, S. (2017) Ikea: criticism of campaigns that champion diversity only pushes us on, *Marketing Week*, 14 November, retrieved 16 November 2017 from https://www.marketing week.com/2017/11/14/ikea-on-facing-criticism-for-diverse-campaigns/

White, R. (2000) Chameleon brands: tailoring brand messages to consumers, *Admap*, July/ August, 8–40.

The marketing communications mix

This is the largest part in the book, configured as three sections, which looks at the various elements that constitute the marketing communications mix. The first section examines the tools or disciplines, the second, messages and creativity issues, and the third considers the media.

Chapter 13 is about advertising and considers the role, use and types of advertising. Ideas about selling propositions are explored and how emotion can be used precedes an exploration of the way advertising might work. Here consideration is given to some of the principal models and frameworks that have been published to best explain the process by which advertising might influence audiences.

Chapter 14 examines the role and characteristics of public relations, including a review of the various methods used in public relations, and crisis communications. Chapter 15 is about sponsorship and considers some of the theoretical aspects of sponsorship and different types of sponsorship activity. Chapter 16 examines both direct marketing and personal selling.

Chapters 17 and 18 both consider a range of disciplines. The first considers the principles and techniques of sales promotion, field marketing and brand experience. The second explores brand placement, exhibitions, packaging and brand licensing.

Chapter 19 examines the second element of the mix, messages and creativity. Attention is first given to the message source, issues relating to source credibility, and the use of spokespersons, either as the face of a brand or as an endorser. This is followed by a review of the need to balance the use of information and emotion in messages, and the way messages are constructed, before finally exploring the various appeals and ways in which messages can be presented.

The focus then changes to explore the nature, role and processes organisations use to manage the creative process. Here ideas about message framing and storytelling are developed before concluding with a review of a more contemporary perspective of content generation and creativity – namely user-generated content.

The third and final element consists of three chapters that explore the nature, role and issues associated with managing the media. Chapter 20 considers the principles and practice associated with the media. In particular, time is spent considering the way media can best be categorised. Here we introduce the notion of linear and interactive media in order to overcome some of the current classification issues.

Chapter 21 opens with an exploration of a range of interactive advertising formats, including behavioural targeting and native advertising, before considering the characteristics of search engine marketing, social media and various other formats. The final chapter, Chapter 22, considers ideas and theories associated with media planning and the way in which people use media. In addition to the conventional planning concepts usually associated with linear media, time is spent considering how automation, and programmatic advertising in particular, impacts on the delivery of interactive media.

03

The tools

Content

The media

Advertising: role, forms and strategy

Advertising is an integral part of society and affects people in many ways: commercially, culturally and psychologically at an individual level. Indeed, advertising is a powerful force, one that can shape perceptions, feelings, emotions, attitudes, understanding, and patterns of individual and group behaviour.

While academics and marketers acknowledge that advertising is a powerful communications tool, any attempt to understand what advertising is, how it might work and how it is developing should be tempered with an appreciation of its complexity and inherent contradictions.

Aims and learning objectives

The aims of this chapter are to explore different ideas about advertising and to consider the complexities associated with understanding how clients can best use advertising in the marketing communications mix.

The learning objectives are to enable readers to:

1. consider the role that advertising plays in influencing our thoughts and behaviour;
2. define advertising as an independent discipline;
3. examine the use of selling propositions, and the role of emotion in advertising;
4. identify different types or forms of advertising;
5. explore various models, concepts and frameworks, which have been used to explain how advertising is thought to influence individuals;
6. consider ways in which advertising can be used strategically;
7. review issues associated with consumer-generated advertising.

Introduction

Advertising is considered to be one of the most powerful elements of the marketing communications mix, based on its potential to influence the way people think/feel and behave. The thinking element may be concerned with the utilitarian or aspirational benefits of product ownership, or simply a matter of memorising the brand and its features for future recall. The behavioural element may be seen in terms of buying an advertised brand, visiting a website to enquire about a product's features or even sharing brand-related ideas with a friend or colleague.

Whatever the motivation, the content and delivery of advertising messages are derived from an understanding of the variety of contexts in which the messages are to be used. For example, research might reveal a poor brand image relative to the market leader, or audiences might misunderstand when or how to use a product or service. In both cases the messages are going to be different.

This chapter explores three main advertising issues. The first is about the role and use of advertising, how ideas about selling propositions and emotion can be used in advertising, and the different types or forms of advertising that can be identified.

The second concerns the way advertising might work. Here consideration is given to some of the principal models and frameworks that have been published to best explain the process by which advertising might influence audiences.

The third concerns the way in which advertising can be used strategically as part of a brand's development, and to review the significance of consumer-generated advertising.

The role of advertising

The principal role of advertising is to engage audiences. Whether it is on an international, national, local or direct basis, advertising can engage audiences by creating awareness, changing perceptions/attitudes and building brand values, or by influencing behaviour, often through calls-to-action.

Advertising has the capacity to reach large audiences with simple messages. These messages are intended to enable individuals to comprehend what an offering is, appreciate what its primary benefit is and how this might be of value to an individual. Wherever these individuals are located, the prime goals are to build awareness of a product or an organisation in the minds of the individuals and engage them. Engagement (as explored in Chapter 1) occurs when audiences are stimulated either to think about or take action about featured products, services, brands and organisations.

Having successfully engaged an audience, advertising can be used to achieve a number of DRIP-based outcomes (as set out in Chapter 1). Advertising is excellent at differentiating and positioning brands. It can be used to reinforce brand messages by reminding, reassuring or even refreshing an individual's perception of a brand. Advertising is excellent at informing audiences, mainly by creating awareness or helping them to learn about a brand or how it works. The one part of the DRIP framework where its ability is challenged is persuasion. In this circumstance sales promotion, direct marketing and personal selling are going to be prominent tools in the mix.

Management's control over advertising messages is strong; indeed, of all the tools in the communications mix, advertising has the greatest level of control. The message, once generated and signed off by the client, can be transmitted in an agreed manner and style and at times that match management's requirements. This means that, should the environment change unexpectedly, advertising messages can be 'pulled' immediately. For example, in 2018 Under Armour pulled ads from YouTube amid concerns that ads were appearing on extremist content (Tan, 2018).

Scholars' paper 13.1
Taking an ethical stance

Borau, S. and Nepomuceno, M.V. (2016) The self-deceived consumer: women's emotional and attitudinal reactions to the airbrushed thin ideal in the absence versus presence of disclaimers, *Journal of Business Ethics*, 1–16.

This paper explores the impact of airbrushed 'thin ideal' models in advertising. The authors argue this issue represents major ethical challenges and identify that even when women were aware that a model's image had been airbrushed they still wanted to resemble the model.

See also:

Turnbull, S., Howe-Walsh, L. and Boulanouar, A. (2016) The advertising standardisation debate revisited: implications of Islamic ethics on standardisation/localisation of advertising in Middle East Islamic States, *Journal of Islamic Marketing*, 7(1).

Advertising costs can be considered in one of two ways. On the one hand, there are the absolute costs, which are the costs of buying the space in magazines or newspapers or the time on television, cinema or radio. These costs can be very significant, and they impact directly on cash flow.

On the other hand, there are the relative costs, which are those costs incurred to reach a member of the target audience with the key message. So, if an audience is measured in hundreds of thousands, or even millions on television, the cost of the advertisement spread across each member of the target audience reduces the cost per contact significantly.

Advertising's main tasks are to build awareness and to (re)position brands, by enabling people to make appropriate brand-related associations. These associations may be based on the utility and functional value a brand represents, or on the imagery and psychological benefits that are conveyed. The regular use of advertising, in coordination with the other elements of the communications mix, can be important to the creation and maintenance of these associations and even build a brand personality.

Viewpoint 13.1
This Girl Can

Sport England wanted to find a way to empower 14–70-year-old women to get active. Statistics showed that 1.79 million fewer women than men exercised and Sport England set out to close this gap.

Insight revealed that women were held back by their fear of being judged. To address this barrier, Sport England decided to launch an advertising campaign that would empower women with the confidence to get active, 'This Girl Can'. The campaign championed women with a powerful message to overcome their fear of judgement and get active.

Sport England developed an app that enabled women to create their own This Girl Can posters and exercise selfies. These posters were then

Image 13.1 Sport England launched a campaign to empower women with the confidence to get active
Source: This Girl Can.

Image 13.2 Sport England developed an app for women to create their own This Girl Can posters and exercise selfies
Source: This Girl Can.

converted into digital OOH and used for the nationwide campaign. Poster sites were selected near to where the women live so that the same women could photograph themselves and share the image again. This meant that paid media was converted into earned media and in some cases back into paid media again.

To support the launch, Sport England created a 90-second film for TV, cinema and social seeding. Advertising also appeared in OOH and digital and Wembley asked to show the ad for free.

This Girl Can trended twice on Twitter within days of the campaign launch and appeared in Google's Hot Trends and Top 12 Trending Searches.

The campaign had a significant impact on women's attitude towards exercise. A panel survey found that women who had seen the campaign were more motivated to take part in sport and exercise. A tracking study reported 2.1 million women had been more active as a result of seeing This Girl Can, with 1.4 million women starting or re-starting exercise.

The results showed that within a year, an additional 246,000 women exercised more regularly as a result of the campaign. This Girl Can began to close the exercise gap between men and women from 1.79 million to 1.55 million.

The increased participation of women in exercise was seen to have an economic value to society and health benefits. Sport England used their 'Economic Value of Sport' model to calculate the campaign value and this was estimated to be £387 million. The campaign cost £10.7 million and the return on marketing investment was calculated as £35 for every £1 spent.

The campaign has won over 50 international awards, including the Cannes Grand Prix for Good and the Cannes Glass Lion, which recognises work that addresses issues of gender biases, through the conscious representation of gender in advertising.

Source: Anon (2018); Kemp (2017); This Girl Can (2017).

Insight

Advertising is seen as a very effective means of delivering messages for social change, as it offers wide reach and high coverage. The use of advertising can have a very powerful impact on audiences and often attracts additional media exposure for the organisation and the message. This case highlights the positive impact that advertising can have on society.

Question: Why do you think This Girl Can invited women to make their own ads? Use Table 13.2 to consider your answer.

Task: Find another example of an advertising campaign that is trying to bring about change in society. Using the elaboration likelihood model in Figure 13.2, explain the route taken in the advertising.

Advertising can be used as a barrier, deterring exit from and entry to markets. Some organisations are initially attracted to a new market by the potential profits, but a key entry decision factor will be the weight of advertising, that is the investment or 'spend' necessary to generate demand and a sufficient return on the investment. Many people feel that some brands sustain their large market share by sheer weight of advertising: for example, the washing powder brands of Procter & Gamble and Unilever. In many product categories word-of-mouth communications and the use of digital technologies can stimulate strong levels of awareness. Google is a prime example of a contemporary brand developed without the use of advertising. However, advertising, both offline and online, is still a key driver of both brand values and directing certain behaviour, most notably driving people to a website.

Advertising can create competitive advantage by providing the communications necessary for target audiences to frame a product or service. By providing a frame or the perceptual space within which to categorise a product, target audiences are enabled to position an offering relative to their other significant products much more easily. Therefore, advertising can provide the means for differentiation and sustainable competitive advantage. It should also be appreciated, however, that differentiation may be determined by the quality of the execution of the advertisements, rather than through the content of the messages.

There has also been a shift in focus away from mass communications towards more personalised messages delivered through different, often interactive media. This shift has been demonstrated by the increased use of direct marketing and the Internet by organisations. It can also be argued that the growth in experiential approaches is a response to some of the weaknesses, to do with cost and effectiveness of the other tools, most notably advertising.

The marketing communications mix has expanded and become a more complex concept, but essentially it is now capable of delivering two main solutions. On the one hand it can be used to develop and maintain brand values, and on the other it could be used to change behaviour through the delivery of calls-to-action. From a strategic perspective, the former is oriented to the long term and the latter to the short term.

Organisations, therefore, are faced with a dilemma. While there is the need to create brands that are perceived to be of value, there is also the need to prompt or encourage customers into purchase behaviour. To put it another way, marketing communications should be used to encourage buyers along the purchase decision path, but how should advertising be involved, what is its contribution in creating brand values, and which and how many of an organisation's other, yet scarce, communications resources should be used to prompt behaviour?

Defining advertising

Definitions of advertising have always varied. Richards and Curran (2002) found differences in the way advertising was defined by authors of various textbooks. They also noted that many of the definitions used the same or similar words. These core words were *paid, non-personal, identified sponsor, mass media* and *persuade* or *influence*. This enabled them to propose a definition that encapsulated a general consensus around the essence of these words. They referred to this as a *current* definition:

> **Advertising is a paid, non-personal communication from an identified sponsor, using mass media to persuade or influence an audience.**

This interpretation, however, is debatable. The development of digital technology and the Internet in particular has led to a plethora of new communications techniques and approaches that raises questions about the validity of some of the words in the current definition. Is 'paid' still viable? Can some forms of advertising be unpaid? Surely the use of commercial text messaging indicates that advertising can be 'personal' and the 'mass media' label must therefore be an invalid restriction.

Using a Delphi research approach, which uses experts' judgements, Richards and Curran (2002) sought to develop a more contemporary definition of advertising. After much discussion and re-evaluation of the issues and wording, a consensus formed around the following *proposed* definition:

> **Advertising is a paid, mediated form of communication from an identifiable source, designed to persuade the receiver to take some action, now or in the future.**

These changes might be subtle, but they represent an important and methodical attempt to review and update the meaning of advertising. The word 'mediated' replaces the restriction of 'mass media'. 'Source' replaces 'an identified sponsor', and 'persuasion' replaces the duplication apparent in 'persuade' and 'influence'.

Since Richards and Curran (2002) published their paper, however, the media landscape has changed dramatically and new forms of advertising have emerged. Native advertising for example, which is seen to be 'a form of paid media where the ad experience follows the natural form and function of the user experience in which it is placed' (MMA, 2015: 4), has been criticised for not always being clearly 'identifiable'. As native advertising matches the design of the media format it can sometimes be difficult for consumers to differentiate between paid content and non-paid content, unless clearly indicated.

Defining what is and what is not 'advertising' in online forms has created a big challenge for academics and industry. Campbell et al. (2014) for example highlight the problems identifying which forms of online brand-related content should be seen as advertising and propose a new categorisation of online brand-related content. The authors propose a two-dimensional categorisation, which considers who created the content and whether the content or its creation was paid for.

Some scholars have attempted to produce new working definitions of advertising in an attempt to reflect the broader scope of the discipline (Dahlen and Rosengren, 2016). Schultz (2016) argues that the lack of an acceptable definition results from an absence of boundaries for advertising theory and practice. See Scholars' paper 13.2 for more information.

Scholars' paper 13.2

What is advertising?

Schultz, D. (2016) The future of advertising or whatever we're going to call it, *Journal of Advertising,* **45(3), 276–85.**

The author discusses the challenge of defining advertising and provides three alternative scenarios for the future of advertising: (1) creeping incrementalism, (2) reversal of buyer/seller roles, and (3) reinvention of the field. The author suggests that technology will shape which scenario is developed and argues that the definition of advertising will change in the future.

See also:

Richards, J.I. and Curran, C.M. (2002) Oracles on 'advertising': searching for a definition, *Journal of Advertising,* 31(2), 63–77.

Selling propositions

For a very long time in the advertising world, great emphasis was placed upon the use of unique selling propositions, or USPs. Advertising was thought to work most effectively when the message said something about a product that no competitor brand could offer. For example, Olay claims its products offer 'younger looking skin'. USPs are based on product features and are related to particular attributes that differentiate one product from another, as demonstrated by many washing powders that wash 'whiter', presumably than the competition. If this uniqueness was of value to a consumer then the USP alone was thought sufficient to persuade consumers to purchase.

The reign of the USP, however, was short-lived when technology enabled me-too and own-label brands to be brought to market very quickly and product lifecycles became increasingly short. The power of the USP was eroded and with it the basis of product differentiation as it was known then. In addition, the power and purpose of advertising's role to differentiate was challenged. It is interesting that many people still refer to a product and its advertising in terms of its USP. Some companies believe USP refers to a 'single' selling point. In some cases people refer to USPs, as if a product is capable of having several unique qualities. This is unlikely and is essentially a contradiction in terms.

What emerged were emotional selling propositions or ESPs. Advertising's role became more focused on developing brand values, ones that were based on emotion and imagery. This approach to communications helps build brand awareness, desire and aspirational involvement. However, it often fails to provide customers with a rationale or explicit reason to purchase, what is often referred to as a 'call-to-action'. Other tools were required to provide customers with an impetus to act and sales promotions, event marketing, road shows and, later, direct marketing evolved to fulfil this need. These tools are known collectively as *below-the-line communications tools* and their common characteristic is that they are all capable of driving action or creating behavioural change.

The use of emotion in advertising

The role of emotion in advertising is very important. For a long time advertising was thought to work by people responding to advertising in a logical, rational and cognitive manner. This indicated that people only take out the utilitarian aspect of advertising messages (cleans better, smells fresher). This is obviously not true and there is certainly a strong case for the use of emotion in advertising in order to influence and change attitudes through the affective component of the attitudinal construct (see Chapter 4).

Most advertised brands are not normally new to consumers as they have had some experience of the brand, whether that be through use or just through communications. This experience affects their interpretation of advertising as memories have already been formed. The role of feelings in the way ads work suggests a consumerist interpretation of how advertising works rather than the rational view, which is much more a researcher's interpretation (Ambler, 1998).

Consumers view advertising in the context of their experience of the category and memories of the brand. Aligned with this approach is the concept of likeability (discussed in Chapter 10), where the feelings evoked by advertising trigger and shape attitudes to the brand and attitudes to the advertisement (Vakratsas and Ambler, 1999). Feelings and emotions play an important role in advertising, especially when advertising is used to build awareness levels and brand strength. The case study of John Lewis's Christmas campaign in Chapter 19 highlights the effectiveness of using emotion in advertising.

Most of the models presented later in this chapter are developed on the principle that individuals are cognitive processors and that ads are understood as a result of information processing. The best examples of these are the sequential models referred to earlier (see Chapter 6) where information is processed step by step. This view is not universally accepted. Researchers such as Krugman (1971), Ehrenberg (1974), Corke and Heath (2004), Heath and Feldwick (2008) and Heath et al. (2009) all dispute the importance of information processing, denying that attention is necessary for people to understand ads and that the creativity within an ad is more important in many circumstances than the rational message the ad purports to deliver.

Types of advertising

There are many ways of categorising advertising, but five perspectives encapsulate the variety of types available. These are the source, the message, the recipient, the media and place (see Figure 13.1).

The source or sender of a message results in different forms of advertising. Using the value chain as a frame, we can identify manufacturers, who in turn will use *manufacturing advertising* to promote their brands to end-users, and retailers who use advertising to attract consumers, *retail advertising*. On some occasions manufacturers collaborate with retailers and use *cooperative advertising*.

Outside the commercial arena, governments use *collective advertising* to communicate with nations, regions and districts, while many not-for-profit organisations use

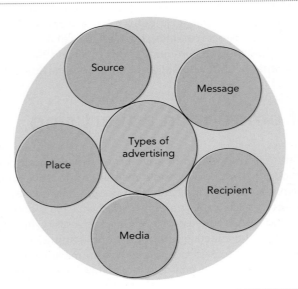

Figure 13.1 Types of advertising
Source: Adapted from De Pelsmacker, P., Geuens, M. and Van Den Berg, J. (2016). Marketing Communications.
A European Perspective (6th ed). Pearson Education.

idea-based advertising. Viewpoint 13.1 provides an example of how advertising is used in a non-commercial context.

The message can provide a further way of categorising advertising. Informational advertising uses messages that predominantly provide information about product and service attributes and features. *Transformational advertising* uses messages that are essentially emotional and which have the capacity to transform the way an individual feels about a product or service. An extreme form of transformational advertising is shock advertising.

Institutional or corporate advertising is undertaken by organisations to express values, intentions, position or other organisation-based issues. This type of advertising can also be used to build reputation, goodwill and relationships, at either a product/service or corporate level.

Theme advertising is most easily represented by ads designed for employee recruitment, or to attract people to events and entertainment venues. The origins of recruitment advertising are of course rooted in hiring help and employees in order to develop an organisation. However, more recently some employers have started to use this type of advertising as a form of reputational instrument. Whether it is through broadcast, print, or online and social network media, advertising is used to influence corporate image and reputation in order to create perceptions that the organisation is a desirable place to work. This might be to sow the seeds and build relationships, in order to recruit at some point in the future, rather than now.

Generic advertising is used to promote a category of products such as dog food, New Zealand lamb or South African wine. For example, the Almond Board of California represents over 6,000 almond growers and uses generic advertising to communicate the health and nutritional benefits of Californian almonds (Almond Board of California, 2018).

Finally in this section, direct-response advertising is used to provoke action. Sometimes referred to as call-to-action advertising, this approach is often used to support sales promotion programmes.

The recipient of advertising messages may be *consumers (advertising)* or *businesses*. The latter can be broken down to industrial and trade advertising. The former represents advertising for products that are used within production and manufacturing processes, whereas the latter concerns products that are resold down the supply chain.

The media category refers to the type of media used to carry advertising messages. For example, *broadcast advertising* refers to the use of television and radio, *print advertising* to newspapers and magazines, *out-of-home* to billboards, posters, transport and terminal buildings, *digital* to internet, mobile and online advertising. In addition, there is *ambient advertising* (petrol pump nozzles, golf holes, washrooms) and cinema advertising. Each of these media is explored in greater detail later in the book. Related to this are display ads that are placed in media for recipients to view, consider, process and form views. These might be magazine or newspaper ads, or banners and pop-ups. Digital media enable interactivity and here both search and social media advertising have become prominent types of advertising.

Place advertising is most commonly represented by *international advertising*. Reference is normally made to *standardised advertising*, where a single message is used in all countries and regions, and to *adapted advertising* where messages and media are altered and amended to reflect local needs and customs.

Advertising models and concepts

For many years a large number of researchers have attempted to determine how advertising works. Finding a real answer would bring commercial success. We know that for a message to be communicated successfully it should be meaningful to the recipient. Messages need to be targeted at the right audience, be capable of gaining attention, be understandable, relevant and acceptable.

One approach to answering this question has been to model the advertising process. From such a model it should be possible to test the linkages and deduce how advertising works. Unfortunately, despite the effort of many researchers over many years, no single model has attracted widespread agreement. However, from all the work undertaken in this area some views have been prominent. The following sections seek to present some of these more influential perspectives.

The elaboration likelihood model

What should be clear from the preceding sections is that neither the purely cognitive nor the purely emotional interpretation of how marketing communications works is realistic. In effect, it is probable that both have an important part to play in the way the various tools, and advertising in particular, work. The degree of emphasis, however, should vary according to the context within which the marketing communications message is expected to work.

One approach to utilise both these elements has been developed by Petty and Cacioppo (1983). The elaboration likelihood model (ELM) has helped to explain how cognitive processing, persuasion and attitude change occur when different levels of involvement are present. Elaboration refers to the extent to which an individual needs to develop and refine information necessary for decision making to occur. If an individual has a high level of motivation or ability to process information, elaboration is said to be high. If an individual's motivation or ability to process information is poor, then the level of elaboration is said to be low. The ELM distinguishes two main cognitive processes, as depicted in Figure 13.2.

Under the central route the receiver is viewed as very active and involved. As the level of cognitive response is high, the ability of the message (advertisement) to persuade will depend on the quality of the argument rather than executional factors. For example, the purchase of a consumer durable such as a car or washing machine normally requires a high level of involvement. Consequently, potential customers would be expected to be highly

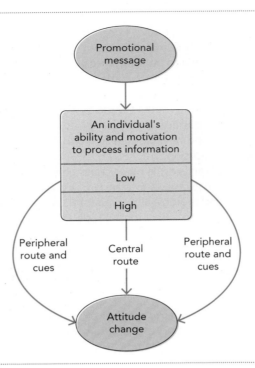

Figure 13.2 The elaboration likelihood model
Source: Based on Petty and Cacioppo (1983); Petty et al. (1983).

involved and willing to read brochures and information about the proposed car or washing machine prior to demonstration or purchase. Their decision to act would depend on the arguments used to justify the model as suitable for the individual. For the car purchase these might include the quiet and environmentally friendly engine, the relatively excellent fuel consumption and other safety and performance indicators, together with the comfort of the interior and the effortless driving experience. Whether the car is shown as part of a business executive's essential 'kit' or the commercial is flamboyant and rich will be immaterial for those in the central route.

Under the peripheral route, the receiver is seen to lack the ability to process information and is not likely to engage cognitive processing. Rather than thinking about and evaluating the message content, the receiver tends to rely on what have been referred to as 'peripheral cues', which may be incidental to the message content. Panasonic uses peripheral cues to attract attention to its brand. This is because most people have low levels of elaboration concerning picture technology and electronics.

In low-involvement situations, a celebrity may serve to influence attitudes positively. This is based upon the creation of favourable attitudes towards the source rather than engaging the viewer in the processing of the message content. For example, Gary Lineker has been the celebrity spokesperson used to endorse Walkers crisps for many years. Gary Lineker, former Tottenham and England football hero and now BBC sports presenter, was an important peripheral cue for Walkers crisps (more so than the nature of the product), in eventually persuading a consumer to try the brand or retaining current users. Think crisps, think Gary Lineker, think Walkers. Where high involvement is present, any celebrity endorsement is of minor significance to the quality of the message claims.

Viewpoint 13.2
Puppy Monkey Baby

Image 13.3 Puppy Monkey Baby featured a hybrid creature, combining a puppy, a monkey and a baby
Source: PepsiCo.

The Super Bowl is the annual championship of the National Football League (NFL). It is one of the biggest sporting events in the US and attracts very large TV audiences. Because of the high viewership, advertising rates are high and advertisers have been known to go to great lengths to produce stand-out advertising. As a result there is always a lot of anticipation around the ads that run, from both media and consumers.

Mountain Dew hadn't advertised during the Super Bowl for 15 years and the beverage company returned to this iconic advertising event with a 30-second spot, 'Puppy Monkey Baby'.

The ad was created for the company's new brand, Kickstart, which combines three ingredients; Mountain Dew, juice and caffeine. The ad, Puppy Monkey Baby, featured a hybrid creature, combining three things; a puppy, a monkey and a baby.

The ad also shows three friends having a quiet night in, when Puppy Monkey Baby arrives with a bucket of Mountain Dew's new beverage, Kickstart. The creature has the head of a puppy, the legs of a baby and the body of a monkey and wears a baby's nappy. The creature is cute, but strange.

After moving around the room and chanting 'puppy monkey baby', the creature licks one of the men's faces.

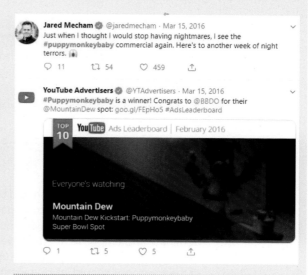

Image 13.4 The audiences' response was mixed
Source: Screenshot © Twitter Inc.

The audiences' response was mixed, with some loving Puppy Monkey Baby and others less impressed. However, the ad got everyone talking. The media were discussing it on live TV and the #PuppyMonkeyBaby trended on Twitter.

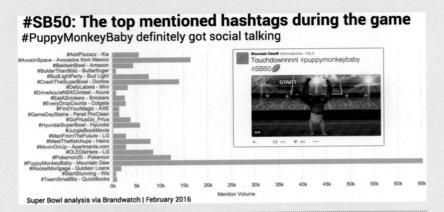

Image 13.5 Puppy Monkey Baby got audiences talking
Source: Screenshot © Twitter Inc.

Source: O'Reilly (2016a); Puppy Monkey Baby (2016); Saeed (2016).

Insight

The ad makes us challenge how advertising works. Puppy Monkey Baby undoubtedly stood out from the rest of the ads shown during Super Bowl and engaged audiences in conversations.

The example also highlights the importance of creative ideas being novel if they are to be effective.

Question: Why do you think Mountain Dew chose to use the Puppy Monkey Baby ad for the Super Bowl? Which route within the elaboration likelihood model (ELM) does this suggest Mountain Dew's consumers follow when purchasing beverages?

Task: Find three examples of other beverage advertising and explain the ELM route assumed by each.

Communications strategy should be based upon the level of cognitive processing that the target audience is expected to engage in and the route taken to affect attitudinal change. If the processing level is low (low motivation and involvement), the peripheral route should dominate and emphasis needs to be placed on the way the messages are executed and on the emotions of the target audience (Heath, 2000). If the central route is expected, the content of the messages should be dominant and the executional aspects need only be adequate.

The ELM model has not been without criticism, however, and a recent review of the model by Kitchen et al. (2014) questions the validity and relevance of the model in modern communications contexts. The authors raise concerns over the model's assumptions and descriptive nature (Kitchen et al., 2014).

Scholars' paper 13.3
The ELM model

Petty, R.E. and Cacioppo, J.T. (1984) Source factors and the elaboration likelihood model of persuasion, *Advances in Consumer Research*, 11(1), 668–72.

This is an important paper because it introduces the elaboration likelihood model. This is based on ideas about how people process ads, relative to how motivated they are to process the information. When people lack motivation and are unable to process a message, they prefer to rely on simple cues in the persuasion context, such as the expertise or attractiveness of the message source. When people are highly motivated and able to process the arguments in a message, they are interested in reviewing all the available information.

See also:

Kitchen, P.J., Kerr, G., Schultz, D.E., McColl, R. and Pals, H. (2014) The elaboration likelihood model: review, critique and research agenda, *European Journal of Marketing*, 48(11/12), 2033–50.

Eclectic models of advertising

A number of new frameworks and explanations have arisen, all of which claim to reflect practice. In other words, these new ideas about how advertising works are a practitioner reflection of the way advertising is considered to work, or at least be used, by advertising agencies. The first to be considered here are four main advertising frameworks developed by O'Malley (1991) and Hall (1992). These reflect the idea that there are four key ways in which advertising works, depending on context and goals. This also says that different advertising works in different ways; there is no one all-embracing model. These were updated by Willie (2007) to incorporate the impact of digital media and interactivity. Figure 13.3 depicts the essence of all of these ideas. The essential point is that advertising cannot be explained by a single interpretation or model.

Each of the following sections has two components. The first refers to the original interpretation, and the second to the work of Willie and the digital element.

1. The persuasion framework

Analogue – the first framework assumes advertising works rationally, and that a 'brand works harder for you'. This is based on messages that are persuasive, because they offer a rational difference, grounded in unique selling propositions (USPs). Persuasion is effected by gradually moving buyers through a number of sequential steps, as depicted through hierarchy of effects models such as AIDA.

Digital – digitisation enables persuasion to be extended into opportunities for exploration, as individuals can now be encouraged to search, 'go to', and to find out more. Willie (2007) points out that this is still persuasion, but it occurs through guided exploration, rather than mere narration.

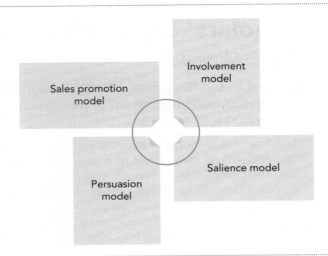

Figure 13.3 Four interpretations of how different ads work

2. The involvement framework

Analogue – involvement-based advertisements work by drawing the audience into the advertisement and eliciting a largely emotional form of engagement. Involvement with the brand develops because the messages convey that the 'brand means more to you'. As Willie (2007) indicates, involvement can be developed through shared values (Dove), aspirational values (American Express) or by personifying a brand, perhaps by using celebrities (Adidas).

Digital – today digitisation develops the notion of involvement by encouraging people to play. This is about content creation and consumers controlling brands. User-generated content can be seen through ads (crowdsourcing), blogs, wikis, videos and social networking, for example. The example of This Girl Can in Viewpoint 13.1 shows how involving consumers in the process works.

3. The salience framework

Analogue – this interpretation is based upon the premise that advertising works by standing out, by being different from all other advertisements in the product class. The ads used by brands such as Cillit Bang, GoCompare.com, Injurylawyers4u and Sheila's Wheels were deemed by consumers to be irritating, partly because the messages make people think about the brand more frequently than they would prefer.

Digital – contemporary interpretations of salience incorporate ideas about sharing messages about the brand either directly or virally, and getting the brand discussed, mentioned and talked about. The Puppy Monkey Baby Super Bowl ad discussed in Viewpoint 13.2 is a good example of this.

4. The sales promotion framework

Analogue – this view holds that advertising activities are aimed ultimately at shifting product: that is, generating sales. Messages are invitations to participate in promotions, sales and various forms of price deals. This framework, oriented mainly to direct-response work, is based on the premise that the level of sales is the only factor that is worth considering when measuring the effectiveness of an advertising campaign.

Digital – digitisation has not affected this framework, simply because sales promotion was always a 'do' or behavioural model. However, campaigns such as SNICKERS HUNGERITHM highlight how digital sales promotion campaigns can increase engagement.

Table 13.1   Digital and analogue advertising messages

Analogue-delivered messages say	Framework	Digitally delivered messages encourage
This is the reason why this brand is different	Persuasion	People to explore a brand such as search
Imagine you are associated with the brand	Involvement	People to play and create content
Please think about this brand	Salience	People to talk and share information about a brand
Act now because you will be rewarded	Promotion	People to act now because they will be rewarded

The analogue-based frameworks represent communications that induce a thinking, value-based response. The digital-based frameworks represent a behavioural response that is related to the brand, not the communications. These two fundamentally different types of response can be seen in Table 13.1. Furthermore, the models bring to attention two important points about people and advertising. Advertisements are capable of generating two very clear types of response: a response to the advertisement itself and a response to the featured brand. Both have clear roles to play in advertising strategy.

The Strong and the Weak theories of advertising

Many of the explanations offered to date are based on the premise that advertising is a potent marketing force, one that is persuasive and which is done to people. More recent views of advertising theory question this fundamental perspective. The second group of eclectic interpretations about how advertising works concerns ideas about advertising as a force for persuasion and as a force for reminding people about brands. Prominent among these theorists are Jones, McDonald and Ehrenberg, some of whose views will now be presented. Jones (1991) presented the new views as the Strong theory of advertising and the Weak theory of advertising.

The Strong theory of advertising

All the models presented so far are assumed to work on the basis that they are capable of affecting a degree of change in the knowledge, attitudes, beliefs and, sometimes, the behaviour of audiences. Jones refers to this as the Strong theory of advertising, and it appears to have been universally adopted as a foundation for commercial activity.

According to Jones, exponents of this theory hold that advertising can persuade someone to buy a product that they have never previously purchased. Furthermore, continual long-run purchase behaviour can also be generated. Under the Strong theory, advertising is believed to be capable of increasing sales at the brand and class levels. These upward shifts are achieved through the use of manipulative and psychological techniques, which are deployed against consumers who are passive, possibly because of apathy, and are generally incapable of processing information intelligently. The most appropriate theory would appear to be the hierarchy of effects model, where sequential steps move buyers forward to a purchase, stimulated by timely and suitable promotional messages.

The Weak theory of advertising

Increasing numbers of European writers argue that the Strong theory does not reflect practice. Most notable of these writers is Ehrenberg (1988, 1997), who believes that a consumer's pattern of brand purchases is driven more by habit than by exposure to promotional messages. The framework proposed by Ehrenberg is the awareness–trial–reinforcement (ATR) framework. Awareness is required before any purchase can be made, although the elapsed time between awareness and action may be very short or very long. For the few people intrigued enough to want to try a product, a trial purchase constitutes the next phase. This may be stimulated by retail availability as much as by advertising, word-of-mouth or personal selling stimuli. Reinforcement follows to maintain awareness and provide reassurance to help the customer to repeat the pattern of thinking and behaviour and to cement the brand in the repertoire for occasional purchase activity. Advertising's role is to breed brand familiarity and identification (Ehrenberg, 1997) and is considered to be a weak force.

Following on from the original ATR model (Ehrenberg, 1974), various enhancements have been suggested. However, Ehrenberg added a further stage in 1997, referred to as the nudge.

He argues that some consumers can 'be nudged into buying the brand more frequently (still as part of their split-loyalty repertoires) or to favour it more than the other brands in their consideration sets'. Advertising need not be any different from before; it just provides more reinforcement that stimulates particular habitual buyers into more frequent selections of the brand from their repertoire.

According to the Weak theory, advertising is capable of improving people's knowledge, and so is in agreement with the Strong theory. In contrast, however, consumers are regarded as selective in determining which advertisements they observe and only perceive those that promote products that they either use or have some prior knowledge of. This means that they already have some awareness of the characteristics of the advertised product. It follows that the amount of information actually communicated is limited. Advertising, Jones continues, is not potent enough to convert people who hold reasonably strong beliefs that are counter to those portrayed in an advertisement. The time available (30 seconds in television advertising) is not enough to bring about conversion and, when combined with people's ability to switch off their cognitive involvement, means there may be no effective communications. Advertising is employed as a defence, to retain customers and to increase product or brand usage. Advertising is used to reinforce existing attitudes, not necessarily to change them drastically.

Unlike the Strong theory, this perspective accepts that, when people say that they are not influenced by advertising, they are in the main correct. It also assumes that people are not apathetic or even stupid, but capable of high levels of cognitive processing.

In summary, the Strong theory suggests that advertising can be persuasive, can generate long-run purchasing behaviour, can increase sales and regards consumers as passive. The Weak theory suggests that purchase behaviour is based on habit and that advertising can improve knowledge and reinforce existing attitudes. It views consumers as active problem-solvers.

These two perspectives serve to illustrate the dichotomy of views that has emerged about this subject. They are important because they are both right and they are both wrong. The answer to the question 'How does advertising work?' lies somewhere between the two views and is dependent upon the particular situation facing each advertiser. Where elaboration is likely to be high if advertising is to work, then it is most likely to work under the Strong theory. For example, consumer durables and financial products require that advertising urges prospective customers into some form of trial behaviour. This may be a call for more information from a sales representative or perhaps a visit to a showroom. The vast majority of product purchases, however, involve low levels of elaboration, where involvement is low and where people select, often unconsciously, brands from an evoked set.

New products require people to convert or change their purchasing patterns. It is evident that the Strong theory must prevail in these circumstances. Where products become established, their markets generally mature, so that real growth is non-existent. Under these circumstances, advertising works by protecting the consumer franchise and by allowing users to have their product choices confirmed and reinforced. The other objective of this form of advertising is to increase the rate at which customers reselect and consume products.

If the Strong theory were the only acceptable approach then, theoretically, advertising would be capable of continually increasing the size of each market, until everyone had been converted. There would be no 'stationary' markets.

Considering the vast sums that are allocated to advertising budgets, not only to launch new products but also to pursue market-share targets aggressively, the popularity and continued implicit acceptance of the power of advertising suggest that a large proportion of resources is wasted in the pursuit of advertising-driven brand performance. Indeed, it is noticeable that organisations have been switching resources out of advertising into digital, brand experiences and sales promotion activities. There are many reasons for this, but one of them concerns the failure of advertising to produce the expected levels of performance: to produce market share. The Strong theory fails to deliver the expected results, and the Weak theory does not apply to all circumstances. Reality is probably a mixture of the two.

Viewpoint 13.3
Google Home of the Whopper

Image 13.6 The TV ad triggered audiences' Google Home devices
Source: Rob Wilson/Shutterstock.

The Whopper is well known as Burger King's signature burger. Burger King have always been keen to boast of the Whopper's fresh ingredients, great taste and flame-grilled preparation. A short 30-second TV ad, however, is not always long enough to get all these messages across.

Google Home provided Burger King with the perfect way to deliver these important Whopper messages to consumers in a 15-second ad. Identifying that many consumers have Google Home, the brand realised that all they needed to do was create a 15-second TV ad that spoke directly to Google Home. As many consumers keep their Google Home devices near their TVs, Burger King created an ad, which activated Google Home to answer the questions they posed on TV. By doing this, the ad was extended to 30 seconds.

Burger King ran TV spots that asked: 'OK Google, what is in the Whopper Burger?' to trigger audiences' Google Home devices to respond with the entire list of ingredients from Wikipedia's entry for the Whopper.

The campaign had 9.3 billion global impressions and trended globally on YouTube, Facebook, Twitter and Google Trends. Google Home of the Whopper was the most talked about ad in the brand's history. The campaign also led to Google Home changing its software to react to only six voices.

Other results were:

- $135 million in earned media;
- a 500 per cent increase in brand mentions;

- 10 million organic views online within the first 48 hours;
- 15 million online-only views, vs the 700,000 Google Home devices targeted through paid media.

Source: Diaz (2017); Google Home of the Whopper (2017); Monllos (2017).

Insight

Burger King was the first brand to use voice-activated technology in advertising and showed how technology can be disrupted to engage audiences. The campaign corresponds with Willie's (2007) interpretation of advertising and highlights how consumers are willing to talk about and share advertising.

Question: What are the advantages and disadvantages of using voice-activated technology in advertising? Consider this from both the brand and consumer perspective.

Task: Find another example of an advertising campaign that has used voice-activated technology. How likely is it that this ad will be shared and talked about? Justify your reasons for this answer.

Scholars' paper 13.4
How advertising really works

Nyilasy, G. and Reid, L.N. (2009) Agency practitioner theories of how advertising works, *Journal of Advertising*, **38(3), 81–96.**

This is an interesting paper because it explores how those in the industry think advertising works and helps us to understand more about the academician–practitioner gap that exists. The study suggests practitioners have their own core theories about how advertising works, which includes a two-step 'break through and engage' process and a longer-term 'mutation of effects' concept. The findings also highlight the important role of emotion in advertising and the value attributed to creativity in advertising.

See also:

Vakratsas, D. and Ambler, T. (1999) How advertising works: what do we really know? *Journal of Marketing*, 63(1), 26–43.

Using advertising strategically

There are many varied and conflicting ideas about the strategic use of advertising. For a long time the management of the tools of the communications mix was considered strategic. Indeed, many practitioners still believe in this approach. However, ideas concerning integrated marketing communications (see Chapter 12) and corporate identity have helped provide a fresh perspective on what constitutes advertising strategy, and issues concerning differentiation, brand values and the development of brand equity have helped establish both a strategic and a tactical or operational aspect associated with advertising.

One of the first significant attempts to formalise advertising's strategic role was developed by Vaughn when working for an advertising agency, Foote, Cone and Belding (FCB). These ideas (see below) were subsequently debated and an alternative model emerged from Rossiter and Percy. Both frameworks have been used extensively by advertising agencies, and although their influence has now subsided, the underlying variables and approach remain central to strategic advertising thought.

The FCB matrix

Vaughn (1980) developed a matrix utilising involvement and brain specialisation theories. Brain specialisation theory suggests that the left-hand side of the brain is best for handling rational, linear and cognitive thinking, whereas the right-hand side is better able to manage spatial, visual and emotional issues (the affective or feeling functions).

Vaughn proposed that by combining involvement with elements of thinking and feeling, four primary advertising planning strategies can be distinguished. These are informative, affective, habitual and self-satisfaction (see Figure 13.4). According to Vaughn, the matrix is intended to be a thought provoker rather than a formula or model from which prescriptive solutions are to be identified. The FCB matrix is a useful guide to help analyse and appreciate consumer/product relationships and to develop appropriate communications strategies. The four quadrants of the grid identify particular types of decision-making and

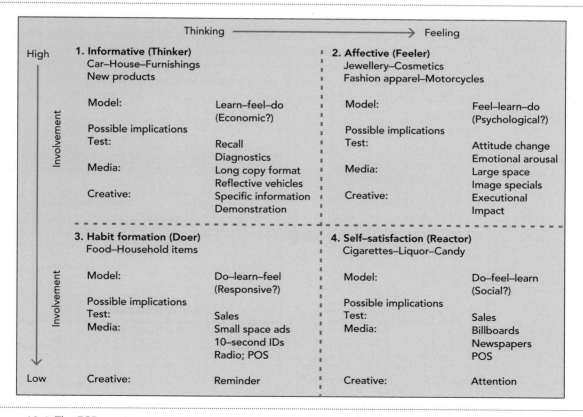

Figure 13.4 The FCB matrix
Source: Vaughn (1980). Used with kind permission from WARC.

each requires different advertising approaches. Vaughn suggests that different orderings from the learn–feel–do sequence can be observed. By perceiving the different ways in which the process can be ordered, he proposed that the learn–feel–do sequence should be visualised as a continuum, a circular concept. Communications strategy would, therefore, be based on the point of entry that consumers make to the cycle.

Some offerings, generally regarded as 'habitual', may be moved to another quadrant, such as 'responsive', to develop differentiation and establish a new position for the product in the minds of consumers relative to the competition. This could be achieved by the selection of suitable media vehicles and visual images in the composition of the messages associated with an advertisement. There is little doubt that this model, or interpretation of the advertising process, has made a significant contribution to our understanding of the advertising process and has been used by a large number of advertising agencies (Joyce, 1991).

The Rossiter–Percy grid

Rossiter et al. (1991), however, disagree with some of the underpinnings of the FCB grid and offer a new one in response (revised 1997) (see Figure 13.5). They suggest that involvement is not a continuum because it is virtually impossible to decide when a person graduates from high to low involvement. They claim that the FCB grid fails to account for situations where a person moves from high to low involvement and then back to high, perhaps on a temporary basis, when a new variant is introduced to the market. Rossiter et al. regard involvement as the level of perceived risk present at the time of purchase. Consequently, it is the degree of familiarity buyers have at the time of purchase that is an important component.

A further criticism is that the FCB grid is an attitude-only model. Rossiter et al. identify the need for brand awareness to be built into such grids as a prerequisite for attitude development. However, they cite the need to differentiate different purchase situations. Some brands require awareness recall because the purchase decision is made prior to the act of purchasing. Other brands require awareness recognition at the point of purchase, where the buyer needs to be prompted into brand choice decisions. Each of these situations requires different message strategies, which are explored in Chapter 19.

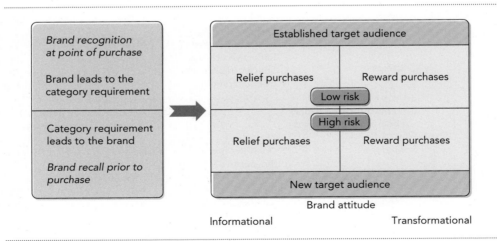

Figure 13.5 The Rossiter–Percy grid
Source: Adapted from Rossiter and Percy (1997). Used with kind permission.

The other major difference between the two grids concerns the 'think–feel' dimension. Rossiter et al. believe that a wider spectrum of motives must be incorporated, as the FCB 'think–feel' interpretation fails to accommodate differences between product category and brand purchase motivations. For example, the decision to use a product category may be based on a strictly functional and utilitarian need. The need to travel to another country often requires air transport. The choice of carrier, however, particularly over the North Atlantic, is a brand choice decision, motivated by a variety of sensory and ego-related inputs and anticipated outputs. Rossiter et al. disaggregate motives into what they refer to as *informational* and *transformational*. By detailing motives into these classifications, a more precise approach to advertising tactics can be developed. Furthermore, the confusion inherent in the FCB grid, between the think and involvement elements, is overcome.

It should be understood that these 'grids' are purely hypothetical, and there is no proof or evidence to suggest that they are accurate reflections of advertising. It is true that both models have been used as the basis for advertising strategy in many agencies, but that does not mean that they are totally reliable or, more importantly, that they have been tested empirically so that they can be used in total confidence. They are interpretations of commercial and psychological activity and have been instrumental in advancing our level of knowledge. It is in this spirit of development that these models are presented in this text.

There are parts in both of these frameworks that have a number of strong elements of truth attached to them. However, for products that are purchased on a regular basis, pull strategies should be geared to defending the rationale that current buyers use to select the brand. Heavy buyers select a particular brand more often than light users do from their repertoire. By providing a variety of consistent stimuli, and by keeping the brand alive, fresh buyers are more likely to prefer and purchase a particular brand than those that allow their brands to lose purchase currency and the triggers necessary to evoke memory impressions.

For products purchased on an irregular basis, marketing communications needs only touch the target audience on a relatively low number of occasions. Strategies need to be developed that inform and contextualise the purchase rationale for consumers. This means providing lasting impressions that enable consumers to understand the circumstances in which purchase of a particular product/brand should be made once a decision has been made to purchase from the product category. Here the priorities are to communicate messages that will encourage consumers to trust and bestow expertise on the product/ brand that is offered.

Traditionally advertising has been used to develop brand identities by stimulating awareness and perception. Advertising had evolved to a point in the 1980s where the focus on developing brand identities and brand values alone was commercially insufficient for clients. The subsequent growth of direct marketing approaches and one-to-one, preferably interactive, communications have become paramount. Marketing budgets have swung in sympathy, and are now very often allocated towards communications that drive a call-to-action; in particular, online communications have been taking a progressively larger share of advertising budgets over the last decade. Consequently, the imperative today is about generating a behavioural rather than an attitudinal response to advertising and other marketing communications campaigns.

So, in this context, what is the role for advertising and what strategies should be used in the contemporary media landscape? One approach would be to maintain current advertising strategies on the grounds that awareness and perception are always going to be key factors. Another approach would be to call for advertising to be used solely for direct-response work. Neither of these two options seems appropriate or viable in the twenty-first century.

In an age where values and response are both necessary ingredients for effective overall communications, advertising strategy in the future will probably need to be based on emotional engagement and an increased level of integration with a range of other forms of communications. Customers will want to engage with the values offered by a brand that are significant to them individually. However, clients will also need to engage with them at a behavioural level and to encourage individuals to want to respond to advertising. Advertising strategy should therefore reflect a brand's context and be adjusted according to the required level of engagement regarding identity development and the required level of behavioural response. Advertising will no longer be able to assume the lead role in a campaign and should be used according to the engagement needs of the audience first, the brand second and the communications industry third, in that order. One of the more integrative approaches concerns the need to use advertising to drive web traffic. This offline/online bridge is a critical aspect of many communications strategies. The examples given in Viewpoints 13.1 and 13.2 highlight how advertising can drive online conversations.

Viewpoint 13.4
Shot on iPhone

Image 13.7 Images are sourced from iPhone users around the globe
Source: Bon Appetit/Shutterstock.

Apple's 'Shot on iPhone' campaign is seen to be one of the best examples of consumer-generated advertising in recent years. Apple wanted to demonstrate the quality of the camera on their iPhone and source images from users around the globe. Asking users to generate the images for the advertising using their iPhones provides credibility and authenticity to the campaign.

The idea behind the campaign is very simple. Apple search for photos taken by iPhone users on Instagram and Flickr using the 'Shot on iPhone' hashtag and the photographs are selected to be used in Apple's advertising. Apple contacts the photographers by email and advises them that their photos have been chosen for the Apple World Gallery.

The users' photographs have been displayed on over 10,000 billboards across 25 countries. Photographs are also used on print posters, TV and online. This mobile gallery of photography brings together users' images taken on their iPhones and creates a unique collection of photos from around the globe.

For the users whose photos are chosen, this gives them the chance to have their photos on display in some exciting locations and provides an opportunity to take part in a global advertising campaign. Many of the photographers have found the experience of having their photo selected life changing and have shared their journeys online.

Sources: Nudd (2017); O'Reilly (2016b).

Insight

Apple's 'Shot on iPhone' campaign highlights some of the advantages of sourcing photography from users for advertising. Apple is able to select from a large number of images taken all over the world, without having to pay a photographer to travel. The process for selection is tightly managed and this reduces the risk of loss of control on the brand message. There is also the advantage that selected users generate online conversations around their own images being selected.

Question: Why did iPhone users want to participate in this campaign? List the possible motivations using Table 13.2 as a guide.

Task: Find another example of a user-generated campaign. List the advantages and disadvantages of participating for both brand and consumer.

Consumer-generated advertising

To conclude this chapter and the strategic perspective on advertising, attention needs to be given to the inexorable rise in user- or consumer-generated advertising (CGA). Shulga et al. (2018: 214) define consumer-generated advertising (CGA) as 'User-generated brand-related content that has components, form and the intent of traditional advertising'. In other words, CGA looks the same as any other advertising, but is made by the public. (UGC is considered in Chapter 19 on messages and creativity, and that material will not be repeated here.)

Much of the advertising explored in this chapter is based on the brand-to-consumer dynamic, a unidirectional interpretation, anchored in a client-agency origin. Increasingly today consumers not only reject this passive-response-based model but are now creating and distributing their own ads, very often as videos hosted on video-sharing sites such as YouTube. The growth in video is seen to be fuelling a revolution in advertising (Campbell et al., 2011).

While many brands are not comfortable with the lack of control that CGA represents and prefer to maintain a tighter control on their brand messages, others have fully embraced the phenomenon. Doritos is one brand that has taken advantage of the opportunity to encourage CGA and ran a series of competitions for consumers to make their own ads for the Super Bowl. The brand's 'Crash the Super Bowl' competition offered a prize and the chance for the winner to make the ad, which was broadcast during the Super Bowl commercial break (Castillo, 2015).

From a brand's perspective there are a number of potential advantages of using CGA, including the generation of a large number of ideas at a lower cost than traditional agency routes and the opportunities to generate media coverage. The reasons why consumers create and broadcast ads has been explored by Berthon et al. (2008) who identified three fundamental motivations: intrinsic enjoyment, self-promotion and perception change. These are explained in Table 13.2.

Brands also need to be aware of the potential drawbacks of involving consumers in advertising development. Thompson and Malaviya (2013) warn against the loss

Table 13.2   Three consumer motivations to create ads

Dominant motivation	Explanation
Intrinsic enjoyment	Here people are primarily creative and enjoy the process for the satisfaction and personal reward the activity brings. They are not so interested in what becomes of their work.
Self-promotion	In this situation people generate advertising materials as a means to an end. It may be that the activity is part of the process of attracting the attention of others, possibly a potential employer.
Perception change	Rather than achieve a tangible outcome, some advertising is generated by people in order to influence the way others think or feel, intangible outcomes. The goal is to change opinions, sentiments or attitudes but for altruistic reasons rather than personally driven, career-based goals.

Source: Based on Berthon et al. (2008).

of control and brand inconsistency. Additionally, the authors' research identified that consumer-generated advertising can undermine message persuasiveness and in cases of contest ads, prompt negative responses from consumers.

Campbell et al. (2011) explored responses to CGA and suggest these can be considered on two broad dimensions. The first dimension spans the *conceptual* – that is, curiosity in how or who created the ad – and *emotion* – how responses to the ad are driven essentially by emotion rather than reason. The second dimension concerns how a consumer's response to the ad either can be collaborative, where the viewer supports the ad's creator, or is in opposition and is hostile towards the ad, and/or its creator. From these dimensions four achetypes of CGA advertising are identified: inquiry, laudation, debate and flame.

Enquiry refers to responses that say: 'That is interesting, tell me more.' Laudation is about how good the ad is thought to be, the praise viewers give it. Debate concerns the different voices and divergent views or opinions on the topic of interest. Finally, flame concerns the outpouring of emotions, the diatribe that occurs when the debate becomes inflamed and hostile (Campbell et al., 2011).

Research by Campbell et al. (2011) identified that while viewers of CGA consider it to be a reliable source of word of mouth, most conversations driven by CGA were often not predominantly about the brand. Their study found that most conversations were around the music in the ad, the creators of the ad, 'and larger social themes such as international justice, globalisation, poverty, and corporate social responsibility'. This could have an important bearing on advertising messages and appeals in the future, especially for functional brands.

Key points

- The role of advertising in most marketing communications campaigns is to engage audiences and enable people to make brand-oriented associations. Engagement is enabled either by informing, changing perceptions and building brand values, or by encouraging a change in behaviour.
- A few of the established definitions have been perpetuated both by practitioners and by academics. These have generally failed to accommodate the changing media landscape and so a new definition is presented.
- Advertising is a paid, mediated form of communications from an identifiable source, designed to persuade the receiver to take some action, now or in the future.

- The idea that a product might have a unique selling proposition is in many cases totally misplaced and inaccurate. The rise of emotional selling points (ESPs) is much more realistic and practised by leading brands. This approach to communications helps build brand awareness, desire and aspirational involvement. However, it often fails to provide customers with a rationale or explicit reason to purchase, what is often referred to as a 'call-to-action'.

- The use of emotion in advertising is considered to be more important, and effective, than the use of information-based messages. Feelings and emotions play an important role in advertising, especially when advertising is used to build awareness levels and brand strength.

- There are many ways of categorising advertising, but five perspectives encapsulate the variety of types available. These are the source, the message, the recipient, the media and place.

- The elaboration likelihood model (ELM) has helped to explain how cognitive processing, persuasion and attitude change occur when different levels of involvement are present. Elaboration refers to the extent to which an individual needs to develop and refine information necessary for decision-making to occur. If an individual has a high level of motivation or ability to process information, elaboration is said to be high and central route processing is used. If an individual's motivation or ability to process information is poor, then the level of elaboration is said to be low, and peripheral processing is appropriate.

- Many of the ideas about how advertising works are a practitioner reflection of the way advertising is considered to work, or at least is used, by advertising agencies. The first to be considered here are the frameworks developed by O'Malley (1991) and Hall (1992), and later supplemented by Willie (2007). They suggest that there are four core advertising frameworks: persuasion/exploration, sales/do, salience/sharing and involvement/play.

- The Strong theory of advertising indicates that advertising is a strong influencing force and reflects the persuasion concept. The Weak theory suggests that advertising has little influence and that advertising should be regarded as a means of defending customers' purchase decisions and for protecting markets, not building them. Reality suggests that the majority of advertising cannot claim to be of significant value to most people and that the Strong and the Weak theories are equally applicable, although not at the same time nor in the same context.

- The FCB and Rossiter–Percy grids represent formalised attempts to interpret the strategic use of advertising. Intended to provide agencies with a method that might ensure consistency, meaning and value with respect to their clients' brands, these are no longer considered by agencies to be sufficiently flexible, rigorous or representative of how contemporary advertising performs. A more current perspective on advertising strategy suggests that advertising should become more engaged with the customer's experience of the brand and not be rooted just in the development of brand values.

- Consumer-generated advertising (CGA) concerns ads developed by members of the public about recognised brands. There are three fundamental motivations that consumers have for creating and broadcasting ads: intrinsic enjoyment, self-promotion and perception change. The critical issue associated with CGA concerns control and the ability of organisations to control the messages surrounding their brands.

Case study

Bolia.com: selling sofas in a financial meltdown

Lars Samuelsen, UNCLEGREY, Copenhagen, Denmark
Matthew Gladstone, GREY, London, UK
Mark Stockdale, The Effectiveness Partnership, London, UK

Image 13.8 Bolia.com introduced highly stylised fashion imagery
Source: Bernie Epstein/Alamy Stock Photo.

Bolia.com is a furniture retailer, founded in Aarhus, Denmark in 2000. It's a youthful brand and offers what it calls 'New Scandinavian Design' to an audience of ambitious, savvy young adults, selling through a modern, seamlessly integrated blend of online and physical stores originally in Denmark, then Norway, Sweden and beyond.

Bolia.com's offering was a winning formula and succeeded beyond all expectations for the first seven years. But then two things happened that changed Bolia.com's fortunes dramatically.

The first of these was the 2008 financial crisis, which unsurprisingly hit the housing market. Property sales across Denmark slumped. This was a major problem for Bolia.com because furniture sales have traditionally been closely bound-up with house sales – roughly a third of new furniture is bought by people who've just moved home. Worse still, it was the highest earners who cut back most, hitting premium brands and 'big ticket' items like sofas hardest. As a premium brand with 75 per cent of its sales accounted for by exactly these big-ticket items, Bolia.com was thus facing a proverbial double-whammy.

The second problem was the price cutting that ensued. Other furniture retailers were hurting too, and in their desperation to get people buying again they started dropping prices, undercutting

Bolia.com. And when that didn't work, they slashed prices even further – in some cases by up to 70 per cent. Bolia.com was now in serious trouble.

As the recession took hold Bolia.com's revenue stalled alarmingly, sales falling for the first time in the company's history. Worse, the business had started to lose a lot of money, profits evaporating almost overnight as they struggled to compete.

Bolia.com knew they couldn't continue 'scrapping it out' like this, and calculated that they had no more than two years to reverse their disastrous commercial performance.

Bolia.com refused to follow the herd and slash prices even deeper and harder. They'd probably end up just another discount furniture warehouse. The more they thought about it, the more convinced they became that the solution lay not in abandoning their vision but in staying true to what had driven their early success: New Scandinavian Design.

The solution

Bolia.com's customers are typically under 45, the biggest proportion being in their 30s. They're not yet settled in life, and feel driven to make their mark on the world.

Qualitative research revealed that their pain wasn't just economic, it was emotional too. For them, moving to a new home wasn't about simple functional things like a better location or more space. Each move signified their achievements, a sign they were making their mark. And how they furnished their new home was the icing on the cake – a clear, overt statement of who they'd become. So their furniture-buying wasn't functional, it was emotional. So not being able to move was hurting them – they felt they'd stopped 'making it'.

And this understanding opened up a big opportunity for Bolia.com, whose rivals were locked into thinking functionally, desperately hoping that if they kept on slashing prices someone, somewhere, would eventually buy something. But we'd come to realise that what our audience really wanted was emotional: they wanted their homes to reflect how they saw themselves and to display that to others.

Our opportunity was therefore to reposition the role of buying new furniture: not as a functional purchase triggered by moving home, but as the means to make your existing home say what you want it to say about you.

And so we came to think of furniture in the same way we would clothing or perfume or any other fashion item that powerfully expresses personal identity – what sofa do you want to 'put on', and what do you want it to say about you?

Communications

Bringing about this attitude change required a two-pronged role for communications:

1. We needed to change how young adults saw new furniture, breaking its traditional tie with house moving, and positioning it instead as the means to create a new home without moving – furniture as a personal statement, driven by the same deeply personal emotional drivers as any other fashion brand.

2. We needed to establish Bolia.com as the brand most able to deliver the furniture that signifies what you want your home to say about you – the best quality, most stylish and desirable, modern and fashionable furniture that you'll happily pay a premium for because it says exactly what you want it to say about you.

To succeed we'd have to attract new young adult shoppers, irrespective of whether they were moving house; and do so in sufficient numbers to reverse our sales decline.

The campaign was thus developed to meet the following tough objectives:

The creative work unashamedly aped fashion campaigns and wouldn't have looked out of place advertising perfume or designer suits. For the conservative, increasingly price-focused Danish furniture category, this was quite simply radical.

The new creative platform was summed up in a powerful statement that unequivocally expressed our insight into how the target audience felt about their homes.

Showcasing New Scandinavian Design was critical, but we needed to go further. Merely featuring lots of photos of lovely-looking sofas, tables and chairs, with relentless close-ups of gorgeous wood-grain and sexy handles and so forth, wasn't going to be enough. To succeed, the creative needed to make a fundamental shift in how new furniture was being marketed.

So we introduced cutting-edge fashion models and highly stylised fashion imagery, along with a sophisticated, contemporary tone-of-voice that spoke with the sort of wit and insight we knew would appeal to our audience. This was woven through all shopper contact-points – not just in advertising but

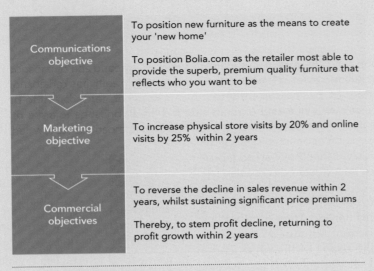

Communications objective	To position new furniture as the means to create your 'new home' To position Bolia.com as the retailer most able to provide the superb, premium quality furniture that reflects who you want to be
Marketing objective	To increase physical store visits by 20% and online visits by 25% within 2 years
Commercial objectives	To reverse the decline in sales revenue within 2 years, whilst sustaining significant price premiums Thereby, to stem profit decline, returning to profit growth within 2 years

Image 13.9 Bolio.com set clear objectives for the campaign to change how young adults saw new furniture
Source: Bolia International.

Image 13.10 Bolia.com's new creative platform
Source: Bolia International.

Image 13.11 Bolia.com's uber-contemporary quirky look, feel and personality was carried through to even the most 'straight' furniture and furnishings shots
Source: Bolia International.

also the physical stores, the website, the catalogue, social media . . . everything.

Implementation

The biggest shift we made was to commit to a vast increase in TV and online investment. TV brought to life the idea that 'the spaces we create are who we are' for our audience, supported by a host of digital activities (such as display ads, search, social media and mobile).

We moved from 'old fashioned' static media like posters into richer, more engaging formats in communications channels and touchpoints essentially owned by the brand – such as visually stunning brand catalogues, beautiful 'coffee table books' (sold in the stores for €50) and interactive in-store experiences.

Previously the media budget had been split 60 per cent tactical print and posters versus 40 per cent TV. The new approach had driven a shift to 65 per cent TV and 35 per cent digital, alongside significant investment in rich and engaging formats in our own channels and touchpoints.

Our creative solution presented a challenge – fashion imagery has a certain look and feel with very high production values, so scrimping and cutting corners wasn't an option.

Budgets therefore had to work harder than ever, so costs were minimised by redesigning the entire production process. Instead of four individually planned and executed productions a year we moved to one fully integrated set-up that would in effect roll seamlessly from one execution to the next. This enabled us not only to manage costs down, but also to work with world-class photographers, stylists and film production companies, dramatically step-changing our production values.

The results

Almost immediately the new campaign launched, sales began to recover, and they've continued to grow strongly ever since. After two years of decline, revenue returned to sustained growth and a stronger, more aspirational brand emerged, supported by an average 22 per cent price increase. Profits increased tenfold between 2010 and 2015, far exceeding targets. Despite the continued drop in house moving, the number of people visiting Bolia.com's physical and online stores rocketed, and brand perceptions improved dramatically – the brand was seen to be more modern and aspirational, and worth the price premium.

This case study is an edited version of a paper submitted to the IPA Effectiveness Awards 2016. It has been reproduced here with the kind permission of the IPA, WARC, Bolia.com and the agencies Grey and The Effectiveness Partnership, who wrote the original paper.

Review questions

Bolia.com case questions

1. How might the elaboration likelihood model be used to interpret how Bolia.com advertising works?

2. Discuss whether the Bolia.com advertising is predominantly trying to persuade audiences or designed to reinforce brand values.

3. Which of the eclectic models of advertising could be used to explain how Bolia.com advertising works?

4. What role does emotion play in this advertising?

5. Consider whether consumer-generated advertising would be appropriate for Bolia.com in the future. Discuss the advantages and disadvantages of using this approach.

General questions

1. Find three different advertisements and write notes explaining how they depict the thinking and feeling aspect of advertising, and the behavioural aspect of advertising.

2. Select an organisation of your choice and find three advertisements it has used recently. Are the ads predominantly trying to persuade audiences or are they designed to reinforce brand values?

3. What are the essential differences between the involvement and salience frameworks of advertising?

Find four advertisements (other than those described in this book) that are examples of these two approaches.

4. Write a short presentation explaining the differences between the Strong and Weak theories of advertising.

5. Draw the FCB grid and place on it the following product categories: shampoo, life assurance, sports cars, kitchen towels, a box of chocolates.

References for Chapter 13

Almond Board of California (2018) *About the Almond Board,* retrieved 10 April 2018 from www.almonds.co.uk/consumers/about-almond-board

Ambler, T. (1998) Myths about the mind: time to end some popular beliefs about how advertising works, *International Journal of Advertising,* 17, 501–9.

Anon (2018) This Girl Can. *FCBinferno,* retrieved 28 May 2018 from http://www.fcbinferno.com/work/case-studies/sport-england-tgc-new/

Berthon, P.R., Pitt, L.F. and Campbell, C. (2008) Ad lib: when customers create the ad, *California Management Review,* 50(4), 6–30.

Borau, S. and Nepomuceno, M. V. (2016) The self-deceived consumer: women's emotional and attitudinal reactions to the airbrushed thin ideal in the absence versus presence of disclaimers, *Journal of Business Ethics,* 1–16.

Campbell, C., Pitt, L.F., Parent, M. and Berthon, P.R. (2011) Understanding consumer conversations around ads in a Web 2.0 world, *Journal of Advertising,* 40(1), 87–102.

Campbell, C., Cohen, J. and Ma, J. (2014) Advertisements just aren't advertisements anymore: a new typology for evolving forms of online advertising, *Journal of Advertising Research,* 54(1), 7–10.

Castillo, M. (2015) Doritos reveals 10 'Crash the super bowl' ad finalists: which one of these will score the coveted TV spot? *Adweek,* 5 January, retrieved 23 May 2015 from www.adweek.com/news-gallery/advertising-branding/doritos-announces-10-crash-super-bowl-ad-finalists-162162

Corke, S. and Heath, R.G. (2004) The hidden power of newspaper advertising, *Media Research Group Conference,* Madrid (November).

Dahlen, M. and Rosengren, S. (2016) If advertising won't die, what will it be? Toward a working definition of advertising, *Journal of Advertising,* 45(3), 334–45.

De Pelsmacker, P., Guens, M. and Van den Bergh, J. (2010) *Marketing Communications: A European Perspective,* 4th edn, Harlow: Financial Times/Prentice Hall.

Diaz, A.-C. (2017) Burger King's Google Home hack wins Cannes Grand Prix in Direct. *Adage,* 20 June, retrieved 10 May 2018 from http://adage.com/article/special-report-cannes-lions/burger-king-s-google-home-hack-takes-grand-prix-direct/309506/

Ehrenberg, A.S.C. (1974) Repetitive advertising and the consumer, *Journal of Advertising Research,* 14 (April), 25–34.

Ehrenberg, A.S.C. (1988) *Repeat Buying,* 2nd edn, London: Charles Griffin.

Ehrenberg, A.S.C. (1997) How do consumers come to buy a new brand? *Admap,* March, 20–4.

Google Home of the Whopper (2017) Cannes Lions Archive, retrieved 10 January 2018 from http://www.canneslionsarchive.com/Home/PublicHome

Hall, M. (1992) Using advertising frameworks, *Admap,* March, 17–21.

Heath, R. (2000) Low involvement processing – a new model of brands and advertising, *International Journal of Advertising,* 19(3), 287–98.

Heath, R. and Feldwick, P. (2008) 50 years using the wrong model of TV advertising, *International Journal of Market Research,* 50(1), 25–59.

Heath, R.G., Nairn, A.C. and Bottomley, P.A. (2009) How effective is creativity? Emotive content in TV advertising does not increase attention, *Journal of Advertising Research,* September, 450–63.

Jones, J.P. (1991) Over-promise and under-delivery, *Marketing and Research Today,* November, 195–203.

Joyce, T. (1991) Models of the advertising process, *Marketing and Research Today*, November, 205–12.

Kemp, N. (2017) 'This girl can' targets older women with new campaign, *Campaign*, 30 January, retrieved 10 February 2018 from https://www.campaignlive.co.uk/article/this-girl-can-targets-older-women-new-campaign/1422505

Kitchen, P.J., Kerr, G., Schultz, D.E., McColl, R. and Pals, H. (2014) The elaboration likelihood model: review, critique and research agenda, *European Journal of Marketing*, 48(11/12), 2033–50.

Krugman, M.E. (1971) Brain wave measurement of media involvement, *Journal of Advertising*, 11(1), 3–9.

MMA (2015) *The Mobile Native Ad Formats*, retrieved 20 May 2015 from www.mmaglobal.com/documents/mobile-native-ad-formats

Monllos, K. (2017) Burger King's 'Outstanding, Outrageous' Google Home stunt snags Direct Grand Prix at Cannes. *Adweek*, 20 June, retrieved 10 May 2018 from https://www.adweek.com/creativity/burger-kings-outstanding-outrageous-google-home-stunt-snags-direct-grand-prix-at-cannes/

Nudd, T. (2017) Apple celebrates summer with joyful worldwide 'Shot on iPhone' out-of-home campaign, *Adweek*, 28 June, retrieved 10 May 2018 from https://www.adweek.com/creativity/apple-celebrates-summer-with-joyful-worldwide-shot-on-iphone-out-of-home-campaign/

Nyilasy, G. and Reid, L.N. (2009) Agency practitioner theories of how advertising works, *Journal of Advertising*, 38(3), 81–96.

O'Malley, D. (1991) Sales without salience? *Admap*, September, 36–9.

O'Reilly, L. (2016a) Mountain Dew's weird 'Puppy Monkey Baby' Super Bowl ad completely split viewers' opinions, *Business Insider*, retrieved 27 May 2018 from http://uk.businessinsider.com/mountain-dews-weird-puppy-monkey-baby-super-bowl-ad-completely-split-viewers-opinions-2016-2

O'Reilly, L. (2016b) Why Apple is rebooting its 'game-changer' billboard ads, *Business Insider*, 3 February, retrieved 10 January 2018 from http://uk.businessinsider.com/why-apple-is-re-running-its-shot-on-iphone-ad-campaign-2016-2

Petty, R.E. and Cacioppo, J.T. (1983) Central and peripheral routes to persuasion: application to advertising, in *Advertising and Consumer Psychology* (eds L. Percy and A. Woodside), Lexington, MA: Lexington Books, 3–23.

Petty, R.E. and Cacioppo, J.T. (1984) Source factors and the elaboration likelihood model of persuasion, *Advances in Consumer Research*, 11(1), 668–72.

Petty, R.E., Cacioppo, J.T. and Schumann, D. (1983) Central and peripheral routes to advertising effectiveness: the moderating role of involvement, *Journal of Consumer Research*, 10(2), 135–46.

Puppy Monkey Baby (2016) *Cannes Lions Archive*, retrieved 10 January 2018 from http://www.canneslionsarchive.com/Home/PublicHome

Richards, J.I. and Curran, C.M. (2002) Oracles on 'advertising': searching for a definition, *Journal of Advertising*, XXXI(2), 63–77.

Rossiter, J.R. and Percy, L. (1997) *Advertising Communications and Promotion Management*, 2nd edn, New York: McGraw-Hill.

Rossiter, J.R., Percy, L. and Donovan, R.J. (1991) A better advertising planning grid, *Journal of Advertising Research*, October/November, 11–21.

Saeed, Z. (2016). A puppy, monkey, baby come together in one odd hybrid for Mountain Dew's Super Bowl return, *Campaign*, 3 February, retrieved 10 May 2018 from https://www.campaignlive.co.uk/article/puppy-monkey-baby-together-one-odd-hybrid-mountain-dews-super-bowl-return/1382209

Schultz, D. (2016) The future of advertising or whatever we're going to call it, *Journal of Advertising*, 45(3), 276–85.

Shulga, L.V., Busser, J.A. and Bai, B. (2018) Factors affecting willingness to participate in consumer generated advertisement, *International Journal of Hospitality Management*, 74, 214–23.

Tan, E. (2018) Under Armour pulls ads from YouTube as 300 brands' ads found on extremist content, *Campaign*, 20 April, retrieved 29 May 2018 from https://www.campaignlive.co.uk/article/armour-pulls-ads-youtube-300-brands-ads-found-extremist-content/1462691

This Girl Can (2017) Cannes Archive, retrieved 10 January 2018 from http://www.canneslions-archive.com/Home/PublicHome

Thompson, D.V. and Malaviya, P. (2013) Consumer-generated ads: does awareness of advertising co-creation help or hurt persuasion? *Journal of Marketing*, 77(3), 33–47.

Turnbull, S., Howe-Walsh, L. and Boulanouar, A. (2016) The advertising standardisation debate revisited: implications of Islamic ethics on standardisation/localisation of advertising in Middle East Islamic State, *Journal of Islamic Marketing*, 7(1).

Vakratsas, D. and Ambler, T. (1999) How advertising works: what do we really know? *Journal of Marketing*, 63(1), 26–43.

Vaughn, R. (1980) How advertising works: a planning model, *Journal of Advertising Research*, October, 27–33.

Willie, T. (2007) New models of communication for the digital age, *Admap*, October, 487, retrieved 23 July 2010 from https://www.warc.com/content/article/A87104_New_models_of_communication_for_the_digital_age/87104

Public relations: principles and practice

Public relations is a communications discipline used to help shape the attitudes and opinions held by an organisation's stakeholders. Through interaction and dialogue with these stakeholders an organisation seeks to adjust its own position and/or strategy.

There is an attempt therefore to identify with, and adjust an organisation's policies to, the interests of its stakeholders. To do this it formulates and executes a programme of action to develop mutual goodwill and understanding.

Aims and learning objectives

The aim of this chapter is to explore the role and characteristics of public relations in the context of profiling organisations and their products.

The learning objectives are to enable readers to:

1. explain the nature and characteristics of public relations;
2. highlight the main audiences to which public relations activities are directed;
3. discuss the role of public relations in the communications mix;
4. appreciate ways in which public relations works;
5. provide an overview of some of the main methods and approaches used by public relations;
6. examine the nature and context of crisis management.

carry greater perceived credibility than those messages transmitted through paid media, such as advertising.

The degree of trust and confidence generated by public relations singles out this tool from others in the marketing communications mix as an important means of reducing perceived risk. While credibility may be high, however, the amount of control that management is able to bring to the transmission of a public relations message is very low. For example, a press release may have been carefully prepared in-house, but as soon as it is passed to the editor of an online or offline magazine or newspaper, a possible opinion former, all control is lost. The release may be destroyed (highly probable), published as it stands (highly unlikely) or changed to fit the available space in the media vehicle (almost certain, if it is decided to use the material). This means that any changes will not have been agreed by management, so the context and style of the original message may be lost or corrupted.

The costs associated with public relations also make this an important discipline in the marketing communications mix. The absolute costs are minimal, except for those organisations that retain an agency, but even then their costs are low compared with those of advertising. The relative costs (the costs associated with reaching each member of a target audience) are also very low. The main costs associated with public relations are the time and opportunity costs associated with the preparation of press releases, videos and associated materials. If these types of activity are organised properly, many small organisations could develop and shape their visibility much more effectively and in a relatively inexpensive way.

A further characteristic of this tool is that it can be used to reach specific audiences in a way that paid media cannot. With increasing media fragmentation and finer segmentation (customisation) of markets, the use of public relations represents a cost-effective way of reaching such markets and audiences.

Digital technology has played a key role in the development and practice of public relations. Back in 2004 Gregory referred to the Internet and electronic communications as 'transforming public relations', and identified two main practitioner approaches. One refers to those who use the Internet as an extension to their established, traditional forms of communications. The second uses the Internet to develop two-way, enhanced communications. Today this demarcation is harder to observe as interactive media are woven into campaigns in order to achieve specific outcomes. There can be little doubt that digital technology has improved the transparency, speed and reach of public relations messages, while at the same time enabling more interactive communications between an organisation and its specific audiences.

Viewpoint 14.1

Chips or Mash?

Image 14.1 Pukka Pies launched a national debate around pies
Source: (a) Sergii Gnatiuk/123RF (b) Tobi/123RF

Pukka Pies wanted to build its brand fame during British Pie Week. The event is an important week for all British pie manufacturers and Pukka Pies wanted to make sure they stood out from their competitors. Working with a limited budget (£85,000) they created a PR-led campaign that sparked a debate around one of the hardest decisions for the British public to make, what to eat with their pie – chips, or mash?

Pukka Pies launched 'The great British pie debate' through a national poll on pie-week.com to find out which is Britain's favourite, chips or mash. Supported with outdoor, radio and social media, the campaign asked the British consumer to choose between mash and chips.

Twitter was used to encourage debate with daily posts and around-the-clock tweets. To start with, the brand created a list of 150 influencers, bloggers and existing Pukka Pie fans. Radio DJs from local stations such as Gem 106 and Capital FM were sent Pukka Pie goodie hampers and asked to join in the debate. Pukka Pies partnered with pie-loving cricketer Freddie Flintoff, who posted a sponsored tweet to encourage his two million followers to vote for their choice.

To build more excitement, Pukka Pies included a competition to win the t-shirt Freddie Flintoff wore in his post.

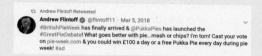

Image 14.2 Freddie Flintoff posted encouragement to his two million social media followers to vote for their choice
Source: Screenshot © Twitter Inc

The campaign ignited a national conversation around pies, with over 5 million impressions and 15,000 likes, comments and shares on social media. The brand created over 150 conversations and even Paddy McGuinness joined in the debate.

Image 14.3 Paddy McGuinness joined the conversation around pies
Source: Screenshot © Twitter Inc

The hashtag trended on Twitter on the Monday and Tuesday of British Pie Week. After five days, the campaign had gained coverage across a range of media, including *Metro Online, the Sun, Daily Star, Take A Break* and Absolute FM.

The poll received over 10,000 votes and the result was announced on radio interviews and through social media. The campaign saw Pukka Pies dominate British Pie Week and the brand sold 1.3 million pies over the seven days.

And, just in case you were wondering – chips won the poll, with 56 per cent of the vote.

Source: Anon (2018); Redmond (2018); Tan (2018).

Insight

Developments in digital media have been instrumental in assisting public relations' move from a predominantly one-way model of communications to an interactive model. Pukka Pies' campaign during British Pie Week highlights how public relations is taking the lead in integrated campaigns and connecting with publics across multiple platforms.

Question: Who were Pukka Pies' main stakeholder audiences? Identify each group using Table 14.1 as a guide.

Task: List the main stakeholder audiences for the launch of a new airline in the UK.

A framework of public relations

Communications with such a wide variety of stakeholders need to vary to reflect different environmental conditions, organisational objectives and forms of relationship. Grunig and Hunt (1984) have attempted to capture the diversity of public relations activities through a framework. They set out four models to reflect the different ways in which public relations is, in their opinion, considered to work. These models, based on their experiences as public relations practitioners, constitute a useful approach to understanding the complexity of this form of communications. The four models are set out at Figure 14.1.

The press agentry/publicity model

The essence of this approach is that communications are used as a form of propaganda. That is, the communications flow is essentially one-way, and the content is not bound to be strictly truthful as the objective is to convince the receiver of a new idea or offering. This can be observed in the growing proliferation of media events and press releases.

The public information model

Unlike the first model, this approach seeks to disseminate truthful information. While the flow is again one-way, there is little focus on persuasion, more on the provision of information. This can best be seen through public health campaigns and government advice communications in respect of crime, education and health.

Characteristic	Model			
	Press agentry/publicity	Public information	Two–way asymmetric	Two–way symmetric
Purpose	Propaganda	Dissemination of information	Scientific persuasion	Mutual understanding
Nature of communication	One way; complete truth not essential	One way; truth important	Two way; imbalanced effects	Two way; balanced effects
Communication model	Source →Rec.*	Source →Rec.*	Source ⇄Rec.* Feedback	Group ⇄ Group
Nature of research	Little; 'counting house'	Little; readability, readership	Formative; evaluative of attitudes	Formative; evaluative of understanding
Leading historical figures	P.T. Barnum	Ivy Lee	Edward L. Bernays	Bernays, educators, professional leaders
Where practised today	Sports, theatre, product promotion	Government, not-for-profit associations, business	Competitive business, agencies	Regulated business, agencies

* Receiver.

Figure 14.1 Models of public relations
Source: Grunig and Hunt (1984). Used with kind permission.

The two-way asymmetric model

Two-way communications are a major element of this model. Feedback from receivers is important, but as power is not equally distributed between the various stakeholders and the organisation, the relationship has to be regarded as asymmetric. The purpose remains to influence attitude and behaviour through persuasion.

The two-way symmetric model

This represents the most acceptable and mutually rewarding form of communications. Power is seen to be dispersed equally between the organisation and its stakeholders and the intent of the communications flow is considered to be reciprocal. The organisation and its respective publics are prepared to adjust their positions (attitudes and behaviours) in the light of the information flow. A true dialogue emerges through this interpretation, unlike any of the other three models, which see an unbalanced flow of information and expectations.

Scholars' paper 14.1
Models of public relations

Grunig, J. (1992) Models of public relations and communication, in *Excellence in Public Relations and Communications Management* (eds J.E. Grunig, D.M. Dozier, P. Ehling, L.A. Grunig, F.C. Repper and J. Whits), Hillsdale, NJ: Lawrence Erlbaum, 285–325.

Although first announced in 1976, and then published fully in 1984, this 1992 chapter is an essential work with which all serious readers of public relations should be conversant. The four primary models of public relations developed by Grunig are considered by most scholars to be the theoretical anchor for the subject.

See also:

Macnamara, J. (2016) Organizational listening: addressing a major gap in public relations theory and practice, *Journal of Public Relations Research*, 28(3–4), 146–69.

The Grunig model has attracted a great deal of attention and has been reviewed and appraised by a number of commentators (Laskin, 2009; Miller, 1989). As a result of this and a search for excellence in public relations, Grunig (1992) revised the model to reflect the dominance of the 'craft' and the 'professional' approaches to public relations practices. That is, those practitioners who utilise public relations merely as a tool to achieve media visibility can be regarded as 'craft'-oriented.

Those organisations whose managers seek to utilise public relations as a means of mediating their relationships with their various stakeholders are seen as 'professional' practitioners. They are considered to be using public relations as a longer-term and proactive form of planned communications. The former see public relations as an instrument, the latter as a means of conducting a dialogue.

These models are not intended to suggest that those responsible for communications should choose among them. Their use and interpretation depend upon the circumstances

Table 14.2 Dimensions of public relations

Dimension of public relations	Explanation
Direction	Refers to whether communications are one-way (disseminating) or two-way (exchange).
Purpose	Purpose refers to degree to which there are communications effects on both parties. Symmetry refers to communications effects on both sides, leading to collaboration, whereas asymmetry leads to one-sided effects and, in turn, advocacy.
Channel	Interpersonal communications refer to direct, face-to-face communications. Mediated communications are indirect and routed through the media.
Ethics	The degree to which public-relations-based communications are ethical. Grunig (1997) refers to three sub-dimensions: teleology (the consequences), disclosure (whose interests do the communications serve?) and social responsibility (who is affected?).

Source: After Yun (2006).

that prevail at any one time. Organisations use a number of these different approaches to manage the communications issues that exist between them and the variety of different stakeholder audiences with whom they interact. However, there is plenty of evidence to suggest that the press/agentry model is the one most used by practitioners and that the two-way symmetrical model is harder to observe in practice.

These models have been subjected to further investigation and Grunig (1997) concluded that these four models are not independent but coexist with one another. Therefore, it is better to characterise public relations as dimensions of communications behaviour (Yun, 2006). These dimensions are direction, purpose, channel and ethics, and are explained in Table 14.2.

Public relations and relationship management

It is important to remember that the shift to a relationship management perspective effectively alters the way public relations is perceived and practised by organisations. Kent and Taylor (2002) and Bruning and Ledingham (2000) suggest that it is the ability of organisations to encourage and practise dialogue that really enables truly symmetrical relationships to develop. What follows from this is a change in evaluation, from measuring the dissemination of messages to one that measures audience influence and behavioural and attitudinal change and, of course, relationship dynamics. Bruning and Ledingham describe this as a change from measuring outputs to one that measures outcomes.

In addition to this discernible shift in emphasis, there has been a change in the way public relations is used by organisations. Traditionally, public relations has been used as a means of managing communications between parties, whereas now communications are regarded as a means of managing relationships (Kent and Taylor, 2002). In order to use communications to develop the full potential within relationships many argue that dialogic interaction should be encouraged. There are five tenets of dialogue: mutuality, empathy, propinquity, risk and commitment (see Chapter 6). These have been offered by Kent and Taylor as the elements that may form a framework through which dialogue may be considered and developed. On a practical level, they argue that organisations should place email, web addresses, contact telephone numbers, Twitter and organisational addresses prominently in all forms of external communications, most notably advertisements and websites, to enable dialogue.

In consideration of the role of public relations, namely to build relationships that are of mutual value, Bruning et al. (2008) conclude that input, interaction and participation of key public members in the organisation–public dynamic are critically important. In other words, dialogue arising through interaction and the personalisation of communications is important for relationship development.

Viewpoint 14.2
Pestaurant Harriet Rich, Joint Managing Director, Brands2Life

Image 14.4 Grubbing around at the Pestaurant
Source: Brands2life

Rentokil is one of the largest pest control companies in the world, operating in 60 countries. The company provides services to both private and commercial clients and has been servicing the UK market for nearly 90 years.

Rentokil approached Brands2Life with the task of engaging professionals and householders with the brand. Our main objective was to deliver a creative PR campaign that would create a buzz and spark conversations, both on- and offline. The result was a creative public relations campaign that gave pest control a 'talkability' factor and became a global sensation.

Driving conversations about pest control was a challenging brief for a number of reasons. First, bugs and pests are not creatures that the public generally finds endearing. Indeed the opposite is true, with most people trying to avoid them. Second, pest control is not a topic most consumers or professionals talk about, unless they have to deal with a particular pest problem. To address this challenge we considered ways that we could engage the public with pests in a fun way.

We saw an opportunity to capitalise on a growing national fascination with eating 'pests', encouraged by TV shows such as I'm a Celebrity. . . Get Me Out of Here! and came up with the idea of the world's first pop-up pest-only restaurant.

The first Pestaurant appeared in London and we developed a menu to showcase Rentokil's tasty pest treats. The menu featured dishes such as sweet chilli pigeon burgers, salt and vinegar crickets, mexican spice mealworms, roasted locusts and insects dipped in chocolate. Manned by Rentokil experts and chefs, the Pestaurant cooked these edible pest treats and handed them out to passers-by.

We decided to enlist the support of Rentokil experts at the events to provide them with an

Image 14.5 The menu featured insects
Source: Brands2life

opportunity to meet potential customers and share their top tips for avoiding pest problems. The one day event attracted over 3,000 visitors, many of whom were brave enough to taste the pests on offer. As well as delighting visitors to the Pestaurant, the edible pest menu caught the attention of both the national and international media.

We secured significant media coverage from the event in the UK, including 18 articles in *the Sun, Daily Mail, Guardian, Express, Metro and Time Out* as well as articles on BBC online. We also achieved standalone pieces in the *Evening Standard and Stylist,* and broadcast interviews with STV and LBC. As well as the national media, the story received international coverage including a 3-minute standalone feature on Brazilian TV and broadcast interviews on news channels in France, India, New Zealand, Singapore and the USA.

In addition to the media coverage there was considerable social buzz. On the day, the campaign trended on Twitter with over 2,000 mentions, with retweets providing an estimated 58.7 million impressions. Rentokil's own website experienced a 22 per cent increase in visitors on the day of the event.

Following the initial success of the one day pop-up Pestaurant in London, we have rolled out the bug menu to a number of other UK locations, including Edinburgh and Manchester. The Pestaurant has also gone global with events in 13 different countries including Australia, Brazil, Germany, Lithuania, South Africa and the USA. This has resulted in over 13,000 people experiencing the Rentokil pop-up Pestaurant and over 1,300 pieces of media coverage.

Insight

Rentokil clearly recognises the role that public relations can play in its communications. It used events and media coverage to create visibility and interest in the brand and through this it engaged various stakeholders. From this it was able to drive conversations, often through social media, with the result that they raised its profile and understanding about who it is and what it represents. Not only did Rentokil generate goodwill and positive feelings, but it also built relationships with critical stakeholder audiences.

Question: Considering Grunig and Hunt's 1984 models of public relations in Figure 14.1, what type of model do you think best reflects Pestaurant?

Task: Write a brief paper on how you would evaluate the success of Pestaurant.

Objectives of public relations

As established, the main reasons for using public relations are to provide visibility for the corporate body and to support the marketing agenda at the product level. The marketing communications objectives, established earlier in the plan, will have identified issues concerning the attitudes and relationships stakeholders have with an organisation and its products. Decisions will have been made to build awareness and to change perception, preferences or attitudes. The task of public relations is to deliver a series of coordinated activities that complement the overall marketing communications strategy and which develop and enhance some of the identity cues used by stakeholders. The overall goal should be to develop the relationship that various audiences have with the organisation.

Public relations can be used to develop understanding, perceptions and positive attitudes towards the organisation. Public relations can also contribute to the marketing needs of the organisation and will therefore be focused at the product level and on consumers, seeking to change attitudes, preferences and awareness levels with respect to products and services offered. Therefore, a series of programmes is necessary – one to fulfil the corporate requirements and another to support the marketing of products and services.

Cause-related marketing

One major reason for the development of public relations and associated corporate reputation activities has been the rise in importance and use of cause-related marketing activities. This has partly been due to the increased awareness of the need to be perceived as credible, responsible and ethically sound. Developing a strong and socially oriented reputation has become a major form of differentiation for organisations operating in various markets, especially where price, quality and tangible attributes are relatively similar. Being able to present corporate brands as contributors to the wider social framework, a role beyond that of simple profit generators, has enabled many organisations to achieve stronger, more positive market positions.

Cause-related marketing (CRM) is a commercial activity through which profit-oriented and not-for-profit organisations form partnerships to exploit, for mutual benefit, their association in the name of a particular cause.

The benefits from a properly planned and constructed cause-related campaign can accrue to all participants. Cause-related marketing helps improve corporate reputation, enables product differentiation and appears to contribute to improved customer retention through enhanced sales. In essence, cause-related marketing is a means by which relationships with stakeholders can be developed. As organisations outsource an increasingly large part of their business activities and as the stakeholder networks become more complex, so the need to be perceived as (and to be) socially responsible becomes a critically important dimension of an organisation's image.

A public relations programme consists of a number of planned events and activities that seek to satisfy communications objectives. Some of the broad tools and techniques associated with public relations are considered in this chapter, but it should be noted that the list is not intended to be comprehensive.

Public relations: methods and techniques

Public relations provides some of the intentional or deliberate cues that enable stakeholders to develop images and perceptions through which they recognise, understand, select and converse with organisations.

The range of public relations cues or methods available to organisations is immense. Different organisations use different permutations in order that they can communicate effectively with their various stakeholder audiences. For the purposes of this text, a general outline is provided of the more commonly used methods. Cues are to some extent interchangeable and can be used to build credibility or to provide visibility for an organisation. It is the skill of the public relations practitioner that determines the right blend of techniques. The various types of cue are set out in Table 14.3.

While there is general agreement on a definition, there is a lower level of consensus over what constitutes public relations. This is partly because the range of activities is diverse and categorisation problematic. The approach adopted here is that public relations consists of a range of communications activities, of which media relations, publicity and event management appear to be the main ones used by practitioners.

Table 14.3   Cues used to generate credibility and visibility

Cues to build credibility	Cues to signal visibility
Product quality	Sales literature and company publications
Customer relations	Publicity and media relations
Community involvement	Speeches and presentations
Strategic performance	Event management
Employee relations	Marketing communications/messages
Crisis management skills	Media mix
Third-party endorsement	Design (signage, logo, letterhead)
Perceived ethics and environmental awareness	Dress codes Video
Architecture and furnishing	Exhibitions/seminars; sponsorships

Media relations

Media relations consist of a range of activities designed to provide media journalists and editors with information. The intention is that they relay the information, through their media, for consumption by their audiences. The greater the coverage, the greater the awareness of the organisation, which in turn improves understanding, appreciation and eventually relationship development. Obviously, the original message may be changed and subject to information deviance as it is processed, but audiences perceive much of this information as highly credible simply because opinion formers have bestowed their judgement on the item. Of the various forms of media relations, press releases, interviews, offering content (e.g. through press kits), press conferences and responding to media queries are, according to Waters et al. (2010), the most used.

Press releases

The press release is a common but increasingly ineffective form of media relations activity. A written report concerning a change in the organisation is sent to various media houses for inclusion in the media vehicle as an item of news. The media house may cover a national area, but very often a local house will suffice. These written statements concern developments in the organisation, such as promotions, new products, awards, prizes, new contracts and customers. The statement is deliberately short and written in such a style that it attracts the attention of the editor. Further information can be obtained if it is to be included within the next publication or news broadcast. The goal of this activity is primarily to create 'mentions' in a variety of targeted media, including other websites. This is important for establishing links and achieving higher search engine rankings. It is also important to build relationships, both with the target stakeholder groups and with journalists and others in the media.

Previously, press releases were faxed to designated journalists. Now press releases are posted on a website and emailed as attached files to specified individuals on mailing lists. All those interested can view the files at their discretion and initiative, and then choose to enter into an interaction or even dialogue, in order to expand on the information provided. Email is regarded as essential by journalists, broadcasters and bloggers.

In many ways e-newsletters and white papers are a natural extension of email communications. The differences concern content and goals. Email communications are sales-driven with product-related content. Newsletters and white papers are reputation-driven, with a diverse range of content concerning organisational and/or technical-related material. These communications can be an essential part of the 'stickiness' that good websites seek to develop. Recipients who find these communications of value either anticipate their release or return to the host's website to search in archived files for past copies and items of interest.

Most large organisations provide online newsroom facilities, but the quality of information provided and their orientation has been found to be less than satisfactory. Capriotti and González-Herrero (2013) for example found that online press rooms are more oriented towards disseminating information and less concerned with engaging journalists in dialogue. There has also been criticism that newsrooms do not accommodate the needs of bloggers, social media influencers and the general public (Capriotti and González-Herrero, 2017).

Capriotti and González-Herrero (2017) report that some organisations such as Dupont, IBM, NASA and Red Bull no longer use the term 'press releases', but rather 'news releases' or 'news' to reflect the broader range of stakeholders who may be searching for information about the company to disseminate through social media, such as Twitter or Facebook.

At the beginning of this section we stated that press releases are becoming increasingly ineffective. This is largely due to changes in what type of news material is being used by media and other stakeholders. In contrast to text-only press releases, journalists and bloggers are looking for visual stories and therefore images and videos are more useful to them (Heckler, 2016).

Multimedia usage in media relations

Traditionally public relations has been channelled through print and broadcast media. Editors selected and shaped the content they received through press releases and other forms of content gathering. As discussed earlier, developments in digital technology and the media environment have impacted on public relations, however. Of these the use of social media and video have been most prominent as increasingly practitioners use interactive media to build relationships based on interaction and dialogue.

The use of video within media relations has become a crucially important form of communications with a variety of audiences. For example, video offers opportunities for interaction driven by consumer audiences contributing user-generated content. The material, often disseminated as a press release, an interview with the CEO, or a press conference with the CMO, are now commonly distributed through video. In addition there is opinion-leadership content, which again is often distributed through video format. These recordings are accessible on the home organisation's website, social media pages, most notably Facebook and YouTube, and other community-based pages.

It is through social media that individuals can learn about new products, consider various user reviews and post their own comments, questions and experiences regarding companies and brands. The interactional capability within digital media complements the core characteristic of public relations. Social networking sites and video-sharing platforms represent a significant opportunity for organisations to engage with their publics (Mamic and Almaraz, 2013). The extent to which they do engage successfully through social media is questionable as listening to/observing the various interactions between stakeholders is said by some to be quite low.

To satisfy the demand for images and film, there is increasing multimedia usage in press releases (Heckler, 2016). Including video and image content allows journalists and bloggers to use the raw material to create their own unique visual stories, and social media users can post and re-post content. This means that press releases including imagery and film have a much higher chance of being shared across social networks (Heckler, 2016).

There are a number of ways organisations can increase their visual content in press releases, such as the inclusion of screenshots, visualised quotes, charts, infographics, GIFs and memes, as well as embeds of quotes from Twitter or other social networks (Anon, 2018b).

Viewpoint 14.3

Google Sheep View

Image 14.6 A story was created around the efforts of a young Faroese woman to get the islands' landscape onto Google Street View
Source: Polhansen/Shutterstock

The Faroe Islands is an archipelago in the North Atlantic and with only 50,000 inhabitants, is one of the smallest countries in the world. Despite their stunning scenery, these unspoilt islands have remained off the tourist map and until 'Sheep View' came along, the islands were also off Google Street View.

To attract more visitors, the islands' tourism board, Visit Faroe Islands, decided they would create their own Google Street View and share images of their beautiful country with the whole world.

The campaign was based around the story of a young Faroese woman's mission to get the islands' landscape onto Google Street View and her efforts to use the local sheep to create 'Sheep View 360'. As sheep outnumber people by 2:1 on the island there were plenty of them at hand to help record images of the scenery. And as the name Faroe Islands actually translates to 'sheep islands', using sheep as ambassadors seemed a natural choice.

To get things started, the sheep were fitted with 360-degree cameras on their backs, together with a solar panel and a cell phone, enabling them to film as they wandered around. Images were uploaded from the cell phones through to Google.

Image 14.7 Sheep were fitted with 360-degree cameras to film as they wandered around the islands
Source: stefano cellai/Shutterstock

To help with the filming, 360-degree cameras were also lent out to tourists and the Faroese people.

A simple film about the efforts to film the scenery using sheep and images was posted on social media. Additional film and images from the sheep were also uploaded.

To engage the international media, the tourist board identified key media and sent them Google Cardboard glasses so they could enjoy the film in 360 degrees. They also invited them to join an online press conference held by the sheep.

The film, 'Sheep View' was quickly picked up by the media and only 20 minutes after the campaign was launched, the story appeared on *the Guardian*, the BBC, CNN, Al Jazeera, *Daily Mail*, *The Washington Post* and Sky News.

The tourist board created a blog with updates on the progress and a petition to ask Google to put the island on Google Street View. Thousands of people signed up to the petition and Google were invited to the island.

The PR campaign generated 2 billion media impressions and an estimated PR value of $50 million. For a campaign that had a total budget of only $280,000 and no media allocation, 'Sheep View' had captured the interest of the media around the world.

The campaign resulted in over 2 million news stories, the story appeared on over 7,000 websites and generated more than a 42 per cent increase on Google search for 'Faroe Islands'.

Google also came onboard and agreed to provide equipment to the island and with the help of the Google Street View team and island volunteers, they have now created Street View using Sheep View. The campaign won Visit Faroe Islands a number of awards, including two Gold Lions and one Bronze Lion at Cannes.

Sources: Birkner (2016); Dixon (2017); Google Sheep View (2017).

Insight

The campaign is a good example of multimedia usage in media relations. Including video and images provides journalists and bloggers with the raw matrial to create their own stories and re-post content. Identifying key media was an important aspect for the campaign as this allowed the tourist board to build a relationship with journalists by sending them Google Cardboard glasses.

Question: Why do you think the media picked up this story so quickly? Explain your reasons.

Task: Find five examples of the media coverage for this story online. For each, list how many images or films are included.

Press conferences

Press conferences are used when a major event has occurred and where a press release cannot convey the appropriate tone or detail required by the organisation. Press conferences are used regularly by politicians, and sports players and managers, but organisations in crisis (e.g. accidents and mergers) and individuals appealing for help (e.g. police requesting assistance from the public with respect to a particular incident) also use these forms of communications. The availability of press kits containing a full reproduction of any statements, photographs and relevant background information is considered important.

Interviews

Interviews with representatives of an organisation enable news and the organisation's view of an issue or event to be conveyed. These are normally disseminated through news channels and posted on websites. Associated formats include bylined articles (articles written by a member of an organisation about an issue related to the company and offered for publication), speeches, video, letters to the editor, and photographs and captions.

Media relations can be planned and controlled to the extent of what is sent to the media and when it is released. While there is no control over what is actually used, media relations allow organisations to try to convey information concerning strategic issues and to reach particular stakeholders.

The quality of the relationship between an organisation's public relations manager/staff and the editor and journalists associated with both the press and the broadcast media dramatically affects the impact and dissemination of news and stories released by an organisation.

Publicity and events

Control over public relations events is not as strong as that for media relations. Indeed, negative publicity can be generated by other parties, which can impact badly on an organisation by raising doubts about its financial status or perhaps the quality of its products. Three main event activity areas can be distinguished: product, corporate and community events (also see Chapter 18).

Media catching

Public relations is concerned with maximising opportunities to present an organisation, and its products and services, in a positive manner. One of the goals is to create 'mentions' in a variety of targeted media, including other websites, and social media such as social networks, blogs and Twitter. This is important for establishing links and achieving higher search engine rankings.

Another goal involves creating opportunities for interaction and dialogue with stakeholders – in particular, journalists. The stronger the communications tie, the more likely the relationship will grow and provide an effective means of distributing content and client materials. It is important to build relationships, both with the target stakeholder groups and with journalists and others in the media. We know that interpersonal relationships between public relations practitioners and journalists can have a substantial influence on the effectiveness of an organisation's media relations performance (Shin and Cameron, 2003). Indeed, there is clear evidence that journalists are no longer the passive recipients of news releases and media kits from practitioners who are striving to generate publicity for their organisation.

As a general rule, public relations has been considered to work through the 'content throw' pattern of communications. In this approach organisations use public relations as a means of contacting journalists, broadcasters and bloggers in the hope of gaining media comment and placements to disseminate news content. A more contemporary approach is referred to as 'media catching'. Using digital media, this pattern of communications involves reversing the content throw approach. Now practitioners are being contacted by journalists and others for specific material for inclusion in stories, articles, blogs and websites where there are pressing deadlines. Rather than 'Here is a story/content please run it', media catching is about 'Do you have a story/content please?'

Erzikova et al. (2018) discuss this reversal of roles between media sources and journalists and argue that media requests services such ProfNet and Help a Reporter Out (HARO) are advantageous to both the organisation and the news outlet. The authors suggest however that reaching out to organisations for help with news stories is not a new practice, but the emergence of news request services have enabled journalists to reach out to a much larger number of organisations.

News request services, such as Help a Reporter Out (HARO), which is the largest English language media request service, has more than 55,000 journalists and bloggers subscribed, over 800,000 sources and circulates over 50,000 media requests every year (HARO, 2018).

Zerfass et al. (2016) argue that the changing use of media by organisations and in particular the emergence of new practices such as content marketing, native advertising and brand journalism has led to the emergence of a new form of media relations. The authors suggest traditional media relations strategies are being replaced by 'strategic mediatization'. More can be read about this emergent concept in Scholars' paper 14.2.

Scholars' paper 14.2
Mediatization

Erzikova, E., Waters, R. and Bocharsky, K. (2018) Media catching: a conceptual framework for understanding strategic mediatization in public relations? *International Journal of Strategic Communication,* **1–15.**

The authors outline the concept and practice of media catching and report on the findings of their study undertaken with journalists in Russia. They examine journalists' queries submitted through Pressfeed.ru to understand how media catching operates in Russia. Patterns between Russia and the US media-catching service, Help a Reporter Out, is discussed.

See also:

Zerfass, A., Verčič, D. and Wiesenberg, M. (2016) The dawn of a new golden age for media relations? How PR professionals interact with the mass media and use new collaboration practices, *Public Relations Review,* 42(4), 499–508.

Forms of public relations

In addition to these key activities the following are important forms of public relations:

1. lobbying (out of personal selling and publicity);
2. sponsorship (out of event management and advertising) (see Chapter 15);
3. corporate advertising (out of corporate public relations and advertising);
4. crisis management (which has developed out of issues management, a part of corporate public relations).

Lobbying

The representation of certain organisations or industries within government is an important aspect of public relations for many organisations (Davidson, 2015; Myers, 2018). While legislation is being prepared, lobbyists provide a flow of information to their organisations to keep them informed about events (as a means of scanning the environment), but they also ensure that the views of the organisation are heard in order that legislation can be shaped appropriately, limiting any potential damage that new legislation might bring.

Moloney (1997) suggests that lobbying is inside public relations as it focuses on the members of an organisation who seek to persuade and negotiate with its stakeholders in government on matters of opportunity and or threat. He refers to in-house lobbyists (those members of the organisation who try to influence non-members) and hired lobbyists contracted to complete specific tasks.

His view of lobbying is that it is one of:

monitoring public policy-making for a group interest; building a case in favour of that interest; and putting it privately with varying degrees of pressure to public decision makers for their acceptance and support through favourable political intervention. (Moloney, 1997: 173)

The Chartered Institute of Public Relations (CIPR, 2018) suggests a broader-based definition of lobbying to cover activities surrounding influencing government:

> Lobbying services means activities which are carried out in the course of a business for the purpose of influencing government or advising others how to influence government.

Where local authorities interpret legislation and frame the activities of their citizens and constituent organisations, the government determines legislation and controls the activities of people and organisations across markets.

This control may be direct or indirect, but the power and influence of government are such that large organisations and trade associations seek to influence the direction and strength of legislation, because any adverse laws or regulations may affect the profitability and the value of the organisation. Not surprisingly, 'firms use multiple channels of potential political influence to influence regulatory and policy outcomes' (Hill et al., 2013). The pharmaceutical industry has been actively lobbying the European Union with respect to legislation on new patent regulations and the information that must be carried in any marketing communications message. The tobacco industry is well known for its lobbying activities, as are chemical, transport and many other industries.

Although lobbying is a legitimate, interactive communications process, a number of moral and ethical issues can arise from an abuse of lobbying practice (Kale, 2017). Bauer (2014: 64) rightly makes the point that organisations run risks concerning a 'disproportionate influence on law-making'. She refers to firms without a democratic mandate attempting to the influence the behaviour of policy-makers who have been elected on a democratic platform. As a result of some high-profile breaches of what might be regarded as legitimate lobbying behaviour, public scrutiny of this activity is becoming more intense. This, she argues, has led to organisations appearing to recognise the importance of ethical restraints so that relationships built on understanding and trust can evolve.

Scholars' paper 14.3
Responsible lobbying

Anastasiadis, S., Moon, J. and Humphreys, M. (2018) Lobbying and the responsible firm: agenda setting for a freshly conceptualized field, *Business Ethics: A European Review*, 27(3), 207–21.

The paper provides a review of the literature on lobbying and defines the concept of responsible lobbying. The authors argue responsible lobbying should consider the content, process, organisation and environment, and suggest a conceptual model to include these conditions.

See also:

Lock, I., Seele, P. and Heath, R. L. (2016) Where grass has no roots: the concept of 'shared strategic communication' as an answer to unethical astroturf lobbying, *International Journal of Strategic Communication*, 10(2), 87–100.

Investor relations

The role of investor relations is seen to be of strategic importance, and one which requires clarity and transparency, with communications, not finance, as a central tenet of investor relations (Laskin, 2009).

Strauß (2018: 12) supports the strategic view of investor relations and suggests it needs to provide 'honest, transparent, comprehensive and coherent information, to be continuous, direct and mutual contact with stakeholders (e.g. investors, analysts, CEOs) and to give a fair representation of the company in the media and among the public'.

Partly as a result of deregulation, the number of target audiences for financial services and related communications has grown. On the one hand, there are large institutional investors such as the government, multinational organisations and agencies such as stock exchanges, all of which require financially related information. On the other hand, there are increasing numbers of individual investors who wish to invest part of their savings in various funds, equities and savings plans. In addition to these there are the financial press, shareholders, investment analysts, financial advisers and fund managers. This means that communications, and the provision of timely, transparent and accurate information, should have become significant factors in the marketplace.

Cutlip et al. define investor relations as 'a specialized part of corporate public relations that builds and maintains mutually beneficial relationships with shareholders and others in the financial community to maximize shareholder value' (1999: 21). The UK Investor Relations Society (2018) describes investor relations as follows:

> **Investor Relations is the communication of information and insight between a company and the investment community. This process enables a full appreciation of the company's business activities, strategy and prospects and allows the market to make an informed judgement about the fair value and appropriate ownership of a company.**

Interestingly, the former stresses the maximisation of shareholder value and relationships, while the latter emphasises fair value rather than maximisation, and implicitly stresses the significance of one-way communications, which are not suitable for relationship development. In practice, the core activity of investor relations is to react to requests for information although the development and use of websites has helped to make the discipline more proactive.

If investor relations are to have an enhanced communications focus, a variety of public relations strategies are necessary to reach different target audiences. Hanrahan (1997) highlights four particular strategies: expansive, defensive, creative and adaptive.

Expansive strategies are followed during periods of growth, when the size of product portfolios increases. In this context competition can be aggressive, so it is critical that awareness, recognition and trust are developed. This can be achieved through serving on committees and public interest groups, publishing white papers, speaking at conferences, writing articles, sponsorship and other activities that serve to raise the profile and credibility of the organisation.

Defensive strategies are needed in times of crisis, such as a recession, very poor trading performance, when accused of malpractice or irregular reporting, or when faced by a hostile takeover bid. In these situations the timely provision of the correct information, perhaps as a separate report, is important.

Creative strategies involve the use of digital technologies to deliver the corporate identity in novel and interesting ways. This might be through the use of interviews, which can be beamed across the television world instantly, if necessary, across the Internet and through Reuters and world services. With information and analysis instantly available, 24/7, the prime role of the press has shifted to one focused on the provision of comment and interpretation.

Adaptive strategies are used when an organisation experiences considerable change. Moving into new financial product and/or geographic markets, merging with another organisation or simply developing key services, all warrant strategies that are flexible and can adapt to local press and media needs. Corporate advertising, adapted for local use, has been a significant tool. Today, one of the roles of the website is to provide fast, localised information that can be targeted at particular opinion leaders and formers.

Corporate advertising

In an attempt to harness the advantages of both advertising and public relations, corporate advertising has been seen by some as a means of communicating more effectively with a range of stakeholders. The credibility of messages transmitted through public relations is high, but the control that management has over the message is limited. Advertising, however, allows management virtually total control over message dispersion, but the credibility of these messages is usually low. Corporate advertising is the combination of the best of advertising and the best of public relations.

The main purpose of corporate advertising appears to be the provision of cues by which stakeholders can identify and understand an organisation. This is achieved by presenting the personality of the organisation to a wide range of stakeholders, rather than presenting particular functions or products that the organisation markets.

Reasons for the use of corporate advertising

Ho et al. (2017) suggest that there are two types of corporate advertising and organisations will have different reasons for using each. The first, image advertising, is to communicate an organisation's view on a topic and Ho et al. (2017) suggest one of the best examples of this category is a 1970s Mobil ad defending the oil industry. The second, corporate image advertising, is used to improve public attitude towards the organisation.

There are particular occasions when organisations need to use corporate advertising. These are set out in Table 14.4.

Table 14.4 Reasons to use corporate advertising

Reason for use	Explanation
During change and transition	To convince stakeholders, particularly shareholders, of the value of the organisation and of the need not to accept hostile offers, before, during and after a takeover or merger.
To change a poor image	To correct any misunderstanding that stakeholders might have of an organisation. For example, financial analysts may believe that an organisation is underperforming, but reality indicates that performance is good.
Product support	To assist the launch of new products by establishing a strong, good reputational equity and so lowering costs.
Recruitment	To recruit employees by creating a positive and attractive image of the organisation.
Repositioning	To refocus the way stakeholders regard an organisation.
Advocacy	To inform stakeholders of the position or stand that an organisation has on a particular issue of social concern.

Crisis communications

Organisational crises are low-probability, high-impact events (Pearson and Clair, 1998) that threaten the existence of an organisation. Crises can occur because of a simple or minor managerial mistake, an incorrect decision, a technology failure, or because of a seemingly distant environmental event. All organisations face the prospect of managing a crisis, indeed some commentators ominously suggest that all organisations have a crisis just around the corner (Fink, 2000).

The impact of crises is very often considered from an external perspective but crises can be of concern to specific areas such as social media environments (Pace et al., 2017), business relationships (Rad, 2017), employees (Halkos and Bousinakis, 2017) and investors (Dillingham and Ivanov, 2017).

Crises are emerging with greater frequency as a result of a number of factors. Table 14.5 sets out some of the main factors that give rise to crises for organisations. For example, Brown et al. (2017) report on the growing incidence of cybercrime and the costs of recovery. The authors refer to the WannaCry ransomware attack in May 2017 and the NotPetya attack in June 2017 as two incidences of cybercrime and suggest such attacks cost the global economy $445 billion annually (Brown et al., 2017). Organisations also need to consider the costs incurred by investors losing confidence as a result of the quality of response to the incident.

Figure 14.2 is used to present organisational crises in the context of two key variables. On the horizontal axis is the degree to which management has control over the origin of the crisis. Is the origin of the crisis outside management's control, such as an earthquake, or is it within its control, such as those crises associated with poor trading results? The vertical axis reflects the potential impact that a crisis might have on an organisation. All crises, by definition, have a potential to inflict damage on an organisation. However, some can be contained, perhaps on a geographic basis, whereas others have the potential to cause tremendous damage to an organisation, such as those experienced through product tampering and environmental pollution.

Table 14.5 Common causes of disasters

Origin of crisis	Explanation
Economic	As new economies emerge (e.g. BRIC), so many established industries in developed economies decline – for example, the UK's steel and shipbuilding industries.
Managerial	Human error and the pursuit of financial goals by some organisations give rise to the majority of disasters. For example, various banks such as RBS and the Co-operative Bank, and those organisations associated with cutting costs at the expense of safety and repair of systems.
Political	Issues concerning war, religious extremism and terrorism have encouraged kidnapping, as well as organisations having to change the locations of their business.
Climate	The climate is changing substantially in certain parts of the world, and this has brought disaster to those who lie in the wake of natural disturbances. For example, the volcanic eruption in Hawaii in 2018.
Technology	The rate at which technology is advancing has brought about crises such as those associated with transportation systems, aircraft disasters and cybercrime. Human error is also a significant factor, often associated with the rate of technological change. Examples include cyber-attacks on the NHS.
Consumer groups	The rise of consumer groups (e.g. Amnesty International and Greenpeace) and their ability to investigate and publicise the operations and policies of organisations. For example, the campaign led by the pressure group 38 Degrees to disassociate LEGO from Shell and the latter's quest to drill for oil in the Arctic.

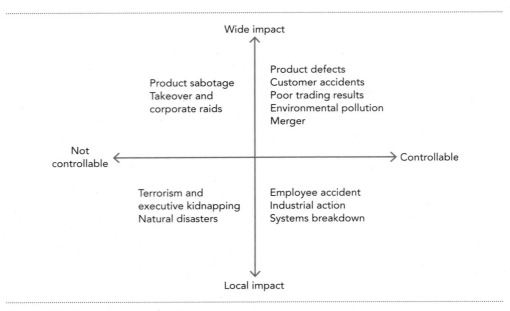

Figure 14.2 An organisational crisis matrix

The increasing occurrence of crises throughout the world has prompted many organisations to review the manner in which they anticipate managing such events, should they be implicated. It is generally assumed that those organisations that take care to plan in anticipation of disaster will experience more favourable outcomes than those that fail to plan. The extent to which this is correct is questionable.

The second reason concerns the expectations of those who design and implement crisis plans. It is one thing to design a plan; it is entirely another to implement it. Crisis planning is about putting into position those elements that can affect speedy outcomes to the disaster sequence. When a crisis strikes, it is the application of contingency-based tactics by all those concerned with the event that will determine the strength of the outcome. Choi and Lee's (2018) study identified that Toyota responded slowly and dishonestly to the recall crisis and highlighted the need for the manufacturer to have been better prepared.

Whatever the cause, whatever the level of preparation, contemporary forms of communications including websites, social media and mobile technologies play a critical role in crisis management (Ye and Ki, 2017). News of an organisational crisis or disaster can spread around the globe instantly, while managers of an afflicted organisation can post up-to-date information quickly, by providing pertinent information or directing visitors to information and associated facilities.

Crisis phases

The number of phases through which a crisis passes varies according to author and the management model being proposed. For example, Penrose (2000) mentions Littlejohn's six-step model, Fink's audit, Mitroff's portfolio planning approach and Burnett's crisis classification matrix. The number of phases is also influenced by the type of crisis management an organisation uses. Essentially there are two main models, as presented in Figure 14.3: organisations that plan in order to manage crisis events and in doing so attempt to contain the impact; and then organisations that fail to plan, and manage by reacting to crisis events.

The differences between these two approaches are that there are fewer phases in the shorter 'reactionary' model and that the level of detail and attention given to the anticipation, management and consideration of crisis events is more deliberate in the planning

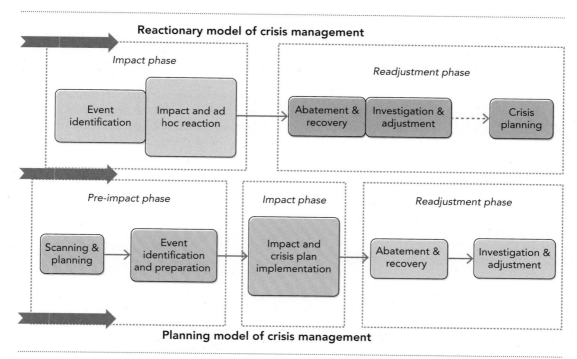

Figure 14.3 Twin models of crisis management

model. Time is spent here considering the sequence of events within the planning model. A three-phase (and five-episode) framework is adopted: pre-impact, impact and readjustment phases. It should be remembered that the duration of each phase can vary considerably, depending upon the nature of the crisis and the manner in which management deals with the events associated with the crisis.

The first period is referred to as the pre-impact phase and consists of two main episodes: scanning and planning; and event identification and preparation. Good strategic management demands that the environment be scanned on a regular basis to detect the first signs of significant change. Organisations that pick up signals that are repeated are in a better position to prepare for disaster than those that do not scan the environment. Penrose (2000) reports that those who perceive the impact of a crisis to be severe or very damaging and plan accordingly tend to achieve more successful outcomes. Those that fail to scan are often taken by surprise and have to react with less time and control to manage the events that hit them. Even if they do pick up a signal, many organisations not only ignore it but also attempt to block it out (Pearson and Mitroff, 1993). It is as if management is attempting to deny the presence of the signals in order that any stability and certainty they may have can continue.

Many of the signals detected during the pre-impact phase wither and die. Some gather strength and develop with increasing force. The next episode is characterised by the identification of events that move from possible to probable status. There is increasing activity and preparation in anticipation of the crisis, once its true nature and direction have been determined. Much of the activity should be geared to training and the preparation and deployment of crisis teams. The objective is not to prevent the crisis but to defuse it as much as possible, to inform significant stakeholders of its proximity and possible effects, and finally to manage the crisis process.

The impact phase is the period when the 'crisis breaks out' (Sturges et al., 1991). Management is tested to the limit and if a plan has been developed it is implemented with the expectation of ameliorating the damage inflicted by the crisis. One method of reducing the impact is to contain or localise the crisis. Neutralising and constraining the event can prevent it from contaminating other parts of the organisation or stakeholders. Pearson and tMitroff (1993) suggest that the containment of oil spills and the evacuation of buildings and aircraft are examples of containment and neutralisation. Through the necessity to talk to all stakeholders, management at this point will inevitably reveal its attitude towards the crisis event. Is its attitude one of genuine concern for the victims and stakeholders? Is the attitude consistent with the expectations that stakeholders have of the management team? Alternatively, is there a perception that management is making lame excuses and distancing itself from the event, and is this consistent with expectations? Readers should note that, within the reactionary model, the pre-impact and impact phases are merged into one, simply because there is little or no planning, no scanning and, by definition, no preparation in anticipation of a crisis.

Viewpoint 14.4

The Cornish cream tea crisis

Image 14.8 The National Trust posted an ad on Facebook for Lanhydrock House showing a scone with jam and cream
Source: Marcin Jucha/123RF

For many, it may seem like a storm in a tea cup, but if you're Cornish it is a big deal. The order in which the jam and cream goes on a scone really matters. In Cornwall, the jam must go on the scone first. It's what makes a Cornish cream tea Cornish.

So when the National Trust posted an ad on Facebook for one of Cornwall's historic houses, Lanhydrock House, showing a photograph of a scone with the cream on first, rather than the jam, they immediately found themselves in hot water.

There was an immediate outcry and the people of Cornwall took offence. The National Trust received around 300 angry responses from those who viewed the ad as 'horrifying', 'shocking' and even 'blasphemy'. Some went further and threatened to cancel their National Trust membership, with others suggesting a boycott.

The National Trust found themselves in the middle of a social media backlash. And it didn't take long for the national media to get their hands on this story and headlines started to appear such as:

'Lanhydrock National Trust cream tea advert sparks outrage' (BBC).

'The "disgusting" Mother's Day cream tea advert that's sparked outrage in Cornwall' (CornwallLive).

'Everyone in Cornwall has totally lost the plot over this cream tea advert' (The Herald).

The debate continued on BBC Breakfast and Good Morning Britain with discussion about whether it was right to put the jam or cream on first and #jamfirst trended on Twitter.

In response to the outcry, the National Trust posted a Facebook response that began with 'We'd like to sincerely apologise'. After this serious beginning the post was more lighthearted and suggested the member of staff who had committed the mistake had been 'marched back over the Tamar'. The apology post showed an image of scones, this time with the scones in the foreground with the jam on first. Unfortunately, the scones in the background once again showed scones with the cream on first, causing the debate to continue.

Sources: Anon (2018c); Fisher (2018); Merrington (2018); Merrington and Lewis (2018).

Insight

This example shows how quickly a crisis can develop and how fast news of a mistake can spread. The National Trust were quick to respond and to apologise for their error, which suggests they undertake crisis management planning. The case also highlights that a well-respected organisation like the National Trust are likely to find it easier to restore trust with its publics.

Question: Using the organisational crisis matrix in Figure 14.2, explain the level of impact and the level of controllability of the cream tea crisis.

Task: Interpret the way the National Trust managed this crisis using the approaches outlined in Figure 14.4.

The readjustment phase within the planning model consists of two main episodes. The period concerns the recovery and realignment of the organisation and its stakeholders to the new environment, once the deepest part of the crisis event has passed. The essential tasks are to ensure that the needs of key stakeholders can still be met and, if they cannot, to determine what must be done to ensure that they can be. For example, continuity of product supply is critically important. This may be achieved by servicing customers from other locations. Common characteristics of this phase are the investigations, police inquiries, public demonstrations, court cases and media probing that inevitably follow major crises and disasters. The manner in which an organisation handles this fallout and tries to appear reasonable and consistent in its approach to such events can have a big impact on the perception that other stakeholders have of the organisation.

The rate at which organisations readjust depends partly on the strength of the image held by stakeholders prior to the crisis occurring. If the organisation had a strong reputation then the source credibility attributed to the organisation will be high. This means that messages transmitted by the organisation will be received favourably and trusted. However, if the reputation is poor, the effectiveness of any marketing communications is also going to be low. The level of source credibility held by the organisation will influence the speed with which stakeholders allow an organisation to readjust and recover after a crisis.

Benoit (1997) developed a theory concerning image restoration in the light of an organisational crisis. The theory states that there are five general approaches: denial, evade responsibility, reduce offensiveness, use corrective action and, lastly, mortification (see Figure 14.4). Benoit has used these approaches to evaluate the responses given by a variety of organisations when faced by different disasters and crises.

Organisations that have not planned their management of crisis events and have survived a disaster may decide to instigate a more positive approach in order to mitigate the impact of future crisis events. This is not uncommon and crisis management planning may occur at the end of this cycle.

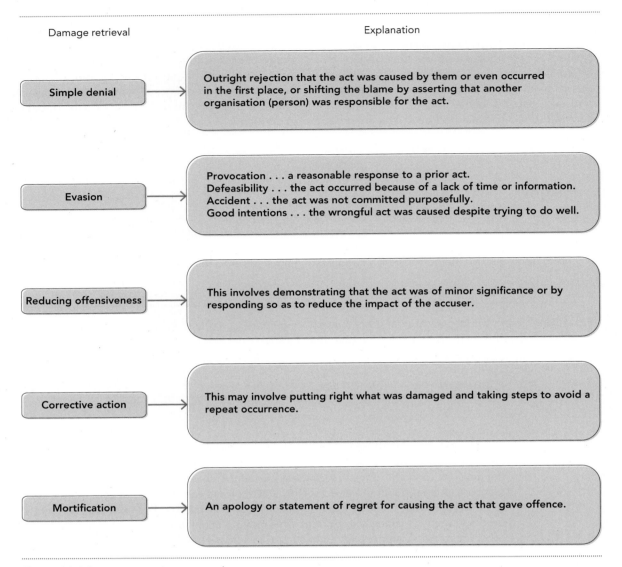

Damage retrieval | Explanation

Simple denial → Outright rejection that the act was caused by them or even occurred in the first place, or shifting the blame by asserting that another organisation (person) was responsible for the act.

Evasion → Provocation . . . a reasonable response to a prior act.
Defeasibility . . . the act occurred because of a lack of time or information.
Accident . . . the act was not committed purposefully.
Good intentions . . . the wrongful act was caused despite trying to do well.

Reducing offensiveness → This involves demonstrating that the act was of minor significance or by responding so as to reduce the impact of the accuser.

Corrective action → This may involve putting right what was damaged and taking steps to avoid a repeat occurrence.

Mortification → An apology or statement of regret for causing the act that gave offence.

Figure 14.4 Image restoration approaches

Framing for crisis communications

Framing involves the selection and prominence of specific topics that are communicated and promoted through an organisation's communications processes (Romenti et al., 2014). The use of framing can shape the way stakeholders perceive an organisation and the associated crisis (Choi and Lee, 2017; Sjöberg, 2018) (see Chapter 19 for a deeper insight into the framing concept).

Crises can be categorised by type (Coombs, 2007) and the type provides the frame through which stakeholders pick up clues about how to interpret the event. Coombs identifies three main types: the extent to which the event was caused by an uncontrollable external force or agent; whether it was the result of an intentional or accidental action by the organisation; or if it was caused by human or technical error. The frame, therefore, enables stakeholders to determine the extent to which the organisation was responsible for the crisis occurring in the first place. From these three, clusters of types of crisis can be identified: victim, accident and preventable clusters (see Table 14.6).

Table 14.6   Crisis types by crisis clusters

Crisis clusters	Explanation
Victim cluster	The organisation is seen as a victim of the crisis. Stakeholders attribute little responsibility to the organisation, so there is only a mild reputational threat. Common events include natural disasters, rumours, workplace violence and product tampering.
Accident cluster	The actions of the organisation leading to the crisis were minimal and the threat to reputational status is moderate. Typical events include stakeholder challenges to the operations, technical-error accidents and technical errors resulting in product defect and subsequent recall.
Preventable cluster	The organisation deliberately placed people at risk, took inappropriate actions or violated regulations and in doing so caused a strong threat to the reputation. Typical events include human-error accidents and product harm/defects, deception, misconduct and actions that lead to injury.

Source: After Protecting organization reputations during a crisis: the development and application of situational crisis communication theory, *Corporate Reputation Review*, 10(3), pp. 163–176 (Coombs, W.T. 2007), reprinted by permission from Macmillan Publishers Ltd.

Coombs (2006) claims that, in order to repair reputation, crisis response strategies are necessary to shape the perceptions of those responsible, change perceptions of the organisation and reduce the negative effects caused through the crisis event. He identifies three main forms of response based on the perceptions of those responsible for the crisis. The first are denial strategies, which attempt to remove connections between the organisation and the crisis. The second are diminish strategies, which argue that the organisation did not lack control over the crisis and that it is not as bad as is claimed by others. The third are rebuild strategies, which involve offering compensation or an apology to victims. Coombs develops a situational crisis communications theory, which anticipates how stakeholders will perceive a crisis and how they will react to various response strategies. He argues that his approach bridges deficiencies in Benoit's image restoration theory, which offers 'no conceptual links between the crisis response strategies and elements of the crisis situation' (Coombs, 2007: 171).

Scholars' paper 14.4

How is a crisis framed?

Choi, J. and Lee, S. (2017) Managing a crisis: A framing analysis of press releases dealing with the Fukushima nuclear power station crisis, *Public Relations Review*, 43(5), 1016–24.

This paper examines press releases from the Tokyo Electric Power Company (TEPCO) after the Japanese earthquake in 2011. The study highlights the importance of keeping publics informed during a crisis and in particular the need to provide information to media outlets.

See also:

Sjöberg, U. (2018) It is not about facts – it is about framing. The app generation's information seeking tactics: proactive online crisis communication, *Journal of Contingencies and Crisis Management*, 26(1), 127–37.

Key points

- Public relations is a communications discipline that can develop and maintain a portfolio of relationships with a range of key stakeholder audiences. The use of public relations does not require the purchase of airtime or space in media vehicles. The decision on whether an organisation's public relations messages are transmitted or not rests with those charged with managing the media resource.

- The main characteristics of public relations are that it represents a very cost-effective means of carrying messages with a high degree of credibility. However, the degree of control that management is able to exert over the transmission of messages can be limited.

- Public relations can be used to communicate with a range of publics (or stakeholders). These vary from employees (internal public relations), financial groups (financial or investor relations), customers (media relations), organisations and communities (corporate public relations) and media (media relations).

- Public relations enables organisations to position themselves and provide stakeholders with a means of identifying and understanding them. This may be accomplished inadvertently through inaction or deliberately through a planned presentation of a variety of visual cues.

- Public relations can be seen to work at a practitioner level where it is used as a tool to achieve media visibility. At a different level public relations is seen as a means of mediating the relationships organisations develop with various stakeholders. Here, public relations is perceived as a longer-term and proactive form of planned communications. In the former view, public relations is seen as an instrument, in the latter, as a means of conducting dialogue.

- Grunig and Hunt (1984) have attempted to capture the diversity of public relations activities through a framework. They set out four models to reflect the different ways in which public relations is, in their opinion, considered to work.

- There are four dimensions of communications behaviour. These dimensions are direction, purpose, channel and ethics. Using predetermined campaign objectives, ranging from publicity, through press releases, to the manner in which customers are treated and products perform, events are managed and expectations are met.

- Public relations consists of a range of communications activities, of which media relations, publicity and event management appear to be the main ones used by practitioners. However, in addition investor relations, lobbying, corporate advertising and crisis communications form an important aspect of public relations activities.

- Public relations plays an important role in preparing for and constraining the impact of a crisis and re-establishing an organisation once a crisis has passed. Crisis planning is about putting into position those elements that can affect speedy outcomes.

- Public relations has three major roles to play within the communications programme of an organisation: the development and maintenance of corporate goodwill; the continuity necessary for good product support; and, through these, the development and maintenance of suitable relationships. These roles can be accomplished more easily when public relations is integrated with the other tools and media of the communications mix.

Case study

The Swedish Number

Image 14.9 The Swedish Number allowed foreigners to connect with a random Swede
Source: The Swedish Number

The Swedish Tourist Association (STF) was set up in 1885 and has become one of the largest volunteer organisations in Sweden. The organisation has pioneered the discovery of Sweden and runs over 250 accommodation sites all over Sweden. As well as hotels and hostels, STF offers visitors the chance to stay in lighthouses, mountain stations and ships as part of their mission to help people discover Sweden.

The STF saw a decrease in their membership between 2007 and 2015, which made them realise they needed to find a way to generate interest in Sweden and boost visitors to the country. Their objective was simple, to slow down the decline in membership by 25 per cent.

Their research showed that young tourists were not interested in visiting Sweden, preferring the rest of the world, so they needed to find a way to get people talking about Sweden in a way that would engage younger audiences.

The solution came from insight about Swedes themselves. By nature Swedes are not very nationalistic and seen as reluctant to show pride in their country. However, research also showed that while Swedes don't like showing national pride when talking to each other, they are happy to share their pride about Sweden with foreigners.

The solution came in the form of a phone number. STF gave Sweden its own phone number that allowed foreigners calling from abroad to connect with a random Swede. Foreign callers were directed through a switchboard to a 'telephone ambassador' somewhere in Sweden.

All Swedes were invited to become a 'Telephone Ambassador' by downloading The Swedish Number App from the App store and registering to take calls. This created a platform for the Swedish people to sell Sweden for themselves. It also provided an opportunity for callers to discover what Sweden was like, from the people that know it best. And Swedes could talk about anything they liked.

The idea of talking freely resonated with Swedes, who in the same year were celebrating the 250-year anniversary of the abolishment of censorship. More than 26,000 signed up to become Telephone Ambassadors for The Swedish Number and the campaign even saw the Swedish Prime Minister take part in answering calls.

This was a PR-led campaign and there was no media budget. This meant that all media had to be earned. The campaign was divided into two separate PR launches, one for national and one for international.

Recognising that Swedes often read international publications and the national media report on what the international media write, the media strategy was to use international press to feed stories to the national media.

The world's first telephone number for a country caught the attention of the international media. Many of the world's media called The Swedish Number and reported live on conversations held with the random Swede who answered the call. As every Swede had their own view about Sweden and each answered questions in a unique way, this made for great live TV and radio around the world.

TV shows and news channels all over the world were talking about The Swedish Number. News also spread in newspaper articles and in blogs, on Twitter and on Facebook. It wasn't long before the phone calls were coming in by the hundreds, with international callers wanting to get a chance to speak to a random Swede about their country.

The web page, theswedishnumber.com, provided media with a film and statistics in real time, allowing them to report on the number of calls that had taken place, the last country that had called and average calling time.

Over the 73-day campaign, The Swedish Number received 197,678 phone calls. Calls were received from 190 countries (of 194 in the world). The accumulated calling time was 367 days and the longest call lasted 3h 42min.

The campaign objective had been to slow down the decline in STF membership by 25 per cent. The outcome of the campaign exceeded this aim and halted the decline in membership by 50 per cent. Membership saw an increase of 7.5 per cent in membership online and 41.6 per cent of new members joined during the three-month campaign.

New membership from younger audiences was increased significantly. Membership from the 16–25-year age segment grew by 70 per cent and the 25–30-year age segment increased by 35 per cent. Membership renewal also increased.

The financial impact of the campaign provided a return on marketing investment (ROMI) of 6,912 per cent.

The Swedish Number connected Sweden to the rest of the world. The phone line facilitated 197,678 personalised and authentic conversations between Swedes and people from nearly every country in the world.

The campaign became one of the most talked about by media and social media, generating 9,324 billion media impressions and resulted in earned media with an estimated PR value of over $146 million.

The Swedish Number won a Titanium and Grand Prix at Cannes, and three Gold, six Silver and two Bronze Lions.

Sources: Nudd (2016); The Swedish Number (2017); The Swedish Number (2018).

Image 14.10 The world's first telephone number for a country
Source: The Swedish Number

Review questions

The Swedish Number case questions

1. Identify the main publics for The Swedish Number public relations campaign.

2. Highlight the main objectives of using public relations. How were these realised in The Swedish Number?

3. How might the success of The Swedish Number be evaluated?

4. Write a brief paper describing the main methods used by The Swedish Number to manage the media relations.

5. Find three pieces of media coverage of The Swedish Number. Compare the type of material used for each, i.e. text-only, images, audio, etc.

General questions

1. Define public relations and set out its principal characteristics.

2. Identify the different strategies associated with investor relations.

3. Identify the main phases associated with crisis management.

4. Suggest how the responses made by The National Trust (Viewpoint 14.4) can be interpreted through use of Benoit's 'approaches to image restoration'.

5. What roles might stakeholders adopt when a crisis occurs?

References for Chapter 14

Anastasiadis, S., Moon, J. and Humphreys, M. (2018) Lobbying and the responsible firm: agenda setting for a freshly conceptualized field, *Business Ethics: A European Review*, 27(3), 207–21.

Anon (2018a) Don't give mash a chance. Vote for chips and join the Great Pie Debate! PukkaPies.co.uk, 5 March, retrieved 1 May 2018 from https://www.pukkapies.co.uk/news/dont-give-mash-chance-vote-chips-join-great-pie-debate/

Anon (2018b) The best multimedia content guide for PR success, PR Newswire, retrieved 20 May 2018 from http://www.cision.ca/resources/white-papers/multimedia-storytelling-lp/

Anon (2018c) Lanhydrock National Trust cream tea advert sparks outrage, BBC News, 11 March, retrieved 20 May 2018 from http://www.bbc.co.uk/news/uk-england-cornwall-43363435

Bauer, T. (2014) Responsible lobbying: a multidimensional model, *Journal of Corporate Citizenship*, 14(53), 61–76.

Benoit, W.L. (1997) Image repair discourse and crisis communications, *Public Relations Review*, 23(2), 177–86.

Bernays, E.L. (1928) *Propaganda*, New York: Horace Liveright.

Birkner, C. (2016) These tiny islands turned sheep into videographers to literally put itself on the map, *Adweek*, 21 November, retrieved 10 February 2018 from http://www.adweek.com/brand-marketing/these-tiny-islands-turned-sheep-videographers-literally-put-itself-map-174720/

Brown, B., Ennis, D., Kaplan, J. and Rosenthal, J. (2017) To survive in the age of advanced cyberthreats, use 'active defense', *McKinsey and Company*, November, retrieved 10 January 2018 from https://www.mckinsey.com/business-functions/digital-mckinsey/our-insights/to-survive-in-the-age-of-advanced-cyberthreats-use-active-defense

Bruning, S.D. and Ledingham, J.A. (2000) Perceptions of relationships and evaluations of satisfaction: an exploration of interaction, *Public Relations Review*, 26(1), 85–95.

Bruning, S.D., Dials, M. and Shirka, A. (2008) Using dialogue to build organisation–public relationships, engage publics, and positively affect organizational outcomes, *Public Relations Review*, 34, 25–31.

Capriotti, P. and González Herrero, A. (2013) Managing media relations in museums through the internet: a model of analysis for online press rooms in museums, *Museum Management and Curatorship*, 28(4), 413–29.

Capriotti, P. and González Herrero, A. (2017) From 1.0 online pressrooms to 2.0 social newsrooms at museums worldwide, *Comunicación y Sociedad*, 30(2), 113.

Choi, J. and Lee, S. (2017) Managing a crisis: a framing analysis of press releases dealing with the Fukushima nuclear power station crisis, *Public Relations Review*, 43(5), 1016–24.

Choi, J. and Lee, S. (2018) Lessons from a crisis: an analysis of Toyota's handling of the recall crisis, *Journal of Public Affairs*, 18(2), e1688.

CIPR (2018) FAQs, CIPR.co.uk, retrieved 20 May 2018 from https://www.cipr.co.uk/content/policy/policy/lobbying/faqs

Coombs, W.T. (2006) The protective powers of crisis response strategies: managing reputational assets during a crisis, *Journal of Promotion Management*, 12, 241–59.

Coombs, W.T. (2007) Protecting organization reputations during a crisis: the development and application of situational crisis communications theory, *Corporate Reputation Review* 10(3), 163–76.

Cutlip, S.M., Center, A.H. and Broom, G.M. (1994) *Effective Public Relations*, Englewood Cliffs, NJ: Prentice Hall.

Cutlip, S.M., Center, A.H. and Broom, G.M. (1999) *Effective Public Relations*, 8th edn, Englewood Cliffs, NJ: Prentice Hall.

Davidson, S. (2015) Everywhere and nowhere: theorising and researching public affairs and lobbying within public relations scholarship, *Public Relations Review*, 41(5), 615–27.

Dillingham, L.L. and Ivanov, B. (2017) Inoculation messages as a preemptive financial crisis communication strategy with inexperienced investors, *Journal of Applied Communication Research*, 45(3), 274–93.

Dixon, R. (2017) Not so sheepish now: Google Street View adds the Faroe Islands, *Guardian*, 2 November, retrieved 10 May 2018 from https://www.theguardian.com/travel/2017/nov/02/faroe-islands-added-to-google-street-view-sheep-cameras

Erzikova, E., Waters, R. and Bocharsky, K. (2018) Media catching: a conceptual framework for understanding strategic mediatization in public relations? *International Journal of Strategic Communication*, 1–15.

Fink, S. (2000) *Crisis Management Planning for the Inevitable*, New York: AMACON.

Fisher, A. (2018) Response shows how to handle a storm in a tearoom, mediafirst, 12 March, retrieved 18 May 2018 from http://mediafirst.co.uk/our-thinking/response-shows-how-to-handle-a-storm-in-a-tearoom/

Google Sheep View (2017) Cannes Archives, retrieved 20 February 2018 from http://player.canneslions.com/index.html#/works

Greenwood, C.A. (2011) Evolutionary theory: the missing link for conceptualizing public relations, *Journal of Public Relations Research*, 22(4), 456–76.

Gregory, A. (2004) Scope and structure of public relations: a technology driven view, *Public Relations Review*, 30(3), 245–54.

Grunig, J. (1992) Models of public relations and communication, in *Excellence in Public Relations and Communications Management* (eds J.E. Grunig, D.M. Dozier, P. Ehling, L.A. Grunig, F.C. Repper and J. Whits), Hillsdale, NJ: Lawrence Erlbaum, 285–325.

Grunig, J.E. (1997) A situational theory of publics: conceptual history, recent challenges and new research, in *Public Relations Research: An International Perspective* (eds D. Moss, T. MacManus and D. Verčič), London: Thomson.

Grunig, J. and Hunt, T. (1984) *Managing Public Relations*, New York: Holt, Rineholt & Winston.

Halkos, G. and Bousinakis, D. (2017) The effect of stress and dissatisfaction on employees during crisis, *Economic Analysis and Policy*, 55, 25–34

Hanrahan, G. (1997) Financial and investor relations, in *Public Relations Principles and Practice* (ed. P. Kitchen), London: Thomson.

HARO (2018) About us, retrieved 20 May 2018 from https://www.helpareporter.com/about/

Heckler (2016) The state of multimedia in press releases [Study + Infographics], *PR Newswire*, 27 January, retrieved 30 August 2018 from https://www.prnewswire.com/blog/2016/the-state-of-multimedia-in-press-releases-study-and-infographic.html

Hill, M.D., Kelly, G.W., Lockhart, G.B. and Ness, R.A. (2013) Determinants and effects of corporate lobbying, *Financial Management*, 42(4), 931–57.

Ho, B., Shin, W. and Pang, A. (2017) Corporate crisis advertising: a framework examining the use and effects of corporate advertising before and after crises, *Journal of Marketing Communications*, 23(6), 537–51.

Kale, S. (2017) I used to work at Bell Pottinger – so I can tell you why good people end up doing immoral things in lobbying, *Independent*, 18 September, retrieved 10 February 2018 from https://www.independent.co.uk/voices/bell-pottinger-pr-scandal-lobbying-government-journalists-fake-news-good-people-immoral-a7952706.html

Kent, M.L. and Taylor, M. (2002) Toward a dialogic theory of public relations, *Public Relations Review*, 28(1), 21–37.

Laskin, A.V. (2009) The evolution of models of public relations: an outsider's perspective, *Journal of Communication Management*, 13(1), 37–54.

Lock, I., Seele, P. and Heath, R.L. (2016) Where grass has no roots: the concept of 'shared strategic communication' as an answer to unethical astroturf lobbying, *International Journal of Strategic Communication*, 10(2), 87–100.

Macnamara, J. (2016) Organizational listening: addressing a major gap in public relations theory and practice, *Journal of Public Relations Research*, 28(3–4), 146–69.

Mamic, L.I. and Almaraz, I.A. (2013) How the larger corporations engage with stakeholders through Twitter, *International Journal of Market Research*, 55(6), 851–72.

Merrington, J. (2018) The 'disgusting' Mother's Day cream tea advert that's sparked outrage in Cornwall, *CornwallLive*, 10 March, retrieved 20 May 2018 from https://www.cornwalllive.com/whats-on/food-drink/disgusting-mothers-day-cream-tea-1322429

Merrington, J. and Lewis, J. (2018) Everyone in Cornwall has totally lost the plot over this cream tea advert, *The Herald*, 10 March, retrieved 10 May 2018 from https://www.plymouthherald.co.uk/whats-on/everyone-cornwall-totally-lost-plot-1322629

Miller, G. (1989) Persuasion and public relations: two 'Ps' in a pod, in *Public Relations Theory* (eds C. Botan and V. Hazelton), Hillsdale, NJ: Lawrence Erlbaum.

Moloney, K. (1997) Government and lobbying activities, in *Public Relations: Principles and Practice* (ed. P.J. Kitchen), London: International Thomson Press.

Myers, C. (2018) Public relations or 'grassroots lobbying'? How lobbying laws are re-defining PR practice, *Public Relations Review*, 44(1), 11–21.

Nudd, T. (2016) Sweden just got its own phone number. A funny thing happened when we called it, *Adweek*, 7 April, retrieved 20 May 2018 from http://www.adweek.com/creativity/sweden-just-got-its-own-phone-number-heres-what-happened-when-we-called-170659/

Pace, S., Balboni, B. and Gistri, G. (2017) The effects of social media on brand attitude and WOM during a brand crisis: evidences from the Barilla case, *Journal of Marketing Communications*, 23(2), 135–48.

Pearson, C.M. and Clair, J.A. (1998) Reframing crisis management, *Academy of Management Review*, 23, 59–76.

Pearson, C.M. and Mitroff, I. (1993) From crisis prone to crisis prepared: a framework for crisis management, *Academy of Management Executive*, 7(1), 48–59.

Penrose, J.M. (2000) The role of perception in crisis planning, *Public Relations Review*, 26(2), 155–71.

Rad, A. (2017) The importance of trust for inter-organizational relationships: a study of inter-bank market practices in a crisis, *Qualitative Research in Accounting & Management*, 14(3), 282–306.

Redmond, A. (2018) How Twitter engagement led Pukka Pies to own #BritishPieWeek, *We Think*, 10 April, retrieved 1 May 2018 from http://blog.togetheragency.co.uk/2018/04/

Romenti, S., Murtarelli, G. and Valentini, C. (2014) Organisations' conversations in social media: applying dialogue strategies in times of crises, *Corporate Communications: An International Journal*, 19(1), 10–33.

Shin, J.H. and Cameron, G.T. (2003) Informal relations: a look at personal influence in media relations, *Journal of Communication Management*, 7, 239–53.

Sjöberg, U. (2018) It is not about facts – it is about framing: the app generation's information-seeking tactics: proactive online crisis communication, *Journal of Contingencies and Crisis Management*, 26(1), 127–37.

Strauß, N. (2018) The role of trust in investor relations: a conceptual framework, *Corporate Communications: An International Journal*, 23(1), 2–16.

Sturges, D.L., Carell, B.J., Newsom, D.A. and Barrera, M. (1991) Crisis communication management: the public opinion node and its relationship to environmental nimbus, *SAM Advanced Management Journal*, Summer, 22–7.

Tan, E. (2018) How Pukka Pies put an end to one of Britain's big debates: pie with mash or chips? *Campaign*, 3 April, retrieved 1 May 2018 from https://www.campaignlive.co.uk/article/pukka-pies-put-end-one-britains-big-debates-pie-mash-chips/1460679

The Swedish Number (2017) *Cannes Lions Archive*, retrieved 10 March 2018 from http://player.canneslions.com/index.html#/works

The Swedish Number (2018) theswedishnumber.com, retrieved 10 April 2018 from https://www.theswedishnumber.com

UK Investor Relations Society (2018) retrieved 23 March 2011 from www.irsociety.org.uk/about

Waters, R.D., Tindall, N.T.J. and Morton, T.S. (2010) Media catching and the journalist–public relations practitioner relationship: how social media are changing the practice of media relations, *Journal of Public Relations Research*, 22(3), 241–64.

Ye, L. and Ki, E.J. (2017) Organizational crisis communication on Facebook: a study of BP's Deepwater Horizon oil spill, *Corporate Communications: An International Journal*, 22(1), 80–92.

Yun, S.-H. (2006) Toward public relations theory-based study of public diplomacy: testing the applicability of the excellence study, *Journal of Public Relations Research*, 18(4), 287–312.

Zerfass, A., Verčič, D. and Wiesenberg, M. (2016) The dawn of a new golden age for media relations? How PR professionals interact with the mass media and use new collaboration practices, *Public Relations Review*, 42(4), 499–508.

Sponsorship

Sponsorship has traditionally been seen as a means of supporting primary media activities and raising a brand's visibility. More recently, however, sponsorship has become a powerful marketing communications tool in its own right and sponsors are taking advantage of opportunities to leverage their partnerships for more tangible returns on their investment.

Sponsorship is being used in a more strategic manner with sponsor partners working together to develop new brands and new broadcast opportunities. In addition, sponsors are taking advantage of benefits such as stadium naming rights, team name titles and access to the sponsored organisation's database. Sponsorship has evolved into a powerful marketing communications tool and this is reflected in the steady increase in sponsorship spending globally.

Aims and learning objectives

The aims of this chapter are to introduce and examine sponsorship as an increasingly significant form of marketing communications.

The learning objectives are to enable readers to:

1. explain how sponsorship activities have developed and understand the main characteristics of these forms of communications;
2. consider reasons for the use of sponsorship and the types of objectives that might be set;
3. appraise how sponsorship might work;
4. examine some of the conceptual and theoretical aspects of sponsorship;
5. appreciate the variety and different forms of sponsorship activities;
6. understand the reasons why sponsorship has become an important part of the communications mix.

Introduction

Sponsorship has become an increasingly popular element of the communications mix. The sponsorship activities of global organisations like Emirates outlined in the case study at the end of this chapter demonstrates not only the importance to brands of being associated with a major sporting team, but also the role sponsors can play in supporting teams. In other words, sponsorship can be mutually rewarding.

Image 15.1 In 2006, O_2 acquired the naming rights to the 'Millennium Dome' in Greenwich, London. The sponsorship associates O_2 with music and entertainment and provides O_2 customers the opportunity to purchase tickets 48 hours in advance of the general public. The partnership provides the venue direct contact with millions of O_2 customers.
Source: Telefónica UK Limited.

Global sponsorship spending has seen a steady increase in expenditure over the last 20 years (Meenaghan, 2013) and current forecasts from the International Events Group (IEG 2018) suggest that this trend will continue with a projected $65.8 billion to be spent on sponsorship rights globally in 2018 (IEG, 2018, cited in McDonald, 2018) (see Table 15.1).

This increase is not surprising considering the high levels of visibility that sponsorship offers and the increased opportunities for activation, especially through social media channels. According to IEG, sponsorship now accounts for an average of 17 per cent of an

Table 15.1 Annual global sponsorship spend

Year	US$ billion
2014	55.3
2015	57.5
2016	60.1
2017	62.7*e
2018	65.8*f

Notes: *e = estimated, *f = forecast
Source: IEG (2018), cited by WARC Data Points, January 2018 (McDonald, 2018).

organisation's overall marketing budget (IEG, 2018). The report published by IEG identi-fied the value attributed to sponsorship and found that as well as benefits such as on-site signage, broadcast advertising opportunities, tickets and hospitality, rights to content for digital use, property marks, logos and co-branded products, sponsors value access to fans and talent and opportunities for activation (IEG, 2018). While category exclusivity was seen to be the most valuable factor, a presence in digital media, social and mobile media has become the second most valuable sponsorship benefit (IEG, 2018). The opportunities to activate sponsorship on digital platforms may in part explain the increase in sponsorship spending.

Sponsorship has traditionally been seen as a mix of advertising, with its capacity for high visibility, high reach and message control, and public relations with its potential for high levels of credibility and message diffusion, directed through or with a third party. So, in this sense, sponsorship lacks the harshness of advertising and the total lack of control that characterises much of the work of public relations.

While many organisations are very active in sponsoring local cultural and sporting events and teams to demonstrate their commitment to the local community, for most global companies sponsorship is now a strategic business activity that is evaluated for its effectiveness against business and brand objectives, using key performance indicators (KPIs) (Kourovskaia and Meenaghan, 2013; Meenaghan, 2013). This reflects the increased value that is seen to be leveraged from sponsorship and the range of opportunities that partnerships with sponsored organisations can offer.

Sponsorship offers an opportunity for organisations to engage with both internal and external audiences and can provide a number of benefits for the sponsor:

1. *Brand awareness.* Sponsor exposure provides an opportunity to raise visibility of the organisation among particular audiences that each event or team attracts. This may mitigate any negative effects associated with traditional mass media and direct persuasion.

2. *Brand association.* Sponsorship suggests to target audiences that there is an asso-ciation between the sponsor and the sponsored organisation and that, by impli-cation, this association may be of interest and/or value. Sponsors are often given rights to use property marks and logos as part of their sponsorship to support the association.

3. *Campaign support.* Sponsoring an event or sport may provide sponsors with the oppor-tunity to blend a variety of tools in the communications mix and use resources more efficiently and, arguably, more effectively. A sponsorship may also provide additional advertising opportunities.

4. *Exclusive rights.* Having exclusive sponsorship rights for an event or team can act as a barrier to entry to competitors.

5. *Access to audiences and resources.* Access to databases of fans or other audiences allows sponsors to leverage their association. Additionally, sponsorship can provide access to talent such as sportsmen and women, who can be featured for marketing purposes.

6. *Hospitality at events.* Access to tickets and hospitality at events for sponsors to entertain clients and prospects.

7. *New products and services.* A sponsorship may include opportunities to develop co-branded products or services.

From this it is possible to define sponsorship as a commercial activity in which one party permits another an opportunity to exploit an association with a target audience in return for funds, services or resources. It also highlights the mutual benefits that can be gained from partnerships.

Viewpoint 15.1

ŠKODA *Tour de Celeb* – engaging audiences through social media

Image 15.2 *Tour de Celeb* was a unique broadcast sponsorship for ŠKODA
Source: STV.

ŠKODA started life as a cycle company over 120 years ago and throughout its history, cycling has remained an important part of the brand's identity. The company retains strong links with its cycling heritage through its sponsorship of many cycling events around the world.

To increase awareness of ŠKODA's existing association with cycling and to extend appeal to a wider audience, the brand partnered with STV productions and Channel 5 to create *Tour de Celeb*. The original TV show followed the cycling highs and lows of eight celebrities as they took on one of the toughest stages of the Tour de France, L'etape du Tour. Celebrities such as Jodie Kidd and Louie Spence took part in the show, which saw them complete a 146km cycle ride through the French Alps from Megève to Morzine.

Tour de Celeb took broadcast sponsorship to a new level. While the celebrity involvement guaranteed media interest, there were significant benefits that came with being involved up front with the design of the programme. ŠKODA was able to provide support cars for the series, offering increased opportunities for brand exposure during the show. Additionally, ŠKODA branding was designed as an integral part of the show's brand logo, rather than being a later add-on.

ŠKODA had opportunities to leverage the sponsorship beyond the show with the launch of a cycling platform, *Life on Two Wheels*, which included tutorials on cycling topics. Content was also developed to support social activation. *Tour de Celeb* was a unique broadcast sponsorship that reached an audience of more than two million and ŠKODA saw purchase intent rise by 100 per cent.

Sources: Agar (2017); ESA (2017a).

Insight

This highlights how sponsorship partnerships can be created by brands to help them connect with audiences. While traditional broadcast sponsorship provides brand association, working closely with partners can allow for unique sponsorship opportunities to emerge.

Question: How relevant was this programme for ŠKODA? Consider the degree of fit using the grid provided in Figure 15.1 and state the type of match this provided from both a functional and image perspective.

Task: Find three other examples of programme sponsorship and consider for each the degree of fit. Using Figure 15.1 state the type of match each sponsorship presents.

It is necessary to clarify the distinction between sponsorship and charitable donations. The latter are intended to change attitudes and project a caring identity, with the main returns from the exercise being directed to society or the beneficiaries. The beneficiaries have almost total control over the way in which funds are used. When funds are channelled through sponsorship the recipient has to attend to the needs of the sponsor by allowing it access to the commercial associations that are to be exploited, partly because they have a legal arrangement, but also to ensure that the exchange becomes relational and longer-term; in other words, there is repeat purchase (investment) activity. The other major difference is that the benefits of the exchange are intended to accrue to the participants, not society at large.

Normally sponsorship involves two parties, the sponsor and the sponsored organisation. The degree of fit between these two parties partly determines the relative effectiveness of the relationship (Poon and Prendergast, 2006). The degree of fit, or product relevance, as proposed by McDonald (1991) and cited by Poon and Prendergast (2006), can be considered in terms of two main dimensions. Function-based similarity occurs when the product is used in the event being sponsored. For example, function-based similarity occurs when a piano manufacturer such as Bösendorfer sponsors a Viennese piano recital. The second dimension concerns image-based similarities, which reflect the image of the sponsor in the event. Here Airbus's sponsorship of a major technical or even artistic exhibition serves to bestow prestige on all parties. Prendergast et al. (2010) identify two levels (high and low) of functional and image-based congruence, before offering a four-quadrant classification (see Figure 15.1).

To illustrate how this works, these authors give as an example an airline's sponsorship of environmental activities. This, they say, is low in both functional and image congruence and there is no clear link to the airline's function or image other than to rectify the situation. The airline has a limited travel scheme, called 'Miles for Kids in Need'. This gives assistance to children who are seriously ill and in need of emergency medical treatment. This equates to high functional congruence but low image congruence (F-MATCH). Low functional congruence with high image congruence (I-MATCH) occurs with the airline's sponsorship of a variety of cultural events. The final quadrant (MATCH) occurs through the

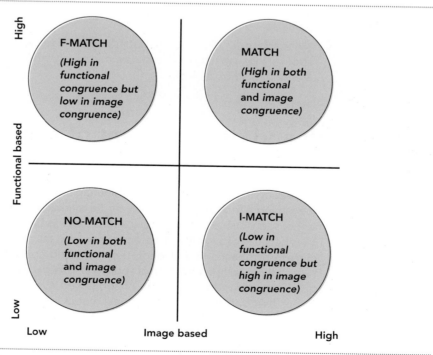

Figure 15.1 Four types of integrated congruence
Source: Based on Prendergast et al. (2010). Used with permission from WARC.

airline's travel sponsorship of a symphony orchestra, as this generates both high functional and image congruence.

Building on Poon and Prendergast's paper in 2006, Prendergast et al. (2010) examined the importance of congruence between a sponsor and the venue being sponsored. They identified that sponsorships involving low functional and low image congruence did little to create favourable communications outcomes for the sponsor and suggest that outcomes were the same as if there were no sponsorship.

Coppetti et al. (2009) emphasise the value of congruence but also demonstrate that even when there is a lack of fit, the effectiveness of the sponsorship can be enhanced by involving the audience in what they refer to as 'attractive sponsor activities'. This suggests that by building in experiences for the audience and encouraging its participation, and by using advertising before and after the sponsorship event, such integration can serve to increase the value of the communications programme.

Scholars' paper 15.1

What makes a good sponsorship opportunity?

Prendergast, G.P., Poon, D. and West, D.C. (2010) Match game: linking sponsorship congruence with communication outcomes, *Journal of Advertising Research,* **50(2), 214–26.**

This is an important paper for those requiring an in-depth understanding of sponsorship. Building on the 2006 paper by Poon and Prendergast, the authors seek to develop the debate about the importance of congruence between a sponsor and the event being sponsored. Their research into the subject found no evidence of interaction effects between functional and image congruence. They determined that sponsorships involving low functional and low image congruence did as little to create favourable communications outcomes as if there were no sponsorship.

See also:

Meenaghan, T., McLoughlin, D. and McCormack, A. (2013) New challenges in sponsorship evaluation actors, new media, and the context of praxis, *Psychology & Marketing,* 30(5), 444–60.

The growth and development of sponsorship

Many researchers and authors agree that the use of sponsorship by organisations is increasing (Mazodier et al., 2017; Meenaghan, 2013; Walraven et al., 2012) and that it is becoming a more significant part of the marketing communications mix. The development of sponsorship as a communications tool has been spectacular since the early 1990s. This is because of a variety of factors, but among the most important are the government's policies on tobacco and alcohol, the escalating costs of advertising media during the 1990s, the proven effectiveness of sponsorship, new opportunities due to increased leisure activity, greater media coverage of sponsored events and the recognition of the inefficiencies associated with the traditional media (Meenaghan, 1991). In addition, changes in broadcast regulations since the early 1990s have allowed programme sponsorship in commercial television and radio. In 2006 Ofcom, the independent regulator and competition authority for the UK communications industry, extended programme sponsorship to commercial television channels and radio services, opening up new opportunities for channel sponsorship (Ofcom, 2006). Table 15.2 highlights some of the main reasons for the

Table 15.2 Factors promoting growth and development of sponsorship

Increased media coverage of events
Relaxation of government and industry regulations
Increased incidence of sponsorship event supply (and demand)
Relationship orientation and association between sponsorship participants
Positive attitude change towards sponsorship by senior management
Awareness and drive towards integrated marketing communications
Increasing rate of other media costs
Need to develop softer brand associations and to reach niche audiences
Increased opportunities to activate social media engagement

growth of sponsorship and Viewpoint 15.1 provides an example of a unique association that developed between a sponsor and a TV broadcaster.

Sponsorship, a part of public relations, should be used as an element of an integrated approach to an organisation's communications. In other words, sponsorship needs to be harnessed strategically. For example, many companies and brands originating in the Middle East, South-East Asia and the Pacific regions have used sponsorship as a means of overseas market entry in order to develop name or brand awareness. Panasonic, JVC and Daihatsu have used this approach, as indeed many companies are now doing in an attempt to become established in the BRIC countries.

Sponsorship objectives

Any organisation developing a sponsorship strategy should always include well-defined objectives and where the sponsorship allows the sponsor to connect with a range of stakeholder groups, according to Meenaghan et al. (2013), specific objectives need to be set for each group. Figure 15.2 provides an outline of the main stakeholder groups identified by Meenaghan et al. (2013) who suggests a broader focus of stakeholders is a key change within the industry.

There are both primary and secondary objectives associated with using sponsorship. The primary reasons are to build awareness, to develop relationships, possibly through loyalty, and to improve perception (image) held of a brand or organisation. Secondary reasons are more contentious, but generally they can be seen to be to attract new users, to support dealers and other intermediaries, and to act as a form of staff motivation and morale building. A recent survey of brand marketers by IEG identified the importance of different objectives for sponsors (IEG, 2018). Figure 15.3 highlights that creating awareness/visibility, increasing brand loyalty and changing/reinforcing image are the top three reasons cited by marketers.

Sponsorship is normally regarded as a communications tool used to reach external stakeholders. However, if chosen appropriately, sponsorship can also be used effectively to reach internal audiences (Khan and Stanton, 2010). Edwards (2016) examined the effect that Olympic sponsorship support had on an organisation's employees and identified sponsorship increased organisational pride and corporate social responsibility (CSR) perceptions.

A number of organisations have used their sponsorship to engage internal audiences. In 2016, Heineken UK sponsored an employee event, Race to the Tower, as part of an internal employee campaign to support employee engagement (ESA, 2017b). The sponsorship helped to demonstrate the organisation's commitment to employee wellbeing and resulted in 10 per cent of employees walking a double marathon within one year. Similarly, Sainsbury's engaged employees with their sponsorship of the

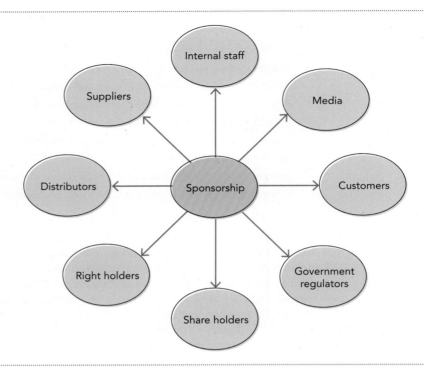

Figure 15.2 The main stakeholder groups within sponsorship
Source: Meenaghan et al. (2013).

2012 Paralympic Games in London. As part of the sponsorship, the supermarket chain selected 150 customers and employees to take part in the torch relay and held, 'Turn the Park Orange', by inviting over 5,000 employees to the Olympic Park to watch the events (Sher, 2016).

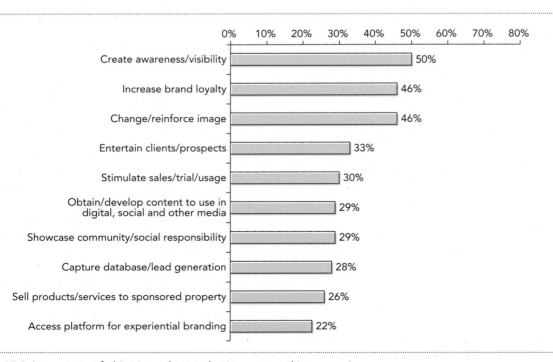

Figure 15.3 Importance of objectives when evaluating sponsorship properties
Source: IEG (2108).

Viewpoint 15.2

The McDonald's EURO Cup

Image 15.3 The McDonald' s EURO Cup saw 180 employees compete
Source: McDonald's.

Sponsorship can be a powerful tool to communicate with internal audiences. Organisations are using sponsorship to engage with employees in much the same way as they do to build relationships with external audiences. In particular, internal sponsorship can be effective in engaging internal audiences with external sponsorship.

McDonald's has a long-standing association with football sponsorship and in addition to being a global partner for both UEFA EURO 2012 and UEFA EURO 2016, the restaurant chain has sponsored the UEFA European Under-21 Championship (2011, 2013, 2015 and 2017), the UEFA European Women's Championship (2013 and 2017) and the UEFA European Futsal Championship (2012, 2014 and 2016).

The partnership with UEFA has allowed McDonald's to benefit from exclusive marketing rights and the restaurant chain has activated their sponsorship to give customers the chance to win tickets for the tournament matches.

To engage internal audiences with their Euro 2016 sponsorship, McDonald's Europe decided to create a unique football sponsorship to drive engagement with their employees. The chain created McDonald's EURO Cup, a sponsored employee event providing the opportunity for their workforce to enter a football tournament.

The sponsorship was launched by inviting all 10,000 of McDonald's Europe's employees to enter the tournament and compete in a special three-day tournament to be held in France. Employees responded from 13 countries and McDonald's saw 180 employees register to compete for their country as part of a six-member team.

Competing in France wasn't the only incentive to take part. The winning team were given tickets to watch a World Cup match in Rio de Janeiro and the opportunity to meet Brazilian legend Cafu.

As well as the response to compete in the tournament itself, McDonald's Europe found that 69 per cent of their workforce reported feeling more connected to McDonald's EURO 2016 sponsorship as a result of the EURO Cup.

Sources: Condon (2014); ESA (2016); UEFA (2010).

Insight

This highlights how sponsorship can be an effective tool for engaging internal audiences. The McDonald's EURO Cup created a unique sponsorship for the organisation and enabled McDonald's to connect their internal audiences with the company's sponsorship of EURO 2016.

Question: Using Figure 15.3 as a guide, what were McDonald's objectives for the sponsorship of McDonald's EURO Cup?

Task: Find three other examples of employee sponsorship. Consider for each what the objectives may have been.

Following on from this is the issue of whether sponsorship is being used to support a product or the organisation. Corporate sponsorships, according to Thwaites (1994), are intended to focus on developing community involvement, public awareness, image, goodwill and staff relations. Product or brand-based sponsorship activity is aimed at developing media coverage, sales leads, sales/market share, target market awareness and guest hospitality. What is important is that sponsorship is not a tool that can be effective in a standalone capacity. The full potential of this tool is only realised when it is integrated with some (or all) of the other tools of the communications mix. As Tripodi (2001) comments, the implementation of integrated marketing communications is further encouraged and supported when sponsorship is an integral part of the mix in order to maximise the full impact of this communications tool.

How sponsorship might work

Interpretations of how sponsorship might work are varied, and research limited. However, assuming a cognitive orientation, sponsorship works through associations that consumers make with a brand. These associations will be an accumulation of previous advertising and other communications activities, and the event being supported. In addition, people make a judgement based on the fit between the event and sponsorship such that the greater the degree of compatibility, the more readily acceptable the sponsorship will be. Poon and Prendergast (2006) argue that sponsorship outcomes can best be understood in terms of the attitude construct and cite product quality, attitude to the brand and purchase intention as representative of the cognition, affection and conation components.

If a behavourist orientation is used to explain how sponsorship works, then sponsorship should be perceived as reinforcement of previous brand experiences. An event generates rewards by reminding individuals of pleasurable brand experiences. However, this assumes that individuals have previous brand experience, and fails to explain adequately how sponsorship works when launching new products.

For many organisations sponsorship plays a supporting or secondary role in the communications mix. This is largely because the communications impact of sponsorship is limited, as sponsorship only reinforces previously held corporate (or product) images (positive or negative) rather than changing them (Javalgi et al., 1994). It is also suggested that the only significant relationship between sponsorship and corporate image occurs where there has been direct experience of the brand. This in turn raises questions about whether sponsorship should be used to influence the image of the product category and its main brands in order to be of any worthwhile effect (Pope and Voges, 1999).

As Dolphin (2003) suggests, the range of activities, events, goals and the variety of ways in which it is used by organisations suggests that it is not entirely clear how sponsorship might best be used to help an organisation achieve its business goals. It is used to shape and assist corporate image, develop name association and awareness, drive product sales, build brands, help with recruitment, defend against hostile competitors and as a means of developing and providing opportunities for corporate hospitality. However, the primary goal for its use will generally reflect the context within which it is used. In situations where transactional exchanges are predominant within the target audience, broad-based sponsorship activities are likely to be preferred. In contexts where the target audience is relatively small or geographically discrete and where relational exchanges are preferred or sought, then relationship development sponsorship activities are more likely to be successful.

Scholars' paper 15.2
The role of sponsorship

Meenaghan, T. (1991) The role of sponsorship in the marketing communications mix, *International Journal of Advertising*, 10(1), 35–47.

This is a classic paper written by one of the early leading researchers and authors about sponsorship and sets out some of the initial perspectives on sponsorship.

See also:

Nickell, D., Cornwell, T.B. and Johnston, W.J. (2011) Sponsorship-linked marketing: a set of research propositions, *Journal of Business & Industrial Marketing*, 26(8), 577–89.

Theoretical aspects of sponsorship

The limited amount of theoretical research into sponsorship suggests that the role of sponsorship within the marketing communications mix has not yet been fully understood. Problems associated with goals, tools and measurement methods and approaches have hindered both academics and practitioners. However, two developments have helped resolve some of these dilemmas. First, the development of relationship marketing and an acknowledgement that there are different audiences, each with different relationship needs, has helped understanding about which types of sponsorship should be used with which type of audience. Second, our understanding of the nature and role of integrated marketing communications within relationship marketing has helped focus thinking about the way in which sponsorship might contribute to the overall communications process.

Relationship marketing is concerned with the concept of mutual value rather than the mere provision of goods and services (Gummesson, 1996) and is therefore compatible in many ways with the characteristics and range of benefits, both expected and realised, associated with sponsorship (Farrelly et al., 2003). Sponsorship represents a form of collaborative communications, in the sense that two (or more) parties work together in order that one is enabled to reach the other's audience. Issues regarding the relationship between the parties involved will impact on the success of a sponsorship arrangement and any successive arrangements. As Farrelly et al.(2003) quite rightly point out, further work concerning the key drivers of sponsorship and relationship marketing is required as sponsorship matures as an increasingly potent form of marketing communications.

Olkkonen (2001) adopted a similar approach as he considered sponsorship within interactional relationships and ultimately a network approach. The network approach considers the range of relationships that impact on organisations within markets and, therefore, considers non-buyers and other organisations – indeed, all who are indirectly related to the exchange process. This approach moves beyond the simple dyadic process adopted by the interaction interpretation. Some scholars have advanced a broad conceptual model within which to consider inter-organisational networks (Hakansson and Snehota, 1995, cited by Olkkonen). These are actors, activities and resources and are set out in Table 15.3.

A relationship consists of activity links based on organisations working together. Some of the activities will use particular resources in different configurations and differing levels of intensity. These activities will impact on other organisations and affect the way they use resources.

In addition, organisations try to develop their attractiveness to other organisations in order to access other resources and networks. This is referred to as network identity and is a base for determining an organisation's value as a network partner. Sponsorship, therefore, can be seen as a function of an organisation's value to others in a network. The sponsored and the sponsor are key actors in sponsorship networks but agencies, event organisers, media networks and consultancies are also players, each of whom will be connected (networked) with the sponsor and sponsored.

Sponsorship has, traditionally, lacked a strong theoretical base, relying on managerial cause-and-effect explanations and loose marketing communications mix interpretations. The network approach may not be the main answer, but it does advance our thought, knowledge and research opportunities with respect to this subject.

Table 15.3 Basic variables underpinning inter-organisational networks

Network variable	Explanation
Actors	These are organisations and individuals who are interconnected; they control the other two variables.
Activities	Activities are created through the use of resources, and complex activity chains arise with different organisations (actors) contributing in different ways.
Resources	There are many different types of resource that can be combined in different ways to create new resources. The relationships that organisations develop create resource ties and these ties become shaped and adapted as the relationship develops.

Source: Based on Olkkonen (2001).

Scholars' paper 15.3

What don't we know about sponsorship?

Walliser, B. (2003) An international review of sponsorship research: extension and update, *International Journal of Advertising*, 22(1), 5–40.

This paper provides an overview of the research on sponsorship and highlights some of the theoretical frameworks that have been used in studies in the past. The paper suggests that given the increasing number of brands associated with individual events, network concepts could provide useful frameworks in future research.

See also:

Meenaghan, T. (2013) Measuring sponsorship performance: challenge and direction, *Psychology & Marketing*, 30(5), 385–93.

One concept that has been established in the literature concerns emotional intensity. This concerns the audience's attention, and associated cognitive orientation, towards the stimulus that is provoking the emotion (Bal et al., 2007). So, if the event becomes dramatic and highly engaging, it is probable that attention will be diverted from the sponsors and any information they might provide (e.g. ads). What this means is that a strongly emotional event (sport, exhibition, programme, film) is likely to reduce the awareness scores associated with the sponsor.

Several studies have examined image-transfer to explain how sponsorship can leverage brand associations (Gross and Wiedmann, 2015). Mazodier et al. (2017) use an image-transfer model to examine how sponsors leverage communications about their sponsorship with consumers. They identified that event associations were only transferred when event-related advertising was used. So, if the advertising messages were typical of the event the image was transferred.

Research by Farrelly et al. (2006), undertaken to better understand how value is perceived by parties to sponsorship agreements, has identified three key marketing competences necessary for the maintenance of successful sponsorship relationships. These are: reciprocal commitment, building capabilities and collaborative capabilities. These are set out in Table 15.4.

Table 15.4 Sponsorship relationship capabilities

Competence	Explanation
Reciprocal commitment	In sponsorship arrangements, each party expects the other to reciprocate the investment made. The greater the level of reciprocity, the greater the level of commitment between parties.
Building capabilities	Sponsorship is seen to provide strategic brand value. Consideration should be given to the extent to which parties align their sponsorship with the overall marketing objectives of the organisation.
Collaborative capabilities	The extent to which parties collaborate to develop the future relationship. How proactive for example is the sponsee in the relationship and what consideration has been given to the future development of the sponsor's brand.

Source: Farrelly et al. (2006).

Types of sponsorship

It is possible to identify particular areas within which sponsorship has been used. These areas are sports, broadcast, the arts and others that encompass activities such as wildlife/ conservation and education. Of all of these, sport has attracted the most attention and sponsorship spending.

Sports sponsorship

Sports activities have been very attractive to sponsors, partly because of the high media coverage they attract, and receive the largest amount of sponsorship spending (IEG, 2018). Sport is the leading type of sponsorship, mainly for the following reasons:

- Sport has the propensity to attract large audiences, not only at each event but, more importantly, through the media that attach themselves to these activities.
- Sport provides a simplistic measure of segmentation, so that as audiences fragment generally, sport provides an opportunity to identify and reach often large numbers of people who share particular characteristics.
- Visibility opportunities for the sponsor are high in a number of sporting events because of the duration of each event (e.g. the Olympics or the FIFA World Cup).

In football, Emirates' sponsorship of the FA Cup and MasterCard's sponsorship of the UEFA Champions League has been motivated partly by the attraction of large and specific target audiences with whom a degree of fit is considered to exist. The Champions League, for example, is estimated to reach 4.2 billion people (Oakes, 2017). The constant media attention enables the sponsors' names to be disseminated to distant audiences, many of them overseas.

Additionally, sports sponsorship offers opportunities for brands to leverage their association with sporting teams and events and provide opportunities for social interaction. Sher (2016) highlights how sponsors can leverage their sports partnerships through content on their social media channels using hashtags, live chats and behind-the-scenes content (Sher, 2016). IBM, for example, developed 'SlamTracker' to activate its sponsorship with Wimbledon and enhance the fan experience. As well as providing fans with real-time scores, statistics and match analysis, IBM is able to demonstrate their mobile capability (Sher, 2016).

Golf has attracted a great deal of sponsorship money, mainly because it has a global upmarket appeal and generates good television and press coverage. Golf clubs are also well suited for corporate entertainment and offer the chance of playing as well as watching. The World Golf Championships are seen as golf's most prestigious global competition, a series of events sanctioned by all six of the six major golf tours (the PGA TOUR, European Tour, Japan Golf Tour, PGA Tour of Australasia, Sunshine Tour and the Asian Tour). Collectively these form the International Federation of PGA Tours, which is supported financially by a few umbrella sponsors: Grupo Salinas, Dell Technologies, Bridgestone and the HSBC Group.

Rugby is a sport that has attracted significant sponsorship over the last few decades. Emirates, for example, sponsors a portfolio of rugby events and teams. They have been the Title Sponsor of the Emirates Airline Dubai Rugby Sevens for over 20 years, helping to establish the tournament as one of the best events on the HSBC Sevens World Series circuit. Emirates first sponsored the Rugby World Cup (RWC) in 2007 in France as a Tournament Sponsor, and then became a Worldwide Partner for RWC 2011 in New Zealand. They then became the first Worldwide Partner to sign an agreement for both the Rugby World Cup that was held in England in 2015 and the tournament to be held in Japan in 2019. Emirates also sponsor the International Rugby Board's (IRB) elite panel of referees, who always take to the field in their 'Fly Emirates' officials' kit (Long, 2014, Nel, 2014).

In 2014, Emirates signed a five-year sponsorship agreement with one of South Africa's most popular and successful Super Rugby teams, the 'Lions', now known as 'Emirates Lions', and the iconic 'Fly Emirates' logo now appears on players' match shirts and training jerseys. The sponsorship agreement has also allowed Emirates to re-name Ellis Park, the scene of South Africa's famous victory in the 1995 RWC Final, as 'Emirates Airline Park'. Emirates agreed in-stadia hospitality arrangements, allowing them to provide important corporate hospitality to travel agents, cargo agents, corporate accounts and other key partners in the country and wider Southern African region (Long, 2014; Nel, 2014).

Viewpoint 15.3

Sponsorship in ITF Taekwon-Do

James M. Crick, Lecturer, Loughborough University

Image 15.4 Taekwon-Do relies on sponsors to support tournaments
Source: Nayladen/Shutterstock.

Taekwon-Do is a martial art practised by approximately eight million people, in over 200 countries. The martial art was formally created in 1946 by the late General Choi Hong Hi, IX Degree Black Belt (1918–2002). There are two main styles of Taekwon-Do, namely the International Taekwon-Do Federation (ITF) style (formed in 1961) and the World Taekwondo Federation (WTF) style (established in 1973).

Sponsors play a vital role in ITF Taekwon-Do as they provide clubs and associations (i.e. regional, national and international-level Taekwon-Do bodies) with the financial resources to operate, in return for promoting and facilitating awareness of the sponsor. While ITF Taekwon-Do is not a well-funded sport (compared to the likes of football, rugby union and cricket), sponsors are used to obtain financial support, and in return, promote sponsors' companies. Specifically, in ITF Taekwon-Do, sponsorship is seen mainly through sporting equipment manufacturers (e.g. Top Pro and Mightyfist) supplying certain goods, such as sparring gloves and shoes, as well as rebreakable plastic boards for testing power.

Sponsors fund major sporting ITF Taekwon-Do tournaments at local, national and international levels, and provide equipment at such events. A recent example is in New Zealand, where an equipment supplier called Fuji Mae sponsors a range of local and national-level tournaments, through helping finance such events and via providing equipment. For those engaging in Taekwon-Do as a martial art (e.g. competing at tournaments), sponsors allow the events to take place, typically by funding a large proportion of the cost for the events and providing equipment.

Sources: Crick and Crick (2016); Crick (2014); Gillis (2011).

Insight

The examples given in this case of equipment suppliers sponsoring ITF Taekwon-Do provide a good illustration of function-based similarity, where the product is used in the event being sponsored. The brands are all used in the events and hence there is a clear functional fit between the sponsor and the sport.

Question: Considering the relationship capabilities outlined in Table 15.4, what types of commitment and capabilities could ITF Taekwon-Do expect from a sponsor?

Task: Find examples of local sports sponsorships within your community. Make a list of the sponsor's reasons for sponsorship using Figure 15.3 as a guide.

Broadcast sponsorship

Broadcast sponsorship has seen significant growth in the UK since the late 1990s when broadcast regulations were relaxed. Before this time, the visibility that each sponsor was allowed was strictly controlled, being restricted to certain times: before, during the break and after each programme with the credits. This was changed so that, while sponsors are not allowed to influence the content or scheduling of a programme so as to affect the editorial independence and responsibility of the broadcaster, it is now permissible to allow the sponsor's product to be seen along with the sponsor's name in bumper credits and to allow greater flexibility in terms of the use of straplines. There is a requirement on the broadcaster to ensure that the sponsored credit is depicted in such a way that it cannot be mistaken as a spot advertisement.

There are a number of reasons why broadcast sponsorship is appealing. First, it allows clients to avoid the clutter associated with spot advertising. In that sense it creates a space, or mini-world, in which the sponsor can create awareness and provide brand identity cues unhindered by other brands. Second, it represents a cost-effective medium when compared with spot advertising. Although the cost of broadcast sponsorship has increased as the value of this type of medium has appreciated, it does not command the high rates required for spot advertising. Third, the use of credits around a programme offers opportunities for the target audience to make associations between the sponsor and the programme.

For sponsorship to work well there needs to be a linkage between the product and the programme. Links that are spurious, illogical or inappropriate are very often rejected by viewers. For example, a branded soft drink might work well with a youth-oriented programme, but a financial services brand supporting a sports programme or film series would not have a strong or logical linkage. Di Falco (2012) suggests that organisations that get the most out of their sponsorship are those that integrate their brands with the editorial environment of the programme. He cites Schwarzkopf LIVE Colour XXL's sponsorship of *Big Brother* on Channel 5 as a good example of this. As well as being the broadcast sponsor for the show, XXL was placed in the bathroom in the *Big Brother* house allowing housemates the opportunity to use the product. Housemates tried the products and walked around the *Big Brother* house with their newly dyed hair, which made great entertainment.

The line between product placement, brand entertainment and programme sponsorship has become increasingly blurred. However, programme sponsorship is not a replacement for advertising. The argument that sponsorship is not a part of advertising is clearly demonstrated by the point that many sponsors continue with their spot advertising when running major sponsorships.

Arts sponsorship

Sponsorship of the arts has moved from being a means of supporting the community to a sophisticated means of targeting and positioning brands. Many organisations sponsor the arts as a means of enhancing their corporate status and of clarifying their identity. Another important reason organisations use sponsorship is to establish and maintain favourable contacts with key business people, often at board level, together with other significant public figures. Through related corporate hospitality, companies can reach substantial numbers of their targeted key people.

Louis Vuitton, the luxury brand, regarded as inventors of 'the art of travel' has worked with painters, photographers, designers and other craftsworkers to maintain strong links with the art world. In 2012, Louis Vuitton partnered with famous Japanese artist Yayoi Kusama in one of the biggest exchanges between the art and fashion worlds in recent times. The brand sponsored a travelling exhibition of the artist's work that visited Museo Nacional Centro de Arte Reina Sofia, Madrid; Centre Pompidou, Paris; London's Tate Modern and New York's Whitney Museum of American Art. To support the collaboration, Louis Vuitton set up a concept boutique in London's Selfridges store. The in-store display together with a takeover of 24 of the Oxford Street store's windows exhibited a capsule collection designed by Louis Vuitton in collaboration with Yayoi Kusama. The range included handbags, travel bags, shoes, accessories and ready-to-wear clothing, all featuring Kusama's signature designs (Tate Modern, 2012; Whitney Museum of American Art, 2012).

Similarly, MasterCard is seen to be a supporter of the arts with their range of arts sponsorships. One of MasterCard's many sponsorships is The Olivier Awards. Partnering with The Society of London Theatre since 2010, MasterCard is the headline sponsor of the awards and sponsor of the MasterCard Best New Musical award (MasterCard, 2018).

Viewpoint 15.4
Vodafone Comedy Festival

Vodafone is one of the world's largest telecommunications companies and has worked long term with festival promoters, Aiken Promotions, to grow the Vodafone Comedy Festival held every year in Dublin into a leading comedy event.

Bringing an international line up of comedy stars, the annual Vodafone Comedy Festival attracts around 20,000 people. Aligned to Vodafone's brand purpose, 'to connect everybody to live a better today and build a better tomorrow', the festival enables Vodafone to connect with younger audiences, especially 18–30-year-olds.

The three-day festival held in Iveagh Gardens, Dublin, features comedians from around the world and the festival also runs a series of free shows through the Vodafone Laughter Lab.

The sponsorship connects Vodafone to a fun event that provides a number of opportunities for brand activation. Comedy is used across a number of platforms to connect with audiences.

Image 15.5 Vodafone Comedy Festival
Source: WENN Rights Ltd/Alamy Stock Photo.

Sources: Bruton (2017); Vodafone (2017).

Insight

The Vodafone Comedy Festival highlights how brands are targeting events to connect with audiences and how event sponsorship can provide opportunities for social interaction.

Question: Using Figure 15.1, identify the level of functional and image-based congruence for Vodafone's sponsorship of the Vodafone Comedy Festival. Explain your answer.

Task: Find two other examples of festival sponsorship and explain for each the degree of fit.

Other forms of sponsorship

The sponsorship of causes is growing with sponsors keen to support their local communities or causes that are of interest to them and their audiences. Such sponsorship offers organisations an opportunity to enter into dialogue with audiences around causes that are seen to be mutually important. Events such as Climate Week provide sponsors with opportunities to demonstrate what actions they are taking with regard to climate change and sustainability. Sponsors can access high-profile events and network with other organisations (The Climate Group, 2018).

Festivals, fairs and annual events are another type of sponsorship category. In particular, festivals have attracted sponsors who are keen to connect with millennials. McCormack (2015) suggests that brands like Hunter, who set up a welly-exchange at Glastonbury in 2013, are among those who are getting the most out of their festival sponsorship. The brand offered festival-goers a new pair of its orange Hunter Headliner Boots in exchange for their old shoes and resulted in its giving away over 3,000 pairs of wellies. This fun giveaway was amplified through social media as festival-goers took pictures of their new boots and shared these across social media platforms. McCormack (2015) also cites Mulberry's sponsorship at the Wilderness festival as an example of good practice and describes how the luxury handbag brand set up a craft workshop at the festival to showcase the craftwork behind their bags. The 'Mulberry loves craft' tent allowed festival-goers to meet the craftsworkers who make the Bayswater bag and interact with bag designers such as Cara Delevingne. Festival-goers were also given the opportunity of customising and monogramming their own leather bracelets, which was shared across social media by festival-goers.

Some brands use sponsorship to own a particular space. Some brands have used sponsorship to own a physical space or forms of transport. Recent examples include Coca-Cola's sponsorship of London landmark The London Eye (Bold, 2015), which saw Europe's tallest Ferris wheel lit up in red. In 2015 Santander spent £43.75 million on its sponsorship deal for Boris bikes, which have been re-named 'Santander cycles' (Ghosh, 2015). More ambitiously, Emirates sponsored the entire London Transport cable car across the River Thames, The Emirates Air Line. As well as the naming rights to the cable car itself the deal included the sponsorship of two new stations, Emirates Greenwich Peninsula and Emirates Royal Docks, which were added to the London tube map (Reynolds, 2011).

Sponsored content is a fast-growing area of sponsorship. MasterCard have been the headline sponsor of The Brit Awards for the last 20 years and in 2012, extended their association with the event to sponsor The Brit Awards ceremony coverage on The Brits Vevo channel. Vevo, the online music video platform, was appointed as the first online video partner for the awards event and MasterCard sponsored the channel. The Brits Vevo channel hosted nomination videos, as well as live coverage of the awards ceremony and performances. Additionally, the channel ran extra content such as interviews filmed with artists backstage. MasterCard's sponsorship of the online platform allowed the brand to extend their association with the event and provided a further opportunity to engage with Brit fans during the ceremony (MasterCard, 2018; McCabe, 2012).

As well as in music, brands have sponsored content in sports channels. Kia Motors' sponsorship of the Ashes content on TalkSPORT shows how brands are able to engage with sports fans (Nias, 2013). Kia's multi-platform sponsorship agreement covered all the content for the 2013 Ashes series between the England and Australia cricket teams, including interviews, score updates, on-air editorial, as well as outside broadcasts from the Kia Oval. The deal included Kia branding running across the talksport.co.uk site and on all cricket coverage in the site's sister publication, *Sport* magazine, for the duration of the Ashes series, as well as Kia-branded features and a competition on TalkSPORT's *Drive Time* show (Nias, 2013). The partnership between Kia and TalkSPORT is just one of many sports content sponsorships that have taken place over the last few years and shows how brands are using this form of sponsorship to engage audiences in conversations around specific sports and sporting events.

The majority of sponsorships, regardless of type, are not the sole promotional activity undertaken by the sponsors. They may be secondary and used to support above-the-line work or they may be used as the primary form of communications but supported by a range of off-screen activities, such as sales promotions and (in particular) competitions. For example, Sony Pictures developed a programme to encourage school pupils to be innovative and to develop their interest in science. It used an unbranded animated film, *Cloudy with a Chance of Meatballs,* to provide a context for activities, quizzes and competitions (Thomas, 2009). More of a partnership than a straight sponsorship, the relationship furthered Sony's positioning as an innovator.

Ambush marketing

Although ambush marketing has been in existence and used by brands for over 30 years, ambushes are becoming increasingly common and more creative (Burton and Chadwick, 2017). Ambush marketing occurs when an organisation deliberately seeks an association with a particular event but does so without paying advertising or sponsorship fees.

Table 15.5 Three types of ambush marketing

Type of ambushing	Nature of ambush	Example
Incursive ambushing	'aggressive, predatory, or invasive activities'	Pepsi 'Refresh Your World' campaign (2010 FIFA World Cup)
Obtrusive ambushing	'prominent or undesirably visible marketing activity' (deliberate or accidental)	Tyskie's 'Fifth Stadium' (2012 UEFA European Championship)
Associative ambushing	'imply or create an illusion that it [brand] has a connection'	Lufthansa 'LH2006' (2006 FIFA World Cup Finals)

Source: Burton and Chadwick (2017).

Such hijacking is undertaken to get free publicity by communicating the brand, unofficially, in places where spectators, cameras or reporters are present, will see it, and pass on the message. The purpose therefore is to influence the audience to the extent that people believe the ambusher is legitimate. Brands need to consider the obvious ethical considerations of using ambush marketing.

A number of studies have examined the nature of ambush marketing activity, including Burton and Chadwick (2017) who identify three different types of ambush marketing; incursive, obtrusive and associative. Each of these types is more fully explained in Table 15.5. Although the authors suggest three types of ambushing exist, they argue the main objective of any ambush marketing is to provide benefits to the brand that are similar to the official sponsor of the event. The authors suggest a number of ways that event owners can limit ambush opportunities, including design of venues and increased ticketing regulation (Burton and Chadwick, 2017).

At the 2010 World Cup in South Africa, 36 orange-clad women were ejected from the Netherlands versus Denmark game. They were accused of participation in an unofficial campaign to promote the Dutch brewery, Bavaria. Anheuser Busch's Budweiser was the official beer for the tournament. There had been a similar incident at the 2006 World Cup finals in Germany. On that occasion, the football governing body FIFA ordered that a number of Dutch men take off orange lederhosen which bore the name 'Bavaria' (Anon, 2010).

In 2012, JUST-EAT staged a creative ambush marketing campaign that saw Italian takeaway chef Mr Mozzarella, from an invented 'Don't Cook Party', stand for election at the Corby Parliamentary by-election (Parkinson, 2013). This was a high-profile by-election with all major political parties fighting hard to win the Parliamentary seat and therefore it was certain to receive significant media coverage. Such guaranteed media attention provided a perfect opportunity for JUST-EAT to ambush the event and gain high visibility for their brand both locally and nationally. The JUST-EAT campaign provides a good example of how when planned and executed with creativity an ambush campaign can be highly effective in gaining high visibility for a brand.

The role of sponsorship in the communications mix

Whether sponsorship is a part of advertising, sales promotion or public relations has long been a source of debate. It is perhaps more natural and comfortable to align sponsorship with advertising. Since awareness is regarded as the principal objective of using sponsorship, advertising is a more complementary and accommodating part of the mix. Sales promotion from the sponsor's position is harder to justify, although from the perspective of the sponsored the value-added characteristic is interesting. The more traditional home for sponsorship is public relations (Witcher et al., 1991). The sponsored, such as a football team, a racing car manufacturer or a theatre group, may be adjudged to perform the role of opinion former. Indirectly, therefore, messages are conveyed to the target audience with the support of significant participants who endorse and support the sponsor. This is akin to public relations activities.

Exploratory research undertaken by Hoek et al. (1997) suggests that sponsorship is better able to generate awareness and a wider set of product-related attributes than advertising when dealing with non-users of a product, rather than users. There appears to be no discernible difference between the impact that these two promotional tools have on users.

Hoek et al. (1997) claim that sponsorship and advertising can be considered to work in approximately the same way if the ATR (attention, trial, reinforcement) model developed by Ehrenberg (1974) is adopted (Chapter 13). Through the ATR model, purchase behaviour and beliefs are considered to be reinforced by advertising rather than new behaviour patterns being established. Advertising offers a means by which buyers can meaningfully defend their purchase patterns. Hoek et al. (1997) regard this approach as reasonably analogous to sponsorship. Sponsorship can create awareness and is more likely to confirm past behaviour than prompt new purchase behaviour. The implication, they conclude, is that, while awareness levels can be improved with sponsorship, other communications tools are required to impact upon product experimentation or purchase intentions. Indeed, Smolianov and Aiyeku (2009) make the point that integrated TV and major event sponsorship appear to work by influencing markets through TV audiences.

It was suggested earlier in this chapter that one of the opportunities that sponsorship offers is the ability to suggest that there is an association between the sponsored and the sponsor that may be of value to the message recipient. This implies that there is an indirect form of influence through sponsorship. This is supported by Crimmins and Horn (1996), who argue that the persuasive impact of sponsorship is determined in terms of the strength of links that are generated between the brand and the event that is sponsored.

These authors claim that sponsorship can have a persuasive impact and that the degree of impact that a sponsorship might bring is as follows:

$$\begin{array}{c}\text{Persuasive}\\\text{impact}\end{array} = \begin{array}{c}\text{strength}\\\text{of link}\end{array} \times \begin{array}{c}\text{duration}\\\text{of the link}\end{array} \times \left\{\begin{array}{c}\text{gratitude felt}\\\text{due to the link}\end{array} + \begin{array}{c}\text{perceptual change}\\\text{due to the link}\end{array}\right\}$$

The *strength* of the link between the brand and the event is an outcome of the degree to which advertising is used to communicate the sponsorship itself. Sponsors that failed to invest in advertising during the Olympic Games have been shown to be far less successful in building a link with the event than those who chose to invest.

The *duration* of the link is also important. Research based on the Olympic Games shows that those sponsors who undertook integrated marketing communications long before the event itself were far more successful than those who had not. The use of mass-media advertising to communicate the involvement of the sponsor, the use of event graphics and logos on packaging, and the creative use of promotional tie-ins and in-store, event-related merchandising, facilitated the long-term linkage with the sponsorship and added value to the campaign.

Gratitude exists if consumers realise that there is a link between a brand and an event. For example, 60 per cent of US adults said that they 'try to buy a company's product if they support the Olympics'. They also stated that 'I feel I am contributing to the Olympics by buying the brands of Olympic sponsors.'

Perceptual change occurs as a result of consumers being able to understand the relationship (meaning) between a brand and an event. The sponsor needs to make this clear, as passive consumers may need the links laid out before them. The link between a swimwear brand and the Olympics may be obvious, but it is not always the case. Crimmins and Horn (1996) describe how Visa's 15 per cent perceived superiority advantage over MasterCard was stretched to 30 per cent during the 1992 Olympics and then settled at 20 per cent ahead one month after the Games had finished. The perceptual change was achieved through the messages that informed audiences that Visa was the one card that was accepted for the Olympic Games; American Express and MasterCard were not accepted.

This research, while based only upon a single event, indicates that sponsorship may bring advantages if care is taken to invest in communications long before and during the event to communicate the meaning between the brand and the event, which will leverage gratitude from a grateful audience. Similarly, Olson and Thjømøe (2009) found that combining television advertising increases the effectiveness of a sponsorship activity. Nickell et al. (2011) go further and argue that leveraging sponsorships – that is, using other marketing communications activities to realise the full potential of the investment – is absolutely necessary.

Activating sponsorship through other forms of communications is therefore seen to be a key to the success of any sponsorship. A recent study by IEG suggests that nine out of ten sponsors include social media in their leveraging mix, with other forms of communications such as public relations, on-site interaction and traditional advertising also being seen to be highly important (IEG, 2018) (see Figure 15.4).

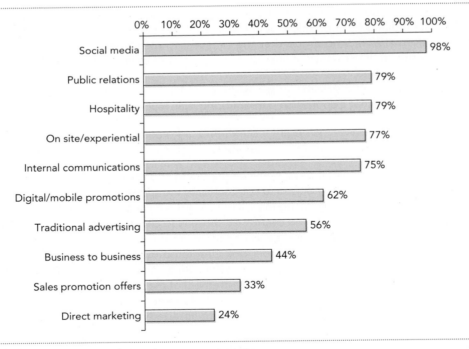

Figure 15.4 Channels used by sponsors to leverage sponsorships
Source: IEG (2018).

Key points

- Sponsorship permits one party an opportunity to exploit an association with a target audience of another organisation, in return for funds, services or resources.

- Sponsorship suggests to target audiences that there is an association between the sponsor and the sponsored organisation and that by implication this association may be of interest and/or value.

- Some organisations use sponsorship, particularly sports activities, as a means of reaching wider target audiences. Sponsorship can provide exposure to particular audiences that each event attracts in order to convey simple, awareness-based brand messages. In particular, sponsorship is an effective way to prepare markets for the arrival of new brands.

- Sponsorship works through associations that consumers make with a brand (which will be an accumulation of previous advertising and other promotional activities) and the event being supported. In addition, people make a judgement based upon the fit between the event and sponsorship in such a way that the greater the degree of compatibility, the more readily acceptable the sponsorship will be.

- Sponsorship represents a form of collaborative communications, in the sense that two (or more) parties work together in order that one is enabled to reach the other's audience. Issues regarding the relationship between the parties concerned will impact on the success of a sponsorship arrangement and any successive arrangements.

- Sponsorship can be seen as a function of an organisation's value to others in a network. The sponsored and the sponsor are key actors in sponsorship networks, but agencies, event organisers, media networks and consultancies are also actors, each of whom will be connected (networked) with the sponsor and sponsored.

- Sponsorship is used in three key areas. These are sports, broadcast and the arts. There is also growing interest in cause sponsorship, festivals, fairs and annual events. Of all of these, sport has attracted most attention and sponsorship spending.

- Some organisations use ambush marketing to deliberately seek an association with a particular event without paying advertising or sponsorship fees.

- Sponsorship has become an important part of the mix as it allows brands to be communicated without the clutter and noise associated with advertising. At the same time, sponsorship enables associations and linkages to be made that add value for all the participants in the communications process.

- It is perhaps more natural and comfortable to align sponsorship with advertising, but it has also been associated with sales promotion and public relations. Since awareness is regarded as the principal objective of using sponsorship, advertising is a more complementary and accommodating part of the mix.

Case study

Emirates: activating football sponsorship

Image 15.6 Emirates 380 crew showcase their football skills
Source: The Emirates Group.

Since Emirates started in Dubai in 1985, the airline has been committed to sports sponsorship and has developed long-standing partnerships with events and teams all around the world. Today their portfolio includes some of the world's iconic sporting events and leading teams in football, cricket, sailing, horseracing, golf, tennis, motorsports and rugby. Emirates' association with these global sports has enabled the airline to connect with audiences around the world and support teams within nations that they fly to. As well as raising the awareness of the Emirates brand and helping to position Dubai as an international destination for sport, their sponsorship helps them to connect with consumers across the globe.

Emirates sponsors a number of football teams around the world and in 2015, the airline became the title partner of the FA Cup, the world's most prestigious domestic cup competition. The partnership agreement between Emirates and The Football Association was extended in 2017, seeing the tournament continue to be named The Emirates FA Cup through until 2021.

The Emirates FA Cup competition reaches over 912 million fans worldwide, providing an opportunity to raise the visibility of the Emirates brand worldwide. As well as increasing brand awareness for the airline, the partnership has helped the competition connect with fans around the world.

To help activate the sponsorship, Emirates branded one of their A380 aircraft with the Emirates FA Cup logo, ensuring that wherever the aircraft landed throughout its network, fans would be reminded of the Emirates FA Cup competition. Additionally, Emirates took the cup on its first ever visit to Africa, with a tour of Ghana and Kenya, providing schools and training centres with an opportunity to get a glimpse of the trophy. With plans to tour the cup to more countries on the airline's network, the partnership between Emirates and The Football Association is helping to connect fans to the competition and inspire new generations of fans.

Emirates have also club-themed many of their other aircraft to activate their sponsorship of club football. Since 2015, the airline has been featuring club crests and first-team players on their aircraft to showcase their football partnerships, including AC Milan, Real Madrid, Paris Saint-Germain and HSV.

As well as using their own aircraft, Emirates has staged stunts with their cabin crew to activate their sports sponsorships. In 2015, Emirates signed as the main sponsor of Portugal's biggest football club, SL Benfica, which has 14 million fans worldwide. To raise awareness of the sponsorship the airline choreographed a special 'pre-match' safety demonstration for SL Benfica fans.

Before the start of one of the biggest matches on the team's calendar, the SL Benfica vs Sporting CP derby, the stadium speaker announced to fans that they would be showing a safety demonstration on the screens. Around 65,000 fans watched as eight Emirates cabin crew members came onto the pitch and performed an entertaining 'pre-match' safety demonstration, which had been created for the stunt. The Emirates stunt was broadcast live on Benfica TV and later shared with millions of fans online on Emirates and SL Benfica's YouTube channels and on Facebook.

This was the first time any football sponsor had ever engaged so directly on the pitch with fans and the safety demonstration soon went viral. Within a week, the stunt video had reached 50 million fans and been watched more than 24 million times. The stunt generated more than 50,000 comments in the first week and saw 300,000 shares on Facebook, Twitter and YouTube all around the world.

Since the first Emirates stunt performed at Benfica, the airline's cabin crew have appeared at a number of other sporting events. In Volkparkstadion in Hamburg, home of HSV, Emirates staged a pre-game safety drill in front of 57,000 fans. Much to the delight of the onlooking fans, the crew performed some impressive ball skills and completed with a showcase of their penalty shooting.

In 2018, the airline extended their sports sponsorship activation with the launch of Emirates #OneTeam

Image 15.7 Emirates branded one of their A380 aircraft with the Emirates FA Cup logo
Source: The Emirates Group.

Image 15.8 Emirates have club-themed many of their aircraft with club crests and first-team players
Source: The Emirates Group.

campaign. The campaign highlights the values Emirates share with their sponsored clubs. Values such as teamwork, ambition, innovation and passion for sports are showcased in a series of videos filmed for the campaign. For example, players from Paris Saint-Germain are featured alongside Emirates crew in a video that demonstrates the football skills of both crew and club.

The Emirates #OneTeam campaign activates the airline's sponsorship of Real Madrid with a one-minute film featuring some of the team's players on a flight from Dubai to Madrid. The film includes Sergio Ramos, Gareth Bale, Marcelo, Karim Benzema, Toni Kroos and Casemiro relaxing onboard an Emirates A380. As well as showing Ramos enjoying the luxury of the First Class Shower Spa, the film showcases some of the Emirates crews' football skills. The film ends showing the Emirates crew joining Real Madrid in the locker rooms on match day and walking out onto the stadium alongside the players in Real Madrid kit.

The films have been shared with audiences across Emirates' Facebook, Instagram, Twitter and YouTube channels.

Sources: Briley (2018); SL Benfica Emirates (2017); Emirates Group (2017a); Emirates Group (2017b).

Review questions

Emirates case questions

1. Explain why football sponsorship is seen to be a good fit for the Emirates brand.
2. What are the advantages for Emirates of sports sponsorship over other forms of sponsorship?
3. Explain how Emirates could evaluate the return on their investment in the Emirates FA Cup sponsorship.
4. Discuss how Emirates could leverage their sponsorship of the Emirates FA Cup to employees.
5. Identify the extent to which Emirates has demonstrated collaborative commitment to the Emirates FA Cup.

General questions

1. To what extent is sponsorship more a leap of faith than a calculated marketing investment?
2. If the objective of using sponsorship is to build awareness (among other things), then there is little point in using advertising. Discuss this view.
3. Why is sport more heavily sponsored than the arts or television programmes?
4. Choose eight sporting events and name the main sponsors. Why do you think they have maintained their associations with the events?
5. Explain the role of sponsorship within the marketing communications mix.

References for Chapter 15

Agar, B. (2017) Tour de Celeb: riding high with Škoda on Channel 5, Mediacom beyond advertising, 18 January, retrieved 10 January 2018, from http://mediacombeyondadvertising.com/riding-high-skoda-channel-5/

Anon (2010) World Cup 2010: women arrested over 'ambush marketing' freed on bail, *Guardian*, Wednesday 16 June, retrieved 7 November 2011 from www.guardian.co.uk/football/2010/jun/16/fifa-world-cup-ambush-marketing

Bal, C., Quester, P.G. and Boucher, S. (2007) *Admap*, 486 (September), 51–2.

Bold, B. (2015) What do people think of Coca-Cola's sponsorship of The London Eye? *Brand Republic*, retrieved 15 March 2015 from www.brandrepublic.com/article/1330961/watch-people-think-coca-colas-sponsorship-london-eye

Briley, S. (2018) Real Madrid players find new teammates on board the Emirates A380, Emirates Group, 5 March, retrieved 10 April 2018 from https://www.emirates.com/media-centre/real-madrid-players-find-new-teammates-on-board-the-emirates-a380

Bruton, L. (2017) Vodafone Comedy Festival: here's everything you need to know, *The Irish Times*, 26 July, retrieved 10 April 2018 from https://www.irishtimes.com/culture/stage/vodafone-comedy-festival-here-s-everything-you-need-to-know-1.3168647

Burton, N. and Chadwick, S. (2017) Ambush marketing is dead; long live ambush marketing: a redefinition and typology of an increasingly prevalent phenomenon, *Journal of Advertising Research*, JAR-2017-014.

Condon, J. (2014) McDonald's kicks off employee soccer tournament, Leo Burnett, 11 August, retrieved 10 January 2018 from http://leoburnett.com/articles/news/mcdonalds-kicks-off-employee-soccer-tournament/

Coppetti, C., Wentzel, D., Tomczak, T. and Henke, S. (2009) Improving incongruent sponsorships through articulation of the sponsorship and audience participation, *Journal of Marketing Communications*, 15(1), 17–34.

Crick, J.M. (2014) Defending ourselves and our organization, *Taekwon-Do Talk*, 2(1), 26–7.

Crick, D. and Crick, J.M. (2016) Coopetition at the sports marketing/entrepreneurship interface: a case study of a Taekwon-Do organization, *Marketing Intelligence & Planning*, 34(2), 169–87.

Crimmins, J. and Horn, M. (1996) Sponsorship: from management ego trip to marketing success, *Journal of Advertising Research*, July/August, 11–21.

Di Falco, A. (2012) Double standards – how should brands tackle media sponsorships? *Brand Republic*, 18 October, retrieved 17 February 2015 from www.brandrepublic.com/article/1155306/double-standards-brands-tackle-media-sponsorships

Dolphin, R.R. (2003) Sponsorship: perspectives on its strategic role, *Corporate Communications: An International Journal*, 8(3), 173–86.

Edwards, M.R. (2016) The Olympic effect: employee reactions to their employer's sponsorship of a high profile global sporting event, *Human Resource Management*, 55(4), 721–40.

Ehrenberg, A.S.C. (1974) Repetitive advertising and the consumer, *Journal of Advertising Research*, 14 (April), 25–34.

Emirates Group (2017a) The Emirates Group Annual Report 2016–17, Emirates Group, retrieved 10 April 2018 from https://cdn.ek.aero/downloads/ek/pdfs/report/annual_report_2017.pdf

Emirates Group (2017b) The Emirates FA Cup sponsorship extended until 2021, Emirates Group, retrieved 10 January 2018 from https://www.emirates.com/media-centre/the-emirates-fa-cup-sponsorship-extended-until-2021

ESA (2016) McDonald's EURO Cup 2016, ESA Excellence Awards, retrieved 10 January 2018 from https://sponsorship.org/awards/2016-shortlist/mcdonalds-euro-cup-2016/

ESA (2017a) ŠKODA Tour De Celeb, ESA excellence awards, retrieved 10 January 2018 from https://sponsorship.org/awards/2017-shortlist/skoda-tour-de-celeb/

ESA (2017b) Heineken Race to the Tower, ESA Excellence Awards, retrieved 10 January 2018 from https://sponsorship.org/awards/2017-shortlist/heineken-race-to-the-tower/

Farrelly, F., Quester, P. and Mavondo, F. (2003) Collaborative communication in sponsor relations, *Corporate Communications: An International Journal*, 8(2), 128–38.

Farrelly, F., Quester, P. and Burton, R. (2006) Changes in sponsorship value: competencies and capabilities of successful sponsorship relationships, *Industrial Marketing Management*, 35(8), November, 1016–26.

Ghosh, S. (2015) Boris bikes rebranded 'Santander Cycles' in £44m deal, *Brand Republic*, retrieved 15 March 2015 from www.brandrepublic.com/article/1336019/boris-bikes-rebranded-santander-cycles-44m-deal

Gillis, A. (2011) *A Killing Art: The Untold History of Taekwon-Do,* Toronto: ECW Press.

Gross, P. and Wiedmann, K.P. (2015) The vigor of a disregarded ally in sponsorship: brand image transfer effects arising from a cosponsor, *Psychology & Marketing,* 32(11), 1079–97.

Gummesson, E. (1996) Relationship marketing and imaginary organisations: a synthesis, *European Journal of Marketing,* 30(2), 31–45.

Hakansson, H. and Snehota, I. (1995) *Developing Relationships in Business Networks,* London: Routledge.

Hoek, J., Gendall, P., Jeffcoat, M. and Orsman, D. (1997) Sponsorship and advertising: a comparison of their effects, *Journal of Marketing Communications,* 3, 21–32.

IEG (2018) *What sponsors want & where dollars will go in 2018,* retrieved 15 January 2018 from http://www.sponsorship.com/IEG/files/f3/f3cfac41-2983-49be-8df6-3546345e27de.pdf

Javalgi, R.G., Traylor, M.B., Gross, A.C. and Lampman, E. (1994) Awareness of sponsorship and corporate image: an empirical investigation, *Journal of Advertising,* 24 (June), 1–12.

Khan, A.M. and Stanton, J. (2010) A model of sponsorship effects on the sponsor's employees, *Journal of Promotion Management,* 16, 1–2.

Kourovskaia, A.A., and Meenaghan, T. (2013) Assessing the financial impact of sponsorship investment, *Psychology & Marketing,* 30(5), 417–30.

Long, M. (2014) Ellis Park renamed as Emirates lands major Lions deal, *SportsPro,* 11 December, retrieved 1 November 2015 from http://www.sportspromedia.com/news/ellis_park_renamed_as_emirates_lands_major_lions_deal

MasterCard (2018) The BRIT Awards, MasterCard website, retrieved 18 January 2018 from https://www.mastercard.co.uk/en-gb/consumers/offers-promotions/brit-awards.html

Mazodier, M., Corsi, A.M. and Quester, P.G. (2017). Advertisement typicality: a longitudinal experiment: can sponsors transfer the image of a sporting event to their brand? *Journal of Advertising Research,* JAR-2017-031.

McCabe, M. (2012) MasterCard sponsors The Brits content on Vevo, *Brand Republic,* 13 January, retrieved 10 December 2014 from www.brandrepublic.com/article/1111999/mastercard-sponsors-brits-content-vevo

McCormack, G. (2015) Unpredictable brands are the headline act for festival sponsorship, *Brand Republic,* 19 January, retrieved 15 March 2015 from www.brandrepublic.com/article/1329801/unpredictable-brands-headline-act-festival-sponsorship

McDonald, C. (1991) Sponsorship and the image of the sponsor, *European Journal of Marketing,* 25(11), 31–8.

McDonald, J. (2018) Global ad trends, January 2018, retrieved 1 February 2018 from www.warc.com/content/article/warc-data/global_ad_trends,_january_2018/119719

Meenaghan, T. (1991) The role of sponsorship in the marketing communications mix, *International Journal of Advertising,* 10, 35–47.

Meenaghan, T. (2013) Measuring sponsorship performance challenge and direction, *Psychology & Marketing,* 30(5), 385–93.

Meenaghan, T., McLoughlin, D. and McCormack, A. (2013) New challenges in sponsorship evaluation actors, new media, and the context of praxis, *Psychology & Marketing,* 30(5), 444–60.

Nel, B. (2014) Emirates set to sponsor Lions, *SuperSport,* 10 December, retrieved 1 November 2015 from http://www.supersport.com/rugby/sa-rugby/news/141210/Emirates_set_to_sponsor_Lions

Nias, S. (2013) Kia to sponsor Ashes content on TalkSport, *Brand Republic,* 19 June, retrieved 7 March 2015 from www.brandrepublic.com/article/1187021/kia-sponsor-ashes-content-talksport

Nickell, D., Cornwell, T.B. and Johnston, W.J. (2011) Sponsorship-linked marketing: a set of research propositions, *Journal of Business & Industrial Marketing,* 26(8), 577–89.

Oakes, O. (2017) Heineken extends Champions League football sponsorship, *Campaign,* retrieved 1 December 2017 from https://www.campaignlive.co.uk/article/heineken-extends-champions-league-football-sponsorship/1422861

Ofcom (2006) Ofcom consults on the use of sponsorship in commercial television, retrieved 3 April 2015 from http://media.ofcom.org.uk/news/2006/ofcom-consults-on-the-use-of-sponsorship-in-commercial-television/

Olkkonen, R. (2001) Case study: the network approach to international sport sponsorship arrangement, *Journal of Business & Industrial Marketing*, 16(4), 309–29.

Olson, E.L. and Thjømøe, H.M. (2009) Sponsorship effect metric: assessing the financial value of sponsoring by comparisons to television advertising, *Journal of the Academy of Marketing Science*, 37, 504–15.

Parkinson, J. (2013) Mr Mozzarella's anti-cooking by-election campaign gets £72,000, *BBC News*, 20 February, retrieved 10 September 2018 from www.bbc.co.uk/news/uk-politics-21521130

Poon, D.T.Y. and Prendergast, G. (2006) A new framework for evaluating sponsorship opportunities, *International Journal of Advertising*, 25(4), 471–87.

Pope, N.K.L. and Voges, K.E. (1999) Sponsorship and image: a replication and extension, *Journal of Marketing Communications*, 5, 17–28.

Prendergast, G.P., Poon, D. and West, D.C. (2010) Match game: linking sponsorship congruence with communication outcomes, *Journal of Advertising Research*, 50(2), 214–26.

Reynolds, J. (2011) Mayor Johnson to announce Emirates as cable car sponsor, *Brand Republic*, retrieved 15 March 2015 from www.brandrepublic.com/article/1097675/mayor-johnson-announce-emirates-cable-car-sponsor

Sher, M. (2016) 7 routes to more effective sports sponsorship, *Admap*, February 2016, retrieved 10 September 2018 from https://www.warc.com/content/paywall/article/admap/7_routes_to_more_effective_sports_sponsorship/106665

SL Benfica Emirates (2017) Cannes Archive, retrieved 5 March 2018 from http://www.canneslionsarchive.com/Home/PublicHome

Smolianov, P. and Aiyeku, J.F. (2009) Corporate marketing objectives and evaluation measures of integrated television advertising and sports event sponsorships, *Journal of Promotion Management*, 15(1–2), 74–89.

Tate Modern (2012) Yayoi Kusama press release, retrieved 15 February 2015 from www.tate.org.uk/about/press-office/press-releases/yayoi-kusama

The Climate Group (2018) Sponsor our work, retrieved 10 January 2018 from https://www.theclimategroup.org/sponsorship

Thomas, J. (2009) Sony Pictures in school science tie, *Marketing*, 23 September, 10.

Thwaites, D. (1994) Corporate sponsorship by the financial services industry, *Journal of Marketing Management*, 10, 743–63.

Tripodi, J.A. (2001) Sponsorship: a confirmed weapon in the promotional armoury, *International Journal of Sports Marketing and Sponsorship*, 3(1), 1–20.

UEFA (2010) McDonald's signed up as official EURO sponsor, UEFA, retrieved 10 January 2018 from http://www.uefa.com/insideuefa/about-uefa/administration/marketing/news/newsid=1492650.html?redirectFromOrg=true

Vodafone (2017) Vodafone Comedy Festival unveils its most exciting and diverse line-up yet! 14 June, retrieved 10 December 2017 from https://n.vodafone.ie/aboutus/press/vodafone-comedy-festival-unveils-its-most-exciting-and-diverse-line-up-yet.html

Walliser, B. (2003) An international review of sponsorship research: extension and update, *International Journal of Advertising*, 22(1), 5–40.

Walraven, M., Koning, R.H. and van Bottenburg, B. (2012) The effects of sports sponsorship: a review and research agenda, *The Marketing Review*, 12(1), 17–38.

Whitney Museum of American Art (2012) Career retrospective of Yayoi Kusama to open at the Whitney, retrieved 15 February from http://press.whitney.org/file_columns/0003/2161/kusama_press_release_final.pdf

Witcher, B., Craigen, G., Culligan, D. and Harvey, A. (1991) The links between objectives and functions in organisational sponsorship, *International Journal of Advertising*, 10, 13–33.

Direct marketing and personal selling

Direct marketing is a strategy used to create a personal and intermediary-free dialogue with customers. This should be a measurable activity and it is very often media-based, used with a view to creating and sustaining a mutually rewarding relationship.

Personal selling involves a face-to-face dialogue between two persons or between one person and a group. Message flexibility is an important attribute, as is the immediate feedback that often flows from use of this promotional tool.

Aims and learning objectives

The aims of this chapter are first to consider the characteristics of direct marketing and second to explore some of the principal issues and concepts associated with personal selling.

The learning objectives are to enable readers to:

1. define direct marketing and set out its key characteristics;
2. describe the different methods used to implement direct marketing;
3. explain the significance of the database and Big Data in direct marketing and consider different direct-response media;
4. identify the different types, roles and tasks of personal selling;
5. discuss the role and evolution of social media within personal selling;
6. consider the characteristics of strategic account management.

Introduction

This chapter explores both direct marketing and personal selling, topics that complement each other in that they are both characterised by their personal and relatively transparent direct nature.

Direct marketing is a term used to refer to all media activities that generate a series of communications and responses with an existing or potential customer. Direct marketing is mainly concerned with the management of customer behaviour and is used to complement the strengths and weaknesses of the other communications disciplines. To put this another way, advertising and public relations provide information and develop brand values, but sales promotion, direct marketing and personal selling drive response, most notably behaviour. Both direct marketing and personal selling have the potential to engage customers directly, explicitly and provide both an intellectual and emotional basis upon which interaction and dialogue can be developed.

The role of direct marketing

Direct marketing is a tool of marketing communications used to create and sustain personal and intermediary-free communications with customers, potential customers and other significant stakeholders. There are a number of important issues associated with this definition. The first is that the activity should be measurable. That is, any response(s) must be associated with a particular individual, a particular media activity and a particular outcome, such as a sale or enquiry for further information. The second issue concerns the rewards that each party perceives through participation in the communications episode. Each customer receives a variety of tangible and intangible satisfactions. These include shopping convenience, time utility and the satisfaction and trust that can develop between customers and a provider of quality products and services when the customers realise and appreciate the personal attention they appear to be receiving.

Direct marketers derive benefits associated with precision target marketing and minimised waste, increased profits and the opportunities to provide established customers with other related products, without the huge costs of continually having to find new customers. There are no channel intermediaries, at least from the initial communications, it reduces costs, and improves the quality and speed of service for customers. Organisations such as Churchill, Everest, Direct Line and First Direct have all used direct marking to secure strong positions in the UK market.

Types of direct brand

Direct marketing is assumed to refer to direct communications mix activity, but this is only part of the marketing picture. Using direct-response media in this way is an increasingly common activity used to augment the communications activities surrounding a brand and to provide a new dimension to the context in which brands are perceived. However, direct marketing can be used by organisations in a number of different ways, very often reflecting the business strategy of the organisation. Four types can be identified and they should not be regarded as hierarchical, in the sense that there has to be progression from one type to another. They are reflections of the ways different organisations use direct marketing and the degree to which the tool is used strategically.

Type 1: complementary tool

At this level, direct-response media are used to complement the other communications mix activities used to support a brand. Their main use is to generate leads and to some extent awareness, information and reinforcement. For example, financial services companies, tour operators and travel agents use direct response television (DRTV) to stimulate enquiries, loans and bookings, respectively.

Type 2: primary differentiator

Rather than be one of a number of communications mix tools, at this level direct-response media are the primary forms of communications. They are used to provide a distinct point of differentiation from competitor offerings. They are the principal forms of communications. In addition to the Type 1 advantages they are used to cut costs, avoid the use of intermediaries and reach finely targeted audiences (e.g. book, music and wine clubs).

Type 3: sales channel

A third use for direct marketing, and telemarketing in particular, concerns its use as a means of developing greater efficiency and as a means of augmenting current services. By utilising direct marketing as a sales tool, multiple sales channels can be used to meet the needs of different customer segments and so release resources to be deployed elsewhere and more effectively.

Type 4: brand vehicle

At this final level, brands are developed to exploit market space opportunities. The strategic element is most clearly evident at this level. Indeed, the entire organisation and its culture are normally oriented to the development of customer relationships through direct marketing activities. Prime examples are lastminute.com and Amazon.

The growth of direct marketing

There can be little doubt that, of all the tools in the marketing communications mix, direct marketing has experienced the most growth in the last 20 years. The reasons for this growth are many and varied, but there have been three essential drivers behind the surge in direct marketing: technological advances; changing buyer lifestyles and expectations; and organisational expectations (see Figure 16.1). These forces for change demonstrate quite dramatically how a change in context can impact on marketing communications.

Growth driver 1: technology

Rapid advances in technology have heralded the arrival of new sources and forms of information. Technology has enabled the collection, storage and analysis of customer data to become relatively simple, cost-effective and straightforward. Furthermore, the management of this information is increasingly available to small businesses as well as the major blue chip multinational organisations. Computing and data storage costs have plummeted, while there has been a correspondingly enormous increase in the power that technology can deliver.

The technological surge has in turn stimulated three major developments. The first concerns the ability to capture information, the second to process and analyse it, and the

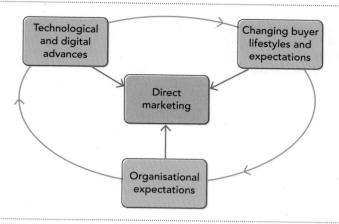

Figure 16.1 Three forces for direct marketing
Source: From *Essentials of Marketing Communications,* Pearson Education (Fill, C. 2011) Figure 11.1, p. 280.

third to represent part or all of the information as forms of communications to stimulate interaction and perhaps dialogue to collect further information. For example, some organisations are incorporating quick response (QR) codes and image recognition technologies to make a bridge between offline and online using smartphones.

Viewpoint 16.1
The British Army – This is Belonging

Image 16.1 The campaign creative was built around a universal need for individuals to belong
Source: THE BRITISH ARMY.

The British Army wanted to extend its recruitment to a broader pool of applicants. At the same time, they needed to increase engagement across social platforms and increase efficiency on cost per application.

They began by matching a data sample of previously successful applicants against their Continuum datapool, a proprietary database drawn from 48 million adults in the United Kingdom. This analysis provided insight into the demographics of the applicants and identified their drivers for applying. Additionally, neurolinguistics and online behaviours were used to model interests and behaviours. This enabled the British Army to develop an algorithm that could be used to inform which media to use and when to use it.

Using tagging technology, AI and machine learning, the campaign created personalised content, based on the theme of belonging, but tailored to each individual's identified drivers.

This meant that messages were personalised to appeal to the individual that it was served to. Additionally, the timing of the campaign was planned to reach potential candidates at times that would be the most effective.

The campaign creative was built around a universal need for individuals to belong. 'This is Belonging' delivered a range of digital content that was designed to drive potential recruits to the British Army website and make an application.

This direct campaign delivered a significant increase in applications for the British Army. Compared to previous years, applications for regular officers increased by 139 per cent, reserve soldiers increased by 80 per cent and applications for regular soldiers increased by 58 per cent.

Sources: Anon (2017a), DMA (2017a), Gwynn (2017a).

Insight

This is Belonging shows how technology is being used to create highly effective communication campaigns. Using advanced data-analytical approaches enables organisations to target specific audiences at a time and in a space where they are likely to be most receptive to the message.

Question: Explain why the British Army chose such a personalised approach for their campaign.

Task: Find two examples of companies using direct marketing and list the tools and media used.

Growth driver 2: changing market context

The lifestyles of people in industrialised economies, in particular, have evolved and will continue to do so. Generally, the brash phase of *selfishness* in the 1980s gave way to a more caring, society-oriented *selflessness* in the 1990s. The first decade of the twenty-first century reverted to a more *self-oriented* lifestyle, reflected in short-term brand purchase behaviour, and self-centred brand values and society behaviour. The second decade has seen further change as the global economy stumbled into a major recession. Some brands have struggled to work with the various forces acting on societies, such as those for environmental care, responsible food production, healthy eating, and the continual expectation that people should seek relationships and even minor celebrity status through social media. The values that are deemed appropriate appear confused as witnessed by various celebrity misbehaviours and the plummeting reputations of various established brands such as banks, supermarkets and technology companies. This destabilisation does not help people to see clearly their role within a society and has not helped brands to interact with their audiences in any meaningful way. The continual shift towards audience fragmentation and associated buyer behaviours is reflected in the diverse ways that the media enable organisations to contact their audiences.

Direct marketing offers a solution to this splintering and micro market scenario and addresses some of the changing needs of customers, such as personalised, permission-based and informed communications. Management also benefits as direct marketing enables improved speed of response, lower waste, and justification for the use and allocation of resources.

Growth driver 3: changing organisational expectations

Organisations can expect to continue experiencing performance pressures. These vary from the expectations of shareholders who may demand short-term returns on their investments, to the impact this can have on managers. They are having to cope with an increasing cost base caused by demands within the supply chain and claims on resources by developing economies, and a downward pressure on prices due to intense competition. This pressure on margins requires new routes to markets to reduce costs. Direct marketing addresses some of these changing management needs as there are no intermediary costs, there is fast access to markets (and withdrawal) plus opportunities to respond quickly to market developments and also justify their use and allocation of resources.

The impact of these drivers can be seen within the emergence of ideas about integrated marketing communications and an overall emphasis on relationship marketing principles. The enhanced ability of organisations to collect, store and manage customer lifestyle and transactional data, to generate personalised communications and their general enthusiasm for retention and loyalty schemes have combined to provide a huge movement towards an increased use of direct and interactive marketing initiatives.

The role of data

Data is critical for direct marketing. Without data there is no means of knowing which audiences to connect with, how to reach them or what message will engage them most (Hemphill, 2018).

The critical role that data now plays in marketing across all channels has led to a growing focus by organisations on how best to manage and optimise data. The WARC's Toolkit 2018 survey identified that 'digital transformation' is a key issue for both agencies and brands, and identified data analysis and data management as two of the three top priorities for organisations (WARC, 2018).

As well as the need to ensure data management works best for marketing, the introduction of the EU's General Data Protection Regulation (GDPR) in May 2018 led to organisations reviewing their data policies to ensure they met the tighter data regulations. One outcome of this has been the recognition of the need for better control of data and some brands are now looking at introducing data management platforms (DMPs) in-house (WARC, 2018).

The GDPR has strengthened existing regulations, particularly in respect of territorial scope, penalties and consent needed (see Table 16.1).

Table 16.1 Summary of main changes introduced by GDPR

Main changes and data subject rights	Implications
Increased territorial scope	The new regulations now apply to 'all companies processing the personal data of data subjects residing in the Union, regardless of the company's location'.
Penalties	Penalties: non-compliance will incur heavy fines as 'breach of GDPR can be fined up to 4% of annual global turnover or € 20 Million (whichever is greater)'.
Consent	'Consent must be clear and distinguishable from other matters and provided in an intelligible and easily accessible form, using clear and plain language. It must be as easy to withdraw consent as it is to give it'.
Breach notification	Where a data breach is likely to 'result in a risk for the rights and freedoms of individuals', notification needs to be done within 72 hours of the breach.

(continued)

Table 16.1 Summary of main changes introduced by GDPR (*Continued*)

Main changes and data subject rights	Implications
Right to access	Includes 'the right for data subjects to obtain from the data controller confirmation as to whether or not personal data concerning them is being processed, where and for what purpose. Further, the controller shall provide a copy of the personal data, free of charge, in an electronic format'.
Right to be forgotten (also called data erasure)	Includes the right for 'the data subject to have the data controller erase his/ her personal data, cease further dissemination of the data, and potentially have third parties halt processing of the data'.
Data portability	Includes the 'right for a data subject to receive the personal data concerning them'.
Privacy by design	This 'calls for the inclusion of data protection from the onset of the designing of systems, rather than an addition'.
Data protection officers	Changes to reporting mechanisms and processes with regard to local data protection officers and greater internal record keeping.

Source: EU GDPR (2018).

Viewpoint 16.2
What does the GDPR mean for marketers?

Image 16.2 The 'Right to be Forgotten' is one of the data subject rights included in GDPR
Source: Stas Ponomarencko/Shutterstock.

The Data Protection Directive 95/46/EC was introduced in 1995 to protect EU citizens from privacy and data breaches. Since it was introduced, the data landscape has changed significantly and this led the European Parliament to overhaul the regulations.

On 25 May 2018, a new set of regulations came into force. The EU General Data Protection Regulation (GDPR) introduced the biggest changes to data regulation in over two decades, forcing organisations to review their use of data and revise data management policies and practices.

Three of the biggest changes related to increased scope, penalties and consent. The increased scope of the regulations under GDPR means that even if companies are not located in Europe they will still need to comply with GDPR. The GDPR also increased penalties for non-compliance and clearer guidelines on consent were introduced.

GDPR introduced stricter regulations on the conditions of consent. Organisations need to use clear wording on the request for consent and must not use 'long illegible terms and conditions full of legalese'.

The purpose for data processing must also be attached with the consent.

The GDPR increased data subject rights significantly to include tighter regulations on notification of a data breach, access to data and the 'Right to be Forgotten'. Additionally, GDPR strengthened regulations on portability and privacy, and changed the reporting mechanisms.

Sources: DMA (2018a); EU GDPR (2018).

Insight

GDPR has greatly increased the regulation around data management and given greater rights to data subjects. The conditions for consent mean that organisations need to make it as easy for individuals to withdraw consent as it is to give it in the first place. The strengthening of data subject rights is considerable and means that there is greater data transparency.

Question: Why was GDPR introduced in 2018? Discuss with examples.

Task: Find three examples of recent email marketing campaigns sent to you and consider for each how they comply with GDPR regulations on consent. Explain why.

Central to successful direct marketing activities has been the database. A database is a collection of files held on a computer that contain data. The data on databases can be related to other data and can reproduce information in a variety of formats. Normally the data consists of information collected about prospects and customers that are used to determine appropriate segments and target markets, and to record responses to communications conveyed by the organisation.

Databases therefore have a storage, sorting and administrative role designed to assist direct and personalised communications. The stored information is gathered from transactions undertaken and information provided by customers. This is insufficient on its own and a further layering of data is required. The recency/frequency/monetary (RFM) model provided a base upon which lifestyle data, often bought in from an agency list, was used to further refine the information held and which enabled more effective targeting and communications.

It should be noted that databases often store data in a highly structured format. Kuechler observed, in 2007, that data was beginning to be stored as streams of data gathered from a variety of sources. These include audio, video, organisational documents and web pages, email, customer comments, plus the major internet platforms such as Facebook, Amazon, Twitter, Google, Apple and others. From these sources a more unstructured format has evolved.

Much of this sophisticated information has arisen through what is referred to as 'Big Data'. The dominant internet platforms referred to earlier accumulate vast amounts of information on consumers, including purchases, interests, activities and overall behaviour. When this information is merged with privately held data, Big Data is the result. Nunan and Di Domenico (2013) consider the impact of Big Data through three perspectives. These are:

1. the technological issues associated with storing, securing and analysing the vast and increasing volumes of data being gathered by organisations, and also including new types of database and 'cloud' storage, which enable innovative forms of analysis;

2. the added commercial value offered through the generation of more effective consumer insights;

3. societal influences such as privacy, freedom of speech, regulation, and suitable guidelines for the ethical commercial use of this data.

Scholars' paper 16.1

Big Data

Hofacker, C.F., Malthouse, E.C. and Sultan, F. (2016) Big data and consumer behavior: imminent opportunities, *Journal of Consumer Marketing*, 33(2), 89–97.

This paper looks at how Big Data can contribute to our understanding of consumer behaviour. The paper explores the potential opportunities for Big Data to increase our knowledge of the consumer decision-making process. The authors also discuss the change in skill set for the workforce of the future and argue that Big Data analytics will be needed.

See also:

Krafft, M., Arden, C.M. and Verhoef, P.C. (2017) Permission marketing and privacy concerns – why do customers (not) grant permissions? *Journal of Interactive Marketing*, 39, 39–54.

Direct-response media

The choice of media for direct marketing can be very different from those selected for general advertising purposes. The main reason for using direct-response media is that direct contact is made with prospects and customers in order that a direct response is solicited and a dialogue stimulated or maintained.

While direct mail, telemarketing and door-to-door activities have been the main forms of offline media in the past and are still popular today, email, mobile and social media have presented marketers with new ways to engage audiences. As well as allowing for personal and direct communications, online media presents new opportunities to connect faster with consumers, in new settings and using new forms of engagement.

Direct marketing channels, however, should not be seen as stand-alone tools and are most effective when used as part of an integrated campaign. When planning a multi-channel campaign it is important to consider how customers want to interact with organisations and allow them to choose for themselves (DMA, 2018b).

Email

Email has become the most popular means of initiating online engagement with customers and is seen to provide the highest rate of return on investment. The industry body, the DMA, suggests that email marketing's return on investment (ROI) is £32.28 for every £1 spent (Anon, 2018a).

As well as delivering on investment, email's increasing popularity is in part due to the frequency with which consumers check their email accounts. Research identifies that 99 per cent of consumers check their personal email accounts every day and their home, work and mobile inbox 20 times a day (DMA, 2017b). This provides opportunities for organisations to connect daily with consumers in a personal and direct way.

The design of emails is important and a number of techniques can be used to encourage the receiver to open the email, which is vital for campaign success. For example, the choice of words in the subject line or the inclusion of an emoji can make all the difference as to whether an email is opened or not. The tone-of-voice used is another consideration and this needs to be contextualised to meet the needs of the consumer.

Email should be seen as part of an overall strategy and it is important that organisations do not assume that recipients of an email will also be engaging with a brand on other channels, although messages should be consistent across communications (DMA, 2017b).

Mobile

Mobile has been one of the most exciting new channels for direct marketing over the last decade. Mobile phones seem to be the first thing consumers check in the morning when they wake up and the last thing they see before they go to bed. Mobile is omnipresent, providing brands with new opportunities to connect with audiences while they are out shopping, sat watching TV or taking a walk in the park.

While the characteristics of mobile are explored in more depth in Chapter 21, it is worth highlighting some key aspects of mobile that are important to consider when planning a direct campaign. The frequency with which messages are sent is a key consideration. This will depend on the audience themselves and their preferences. Guidelines issued by the Direct Marketing Association (DMA, 2016a) suggest that organisations need to respect reasonable hours when using mobile. In particular they recommend messaging between 8am and 8pm and avoiding Sundays, or public or religious holidays.

The availability of GPS-enabled smartphones makes location-based mobile marketing a new possibility for marketers and provides opportunities to connect with customers in a variety of environments, including point of purchase. This allows campaigns to be highly targeted geographically and presents opportunities for including promotional offers.

Apps provide an opportunity to connect with audiences in a highly targeted way and provide a functional experience for consumers. App-based services such as Groupon and Foursquare permit users to 'check in' at locations, enabling them to receive promotional offers (DMA, 2016a). Similarly, augmented reality can be triggered by posters, press ads or packaging to further engage audiences and quick response (QR) codes can connect audiences directly to brand websites (DMA, 2016a). For example, Fanta placed QR codes on limited edition Halloween packaging, which when scanned provided customers with access to branded Snapchat filters and lenses (Gwynn, 2017b).

Mobile is also used to create interactive opportunities within integrated campaigns. For example, Audi's 'Send in the Clowns' TV ad invited audiences to Shazam and download the music from the ad (Carter, 2017). Shazam was also used by Lipton in Turkey, where audiences were asked to Shazam the TV jingle to get a free sample of Lipton's tea (Anon, 2017b).

Social

Social media is considered in Chapter 21 and provides a detailed discussion of the advantages and disadvantages of social channels. However, it is worth discussing the nature of social media here briefly in the context of how it enables organisations to connect directly with audiences.

Social media is built around connecting people directly with each other and therefore it is by design a highly effective direct-response medium. As well as providing platforms for friends, families, employers and businesses to connect with each other, social media also allows brands to engage with large audiences very quickly (DMA, 2016b). There are opportunities to encourage dialogue with customers and develop closer relationships across customer segments.

Organisations need to set clear guidelines for each social network on how they will be used for marketing and selling to ensure there is a degree of fit between network content and campaign content. For example, using Pinterest which is a highly image-based network would be more appropriate for image-led campaigns such as holiday brands or florists, in comparison to business-to-business (B2B) campaigns with an information-based message (DMA, 2016b).

Image 16.3 During the European Football Championships, Cornetto brand Mini Mix featured Shazam on packaging and invited consumers to use their phone to access a microsite. This allowed them to take selfies and, using country themed objects, customise their photos
Source: Unilever.

This does not mean, however, that image-led social media networks are not suitable for B2B and many B2B brands are using images effectively to engage customers on networks such as Instagram. For example, FedEx use images effectively on Instagram to create a strong profile, showing their couriers in different colourful locations and telling an interesting visual story about the brand (Williams, 2017).

Scholars' paper 16.2
Connecting with audiences on social

Swani, K., Milne, G.R., Brown, B.P., Assaf, A. G. and Donthu, N. (2017) What messages to post? Evaluating the popularity of social media communications in business versus consumer markets, *Industrial Marketing Management*, 62, 77–87.

This paper considers the reasons why Facebook users 'like' and 'comment'. The authors choose a business-to-business context for the study and select Fortune 500 companies to explore the factors that contribute towards these brand popularity metrics. This provides a better understanding of how to connect with audiences on social platforms.

See also:

Ferguson, D.A. and Greer, C.F. (2018) Visualizing a non-visual medium through social media: the semiotics of radio station posts on Instagram, *Journal of Radio & Audio Media*, 25(1), 126–41.

Direct mail

Direct mail refers to personally addressed advertising that is delivered through the postal system. It can be personalised and targeted with great accuracy, and its results are capable of precise measurement.

Direct mail has a number of advantages over other media. The physical nature of direct mail and its ability to stand out from the clutter of online advertising are some of the main reasons why it is seen to be so effective (Cerna, 2018). Additionally, direct mail's ability to generate enquiries and leads, together with the intention of building a personal relationship with customers are important factors.

Management should decide whether to target direct mail at current customers with the intention of building loyalty and retention rates, or whether it should chase new customers. The decision, acquisition or retention, should be part of the marketing plan but often this aspect of direct marketing lacks clarity, resulting in wastage and inefficiency. Direct mail can be expensive; it should, therefore, be used selectively and for purposes other than creating awareness.

Organisations in the financial services sector have been heavy users of this medium and the financial health of the sector is dependent to a large extent on some of the major financial services companies maintaining their spend on direct mail. An increasing number of other organisations, however, are experimenting with this approach, as they try to improve the effectiveness of their investment in the communications mix and seek to reduce television advertising costs.

Telemarketing

Telemarketing is a valuable direct marketing tool. It provides for interaction, is flexible and permits immediate feedback and the opportunity to overcome objections, all within the same communications event.

The personalised nature of telemarketing provides a unique opportunity to deliver a highly relevant and individual offer to customers. If planned and executed well, campaigns can be very successful and assist in the development and maintenance of customer relationships.

A one-to-one phone call is an effective way to build rapport with clients and manage enquiries. It also allows for orders to be taken and support to be given to retailers and distributors (DMA, 2016c). Telemarketing provides opportunities to cross-sell products and services to existing customers, as well as introduce new products and promotions. The personal nature of a phone call allows the offers to be tailored to meet the customer's needs.

Telemarketing is seen to be a cost-effective alternative to personal selling. While personal selling shares many of the interactive benefits of telemarketing, using a phone rather than face-to-face meetings reduces costs. The cost advantage and the ability to accurately measure its effectiveness has made telemarketing an attractive medium to marketers.

Telemarketing is used for a number of different activities, including building rapport with customers, gaining feedback, and research and sales activities. Table 16.2 highlights some of the many uses of telemarketing.

Inserts

Inserts are media materials that are placed in magazines or direct mail letters. These not only provide factual information about the product or service but also enable the recipient to respond to the request of the direct marketer. This request might be to place an order or post back a card for more information, such as a brochure.

Inserts have become more popular because of their effectiveness as a lead generator, but their cost is substantially higher than a four-colour magazine ad in which the insert

Table 16.2 Telemarketing activities

Telemarketing activity	Examples
Telephone account management (TAM)	Building rapport with customers, customer liaison, enquiry management, order taking, new product launches, and point of sale and promotional support to retailers and distributors.
Customer satisfaction index (CSI)	Gaining customer feedback on services and products.
Inside sales representatives (ISR)	Increasing awareness of products and promotions.
Lead generation and profiling	Identifying leads and customer profiling.
Appointment setting	Making appointments for customer meetings or test drives.
Follow-up calls and customer care	Resolving customer complaints or dealing with enquiries.
Research	Undertaking qualitative or quantitative surveys to gain customer insights.
Customer relationship management (CRM) and sales	Sales activities, cross-selling and up-selling, building customer relationships, reactivating lapsed customers, customer retention.

Source: DMA (2016c).

is carried. Additionally, the time needed to create and print the inserts means they have longer lead times than other media, such as email.

There are a number of different types of inserts that can be used, each offering unique opportunities for creativity. Some inserts such as special covers can allow the brand to dominate the publication, while others provide opportunities for sampling. The main types of inserts are outlined in Table 16.3.

Print

There are two main forms of direct-response advertising through the printed media: first, catalogues and second, magazines and newspapers.

Catalogues mailed direct to consumers have been an established method of selling products for a long time. Mail-order organisations for a range of products from clothing and music to gardening and cosmetics continue to exploit this form of direct marketing. The size of each catalogue and the range of products included have been slimmed down so that mini-catalogues are popular. IKEA's catalogue is an example of how effective this route continues to be, with the retailer printing 38 editions in 17 languages for 28 countries around the world (Anon, 2018b).

Table 16.3 Main insert types

Type of insert	Description
Furnished outserts	These are attached to the outside covers of publications such as magazines and often include free samples.
Loose inserts	These range from a single inserted sheet to a catalogue.
Furnished inserts	These are glued to the inside of the publication.
Bound-in inserts	These are fixed into the main publication and usually the only insert included.
Tip-on inserts	These are glued inserts that are placed on the relevant page inside a publication.
Brochure	These can be full brochures or mini-catalogues placed within the publication.
Post-it	These are glued onto a relevant ad on a specified page inside the publication.
Bellyband	These are belts of paper wrapped around the publication.
Special covers	These are additional covers over the top of the real front cover of the publication.

Source: DMA (2016d).

Image 16.4 The IKEA Catalogue is printed in 17 different languages
Source: © Inter IKEA Systems B.V.

Business-to-business marketers also use this medium, and organisations such as Dell and IBM now use online and offline catalogues, partly to save costs and partly to free valuable sales personnel so that they can concentrate their time selling into larger accounts. Direct-response advertising through the press is similar to general press advertising except that the advertiser provides a mechanism for the reader to take further action. The mechanism may be a telephone number (call free) or a coupon or cut-out reply slip requesting further information. Dell transformed its marketing strategy to one that is based around building customised products for both consumers and business customers. Consumer direct print ads which offer an incentive are designed explicitly to drive customers to the Dell website, where transactions are completed without reference to retailers, dealers or other intermediaries.

Viewpoint 16.3

Virgin Holidays: Ready to Travel

Virgin Holidays identified that consumers found getting ready to go on holiday was stressful. They also found that their communication to customers was making matters worse. In some cases, they had been sending 35 messages to customers from different departments. This insight led them to think about what they could do to alleviate the stress and focus on how they could provide a smoother pre-departure service for their customers.

The result was the 'Ready To Travel' programme. Virgin Holidays developed a communication plan that was intended to allow customers to focus on the excitement of going on holiday, rather than be stressed about the preparation.

To ensure customers weren't overwhelmed by emails from Virgin Holidays, communication was divided into two distinct types. The first type was purely informational and the second was aimed at exciting customers about their holiday.

Virgin Holidays used Ready To Travel as a way to connect with customers and engage them in the positive aspects of their holiday. From the moment of booking, when customers received a singing receipt holder, the campaign encouraged

Image 16.5 Virgin Holidays developed their Ready To Travel programme to build excitement in the pre-departure stage
Source: NextNewMedia/Shutterstock.

excitement. Personalised emails linked customers to a microsite providing information about the destination and services. The site includes travel tips and destination 'must sees'.

Virgin Holidays continued to build excitement within the pre-departure stage with personalised, shareable GIFs, which included customers' names. Instagram photos of reps from the resorts booked were also used to excite customers about their destination. Local reps provided information about the resort and suggested itineraries to meet individual preferences.

Throughout the pre-departure stage customers were kept informed about the status of their booking and what to expect next from Virgin Holidays.

Sources: Anon (2018c); DMA (2017c).

Ready To Travel was well received by customers and the campaign had an open rate of 84 per cent in email and 92 per cent click-through rates. Traffic to the Virgin Holidays concierge pages to find more information about destinations rose by 800 per cent and scores for customer satisfaction increased by 5 per cent.

The programme also found that Ready To Travel customers spent more on 'extras' for their holiday and this saw customers on the programme spending 11 per cent more than those who had not been included. This additional customer spend was estimated to have generated an additional £1.35 in revenue for the year. The return on investment for the campaign was £16.20:1.

Insight

The Virgin Holidays campaign highlights how direct, personalised campaigns can be used to engage customers. Building a unique engagement journey for customers, which embedded their pre-departure information needs as well as exciting them about their upcoming holiday allowed Virgin Holidays to connect in a more streamlined way.

Question: What were the benefits of engaging customers? Consider the benefits to both Virgin and the customer.

Task: Think about when you made your university choice. How could the university have made your own 'pre-departure' journey more engaging? Provide examples.

Door-to-door

This delivery method can be much cheaper than direct mail as there are no postage charges to be accounted for. However, if the costs are much lower, so are the response rates. Responses are lower because door-to-door drops cannot be personally addressed, as can direct mail, even though the content and quality can be controlled in the same way.

Avon (Cosmetics) and Betterware are traditionally recognised as professional practitioners of door-to-door direct marketing. Other organisations, such as the utility companies (gas, electricity and water) and the domestic cleaning company, Molly Maid, are using door-to-door to create higher levels of market penetration.

Radio and television

Of the two main forms discussed earlier, radio and television, the former is often used as a support medium for other advertising, usually by providing enquiry numbers and website addresses. Television has greater potential because it can provide the important visual dimension. The original DRTV model involved generating response to 0800 numbers and a call to immediate action.

Now that consumers practise multiscreening, the model has moved to one that harnesses brand search activity through mobile devices, which in turn drives spontaneous purchases. Instead of a phone number this activity is stimulated through the use of compelling content that consumers want to share. These links boost natural search rankings.

Viewpoint 16.4
Pet Perks

Image 16.6 The Pets at Home app was personalised to pets and their owners
Source: Chendongshan/Shutterstock.

Pets at Home is the leading UK omnichannel pet retailer, offering pet owners everything from pet food to vet and grooming services. In 2012, the retailer launched a VIP loyalty club. Data collected from its members since the launch showed that those who used multiple services from Pets at Home were more likely to remain a VIP member.

To strengthen the relationship with members, Pets at Home launched an app, which allowed the brand to deliver more personalised content such as offers, expert advice and tips specific to the type of pet the member owned. These 'Pet Perks' meant that pet owners received offers that were tailored specifically to them and their pets.

Members who signed up were offered a 10 per cent off welcome offer and vouchers were sent directly to members' phones giving them savings and tailored offers to suit their pets' type, size and life stage.

The app allowed members to register their pets' date of birth and personalise the app with pictures of their cat, dog, bird, fish, guinea pig, rabbit, horse or hamster.

Source: Anon (2018d); DMA Awards (2017); Pickwick (2016).

The app also gave members the chance to collect and donate points to animal charities and linked them to the 'Golden Paws' puppy initiative, which encourages responsible puppy ownership.

The app offered an exclusive lost pet finding service, 'Find My VIP' and 'Save Flea', giving VIP members access to a specialist service that delivers flea treatment to members' homes.

The campaign increased the total number of VIP members to over six million and resulted in 163,000 VIP members downloading the app.

Insight

The Pets at Home app allowed the brand to connect with members in a more targeted and personalised way. Tailoring offers and information to members' specific needs delivered value to both the customer and the brand. The app acted as an excellent acquisition tool for the brand and attracted many new members to the VIP programme.

Question: What other forms of direct marketing could Pets at Home have used to build stronger relationships with customers? Explain why you think the retailer chose to launch an app.

Task: Find an example of another customer app in the retail sector. Make a list of all the benefits the app offers customers.

Personal selling

The traditional image of personal selling is one that embraces the hard sell, with a brash and persistent salesperson delivering a volley of unrelenting, persuasive messages at a confused and reluctant consumer. Fortunately this image has receded as the professionalism and breadth of personal selling has become more widely recognised and as the role of personal selling becomes even more important in the communications mix.

Personal selling activities can be observed at various stages in the buying process of both the consumer and B2B markets. This is because the potency of personal communications is very high, and messages can be adapted on the spot to meet the requirements of both parties. This flexibility, as we shall see later, enables objections to be overcome, information to be provided in the context of the buyer's environment, and the conviction and power of demonstration to be brought to the buyer when the buyer requests it.

Personal selling is different from other forms of communications in that the transmitted messages represent, mainly, dyadic communications. This means that there are two persons involved in the communications process. Feedback and evaluation of transmitted messages are possible, more or less instantaneously, so that these personal selling messages can be tailored and be made much more personal than any of the other methods of communications.

Using the spectrum of activities identified by the hierarchy of effects, we can see that personal selling is close enough to the prospective buyer to induce a change in behaviour. That is, it is close enough to overcome objections, to provide information quickly and to respond to the prospects' overall needs, all in the context of the transaction, and to encourage them directly to place orders.

Scholars' paper 16.3
How ethical are salespeople?

Bush, V., Bush, A.J., Oakley, J. and Cicala, J.E. (2017) The sales profession as a subculture: implications for ethical decision making, *Journal of Business Ethics*, **142(3), 549–65.**

The authors suggest that salespeople tend to work in isolation and with little daily contact with other employees from the same organisation. They explore the phenomena of an ethics subculture in the sales domain and recommend ethics training be part of an ongoing process for salespeople.

See also:

Serviere-Munoz, L. and Mallin, M.L. (2013) How do unethical salespeople sleep at night? The role of neutralizations in the justification of unethical sales intentions, *Journal of Personal Selling and Sales Management*, 33(3), 289–306.

The tasks of personal selling

The generic tasks to be undertaken by the sales force have been changing because the environment in which organisations operate is shifting dramatically. These changes, in particular those associated with the development and implementation of new technologies, have had repercussions on the activities of the sales force and are discussed later in this chapter.

The tasks of those who undertake personal selling vary from organisation to organisation and in accord with the type of selling activities on which they focus. It is normally assumed that they collect and bring into the organisation orders from customers wishing to purchase products and services. In this sense the order aspect of the personal selling tool can be seen as one of four order-related tasks:

1. *Order takers* are salespersons to whom customers are drawn at the place of supply. Reception clerks at hotels and ticket desk personnel at theatres and cinemas typify this role.

2. *Order getters* are sales personnel who operate away from the organisation and who attempt to gain orders, largely through the provision of information, the use of demonstration techniques and services, and the art of persuasion.

3. *Order collectors* are those who attempt to gather orders without physically meeting their customers. This is completed electronically or over the telephone. The growth of telemarketing operations was discussed earlier in this chapter but the time saved by both the buyer and the seller using the telephone to gather repeat and low-value orders frees valuable sales personnel to seek new customers and build relationships with current customers.

4. *Order supporters* are all those people who are secondary salespersons in that they are involved with the order once it has been secured, or are involved with the act of ordering, usually by supplying information. Order processing or financial advice services typify this role. In truly customer-oriented organisations all customer-facing employees will be an order supporter.

However, this perspective of personal selling is narrow because it fails to set out the broader range of activities that a sales force can be required to undertake. Salespeople do more than get or take orders. The tasks listed in Table 16.4 provide direction and purpose, and also help to establish the criteria by which the performance of members of the personal selling unit can be evaluated. The organisation should decide which tasks it expects its representatives to undertake.

It is argued that the personal selling process should be seen as something beyond simply a series of buyer–seller interactions (Shannahan et al., 2013). By understanding the personal selling process as an interpretation system comprising individuals whose goal is to reduce uncertainty with respect to the activities within the selling process, a wider, more relational perspective can be appreciated.

Personal selling is the most expensive element of the communications mix and it is generally agreed that personal selling is most effective at the later stages of the hierarchy of effects or buying process, rather than at the earlier stage of awareness building.

Therefore, each organisation should determine the precise role the sales force is to play within the communications mix.

The role of personal selling

Personal selling is often referred to as interpersonal communications and from this perspective Reid et al. (2002) determined three major sales behaviours, namely getting, giving and using information:

Table 16.4 Tasks of personal selling

Prospecting	Finding new customers
Communicating	Informing various stakeholders and feeding back information about the market
Selling	The art of leading a prospect to a successful close
Information gathering	Reporting information about the market and reporting on individual activities
Servicing	Consulting, arranging, counselling, fixing and solving a multitude of customer 'problems'
Allocating	Placing scarce products and resources at times of shortage
Shaping	Building and sustaining relationships with customers and other stakeholders

1. Getting information refers to sales behaviours aimed at information acquisition, for example gathering information about customers, markets and competitors.

2. Giving information refers to the dissemination of information to customers and other stakeholders, for example sales presentations and seminar meetings designed to provide information about products and an organisation's capabilities and reputation.

3. Using information refers to the salesperson's use of information to help solve a customer's problem. Associated with this is the process of gaining buyer commitment through the generation of information (Thayer, 1968, cited by Reid et al., 2002).

These last authors suggest that the using information dynamic appears to be constant across all types of purchase situations. However, as the complexity of a purchase situation increases so the amount of giving information behaviours decline and getting information behaviours increase. This finding supports the need for salespeople to be able to recognise particular situations in the buying process and then to adapt their behaviour to meet a buyer's contextual needs.

However, salespeople undertake numerous tasks in association with communications activities. Guenzi (2002) determined that some sales activities are generic simply because they are performed by most salespeople across a large number of industries. These generic activities are selling, customer relationship management and communicating to customers. Other activities such as market analysis, pre-sales services and the transfer of information about competitors to the organisation are industry-specific. Interestingly he found that information-gathering activities are more likely to be undertaken by organisations operating in consumer markets than in B2B, possibly a reflection of the strength of the market orientation in both arenas.

The role of personal selling is largely one of representation. In B2B markets sales personnel operate at the boundary of the organisation. They provide the link between the needs of their own organisation and the needs of their customers. This linkage, or boundary spanning role, is absolutely vital, for a number of reasons that will be discussed shortly, but without personal selling, communications with other organisations would occur through electronic or print media and would foster discrete closed systems. Representation in this sense therefore refers to face-to-face encounters between people from different organisations.

Many authors consider the development, organisation and completion of a sale in a market exchange-based transaction to be the key part of the role of personal selling. Sales personnel provide a source of information for buyers so that they can make the right purchase decisions. In that sense they provide a good level of credibility, but they are also perceived, understandably, as biased. The degree of expertise held by the salesperson may be high, but the degree of perceived trustworthiness will vary, especially during the formative period of the relationship, unless other transactions with the selling organisation have been satisfactory. Hamwi et al. (2013) found that a buyer's commitment to and trust in a salesperson increase when the expected number of sales calls, as perceived by the buyer, is met. This improves the relational dimension and length of a buyer–seller relationship.

As the costs associated with personal selling are high, it is vital that sales personnel are used effectively. To that end, some organisations are employing other methods to decrease the time that the sales force spends on administration, travel and office work and to maximise the time spent in front of customers, where its specific selling skills can be used.

The amount of control that can be exercised over the delivery of the messages through the sales force depends upon a number of factors. Essentially, the level of control must be regarded as low, because each salesperson has the freedom to adapt messages to meet changing circumstances as negotiations proceed. In practice, however, the professionalism and training that many members of the sales force receive and the increasing accent on measuring levels of customer satisfaction mean that the degree of control over the message can be regarded, in most circumstances, as very good, although it can never, for example, be as high as that of advertising.

This flexibility is framed within the context of the product strategy. Decisions that impact upon strategy are not allowed. There is freedom to adapt the manner in which products are presented, but there is no freedom for the sales representatives to decide the priority of the products to be detailed.

Scholars' paper 16.4
What is selling?

Hartmann, N.N., Wieland, H. and Vargo, S.L. (2018) Converging on a new theoretical foundation for selling, *Journal of Marketing*, 82(2), 1–18.

The authors suggest selling exists within a broader service ecosystem where selling is a core activity engaging many actors. The paper argues that participation in the ecosystem is changing and discusses the management of intrafirm relationships and sales performance.

See also:

Lacoste, S. (2018) From selling to managing strategic customers – a competency analysis, *Journal of Personal Selling & Sales Management*, 38(1), 92–122.

When personal selling should be a major part of the communications mix

In view of the role and the advantages and disadvantages of personal selling, when should it be a major part of the communications mix? Table 16.5 indicates some key factors using advertising as a comparison.

Table 16.5 When selling is a major element of the communications mix

	Advertising relatively important	Personal selling relatively important
Number of customers	Large	Small
Buyers' information needs	Low	High
Size and importance of purchase	Small	Large
Post-purchase service required	Little	A lot
Product complexity	Low	High
Distribution strategy	Pull	Push
Pricing policy	Set	Negotiate
Web-enabled communications and exchanges	High	Low
Resources available for promotion	Many	Few

Source: Adapted from Cravens (1987).

The following is not an exhaustive list, but is presented as a means of considering some of the important issues: complexity, network factors, buyer significance and communications effectiveness.

Complexity

Personal selling is very important when there is a medium to high level of relationship complexity. Such complexity may be associated either with the physical characteristics of the product, such as computer software design, or with the environment in which the negotiations are taking place. For example, decisions related to the installation of products designed to automate an assembly line may well be a sensitive issue. This may be due to management's attitude towards the operators currently undertaking the work that the automation is expected to replace.

When the complexity of the offering is high, advertising and public relations cannot always convey benefits in the same way as personal selling. Personal selling allows the product to be demonstrated so that buyers can see and, if necessary, touch and taste it for themselves. Personal selling also allows explanations to be made about particular points that are of concern to the buyer or about the environment in which the buyer wishes to use the product.

Buyer significance

The significance of the product to the buyers in the target market is a very important factor in the decision on whether to use personal selling. Significance can be measured as a form of risk, and risk is associated with benefits and costs.

The absolute cost to the buyer will vary from organisation to organisation and from consumer to consumer. The significance of the purchase of an extra photocopier for a major multinational organisation may be low, but for a new start-up organisation or for an established organisation experiencing a dramatic turnaround, an extra photocopying machine may be highly significant and subject to high levels of resistance by a number of different internal stakeholders.

Communications effectiveness

There may be a number of ways to satisfy the communications objectives of a campaign, other than by using personal selling. Each of the other communications tools has strengths and weaknesses; consequently differing mixes provide different benefits. Have they all been considered?

One of the main reasons for using personal selling occurs when advertising alone, or any other medium, provides insufficient communications. The main reason for this inadequacy surfaces when advertising media cannot provide buyers with the information they require to make their decision. For example, someone buying a new car may well observe and read various magazine and newspaper advertisements through which an emotional disposition towards a brand might be created. Then people go online and look at detailed information and comparison tests. The decision to buy, however, requires information and data upon which a balanced decision can be made. The rationality and emotional elements are brought together through experience of the car, through a test drive perhaps.

The decision to buy a car normally evokes high involvement, therefore car manufacturers try to provide a rich balance of emotional and factual information in their literature. From this perspective buyers seek further information at the website and seek experience and reassurance at a dealership. Car buyers sign orders with the presence and encouragement of salespersons. Very few cars are bought on a mail-order basis, although some, mainly used cars, are bought online.

Personal selling provides a number of characteristics that make it more effective than the other elements of the mix. As discussed, in B2B marketing the complexity of many products requires salespeople to be able to discuss with clients their specific needs; in other words, to be able to talk in the customer's own language, to build source credibility through expertise and hopefully trustworthiness, and build a relationship that corresponds with the psychographic profile of each member of the decision-making unit (DMU). In this case, mass communications would be inappropriate.

Channel network factors

When the number of members in a network is limited, the use of a sales force is advisable, as advertising is inefficient. Furthermore, the opportunity to build a close collaborative relationship with members may enable the development of a sustainable competitive advantage.

There are two further factors that influence the decision to use personal selling as part of the communications mix. When the customer base is small and dispersed across a wide geographic area it makes economic sense to use salespersons, as advertising in this situation is inadequate and ineffective.

Personal selling is the most expensive element of the communications mix. It may be that other elements of the mix may provide a more cost-effective way of delivering the message.

The role of social media in personal selling

There is general agreement that a salesperson's selling behaviours are important when building a buyer's trust. There are ramifications in terms of longer-term sales performance and customer loyalty. This means that the development of relationship marketing skills through the use of a customer-oriented selling approach by salespeople, is critical if sales performance and customer loyalty targets are to be achieved (Chakrabarty et al., 2013).

The development and implementation of social media, within a business-to-business selling context, has been an important means of adopting a customer-oriented selling approach. In addition to moderating the high costs of personal selling, the use of social media can also enhance customer relationships. The incorporation of interactive media, and social media in particular, within the selling process has evolved through time, from simply generating awareness, to driving customers to a firm's social media pages, and through to facilitating learning, the co-creation of value, and undertaking a fully integrated role within sales strategy.

The use of social media has changed how buyers and sellers interact. Agnihotri et al. (2015) argue that by using social media to facilitate their behaviours, salespeople can improve buyer engagement, and involvement, and can positively impact both information communication and customer responsiveness.

This facilitation can be undertaken within each stage of the sales process. As Andzulis et al. (2012) rightly observe social media can have a distinct role to play within each step of the sales process. These steps, or sales episodes, include understanding the customer, the approach, needs discovery, presentation, close and the follow-up. Within each of the steps key sales tasks can be accomplished using a particular combination of social media skills.

Pallouras and Siakas (2017) suggest that Customer Relationship Management (CRM) has evolved through e-CRM and now to Social CRM. They argue that two-way communication with customers through social media sites, such as Facebook, LinkedIn, and Twitter, enable organisations to interact directly with customers and potential customers, track all relevant customer interactions, and monitor their social influence. At the same time understanding and trust develops which in turn helps the development of stronger, longer lasting marketing relationships.

Strategic account management

One of the major issues concerning the development and maintenance of inter-organisational relationships is the method by which very important and/or valuable customers are managed. Two main forms are considered here in turn, key account management and the emerging global account management disciplines.

Key account management

The increasing complexity of both markets and products, combined with the trends towards purchasing centralisation and industrial concentration, mean that a small number of significant accounts have become essential for the survival of many organisations. The growth in the significance of key account management (KAM) is expected to continue and one of the results will be the change in expectations of buyers and sellers, in particular the demand for higher levels of expertise, integration and professionalism of sales forces.

It has long been recognised that particular customer accounts represent an important, often large, proportion of turnover. Such accounts have been referred to variously as national accounts, house accounts, major accounts and key accounts. Millman and Wilson (1995) argue that the first three are sales-oriented, tend to the short term and are often only driven by sales management needs. However, Ojasalo (2001) sees little difference in the terminology KAM, national account marketing (NAM) and strategic account management (SAM).

Key accounts may be of different sizes in comparison to the focus organisation, but what delineates them from other types of 'account' is that they are strategically important. Key accounts are customers who, in a B2B market, are willing to enter into collaborative exchanges and who are strategically important to the focus organisation.

There are two primary issues that arise. The first is that both parties perceive relational exchanges as a necessary component and that the relationship is long term. The second aspect refers to the strategic issue. The key account is strategically important because it might offer opportunities for entry to new markets, represent access to other key organisations or resources, or provide symbolic value in terms of influence, power and stature.

The importance of the long-term relationship as a prime element of key account identification raises questions about how they are developed, what resources are required to manage and sustain them, and what long-term success and effectiveness results from identifying them.

In many ways KAM programmes are a means to reduce the various complexities and uncertainties that arise from the external and internal forces acting on both the selling and buying organisations. Brehmer and Rehme (2009) deduce that KAM-oriented complexity can be considered across two dimensions. The first is structural complexity, which is concerned with the number, location and geographical dispersion of a customer's units. The second is operational complexity, and concern here is focused on the variety of product lines, services, systems, fulfilment facilities and commercial solutions.

There are three forms of uncertainties experienced by buyers according to Håkansson et al. (1977). These are *need uncertainty*, which concerns levels of demand, and whether increased interaction might increase or decrease the level of uncertainty. *Market uncertainty* concerns suppliers and perceptions of instability and the assumptions upon which decisions are made. The third element is *transaction uncertainty*, which is related to the physical transfer of products from supplier to buyer.

A primary goal of KAM programmes should therefore be one of reducing a buyer's uncertainties by coordinating an offer according to the prevailing complexities. To do this Brehmer and Rehme (2009) formulate a grid, which they refer to as the 'Sales complexity management matrix' (see Figure 16.2).

By focusing on the operational and structural complexities experienced by organisations, KAM programmes can be formulated to meet the coordination needs of buyers.

In order for these coordination activities to be designed and implemented a decision about who in the organisation should be responsible for these key accounts needs to be made. Generally speaking, there are three main responses: to assign sales executives, to create a key account division or to create a key account sales force (see Table 16.6).

Global account management

The development of KAM approaches highlighted the strategic importance that some customers represent to organisations. KAM represents an attempt to meet the needs of these customers in a customised and personal way. However, there are many organisations whose customers are located in many different countries, regions and even on different continents, and the management of their needs demands different skills and resources from those adopted for KAM. The management of these customers is referred to as global account management (GAM) and in many ways is evidence of a new strategic approach to business development and marketing management in B2B organisations.

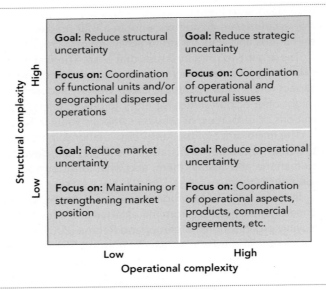

Figure 16.2 The sales complexity management matrix
Source: Brehmer and Rehme (2009). Used with permission.

Table 16.6 Three ways of managing key accounts

KAM management	Explanation
Assigning sales executives	Common in smaller organisations that do not have large resources. Normally undertaken by senior executives who have the flexibility and can provide the responsive service often required. They can make decisions about stock, price, distribution and levels of customisation. There is a tendency for key accounts to receive a disproportionate level of attention, as the executives responsible for these major customers lose sight of their own organisation's marketing strategy.
Creating a key account division	The main advantage of this approach is that it offers close integration of production, finance, marketing and sales. The main disadvantage is that resources are duplicated and the organisation can become very inefficient. It is also a high-risk strategy, as the entire division is dependent upon a few customers.
Creating a key account sales force	This is adopted by organisations that want to differentiate through service and they use their most experienced and able salespersons and provide them with a career channel. Administratively, this structure is inefficient, as there is a level of duplication similar to that found in the customer-type structure discussed earlier. Furthermore, commission payable on these accounts is often a source of discontent, both for those within the key account sales force and for those aspiring to join the select group.

Understanding the nature of GAM is helped by Hennessey and Jeannet (2003: 1), who provide a useful definition:

> Global accounts are large companies that operate in multiple countries, often on two or more continents, are strategically important to the supplier and have some form of coordinated purchasing across different countries.

One of the characteristics of global accounts is that their decision-making units are influenced through inputs from various geographical locations. Wilson et al. (2000) highlight the important characteristics associated with the strategic coordination associated with GAM. To them, a strategic global account is characterised as representing a major part of a supplier's corporate objectives and where the account expects the supplier to offer an integrated global product service offering.

It would therefore be a mistake to think that KAM and GAM are the same. Indeed, Birkinshaw (2003) makes the point that global and key accounts are not identical. He argues that the roots of GAM are to be found in supply chain management, unlike KAM, which has been influenced by the sales management perspective. Hennessey and Jeannet (2003) believe that national account managers are relationship managers, whereas global account managers have a greater focus on strategic issues and coordination of personnel in different countries. Millman and Wilson (1998) refer to the importance and significance of cultural diversity and organisational issues when adopting a GAM programme.

Wilson et al. (2000) consider how global account programmes can be delivered. They identified the need for three main global competences:

1. a coordinated, globally competent supply chain;
2. management of the interaction process *within* the supplying company, particularly the information and communications flows;
3. the establishment of a forum, with the customer, of a collaborative design process.

This suggests that relationship management skills, in particular the use of interaction and collaboration to develop dialogue, are critical factors associated with GAM. Wilson et al. (2000) identify many competences that are necessary for GAM to be successful, ranging from strong communications and relationship management skills through cultural empathy and business and financial acumen. However, they make the point that global account managers need strong political skills, especially in view of the fact that they often operate without direct authority, particularly with regard to resources and processes. They refer to this role as 'political entrepreneur'.

Understanding the nature of GAM, its management and indeed associated research are at an early stage as the discipline is very young. Early work in the area suggests that there is no fixed strategic model that represents GAM, if only because GAM needs to be flexible and dynamic as engagement with key global customers evolves.

Key points

- Direct marketing is a tool of marketing communications used to create and sustain personal and intermediary-free communications with customers, potential customers and other significant stakeholders.
- It is concerned with the management of customer behaviour and is used to complement the strengths and weaknesses of the other communications disciplines.
- Four main forms of direct marketing can be identified: as a complementary tool, a primary differentiator, as a sales channel and as a brand vehicle.
- There have been three essential drivers behind the surge in direct marketing: technological advances; changing buyer lifestyles and expectations; and organisational expectations.
- Databases and Big Data play a central role as storage, sorting and administrative devices to assist strategy formulation, cross-selling, plus direct and personalised communications.
- Email, mobile and social media are the main online forms of direct-response media, as they allow more personal, direct and evaluative means of reaching precisely targeted customers.
- Direct mail, telemarketing, inserts, print, door-to-door activities, and radio and TV are the main offline forms of direct-response media.
- Personal selling activities can be observed at various stages in the buying process of both the consumer and business-to-business (B2B) markets.
- Personal selling can be considered in terms of four different tasks: order takers, order getters, order collectors and order supporters.
- Some of the issues associated with the deployment of personal selling include: complexity, network factors, buyer significance and communications effectiveness.
- Key account management (KAM) programmes are a means of reducing the various complexities and uncertainties that arise from the external and internal forces that act on both selling and buying organisations.

Direct Line: we solve problems
Carl Bratton and Ann Constantine, Direct Line Group
Nic Pietersma, Ebiquity

Image 16.7 Direct Line faced new challenges in the insurance market

Source: U K Insurance Limited.

In 1985 Direct Line revolutionised insurance by cutting out the middle-man. The direct revolution propelled us to market leader inside 12 years, so that by 1997 we were insuring one in ten private cars. By 2012 we had a large customer base and cash flow was stable, and Direct Line was still one of the largest direct insurers in the UK for car and home insurance.

But as a business, we had an urgent problem to solve. The marketing model that we had effectively invented in the 1980s, direct response insurance, was broken. Price comparison websites (PCWs) had changed the face of insurance. PCWs didn't just steal market share. They also put the middle-man back into insurance, put pressure on margins, added to transaction costs, reduced loyalty and commoditised the product. This technologically led revolution was a specific threat to Direct Line because the centre of gravity for our brand had always been 'going direct'. In effect, PCWs broke Direct Line's business model. Our quotes and sales were reliably and predictably

in decline year after year. We had a declining share of a declining market.

The decline can in part be explained by reduced above-the-line adspend from 2013. But it also aligns with the launch of our 2012 'Take the Direct Line' creative platform. This was an attempt to update the look and feel of the brand and to stem the decline. We wanted to present ourselves to the world as a slick, modern business. We wanted to demonstrate scale. It needed to make us look 'big'.

However, the message that Direct Line is 'big' doesn't really convey a benefit to the consumer. Nothing about the creative was disruptive. Some of the executions were simply communicating price signals, but for car insurance the price signals were particularly weak with only 10 per cent to 20 per cent discount on offer. The product had become commoditised and the momentum was against direct brands. Unless we could differentiate our brand and rebuild trust with the consumer, we couldn't reasonably expect consumers to choose us over any cheaper competitor.

We didn't just have an advertising problem or indeed a marketing problem. In fact, there was a problem with the brand itself. Our 'go direct' raison d'être was no longer meaningful or sufficient. To stem the decline we needed to rethink our identity, our propositions, how we did business. Direct Line, in its current form, was no longer sustainable.

Finding a solution

Qualitative research pointed us towards an attitudinal group who tend to be assertive and look for a product that they can be confident in, that is flexible and

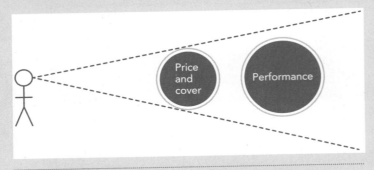

Image 16.8 Direct Line's need to encourage consumers to see beyond price

that offers good value. These consumers are time poor and they resent having to spend their time on insurance. They plan ahead. They want control over their affairs, but they also want reduced complexity. They want insurance that will just fix the problem and let them get back on track with their lives.

Efficiency and simplicity were considered the most achievable 'ways in' to this target audience. For most consumers insurance is a commodity, but this audience are sufficiently motivated to pay an 'acceptable' premium for a product that frees them from the unnecessary worry and hassle that surrounds insurance.

The brand positioning 'hassle-free insurance that just works' was tested and approved. Crucially, no other brand owned this space. Our research suggested that seven out of ten complaints related to timescales of settling a claim or failure to keep customers informed. That was when we knew.

For the first time in a long time we knew what we wanted to be, we knew our role in the world. We knew our archetype. We're Fixers, we put things right when they go wrong. We take the worry and hassle out of insurance.

Moving forward

We undertook the creation of a pipeline of new propositions, the first new proposition being: 'your car fixed in seven days or we pay you £10 a day until the job is done'. Home insurance had a similar: 'claims settled in eight hours' promise. What we liked about these propositions is that they act as a proof point to the efficiency of our service. No other insurer automatically provides goodwill payments.

In order to 'walk the walk' we kicked off a significant operational change programme that saw

the number of repairs completed within seven days jump from 35 per cent to 70 per cent. To 'signal' the quality of our insurance we also restructured our call centres so that cross-brand Direct Line Group agents became dedicated Direct Line Fixers. We stopped charging amendment fees. We made our website easier to use.

PCWs had simplified decision-making in insurance to the point where the only things that people cared about were price and cover at the point of purchase. The creative strategy needed to change the conversation to get around the communications eclipse that PCWs had created.

By repositioning Direct Line as 'high performance insurance' the campaign aimed to return the category back to a conversation about insurance's fundamental role – fixing problems and getting life back on track. We needed an archetype to lead the campaign. Quentin Tarantino's *Pulp Fiction* character, Winston Wolf, is the embodiment of The Fixer. He comes into the story, fixes a problem, and then leaves. Quickly and efficiently.

Image 16.9 Direct Line's Fixer Creative
Source: U K Insurance Limited.

To us the Wolf was a superb parallel for the way great insurance works – a call away, knows exactly what to do, executes it without fuss, puts things right and gets out of your life.

Execution

Our annual marketing spend had fallen by 46 per cent between 2011 and 2015. We had to do more with less. To achieve this, we looked at the efficiency of our current activities. As a result, we found that leaflets were only recovering about 55 per cent of their cost so we reduced the annual spend by 97 per cent. We reduced our annual investment in banner advertising by 50 per cent, the DM budget by 51 per cent, and the DRTV spend was cut by 60 per cent between 2011 and 2015.

With these savings we launched the Fixer Reboot campaign as it was known internally. TV was crucial for delivering the impact that was needed. Mediacom launched with *The X Factor,* as the programme delivered the highest reach (8 million) and was best positioned to generate buzz. It was the first show of the season for *The X Factor* – we owned the night by flighting Car, Home and Landlord ads in consecutive breaks. The strategy was to generate buzz and cut-through rather than efficient reach. The fact that Direct Line was 'trending on Twitter' on the night suggests we achieved this.

Following the initial phase, the goal shifted from generating buzz to supporting each product as efficiently as possible. Mediacom aimed to hit our target audience three to four times within a month. While TV ensured that we reached a broad audience, adding a seven-week cinema campaign to the launch helped target a highly engaged and desirable audience. It also leveraged the fantastic 'cinematic' property we had in Tarantino's Mr Wolf.

Our new digital strategy aimed to make more use of social and content marketing. In brief the digital launch had three strands:

* Social VOD: 'How To …' videos on YouTube featuring Winston Wolf and side-kick Billy solving everyday problems like getting rid of red wine stains. Resulting in 1.7 million views at a 15 per cent completion rate (vs an industry benchmark of 12 per cent).
* *Guardian* Fixology: a content partnership microsite featuring 100 fixes to everyday problems. Seen by 600,000 people in the first three months of the campaign.
* Buzzfeed: animated GIFs featuring people who are 'totally on it'. Resulting in 200,000 views.

Between TV, cinema, digital and press we reached 85 per cent of the population within the first month of the campaign.

Results

By February 2016 we had achieved 10 per cent annual growth in car insurance and 16 per cent in home insurance. By February 2016 we had halted five consecutive years of decline.

The Fixer campaign also stemmed the decline in the awareness, consideration, and most crucially, the preference metrics. People were getting the message that Direct Line offer a better product or 'hassle-free insurance that just works'. The Fixer Reboot changed how people saw us. The majority of our brand metrics saw significant improvement.

Recasting ourselves as 'Fixers' has helped Direct Line take the No. 1 spot in the UK. We have a new raison d'être. We're Fixers. This has become the organising principle of our business. Once we discovered our archetype, we knew what to do next.

This case study is an edited version of a paper submitted to the IPA Effectiveness Awards 2016. It has been reproduced here with the kind permission of the IPA, WARC, and the Direct Line Group, and Ebiquity who wrote the original paper.

Review questions

Direct Line case questions

1. Identify the key success factors underpinning the Direct Line campaign.

2. Explain how the use of rational and emotional benefits in their advertising helps Direct Line in their direct marketing.

3. Identify the different types of direct marketing used by Direct Line.

4. Explain the role of social media and content in the campaign.

5. Why was Winston Wolf chosen to lead the campaign? List the advantages and possible disadvantages of using this character.

General questions

1. Write brief notes explaining the reasons why usage of direct marketing has grown in recent years.

2. List the advantages and disadvantages of using email and door-to-door media as direct marketing media.

3. How can mobile be used to create interactive opportunities within integrated campaigns?

4. Which industries might use personal selling as a primary element of their marketing communications mix?

5. What are the different types of personal selling and what are the tasks that salespeople are normally expected to accomplish?

References for Chapter 16

Andzulis, J.M., Panagopoulos, N.G. and Rapp, A. (2012) A review of social media and implications for the sales process, *Journal of Personal Selling & Sales Management*, 32(3), 305–16.

Anon (2017a) 2017 Winners, CMA, *CMA.com*, retrieved 3 April 2018 from http://the-cma.com/awards/winners2017/

Anon (2017b) Lipton: the unique position of tea in Turkey, WARC, retrieved 10 May 2018 from https://www.warc.com/content/article/mma-smarties/lipton_the_unique_position_of_tea_in_turkey/118407

Anon (2018a) Email's ROI increases, despite concerns about testing and GDPR, 8 February, *DMA website*, retrieved 10 September 2018 from https://dma.org.uk/press-release/emails-roi-increases-despite-concerns-about-testing-and-gdpr

Anon (2018b) About IKEA catalogue, IKEA.com, retrieved 10 May 2018 from https://www.ikea.com/ms/en_JP/customer_service/faq/help/about_ikea/ikea_catalogue.html

Anon (2018c) Virgin Holidays: before the destination, there's the journey, *Proximity*, retrieved 1 May 2018 from https://www.proximitylondon.com/work/before-the-destination-there-s-the-journey

Anon (2018d) Want to join the VIP Club? Pets at Home website, retrieved 10 September 2018 from https://vip.petsathome.com/

Birkinshaw, J.M. (2003) *The Blackwell Handbook of Global Management*, Boston, MA: Blackwell.

Brehmer, P.O. and Rehme, J. (2009) Proactive and reactive: drivers for key account management programmes, *European Journal of Marketing*, 43(7/8), 961–84.

Bush, V., Bush, A.J., Oakley, J. and Cicala, J.E. (2017) The sales profession as a subculture: implications for ethical decision making, *Journal of Business Ethics*, 142(3), 549–65.

Carter, M. (2017) Behind the scenes of Audi's 'Clowns', *Campaign*, 18 December 2017, retrieved 10 January 2018 from https://www.campaignlive.co.uk/article/behind-scenes-audis-clowns/1455482

Cerna, N. (2018) Top 5 reasons to use direct mail, dma.org.uk, 23 April, retrieved 10 May 2018 from https://dma.org.uk/article/top-5-reasons-to-use-direct-mail

Chakrabarty, S., Brown, G. and Widing II, R.E. (2013) Distinguishing between the roles of customer-oriented selling and adaptive selling in managing dysfunctional conflict in buyer–seller relationships, *Journal of Personal Selling & Sales Management,* 33(3), 245–60.

Cravens, D.W. (1987) *Strategic Marketing,* Homewood, IL: Irwin.

DMA (2016a) *DMA Mobile Guide,* March, dma.org.uk, retrieved 5 December 2017 from https://www.theidm.com/getmedia/03e7b74d-4208-4317-aa97-3ec1fed583bd/Mobile-DMA-guide.pdf

DMA (2016b) *DMA Social Media Guide,* March, dma.org.uk, retrieved 5 December 2017 from https://www.theidm.com/content-resources/best-practice-guides/dma-social-media-guide

DMA (2016c) *DMA Telemarketing Guide,* March, dma.org.uk, retrieved 5 December 2017 from https://www.theidm.com/getmedia/3c8bcb4d-42c3-4783-80b2-4fbe9c4fd3d5/Telemarketing-DMA-guide.pdf

DMA (2016d) *DMA Inserts Guide,* March, dma.org.uk, retrieved 5 December 2017 from https://www.theidm.com/getmedia/35ea8d39-d82d-4292-b083-2e375c0ea825/Inserts_DMA-guide.pdf

DMA (2017a) 2017 Gold Best data strategy (2017), DMA, 4 December, retrieved 10 January 2018 from https://dma.org.uk/awards/winner/2017-gold-best-data-strategy

DMA (2017b) DMA insight: consumer email tracker 2017, dma.org.uk, 12 January, retrieved 10 February 2018 from https://dma.org.uk/research/dma-insight-consumer-email-tracker-2017

DMA (2017c) Virgin Holidays Ready to Travel, 2017 Gold Travel and Leisure, dma.org.uk, 4 December 2017, retrieved 10 January 2018 from https://dma.org.uk/awards/winner/2017-gold-travel-and-leisure

DMA (2018a) GDPR, email marketing and seeking consent, dma.org.uk, 10 May, retrieved 11 May 2018 from https://dma.org.uk/article/gdpr-email-marketing-and-seeking-consent

DMA (2018b) Email's ROI increases, despite concerns about testing and GDPR, dma.org.uk, 8 February, retrieved 10 May 2018 from https://dma.org.uk/press-release/emails-roi-increases-despite-concerns-about-testing-and-gdpr

DMA Awards (2017) 2017 Bronze Best Loyalty or CRM Programme, dma.org.uk, 4 December, retrieved 31 May 2018 from https://dma.org.uk/awards/winner/2017-bronze-best-loyalty-or-crm-programme

Dwyer, F.R., Shurr, P.H. and Oh, S. (1987) Developing buyer–seller relationships, *Journal of Marketing,* 51(2), 11–28.

EU GDPR (2018) *GDPR Key Changes,* retrieved 2 May 2018 from https://www.eugdpr.org/key-changes.html

Ferguson, D.A. and Greer, C.F. (2018) Visualizing a non-visual medium through social media: the semiotics of radio station posts on Instagram, *Journal of Radio & Audio Media,* 25(1), 126–41.

Guenzi, P. (2002) Sales force activities and customer trust, *Journal of Marketing Management,* 18, 749–78.

Gwynn, S. (2017a) Army appeals to human need to belong in new integrated recruitment campaign, *Campaign,* 6 January, retrieved 16 January 2018 from https://www.campaignlive.co.uk/article/army-appeals-human-need-belong-new-integrated-recruitment-campaign/1419994

Gwynn, S. (2017b) Fanta creates elevator-crash VR experience and Snapchat-enabled packs for Halloween, *Campaign*, 20 October, retrieved 10 February from https://www.campaignlive.co.uk/article/fanta-creates-elevator-crash-vr-experience-snapchat-enabled-packs-halloween/1447940

Håkansson, H., Johansson, J. and Wootz, B. (1977) Influence tactics in buyer-seller processes, *Journal of Marketing Management*, 5(6), 319–32.

Hamwi, G.A., Rutherford, B.N., Barksdale Jr, H.C. and Johnson, J.T. (2013) Ideal versus actual number of sales calls: an application of disconfirmation theory, *Journal of Personal Selling & Sales Management*, 33(3), 307–18.

Hartmann, N.N., Wieland, H. and Vargo, S.L. (2018) Converging on a new theoretical foundation for selling, *Journal of Marketing*, 82(2), 1–18.

Hemphill, B. (2018) Trend report: data management in the 'mass personalisation' era, WARC, 18 February, retrieved 5 May 2018 from https://www.warc.com/content/article/warc-exclusive/trend_report_data_management_in_the_mass_personalisation_era/120318

Hennessey, D.H. and Jeannet, J.-P. (2003) *Global Account Management: Creating Value*, Chichester: Wiley.

Hofacker, C.F., Malthouse, E.C. and Sultan, F. (2016) Big data and consumer behavior: imminent opportunities, *Journal of Consumer Marketing*, 33(2), 89–97.

Kaplan, A. and Haenlein, M. (2010) Users of the world, unite! The challenges and opportunities of social media, *Business Horizons*, 53(1), 59–68.

Krafft, M., Arden, C.M. and Verhoef, P.C. (2017) Permission marketing and privacy concerns – why do customers (not) grant permissions? *Journal of Interactive Marketing*, 39, 39–54.

Kuechler, W. (2007) Business applications of unstructured text, *Communications of the ACM*, 50(10), 86–93.

Lacoste, S. (2018) From selling to managing strategic customers – a competency analysis, *Journal of Personal Selling & Sales Management*, 38(1), 92–122.

Millman, T. and Wilson, K. (1995) From key account selling to key account management, *Journal of Marketing Practice: Applied Marketing Science*, 1(1), 9–21.

Millman, T. and Wilson, K. (1998) Global account management: reconciling organisational complexity and cultural diversity, in *The 14th Annual Industrial Marketing and Purchasing (IMP) Group Conference*, Turku School of Economics and Business Administration.

Nunan, D. and Di Domenico, M.L. (2013) Market research and the ethics of big data, *International Journal of Market Research*, 55(4), 505–20.

Ojasalo, J. (2001) Key account management at company and individual levels in business-to-business relationships, *Journal of Business and Industrial Marketing*, 16(3), 199–220.

Pickwick, K. (2016) Pets at Home unleashes new app, *Pet Business World*, 3 August, retrieved 30 May 2018 from https://www.petbusinessworld.co.uk/news/feed/pets-at-home-unleashes-new-app

Reid, A., Pullins, E.B. and Plank, R.E. (2002) The impact of purchase situation on sales-person communication behaviors in business markets, *Industrial Marketing Management*, 31(3), 205–13.

Serviere-Munoz, L. and Mallin, M.L. (2013) How do unethical salespeople sleep at night? The role of neutralizations in the justification of unethical sales intentions, *Journal of Personal Selling & Sales Management*, 33(3), 289–306.

Shannahan, R.J., Bush, A.J., Moncrief, W.C. and Shannahan, K.L.J. (2013) Making sense of the customer's role in the personal selling process: a theory of organizing and sense making perspective, *Journal of Personal Selling & Sales Management*, 33(3), 261–75.

Swani, K., Milne, G.R., Brown, B.P., Assaf, A.G. and Donthu, N. (2017) What messages to post? Evaluating the popularity of social media communications in business versus consumer markets, *Industrial Marketing Management*, 62, 77–87.

Thayer, L. (1968) *Communication and Communication Systems*, Homewood, IL: Irwin.

WARC (2018) Toolkit 2018, WARC, retrieved 10 March 2018 from https://www.warc.com/content/article/Toolkit_2018_How_brands_can_respond_to_the_yearamp;39;s_biggest_challenges/117399

Williams, H. (2017) Instagram: content creation, dma.org.uk, 21 July, retrieved 1 January 2018 from https://dma.org.uk/article/instagram-content-creation

Wilson, K., Croom, S., Millman, T. and Weilbaker, D.C. (2000) *Global Account Management Study Report*, Southampton: The Sales Research Trust.

Sales promotion, field marketing and brand experience

Sales promotion provides an incentive to encourage consumers to buy a product or service now, rather than at some point in the future. The incentive can come in many forms, including a price deal or piggy-back gift and is seen to add value. Sales promotion techniques can be a source of advantage, one that has a short, rather than a long-run, orientation.

Field marketing provides a range of support activities for the sales force and merchandising personnel. Techniques may include sampling or research and are a key aspect of marketing communications, especially in grocery markets.

Brand experiences or experiential marketing allow organisations to create face-to-face experiences with consumers, that are physically and emotionally engaging.

Aims and learning objectives

The aims of this chapter are to consider the role and techniques of sales promotion and field marketing and to appraise their contributions to the marketing communications mix.

The learning objectives are to enable readers to:

1. understand the value and the role of sales promotions;
2. discuss the ways in which sales promotion is thought to work;
3. evaluate the merits of loyalty and retention programmes;
4. explain the different sales promotion methods and techniques;
5. explore ideas associated with field marketing and related activities;
6. describe the principles associated with brand experience.

Introduction

Sales promotion, field marketing and brand experiences offer some exciting opportunities for brand activation. This chapter will consider the characteristics of each of these tools and look at some of the ways they have been used by brands to engage audiences.

The first part of this chapter discusses sales promotion, whose main task it is to encourage the target audience to behave in a particular way, often to buy a product. Advertising, on the other hand, is usually geared towards developing market awareness. These two tools set out to accomplish tasks at each end of the attitudinal spectrum: the conative and cognitive elements respectively. Just as advertising is used to work over the long term, sales promotion can achieve upward shifts in sales in the short term.

Sales promotion offers buyers additional value, as an inducement to generate an immediate sale. These inducements can be targeted at consumers, distributors, agents and members of the sales force. A whole range of network members can benefit from the use of sales promotion.

This tool is traditionally referred to as a form of below-the-line communications because, unlike advertising, there are no commission payments from media owners with this form of communications. The costs are borne directly by the organisation initiating the activity, which in most cases is a manufacturer, producer or service provider.

The second part of this chapter considers field marketing and brand experience. Field marketing has emerged out of what was formally referred to as merchandising but now encompasses a wider range of activities. Brand experience provides an opportunity for brands to interact with consumers face-to-face, encouraging deeper engagement.

Understanding the value of sales promotions

There are many sales promotion techniques, but they all offer a direct inducement or an incentive to encourage receivers of these promotional messages to buy a product/service sooner rather than later. The inducement (e.g. price deals, coupons, premiums) is presented as an added value to the basic offering, one that is intended to encourage buyers to act 'now' rather than later. Sales promotion, therefore, is principally a means to accelerate sales. The acceleration represents the shortened period of time in which the transaction is completed relative to the time that would have elapsed had there not been a promotion. This action does not mean that an extra sale has been achieved, just that a potential future exchange is confirmed and transacted upon now.

Sales promotions consist of a wide range of tools and methods. These instruments are considered in more detail later in this chapter, but consideration of what constitutes sales promotion methods is important. In many cases, price is the determinant variable and can be used to distinguish between instruments. Sales promotions are often perceived purely as a price discounting mechanism through price deals and the use of coupons. This is not the whole picture, however, as there are many other ways in which incentives can be offered to buyers.

Reference has already been made to the idea that sales promotions are a way of providing value, and it is this value orientation that should be used when considering the nature and essential characteristics of sales promotions. Peattie and Peattie (1994) established a useful way of discriminating between price and non-price sales promotion instruments. These are set out in Table 17.1 where reference is made to sales promotions that are value-increasing and sales promotions that are value-adding.

Image 17.1 Pringles use value-adding promotions by offering prizes to augment the product offering.
Source: Designs by Jack/Shutterstock.

Table 17.1   A value orientation of sales promotions

Value element	Explanation
Value-increasing	Value is increased by offering changes to the product quantity/quality or by lowering the price. Generally used and perceived as effective over the short term.
Value-adding	Value is added by offering something to augment the fundamental product/price offering. Premiums (gifts), information or opportunities can be offered as extras and the benefits realised over different periods of time: delayed (postal premiums), accumulated (loyalty programmes) or instant (scratch and win competitions). These have the potential to add value over the longer term.

Source: Peattie and Peattie (1994).

This demarcation is important because a large amount of research into sales promotion has been based on value-increasing approaches, most notably price deals and coupons (Drechsler et al., 2017; Guissoni et al., 2018; Kivetz, and Zheng, 2017; Simpson, 2006). This tends to distort the way sales promotions are perceived and has led to some generalisations about the overall impact of this promotional discipline. There is a large range of other sales promotion instruments that add value, enhance the offering and provide opportunities to drive longer-term benefits (see Table 17.2). Research into the long-term effects of sales promotion has been limited however (Karray et al., 2017).

As a result of this diversity of sales promotion instruments it should be no surprise to learn that they are used for a wide range of reasons. Sales promotions can be targeted, with considerable precision, at particular audiences and there are three broad audiences at whom sales promotions can be targeted: consumers, members of the distribution or channel network, and the sales forces of both manufacturers and resellers. It should be remembered that the accuracy of these promotional tools means that many sub-groups within these broad groups can be reached quickly and accurately.

Table 17.2   A typology of sales promotion

Value-increasing (alters price/quantity or price/quality equation)	Value-adding (offers 'something extra' while leaving core product and price unchanged)
Discount pricing	Samples
Money-off coupons	Special features (limited editions)
Payment terms (e.g. interest-free credit)	Valued packaging
Refunds	Product trial
Guarantees	In-pack gifts
Multipack or multi-buys	In-mail gifts
Quantity increases	Piggy-back gifts
Group buying	Gift coupons
Buybacks	Information (e.g. brochure, catalogue) Clubs or loyalty programmes Competitions/prize draws

Table 17.3   Reasons for the use of sales promotions

Reason	Explanation
Reach new customers	They are useful in securing trials for new products and in defending shelf space against anticipated and existing competition.
Reduce distributor risk	The funds that manufacturers dedicate to them lower the distributor's risk in stocking new brands.
Reward behaviour	They can provide rewards for previous purchase behaviour.
Retention	They can provide interest and attract potential customers and in doing so encourage them to provide personal details for further communications activity.
Add value	They can encourage sampling and repeat purchase behaviour by providing extra value (superior to competitors' brands) and a reason to purchase.
Induce action	They can instil a sense of urgency among consumers to buy while a deal is available. They add excitement and interest at the point of purchase to the merchandising of mature and mundane products.
Preserve cash flow	Since sales promotion costs are incurred on a pay-as-you-go basis, they can spell survival for smaller, regional brands that cannot afford big advertising programmes.
Improve efficiency	They allow manufacturers to use idle capacity and to adjust to demand and supply imbalances or softness in raw material prices and other input costs, while maintaining the same list prices.
Integration	They can provide a means of linking together other tools of the promotional mix.
Assist segmentation	They allow manufacturers to price-discriminate among consumer segments that vary in price sensitivity. Most manufacturers believe that a high-list, high-deal policy is more profitable than offering a single price to all consumers. A portion of sales promotion expenditures, therefore, consists of reductions in list prices that are set for the least price-sensitive segment of the market.

The reasons why organisations use sales promotions are set out in Table 17.3.

As if in an attempt to categorise and manage this list, Lee (2002) suggests that the main reasons for the use of sales promotions can be reduced to four:

1. as a reaction to competitor activities;
2. as a form of inertia – this is what we have always done;
3. as a way of meeting short-term sales objectives;
4. as a way of meeting long-term objectives.

The first three are used widely and Lee (2002) comments that many brand owners use sales promotions as a panic measure when competitors threaten to lure customers away. Cutting prices is undoubtedly a way of prompting a short-term sales response but it can also undermine a longer-term brand strategy.

Although the overall use of certain sales promotion methods such as coupons has declined, sales promotion activities in the form of temporary price reductions (TPRs) have become the 'dominant marketing instrument of consumer packaged goods manufacturers and retailers' (Guyt and Gijsbrechts, 2014: 753). These researchers claim that price cuts supported by feature advertising are very effective. In the UK, supermarkets negotiate a price discount with suppliers, over and above the contracted price. This enables the supermarkets to offer a lower price for their customers. The additional earnings derived from the gap between a supplier's original and promotional costs are referred to as 'commercial income'. It was the accounting procedures associated with these sums that led Tesco to announce that it had overstated its profits for three years from 2011, and which led to negative media comment and reputational damage.

The use of interactive media and the integration of sales promotion within other campaigns has been successful. SMS, email, viral campaigns, apps and the Internet are being used increasingly to drive sales by providing a 'call-to-action', for a long time the province of sales promotion activities. Mobile technology has also enabled the delivery of e-coupons within particular geographic areas, such as shopping centres and malls. Viewpoint 17.1 shows how brands are building creative sales promotion campaigns around mobile.

Viewpoint 17.1

Hungerithm

Image 17.2 Snickers HUNGERITHM monitored the mood online and changed the price of Snickers
Source: WAYHOME studio/Shutterstock.

In Australia, more than half of all convenience store purchases of chocolate bars are driven by promotion. This insight led to Snickers needing to find a way to stand out from the promotion clutter with a campaign that both aligned to the brand's 'You're Not You When You're Hungry' platform, but also built excitement around price.

Snickers' 'You're Not You When You're Hungry' is based on a suggestion that when you're hungry, you get angry and that eating a Snickers bar can restore you to normal. Building on this platform, the brand created the Snickers HUNGERITHM: a hunger algorithm that monitored the mood online and adjusted the price of Snickers at 7-Eleven stores according to the mood of the Internet. This meant that the angrier the mood on the Internet, the cheaper Snickers became.

Built on a 3,000-word lexicon, Snickers HUNGERITHM analysed more than 14,000 social media posts daily and updated the price of Snickers bars over 144 times each day. This sophisticated price promotion ran 24/7 for five weeks. In this time, the price of Snickers bars changed over 5,000 times.

The price was set on ten price points which varied from AU$1.75 when the Internet mood was 'PRETTY CHILL' down to only 50 cents when the mood was 'LOSING IT'. Consumers were able to track the price online and download a barcode to their mobile to redeem against a Snickers bar.

To launch the promotion, Snickers posted a 30-second film on Facebook video and Spotify radio was used to explain the promotion. Promoted tweets were used and digital displays and signage activated the promotion in-store.

In the media and online, people were talking about the brand. Snickers mentions in social media increased by 120 per cent and the campaign delivered 71 million impressions, with more than 50 per cent being earned. 70,000 consumers visited the website to download a barcode.

The promotion campaign increased sales in 7-Eleven by 19.25 per cent and saw over 67 per cent more Snickers bars sold than in the same period the previous year. The promotion not only grew the Snickers brand, but also the category for 7-Eleven.

Snickers HUNGERITHM was reported in over 150 articles around the world in media such as Gizmodo and Mashable. The campaign has received numerous awards around the world, including five Gold Lions.

Sources: Anon (2018a); Nudd (2016); Snickers HUNGERITHM (2017).

Insight

Snickers HUNGERITHM demonstrates how sales promotion can be used as a lead campaign tool to drive customer engagement. While the campaign was in essence a price promotion, the interactive nature of the coupon offer built excitement. The value of this promotion reached beyond the sales uplift it achieved, delivering a significant level of earned media for the brand.

Question: Considering Peattie and Peattie's (1994) value orientation of sales promotions explained in Table 17.1, explain whether Snickers HUNGERITHM was a value-increasing or value-adding promotion. Justify your answer.

Task: Find a recent example of both a value-increasing and a value-adding sales promotion. List the reasons why you think the brands have used each type of promotion.

The role of sales promotion

The role of sales promotion has changed significantly over recent years. At one time, when the largest proportion of communications budgets was normally allocated to advertising, the role of sales promotion was essentially behavioural, that is selling. Now, at a time when advertising is not always the dominant discipline, the role of sales promotion has become oriented towards engagement. This can be achieved through adding value to a brand as well as still selling product. In situations where sales promotion has assumed the focus of the communications spend, for reasons that are set out below, the role is also to help integrate aspects of a campaign. This is particularly evident in consumer markets that are mature, have reached a level of stagnation, and where price and promotion work are the few ways of inducing brand-switching behaviour.

Short termism

The short-term financial focus of many developed economies has garnered a managerial climate, one that is geared to short-term performance and evaluation, over periods as short as 12 weeks. To accomplish this, communications tools are required that work quickly and impact directly upon sales. Many see this as leading to an erosion of the brand franchise.

Managerial accountability

Following on from the previous reason is the increased pressure on marketing managers to be accountable for their communications expenditure. The results of sales promotion activities are more easily justified and understood than those associated with advertising. The number of codes activated online and the number of bonus packs purchased can be calculated quickly and easily, with little room for error or misjudgement. Advertising, however, cannot be so easily measured in either the short or the long term. The impact of this is that managers can relate the promotional expenditure to the bottom line much more comfortably with sales promotion than with advertising.

Brand performance

Technological advances have enabled retailers to track brand performance more effectively. This in turn means that manufacturers can be drawn into agreements that promulgate in-store promotional activity at the expense of other more traditional forms of mass-media promotion. Developments in technology have facilitated tighter buying, delivery, stock control and tracking of merchandise, meaning that brand managers can be held responsible much more quickly for below-par performance.

Brand expansion

As brand quality continues to improve and as brands proliferate on the shelves of increasingly larger supermarkets, so the number of decisions that a consumer has to make also increases. Faced with multiple-brand decisions and a reduced amount of time to complete the shopping expedition, the tension associated with the shopping experience has increased considerably over the last decade.

Promotions make decision-making easier for consumers: they simplify a potentially difficult process. Thus, as brand choice increases, so the level of shopping convenience falls. The conflict this causes can be resolved by the astute use of sales promotions.

Some feel that the cognitive shopper selects brands that offer increased value, which makes decision-making easier and improves the level of convenience associated with the shopping experience. However, should there be promotions on two offerings from an individual's repertoire then the decision-making is not necessarily made easier.

Competition for shelf space

The continuing growth in the number of brands launched and the fragmentation of consumer markets mean that retailers have to be encouraged to make shelf space available. Sales promotions have helped manufacturers win valuable shelf space and assist retailers to attract increased levels of store traffic and higher utilisation of limited resources, but this approach is not always viable today.

The credibility of this promotional tool is low, as it is obvious to the receiver what the intention is of using sales promotion messages. However, because of the prominent and pervasive nature of the tool, consumers and members of the trade understand and largely accept the direct sales approach. Sales promotion is not a tool that hides its intentions, nor does it attempt to be devious (which is not allowed, by regulation).

The absolute costs of sales promotion are low, but the real costs need to be evaluated once a campaign has finished and all redemptions received and satisfied. The relative costs can be high, as not only do the costs of the premium or price discount need to be determined, but also the associated costs of additional transportation, lost profit, storage and additional time spent organising and administering a sales promotion campaign need to be accounted for.

In its favour, sales promotion allows for a high degree of control. Management is able to decide just when and where a sales promotion will occur and also estimate the sales effect. Sales promotions can be turned on and off quickly and adjusted to changed market conditions.

The intended message is invariably the one that is received, as there is relatively little scope for it to be corrupted or damaged in transmission. However, this view needs to be tempered by some of the problems companies have experienced by not thinking through the sales promotion exercise in the first place, only to find themselves exposed to exploitation and financial embarrassment. Sales promotion campaigns can backfire. When KFC offered a downloadable coupon that was endorsed by Oprah Winfrey, franchises could not keep pace with demand, especially as KFC had not placed any control on or limit to the number of coupons that could be downloaded.

Scholars' paper 17.1
Double jeopardy

Ehrenberg, A.S.C., Goodhardt, G.J. and Barwise, T.P. (1990) Double jeopardy revisited, *Journal of Marketing*, 54 (July), 82–91.

The double jeopardy phenomenon is well established. This paper describes and explains the wide range of empirical evidence for the existence of double jeopardy, the various theories that account for its occurrence, the issues and practical implications.

See also:

Jones, P.J. (1990) The double jeopardy of sales promotions, *Harvard Business Review*, September/October, 145–52.

Sales promotion plans: the objectives

The objectives of using this tool are sales-oriented and geared to stimulating buyers either to use a product for the first time or to encourage use on a routine basis. As Viewpoint 17.1 highlights however, brands are increasingly using sales promotion to connect with customers and are used as part of a wider integrated campaign.

One objective of sales promotion activity is to prompt buyers into action, to initiate a series of behaviours that result in long-run purchase activity. These actions can be seen to occur in the conative stage of the attitudinal set. They reflect high or low involvement, and indicate whether cognitive processing and persuasion occur via the central or peripheral routes of the ELM (see Chapter 13). If the marketing objectives include the introduction of a new product or intention to enter a new market, then the key objective associated with low-involvement decisions and peripheral route processing is to stimulate trial use as soon as possible. When high-involvement decisions and central route processing are present, then sales promotions need to be withheld until a suitable level of attitudinal development has been undertaken by public relations and advertising activities.

If a product is established in a market, then a key objective should be to use sales promotions to stimulate an increase in the number of purchases made by current customers and to attract users from competing products (see Figure 17.1). The objectives, therefore, are either to increase consumption for established products or to stimulate trial by encouraging new buyers to use a product. Once this has been agreed, the desired trial and usage levels need to be determined for each of the target audiences. Before discussing these aspects, it is necessary first to review the manner in which sales promotions are thought to influence the behaviour of individuals.

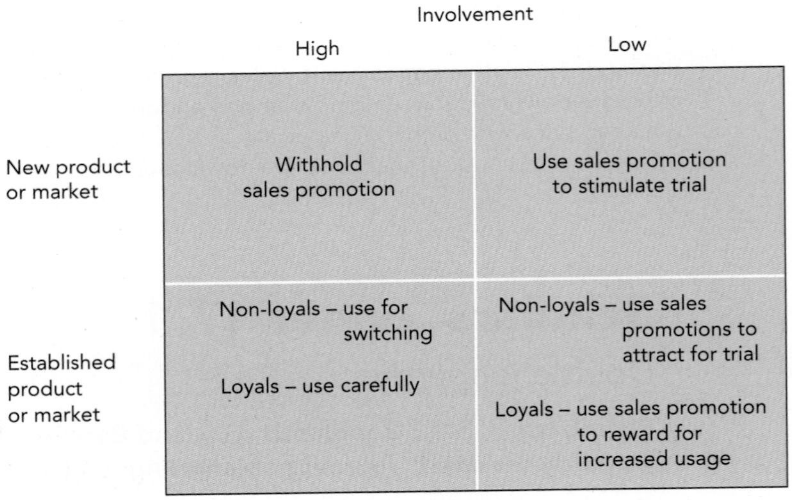

	Involvement	
	High	**Low**
New product or market	Withhold sales promotion	Use sales promotion to stimulate trial
Established product or market	Non-loyals – use for switching Loyals – use carefully	Non-loyals – use sales promotions to attract for trial Loyals – use sales promotion to reward for increased usage

Figure 17.1 A sales promotion objectives grid

An overview of how sales promotions work

If the overriding objectives of sales promotions are to accelerate or bring forward future sales, the implication is that a behavioural change is required by the receiver for the sales promotion to be effective. The establishment of new behaviour patterns is the preferred outcome. If sales promotions are to work over the longer term, that is to bring about repeat purchase behaviour, then the new behaviour patterns need to be learned and adopted on a permanent basis.

This is a complex task, and is referred to by behaviourists as shaping. The behaviourists' view is advocated by Rothschild and Gaidis (1981). They suggest that by breaking the overall task into its constituent parts a series of smaller sequential tasks can be learned. When the successive actions are aggregated the new desired pattern of behaviour emerges. This view emphasises the impact of external stimuli in changing people's behaviour.

The cognitive view of the way sales promotions operate is based on the belief that consumers internally process relevant information about a sales promotion, including those of past experiences, and make a reasoned decision in the light of the goals and objectives that individuals set for themselves.

The ELM suggests that individuals using the peripheral route will only consider simplistic cues, such as display boards and price reduction signs. Individuals using the central route of the ELM have a higher need for information and will develop promotional signals to evaluate the value represented by the relative price and the salient attributes of the promoted product, before making a decision (Inman et al., 1990).

Related to this approach are ideas about how price promotions work. The use of these is widespread as it is regarded as the optimal way of generating short-term sales increases. It has been assumed that it works because it discourages purchase processing deliberation. This is because paying a lower price removes the need for additional thought or consideration of any other purchase-related factors (Aydinli et al., 2014). Consumer purchase decisions are made through the assimilation of two types of thinking. The first is automatic and loaded with emotions and feelings. The second is deliberate and controlled, dominated by access to memory and previously stored experiences and information. Aydinli et al. (2014) suggest that the switch from the former to the latter is triggered by the need for decision-making accuracy in order to avoid the risks and consequences arising from a poor decision. They argue that price promotions can trigger this switch.

An alternative view considers the role of information processing and the mental budgets people make when shopping. This involves the psychological allocation of money to different account categories, such as food, clothing, drink and entertainment, in a person's mind. Once each mental budget is exhausted consumers resist further spending in that category. However, there are opportunities to trade off an under spend in one category to support additional purchases in another.

Research also shows that consumers use mental budgeting processes for grocery shopping trips. These are expectations based on experiences developed through previous shopping excursions. From these experiences Stilley et al. (2010a) suggest that consumers allocate an itemised portion of their mental budget for planned, anticipated brand or category purchases. Consumers also allocate a proportion of their mental budget for in-store, unplanned decisions, as if they are preparing to take advantage of store suggestions and promotional offers. Of the many issues that arise, one concerns what shoppers do with what might be saved from both the planned and unplanned mental budgets and whether this influences their purchasing activities and willingness to take advantage of sales promotions.

Reinforcing work by Heilman et al. (2002), Stilley et al. (2010b) agree that savings derived from the planned mental list 'only increases spending on unplanned items after in-store slack is depleted'. Another finding is that some promotions can encourage unplanned purchases, but savings from other promotions are just taken into the in-store slack. Stilley et al. (2010b) suggest that there are benefits for retailers arising from an understanding of mental budgets. For example, store layout should incorporate the placement of displays of full-price, high-margin unplanned items early in the path a customer takes around a store. Other low-margin unplanned promotional items should be placed later in the store path.

The main difference between the views of the behaviourists and those of the cognitive school of thought is that the former stress the impact of externally generated stimuli, whereas the latter emphasise the complexity of internal information processing.

The increasing proportion of budgets being allocated to sales promotions, and temporary price reductions (TPRs) in particular, has prompted concern about the costs and overall impact of these activities. It might be reasonable to expect that the sales curve following a price-based promotion would look like that depicted in Figure 17.2. There is plenty of evidence that sales volumes can be increased following use of a TPR (Ehrenberg, 2000). However, a long-term upward shift in demand is unrealistic, particularly in mature markets. Extra stock is being transferred to consumers, and therefore they have more than they require for a normal purchase cycle. Ehrenberg suggests that most people who use TPRs are actually infrequent purchasers of a given category. Research suggests that these types of promotion do not attract new buyers.

The graph shown in Figure 17.3 is more likely to occur with sales volume falling in the period when buyers are loaded with stock and temporarily removed from the market. However, Dawes (2004) found that there were as many buyers in a market in the period following a promotion as there were when the TPR was running.

Promotional activity does not take place in a vacuum with new products: competitors will be attracted and some customers lost to competitive offerings; in mature markets, non-loyals will take advantage of a sales promotion and then revert to competitors' sales promotions when they re-enter the market. So, the third scenario is shown in Figure 17.4. The result is that overall demand for a brand *may* be reduced owing to the combined effects of competitive promotional activity. However, Dawes found that price promotions have a neutral impact on a brand, with the benefits of volume increases being countered by the consequent fall in profitability. It may be, therefore, that the second scenario is the more accurate interpretation.

Promotions give a brand presence through extra facings, but they also incur difficulties for retailers. This is because of the impact promotions can have on the relatively stable

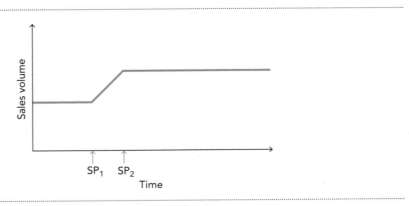

Figure 17.2 Expected response to a sales promotion event: SP_1 is the start of the event; SP_2 is the end

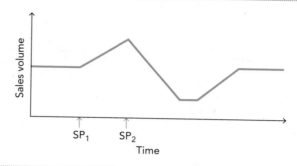

Figure 17.3 Realistic response to a sales promotion event

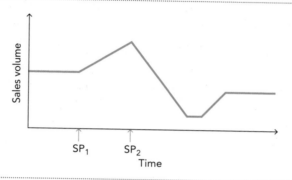

Figure 17.4 The destructive effect of competitive sales promotions

logistics associated with normal trading patterns. The capacity that stores and lorries have is finite and known. Goods are moved from warehouses, with lorries to stores whose sales performance is known. If a promotion is added to this mix these logistics patterns are thrown into temporary chaos as both the stores and the transportation create room for the promotion at the expense of other items and higher margins.

These activities suggest that the relationship between the members of the network is market-oriented rather than relational. However, many of these extra costs are unknown, and the resellers are unaware of the costs they are absorbing as a result of the deal. In the future, resellers and manufacturers should work together on such promotions and attempt to uncover all the costs involved to ensure that the exercise is successful for both parties.

Some retailers choose not to use price promotions of any kind as they see them as unfair and argue there are hidden costs associated with discounting. For example, US e-commerce company Tuft & Needle believe every customer should pay the same price for products and argue promotions are unfair to those customers who have paid the full price (Maridou, 2017). They also argue that there are hidden costs associated with price discounting, such as additional manpower to deal with increased orders, and an increased likelihood of products being returned (Maridou, 2017).

Not only the short-term costs associated with a sales promotion but also the long-term costs must be evaluated. Jones (1990) refers to this as the double jeopardy of sales promotions. He argues that manufacturers who participate extensively in short-term sales promotions, mainly for defensive reasons, do so at the expense of profit. The generation of sales volume and market share is at the expense of profit. The long-term effects are equally revealing. As the vast majority of sales promotions are TPRs, the opportunity to build a consumer franchise, where the objective is the development of brand identity and loyalty, is negated. Evidence shows that as soon as a sales promotion is switched off, so any increased sales are also terminated until the next promotion. The retaliatory effect that TPRs have on competitors does nothing to stabilise what Jones calls volatile demand, where the only outcome, for some products, is decline and obscurity.

Sales promotions can lead consumers to depend on the presence of a promotion before committing to a purchase. If the preferred product does not carry a coupon, premium or TPR, then they may switch to a competitor's product that does offer some element of increased value. A related issue concerns the speed at which sales promotions are reduced following the introduction of a new product. If the incentives are removed too quickly, it is probable that consumers will have been unable to build a relationship with the product. If the incentives are sustained for too long, then it is possible that consumers have only identified a product by the value of the incentive, not the value of the product itself. The process by which a sales promotion is removed from a product is referred to as fading, and its rate can be crucial to the successful outcome of a product launch and a sales promotion activity.

The use of free-trial offers is common among many service companies, such as video streaming services (Netflix). These are used to encourage risk-free trial before signing up as a paid-for customer. Research by Datta et al. (2015) found that the higher churn rate associated with free-trial customers makes them worth nearly 60 per cent less than regular customers. Free-trial customers have underdeveloped relationships with the firm, and are more uncertain about the service benefits. This, according to the researchers, makes them more likely to rely on marketing communications and their own usage behaviour when deciding whether to retain the service. This indicates that compared with regular customers, free-trial customers are considerably more responsive to direct marketing, advertising, flat-rate usage and pay-per-use usage. Direct marketing and advertising are more appropriate disciplines to reach free-trial customers. Companies should therefore remind free-trial customers about their usage rates, especially when they are high, as this should encourage them to retain the service.

Viewpoint 17.2
Getting to know Joe

Image 17.3 Customers could win Joe the Mug
Source: Nestlé.

Following on from the success of the KitKat personalised pack promotion in 2017, which saw 57,000 prizes given away to customers, the brand launched Joe the Mug.

KitKat has always been associated with hot drinks and so giving customers the chance to win Joe the Mug, a limited edition, heat-reactive mug that displays different personalities when hot drinks are added was the perfect brand promotion.

The promotion gave customers the chance to win one of the special 50,000 mugs. By purchasing one of the promotional KitKat packs, consumers could enter the promotion to win a Joe the Mug, which came to life with the addition of a hot drink to reveal eight different designs.

The promotion was supported with a dedicated microsite, where customers could spend time 'getting to know Joe' through a 'Which Joe are You?' quiz. The fun quiz asked customers five questions, such as 'What do you spend your break doing?' The results matched customers to the one of Joe's eight personalities that best suited their break. Customers were given results of 'Glam Joe', 'Original Joe', 'Flirty Joe', 'Brainy Joe', 'Dapper Joe', 'Dreamy Joe', 'Cheeky Joe', or 'Chatty Joe'.

The digital support for the on-pack promotion helped activate the campaign across social platforms and customers used a gamified Snapchat filter to engage further with the campaign. Additional support came from online web banners.

Sources: Anon (n.d.a); Anon (n.d.b).

Image 17.4 Joe the Mug had eight different personalities
Source: Nestlé.

Image 17.5 The promotion was supported with a dedicated microsite
Source: Nestlé.

Insight

The KitKat Joe the Mug promotion provides a good example of how a non-price-based promotion can offer value to brands. The development of a microsite and activations across social platforms provided opportunities for brand engagement with customers. In the longer term, the promotion further aligned KitKat and hot drinks, helping KitKat to continue to own the break occasion.

Question: What was the goal of Joe the Mug promotion? Use Table 17.4 to guide your answer.

Task: Find three other examples of on-pack promotions. Using Table 17.4 as a guide, list the principal audiences and sales promotion goals for each promotion.

Scholars' paper 17.2
Inside promotions

Guissoni, L.A., Sanchez, J.M. and Rodrigues, J.M. (2018) Price and in-store promotions in an emerging market, *Marketing Intelligence & Planning*, **36(4), 498–511.**

The authors provide an account of the effects on sales of price and in-store temporary displays of promoted products in Brazil, an emerging economy. The study identifies the structural format of the store and the visibility of the temporary displays of promoted products are important considerations for the success of sales promotions.

See also:

Stilley, K.M., Inman, J.J. and Wakefield, K.L. (2010b) Spending on the fly: mental budgets, promotions, and spending behavior, *Journal of Marketing*, 74(3), 34–47.

Sales promotions: methods and techniques

As established earlier, sales promotions seek to offer buyers additional value, as an inducement to generate an immediate sale. These inducements can be targeted at consumers, distributors, agents and members of the sales force. A whole range of network members can benefit from the use of sales promotion.

The range and variety of techniques that are used to add value and induce a sale sooner rather than later mean that different techniques work in different ways to achieve varying objectives. Here, consideration is given to the range of tasks that need to be accomplished among two key audiences: resellers and consumers.

The range of techniques and methods used to add value to offerings is enormous but there are growing doubts about the effectiveness and profitability associated with some sales promotions. Sales promotions used by manufacturers to communicate with resellers are aimed at encouraging resellers either to try new products or to purchase more of the ones they currently stock. To do this, trade allowances, in various guises, are the principal means.

The majority of sales promotions are those used by manufacturers to influence consumers. Again, the main tasks are to encourage trial or increase product purchase. A range of techniques, from sampling and coupons to premiums, contests and sweepstakes, are all used with varying levels of success, but there has been a distinct shift away from traditional promotional instruments to the use of interactive media in order to reflect consumers' preferences and media behaviour.

The following two tables set out information about key sales promotion techniques used between manufacturers and their intermediary partners, and with consumers. It should also be appreciated that sales promotions are used by retailers to influence consumers and between manufacturers and dealer sales force teams, although these are not itemised here. Table 17.4 depicts information about the audiences and reasons for using sales promotions. Table 17.5 provides information about the various sales promotion methods and techniques.

Group-buying agents such as Groupon, Treatwell and LivingSocial have spearheaded the rise of this form of discounting. Clark (2010) refers to Groupon as the leading provider, which originated in Chicago where coupon use is a natural part of everyday buying, unlike the UK and Europe where coupon usage is a minority activity and often favoured by deal chasers. Groupon has 53.2 million users, of which approximately 5 million are in the UK (Wood, 2014).

Table 17.4   Principal audiences and sales promotion goals

Audience	Objectives	Explanation	Methods
Manufacturers to resellers	For new products: *Sampling and trial*	For new products it is important to create adequate channels of distribution in anticipation of consumer demand. The task of marketing communications is to encourage resellers to distribute a new product and to establish trial behaviour.	Allowances: *Buying Count and recount* *Buy back Advertising*
	For established products: *Usage*	One of the key objectives of manufacturers is to motivate distributors to allocate increased shelf space to a product thereby (possibly) reducing the amount of shelf space allocated to competitors. The task of marketing communications, therefore, is to encourage resellers to buy and display increased amounts of the manufacturer's products and establish greater usage.	Dealer contests Dealer conventions and meetings Training and support
Manufacturers to consumers	For new users: *Stimulate trial*	Before customers buy a product they need to test or trial the product. Through the use of coupons, sampling and other techniques (see below), sales promotions have become an important element in the new product launch and introduction processes.	Sampling Coupons Price offs Bonus packs Refunds and rebates
	For established customers: *Increase product usage*	In mature markets customers need to be encouraged to keep buying a product. This can be achieved by attracting users from competitive brands, by converting non-users and by developing new uses.	Premiums Contests and sweepstakes

Table 17.5   Principal audiences and sales promotion methods

Audience	Method	Explanation
Manufacturers to resellers	Advertising allowance	A percentage allowance is given against a reseller's purchases during a specified campaign period. Instead of providing an allowance against product purchases, an allowance can be provided against the cost of an advertisement or campaign.
	Buying allowance	In return for specific orders between certain dates, a reseller will be entitled to a refund or allowance of x per cent off the regular case or carton price.
	Count and recount	Manufacturers may require resellers to clear old stock before a new or modified product is introduced. One way this can be achieved is to encourage resellers to move stock out of storage and into the store. The count and recount method provides an allowance for each case shifted into the store during a specified period of time.
	Buy back	Purchases made after the count and recount scheme (up to a maximum of the count and recount) are entitled to an allowance to encourage stores to replenish their stocks (with the manufacturer's product and not that of a competitor).
	Dealer contests	Used to hold a reseller's attention by focusing them on a manufacturer's products, not a competitor's.
	Dealer conventions and meetings	These enable informal interaction between a manufacturer and its resellers and can aid the development and continuance of good relations between the two parties.
	Training and support	This is an important communications function, especially when products are complex or subject to rapid change, as in IT markets. This can build stronger relationships and manufacturers have greater control over the messages that the resellers transmit.

(continued)

Table 17.5 Principal audiences and sales promotion methods (*Continued*)

Audience	Method	Explanation
Manufacturers to consumers	Sampling	Although very expensive, sampling is an effective way of getting people to try a product. Trial-size versions of the actual product are given away free. Sampling can also take the form of demonstrations, trial-size packs that have to be purchased or free use for a certain period of time.
	Coupons	These are vouchers or certificates that entitle consumers to a price reduction on a particular product. The value of the reduction or discount is set and the coupon must be presented at purchase.
	Price offs	These are a direct reduction in the purchase price, with the offer clearly labelled on the package or point of purchase display.
	Bonus packs	These offer more product for the regular pack price, typically a 2 for 1 offer. They provide direct impact at the point of purchase and represent extra value.
	Refunds and rebates	Used to invite consumers to send in a proof of purchase and in return receive a cash refund.
	Premiums	Items of merchandise that are offered free or at a low cost in return for product purchase.
	Contests and sweepstakes	A contest is a customer competition based on skill or ability. Entry requires a proof of purchase and winners are judged against a set of predetermined criteria. A sweepstake determines winners by chance and proof of purchase is not required. There is no judging and winners are drawn at random.

Retention programmes

Despite questions about the use of sales promotions to build loyalty, the growth of retention programmes has been a significant promotional development in recent years, as demonstrated by the Tesco and Nectar programmes. The growth of retention, or loyalty, schemes has been encouraged by the widespread use of swipe cards. Users are rewarded with points each time a purchase is made. This is referred to as a 'points accrual programme', whereby loyal users are able to build up the necessary points, which are stored (often) on a card, and 'cashed in' at a later date for gifts or merchandise. The benefit for the company supporting the scheme is that the promised rewards motivate customers to accrue more points and in doing so increase their switching costs, effectively locking them into the loyalty programme and preventing them from moving to a competitor brand. Smart cards, which have a small microprocessor embedded, can record enormous amounts of information, which is updated each time a purchase is made. However, some people have so many cards that a large number of loyalty cards are never used, or even scrapped.

Not only have loyalty schemes for frequent flyers been very successful, but the cards are also used to track individual travellers. Airlines are able to offer cardholders particular services, such as special airport lounges and magazines. Through its links to a database, the card also enables a traveller's favourite seat and dietary requirements to be offered. In addition, the regular accumulation of air miles fosters continuity, and hence loyalty, through which business travellers can reward themselves with leisure travel.

Perhaps the attention given to loyalty and retention issues is misplaced because marketing is concerned with customer management, and that involves the identification, anticipation and satisfaction of customer needs. If these needs are being met properly it might be reasonable to expect that customers would return anyway, reducing the need for overt 'loyalty' programmes. The withdrawal by Debenhams from the Nectar scheme in 2008 was made in order to better reward store-card holders, at a time when the trading environment was getting tighter. There is an argument that these schemes are important not because of the loyalty aspect, but because the programme allows for the collection of up-to-date customer information and then the use of the data to make savings in the supply chain.

It is interesting to note that there is little evidence to support the notion that sales promotions, and in particular the use of premiums, are capable of encouraging loyalty, whether that be defined as behavioural and/or attitudinal. Loyalty schemes do enable organisations to monitor and manage stock, use direct marketing to cross- and up-sell to customers, and manage their portfolio in order to consolidate/increase customer spending in a store. Whether loyalty is being developed by encouraging buyers to make repeat purchases, or whether the schemes are merely sales promotion techniques that encourage extended and consistent purchasing patterns, is debatable. Customer retention is a major issue and a lot of emphasis, possibly misplaced, has been given to loyalty schemes as a means of achieving retention targets.

There are views that loyalty schemes not only are misguided but have cost industry a huge amount of money. Hastings and Price (2004), for example, have expressed strong views about the notion and viability of so-called loyalty and points-based schemes. They claim that loyalty schemes are misunderstood for two main reasons. First, there is the assumption that loyalty can be bought when, like love, true loyalty can only be given. Second, there is an assumption that points-based schemes can be profit centres.

A major study involving in excess of 600,000 in-depth consumer interviews identified different levels of loyalty and concluded that significant financial returns were only gained when the highest level of loyalty was achieved (Hallberg, 2004). These levels of loyalty are set out in Figure 17.5. Hallberg (2004) refers to the impact of emotional loyalty, a non-purchase measurement of attachment to a brand:

- At the 'no presence' level consumers are unaware of a brand and so there is no emotional loyalty.

- At the 'presence' level there is awareness but emotional loyalty is minimal.

- At the 'relevance and performance' level consumers begin to feel that the brand is acceptable in terms of meeting their needs.

- At the 'advantage' level consumers should feel that the brand is superior with regard to a particular attribute.

- At the 'bonding' level emotional loyalty is at its highest because consumers feel the brand has several unique properties. They love the brand.

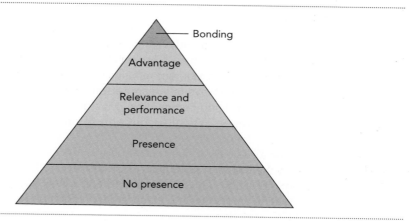

Figure 17.5 The brand emotional loyalty pyramid
Source: Hallberg (2004). Used with permission.

Table 17.6   Five loyalty trends

Trend	Explanation
Ubiquity	Loyalty programmes have proliferated in most mature markets and many members have little interest in them other than the functionality of points collection. Managers are trying to reduce communications costs by moving the scheme online but also need to be innovative.
Coalition	Schemes run by a number of different organisations in order to share costs, information and branding (e.g. Nectar) appear to be the dominant structure industry model.
Imagination	Opportunities to exploit technologies and niche markets will depend on creativity and imagination in order to get customer data to feed into the loyalty system.
Wow	To overcome consumer lethargy and boredom with loyalty schemes, many rewards in future will be experiential, emotional, unique in an attempt to appeal to life stage and aspirational lifestyle goals – wow them. Differentiate to stand out.
Analysis	To be competitive the use of customer data analytics and business intelligence is becoming critical, if only to feed CRM programmes. Collect and analyse customer information effectively.

Source: Adapted from Capizzi et al. (2004).

Loyalty schemes are exponentially effective when consumers reach the bonding stage. Although sales generally increase the further up the pyramid consumers move, it is only at the 'bonding' stage that sales start to reflect the emotional attachment people feel towards the brand.

There is a proliferation of loyalty programmes to the extent that Capizzi et al. (2004) suggest that the market is mature. They also argue that five clear trends within the loyalty market can be identified (see Table 17.6).

These trends suggest that successful sales promotion schemes are those that enable members to perceive significant value associated with their continued association with a scheme. That value will be driven by schemes run by groups of complementary brands, which use technology to understand customer dynamics and communications that complement their preferred values. The medium-term goal might be that these schemes should reflect customers' different relationship needs and recognise the different loyalty levels desired by different people.

Field marketing

Field marketing provides support for the sales force and merchandising personnel together with data collection and research facilities for clients.

Although this element remains important, field marketing has evolved so that it now encompasses ways in which people can experience a brand. This reflects an overall shift in marketing communications from one based largely on developing brand values through an emotional proposition to one that emphasises changes in behaviour and calls-to-action.

At a basic level, field marketing is concerned with getting free samples of a product into the hands of potential customers. At another level, field marketing is about creating an interaction between the brand and a new customer. At yet another level, it is about creating a personal and memorable brand experience for potential customers. The key to field marketing is the flexibility of services provided to clients. Sales forces can be hired on short-term contracts and promotional teams can be contracted to launch new products, provide samples (both in-store and door-to-door) and undertake a range of other activities that are not part of an organisation's normal promotion activities.

Table 17.7 sets out the range of activities undertaken in the name of field marketing (FM). To some extent it consists of tasks pulled from some of the five main promotional tools, repackaged and presented under a more contemporary title; for example, door-to-door and sales activities from personal selling, merchandising from both personal selling and sales promotion, sampling (which is a straight sales promotion task) and event marketing from public relations. Field marketing is a response to market needs and is a development practitioners have pioneered to fulfil a range of customer needs that presumably had not been adequately satisfied.

Perhaps merchandising lies at the root of field marketing. This is concerned with the presentation and display of products in-store, in order to maximise impact, attention and 'pick-up' opportunities. Referred to as point-of-sale (POS), these activities occur where a decision to purchase is made – normally this will be in the aisles.

POS is essentially about persuasion. This might be to reinforce a consumer's brand decision at the point of purchase or about using sampling to encourage customers to switch brands.

Merchandising ensures brands are visible in-store. Of central interest in merchandising is how and where products should be allocated within a scarce resource, namely the capacity and location of shelf space. Academics are attracted by the theoretical, problem-solving and statistical issues, while practitioners and retailers, seek increased efficiency and profitability.

There has been extensive research, most of which concludes that the location of a product on a shelf has no major effect on the sales of a product (Russell and Urban, 2010). However, research by Drèze et al. (1994), cited by Russell and Urban, found that the 'vertical and horizontal positioning on the shelves for a number of (product) categories, led to an average difference in sales of 59 per cent from the worst to the best position on the shelves. They also found that half of the categories had increased sales on the end of the display, while the other half favored the center'.

Field marketing can take place virtually anywhere, but common locations are in shopping centres and supermarkets where footfall is greatest. Typically these events require agency staff to dress up in an eye-catching way in order to form associations between the clothing and the brand (e.g. dressed in Mexican ponchos and sombreros to give out free samples of Pot Noodle in a supermarket). It is regarded as a cost-effective way of demonstrating a product,

Table 17.7 Essential features of field marketing activities

Core activities	Essential features
Sales	Provides sales force personnel on either a temporary or a permanent basis. This is for business-to-business and direct to the public.
Merchandising	Generates awareness and brand visibility through point-of-purchase placement, in-store staff training, product displays and leaflets.
Sampling	Mainly to the public at shopping centres and station concourses but also for business-to-business purposes.
Auditing	Used for checking stock availability, pricing and positioning.
Mystery shopping	Provides feedback on the level and quality of service offered by retail- and services-based staff.
Event marketing	Used to create drama and to focus attention at sports events, open-air concerts and festivals. Essentially theatrical or entertainment-based.
Door-to-door (home calls)	A form of selling where relatively uncomplex products and services can be sold through home visits.

Source: Adapted from McLuhan (2000). Reproduced from *Marketing* magazine with the permission of the copyright owner, Haymarket Business Publications Limited.

getting stand-out and creating opportunities for customers to trial a product with minimum risk. Field marketing is also used to sell relatively complex products where a degree of explanation is required (e.g. computers, broadband, TV and related products, or mobile phones).

One of the reasons field marketing can take place at any location is due to digital technology. The use of apps and cloud technology in particular are helping to change the way in which the business works. Originally field marketing was about stock control and shelf positioning. These are essentially low-level jobs. The use of technology now allows field force agents to engage with in-store employees and this is enabled by real-time data and analysis. Through cloud technologies data can be accessed on demand. Without the need to manage hardware and software, field agents can present training materials, web-based instruction tools, the latest product information, and even use tablets to present data about sales of brands in similar stores (Ryan, 2012). The use of real-time sales data allows for the identification of stores that show stock irregularities. Staff can then be sent out to the stores and locations where a problem needs to be fixed.

The second development, the use of apps (with tablets and smartphones), helps agents check that stores are stocking and presenting brands in the right way. Now they are able to photograph merchandising on shelves and record data. So, although field marketing is a more sophisticated business than it was originally, the operating margins have become much tighter, in turn generating a need to find alternative high-margin activities.

One way around this margin issue is to reduce costs, and the use of apps is a route forward some agencies are pursuing. So, rather than give a smartphone and an app to a paid agent, the new approach is to encourage the public to go into stores and get them to take pictures of stock and record simple information about the way products are displayed. They then upload the data for analysis by brand owners, and get paid a small fee for their time and contribution. In a sense this is a variant on crowdsourcing and has raised alarm bells within the industry. Issues about consistency, coverage and ethics are voiced by those against this development. For field marketing agencies and their clients, costs are halved.

Viewpoint 17.3
Van Gogh's Bedrooms

Image 17.6 The Art Institute of Chicago recreated Van Gogh's bedroom
Source: Tribune Content Agency LLC/Alamy Stock Photo.

The Art Institute of Chicago (AIC) is one of America's biggest art museums and a top tourist attraction in Chicago. While the museum is one of the most popular destinations for visitors to Chicago, local Chicagoans were less frequent visitors. Visitor statistics showed that 75 per cent of visitors to AIC were from outside the city and insight suggested that Chicagoans saw the museum as intimidating, preferring instead to spend a day out at attractions such as the zoo.

To change perceptions of the museum and encourage Chicagoans to visit an upcoming Van Gogh exhibition featuring the artist's iconic bedroom paintings, AIC launched a unique experience in partnership with Airbnb, 'Van Gogh's Bedrooms: Let yourself in'.

To connect visitors with the artist's work and life, AIC brought to life Van Gogh's iconic 1888 bedroom painting, literally. AIC created an exact reconstruction of Van Gogh's bedroom and invited visitors to spend a night in the room. This meant that visitors could not only see Van Gogh's famous bedroom in his paintings, but were also able to experience his bedroom for themselves.

The experience was launched with a single media post announcing the first block of nights available for booking and was featured on Airbnb, where visitors could book a night in the room.

Rooms were made available in blocks of three to four weeks and each block sold out within minutes of being released.

'Van Gogh's Bedrooms' was the highest attended exhibition for the Art Institute of Chicago in 15 years. Pre-sale tickets increased by 250 per cent and in the first six weeks of opening, the exhibition saw on average of 4,700 visitors every day. The exhibition had 54 per cent more visitors than previous exhibits and some daily attendance numbers were 70 per cent higher than other shows.

Importantly, the exhibition saw an increase in local visitor numbers, with local attendance increasing by 97 per cent. In total the exhibition attracted 234,415 Chicagoans, over 50 per cent of the total visitors for the exhibition.

From an investment cost of $31,000 to build Van Gogh's bedroom replica, the campaign earned The Art Institute of Chicago $6 million in earned media. The campaign was covered in media in over 100 countries and resulted in 623 million earned media impressions. The campaign has won a number of awards for creativity, including seven Gold Lions and seven Silver Lions at Cannes 2017.

The experience drove visitor attendance and yielded $6.6 million in museum revenue, 36 per cent higher than the museum's last most successful exhibit.

Sources: Griner (2017); Van Gogh's Bedrooms: Let Yourself In (2017); Wohl (2016).

Insight

The campaign gave visitors the chance to experience a memorable night's stay in 'Van Gogh's Bedroom'. Creating this unusual experience encouraged sharing and drove online conversations. For visitors to the exhibit, the experience connected them with Van Gogh in a personal way and the campaign drove sales for the museum.

Question: What were the advantages for The Art Institute of Chicago of creating the 'Van Gogh's Bedrooms' experience? Explain why creating this experience was chosen over other forms of marketing communication.

Task: Find three examples of recent brand experiences. Consider for each how they rate against Smith and Hanover's (2016) experiential pillars: remarkable, shareable, memorable, measurable, relatable, personal, targetable, connectable, flexible, engageable, believable.

Brand experience

Creating brand experiences that engage directly with current and potential customers, also known as experiential marketing, is a growth area. The IPA Bellwether Report (IPA, 2018) suggests event marketing budgets, which include experiential marketing, have been raised every year over the last four and a half years.

Smilansky (2017) argues that experiential marketing should be seen as an integrated approach that brings value to audiences through two-way communications. The notion of value provided to the target audience through the experience may in part explain why experiential marketing has undergone such significant growth.

Smith and Hanover (2016) suggest there are seven main factors that help to account for the increasing popularity of the use of experiential marketing:

1. 'It Carries the Strength of Many': experiential campaigns can choose the best aspects of each tool and media for more effective integrated campaigns.
2. 'It's Unstoppable': face-to-face experiences are difficult for consumers to block, unlike other forms of communications, which consumers are increasingly avoiding.
3. 'It's the First Singular Converter': marketers are increasingly moving away from the view that marketing channels have distinct roles and multi-silo marketing campaigns.
4. 'It's an Accelerant': experiential campaigns can move consumers faster through the purchase funnel, leading them to a purchase decision more quickly than other forms of marketing.
5. 'It Drives Lifetime Value': experiential marketing creates an immediate connection with consumers and builds relationships.
6. 'It's an Engagement Multiplier': consumers become more engaged in experiential campaigns and this increases brand affinity. They are also more likely to share their experience.
7. 'It's the Marketing Mix's Charger': experiential-led campaigns improve effectiveness in other areas of the marketing mix.

While many in the industry see their role as delivering brand experience opportunities for their clients' customers, experiential marketing can be differentiated from other marketing activities, as it requires very precise targeting, and it is more emotionally and physically engaging than sampling and many events or roadshows.

Image 17.7 The Ford Rouge Factory Tour
Source: Jim West/Alamy Stock Photo.

Scholars' paper 17.3
Fantasy and fun

Holbrook, M.B. and Hirschman, E.C. (1982). The experiential aspects of consumption: consumer fantasies, feelings, and fun, *Journal of Consumer Research*, **9(2), 132–40.**

This seminal paper on experiential consumption argued for a broader view of consumer behaviour to include the symbolic, hedonic and aesthetic nature of consumption. The authors view consumption experience as a phenomenon directed towards the pursuit of fantasies, feelings and fun.

See also:

Gilovich, T., Kumar, A. and Jampol, L. (2015) A wonderful life: Experiential consumption and the pursuit of happiness, *Journal of Consumer Psychology*, 25(1), 152–65.

Smith and Hanover (2016) provide an anatomy of experiential marketing campaigns. Composed of 11 experiential pillars: remarkable, shareable, memorable, measurable, relatable, personal, targetable, connectable, flexible, engageable and believable; the authors suggest these are all essential elements of a successful experiential campaign. Viewpoint 17.3 provides an example of how The Art Institute of Chicago created a memorable experience for visitors to connect with their Van Gogh exhibit.

Some brands have created permanent brand homes for their brand experience. For example, The Ford Rouge Factory Tour is a partnership between The Henry Ford and Ford Motor Company, providing an opportunity for visitors in the US to tour the birthplace of the Model A, the V-8, the Mustang and the Thunderbird. Visitors are also treated to an inside look at how the iconic Ford F-150 is manufactured. As well as experiencing the scale of a real factory floor, visitors are treated to a multisensory film experience that includes vibrating seats, gusts of wind, 3D projection mapping and winking robots to complete the experience (Anon, n.d.c).

Associated with this experience element is the growing use of events as a form of marketing communications, as demonstrated through the Lucozade example in Viewpoint 17.4. Events are a part of several aspects of marketing communications, including brand experience considered here but also product and corporate branding, and sponsorship (Chapter 15). However, a deeper insight into the nature and characteristics of events can be found in Chapter 18, which incorporates a section about exhibitions and trade shows.

Finally, some consumers experience brands in unexpected ways. Through increasingly open communications, typically Twitter and social networks, some companies can sense moods, intentions, desires and consumer frustrations and intervene to help people with personalised gifts or solutions. These activities are known as 'random acts of kindness' and can result in positive word of mouth and improvements to brand image. For example, when the owner of a toy company saw on Facebook that a child's birthday present had been lost in the post he sent her a toy bunny, free of charge, and a note that said 'Sorry Royal Mail let you down, hopefully this will put a smile on your little girl's face' (Behrman, 2012).

Other examples include sending restaurant vouchers to customers picked at random, upgrading to next-day free delivery, sending out personalised key rings and including free gifts with an order. A Scottish brewery might give away a box of beer one day, and then give someone £200-worth of shares in the company through its fan investor scheme. For a few months, staff at airline KLM selected eight Twitter followers who were feeling low or in need of a break, and gave them a free return flight to Amsterdam. The campaign resulted in an increase of 784 followers for KLM's UK Twitter feed.

Scholars' paper 17.4
Managing the experience

Homburg, C., Jozić, D. and Kuehnl, C. (2017) Customer experience management: toward implementing an evolving marketing concept, *Journal of the Academy of Marketing Science,* **45(3), 377–401.**

The paper introduces the concept of customer experience management (CEM). The authors argue their conceptualisation of CEM differs from other marketing management concepts and identifies CEM patterns collected from 52 managers engaging in CEM.

See also:

Schmitt, B. (1999). Experiential marketing; *Journal of Marketing Management,* 15(1–3), 53–67.

Viewpoint 17.4
Lucozade Sport Conditions Zone
Andrew Orr

Image 17.8 The Lucozade Sport Conditions Zone
Source: TRO Group.

The 2014 FIFA World Cup finals gave Lucozade Sport the perfect platform to communicate to its target audience in an innovative, immersive and credible way.

The key objective of the campaign was to create a World Cup-relevant experiential event, bringing to life the claim that Lucozade Sport 'Enhances Hydration, Fuels Performance'.

At its heart was experiential marketing, devised to create dynamic and credible content. The idea and execution had to be bold and relevant to gain cut-through, at a time when many brands would be competing for share of voice, and, crucially, to resonate with the target audience.

With the 2014 World Cup being hosted in Brazil, and England's opening game taking place in Manaus – with average conditions of 32°C and 76 per cent humidity – Lucozade Sport had the unique opportunity to drive the conversation around the importance of fuel and hydration.

Lucozade Sport created the 'Lucozade Sport Conditions Zone' – a bespoke, state-of-the-art immersive experience in London's Canary Wharf – offering grassroots footballers the chance to play five-a-side football in the same extreme conditions as England's opening World Cup game in Manaus, Brazil.

Lucozade Sport replicated the extreme conditions by designing and building a venue with the 'wow' factor for all consumers and media who attended. The Conditions Zone was situated in Canary Wharf for three weeks throughout June 2014, and received over 4,000 visitors. The bespoke structure housed a heated football pitch in an enclosed space (maintained at 32°C and 76 per cent humidity), and included a registration area, changing rooms and science lab.

Buzz and excitement for the Conditions Zone and Lucozade Sport was created through a multichannel integrated communications strategy that used all channels to deliver effectiveness at grassroots, social, digital and traditional media, PR, as well as paid-for media. From the pre-launch activity through to media launch day, the Conditions Zone developed a huge momentum of its own.

The Conditions Zone involved a 2.5-hour experience with education around Lucozade Sport's hydration properties at its core, hosted by an MSc qualified sports scientist.

Before playing, participants entered The Laboratory to have their key statistics recorded (resting heart rate, core body temperature and weight) and a urine test to ensure satisfactory hydration levels. Players were fitted with STATSport kit, used by the England Football Team, to monitor heart rates and track distance covered via GPS. Then the sports scientist took players through a presentation educating them on the science behind fuel and hydration.

Image 17.9 Grassroots footballers were given the chance to play in the same extreme conditions as in Manaus, Brazil
Source: TRO Group.

The pitch was housed within a heat and humidity-controlled chamber – and dramatically brought to life the Manaus conditions. A 50-minute match ensued with key stats delivered in real time and displayed on screens throughout. Chilled bottles of Lucozade Sport were provided, and players were encouraged to hydrate and measure how much they drank.

Post-match players went into The Comparison Zone where they were weighed to ascertain how much sweat they had lost – in some cases up to 2 litres! NFC (Near Field Communications) throughout the experience ensured everything integrated seamlessly with Facebook and allowed players to compare and share their statistics. On leaving the experience each player was given Lucozade Sport to ensure they continued to rehydrate on their journey home.

Insight

The 'Lucozade Sport Conditions Zone' gave Lucozade Sport a credible and relevant story to talk about during a time when many other brands were competing for share of voice. Leveraging cultural and sporting momentum, Lucozade was able to build a unique brand experience that engaged visitors and national media. The campaign received 114 pieces of UK media, over 32 million impressions on social media and helped Lucozade achieve a record summer contributing to a 12 per cent rise in sales.

Question: What might have been the motivation for Lucozade Sport to host this experiential event?

Task: Find one example of another experiential event organised by Lucozade Sport. Consider why the event might have resulted in earned media.

Key points

- Sales promotions offer a direct inducement or an incentive to encourage audiences to buy a product/service sooner rather than later. The inducement (e.g. price deals, coupons, premiums) is presented as an added value to the basic product, one that is intended to encourage buyers to act 'now' rather than later.

- The role of sales promotion is to engage audiences and to motivate them so that they are persuaded to behave now rather than at a later stage.

- The objective of sales promotion is to stimulate action. This can be to initiate a series of behaviours that result in long-run purchase activity, but the goal of sales promotion is to drive short-term shifts in sales. These actions can be seen to occur in the conative stage of the attitudinal set.

- The cognitive view of the way sales promotions operate is based on the belief that consumers internally process relevant information about a sales promotion, including those of past experiences, and make a reasoned decision in the light of the goals and objectives that individuals set for themselves.

- The behaviourists' view is that when the various actions that are embedded within a sales promotion activity are aggregated, a new desired pattern of behaviour emerges.

- Many organisations have developed schemes designed to retain customers based on the notion that they, the customers, are loyal. This brings into debate the notion of what is loyalty. In many ways these schemes are a function of customer convenience and all that they achieve is sufficient leverage to hold onto a customer a fraction longer than might have been possible in the absence of the scheme.

- The range of techniques and methods used to add value to offerings is enormous and runs from sampling and coupons to premiums, contests and sweepstakes, all used with varying levels of success. However, there has been a distinct shift away from traditional promotional instruments to the use of digital media in order to reflect consumers' preferences and media behaviour.

- Field marketing is a relatively new sector and seeks to provide support for the sales force and merchandising personnel along with data collection and research facilities. A key aspect of field marketing concerns the growing interest in what is referred to as experiential marketing or brand experience.

- Brand experiences or experiential marketing allow organisations to create physically and emotionally engaging face-to-face experiences with consumers.

- Experiential marketing should be seen as an integrated methodology that brings value to audiences through two-way communications that add value to the target audience.

Doors of Thrones

Image 17.10 The Doors of Thrones experience was created by Tourism Northern Ireland
Source: Discover Northern Ireland.

Game of Thrones has been filmed in Northern Ireland for 10 years. Fans of the epic HBO series have enjoyed the spectacular scenery of Northern Ireland as Westeros and locations such as The Dark Hedges have become better known to audiences as Kingsroad, the highway in the Seven Kingdoms that leads to the mythical King's Landing.

With 26 *Game of Thrones* filming locations in Northern Ireland, Tourism Northern Ireland decided to use this association to attract more fans to visit the country. They wanted to create a physical experience in the country that would allow fans to link destinations with the scenes shot at the location, and encourage visitors to travel around Northern Ireland and increase dwell time.

The fans of the series create a large volume of online discussion themselves about the show and so Tourism Northern Ireland knew that it would be difficult to compete through digital channels for their attention. They also knew that they needed to avoid merely piggybacking the show, which risked the contempt of the fans. Tourism Northern Ireland decided it would create an experience for fans that

they would value and be keen to share throughout their fan-run social channels.

Tourism Northern Ireland wanted to link the experience to the iconic Dark Hedges filming location, which had become a key attraction for fans. Following a terrible storm that hit Ireland, some of the trees from The Dark Hedges were blown over. While this was a terrible event, Tourism Northern Ireland decided to use the wood from these iconic trees to create 10 unique pieces of artwork. The wood was transformed into 10 beautifully crafted doors, each intricately carved to tell the story of Season 6, with each door depicting an episode from the series.

The doors were designed by world-class illustrators who were given the storylines a few days before each episode aired. The illustrators were asked to produce a design for the door that would reflect the plot, but not give away the exact storyline in advance. They used imagery from the series, but also drew heavily from Celtic symbolism for their designs. When completed, the designs were given to CGI artists to convert into 3D and these were then carved into the doors made with wood from The Dark Hedges.

Each door was then hung in a pub or restaurant location in Northern Ireland and unveiled the day after the corresponding episode aired on TV. Tourism Northern Ireland engaged with the biggest fan sites and bloggers first, which ensured the weekly unveiling of doors created a lot of excitement with fan conversations online.

The positioning of doors across Northern Ireland near to filming locations and connecting 10 pubs and restaurants in a national pub crawl, created the *Game of Thrones* trail.

With fans keen to engage with the series beyond the screen episodes, Tourism Northern Ireland created the perfect way for fans to immerse themselves in the locations and experience the land of Westeros for real. Every time a visitor came across a door they knew they were in *Game of Thrones* territory.

Once all ten doors were revealed, Tourism Northern Ireland created the Journey of Doors Passport, which is available at each of the venues and Visitor Information Centres. Fans are also able to download the passport from the Tourism Northern Ireland's website and can present their passport at each of the 10 locations to receive a stamp. The 10 doors within the passport are located in:

1. *The Cuan, Strangford, Co. Down.* Nearby filming locations: Castle Ward, Audley's Field, Quoile River and Inch Abbey. Castle Ward was the location for Winterfell and key scenes in Season 1.

2. *Fiddler's Green, Portaferry, Co. Down.* Nearby filming location: Quintin Bay, the location for Stokeworth in Season 5.

3. *Percy French, Newcastle, Co. Down.* Nearby filming locations: Tollymore Forest and Leitrim Lodge. Tollymore Forest Park was used in Season 1.

4. *Blakes of the Hollow, Enniskillen, Co. Fermanagh.* Nearby filming location: Pollnagollum Cave used in Season 3 as Hollow Hill in the Riverlands.

5. *Owens, Limavady, Co. Londonderry.* Nearby filming locations: Downhill Beach, Binevenagh and Portstewart Strand. Binevenagh was the location for the Dothraki Grasslands in Season 5.

6. *Fullerton Arms, Ballintoy, Co. Antrim.* Nearby filming locations: Ballintoy Harbour and Larrybane. Ballintoy Harbour is known to fans as Pyke and the Iron Islands in Season 2 and was also represented as Dragonstone in Season 4.

7. *Gracehill House, Stranocum, Co. Antrim.* Nearby filming location: The Dark Hedges. The Dark Hedges were seen in Season 2 as the Kingsroad.

8. *Mary McBride's, Cushendun, Co. Antrim.* Nearby filming locations: Cushendun Caves, above Murlough Bay, Murlough Bay, Carnlough Harbour and The Glens of Antrim. Cushendun Caves were used in Season 2 as a cove in the Stormlands.

9. *Ballygally Castle, Ballygally, Co. Antrim.* Nearby filming locations: Cairncastle, Carnlough Harbour, The Glens of Antrim, Sallagh Braes and Shillnavogy Valley. The countryside of Cairncastle in Larne, County Antrim has featured in some of the most memorable scenes in *Game of Thrones* in Season 1, and also The Neck on the road to Moat Cailin in Season 5.

10. *The Dark Horse, Belfast, Co. Antrim.* This door is a tribute to all the filming in Belfast.

Image 17.11 The first door can be found in The Cuan, Strangford, Co. Down. Nearby film locations include Castle Ward, the location for Winterfell.
Source: Discover Northern Ireland.

Image 17.12 To help fans navigate their way around the filming locations, Tourism Northern Ireland launched the Game of Thrones Filming Locations Northern Ireland app
Source: Discover Northern Ireland.

As well as a passport, visitors can download an app to help them to plan their visit to Northern Ireland.

The results

Tourism Northern Ireland generated more than €17 million in earned media from a €140,000 budget. The coverage has reached more than 126 million people, received 17.5 million views and over 250,000 engagements.

> MTV: 'The Irish Game of Thrones pub crawl is literally everything'

> *Cosmopolitan*: 'You NEED to know about this Game of Thrones pub crawl'

In 2016, when the Doors of Thrones experience was launched, Northern Ireland had a record number of visitors and an 8 per cent increase on the previous year. Ireland.com had an additional 300,000 clicks.

A number of tour companies such as Contiki now run tours of all 10 doors, receiving bookings from as far as Japan, the US and Australia. The pubs and restaurants where the doors are hung report a doubling of profits since the doors were installed.

The campaign has been awarded with Gold, Silver and Bronze Lions.

Sources: Anon (2018B); Doors of Thrones (2017).

Review questions

Doors of Thrones case questions

1. What might have been the motivation for Tourism Northern Ireland to use such an experiential route to engage *Game of Thrones* fans?

2. Why would visitors to Northern Ireland want to share their experience of the *Game of Thrones* trail?

3. Why do you think the campaign generated so much earned media?

4. Consider what the lifetime of this campaign is likely to be. How could Tourism Northern Ireland extend the campaign in the future?

5. Write a brief note explaining the advantages of creating brand experiences, using examples from the case.

General questions

1. List the main sales promotion methods.

2. Identify the major differences between the behavioural and the cognitive explanations of how sales promotions work.

3. Write brief notes outlining some of the issues associated with loyalty programmes and customer retention initiatives.

4. Name five core activities associated with field marketing and explain their essential features.

5. Find three brand experience events and make notes of the main points of similarity.

References for Chapter 17

Anon (n.d.a) Have a break with Zeal and Kitkat, Zeal Creative, retrieved 1 May 2018 from http://www.zealcreative.com/work/

Anon (n.d.b) KitKat.co.uk, retrieved 1 May 2018 from https://www.kitkat.co.uk/joe-the-mug/Public/Register.aspx

Anon (n.d.c) Discover your drive, thehenryford.org, retrieved 10 May 2018 from https://www.thehenryford.org/visit/ford-rouge-factory-tour/

Anon (2018a) When the internet got angry, Snickers bars became cheaper, MediaCom, retrieved 10 February 2018 from https://www.mediacom.com/en/work/hungerithm

Anon (2018b) Game of Thrones: Doors of Thrones, discovernorthernireland.com, retrieved 30 May from https://discovernorthernireland.com/things-to-do/attractions/game-of-thrones/journey-of-doors/

Aydinli, A., Bertini, M. and Lambrecht, A. (2014) Price promotion for emotional impact, *Journal of Marketing*, 78 (July), 80–96.

Behrman, D. (2012) Work: better business: acts of kindness, *Guardian*, 13 April, 2.

Capizzi, M., Ferguson, R. and Cuthbertson, R. (2004) Loyalty trends for the 21st century, *Journal of Targeting Measurement and Analysis for Marketing*, 12(3), 199–212.

Clark, N. (2010) The power of the crowd, *MarketingMagazine*, 24 August, retrieved 18 October 2011 from www.brandrepublic.com/features/1023618/power-crowd/?dcmp=ilc-search

Datta, H., Foubert, B. and van Heerde, H.J. (2015) The challenge of retaining customers acquired with free trials, *Journal of Marketing Research*, 52(2), 217–34.

Dawes, J. (2004) Assessing the impact of a very successful price promotion on brand, category and competitor sales, *Journal of Product and Brand Management*, 13(5), 303–14.

Door of Thrones (2017) *Cannes Archive*, retrieved 10 February 2018 from http://www.canneslionsarchive.com/Home/PublicHome

Drechsler, S., Leeflang, P.S., Bijmolt, T.H. and Natter, M. (2017) Multi-unit price promotions and their impact on purchase decisions and sales, *European Journal of Marketing*, 51(5/6), 1049–74.

Drèze, X., Hoch, S.J. and Purk, M.E. (1994) Shelf management and space elasticity, *Journal of Retailing*, 70(4), 301–26.

Ehrenberg, A.S.C. (2000) Repeat buying: facts, theory and application, *Journal of Empirical Generalisations in Marketing Science*, 5(2).

Ehrenberg, A.S.C., Goodhardt, G.J. and Barwise, T.P. (1990) Double jeopardy revisited, *Journal of Marketing*, 54 (July), 82–91.

Gilovich, T., Kumar, A. and Jampol, L. (2015) A wonderful life: Experiential consumption and the pursuit of happiness, *Journal of Consumer Psychology*, 25(1), 152–65.

Griner, D. (2017) What a Chicago museum and agency learned by creating one of the world's favorite ads, *Adweek*, 9 June, retrieved 10 December 2017 from http://www.adweek.com/creativity/what-a-chicago-museum-and-agency-learned-by-creating-one-of-the-worlds-favorite-ads/

Guissoni, L.A., Sanchez, J.M. and Rodrigues, J.M. (2018) Price and in-store promotions in an emerging market, *Marketing Intelligence & Planning*, 36(4), 498–511.

Guyt, J.Y. and Gijsbrechts, E. (2014) Take turns or march in sync? The impact of the National Brand promotion calendar on manufacturer and retailer performance, *Journal of Marketing Research*, 51(6), 753–72.

Hallberg, G. (2004) Is your loyalty programme really building loyalty? Why increasing emotional attachment, not just repeat buying, is key to maximizing programme success, *Journal of Targeting Measurement and Analysis for Marketing*, 12(3), 231–41.

Hastings, S. and Price, M. (2004) Money can't buy me loyalty, *Admap*, 39(2), 29–31.

Heilman, M.C., Nakamoto, K. and Rao, A.G. (2002) Pleasant surprises: consumer response to unexpected in-store coupons, *Journal of Marketing Research*, 34 (May), 242–52.

Holbrook, M.B. and Hirschman, E.C. (1982) The experiential aspects of consumption: consumer fantasies, feelings, and fun, *Journal of Consumer Research*, 9(2), 132–40.

Homburg, C., Jozić, D. and Kuehnl, C. (2017) Customer experience management: toward implementing an evolving marketing concept, *Journal of the Academy of Marketing Science*, 45(3), 377–401.

Inman, J., McAlister, L. and Hoyer, D.W. (1990) Promotion signal: proxy for a price cut? *Journal of Consumer Research*, 17 (June), 74–81.

IPA (2018) Q1 2018 Bellwether Report, IPA, 18 April, retrieved 10 May 2018 from http://www.ipa.co.uk/document/q1-2018-bellwether-report#.WvqQK2gvyHs

Jones, P.J. (1990) The double jeopardy of sales promotions, *Harvard Business Review*, September/October, 145–52.

Karray, S., Martin-Herran, G. and Sigué, S.P. (2017) Cooperative advertising for competing manufacturers: the impact of long-term promotional effects, *International Journal of Production Economics*, 184, 21–32.

Kivetz, R. and Zheng, Y. (2017) The effects of promotions on hedonic versus utilitarian purchases, *Journal of Consumer Psychology*, 27(1), 59–68.

Lee, C.H. (2002) Sales promotions as strategic communications: the case of Singapore, *Journal of Product and Brand Management*, 11(2), 103–14.

Maridou, E. (2017) The hidden cost of discounts, tuftandneedle.com, 17 May, retrieved 10 May 2018 from https://www.tuftandneedle.com/hidden-cost-of-discounts

McLuhan, R. (2000) Fighting for a new view of field work, *Marketing*, 9 March, 29–30.

Nudd, T. (2016) Snickers 'Hungerithm' sets the candy's in-store price based on the internet's mood, *Adweek*, 25 May, retrieved 10 December 2017 from http://www.adweek.com/creativity/snickers-hungerithm-sets-candys-store-price-based-internets-mood-171674/

Peattie, S. and Peattie, K.J. (1994) Sales promotion, in *The Marketing Book* (ed. M.J. Baker), 3rd edn, London: Butterworth-Heinemann.

Rothschild, M.L. and Gaidis, W.C. (1981) Behavioural learning theory: its relevance to marketing and promotions, *Journal of Marketing Research*, 45(2), 70–8.

Russell, R.A. and Urban, T.L. (2010) The location and allocation of products and product families on retail shelves, *Annals of Operations Research*, 179(1), 131–47.

Ryan, M. (2012) Forward thinking essays 2012: access all areas, *Marketing*, retrieved 17 February 2012 from https://www.campaignlive.co.uk/article/forward-thinking-essays-2012-access-areas-martin-ryan-cpm-uk/1112655

Schmitt, B. (1999) Experiential marketing, *Journal of Marketing Management*, 15(1–3), 53–67.

Simpson, L.S. (2006) Enhancing food promotion in the supermarket industry: a framework for sales promotion success, *International Journal of Advertising*, 25(2), 223–45.

Smilansky, S. (2017) *Experiential marketing: A practical guide to interactive brand experiences*, 2nd edn, London: Kogan Page.

Smith, K. and Hanover, D. (2016) *Experiential Marketing: Secrets, Strategies, and Success Stories from the World's Greatest Brands*, Hoboken: Wiley.

Snickers HUNGERITHM (2017) *Cannes Archive*, retrieved 5 April 2018 from http://player.canneslions.com/index.html#/works?category=cyber&entry=808587&festival=CL

Stilley, K.M., Inman, J.J. and Wakefield, K.L. (2010a) Planning to make unplanned purchases? The role of in-store slack in budget deviation, *Journal of Consumer Research*, 37(2), 264–78.

Stilley, K.M., Inman, J.J. and Wakefield, K.L. (2010b) Spending on the fly: mental budgets, promotions, and spending behavior, *Journal of Marketing*, 74(3), 34–47.

Van Gogh's Bedrooms: Let Yourself In (2017) *Cannes Lions Archive*, retrieved 10 March 2018 from http://www.canneslionsarchive.com/Home/PublicHome

Wohl, J. (2016) Want to rent Van Gogh's 'Bedroom'? *AdAge*, 7 April, retrieved 10 December 2017 from http://adage.com/article/creativity/art-instti/303425/

Wood, Z. (2014) Groupon revamps UK deals site in bid to become retail marketplace, *Guardian*, 19 August, retrieved 1 April 2015 from www.theguardian.com/technology/2014/aug/19/groupon-revamps-uk-site-bid-to-beomce-retail-marketplace

Chapter 18

Brand placement, exhibitions, packaging and licensing

Brand placement enables brands to be seen in context and used by appropriate role models in order to help form effective brand associations. Exhibitions can be a significant part of a consumer marketing communications mix, while trade shows are a major part of the way B2B marketing is conducted. Packaging is always an important factor in the way consumer goods, which generally evoke low involvement, are presented. Licensing, a means of using another party's assets, has become a more common activity in the twenty-first century.

Aims and learning objectives

The aims of this chapter are to consider a range of marketing communications activities that have no specific designation, yet which can make a major contribution to a marketing communications campaign. These activities are applied to both the B2B and B2C markets.

The learning objectives are to enable readers to:

1. understand the concept and issues associated with brand placement;
2. explore the differences and significance of exhibitions and trade shows;
3. consider the main advantages and disadvantages of using exhibitions as part of the communications mix;
4. examine the role and key characteristics of packaging as a form of marketing communications;
5. describe the principles and issues associated with licensing.

Introduction

Most of the tools presented so far are regarded as the primary instruments of the marketing communications mix. In order to provide a difference, however, and to cut through the noise of competing brands, it is necessary to provide additional resources and, preferably, integrated communications, right up to the point when customers make decisions. This chapter considers several other important means of communicating with both customers and distributors: brand placement, exhibitions and trade shows, packaging and licensing.

'Brand placement' enables a brand to be observed in a more natural environment than if viewed on a shelf, online or in a shop window. Unsurprisingly, this part of marketing communications is growing and provides income for film producers and broadcasters, as well as authenticity for brand managers and relief from advertising for consumers.

Exhibitions enable customers to become familiar with new developments, new products, services and leading-edge brands. Very often these customers will be opinion leaders and will use word-of-mouth communications to convey their feelings and product experiences to others. In the B2B market, exhibitions and trade shows are very often an integral and important component in the communications mix. Meeting friends, customers, suppliers, competitors and prospective customers is an important sociological and ritualistic event in the communications calendar for many companies. In the consumer sector, and in particular the FMCG market, it is important to provide a point of difference and offer continuity for those people who make the brand choice decisions at the point of purchase.

In addition, the way products are packaged not only influences brand perception but can also be an integral part of the customer purchasing process. Packaging moves with a brand back into the home and can be present while a brand is consumed. This provides a constant visibility and reinforcement of the brand, something other forms of communications cannot do.

Brand licensing has become an important element in industries such as the music business and communicates with stakeholders. Licensing is a commercial arrangement whereby one party, who holds certain property rights or a trademark, grants permission to particular others – a manufacturing company, for example – to allow them the right to carry the designated logo or trademark. Some might see this as a variant of brand extension, but licensing has become a significant communications activity in its own right.

Brand placement

The growth in brand placement in recent years has largely been due to the rise in on-demand, catch-up and an increase in recording TV programmes and films (Sweney, 2018). With increased advertising avoidance, brands have been forced to consider new ways to reach audiences and one solution has been brand placement.

Dens et al, (2018) highlight the growth in the global brand placement industry over the last decade and suggest brand managers should view brand placement as part of their marketing communications strategy, rather than using placement in isolation. Their study identified that when combined with programme sponsorship, brand placement can have a greater impact on brand awareness than if used on its own.

The practice of placing a product within a film or programme is not a recent practice, however, and was originally referred to as *product* placement. The change in name came about due to the changing nature of the practice and in recognition that it is not products that are placed within the media, but brands with identities and associated brand meanings and messages (Kandhadai and Saxena, 2014).

Chen and Haley (2014: 286) use the following definition: the 'intentional, paid inclusion of products, services, brands, or/and brand identifiers into media content'. Kandhadai and Saxena (2014: 241) define it in terms of identities, as 'the paid inclusion of communicative brand identities, via management of intensities, in the creative content of any media, and is an audience-driven strategic communication process, managed by stakeholders for a desired outcome'.

A wide variety of products can be placed in this way, including drinks (both soft and alcoholic), confectionery, newspapers, cars, airlines, perfume and even holiday destinations and sports equipment. However, the development of brand placement has inevitably led to new formats and fresh approaches, some of which only serve to muddy the waters.

Scholars' paper 18.1
Is this product placement?

Gillespie, B., Muehling, D.D. and Kareklas, I. (2018) Fitting product placements: affective fit and cognitive fit as determinants of consumer evaluations of placed brands, *Journal of Business Research*, 82, 90–102.

This paper considers the importance of ensuring product placements are a good fit within the storyline in which they are placed. The authors identify that when product placements fit well with both the storyline (cognitive fit) and the tone of the narrative (affective fit), brand attitudes are more favourable. The paper highlights the importance of how brands consider 'fit' within a product placement.

See also:

Kandhadai, R. and Saxena, R. (2014) Brand placement: new perspectives and a comprehensive definition, *The Marketing Review*, 14(3), 231–44.

Hudson and Hudson (2006) set out the development of brand placement. Early forms of placement concerned brand owners making deals with film producers and film stars openly to endorse a brand. The brand owner would fund props and facilities for the film in return for spoken and visual endorsement. Some of the first television programmes were named after the brands that sponsored them, for example *The Colgate Comedy Hour* and the *Kraft Television Theatre* (Hudson and Hudson, 2006).

The establishment of brand placement agencies in the 1980s helped formalise the process and removed much of the barter and haggling that had typified arrangements. The turning point occurred when the film *ET* depicted an alien being lured by Reese's Pieces. Hershey, the manufacturer, saw sales rise over 60 per cent following the release of the film, and since then brand placement has grown year on year.

Two distinct forms of placement-related activity have emerged, partly as a result of the proliferation of the media, the consequential surge in the production of entertainment programmes and the media industries' need to generate income streams. Rather than place a brand within a film, television or radio programme where it assumes a passive role, hoping to get noticed, a new approach sees whole entertainment programmes built around a single brand. In contrast to the passivity of brand placement, here a brand is actively woven into the theme or the plot of the programme. This latter approach has been labelled 'branded entertainment'. Hudson and Hudson (2006) depict this as a continuum (represented in Figure 18.1).

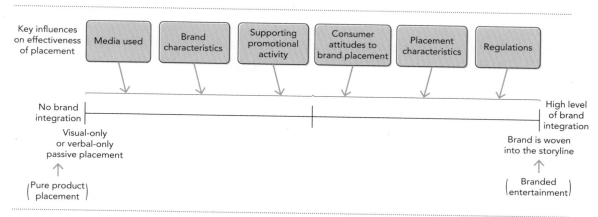

Figure 18.1 A spectrum of brand placement opportunities
Source: Hudson and Hudson (2006). Reproduced with permission.

Viewpoint 18.1

Coronation Street opens a Costa and a Co-op

Image 18.1 Coronation Street has signed an agreement with Costa Coffee and the Co-op to allow product placement
Source: Costa Coffee.

Product placement on UK TV has been allowed since 2011 when the media regulator, Ofcom, relaxed the regulations to permit brands to pay for their products to appear on TV programmes. ITV1 was the first channel to include a paid product placement deal on TV in the UK and on the day restrictions were relaxed, the *This Morning*

show featured Nestlé's Dolce Gusto brand. In the same year, Nationwide signed a product placement deal with *Coronation Street*, one of the UK's longest-running and most popular soap operas.

Coronation Street has a large fan base and some episodes attract more than 8.5 million viewers. The Nationwide placement deal, which was the first paid product placement for a peak-time TV show in the UK, was estimated to have cost £100,000. The show placed a Nationwide ATM inside Dev Alahan's *Coronation Street* shop, bringing the building society into the homes of millions of viewers three nights a week. In addition to the cashpoint machine installed inside the shop, the deal saw a Nationwide swing board placed outside the shop, increasing the brand's presence on the set.

In 2018, *Coronation Street* announced the show's biggest product placement deal to date, with Co-op and Costa Coffee opening shopfronts on the famous streets of the show. The agreement also allows for the stores' posters, bags and cups to appear on the set to further integrate the product placement and access to *Coronation Street*'s off-air channels. This paid product placement deal will see both brands become an inherent part of daily life on the set of the UK's most loved soap.

Sources: Banham (2011); Gwynn (2018).

Insight

While paid product placement on UK TV is relatively new, this example reflects how brands are taking advantage of the opportunities to be associated with some of the nation's most loved national shows. Placement deals, such as those given to the Co-op and Costa, allow brands to become an integral part of the show. The exposure on the set helps to build brand awareness, reinforces brand image and improves source credibility. However, brands need to consider the ways their products might be used in the show and impact this may have on the brand.

Question: Consider where on Hudson and Hudson's (2006) spectrum of brand placement (shown in Figure 18.1) you would place the *Coronation Street* placements.

Task: Watch a recent episode of *Coronation Street* and count the number of brand placements.

Brand placement is not restricted to offline communications. For example, the growing popularity of social gaming, such as Mafia Wars, which are run on social network platforms, has also attracted an increasing number of placements (Chen and Haley, 2014). The toothpaste brand Pearl Drops was written into the plotline and integrated into the social network of Bebo's interactive drama, *Sofia's Diary*, a teen-targeted programme.

Eagle and Dahl (2018) highlight the growing use of product placement on social media platforms such as Facebook, Twitter and YouTube, and in console-based video games, online advergames and on mobile phone apps. The authors suggest games provide an opportunity for brands to be seen many times as consumers may play more than once.

Characteristics of brand placement

Strengths

By presenting a brand as an integral part of a film, not only is it possible to build awareness, but source credibility can be improved significantly and brand images reinforced. The audience is assisted to identify and associate itself with the environment depicted in the film or with the celebrity who is using the brand.

Levels of impact can be very high, as cinema audiences are very attentive to large-screen presentations. Rates of exposure can be high, particularly now that cinema films and television shows are released through video outlets, various new regional cable and television organisations, and streaming providers such as Netflix, Amazon Instant Video and Now TV.

Brand placement is often used as an integral part of an international marketing strategy. This is because, as McKechnie and Zhou (2003) observe, films are often produced for and play to audiences across cultures. However, it should be recognised that this approach constitutes a standardised marketing strategy, since it is difficult to customise across cultures because media content and placed brands are identical (Nelson and Devanathan, 2006).

Perhaps the major advantage is that the majority of audiences, worldwide, appear to approve of this form of marketing communications. Davtyan and Cunningham (2017) found that consumers' attitude towards brand placement was more positive than their attitude towards TV commercials. This may be because it is unobtrusive and integral to the film (Nebenzahl and Secunda, 1993). Audiences appear to have a positive attitude towards brand placement when they believe that the placement content enhances realism. In addition, audiences believe that the naturalistic representation of products serves to reinforce the integrity of fictionalised storylines and reflects the 'real-life' experiences of the audience in the entertainment media setting (Lee et al., 2011a).

Consumers also appear to approve of product placement on the radio. Van Reijmersdal (2011) found that placements on radio are perceived not only to be liked more than ads, but also as more credible than ads. This, in turn, affects brand recall positively. Thanks to the credibility issue, it is contended that brand placement receives more attention from listeners and so has a higher chance of being processed and recalled than commercials.

Brand placement is not confined to cinema films. Music videos, television plays, dramas and soap operas can also use this method to present advertisers' brands. The novel *The Sweetest Taboo*, written by novelist Carole Matthews, includes frequent references to various Ford cars, which is not surprising as Ford paid her to mention their cars in her work (Plaut, 2004).

Weaknesses

Having achieved a placement in a film, there is still a risk that the brand will run unnoticed, especially if the placements coincide with distracting or action-oriented parts of the film. Associated with this is the lack of control the advertiser has over when, where and how the brand will be presented. If the brand is noticed, a small minority of audiences claim that this form of communications is unethical; it is even suggested that it is subliminal advertising, which is, of course, illegal. Gould et al. (2000) suggest that placements involving ethically charged brands, those that might be deceptive, that encroach upon artistic licence, are subliminal or excessively commercial, are perceived negatively.

The absolute costs of brand placement in films can be extremely high, counteracting the low relative costs or cost per contact. For example, Barber (2015) suggests $45 million has been cited as the figure Heineken paid for product placement within *Skyfall*. In addition to the high cost of placement, Eagle and Dahl (2018) warn that in some films the level of product placement is excessive and can lead to ridicule.

Gillespie et al. (2018) discuss the importance of 'product placement fit' and argue that for product placement to be effective, it should have both cognitive fit and affective fit. Cognitive fit ensures the product placement is aligned to the story or characters. Affective fit represents the alignment with the emotional state created by the story. They use the example of Pepsi's placement within *World War Z*, where the character stops at a Pepsi vending machine for a drink before saving mankind, as irrelevant to the storyline and having low cognitive fit.

Pervan and Martin (2002) found that brand placement in US and New Zealand television soaps was an effective communications activity. They also concluded that the way a product is used in the soap (i.e. positive and negative outcomes) may well have important implications for the attitudes held towards these products. In addition, they suggested that organisations should study the consumption imagery associated with placed brands as this might yield significant information about the way in which these products are actually consumed.

The final major drawback of this form of communications concerns its inability to provide explanation, detail or indeed any substantive information about the brand. The brand is seen in use and, it is hoped, associated with an event, person(s) or objects that provide a source of pleasure, inspiration or aspiration for an individual viewer.

Image 18.2 If a UK programme contains product placement it has to show this logo to let viewers know that the channel has been paid to feature products in the show. The P logo must be shown at the start of the show, after any ad breaks and again at the end of the programme
Source: Ofcom 2018.

Scholars' paper 18.2

Are we doing enough to regulate product placement?

Eagle, L. and Dahl, S. (2018) Product placement in old and new media: examining the evidence for concern, *Journal of Business Ethics,* **147(3), 605–18.**

This paper provides an overview of the development that has taken place in product placement. The authors review both traditional and digital media and raise a number of concerns over current regulations. In particular, they highlight the impact of product placement on children and young adults.

See also:

Redondo, I., Russell, C.A. and Bernal, J. (2018) To brand or not to brand a product placement? Evidence from a field study of two influence mechanisms of positive portrayals of alcohol in film, *Drug and Alcohol Review,* 37(S1), S366–S374.

Placement issues

The nature of a placement and the impact it has on the audience appear to be affected by a number of variables. Important issues concern: the nature of the placement (Sung et al., 2009) and its association with the storyline; whether the actors use the brand or if it remains a background object; whether the brand fits the plot; the degree to which the brand is prominently displayed; the medium used (de Gregorio and Sung, 2010); and the amount of time that the brand is actually exposed.

For example, research by Kamleitner and Jyote (2013) into the relative effectiveness of different types of placement in films found that those involving character–product interaction (where a character in a film has some physical interaction with a branded product) generate far stronger and more positive attitude changes in comparison to static placements where there is similar visual prominence.

Research into brand placement appears to have focused on three main issues concerning consumer opinion. Lee et al. (2011b) refer to the perceived realism, ethicality and influence of a brand placement. There is strong agreement that placements:

- can enhance the realism of film and TV content (Nebenzahl and Secunda, 1993; Gupta et al., 2000);

- have the potential to reinforce the integrity of a film and help viewers to become absorbed within the storyline (DeLorme and Reid, 1999);

- are perceived to be ethical, even if they are considered to be advertisements in disguise (Sung and de Gregorio, 2008).

Karrh et al. (2003) refer to the relative lack of control that marketers have over placement activities, but confirm that in comparison to advertising equivalents, brand placement can have a far greater impact on audiences and in most cases at a fraction of the cost of a 30-second advertisement.

Cultural background and ethical disposition can influence an audience's perception of brand placements (Nelson and Devanathan, 2006) while Russell and Belch (2005) refer to difficulties relating to the way the value of a placement is perceived. Chen and Haley (2014) reinforce the point that the meanings attributed by consumers to brand placements are determined contextually, the same way as advertising (Hirschman and Thompson, 1997). The message and the medium within brand placements combine to deliver intertextual brand image/meaning.

There is a view, held by creative and media agencies, that the 'number of seconds on screen' is a valid measurement of effectiveness. Many do not agree and prefer to consider the context of the placement and the level of continuity within a defined communications strategy as more meaningful measures.

Brand placement can take varying forms but two main forms are considered in the literature: subtle versus prominent types of placements, or *implicit* and *explicit* brand placements (D'Astous and Séguin, 1999). The premise is that prominent/explicit placements are more persuasive (in terms of attitude change) than subtle/implicit placements, owing to their attention-getting power. However, prominence raises issues about distraction, irritation and perceptions about self-serving that can inhibit persuasion. Research indicates that brand placement can impact on attitudes through mere exposure (Hang, 2012). Homer (2009) found that attitudes decrease with prominent/explicit placements and are maintained where the placement is subtle/implicit.

Following research by Smit et al. (2009) into how brand placement is used in the Netherlands, their results revealed that a quarter of Dutch television contained a mixture of brand sponsorship announcements, commercials and brand placement programmes. They also found that approximately 10 per cent of programmes, excluding sports, news, foreign movies and foreign soap operas, included brand placements. They identified that human-interest programmes, soap operas, games and quiz shows were the most popular brand placement.

Practitioners perceive brand placement and brand-integrated programmes as the future of television advertising. Sponsors are enthusiastic about brand-integration simply because they see this format as more effective than a traditional 30-second commercial.

Brand placement is normally undertaken through specialised agencies and by dedicated professionals. Some practitioners believe that the emergence of these placement agencies might eventually weaken the position of advertising agencies.

The use of brand placement as a part of an international marketing strategy has several advantages. However, as Lee et al. (2011b) suggest, local contextual elements such as the cultural environment, legal conditions, media infrastructure, plus public sentiment, all need to be considered when using brand placement on a global basis. They also warn that technologically sophisticated audiences are increasingly watching a range of content (soap operas, sitcoms and news programmes) via podcasts, mobile television (i.e. digital multimedia broadcasting) and interactive television (i.e. internet protocol television) (Kwak etal., 2009). It is therefore important to understand the way consumers use television (active, passive and multitasking behaviours) and the impact this might have on the effectiveness of brand placement in different cultural contexts.

Trade shows and exhibitions

Trade shows and exhibitions fulfil a role for customers by enabling them to become familiar with new developments, new products and leading-edge brands. Very often these customers will be opinion leaders and will use word-of-mouth communications to convey their feelings and both product and exhibition experiences to others. The role of trade fairs is to enable manufacturers, suppliers and distributors to meet at a designated location. As these are drawn from a particular industry or related industries, the purpose is to exchange information about products and services and to build relationships. These events normally exclude consumers. Exhibitions are attended by consumers.

In the B2B market, trade shows are very often an integral and important component in the communications mix. Meeting friends, customers, suppliers, competitors and prospective customers is an important sociological and ritualistic event in the communications calendar for many companies. In the consumer sector, exhibitions provide a point of difference and offer continuity for those people who make the brand choice decisions at the point of purchase.

The idea of many suppliers joining together at a particular location to set out their products and services so that customers may meet, make comparisons and place orders is far from new. Indeed, not only does this form of promotional activity stretch back many centuries, but it has also been used to explain the way the Internet works (Bertheron et al., 1996).

Reasons to use exhibitions

There are many reasons to use exhibitions, but the primary ones appear not to be 'to make sales' or 'because the competition is there' but because these events provide opportunities to meet potential and established customers and to create and sustain a series of relational exchanges. Sarmento and Simões (2018) stress that the impact of trade shows on the development of valuable, long-term buyer–seller relationships is important.

The main aims are, therefore, to develop and strengthen relationships with customers (Sarmento et al., 2015; Yuksel and Voola, 2010). This implies that exhibitions should not be used as isolated events, but that they should be integrated into a series of activities, which serve to foster long-term relationship building.

Sarmento and Simões (2018) identify that exhibitors use exhibitions to launch new products and to internationalise. International exhibitions, such as the World Travel Market (WTM) highlighted in Viewpoint 18.2, attended by global buyers and media provide an excellent opportunity for organisations to announce new products and services.

Exhibitions also allow organisations to gather current market intelligence and exchange information about industry issues (Sarmento and Simões, 2018). The sharing of information, both formally and informally, encourages innovative practices at both organisational and industry levels.

Costs can be reduced by using private exhibitions. The increased flexibility allows organisations to produce mini or private exhibitions for their clients at local venues (e.g. hotels). This can mean lower costs for the exhibitor and reduced time away from their businesses for those attending. The communications 'noise' and distraction associated with the larger public events can also be avoided by these private showings.

Viewpoint 18.2
The World Travel Market

Image 18.3 The World Travel Market attracts exhibitors from across the globe
Source: WTM London.

The World Travel Market (WTM) is one of the largest trade shows in the world. Started over 40 years ago, the event takes place every year in London and attracts exhibitors from all over the globe. For national and regional tourist boards, global airlines and travel brands, the WTM is a key fixture on their event calendar and provides them with an opportunity to showcase new products and services.

The chance to meet up with customers and partners from all over the world is one of the main advantages of WTM and the organisers estimate that over 935,000 business meetings take place during the three-day event. As well as networking opportunities with over 10,000 industry buyers, the show reportedly generates over £3 billion in travel and tourism deals.

Many exhibitors choose to use WTM to launch new products and with an attendance of over 51,000 visitors from over 185 countries, the show provides a good platform to reach existing and new customers. The broad visitor base also allows exhibitors and visitors to gather market intelligence. This may be information about new industry trends or even finding out what competitors are planning.

Many exhibitors have elaborate stands and use these to host events during the show. As well as providing entertainment for the visitors and business guests, with over 1,600 global press in attendance at WTM, such events are guaranteed to attract media attention. For example, regional and national tourist boards often stage dance shows featuring traditional dancers and local foods.

Running alongside the show are a series of over 80 seminar events on topics ranging from destination weddings, creative tourism and youth tourism to responsible tourism. With industry speakers providing insights into current issues and developing sectors, the seminars provide an opportunity for visitors to gather information on emergent trends.

Sources: Visit Britain (2018); WTM (2018).

Insight

The WTM provides an example of the advantages afforded to both exhibitors and visitors of attending a global trade exhibition. As well as the networking opportunities, the exhibition allows exhibitors to gather data on existing and new customers through competitions and promotions. However, exhibiting at an international trade show requires significant planning ahead of time and is likely to require significant investment.

Question: How would you use marketing communications to attract visitors to an exhibition such as WTM?

Task: Make a list of the 10 critical activities associated with organising a trade show.

Characteristics of exhibitions and trade fairs

The main reasons for attending exhibitions and trade fairs are that they enable organisations to meet customers (and potential customers) in an agreeable environment – one where both have independently volunteered their time to attend in order to place/take orders, to generate leads and to gather market information. The reasons for attending exhibitions are set out in Table 18.1.

From this it is possible to distinguish the following strengths and weaknesses of using exhibitions as part of the marketing communications programme.

Strengths

The costs associated with exhibitions, if controlled properly, can mean that this is an effective and efficient means of communicating with customers. The costs per enquiry need to be calculated, but care needs to be taken over who is classified as an enquirer, as the quality of the audience varies considerably. Costs per order taken are usually the prime means of evaluating the success of an exhibition. This can paint a false picture, as the true success can never really be determined in terms of orders because of the variety of other factors that impinge upon the placement and timing of orders.

Products can be launched at exhibitions and, when integrated with a good PR campaign, a powerful impact can be made. This can also be used to reinforce corporate identity. Exhibitions are an important means of gaining information about competitors, buyers and technical and political developments in the market, and they often serve to facilitate the recruitment process. Above all else, exhibitions provide an opportunity to meet customers on relatively neutral ground and, through personal interaction, develop relationships. Products can be demonstrated, prices agreed, technical problems discussed and trust and credibility enhanced.

Table 18.1   Reasons exhibitors choose to attend exhibitions

To meet existing customers
To take orders/make sales
To get leads and meet prospective new customers
To meet lapsed customers
To meet prospective members of the existing or new marketing channels
To provide market research opportunities and to collect marketing data

Weaknesses

One of the main drawbacks associated with exhibition work is the vast and disproportionate amount of management time that can be tied up with the planning and implementation of exhibitions. However, good planning is essential if the full potential benefits of exhibition work are to be realised.

Taking members of the sales force 'off the road' can also incur large costs. Depending on the nature of the business, these opportunity costs can soar. Some pharmaceutical organisations estimate that it can cost approximately £5,000 per person per week to divert salespeople in this way.

The expected visitor profile must be analysed in order that the number of quality buyers visiting an exhibition can be determined. The variety of visitors attending an exhibition can be misleading, as the vast majority may not be serious buyers or, indeed, may not be directly related to the industry or the market in question. Research by Gopalakrishna et al. (2010) has found that approximately 40 per cent of first-time exhibitors, spanning a range of industries, do not return to the same show the following year. As Gopalakrishna et al. (2010) point out, a growing concern for managers is the ability to reach relevant decision-makers. The researchers' response was to attempt an understanding of attendee behaviour, as this would help trade show organisers segment their audiences. From their research data they determined a typology of business show visitors. These are depicted in Table 18.2.

Exhibitions as a form of marketing communications

As a form of marketing communications, exhibitions enable products to be promoted, they can build brands and they can be an effective means of demonstrating products and building industry-wide credibility in a relatively short period of time. Attendance at exhibitions may also be regarded from a political standpoint, in that non-attendance by competitors may be taken as an opportunity by attendees to suggest weaknesses.

Table 18.2   A typology of trade show visitors

Segment name	Key characteristics
The basic shopper (39%)	Basic shoppers make about 7 'serious' visits to booths, 75% are planned and 70% of visits are made to standalone booths, which are accessible on all four sides.
The enthusiast (17%)	Enthusiasts make an average of 24 visits while at the trade show, more than three times that of the basic shopper; 80% of their visits are planned and they prefer to be 'where the action is'.
The niche shopper (17%)	The niche shopper makes an average of 9.2 visits, which is greater than the basic shopper but lower than the enthusiast. The key characteristic of this type of shopper is that 40% of their serious visits are made to small-sized booths. The niche shopper prefers to work with speciality exhibitors who do not have a big presence at the show.
The brand shopper (16%)	Brand shoppers make about 10 serious visits and show the highest preference for large booths. They are the most thorough in planning which booths to attend, reflecting their need to plan and make their visit to the show as efficient as possible.
The apathetic shopper (11%)	Only 33% of the apathetic shoppers' booth visits are planned. They also prefer booths that are open on three sides, and which have a wide selection of products. The suggestion is that apathetic shoppers might represent 'newcomers' or attendees who are unfamiliar with the trade show.

Source: Based on Gopalakrishna et al. (2010). © Emerald Group Publishing Limited. All rights reserved.

In the B2B sector new products and services are often introduced at trade shows, especially if there are to be public relations activities and events that can be spun off the launch. In other words, exhibitions are not activities independent of the other communications tools. Exhibitions, if used effectively, can be part of an integrated communications campaign.

Advertising prior to, during and after a trade show can be dovetailed with public relations, sponsorship and personal selling. Sales promotions can also be incorporated through competitions among customers prior to the show to raise awareness, generate interest and to suggest customer involvement. Competitions during a show can be focused on the sales force to motivate and stimulate commercial activity and among visitors to generate interest in the stand, raise brand name awareness, encourage focus on particular products (new, revised or revolutionary) and generate sales leads and enquiries.

Perhaps above all else, trades shows and exhibitions play a major role in the development of relationships.

Multimedia and trade shows

In many ways the use of a website as brochureware represented a first attempt at an online exhibition. In these situations, commercial organisations provided opportunities for people who could not physically get to see a product to gain some appreciation of its size, configuration and capability (through text).

Online trade shows are web-based platforms giving manufacturers, suppliers and distributors an opportunity to exchange information, virtually. As noted by Geigenmüller (2010), online show visitors can call on virtual halls and booths to obtain information about a firm's products and its services. Interaction between buyers and sellers occurs through chat rooms or video conferences, and forums. Online diaries or blogs are also used to discuss issues or leave messages for other participants.

However, the development of multimedia technologies has given not only commercial but also not-for-profit organisations the opportunity to showcase their wares on a global basis. One type of organisation to explore the use of this technology has been museums and art collections (static exhibits). Dumitrescu et al. (2014) argue that virtual exhibitions are currently used as an extension to physical exhibitions. Their capacity to engage visitors with multiple forms of multimedia content, regardless of location, suggests that virtual exhibitions will become the established format.

The use of multimedia technologies enables audiences across the world to access these collections and with the use of audio, video clips and streaming video, in addition to pictures and extensive text, these exhibitions can be brought to life, visited repeatedly, focus given to particular exhibits, materials updated quickly and unobtrusively, and links made to other similar facilities (Foo, 2008). Referred to as virtual exhibitions, the key difference with previous brochureware-type facilities is the feeling of virtual reality, the sense that a digital visitor is actually in the exhibition, even though seated several thousand miles away.

The use of e-commerce and digital media in the management and presentation of exhibitions is increasing. It is unlikely that online exhibitions will ever replace the offline, real-world version, if only because of the need to form relationships and to network with industry members, to touch and feel products, and to sense the atmosphere and vitality that exhibitions generate. However, there is huge scope to develop specialised exhibitions, and to develop online showcases that incorporate exhibits (products and services) from a variety of geographically dispersed locations.

Marketing management of exhibitions

Good management of exhibitions represents some key aspects of marketing communications in general. Successful events are driven by planning that takes place prior to the exhibition, with communications inviting a range of stakeholders, not just customers, in advance of the exhibition event. Stands should be designed to deliver key messages and press releases and press information packs should be prepared and distributed appropriately.

During the event itself staff should be well briefed, trained and knowledgeable about their role in terms of the brand and in the exhibition process. After the exhibition it is vital to follow up on contacts made and discussions or negotiations that have been held. In other words, the exhibition itself is a planned marketing communications activity, one where activities need to be planned prior to, during and after the event. What is key is that these activities are coordinated, themed and supported by brand-oriented staff.

Above all else, exhibitions are an important way of building relationships and signalling corporate identity. Trade shows are an important means of providing corporate hospitality and showing gratitude to all an organisation's customers, but in particular to its key account customers and others of strategic interest. Positive relationships with customers, competitors and suppliers are often reinforced through face-to-face dialogue that happens both formally in the exhibition hall and informally through the variety of social activities that surround and support these events.

Hospitality and events

As mentioned in the previous chapter, event management is closely connected with brand experience, public relations, sponsorship and branding. It is considered here as an adjunct to the experiences associated with attending exhibitions or trade shows. Prospective purchasers visit a designated area or location where, unlike an exhibition, a single brand is available to be tried, sampled and experienced or just enjoyed as an unobtrusive support.

Product events

Product-oriented events are normally focused on increasing sales. Cookery demonstrations, celebrities autographing their books and the opening of a new store by the CEO or local MP are events aimed at generating attention, interest and sales of a particular product. Alternatively, events are designed to attract the attention of the media and, through stories and articles presented in the news, are able to reach a wide audience.

Corporate events

Events designed to develop the corporate body are often held by an organisation with a view to providing some entertainment. These can generate considerable local media coverage, which in turn facilitates awareness, goodwill and interest. For example, events such as open days, factory visits and donations of products to local events can be very beneficial.

Community events

These are activities that contribute to the life of the local community. Sponsoring local fun runs and children's play areas, making contributions to local community centres and the disabled are typical activities. The organisation attempts to become more involved with the local community as a good employer and good member of the community. This helps to develop goodwill and awareness in the community.

The choice of events an organisation becomes involved with is critical. The events should have a theme and be chosen to satisfy objectives established earlier in the communications plan.

Scholars' paper 18.3

Trade fairs

Sarmento, M. and Simões, C. (2018) The evolving role of trade fairs in business: A systematic literature review and a research agenda, *Industrial Marketing Management*, **73 (August), 154–70.**

The authors provide a comprehensive review of studies on trade fairs, trade shows and exhibitions in the period from 1927 to 2016. They identify the evolving role of exhibitions over nine decades from the perspectives of organisers, exhibitors and visitors.

See also:

Brown, B. P., Mohan, M. and Boyd, D.E. (2017) Top management attention to trade shows and firm performance: a relationship marketing perspective, *Journal of Business Research*, 81, 40–50.

Packaging

Packaging has long been considered a means of protecting and preserving products during transit and while they remain in store or on the shelf prior to purchase and consumption. In this sense, packaging can be regarded as an element of product strategy. To a certain extent this is still true; however, technology has progressed considerably and, with consumer choice continually widening, packaging has become a means by which buyers, particularly in consumer markets, can make significant brand choice decisions. Stewart (2007) suggests that packaging has a role to play in marketing, 'selling the product, and representing the brand'. Indeed, Rundh (2016) identified packaging as a source of competitive advantage for products and found creative packaging provided a means of differentiation.

Nørgaard Olesen and Giacalone (2018) found that even for unbranded products such as carrots, packaging impacted consumer choice. Their study found that box packaging was associated with higher-quality produce than bags and identified consumers were willing to consider paying a higher price for boxed carrots. In contrast, a study of packaging for fresh cod in Norway identified consumers that find informational attributes, such as freshness statements, information on taste and convenience, of greater importance than visual aspects of the packaging (Heide and Olsen, 2017).

Low-involvement decision-making often requires peripheral cues to stimulate buyers into action. It has already been noted that decisions made at the point of purchase, especially those in the FMCG sector, often require buyers to build awareness through recognition. The design of packages and wrappers is important, as continuity of design, combined with the power to attract and hold the attention of prospective buyers, is a vital part of point-of-purchase activity. The degree of importance that manufacturers place upon packaging and design can be seen in the increasing frequency with which brands seek legal redress when they feel their brand (packaging) has been copied (Satomura et al., 2014).

Although it is agreed that packaging can provide a strong point of differentiation, one that is increasingly recognised by food manufacturers and producers (Wells et al., 2007), the implementation of suitable packaging for different consumers is far from satisfactory.

Sudbury-Riley (2014) found that packaging is regarded in many organisations as a technically based task, one where the goal is to develop particular functional specifications. Her research into the perceptions and experiences of packaging by senior citizens reveals that in addition to problems associated with wastage and mess, some forms of packaging were perceived to be 'difficult, time-consuming and frustrating' (p. 673). Part of her conclusion is that this serves to demonstrate that too few organisations appear to adopt a user-led orientation into the design of packaging and that this represents a major opportunity for companies.

While packaging should have functional value, such as the protection of the product, it is able to convey persuasive information and be part of the decision-making process and as such is an important means of marketing communications in particular markets, such as FMCG.

The communications dimensions of packaging

There are a number of dimensions that can affect the power and utility of a package. Colour is influential, as the context of the product class can frame the purchase situation for a buyer. This means that colours should be appropriate to the product class, to the brand and to the prevailing culture if marketing overseas. For example, red is used to stimulate the appetite, white to symbolise purity and cleanliness, blue to signal freshness, and green is increasingly being used to denote an environmental orientation and natural ingredients. From a cultural aspect, colours can be a problem. In China red is used to depict happiness; in Germany bright bold colours are regarded as appropriate for baby products, whereas in the UK pastel shades are more acceptable.

The shape may also provide information about how to open and use the product, while some packages can be used for other purposes after the product has been consumed. For example, some jars can be reused as food containers, thereby providing a means of continual communications for the original brand in the home. Packaging can also be used as a means of brand identification, as a cue by which buyers recognise and differentiate a brand. The supreme example of this is the Coca-Cola contour bottle, with its unique shape and immediate power for brand recognition at the point of purchase. Other iconic packaging includes Toblerone, Heinz Tomato Ketchup and Orangina.

Viewpoint 18.3
Packaging drives social media conversations

Image 18.4 Snickers swopped its own logo for 'hunger' words
Source: Keith Homan/123RF.

Personalised packaging has been used by several FMCG brands to differentiate the brand and drive social media engagement. Providing personalised products by changing logos to first names or special messages encourages conversations around the brand, both on and offline.

Coca-Cola's 'Share a Coke' campaign, which personalised the iconic logo to first names was successful in creating buzz around the brand. Consumers were seeking out bottles with their names on and posting messages to friends, which drove social media for the brand. This increased the number of people talking about the brand online.

Packaging has also been used as extensions of existing campaigns. Snickers altered its packaging to engage consumers by developing Hunger Bars. To extend its, 'You're Not You When You're Hungry' positioning, the chocolate bar swapped its brand name for 21 'hunger' words, such as Cranky, Impatient and Whiny. The words that are associated with hunger replaced the Snickers branding. The name change was supported with an online ad campaign to drive social media further.

To drive online engagement, KitKat changed their packaging on 47 million chocolate bars to include a QR code, which could be scanned on mobile devices. The code linked consumers with 74 YouTube videos, providing entertainment while having a break. The new branded packs of chocolate bars were part of a partnership with Nestlé and Google that included Google's Android system version 4.4 being called 'KitKat'.

Image 18.5 A limited edition KitKat pack was introduced in the UK and Ireland featuring the YouTube logo and QR code
Source: Nestlé.

Sources: Mortimer (2015); Nestlé (2016).

Insight

These examples show how packaging has evolved from more than just a means of protecting and preserving a product, and highlight how it is being used to engage audiences and drive social media for brands. Packaging has a physical presence unlike other media and brands are experimenting with new ways to use to use the space.

Question: How are brands using packaging to drive social media?

Task: Find other brands that have personalised or altered their packaging. Explain how this could be used as part of a wider marketing communications campaign.

Package size is important, as different target markets may consume varying amounts of product. However, the size of a package can also be an important perceptual stimulus. Fernqvist et al. (2015) found in their study of perceptions of potato packaging that consumers considered the size of the packaging within their purchase decision.

However, Folkes and Matta (2004) counter this by referring to *gestalt* theory, which is concerned with holistic perspectives. They say that consumers use multiple dimensions to make judgements about objects (packages). Their research suggests that there is a relationship between the attractiveness of a package and the volume of the package. As a broad generalisation, the greater the attractiveness, the greater is the perceived volume. The implications of this insight have been implicitly known by marketing management for years, judging by the effort that is given to create attractive packaging and shelf stand-out.

Simmonds and Spence (2017) found that packaging that allows the consumer to see the product influences consumer decision making. The authors suggest product images and transparency should be considered for food product packaging as a means to capture consumers' attention and increase purchase intention. Packaging that allows the consumer to see the product itself is clearly favoured, although the study cautions against using transparent packaging for products that are unappealing.

All food packages have to carry information concerning the ingredients, nutritional values and safety requirements, including sell-by and use-by dates. Eco-labels appear to generate positive reactions from consumers, particularly when there is low involvement. Research by Atkinson and Rosenthal (2014) indicates that the addition of eco-labels is likely to drive positive attitudes among consumers about both the product and the source. Traffic light colour-coded nutrition labels are used to signal that a food contains low, medium or high amounts of particular unhealthy ingredients. The intention is to communicate that the product can therefore be consumed regularly (green), most of the time (amber) or only occasionally (red) (Koenigstorfer et al., 2014).

Non-food packages must also attempt to be sales agents and provide all the information that a prospective buyer might need, while at the same time providing conviction that this product is the correct one to purchase. Labelling of products offers opportunities to manufacturers to harmonise the in-store presentation of their products in such a way that buyers from different countries can still identify the brand and remain brand loyal.

Packages carry tangible and intangible messages. The psychological impact that packages can have should not be underestimated. They convey information about the product, but they also say something about its quality and how it differs from competitive offerings. In some cases, where there is little to differentiate products, buyers may use the packaging on its own for decision-making purposes.

Scholars' paper 18.4

Packaging to create value

Rundh, B. (2016) The role of packaging within marketing and value creation, *British Food Journal*, 118(10), 2491–511.

The author discusses the role of packaging within a brand's marketing strategy. The paper highlights the importance of including packaging as part of an integrated marketing approach and argues packaging should be seen as a means of creating value for brands. The view that packaging can create competitive advantage is an important one.

See also:

Simmonds, G. and Spence, C. (2017) Thinking inside the box: how seeing products on, or through, the packaging influences consumer perceptions and purchase behaviour, *Food Quality and Preference*, 62, 340–51.

Licensing

Licensing is not an option open to all organisations, yet of many of those who are able to utilise it, an increasing number are integrating this approach into their communications activities. Spurred by the surge in the numbers of digital characters and digital games, online and mobile games such as Angry Birds, Talking Friends, Moshi Monsters and MovieStarPlanet have, according to Macintosh (2012), not only attracted millions of players worldwide, in just a few years, but have also expanded into toys, clothing, TV shows, magazines and computer games.

The licensing industry has seen significant growth in recent years, with the global licensing industry now valued at $262.9 billion (LIMA, 2017). According to Brand Licensing Europe (2018) the three main sectors of licensing are seen to be character and entertainment, brands and lifestyle, and art, design and image. The largest of these sectors, character and entertainment, generated retail sales of $118 billion in 2016 (Brand Licensing Europe, 2018).

According to Kwon et al. (2008), licensing is a commercial arrangement whereby a licensor, the party that holds the property rights or trademark, grants permission to others, called licensees, such as manufacturing companies, permitting them to manufacture products carrying the licensor's logo or trademark. Another simpler view is that a brand owner (licensor) grants a brand user (licensee) the right to use the brand in association with a defined product or service, for a specific period of time, and within defined terms, areas and territories, in return for the payment of a specific licence fee, royalty, or some such combination of financial rewards (Keller, 2003). Both interpretations are essentially the same, although the second might be closer to considering licensing as a form of brand extension (Weidmann and Ludwig, 2008). This is because the process of extension shifts the brand into a new, albeit slightly dissimilar, marketing context.

This practitioners' interpretation from Brand Licensing Europe (2018: 4) states that licensing is 'the process of leasing a trademarked or copyrighted entity (known as a property) for use in conjunction with a product, service or promotion'.

Licensing is a form of brand alliance, of which there are many types. These are presented in Figure 18.2. Ervelles et al. (2008) provide a useful clarification of brand alliance

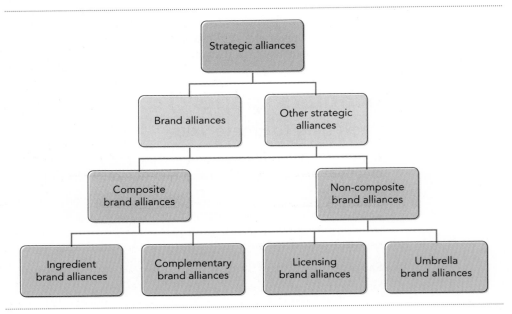

Figure 18.2 Types of brand alliance
Source: Ervelles et al. (2008).

and present a typology of the common types of brand alliances in B2C markets and high-light the differences between strategic alliances and brand alliances, and between brand alliances and co-branding.

A licensed product carries two different brand names or logos simultaneously. These are the brands of the licensor and the licensee. Park et al. (1996) refer to these as a *modifier*, such as a manufacturer's brand, and a *header*, the licensee's brand, such as the name or logo of a sports team. Kwon et al. (2008) cite as an example the licensing agreement between Ohio State University (OSU) and Nike over the OSU's Buckeyes' sweatshirt. Here Nike is the modifier and the header is OSU Buckeyes.

Licensing can benefit business in a number of ways. Weidmann and Ludwig (2008) make the point that licensed products offer opportunities for improved differentiation and stand-out and argue that licensing can:

- expand a product portfolio;
- increase the number of revenue streams;
- increase awareness – especially important when incorporated within an international marketing strategy;
- build brand equity;
- stimulate customer brand loyalty;
- develop partnerships with retailers;
- develop brand positioning.

Licensing enables brands to move into new businesses and markets without the major investment necessary for new manufacturing processes, machinery or facilities. Well-run licensing programmes are characterised by licensor's control over the brand image and how it is portrayed. This is achieved through an effective approvals process and other contractual obligations. The rewards of additional revenue (royalties) and profit are also accompanied by exposure in fresh media channels or even supermarket aisles (Brand Licensing Europe, 2018).

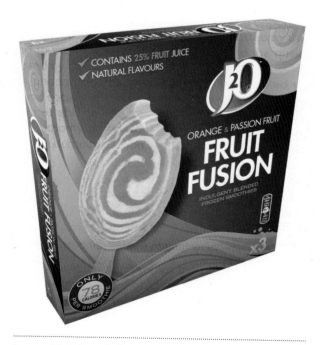

Image 18.6 Brand of Brothers recently launched two ice lollies using the J20 brand
Source: Britvic PLC.

An increasingly important, yet expensive approach is to license a cartoon character, for example from *The Simpsons*, *Rugrats* or *South Park*, or a cyber-person such as Lara Croft who was used by Lucozade. These characters are then used strategically to build brands in order to attract the attention of children and provide the parental agreement necessary for a purchase to be made.

Viewpoint 18.4

How brand licensing influences popular music acts

Dr Ray Sylvester, Anderson University (IN), USA

Image 18.7 High-profile music acts and music entertainment companies agree 360-degree deals
Source: Kevin Winter/Getty Images.

Historically a music act/artist primarily accrued income through music sales paid by record companies, who controlled the production and consumption of physical recorded music (vinyl/cassettes/CDs). Today, digitisation has forever changed the music and entertainment landscape. A popular music act or artist can now control the production, and significantly influence distribution and consumption of their own music. Digital native consumers now predominate. They consume music via annual and/or monthly subscription platforms that enable constant digital music product downloads and streaming service access through sites such as iTunes, Apple Music and Spotify. Today the subscriptions services of Apple Music and Spotify account for around 38m and 70m subscribers respectively.

The digital revolution has created a major change. As the value of physical recorded music has diminished, the value of the music act/ artist has gone up. In recognition of this paradox, record labels, commonly known now as 'entertainment companies', have developed new ways to generate income. A '360-degree deal' is an extended portfolio of income opportunities from the whole realm of commercial value derived from the music act/artist brand. Accordingly, they have now truly moved from their traditional pre-millennial business origin of control of singular rights (recorded music) to the attempt to manage and control multiple (music brand) rights.

These multiple rights deals seek to obtain royalties or usage income from multiple music act/artist brand-derived sources, including digital rights management (DRM), music tours/concerts, public performance royalties, songwriting, lyric display and publishing, ringtone sales, merchandising, TV/film and games music licensing, TV/film appearances and endorsements. These multiple rights deals can provide immediate returns for an entertainment/record label to offset the lucrative advance established artists can command.

Multiple rights income derived from a recognised music act/artist brand is now the standard throughout the music industry today. An act/artist can now be seen as possessing a portfolio of music brand products and/or services. This portfolio is normally made possible through several levels of brand licensing:

- the music brand (live and recorded);
- the extended brand licensing (e.g. fashion);
- the brand partnership (e.g. endorsements).

Several 360-degree deals have been brokered between high-profile popular music acts and music entertainment companies. Robbie Williams signed a deal with the former major label EMI in 2002 for a reputed £80 million, while Madonna received over £100 million for a deal with Live Nation in 2007. A year later Jay-Z received an alleged deal of £150 million over 10 years.

However, today there is now a growing profile of popular music act/artists who are exploiting and managing their own brand value through multiple rights management. Chance the Rapper initially gave away his music for free via online platforms. In 2016 he made history by directly signing a distribution (streaming only) deal with Apple Music that reputedly earned him $500,000 for a two-week streaming exclusive for his album *Coloring Book*. In the first week of release it debuted at number eight in the US charts with its 57.3 million streams equating to 38,000 equivalent album units. The album became the very first stream-only album to chart. The album stayed in the US charts for 33 consecutive weeks and has now surpassed 500,000 streaming album equivalent sales. Chance went on to win three Grammy awards in 2017, including Best New Artist and Best Rap Album'. In 2017 he was ranked as the 5th highest-paid hip-hop artist with an income of $33 million from touring, endorsements (Nike, Nestlé and Twitter) and digital streaming.

Sources: Bahler (2017); Ingham (2017); Sylvester (2013); Sylvester (2016).

Insight

This highlights how brand licensing is being used within the music industry to increase revenue streams. In particular, the examples given illustrate how digital channels have changed licensing and how new streams of income can be generated.

Question: What might be the goals associated with licensing arrangements in the music industry?

Task: Find three examples of recent licensing deals between music acts and music entertainment companies.

Not necessarily the first, but Bass (2004) indicates that the actor Jack Nicholson had a clause in his contract that rewarded him with a percentage of the licensing revenue generated by the film *Batman*. For licensors a common strategy is to license into 'accessory categories'. This occurs when the extension is something that accompanies consumption of the core product. Bass suggests that the strong emotional loyalty or bonding generated by a confectionery brand such as KitKat could lead into a KitKat mug, teaspoon, kettle and teapot.

However, although brand licensing appears to be well established and accepted, there are certain risks associated with this marketing communications activity. For example, product failure, poor quality or just a failure to reach expectations can reflect poorly on the licensor and the brand as a whole. In an age where conversations are a potent form of communications, product reviews, customer feedback, as well as media comment and word-of-mouth communications, can all have a negative impact on a brand. Mattel's experience of poor product quality and associated health risks, when some of its Fisher-Price toys were discovered to be coated with a potentially toxic, lead-based paint, led to a massive product recall and consequential negative conversations (Edwards, 2010). These products, made under licence in China, serve to warn of the issues at stake.

Key points

- Brand placement is the inclusion of products and services in films (or media) for deliberate promotional exposure, often, but not always, in return for an agreed financial sum.
- It is regarded by some as a form of sales promotion, by others as sponsorship, but the most common linkage is with advertising, because the 'advertiser' pays a third party for the opportunity to present the product in their channel.
- There are distinct forms of placement. One involves the passive placement of a brand within the media; the other sees whole entertainment programmes built around a single brand, one where the placement is actively woven into the theme or the plot of the programme. This is known as 'branded entertainment'.
- The main reasons for attending exhibitions (consumer shows) and trade fairs (B2B shows) are that it enables organisations to: meet customers (and potential customers) in an agreeable environment, one where both have independently volunteered their time to attend; place/take orders; generate leads; and gather market information.
- As a form of marketing communications, exhibitions enable products to be promoted, they can build brands and they can be an effective means of demonstrating products and building industry-wide credibility in a relatively short period of time.
- Positive relationships with customers, competitors and suppliers are often reinforced through face-to-face dialogue that happens both formally in the exhibition hall and informally through the variety of social activities that surround and support these events.
- Packages carry tangible and intangible messages and packaging has become a means by which buyers, particularly in consumer markets, can make significant brand choice decisions. Packaging conveys information about the product, but it also makes a statement about the quality of the product and how it differs from competitive offerings.
- Packaging has become a means by which buyers, particularly in consumer markets, can make significant brand choice decisions and constitutes more than a means of preserving product integrity.
- Licensing is a commercial arrangement where a brand owner (licensor) grants a brand user (licensee) the right to use the brand in association with a defined product or service, for a specific period of time, and within defined terms, areas and territories, in return for the payment of a specific licence fee, royalty, or some such combination of financial rewards.

- A licensed product carries two different brand names or logos simultaneously. These are the brands of the licensor and the licensee.
- Licensing enables brands to move into new businesses and markets without the major investment necessary for new manufacturing processes, machinery or facilities.
- Well-run licensing programmes are characterised by the licensor's control over the brand image and how it is portrayed. This is achieved through an effective approvals process and other contractual obligations. The rewards of additional revenue (royalties) and profit are also accompanied by exposure in fresh media channels or even supermarket aisles.

Product placement within your own product: The NFL's brand communications 'Super Bowl LII' strategy

Dr Ray Sylvester, with input and support from both Dr Anna Stumpf and Dr Brock Vaughters, Anderson University (IN), USA

Image 18.8 The NFL created their own Super Bowl commercial
Source: PCN Photography/Alamy Stock Photo.

One of the biggest events on the USA and progressively the world's sporting calendar took place on the 4th February 2018. It was Super Bowl LII (52). The NFL is one of the most popular sports in America. 32 teams compete each year to be crowned Super Bowl champions. The NFL is acknowledged for its brand marketing acumen.

However, the National Football League [NFL] has been facing increasing negativity and challenge to its brand reputation, brand engagement and its overall brand value.

Brand value has been historically dominated by economic measures, yet in recent years the cultural aspect of the brand has become a growing and significant force that ultimately impacts revenue. With the NFL's revenue of around $14 billion in 2017 you could think that such concerns were unfounded. But,

when you examine recent viewing and engagement information about the NFL brand, one can see that there are signs that the once unblemished brand identity is facing difficult times.

According to several reports in 2017 the NFL's TV AD revenue was projected to fall to its lowest since 2008. A survey had pointed to a range of factors that had caused NFL viewing and therefore revenue projections to decline. They included the 2016 election, too much advertising, game delays, off-field image, cord-cutting (subscription cancellation) and anthem protests.

Whatever one's opinion, it is clear that the NFL brand has begun to lose its luster. The response from the sporting giant has been to use its largest and by far most precious asset, namely the Super Bowl. It has previously been used as a channel to do 'product placement' campaign advertising. In other words, its is using some of its own advertising space to promote itself.

In recent years this has included campaigns related to 'Super Bowl Babies Choir' in 2016, which used a reworking of Seal's 'Kiss from a Rose' to chronicle the fact that the celebrating winning cities see a spike in birth rates 9 months following the game. 'Super Bowl Baby Legends' in 2017 extended the lineage thread by reinforcing their 'Football is Family' tagline.

These campaigns were created and produced by Grey New York, the official marketing agency of the NFL since 2009. They were also the agency that dealt with the 'No More' campaign, which aired in both 2015 and 2016 Super Bowls to bring public awareness to domestic violence and sexual assault. These two topics plagued the NFL after the 2014 backlash to the NFL's handling of a player's assault of their fiancée, which was caught on surveillance video.

The commercials were linked to a powerful text campaign, by No More, which was promoted in the Super Bowl commercials and existed to offer help and information to those who needed it. The NFL paid all production costs of the spots in an attempt to placate the public's outrage.

So, the NFL wants to increase awareness of both its values and mission. Their values espoused include reference to responsibility, trust, character, respect, integrity, humility, and togetherness. While the NFL's mission relates to providing all of their stakeholders with world-class sport and entertainment.

With awareness of their own issues and the ability to use their own Super Bowl as a platform, what would the 2018 NFL Super Bowl commercial look like? Arguably, the league could not ignore the controversy of the 2017 season that involved players taking a knee during the playing of the national anthem. It was reported that more than 250 players knelt during the national anthem over one weekend as a nod to peaceful protests for racial equality that former NFL quarterback Colin Kaepernick began in 2016. The protests were reignited prior to that weekend after US President Donald Trump used controversial negative language to describe protesting players and called for their firing.

According to the Grey New York, the 2018 Super Bowl commercial was inspired by the NFL's change of the rules in 2017, that allowed players to celebrate their touchdowns. Grey New York noted that the campaign would create a "celebration of celebrations". The creative direction was to attach fun and positivity to the NFL. It was clear that the campaign was created to offset negativity and bring about a sense of positive community togetherness, which attempts to reflect the NFL mission and values.

The NFL's annual Super Bowl event has very distinctive qualities that relate to the fact that the NFL is tasked with developing and managing the brand of both NFL and the Super Bowl.

So, how did the NFL do with their product placement advertisement in their very own Super Bowl 2018? Well, they decided to instill a fun narrative about the NFL that connected their brand values. They introduced a brand story related to two players from the New York Giants and their own supposed preparations for the now legal touchdown celebration. The first player was Eli Manning, the winner of two Super Bowls and the brother of the recently retired and possibly more popular Peyton Manning. The other Odell Beckham Jr., the wide receiver, who has been one of the most exciting, productive, popular and sometime controversial players both on and off the playing field. The Giants didn't have a great year and their selection for the NFL advertising campaign has been attributed to both their notably humble year as a team and the respective personalities of the two players.

The advert shows Beckham Jr. receiving a touchdown pass from Manning and then a reworking of the famous dance in the iconic film "Dirty Dancing" ensues, with Beckham Jr. running and leaping into Manning's arms as he lifts him into the air. 'To all the touchdowns to come' then appears alongside the NFL shield at the end.

The result was that the Super Bowl advert was recorded as one of the most popular advertising slots of the 2018 Super Bowl. The NFL product placement within its own product was successful. Why? Could it be that they managed to reinforce some of their brand values such as trust and togetherness?

Sources various including

American Marketing Association, Marketing News Staff. (2018, February 5). Marketing News Roundup: Super Bowl LII. Retrieved from https://www.ama.org/publications/eNewsletters/Marketing-News-Weekly/Pages/marketing-news-roundup-super-bowl-lii.aspx

Best, N. (2018) How the Super Bowl LII Eli Manning, Odel Beckham Jr. commercial came about. Available at: https://www.newsday.com/sports/football/super-bowl/super-bowl-eli-manning-odell-beckham-jr-commercial-1.16547651 [Accessed on April 17th 2018]

Bump, P. (2017) What that study about the decline in football viewership actually says. Available at: https://www.washingtonpost.com/news/politics/wp/2017/07/27/what-that-study-about-the-decline-in-football-viewership-actually-says/?utm_term=.f6bfc45b18a8 [Accessed on April 17th 2018]

Crowl, J. (2017) The NFL's Brand Crisis: How It Plans to Market Itself Differently. Available at: https://www.skyword.com/contentstandard/marketing/nfls-brand-crisis-plans-market-differently/ [Accessed on April 17th 2018]

Lafayette, J. (2018, February 5). Super Bowl Generated $414M in Ad Revenue. Retrieved from https://www.broadcastingcable.com/news/super-bowl-generated-414m-ad-revenue-171555

NFL (2017) NFL Company Overview. Available at: https://www.nfl.com [Accessed on April 17th 2018]

Pallotta, F. (2018) Super Bowl ratings are down, but 103 million people watched. Available at: http://money.cnn.com/2018/02/05/media/super-bowl-ratings-index.html [Accessed on April 17th 2018]

Sports Illustrated. (2018, January 11). Super Bowl LII: How Much Does a Commercial Cost? Retrieved from https://www.msn.com/en-us/sports/nfl/super-bowl-lii-how-much-does-a-commercial-cost/ar-AAuzx9k

Swallen, J. (2018, February 5). Super Bowl LII - The Numbers. Retrieved from https://www.kantarmedia.com/us/thinking-and-resources/blog/super-bowl-lii-the-numbers

The case study was written by Dr Ray Sylvester, with input and support from both Dr Anna Stumpf and Dr Brock Vaughters at Anderson University, IN. USA

Review questions

Super Bowl case questions

1. What were the NFL trying to achieve through the Super Bowl campaign?

2. Make notes about the ideal context for the use of product placement.

3. Find three examples of product placement in sport.

4. What opportunities are there for product placement within sporting events?

5. Discuss the possible ethical implications of allowing brands to use product placement in sport.

General questions

1. Identify two strengths and two weaknesses of brand placement. Identify four examples of brand placement and evaluate their effectiveness.

2. Evaluate the differences between consumer- and business-oriented trade shows.

3. As sales manager for a company making plastic mouldings for use in the manufacture of consumer durables, set out the reasons for and against attendance at trade shows and exhibitions.

4. Find three brands where the shape of a package is an integral part of the product.

5. What is the difference between active and passive packaging?

References for Chapter 18

Atkinson, L. and Rosenthal, S. (2014) Signaling the green sell: the influence of eco-label source, argument specificity, and product involvement on consumer trust, *Journal of Advertising*, 43(1), 33–45.

Bahler, K. (2017) How Chance the Rapper, a 24-year-old with no record label, became the youngest person on Fortune's 40 under 40 list, *time.com*, 17 August, retrieved 17 September 2018 from http://time.com/money/4901591/chance-the-rapper-youngest-40-under-40/

Banham, M. (2011) ITV signs Nationwide for first Coronation Street product placement deal, *Campaign*, 31 October 2011, retrieved 10 January 2018 from https://www.campaignlive.co.uk/article/itv-signs-nationwide-first-coronation-street-product-placement-deal/1101366

Barber, N. (2015) Does Bond's product placement go too far? *BBC Culture*, 1 October, retrieved 10 December 2017 from http://www.bbc.com/culture/story/20151001-does-bonds-product-placement-go-too-far

Bass, A. (2004) Licensed extensions – stretching to communicate, *Brand Management*, 12(1), 31–38.

Bertheron, P., Pitt, L.F. and Watson, R.T. (1996) The World Wide Web as an advertising medium, *Journal of Advertising Research*, 6(1), 43–54.

Best, N. (2018) How the Super Bowl LII Eli Manning, Odell Beckham Jr. commercial came about, *Newsday*, 5 February, retrieved 17 April 2018 from https://www.newsday.com/sports/football/super-bowl/super-bowl-eli-manning-odell-beckham-jr-commercial-1.16547651

Brand Licensing Europe (2018) *Brand Licensing Handbook 2018*, retrieved 20 February 2018 from, https://ubm.brandlicensing.eu/licensinghandbook/

Brown, B.P., Mohan, M. and Boyd, D.E. (2017) Top management attention to trade shows and firm performance: a relationship marketing perspective, *Journal of Business Research*, 81, 40–50.

Bump, P. (2017) What that study about the decline in football viewership actually says, *Washington Post*, 27 July, retrieved 17 April from https://www.washingtonpost.com/news/politics/wp/2017/07/27/what-that-study-about-the-decline-in-football-viewership-actually-says/?utm_term=.f6bfc45b18a8

Chen, H. and Haley, E. (2014) Product placement in social games: consumer experiences in China, *Journal of Advertising*, 43(3), 286–95.

Crowl, J. (2017) The NFL's brand crisis: how it plans to market itself differently, *Skyword*, 17 August, retrieved 17 April from https://www.skyword.com/contentstandard/marketing/nfls-brand-crisis-plans-market-differently/

D'Astous, A. and Séguin, N. (1999) Consumer reactions to product placement strategies in television sponsorship, *European Journal of Marketing*, 33(9/10), 896–910.

Davtyan, D. and Cunningham, I. (2017) An investigation of brand placement effects on brand attitudes and purchase intentions: brand placements versus TV commercials, *Journal of Business Research*, 70, 160–67.

de Gregorio, F. and Sung, Y.J. (2010) The influence of consumer socialization variables on attitude toward product placement, *Journal of Advertising*, 39(1), 85–99.

DeLorme, D.E. and Reid, L.N. (1999) Moviegoers' experiences and interpretation of brands in films revisited, *Journal of Advertising*, 28(2), 71–95.

Dens, N., De Pelsmacker, P. and Verhellen, Y. (2018) Better together? Harnessing the power of brand placement through program sponsorship messages, *Journal of Business Research*, 83, 151–59.

Dumitrescu, G., Lepadatu, C. and Ciurea, C. (2014) Creating virtual exhibitions for educational and cultural development, *Informatica Economică*, 18(1), 102–10.

Eagle, L. and Dahl, S. (2018) Product placement in old and new media: examining the evidence for concern. *Journal of Business Ethics*, 147(3), 605–18.

Edwards, H. (2010) The supply-chain reaction, *Marketing*, 19 May, retrieved 1 March 2012 from https://www.campaignlive.co.uk/article/helen-edwards-branding-supply-chain-reaction/1003783?src_site=brandrepublic

Ervelles, S., Horton, V. and Fukawa, N. (2008) Understanding B2C brand alliances between manufacturers and suppliers, *Marketing Management Journal*, 18(2), 32–46.

Fernqvist, F., Olsson, A. and Spendrup, S. (2015) What's in it for me? Food packaging and consumer responses, a focus group study, *British Food Journal*, 117(3), 1122–35.

Folkes, V. and Matta, S. (2004) The effect of package shape on consumers' judgments of product volume: attention as a mental contaminant, *Journal of Consumer Research*, 31(2), 390–402.

Foo, S. (2008) Online virtual exhibitions: concepts and design considerations, *Journal of Library and Information Technology*, 28(4), July, 22–34.

Geigenmüller, A. (2010) The role of virtual trade fairs in relationship value creation, *Journal of Business and Industrial Marketing*, 25(4), 284–92.

Gillespie, B., Muehling, D.D. and Kareklas, I. (2018) Fitting product placements: affective fit and cognitive fit as determinants of consumer evaluations of placed brands, *Journal of Business Research*, 82, 90–102.

Gopalakrishna, S., Roster, C.A. and Sridhar, S. (2010) An exploratory study of attendee activities at a business trade show, *Journal of Business and Industrial Marketing*, 25(4), 241–48.

Gould, S.J., Gupta, P.B. and Grabner-Kräuter, S. (2000) Product placements in movies: a cross-cultural analysis of Austrian, French, and American consumers' attitudes toward this emerging international promotional medium, *Journal of Advertising*, 29(4), 41–58.

Gupta, P.B., Balasubramanian, S.K. and Klassen, M.L. (2000) Viewers' evaluations of product placements in movies: policy issues and managerial implications, *Journal of Current Issues and Research in Advertising*, 22(2), 41–52.

Gwynn, S. (2018) Co-op and Costa come to Coronation Street in ITV's biggest product placement deal, *Campaign*, 30 January, retrieved 10 January 2018 from https://www.campaignlive.co.uk/article/co-op-costa-coronation-street-itvs-biggest-product-placement-deal/1455802

Hang, H. (2012) The implicit influence of bimodal brand placement on children, *International Journal of Advertising*, 31(3), 465–84.

Heide, M. and Olsen, S.O. (2017) Influence of packaging attributes on consumer evaluation of fresh cod, *Food Quality and Preference*, 60, 9–18.

Hirschman, E.C. and Thompson, C.J. (1997) Why media matter: toward a richer understanding of consumers' relationships with advertising and mass media, *Journal of Advertising*, 26(1), 43–60.

Homer, P. (2009) Product placements: the impact of placement type and repetition on attitude, *Journal of Advertising*, 38(3), 21–31.

Hudson, S. and Hudson, D. (2006) Branded entertainment: a new advertising technique or product placement in disguise? *Journal of Marketing Management*, 22(5–6), 489–504.

Ingham, T. (2017) Apple paid Chance The Rapper $500,000 for coloring book exclusive, *Music Business Worldwide*, 19 March, retrieved 17 September 2018 from https://www.musicbusinessworldwide.com/chance-the-rapper-apple-paid-me-500000-for-coloring-book-exclusive/

Kamleitner, B. and Jyote, A.K. (2013) How using versus showing interaction between characters and products boosts product placement effectiveness, *International Journal of Advertising*, 32(4), 633–53.

Kandhadai, R. and Saxena, R. (2014) Brand placement: new perspectives and a comprehensive definition, *The Marketing Review*, 14(3), 231–44.

Karrh, J.A., McKee, K.B., Britain, K. and Pardun, C.J. (2003) Practitioners' evolving views of product placement effectiveness, *Journal of Advertising Research*, 43(2), 138–50.

Keller, K.L. (2003) *Strategic Brand Management: Building, measuring and managing brand equity*, 2nd edn, Upper Saddle River, NJ: Pearson Education.

Koenigstorfer, J., Groeppel-Klein, A. and Kamm, F. (2014) Healthful food decision making in response to traffic light color-coded nutrition labeling, *Journal of Public Policy and Marketing*, 33(1), 65–77.

Kwak, H., Andras, T.L. and Zinkhan, G.M. (2009) Advertising to active viewers: consumer attitudes in the US and South Korea, *International Journal of Advertising*, 28(1), 49–75.

Kwon, H.H., Kim, H. and Mondello, M. (2008) Does a manufacturer matter in cobranding? The influence of a manufacturer brand on sport team licensed apparel, *Sport Marketing Quarterly*, 17, 163–72.

Lee, T., Sung, Y. and Choi, S.M. (2011a) Young adults' responses to product placement in movies and television shows: a comparative study of the United States and South Korea, *International Journal of Advertising*, 30(3), 479–507.

Lee, T., Sung, Y. and de Gregorio, F. (2011b) Cross-cultural challenges in product placement, *Marketing Intelligence & Planning*, 29(4), 366–84.

LIMA (2017) LIMA Annual Global Survey of Licensing Industry 2017, retrieved 20 February 2018 from https://www.licensing.org/news/lima-annual-global-survey-of-licensing-industry-now-available/

MacIntosh, E. (2012) Exploring licensing's new gaming frontier, *Marketing*, 10 February.

McKechnie, S.A. and Zhou, J. (2003) Product placement in movies: a comparison of Chinese and American consumers' attitudes, *International Journal of Advertising*, 22(3), 349–74.

Mortimer, N. (2015) Snickers follows Coke's lead for personalised package design campaign, *The Drum*, 24 September, retrieved 14 December 2017 from http://www.thedrum.com/news/2015/09/24/snickers-follows-coke-s-lead-personalised-package-design-campaign

Nebenzahl, I.D. and Secunda, E. (1993) Consumer attitudes toward product placement in movies, *International Journal of Advertising*, 12, 1–11.

Nelson, M.R. and Devanathan, N. (2006) Brand placements Bollywood style, *Journal of Consumer Behaviour*, 5(3), 211–21.

Nestlé (2016) Nestlé and Google team up for KitKat YouTube partnership, *Nestlé*, 3 May, retrieved 10 December 2017 from https://www.nestle.co.uk/media/pressreleases/nestle-and-google-team-up-for-kitkat-youtube-partnership

NFL (2017) NFL company overview, *NFL*, retrieved 17 April 2018 from http://www.nfl.com/careers/about

Nørgaard Olesen, S. and Giacalone, D. (2018) The influence of packaging on consumers' quality perception of carrots, *Journal of Sensory Studies*, 33(1).

Pallotta, F. (2018) Super Bowl ratings are down, but 103 million people watched, CNN, 5 February, retrieved 17 April 2018 from http://money.cnn.com/2018/02/05/media/super-bowl-ratings/index.html

Park, C., Jun, W.S.Y. and Shocker, A.D. (1996) Composite branding alliances: an investigation of extension and feedback effects, *Journal of Marketing Research*, 33(4), 453–66.

Pervan, S.J. and Martin, B.A.S. (2002) Product placement in US and New Zealand television soap operas: an exploratory study, *Journal of Marketing Communications*, 8, 101–13.

Plaut, M. (2004) Ford advertises the literary way, *BBC News/Business*, retrieved 20 March 2008 from http://news.bbc.co.uk/1/hi/business/3522635.stm

Redondo, I., Russell, C.A. and Bernal, J. (2018) To brand or not to brand a product placement? Evidence from a field study of two influence mechanisms of positive portrayals of alcohol in film, *Drug and Alcohol Review*, 37(S1), S366–S374.

Rundh, B. (2016) The role of packaging within marketing and value creation, *British Food Journal*, 118(10), 2491–511.

Russell, C.A. and Belch, M. (2005) A managerial investigation into the product placement industry, *Journal of Advertising Research*, 45(1), 73–92.

Sarmento, M., and Simões, C. (2018) The evolving role of trade fairs in business: a systematic literature review and a research agenda, *Industrial Marketing Management*, 73 (August), 154–70.

Sarmento, M., Simões, C. and Farhangmehr, M. (2015) Applying a relationship marketing perspective to B2B trade fairs: the role of socialization episodes, *Industrial Marketing Management*, 44, 131–41.

Satomura, T., Wedel, M. and Pieters, R. (2014) Copy alert: a method and metric to detect visual copycat brands, *Journal of Marketing Research*, 51(1), 1–13.

Simmonds, G. and Spence, C. (2017) Thinking inside the box: how seeing products on, or through, the packaging influences consumer perceptions and purchase behaviour, *Food Quality and Preference*, 62, 340–51.

Shamsian, J. (2017) A 23 year old rapper who refuses to sign a record deal just made Grammy history, *Independent*, 13 February, retrieved 18 September 2018 from https://www.independent.co.uk/life-style/chance-the-rapper-grammys-record-deal-a7578031.html

Smit, E., van Reijmersdal, E. and Neijens, P. (2009) Today's practice of brand placement and the industry behind it, *International Journal of Advertising*, 28(5), 761–82.

Stewart, B. (2007) *Packaging Design*, London: Laurence King.

Sudbury-Riley, L. (2014) Unwrapping senior consumers' packaging experiences, *Marketing Intelligence & Planning*, 32(6), 666–86.

Sung, Y. and de Gregorio, F. (2008) Brand new world: a comparison of consumers' attitudes toward brand placement in film, television shows, songs and video games, *Journal of Promotion Management*, 14(1/2), 85–101.

Sung, Y., de Gregorio, F. and Jung, J. (2009) Non-student consumer attitudes towards product placement: implications for public policy and advertisers, *International Journal of Advertising*, 28(2), 257–85.

Sweney, M. (2018) Forget product placement: now advertisers can buy storylines, *Guardian*, retrieved 10 February 2018 from https://www.theguardian.com/media/2018/jan/20/forget-product-placement-advertisers-buy-storylines-tv-blackish

Sylvester, R. (2013) Brand You, in Fitterman Radbill, C. (2013) *Introduction to The Music Industry*, New York: Routledge.

Sylvester, R. (2016) Beyoncé – how brand licensing influences popular music acts, in Fill, C. and Turnbull, S. (2016) *Marketing Communications: discovery, creation and conversations*, 7th edn, Harlow: Pearson.

van Reijmersdal, E.A. (2011) Mixing advertising and editorial content in radio programmes: appreciation and recall of brand placements versus commercials, *International Journal of Advertising*, 30(3), 425–46.

Visit Britain (2018) World Travel Market 2018, retrieved 14 September 2018 from https://www.visitbritain.org/world-travel-market-2018

Weidmann, K.-P. and Ludwig, D. (2008) How risky are brand licensing strategies in view of customer perceptions and reactions? *Journal of General Management*, 33(3), 31–52.

Wells, L.E., Farley, H. and Armstrong, G.A. (2007) The importance of packaging design for own-label food brands, *International Journal of Retail and Distribution Management*, 36(9), 677–90.

WTM (2018) WTM London 2017 facilitates a record £3.1 billion in travel industry deals, WTM, 27 March, retrieved 5 April 2018 from https://news.wtm.com/wtm-london-2017-facilitates-a-record-3-1-billion-in-travel-industry-deals/

Yuksel, U. and Voola, R. (2010) Travel trade shows: exploratory study of exhibitors' perceptions, *Journal of Business & Industrial Marketing*, 25(4), 293–300.

Messages and creativity

The message an organisation conveys is a critical aspect of marketing communications. This means consideration must be given to what organisations say, how they say it and the meaning people are expected to ascribe to these messages. Ensuring that the right balance of information and emotion is achieved and that the presentation of the message is appropriate for the target audience is important. Above all, messages must be creative if they are to get attention from the audiences or publics they are trying to engage.

Aims and learning objectives

The aims of this chapter are to consider some of the ways in which marketing communications messages can be presented.

The learning objectives are to enable readers to:

1. consider the importance and characteristics of source credibility;
2. explain the different ways messages can be constructed;
3. examine the various ways in which advertising appeals can be presented;
4. describe how informational and transformational motives can be used as tactical tools in a communications plan;
5. explore the role of creativity and how the creative process is managed;
6. understand how message framing, storytelling and user-generated content are used in marketing communications.

Introduction

Developing the right messages for the right audience is one of the biggest challenges for brands. The message that is created must engage with the target audience and stand out from competitors and other communications messages if it is to be effective. This means that the message appeal needs to be carefully considered and the organisation and its agency must work together to develop messages that are creative. This chapter considers the variety and forms of the different appeals and the importance of creativity.

The John Lewis campaign described at the end of this chapter illustrates how an emotional appeal has been used to build brand loyalty and demonstrates the power that emotion can bring to communications messages. In addition to resonating with target audiences, breaking away from traditional retail category formats means that the message stands out from others. Being novel and yet appropriate to the target audience is a key aspect of advertising creativity.

This chapter explores four key elements that need to be considered in message appeals and creativity. First, attention is given to the source of a message and issues relating to source credibility. This includes the advantages and disadvantages of using a spokesperson. Second, consideration is given to how messages are constructed and the balance in the use of information and emotion in messages. Third, the chapter explores the various appeals and ways in which messages can be presented and framed, including storytelling. Lastly, consideration is given to creativity: the impact it can have on the effectiveness of a campaign and the management of the creative process.

Message source

Messages are perceived in many different ways and are influenced by a variety of factors. A critical determinant, however, concerns the credibility that is attributed to the source of the message itself. Kelman (1961) believed that the source of a message has three particular characteristics. These are: the level of perceived credibility as seen in terms of perceived objectivity and expertise; the degree to which the source is regarded as attractive and message recipients are motivated to develop a similar association or position; and the degree of power that the source is believed to possess. This is manifested in the ability of the source to reward or punish message receivers. The two former characteristics are evident in various forms of marketing communications, but the latter is directly observable in personal selling situations, and perhaps in the use of sales promotions.

Following this work on source characteristics, three key components of source credibility can be distinguished:

1. What is the level of perceived expertise (how much relevant knowledge is the source thought to hold)?
2. What are the personal motives the source is believed to possess (what is the reason for the source to be involved)?
3. What degree of trust can be placed in what the source says or does on behalf of the endorsement?

No matter what the level of expertise, if the level of trust is questionable, credibility will be adversely affected. Kareklas et al. (2015) investigated the influence of source credibility on the effectiveness of health-related messages, public service announcements (PSAs) and electronic word-of-mouth (eWoM) communications. The findings indicated that online commentators who were perceived by the reader to be a credible source influenced how consumers responded to the health message.

Scholars' paper 19.1
A credible source

Hovland, C.I. and Weiss, W. (1951) The influence of source credibility on communication effectiveness, *Public opinion quarterly,* **15(4), 635–50.**

This early paper is one of the most cited works on source credibility. The study identifies the effects of source credibility on the acquisition and retention of communications. The findings highlight the difference in response to trustworthy and untrustworthy sources.

See also:

Westerman, D., Spence, P.R. and Van Der Heide, B. (2014), Social media as information source: recency of updates and credibility of information, *Journal of Computer-Mediated Communication,* 19(2), 171–83.

Establishing credibility

Credibility can be established in a number of ways. One simple approach is to list or display the key attributes of the organisation or the product and then signal trustworthiness through the use of third-party endorsements and the comments of satisfied users.

A more complex approach is to use referrals, suggestions and association. Trustworthiness and expertise are the two principal elements of source credibility. One way of developing trust is to use spokespersons to speak on behalf of the sponsor of an advertisement and, in effect, provide a testimonial for the product in question. Credibility, therefore, can be established by the initiator of the advertisement or by a spokesperson used by the initiator to convey the message.

Effectively, consumers trade off the validity of claims made by brands against the perceived trustworthiness (and expertise) of the individuals or organisations who deliver the message. The result is that a claim may have reduced impact if either of these two components is doubtful or not capable of verification but, if repeated enough times, will enable audiences to accept that the products are very effective and of sufficiently high performance for them to try.

Credibility established by the initiator

The credibility of the organisation initiating the communications process is important. An organisation should seek to enhance its reputation with its various stakeholders at every opportunity.

However, organisational credibility is derived from the image, which in turn is a composite of many perceptions. Past decisions, current strategy and performance indicators, the level of perceived service and the type of performance of network members (e.g. high-quality retail outlets) all influence the perception of an organisation and the level of credibility that follows.

The need to establish high levels of credibility allows organisations to divert advertising spend away from a focus on brands to one that focuses on the organisation. Corporate advertising seeks to adjust organisation image and to build reputation.

Credibility established by a spokesperson

People who deliver the message are often regarded as the source, when in reality they are only the messenger. These people carry the message and represent the true source or initiator of the message (e.g. manufacturer or retailer). Consequently, the testimonial they transmit must be credible. There are four main types of spokesperson: the expert, the celebrity, the chief executive officer and the consumer.

The expert has been used many times and was particularly popular when television advertising first established itself in the 1950s and 1960s. Experts are quickly recognisable because they either wear white coats and round glasses, or dress and act like 'mad professors'. Through the use of symbolism, stereotypes and identification, these characters (and indeed others) can be established very quickly in the minds of receivers and a frame of reference generated that does not question the authenticity of the message being transmitted by such a person. Experts can also be users of products – for example, professional photographers endorsing cameras, professional hairdressers endorsing shampoos and professional golfers endorsing golf equipment.

Entertainment and sporting celebrities are being used increasingly, not only to provide credibility for a range (e.g. Gary Lineker for Walkers), but also to grab the attention of people in markets where motivation to decide between competitive products may be low. The celebrity enables the message to stand out among the clutter and noise that typify many markets. However, celebrities often demand high costs to appear in campaigns. For example, Nicole Kidman was paid £2 million to appear in Chanel's 2004 No5 TV commercial (Anon, 2015).

There are some potential problems that advertisers need to be aware of when considering the use of celebrities. First, does the celebrity fit the image of the brand and will the celebrity be acceptable to the target audience? Consideration also needs to be given to the longer-term relationship between the celebrity and the brand. Should the lifestyle of the celebrity change, what impact will this change have on the target audiences and their attitude towards the brand? Halonen-Knight and Hurmerinta (2010) argue that celebrity endorsement needs to be seen as a brand alliance with celebrities selected and managed in a similar manner to any other brand alliance partnership.

The second problem concerns the impact that the celebrity makes relative to the brand. There is a danger that those receiving the message remember the celebrity but not the brand that is the focus of the advertising spend. The *celebrity* becomes the hero, rather than the product being advertised.

Brownsell (2009) discusses the problems that can occur when the celebrity is also the CEO of the company. Apple's Steve Jobs provided a good example of the impact that transition in company leadership can have on a brand. Despite the potential issues associated with CEO celebrity endorsement, many heads of organisations have relished the chance to front their brands. Sir Richard Branson has fronted campaigns for a number of brands within the Virgin portfolio including Virgin Media and Virgin Money financial products.

When using consumers as the spokesperson to endorse products, the audience is being asked to identify with a 'typical consumer'. The identification of similar lifestyles, interests and opinions allows for better reception and understanding of the message. Consumers are often depicted testing similar products, such as margarine and butter. The Pepsi Challenge required consumers to select the drink they preferred in blind taste tests of Pepsi and Coca-Cola. Showing someone using the product, who is similar to the receiver, means that the source is perceived as credible and the potential for successful persuasion is considerably enhanced.

Sleeper effects

The assumption so far has been that high credibility enhances the probability of persuasion and successful communications. This is true when the receiver's initial position is opposite to that contained in the message. When the receiver's position is favourable to the message, a moderate level of credibility may be more appropriate.

Whether source credibility is high, medium or low is of little consequence, according to some researchers (Hannah and Sternthal, 1984). The impact of the source is believed to dissipate after approximately six weeks and only the content of the message is thought to dominate the receiver's attention.

Hovland and Weiss (1951) identified that there was a decrease over time in the extent to which individuals agreed with messages coming from a trustworthy source. In contrast, when the message came from an untrustworthy source, the agreement increased. This counter-intuitive effect is called the sleeper effect and suggests that the persuasiveness of a message can increase over time.

Foos et al. (2016) undertook an experimental study to explore the sleeper effect within the current advertising setting. Given the increased availability of positive and negative information about products on the Internet, the study investigated whether the sleeper effect was still relevant in the context of today's advertising environment. The findings confirmed those of previous studies, which identified the existence of a sleeper effect and the notion that the favourability of a message can increase over time, even when information discounts the message.

Structural elements in a message

An important part of any message strategy is a consideration of the best way of communicating the core message or proposition. This needs to be accomplished by structuring messages carefully to avoid encouraging objections and opposing points of view. The following are regarded as some of the important structural features that can shape the pattern of a message.

Message balance

It is evident from previous discussions that the effectiveness of any single message is dependent on a variety of factors. From a receiver's perspective, two elements appear to be significant: first, the amount and quality of the information that is communicated and, second, the overall judgement that each individual makes about the way a message is communicated.

This suggests that the style of a message should reflect a balance between the need for information and the need for pleasure or enjoyment in consuming the message. Figure 19.1 presents the two main forms of appeal. Messages can be product-oriented and rational or customer-oriented and based on feelings and emotions. For example, John Lewis, featured in the case study, originally used a product-oriented information base for its ads, but then changed to one that was customer-oriented and heavily emotional.

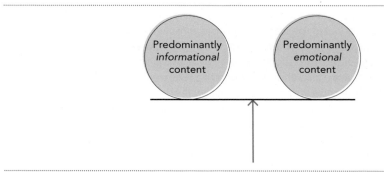

Figure 19.1 The balance of emotions and information provision

It is clear that when dealing with high-involvement decisions, where persuasion occurs through a central processing route, the emphasis of the message should be on the information content, in particular the key attributes and the associated benefits. This style is often factual and product-oriented. If a product evokes low-involvement decision-making, then the message should concentrate on the images that are created within the mind of the message recipient. This style seeks to elicit an emotional response from receivers. Obviously, there are many situations where both rational and emotional messages are needed by buyers in order to make purchasing decisions.

Conclusion drawing

Should the message draw a firm conclusion for an audience or should people be allowed to draw their own conclusions from the content? Explicit conclusions are more easily understood and stand a better chance of being effective (Kardes, 1988). However, it is the nature of the issue, the particular situation and the composition of the target audience that influence the effectiveness of conclusion drawing (Hovland and Mandell, 1952). Whether or not a conclusion should be drawn for the receiver depends upon the following:

1. The complexity of the issue. Healthcare products, central heating systems and personal finance services, for example, can be complex, and in the case of some members of the target audience their cognitive ability, experience and motivation may not be sufficient for them to draw their own conclusions. The complexity of the product requires that messages must draw conclusions for them. It should also be remembered that even highly informed and motivated audiences may require assistance if the product or issue is relatively new.

2. The level of education possessed by the receiver. Better-educated audiences prefer to draw their own conclusions, whereas less-well-educated audiences may need the conclusion drawn for them because they may not be able to make the inference from the message.

3. Whether immediate action is required. If urgent action is required by the receiver, then a conclusion should be drawn very clearly. Political parties can be observed to use this strategy immediately before an election.

4. The level of involvement. High involvement usually means that receivers prefer to make up their own minds and may reject or resent any attempt to have the conclusion drawn for them (Arora, 1985).

One- and two-sided messages

This concerns how the case (or justification) for an issue is presented. One approach is to present the case for and against an issue – a two-sided message. Alternatively, just the case in favour of an issue can be presented – a one-sided message. Research indicates that one-sided messages are more effective when receivers favour the opinion offered in the message and when the receivers are less well-educated.

Two-sided messages, where both the good and the bad points of an issue are presented, are more effective when the receiver's initial opinion is opposite to that presented in the message and when they are well-educated. Credibility is improved by understanding the audience's position and then fashioning the presentation of the message. Faison (1961) found that two-sided messages tend to produce more positive perceptions of a source than one-sided messages.

Order of presentation

Further questions regarding the development of message strategy concern the order in which important points are presented. Messages that present the strongest points at the beginning use what is referred to as the *primacy* effect. The decision to place the main points at the beginning depends on whether the audience has a low or high level of involvement. A low level may require an attention-getting message component at the beginning. Similarly, if the target has an opinion opposite to that contained in the message, a weak point may lead to a high level of counter-argument.

A decision to place the strongest points at the end of the message assumes that the *recency* effect will bring about greater levels of persuasion. This is appropriate when the receiver agrees with the position adopted by the source or has a high positive level of involvement.

The order of argument presentation is more relevant in personal selling than in television or display advertisements. However, as learning through television is largely passive, because involvement is low and interest minimal, the presentation of key selling points at the beginning and at the end of the message will enhance message reception and recall.

Message appeals

The presentation of a message requires that an appeal be made to the target audience. The appeal is important, because unless the execution of the message appeal (the creative) is appropriate to the target audience's perception and expectations, the chances of successful communications are reduced.

There are two main factors associated with the presentation. Is the message to be dominated by the need to transmit product-oriented information or is there a need to transmit a message that appeals predominantly to the emotional senses of the receiver? The main choice of presentation style, therefore, concerns the degree of factual information transmitted in a message against the level of imagery thought necessary to make sufficient impact for the message to command attention and then be processed.

The different approaches are alternatively given the soft-sell, hard-sell demarcation, well established in the academic and practitioner worlds of advertising. A soft-sell appeal is designed to provoke an affective or feelings response from the receiver of the message, one in which human emotions are emphasised. These types of appeal tend to be subtle and indirect, and an image or atmosphere may be conveyed (Okazaki et al., 2010).

A hard-sell appeal is one in which the objective is to induce receivers to think in rational terms about the message. These appeals tend to be direct, emphasising a sales orientation, and often specify the brand name and product recommendations. Factual information, including numerous product (pack) shots, emphasises specific differentiating product features or some other dimension relevant to consumers. These two broad types of appeal are underpinned by three dimensions. These are feeling versus thinking, implicit versus explicit, and image versus fact.

Okazaki et al. (2010) believe that soft-sell appeals lead to more positive attitudes to the ad and to increased ad believability. This suggests that soft-sell appeals can strengthen purchase intentions. Hard-sell advertising appeals can also strengthen purchase intention. However, this is not accomplished directly through the creation of a favourable attitude, but through the formulation of convincing ad content.

Most message appeals should balance the informative and emotional dimensions. Adams and Henderson Blair (1992) confirm that the weight of advertising is relatively unimportant, and that the quality of the appeal is the dominant factor. However, the correct blend of informative and emotional elements in any appeal is paramount for persuasive effectiveness.

There are numerous presentational or executional techniques, but the following are some of the more commonly used appeals.

Information-based appeals

Information or rational appeals can be presented through four main types of appeal. These are factual, slice-of-life, demonstration and comparative appeals.

Factual

Sometimes referred to as the 'hard sell', the dominant objective of these appeals is to provide, often detailed, information. This type of appeal is commonly associated with high-involvement decisions where receivers are sufficiently motivated and able to process information. Persuasion, according to the ELM, is undertaken through the central processing route. This means that ads should be rational and contain logically reasoned arguments and information in order that receivers are able to complete their decision-making processes.

Slice of life

As noted earlier, the establishment of credibility is vital if any message is to be accepted and processed. One of the ways in which this can be achieved is to present the message in such a way that the receiver can identify immediately with the scenario being presented. This process of creating similarity is used a great deal in advertising and is referred to as slice-of-life advertising. For example, advertisers may depict their products in a typical family setting such as a food brand showing their product in use at a family dinner. This technique is simple, well-tried, well-liked and successful.

Demonstration

A similar technique is to present the problem to the audience as a demonstration. The focus brand is depicted as instrumental in the resolution of a problem. Headache remedies, floor cleaners and tyre commercials have traditionally demonstrated the pain, the dirt and the danger respectively, and then shown how the focus brand relieves the pain (Panadol) or removes the stubborn dirt (Flash or Cillit Bang). Whether the execution is believable is a function of the credibility and the degree of life-like dialogue or copy that is used.

Viewpoint 19.1

Send in the clowns

Audi's 'Clowns' ad is an example of how to create an entertaining and visually engaging demonstration ad. The Clowns ad shows circus clowns causing chaos on the roads with their dangerous driving. As well as providing colourful entertainment, the film provides a platform for Audi to showcase some of the manufacturer's hi-tech safety features.

The Clowns ad takes us through many of the manufacturer's intelligent driver assistance features as the Audi avoids colliding with the many clowns who are shown larking around in their cars and buses

Image 19.1 The film provides a platform for Audi to showcase some of the hi-tech safety features
Source: AUDI AG.

and on motorbikes. The film begins by featuring the Audi pre-sense range of predictive technologies, which have been designed to react quickly to sudden obstacles, even if they appear at the rear. We are also shown intelligent features like the LED headlights, which automatically come on if the road ahead suddenly becomes dark and Audi's Park Assist feature that can help drivers park in tight parking spaces.

Audiences are invited to use the Shazam app to identify the music for the ad and the campaign is supported by data-driven OOH. The outdoor sites use data on time and weather to generate appropriate creative.

The film is set to a classic song by Stephen Sondheim, 'Send in the Clowns', which is performed by Lisa Hannigan. Having watched the Audi's technology successfully navigate through all the clowns' antics, the film ends with the tagline 'Audi technology. Clown proof'.

Sources: Audi Intelligent technology (2018); Kiefer (2017).

Insight

Audi's 'Clowns' reminds us that brands often combine a number of appeal techniques. Here we see a demonstration ad, which includes music to set the mood and clowns to add a hint of humour. The film also highlights that product demonstration is still an effective route for brands to choose and how, if used creatively, this type of appeal can help to activate social media and support other marketing communications tools.

Question: Why do you think Audi chose a demonstration route for their campaign? What other types of information-based appeal could have been chosen and why?

Task: Find examples of five other auto manufacturers' ads and identify which style of appeal they have used according to the classifications given in this chapter. Explain why you think each route was taken.

Comparative advertising

Comparative advertising is a popular means of positioning brands. Messages are based on a comparison with either a main competitor brand or all competing brands, with the aim of establishing and maintaining superiority. The comparison may centre on one or two key attributes and can be a good way of entering new markets. Entrants keen to establish a presence in a market have little to lose by comparing themselves with market leaders. However, market leaders have a great deal to lose and little to gain by comparing themselves with minor competitors.

Emotions- and feelings-based appeals

Appeals based on logic and reasons are necessary in particular situations, especially where there is high involvement. As products become similar, however, and as consumers become more aware of what is available in the category, so the need to differentiate becomes more important. Increasing numbers of advertisers are using messages that seek to appeal to the target's emotions and feelings, a 'soft sell'. Cars, toothpaste, toilet tissue and mineral water often use emotion-based messages to differentiate their products' position.

There are a number of appeals that can be used to elicit an emotional response from an individual receiver. Of the many techniques available, the main ones that can be observed to be used most are fear, humour, shock, sex, music and fantasy and surrealism.

Fear

Fear is used in one of two ways. The first way demonstrates the negative aspects or physical dangers associated with a particular behaviour or improper product usage. Drink driving, life assurance and toothpaste advertising typify this form of appeal. The second approach is the threat of social rejection or disapproval if the brand is not used. This type of fear is used frequently in advertisements for such products as anti-dandruff shampoos and deodorants, and is used to support consumers' needs for social acceptance and approval.

There is a great deal of evidence that fear can facilitate attention and interest in a message and even motivate an individual to take a particular course of action: for example, to stop smoking. Fear appeals can be effective in changing attitude, intention and behavior (Witte and Allen, 2000). Vos et al. (2017) studied the effectiveness of fear appeals among at-risk gamblers in Australia and identified threats such as self-esteem, isolation, identity loss and significant financial debt were among the most fear inducing.

Fear appeals need to be constrained, if only to avoid being categorised as outrageous and socially unacceptable. Some authors caution against fear appeals, suggesting the evidence to support the use of fear appeals is inconclusive (Ruiter et al., 2014). Ray and Wilkie (1970), for example, show that, should the level of fear rise too much, inhibiting effects may prevent the desired action occurring. This inhibition is caused by the individual choosing to screen out, through perceptive selection, messages that conflict with current behaviour. The outcome may be that individuals deny the existence of a problem, claim there is no proof or say that it will not happen to them.

Scholars' paper 19.2

Fear appeals

Witte, K. and Allen, M. (2000) A meta-analysis of fear appeals: implications for effective public health campaigns, *Health Education & Behavior*, 27(5), 591–615.

This paper provides a meta-analysis of studies on fear appeals. The study suggests that strong fear appeals can provide high levels of perceived severity and suscepti-bility and are found to be more persuasive than fear appeals that are low or weak. The study provides a good review of all the main theoretical approaches used in fear appeals.

See also:

Ruiter, R.A., Kessels, L.T., Peters, G.J.Y. and Kok, G. (2014) Sixty years of fear appeal research: current state of the evidence, *International Journal of Psychology*, 49(2), 63–70.

Humour

Humour has been a popular appeal used in advertising for over a hundred years (Weinberger et al., 2015). The use of humour as an appeal is attractive because it can attract attention, stimulate interest and foster a positive mood. This can occur because there is less effort involved with peripheral rather than central cognitive processing, and this helps to mood-protect. In other words, the positive mood state is more likely to be maintained if cognitive effort is avoided.

Barry and Graça (2018) found that humour is more effective when there is low rather than high involvement. In their study of social videos, the authors identified that some categories of product use humour more than others. In particular, the authors found that there was a higher ratio of ads using humour in comparison to non-humour for 'little toys and treats', such as snacks and drinks, and the use of humour was proportionately lower for 'big toys', such as luxury cars and travel.

Another form of humour used in advertising is parody. Vanden Bergh et al. (2011) identify parodic advertising as a route that mimics other advertising or cultural work. This style of appeal takes another brand's advertising or other creative work and re-presents it in a humorous manner. It is a popular form of appeal on social media and is widely shared on social media platforms.

Viewpoint 19.2

How funny was that? Using humour in ads

Image 19.2 The Salvation Army's campaign, 'Unwanted Gifts' uses a tagline, 'It may not be perfect for you, but it's perfect for us.'

Source: Print advertisement created by McCann, Brazil for Salvation Army.

Humour can help organisations differentiate themselves from competitors. A recent campaign for The Salvation Army in São Paolo, Brazil uses humour to drive donations. Rather than choosing an emotional, heart-tugging approach in their appeal for donations, 'Unwanted Gifts' uses humour. The campaign features colourful illustrations of global leaders such as Donald Trump and Kim Jong-Un to show that while some gifts may not be suitable for one person, they may be useful for others. The tagline on the ads provides a call-to-action for consumers to donate their unwanted gifts, 'It may not be perfect for you, but it's perfect for us.'

The Unwanted Gifts uses political humour to engage audiences in what would normally be considered quite a dull topic – donating your old gifts to a charity. The humour draws on current political tensions to provide examples of gifts that leaders such as Donald Trump are unlikely to want. In Trump's case he is seen receiving a Mexican Hat.

Humorous appeals can be successful within a single country, but organisations need to be mindful that humour is culturally bound and care needs to be taken to ensure that audiences in different countries will find the advertising humorous. What can be funny in one country may not be understood or may even be seen to be offensive in another. Pre-testing advertising in each country is often undertaken to determine how messages are likely to be received by consumers in the market.

Creating ads that are seen to be funny across cultures is challenging. Volkswagen managed to find a solution with their 'The Force' ad, which broke Super Bowl records as the most viewed auto video. Even before airing on TV the ad had been shared and watched by over 13 million people on YouTube. The film had 2.7 million shares on Facebook and 32 million views within three weeks.

Sources: Cannes Lions Archive (2011); Lyons (2018); WMcCann Brazil (2018).

Insight

Humour is a route that is effective at engaging audiences. The examples given show how brands can use humour to differentiate themselves against competitors. However, we should note that developing a global campaign with a humorous creative platform may be a challenge to ensure that the ads resonate with the local culture.

Question: Why do you think The Salvation Army used a humorous route for their donation campaign? What alternative emotional appeal styles could have been used?

Task: Choose five ads that use a humorous route and identify whether the products are low or high involvement. Consider *why* humour might be less effective for high-involvement products.

Shock

Some advertisers use appeals that are intended to shock their target audiences. This is called shock advertising, which, according to Venkat and Abi-Hanna (1995), 'is generally regarded as one that deliberately, rather than inadvertently, startles and offends its audience'.

Dahl et al. (2003) suggest that shock advertising by definition is unexpected and audiences are surprised by the messages because they do not conform to social norms or their expectations. They argue that audiences are offended because there is 'norm violation, encompassing transgressions of law or custom (e.g. indecent sexual references, obscenity), breaches of a moral or social code (e.g. profanity, vulgarity), or things that outrage the moral or physical senses', for example gratuitous violence and disgusting images (p. 268). The clothing company French Connection's use of the FCUK slogan and the various Benetton campaigns depicting a variety of incongruous situations (e.g. a priest and a nun kissing, and a man dying of AIDS) are examples of norm violation. Shock advertising is not only used by commercial organisations but also by not-for-profit organisations such as the government (anti-smoking, anti-drink-driving), charities (child abuse), climate change (Greenpeace) and human rights campaigners (Amnesty International).

The main reason for using a shock advertising strategy is that it is a good way to secure an audience's attention and achieve a longer-lasting impact than through traditional messages and attention-getting devices. The surprise element of these advertisements secures attention, which is followed by an attempt to work out why an individual has been surprised. This usually takes the form of cognitive engagement and message elaboration in order that the message be understood. Through this process a shocking message can be retained and behaviour influenced. This process is depicted in Figure 19.2.

Shocking ads also benefit from word-of-mouth communications as these messages provoke advertisement-related conversations (Dichter, 1966). These can be distributed orally or digitally as virals. The credibility of word-of-mouth communications impacts on others who, if they have not been exposed to the original message, often seek out the message through curiosity. Associated with this pass-along impact is the generation of controversy, which can lead to additional publicity for an organisation and its advertisements. This 'free' publicity, although invariably negative, is considered to be desirable as it leads to increased brand awareness without further exposure and associated costs. This in turn can give the organisation further opportunities to provide more information about the advertising campaign and generate additional media comment.

The use of shock tactics has spread to viral marketing (a topic discussed in more detail in Chapter 21). Virals delivered through email communications have an advantage over paid-for advertising because consumers perceive advertising as an attempt to sell a product, whereas virals are perceived as fun, can be opened and viewed (repeatedly) at consumer-determined times. Furthermore, virals are not subject to the same regulations that

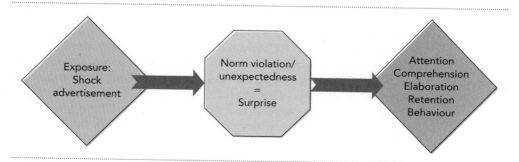

Figure 19.2 A preliminary model of consumer reactions to shock appeals
Source: Dahl et al. (2003). Used with kind permission from WARC.

govern advertising, opening opportunities to convey controversial material. For example, a Volkswagen viral showed a suicide bomber exploding a device inside a car but the vehicle remained in one piece ('small but tough'). Another for Ford Ka showed a cat being decapitated by the sunroof. As Bewick (2006) suggests, joking about terrorism and pets is a sure-fire way of generating shock, and with that comes publicity. However, caution is needed in the use of such shocking appeals as discussed in the Scholars' paper 19.3.

Kadić-Maglajlić et al. (2017) studied controversial ads on social networking sites and found that they can be seen as offensive to consumers with higher religious commitments. The findings suggest that controversial ads can have a negative impact on some consumers' attitudes towards the ad and purchase intentions.

Scholars' paper 19.3

Controversial ads

Sabri, O. (2017) Does viral communication context increase the harmfulness of controversial taboo advertising? *Journal of Business Ethics*, 141(2), 235–47.

This study considers the counter-productive effect of controversial viral ads. The authors suggest that controversial ads do not improve brand attitude and raise concerns over the dangers of taboo imagery being trivialised.

See also:

Kerr, G., Mortimer, K., Dickinson, S. and Waller, D.S. (2012) Buy, boycott or blog: exploring online consumer power to share, discuss and distribute controversial advertising messages, *European Journal of Marketing*, 46(3/4), 387–405.

Sex appeals

Sexual innuendo and the use of sex as a means of promoting products and services are both common and controversial. Using sex as an appeal in messages is excellent for gaining the attention of buyers. Wirtz et al. (2018) identified that sex appeals had a significant positive effect on ad recognition and recall. In contrast, their study found that there was no significant effect on brand recognition and recall. While sex appeals can gain audiences' attention, they may achieve less for the brand.

Research has highlighted the importance of using sex appeals only if the product is related (Paek and Nelson, 2007). Therefore, sex appeals are often used for products such as perfume, clothing and jewellery but provide for poor effectiveness when the product is unrelated, such as cars, photocopiers and furniture. Reichert et al. (2012) identified that low-involvement products in particular use sex as an attention-getting cue and the product categories with the highest sexual content were health/hygiene, beauty, drugs/medicine and clothing.

Other studies have identified that sex appeals do not 'sell' more than any other type of appeal and that as long as the advertising is pleasant, other appeal styles such as humour are just as effective (Das et al., 2015). Culture should also be considered since sexual imagery is less favoured in some countries such as China where consumers are cautious about engaging with sex appeals (Cui and Yang, 2009).

Using sex appeals is an increasingly controversial route to take. There is growing discussion in the industry regarding the negative impact of appeals that objectify either men or women. Viewpoint 19.3 highlights the movement to end the objectification of women in advertising, which has gained significant support within the industry.

Viewpoint 19.3
#WomenNotObjects

Image 19.3 The campaign led with a hard-hitting film that called for greater respect for women in advertising
Source: Tagline of Badger & Winters.

There has been increasing debate in recent years about how women are portrayed in advertising. In particular there is growing concern within the advertising industry about the extent of objectification of women in advertising and harmful effects of this on women. In 2016, Madonna Badger, a principal at Badger & Winters, a USA agency, decided to address the issue and launched a global campaign to raise awareness of the problem. Her mission was to make organisations think differently about how they portrayed women in advertising.

The campaign led with a hard-hitting two-minute film, #WomenNotObjects, calling out ads that show up when you Google the phrase 'objectification of women'. The video had an immediate impact and created a global conversation around the objectification of women. As well as raising awareness of the issue among consumers, the video sent a powerful message to advertisers that objectification of women in ads was no longer acceptable and could damage their brands. Calling for greater respect for women in advertising, the campaign was launched on Facebook and quickly took the Internet by storm. Since it was posted in 2016, the film has received more than 2.45 million views on YouTube.

The impact of the campaign within the industry has been significant. The campaign has sparked a global movement and a conversation around the need to respect women in advertising. Many agency leaders around the world have signed up to the movement and have given their full support to the campaign to put a stop to the objectification of women in advertising. In 2017, in full support of the movement, the Cannes Lions Festival of Creativity advised jurors not to award trophies to any ads that objectified women.

To help organisations understand the impact of the objectification of women in advertising, Badger & Winters partnered with The Girls' Lounge and Advertising Benchmark Index (ABX) to examine the effects on a brand's reputation and consumer purchase intent. The study undertook 3,000 online questionnaires with 13–74-year-olds in the United States and tested an ad that objectifies women and an ad that does not to compare how objectifying stood up against non-objectifying ads. The results of the research showed that ads objectifying women had a significant negative effect on purchase intention and a negative influence on brand reputation. The study also found objectification had a negative effect on awareness of brand message. These findings send a powerful message to brand owners.

Sources: Quantifying the effect of objectifying women in advertising (n.d.); Quenqua (2017); Stein (2016).

Insight

The #WomenNotObjects movement highlights the importance of growing debate around the objectification of women in advertising and challenges the industry to re-examine how they represent women in advertising. While academic studies on sex appeals show that sex does not increase purchase intention, the research undertaken for #WomenNotObjects argues that ads objectifying women are damaging to brands.

Question: Why do you think the research found that ads objectifying women had a negative effect on brand reputation?

Task: Find three examples of recent TV ads that include women. Consider whether you think they show women in a respectful way. Justify your answer.

Music

Music can create a mood for the advertising and differentiate the message. Binet et al. (2013) suggest that the most popular and effective advertising over the last decade has included music, which can facilitate brand and message recall, improve attitudes towards the brand and can influence purchase intention. Many brands are using music to help connect with audiences emotionally.

Music can provide continuity between a series of advertisements and can also be a good peripheral cue. A jingle, melody or tune, if repeated sufficiently, can become associated with the advertisement or brand. This means there is potential for the campaign life to be extended beyond the advertising. Bhattacharya et al. (2017) undertook an electro-physiological study of brain responses to music in advertising and identified that using the same piece of music across advertising campaigns was more impactful than using different music for each new ad.

Some luxury and executive cars are advertised using commanding background music to create an aura of power, prestige and affluence, which is combined with strong visual images in order that an association be made between the car and the environment in which it is positioned. There is a contextual juxtaposition between the car and the environment presented. Readers may notice a semblance of classical conditioning, where the music acts as an unconditioned stimulus. Foxall and Goldsmith (1994) suggest that the stimulus elicits the unconditioned emotional responses that may lead to the purchase of the advertised product. Viewpoint 19.1 discusses how music was used to engage audiences in the Audi 'Clowns' ad.

Fantasy and surrealism

The use of fantasy and surrealism in advertising has grown, partly as a result of the increased clutter and legal constraints imposed on some product classes. In fantasy appeals, associations with certain images and symbols allow advertisers to focus attention on products. The receiver can engage in the distraction offered and become involved with the execution of the advertisement. If this is a rewarding experience it may be possible to affect the receiver's attitudes peripherally. Readers may notice that this links to the earlier discussion on 'liking the advertisement' (see Chapter 6).

Surrealism has been used in advertising since the 1920s and images are seen to have a disruptive effect (Barron-Duncan, 2017). Advertisers can challenge individuals by presenting questions and visual stimuli that demand attention and cognitive response. When individuals respond positively to a challenge, the advertiser can either provide closure (an answer) or, through surreal appeals, leave the receivers to answer the questions themselves in the context in which they perceive the message. One way of achieving this challenging position is to use an appeal that cognitively disorients the receiver (Parker and Churchill, 1986). If receivers are led to ask the question 'What is going on here?' their involvement in the message is likely to be very high. Benetton consistently raises questions through its advertising. By presenting a series of messages that are socially disorienting, and for many disconcerting, Benetton continually presents a challenge that moves away from involving individuals in an approach where salience and 'standing out' predominate. This high-risk strategy, with a risk of rejection, has prevailed for a number of years.

The surrealist approach does not provide or allow for closure. The conformist approach, by contrast, does require closure in order to avoid any possible counter-arguing and message rejection. Parker and Churchill (1986) argue that, when questions are left unanswered, receivers can become involved in both the product and the execution of the advertisement.

Copycat messaging

There are certain occasions where the appeal used by a follower brand can be judged to mimic that of the brand leader. Brands use this if they wish to attack the brand leader in the category to reduce the potency of the competitor's marketing communications. Oakes (2015) refers to Aldi's spoof of the John Lewis 'man on the moon' Christmas ad that showed an old man on the moon comparing the prices of telescopes, with Aldi's telescope being cheaper.

Advertising tactics

The main creative elements of a message need to be brought together in order for an advertising plan to have substance. The processes used to develop message appeals need to be open but systematic.

The level of involvement and combination of the rational/emotional dimensions that receivers bring to their decision-making processes are the core concepts to be considered when creating an advertising message. Rossiter and Percy (1997) devised a deductive framework that involves the disaggregation of the emotional (feel) dimension to a greater degree than that proposed by Vaughn (1980) (see Chapter 13 for details). They claim that there are two broad types of motive that drive attitudes towards purchase behaviour. These are informational and transformational motives and are now considered in turn.

Informational motives

Individuals have a need for information to counter negative concerns about a purchase decision. These informational motives, set out in Table 19.1, are said to be negatively charged feelings. They can become positively charged, or the level of concern can be reduced considerably, by the acquisition of relevant information.

Table 19.1   Informational motives

Motive	Possible emotional state
Problem removal	Anger–relief
Problem avoidance	Fear–relaxation
Incomplete satisfaction	Disappointment–optimism
Mixed approach–avoidance	Guilt–peace of mind
Normal depletion	Mild annoyance–convenience

Transformational motives

Promises to enhance or to improve the user of a brand are referred to as transformational motives. These are related to the user's feelings and are capable of transforming a user's emotional state, hence they are positively charged. Three main transformational motives have been distinguished by Rossiter et al. (1991), presented in Table 19.2. Various emotional states can be associated with each of these motives, and they should be used to portray an emotion that is appropriate to the needs of the target audience.

For example, Cancer Research UK changed the approach it used to communicate with donors. For a while, the campaigns used to convey messages about family loss and in that sense adopted a negative approach. The charity then adopted an 'All Clear' campaign. This conveyed messages about people diagnosed with cancer and their improved chances of recovery due to the benefits of the research. For many people this is low involvement with transformational motives. This means that the use of an emotional-based claim in the message is important. The happy ending, based on people surviving, achieves this while the endline uses a voice-over that requests a donation so that the words 'all clear' can be heard by more people in the future.

One of the key communications objectives, identified earlier, is the need to create or improve levels of awareness regarding the product or organisation. This is achieved by determining whether awareness is required at the point of purchase or prior to purchase. Brand recognition (at the point of purchase) requires an emphasis upon visual stimuli, the package and the brand name, whereas brand recall (prior to purchase) requires an emphasis on a limited number of peripheral cues. These may be particular copy lines, the use of music or colours for continuity and attention-grabbing, frequent use of the brand name in the context of the category need, or perhaps the use of strange or unexpected presentation formats.

Advertising tactics can be determined by the particular combination of involvement and motives that exist at a particular time within the target audience. If a high-involvement decision process is determined, with people using a central processing route, then the types of tactics shown in Figures 19.3 and 19.4 are recommended (Rossiter and Percy, 1997). If a low-involvement decision process is determined, with the target audience using

Table 19.2   Transformational motives

Motive	Possible emotional state
Sensory gratification	Dull–elated
Intellectual stimulation	Bored–excited
Social approval	Apprehensive–flattered

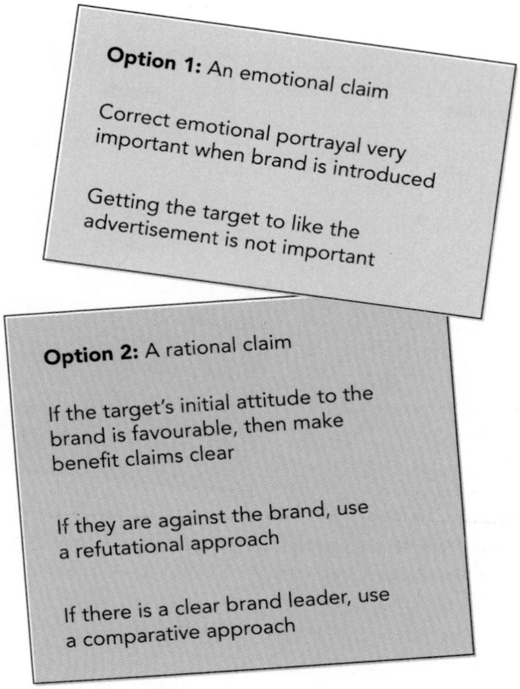

Option 1: An emotional claim

Correct emotional portrayal very important when brand is introduced

Getting the target to like the advertisement is not important

Option 2: A rational claim

If the target's initial attitude to the brand is favourable, then make benefit claims clear

If they are against the brand, use a refutational approach

If there is a clear brand leader, use a comparative approach

Figure 19.3 Message tactics where there is high involvement and informational motives
Source: After Rossiter and Percy (1997). Used with kind permission.

Option 1: An emotional claim

Use emotion in the context of the prevailing lifestyle groups

Identification with the product is as important as liking the advertisement

Option 2: A rational claim

Include information as well

Overstate the benefits but do not understate them

Use repetition for reinforcement

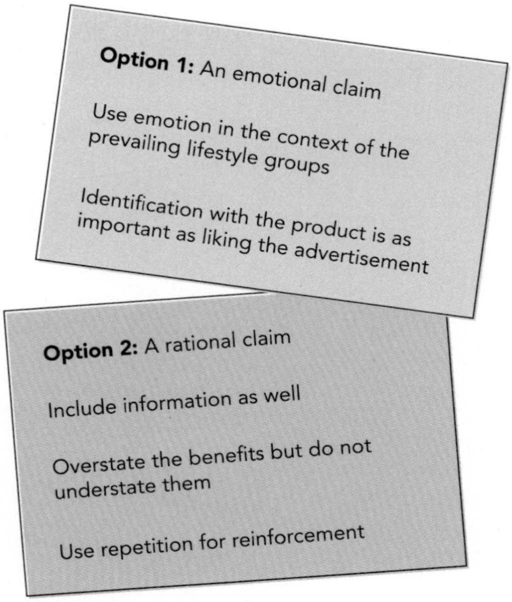

Figure 19.4 Message tactics where there is high involvement and transformational motives
Source: After Rossiter and Percy (1997). Used with kind permission.

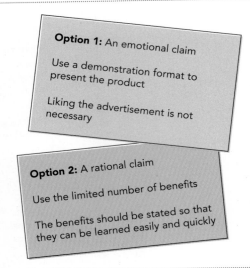

Figure 19.5 Message tactics where there is low involvement and informational motives
Source: After Rossiter and Percy (1997). Used with kind permission.

a peripheral processing route, then the types of tactics shown in Figures 19.5 and 19.6 are recommended.

The Rossiter–Percy approach provides for a range of advertising tactics that are oriented to the conditions that are determined by the interplay of the level of involvement and the type of dominant motivation. These conditions may only exist within a member of the target audience for a certain period. Consequently, they may change and the advertising tactics may also have to change to meet the new conditions. There are two main points that emerge from the work of Rossiter and Percy (1997). The first is that all messages should be

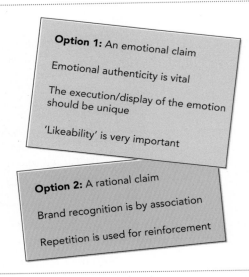

Figure 19.6 Message tactics where there is low involvement and transformational motives
Source: After Rossiter and Percy (1997). Used with kind permission.

designed to carry both rational, logical information and emotional stimuli, but in varying degrees and forms. Second, low-involvement conditions require the use of just one or two benefits in a message, whereas high-involvement conditions can sustain a number of different benefit claims. This is because persuasion through the central processing route is characterised by an evaluation of the alternatives within any one product category.

Creativity

Having considered the different appeal styles available to advertisers, another important element of any marketing communications campaign is creativity. Creativity is seen to increase the effectiveness of a campaign (Hurman, 2016). Some writers argue campaign effectiveness can be increased by up to 10 times (Priest, 2014).

While creativity is an important feature of any marketing communications activity there is no universally agreed definition of what advertising creativity is. Early holistic ideas about creativity considered it to be about a violation of expectations, often expressed through contradictory ideas (Blasko and Mokwa, 1986; Reid and Rotfeld, 1976). These views have given way to a general agreement that creativity in advertising has two main characteristics. The first is that creative ads are divergent, or highly unique or novel, and, second, relevant or meaningful (Smith et al., 2007).

Smith and Yang (2004) suggest that a creative ad uses a divergent appeal (unexpected and unusual, such as fear or humour) to deliver a relevant core message about the brand (such as an attribute or benefit), yet still allows the audience to interpret and assign meaning to the message within the linkage between the fear or humour and the product. Ideas about divergence and relevance have several interpretations and these are represented in Table 19.3, drawn from Smith et al. (2008).

Heath et al. (2009) believe that creativity in contemporary branded advertising involves a variety of elements. These include characters (who express mild emotion, e.g. love, irritation, excitement, boredom, curiosity, amusement), situations (that are considered humorous, poignant or dramatic), visuals (that are elegant or attractive, beautifully shot footage with high production values), and background music (that is pleasant, uplifting or evocative).

Table 19.3 Interpretations of the dimensions of creativity

Dimension	Explanation
Divergence	
Originality	Ads that contain elements that are rare, surprising, or move away from the obvious and commonplace.
Flexibility	Ads that contain different ideas or switch from one perspective to another.
Elaboration	Ads that contain unexpected details or finish and extend basic ideas so they become more intricate, complicated, or sophisticated.
Synthesis	Ads that combine, connect, or blend normally unrelated objects or ideas.
Artistic value	Ads that contain artistic verbal impressions or attractive colours or shapes.
Relevance	
Ad-to-consumer relevance	Refers to situations where the ad contains execution elements that are meaningful to consumers. For example, using Beatles music in an ad could create a meaningful link to baby boomers, thereby making the ad relevant to them.
Brand-to-consumer relevance	Refers to situations where the advertised brand (or product category) is relevant to potential buyers. For example, the advertisement could show the brand being used in circumstances familiar to the consumer.

Source: Derived from Smith et al. (2008).

Creativity and attention

Creativity in advertising is considered to be important because of the common belief that creativity is an effective way of getting people to attend to an ad (Rossiter and Percy, 1998; Yang and Smith, 2009). Kover's (1995) research around the impact of emotive content and attention led to the identification of two attention-getting strategies: forcing and subversion. Forcing strategies involve the use of surprising, irrelevant or perhaps mildly shocking content. He gives as an example the famous Apple ad shown during the 1984 Super Bowl. This strategy is not used so much today. Subversion strategies require an ad to seduce an audience, to slip by it as if unnoticed. Kover uses the words charming and seductive to describe this sort of creativity and refers to ads by O2, Honda and M&S Food campaigns as examples of this approach.

Much research into creativity in advertising is concerned with what is referred to as 'attention effects'. This is related to the links between increased attention to an ad, heightened motivation to process the message, and the depth of processing that follows (Smith and Yang, 2004). Here, as Baack et al. (2008) comment, the amount of attention paid to advertisements is a function of the amount of cognitive capacity allocated to a task. Only when consumers focus more attention on the advertisement itself, rather than divide their attention among multiple tasks, do higher levels of processing occur. The greater the originality or divergence and personal relevance a creative ad displays, the greater the attention it attracts, which leads to a greater depth of message processing. What follows from this are higher recall and recognition scores.

However, Yang and Smith (2009) and Heath et al. (2009) question the proposition that creativity works by increasing attention. They all agree that some attention is necessary, but it is not the direction of attention, but the level of attention, that is important. Yang and Smith had inconclusive results from their research, yet Heath (2010) found that creativity does not increase attention; if anything, it decreases it. This might raise an argument that it would be better to use force-based strategies. However, as Binet and Field (2007) found, emotion-based ads are more successful than information-led campaigns. The conclusion, therefore, is that creative ads enable open-minded message processing, which in turn can increase a willingness to view an ad again.

The importance of context

According to Kim et al. (2010), it is crucial that creative advertising has a product-relevant or audience-relevant context if it is to be effective. This contrasts with fine art where creativity is not bounded by this type of contextual constraint or the setting of objectives by one party, as its goal is to please or stimulate the viewer's senses.

Kim et al. (2010) argue that it is the surrounding culture that influences advertisers, ad creators and consumers when determining what constitutes the contextual component of advertising creativity. They offer the research findings of Koslow et al. (2003: 94) who found that 'creatives perceive advertisements to be more appropriate if the ads are artistic, whereas account executives perceive advertisements to be more appropriate if the ads are strategic'.

The development of advertising materials and associated processes occurs within organisations and is therefore embedded within the prevailing organisational context and culture. Stuhlfaut (2011) refers to clients, agency managers, media specialists and account planners, as well as market conditions, which have all been shown to have varying levels of influence on the creative process and its outputs.

Stuhlfaut (2011) offers an interesting concept, which he refers to as the 'creative code'. Citing Goodenough (1981: 52), the code shapes the development of advertisements that are regarded as cultural artefacts or 'material manifestations of what is learned'. Through this process a sub-cultural creative code is understood and made available to others. In this sense, a creative code serves to direct or limit what internal and external stakeholders believe an acceptable creative might be.

Interpretations of what constitutes advertising creativity, therefore, vary depending on the viewer's context. This may be relative to role (a client striving to meet market share targets), culture (the societal values and norms of behaviour) or perspective (media commentator or blogger).

The creative process

The creative process has been studied in a variety of contexts outside advertising (Amabile, 1996), but there have been only a limited number of studies undertaken in an advertising context. Among those there have been a number of studies on idea generation (Stuhlfaut and Vanden Bergh, 2014), agency decision-making systems (Na et al., 2009), and the stages that take place between the agency and the client (Hill and Johnson, 2004).

One of the few studies that have been undertaken within advertising agencies themselves has been Turnbull and Wheeler's (2017) study of the advertising creative process within advertising agencies. The study explores the stages that occur from when the client first mentions the need for advertising to the agency, up to the moment when the concepts are approved and ready to go into production. They offer a seven-step model of the advertising creative process (see Table 19.4).

These researchers found that agencies customise the advertising creative process to meet the needs of the advertising task. In cases where the advertising brief has a limited response time, agencies were found to set up 'drive-by' briefs, which allowed the entire agency to think about creative ideas rather than just a selected creative team. The study also found that in cases where the creative was for a new business client, agencies held Chemistry Meetings, and set up a War Room within the agency, to manage the process of creative development.

Tevi and Koslow (2018) consider the use of rhetoric theory as a lens to view the creative development process. They argue that the stages of creative development (message strategy, idea generation, execution, media and production) can be compared to the canons of rhetoric (invention, style, arrangement, memory and delivery).

Table 19.4   The advertising creative process

Stage	Process
Stage one	Task identification
Stage two	Agreement of task objectives
Stage three	Ideation
Stage four	Response
Stage five	Validation – internal review (Agency Creative Director and WIP meetings)
Stage six	External review (Client Tissue Sessions and consumer qual and quant pre-testing).
Stage seven	Decision

Source: Adapted from Turnbull and Wheeler (2017).

As with any professional service, the level of interaction between client and provider plays an important role in the output of the service. The relationship between the client and advertising agency is seen to influence the creative output (Koslow et al., 2006). There is a need not only for the client and agency to share information but for the client to provide information that can assist the development of creative advertising. The quality of the communications brief given to the agency is seen to influence greatly the creative output (Koslow et al., 2006; Sutherland et al., 2004).

There are many other possible influences on the creative process. One major factor concerns the prevailing regulations and industry standards about what is acceptable behaviour. The amount of risk the client is prepared to take (El-Murad and West, 2004), access to consumer research and sufficient development time are seen to be important factors in determining the level of creative output (Koslow et al., 2006).

O'Connor et al. (2017) explored the drivers of creativity within agencies and in particular the influence of structural configuration on creative development. Their study identified that increasing staff resource does not always lead to more creative work and suggested that in some cases fewer staff may produce better results.

Scholars' paper 19.4

The creative process

Turnbull, S. and Wheeler, C. (2017) The advertising creative process: a study of UK agencies, *Journal of Marketing Communications*, 23(2), 176–94.

The process of developing creative work can be complex and challenging. The authors explore the stages used in UK advertising agencies when developing new creative work. Interviews with advertising account managers in London agencies provide a rare insight into the world of advertising agency creative development.

See also:

Stuhlfaut, M.W. and Windels, K. (2017) Altered states: the effects of media and technology on the creative process in advertising agencies, *Journal of Marketing Communications*, 1–27.

Message framing

The principle of building a border around an idea or story, and then presenting a contained and managed view of an issue, is well known and practised regularly by politicians, and advertising and public relations professionals. Known as *framing*, the concept has roots in communications studies, psychology and sociology. As with a number of concepts, there is little agreement on what framing is and, as Tsai (2007) indicates, it is controversial and empirically unproven. However, of the many definitions, Dan and Ihlen (2011) cite Entman's (1993: 52) as one definition quoted more often than others. To frame is to:

> select some aspects of a perceived reality and make them more salient in a communicating context, in such a way as to promote a particular problem definition, causal interpretation, moral evaluation, and/or treatment recommendation.

By cropping and framing an item any distracting or contradictory elements are removed and focus can be given to the interpretation intended by the source. Gamson and Modigliani (1989) indicate that those who use framing to influence public opinion often compete with each other to frame the issues of interest. The goal of these *framing contests* (Pan and Kosicki, 2001) is to get, first, the media to adopt that particular frame and then the audience.

The framing principle is used in advertising to present predetermined brand elements. Competitors frame their messages and stories in order that their brands stand out, have clarity and focus, and be positioned distinctly and clearly.

Message framing works on the hedonic principles of our motivation to seek happiness and to avoid pain. So, messages can be framed either to focus a recipient's attention on positive outcomes (happiness) or to take them away from the possible negative outcomes (pain). For example, a positively framed message might be a yogurt that is presented as 'contains real fruit' or a car as 'a stylish design'. Conversely, messages could be presented as 'contains only 5 per cent fat' and 'low carbon emissions'; these are regarded as negatively framed.

Many practitioners work on the basis that positive are better than negative messages, whereas others believe negative framing promotes deeper thinking and consideration. However, there is little empirical evidence to support any of these views. Therefore, in an attempt to understand when it is better to use positive or negative framing, Tsai argues that it is necessary to develop a holistic understanding of the target audience. This involves considering three factors: self-construal; consumer involvement; and product knowledge. These are explained in Table 19.5.

Tsai believes that these three factors moderate an individual's response when they are exposed to positively or negatively framed brand messages. In turn, these influence the three main dimensions of a brand's communications. These are generally accepted by researchers such as MacKenzie and Lutz (1989) and Lafferty, Goldsmith and Newell (2002) to be attitude to the ad, attitude to the brand and purchase intention. Tsai develops a conceptual model to demonstrate this, through which he argues brand communications persuasiveness is moderated by these three factors.

Table 19.5 Factors associated with message framing

Factor	Range	Explanation	Positive message framing	Negative message framing
Self-construal	Independent	Individuals (the self) seek to distinguish themselves from others. These individuals respond best to positive framing.	Independent	
	Interdependent	Individuals (the self) try not to distinguish themselves from others. These individuals respond best to negative framing.		Interdependent
Consumer involvement	High/low	Refers to the extent to which personal relevance and perceived risk influence decision-making within a product category. When high, negative framing is preferred; when low, positive framing is preferred.	Low	High
Product knowledge	High/low	Product knowledge consists of two elements: behavioural (usage) experience and mental (search, exposure and information). Message framing is more suitable where product knowledge is low.	Low	Low

Source: Based on Tsai (2007).

His research concludes that positive message framing should be used under the following conditions:

Independent self-construal × low consumer involvement × low product knowledge

Negative framing should be used in the case of:

Interdependent self-construal × high consumer involvement × low product knowledge

Storytelling

Stories are considered to be an integral part of the way we lead our lives. This is because they enable us to make sense of our perceived world and our role within it, the events that we encounter, and meaning we derive from our relationships and social activities (Merchant et al., 2010). In many ways stories enable us to frame core messages. Stories are embedded in music, novels, fairytales, films, news, religion, politics and plays. They work because they fit or match the way people think and retrieve information from memory.

Stories are the foundation of word-of-mouth communications and a significant dimension of brands and the advertising used to support them, yet they are often an understated aspect of marketing communications.

The versatility of storytelling is recalled by Barker and Gower (2010). They believe that in addition to helping to sell products (Wylie, 1998), storytelling is used by organisations for communications (Jones and LeBaron, 2002), to introduce and manage change (Boje, 1991), for leadership (Marshall and Adamic, 2010), organisational learning (Lämsä and Sintonen, 2006), and even design management (DeLarge, 2004). Woodside et al. (2008) refer to the use of storytelling through blogs, suggesting it may be a more effective way of driving purchase intentions than traditional websites.

Carnevale et al. (2018) identified that meaningful stories shared by brands are more likely to result in positive brand attitudes than just happy stories. The suggestion here is that brands need to ensure that the stories they share have a purpose. This echoes the findings of McKee and Fryer (2003) who argue that stories are effective at persuasion because they involve people emotionally.

Stories consist of a theme and a plot, the latter conveying the former. Papadatos (2006) refers to themes within stories, and identifies three main elements: hardship, reciprocity and a defining moment. Each story has a sequence of events, or plot. The normal sequence starts with anticipation, and then progresses through a crisis, getting help, and then achieving a goal. See Table 19.6 for more information about these elements.

Stories are used to frame our understanding and to encourage individuals to want to become a part of the story itself and to identify with a brand and/or its characters. Strong brands are built around a core theme or platform from which a series of linked stories can be developed. Cordiner (2009) refers to brands having a moral premise (platform): Honda's power of dreams, and Starbucks' 'third space' about having somewhere for each of us between work and home. Virgin's platform is to challenge the establishment, and Google's is to set information free and connect people.

Stories can be understood in terms of four main categories. These are:

1. *Myths and origins* can be used to recall how a company started and what its principles are, but very often the focus is on how it overcame early difficulties and achieved success. The current values can often be seen embedded in these stories. For example, the founders of HP started the company in a garage. As the company grew, so a stream of stories centred on the garage developed. These referred to the roots of the company, and became a central and controlling element in the culture of the company.

Table 19.6 Elements of storytelling

	Element	Explanation
Theme	Hardship	In order to overcome obstacles perseverance and determination in the face of these difficulties and hardship are critical so that the end product has a sense of being earned.
	Reciprocity	An appreciation that there is a fair or equal exchange, that the give and take of life is present.
	Defining moments	Human experience is punctuated with moments that stand out, or even change lives, and these are the moments that are remembered and treasured.
	Anticipation	Stories begin with a sense of hope for the future – a new job, home, baby, activity, all of which represent anticipation about the future.
Plot	Crisis	The feeling of anticipation is often followed by a negative, an unanticipated event or crisis that disrupts the path to the future.
	Help along the way	The crisis is mediated by the arrival of unexpected help. This might be in the form of advice from a new person or organisation, a tip from a friend or information from a specialist such as a mentor, an experienced teacher, protector, or trusty sage. As a result, there is a period of hard work and endurance.
	The goal is achieved	Following much discomfort and many obstacles, stories conclude with the goal accomplished and, for many, muted celebration.

Source: Based on Papadatos (2006).

2. *Corporate prophecies* are predictions about an organisation's future, which are often based on past stories or stories about other organisations.

3. *Hero stories* recall people from the organisation who confronted and overcame a dilemma. The story provides a set of behaviours and values to be copied by others, especially during periods of crisis. These stories help people establish priorities and make decisions.

4. *Archived narratives* are an organisation's collection of stories, which trace its history and development. With organisations changing names, being merged, bought out and reconstituted, there is an increasing need to access key stories from the past in order to provide a sense of history.

Viewpoint 19.4

Samsung delivers an emotional story

Samsung India's customer service film, *We'll Take Care of You, Wherever You Are* uses storytelling as a device to engage target audiences emotionally with the brand. Developed to raise awareness of Samsung's initiative in India to deliver customer service to all corners of the country, the four-minute film tells the story of a Samsung service engineer who is responding to a girl's call about her broken television set.

The ad draws on many traditional narrative devices used in storytelling. The film relates the story of the young engineer and his efforts to reach a remote village in India. The young man provides us with a hero for the story, living up to our expectations of all good heroes by overcoming the hardship he is confronted with. We see his Samsung van crossing bridges and navigating high mountain roads and witness the efforts he

Image 19.4 Samsung uses a simple storytelling plot in their film
Source: d_odin/Shutterstock.

makes to get past fallen trees and herds of sheep. He is determined to reach the girl despite all the difficulties he faces. When he finally reaches the girl, he discovers he is making a very special house call.

The film uses a simple plot. The girl's broken television provides the crisis and the engineer provides the heroic figure who conquers all to achieve his goal in the face of adversity. The conclusion to the story is when the television is repaired and the goal achieved. Drawing on audiences' childhood memories of narratives from fairytales and myths, the ad provides a familiar plot that audiences can easily relate to.

And everyone loves a good story. The film was the most watched video globally on YouTube in 2017 and has been viewed over 208 million times.

Sources: Nudd (2017); Samsung India (2017); Samsung Newsroom India (2017).

Insight

The Samsung film highlights how effective story telling can be for brands to deliver their own story. In this case the story is a *hero story* and tells the tale of how an employee overcame a dilemma. The story invites viewers to make an association between the dedication and empathy shown by the service engineer and the brand.

Question: Watch the Samsung film, *We'll Take Care of You, Wherever You Are* and make a list all the elements of storytelling you can identify using the Papadatos (2006) framework.

Task: Find another example of storytelling in advertising and explain what elements of storytelling are used.

User-generated content (UGC)

So far in this chapter attention has been given to the issues associated with organisation-driven creativity. However, it is important to consider the increasing numbers of messages that are developed and communicated by ordinary individuals. Not only are these used to communicate with organisations of all types and sizes but they are also shared with peers, family, friends and others in communities such as social networks and specialist interest online communities (e.g. reunion and family history sites). This is referred to as *user-generated content* (UGC) and it can be seen in action at YouTube, Flickr, Twitter, DIGG, Instagram, Pinterest and in all the millions of blogs and vlogs.

UGC can be considered to be all of the ways in which people make use of social media (Kaplan and Haenlein, 2010) and describes the various forms of media content that are publicly available and created by end-users. According to Christodoulides et al. (2011), one interpretation of UGC requires that three core conditions need to be met. First, the content needs to be published either on a publicly accessible website or on a social networking site accessible to a selected group of people. Second, the material needs to show some creative effort and, finally, it has to have been created outside of professional routines and practices.

Malthouse et al. (2016) found that if the content requires consumers to think about a personal goal that is related to the brand, it will increase purchase behaviour. This highlights both the importance of audience engagement and the need for brands to request relevant content.

Discussion boards and online forums can only work through consumer participation and UGC. One of the more common forms of UGC is blogging. This involves individuals, sometimes in the name of organisations, but more often as independent consumers, posting information about topics of personal interest. Sometimes these people develop opinion leader status and organisations feed them information about the launch of new brands, so that they pass on the information to opinion followers.

Social networks thrive on the shared views, opinions and beliefs, often brand-related, of networked friends. YouTube, Instagram and Flickr provide opportunities for consumers to share video and photos respectively, with all material posted by users. Users post their content and respond to the work of others, often by rating the quality or entertainment value of content posted by others.

Although people understand the rules and norms associated with communicating across peer groups and social networks, organisations have yet to master these new environments. Firms are not able to use traditional forms of free communications with as much credibility and authority as individuals regularly do within these contexts. One of the reasons for this is the democratisation of the media and the language codes that have emerged.

Sourcing content

UGC can be derived through one of three main processes:

1. *Crowdsourcing* – organisations can prompt the public into action, via the web community, to develop specific types of content and materials. Where organisations deliberately invite the entire web community to suggest material that can be used commercially, in return for a reward, the term *crowdsourcing* is used. In this circumstance the crowd may consist of amateurs or businesses. The difference between crowd-sourcing and outsourcing is that the latter is directed at a predetermined, specific organisation.

2. *Open-source materials* – the public may take the initiative themselves and communicate with a specific organisation or industry. Where a group of people voluntarily offer ideas and materials, without invitation, prompting or seeking a reward from an organisation, the term *open-source materials* is used.

3. *Friendsourcing* – the public may exchange information and ideas amongst themselves, without any direct communications with an organisation or brand owner. This occurs when friends and families communicate and share ideas and materials among themselves, for their own enjoyment, bonding and enrichment.

Some marketers are using the increasing occurrence of UGC as an opportunity to listen to and observe consumers and to find out what meanings they attribute to products, brands and company actions. Some companies invite consumers to offer content (ads): crowdsourcing. Unilever dissolved its 16-year-old relationship with its ad agency Lowe London, in order to embark on a crowdsourcing strategy. Focusing on the Peperami brand, Unilever searched for material to support a TV and print campaign. The result was 1,185 ideas, and the winner won £6,000 (Charles, 2009).

Ideas about co-creation and collaboration now pervade marketing communications. There is an increasing role for messages to be shared with audiences, not sent to or at them (Earls, 2010). Understanding the relationships audiences prefer with product categories and brands enables the identification of opportunities to share and collaborate.

Key points

- Source credibility consists of three key elements: the level of perceived expertise; the personal motives the source is believed to possess; and the degree of trust that can be placed in what the source says or does on behalf of the endorsement.

- A spokesperson can provide credibility and four main types of spokesperson are identified: the expert, the celebrity, the chief executive officer and the consumer.

- Arguments for a brand or issue can be presented for and against an issue – a two-sided message. Alternatively, just the case in favour of an issue can be presented – a one-sided message. Credibility is improved by understanding the audience's position and then fashioning the presentation of the message.

- Messages that present the strongest points at the beginning use the primacy effect. Placing the strongest points at the end of the message assumes that the recency effect will bring about greater levels of persuasion. This is appropriate when the receiver agrees with the position adopted by the source or has a high positive level of involvement.

- Messages can use informational/rational or emotional appeals. Information or rational appeals use factual, slice-of-life, demonstration and comparative style. Emotional appeals use fear, humour, sex, music, fantasy and surrealism.

- There are two broad types of motive that drive attitudes towards purchase behaviour. These are informational and transformational motives. Individuals have a need for information to counter negative concerns about a purchase decision. These informational motives are said to be negatively charged feelings. They can become positively charged, or the level of concern can be reduced considerably, by the acquisition of relevant information.

- Promises to enhance or to improve a brand are referred to as transformational motives. These are related to the user's feelings and are capable of transforming a user's emotional state, hence they are positively charged.

- Creativity in advertising is seen to enhance the effectiveness of an ad. This can lead to improved motivation to process a message, and from this higher recall and recognition scores can develop.

- Creativity in advertising has two main characteristics: first, ads are divergent, or highly unique or novel; and second, they are relevant or meaningful to the audience. The higher the originality or divergence and the more personally relevant, the greater the attention the ad attracts.

- Agencies, and all those working within creative departments, work within and are constrained by the prevailing organisational culture. Stuhlfaut (2011) identifies the existence of a creative code which shapes the development of advertisements.

- The creative process in advertising agencies is seen to progress through a number of stages which include internal and external review meetings such as Chemistry Meetings and can involve setting up War Rooms and undertaking consumer research.

- Framing is concerned with the selection of particular elements in order to restrict and focus the way people perceive a problem, brand, issue or communications event.

- People use storytelling to help make sense of their lives and the events that they encounter and to derive meaning from their relationships and social activities. Stories consist of themes (hardship, reciprocity and a defining moment) and plots (a sequence of events; anticipation, crisis, getting help, and achieving a goal).

- User-generated content (UGC) considers how messages are developed by consumers. UGC has three primary characteristics: the content needs to be published either on a publicly accessible website or on a social networking site accessible to a selected group of people; the material needs to demonstrate some creative effort; and it has to have been created outside of professional routines and practices.

Case study

John Lewis: Buster the Boxer
This case is endorsed by adam&eveDDB

Image 19.5 John Lewis launched a series of campaigns that tapped into consumers' emotions
Source: Pajor Pawel/Shutterstock.

Founded in 1864, John Lewis are the UK's largest department store retailer, with 31 department stores, 10 home shops and an established online business. With a vast range of products on sale, from tights to home insurance, the chain's target market is broad.

In 2009 the British economy was in recession, unemployment had risen and consumer spending was falling. John Lewis found their sales were in decline and realised they needed to take action. Although before 2009 little advertising had been done by the retailer apart from supporting new store openings, John Lewis recognised that advertising had the power to influence consumers and could help in increasing consumer spending and attract new customers. They approached their agency with a brief to re-engage customers with the brand and drive greater brand loyalty.

Research showed John Lewis that emotional affinity was a key driver of customer loyalty and this made the communications strategy clear. They realised very early on in the process that they needed to engage consumers emotionally with the brand. With Christmas approaching, which is a key trading period for retailers in the UK with consumers buying gifts for family and friends, this was the time to put their new strategy to the test. In the past, most retailers have used their advertising to showcase their range of gifts, with advertising acting like 'video catalogues', and merchandise displayed in a Christmas setting. They realised that to grow their share of this seasonal spend their message needed to stand out from their competitors and engage consumers differently.

In 2009, John Lewis launched their first Christmas ad in what has become an iconic series of emotionally led campaigns, based on a new positioning strategy of 'thoughtful giving'. The idea of using a story about thoughtful giving was derived from consumer insight. Focus group research had identified how stories about finding gifts for someone you love resonated with the target audience. This insight was used to develop a creative platform about giving that was seen to be authentic and tapped into consumers' emotions.

The first Christmas campaign using this new platform, 'Remember the Feeling' was a huge success. As well as improving brand perception, the campaign delivered increased penetration, frequency and spend for the retailer, which directly contributed towards sales and profitability. John Lewis showed that they were able to activate emotional engagement with the brand through advertising. Since the first Christmas ad for John Lewis ran in 2009 the retailer has continued with the strategy of 'thoughtful giving' as a campaign.

John Lewis' Christmas ads have now become synonymous with Christmas and are one of the most anticipated events of the festive season. In 2016, John Lewis released, 'Buster the Boxer' the next in a line of award-winning campaigns. The ad tells the story of young girl called Bridget who loves to bounce and her pet dog, Buster. When Bridget's parents buy her a trampoline for Christmas, we discover it is not only Bridget who enjoys bouncing. Using CGI to create a host of garden animals, the film entertains us with their antics on Bridget's trampoline. Bridget's dog, Buster watches on enviously and on Christmas morning he is the first to rush out and have a bounce himself on the new trampoline.

Prior to broadcasting the ad on TV and online, John Lewis ran a teaser campaign using three short teaser films on social media to build a sense of anticipation. The retailer partnered with Sky to allow audiences to download the film and watch it using Sky+ planner. Additionally, a branded Snapchat lens was used to extend the campaign.

The two-minute ad was launched on John Lewis's social media channels and within 24 hours it had received 721,000 combined unique downloads. The ad received 900,000 views in the first weekend alone.

Previous Christmas campaigns have identified the importance of social engagement for John Lewis and this strategy was continued for 'Buster the Boxer'. The ad had 64.36 million views on social and went viral as 93 per cent of online views coming from mobile were organic. The ad became #1 global trend on Twitter 50 minutes after its release and was a trending topic on Facebook. The retailer saw 'Buster the Boxer' #1 viewed Christmas advert on YouTube.

On the day of the launch the ad was trending ahead of the US election results from the previous day and broke the Sky 24-hour download record.

It did not take long for 'Buster the Boxer' to become part of the national conversation and enter popular culture. The campaign was discussed on a number of TV shows including, *This Morning, Have I Got News For You*, and *Lorraine*. Within days parodies appeared on YouTube, the most popular one featured the US presidential candidates as Bridget and Buster and was viewed 1.9 million times.

Image 19.6 Window displays supported the in-store activation
Source: Elena Rostunova/Shutterstock.

The campaign message was amplified beyond the TV campaign using interactive experiential marketing. A fully immersive VR trampoline experience was set up in the John Lewis flagship store. Additionally, a 360-degree video on Google Cardboard VR provided an in-store experience for younger children.

Further in-store activations included window displays and a range of official merchandise, including books and branded bags inspired by Buster.

Although the impact of the campaign was evident in the media, the success of the campaign is reflected in John Lewis's trading results with the retailer enjoying sales increases of 4.9 per cent in the last six weeks of the year.

Sources: Cannes Lions Archive (2017); Gwynn (2017).

Review questions

John Lewis case questions

1. Why was an emotional appeal used by John Lewis in its Christmas advertising campaign? Explain why you think an information-based appeal was not used.

2. Which elements in 'Buster the Boxer' help to develop the emotional appeal?

3. Watch 'Buster the Boxer' for yourself and identify the elements of storytelling that are evident in the TV ad.

4. Discuss why you think 'Buster the Boxer' is seen to be a creative ad. Evaluate the ad against the terms 'divergence' and 'relevance'.

5. Find examples of Christmas advertising from three other retailers and decide whether they have used an emotional-based appeal or an information-based appeal.

General questions

1. Why is source credibility seen as important? Find examples of each type of spokesperson.

2. Explain the difference between informational and transformational motivations.

3. What do forcing and subversion mean in the context of creativity? Find a current example of each approach.

4. Outline the principles associated with framing. How does this concept assist those responsible for marketing communications?

5. Using different media, find three examples of user-generated content.

References for Chapter 19

Adams, A.J. and Henderson Blair, M. (1992) Persuasive advertising and sales accountability, *Journal of Advertising Research*, 32(2), 20–5.

Amabile, T.M. (1996) *Creativity in Context*, Boulder, CO: Westview Press.

Anon (2015) No 132: the world's most expensive TV commercial, *Campaign*, 15 May, 13.

Arora, R. (1985) Consumer involvement: what it offers to advertising strategy, *International Journal of Advertising*, 4, 119–30.

Audi Intelligent technology (2018) Audi, retrieved 10th January 2018 from https://www.audi.co.uk/audi-innovation/advanced-technologies.html

Baack, D.W., Wilson, R.T. and Till, B.D. (2008) Creativity and memory effects: recall, recognition, and an exploration of nontraditional media, *Journal of Advertising*, 37(4), 85–94.

Barker, R.T. and Gower, K. (2010) Strategic application of storytelling in organizations toward effective communication in a diverse world, *Journal of Business Communication*, 47(3), 295–312.

Barron-Duncan, R. (2017) Transatlantic translations: surrealist modes of advertising in France and the United States of America, *Visual Resources*, 1–33.

Barry, J.M. and Graça, S.S. (2018) Humor effectiveness in social video engagement, *Journal of Marketing Theory and Practice*, 26(1–2), 158–80.

Bewick, M. (2006) Pushing the boundaries, *The Marketer*, September, 25.

Bhattacharya, J., Zioga, I. and Lewis, R. (2017) Novel or consistent music? An electrophysiological study investigating music use in advertising, *Journal of Neuroscience, Psychology, and Economics*, 10(4), 137.

Binet, L. and Field, P. (2007) *Marketing in the Era of Accountability*, Henley-on-Thames: Institute of Practitioners in Advertising/WARC.

Binet, L., Müllensiefen, D. and Edwards, P. (2013) The power of music, *Admap*, October, 10–13.

Blasko, V.J. and Mokwa, M.P. (1986) Creativity in advertising: a Janusian perspective, *Journal of Advertising*, 15(4), 43–50.

Boje, D.M. (1991) The storytelling organization: a study of story performance in an office-supply firm, *Administrative Science Quarterly*, March, 106–26.

Brownsell, A. (2009) When personalities become bigger than their brands, *Brand Republic*, retrieved 10 January 2015 from www.brandrepublic.com/article/872886/when-personalities-become-bigger-brands

Cannes Lions Archive (2011), The Force, retrieved 20 March 2018 from http://www.canneslionsarchive.com

Cannes Lions Archive (2017) Buster The Boxer, retrieved 20 March 2018 from http://www.canneslionsarchive.com

Carnevale, M., Yucel-Aybat, O. and Kachersky, L. (2018) Meaningful stories and attitudes toward the brand: the moderating role of consumers' implicit mindsets, *Journal of Consumer Behaviour*, 17(1).

Charles, G. (2009) Peperami ad will be test case for crowd-sourcing, *Marketing*, 4 November, 2.

Christodoulides, G., Jevons, C. and Blackshaw, P. (2011) The voice of the consumer speaks forcefully in brand identity: user-generated content forces smart marketers to listen, *Journal of Advertising Research*, Supplement, March, 101–8.

Cordiner, R. (2009) Set free your core narrative: the brand as storyteller, *Admap*, October, retrieved 8 July 2010 from https://www.warc.com/content/paywall/article/admap/set_free_your_core_narrative_the_brand_as_storyteller/90075

Cui, G. and Yang, X. (2009) Responses of Chinese consumers to sex appeals in international advertising: a test of congruency theory, *Journal of Global Marketing*, 22, 229–45.

Dahl, D.W., Frankenberger, K.D. and Manchanda, R.V. (2003) Does it pay to shock? Reactions to shocking and nonshocking advertising content among university students, *Journal of Advertising Research*, 43(3), 268–81.

Dan, V. and Ihlen, Ø. (2011) Framing expertise: a cross-cultural analysis of success in framing contests, *Journal of Communications Management*, 15(4), 368–88.

Das, E., Galekh, M. and Vonkeman, C. (2015) Is sexy better than funny? Disentangling the persuasive effects of pleasure and arousal across sex and humour appeals, *International Journal of Advertising*, 34(3), 406–20.

DeLarge, C.A. (2004) Storytelling as a critical success factor in design processes and outcomes, *Design Management Review*, 15(3), 76–81.

Dichter, E. (1966) How word-of-mouth advertising works, *Harvard Business Review*, 44 (November/December), 147–66.

Earls, M. (2010) Collaboration: the wisdom of crowds, *Admap*, May, retrieved 10 May 2010 from https://www.warc.com/content/paywall/article/admap/collaboration_the_wisdom_of_crowds/91816

El-Murad, J. and West, D.C. (2004) The definition and measurement of creativity: what do we know? *Journal of Advertising Research*, 44(2), 188–201.

Entman, R.M. (1993) Framing: toward clarification of a fractured paradigm, *Journal of Communications*, 43(4), 51–8.

Faison, E.W. (1961) Effectiveness of one-sided and two-sided mass communications in advertising, *Public Opinion Quarterly*, 25 (Autumn), 468–9.

Foos, A.E., Keeling, K. and Keeling, D. (2016) Redressing the sleeper effect: evidence for the favorable persuasive impact of discounting information over time in a contemporary advertising context, *Journal of Advertising*, 45(1), 19–25.

Foxall, G.R. and Goldsmith, R.E. (1994) *Consumer Psychology for Marketing*, London: Routledge.

Gamson, W.A. and Modigliani, A. (1989) Media discourse and public opinion on nuclear power: a constructionist approach, *American Journal of Sociology*, 95, 1–37.

Goodenough, W.H. (1981) *Culture, Language, and Society*, Menlo Park, CA: Benjamin Cummings.

Gwynn, S. (2017) John Lewis grows Christmas sales but staff bonus cut as dark clouds loom, *Campaign*, 12 January, retrieved 10 January 2018 from https://www.campaignlive.co.uk/article/john-lewis-grows-christmas-sales-staff-bonus-cut-dark-clouds-loom/1420686

Halonen-Knight, E. and Hurmerinta, L. (2010) Who endorses whom? Meanings transfer in celebrity endorsement, *Journal of Product & Brand Management*, 19(6), 452–60.

Hannah, D.B. and Sternthal, B. (1984) Detecting and explaining the sleeper effect, *Journal of Consumer Research*, 11 (September), 632–42.

Heath, R.G. (2010) Creativity in TV ads does not increase attention, *Admap*, January, retrieved 23 October 2011 from https://www.warc.com/content/paywall/article/admap/creativity_in_tv_ads_does_not_increase_attention/90677

Heath, R.G., Nairn, A.C. and Bottomley, P.A. (2009) How effective is creativity? Emotive content in TV advertising does not increase attention, *Journal of Advertising Research*, September, 450–63.

Hill, R. and Johnson, L.W. (2004) Understanding creative service: a qualitative study of the advertising problem delineation, communication and response (APDCR) process, *International Journal of Advertising*, 23(3), 285–307.

Hovland, C.I. and Mandell, W. (1952) An experimental comparison of conclusion drawing by the communicator and by the audience, *Journal of Abnormal and Social Psychology*, 47 (July), 581–8.

Hovland, C.I. and Weiss, W. (1951) The influence of source credibility on communication effectiveness, *Public Opinion Quarterly*, 15(4), 635–50.

Hurman, J. (2016) *The Case for Creativity*, 2nd edn, London: AUT Media.

Jones, S.E. and LeBaron, C.D. (2002) Research on the relationship between verbal and nonverbal communication: emerging integrations, *Journal of Communication*, 52(3), 499–521.

Kadić-Maglajlić, S., Arslanagić-Kalajdžić, M., Micevski, M., Michaelidou, N. and Nemkova, E. (2017) Controversial advert perceptions in SNS advertising: the role of ethical judgement and religious commitment, *Journal of Business Ethics*, 141(2), 249–65.

Kaplan, A.M. and Haenlein, M. (2010) Users of the world, unite! The challenges and opportunities of Social Media, *Business Horizons*, 53(1), 59–68.

Kardes, F.R. (1988) Spontaneous inference processes in advertising: the effects of conclusion omission and involvement on persuasion, *Journal of Consumer Research*, 15 (September), 225–33.

Kareklas, I., Muehling, D.D. and Weber, T.J. (2015) Reexamining health messages in the digital age: a fresh look at source credibility effects, *Journal of Advertising*, 44(2), 88–104.

Kelman, H. (1961) Processes of opinion change, *Public Opinion Quarterly*, 25 (Spring), 57–78.

Kerr, G., Mortimer, K., Dickinson, S. and Waller, D.S. (2012) Buy, boycott or blog: exploring online consumer power to share, discuss and distribute controversial advertising messages, *European Journal of Marketing*, 46(3/4), 387–405.

Kiefer, B. (2017) Audi sends in the clowns for big-budget tech campaign, *Campaign*, 28 September, retrieved 10th January 2018 from www.campaignlive.co.uk/article/audi-sends-clowns-big-budget-tech-campaign/1445813#KBD5chfHZ4SrJbH1.99

Kim, B.H., Han, S. and Yoon, S. (2010) Advertising creativity in Korea: scale development and validation, *Journal of Advertising*, 39(2), 93–108.

Koslow, S., Sasser, S.L. and Riordan, E.A. (2003) What is creative to whom and why? Perceptions in advertising agencies, *Journal of Advertising Research*, 43 (March), 96–110.

Koslow, S., Sasser, S.L. and Riordan, E.A. (2006) Do marketers get the advertising they need or the advertising they deserve? *Journal of Advertising*, 35(3), 81–101.

Kover, A.J. (1995) Copywriters' implicit theories of communication: an exploration, *Journal of Consumer Research*, 21(4), 596–611.

Lafferty, B.A., Goldsmith, R.E. and Newell, S.J. (2002) The dual credibility model: the influence of corporate and endorser credibility on attitudes and purchase intentions, *Journal of Marketing Theory and Practice*, 10(3), 1–12.

Lämsä, A. M. and Sintonen, T. (2006) A narrative approach for organizational learning in a diverse organization, *Journal of Workplace Learning*, 18(2), 106–20.

Lyons, E. (2018) Brazil's Salvation Army uses political humour to draw donations, *Marketing Week*, 5 April, retrieved 5 May 2018 from https://www.marketingweek.com/2018/04/05/target-trials-voice-activated-coupon/

MacKenzie, S.B. and Lutz, R.L. (1989) An empirical examination of the structural antecedents of attitude toward the ad in an advertising pretesting context, *Journal of Marketing*, 53, 48–65.

Malthouse, E.C., Calder, B.J., Kim, S.J. and Vandenbosch, M. (2016) Evidence that user-generated content that produces engagement increases purchase behaviours, *Journal of Marketing Management*, 32(5-6), 427–44.

Marshall, J. and Adamic, M. (2010) The story is the message: shaping corporate culture, *Journal of Business Strategy*, 31(2), 18–23.

McKee, R. and Fryer, B. (2003) Storytelling that moves people, *Harvard Business Review*, 81(6), 51–5.

Merchant, A., Ford, J.B. and Sargeant, A. (2010) Charitable organizations' storytelling influence on donors' emotions and intentions, *Journal of Business Research*, 63(7), 754–62.

Na, W., Marshall, R. and Woodside, A.G. (2009) Decision system analysis of advertising agency decisions, *Qualitative Market Research: An International Journal*, 12(2), 153–70.

Nudd, T. (2017) Ad of the day: see the sweet Samsung ad that's become a major hit in India, *Adweek*, 11 January, retrieved 15 January 2018 from http://www.adweek.com/brand-marketing/ad-day-see-sweet-samsung-ad-thats-become-major-hit-india-175484/

Oakes, O. (2015) Aldi spoofs John Lewis Christmas ad with its own man on the moon, *Campaign*, 26 November, retrieved 15 January 2018 from https://www.campaignlive.co.uk/article/aldi-spoofs-john-lewis-christmas-ad-its-own-man-moon/1374591

O'Connor, H., Kilgour, M., Koslow, S. and Sasser, S. (2017) Drivers of creativity within advertising agencies: how structural configuration can affect and improve creative development, *Journal of Advertising Research*, JAR-2017-015.

Okazaki, S., Mueller, B. and Taylor, C.R. (2010) Measuring soft-sell versus hard-sell advertising appeals, *Journal of Advertising*, 39(2), 5–20.

Paek, H.-J. and Nelson, M.R. (2007) A cross-cultural and cross media comparison of female nudity in advertising, *Journal of Promotion Management*, 13(1/2), 145–67.

Pan, Z. and Kosicki, G. (2001) Framing as a strategic action in public deliberation, in *Framing Public Life: Perspectives on Media and Our Understanding of the Social World* (eds S.D. Reese, O.H. Gandy and A.E. Grant), Mahwah, NJ: Lawrence Erlbaum, 35–65.

Papadatos, C. (2006) The art of storytelling: how loyalty marketers can build emotional connections to their brands, *Journal of Consumer Marketing*, 23(7), 382–4.

Parker, R. and Churchill, L. (1986) Positioning by opening the consumer's mind, *International Journal of Advertising*, 5, 1–13.

Priest, I. (2014) Client-agency relationship: seven principles for better commercial creativity, *Market Leader*, Quarter 3, retrieved 10 December 2014 from www.warc.com/Content/ContentViewer.aspx?MasterContentRef=7654819d-4ed7-47f7-9323-f039e5cc8ec4&q=priest&CID=A102137&PUB=MKT.

Quantifying the effect of objectifying women in advertising (n.d.) #WomenNotObjects retrieved 10 January 2018 from https://static1.squarespace.com/static/56af7d21fd5d081beb0b25a4/t/57e308f7440243d14d591fb6/1474496760559/B%26W_Objectifying+Women+in+Advertising.pdf

Quenqua, D. (2017) 1 year later: Badger and Winters on #WomenNotObjects in the age of Trump, *Campaign*, 13 February, retrieved 10 January 2018 from https://www.campaign-live.co.uk/article/1-year-later-badger-winters-womennotobjects-age-trump/1423996

Ray, M.L. and Wilkie, W.L. (1970) Fear: the potential of an appeal neglected by marketing, *Journal of Marketing*, 34 (January), 54–62.

Reichert, T., Childers, C.C. and Reid, L.N. (2012) How sex in advertising varies by product category: an analysis of three decades of visual sexual imagery in magazine advertising, *Journal of Current Issues & Research in Advertising*, 33(1), 1–19.

Reid, L.N. and Rotfeld, H.J. (1976) Toward an associative model of advertising creativity, *Journal of Advertising*, 5(4), 24–9.

Rossiter, J.R. and Percy, L. (1997) *Advertising and Promotion Management*, 2nd edn, New York: McGraw-Hill.

Rossiter, J. and Percy, L. (1998) *Advertising, Communications, and Promotion Management*, Singapore: McGraw Hill, International Editions.

Rossiter, J.R., Percy, L. and Donovan, R.J. (1991) A better advertising planning grid, *Journal of Advertising Research*, October/November, 11–21.

Ruiter, R.A., Kessels, L.T., Peters, G.J.Y. and Kok, G. (2014) Sixty years of fear appeal research: current state of the evidence, *International Journal of Psychology*, 49(2), 63–70.

Sabri, O. (2017) Does viral communication context increase the harmfulness of controversial taboo advertising? *Journal of Business Ethics*, 141(2), 235–47.

Samsung India (2017) Samsung India Service (SVC) – Most Watched Video in 2017 – We'll take care of you, wherever you are, *YouTube*, retrieved 11 January 2018 from https://www.youtube.com/watch?v=779KwjAYTeQ

Samsung Newsroom India (2017) Samsung India's customer service film creates world record with 100 million hits, *Samsung*, 21 February, retrieved 10 January 2018 from https://news.samsung.com/in/samsung-indias-customer-service-film-creates-world-record-with-100-million-hits

Smith, R.E. and Yang, X. (2004) Toward a general theory of creativity in advertising: the role of divergence, *Marketing Theory*, 4(1/2), 31–58.

Smith, R.E., Chen, J. and Yang, X. (2008) The impact of advertising creativity on the hierarchy of effects, *Journal of Advertising*, 37(4), 47–61.

Smith, R.E., MacKenzie, S.B., Yang, X., Buchholz, L.M. and Darley, W.K. (2007) Modelling the determinants and effects of creativity in advertising, *Marketing Science*, 26(6), 819–33.

Stein, L. (2016) #WomenNotObjects ignites crucial advertising industry conversation, *Adage*, 27 January, retrieved 5 January 2018 from http://adage.com/article/agency-news/womennotobjects-ignites-crucial-ad-industry-conversation/302379/

Stuhlfaut, M. (2011) The creative code: an organisational influence on the creative process in advertising, *International Journal of Advertising*, 30(2), 283–304.

Stuhlfaut, M.W. and Vanden Bergh, B.G. (2014) Creativity is … a metaphoric model of the creative thought process, *Journal of Marketing Communications*, 20(6), 383–96.

Stuhlfaut, M.W. and Windels, K. (2017) Altered states: the effects of media and technology on the creative process in advertising agencies, *Journal of Marketing Communications*, 1–27.

Sutherland, J., Duke, L. and Abernethy, A. (2004) A model of marketing information flow: what creatives obtain and want to know from clients, *Journal of Advertising*, 33(4), 39–52.

Tevi, A. and Koslow, S. (2018) How rhetoric theory informs the creative advertising development process: reconciling differences between advertising scholarship and practice, *Journal of Advertising Research*, 58(1), 111–28.

Tsai, S.-P. (2007) Message framing strategy for brand communication, *Journal of Advertising Research*, 47(3), 364–77.

Turnbull, S. and Wheeler, C. (2017) The advertising creative process: a study of UK agencies, *Journal of Marketing Communications*, 23(2), 176–94.

Vanden Bergh, B.G., Lee, M., Quilliam, E.T. and Hove, T. (2011) The multidimensional nature and brand impact of user-generated advertising parodies in social media, *International Journal of Advertising*, 30(1), 103–31.

Vaughn, R. (1980) How advertising works: a planning model, *Journal of Advertising Research*, 20(5), 27–33.

Venkat, R. and Abi-Hanna, N. (1995) Effectiveness of visually shocking advertisements: is it context dependent? *Administrative Science Association of Canada Proceedings*, 16(3), 139–46.

Vos, S., Crouch, R., Quester, P. and Ilicic, J. (2017) Examining the effectiveness of fear appeals in prompting help-seeking: the case of at-risk gamblers, *Psychology & Marketing*, 34(6), 648–60.

Weinberger, M.G., Gulas, C.S. and Weinberger, M.F. (2015) Looking in through outdoor: a socio-cultural and historical perspective on the evolution of advertising humour, *International Journal of Advertising*, 34(3), 447–72.

Westerman, D., Spence, P.R. and Van Der Heide, B. (2014) Social media as information source: recency of updates and credibility of information, *Journal of Computer-Mediated Communication*, 19(2), 171–83.

Wirtz, J.G., Sparks, J.V. and Zimbres, T.M. (2018) The effect of exposure to sexual appeals in advertisements on memory, attitude, and purchase intention: a meta-analytic review, *International Journal of Advertising*, 37(2), 168–98.

Witte, K. and Allen, M. (2000) A meta-analysis of fear appeals: implications for effective public health campaigns, *Health Education and Behavior*, 27(5), 591–615.

WMcCann Brazil (2018) Salvation Army uses political humor to generate donations in Brazil, Press Release, 3 April.

Woodside, A.G., Sood, S. and Miller, K.E. (2008) When consumers and brands talk: storytelling theory and research in psychology and marketing, *Psychology & Marketing*, 25(2), 97–145.

Wylie, A. (1998) Storytelling, *Communication World*, 15(3), 30–2.

Yang, X. and Smith, R.E. (2009) Beyond attention effects: modeling the persuasive and emotional effects of advertising creativity, *Marketing Science*, 28(5), 935–49.

Media: principles and practice

The selection and use of particular media is necessary in order to channel messages to, from, and among particular groups of consumers and organisations. This is necessary to engage audiences and to enable conversations. Although the array of available media is continually growing, each has its characteristics that impact on the quality, effectiveness and the meaning attributed to a message by an audience.

Aims and learning objectives

The aim of this chapter is to identify and explore the principal characteristics of the main types of media. This will assist understanding of the management processes by which media are selected and scheduled to deliver messages and influence audiences.

The learning objectives are to enable readers to:

1. appreciate the three main ways in which media can be classified;
2. evaluate the different characteristics associated with interactive media, and comprehend what interactive media enable people to do;
3. describe the trends and primary characteristics of each type of linear media;
4. explain the issues associated with multichannel campaigns and explore the role of media within a retailing context;
5. understand the differences between linear and interactive media.

Introduction

The media constitute the third major element of the marketing communications mix. The primary role of the media is to enable planned and unplanned messages to be channelled to, from and among audiences.

The range and variety of media available to organisations has been expanding rapidly. In addition to the traditional list of media, namely newspapers, magazines, radio, television, outdoor and film, Sundar and Limperos (2013: 505) refer to the 'plethora of devices (smartphones, robots) to channels (mobile, cable) to venues on those channels (social networking sites, home shopping networks) and/or devices (smartphone apps), affording users the ability to not only interact with these 'media' (human-computer interaction) but also interact through them to communicate with other users (computer-mediated communications)'. In other words, the range of media available to consumers, and advertisers, is now enormous, and still growing.

Attempts to classify them as simply *traditional* and *new*, or *conventional* and *digital*, are misplaced because these terms are too broad, vague and misleading. What constitutes new and old depends largely on arbitrary timelines and, in any case, digital media are used within traditional formats.

A more meaningful classification is to consider the media in terms of their physicality or location as depicted in Figure 20.1. Here 'broadcast' and 'outdoor' describe what these media are and how they work. This is a static perspective so an alternative approach is to consider the media in terms of their origin or ownership. Here media owned by others are segregated from media that the clients own themselves.

A third type of classification, one based on their communications function, is examined and used as the foundation for exploring media in the remaining part of this and Chapters 21 and 22.

Media classification – by form

When classifying media in terms of their form, six main *classes* can be identified. These are broadcast, print, outdoor, digital, in-store and other media classes. Within each of these classes there are particular *types* of media. For example, within the broadcast class there are television and radio, and within the print class there are newspapers and magazines.

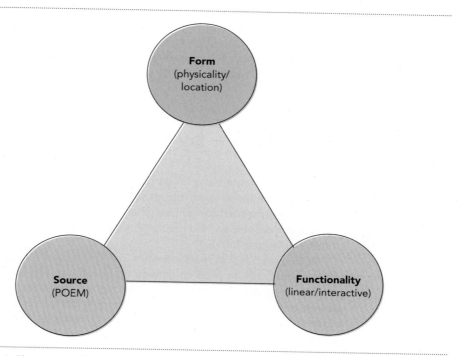

Figure 20.1 Three ways of classifying media

Table 20.1 Summary chart of the main forms of media by form

Class	Type	Vehicles
Broadcast	Television Radio	*Coronation Street*, *The X Factor*, *Game of Thrones* Capital Xtra

Print	Newspapers
	Magazines:
	  consumer
	  business
		The Sunday Times, *Daily Mirror*, *The Telegraph*
		
		Cosmopolitan, *Red*, *Country Life*
		Plumbing News, *The Grocer*

Out-of-home	Billboards Street furniture Transit	96-, 48- and 6-sheet Adshe l Underground stations, airport buildings, taxis, hot-air balloons
Interactive media	Internet Social media Search	Websites, email, apps, RSS, intranets Networks, communities, blogs Organic, sponsored links
In-store	Point-of-purchase Experiences Packaging	Bins, signs and displays Theatre (Lego) The Coca-Cola contour bottle
Other	Cinema Exhibitions and events Product placement Ambient Guerrilla	Pearl & Dean Ideal Home Show, The London Motor Show Films, TV, books Litter bins, golf tees, petrol pumps, washrooms Flyposting

Within each type of media there are a huge number of different media *vehicles* that can be selected to carry an advertiser's message. For example, within UK television there are the terrestrial networks (Independent Television Network, Channel 4 and Channel 5) and the satellite (BSkyB) and cable (e.g. Virgin Media) networks. In print, there are consumer and business-oriented magazines, and the number of specialist magazines is expanding rapidly. These specialist magazines are targeted at particular activity and interest groups, such as *Amateur Photographer*, *Golf Monthly*, and the infamous *Airliner World*! This provides opportunities for advertisers to send messages to well-defined homogeneous groups, which improves effectiveness and reduces wastage in the communications spend. Table 20.1 sets out the three forms of media – classes, types and vehicles – with a few examples.

Media classification – by source

The traditional demarcation regards media in terms of purely paid-for channels, used to support conventional, linear-based advertising. The second classification of the media, by source, was presented earlier (see Chapter 1). Popularly known as POEM, which stands for paid-for, owned and earned media, this classification reflects a practitioner's interpretation of the media (see Table 20.2).

POEM assumes that media are not just about paid-for media but media that embrace all items that can be used to convey brand-oriented messages, regardless of whether a payment is necessary. With the rapid growth of digital technology and formats, reconfiguration of the media landscape and changing consumer behaviours, POEM reflects the increasing scope of contemporary media and the range of media opportunities to engage audiences.

Table 20.2   POEM – a classification of the media by source

Type of media		Explanation
P	Paid-for	Advertising traditionally requires that media time and space are rented from a media owner, in order to convey messages and reach target audiences. The selection of the media mix is planned, predetermined and measured in terms of probable size of audience, costs and scheduling.
O	Owned	Organisations have a range of assets that they can use to convey messages to audiences, and through which they can develop conversations. Ownership means that there are no rental costs as with paid-for media. For example, a brand name or product display on a building, a telephone number or URL on a vehicle, or the use of the company website and its links to other sites, do not incur usage fees.
E	Earned	Earned media refers to comments and conversations, both offline and online, in social media, in the news, or through face-to-face communications, about a brand or organisation. These comments can be negative or positive but the media carrying them are diverse and can be referred to as 'unplanned', although many campaigns seek to stimulate strong word-of-mouth communications through earned media.

The POEM categorisation has recently been supplemented by the notion of shared media. This is similar to earned media because just as WoM communications involve getting others to advocate your brand, shared media focuses on the sharing of your content within social networks. Brands can provoke sharing by providing tools for their audience to create and share branded marketing with their peers. As Guest (2016) observes, Snapchat enables users to create and share branded videos or selfies with friends. As they then share your content, more people see it, and more leads might be generated. Shared media has also become important because it impacts search results. This is because Google is interested in how often content is shared, as the more people share content, the simpler it is to find.

Whatever the classification it is important that media are considered to be more than just a technological platform. Each medium generates its own individual sets of meanings and, as Gould and Gupta (2006) indicate, it is through these that consumers forge associations by interpreting and reacting to the content that the medium delivers. Chen and Haley (2014) argue and reinforce the research of Hirschman and Thompson (1997), that the relationships consumers have with the media are a fundamental element through which the perceived meaning of commercial messages is derived.

Scholars' paper 20.1
The impact of POE on brands

Lovett, M. and Staelin, R. (2016) The role of paid, earned, and owned media in building entertainment brands: reminding, informing, and enhancing enjoyment, *Marketing Science*, Jan/Feb, 35(1), 142–57.

These researchers consider the elements of POE media to determine the roles these media types play in reminding (i.e. activating memory), informing (i.e. learning their tastes for the brand), or enhancing enjoyment (e.g. gaining additional utility from socialising about the brand) with regard to branding.

Media classification – by function

Another way of classifying the media is to adopt the principles of communications theory. By incorporating the principal functionality offered by individual media, and relating this to the forms embedded within communications theory, so more meaningful classifications emerge.

The reason for looking at a different approach is to provide more helpful terminology, one that overcomes the ubiquity and senseless use of the word 'digital'. As Goodwin (2014) so aptly puts it, 'technically a TV spot is digital advertising, as is a video pre-roll, interactive bus stop poster and print ad in the Wired iPad app, but a YouTube channel, tweet, Facebook page, website, viral film or an app are all not digital advertising. Now to draw the line between these outputs is absurd'.

Early theories about communications refer to a linear, mass-media interpretation, where the primary media were essentially broadcast and print. These were used to deliver messages to audiences, and communications were considered to happen as a series of stages (source, encoding, decoding and receiver). Contemporary communications models embrace the responses, relationships and interaction that occur between a network of participants. Sundar and Bellur (2011) refer to the gratifications that users experience from media usage, one of which is interactivity.

From this, two main classifications can be identified. The first is 'linear', which reflects media that are characterised by monologic, one-way communications. The second is 'interactive', which reflects media that, to varying levels, enable response, participation and interaction, which can lead to dialogue.

Using this understanding we refer to 'interactive' media and 'linear' media to structure our exploration of this element of the mix.

Interactive media

This section defines interactive media, identifies the various forms of interactive media, and concludes with a consideration of the benefits these bring to people and organisations.

So, what are interactive media?

England and Finney (2011) refer to the various terms that were used to highlight changes in the development of digital technology. The issue associated with the term 'digital media' is that it is too general, and the term 'new' media is made redundant very quickly as innovations are announced on a regular basis. What binds certain media together is their functionality, namely their interactive capability. The term 'interactive media' highlights media that differentiate them from older style (linear) media (England and Finney, 2011). The term refers to media that provide interactive properties that are accessible across a variety of delivery channels or 'platforms'.

Interactive media are defined as:

> the integration of digital media including combinations of electronic text, graphics, moving images, and sound, into a structured digital computerised environment that allows people to interact with the data for appropriate purposes. (England and Finney, 2011)

Core technologies

There are three evolving core technologies that support interactive media. These are the Internet, databases and Big Data, and mobile.

The Internet provides a wide variety of activities, including electronic mail, global information access and retrieval systems, discussion groups, multiplayer games and file transfer facilities, all of which have not only helped to transform the way we manage marketing communications, but also impacted on business strategy, marketing channel structures, inter-organisational relationships and the configuration of the marketing communications mix.

The Internet is an important way of providing product and service information and can enable organisations to provide frequent and intensive levels of customer support. With it come doubts about its ability to deliver competitive advantage and whether it could offer suitable levels of privacy, security and measures of advertising effectiveness.

Mobile phone technologies have advanced considerably and have enjoyed huge commercial success. Wireless application protocol, or WAP, phones possess the usual email and text information services, but they also have an internet browser facility and a camera. As a result, messages can be not only location-, but also time-specific.

A marketing database is a collection of records that can be related to one another in multiple ways and from which information, usually customer-related, can be obtained in a variety of formats. This can be analysed to determine appropriate segments and target markets and used to stimulate and record individual responses to marketing communications. It, therefore, plays a role as a storage, sorting and administrative device to assist direct, personalised communications.

When customer-related transactional and response data are combined with additional information from external sources, such as a list broker, the database can become a potent source for marketing communications activities. Indeed, the increasing sophistication of information retrieval from databases and Big Data enables much more effective targeting and communications. (For more information about Big Data see Chapters 2 and 16.)

Characteristics of interactive media

Arising from these core technologies are interactive media which have some distinguishing characteristics, and which influence the way marketing communications is used by organisations and consumers. From a user perspective, these characteristics include speed, efficiency, interactivity, independence, personalisation and enhanced relationships. See Figure 20.2.

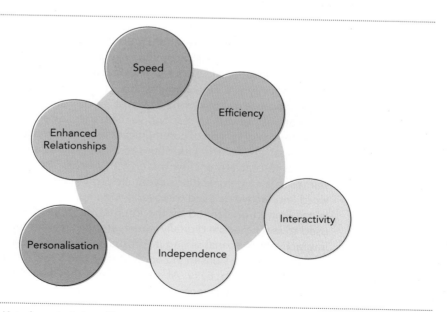

Figure 20.2 Key characteristics of interactive media

Speed

Interactive media enable marketing communications to be conducted at high speed – indeed, electronic speeds. This impact is manifest in direct communications with end-users and in the production process itself. Draft documents, film and video clips, contracts, address lists, and research and feedback reports, to name but a few, can all now be transmitted and shared electronically, saving processing time and reducing the elapsed production time necessary to create and implement marketing communications activities and events.

Efficiency

Efficiency is a broad term used to encompass a wide array of issues. New technology helps organisations to target their messages accurately to discrete groups or audiences. Indeed, one-to-one marketing is possible and, when compared with linear media and broad audiences, it is clear that interactive media offer huge opportunities for narrowcasting and reduced communications waste. Rather than shower audiences with messages that some of them do not wish to receive, direct marketing should, theoretically, enable each message to be received only by those who are favourably disposed to the communications.

This principle of narrowcasting applies equally well to communications costs. Moving away from mass media to direct marketing and one-to-one communications reduces the absolute costs associated with campaigns. The relative costs may be higher, but these richer communications facilitate interactive opportunities with a greater percentage of the target audience than previously experienced in the mass broadcast era.

A further type of efficiency can be seen in terms of the accuracy and precision of the messages that are delivered. Marketing communications delivers product information, specifications and service details, contracts, designs, drawings and development briefs when customising to meet customer needs. The use of digital technology can help organisations provide customers with precise information and reduce opportunities for information deviance.

Interactivity

Back in 1995 Deighton and Grayson speculated, correctly, about the impact of the move towards digital-based marketing communications and how electronic dialogue would make marketing communications more conversational. Well, the conversational movement is now a central marketing communications activity for many organisations. What enables these conversations is the interactive capacity within 'digital' media.

Interactivity is a key characteristic of contemporary marketing communications. It is crucial because it signifies the available functionality, the ability of all participants in a communications network to respond to messages, often in real time. It is also key because it indicates that this type of communications environment is open – that is, more democratic than linear media. The latter tend to be one-sided and driven primarily by organisations and the satisfaction of their more overt needs. The word 'interactivity' suggests that all parties to a communications event are legitimately enabled to communicate. Finally, the word 'interactive' is used to cover a wide spectrum of electronic environments, one that is not limited or defined by the Internet. For example, mobile communications can be used to reach people digitally wherever they are, and have the potential to engage them interactively. Personal selling incorporates interactive behaviours.

Two researchers based in Zagreb, Vlasic and Kesic (2007), considered the various interpretations of interactivity. At a simple level they found that it is about the interchanging roles of senders and receivers within a communications event. This view however, casts little light on the depth and significance of the topic. They cite Hoey (1998) who, among others, sees it as direct communications without time/space constraints.

Image 20.1 Look at Me–interactivity within ads

This interactive ad was used to support International Women's Day. Facial recognition technology recognized when people were paying attention to the image of a bruised woman. As more people looked at the ad, the faster her bruises and cuts healed. This synergy expressed the importance of not turning a blind eye.
Source: Rankin/WCRS.

Some authors stress the measurability element (Morowitz and Schmittlein, 1998), while others focus on the communications and information control perspective (Liu and Shrum, 2005; Lockenby, 2005) and the influence the communications bestow on parties to the communications process. Vlasic and Kesic (2007: 111) deduce that interactivity brings benefits concerning 'convenience, diversity, relationship and intellectual challenges alongside the very important aspect of control of communications and relationships'.

Considering these perspectives, it can be concluded that interactive media concern processes through which individuals and organisations attempt to engage others with messages that are delivered primarily, but not exclusively, through electronic channels, and which offer all parties an opportunity to respond. Interaction can occur through the same or a different channel from that used to convey the previous message. The purpose is to build and sustain relationships that are based on mutual satisfaction, achieved through the exchange of information, goods or services that are of value to those involved.

Perhaps the strongest characteristic of interactive media is that they enable communications to move from one-way and two-way models to one where communications flow in real time. Interactivity normally precedes the establishment of dialogue between participants in the communications process. This, in turn, enables all participants to contribute to the content that is used in the communications process. This is referred to as *user-generated content*.

An emerging interactive strategy involves 'choose-your-own-adventure story'. One of the first to experiment with this format was Netflix who, in partnership with several major entertainment brands, used a storytelling app called Episode. Clothing company Hanes ran a choose-your-own-adventure on Facebook (Tode, 2017). See Viewpoint 20.1 to see how M&M's have used this format.

Viewpoint 20.1
M&M's use interactivity to tell ghost stories

M&M's used Facebook, Instagram and Twitter to tell an interactive ghost story. Told through weekly instalments leading up to Halloween, the 'Millie & Max: A Ghost Story' unfolded over seven chapters. Each of the 30-second animated videos concluded by asking viewers to vote on one of two possible decisions the main character should make. The following week's instalment was then structured around the most popular choice.

The story was based around a 15-year-old girl called Millie who had moved to New York from the West Coast. With eerie music and spooky scenery, she encountered different scenarios in her new house. At different points, Millie had to decide which trail of M&M's to follow and which flavour to take. The first video had 2,000 views but Chapter five had over 17,000 views.

'Help us create Ch. 6!'

'Does Millie choose
A) M&M's Ghoul's Mix
B) M&M's White Candy Corn?'

Source: Tode (2017).

Insight

Storytelling is an integral part of contemporary messaging. Traditionally storytelling was used in broadcast media, primarily television. Today, storytelling is used throughout different advertising formats, even 6-second videos. In this example the format is 30 seconds but the distinguishing factor is the participation of users. Through user-generated content, stories remain fresh but they are also subject to user amplification as WoM is used to share experiences (and the brand) with friends, many on social media.

Question: To what extent is interactivity an absolute requirement in all marketing communications?

Task: Find another campaign that utilises user-generated content, and compare the way it has been used with the M&Ms campaign.

This form of interactivity symbolises a shift in the way in which marketing communications has developed. When the maintenance of 'relationships' is a central marketing activity it is possible to conclude that interactive marketing communications has an important role to play.

In addition to the Internet, technological advances have enabled a range of other interactive communications opportunities. These include television: one of the biggest factors accelerating the use of digital television is the variety of entertainment possibilities that the Internet can provide. The development of iPlayers and time-shifted recording facilities have helped shape consumer behaviour and the consumption of television programmes. This is now evolving as people are increasingly downloading or streaming their entertainment, and consuming it at times and places convenient to them. Other areas include home shopping, financial services, entertainment, education, fashion and, of course, mobile and the ability to reach individuals with personalised messages when they are in the proximity of a store, or when passing an outdoor poster site.

This technology and the contemporary communications infrastructure offer increasing numbers of people the opportunity to experience interactive marketing communications. This may impact on their expectations and bring changes to the way in which people lead their lives, including their purchase decision behaviour and their associated values and responsibilities.

Independence

Digital technologies support a range of mobile devices. These include smartphones, readers, tablets and wearables such as Panasonic's high-quality ear camera, a range of interactive clothing and the Apple Watch. The prevailing usage is built around short message services (SMSs), multimedia messaging, wireless application protocol (WAP), mobile internet and WAP push services, and full multimedia, third- and fourth-generation (3G and 4G) services for both product promotion and entertainment purposes.

Mobile marketing communications, to give it its full title, involves the delivery of direct marketing messages to mobile devices using wireless technologies, which enable people to be independent of fixed or permanent computing facilities. Independence is also enabled by people having increasing levels of control over when, where and how they are reached through marketing communications.

The delivery of personalised and pertinent information plus inducements and promotional offers in order to encourage specific purchase behaviour can have greater impact.

Apart from the sheer volume of users, there are several reasons why the use of mobile communications has grown:

- *Interactivity*: the use of SMS, for example, provides recipients with the opportunity to respond directly to incoming requests. Simple yes/no answers are quick and easy to execute while opportunities to encourage interaction with brands exist 24/7, whether that be in- or out-of-home.

- *Smartphone technologies*: developments in smartphone technologies have spurred a huge growth in usage. Among these are social media, and downloadable apps, which provide particular functionality or entertainment.

- *Personalisation*: mobile communications enable messages to be customised to the personal needs of users. This means information can be highly targeted and contain relevant information, delivered at the right time.

- *Ubiquity*: the portability of mobiles means that it is possible to reach users at virtually any location, at any time and send them location-specific information. For example, following the launch of Camelot's mobile payment facility, mobile now accounts for roughly half of all interactive National Lottery sales (Rogers, 2016).

- *Integration*: the effectiveness of mobile communications is optimised when they are used as a part of an integrated communications campaign.

- *Accountability*: the volume and nature of SMS responses can be measured, which is important from an investment perspective. In addition, it is possible to measure the contribution that different media make to drive responses. This in turn helps organisations optimise their media spend and pursue integrated communications.

- *Cultural expectations*: as the number of mobile phones in circulation reaches saturation point, and as technology develops, enabling more efficient communications, so peer-group pressure and the entertainment industry encourage use of mobile phones. For example, presenters of television and radio programmes encourage their audiences to engage with them through text and mobile facilities in response to news items, quizzes and general topics of current interest. For many these forms of communications and involvement have become a normal element of their leisure and entertainment expectations.

The key attributes of mobile communications are that they are a personal, independent channel, one that enables direct, targeted and interactive communications, which can occur at any time and any place. Social media and SMS communications have underpinned this growth and are used not just for direct response-based advertising, but also as an effective way of delivering publicity material and sales promotions, such as announcing special offers and 'text and win' events.

The potential to develop mobile communications is enormous, simply because the channel can deliver direct marketing messages related to advertising, sales promotion and public relations to individuals, regardless of location. These messages can be used to develop brand awareness, support product launches, incentivise customers through competitions and promotions, and promote trade and distributor involvement, as well as provide branded entertainment. However, as with email, it is also important to consider the potential privacy concerns of customers, especially as the receipt of unwanted messages (i.e. spam) may well increase.

QR codes demonstrate the richness of interactivity through mobile technology. By taking a picture of a QR code using a camera phone with a built-in QR code reader, consumers can access further brand-related material that is linked to the code.

An emerging technology, likely to change a raft of behaviours, is called near field communication (NFC). NFC involves a small chip that is being embedded in smartphones, and is now in most new credit cards. By presenting a phone to an advert, or signage that has an NFC symbol, information is automatically transferred to the phone. The applications are numerous, including access facilities (turnstiles at stations, offices and stadia), paying for car parking, getting information through ads (events, hotels, taxis), making credit card payments for store purchases, logging into computers and security systems, travel ticket payments, and even the exchange of business cards by touching phones.

Personalisation

Personalisation involves the delivery of tailored messages, on a one-to-one basis, through the use of data and technology in order to satisfy an individual's current or future needs. The use of personalised messages is not new and it can take many forms. These range from the incorporation of names on products, emails and correspondence, ads on social media based on profile data, the use of display advertising founded on search history and browsing behaviours, and personalised discounts informed by smartphones, beacons and geolocation (Whiteside, 2016).

Interactive media have empowered organisations to personalise content, messages and communicate with consumers on a one-to-one basis, and on a scale that is commercially viable. This has reshaped the basis on which organisations target and segment markets, stimulated interaction and dialogue, brought about a raft of new strategies and challenged the conventional approach to mass marketing and branding techniques. Netflix, Airbnb, and Uber typify this approach giving consumers what they want, when they want it, and do so by communicating at the right time with the right tone, providing a totally personalised experience (Schriber, 2017).

The huge changes in the media landscape have fuelled the amount and quality of data required for personalisation strategies. This is derived from smartphones and mobile devices, interactions within social media, and search and viewing behaviours. This data is then anlaysed through the use of data management platforms (DMPs) and delivered to individuals through programmatic technologies. (These issues are considered further in Chapters 2, 21 and 22.)

Communications enable a high degree of personalisation, and in order to personalise messages, it is necessary to understand the attitudinal and behavioural characteristics of each audience. This is because this knowledge can influence the degree of personalisation that is given to ads, email, text and welcome messages.

Many people now expect a high level of personalisation and virtual recognition, as the number of opportunities arising through 'personalisation' have grown. Personalisation is a sensitive area, often twinned with privacy and irritation issues, witnessed by the growing use of adblockers and other ad avoidance techniques.

Personalisation is an integral aspect of relationship marketing. The degree of personalisation can vary over a customer lifecycle and become more intimate as a relationship matures. This variance can be neutralised using social selling, which is starting to change the way organisations manage personal selling at scale (Schriber, 2017). (See Chapter 4 for more information about social selling.)

Scholars' paper 20.2
Strategic issues arising from intrusion

Truong, Y. and Simmons, G. (2010) Perceived intrusiveness in digital advertising: strategic marketing implications, *Journal of Strategic Marketing*, 18(3), 239–56.

Following the increasing amount of advertising on digital media, concern has started to be expressed about negative consumer perceptions concerning its intrusiveness. This may be a challenge to the claimed added value of this medium over traditional media. From this the authors explore the strategic marketing issues that have arisen and, among other things, confirm previous findings that pushed internet and mobile digital advertisements are seen as intrusive.

Enhanced relationships

Through the use of databases and interactive media, organisations seek to develop longer-term relationships with customers, with programmes and strategies that are dubiously termed 'customer loyalty schemes'. While there may be doubt about the term 'loyalty', and the effectiveness of campaigns designed to increase loyalty (Binet and Field, 2007), there can be no doubt that interactive media have helped develop new forms of sales promotion and have influenced customer relationships.

Some customer-service interface functions have been replaced with technology in the name of greater efficiency, cost savings and improved service. Financial services organisations are able to inform customers of their bank balances and transaction histories automatically, without human intervention.

The rapid development of social media, and social networks in particular, has added a new dimension to the way brands and their customers interact and the way in which brand-based relationships are fashioned. Relationships with intermediaries have also been affected by new technology. The development of e-commerce has given rise to channel strategies that either result in channel functions and hence, members being discarded, or give rise to opportunities for new functions and members. These processes, disintermediation and reintermediation respectively, are both dynamic and potentially disruptive for organisations and their partners.

Some of the more prominent interactive media are set out in Figure 20.3. The limited amount of space in this book precludes a detailed examination of each of these types of interactive media. Some are explored in Chapter 21 and a description of each can be found in the online resources that support this book.

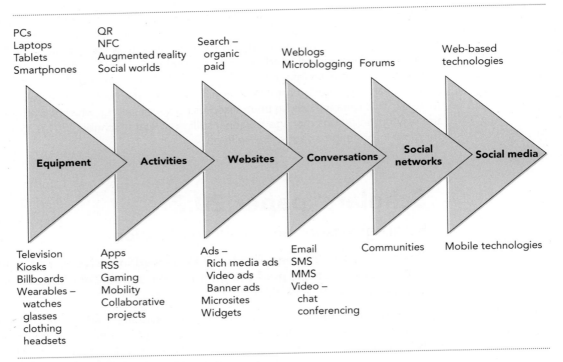

Figure 20.3 A range of interactive media

What interactive media enable users to do

Having determined what interactive media are, and considered their characteristics, we turn our attention to some of the benefits and opportunities interactive media offer and the ways in which they influence marketing communications. As noted earlier, interactive media enable users to fulfil an increasing variety of activities that encompass their work, home and leisure environments. Interactive media enable people to explore and discover new things, to play and be entertained, to share with like-minded tribes and communities, and to engage in order to do things and shape their behaviour (see Figure 20.4):

- *Discovery* – by enabling exploration people can search and find information about a wealth of subjects. Whereas linear media deliver pre-structured information in a 'tell' format, interactive media enable information mining, development and richness through interrogation (interaction) to answer specific questions on a personal basis. Search, websites and online chat facilities are at the heart of the discovery mode but email, social media, kiosks, video conferencing, augmented reality and RSS also embody this approach.

- *Play* – people use interactive media as entertainment. Interactive television and online and video gaming are obvious examples, but at a deeper level people are entertained through the interaction experienced when creating (user-generated) content, blogging, visiting online communities and forums, creating and uploading videos, streaming music and film, and engaging others through social networks. Brands attempt to communicate their messages either through or by associating themselves with these play environments, with varying levels of success and at the same time risking the trust and reputation that may have been developed.

- *Sharing* – opportunities to share ideas, thoughts, memories and knowledge have been enhanced considerably. Offline word-of-mouth communications are now complemented by online, viral communications. Organisations actively encourage people

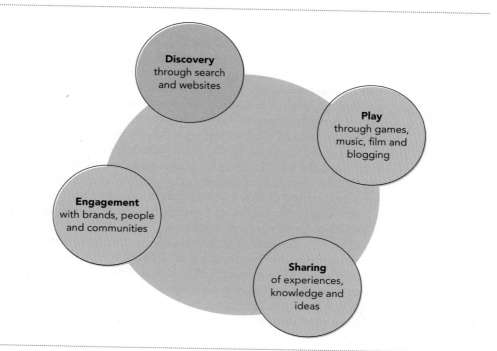

Figure 20.4 The influential scope of interactive media

to share their brand-related experiences either through social media such as networks, blogs or communities, or, alternatively, directly to them as user feedback. Marketing communications is designed to encourage people to participate and share their experiences.

• *Engagement* – interactive media have had a profound impact on the way people and organisations engage with one another. On the one hand, interactive media enable people to develop their understanding and knowledge about brands and how they work through the provision and depth of information that can be accessed. On the other, behaviour is influenced, through prompts to interrogate a website, to provide personal information, to submit and upload content and often through direct marketing and sales promotions.

Linear media

Earlier in this chapter we introduced the notion that media can be classified as either linear or interactive. We have explained the characteristics of interactive media and now we turn our attention to understanding linear media.

This part of the chapter explores the main types of linear media. These include print, broadcast, outdoor, in-store, cinema and ambient.

Print media

Newspapers and magazines are the two main types of print media. They attract advertisers for a variety of reasons, but the most important is that print media are very effective at delivering a message to a target audience.

An increasing number of people however, do not read newspapers and press advertising spend is declining as budgets are shifted to other media, most notably the Internet and mobile.

People who do use printed media tend to have consistent reading habits and buy or borrow the same media vehicles regularly. For example, most people who read tend to buy the same type of newspaper(s) each day and their regular choice of magazine reflects either their business or leisure interests, which are normally quite stable. This means that advertisers, through marketing research, are able to build a database of the main characteristics (a profile) of their readers. This in turn allows advertisers to buy space in those media vehicles that will be read by the sort of people they think will benefit from their product or service.

The printed word provides advertisers the opportunity to explain their message in a way that most other media cannot. Such explanations can be in the form of either a picture or a photograph, perhaps demonstrating how a product is to be used. Alternatively, the written word can be used to argue why a product should be used and detail the advantages and benefits that consumption will provide the user. In reality, advertisers use a combination of these two forms of communications.

Print media are most suitable for messages designed when high involvement is present in the target market. These readers not only control the pace at which they read a magazine or newspaper, but also expend effort to read advertisements because they care about particular issues. Where elaboration is high and the central processing route is preferred, messages that provide a large amount of information are best presented in the printed form.

Unlike most print media, the performance of customer magazines is improving. They differ from consumer magazines because they are sent to customers direct, often without charge, and contain highly targeted and significant branded content. These have made a big impact in recent years and, partly because of high production values, have become a significant aspect of many direct marketing activities. This medium is very popular with most of the supermarkets offering their own magazine such as *Sainsbury's Magazine, Tesco Magazine*, Asda's *Good Living* and *Waitrose Food*. The aim of the latter is to encourage customers to buy two or three items they wouldn't otherwise have bought. For example, Tilda Brown Basmati and Quinoa experienced an uplift of 189 per cent after it was featured in the magazine. Red Bull publishes *The Red Bulletin,* a magazine that gives customers another opportunity to identify themselves and bond with the brand. See Viewpoint 20.2 for another example of customer magazines.

Sales of magazines in pure hardcopy print format are falling. The magazine sector is in transition as digital formats evolve. Publishers are having to innovate and develop their titles as media brands and extend reader relationships across mobile, tablet and the Web. Customer magazines and campaigns that integrate a variety of media, perhaps with social networks, microblogging, QR codes and augmented reality, reflect some of the ways publishers are changing their approach to reaching and engaging their audiences.

Scholars' paper 20.3

Newspaper as media efficacy

Danaher, P. and Rossiter, J. (2011) Comparing perceptions of marketing communication channels, *European Journal of Marketing,* **45(1/2), 6–42.**

Danaher and Rossiter's research demonstrates that clutter in newspapers is less bothersome to newspaper readers than clutter in other media. Their research concluded that print ads in newspapers are less intrusive than other forms of media (such as the 'interruptive' quality of radio and TV) and that consumers who read newspapers feel that engagement with the traditional print medium is a good use of their time.

Broadcast media

There are two main forms of broadcast media: television and radio. Advertisers use this class of media because they can reach mass audiences with their messages at a relatively low cost per target reached.

Approximately 99 per cent of the population in the United Kingdom, and most developed economies, have access to a television and a similar number have radio. The majority of viewers use television passively, as a form of entertainment. New technological applications however, have the potential to change this, so that television could be used proactively for a range of services, such as banking and shopping. Radio demands active participation, and can reach people who are out of the home environment.

Broadcast media allow advertisers to add visual and/or audio dimensions to their messages. The opportunity to demonstrate or to show the benefits or results that a particular product can bring gives life and energy to an advertiser's message. Television uses image, audio and movement, whereas radio can only use its audio capacity to convey meaning, but it does stimulate a listener's imagination and thus can involve audiences in a message. Both media have the potential to tell stories and to appeal to people's emotions. These are dimensions that print media find difficulty in achieving effectively within the time allocations that advertisers can afford.

Advertising messages transmitted through the broadcast media use a small period of time, called 'spots', normally 60, 30, 20 or 10 seconds, that are bought from the owners of the medium. Research by Southgate (2014) helps understanding about how to utilise the length of different lengths of video/film ads. These are summarised in Table 20.3.

The cost of the different time spots varies throughout a single transmission day and with the popularity of individual programmes. The more listeners or viewers a programme attracts, the greater the price charged for a slice of time to transmit an advertising message. Costs also vary according to region, the length of the commercial, the time of day it is screened, the programming environment, the time of year, the target audience and volume of view.

The time-based costs for television can be extremely large. For example, the UK rate card cost of a nationwide 30-second spot in the middle of a popular soap is approximately £60,000, but this large, single cost needs to be put in perspective. The actual cost of reaching individual members of the target audience is quite low, simply because all the costs associated with the production of the message and the purchase of time to transmit the message can be spread across a mass of individuals.

Table 20.3 When to use different ad lengths

Length of ad	Suited for
6-second spots	These micro-videos or 'vines' are considered best for the delivery of simple, explicit and authentic messages. Good for use within social networks. The ad should involve the brand as part of the story.
15-second spots	Suitable for stretching TV budgets, for simple messages or reinforcing more complex messages from longer executions, where these are well established and the shorter ad will trigger memories of the full creative.
30-second spots	Best for more complex messages, including new product launches, a new campaign or after a brand has been out of the spotlight for a long time.
60-second spots	These should seek to tell complex brand stories which engage viewers emotionally. This requires a high degree of involvement whilst the ad generates event status.
60 seconds to 5 minutes	This type of long-form format, typically found on YouTube and other video platforms, is ideal for fans who are immersed in a brand and its entertainment. The inspirational content should be regarded as a reward for advocates and other brand-loyal customers.

Source: Based on Southgate (2014).

The costs associated with radio transmissions are relatively low when compared with television. This reflects radio's lack of prestige and the pervasiveness of television. Radio, however, is regarded as the most trusted medium for news and information, across the UK and Europe (Radiocentre, 2017), important at a time when fake news and misinformation are becoming more apparent.

People are normally unable, and usually unwilling, to become actively involved with broadcast advertising messages. They cannot control the pace at which they consume advertising messages and as time is expensive and short, so advertisers do not have the opportunity to present detailed information. The result is that this medium is most suitable for messages where there is low involvement. Where the need for elaboration is low and the peripheral processing route is preferred, messages transmitted through electronic media should seek to draw attention, create awareness and improve levels of interest.

As the television and radio industries become increasingly fragmented, reaching particular market segments has become more challenging, as the target audience is often dispersed across other media. This means that the potential effectiveness of advertising through these media decreases. These media can reach large consumer audiences, but there is often considerable wastage and inefficiency. The result is that advertisers have been shifting the balance of their advertising spend, most notably to online and mobile media. In essence the role of television is changing, especially among younger age groups. Television is perceived to be good at brand awareness and engagement, but should be complemented with other media, and in particular social media and online video, in order to drive subsequent reach, frequency and content.

The death of television as an advertising medium has been predicted frequently and erroneously, as the statistics reveal that the number of hours people watch television has remained relatively stable. Mark Ritson argues that the number of customers a brand has dwarfs those who are 'followers', especially those followers who have engaged with a brand in the last seven days. The relative impact of a brand tweet, even if amplified through retweeting has, therefore, minor economic and communicative significance compared to the power of television and radio (Joy, 2015).

Viewpoint 20.2
Traditional media still has a role

TD Ameritrade's customer magazine is *think-Money*, and is targeted at options traders, a niche market within the financial world. These people are comfortable taking risks, are clever, and prone to making investment decisions that deliberately contradict the wisdom and actions of mainstream investors. This leads to a magazine with a look, feel, and tone that appeals to this discriminating audience. Only editors and writers who are active traders are recruited by *thinkMoney*. The design of the magazine is completely original, with the magazine's covers using bold visuals, subtle humour and a side wink. The result is regarded as a beautifully executed publication.

Sofa experts DFS have always used television as their lead medium. This had helped make the brand well-known throughout the UK. To move the brand on they wanted to become well-loved. The move from well-known to well-loved had to be accomplished without dropping a single sale.

The answer was to continue using television but to use it differently. Fusing first-party data from a newly developed interactive microsite and second-party data, DFS not only improved its targeting but also increased its conversion rate. DFS also partnered ITV's Text Santa with a 'Knitted Ad Break', which featured knitted versions of DFS factory staff. The media mix included product placement in the ITV *This Morning* studio, and partnerships were arranged with Channel 5 (channel idents), Aardman (teaser ads), and Thinkbox (Boxing Day alien ad).

Image 20.2 HOG - The magazine of the Harley-Davidson Community
Source: © 2018 H-D.

Image 20.3 DFS use TV as their main media
Source: to follow.

Sources: (a) Justin Kase zninez / Alamy Stock Photo (b) Jevanto Productions/Shutterstock

Insight

Customer magazines are provided for current customers and deliver opportunities for developing and strengthening brand relationships. The critical factor is the content. It needs to be relevant and of value to the reader, otherwise the touchpoint opportunity will be missed. Using television as the lead medium can provide a strong return. This is because television is best at creating brand fame and because it can deliver high emotional messaging. Through the use of a strong creative and innovative scheduling both brands were able to cut through to their target audiences. Note how data and interactive media was used to support the campaign.

Question: Why was social media not a major element in these campaigns?

Task: Go to the www.Thinkbox.tv site and read some of the other television case studies. Make a list of the elements that appear central in the ones you choose.

Scholars' paper 20.4

Emotional television works

Heath, R. (2009) Emotional engagement: how television builds big brands at low attention, *Journal of Advertising Research*, 29(1), 62–73.

This paper is principally concerned with engagement and the way in which television can build brands through low attention. An interesting and thought-provoking article, and one which those interested in advertising and media should read.

Outdoor media

Outdoor media (also referred to as out-of-home) consist of three main formats: street furniture (such as bus shelters); billboards (consisting primarily of 96-, 48- and 6-sheet poster sites); and transit (which covers the underground/metro, lorries, buses and taxis). The range of outdoor media encompasses a large number of different formats, each characterised by two elements. First, they can be observed at locations away from home. Second, they are normally used to support messages that are transmitted through primary media: online, broadcast and print. Outdoor can therefore, be seen as secondary but important support media for a complementary and effective communications mix.

Other reasons to use outdoor advertising are that it can reinforce messages transmitted through primary media, act as a substitute medium when primary media are unavailable due to regulatory or budgetary reasons, and provide novelty and interest (electronic, inflatable and three-dimensional billboards), which can help avoid the clutter caused by the volume of advertising activity. Outdoor has now embraced digital, transforming the medium into an increasingly dynamic, adaptive, innovative and interactive medium.

According to Fitch (2007) the use of outdoor media must take into account the following variables: 'the length of the ad exposure (viewer 'dwell time' in relation to the ad), the ad's intrusiveness on the surrounding environment, and the likely mood and mindset of the consumers who will encounter the ad'. It is the interaction of these variables that shapes each individual's experience of outdoor media and hence the effectiveness of these communications.

Billboards and street furniture

These are static displays and, as with out-of-home media generally, are unable to convey a great deal of information in the short period of time available in which people can attend to the messages. However, advances in technology permit precise targeting of poster campaigns on a national, regional or individual audience basis, or by their proximity to specific outlets, such as banks, CTNs (confectioners, tobacconists and newsagents) and off-licences.

A key development in the industry concerns the increasing use of digital boards and the scope for interactivity and improved measurement. New projection technology was piloted late in 2017 by Marriott Hotels in London. The technique creates an optical illusion of images projected into the night sky. Marriott 'projected' images at London's South Bank of the Eiffel Tower and Rome's Colosseum, complementing the brand's 'Travel Brilliantly' campaign (Gwynn, 2017). See Viewpoint 20.3 for an example of billboard-based interactivity.

Transit

The names, signs and symbols that are displayed on the sides of lorries and taxis best represent transit or transport advertising. These moving posters, which travel around the country, serve to communicate names of organisations and products to all those who are in the vicinity of the vehicle. Indeed, transport advertising includes all those vehicles that are used for commercial purposes. In addition to lorries and taxis, transit media include buses, the Underground and Metro (trains, escalators and walkways), aeroplanes, blimps and balloons, ferries and trains, plus the terminals and buildings associated with the means of transport, such as airports and railway stations.

The difference between outdoor and transport media is arbitrary, although the former are media static and the latter are media mobile.

Viewpoint 20.3
Look, compassion farming

Image 20.4 Compassion in World Farming – "The World's First Really Live Feed"
Source: Ocean Outdoor UK Limited.

The mission of Compassion in World Farming is to replace the inherent cruelty associated with factory farming with free-range methods. In order to show people why free-range methods are best, help them to make people feel good about the food they eat, and to show where it comes from, high-impact interactive technology was used to show free-range farming in central London.

Shoppers at Westfield London were invited to feed free-range pigs. This was achieved by people donating through their smartphones. A link to a free-range pig farm in Buckinghamshire via an electronic billboard in central London enabled these shoppers to feed pigs live.

People could throw apples directly to the hungry pigs. This was accomplished using an accelerometer in people's phones connected via an app to a feed machine on the farm.

The campaign worked in real time and delivered a personalised brand experience that transported consumers from an urban environment directly into the countryside. There was a 37 per cent increase in traffic to this small charity's website, and over 5,000 interactions and donations over the 'live' days.

Source: Anon (2017b).

Insight

Increasingly billboards are becoming digitised, and in this case interactive. This creates opportunities to enhance customer experiences and, in this case, stand out from the clutter. In this example consumers not only experienced an interactive event but they were informed within the context of active learning.

Question: To what extent is this type of interactive billboard more effective than the conventional, static outdoor facilities?

Task: Find a similar outdoor billboard where there is interaction with the immediate environment, and not with the public.

Scholars' paper 20.5

Outdoor, out-of-home? . . . Whatever, it works

Roux, A.T. (2016) Practitioners' view of the role of OOH advertising media in IMC campaigns, *Management*, 21(2), 181–205.

There are few papers on outdoor advertising so these three are recommended not only for their content but also for their scarcity. This one considers the neglected role of OOH within IMC from a practitioners' perspective, and provides some interesting insights.

See also:

van Meurs, L.and Aristoff, M. (2009) Split-second recognition: what makes outdoor advertising work? *Journal of Advertising Research*, 49(1), 82–92.

Taylor, C.R., Franke, G.R. and Bang, H.-K. (2006) Use and effectiveness of billboards: perspectives from selective-perception theory and retail-gravity models, *Journal of Advertising*, 35(4), 21–34.

In-store media

As an increasing number of brand choice decisions are made during the shopping experience, advertisers have become aware of the need to provide suitable in-store communications. The primary objective of using in-store media is to direct the attention of shoppers and to stimulate them to make purchases. The content of messages can be easily controlled by either the retailer or the manufacturer. In addition, the timing and the exact placement of in-store messages can be equally well controlled.

As mentioned previously, both retailers and manufacturers make use of in-store media although, of the two main forms (point-of-purchase displays and packaging), retailers control the point-of-purchase displays and manufacturers the packaging. Attention is given here to point-of-purchase, while a consideration of packaging issues can be found in Chapter 18.

There are a number of POP techniques, but the most used are window displays, floor and wall racks to display merchandise, posters and information cards, plus counter and checkout displays. Overhead electronic signage, in-store videos and check-out driven coupons represent some of the more recent developments. The most obvious display a manufacturer has at the point of purchase is the packaging used to wrap and protect the product until it is ready for consumption.

Indirect messages can also play a role in in-store communications: for example, fresh bread smells can be circulated from the supermarket bakery at the furthest side of the store to the entrance area, enticing customers further into the supermarket. Some aroma systems allow for the smell to be restricted to within just 45 cm (18 inches) of the display.

End-of-row bins and cards displaying special offers are POP media that aim to stimulate impulse buying. With over 75 per cent of supermarket buying decisions made in store, a greater percentage of communications budgets will be allocated to POP items.

Increasingly stores are using branded retail apps to complement consumer use of mobiles in-store. These can be used to offer deals to customers directly in-store, generate loyalty by providing rewards and to give customers a chance to share and provide feedback about their experiences.

Cinema

The overall growth in cinema attendances in the past 10 years can be attributed to many factors, including bad summer weather and the increase in the number of multiplex cinemas (multiple screens at each site). Advertisers have consistently increased the adspend in this medium, especially as research shows that cinema audiences remember more detail than television audiences and, since they are a captive audience, there are no distractions.

Advertising messages transmitted in a cinema have all the advantages of television-based messages. Audio and visual dimensions combine to provide high impact. However, the audience is more attentive because the main film has yet to be shown and there are fewer distractions or noise in the communications system. The implication is that cinema advertising has greater power than television advertisements. This power can be used to heighten levels of attention and, as the screen images are larger than life and because they appear in a darkened room that is largely unfamiliar to the audience, the potential to communicate effectively with the target audience is strong.

Ambient media

Ambient media represent those media that fail to fit any of the established outdoor media categories. Typically, ambient media comprises:

- Standard posters, e.g. washrooms, shopping trolleys.
- Distribution, e.g. tickets, receipts, carrier bags.

- Digital, e.g. video screens, projections, LED screens.
- Sponsorships, e.g. playground furniture, golf holes, petrol pump nozzles.
- Mobile posters, e.g. cycles, barges, sandwich boards.
- Aerials, e.g. balloons, blimps, towed banners.

Of these, standard posters account for over 50 per cent of ambient activity.

Guerrilla tactics

Guerrilla media tactics are an attempt to gain short-term visibility and impact in markets where the conventional media, normally linear, are cluttered and the life of the offering is very short.

Traditionally, flyposting was the main method, practised most often by the music business. Now the term refers to a range of activities that derive their power and visibility from being outside the jurisdiction of the paid-for media. Sabotage is a stronger interpretation, as the tactics require the hijacking of conventional media events.

Multichannel campaigns

Having considered some of the characteristics associated with both interactive and linear media we now explore the strategic opportunity arising from the use of multiple media channels to reach audiences. Data-driven social media and mobile advertising, telemarketing, direct mail and email are now used in combination with television ads, field marketing, personal, retail and catalogue selling. Now organisations can determine which customers prefer which channels, and which are the most effective and profitable.

This in turn enables organisations to allocate resources far more effectively and to spread the customer base upon which profits are developed. A multichannel strategy should accommodate customers' channel preferences, their usage patterns, needs, price sensitivities, and preferred point of product and service access. So, as Stone and Shan (2002) put it, the goal is to manage each channel profitably while optimising the attributes of each channel so that they deliver value for each type of customer.

Multichannel strategies have added new marketing opportunities, and enabled audiences to access products and services in ways that best meet their own lifestyle and behavioural needs. For organisations this has reduced message wastage, used media more efficiently and, in doing so, reduced costs and improved communications effectiveness.

Research undertaken by the IPA indicates that adults consume a portfolio of media that embraces 10–15 television channels, 10–15 websites and a similar number of magazines. This does not account for a wealth of other media such as radio and cinema. In addition, people are consuming media through time and place, shifting and using their portfolio of media in an integrated format (Binet and Field, 2007).

Their analysis also found that when advertising is coupled with sponsorship or public relations the strongest measures of effectiveness, in terms of communications goals, was achieved. What is also clear is that multichannel campaigns are more effective than single-channel activity.

Of course, the possible number of channel combinations is huge and too numerous for each to be considered here. However, the use of three advertising media was considered optimal, although for large brands this might need to be increased. Integrated multimedia campaigns have been shown by the IPA to be more effective and efficient than single-channel campaigns (Binet and Field, 2007).

In 2011, the IPA's analysis of the most successful campaigns during the period 2004 to 2010 supports the findings of Binet and Field (2007) concerning the optimum number of channels. To achieve business goals (profit, market share, etc.), diminishing returns set in once the number of advertising media used reaches three. When interactive and web channels, plus direct marketing, sales promotion and public relations are included in the mix, there does not appear to be a limit, apart from budget, to achieve both business and communications effects.

Broadbent (2011) considered these outcomes and suggests two reasons to explain why campaigns using many channels are less likely to be effective. The first is that the evidence indicates that brands that under spend in a channel, relative to their market share, struggle to grow. The second concerns the extent to which multichannel campaigns have integrated content. Broadbent explains that many campaigns run with seven channels and each requires content. The way each is produced, who produces it and under what brief and guidance vary considerably and consequently it is really hard to integrate the content of a three-channel campaign, let alone seven.

Retailing in a multichannel environment

Retailers are faced with particular problems that concern the amount of property/freehold they possess and the emerging patterns of consumer online/mobile shopping behaviour.

Some believe that retailers should dispose of their fixed assets and transfer activities into e-commerce, or perhaps reconfigure their store layouts. In most cases, the solution is to develop a multichannel solution whereby a range of media and experiences is offered to consumers. Some prefer online, some the high street, some mobile, others will use television, and some prefer catalogue shopping. Most use a combination of two or more channels.

'Showrooming' concerns the use of smartphones when visiting a store to compare prices, and then leave the store empty handed to buy online. This was considered to be a major threat to high-street retailers, who responded with various tactics that included providing shoppers with their own free in-store Wi-Fi to drive them to their own websites. In addition, retailers have exploited the skills and knowledge of their sales staff, used the store for the pick-up of online orders, provided smartphone discounts to prod showroomers to buy in-store (Alder, 2014) and used networks such as Snapchat to engage consumers around the store and the brand (Emig, 2015).

Image 20.5 Showrooming has become a common aspect of consumer behaviour
Source: Stanisic Vladimi/123RF.

Retailers have also developed 'reverse showrooming', or 'webrooming'. This involves consumers researching products online, but then physically visiting a bricks-and-mortar store to complete the purchase (Alder, 2014). Although not new, this approach is now actively utilised by retailers to drive revenue.

Most consumers use a mix of these various approaches, dependent on category and need. What is good is that this approach puts customers' needs first by determining their preferred channels.

What may happen is that shopping activities become divided into categories that reflect particular channel options. Routine, unexciting purchases may be consigned to online and interactive channels, and the more explorative, stimulating and perhaps socially important purchases are prioritised for physical shopping expeditions. Many stores have recognised the need to adapt and provide more value (than a current product focus). Related benefits and enhanced services are important as they help differentiation and attract customers. For example, Chapman (2017) reports that luxury design house Kate Spade used an augmented reality campaign to publicise the launch of its Paris store. The experience included 'Joy Walks'. Using augmented reality (AR) it allowed people to see real-world Parisian locations with a Kate Spade twist, including unexpected moments such as pink flamingos frolicking in the Seine and a New York City yellow cab bustling down a Parisian street. See Viewpoint 20.4.

Viewpoint 20.4

John Lewis provide an in-store home experience

Image 20.6 The John Lewis in-store experience – "The Residence"
Source: John Lewis & Partners.

John Lewis created a series of fully furnished in-store apartments, enabling people to stay over or host a private dinner party for the 'ultimate try before you buy' experience. Called 'The Residence', people could experience John Lewis products first-hand, for example, by rearranging the location of a sofa or table in a living room.

Different stores had different layouts. So, The Cambridge and Liverpool Residences had a living and dining area, and a bedroom. The Oxford Street store also featured a fitted kitchen with matching wine cooler, a study and an indoor terrace overlooking Cavendish Square.

The Residence, which incorporated a one-hour private shopping experience, included a range of atmospheric features such as fresh coffee, its own scent, and a radio playing in the background. The cupboards and wardrobes held the latest autumn/winter fashion products. In addition to the availability of a concierge and Waitrose snacks, guests had a checklist of products they could choose to try overnight such as pillows, scent and beauty products.

In the morning, a Waitrose breakfast basket was available in addition to various newspapers.

Customers could also host brunch at the Liverpool or Cambridge locations, or even have a dinner party for up to 10 people at the Oxford Street store.

In addition to this, John Lewis hosts a range of workshops designed to help customers learn a new skill. These include how to choose the right bedding, dinner party tips, and even how to understand lighting from a mood and design perspective.

Sources: Berrington (2017); Degun (2017); www.johnlewis.com/.

Insight

It might be argued that John Lewis are just making their store assets work a little harder. At another level it could be said that The Residence project seeks to use the principles associated with relationship marketing. This indicates that brand sympathies, if not loyalties, are used to make stronger bonds through excitement, entertainment and a stimulating brand experience.

Question: If providing customer experiences is considered vital, does that make public relations an even more important part of the communications mix?

Task: Make a list of the advantages and disadvantages of staging this type of brand experience.

Scholars' paper 20.6
Multichannel communications

Godfrey, A., Seiders, K. and Voss, G.B. (2011) Enough is enough! The fine line in executing multichannel relational communications, *Journal of Marketing*, 75 (July), 94–109.

Increasingly organisations are developing their relationships with customers across a range of channels. This involves the use of personalised messages and constitutes multichannel relational communications. These authors provide some interesting insights into this strategy, and consider three key drivers of relational communications effectiveness: volume of communications, mix of communications channels, and alignment of those channels with customers' preferences. From their research they argue that reciprocity explains response to lower levels of communications, and reactance explains response to higher levels of communications.

Experience shows that high-street shopping is not about to die, but is revising its shape, form and role. Indeed, research shows the importance of having a physical presence. Hero have found that e-commerce brands, based in the US, and which received funding of over $6 million, went on to open a physical store (Chapman, 2017).

Many retailers now seek to provide customers with a memorable store experience. Some malls are increasing the number of leisure and entertainment facilities, while seeking to attract destination stores. In some stores, firms like Lego are providing a form of theatre around the brand with a view to creating a retail experience for customers.

Key differences between linear and interactive media

Having considered the characteristics of both linear and interactive media we now compare them. The contrast is interesting, as set out in Table 20.4. Space (or time) within linear media is limited and costs rise as demand for the limited space/time increases. In interactive media, especially the Internet, space is unlimited, so absolute costs remain very low and static, while relative costs plummet as more users participate. Another aspect concerns the focus of an advertising message. Traditionally, advertisers tend to emphasise the emotional rather than the information aspect, particularly within low-involvement categories. Interactive media allow focus on the provision of information, so the emotional aspect of advertising messages tends to have a lower significance. As branding is becoming a more important aspect of internet activity, so there will be a greater use of emotions, especially when the goal is to keep people at a website, rather than just driving them to it.

Apart from the obvious factor that interactive media, and the Internet in particular, provide interactive opportunities that linear media cannot provide, it is important to remember that opportunities-to-see are generally driven by customers rather than by an advertiser disrupting viewing or reading activities. People drive interactions at a speed that is convenient to them; they are not driven by others.

Management control over internet-based marketing communications is relatively high, as not only are there greater opportunities to control the position and placement of advertisements, promotions and press releases, but it is also possible to change the content of these activities much more quickly than is possible with linear media. The goals outlined above indicate the framework within which advertising needs to be managed.

As mentioned earlier, interactive media are superior at providing rational, product-based information, whereas linear media are much better at conveying emotional brand values. The former have a dominant cognition orientation and the latter an emotional one. There are other differences, but the predominant message is that these types of media are,

Table 20.4   Comparison of interactive and linear media

Interactive media	Linear media
One-to-one and many-to-many	One-to-many
Dialogic format	Monologue format
Passive provision Lifestyle compatible	Active provision Interruptive
Individualised marketing	Mass marketing
Information	Branding
Communities	Segmentation
Personal	Impersonal
Frequent	Infrequent

to a large extent, complementary, suggesting that they should be used together, not one independently of the other.

To conclude this chapter, it is worth trying to keep all of these developments in perspective. The digital technologies, applications and interactive media considered here constitute a dynamic environment. Continual change and disruption characterises the industry and helps to reshape the form and structure of digital-based marketing communications. The changes experienced so far, from 'fixed to mobile, limited media to rich media, limited interaction to real time interaction' (England and Finney, 2011), are only steps in the development of digital technology and interactive media. Linear media still fulfil important roles in many campaigns, as witnessed by the amount and proportion of budget still spent on television by clients. Linear and interactive media should be considered and used as complementary channels.

Key points

- There are three main ways of classifying the media: form, source, and function of a media vehicle.

- Media classified according to their functionality refer to media that only enable one-way communications – linear media. Media that enable two-way or interactive communications are referred to as interactive media.

- The rich array of characteristics that each type of medium possesses serve to engage audiences in different ways. These represent opportunities for organisations to make sure they use the right mix of media to deliver against different goals.

- The principal use of the media is to convey one of two types of message: one is oriented towards the development of brands and attitudes; the other is aimed at provoking a physical (and mental) response. It follows that attitude- and response-based communications require different media.

- There is a growing body of evidence that shows that the effectiveness of the media increases considerably when media are used in combination. The use of multichannel campaigns has been spurred by interactive media, and research indicates that adults consume a portfolio of media, which embraces 10–15 websites and 10–15 television channels.

- People are consuming media through time and place shifting, and using their portfolio of media in an integrated format.

- Retailers are having to adjust their mix of media in order to accommodate consumers' use of online, mobile and offline media. Many retailers now seek to provide customers with a memorable experience, through whichever channel they prefer to use.

- As a broad generalisation interactive media are superior at providing rational, product-based information, whereas linear media are much better at conveying emotional brand values. The dramatic increase in the use of video however, is enabling interactive media to deliver emotional brand messages.

- It is becoming apparent that interactive and linear media should be used together, not independently of each other.

Dumb Ways to Die

How Metro Trains Melbourne used earned media and games to improve rail safety

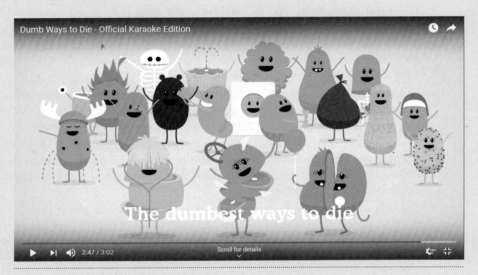

Image 20.7 Melbourne's Metro Trains ad

Cartoon characters were used to show some of the 'Dumb Ways to Die'
Source: Metro Trains Melbourne.

Engaging audiences in public safety announcements has always been one of the most challenging communications tasks. First, there is the challenge of finding a creative strategy that is not too serious, but can still deliver an important safety message. Second, there is the challenge of selecting the right media to ensure the message is delivered to an often hard-to-reach audience. These were the key tasks facing Metro Trains in 2012 when they needed a new rail safety campaign to reach the youth of Melbourne.

Metro Trains had identified 14–18-year-olds as being the age group most at risk of being involved in a serious accident or a near miss on their network. To increase awareness about rail safety among this key target group Metro Trains Melbourne launched, 'Dumb Ways to Die', a three-minute online music video with friendly cartoon characters showing some of the dumber ways that people could die. The animated film using dark humour showed characters performing dumb acts such as sticking forks in toasters and eating tubes of superglue, as well as standing too close to train platform edges and dodging the barriers at level crossings. The video was accompanied by an upbeat tune and lyrics with a catchy chorus of 'Dumb Ways to Die'.

The broad-based media mix included television, cinema, radio, internet, microsites, widgets, radio and ambient media. However, a restricted budget of AU$300,000 meant that Metro Trains had to incorporate earned and owned media if they were to achieve their target of 15 per cent awareness. To that end social media had to play a significant role.

Seeding the film on Tumblr and with the use of the Metro Trains website and YouTube, the campaign soon went viral. Facebook, Twitter, Instagram and Pinterest were also used to provide content and amplification. Reach was further extended when the song was released on iTunes and SoundCloud.

Other assets were produced to promote virality, including a karaoke version to encourage parodies and spin-offs. Posters and ambient media allowed audiences of all ages to engage with the campaign by taking shots of themselves with the characters and posting images and messages on Instagram and social media platforms.

The strategy to create an ad that audiences would find entertaining and generate earned media was a success. Within 24 hours of the campaign launch, the Dumb Ways to Die song reached the top 10 iTunes charts. Within the first month the campaign reached 46 per cent of the target audience and earned $60 million media impressions. By 2015, Dumb Ways to Die had become the third most shared ad of all time. The video has now been watched on YouTube over 162 million times and 127 million people have pledged to stay safer around trains.

The ad entered popular culture and became a global phenomenon, with a number of global parodies and tributes. Some of the most watched parodies and YouTube videos have amassed nearly 22 million views.

Following on from the success of the launch campaign and building on media insights gained from how audiences were engaging with content, particularly on mobile devices, Metro Trains sought to extend Dumb Ways to Die. Seeking to expand on the peer to peer sharing that had proved so effective in the launch campaign, in 2013 Metro Trains launched, an app, Dumb Ways to Die: The Games. Launched through YouTube and Metro Trains' own outdoor and poster sites, the app, available free on iOS, Android and Windows platforms, featured a host of new characters competing to stay alive in different sports, as well as a number of train safety messages included as mini games. Allowing players to share their scores and their deaths encouraged engagement and sharing.

Dumb Ways to Die – The Games' quickly shot to number one in the app charts in 22 countries including the US, UK, Canada and Australia, and has over 120 million downloads and three billion unique plays from all over the globe. Although the app was free to download, Metro Trains included in-app purchases to support the campaign funding. This was a unique aspect of the campaign and has allowed for future generations of the app to be developed.

In 2014, Metro Trains launched a second app, Dumb Ways to Die 2: The Games, further extending the safety message to audiences. This second app became the top app in 83 countries. With over 75 million downloads, over 1.2 billion unique plays and four billion mini-game plays in the first three

Image 20.8 DWTD used posters

Posters were used to encourage audiences to share DWTD messages on social media platforms

Source: Metro Trains Melbourne.

Image 20.9 Annoying Orange

One of the many hundreds of 'Dumb Ways to Die' parodies on YouTube

Source: Metro Trains Melbourne.

months, the app has engaged an even larger global audience. More significantly, the app has resulted in more than 80 million people pledging to keep themselves safe around trains. The third app in the series, Dumb Ways to Die 3: World Tour, which features the rebuilding and safeguarding of the town 'Dumbville' has brought the combined number of downloads for the Dumb Ways to Die apps to 200 million.

Dumb Ways to Die shows how creativity combined with careful media planning built on consumer insight can deliver effective campaign results. The primary objective was to increase public awareness of rail safety by 15 per cent. In 2017 85 per cent awareness had been achieved, and over 105 million promises had been made to keep safe around trains.

The case has highlighted not only how media planners are using existing forms of media, but how they are creating new self-funding owned-media platforms to reach audiences.

Sources: Anon (2017c); Bates et al. (2013); Brownsell (2013); Diaz (2013); Dumb Ways to Die (2018); Faull (2012); McCANN (2018).

Review questions

Dumb Ways to Die case questions

1. Use the DWTD case to explain the differences between media classes, types and vehicles.

2. How might DWTD use of the media be interpreted through the use of POEM?

3. Explain the differences between linear and interactive media, making reference to the DWTD case.

4. Which of the four activities that interactive media enable people to achieve might have enabled the DWTD campaign?

5. Discuss the ways in which interactivity is demonstrated through the DWTD campaign.

General questions

1. What are the reasons that explain the growth in mobile communications from a marketing perspective?

2. Discuss the view that outdoor media are the last true broadcast media.

3. What are the three core technologies that underpin the use of interactive media?

4. Under which circumstances should cinema be used as the primary medium?

5. What are the characteristics of a multichannel campaign and what is considered to be the optimal number of channels?

References for Chapter 20

Alder, E. (2014) Reverse showrooming: bricks-and-mortar retailers fight back, *Business Insider*, 13 July, retrieved 28 January 2015 from www.businessinsider.com/reverse-showrooming-bricks-and-mortar-retailers-fight-back-2-2014-2?IR=T

Anon (2017a) Mediacom & DFS – Grand Prix Winner, *Thinkbox TV Planning Awards 2017: Roll of Honour*, 6–7.

Anon (2017b) From the idea to the big screen: 'The World's First Really Live Feed', *Campaign*, 2 August, retrieved 6 August 2017 from www.campaignlive.co.uk/article/idea-big-screen-the-worlds-first-really-live-feed/

Anon (2017c) Metro Trains Melbourne: Dumb Ways To Die: The Games, WARC, retrieved 2 February 2018 from https://www.warc.com/content/article/cannes/metro_trains_melbourne_dumb_ways_to_die_the_games/111498

Bates, K., Mills, A. and Chan, D. (2013) Metro Trains Melbourne: Dumb Ways to Die, WARC, retrieved 2 February 2018 from https://www.warc.com/content/article/warc-prize/metro_trains_melbourne_dumb_ways_to_die/99231

Berrington, K. (2017) John Lewis offers in-store sleepovers (yes, you heard right), *Vogue*, 15 September, retrieved 23 October 2017 from http://www.vogue.co.uk/gallery/john-lewis-the-residence-sleepover-in-store

Bidlake, S. (2018) How MediaCom's TV ad innovations sold £1bn worth of DFS sofas, *Campaign*, 15 February, retrieved 12 September 2018 from https://www.campaignlive.co.uk/article/mediacoms-tv-ad-innovations-sold-1bn-worth-dfs-sofas/1457287

Binet, L. and Field, P. (2007) *Marketing in an Era of Accountability*, Henley: IPA-WARC.

Broadbent, T. (2011) Channel planning: effectiveness lies in channel integration, *Admap* (January), retrieved 17 May from www.warc.com/Content/ContentViewer.aspx?MasterContentRef=fbf731f8-4087-449f-a232-0f69f2863b17&q=direct+marketing

Brownsell, A. (2013) 'Dumb Ways to Die': the story behind a global marketing phenomenon, *Campaign*, 20 June, retrieved 1 February 2018 from www.campaignlive.co.uk/article/dumb-ways-die-story-behind-global-marketing-phenomenon/1187124?src_site=marketingmagazine

Chapman, M. (2017) How retail marketers are transforming tomorrow's shopper experience, *Campaign*, 26 October, retrieved 15 December 2017 from www.campaignlive.co.uk/article/retail-marketers-transforming-tomorrows-shopper-experience/1446949#ULRw6BQzPHiLXHO6.99

Chen, H. and Haley, E. (2014) Product placement in social games: consumer experiences in China, *Journal of Advertising*, 43(3), 286–95.

Danaher, P. and Rossiter, J. (2011) Comparing perceptions of marketing communications channels, *European Journal of Marketing*, 45(1/2), 6–42.

Degun, G. (2017) John Lewis invites customers to stay over to experience its products, *Campaignlive*, 15 September, retrieved 23 October 2017 from https://www.campaignlive.co.uk/article/john-lewis-invites-customers-stay-experience-its-products/1444678

Deighton, J. and Grayson, K. (1995) Marketing and seduction: building exchange relationships by managing social consensus, *Journal of Consumer Research*, 21(4), 660–76.

Diaz, A.-C. (2013) How 'Dumb Ways to Die' won the internet, became the no.1 campaign of the year, *Adage*, 11 November, retrieved 1 February 2018 from http://adage.com/article/special-report-the-awards-report/dumb-ways-die-dissected/245195/

Dumb Ways to Die (2018) accessed 2 February 2018 from http://www.dumbwaystodie.com/

Emig, J. (2015) How Snapchat can help retailers kill 'showrooming', *Adage*, 14 January, retrieved 28 January 2015 from http://adage.com/article/digitalnext/snapchat-retailers-kill-showrooming/296593/

England, E. and Finney, A. (2011) Interactive media – what's that? Who's involved? *ATSF White Paper – Interactive Media UK*, retrieved 27 October 2014 from www.atsf.co.uk/atsf/interactive_media.pdf

Faull, J. (2012) Dumb Ways to Die: Metro Trains Melbourne safety campaign goes viral, *The Drum*, 1 December, retrieved 1 February 2018 from http://www.thedrum.com/news/2012/12/01/dumb-ways-die-metro-trains-melbourne-safety-campaign-goes-viral

Fitch, D. (2007) Outdoor advertising, retrieved 20 January 2008 from www.millwardbrown.com/Sites/MillwardBrown/Content/News/EPerspectiveArticles.aspx?id=%2f200711010001

Godfrey, A., Seiders, K. and Voss, G.B. (2011) Enough is enough! The fine line in executing multichannel relational communications, *Journal of Marketing*, 75 (July), 94–109.

Goodwin, T. (2014) Is vagueness killing advertising? *Adweek*, 30 November, retrieved 23 January 2015 from www.adweek.com/news/advertising-branding/vagueness-killing-advertising-161638

Gould, S.J. and Gupta, P.B. (2006) Come on down: how consumers view game shows and products placed in them, *Journal of Advertising*, 35(1), 65–81.

Guest (2016) Shared media' is the future and will disrupt media buying as we know it, *Adweek*, 22 August, retrieved 30 January 2018 from http://www.adweek.com/digital/katherine-hays-vivoom-guest-post-shared-media/

Gwynn, S. (2017) Marriott to be first advertiser to use Echo outdoor ad technology, *Campaign*, 21 December, retrieved 22 December from https://www.campaignlive.co.uk/article/marriott-first-advertiser-use-echo-outdoor-ad-technology/1453299

Heath, R. (2009) Emotional engagement: how television builds big brands at low attention, *Journal of Advertising Research*, 29(1), 62–73.

Hirschman, E.C. and Thompson, C.J. (1997) Why media matter: toward a richer understanding of consumers' relationships with advertising and mass media, *Journal of Advertising*, 26(1), 43–60.

Hoey, C. (1998) Maximizing the effectiveness of web based marketing communications, *Marketing Intelligence and Planning*, 16(1), 31–7.

Joy, S. (2015) Why social media is mostly a waste of time for marketers: Mark Ritson presentation, *Marketing Week*, 14 January, retrieved 16 February 2015 from www.marketingweek.com/2015/01/14/why-social-media-is-mostly-a-waste-of-time-for-marketers-mark-ritson-presentation/

Liu, Y. and Shrum, L.J. (2005) Rethinking interactivity, in *Advertising, Promotion and New Media* (eds M.R. Stafford and R.J. Faber), New York: M.E. Sharpe, 103–24.

Lockenby, J.D. (2005) The interaction of traditional and new media, in *Advertising, Promotion and New Media* (eds M.R. Stafford and R.J. Faber), New York: M.E. Sharpe, 13.

Lovett, M. and Staelin, R. (2016) The role of paid, earned, and owned media in building entertainment brands: reminding, informing, and enhancing enjoyment, *Marketing Science*, Jan/Feb, 35(1), 142–57.

McCANN (2018) Dumb Ways to Die, retrieved 2 February 2018 from http://mccann.com.au/project/dumb-ways-to-die/

McDermott, C. (2017) Print's very much alive: magazine examples from 9 brands, *Content Marketing Institute*, 16 June, retrieved 23 October 2017 from http://contentmarketinginstitute.com/2017/06/magazine-examples-brands/

Mills, D. (2017) Customer magazines: hardy, perennial performers, *Content Marketing Association*, 4 September, retrieved 23 October 2017 from http://the-cma.com/news/customer-magazines-hardy-perennial-performers/

Morowitz, V.G. and Schmittlein, D.C. (1998) Testing new direct marketing offerings: the interplay of management judgement and statistical models, *Management Science*, 44(5), 610–28.

Radiocentre (2017) Breaking News, Radiocentre, 21 November, retrieved 22 November 2017 from https://www.radiocentre.org/policy/breaking-news/

Rogers, C. (2016) Camelot celebrates 'stellar' year as mobile helps drive record sales, *Marketing Week*, 24 May, retrieved 21 February 2018 from https://www.marketingweek.com/2016/05/24/camelot-celebrates-stellar-year-as-mobile-helps-drive-record-sales/

Roux A.T. (2016) Practitioners' view of the role of OOH advertising media in IMC campaigns, *Management*, 21(2), 181–205.

Schriber, J. (2017) How B2B sellers are offering personalization at scale, *Harvard Business Review*, 12 July, retrieved 19 July 2017 from https://hbr.org/2017/07/how-b2b-sellers-are-offering-personalization-at-scale

Southgate, D. (2014) The agony of choice, *Contagious.com*, 20 October, retrieved 2 February 2015 from www.contagious.com/blogs/news-and-views/15676936-the-agony-of-choice

Stone, M. and Shan, P. (2002) Transforming the bank branch experience for customers, *What's New in Marketing*, 10 (September), retrieved 23 August 2004 from www.wnim.com/archive/

Sundar, S.S. and Bellur, S. (2011) Concept explication in the internet age: the case of interactivity, in *Sourcebook for Political Communication Research: Methods, measures, and analytical techniques* (eds E.P. Bucy and R.L. Holbert), New York: Routledge, 485–500.

Sundar, S.S. and Limperos, A.M. (2013) Uses and grats 2.0: new gratifications for new media, *Journal of Broadcasting and Electronic Media*, 57(4), 504–52.

Taylor, C.R., Franke, G.R. and Bang, H.-K. (2006) Use and effectiveness of billboards: perspectives from selective-perception theory and retail-gravity models, *Journal of Advertising*, 35(4), 21–34.

Tode, C. (2017) Campaign trail: M&M's tells interactive ghost story; Snapchat brings dancing hot dog to life; Bud Light parodies hipsters, *Marketing DIVE*, 20 October, retrieved 20 October 2017 from http://www.marketingdive.com/news/campaign-trail-mms-tells-interactive-ghost-story-snapchat-brings-dancin/507721/

Truong, Y. and Simmons, G. (2010) Perceived intrusiveness in digital advertising: strategic marketing implications, *Journal of Strategic Marketing*, 18(3), 239–56.

van Meurs, L. and Aristoff, M. (2009) Split-second recognition: what makes outdoor advertising work? *Journal of Advertising Research*, 49(1), 82–92.

Vlasic, G. and Kesic, T. (2007) Analysis of customers' attitudes toward interactivity and relationship personalization as contemporary developments in interactive marketing communications, *Journal of Marketing Communications*, 13(2), 109–29.

Whiteside, S. (2016) Heineken embraces 'moment marketing', WARC, Warc Reports, March, retrieved 8 February 2018 from: https://www.warc.com/Content/62206ab8-c6ce-4a06-8c9e-ae9f370bb738

Digital and other interactive media

The significant changes in consumer behaviour, technology, media usage and digital formats experienced in recent years continue to have a significant impact on the way organisations use marketing communications.

Interactive media, which include search and social media, represent a democratisation of the media landscape as new forms of communications, relationships and behaviours develop.

Aims and learning objectives

The aims of this chapter are to explore ways in which interactive media are used in advertising, search marketing, social media and other types of marketing communications.

The learning objectives are to enable readers to:

1. understand how advertising can be used in interactive contexts;
2. evaluate search engine marketing and distinguish the main features of both pay-per-click and search engine optimisation, and consider the impact of voice technologies;
3. explore the characteristics and value of marketing communications through social media;
4. explain how social networks can be used in marketing communications;
5. understand and identify the characteristics associated with viral marketing, weblogs and microblogging, and online communities;
6. appraise the features of email, SMS, apps, affiliate marketing, and augmented and virtual reality within marketing communications.

Introduction

The current communications landscape is more decentralised and democratic than it has ever been. This reconfigured network has fuelled interactivity and enables consumers to connect, collaborate and create online communities (Garrett et al., 2017) with one another, and to choose what, when and how they communicate with brands.

Interactivity represents a critical shift in communications format, a move from a one-way model to one that is literally 'interactive'. We mentioned previously in Chapter 20, that interactivity normally precedes the establishment of dialogue between participants in a communications process, and this enables all participants to contribute to the content. This is referred to as *user-generated content,* as demonstrated by people uploading videos to YouTube, tweeting, texting, sharing images, and emailing comments to friends and contacts, as well as to radio and television programmes, or submitting ads to competitions, or events such as the Doritos Super Bowl competition. This represents a significant shift in the way in which marketing communications has developed.

This chapter builds on the introduction to media in Chapter 20, and considers a variety of interactive facilities and their role within marketing communications. We start with a consideration of interactive media advertising, including display (banners), behavioural targeting, video and other interactive advertising formats. This is followed by a consideration of search engine marketing and two advertising approaches – organic and sponsored links.

The third main section explores social media, and in particular social networks, viral marketing, blogging, including microblogging (Twitter), and online communities. The chapter concludes with an exploration of email, SMS, apps, affiliates, and both virtual and augmented reality.

Interactive media advertising

Interactive media advertising embraces ads that are bought and placed on websites where members of the target market are anticipated to pass. Once viewed the goal is to prompt a click-through to the advertiser's own designated site. So, in addition to the normal engagement elements, these ads serve to redirect people by interrupting or accelerating their goal-directed browsing behaviour. Ironically, this is a criticism often levelled at broadcast, and television advertising in particular.

Interactive media ads are used to achieve one of two main tasks:

1. to create brand awareness and make a favourable impression such that the reader develops a positive image of the brand;

2. to provoke behaviour, a direct response, which is used to provide readers with a call-to-action. This may be a click-through to the advertiser's destination site, a video, or a prompt to make a purchase or phone call.

The vast majority of interactive ads are direct-response, making use of the two-way capacity to provide immediate measurement of the relative success of each campaign. For many brands, offline communications are used to create brand images while interactive media ads are used to generate a call-to-action. Figure 21.1 depicts the interactive media ad formats discussed below.

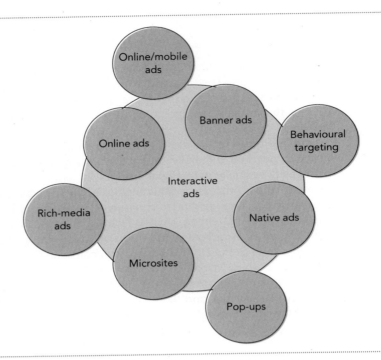

Figure 21.1 Interactive media – ad formats

The most common forms of ads are referred to as 'banner ads', but as technology and marketing knowledge have evolved, so more sophisticated versions of the banner ad have evolved. Some of these are outlined below.

Banner ads

Referred to generically as *display advertising,* banners are the dominant form of paid-for online advertising (Lobschat et al., 2017). Although effective as a standalone ad, banner ads are linked through to an advertiser's chosen destination and therefore act as a gateway to other websites. Banners are said to signpost, whereas rich media content, explored later, provides action. These allow for a greater depth of material and online interactions and transactions. Increasing numbers of these ads incorporate Flash, rich media, multipurpose units and skyscrapers (very tall banner ads) as these formats generate better recall scores than the standard banners.

Instead of transferring visitors to an orthodox website, banner ads can also be used to transfer visitors to a games or a competition site. These provide entertainment, seek to develop user involvement and can act as an incentive to return to the site at a later date. In addition, data about the user can be captured in order to refine future marketing offers. These ads can be saved for later use and are, therefore, more adaptable and convenient than interstitial ads (ones that pop-up as users move between websites) and cannot be controlled by the user. Banner ads can also be used to transfer users to an interactive microsite.

The aim of using banner ads is to attract attention and stimulate interest, but the problem is that click-through rates are very low, at around 0.05 per cent. This figure helps explain why advertisers have moved their adspend away from banners to video and other formats.

Click-through rates can be improved when online ads are integrated with a sales promotion device that is designed to reward behaviour. Special offers, competitions and other powerful calls-to-action can encourage engagement incentives, which can increase rates. Hughes (2018) suggests branding the shortened links to establish credibility, and using the link slugs (the end part of URL) to briefly and accurately describe the content optimising, as this improves transparency.

Banners have been successful for several reasons. Banners are thought to be more effective when used within a re-targeting programme, which occurs when ads are placed within the browsing patterns of target audiences who have already visited a website. Another is integration. The integration of banners into social and mobile strategies and rewarding customers through loyalty programmes when they engage with these richer ads, has given banners a renewed role to play. A third reason concerns 'contextual advertising' and the placing of these ads. Rather than place banners on various sites that the target audiences are known or thought to frequent, it was found to be more effective to place them on sites that are relevant to the product/service offering. Saenger et al. (2017) have shown that web-based contextual advertising can increase brand recognition, and foster positive attitudes towards the ad and attributes of the advertised brand.

Research has shown that banners can be used to increase offline sales for organisations whose primary commercial activities are offline (Lobschat et al., 2017).

Online behavioural advertising

Online behavioural advertising, sometimes referred to as behavioural targeting, involves the use of information about an individual's web-browsing behaviour in order to display ads that are considered personally relevant and of particular interest to the user. To implement this, Boerman et al. (2017: 364) refer to the capture of 'web browsing data, search histories, media consumption data (e.g., videos watched), app use data, purchases, click-through responses to ads, and communication content, such as what people write in e-mails (e.g., via gmail) or post on social networking sites'.

Trying to determine the optimum context for presenting online behavioural ads is less of an issue than with display advertising. For example, travel brands might previously have targeted ads specifically to travel sites, but with behavioural targeting ads can be presented on various websites that are specific to a user's online browsing interests. However, ensuring that ads appear only on sites that match both campaign and brand goals is an issue that threatens *brand reputation*. This highlights an important issue. Display ads incur waste as a percentage of the ads are seen by people who are not part of the target audience. Behavioural targeting only delivers messages to people who have expressed recent interest in the category or the brand. As a result, behavioural targeting carries a pricing premium as there is little wastage.

Many brands use behavioural advertising for direct-response-based campaigns, mainly because of the superior click-through rates that behavioural targeting triggers (Summers et al., 2016). However, it is beginning to be extended to branding campaigns. Regardless of purpose, a growing concern is the intrusion and abuse of an individual's privacy that behavioural targeting represents. With so much data being collected, often without consumer consent or knowledge, this approach to advertising has caused substantial unrest and the introduction of regulations designed to empower users. This is often shaped in the form of an opt-in notice regarding the use of cookies.

Scholars' paper 21.1
Is social media a friend of online shopping?

Zhang, Y., Trusov, M., Stephen, A.T. and Jamal, Z. (2017) Online shopping and social media: friends or foes? *Journal of Marketing*, 81 (November), 24–41.

Social network usage has increased considerably and this paper explores the relationship with online shopping. The authors find a positive relationship between greater cumulative usage of social networking sites and online shopping activity. However, they also find a short-term negative relationship, such that immediately after a period of increased usage of social networking sites, online shopping activity appears to be lower.

See also:

Summers, C.A., Smith, R.W. and Reczek, R.W. (2016) An audience of one: behaviorally targeted ads as implied social labels, *Journal of Consumer Research*, 43(1), June, 156–78.

Chen, J. and Stallaert, J. (2014) An economic analysis of online advertising using behavioral targeting, *MIS Quarterly*, 38(2), 429–49.

Native advertising

Native advertising is considered to be 'paid advertising where the ad matches the form, feel and function of the content of the media on which it appears' (Vinderslev, 2018). Advertorials in newspapers and magazines, advertiser-funded TV programming, sponsored or promoted posts on social media such as Facebook, Twitter and LinkedIn, plus other 'in-stream' ads, are all examples of what constitutes 'native advertising'. In the same way, ads from golf equipment manufacturers within golf magazines, fashion and beauty ads in *Cosmopolitan* or *Vogue,* and car ads in automotive magazines all represent native advertising.

The native advertising format has grown significantly, partly because, like behavioural ads, native ads can be bought through programmatic processes (as explained in Chapter 22), and partly because of the surge in mobile usage. They are often, but erroneously, compared with content marketing (as explored in Chapter 6). The Mobile Marketing Association (MMA) identifies that there are various types of native advertising, ranging from search advertising, the earliest form of native, and in-stream advertising, to in-game native formats and others. There are several native ad formats specific to the mobile channel. These are in-feed social, in-feed content, in-map, in-game, paid search, recommendation widgets and custom (MMA, 2015).

Pop-ups

Also known as *transitional online ads,* pop-ups appear in separate browser windows, when web pages are being loaded or closed. Originally they were intended to appear as a relief to the boredom that can set in when downloading files took a long time. As broadband speeds and computer technology have accelerated, and 'waiting' times minimised, pop-ups are now generally regarded as an irritation.

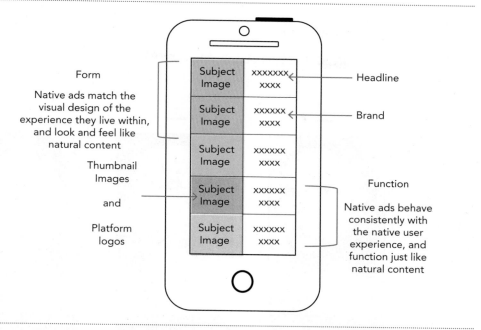

Figure 21.2 The form and nature of native advertising
Source: Based on images developed by the MMA.

Video

The use of video advertising has grown enormously, partly because it can be used in a number of different ways apart from simply showing ads at the beginning or end of programmes. Online video was reported to be a key channel for creative effectiveness, following research of the 122 campaigns entered for the Creative Effectiveness Lions in 2017 (Anon, 2017a). Video in all formats was integral to effective campaigns, reflecting moves towards a visual vocabulary (see Chapter 5). The Christmas ads by UK retailer John Lewis (*Moz, Buster, Monty*) and the Spanish lottery ticket brand Loterias Y Apuestas del Estado (*Justino*) are considered to be excellent examples of optimising video usage across screens and platforms, both online and offline.

At the outset, online video content played in an unstoppable loop, so the ads were unavoidable, and extremely annoying for users. In addition, advertisers placed ads within video streams, which also prevented users from avoiding them. Video ads can also be embedded within web pages and online articles, relating closely to the site content. In the early days many online ads were derived directly from television ads, but the 30-second format is not appropriate for the online environment, so now specific content for online ads has been developed.

Recognising the importance of generating great (better) user experiences brands now use platform- and content-specific advertising, having seen the value of Snapchat-specific vertical ads. Wohlwend (2017) observes that brands now tailor their ads to accommodate the behaviours of social media users, and platform characteristics, and this means ads are delivered in auto-play, with the sound off and in-feed.

Other changes designed to improve user experiences include Trueview messaging, a format that allows viewers to skip an ad after five seconds. If the ad is served contextually, however, it is more likely to be relevant, less disruptive, and increases the probability that the ad will not be skipped (Wohlwend, 2017).

Viewpoint 21.1

L'Oréal move into interactive media

Image 21.1 L'Oréal's Makeup Genius
Source: L'Oréal.

L'Oréal's digital transformation was initiated by the recognition that digital, and mobile in particular, was changing buyer behaviour. The way people use media, develop brand preferences and choose products was changing rapidly. This required a digital transformation to reinvent the way they met their consumers' needs at the point it was required.

The transformation at L'Oréal considered three core elements: personal, data, and storytelling.

Make it personal

Mobile gives consumers a personal stylist, a hair-dresser and a makeup artist at their fingertips, 24/7. This requires not just customised products, but a personalised digital experience. To meet this goal L'Oréal launched *Makeup Genius*, a mobile app that allows consumers to try on makeup, virtually.

The app scans a customer's face, analyses over 60 characteristics, and then virtually displays how various products can be used to achieve different looks, all in real time. Consumers can select a look they like, and directly order the right products with a simple click. The app then tracks how a customer uses it, what they buy, learns their preferences, makes inferences based on similar customers' choices, and tailors its responses.

This app is a branded channel for engaging over 20 million customers. It allows L'Oréal to understand the needs of loyal users and tailor meaningful experiences for them.

Harness the power of data

The launch of the Maybelline Master Contour makeup line was partnered with Google in order to learn about the concerns consumers had and, specifically, their contouring questions. This helped L'Oréal to identify, predict and meet their needs.

Of the three audience segments identified it was decided to focus on the 'contour-me-quick' con-sumers. These are women who desire contouring skills, but think it's too hard or time-consuming for them to learn. A series of quick how-to YouTube videos about the art of contouring, in three simple steps, were posted. The videos were personalised by intent and demographics, to ensure a shopper's primary question was addressed, and gave them the best advice for their skin colour and type.

This data-driven approach helped reach more than nine million people across this key customer segment.

Reimagine storytelling

For consumers to engage with a story, its relevance must be established within seconds. L'Oréal

Sources: Gulin-Merle (2017); Petrova (2017).

not only had to align their message, creative and media in a compelling way, but they also had to speed up their storytelling.

When they launched their Root Cover Up spray, they created a bumper ad on YouTube that demonstrated the core value and product usefulness within the first six seconds. Consumers were then able to watch the full video if they wished.

Insight

L'Oréal demonstrate that the use of a variety of interactive media, and an understanding of the objectives and context, is important when deciding which route to follow. Here we can see the use of apps, mobile, bumpers and data-driven strategies, all of which have been used to achieve different goals, in different contexts.

Question: Does this use of interactive media provide L'Oréal with a competitive advantage or just enable them to stay competitive?

Task: Find another independent fashion or beauty retailer and list the media they use to reach their customers.

Bumpers

In 2016 Google introduced a brand-new ad format on YouTube called bumper ads. These run for six seconds, cannot be skipped, and are intended to attract the attention of impatient mobile users. Rather than try to cram a large message into six seconds, successful bumpers are rooted in the creation of three distinct ads, with each focusing on a single element, and then linking them together.

Bumpers are used primarily to aid ad recall and awareness among users embarking on purchase journeys. They amplify existing messages, and are used to tease an upcoming campaign or launch, running a few weeks before the official release. See Viewpoint 21.1 where L'Oréal have used bumpers successfully.

Online gaming

The development of game technology has prompted enormous growth in the numbers of consumers who play online games. This in turn has attracted advertisers. It should be noted that there are two forms of game-based advertising.

In-game advertising (IGA)

Yang et al. (2006: 63) refer to in-game advertising (IGA) as 'the placement of brands in games (usually in the form of billboards, posters, or sponsor signage in sports and racing games)'.

In many ways this resembles the model through which brand placement is considered to work. However, as Cauberghe and De Pelsmacker (2010) point out, the interactive context of in-game brand placements can evoke cognitively involving experiences for players. This is something which the static nature of traditional product placements in television programmes and films cannot achieve.

Hwang et al. (2017) note that the degree of game difficulty is an important factor when considering brand placement in sports video games. The logic is that the higher the level of game difficulty, the greater the number of cognitive resources that need to be deployed and in doing so narrow the field of attention. Their research found that game difficulty influenced recognition but not recall.

In addition to game difficulty the effectiveness of IGA can be improved when two main elements are attended to. First, the advertising needs to be integrated into the game. They found that the sense of realism felt by players is not disturbed or can even be improved when the advertising is an integral part the game. Hwang et al. (2017) suggest that advertisers should find ways in which the advertised brand becomes part of a primary task in any gaming experience, such as a branded car in a racing game.

The second element concerns the selection of an appropriate game in which the advertising is to be placed. By selecting a game with attributes that are similar to those of the advertised brand, such as sports brands with sports-based games, the media vehicle, the game, can enhance advertising effects. Interestingly, Hwang and his colleagues suggest that novelty and 'incongruency relative to brand placement may be an effective means to achieving desired advertising results' (2017: 492).

Advergaming

Companies use promotional games to influence customer behaviour, build brand awareness, and in time, increase market share as a result of a participant's positive experiences (Renard and Darpy, 2017). Advergaming can be distinguished on the basis that 'the game is specially made to promote the brand' (Cauberghe and De Pelsmacker (2010: 5). These games tend to be relatively simple in design, with few rules and are easy to play. This is mainly because advergames are distributed across different platforms, such as websites, viral marketing, mobiles, and commercials on interactive digital television.

Mainstream advertising works partly on the principle of association, and IGA works on there being a positive association between an advertiser and the game. Chang et al. (2010) conclude that to be successful it is important to integrate the advertising closely into a game. This means embedding it as an integral part of the activity, not at the periphery or as an add-on. This helps to enhance the sense of realism for players.

Image 21.2 Advergaming works by association
Source: ADVERGAMING.

They also recommend that it is important to select an appropriate game as the advertising vehicle. Player annoyance can be reduced if there is a close alignment between the game's attributes and those of the brand being advertised. In much the same way, each player has a psychological profile. So those playing sports games are more predisposed to sports brands being integrated into the game.

Cauberghe and De Pelsmacker's (2010) research results are interesting because they find that brand prominence affects recall. Prominence in an advergame refers to the extent to which a brand is an integral and dynamic part of the game. Brands that are placed prominently in a game are likely to benefit from a player's focus on the interactive content and consequent intensive processing of ads. The result is higher brand recall (Schneider and Cornwell, 2005). This works for products that evoke both high and low involvement.

Search engine marketing

Websites need visitors and the higher the number of visitors, the more effective the website is likely to be. Many people know of a particular site and simply type in the address or use a bookmark to access it. The majority of people however, arrive at sites following a search using particular keywords and phrases to locate products, services, news, entertainment and the information they need. We do this through search engines, and the results of each search are displayed in rank order. It is understandable, therefore, that those ranked highest in the results lists are visited more often than those in lower positions.

Consequently, from a marketing perspective it is important to undertake marketing activities to attain the highest possible ranking position, and this is referred to as search engine marketing (SEM). There are two main search engine marketing techniques: search engine optimisation (SEO) and pay-per-click (PPC), and ideally both should be used together.

Search engine optimisation

Search engine optimisation (SEO), or *organic search*, is a process used to win a high-ranking page position on major search engines and directories. To achieve top-ranking positions, or least a first-page listing, it is necessary to design web pages using appropriate high-quality content, links with other quality websites, and inputs from social media to enhance the user experience. This enables search engines to match closely a searcher's request with the content of registered web pages.

Search engines use robotic electronic spiders to crawl around registered sites and from this to compile an index of the content they find, placed there by the designer of each website. When a search is activated, it is the database housing the content that is searched, not the millions of World Wide Web pages.

Each search engine, such as Google and Bing in the West, Yandex in Russia, Daum and Naver in Korea, and Baidu in China, all use algorithms to compare the content of relevant site pages with the keywords/phrases used to initiate a search (Jerath et al., 2014). For some time designers believed that 'keyword density' was important. This refers to the number of times a keyword is repeated in the text of a web page. Another key factor was thought to be the number of inbound links. The greater the number of links, the higher the ranking was likely to be. These approaches are now regarded as ineffective with the emphasis now placed on key phrases, overall quality of content, social media interaction and user experience.

In 2013, and in the name of user security, Google started to encrypt all of its searches. While the use of keyword-rich content that matches what users are searching for is an important website design factor, now the process works by looking at longer words, phrases or questions, not just keywords. This means that it is fresh, high-quality relevant content that counts.

In addition to this the Google algorithm has multiple named parts that influence search rankings. Google 'Panda' considers the quality of content, 'Penguin' is specific to the quality of links, and Google 'Hummingbird' handles conversational search queries (Slegg, 2016).

Image 21.3 Google Hummingbird

Google made a radical change to their search algorithm in 2013 and named it Hummingbird to reflect Google's search as 'precise and fast'.
Source: Google LLC.

According to Knauff (2017) a registered site will attain a high ranking by performing on three main criteria: technical SEO, link building, and content:

1. Technical SEO has evolved from simple algorithms based around keyword density, to one that reflects the quality of a user's experience. These include mobile responsiveness, page speed and site dwell time.

2. Link building is now concerned with high-quality content that adds value for users. This means links to legitimate editorial content that reflect strong relationships, where interaction and dialogue is frequent, and which meet Google's webmaster guidelines.

3. Content that engages users is a prerequisite for good search results. If the content is old, irrelevant or simply a reiteration of particular phrases then it will not be of value to users.

It is not surprising that an airline such as easyJet, which sells more than 98 per cent of its seats via the www.easyjet.com website, uses search engine optimisation to drive traffic to its websites across Europe. It is vital that 'easyJet' appears when the search phrases associated with the discount airlines business are used, and content is revised on a daily basis.

Pay-per-click searches

Pay-per-click (PPC) is similar to display advertising found in offline print formats. Ads are displayed when particular search terms are entered into a search engine. These ads appear on the right-hand side of the results page and are often referred to as sponsored links. Unlike offline display ads, however, where a fee is payable in order for the ad to be printed, here a fee is only payable once the display ad is clicked, and the searcher is taken through to the company's web page.

It is important for organisations to maintain high visibility, especially in competitive markets, and they cannot rely on their search engine optimisation skills alone. PPC is a paid search list and, once again, position in the listings (on the right-hand side of the page) is important. The position in the list is determined mainly through a bidding process. Each organisation bids an amount it is willing to pay for each searcher's click, against a particular keyword or phrase. Unsurprisingly, the higher the bid, the higher the position where a search result appears on a page. To place these bids, brokers (or PPC ad networks) are used. Their role is to determine what a competitive cost per click should be for their client. They achieve this through market research to determine probable conversion rates, and from this deduce what the purchase and lifetime value of customers are likely to be. Consideration needs to be given to the quality of the landing page to which searchers are taken (not the home page), and whether the call-to-action is sufficiently strong.

Voice

Voice technologies are becoming embedded within our lives as they help people search, shop, and interact with other companies (Tan, 2017). There are interesting ramifications for brands, in particular categories, as they might not have to invest in packaging and design, but instead have to address issues concerning their identity and the way they are perceived within the new voice context. For example, Google's 'Assistant', Amazon's 'Alexa', and Apple's 'Siri' are voice-powered devices bounded by gender, accent, age, tone and personality. For example, these issues are faced by brands who develop a 'Skill' on Alexa. Vodafone launched a voice-activated 'Skill' that enables customers to check their data balances. Domino's developed a voice ordering service on the same platform (Tan, 2017). These early movers seek to learn from their innovations before refining their voice services.

Image 21.4 Amazon's Alexa

Not everyone is convinced that voice-activated fridges are the future.
Source: David Becker / Stringer/Getty Images North America/Getty Images.

More critically, brands are threatened by automated purchase decisions. So, when consumers request margarine, not a specific brand such as Flora or Bertolli, the technology will make a product decision, perhaps based on price, convenience or other factors. One issue that arises is that brands will have to improve brand name identification, or what is requested of the device. A second issue is the implication that tech companies will own the customer relationship, not the retailer, as they will decide which brand, and from whom it will be purchased (Ritson, 2017).

A related technology, Amazon 'Polly', is a cloud service that converts text into lifelike speech audio. Apart from chatbots, applications for mobile include games, newsreaders, e-learning platforms, applications for visually impaired people, and the rapidly growing segment of Internet of Things, all of which encompass brand messaging opportunities.

Voice technologies have the potential to reduce search time drastically, undertake purchases, and even change the balance of brand relationships. More interestingly they have the potential to remove the need for apps and multiple searches (see Viewpoint 21.2).

The user voice experience can be evaluated in terms of their behaviour in the event of a failed search. As Davies (2017) observes, did the user return to make another query, ask for the next result, or modify their initial query? Other indicators include whether a user returned to traditional search, or if the user's voice was relaxed or agitated, or whether it changed *during* a search.

Viewpoint 21.2

Voice changes search . . . in a big way

Searcher: OK Google. Let's shop for some shoes.

Google Home: Would you like to shop for men's or women's shoes?

Searcher: Men's.

Google Home: Where would you like to see them?

Searcher: Cast them to my TV.

Google Home: Men's shoes displaying on your TV.

Searcher: OK Google. Just show me the black ones.

Google Home: Filter applied to just display black men's shoes. Is there a type of shoe you are looking for?

Searcher: Dress shoes for a wedding.

Google Home: Filter applied to just display men's black dress shoes. Would you like me to add the date of the wedding to your calendar?

Searcher: Yes. It's May 20th.

Google Home: Wedding on May 20th added to calendar.

Searcher: I like the black pair on the top right. Where is it available cheapest?

Google Home: That pair is offered from 13 retailers and is cheapest at Steve Madden. They have free shipping on that order.

Searcher: OK Google. Order that shoe in a size 11 to my house.

Google Home: Order confirmed.

Source: Davies (2017).

Insight

This vision of future voice-based interactions with devices not only shows that the number of results will be limited, perhaps to just one in some circumstances, but that preference will be given to those paying the highest price for that space, rather than fitting the consumer's inner needs.

This also suggests that there will be no need for multiple searches and will bring to an end the need for a first page ranking.

> Question: To what extent do you believe that voice is disrupting search behaviour?
>
> Task: Make a list of the implications voice-based searches could have for both consumers and brands.

Search, as it is currently understood, is in transition. It is evolving for many reasons, but of them all, voice technologies are a very significant factor when matched with artificial intelligence (AI). Voice search will provide faster and more accurate results, based mainly on a combination of user experience and Big Data.

Social media

Social media embrace a range of applications, all of which incorporate a form of word-of-mouth communications. Kietzmann et al. (2011: 1) state that 'Social media employ mobile and web-based technologies to create highly interactive platforms via which individuals and communities share, co-create, discuss, and modify user-generated content'.

The role of opinion formers is much diminished within an interactive media context, especially with digital natives, and the predominant 18–25-year-old user group. For them expert opinion, as represented by opinion formers, is rejected in favour of peer-group and user recommendations (opinion leaders).

The terms 'social media' and 'social networks' have become increasingly prevalent. Although similar, they do not mean the same, yet are often used interchangeably, and mistakenly. Kaplan and Haenlein (2010: 61) define social media as 'a group of Internet based applications that build on the ideological and technological foundations of Web 2.0 and that allow the creation and exchange of user generated content'. In order to understand the range of social media, they develop a classification scheme. To do this, they identify two key elements of social media: first, social presence/media richness and, second, social processes in the form of self-presentation/self-disclosure.

In other words, *social media* refer to a broad range of web-based applications, and social networking sites are just one of the many applications that are available. Others include weblogs, content communities (e.g. YouTube), collaborative projects (e.g. Wikipedia), virtual game worlds (e.g. Call of Duty) and virtual social worlds (e.g. Second Life).

The role and presence that an organisation seeks to adopt in social media is critical. Kietzmann et al. (2011: 242) refer to a 'rich and diverse ecology of social media sites, which vary in terms of their scope and functionality'. This diversity has posed problems for organisations as they attempt to adapt and implement digital strategies, in an environment where their level of control and influence is much reduced. Kietzmann et al. (2011) developed a framework consisting of seven building blocks. These refer to identity, conversations, sharing, presence, relationships, reputation and groups. These blocks are constructs designed to enable insight into the different levels of social media functionality, which in turn, they argue, can help organisations develop more effective configurations and use of social media. See Table 21.1.

Having identified the building blocks, Kietzmann et al. (2011) recommend that organisations develop strategies to monitor, understand and respond to different social media activities. They suggest a framework, called the '4Cs':

1. *Cognise.*

    Each organisation should try to recognise and understand its social media landscape.

Table 21.1 The building blocks of social media

Building blocks	Explanation
Identity	The extent to which users reveal their identities in a social media setting. This can include disclosing information such as name, age, gender, profession, location, and also information that portrays users in certain ways.
Conversations	The enormous number and diversity of social media conversations leads to format and protocol implications for firms that seek to host or track these conversations. Differences in the frequency and content of a conversation can have major implications for how firms monitor and make sense of the 'conversation velocity' – that is, the rate and direction of change in a conversation.
Sharing	Social media users exchange, distribute and receive content. Firms wishing to engage with social media need to evaluate what objects of sociality their users have in common as, without these objects, a sharing network will be primarily about connections between people but without anything connecting them together.
Presence	The extent to which users can know if other users are accessible. It includes knowing where others are, in the virtual world and/or in the real world, and whether they are available. If users prefer to engage in real time, the social media platform should offer a presence or status line indicator, along with a suitable mechanism through which these users can contact each other and interact.
Relationships	This is about the associations users have that lead them to converse, share objects of sociality, meet up, or simply just list each other as a friend or fan. The way users are connected can determine the characteristics of information exchange. Some relationships are fairly formal, regulated and structured (LinkedIn), while others can be informal, unregulated and without structure (Skype).
Reputation	The extent to which users are able to identify the status of others, and themselves, in a social media context. Reputation can be a matter of trust, but this can be based on the number of endorsements from others (LinkedIn), content voting (YouTube) or aggregators (Twitter).
Groups	Users can form communities and sub-communities and so the more 'social' a network becomes, the larger the potential groups (of friends, followers and contacts) become. Organisations should be prepared to help users manage their groups.

Source: Based on Kietzmann et al. (2011).

2. *Congruity.*

   Each organisation should develop strategies that match the different social media functionalities and their goals.

3. *Curate.*

   Each organisation should develop a policy about who should listen to conversations on a social media platform and when.

4. *Chase.*

   Each organisation should undertake environmental scanning to understand the speed of conversations and the information flows that could affect the organisation and the market.

Viewpoint 21.3

B2B use social media as well . . . Powwownow!

Powwownow believes work time can be spent more productively by using technology. Through the use of conference calling, employees are better able to work in a more agile, flexible way. Unfortunately conference calling isn't a riveting subject, so in order to get businesses talking about telecommunications on social media, Powwownow needed to become part of the conversation. To avoid being perceived as serious, and boring, this had to be accomplished

Image 21.5 Powwownow's #Flexie competition

This encouraged people on Twitter and Instagram to take a flexible working selfie.
Source: PowWowNow.

with a light-hearted, tongue-in-cheek tone of voice.

The business goal was to double the growth rate of 20 per cent. For social media, the communications challenge was to increase engagement (click-throughs, reach and website traffic) by 40 per cent. This was achieved through a series of campaigns targeted at UK-based employees who were interested in productivity and more contemporary ways of working.

Using its core social media mix of Twitter, LinkedIn, Facebook and Instagram, Powwownow launched a series of campaigns throughout the year.

'Here's to flexible working' highlighted how traditional nine-to-five office-based hours are outdated and flexible working (combined with technology) enables smarter working. The #FlexibleWorkWin campaign encouraged people to share what flexible working meant for them. Among the ideas shared included a quick gym session instead of their morning commute to work, or being able to take their kids to school.

This sharing of ideas not only encouraged other employees to share their benefits of flexible working, but also helped to amplify Powwownow's advertising campaign.

The 'Smarter working initiative' encouraged businesses to let their staff work flexibly on the first day of the school summer holidays. The #Flexie competition encouraged people on Twitter and Instagram to take a flexible working selfie. This content served to further promote the initiative.

The #WorkWish campaign encouraged individuals at Christmas to make a work-based wish list. Employees who divulged their work wish did not expect Powwownow to actually surprise them at their workplace with their #WorkWish.

With a budget of just £15,000, engagement rose by 2,083 per cent, reach grew by 162 per cent, click-throughs increased by 248 per cent, followers increased by 154 per cent, and traffic to the website via social increased by 350 per cent. There was substantial media coverage of the different initiatives, and the brand won many awards.

Sources: Anon (2016); Anon (2017b); www.powwownow.co.uk

Insight

There are several points about this campaign. Each of the social media initiatives served to involve people and encouraged participants to become engaged with the campaign. This amplification feature is a core characteristic of successful social media activities.

The campaign shows that a small budget can achieve remarkable results. For just £15,000 the 40 per cent target on all the KPIs were exceeded. This initiative demonstrates the relational value of social media through the merit in creating genuinely interesting, fun and engaging campaigns that got the brand into conversations on social media. It lays a strong base on which to build corporate identity. In turn this can develop and strengthen corporate reputation.

Unlike many organisations, Powwownow had a defined goal and developed a social media strategy, around which campaigns were designed and launched.

Question: If Powwownow can develop this level of social media activity, what prevents other B2B firms following a similar strategy?

Task: Apply Kietzmann et al.'s (2011) 4Cs framework to the Powwownow case. How good is the fit?

Figure 21.3 shows the main elements of social media that are explored in the following section.

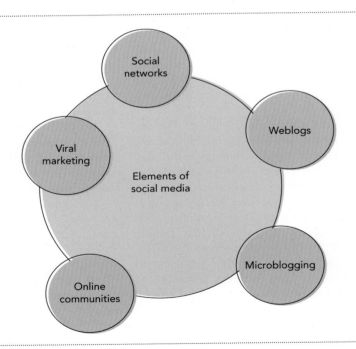

Figure 21.3 The main elements of social media

Scholars' paper 21.2
How can social media be more effective?

Hodis, M.A. Sriramachandramurthy, R. and Sashittal, H.C. (2015)
**Interact with me on my terms: a four segment Facebook engagement
framework for marketers**, *Journal of Marketing Management*, 31(11–
12), 1255–84.

In the light of the chatter about social media and Facebook in particular, this paper
provides a view of the key segments of Facebook users. These are used to build
a marketing strategy framework designed to assist marketers better target their
Facebook consumers and implement more effective Facebook campaigns.

See also:

Kaplan, A.M. and Haelein, M. (2010) Users of the world unite! The challenges and
opportunities of social media, *Business Horizons*, 53(1), 59–68.

Fournier, S. and Avery, J. (2011) The uninvited brand, *Business Horizons*, 54(3),
193–207.

Colliander, J. and Dahlén, M. (2011) Following the fashionable friend: the power of
social media, *Journal of Advertising Research*, 51(1), 313–20.

Social networks

The growing popularity of social networks around the world is reflected in the range of
activities that can be undertaken through the web-based services. Primarily these allow
users to undertake a range of electronic-based activities. At a general level they enable
people to engage in social interaction (e.g. Facebook), exchange small amounts of content very quickly (e.g. Twitter and WhatsApp), develop careers (e.g. LinkedIn), and be
entertained through the sharing of user-generated videos (e.g. YouTube) and photos (e.g.
Instagram) (Keskin et al., 2017).

Social networks are communities of people using the Internet to share lifestyle and
experiences. The critical aspect of social networks is that most of the content is user-generated and this means users own, control and develop content according to their needs,
not those of a third party.

Social networks enable people to share experiences. Typical sites include Google+,
LinkedIn, Qzone, Sina Weibo, YouTube, Tumblr and, of course, Facebook, which has been
the largest Western network in recent years with 2 billion active users in 2017. These sites
provide individuals with an opportunity to reach their friends, generate new ones, and
share experiences, information and insights, electronically.

Social networks enable organisations to assess the health of their brand. Most importantly brands can use these networks to listen to and observe the comments, feelings and
behaviour expressed by a range of people about a brand. In addition they can be used to
measure campaign effectiveness.

Despite these advantages however, questions arise about the effectiveness of ads in
a social networking environment. Many users do not like brand advertising and prefer
to take advice from their online peers in these communities when deciding what to
buy, rather than listen to advertisers. Social networking has become a media channel
in its own right and it is one that is reflecting the voice of consumers instead of those
of brand owners.

Brand-oriented communications within social media should not be invasive, intrusive or interruptive. In order to work, marketing communications needs to become part of the context in which site users interact. Advertising will continue to form a major revenue stream for the owners of these social networking sites and online communities, but increasingly this needs to be supplemented with the use of a mixture of sponsorship, brand placement and public relations.

Weblogs

Weblogs, or *blogs* as they are commonly known, are personal online diaries. Although individual issues are recorded and shared, a large proportion of blogs concern organisations and public issues, and they are essentially free.

The informality of blogs enables information to be communicated in a much more relaxed manner than most other forms of marketing communications. This is typified by the use of podcasting and the downloading of blogs to be 'consumed' at a later, more convenient time, or while multitasking. Blogs represent user-generated content and are often a key indicator of the presence of an influencer.

Blogs can be understood using a number of criteria, other than the basic consumer or corporate demarcation. Typically, the content and the type of media are the main criteria. A blog can be categorised by its content or the general material with which it is concerned. The breadth of content is only limited by the imagination, but some of the more mainstream blogs tend to cover topics such as sport, travel, music, film, fashion and politics. Blogs can also be categorised according to the type of media. For example, 'vlogs' contain video collections, whereas a 'photoblog' is a collection of photos and a 'sketchblog' contains sketches.

Nardi et al. (2004), as cited by Jansen et al. (2009), found five reasons why people choose to blog:

1. documenting their lives;
2. providing commentary and opinions;
3. expressing deeply held emotions;
4. articulating ideas through writing;
5. forming and maintaining communities.

These appear to be a list of outward-facing reasons. What is not mentioned here are inner-directed reasons, such as the need for feedback, or psychological issues relating to the need for self-esteem, reassurance and reinforcement of an individual's identity.

Just as consumers write about their experiences with brands, opportunities exist for organisations to identify emerging trends, needs and preferences, and also to understand how brands are perceived. Blogs provide brands with a potent advertising platform, because, as Segev et al. (2014) point out, they enable contextual advertising. This occurs where advertised objects are relevant to the theme of the blog (context), which in turn are read by consumers who are interested in the content available on the platform.

Organisations can set up *external* corporate blogs to communicate with customers, channel partners and other stakeholders. Many major organisations use external blogs to provide information about company issues and other organisations use blogs to launch brands or attend to customer issues. The other form of corporate blog is the *internal* blog. Here the focus is on enabling employees to write about and discuss corporate policies, issues and developments. Some organisations encourage interaction between their employees and customers and the general public. Although problems can arise through inappropriate comments and observations, blogging is an informal communications device that can serve to counter the formality often associated with planned marketing communications.

Scholars' paper 21.3
Remember, B2B use social media

Andersson, S. and Wikström, N. (2017) Why and how are social media used in a B2B context, and which stakeholders are involved? *Journal of Business & Industrial Marketing*, 32(8), 1098–1108.

A very accessible paper that shows companies in a B2B context use social media to enhance customer relationships, support sales and build brands. However, they also use social media as a recruiting tool, a seeking tool, and a product information and service tool.

See also:

Cawsey, T. and Rowley, J. (2016) Social media brand building strategies in B2B companies, *Marketing Intelligence & Planning*, 34(6), 754–76.

Wang, Y., Rod, M., Ji, S. and Deng, Q. (2017) Social media capability in B2B marketing: toward a definition and a research model, *Journal of Business & Industrial Marketing*, 32(8), 1125–35.

Enabling people to blog, perhaps by creating a dedicated web space, facilitates interaction and communications through people with similar interests. There is also an added attraction in that communities of bloggers can attract advertisers and form valuable revenue streams. Blogs can be used by organisations as a form of public relations in order to communicate with a range of stakeholders. For example, a blog on an intranet can be used to support internal communications, on an extranet to support distributors, and on the Internet to reach and influence consumers.

Microblogging

Microblogging or *nanoblogging*, as it is sometimes referred to, is a short-format version of blogging. Twitter, which appeared in 2006, is probably the best known. A microblog, or tweet, consists of a short comment, a post of 280 characters, which is shared with a network of followers. This makes production and consumption relatively easy in comparison to blogs.

These posts can be distributed through instant messages, email, mobile phones and tablets, or the Web. Therefore, as Jansen et al. (2009) put it, people can share brand-related thoughts at any time, and more or less anywhere, with people who are connected via the Web, smartphone, tablet, or instant messages and email, on an unprecedented scale.

Wood and Burkhalter (2014) indicate that Twitter is used by consumers for a variety of reasons. These include informing family, friends and contacts about what they are doing or thinking, crowdsourcing, and sharing and forwarding information and news articles to others. At a deeper level, ideas about self-expression, personal identity, and a need to participate and to be seen and heard, can be added. They suggest that Twitter is used by organisations to target audiences efficiently, to collect market intelligence in real time, and to provide customer service. To this might be added ideas about engaging audiences, establishing a digital credibility and fostering relationships.

We know that WoM has a particularly significant impact on purchasing decisions, but eWoM can take place close to or even during a purchase process. Although eWoM may be less personal than face-to-face WoM, it has substantially greater reach and has greater credibility because it is in print and accessible by others (Hennig-Thurau et al., 2004).

Table 21.2   Four ways to use Twitter in marketing communications

Twitter format	Explanation
Company organic	A brand to consumer message, at no cost, encouraging consumers to follow it on Twitter.
Company paid	Known as a 'promoted tweet', a company pays to have a tweet inserted in a consumer's twitter feed. Normally these are targeted at people who do not currently follow the brand on Twitter. Promoted tweets are charged on a cost per engagement event or a cost per thousand impressions model. In the case of Twitter, engagement refers to clicks, favourites, retweets and @replies.
Celebrity paid	Sometimes referred to as a 'sponsored tweet', this approach involves a brand paying a celebrity to tweet on its behalf. Through the use of hashtags at the end of a tweet (the symbol # followed by the name of a group) the message discloses that the message is an ad. Each sponsored tweet can cost tens of thousands of dollars.
Celebrity organic	This involves a celebrity tweeting about a brand voluntarily and without compensation. Although this incurs no cost to the brand there is low control and high risk as the brand has no influence over the association with the celebrity tweeter, the content and the timing of these tweets.

Source: Based on Wood and Burkhalter (2014).

The implication of this is that microblogging offers huge potential to marketers, recognised when Twitter announced that it was to allow advertising on its site. However, these are not conventional adverts. These ads are tweets, and are an integral part of the conversations, referred to as 'Promoted tweets'.

There are four main ways in which brands can use microblogging. These are set out in Table 21.2.

Twitter provides organisations with a platform on which to engage audiences and through interaction prompt dialogue. This is possible because Twitter gives users the opportunity to interact through response to others, and make the communications roles interchangeable (Mamic and Almaraz, 2013).

Scholars' paper 21.4

Twittering success

Wood, N.T. and Burkhalter, J.N. (2014) Tweet this, not that: a comparison between brand promotions in microblogging environments using celebrity and company-generated tweets, *Journal of Marketing Communications*, 20(1–2), 129–46.

As the use of Twitter increases, this paper provides an insight into the ways in which Twitter can be used in marketing communications. This paper provides good background information about social media and Twitter, and the results of its research indicate that celebrities in a social media context may be influential in drawing attention to unfamiliar brands.

Viral marketing

Viral marketing involves the peer-to-peer passing of a promotional message among a social network audience. The content is sufficiently informative, humorous, interesting or persuasive that the receiver feels emotionally compelled to send it on to a friend or acquaintance.

The term 'viral marketing' was developed by a venture capital company, Draper Fisher Jurvetson (Jurvetson and Draper, 1997). The term was used to describe the Hotmail email service, one of the first free email address services offered to the general public and one that had grown enormously. According to Jurvetson (2000: 12), they defined the term simply as 'network-enhanced word-of-mouth'.

Viral advertising has been defined as 'a persuasive message distributed by an advertiser through an unpaid channel among peers on interactive digital platforms' (Eckler and Rodgers, 2010). It is argued that these messages are usually seeded through the Internet, are often distributed through independent third-party sites, are usually personal, more credible than traditional advertising, and humour is almost invariably employed in executions (Porter and Golan, 2006).

Kirby (2003) agrees, indicating that there are three key elements associated with viral marketing:

1. *content,* which he refers to as the 'viral agent', is the quality of the creative material and whether it is communicated as text, image or video;
2. *seeding,* which requires identifying websites or people to send email in order to kick-start the virus; and
3. *tracking,* or monitoring, the impact of the virus and in doing so providing feedback and a means of assessing the return on the investment.

There is no doubt that viral marketing is difficult to control and can be very unpredictable, yet despite these characteristics, organisations are incorporating this approach within their marketing communications in order to reach their target audiences. Increasingly organisations are using word-of-mouth communications to generate conversations before the official (re)launch of a brand. The key reasons for this approach are that it helps identify interested communities and consumer groups and it also encourages feedback, in a similar way to test marketing.

Viewpoint 21.4

Repositioning content goes viral for Soberana

Fermín Paús, formerly Soberana Sr. Brand Manager at Heineken

Image 21.6 'Soberana Sessions'

An online video content platform where Soberana empowered its brand ambassadors.
Source: Fermín Paús Formerly Soberana Sr. Brand Manager at Heineken.

Soberana, a traditional beer brand in Panama, needed to renew its base of consumers and recruit an entire new generation, the millennials. To achieve its goal, the brand had to connect emotionally with this segment.

The brand repositioned in 2016 by embracing freedom and authenticity as the core brand values. Through its new creative territory, 'Live a Sovereign Life', Soberana invited consumers to live a free life, full of rights and no obligations.

Panamanian society, like many others, suffers from prejudices and discrimination based on skin colour, tattoos, profession and sexuality, to name a few. Many millennials do not know how to deal with this and often hide the features that make them unique. Soberana took the opportunity to align the brand with these emotions, and be seen to take an active role in helping to fight discrimination and enable consumers to be true to themselves.

We launched 'Soberana Sessions', an online video content platform where Soberana empowered its brand ambassadors (surf and skate national champions) to talk about their experiences and how they dealt with these difficult situations. Their openness and willingness to address these issues helped millennials associate Soberana with a different set of values, including tolerance, optimism, and authenticity.

The results of this new positioning were extraordinary and the content went viral rapidly. With the same level of investment, we had an incredible organic performance. We duplicated our average reach (75 per cent of target consumers) and impressions (2.3 million in total). Furthermore, 60 per cent of reached users interacted with our content (400,000 total interactions) generating an engagement rate of 17 per cent, while our average is between 5 per cent and 7 per cent. The brand achieved the largest number of interactions across the category, within the activation period.

The main equity indicators were tripled, and the Soberana Sessions content became the most virulent of all brands in the category in terms of reach, total interactions and engagement rate. This content has become a powerful tool with which to create emotional connections with millennials.

Insight

At the heart of viral campaigns is content or the 'viral agent'. This is the focus of the message that is communicated as text, image or video. Normally viral material is humorous or at least extraordinary in some way. In this case the content was essentially the openness of the brand ambassadors discussing the issues that they faced and how they had overcome them.

The emotional engagement that this material contained served to heighten the viral dynamic. This was tracked and so the impact of the virus was understood and provided valuable feedback.

Question: To what extent is viral just shared entertainment, and nothing more profound?

Task: Find two viral campaigns that do not seek to entertain viewers with humour-based content.

Online communities

Communities of people who share a common interest(s), who interact, share information, develop understanding and build relationships, all add value, in varying degrees, through their contribution to others involved with the website. In a sense, user groups and special interest groups are similar facilities, but the key with all these variations is the opportunity to share information electronically, often in real time.

Table 21.3   Four types of virtual community

Type of community	Explanation
Purpose	People who are attempting to achieve the same goal or who are experiencing a similar process.
Position	People who are experiencing particular circumstances. These might be associated with life-stage issues (the elderly, the young), health issues or perhaps career development opportunities.
Interest	People who share a hobby, pastime or who are passionately involved with, for example, sport, music, dance, family ancestry, jigsaws, wine, gardening, film, etc.
Profession	People involved with the provision of B2B services. Often created by publishers, these portals provide information about jobs, company news, industry issues and trading facilities, for example auctions.

Durlacher (1999) argues that there are four main types of community, defined by their purpose, position, interest and profession, as set out in Table 21.3.

Communities can be characterised by several determining elements. Muniz and O'Guinn (2001) identify three core components:

1. consciousness of kind: an intrinsic connection that members feel towards one another;

2. the presence of shared rituals and traditions that perpetuate the community's history, culture and consciousness; and

3. a sense of moral responsibility, duty or obligation to the community as a whole and its individual members.

Within these online or virtual communities five particular characteristics can be identified. The first concerns the model of communications, which is essentially visitor-to-visitor and in some cases customer-to-customer. Second, communities create an identity that arises from each individual's involvement and sense of membership and belonging. The more frequent and intense the interaction, the stronger the identity the participants feel with the community.

Third, relationships, even close friendships, develop among members, which in turn can facilitate mutual help and support. The fourth characteristic concerns the language that the community adopts. Very often specialised languages or codes of (electronic) behaviour emerge that have particular meaning to members. The fifth and final characteristic refers to the methods used to regulate and control the behaviour and operations of the community. Self-regulation is important in order to establish acceptable modes of conduct and interaction among the membership.

The role that members assume within these communities and the degree to which they participate also vary. There are members who attend but contribute little, those who create topics, lead discussions, those who summarise and those who perform brokerage or intermediary roles among other members. Edwards (2011) refers to the '1-9-90 rule'. This suggests that 1 per cent of any community are drivers, those who create large amounts of activity. Next, 9 per cent are influencers. These are people who either formally or informally edit, shape, modify and fashion content. The remaining 90 per cent read, observe and consider the community's content; they lurk around the community rather than participate in it. The implication for marketers is that key messages need to reach the drivers and influencers: 10 per cent of the audience.

Szmigin and Reppel (2004) have offered their customer bonding triangle framework, which is built on interactivity, technical infrastructure and service value elements. It is argued by the authors of this framework that it is the fit between the elements that determines the level of bonding between community members.

Table 21.4 Segments in virtual communities

Community segment	Explanation
Insiders	Insiders have strong social ties to other members of the community and consumption and participation is central to their self-image.
Devotees	Devotees participate because of their strong ties and identification with the product.
Minglers	Minglers are tied to some other members but do not have strong associations with the community as a whole or the product.
Tourists	Tourists do not have ties to the product or other members and are transient through the community.

Source: Based on Kozinets (1999).

The knowledge held in virtual communities can be expected to be of significant value when searching for product information. In 1999 Kozinets presented four segments related to virtual communities, based around two dimensions. These are presented in Table 21.4.

Any discussion of social media and branding should consider the important point made by Fournier and Avery (2011: 193), namely that 'the Web was created not to sell branded products, but to link people together in collective conversational webs'.

Scholars' paper 21.5
Looking into virtual communities

Willi, C.H., Melewar, T.C. and Broderick, A.J. (2013) Virtual brand-communities using blogs as communication platforms and their impact on the two-step communication process: a research agenda, *The Marketing Review,* **13(2), 103–23.**

This easy-to-read paper provides excellent coverage of a range of related issues, including blogs, interactive platforms, opinion leadership, the process of adoption, social identity theory and different types of virtual community.

Other forms of interactive media

The final part of this chapter briefly considers other forms of interactive media, as represented in Figure 21.4.

Email marketing

There are two key characteristics associated with email communications. First, they can be directed at clearly defined groups and individuals. Second, email messages can be personalised and refined to meet the needs of individuals. In this sense email is the antithesis of broadcast communications, which are scattered among a mass audience and lack any sense of individualisation, let alone provide an opportunity for recipients to respond. In addition, email can be used with varying levels of frequency and intensity, which is

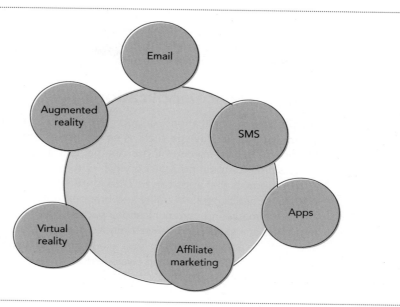

Figure 21.4 Other forms of interactive media

important when building awareness, reinforcing messages or when attempting to persuade someone into a trial or purchase.

Organisations need to manage two key dimensions of email communications: outbound and inbound email. Outbound email concerns messages sent by a company concerning public-relations-based announcements, newsletters and sales promotions, to distribute online catalogues and to trigger responses. The inbound dimension concerns the management of email communications received from customers and other stakeholders. These may have been stimulated by an individual's use of the website, exposure to a news item about the product or organisation, or through product experience, which often entails a complaint.

Managing inbound email represents a huge opportunity not only to build contact lists for use in outbound campaigns, but also to provide high levels of customer service interaction and relationship development. If undertaken properly and promptly, this can help to build trust and reputation, which in turn can stimulate word-of-mouth communications. Activity-triggered emails that incorporate the interests of the target audience and which follow up on audience behaviour are deemed to be more successful and good practice, if only because of the higher conversion rates and return on investment.

Short message service (SMS)

Although different in format, short message service (SMS), or 'texting', can be regarded as an extension of email communications. Apart from pure text, other simple applications consist of games, email notifications, and information-delivery services such as sports and stock market updates.

Yaobin et al. (2010) undertook a study into the reasons why consumers use SMS. The research was based in China, where SMS is used extensively, and the results highlighted three main reasons for use. These concern the perceived utilitarian value of SMS, the level of intrinsic enjoyment and the satisfaction derived from the involvement in communications. The third reason was the relatively low costs of use.

For some time organisations were relatively slow at adopting SMS despite the low costs and high level of user control (target, content and time). However, as organisations recognise these benefits, so SMS has become an integral part of the media mix for many.

Marketers are mindful of the potential concerns of consumers, most notably security and privacy. Just as with email, there is the potential for unwanted messages (i.e. spam) and internet service providers (ISPs) need to manage the increasing numbers of unsolicited messages through improved security systems.

Mobile device applications

Mobile device applications, or apps, are small pieces of software that are downloaded to run on mobile devices such as smartphones and tablets. Apps enable users to do all sorts of things, from finding a cinema, taxi or restaurant, to reading news, providing entertainment, updating a grocery list, or remembering where a car is parked. Goddard (2010) suggests that apps can be categorised into four types. These are campaign-based, popular gimmick, straight utility and branded utility (see Table 21.5).

From a marketing communications perspective, apps enable a brand to be connected regardless of location, and deliver branded content. More importantly Fang (2017) states that apps provide an opportunity to have a logo or brand name displayed on a user's device at all times. This can strengthen brand awareness, and offer opportunities for more frequent interaction and brand engagement. Apps, however, represent an additional channel and, apart from costs, questions arise about ad effectiveness in a multichannel environment. Xu et al. (2014) find that the use of an app can help sustain awareness in a crowded multichannel context. They also suggest that apps and mobile websites may need to have different digital media strategies if a brand is to gain any significant benefits from having to operate with multiple platforms.

Affiliate marketing

Dwivedi, et al. (2017: 33) refer to affiliate marketing as a 'prominent, contemporary type of performance-based internet marketing whereby a firm reimburses affiliates for each customer referred through the affiliate's marketing effort'.

By providing a network of additional distribution points, affiliate marketing provides organisations, such as Amazon, access to a wider range of potential customers. The goal is to drive web traffic to the advertiser, via the affiliate, and to sell products. If a sale is made, only then will the affiliate receive a commission, or other agreed reward.

Table 21.5 Categories of apps

Type of community	Explanation
Campaign-based	Apps which have high brand-value content but little everyday utility. This means they will attract attention in the short term but will not serve to retain users.
Popular gimmick	Apps characterised by low brand value, which are not very useful. Their value lies in supporting short-term campaigns or events, but they can become obsolete when the campaign finishes. Often good for entertainment purposes, but once seen there is little value in repeating.
Straight utilities	Apps that serve as everyday tools. For example, location finders, currency converters, and recipe and menu directories can be useful but competition is high and stand-out opportunities are rare.
Branded utilities	Apps which are both useful and develop the brand promise. These are considered to be the most powerful types of mobile apps, simply because engagement occurs through the functionality which is tied to the essential value of the brand.

Source: Based on Goddard (2010).

Table 21.6   Fraudulent affiliate marketing practices

Type of fraud	Explanation
Adware	Software which sees a user's activity and redirects them through an affiliate's marketing link.
Cookie stuffing	Pages designed to repeatedly attract traffic to particular merchants. If a user makes a purchase from that merchant within a predetermined time, often 7–30 days, the affiliate is credited.
Typostuffing	The registration of domain names that are misspellings of merchants' domain names. When a user misspells a merchant's domain name in the way that the affiliate anticipated, the user is redirected to the affiliate's site.
Loyalty software	The placement of 'loyalty' software on a user's computer to remind them about possible rebates, points or other benefits from purchasing through certain merchants. When a user requests a merchant's site directly the loyalty software automatically sends them through an affiliate's link.

Source: Based on Edelman and Brandi (2015).

Cookies contain information generated by a web server and stored in a user's computer. These provide fast access to a site and are used to track, monitor and record transactions and pay commission plus any agreed charges. As with many online marketing schemes, management can be undertaken in-house or outsourced.

Amazon run a high-profile affiliate marketing scheme and they have thousands of affiliates all driving visitors to the Amazon website. These schemes are popular because they are low-cost operations, paid on a results-only basis and generate very favourable returns on investment.

Affiliate marketing is, however, open to abuse. Edelman and Brandi (2015) refer to particular types of fraud that some affiliates have commonly undertaken. These are set out in Table 21.6.

Augmented and virtual reality

Augmented Reality (AR) and Virtual Reality (VR) are two different technologies, which deliver different effects. Both are receiving massive investment by Google, Facebook and Microsoft. AR is based on inserting virtual objects and information into the real world, and in doing so augmenting the user's experience of it via a smart device. VR immerses the user in a virtual world, via a headset, which serves to isolate the user from the real world (Yaoyuneyonga et al., 2016).

AR, therefore, allows people to see what they look like in different clothes, without having to get changed into them and, with developments in mobile technology, without a change of location. A virtual reality environment (VRE) enables users to 'feel present in the simulated environment in which they are immersed through interaction with virtual objects' (Rosa et al., 2016: 209).

AR technologies are still developing, but they are increasingly used in mobile applications in connection with location facilities. For example, they can be used as virtual wardrobes, shop fronts, store layouts and as a means of locating shops, tube stations, restaurants, pubs and theatres with a mobile phone. Land Rover has used AR to replicate the showroom experience on people's phones, while Fiat and Ford have used the technique to launch new models (Hobbs, 2015).

AR, however, also raises issues concerning privacy and security, particularly in a multi-channel environment (Roesner et al., 2014).

Image 21.7 VR technologies have been taken up by many car manufacturers
Source: SeventyFour/Shutterstock.

Key points

- Social media embrace a range of internet-based applications, all of which are characterised by two key elements. These are social presence/media richness, and, second, social processes in the form of self-presentation/self-disclosure.

- Interactive media advertising comprises mainly of banners, behavioural targeting, native advertising, pop-ups, video, bumpers and online gaming.

- The goal of search engine marketing (SEM) is to drive traffic to websites, and ranking on the search-results page is achieved in two fundamentally different ways. In SEO ranking, searches are based on content, while the PPC approach relies entirely on price as a ranking mechanism.

- Voice technologies have the potential to reduce search time drastically, undertake purchases and even change the balance of brand relationships.

- Social networks are about people using the Internet to share lifestyle and experiences. Participants in these networks also use the interactive capacity to build relationships. The critical aspect of social networks is that the content is user-generated and this means users own, control and develop content according to their needs, not those of a third party.

- Blogs are personal online diaries. Business-related or corporate blogs represent huge opportunities as a form of marketing communications for organisations. This is because blogs reflect the attitudes of the author, and these attitudes can influence others. Microblogging is a short-format version of blogging and Twitter is probably the best known.

- Viral marketing involves the use of email to convey messages to a small part of a target audience where the content is sufficiently humorous, interesting or persuasive that the receiver feels emotionally compelled to send it on to a friend or acquaintance.

- Online communities consist of people who share a common interest(s), who interact, share information, develop understanding and build relationships.

- Augmented reality (AR) is based on inserting virtual objects and information into the real world, and in doing so augmenting the user's experience of it via a smart device. Virtual reality (VR) immerses the user in a virtual world, via a headset, which serves to isolate the user from the real world.

- Other forms of interactive communications include email, SMS, apps and affiliate marketing.

Fridge Raiders: less media, more conversation

Vizeum and Kerry Foods

Mattessons are an established UK firm selling meat products such as specialist hams and smoked pork sausage. The problem we faced was that our sales were in decline and we needed to move into new categories and eating occasions. Fridge Raiders are 100 per cent chicken breast in flavoured snack portions, and represented a major opportunity for us.

The challenge for our brand lies not in the goodness of its product or its great flavours but more the nature of its category: meat snacking is not a 'normal' behaviour. It is a standard habit for hungry teens to tuck into some crisps, chocolate or sweets but not meat. Our main rival is Peperami, who not only dominate the market, but also have a considerable marketing budget, enabling them to outspend us and enjoy greater awareness levels. We needed our small brand to find a big voice.

We set out our objectives as follows:

1. Business objective . . . to increase volume and value of Fridge Raiders' sales.

2. Marketing objective . . . to increase desire for Fridge Raiders as the after-school snack of choice among teens.

3. Communication objective . . . to emotionally engage teenagers with Fridge Raiders during the after-school occasion.

Fridge Raiders are a healthy snack that teens enjoy more than anyone else. To reach this audience we adopted a media strategy of sparking conversations in the digital environments where opinions were formed and new thinking was shared. Having established our goals we needed to spark a legitimate and intimate conversation with teens, our target audience, and this required understanding their behaviours. Research revealed that teens took their after-school gaming seriously but their snacking on salty crisps led to greasy fingers and a downturn in their gaming performance.

We knew that a standard FMCG media channel mix wouldn't work to reach teens and gamers. They spend a lot more time consuming digital media content than they do watching TV, food shopping or listening to the radio. So we decided to ask the gamers themselves, to involve them in the development of a solution.

Gamers are heavy users of Facebook, Twitter and YouTube and influenced by their peers. In turn, games celebrities use social media to promote themselves and their activities, and large communities and influence build up around them. By partnering with one such games celebrity, Fridge Raiders could efficiently target teenage gamers, encourage them to participate in a challenge, and build the brand's awareness and games association among this audience.

To achieve credibility in this new market we partnered with Tom Cassell, an online gaming celebrity, using the name 'The Syndicate Project'. The campaign kicked off with a film on YouTube to start the operation against greasy fingers. We then filmed 'Syndicate Project' opening a mystery box from Fridge Raiders inviting him and his followers to become part of the project. The film was posted on YouTube setting the challenge and inviting solutions to be posted on the Facebook page. Regular updates and announcements were provided online, and 15,000 ideas were submitted.

The community were updated about the short-listed finalists before the winning idea was selected. Saatchi & Saatchi built the 'MMM3K' – the first ever snack-dispensing helmet that could feed gamers Fridge Raiders automatically without the gamer needing to take their hands off the controller. The 'meat-snacking helmet' was then filmed being delivered to the Syndicate Project by the Royal Marines, and then opened and revealed with due ceremony.

Against the objectives, sales volume rose 20 per cent, and sales value by £1.78 million. The desire objective was met as propensity to trial rose from 3 per cent to 11 per cent. In addition, social media comments and support indicate strongly that the campaign engaged teens emotionally. The brand had spent more on 'influencers' than ever before as they built credibility, effectively creating a media channel in their own right. Thanks to the messages they passed on and the reach they commanded, we could invest less in paid media as a result.

Buoyed by the success of combining an influencer with social media amplification, we were able to evolve the media strategy even further, increasing the percentage of total media investment in social from 16 per cent to 21 per cent (a 31 per cent increase year on year and the highest of any Kerry Foods brand) and investing even more in a brand-new influencer. Year 2 of Fridge Raiders' gaming strategy brought a new idea from Saatchi & Saatchi, a gaming artificial intelligence robot called F.R.H.A.N.K (Fridge Raiders Hunger Automated Nutritional Kit). We delivered a two-metre square LED cube to Ali A's back garden. The gaming community legend has 4.7 million followers, who helped him crack a code and reveal an artificially intelligent robot.

Our most recent campaign has built on this momentum to take our brand to the next level. With the digital skills gap in the news, we wanted to excite kids about coding. We used YouTube to create the world's first live hacking adventure in an ambitious campaign that involved six of the gaming community's big stars. We set nine challenges over six weeks, each of which was a lesson in disguise that taught over 77,000 youngsters the basics of Python, the coding language used in schools.

These campaigns showed a clear transformative effect on Fridge Raiders. Levels of engagement with YouTube's biggest community (gamers) were impressive, with 220 gaming reaction videos made by the community in reaction to the campaigns, 218,000 gaming comments generated and 871,000 YouTube gaming unique visitors to Fridge Raiders' sites – with total views of all the content reaching more than 36 million.

Not surprisingly we have reviewed the media mix used across all parts of business. As a result we have reduced the amount spent in traditional media and increased the interactive, and in particular, the social media activity.

This case study is an edited version of a paper submitted to the IPA Effectiveness Awards 2016. It has been reproduced here with the kind permission of the IPA, WARC, Kerry Foods and the agency Vizeum.

Review questions

Fridge Raiders case questions

1. Discuss ways in which brands might imitate Fridge Raiders' use of social media to engage their target audiences.

2. Appraise the concept of influencer communications and consider their use within Fridge Raiders' use of social networks.

3. Make brief notes concerning the ways in which Fridge Raiders might extend their use of social networks.

4. How might Fridge Raiders use SMS to improve operational efficiencies?

5. To what extent might the use of apps assist Fridge Raiders?

General questions

1. Explain the basic principles of search engine marketing.

2. Describe the way in which both search engine optimisation and pay-per-click systems operate.

3. Write a report examining the use of email as a form of marketing communications. Find examples to support the points you make.

4. Goddard (2010) suggests that apps can be categorised into four types. What are they and how are they different?

5. What is a cookie and why are they important to affiliate marketing?

References for Chapter 21

Andersson, S. and Wikström, N. (2017) Why and how are social media used in a B2B context, and which stakeholders are involved? *Journal of Business & Industrial Marketing*, 32(8), 1098–1108.

Anon (2016) Powwownow launches social media campaign to encourage flexible working, *B2B Marketing*, 16 July, retrieved 21 December 2017 from www.b2bmarketing.net/en-gb/resources/news/powwownow-launches-social-media-campaign-encourage-flexible-working

Anon (2017a) Cannes study: video is key for effectiveness, WARC, 7 August, retrieved 9 August 2017 from https://www.warc.com/NewsAndOpinion/News/Cannes_study_Video_is_key_for_effectiveness/39096?utm_source=DailyNews&utm_medium=email&utm_campaign=DailyNews2017807

Anon (2017b) Powwownow increases reach by 2083% with 'smarter working' social media campaign, *B2B Marketing*, 14 November, retrieved 21 December 2017 from http://www.b2bmarketing.net/en-gb/resources/b2b-case-studies/awards-case-study-powwownow-increases-reach-2083-smarter-working-social

Boerman, S.C., Kruikemeier, S. and Borgesius, F.J.Z. (2017) Online behavioral advertising: a literature review and research agenda, *Journal of Advertising*, 46(3), 363–76.

Cauberghe, V. and De Pelsmacker, P. (2010) Advergames: the impact of brand prominence and game repetition on brand responses, *Journal of Advertising*, 39(1), 5–18.

Cawsey, T. and Rowley, J. (2016) Social media brand building strategies in B2B companies, *Marketing Intelligence & Planning*, 34(6), 754–76.

Chang, Y., Yan, J., Zhang, J. and Luo, J. (2010) Online in-game advertising effect: examining the influence of a match between games and advertising, *Journal of Interactive Advertising*, 11(1), 63–73.

Chen, J. and Stallaert, J. (2014) An economic analysis of online advertising using behavioral targeting, *MIS Quarterly*, 38(2), 429–49.

Colliander, J. and Dahlén, M. (2011) Following the fashionable friend: the power of social media, *Journal of Advertising Research*, 51(1), 313–20.

Davies, D. (2017) The death of organic search (as we know it), *Search Engine Journal*, 29 March, retrieved 11 December 2017 from https://www.searchenginejournal.com/death-organic-search-know/189625/

Durlacher (1999) UK on-line community, *Durlacher Quarterly Internet Report*, Q3, 7–11, London.

Dwivedi, Y.K., Rana, N.P.and Alryalat. M.A.A. (2017) Affiliate marketing: an overview and analysis of emerging literature, *Marketing Review*, 17(1), Spring, 33–50.

Eckler, R. and Rodgers, S. (2010) Viral advertising: a conceptualization, paper presented at the Annual Meeting of the Association for Education in Journalism and Mass Communication, Denver, CO.

Edelman, B. and Brandi, W. (2015) Risk, information, and incentives in online affiliate marketing, *Journal of Marketing Research,* 52 (February), 1–12.

Edwards, J. (2011) Influencer metrics are getting a Klout, *B2B Marketing,* November/December, 14.

Fang, Y.-H. (2017) Beyond the usefulness of branded applications: insights from consumer–brand engagement and self-construal perspectives, *Psychology & Marketing,* 34(1), January, 40–58.

Fournier, S. and Avery, J. (2011) The uninvited brand, *Business Horizons,* 54(3), 193–207.

Garrett, A., Straker, K. and Wrigley, C. (2017) Digital channels for building collaborative consumption communities, *Journal of Research in Interactive Marketing,* 11(2), 160–84.

Goddard, M. (2010) Sizing up a proposed app, *ABA Bank Marketing,* 42(4), 20–23.

Gulin-Merle, M. (2017) L'Oréal's digital transformation, *Think with Google,* April, retrieved 22 October from https://www.thinkwithgoogle.com/marketing-resources/loreal-mobile-digital-marketing-strategy/?utm_medium=email-d&utm_source=content-alert&utm_team=twg-us&utm_campaign=20170418-twg-us-advertising-alert

Hennig-Thurau, T., Gwinner, K.P., Walsh, G. and Gremler, D.D. (2004) Electronic word-of-mouth via consumer-opinion platforms: what motivates consumers to articulate themselves on the internet? *Journal of Interactive Marketing,* 18(1), 38–52.

Hobbs, T. (2015) 'Augmented reality can replace the showroom' says Land Rover marketing chief, *Marketing Week,* 2 February, retrieved 3 February 2015 from www.marketingweek.com/2015/02/02/augmented-reality-can-replace-showroom-says-land-rover/

Hodis, M.A. Sriramachandramurthy, R. and Sashittal, H.C. (2015) Interact with me on my terms: a four segment Facebook engagement framework for marketers, *Journal of Marketing Management,* 31(11–12), 1255–84.

Hughes, J. (2018) Click-through rates: what they are and how to improve yours, *Pretty Links,* 12 January, retrieved 9 April 218 from https://prettylinks.com/2018/01/improve-click-through-rates/

Hwang, Y., Ballouli, K., So, K. and Heere, B. (2017) Effects of brand congruity and game difficulty on gamers' response to advertising in sport video games, *Journal of Sport Management,* 31, 480–96.

Jansen, B.J. and Molina, P.R. (2006) The effectiveness of web search engines for retrieving relevant e-commerce links, *Information Processing and Management,* 42(4), July, 1075–98.

Jerath, K., Ma, L. and Park, Y.H. (2014) Consumer click behavior at a search engine: the role of keyword popularity, *Journal of Marketing Research,* 51 (August), 480–6.

Jurvetson, S. (2000) *What is Viral Marketing?* Draper Fisher Jurvetson website, retrieved 12 March 2006 from https://pdfs.semanticscholar.org/937d/5bf28040bdf9cbb3c1a47da8853118eb49a7.pdf

Jurvetson, S. and Draper, T. (1997) *Viral marketing,* Draper Fisher Jurvetson website, retrieved 12 March 2006 from https://www.scribd.com/document/133798561/08-Tim-Draper-on-Viral-Marketing

Kaplan, A.M. and Haelein, M. (2010) Users of the world unite! The challenges and opportunities of social media, *Business Horizons,* 53, 59–68.

Keskin, H., Akgun, A.E., Ayar, H. and Etlioglu, T. (2017) Persuasive messages and emotional responses in social media marketing, *Journal of Management, Marketing and Logistics,* 4(3), 202–8.

Kietzmann, J.H., Hermkens, K., McCarthy, I.P. and Silvestre, B.S. (2011) Social media? Get serious! Understanding the functional building blocks of social media, *Business Horizons,* 54(3), 241–51.

Kirby, J. (2003) The message should be used as a means to an end, rather than just an end in itself, *VM-People,* 16 October, retrieved 31 August 2007 from http://virus-marketing.de/de/vmknowledge/interviews/interviews_detail.php?id=14

Knauff, J. (2017) I, Search: how AI will transform the landscape of SEO, *Search Engine Journal,* 16 February, retrieved 11 December 2017 from https://www.searchenginejournal.com/search-ai-will-transform-landscape-seo/185531/

Kozinets, R.V. (1999) E-tribalized marketing: the strategic implications of virtual communities on consumption, *European Management Journal,* 17(3), 252–64.

Lobschat, L., Osinga, E.C. and Reinartz, W.J. (2017) What happens online stays online? Segment-specific online and offline effects of banner advertisements, *Journal of Marketing Research,* 54(6), December, 901–13.

Mamic, L.I. and Almaraz, I.A. (2013) How the larger corporations engage with stakeholders through Twitter, *International Journal of Market Research,* 55(6), 851–72.

MMA (2015) The mobile native ad formats, *Mobile Marketing Association,* retrieved 1 June 2015 from www.mmaglobal.com/files/documents/the_mobile_native_formats_final.pdf

Muniz Jr, A.M. and O'Guinn, T.C. (2001) Brand community, *Journal of Consumer Research,* 27(4), 412–32.

Nardi, B.A., Schiano, D.J., Gumbrecht, M. and Swartz, L. (2004) Why we blog, *Communications of the ACM,* 47(12), 41–6.

Petrova, E. (2017) 3 ways brands are innovating with YouTube bumper ads, *think with Google,* May, retrieved 11 December 2017 from https://www.thinkwithgoogle.com/advertising-channels/video/youtube-bumper-ads-six-second-format/

Porter, L. and Golan, G.J. (2006) From subservient chickens to brawny men: a comparison of viral advertising to television advertising, *Journal of Interactive Advertising,* 6(2), 30–8.

Renard, D. and Darpy, D. (2017) What makes online promotional games go viral? *Journal of Advertising Research,* June, 57(2), 173–81.

Ritson, M. (2017) Voice search spells trouble for both brands and retailers, *Marketing Week,* 11 October, retrieved 19 December 2017 from https://www.marketingweek.com/2017/10/11/mark-ritson-voice-search/

Roesner, F., Kohno, T. and Molna, D. (2014) Security and privacy for augmented reality systems, *Communications of the ACM,* 57(4), 88–96.

Rosa, P.J., Morais, D., Gamito, P., Oliveira, J. and Saraiva, T. (2016) The immersive virtual reality experience, *Cyberpsychology, Behavior, and Social Networking,* 19(3), 209–16.

Saenger, C., Jewell, R.D. and Grigsby, J.L. (2017) The strategic use of contextual and competitive interference to influence brand-attribute associations, *Journal of Advertising,* 46(3), 424–39.

Schneider, L.P. and Cornwell, B.B. (2005) Cashing in crashes via brand placement in computer games, *International Journal of Advertising,* 24(3), 321–43.

Segev, S., Wang, W. and Fernandes, J. (2014) The effects of ad-context congruency on responses to advertising in blogs, *International Journal of Advertising,* 33(1), 17–36.

Slegg, J. (2016) A complete guide to Panda, Penguin, and Hummingbird, *Search Engine Journal,* 11 August, retrieved 22 October 2017 from https://www.searchenginejournal.com/seo-guide/panda-penguin-hummingbird/

Summers, C.A., Smith, R.W. and Reczek, R.W. (2016) An audience of one: behaviorally targeted ads as implied social labels, *Journal of Consumer Research,* 43(1), June, 156–78.

Szmigin, I. and Reppel, A.E. (2004) Internet community bonding: the case of macnews.de, *European Journal of Marketing,* 38(5/6), 626–40.

Tan, E. (2017) How voice is changing everything, *Campaign,* October, 56–9.

Vinderslev, A. (2018) The definition of native advertising, *The Native Advertising Institute,* retrieved 13 September 2018 from https://nativeadvertisinginstitute.com/blog/the-definition-of-native-advertising/

Wang, Y., Rod, M., Ji, S. and Deng, Q., (2017) Social media capability in B2B marketing: toward a definition and a research model, *Journal of Business & Industrial Marketing*, 32(8), 1125–35.

Willi, C.H., Melewar, T.C. and Broderick, A.J. (2013) Virtual brand-communities using blogs as communication platforms and their impact on the two-step communication process: a research agenda, *The Marketing Review*, 13(2), 103–23.

Wohlwend, A. (2017) The 6-second impact: bumper ads explained, *AdAge*, 13 March, retrieved 11 December 2017 from http://adage.com/article/digitalnext/impact-bumper-ads-explained/308201/

Wood, N.T. and Burkhalter, J.N. (2014) Tweet this, not that: a comparison between brand promotions in microblogging environments using celebrity and company-generated tweets, *Journal of Marketing Communications*, 20(1–2), 129–46.

Xu, J., Forman, C., Kim, J.B. and van Ittersum, K. (2014) News media channels: complements or substitutes? Evidence from mobile phone usage, *Journal of Marketing*, 78 (July), 97–112.

Yang, M., Roskos-Ewoldsen, D.R., Dinu, L. and Arpen, L.M. (2006) The effectiveness of in-game advertising: comparing college students' explicit and implicit memory for brand names, *Journal of Advertising*, 35(4), 143–52.

Yaobin, L., Deng, Z. and Bin, W. (2010) Exploring factors affecting Chinese consumers' usage of short message service for personal communication, *Information Systems Journal*, 20(2), 183–208.

Yaoyuneyonga, G., Fostera, J., Johnson, E. and Johnson, D. (2016) Augmented reality marketing: consumer preferences and attitudes toward hypermedia print ads, *Journal of Interactive Advertising*, 16(1), 16–30.

Zhang, Y., Trusov, M., Stephen, A.T. and Jamal, Z. (2017) Online shopping and social media: friends or foes? *Journal of Marketing*, 81 (November), 24–41.

Media planning in a digital age

Media, or channel planning as it is referred to by practitioners, is essentially a selection and scheduling exercise. The selection concerns the choice of media vehicles to carry messages on behalf of an advertiser. With media fragmentation, audiences are switching between media with greater regularity, which impacts media scheduling. Decisions regarding the number of occasions, the timing and duration that a message is exposed to the target audience, in selected vehicles, have become increasingly critical.

Automation is having a major impact on media planning, while owned and earned media, plus social media and search in particular, have changed consumer behaviour and the way media is used. Media scheduling and selection is experiencing major changes in the way it should be managed.

Aims and learning objectives

The aims of this chapter are to introduce the principles of media planning, explore the impact of automation, and to set out some of the issues facing media planners.

The learning objectives are to enable readers to:

1. explain the principles associated with media planning and highlight the impact of media and audience fragmentation;

2. evaluate the various theories concerning different media and related switching behaviours;

3. examine the key concepts used principally in linear media selection: reach and cover, frequency, duplication, rating points and CPT;

4. discuss planning issues related to interactive media and scheduling;

5. explore issues associated with the automation of media planning and to become familiar with the nature and characteristics of programmatic advertising.

Introduction

Devising an optimum mix of media channels for the delivery of messages to target audiences is an integral part of effective marketing communications. Media (or channel) planning is normally undertaken by specialists, usually media independents, whose primary function is to buy airtime or space from media owners on behalf of their clients, the advertisers.

Media planning occurs within an environment populated with an ever-increasing number and type of media and ad formats. The resultant clutter affects the choices that consumers make, the placements of ads, and the potency of ads to cut through the clutter and engage the intended audience. As planning specialist Curtis Tingle observes, media planning has become much more complex, largely because of the increasing number of channels, fragmentation of consumers, and the data integration opportunities that have evolved with technological advances (Whitler, 2017).

The increasingly rich array of media opportunities begs many questions but of these one should be whether advertisers need to concentrate on linear or interactive media formats. The answer to this question is that advertisers can improve communications effectiveness by placing ads in both linear and interactive advertising media. Research by Binet and Field (2007) established that optimally, 40 per cent of budget should be allocated to activation or response activities (essentially interactive media), and 60 per cent to brand-building activities (mainly linear media).

This chapter is concerned with the various issues associated with the selection, optimisation and scheduling of media. Ideas about what constitutes media, however, have changed considerably in recent years. The prevalence of digital and interactive media, data management platforms and programmatic technologies, plus the growing significance of owned and earned media, is reshaping media planning.

We commence with a consideration of some media related issues such as media richness and media switching behaviours. We then review some media planning concepts derived from the management of linear media. This serves to set out some of the established principles of media planning. Issues relating to the incorporation and planning associated with interactive media, such as automation and programmatic advertising, are considered next. The chapter concludes with a review of the main elements of a media plan, which incorporates online, mobile and offline media within the context of a consumer purchase journey.

Media planning and the media mix

Traditionally media planning was concerned with the selection and scheduling of paid media vehicles to carry a message on behalf of an advertiser. Indeed, many of the concepts referred to later have their origins in the planning of linear, paid-for media.

Scheduling refers to the number of occasions, timing and duration that a message is exposed, in the selected vehicles, to the target audience. There are several factors, however, that complicate these seemingly straightforward tasks. One is the huge and growing variety of available media. This proliferation of the media is referred to as *media fragmentation*. Although consumers benefit from a wider choice, advertisers and media owners are faced with smaller audiences, known as *audience fragmentation*.

A media planner's task is complicated by another element: money. Clients have restricted financial resources and require their media planners to create schedules that deliver their messages not only effectively but also efficiently, which means within the parameters of the available budget.

The task of a media planner, therefore, is to deliver advertising messages through a selection of media that matches the viewing, reading, listening or search habits of the largest possible number of people in the target audience, within budget, and at the lowest possible cost.

Contemporary media planning is increasingly anchored around the purchase journeys that consumers undertake, something that is explored at the end of this chapter. In order for these tasks to be accomplished, three sets of decisions need to be made, about the choice of media, vehicles and schedules.

Decisions about the choice of media are complex. While choosing a single one is reasonably straightforward, choosing media in combination and attempting to generate synergistic effects is far from easy. Advances in technology have made media planning a much faster, more accurate process, one that is now more flexible and capable of adjusting to fast-changing market conditions.

Another key task of a media planner is to decide which combination of vehicles should be selected to carry the message to a target audience. McLuhan (1966) said that 'the medium is the message'. In other words, the choice of medium (or vehicle or channel) says something about the brand and the message it is carrying. He went on to say that 'the medium is the *massage*, as each medium massages the recipient in different ways and so contributes to learning in different ways'. For example, Krugman (1965) hypothesised that television advertising washes over individuals. He said that viewers, rather than participating actively with television advertisements, allow learning to occur passively. In contrast, magazine advertising requires active participation if learning is to occur. Today, online and interactive advertising actively promote engagement, involvement and participation.

Table 22.1 A summary of media characteristics

Type of paid media	Strengths	Weaknesses
Interactive media	High level of interaction High level of personalisation Immediate response possible Low absolute and relative costs Flexible and easy to update Measurable Ubiquity	Segment-specific Infrastructure constantly evolving Transaction security issues Privacy and transparency issues Placement issues Move from text to visual vocabulary
Print Newspapers	Wide reach High coverage Low costs Very flexible Short lead times Speed of consumption controlled by reader	Short lifespan Advertisements get little exposure Relatively poor reproduction, gives poor impact Low attention-getting properties
Magazines	High-quality reproduction that allows high impact Specific and specialised target audiences High readership levels Longevity High levels of information can be delivered	Long lead times Visual dimension only Slow build-up of impact Moderate costs Declining readership
Television	Flexible format, uses sight, movement and sound High prestige High reach Mass coverage Low relative cost, so very efficient	High level of repetition necessary Short message life High absolute costs Clutter Increasing level of fragmentation (potentially)

(continued)

Table 22.1 A summary of media characteristics (*Continued*)

Type of paid media	Strengths	Weaknesses
Radio	Selective audience, e.g. local Low costs (absolute, relative and production) Flexible Can involve listeners	Lacks impact Audio dimension only Difficult to get audience attention Low prestige
Outdoor	High reach High frequency Low relative costs Good coverage as a support medium Location-oriented	Poor image (but improving) Long production time (non digital) Difficult to measure
Transport	High length of exposure Low costs Local orientation	Poor coverage Segment specific (travellers) Clutter

The various media depicted in Table 22.1 have wide-ranging characteristics. These, and the characteristics of the target audience, should be considered when deciding on the optimal media mix. It should be clear that simply deciding on which media to use is fraught with difficulties, let alone deciding on the optimal combination, how much of each channel should be used, and considering the cost implications. Viewpoint 22.1 demonstrates how the media mix has evolved within the music industry.

Viewpoint 22.1

Evolving mixes within the music industry

Eloise Augustine

Image 22.1 Evolution of music media
Source: KerdaZz/Shutterstock.

Music artists and their record labels use a variety of media to reach their audiences. Live music has always been popular and in the 1940s and 1950s print media was prominent. Using local, regional and national advertising in newspapers and spe-cialist magazines, plus the use of posters and billboards, big bands and music artists were able to publicise their events. Radio also enabled fans to listen to their favourite music from home.

Broadcast media became the dominant format in the 1960s and 1970s. First, commercial radio (pirate) stations such as Radio Luxembourg and Radio Caroline enabled people to listen to popular music. But, as BBC Radio 1 became established and as television ownership increased, so programmes such as *Top of the Pops* and *Ready, Steady, Go!* provided additional, important routes to mass audiences for bands such as The Beatles and Fleetwood Mac, and artists such as Bob Dylan, Dionne Warwick and Cher.

Underground genres such as Punk, most notably the Sex Pistols, and New Romantic artists, used broadcast and print media, but they also developed the use of outdoor media. They used posters as a low-key and cost-effective way of targeting audiences for promotional gigs and acoustic nights. Visual art was a key medium within the subculture, and extremely important for marketing the punk aesthetic. At this time, highly visual (vinyl) record covers were an important in-store medium in retail record shops. These provided important packaging services but they were also regarded as an important medium for helping to differentiate artists and provide added value.

The rise of the digital era and the CD meant that fans could now listen to their favourite artists on the go. The MP3 download meant that music could be downloaded anywhere, any time.

Other forms of both indoor and outdoor communications include the use of guerrilla marketing. Used by artists and companies with low funds, they use a mix of graffiti, stickers, flash mobs and publicity stunts to make their product and services stand out.

Nowadays, there is a multitude of media channels available to artists. Print, broadcast, especially TV music-video channels, and digital through social media and specific music websites, provide a rich array for audiences to access music. YouTube, for example, offers an unlimited amount of music videos, a large proportion of which are posted by fans.

The latest additions to the media mix are streaming services. With a connection through social networks, these services allow people to see what music their friends, family and colleagues are listening to. Streaming services such as Spotify and Pandora have dramatically changed the way music is consumed. Streaming has also reduced the rate of illegal downloads.

The evolution of the media mix has increased the reach and frequency with which audiences can be entertained by their preferred music artists. Fans can now control and access their preferred music whenever they like. They can share it globally, 24/7. Gone are the days when access to music was controlled by those who owned particular media, and with them the days when tight planning was possible across the whole media mix.

Sources: Anon (2015); Mansfield (2012); Poynor (2012); Sylvester (2013).

This Viewpoint was written by Eloise Augustine when she was a student at Buckinghamshire New University.

Insight

The nature and characteristics of each media mix vary according to a range of factors. These include the objectives that a campaign is set to achieve, the context and situational issues and, of course, the budget that is available. This viewpoint shows how the mix has evolved through time to accommodate current technologies. It is also interesting to note the way in which music ownership and media planning have become more relaxed at a time when the volume of associated fraud has been reduced.

Question: Why is the media mix harder to plan and implement today?

Task: Select an album or gig/tour of a preferred music artist and list the media used to promote the artist.

For a long time, television has been used as the lead channel for major FMCG brands, when developing campaigns. WARC reported that in 2016 social media was found to be the second most frequently used lead channel. This collapsed in 2017 when it was found that social media had a more supportive or amplifying role, one designed to increase reach, often in support of other channels, rather than being used as a central strategy (Anon, 2017).

Media switching behaviour

Even before the arrival of interactive media, researchers had recognised that different media have different capabilities and that media were not completely interchangeable. In other words, different tasks can be accomplished more effectively using particular media. This implies that there is a spectrum of media depending on the content they carry.

Increasingly people multitask and use multiple media. As explored in Chapter 5, this is known as media stacking and media meshing, and it is these and other behaviours that require planners to understand why particular media are chosen in any one communications context. Various theories have been proposed but as George et al., (2013) affirm, no single complete theory has yet been identified that explains media choice.

Daft and Lengel (1984) were the first to propose that this content issue concerned the richness of the information conveyed through each medium. As a result, one of the tasks facing planners is selecting the right fit between the most appropriate media and the richness of the information. Four main criteria are used to determine the level of richness a medium possesses:

- the availability of instant feedback;
- the capacity to transmit multiple cues;
- the use of natural language;
- the degree of personal focus.

Media richness theory (MRT) holds that there is a hierarchy or spectrum of media ranging from personal or face-to-face encounters as the richest media, through to single sheets of text-based information as lean media at the other end. Rich media facilitate feedback, dialogue iteration and an expression of personal cues such as tone of voice, body language and eye contact that, in turn, help establish a personal connection. In descending order of richness, the other media are telephone, email, letter, note, memo, special report, fliers and bulletins. At this end of the richness scale numeric and formal written communications are slow, often visually limited and impersonal.

MRT suggests that rich media reduce ambiguity more effectively than others, but are more resource-intensive than lean media. If rich media allow for more complex and difficult communications, then lean media are more cost-effective for simple or routine communications.

Social influence theory (SIT) was developed by Fulk et al. (1990). This is intended to complement MRT as it also assumes that the relatively objective features of media do influence how individuals perceive and use media. These researchers, however, argue that SIT has a strong social orientation because different media properties (such as ability to transmit richness) are subjective and are influenced by attitudes, statements and the behaviour of others. This approach recognises that members of groups influence other people in terms of their perceptions of different media. The main difference between MRT and SIT is that MRT identifies rich media as inefficient for simple or routine communications whereas SIT suggests rich media can be just as appropriate for simple messages as they are for ambiguous communications.

A third approach, the technology acceptance model (TAM), relates to the utility and convenience a medium offers. The perceived usefulness and perceived ease of use are regarded as the main issues that are considered when selecting media (King and Xia, 1997). Perceived usefulness refers to the user's subjective assessment that using a specific computer application will improve their job performance. Perceived ease of use addresses the degree to which a user expects the identified application to be free of effort.

Scholars' paper 22.1

Theoretical insights into media choice

Armengol, X., Fernandez, V., Simo, P. and Sallan, J.M. (2017) An examination of the effects of self-regulatory focus on the perception of the media richness: the case of email, *International Journal of Business Communication*, 54(4), 394–407.

The authors consider media richness theory and channel expansion theory, among others, and their influence regarding the selection and use of communication media in organisations. They find that a perception of media richness is influenced by the experience with the communication partner, the experience with the medium, the experience with the topic and the social influence.

See also:

George, J.F., Carlson, J.R. and Valacich, J.S. (2013) Media selection as a strategic component of communication, *MIS Quarterly*, 37(4), 1233–51.

Vehicle selection

In addition to using their owned media, organisations need to use media that are owned by others in order to convey their messages effectively. These paid-for media have particular characteristics and ability to deliver rich or lean content. Our discussion now moves on to consider different paid-for media and the ways in which organisations develop a media mix to meet their communications needs.

Increasingly organisations are required to prove how advertising adds value to the bottom line. While this is not a new question, it is one that is being asked more often and in such a way that answers are required. As advertisers attempt to demonstrate effectiveness, contribution and return on investment, senior managers are increasingly haunted by questions concerning the choice of media, how much should be spent on message delivery and how financial resources are to be allocated in a multichannel environment.

Attention towards media decision-making has increased as the media have become more visible and significantly more important. Organisations such as BT, IKEA and RBS need to use media strategically in order to reach the right audience, in the right context, at the right time and at an acceptable cost. The media scheduling shown in Figure 22.1 for the British Heart Foundation's 'Vinnie campaign' shows how media can be used to build engagement to achieve specific goals.

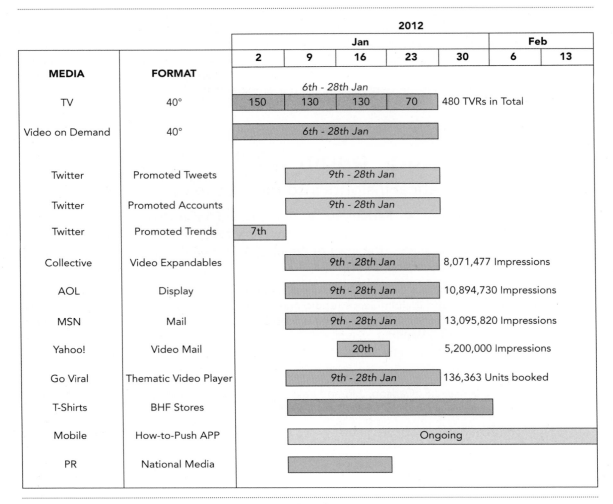

Figure 22.1 Overall activity used by the British Heart Foundation in their Vinnie campaign

Media planning concepts

There are several fundamental concepts that underpin the way in which linear media should be selected and incorporated within a media plan. These are reach, frequency, gross rating points, duplication and effective frequency.

Reach and coverage

Reach refers to the percentage of the target audience exposed to a message at least once during the relevant time period. Where 80 per cent of the target audience has been exposed to a message, the figure is expressed as an '80 reach'.

Coverage, a term often used for reach, should not be confused or used in place of reach. Coverage refers to the size of a potential audience that might be exposed to a particular media vehicle. For media planners, therefore, coverage (the size of the target audience) is very important. Reach will always be lower than coverage, as it is impossible to reach 100 per cent of a target population (the universe).

Building reach within a target audience is relatively easy, as the planner needs to select a range of different media vehicles. This will enable different people in the target audience to have an opportunity to see the media vehicle. There will come a point however, when it becomes more difficult to reach people who have not been exposed. As more vehicles are added, so repetition levels (the number of people who have seen the advertisement more than once) also increase.

Frequency

Frequency refers to the number of times a member of the target audience is exposed to a media vehicle (not the advertisement) during the relevant time period. It has been stated that targets must be exposed to the media vehicle, but to say that a target has seen an advertisement simply because they have been exposed to the vehicle is incorrect. For example, certain viewers hop around channels as a commercial break starts, referred to by Lloyd and Clancy, (1991) as 'channel grazing'. Individuals have different capacities to learn and to forget, and how much of a magazine does a reader have to consume to be counted as having read an advertisement? These questions are still largely unanswered, so media planners have adopted an easier and more consistent measure – opportunities to see (OTS).

This is an important point. The stated frequency level in any media plan will always be greater than the advertisement exposure rate. The term 'OTS' is used to express the reach of a media vehicle rather than the actual exposure of an advertisement. However, a high OTS could be generated by one of two different events. First, a large number of the target audience are exposed once (high reach) or, second, a small number are exposed several times (high frequency).

This then raises a major issue. As all campaigns are restricted by time and budget limitations, advertisers have to trade off reach against frequency. It is impossible to maximise both elements within a fixed budget and set period of time.

To launch a new product, it has been established that a wide number of people within the target audience need to become aware of the product's existence and its salient attributes or benefits. This means that reach is important but, as an increasing number of people become aware, so more of them become exposed a second, third or fourth time, perhaps to different vehicles. At the outset, frequency is low and reach high, but as a campaign progresses so reach slows and frequency develops. Reach and frequency are inversely related within any period of time, and media planners must know the objective of a campaign: is it to build reach or develop frequency?

Scholars' paper 22.2
Digital says no to reach and frequency

Cheong, Y., De Gregorio, F. and Kim, K. (2011) The power of reach and frequency in the age of digital advertising: offline and online media demand different metrics, *Journal of Advertising Research*, 50(4), 403–15.

This empirical paper explored the use of reach and frequency concepts. The findings are that the concepts are still used to evaluate offline media schedules. However, the use and practicality in online contexts is more limited, with agencies using qualitative and cost-based measures.

Gross rating point

To decide whether reach or frequency is the focus of the campaign objective, a more precise understanding of the levels of reach and frequency is required. The term *gross rating point* (or broadly in television a TVR) is used to express the relationship between these two concepts. GRPs are a measure of the total number of exposures (OTS) generated within a particular period of time. The calculation itself is simply reach × frequency:

$$reach \times frequency = gross\ rating\ point$$

Media plans are often determined on the number of GRPs generated during a certain time period. For example, the objective for a media plan could be to achieve 450 GRPs in a burst (usually four or five weeks). However, as suggested earlier, caution is required when interpreting a GRP, because 450 GRPs may be the result of 18 message exposures to just 25 per cent of the target market. It could also be an average of nine exposures to 50 per cent of the target market.

Rating points are used by all media as a measurement tool, although they were originally devised for use with broadcast audiences. GRPs are based on the total target audience (e.g. all women aged 18–34, or all adults) that might be reached, but a media planner needs to know, quite rightly, how many GRPs are required to achieve a particular level of effective reach and what levels of frequency are really required to develop effective learning or awareness in the target audience. In other words, how can the effectiveness of a media plan be improved?

Viewpoint 22.2
Media mixes

Knorr's 'Love at First Taste' campaign involved creating a content film, a Flavour Profiler derived from answers to a quiz, and personalised recipes. These were delivered through a multi-channel ecosystem. This included YouTube to drive video views, Facebook to drive sharing, and Twitter to drive conversation. Knorr also ran content partnerships with Playbuzz and Tastemade to create promoted recipe videos in social media.

When Kärcher launched their Window Vac in the UK they used TV as the lead channel. This medium enabled them to demonstrate the convenience and performance of the Vac. In addition, press, radio, online and VOD were used to provide more information. Press was highly targeted via niche magazines and was supported by digital advertising. Radio was timed to reach consumers in their cars or at the weekend, when they were most likely to be visiting outlets that stocked Window Vac. In-store displays and demonstrations were also important.

The traditional channel mix used by Anglian, the home improvement company, includes press, DRTV, direct mail and door drops. Direct mail works best when implemented at the end of a television campaign, as awareness levels have been raised. Television works best when used with press and door drops, and direct mail works best with current customers.

Sources: Morgan (2017); Springall (2016).

Insight

These few examples serve to demonstrate that the configuration of the channel mix should vary according to various contextual factors. These include the campaign objectives, the customers' purchase journey and preferred media, plus time of year, weather and other applicable variables.

Question: Why do you think television is no longer the automatic lead channel for those brands that can afford it?

Task: Find two campaigns that do not use mass media. Make a list of the channels they do use and identify any similarities or differences.

Effective frequency

Frequency refers to the number of times members of the target audience are exposed to a vehicle. It says nothing about the quality of the exposures and whether any impact was made. The contemporary version of this issue is referred to as 'viewability' of display ads in interactive media (see Chapter 2).

Effective frequency refers to the number of times an individual needs to be exposed to an advertisement before communications are effective. Being exposed once or possibly twice is unlikely to affect the disposition of a receiver. But the big question facing media planners is: how many times should a message be repeated for effective learning to occur? The level of effective frequency is generally unknown, but there has been some general agreement following work by Krugman (1972) that, for an advertisement to be effective (to make an impact), a target should have at least three OTS, the three-hit theory. The first exposure provokes a 'What is this?' reaction, the second reaction is 'What does this mean to me?' The reaction to the third is 'Oh, I remember' (du Plessis, 1998). The three-exposure theory is based on messages that first provide understanding, second, provide recognition and, third, actually stimulate action. More than 10 exposures is regarded as an ineffective plan and hence a waste of resources.

Determining the average frequency partially solves the problem. This is the number of times a target reached by the schedule is exposed to the vehicle over a particular period of time. For example, a schedule may generate the following:

10 per cent of the audience is reached ten times ($10 \times 10 = 100$)

25 per cent of the audience is reached seven times ($25 \times 7 = 175$)

65 per cent of the audience is reached once ($65 \times 1 = 65$)

Total = 340 exposures

Average frequency = $340/100 = 3.4$

Average frequency is misleading because different groups of people have been reached with varying levels of frequency. In the example above, an average frequency of 3.4 is achieved but 65 per cent of the audience is reached only once. This means that the average frequency, in this example, may lead to an audience being underexposed.

People do not visit a single website, buy and read just one magazine or watch a single television programme. Consumer media habits are complex, and although distinct patterns can be observed, it is likely that a certain percentage of the target audience will be exposed to an advertisement if it is placed in two or more media vehicles. Those who are exposed once constitute unduplicated reach. Those who are exposed to two or more of the advertisements are said to have been duplicated. Such overlapping of exposure, shown in Figure 22.2, is referred to as duplicated reach.

Duplication provides an indication of the levels of frequency likely in a particular media schedule. Duplication also increases costs, so if the objective of the plan is unduplicated reach, duplication brings waste and inefficiency. So media plans need to specify levels of duplicated and unduplicated reach.

Nevertheless, it is generally agreed that a certain level of GRPs is necessary for awareness to be achieved. It is also accepted that increased GRPs are necessary for other communications effects to be achieved. These levels of GRPs are referred to as *weights*, and the weight of a campaign reflects the objectives of the campaign. For example, a burst designed to achieve 85 per cent coverage with eight OTS would make a 680 rating, which is considered to be heavy. Such high ratings are often associated with car launches and, for example, products that are market leaders in their class, such as Nescafé or Pantene. An average rating would be one set to achieve a 400 rating, through 80 per cent coverage and five OTS over the length of a five-week period.

Our understanding about how learning works can assist the quest for effective frequency levels. The amount of learning in individuals increases up to a certain point, after

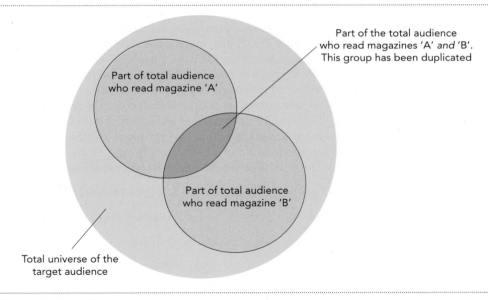

Part of total audience
who read magazine 'A'

Part of the total audience
who read magazines 'A' *and* 'B'.
This group has been duplicated

Part of total audience
who read magazine 'B'

Total universe of the
target audience

Figure 22.2 Duplicated reach

which further exposure to material adds little to our overall level of knowledge. The same applies to the frequency level and the weightings applied to exposures.

Recency planning

To counter the effective frequency model *recency planning* was developed at a time when the weak theory of advertising started to gain acceptance as the most viable general interpretation of how advertising works. There was also a growing general acceptance that the timing and presentation of advertising messages need to be reconsidered in the light of the way advertising was thought to work.

If it is accepted that consumer decision-making is more heavily influenced by 'running out' of particular products (opening empty fridges and store cupboards), than by exposure to advertising messages that are repeated remorselessly, then it follows that advertising needs to be directed at those people who are actually in the market and prepared to buy (Ephron, 1997).

As many fast-moving consumer goods products are purchased each week, Jones (1995) argues that a single exposure to an advertising message in the week before a purchase is to be made is more important than adding further messages, thereby increasing frequency. Recency planning considers reach to be more important than frequency.

The goal of this approach was to reach those few consumers who are ready to buy (in the market). To do this the strategy requires reaching as many consumers as possible in as many weeks as possible (as far as the budget will extend). This requires a lower weekly weight and an extended number of weeks for a campaign. Advertising budgets are not cut; the fund is simply spread over a greater period of time. According to Ephron, this approach is quite different from effective frequency models and quite revolutionary. See Table 22.2.

The debate about the efficacy of recency planning and effective frequency has been arrested mainly due to Big Data, data management platforms (DMPs) and programmatic advertising. Now planners have real-time insight into actual purchase behaviours and can use personalised advertising based on real usage and exposure figures. This is explored later.

Table 22.2 The differences between effective frequency and recency planning

Recency planning model	Effective frequency model
Reach goal	Frequency goal
Continuity	Burst
One-week planning cycle	Four-week planning cycle
Lowest cost per reach point	Lowest cost per thousand
Low ratings	High ratings

Source: Adapted from Ephron (1997). Used by permission of WARC.

Media usage and attitudes

A large number of people have a negative attitude towards advertising, which they see as both intrusive and pervasive. Today the increasing use of adblockers is testimony to this negative attitude. Back in 1997, Beale developed a four-part typology of personality types based upon respondents' overall attitudes towards advertising (see Table 22.3). Through an understanding of the different characteristics, it is possible to make better (more informed) decisions about the most appropriate media channels to reach target audiences.

It was common for advertisers and media planners to discuss target markets in the context of heavy, medium, light and non-users of a product. In much the same way media planners consider the usage levels of audiences. So, television audiences can be categorised as heavy, medium and light users based on the amount of time they spend watching television. One of the implications of this approach is that if light users consume so little television, then perhaps it is not worthwhile trying to communicate with them and resources should be directed to the medium and heavy user groups. The other side of the argument is that light users are very specific in the programmes that they watch. It should be possible, therefore, to target messages at them and a heavy number of GRPs should be used. However, questions still remain about the number of ratings necessary for effective reach in each of these categories.

Ostrow (1981) was the first to question how many rating points should be purchased. He said that, rather than use average frequency, a decision should be made about the minimum level of frequency necessary to achieve the objectives and then maximise reach at that level. Ostrow (1984) suggested that consideration of the issues set out in Table 22.4 would also assist.

Table 22.3 Advertising attitudes for media determination

Cynics (22 per cent)	Enthusiasts (35 per cent)
This group perceives advertising as a crude sales tool. They are resentful and hostile to advertisements, although they are more likely to respond to advertisements placed in relevant media.	Enthusiasts like to get involved with advertising and creativity is perceived as an important part of the process. Apart from newspapers, which are regarded as boring, most types of media are acceptable.
Ambivalents (22 per cent)	**Acquiescents (21 per cent)**
While creativity is seen as superfluous and irrelevant, ambivalents are more disposed to information-based messages or those that promise cost savings. The best advertisements are those that use media that reinforce the message.	As the name suggests, this group of people has a reluctant approach to advertising. This means that they see advertising as unavoidable and an inevitable part of their world. Therefore, they are open to influence through a variety of media.

Source: Adapted from Beale (1997). Reproduced with the permission of the copyright owner, Haymarket Business Publications Limited.

Table 22.4 Issues to be considered when setting frequency levels

Issues	Low frequency	High frequency
Marketing issues		
Newness of the brand	Established	New
Market share	High	Low
Brand loyalty	Higher	Lower
Purchase and usage cycle times	Long	Short
Message issues Complexity	Simple	Complex
Uniqueness	More	Less

Issues	Low frequency	High frequency
Image versus product sell	Product sell	Image
Message variation	Single message	Multiple messages
Media plan issues Clutter	Less	More
Editorial atmosphere	Appropriate	Not appropriate
Attentiveness of the media in the plan	Holds	Fails to hold
Number of media in the plan	Less	More

Source: Adapted from Setting frequency levels: an art or a science? Marketing and Media Decisions, 24(4), pp. 9–11 (Ostrow, J.W. 1984), The Nielsen Company.

The traditional approach of using television to reach target audiences to build awareness and brand fame is still actively used. For example, Procter & Gamble, Unilever, Nestlé, Kellogg's and BT all spend the majority of their budgets, albeit a declining proportion, on television advertising. However, many major advertisers have moved the balance of their media budgets to incorporate interactive, largely social, media to increase frequency. These media are sometimes referred to as 'targeted media' (Gates-Sumner, 2014) with online video, mobile, gaming and social media sites prominent.

Efficiency

All campaigns are constrained by a budget. Therefore, a trade-off is required between the need to reach as many members of the target audience as possible to create awareness, and the need to repeat the message to achieve effective learning in the target audience. The decision about whether to emphasise reach or frequency is assisted by a consideration of the objectives, and the costs involved in each proposed schedule or media plan.

There are two main types of cost. The first of these is the *absolute cost*. This is the cost of the space or time required for the message to be transmitted. For example, the cost of a full-page, single-insertion, black and white advertisement, booked for a firm date in the *Sunday Times*, is £60,690 (Newsworks, 2018). Cash flow is affected by absolute costs.

In order that an effective comparison be made between media plans the *relative costs* of the schedules need to be understood. Relative costs are the costs incurred in making contact with each member of the target audience.

Traditionally, the magazine industry has based its calculations on the cost per thousand people reached (CPT). The original term derived from the print industry is CPM, where the 'M' refers to the Roman symbol for thousand. This term still has limited use but the more common term is CPT:

$$CPT = space\ costs\ (absolute) \times 1,000/circulation$$

The newspaper industry has used the milline rate, which is the cost per line of space per million circulation.

Broadcast audiences are measured by programme ratings (USA), and television audiences in the UK are measured by television ratings or TVRs. They are essentially the same in that they represent the percentage of television households that are tuned to a specific programme. The TVR is determined as follows:

$$TVR = number\ of\ target\ TV\ households\ tuned\ into\ a\ programme$$
$$\times 100/total\ number\ of\ target\ TV\ households$$

A single TVR, therefore, represents 1 per cent of all the television households in a particular area that are tuned into a specific programme.

A further approach to measuring broadcast audiences uses the share of televisions that are tuned into a specific programme. This is compared with the total number of televisions that are actually switched on at that moment. This is expressed as a percentage and should be greater than the TVR. Share, therefore, reveals how well a programme is perceived by the available audience, not the potential audience. The question of how to measure relative costs in the broadcast industry has been answered by the use of the rating point or TVR. Cost per TVR is determined as follows:

$$Cost\ per\ TVR = time\ costs(absolute\ costs)/TVR$$

Intra-industry comparison of relative costs is made possible by using these formulae. Media plans that only involve broadcast or only use magazine vehicles can be evaluated to determine levels of efficiency. However, members of the target audience do not have discrete viewing habits; they have, as we saw earlier, complex media consumption patterns that involve exposure to a mix of media classes and vehicles. Advertisers respond to this mixture by placing advertisements in a variety of media, but have no way of comparing the relative costs on an inter-industry basis. In other words, the efficiency of using a *News at Ten* television slot cannot be compared with an insertion in *The Economist*.

Finally, some comment on the concept of CPT is necessary, as there has been speculation about its validity as a comparative tool. There are a number of shortcomings associated with the use of CPT. For example, because each media class possesses particular characteristics, direct comparisons based on CPT alone are dangerous. The levels of wastage incurred in a plan, such as reaching people who are not targets or by measuring OTS for the vehicle and not the advertisement, may lead to an overestimate of the efficiency that a plan offers.

Similarly, the circulation of a magazine is not a true representation of the number of people who read or have an opportunity to see. Therefore, CPT may underestimate the efficiency unless the calculation can be adjusted to account for the extra or pass-along readership that occurs in reality. Having made these points, media buyers in the UK continue to use CPT and cost per rating point (CPRP) as a means of planning and buying time and space.

Target audiences and television programmes are priced according to the ratings they individually generate. The ratings affect the cost of buying a spot. The higher the rating, the higher the price will therefore be to place advertisements in the magazine or television programme.

Scholars' paper 22.3
Media planning for radio

De Pelsmacker, P., Geuens, M. and Vermeir, I. (2004) The importance of media planning, ad likeability and brand position for ad and brand recognition in radio spots, *International Journal of Market Research,* **46, Quarter 4, 465–78.**

These authors consider a range of issues associated with radio advertising in Belgium. The paper is welcome not only because it considers radio, which is often overlooked, but also because it explores media planning issues in the light of ad likeability. Among other things, they find that radio campaigns are more effective if the other instruments of the marketing mix are used to build a strong position for the brand and that likeable ads enhance the effectiveness of radio advertising.

Automation and the block plan

The prevailing media buying system involves the purchase of ad placements in blocks of thousands or millions of impressions in anticipation of market demand. These blocks are based on the placement (of ads) within content. It is a hands-on process involving phone calls, emails, discussions about the nature of the target audience and negotiating a price. This works but there is waste and inefficiency. Tad Smith, Cablevision's president of local media (cited by WARC, 2013) described the process for buying TV ads as 'labour intensive, very complicated, expensive, and challenging and not very user friendly'.

The block plan

The 'interruption' model of advertising placement has traditionally been based on the use of linear media. This is predicated on the idea that the media manage audiences, influence what they see and when they see it, and shape the pattern of their media behaviour. Advertisers therefore, interrupted their audiences' viewing or listening to deliver product and branded messages, for which, according to the advertiser's segmentation analysis, they were suitable recipients.

The media planning concepts referred to in this chapter (reach, frequency, etc.) evolved to manage linear media and the interruption approach. Planning has been based around the development of the 'block plan'. In this approach the goal was to place messages in locations where the 'target' audience was most likely to notice and be receptive to them. To help achieve this, planners constructed a complex, coloured spreadsheet, referred to as a block plan. This contained detail about each of the channels to be used in the campaign, when they were to be activated over the campaign period, their phasing, costs, and their expected reach and frequency (Morris, 2011). The block plan accounted for the use of paid media, that is, space and time rented from media owners.

Changes in the media landscape have altered the way people now use media. Now people use linear media for information and some entertainment, and interactive media for active participation to enable user-generated content through search, downloading, sharing, publication and involvement in virtual communities. The task now is not to interrupt participants but to augment experiences, listen and facilitate interaction. People use interactive media to discover new things, to play and be entertained, to share with like-minded tribes and communities, and to engage and express themselves. Most people consume a mixture of linear and interactive media, with particular audiences skewed more to one rather than the other.

It is noticeable that print magazines and newspapers have experienced a decline in sales, but the argument that linear media advertising is in permanent decline is a fallacy. The continuing investment by a huge range of brands in television advertising is evidence of a thriving sector. Indeed, there is considerable evidence that the use of digital with television substantially improves effectiveness. Digital's ability to amplify messages improves effectiveness considerably. There has certainly been a readjustment of media budgets to reflect contemporary media usage, but the new is not wiping out the old.

The early years of online and interactive media saw attempts to use the established methods of measurement and evaluation. It became clear, however, that these methods were not entirely suitable, simply because interactive media are used differently. Instead of measuring how often a message is delivered or the share of audience reached with a message, it becomes more important to measure consumers' expectations and their interaction with brands. Put another way, these might be considered as dwell time (the amount of time consumers spend with a brand), dwell quality (a consumer's perceived richness resulting from brand interaction) and dwell insight (what motivates a consumer to spend time with a brand).

One further issue concerns the time a campaign is expected to work. Block plans were designed to work when communications ran over a typical six-week campaign period. A campaign burst. Today communications are not so delineated by time as they are increasingly 'on 24/7', as a new activity meshes into the previous one in online, social and mobile media.

Paid media is now augmented with earned and owned media, so what does this mean for the block plan? It means that media work continually, not just at particular campaign points or bursts of six weeks. With communications continually switched 'on', all the paid, owned and earned media need to be interlinked, or integrated. It is often the case that the role of paid media changes from one of leading communications activities to one that supplements the entire media activity designed to reflect an audience's relationship, levels of advocacy and journey with a brand. A block plan cannot reflect this and although it continues to have a presence within agencies as a support for paid and owned media activities, it does not support earned media, and although still important, it is not the bedrock of media planning that it once was.

Automation and programmatic technologies

Programmatic targets the placement of advertising using real time data based on actual behaviour, rather than claimed audience behavior (Perkin, 2017). This is founded on the principles of behavioural targeting, considered in Chapter 21. Instead of buying programmes, in which to insert ads and interrupt audiences, programmatic is about buying audiences, wherever they appear. This represents a totally new approach for communication planning.

Programmatic offers highly targeted advertising, which is relevant to the audience, and it also makes media buying much more efficient. This is because the use of technology and data to automate the media buying process makes it easier and cheaper for a brand to reach its target audience (Roderick, 2017). It also reduces the wastage associated with traditional planning approaches where too many messages are received by people who are not realistic targets.

Programmatic advertising in the UK was worth over £3.4 billion in 2017 (Tan, 2017a), with 78 per cent of this spent on mobile. Programmatic involves the automation of large sections of the media planning, buying and selling process and it also impacts on the creative element that is presented. As Rogers (2017a) reports, programmatic is about buying digital advertising space automatically, with computers using data to decide which ads to buy and how much to pay for them, often in real time (*Source*: Kenneth Kulbok, LinkedIn Programmatic).

A variation of programmatic is real-time bidding (RTB), the auction dimension. This allows advertisers to buy on an impression-by-impression basis and to target specific online audiences on web pages as they browse. RTB also reduces operational issues associated with invoicing individual campaigns and tagging buying space when buying from several hundred companies.

The efficiency and effectiveness of automated planning and programmatic technologies is reflected in the way plans are now optimised. Muir (2015) refers to Simon Harris, programmatic director at iProspect, who comments on how the real-time, continuous feedback of data into the planning process enables planners to understand what is working well and what isn't. This allows budget to be shifted to media that can improve the return of the overall activity.

This ability to optimise a plan can also be observed with the use of personalised creatives. The DMP can be loaded with a range of messages, which means that individual ads are automatically presented to different users depending upon how they interact with the material.

Programmatic systems enable scanning of the competitive environment. This helps planners to see what other brands are doing, how others are bidding, and whether their results are affecting the performance of their client's brand. Planners can use programmatic to test different combinations of ads and audiences across multiple channels, to determine what works best and then optimise based on what is learned. All of this happens with real audiences in live market conditions, not with an isolated test sample.

In essence, programmatic technologies allow media planners to input the characteristics of the target audience and the broad parameters of the budget, and to then observe and monitor as the system automatically bids, buys, places, and optimises the budget and all of the creative materials.

The development and use of automated media buying platforms was initially focused on online display ads, but this has been extended into TV and linear media, outdoor, video, and mobile. This growth is due to the time and resources that can be saved, the reduction in human error and waste, and the improved targeting and facility to run campaigns across a greater number of media (see Viewpoint 22.3).

Viewpoint 22.3

Brands use programmatic media buying

Image 22.2 Missing People uses programmatic out-of-home advertising
Source: Anthony Devlin - PA Images/Getty Images.

Brands have been increasing their investment in programmatic as their confidence in the technology has grown.

Topman's khaki 'look' was photographed on five different models. Each matched one of the retailer's core customer types. These included an understated man who wants to look stylish but not fashionable, 'aspiring fashionistas' and 'extreme fashionistas'. Multiple creative executions were then developed and run in parallel online media

placements. The creative that attracted the most interaction was then optimised.

IHG, the hotel group which owns the Holiday Inn and Intercontinental chains, undertook data analysis to reveal how people book hotels. They found that 20 per cent of direct sales were lost as people completed their booking at price comparison sites or third-party sellers such as Booking.com and Expedia. IHG launched a programmatic campaign targeted at people who were considering a reservation to encourage consumers to book direct. This was achieved through the use of an ad which included a 'book direct price' option.

The charity 'Missing People' used out-of-home media for many years but budget restrictions limited their reach and effectiveness as they were only able to advertise one appeal a week for a missing child across the whole UK. The out-of-home industry now donates £10m worth of advertising space each year for appeals for missing children. Now, through the use of programmatic, the charity runs more targeted campaigns, which are location specific. As soon as a missing child is found a new appeal can be created immediately. Before the use of programmatic, 50 per cent of children appealed for were found alive. Following the switch to a programmatic approach the response rate has risen to 70 per cent.

AI platform 'Albert' was used by lingerie retailer Cosabella as a replacement for its digital agency. Albert automatically builds and serves programmatically a variety of ads and KPIs provided by the brand. Within the first month, adspend decreased 12 per cent, yet search and social return-on-adspend increased 50 per cent.

Source: Tan (2017b); Tesseras (2017).

Insight

The cases shown here demonstrate some of the ways in which media planning and automated delivery can drive advertising effectiveness, in both the profit and not-for-profit sectors. From listening, timing, and presenting near customised messages to specific people, programmatic cuts waste, improves efficiency and effectiveness and avoids the interruption associated with the block-plan.

Question: Why might brands be wary of programmatic advertising?

Task: Choose a category (e.g. haircare, fast food, cars) and find out the extent to which brands used programmatic ads last year, compared with the previous year.

Apart from these efficiency gains, the growth of automated media buying for linear media is likely to impact on media planners as there is less hands-on activity, and a need for increased strategic and advisory roles.

The decision to place interactive ads is complicated, not just deciding which of the various formats should be used, but also where, when and how the ads need to be placed. The number of options is huge and includes portals, social media and community sites, plus search engines, online magazines, and shopping comparison sites.

Programmatic planning issues

So far, we have presented programmatic technologies in a positive light. There are however, several planning-related issues that arise from their use. These include transparency, ad fraud, viewability and brand safety, which were considered in Chapter 2. These concern the actual price of the ads, where they should be placed, and what and how they should be measured in the light of the vast number of fake ads, fake sites and fraudulent counting. Spanier (2017) suggests that 60 per cent of programmatic ad spend is wasted. This is because the majority of these ads fail to reach consumers, due to fraud, a lack of viewability and the use of non-human traffic (bots), all of which serve to reduce the value of the investment. For more on ad fraud see Viewpoints 10.4 and 22.4

Optimisation leads to reduced wastage and improved efficiency, but the huge amount of available data leads to issues concerning data analysis, the validity of metrics, counting and insight. Put simply, more data is useless unless it's better data. Agencies are also having to adapt. For example, the established TV department has been relabelled the AV department at some agencies. More deeply, agencies are restructuring and are having to find new skills sets, as they search for staff to fill the increasingly specialist digital roles. The planning process is speeding up as the testing of new creative can be completed in days, not months.

In addition, programmatic is closely associated with short-termism. This is because the system draws on short-term real-time data such as clicks, views and conversions. This distracts from driving longer-term behavioural changes and from strengthening long-term brand health (Binet and Field, 2013).

Viewpoint 22.4
Programmatic ad fraud

Image 22.3 Ad fraud

Danish agency Adforum uncovered the Hyphbot ad fraud scheme
Source: VStock / Alamy Stock Photo.

An advertising-fraud operation that used 'domain spoofing', was revealed by Danish firm Adform. The scheme, named as 'Hyphbot', used fake websites and infected domestic computers to scam advertisers and publishers. Adform claimed the fraudsters created in excess of 34,000 different domain names and more than a million different URLs.

These were designed to trick advertisers into believing they were buying ad inventory from publishers such as *The Economist*, the *Financial Times*, *The Wall Street Journal* and CNN.

The next step was to generate a wave of non-human, or 'bot' traffic that loaded the fraudulent sites. The suspicious URLs presented themselves in ad auctions through at least 14 different ad exchanges, at a rate of up to 1.5 billion requests to ad buyers a day.

Video ads were used as these are more lucrative than other online display ads. It was estimated that the scheme was making at least $500,000 a day.

Since its exposure there has been a reduction in the volume of fraudulent traffic, although Hyphbot was still believed to be active when the article was first written. It is estimated that $6.5 billion in adspend was wasted in 2017 due to ad fraud alone.

Sources: O'Reilly (2017); Shields (2017).

Insight

Hyphbot used approximately 500,000 computers rather than a data centre. This made the operation more difficult to detect, because the wider the bot network is distributed, the harder it is to spot signs of fraudulent activity. Fake traffic is a serious issue for advertisers. This is because they waste money buying ads that were served to computer programs, rather than real people. This means there are no product purchases and real publishers get cheated out of potential advertising revenue.

Question: To what extent should society prioritise ad fraud over other online criminal activities?

Task: The next biggest fraud to be found was Methbot. Find similarities between the two.

Automation through the use of DMPs and programmatic technologies is disrupting the established media planning process. Data has become the focal point and with that the planning processes and issues are evolving at a rapid pace.

Blockchains

The development of blockchain technologies presents major opportunities for a variety of organisations, including agencies, to overcome fraud and corruption within media ecosystems. Blockchain enables data to be shared, updated on a continuous basis, and encrypted within a distributed format, rather than in a centralised and administered storage area (Wootton, 2017). Each individual data record, or block, is distributed across a network with a link to the previous block. This means that data can only be changed if all those empowered to amend the data agree. All changes made on a blockchain are registered and can be traced back to source. This means that a blockchain disrupts the current flawed approach to the management of data, especially when intermediaries are involved, and provides a secure, verifiable and highly transparent platform (Rogers, 2017b).

Scholars' paper 22.4

How does programmatic deliver the right ad, to the right person, at the right time?

Gertz, O. and McGlashan, D. (2016) Programming the purchase funnel, *Journal of Brand Strategy*, 5(3), Winter, 275–81.

Although these authors are not scholars in the true sense, their paper provides an interesting and accessible view of the development of programmatic technology and how it can now be used to reach consumers at every point of the purchase funnel. It explains the difference programmatic makes to media planning.

The cross-media mix

Advertisers selecting media across the linear and interactive spectrum face numerous complex decisions. Cross-media campaigns seek to maximise sales effectiveness yet research by Taylor et al. (2013) shows that although both online and television advertising can drive sales among those who are reached, they found no evidence of cross-media synergy effects. What they found was that a 'mixed-media campaign could well be successful if it broadens reach cost effectively but still may not generate additional sales synergies' (p. 209).

As technology advances and the number of interactive media increases, how should management develop its media mix so that it remains current yet meets consumers' changing media behaviours? Any change to an established media mix can be risky and making a judgement about different options and permutations consumes resources. Using ideas advanced at Coca-Cola for managing content, Southgate and Svendsen (2015) reinforce the use of the 70/20/10 formula.

The 70 per cent zone requires that budget is used to support a mix of low-risk, safe, established media. These are likely to involve a proven mix of media channels, which will vary across categories and countries. So, a new service brand in Japan might use TV, event sponsorship, mobile display and QR codes, whereas a brand in a considered-purchase category in Germany could well use a mix of print, sports sponsorship, online search and online display (Southgate and Svendsen, 2015).

The 20 per cent zone of the budget should be allocated to the use of innovative, yet low-risk media. This should include the adoption of media that are known to be effective, but the risk involves increasing the amount allocated. Another approach might be to adopt a channel that was experimented with previously, or where there is little research evidence to support the initiative. For many this could include social media where questions about what the return on investment should be, or what is the right content, remain unanswered for many organisations. It might involve branching out within a familiar channel. For example, sponsoring a music festival for the first time when you have previously been known for associations with sport.

Southgate and Svendsen (2015) argue that the 10 per cent zone is for pure experimentation with new and emerging channels. Typically, mobile, apps, QR codes and Pinterest pages would fall into this zone, at the time of writing, but whatever the media activity, it should always complement brand and campaign objectives. The goal is to use deliberately allocated time and money to experiment with and increase knowledge about unknown, new and ground-breaking media. It could be that media in this zone transfer next year to the 20 per cent zone.

Scholars' paper 22.5
Cross-media synergies

Assael, H. (2010) From silos to synergy: a fifty-year review of cross-media research shows synergy has yet to achieve its full potential, *Journal of Advertising Research,* 27(4), 63–9.

An important paper for all of those interested in cross-media activities, including their evolution, measurement, form, research and in particular the synergies that might be generated. The paper also touches on IMC.

See also:

Taylor, J., Kennedy, R., Mcdonald, C., Larguinat, L., El Ouarzazi, Y. and Haddad, N. (2013) Is the multi-platform whole more powerful than its separate parts? *Journal of Advertising Research,* 53(2), 200–11.

Campaign media planning

In Chapter 7 we considered issues concerning marketing communications strategy and planning. Here we review the principles and activities associated with media planning.

For a long time, planning was based on choosing media channels according to the percentage of the audience that engages with a channel and its content. Now, planning is increasingly based around consumer purchase journeys, and three broad stages can be identified. Understanding these stages can help planners frame their communications within the plan, to play particular roles. These stages are pre-store, in-store and post-store.

Pre-store

During a consumer's purchase research phase, the plan needs to ensure that a brand is visible where and whenever consumers are looking. Devices are used in various ways. With the majority of tablets used at home, users often undertake extensive research and engage in deep interactive experiences. Smartphones are used more functionally and are used to find product and store information, often when away from home.

At this stage planning is about utilising three types of data: search, device, and location:

- **Search data** can be considered to reveal signs of purchase intention and can be used to make communications more relevant and personalised.
- **Device data** can expose differences in consumer behaviour, and use context and purchase trends. This means that messaging needs to be varied by type of device.
- **Location data** can drive more relevant messaging, such as the delivery of promotions when target consumers are near retail locations, or to serve discount offers when they are near competitor locations.

In-store

The use of mobiles in-store is now commonplace, and very often used for price comparisons. Planners therefore, seek to provide additional product detail at this stage to encourage purchase. This product detail can be as product specifications, warranty information and product reviews. In addition, purchase action can be provoked through discounts and offers, plus added value through reward points, extended warranties, and even product samples.

Post-store

Many customers are willing to share their purchase history and product preferences, in return for relevant and personalised content. Repeat purchases are more likely when consumers are provided with appropriate product suggestions and when offered benefits.

These can be delivered through loyalty programmes, which should provide added-value promotions and discounts, through regular communications. Social media is an important channel as it encourages interaction with branded content, which can be a valuable source of news and information.

The plan

Using information from a variety of sources, including those structured around the three stages outlined above, planners seek to develop, implement and measure media plans that deliver value for their clients. Planning and managing communications consists of a series of activities, not all of which are necessarily undertaken in a sequential manner. Figure 22.3 sets out these activities.

Media planning, and other communication-related exercises, start with a brief and once agreed, a set of SMART objectives are determined.

It is at this point that media planners prepare two key documents. The first is referred to as the 'ecosystem' and the second the 'schematic'.

- An 'ecosystem' is a holistic view of all the selected touchpoints and the content that will form part of the plan. Linkages and interdependencies between the touchpoints are also set out.

- A 'schematic' is a visual statement of the investment or budget allocated to each touchpoint. Essentially this is an updated block plan.

Agencies have different tools and processes associated with the way these documents are prepared. There is no definitive approach, partly because of the quickly evolving media landscape.

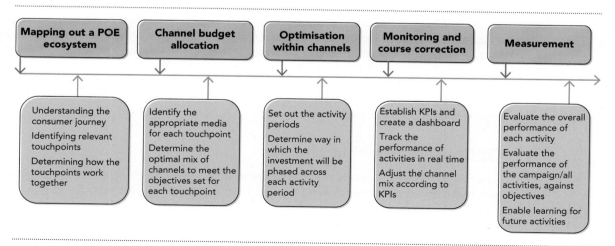

Figure 22.3 The core activities associated with contemporary media planning

The ecosystem

At the core of a media plan is an understanding of a consumer's purchase journey, as considered in Chapter 4. Throughout a purchase journey a variety of touchpoints can be identified. These are the points at which a consumer comes into contact with a brand during their purchase journey. At each of these fixed destinations, within online, mobile and offline journeys, both media and content need to be aligned with a consumer's need at that point.

Ecosystems are a web or network of carefully balanced, interconnected elements, within a particular environment. In this context ecosystems bring together the paid, owned and earned touchpoints, as well as content, that will underpin the plan for a brand. Ecosystems are used to help identify how the various touchpoints link together, and help planners make effective use of them all. This supports the delivery of an integrated campaign.

Communications planners set out all of the potential touchpoints and select those that work together, and which, in sum, deliver a particular consumer experience. The selection of touchpoints should reflect a particular combination of paid, owned and earned media used during the journey. The selection needs to be made using a combination of elements. These include historic data, device, location, media exposure, the purchase journey and whether it is an 'always on' or a fixed period campaign.

The resulting ecosystem enables clients to see how all of the touchpoints work together in their own unique ecosystem. For example, Barley (2017) reports that John Lewis discovered that the journeys undertaken by their customers crisscrossed different channels and devices: 40 per cent of sales were derived from online channels, with 50 per cent from tablets and smartphones; 25 per cent of orders involved both in-store and online interaction; 35 per cent of customers arrived at its website through a product page rather than the home page; and dwell times and browsing paths varied by device. Importantly, data indicates that there is no single, or typical journey. Customers use different devices at different stages, with no obvious pattern. It is important to understand that no consumer journey is the same and, therefore, each campaign needs to have a bespoke ecosystem designed, based on the target audience and objectives it needs to deliver.

The schematic

Having determined the optimal channel mix, which meets the objectives, the next activity requires allocating the client's budget across the selected channels that make up the ecosystem. Some of the budgeting techniques used to accomplish this are considered in Chapter 9.

The block plan or 'schematic' breaks down the investment by touchpoint, and provides a recommendation of how that investment is phased over time. A schematic, is created in order to prioritise budget against paid touchpoints in the best way possible to deliver the activity against the objectives. By allocating budget in this way, clients can not only see how their investment is being used but they can also calculate the impact of either adding or removing touchpoints. It should not be forgotten however, that schematics only accommodate paid and owned media.

Optimisation within channel

Whereas ecosystems illustrate the links between all touchpoints, the schematic helps planners make adjustments midstream, referred to as optimisation. This includes re-phasing activities, adjusting for seasonal influences, managing budget changes and changes in an audience's media consumption behaviours.

Having allocated the budget across the selected media channels the next step is to consider *when* the investment should be used during the activity period. For example, should it be spent up front, spread out evenly, or concentrated at the end of the period? To achieve effective phasing, it is important to consider the particular objectives that are to be achieved at each touchpoint within a purchase journey. This requires use of the core media-planning principles considered earlier in this chapter, such as reach, impressions, effective frequency and coverage.

Monitoring and course correcting

Planners use a dashboard in order to understand the impact that communications are having as activity unfolds. These dashboards, often in key performance indicator (KPI) format, are particular to each ecosystem and set of objectives. This helps planners to monitor each part of the ecosystem, and to determine which are working, which need to improve or be removed, or where budget needs to be redirected. This redirecting of budget, which can take place in real time within programmatic programmes, is referred to as course correction.

Measurement

When trying to understand whether a campaign was successful, four elements should be considered:

1. Outputs – what did the campaign deliver against the given budget? Measures include reach, frequency, impressions, etc.
2. Intermediate measures – how did the activity impact target audience attitudes or perceptions, and what changed as a result of the campaign? Measures include awareness, consideration and relevance.
3. Hard behavioural measures – what did the target audience do as a result of exposure to the campaign? Measures include clicks, sign ups and phone calls.
4. Hard business measures – how did the campaign impact the client's business? Measures include sales and shipments.

Reporting against these four outcomes and linking them to the objectives provides a clear view of the effectiveness of a communication activity and assists the development of future communications.

Key points

- Media or channel planning is concerned with the selection and scheduling of media vehicles designed to carry an advertiser's message.
- The variety of media is rapidly increasing and is referred to as 'media fragmentation'. This makes the media planner's task increasingly complicated because the size of audience available to each medium reduces, making the number of media vehicles required to reach a target audience increasingly large.
- Media richness theory (MRT) holds that there is a hierarchy of media ranging from the richest media such as personal or face-to-face encounters, through to lean media typified by single sheets of text-based information.
- Social influence theory (SIT) complements MRT as it also assumes that the relatively objective features of media do influence how individuals perceive and use them. The technology acceptance model (TAM) relates to the perceived usefulness and perceived ease of use as the main issues that are considered when selecting media.

- There are several fundamental concepts that underpin the way in which media should be selected and included in a media plan. These concepts refer to the percentage of the target audiences reached, the number of times they receive a message, the number of media they are exposed to and various measures associated with the efficiency with which media deliver messages.

- The greater the number of exposures, the more likely an individual is to learn about the message content. The question is how many times should a message be repeated for effective learning to occur (i.e. what is the effective frequency)?

- Recency planning is a reach-based model and argues that a single exposure to an advertising message in the week before a purchase is more important than adding further messages, thus increasing frequency. Recency planning considers reach to be more important than frequency.

- The efficiency of a schedule refers to the costs involved in delivering messages. There are two main types of cost. The first of these is the *absolute cost,* which is the cost of the space or time required for the message to be transmitted. The second concerns the costs incurred in making contact with each member of the target audience. These are referred to as the *relative costs* and are used to compare different media schedules.

- Developing a block plan to manage the media mix is only applicable to managing paid media. The incorporation of social media and search render the block plan redundant.

- Ecosystems represent all the touchpoints that customers experience when following their purchase journeys. POE media and content are designed to meet the different needs customers have at individual touchpoints.

- The schematic overlays the cost of the media investment at each point within the ecosystem.

Case study

Narellan Pools: diving into data makes a big splash

Image 22.4 Swimming pools complement the Australian climate

Swimming pools are an important asset for many families in Australia. Competitive conditions in the Australian home swimming market tightened after 2008 forcing market leader Narellan Pools, to review their approach to the market
Source: Jodie Johnson/Shutterstock.

For many Australians, buying a pool has been traditionally high on the priority list of what to achieve after buying their home. Narellan is one of Australia's largest pool builders. It's a franchisee-based business that operates in 49 different defined regional and metro centres. Collectively they sell thousands of pools every year and the average sale price is approximately AU$50,000. Narellan's sales have declined year-on-year for the last seven years.

There are several reasons for this decline, including demographic shifts, housing affordability and a big rise in competition.

Demographic shifts – the increasing proportion of people living in apartments means that the pool-buying market halved from 1992 to 2011.

Housing affordability – more Australians are renting their homes than ever before, due mainly to the high cost of ownership. This means the opportunity for major household improvement vendors is increasingly diminishing.

Household debt – the proportion of Australian household debt to GDP has reached a record high. This means that home owners, after paying their mortgage, have a lower disposable income to improve their homes.

It is not surprising that our research found fewer Australians searching for the keyword term 'pool builder'.

In addition to a shrinking pool-buyer market, the cost of entry to being a pool builder has dropped substantially. Many new, small solo operators have found it lucrative to promote themselves as pool providers with many generalist builders turning to pools to supplement their incomes.

In regional areas Narellan now competes with as many as 28 different providers, whereas previously this was less than a handful. Solo operators can easily undercut Narellan's pricing.

Our brief was to arrest the decline and bring sales back to 2008 levels, with a media budget of AU$495,000. Prior to our appointment, Narellan had deployed a traditional media strategy focused around mass-awareness channels of TV and print, with search rounding out the rest.

Over the course of 2014 we helped deliver one of the highest ever sales results for Narellan and certainly reversed their downward sales performance. It was on these strong results that Narellan set us an ambitious target in 2015 to increase leads by a further 10 per cent and conversion to sales by 5 per cent.

We knew that after a year of optimisation, the digital 2014 strategy had reached its maximum usefulness. We needed to change things radically to deliver on our client's challenging objectives.

Our first step was to talk to pool buyers to gain a deeper understanding of drivers of pool purchase coupled, with an aim to identify a tipping point to sale in Narellan's first-party data. After conducting qualitative research with recent Narellan pool buyers we found that the aspiration of their first 'dive-in moment' in their own pool is one of the most powerful motivators for buying. So we crafted creative around this insight, celebrating the moment of the first dive on a shoestring budget.

Meanwhile, our data team went to work to find insights that would best utilise Narellan Pools' limited media spend. Our goal was to identify the all-important tipping point for when people shift from wanting a pool to actually purchasing a pool – and we unearthed something amazing.

Our first task was to do a full CRM audit, where we identified the average path to sale was between three to nine months. While there we saw the expected seasonal uplift in leads in warmer months, we also found that there were some interesting and unexplained changes in behaviour. On some days within the focus months there were pronounced increases in leads, as well as massive spikes in conversion of those leads with no clear causation. So we'd discovered an unexplained anomaly – conversion rates were spiking up to 800 per cent on certain days in each month for a period of up to four days.

We started by overlaying Narellan's first-party data including leads, sales, conversion rates, marketing and promotional plans along with website analytics such as traffic, time on site and visit-to-enquiry conversion rates. We then further compared this with third-party data including consumer confidence, interest rates, CPI, building approvals, search volumes for pool quotes and related keywords, and weather. This data was mapped over a five-year period. We undertook an intensive process to gather and compile the data into a structured format ready to analyse. In total this amounted to over seven terabytes of data and resulted in data tables with over 100 million rows.

We analysed the data across all 49 territories where we found that temperature was the important determinant in successful lead generations and conversion to sales. But the eureka moment was in the detail. Temperature being higher on a given day or across a month did not in itself affect leads and conversions. We discovered that if the temperature was higher than the mean monthly rolling average for more than two consecutive days, we saw a spike in sales conversion rates.

To be clear, the temperature effect wasn't creating pool buyers that hadn't been thinking of buying a pool previously. It simply acted as the tipping point for taking the next critical step in their path to purchase: picking up the phone or making a web enquiry for a quote.

Not only were we seeing more leads, the quality of these leads were significantly higher. When we analysed the Narellan CRM data, we found that leads coming through under these conditions were up to 800 per cent more likely to buy a pool from Narellan. We also found that these leads had a considerably shorter buying path or latency. Finally, we observed the increase in quality and conversion phenomenon lasted for a total period of four days, inclusive of the second day over the mean average temperature.

Knowing that qualified potential pool purchasers were more likely to act every time these specific temperature conditions occurred, we delivered our 'dive-in moment' creative message. If the specific temperature conditions were met in any of our 49 targeted regions, we activated the media spend for our creative campaign ,which included pre-roll video, banners, search and social.

We created rules in our programmatic buying tools to set the campaign live based on the following rules:

- if the temperature yesterday was higher than the mean monthly rolling average temperature;
- and the forecast/real-time temperature for today is higher than the mean monthly rolling temperature;
- set campaign live and turn off after four days, unless the conditions were met again in that period.

To deliver this, we built an innovative and intricate weather-polling app to seamlessly feed forecast and real-time temperature data from 49 different regions into our real-time buying platforms. We then hacked programmatic buying tools to activate spend, only when our specific conditions were met.

Turning the campaign on and off in real-time based on specific weather conditions – so that we only ran advertising when we'd have the greatest effect is, to our knowledge, a world first. By spending only when these conditions were met, we delivered some unprecedented results for Narellan.

Despite being asked to deliver a 10 per cent increase in target in the context of a diminished market size, less media spend and increased competition, we smashed our goals.

We increased direct leads by 11 per cent and increased sales by 23 per cent year-on-year (a whopping 360 per cent of our goal). In 2015 we helped Narellan deliver its highest sales result in over a decade. This was achieved using just 70 per cent of the media budget.

This case study is an edited version of a paper submitted to the IPA Effectiveness Awards 2016. It has been reproduced here with the kind permission of the IPA, WARC, Narellan Pools, and Infinity their agency who wrote the original paper.

Review questions

Narellan Pools case questions

1. Identify the key contextual elements facing Narellan's media selection decisions.
2. What were the main media planning tasks facing Narellan and how did they overcome them?
3. What role did conventional media play within the media strategy?

4. How might planning for interactive media differ from that for linear media? How did these two media formats complement each other in the Narellan campaign?
5. How might an understanding of reach and frequency influence the use of media in the Narellan campaign?

General questions

1. Explain the concept of effective frequency and why frequency levels are so important.
2. Compare media richness theory, social influence theory and the technology adoption model.
3. To what extent do programmatic technologies enhance media planning?

4. Explain the nature and role of an ecosystem in contemporary media planning.
5. What are the essential differences between buying media through a block plan and programmatically?

References for Chapter 22

Anon (2015) The Sex Pistols, *Punk 77*, issue 18, retrieved 3 May 2015 from www.punk77. co.uk/groups/sex.htm

Anon (2017) Cannes study: video is key for effectiveness, WARC, 7 August, retrieved 9 August 2017 from https://www.warc.com/NewsAndOpinion/News/Cannes_study_ Video_is_key_for_effectiveness/39096?utm_source=DailyNews&utm_medium=e- mail&utm_campaign=DailyNews2017807

Armengol, X., Fernandez, V., Simo, P. and Sallan, J.M. (2017) An examination of the effects of self-regulatory focus on the perception of the media richness: the case of email, *International Journal of Business Communication*, 54(4), 394–407.

Assael, H. (2010) From silos to synergy: a fifty-year review of cross-media research shows synergy has yet to achieve its full potential, *Journal of Advertising Research*, 27(4), 63–9.

Barley, E. (2017) John Lewis: ten things we've learnt about mobile shopping, WARC, retrieved 23 June 2018 from https://www.warc.com/content/article/event-reports/john_lewis_ten_things_weve_learnt_about_mobile_shopping/110924

Beale, C. (1997) Study reveals negativity towards ads, *Campaign*, 28 November, 8.

Binet, L. and Field, P. (2007) *Marketing in the Era of Accountability*, Henley-on-Thames: World Advertising Research Centre/IPA.

Binet, L. and Field. P. (2013) *The Long and the Short of It*. London: IPA, 18.

Cheong, Y., De Gregorio, F. and Kim, K. (2011) The power of reach and frequency in the age of digital advertising: offline and online media demand different metrics, *Journal of Advertising Research*, 50(4), 403–15.

Daft, R.L. and Lengel, R.H. (1984) Information richness: a new approach to managerial behavior and organizational design, in *Research in Organizational Behavior*, 6 (eds L.L. Cummings and B.M. Straw), Homewood, IL: JAI Press, 191–233.

De Pelsmacker, P. de Geuens, M. and Vermeir, I. (2004) The importance of media planning, ad likeability and brand position for ad and brand recognition in radio spots, *International Journal of Market Research*, 46, Quarter 4, 465–78.

du Plessis, E. (1998) Memory and likeability: keys to understanding ad effects, *Admap*, July/August, 42–6.

Ephron, E. (1997) Recency planning, *Admap*, February, 32–4.

Ephron, E. (2003) The paradox of product placement, *Mediaweek*, 2 June, 20.

Fulk, J., Schmitz, J.A. and Steinfield, C.W. (1990) A social influence model of technology use, in *Organizations and Communication Technology* (eds J. Fulk and C. Steinfield), Newbury Park, CA: Sage.

Gates-Sumner, L. (2014) Sharpening the arrow: the value of modern targeting approaches, *Millward Brown*, retrieved 14 November 2014 from http://www.millwardbrown.com/docs/default-source/insight-documents/articles-and-reports/Millward_Brown_Targeted_Media.pdf

George, J.F., Carlson, J.R. and Valacich, J.S. (2013) Media selection as a strategic component of communication, *MIS Quarterly*, 37(4), 1233–51.

Gertz, O. and Mcglashan, D. (2016) Programming the purchase funnel, *Journal of Brand Strategy*, 5(3), Winter, 275–81.

Jones, P. (1995) *When Ads Work: New Proof that Advertising Triggers Sales*, New York: Simon & Schuster, Free Press/Lexington Books.

King, R.C. and Xia, W. (1997) Media appropriateness: effects of experience on communication media choice, *Decision Sciences*, 28(4), 877–909.

Krugman, H.E. (1965) The impact of television advertising: learning without involvement, *Public Opinion Quarterly*, 29 (Fall), 349–56.

Krugman, H.E. (1972) How potent is TV advertising? cited in du Plessis (1998).

Lloyd, D.W. and Clancy, K.J. (1991) CPMs versus CPMIs: implications for media planning, *Journal of Advertising Research*, 31(4), 34–44.

Mansfield, B. (2013) Elvis Presley tops list of digitally streamed artists, *USA Today*, 3 October, retrieved 3 May 2015 from www.usatoday.com/story/life/music/2013/10/03/elvis-presley-tops-digitally-streamed-artists-soundexchange/2909811/.

McLuhan, M. (1966) *Understanding Media: The Extensions of Man*, New York: McGraw-Hill.

Morgan, R. (2017) Case study: how Knorr's 'Love at first taste' bonded the brand with millennials, *Campaignlive*, 14 April, retrieved 14 March 2018 from https://www.campaignlive.co.uk/article/case-study-knorrs-love-first-taste-bonded-brand-millennials/1430457#OuMpdjaq06g9rPeX.99

Morris, R. (2011) The modern media mix, *Campaignlive*, 8 July 2011, retrieved 23 April 2012 from www.brandrepublic.com/features/1079039/Modern-Media-mix/?DCMP=ILC-SEARCH

Muir, R. (2015) How programmatic has changed media planning, *Exchangewire*, 12 November, retrieved 3 January 2018 from www.exchangewire.com/blog/2015/11/12/how-programmatic-has-changed-media-planning

Newsworks (2018) *The Sunday Times*, retrieved 12 March 2018 from http://www.newsworks.org.uk/the-sunday-times

O'Reilly, L. (2017) Fake-ad operation used to steal from publishers is uncovered, *The Wall Street Journal*, 21 November, retrieved 3 January 2018 from https://www.wsj.com/articles/fake-ad-operation-used-to-steal-from-publishers-is-uncovered-1511290981?mod=djemCMOToday

Ostrow, J.W. (1981) What level of frequency? *Advertising Age*, November, 13–18.

Ostrow, J.W. (1984) Setting frequency levels: an art or a science? *Marketing and Media Decisions*, 24(4), 9–11.

Perkin, N. (2017) *The Future Strategist/Planner*, 20 March, retrieved 24 January 2018 from http://www.onlydeadfish.co.uk/only_dead_fish/2017/03/google-firestarters-23-the-future-strategistplanner-the-event.html

Poynor, R. (2012) The art of punk and the punk aesthetic, *Design Observer*, 14 October, retrieved 3 May 2015 from http://designobserver.com/feature/the-art-of-punk-and-the-punk-aesthetic/36708

Roderick, L. (2017) The state of programmatic advertising, *Campaignlive*, 27 March, retrieved 26 October 2017 from https://www.marketingweek.com/2017/03/27/state-programmatic-advertising/

Rogers, C. (2017a) What is programmatic advertising? A beginner's guide, *Marketing Week*, 27 March, retrieved 14 September 2018 from https://www.marketingweek.com/2017/03/27/programmatic-advertising/

Rogers, C. (2017b) Why marketers need to get to grips with Blockchain, *Marketing Week*, 5 April, retrieved 4 April 2018 from https://www.marketingweek.com/2017/04/05/marketers-need-know-blockchain/

Shields, R. (2017) Inside Adform's 'Hyphbot' ad fraud takedown, *The Drum*, 29 November, retrieved 22 January 2018 from http://www.thedrum.com/news/2017/11/29/inside-adform-s-hyphbot-ad-fraud-takedown-0

Southgate, D. and Svendsen, J. (2015) Changing channels with confidence: a structure for innovation, *Millward Brown*, retrieved 30 January 2015 from www.millwardbrown.com/Insights/Point-of-View/Changing_Channels_with_Confidence/default.aspx

Spanier, G. (2017) Marketers must tell their boards '60% of programmatic spend is wasted', *Campaignlive*, 28 March, retrieved 12 March 2018 from https://www.campaignlive.co.uk/article/marketers-tell-boards-60-programmatic-spend-wasted/1428837

Springall, P. (2016) Case study: Karcher: Window Vac, in Fill, C. and Turnbull, S. (2016) *Marketing Communications*, 7th edn, Harlow: Pearson.

Sylvester, R. (2013) Brand you, in Fitterman Radbill, C. (2013) *Introduction to the Music Industry: An Entrepeneurial Approach*, New York: Routledge.

Tan, E. (2017a) UK programmatic market to grow 23.5% this year, *Campaignlive*, 12 December, retrieved 12 March 2018 from https://www.campaignlive.co.uk/article/uk-programmatic-market-grow-235-year/1452593

Tan, E. (2017b) Why Cosabella replaced its agency with AI and will never go back to humans, *Campaign*, retrieved 22 January 2018 from: http://www.campaignlive.co.uk/article/why-cosabella-replaced-its-agency-ai-will-go-back-humans/1427323

Taylor, J., Kennedy, R., McDonald, C., Larguinat, L., El Ouarzazi, Y. and Haddad, N. (2013) Is the multi-platform whole more powerful than its separate parts? *Journal of Advertising Research*, 53(2), 200–11.

Tesseras, L. (2017) Five of the best programmatic ad campaigns, *Marketing Week*, 3 April, retrieved 26 October 2017 from https://www.marketingweek.com/2017/04/03/programmatic-best-campaigns/

WARC (2013) Automated TV buying moves closer, retrieved 14 September 2018 from https://www.warc.com/NewsAndOpinion/News/31820

Whitler, K.A. (2017) How traditional media planning is changing, and what marketers can do about it, *Forbes*, 28 May, retrieved 6 February 2018 from https://www.forbes.com/sites/kimberlywhitler/2017/05/28/how-traditional-media-planning-is-changing-and-what-marketers-can-do-about-it/#8bfce67c499b

Wootton, B. (2017) Can Blockchain clean up the ad industry? *Marketing Week*, 17 August, retrieved 4 April 2018 from https://www.marketingweek.com/2017/08/15/bob-wootton-blockchain/

Author index

Subject index